ANNOTATED INSTRUCTOR'S EDITION

The

St. Martin's

HANDBOOK

Andrea Lunsford
Ohio State University

Robert Connors
University of New Hampshire

Prepared by

Cheryl Glenn
Roger C. Graves
R. Gerald Nelms
Dennis Quon

(all of Ohio State University)

ST. MARTIN'S PRESS   New York

Manufactured in the United States of America.
32109
fedcba

For information, write:
St. Martin's Press, Inc.
175 Fifth Avenue
New York, NY 10010

ISBN: 0-312-01949-1

Preface to Annotated Instructor's Edition

When we began this annotated edition, we hoped to create an efficient and accessible resource for instructors. Our first thought was of everyday classroom needs—teaching suggestions, answers to the exercises, and so on. As we began work, however, we came upon materials and ideas for teaching that have, we think, expanded our original horizons, providing not only the *what* to teach but, more importantly, the *how* and the *why*. Our experience mirrors the recent history of composition scholarship. In the past twenty years, the *what* has changed from a product-oriented approach to what is typically referred to as a process approach. Our teaching no longer focuses entirely upon the final text; we now intervene in the course of student writing, and try to embrace the overall procedure as well as the final product. Accompanying this shift in *what* has been increasingly sophisticated pedagogy and research, the *how*, and greater justification, the *why*. In our experience, the *what* cannot be separated from the *how* and the *why*. Without explaining *why* we teach what we do, the *what* remains simply dogma. By not providing information about *how* to teach it, the *what* remains merely abstraction.

Like *The St. Martin's Handbook* itself, the Annotated Instructor's Edition rests on the assumption that writing decisions are never merely mechanical, but are always rhetorical as well. This rhetorical dimension is introduced and explored in the four essays that follow this preface. The essays include an introduction to rhetorical theory and the teaching of writing, a report on research and practice of collaborative writing, a plan for ways of responding to student writing, and a brief history of composition studies. Together, these essays constitute a brief introduction to the field of rhetoric and composition and ground what follows in a theoretical, historical, and practical discussion. On the very practical side, we also offer sample syllabi for semester- and quarter-length courses to help you use *The St. Martin's Handbook*.

Within the text itself, each chapter includes various kinds of annotations. First come sections we call *(Back)grounding*, which present useful historical and theoretical information. *Teaching Practices* offer specific classroom and homework strategies. Strategies for *Writing Together* suggest activities for group work with your students. *Optional Exercises* offer additional opportunities for practice, both in class and at home. Sprinkled throughout are brief pieces called *Writers on Writing* and *Writers Writing*, which provide instructive, provocative, and sometimes just plain entertaining quotations and passages from some of our most quotable writers. These can be used in various ways—to generate discussion about the topic at hand, to illustrate abstract concepts or ideas, even to provide topics for composition. Finally come references to *Useful Readings*, which will lead you to in-depth analysis, description, and development of the ideas and concepts presented in each chapter.

Creating this annotated edition has offered us a rich opportunity to practice what we so often preach. As graduate research and teaching assistants, we have been able throughout this project to test the materials we were creating in the crucible of our classrooms, thereby making the necessary if not always successful connection between theory and practice. Similarly, we have found ourselves collaborating in the same ways we ask our students to do—again making that connection between theory and practice. And like our students, we have struggled with the concept of audience, attempting to address both beginning and experienced instructors of composition.

Our collaboration reaches far beyond our group of four, however, to include a number of friends and colleagues to whom we are indebted. At St. Martin's Press, we wish to thank Virginia Biggar, Marilyn Moller, Nancy Perry, Denise Quirk, and Richard Steins, who have supplied support and encouragement. We are especially grateful to those good friends and generous colleagues who provided clerical support, research assistance, and generous, always valuable criticism: Melinda Bako, Doug Brent, Beverly Bruck, Bob Connors, Heather Graves, Sue Lape, Andrea Lunsford, Jaime Mejia, Roxanne Mountford, Marcia Nelms, Jon Olson, Mike Rose, Cindy Selfe, Kimberly Town, Kelly Vezdos, and Tracy Vezdos. In an important sense, however, this group extends to include all the teachers to whom this book is addressed. Everything in this book is written for you—but in fact much, perhaps most, of it has been inspired by you.

Cheryl Glenn
Roger C. Graves
R. Gerald Nelms
Dennis Quon

Contents

Brief Contents of Student Edition

Rhetorical Theory and the Teaching of Writing

—Andrea Lunsford and Cheryl Glenn

I. RHETORIC AND THE DYNAMIC ELEMENTS OF WRITTEN COMMUNICATION

For some 2,500 years, speakers and writers have re-lied—often unknowingly—on rhetorical theory to achieve successful persuasion and communication or to gain coop-eration. "Rhetorical theory?"—it sounds formidable, perhaps even beside the point. Yet every teacher and every student works out of rhetorical theory, which guides us in the dy-namic process of making meaning, sustains our classroom writing practices, and informs our textbooks.

Long the staple of communication theory, the "com-munication triangle," comprising *sender*, *receiver*, and *mes-sage*, has expanded to incorporate *universe* (or *context*), the fourth component of this rhetorical set of interrelationships. These four elements of meaning not only guide teachers in their teaching choices but also guide writers in their writing choices, choices based on (1) their own values; (2) those of their receivers; (3) the possible range of messages; and (4) the nature of the universe, of reality.

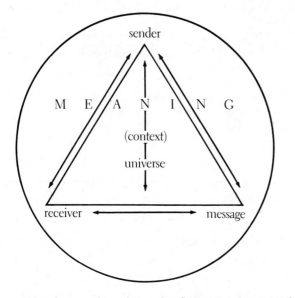

Aristotle may have been the first to separate out the rhetorical elements (the persuasive appeals) of communica-tion when he wrote that the true constituents of the art of rhetoric are *ethos*, the appeals exerted by the speaker (the sender); *pathos*, the appeals to the emotions or values of the audience (the receiver); and *logos*, the appeals to reason of the message itself—with all appeals reflecting or affecting the *universe* (*Rhetoric*, I.2.1356c).[1] Hence, any communication

reveals *all* the elements of the communication triangle even if one leg of the tripod is emphasized. When Aristotle went on to divide public, persuasive discourse into kinds, again the divisions fell into three: ethos being most prominent in *deliberative* oratory, the oratory of public policy that insists on a high degree of probability; pathos, dominating *epideictic* or ceremonial oratory; and logos, foregrounded in *judicial* or courtroom oratory—and again, the discourse reflects, af-fects, or effects the universe or context (I.3; II.1). And his definition of rhetoric as "the faculty of observing in any given case the available means of persuasion" (I.2.1355b) has un-dergirded all rhetorical theory thenceforth, providing schol-ars, critics, and rhetoricians a dependable and expandable base for their own contributions to rhetorical theory and practice.

In his landmark *Theory of Discourse*, James Kinneavy relates Aristotle's rhetorical triangle to fields other than rheto-ric (such as literary theory, anthropology, communication, and semiotics), showing, in each case, just how *any* com-munication can emphasize one particular element of the triangle. Like Aristotle, who demonstrates three purposeful discourses, Kinneavy locates the variable aims of discourse in its emphatic triangulation of author, audience, universe, or in its reflexive emphasis on itself, the text.

Kinneavy refers to the work of literary theorist M. H. Abrams (310-48), whose *Mirror and the Lamp* posits the four elements in the total situation of a work of art: the *work*, the artistic product itself; the *artist*, who produced the work; the *universe*, the subject of the work itself or from which the work is derived; and the *audience* to whom the work is ad-dressed or made available (6-7, passim). Although a work of artistic literature itself always implicitly assumes an author, an audience, a universe, the four coordinates of the work vary in significance according to the theory in which they occur: mimetic theories emphasize art's imitation of the *uni-verse*; pragmatic theories propound art's effect on the *audi-ence*, on getting things done; expressive theories center on the *artist* as cause and criterion of art; and objective theories deal with the work of art itself, in parts and in the mutual relations of its parts. According to Kinneavy, the aim or intention of the communication can be extracted from nei-ther the author[2] ("intentional fallacy") nor the receiver ("af-fective fallacy") but is embodied only in the text itself—given the qualifications of situation and culture (49–50).

Kinneavy also refers to the work of anthropological lin-guists, who, like the literary theorists, evaluate language in terms of its aims: as verbal gesture, *interjectional*; as imitation of reality, *representational*; as a pragmatic symbol for getting things done, *utilitarian*; and as expression of the sender, *poetic* or *play* (51–52). The communication theorists, too, refer to language aims: informative, exploratory, instrumental, and emotive—aims that stress the importance of one rhetorical element (53–54). Communicationists call the elements *encoder, decoder, signal,* and *reality,* and they connect informative communication with the signal or text; exploratory with reality or the universe; instrumental with the decoder or the audience; and emotive with the encoder or the author.

Eminent rhetorician Kenneth Burke extended the grammar of rhetoric to encompass five elements, expanding the rhetorical triangle to a pentad: agent (who?), action (what?), scene (where and when?), purpose (why?), and agency (how?) (*A Grammar of Motives,* passim). Not intended as a heuristic, an aid to discovery or invention, Burke's pentad, nonetheless, supplies writers and readers with a method for establishing the focus of a written or spoken text. His theory of dramatism, focusing as it does on the ratios between the elements in the pentad, calls attention to the ways these representative terms link up. Dramatism is a theory of action that breathes life into a text, humanizing the action. And the key term of Burke's pentad is "act," for it is the starting point for text analysis. When a person's acts are to be interpreted in terms of the circumstances, the scene in which he is acting (as in *Robinson Crusoe, Lord of the Flies,* or *Riddley Walker,* for example), his behavior would fall under the heading of a "scene-act ratio." In *Lord of the Flies,* both Ralph and Jack, leaders of opposing factions, "act" in reaction to the "scene": they are stranded on a desert island without the traditional protection of society. Yet within the "scene-act ratio" would fall a range of behavior that must again be evaluated according to the "agent-act ratio"—what is the correspondence between a person's character and action? between the action and the circumstances? Well-adjusted, optimistic, and athletic, Ralph "naturally" acts out the desire for civilization, while Jack, the cruel and ugly bully, acts out the feral desire for mastery by intimidation and violence. Texts such as *Madame Bovary, Anna Karenina,* and *Portrait of a Lady* reflect a prominent "agency-act ratio," the texts reflecting correspondence between each character and the character of her behavior. Other dynamic relationships, other ratios, disclose still other features of human relations, behavior, and motives. Yet no matter how we look at texts, no matter which theorist's game we play, we always seem to swing around the poles of the original rhetorical triangle.

Like Burke, Wayne Booth also expands the notion of the rhetorical triangle. Burke uses his pentad retrospectively to analyze the motives of language (human) actions—texts or speeches—while Booth stresses the persuasive potential of his triangulated proofs: *ethos,* which is situated in the sender; *pathos,* in the receiver; and *logos,* in the text itself (*Modern Dogma and the Rhetoric of Assent* 144-64). Both their ana-

lytical frameworks can be used two ways: (1) as systems or frames on which to build a text; and (2) as systems of analysis for already-completed texts. Booth's rhetorical triangle provides a framework that can be used to analyze a text, for it is the dynamic interaction of *ethos, pathos,* and *logos* that creates that text. Neither rhetorician considers content alone or the examination of that content sufficient to create meaning; "attitude" overlays that content and enhances the ensuing meaning. To understand the *meaning* of an already-completed text, Booth would examine the content, analyze the audience that is implied in that text, and recover the attitudes expressed by the implied author. The total act of communication must be examined in order to recover the ethos/character of the speaker, authorial attitude and intention, and voice—vital elements, resonant with attitude, that create a text. Burke, too, realized the importance of "attitude" and often talked of adding it to his dramatistic pentad (thereby transforming it into a hexad).

In "The Rhetorical Stance," Booth's message to teachers, he posits a concept of rhetoric that can support an undergraduate curriculum:

> The common ingredient that I find in all of the writing I admire . . . is something that I shall reluctantly call the rhetorical stance, a stance which depends on discovering and maintaining in any writing situation a proper balance among the three elements that are at work in any communicative effort: the available arguments about the subject itself, the interests and peculiarities of the audience, and the voice, the implied character, of the speaker. (27)

Like Aristotle, Booth posits a carefully balanced tripartite division of rhetorical appeals. Ever mindful of the audience being addressed, Booth would have us—as writers—strike such a balance to have a clear relationship with our reader(s) and our texts. As readers, Booth would have us keep this triangulation in mind, too, searching for and analyzing ethical, emotional, and logical appeals as we read. Otherwise, he warns, our reading of the text will be at best insensitive, at worst inaccurate. In *Lord of the Flies,* we analyze Ralph's and Jack's speeches for persuasive appeals, just as we analyze the appeals imbricating the omniscient author's narrative. Like Aristotle, who believed the ethical appeal to be the most effective, Booth wants speakers and writers—teachers and students alike—to examine their assumptions and to inspect the reasons for their strong commitments. Booth would like to reintroduce into education a strong concept of *ethos,* the dynamic start of persuasive communication: in balancing these three elements, the *logos* may determine how far we extend our *ethos* or what *ethos* we use or how much *pathos.* Booth goes on to say that "it is this balance, this rhetorical stance, difficult as it is to describe, that is our main goal as teachers of rhetoric" (27).

The traditional, stable, tricornered dynamics of written communication have been recently expanded. Gone is the notion of one speaker, one listener, one message—one voice. Instead, such univocal discourse has been replaced with many speakers, many listeners, many messages. In most communications, people are both speakers *and* listeners, or there is a multitude of listeners for one speaker; and the message is constantly affected by and adjusted to both speakers and listeners. To complicate communication even further, each listener interprets each speaker differently, even if there is only one speaker. Thus, just as the speaker and listener cannot be univocal, neither can the interpretation. Although the resulting icon is no longer the "rhetorical triangle," the triangular dynamics remain, for the figure becomes one of equilateral triangles with varying but concentric orientations. The familiar triangle has been embellished, but the original three key terms—speaker, listener, subject—remain.

II. WHAT RESEARCH TELLS US ABOUT THE ELEMENTS OF WRITTEN COMMUNICATION

The revival of rhetorical theory witnessed during the last twenty-five years has reacquainted teachers with the primary elements of the rhetorical tradition—ethos/writer; pathos/audience; logos/text—and with the way those elements have been played out in the canon of rhetoric. Although they may not be familiar with the actual names, most teachers are familiar with concepts forming the canons of rhetoric: invention, arrangement, style, memory, and delivery. While this formulation is in some sense reductive, it nevertheless provides a useful framework for investigating the recent contributions of rhetorical theory to the teaching of writing. Close attention to the *writer* during this time has resulted in much important work that attempts essentially to answer this two-fold question: where do a writer's ideas come from and how are such ideas formulated into writing? Such a question demands a new focus on *invention*, the first canon of rhetoric, and has led in two provocative and profitable directions. The first, represented in the work of Richard Young, Janice Lauer, and Richard Larson (to name only a very few) aims at deriving heuristic procedures or systematic strategies that will aid students in discovering and generating ideas about which they might write. Such strategies may be as simple as prompting students to generate ideas about a subject by asking—who, what, when, where, why, and how—the traditional "journalistic formula" mentioned above. Or they can be as complex as the nine-cell matrix presented in Young, Becker, and Pike's *Rhetoric: Discovery and Change*. Essentially, this heuristic asks student writers to look at any subject from nine different perspectives. For example, a student writing about a campus strike might look at it first as a "happening" frozen in time and space, or as the result of a complex set of causes, or as a *cause* of some other effects, or as one tiny part of a larger economic pattern. Looking at the subject in such different ways "loosens up" mental muscles and jogs writers out of unidimensional or tunnel-vision views of a subject.

We see this interest in procedural heuristics as related theoretically to the work of researchers interested in cognition. Linda Flower and coauthor John Hayes are best known for their studies of writers' talk-aloud protocols, tape-recorded documents that catch a writer's *thoughts* about writing while the writing is actually in progress. Like any methodology is bound to be, such methodology is flawed, but it *has* provided a fascinating "window on writers' minds," to use Flower's descriptive phrase. Stephen Witte has recently built on the work of Flower and Hayes in order to study what he calls a writer's "pretext," a writer's "trial locution that is produced in the mind, stored in the writer's memory, and sometimes manipulated mentally prior to being transcribed as written text" (397). Other researchers have attempted to map the relationship of affective factors to a writer's "invention": John Daly, in terms of writing apprehension, and Mike Rose, in terms of writer's block. All of this research aims to help teachers understand the rich, diverse, complex, and largely *invisible* processes student writers go through in writing.

But a renewed interest in student writers had led in another powerful direction as well, notably in the work of Ken Macrorie and, more pervasively, of Peter Elbow. Elbow is interested in how writers establish unique voices, in how they realize individual selves in discourse, and his work with students presents dramatic evidence of such activity. In a series of very influential books (*Writing without Teachers, Writing with Power, Embracing Contraries*), Elbow has focused on how writers come to know themselves—and then share those selves with others.

The researchers and teachers we have been surveying here differ in many ways, but their work is all aimed primarily at that point of the rhetorical triangle that focuses on the writer and his or her powers of invention. They want to know what makes writers tick—and how teachers can help writers "tick" most effectively.

If we shift the focus of our discussion from writer to *text*, we also find that rhetorical theory has much to offer the teacher of writing. Students are often puzzled when teachers don't "get the meaning" they intend. Rhetorical theory helps us explain why such miscommunication takes place and suggests powerful ways to avoid it. One of the simplest to use with students is I. A. Richard's own version of the rhetorical triangle:

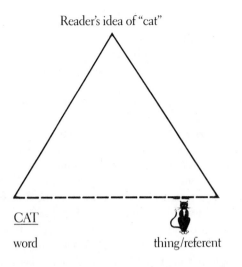

Reader's idea of "cat"

CAT
word   thing/referent

Richards argues that no direct relationship exists between a word—a set of black marks on a page—and its referent in the world (*The Meaning of Meaning* 10–13). That is to say, the meaning of *cat* is not inherent in the little squiggles we call letters nor in the furry, purry pet we may have. Rather, meaning arises in the perceiver—in people—as they filter the linguistic signal *cat* through all their experience with both word and thing. So *cat* may well mean one thing to someone who adores cats and something quite different to someone who was, as a child, badly scratched by a cat.

Richards uses another principle to help us understand how we get meaning from texts. He calls this principle "interinanimation of words," which simply means that any one word is strongly affected by other words around it (*Philosophy of Rhetoric* 47–66). The word *love*, for instance, suggests one meaning when connected to the words *grandparent* and *grandchild*, and another when connected to *husband* and *wife*, and yet another when connected to a business tycoon and his image of himself. Students can put Richards's principle to use by examining a text closely for the ways its words interinanimate one another. And teachers can use the principle of interinanimation to show students that we are all very much *what we say*, that our words work together (interinanimate) to create the people we are, with our individual values, prejudices, and so on.

Three other concepts used by modern rhetorical theorists may help students and teachers get inside the intricacies of any text. Richard Weaver provides one set, what he calls "ultimate" or "God terms" and "Devil terms," to indicate those words or concepts that represent something we will make sacrifices for ("Ultimate Terms in Contemporary Rhetoric" 87–112). In the 1950s, Weaver hypothesized that *Americanism*, *progress*, and *science* served as God terms, large concepts that most people held very dear. He went on to suggest that God or Devil terms set up hierarchical rela-

tionships in texts—that is, that many other related terms are usually clustered under them. Identifying such a central term and then mapping its related clusters of terms can help students get at complex meanings in texts.

Kenneth Burke proposes a somewhat similar enterprise by suggesting that we look at a text (or any discourse, spoken or written) as a *terministic screen* ("Terministic Screen" 59 ff). If you think of a text as a very fine-meshed screen, with every point connected to every other point, you will see what Burke has in mind. The "screen" of the text directs our attention in certain ways, selecting some points for emphasis, deflecting others. And the screen is made up not of wire—but of words or *terms*. Burke challenges us to trace out all the minute interstitial connections among terms in any text/screen as a means of constructing meaning. Students can put Burke's metaphorical screen to work, particularly in the language of advertising but also with the language of any other text. In addition, they take pleasure and profit from examining their *own* terministic screens.

One other key principle deserves our attention in discussing rhetorical theory and texts. That word, a popular one among literary theorists today as well, is *intertextuality*, and it refers to a principle very similar to those we have been discussing. Most simply, intertextuality denotes the great conversation among texts, the way texts refer or allude to one another, build on or parody one another, revolve around one another. The Mel Brooks movie *Young Frankenstein*, for instance, which many of our students know well, is part of an elaborate and extensive conversation stretching back through countless other movies to Mary Shelley's novel (with its subtitle *The Modern Prometheus*) to many poems and plays and mythical accounts of Prometheus, to the creation of Adam in the Bible—or *forward* to the contemporary debate over genetic engineering and our ability to create life. Introducing students to this principle allows them to enter this great conversation and provides them with an effective method for probing textual meaning.

The theorists we have been discussing offer ways to see the "big picture" of a text; they deal with the macrostructure element of the second canon of rhetoric, the *arrangement* of argument. But rhetorical theory offers help on the microstructures of the "little picture" as well. This tradition of research, which focuses on organization, on the relationship between form and function, is extensive and complex. Here we will cite two rhetoricians whose work seems most helpful for the teaching of writing. Many readers of this book may already be familiar with the first, Francis Christensen. In a series of essays, Christensen demonstrated a way to map sentences and paragraphs according to levels of generality and modification. According to Christensen, *periodic* sentences and paragraphs are those that delay or postpone announcing the general main clause/topic until the very end, leading into the topic with supporting or modifying details ("A Generative Rhetoric of the Sentence" 155–56). This kind of structure forces a reader to hold the subject in mind until the very end and keep syntactic tension high. In the hands of skilled writers, periodic structures can keep readers alert for what is to come and make the main idea, when it finally does appear, all the more impressive.

Although structures using various degrees of periodicity can be very effective in challenging and interesting readers, they do not constitute the most frequently used pattern in modern English. Rather, the *cumulative* structure, which adds details after the main clause or announcement of the topic, is the more dominant. Christensen writes:

> The main clause, which may or may not have a sentence modifier before it, advances the discussion; but the additions move backwards, as in this clause, to modify the statement of the main clause or more often to explicate it or exemplify it, so that the sentence has a flowing and ebbing movement, advancing to a new position and then pausing to consolidate it, leaping and lingering as the popular ballad does. (156)

Because the main clause/topic is presented at or near the beginning of the sentence/paragraph, cumulative structures do not require readers to hold the subject in suspense until the end. In one sense, then, these structures may be easier to read than periodic ones, yet the skillful writer can position the most important piece of information at the end. Like all sentence patterns, however, the cumulative sentence can be used either effectively or, like the following example, ineffectively: "The cumulative sentence in unskilled hands is unsteady, allowing a writer to ramble on, adding modifier after modifier, until the reader is almost overwhelmed, because the writer's central idea is lost."

Using exclusively periodic or cumulative structures, of course, would be monotonous. And so the best writers mingle structures—short and long, periodic and cumulative—though never forgetting that the most important ideas naturally deserve the most prominent positions. Our own students can easily test the structures of others' as well as their own texts, relating purpose to structure, and can learn to balance their own prose with purposeful and effective movement between general and specific information.

More recently, Richard Coe has elaborated and extended the work of Christensen, moving toward what he calls a "grammar of passages." In his monograph, Coe takes the traditional syntactic relationships between form and function—coordinate, subordinate, and superordinate—and subdivides them further: (1) coordination: contrasting, contradicting, conjoining, and repeating on the same level of generality; (2) subordination: defining, exemplifying, giving reasons, deducing (deductive conclusion), explaining (making plain by restating more specifically), qualifying; and (3) superordination: drawing conclusion, generalizing (making an inductive inference), commenting on a previously stated proposition (32-33). Then Coe goes on to develop a system for mapping these relationships. This syntactical system has been tested extensively with student writers, in classes ranging from ESL to technical writing, to basic writing, to advanced composition, with dramatic results. Students learn to "map" their own texts and thereby have a means of deciding whether those texts are coherent, whether they "make sense."

But what of the third angle of the rhetorical triangle—that pointing to audience and context? Does rhetorical theory offer any insights into these crucial elements in communication? Of course. As a discipline, rhetoric has always been intensely interested in the effects a writer's intentions, words, texts, have *on people* in varying situations. That is to say, taking a "rhetorical stance" will always place you in a full context. In this regard, rhetorical theory has helped us learn about the psychology of readers (or listeners, interpreters, responders), from Aristotle's discussion of how different types of people react to different subjects and Plato's elegant oration on souls, to contemporary persuasion theorists (Petty, Brock, Ostrom) on the one hand and reader-oriented researchers and critics (Rosenblatt, Bleich, Iser) on the other.

What this research tells us as teachers of writing is simply this: the processes of reading and responding to texts are at least as complex as those of writing a text; that all readers build up frameworks (called schemata), which they use to make sense as they read; that such frameworks are affected both by everything we already know and by what we are (gender, for example, exerts powerful influence on patterns of interpretation and response). As teachers, we must help students understand and theorize about their own such patterns. Doing so leads to the second major point we want to make here. That is, we can often understand our own patterns of response by seeing them *in context*, as related to others' responses and as part of a large social process aimed at negotiating and constructing meaning. If intertextuality is a coin, this is its flip side—inter-reader-ability—the fully contextualized, multiple voices out of which we forge an understanding of texts.

Kenneth Bruffee is probably the best-known composition theorist who argues that knowledge is constructed socially, and his work is related to a large body of research on collaborative writing, reading, and learning. Tori Haring-Smith, for instance, bases arguments for writing-across-the-curriculum efforts on such a collaborative foundation. And a team of researchers at Purdue University (Morgan et al.) has studied collaborative reading and writing in a number of settings, using differing research methodologies. In addition, the work of Andrea Lunsford and Lisa Ede demonstrates that this contextual element—collaboration—characterizes a great deal of the writing and reading on the job.

This research on writers, texts, readers, and contexts holds powerful pedagogical implications, many of which have no doubt already occurred to our readers.

III. PEDAGOGICAL IMPLICATIONS OF A RHETORIC OF WRITTEN COMMUNICATION

A rhetoric of written communication demands a dynamic balancing of speaker, listener, subject (of *ethos*, *pathos*, *logos*). And when a teacher introduces these elements into the writing classroom, she can expect learning to emerge. The interdependency of these elements creates galvanic tension, in terms not only of the rhetorical elements themselves, but also of the students, teacher, and texts.

The pedagogical implications for the teacher are manifold, most prominent being that she must learn to share her authority, thereby enabling students to experience, create, and evaluate their own and others' texts. One of the best ways teachers can share responsibility for learning is to provide "demonstrations," occasions for active learning for their students. In the terms of education researcher Frank Smith, demonstrations provide students opportunities to become so engaged that they really teach themselves; they forget that they are learning and take an active role in their own learning.

In fact, writing teachers can most easily provide students with demonstrations by adjusting writing assignments, making them (to use an overused term) "relevant" to the students' lives. Often, meaningful writing assignments are merely those that provide students with information on their intended audience, their purpose for writing, and the context of the communication—information that encourages students to harness the dynamics of the rhetorical triangle. Other teachers provide demonstrations by building their syllabi on a theme, such as "education" (cf. Bartholomae and Petrosky; Lunsford). A teacher in an Open Admissions college provided his students with demonstrations by building a syllabus on "work." Urging his students to meet in small groups, to speak out loud, to read and respond to one another's writing, to expect concrete details and supporting observations, this teacher watched as his class of low-paid, blue-collar manual workers reinvented their daily lives, sharing their experiences, critically analyzing their situations, and writing persuasively and feelingly about their lives. No longer was learning the retrieval and transmission of static information—from the teacher's head to the students'. Rather, learning became the dynamic interactions of the students, a

demonstration of their abilities to discover and create, think up and communicate their own knowledge. Once they realized their own rhetorical stance, the values and attitudes of their intended audience, and the importance of their message, their rhetorical triangles were balanced. In this case, choice of writing assignments indicated the teacher's willingness to share responsibility for classroom learning.

Hence, such a classroom transforms itself from uni- to polyvocal. The original rhetorical triangle, weighted fully on the teacher/speaker side, becomes a series of phase-shift rotations, rhetorical triangles that constantly achieve, lose, and reestablish rhetorical balance. Each shift, a fusion of rhetoric and dialectic, is determined by whose paper is being featured, who is serving as author, who is serving as audience, and how the in-draft text is being affected and effected by the speaker and audience. And ultimately, that original triangle, in re-creating itself, begins to round out and resemble an expanded circular universe of discourse.

To make the polyvocal, rhetorical classroom "work," students, too, must learn to share responsibility for their learning, and rely no longer solely on their teacher for grades, knowledge, approval, or ego gratification. What may be initially perceived as instability will soon be seen for what it is—dynamics. Once students begin to take advantage of these classroom dynamics—teacher and students alike working as sharers and evaluators—they will realize the potential for their own written communication. No longer will they be contented to serve as repositories for their teacher's knowledge, to write *for* and *to* only their teachers, to remain silent. Yet often and understandably, just transferring their allegiance from their teacher to their peers is difficult for them, accustomed as they are to years of passive learning. Accustomed as teachers are to years of one-way teaching and nearly total responsibility for learning (and teaching), many find relief in newly shared allegiance. Students need to know that in the rhetorical classroom, their teachers are willing to share their work, their responsibility, even their authority.

Student writers have, for too long, been writing in a vacuum: not only have they been given assignments that ask them to write for nobody (no audience) in particular, but those assignments, once completed, were not really read—only corrected, a fact Susan Miller points out in "The Student's Reader Is Always a Fiction." In the rhetorical writing classroom, students will broaden their intended audience from the teacher-evaluator to include their peers, carefully considering the responses and evaluations of those peers, perhaps more than they did those of their teachers. Many students will want to respond orally and in writing to classroom, in-draft texts and to participate in the final evaluation of themselves and their peers. Peers create an actual audience and often a reason for writing, for they provide response—

what Peter Elbow calls "the main experience that makes people want to write more" (130). In *Writing without Teachers*, Elbow writes about one student's thrill of working with her peers: "her words got through to the readers. She sent words out into the darkness and heard someone shout back. This made her want to do it again, and this is probably the most powerful thing that makes people improve their writing" (ibid.).

When students are involved in one another's writings, serving as senders and receivers of communication, as questioners of purpose, as judges of *ethos*, *pathos*, and *logos*, as refiners of style and tone, when they are respectfully attentive of one another's *author*-ity, when students have the opportunity to question responses to their drafts *as they draft*, when they coach as they are being coached, then they are indeed sharing the responsibility for their own learning and incorporating in their learning the dynamics of rhetorical theory.

The implications for a rhetoric of written communication go beyond those for the teacher and her students, however, to affect the very physical structure of the classroom itself. Always, or so it seems, students have sat in neat rows of nailed-down desks, discouraged from making so much as eye contact with their peers, asked to write in solitude. But as teachers and students begin to use rhetorical theory, begin to see that senders need the responses of receivers, that the universe, the "out there," plays an integral part in communication, and that messages are colored by all the elements in the rhetorical triangle, they will be unable to work in the traditional classroom environment. They will want tables or moveable desks so they can sit and work together. They will want to talk on the phone or through their computers both during and after school. They need to be together. And they need time.

Gone should be the days when students are asked to complete their writing in forty-eight minutes or to evaluate the work of their groups in forty-eight minutes. Gone should be the days when one draft—the first and final—is handed in for an unchangeable grade. Many schools, in fact, are moving toward the portfolio method of evaluation, which encourages students to gather up their best revisions for one end-of-the-term grade.[3] Thoughtful writing and thoughtful responding take time, time for planning, thinking, drafting, responding, revising, and polishing. Hence, classrooms themselves must be designed in response to the evolution of classroom practices as well as classroom schedules.

IV. ISSUES RAISED BY A RHETORIC OF WRITTEN COMMUNICATION

Teachers and students committed to examining the dynamic relationship among writers, audiences, texts, and contexts will face a number of important issues, foremost among them the complex question of ethics and language use. If we are not so much what we *eat* as what we say or write, if as Jacques Derrida claims, we don't write language so much as language *writes us*, then words can never ever be "mere" words again (*Of Grammatology* passim). Instead words are, to use Kenneth Burke's term, symbolic *acts* (*Language as Symbolic Action* passim); as Richard Weaver says, a speaker's words have *consequences*, and these consequences affect other people, texts, and context ("Language Is Sermonic" 221 ff). As language users, we thus must be responsible for our words, must take the responsibility for examining our own and others' language and seeing how well, how truly, it represents the speaker. We can do so playfully, through parody or spoofing, or we can do so most seriously, as in an analysis of the consequences of political doublespeak. But we—teachers and students alike—must carry out such analyses consistently and rigorously.

Once students grasp this principle of analytic responsibility, they become rhetors. They see writing and reading not as boring school-bound drills or as ways of packaging static information, but as ways of creating and re-creating themselves through and with others, as a student reported during a recent evaluation of one of our courses:

> When we first started this class, I couldn't *imagine* what you meant by our being rhetoricians, getting rhetorical stances of our own. What's all this, I thought? You're the teacher. You know a whole lot of stuff, and you better just *tell* it to us. Now I know that you really do know a lot of stuff, more even than I thought. But that's not what matters. What matters is what I know. And now I know that I'm making what I know in language, forming, transforming, and reforming myself with other people. What I know is we are all of us learners in progress. Even you! So—*wish me luck.*

Teachers, of course, are the ones who develop and nurture such an atmosphere, who set the terms within which an ethos of the classroom emerges. Building such an atmosphere implies that the teacher becomes a member/participant of the class, providing questions, tasks, and situations that will allow the class to experience what it means not to *reveal* knowledge but to *construct* it, to be learners-in-progress. This role is a demanding one, far more so than traditional teacherly roles have been.

In the final analysis, a rhetorical perspective on the teaching of writing pushes us outside our private selves, beyond our solitary teacherly or writerly desks, to a realization of the ways in which we all use language to create—or destroy—communities, societies, worlds. The writing classroom is one such world. And rhetorical theory provides us, together with our students, with the means of making that world, one that is rich in diversity, complex in meaning, and full of all the life our blended voices can give it.

NOTES

[1]We thank Gerald Nelms for helping with the citations and bibliography. We are also grateful to Jon Olson and Jamie Barlowe Kayes, whose sensible suggestions and supportive criticism helped us rewrite parts of the manuscript.

[2]When Kinneavy says that intention cannot be extracted from the author, he is not using *author* in the same way all other rhetoricians use it. Even rhetoricians and theorists do not always agree on the meanings of terms. While Wayne Booth discusses the "implied author" of a text, an author whose intention is discernible from that text, Kinneavy is talking the actual person who wrote the text, whose intention cannot be known. Theories (such as psychoanalytic, some feminist or Marxist theories) that attempt to or purport to reveal knowledge about real-person authors are *not* rhetorical theories. Yet these theories could not exist if rhetorical theories were not already in place.

[3]The portfolio method of assessment has been most thoroughly documented and argued for by Peter Elbow of University of Massachusetts-Amherst. The largest school to adopt a portfolio method of assessment is University of Minnesota, which, beginning in 1989, plans to use portfolios for evaluation in introductory composition as well as for promotion from junior to senior standing. In addition, they are piloting the use of portfolios for admission to University of Minnesota. Portfolios will soon be used by other members of the Alliance for Undergraduate Education.

WORKS CITED

Abrams, M. H. *The Mirror and the Lamp: Romantic Theory and the Critical Tradition*. New York: Oxford UP, 1953.

Aristotle. *The Rhetoric and the Poetics of Aristotle*. Trans. W. Rhys Roberts. New York: Modern Library, 1984.

Bartholomae, David, and Anthony Petrosky. *Facts, Artifacts, and Counterfacts: Theory and Method for a Reading and Writing Course*. Upper Montclair, NJ: Boynton/Cook, 1986.

Bleich, David. *Subjective Criticism*. Baltimore: Johns Hopkins UP, 1978.

———. *Readings and Feelings: An Introduction to Subjective Criticism*. Urbana, IL: NCTE, 1975.

———. "The Subjective Character of Critical Interpretation." *CE* 36 (1975): 739–55.

Booth, Wayne C. *Modern Dogma and the Rhetoric of Assent*. Chicago: U of Chicago P, 1974.

———. "The Rhetorical Stance." *Now Don't Try to Reason with Me: Essays and Ironies for a Credulous Age*. Chicago: U of Chicago P, 1970.

Bruffee, Kenneth. "Collaborative Learning and the 'Conversation of Mankind.'" *CE* 46 (1984): 635–52.

———. "The Brooklyn Plan: Attaining Intellectual Growth through Peer-Group Tutoring." *Liberal Education* 64 (1978): 447–69.

———. "Collaborative Learning: Some Practical Models." *CE* 34 (1973): 634–43.

Burke, Kenneth. *A Grammar of Motives* and *A Rhetoric of Motives*. Cleveland: World, 1962.

———. "Terministic Screens." *Language as Symbolic Action*. Berkeley: U of California P, 1966. 44–62.

Christensen, Francis. "A Generative Rhetoric of the Sentence." *CCC* 14 (1963): 155–61.

———. "A Generative Rhetoric of the Paragraph." *CCC* 16 (1968): 144–56.

Coe, Richard. *Toward a Grammar of Passages*. Carbondale, IL: Southern Illinois UP, 1987.

Daly, John. "The Effects of Writing Apprehension on Message Encoding." *Journalism Quarterly* 54 (1977): 566–72.

———. "Writing Apprehension and Writing Competency." *Journal of Educational Research* 72 (1978): 10–14.

Derrida, Jacques. *Of Grammatology*. Trans. Gayatri Chakrovorty Spivak. Baltimore: Johns Hopkins UP, 1974.

Ede, Lisa S., and Andrea A. Lunsford. "Collaborative Learning: Lessons from the World of Work." *WPA* 9 (1986): 17–26.

———. "Let Them Write—Together." *English Quarterly* 18 (1985): 119–27.

———. "Why Write . . . Together?" *Rhetoric Review* 1 (1983): 150–57.

Elbow, Peter. *Embracing Contraries*. New York: Oxford UP, 1986.

———. *Writing with Power*. New York: Oxford UP, 1981.

———. *Writing without Teachers*. New York: Oxford UP, 1973.

Flower, Linda, and John R. Hayes. "Uncovering Cognitive Processes in Writing: An Introduction to Protocol Analysis." *Research on Writing*. Ed. P. Mosenthal, S. Walmsley, and L. Tamor. London: Longmans, 1982. 207–20.

Haring-Smith, Tori, ed. *A Guide to Writing Programs, Writing Centers, Peer-Tutoring Programs, and Writing Across the Curriculum*. Glenview, IL: Scott, 1985.

Iser, Wolfgang. *The Act of Reading: A Theory of Aesthetic Response*. Baltimore: Johns Hopkins UP, 1974.

———. *The Implied Reader*. Baltimore: Johns Hopkins UP, 1974.

Kinneavy, James L. *A Theory of Discourse*. New York: Norton, 1971.

Larson, Richard L. "Discovery through Questioning: A Plan for Teaching Rhetorical Invention." *CE* 30 (1968): 126–34.

Lauer, Janice. "Heuristics and Composition." *CCC* 21 (1970): 396–404.

Lunsford, Andrea A. "Assignments for Basic Writers: Unresolved Issues and Needed Research." *Journal of Basic Writing* 5 (1986): 87–99.

Miller, Susan. "The Student's Reader Is Always a Fiction." *Journal of Advanced Composition* 5 (1984): 15–29.

Morgan, Meg, Nancy Allen, Teresa Moore, Dianne Atkinson, and Craig Snow. "Collaborative Writing in the Classroom." *The Bulletin.* (Sept. 1987): 20–26.

Ogden, C. K., and I. A. Richards. *The Meaning of Meaning: A Study of the Influences of Language upon Thought and of the Science of Symbolism.* New York: Harcourt, 1936.

Petty, Richard E., Thomas M. Ostrom, and Timothy Brock, eds. *Cognitive Responses in Persuasion.* Hillsdale, NJ: Earlbaum, 1981.

Richards, I. A. *The Philosophy of Rhetoric.* New York: Oxford UP, 1936.

Rose, Mike. *Writer's Block: The Cognitive Dimension.* Carbondale, IL: Southern Illinois UP, 1984.

Rosenblatt, Louise. *Literature as Exploration.* 3d ed. New York: Barnes, 1976.

Rosenblatt, Louise. *The Reader, the Text, the Poem: The Transactional Theory of the Literary Work.* Carbondale, IL: Southern Illinois UP, 1978.

Smith, Frank. "Research Update: Demonstrations, Engagements, and Sensitivity—A Revised Approach to Language Learning." *Language Arts* 58 (1981): 103–12.

Weaver, Richard M. *Language Is Sermonic: Richard M. Weaver on the Nature of Rhetoric.* Eds. Richard L. Johannesen, Rennard Strickland, and Ralph T. Eubanks. Baton Rouge, LA: Louisiana State UP, 1970.

Witte, Stephen. "Pre-Text and Composing." *CCC* 38 (1987): 397–425.

Young, Richard E., Alton L. Becker, and Kenneth L. Pike. *Rhetoric: Discovery and Change.* New York: Harcourt, 1970.

Let Them Write—Together

—Lisa Ede and Andrea Lunsford

In 1978, the Ford Foundation published a special report on writing as part of its series of Papers About Learning. In this report, *Balance the Basics: Let Them Write* (1978), Donald Graves argued strenuously for the importance of writing in education:

> People want to write. The desire to express is relentless. People want others to know what they hold to be truthful. They need the sense of authority that goes with authorship. They need to detach themselves from experience and examine it by writing. Then they need to share what they have discovered through writing. (p. 4)

He also argued that what he called a "process-conference" approach represents the most efficient and effective way to help students improve their writing skills. In the years since Graves' report, many language arts and English teachers have incorporated this approach, with its emphasis on meaning and communication rather than form and the mastery of discrete language skills, into their classrooms. They have also followed Graves and other scholars, such as James Britton and James Moffett, by including group activities as a regular part of their students' language arts experience.

Despite these innovations, however, most high school and college English teachers still cling to highly traditional assumptions about the nature of writing and of authorship—assumptions so deeply ingrained that they rarely are made explicit, much less critically examined. One such assumption, which informs such diverse pedagogical activities as making assignments, assessing students' writing skills, and responding to student writing, is that writing is necessarily and inevitably a solitary activity. If questioned, many English teachers would undoubtedly say that they know of situations where individuals—members of a scientific research team or business people writing a report—collaborate on a single written product. But most would insist that what one of our colleagues once called real writing, and certainly school writing, can only be an individual enterprise. According to this view, which is common throughout the humanities and which reflects essentially Romantic notions about the relationship between inspiration, individual genius, and the authoring of texts, the authority that "goes with authorship" (Graves, 1978) most genuinely derives from a person's individual struggle to shape meaning through language.

Consequently, except for the very early grades (where a kindergartener or first grader may tell a story which the teacher writes down, thus jointly producing a book, or where slightly older children may work together to write and illus-

trate a narrative), our high school and college students largely experience writing as a solitary—and, hence, for some of them, isolating—activity. They may discuss their ideas with fellow students as part of a brainstorming session, or they may receive formal or informal responses to their writing with suggestions for revision from their peers. But when they sit down to write, they almost always do so alone.

Important research suggests that the concept of authorship as inherently single or solitary is both theoretically naive and pedagogically flawed. It has become almost a truism, for instance, to argue (with Britton, Emig, and others) that students must experience writing as a meaningful, purposive activity if they are to improve as writers, that writing in the schools must function not only as a means of testing but of learning. These researchers, as well as others who study early language acquisition and cognitive-developmental theory, insist that learning always occurs as part of an interaction, either between the learner and the environment or, more frequently, between the learner and peers. Evidence in support of this hypothesis has been provided by Abercrombie, Bruffee, and Garth, who have studied the collaborative learning process in detail. Their studies confirm that students often learn both skills (such as writing) and content material more effectively and efficiently when they do so as part of a group. They do so not because group activities somehow "trick" students into caring about their school work—although group work can indeed be an effective motivational device—but because they all learn most of what is important to them through a process that combines social interaction with individual assimilation.

Finally, recent studies in such disciplines as philosophy, anthropology, literary criticism, and linguistics all recognize, though for different reasons and from different perspectives, that traditional assumptions which represent knowledge as individually derived (Descartes' *I think therefore I am*) are highly questionable. Since the turn of the twentieth century, the image of the solitary individual as the source or foundation of all knowledge, all literature worth the name, has met increasing challenges. Perhaps the most direct assault has come from such philosophers as the later Wittgenstein, Heidegger, and Dewey, all of whom broke from the epistemological tradition to, as Richard Rorty notes in *Philosophy and the Mirror of Nature*, "set aside the notion of 'the mind' common to Descartes, Locke, and Kant—as a special subject of study, located in inner space, containing elements or processes which make knowledge possible" (p. 6). One effect of what we may, without too much exaggeration, call an epistemological revolution is a new view of the role of language, a view which no longer defines language as incidental to the creation of knowledge or belief (a second-best tool which must at times substitute for the more accurate discourse of mathematics and logic) but as itself constitutive of knowledge. This view of language (see, e.g., Geertz, 1983 or Kuhn, 1970) strongly challenges our accepted notions of the nature or authorship. In its more extreme forms, as in some of Derrida's work, the conventional relationship is almost reversed. We do not write language, Derrida and others say; rather, language writes us. Other literary theorists, such as Eagleton in *Literary Theory: An Introduction* (1983), emphasize that our obsession with the solitary "contemplative individual self, bowed over its books, striving to gain touch with experience, truth, reality, history, or tradition" (p. 196) must be replaced by what Eagleton calls a "new" rhetoric based on social relations between "writers and readers, orators and audiences [embedded in their] social purposes and conditions" (Eagleton, 1983, p. 206). In this view, an individual writing alone is still participating in social experience, since the language he or she grows into as a child comes with its own rich history. Even when writing alone in a garret, in other words, the writer is not alone.

The research described above questions the assumption that writing is an inherently solitary activity, challenging teachers to revise pedagogical practices accordingly. We believe, therefore, that for a wide range of theoretical reasons as well as for practical reasons suggested by our own research it is indeed time to let students write—together. In the space remaining, then, we will supplement the theoretical arguments already presented with practical justification for incorporating collaborative writing in the language arts curriculum derived from the research project we have undertaken under the sponsorship of the Fund for The Improvement of Post-Secondary Education's Shaughnessy Scholars Program. In addition, we will detail ways that teachers can build in more opportunities for group writing activities. Any pedagogical strategy has potential drawbacks or problems, of course, and group writing is no exception: we will describe these problems and their appropriate solutions. Finally, we will close by noting the benefits of group writing as we have experienced them both as writers and teachers.

Our original interest in what we have come to call collaborative writing, the production of a single text by co-authors or group authors, grows directly out of our own experiences. Longtime friends, we first began to write together by chance. Since working together seemed both natural and productive, we continued occasionally to write together. What seemed natural to us, however, appeared anything but natural to our colleagues, whose responses to our collaboration, ranging from astonishment to dismay, forced us to examine our experience more critically. Our analysis progressed from casual reading and discussion to a largely anecdotal early article (Ede & Lunsford, 1983) in which we set forth a number of unanswered questions: What specific features distinguish the processes of co-authorship and group authorship (or collaborative writing, as we have since come to call it)? How frequently and in what situations are members of representative professions called upon to write *collaboratively*? Is the emphasis on or weight of various cognitive and rhetorical strategies different when writing collaboratively than when writing alone? What epistemological implications does collaborative writing hold for traditional notions of "creativity" and "originality," terms that almost always refer to single authorship? "What are the pedagogical implications of collaborative writing? These research questions in turn led us to a lengthy formal research project.

This project, now nearing completion, has taught us a number of important lessons. Probably the most significant of these is, quite simply, that people in a range of professions regularly write as part of teams or groups, and that their ability to participate successfully in such collaborative writing efforts is essential both to their productivity and job satisfaction. The evidence for this assertion comes largely from the first stage of our project. In an effort to determine just how many people in the "real world" write collaboratively and the kinds of collaborative writing they do, we surveyed 200 randomly selected members of six professional associations: The American Council of Consulting Engineers, the American Institute of Chemists, the American Psychological Association, the International City Management Association, the Professional Services Management Association, and the Society for Technical Communication. Of the 1200 members surveyed, 530 persons (or almost 50% of our sample), completed the questionnaire. And of these 530 respondents, 87% reported that they have written as part of a team or group.

The extent of this collaboration is perhaps best indicated by participants' responses to a question which asked them to "indicate how frequently, in general, you work on the following types of writing, distinguishing between writing done alone or with one or more persons." We listed thirteen types of writing, from letters and lecture notes to reports, proposals, and books. Although the frequency of response varied from type to type, some participants indicated that they had very often, often, or occasionally worked on each type or writing with one or more persons. Finally, and perhaps most important, 59% of those who had participated in co- or group writing projects indicated that they found such collaboration to be "productive" (45%) or "very productive" (14%).

At present, we are engaged in follow-up studies—a longer, more detailed questionnaire sent to seventy-two carefully selected respondents from the first survey and four to six case studies with people who regularly write collaboratively on the job—which we expect will deepen our understanding of the dynamics of collaborative writing. But even our first survey results, preliminary as they are, provide significant evidence that upon graduation many students will be called upon not just to write, but to write with others. In addition, our own experience as writers tells us that we are constantly collaborating with others as we write, that even in our single-authored essays we are indebted, directly or indirectly, to a whole range of people in ways that we could never fully acknowledge.

Yet, as we have noted, the way we teach writing belies both our experience and our research by positing a model of single authorship, a model strongly reinforced by our system of testing, which of course proscribes any form of collaboration. The question of definition, then, is crucial. Put most briefly, is our current definition of writing, and of authorship, a reductive and hence a constraining one? Theoretical and practical reasons as well as our own experience all suggest that the answer to this question is "yes." As a result, we believe that our efforts should therefore be directed toward understanding those historical and social forces that have led us to define writing as a solitary act and, ultimately, toward providing support for a redefinition which would not only legitimatize but encourage collaboration in writing. In addition to raising questions of definition, our research suggests that collaborative writing draws on different cognitive and procedural strategies than does single authorship. In light of these findings, we need to work toward devising a model of collaborative writing and to ask how such a model might compare to those (such as the cognitive process model proposed by Flower and Hayes) which posit single authorship.

Answering these questions will require a great deal of research time and effort, commodities that many of us find all too scarce. On a more practical level, however, we can act to bring about some changes in our own classrooms by building in more and better opportunities for students to write together. Many teachers are already using the peer response and peer editing groups recommended by Peter Elbow, James Moffett, and Kenneth Bruffee. In such groups, members usually respond to a piece of writing produced by one student (though the means of response varies from one theorist to the next), who then revises the writing on the basis of the peer responses. We believe that using such peer response groups is the best and most effective way to introduce students to collaborative or group writing. Teachers who use such groups in their classes report a number of benefits: group members provide an immediate, concrete audience, often the first one a student has encountered; interest level is generally high, since students are inherently interested in what their peers think; the teacher becomes a helper rather than a judge; and emphasis is put on revision, with its obvious rewards. These benefits seem powerful enough to sug-

gest that peer group response and peer editing can add a dynamic dimension to any writing class.

Once students are comfortable with group work in general, however, we recommend that teachers expand on the collaborative aspect inherent in peer response in one or more of the following ways:

1. Ask student group members to respond to one student's writing and then to work together on revising the draft.
2. Ask students to work in groups to solve a problem or accomplish a task that is already part of the teacher's plan. Provide, for example, a set of data or particulars—in random or scrambled order—and ask the group to use those data to write a well-organized paragraph together.
3. On the basis of class discussion, provide a thesis or proposition which the groups will work on together to work into one or two paragraphs.
4. Pose a question or set of questions that the group will write a response to. Then use these group writings to lead to a class discussion of a particular topic or issue.
5. Ask students to attend some function (another class, a film, a concert, an exhibit) with members of the group and then work together to write a summary of the event.

As Garth (1983) notes in *Learning in Groups*, there are two essential elements to successful collaborative learning: an active learning process involving peer interaction; and faculty guidance. Learning groups themselves may vary in size from two to seven students, though we prefer five as the ideal number. The role that groups can play in any teacher's class may also vary widely. Some teachers structure an entire class around collaborative groups; others use them as a means of carrying out only one specific project. And some teachers use groups mainly as a means of organizing class discussions. Because learning groups must be carefully integrated into any course, only the teacher can decide how best to do so. Nevertheless, the following teaching tips may prove useful to teachers attempting to bring more collaborative learning experiences into their classrooms.

1. The most effective groups generally have members with a variety of viewpoints and skills. Therefore, teachers should form the groups themselves, mixing ability levels, sexes, leadership qualities, etc.
2. As Michaelsen (1983) stresses in his essay in *Learning in Groups*, "Group tasks must be carefully structured so that students understand the kind of 'product' the group is to produce, and sufficiently challenging for information from a majority of group members to be required. Studies have found that groups are more effective than individuals in solving problems that require either the pooling of information or the application of concepts that have been mastered in the abstract" (p. 17).
3. Teachers sometimes use learning groups in less formal or product-centered ways, often to focus class discussion. The

following outline represents one generally successful way of organizing class discussion groups. Unlike groups involved in a long-term class project, the composition of discussion groups may vary throughout the term.

   a. The teacher groups students and poses a problem (based on readings, lectures, etc.) to be discussed.

   b. The groups meet and appoint recorders, who take notes on the discussions and eventually report to the class.

   c. The group discusses the problem or issue posed by the teacher. One goal is to achieve some consensus, without squelching minority opinions.

   d. During the discussion, the teacher moves among the students, helping groups which are having trouble focusing their discussion by posing questions or suggesting possible stratgies.

   e. Once the groups have completed their discussion and agreed with the recorder on his or her conclusions, the class moves back into a single large group.

   f. With the teacher acting as moderator, the recorders report the results of each group's discussion.

   g. Finally, the class as a whole attempts to achieve a consensus, if not on conclusions then at least on major questions and problems.

4. A group grade on a collaborative project is generally necessary to reinforce students' commitment.

5. Group activities early in a term may need to be structured in more specific and detailed ways than later activities. Students who have never participated in collaborative learning experiences previously need time and careful guidance in order to adjust.

6. It is helpful to address students' anxiety about group work (concerns about grades or nervousness about working with peers) directly in class.

The possible assignments we have described briefly here carry the obvious advantage of involving students in writing collaboratively. As the teaching tips indicate, however, they also allow students to practice a number of important skills: arriving at a consensus; looking at an issue from a number of differing viewpoints; learning to listen carefully and to respect the views of others; inferring sound conclusions from particular instances. Such skills are crucial to much that we do, and they appear to be particularly important to successful work-related writing. In addition, such exercises graphically demonstrate the ways in which we learn from and with one another and the ways in which this essentially collaborative process shapes much of what we think.

We believe that these are considerable practical advantages. And yet we do not wish to present group writing as some sort of classroom panacea. In fact as our "teaching tips" suggest, the kinds of group writing tasks we are advocating present a number of problems on which we wish to elaborate. In the first place, students may well resist writing in groups because of their own preconceptions about the nature of writing or for any number of other reasons. The teacher must therefore prepare students for group work, perhaps by demonstrating its effectiveness. In our classes, for instance, students from the previous term often come in to model a group project for students. Another means of encouraging participation in group writing might be to invite one or two people who typically write in groups (a technical writer, for example, or a researcher in almost any scientific field) to come and talk with the students about their experiences with group or collaborative writing.

Once students are predisposed to try group work, however, the teacher faces yet another potential problem: how to structure group writing tasks and define student roles. In our experience, simply putting students in loosely-organized groups too often results in aimless chit-chat among group members, an obvious waste of time. This problem can be avoided by providing the groups with a work sheet or plan of action which describes the problem to be addressed and outlines the steps that must be taken by group members to accomplish the task. As soon as is practicable, the teacher should enlist student participation in designing the group writing projects or "problems" and in working out the necessary plans and assigning the role each member is to play. Once the groups actually begin to work on the task at hand, the teacher can move freely among them, monitoring progress, "troubleshooting," and joining in whenever and wherever necessary. Doing so will help keep the students focused on their task and on the most effective and efficient means of accomplishing it.

A final potential problem involves how to "count" group writing. To be most effective, such writing should eventually be evaluated in some way and a mark or some other form or response given. Ideally, the teacher will begin with one or two ungraded group writing projects, such as those intended to lead to class discussion, and move to a project which requires several drafts to which the teacher responds just as any other group member. Formal group projects can then be evaluated in several ways. The teacher may decide to award one common mark to all members of the group, or to mark each member's contribution separately, according to a set of agreed-upon criteria. On the other hand, the teacher may wish to set up an "evaluation panel" (made up of several students and the teacher) whose job it is to evaluate the group writing according to criteria established in advance by the whole class. Whatever the means of evaluation and/or response, students must be assured that they will have a number of opportunities to write in groups—and hence a number of opportunities to make sure that each member does his or her fair share of the work.

In spite of the very real problems associated with successful group writing projects, the benefits of such writing seem to us to fully justify its use. Perhaps most importantly, group writing demonstrates the way in which we share or collaborate in making sense out of the world around us, in creating our own realities and selves. In such demonstrations, moreover, the teacher becomes in effect another member of the group, thus fostering the kind of student-centered classrooms most of us strive for. Group writing also can provide a powerful socializing force, particularly for students in their middle- and high school years when peer pressures sometimes have negative rather than positive results. In his essay "Collaborative Learning and the 'Conversation of Mankind,'" Kenneth Bruffee (1984) identifies the possible "negative efforts of peer group influence: conformity, anti-intellectualism, intimidation, and leveling-down of quality," and argues that these pitfalls can be avoided by making "social engagement in intellectual pursuits a genuine part of students' educational development" (p. 652).

Another significant benefit to be gained from group writing we have as yet only hinted at. The kind of group writing tasks we are recommending integrate all of the communicative arts—listening, speaking, reading, and writing. Thus a carefully structured group writing project provides practice in each one of these communicative arts at the same time that it demonstrates the ways in which each one builds on all the others. And, finally, group writing offers some very pragmatic benefits for both student and teachers: it allows students to gain some first-hand experience in group dynamics and in a kind of writing our research indicates they will most likely encounter on the job; and group writing tasks save valuable teacher time. The time spent responding to thirty-five individual paragraphs, for instance, is dramatically reduced when only six group-written paragraphs must be read. The time thus saved can then be devoted to working with individuals or groups of students and to structuring additional group projects.

Collaborative writing should, of course, constitute only one part of a student's classroom writing experience. We hope we have provided sufficient evidence to suggest, however, that group writing does deserve to play a part in that experience, for it offers a powerful means of engaging students in the myriad mental, physical, and social acts which the term "writing" includes. We urge teachers to join us, therefore, in going beyond Donald Graves's injunction to "let them write." We say, in addition, let them write—together.

REFERENCES

Abercrombie, M.L.J. (1960). *The anatomy of judgment*. Harmondsworth: Penguin.

Britton, J., Burgess, T., Martin, N., McLeod, A., & Rosen, H. (1975). *The development of writing ability, 11-18*. London: Macmillan.

Bruffee, K. (1984). Collaborative learning and the 'Conversation of mankind', *College English*, 46, 635–652.

Bruffee, K. (1983). Writing and reading as collaborative or social acts. In J.N. Hays (Ed.), *The Writer's Mind*. Urbana, IL: National Council of Teachers of English.

Eagleton, T. (1983). *Literary theory: An introduction*. Minneapolis: University of Minnesota Press.

Ede, L. and & Lunsford, A.A. (1983) Why write—together? *Rhetoric Review*, 2, 150–157.

Emig, J. (1983). *The web of meaning*. Upper Montclair, NJ: Boynton/Cook.

Garth, R. (Ed.). (1983). *Learning in Groups*. San Francisco: Jossey-Bass.

Geertz, C. (1983). *Local knowledge*. New York: Basic Books.

Graves, D. (1978). *Balance the basics: Let them write*. Ford Foundation Report.

Kuhn, T. (1970). *The structure of scientific revolutions* (2nd ed.) Chicago: University of Chicago Press.

Michaelsen, J. (1983). Team learning in large classes. In R. Garth (Ed.) *Learning in groups*. San Francisco: Jossey-Bass.

Moffett, J. (1968). *Teaching the universe of discourse*. Boston: Houghton-Mifflin.

Rorty, R. (1979). *Philosophy and the mirror of nature*. Princeton: Princeton University Press, 1979.

Responding to Student Writing

—Sue V. Lape and Cheryl Glenn

Successful writers would be the first to caution teachers against the ideal of the perfected text, especially as it applies to beginning writers. All writers, however successful, are beginning writers, every time they take up the pen or keyboard.

Professional writers interviewed for the *Writers at Work, Paris Review Series* admit they almost *never* know, before they write, exactly what they want to say. James Thurber warns that a writer shouldn't know "too much where he is going." If he does, he runs into "old man blueprint—old man propaganda." Dorothy Canfield Fisher once compared writing the first draft with skiing down a steep slope she wasn't sure she was clever enough to manage. "Get black on white," was de Maupassant's advice. Write whatever occurs to you and don't worry about neatness.

Experienced writers begin writing to "catch a glimpse of what they may see" and then they "revise—and revise and revise—to make it come clear," says Donald Murray. What these writers know is that by refining their writing through a series of rewrites, or drafts, they will eventually produce a written piece with lucidity and correctness. The problem of responding to student essays, then, lies not so much with the teacher as it does with the system of the *single-draft essay.* How can we as teachers of writing encourage our students to move successfully through the rewriting process, from discovery to final draft? Often, by "shutting up," according to Donald Murray, himself a writer and teacher of writers. Teachers must learn to be still while students are struggling through the early stages of the writing process. The teacher must play the "listening game," as Murray calls it.

The assumptions which underlie the listening teacher approach to writing directly affect the responses the teacher makes on student papers. "The listening teacher believes that his students' papers are the content of the course," according to Murray. The teacher does not "put content" into the students' work, but "draws out what is already there." Students are always respected as writers who are working to fulfill their potential as communicators—in other words, as working writers. There is no "right" way, only the "best" way. That is why many teachers use the portfolio method for evaluating student writing since it encourages students to take responsibility for their writing successes. With the portfolio method, student writers submit only their best work for final evaluation; early drafts are not graded. This system, of course, does not mean that the teacher cannot respond to student writing at the initial draft stage, but he or she must do so with caution. Nancy Sommers points out that appropriation of student texts occurs particularly when teachers "identify er-

rors in usage, diction, and style" in an initial draft. Comments on comma splices and sentence fragments are not appropriate for an exploratory draft that may, at this stage, be nothing more than an extended freewrite. Rather those comments which offer feedback and encourage learning are most appropriate in the early stages of the writing process. The paragraph below is taken from the initial draft of a student writer, Mindy. Although the paragraph displays some obvious surface errors, Mindy's teacher, rather than focusing on the student's weak points at this early stage, has chosen instead to concentrate on the essay's potential strengths because he realizes that student writers often lack self-confidence. Mindy's teacher wants to encourage rather than discourage her growth as a writer.

Strong opening, Mindy. Are you prepared to back it up?

Pit bulls aren't not naturally violent. Its their environment and treatment by their owners that determines how they will act. You shouldn't abuse your dog. Doing so will naturally make him more vicious.

Good examples. Anything else?

Not feeding him, beating on him, keeping him chained up, and not showing him attention or love are things

Terrific! You're writing from experience. Be sure to add your own examples.

that should be avoided. My dog is a pit bull and he is one of the sweetest dogs I know. I would trust this dog around any child. What you put into him is what you will get out of him in the end.

Good Summary Sentence. Sounds as if you've discovered your thesis.

Like Murray's "listening teacher," this instructor has signaled to Mindy that he expects her to examine her own evolving writing and to make choices and changes based upon her best judgment not his. Of course, the student will need the teacher's guidance in learning to make those choices, but this teacher knows that Mindy does not need his constant and overbearing presence to learn to write well. In fact, it may not be the teacher alone who responds to the student's paper, but other student writers as well.

Peer responding in the writing classroom may be one of the most problematic concepts of the new process approach to writing. Not only are modern theorists asking teachers to relinquish their hold on student essays, they are also suggesting that peers assume the role of informed readers in responding to student essays. "How," the teacher wonders, "can students who don't even know what questions to ask about their own texts query another's?" The answer is simple. Show them.

One very effective method for making students aware of strong writing is to reproduce, on a regular basis, examples of student writing (anonymously, of course) taken from journal entries and drafts of essays. Have student writers underline words, phrases, sentences, chunks, and paragraphs they especially like and ask them to explain, *in their own words*, why. Student writers should also practice identifying trouble spots in the text: what's not working and why, again *in their own words*. In this way students become accustomed to effective and less effective use of language. They also, as Mary K. Healy points out, "grow in confidence about their ability to recognize strong writing." Individual responses can be shared with the class either by reading selections aloud or by writing them on the board (an overhead projector works for some people, but the blackboard is less intimidating because it invites student participation). Once students have become accustomed to responding to sample writing in this way, they are ready to work with other writers in the classroom. Of course the teacher may intervene at any time in the responding process, either by collecting and examining student drafts, or by facilitating the exchange between peer reader and student writer.

Healy offers suggestions for the use of student writing response groups in the classroom. She begins with a whole-class writing assignment. When the first drafts are completed, Healy chooses several for reproduction on an overhead projector, being careful to impress upon her students the difference between *evaluation* and *response*. *Evaluation* is the final "assessment" of a work that has gone through a drafting process, and is the teacher's responsibility. *Response*, on the other hand, is a reaction to an initial or working draft in the form of "questions to the writer about the content or form of the piece." Response is the responsibility of both student writers and the teacher.

Shortly after the class responding session, Healy duplicates selected drafts of student papers (always with their permission) and asks groups of students to respond to the papers, writing their responses directly on the duplicate sheets. Healy collects the sheets, examines the responses and then comments on them. In this way she is able to monitor and guide the progress and effectiveness of student comments.

In *Writing without Teachers*, Peter Elbow suggests other effective ways for shifting the responding responsibility from the teacher to groups of students. Students in Elbow's classroom read each text with care; students may even take essays home for a more considered opinion. Once in a dialogue with the writers, peer responders always begin by pointing out the text's strengths; then they react to it, sharing their

valid and richly varied perceptions. Elbow also encourages "criterion-based feedback and reader-based feedback." For the first, the writer confronts the reader with four fundamental questions:

1. What is the quality of the content of my writings: the ideas, perceptions, point of view?
2. How well is the writing organized?
3. How effective is the language?
4. Are there mistakes or inappropriate choices in usage?

For reader-based feedback, the writer asks:

1. What was happening to you moment by moment as you read my work?
2. Summarize the writing: give your understanding of what it says.
3. Make up some images for the writing and the transaction it creates for you.

Teacher responses on paper can also serve as models for student responses, but beware. As a group, English teachers feel well prepared to march lockstep through papers, identify errors, and write appropriate comments. In fact, research shows just the opposite. As a group, we are inconsistent: we neither search out the same kinds of errors nor mark the problems we claim to be interested in solving. Several years ago, Sarah Freedman accounted for these differences in reading student papers. According to her research, we only think we are using a rubric when, in reality, we are influenced by content, organization, mechanics, and sentence structure, in that order. We must also be aware, as teachers, that many of the comments we make are misunderstood by our students: they see no hierarchy in our comments, so they spend energy "fixing" the little, easily repaired problems in their text, unsure of what to do with the larger questions concerning content. Often, students are actually derailed by our comments, trying so hard to please us that they lose their own sense of purpose in writing. Let's look at a "before" and "after" model for responding to student writing taken from Erica Lindemann's *A Rhetoric for Writing Teachers*.

As time changes people's views and outlooks on

life change with it. My parents grew up with completely

sp.   *sp.*
diffrent standards in a completely diffrent time.

Because of the time I grew up in and the time I live

in, my life differs from the lives of my parents.

cliché

Modern society offers more aid to young people—
jobs, school, financial—that my parents could never
receive. Because of this aid my life has been more
free than theirs ever was. I have more free time on
my hands than they ever did. My parents were and
are always working to keep and get, the things needed
for survival.

[handwritten: ?? (above "that my"); rep. (above "free"); circles around "were", "are", and comma]

Note that the comments here simply identify and correct errors, except perhaps for the "clichés," which signal to the student that his prose lacks freshness, but offer no clue as to how to improve it. Without giving David (the writer of this piece) any encouragement for developing his own critical reading skills ("let me do it for you; teacher knows best"), the instructor still expects him to transform his tired language into something new and exciting—a mixed message! The next example demonstrates a much more helpful, and we might add respectful, response to David's paper.

[handwritten: Beginning a paper is tough, isn't it? Notice how the sentences in this first paragraph repeat one basic idea three times.]

As time changes people's views and outlooks on life
change with it. My parents grew up with completely
diffrent standards in a completely diffrent time.
[handwritten checkmarks above "diffrent" twice]

Because of the time I grew up in, and the time I live
[handwritten: How does it differ?]
in, my life differs from the lives of my parents.

Modern society offers more aid to young people—
[handwritten: Do you have a job? Tell me about it.]
jobs, school, financial—that my parents could never
receive. Because of this aid my life has been more
free than theirs ever was. I have more free time on
my hands than they ever did. My parents were, and
are, always working to keep and get things needed for
survival in this life. *[handwritten: Specifically, what did your parents have to worry about that you do not? Do you think having to work hard for a goal might be an advantage?]*

Notice that the teacher has not identified all of the errors in David's first two paragraphs, recognizing that he cannot possibly work on everything at once. The teacher also realizes, as many teachers do not, that David's errors are the result not of carelessness or irrationality, but of thinking; therefore, the teacher's comments don't just "label problems." Instead, they emphasize how and why communication fails. Furthermore, the comments create a dialogue between writer and reader, rather than between student and teacher. The reader's questions and positive comments not only prompt a response from David, they act as a *model*—they encourage him to ask similar questions of himself as he writes; in other words, they enhance learning. But isn't this a lot of work for the teacher? Isn't it much simpler just to rake the page with a red pen? Yes and no. If students are to "learn from what you write in the margins" of their essays, Richard Larson reminds us, and thus become responsible for their own writing successes, "your observations must be clear and self-explanatory." In his article "Training New Teachers of Composition in the Writing of Comments," Larson offers the following advice on responding to student papers, advice which is appropriate for all teachers, regardless of experience.

1. Use marginal comments primarily to call the student's attention to some particular strength or weakness in his or her work—usually a strength or weakness of detail . . . one that can be located *precisely*, and try not to limit your comment to matter of mechanics alone.

2. Use correction symbols only where the error will be obvious to the student once it is pointed out. Avoid letting *Log* stand for an error in Logic; don't just write *cl* if you think the passage is unclear. Instead assume that the student would not have made the error in logic or permitted the lack of clarity if he or she had known it was present. Explain, in a phrase or two, precisely where the difficulty lies and why the passage is open to criticism. Reread your comment and ask yourself: would this comment make the source of the difficulty clear to me, if I had made the mistake without realizing it was a mistake?

3. Avoid using terse queries like "what?" or "how come?" or "so what?" If you feel the student's reason is unsatisfactory, explain your judgment precisely enough to let the student know where the thinking is faulty. Don't leave the student guessing that your notation simply reveals an honest difference of opinion between the two of you, or that your opinions on the point at issue are unjustifiably rigid.

4. In general, avoid arguing with the student. Ask for explanations only when the reasoning is genuinely hidden and needs to be disclosed. Try not to quibble over matters of diction and sentence structure that only reflect differences between your taste and that of the student.

5. Do not hesitate to note places where the student's thinking is especially effective, the style especially telling, the organization notably well handled.

The key here is specificity. Relate the comments to the text and make certain that your responses model clear, concise, writing. In the general comment, which comes at the end of the essay, Larson reminds teachers that their response must "support and be supported by" the marginal comments. Larson also suggests that teachers should:

1. Make the general comment more than a list or summary of errors in mechanics and syntax.
2. Point out the strengths or good features of the essay, rather than focusing exclusively on weaknesses.
3. Let the student know how well he or she had met the substantive, structural, and stylistic problems posed by the assignment.
4. Concentrate on the most important difficulties of substance, structure, and style that affect the paper as a whole. Specify in the comment what the student's principal aims should be in revising.
5. Try to see that the comment is constructive—that it has "transfer value." That is, try to help the student to improve his or her work on future papers.

Finally, Larson cautions teachers to remember that in commenting on student papers, they are neither a proofreader (responsible for normalizing spelling or punctuation) nor an editor (responsible for improving diction, idiom, and possibly syntax) nor a judge (responsible for rendering a verdict of "good" or "bad"), but rather a respectful and therefore respected reader from whom the student can expect to get help in improving his or her reasoning, organization, and style.

We have said a great deal here about the student-centered versus teacher-centered classroom when what we are really advocating is the *writing-centered* classroom. As long as grades are given for academic performance, there is no question as to who is the final "authority" in the class-room. But until the grade must be posted, it is the writing that must be the focus of the composition classroom, as it moves through the various stages of revision from invention to exploratory draft, from first working draft to second until, finally, it comes to rest but never perfection in the final draft.

"Do you rewrite?" Frank O'Connor was asked by an interviewer. "Endlessly, endlessly, endlessly. And keep on rewriting, even after it's published." O'Connor also said that there is "only one person a writer should listen to. It's not any damn critic. It's the *reader*." When the teacher reads and responds as critic, writing suffers and sometimes dies. When the teacher becomes a respectful reader, and models that same concerned response for student readers, writing thrives.

WORKS CITED

Cowley, Malcolm, ed. *The Paris Review Series, Writers at Work.* First Series. New York: Viking, 1953.

Elbow, Peter. *Writing with Power: Techniques for Mastering the Writing Process.* New York: Oxford UP, 1981.

———. *Writing without Teachers.* New York: Oxford UP, 1973.

Healy, Mary K. "Preparing for Small Group Response Sessions." Using Student Writing Response Groups in the Classroom. Curriculum Publication no. 12 (Berkeley: Bay Area Writing Project, University of California, 1980).

Larson, Richard. "Training New Teachers of Composition in the Writing of Comments on Themes." *College Composition and Communication* 17 (1966): 152–155.

Lindemann, Erica. *A Rhetoric for Writing Teachers.* New York: Oxford UP, 1982.

Murray, Donald. "The Listening Eye: Reflections on the Writing Conference." *College English* 41 (1979): 13–18.

———. *A Writer Teaches Writing.* Boston: Houghton, 1968.

A Brief History of American Composition Studies

—R. Gerald Nelms

Classical rhetorical theory, with its emphasis on oratory, remained the centerpiece of education and communication theory through the Middle Ages. However, during the Renaissance it came under attack, was displaced from its central position in education, and was equated simply with oratorical style and delivery—the form of discourse, but not the substance. The colonists who settled in America brought with them this abridged rhetorical theory. Yet, they also brought with them a sense of individualism, based in their belief of their election by God, and they brought a strong oratorical tradition that in practice implied a full rhetorical theory (Guthrie 21).

During the late eighteenth century, the classical tradition experienced a strong revival that can be attributed in part to the recovery during the Renaissance of many classical texts, and partly to increasing emphasis on secular public discourse. The colonies were moving toward a revolution and the creation of a new nation; naturally, there was a growing interest in public affairs. Oral communication remained the dominant rhetorical medium, and oral disputation and public declamations were the most common pedagogical system in schools. In fact, students were promoted through what were called "visitations" or the "sitting solstices," three-week periods in June when students made themselves available for disputations with "all Commers." The major debate within the discipline at the time was not whether writing fell within the scope of rhetorical study but which was the more pedagogically effective, formally composed oratory or extemporaneous debate (Halloran 254).

In the nineteenth and early twentieth centuries, developments in the rise of modern Western culture began to fully influence the institutions of American society. One of the more important global factors involved in the decline of rhetorical theory, in the appearance of what is typically referred to as the "current-traditional paradigm," and in the shift in emphasis to written discourse was the rise of the concept of the autonomous self, "individualism," in Western culture. According to Romano Guardini, the Renaissance, with its increased secularization, brought an increase in individualism. Men (for few women were allowed to become scholars, fewer still recognized) began to question the authority to which they had deferred during the Middle Ages, including that of the Church (Guardini 46). At least partially as a consequence of this new individualism, the middle class and its favored economic system, capitalism, arose; notions of democracy were revived; and artistic endeavor became the province of genius. In the nineteenth century, these changes began to affect American education. But not until the period 1860–1900 can we see clearly the effects upon composition theory.

For education, these social changes meant, for one thing, more students and more colleges. During the period 1820–1850, American colleges experienced tremendous growth and enrollments skyrocketed, outrunning the number of available teachers and causing significant pedagogical problems. Schools were forced to hire relatively untrained teachers, and there was a rise in specialization. Whereas before 1800, one teacher taught all subjects to the same class of ten to twelve boys throughout their college careers, by the 1840s, typical college faculties had several professors, each responsible for a department and the teaching of one part of the curriculum. Professors were assisted by often minimally trained tutors. Disputations suddenly became an inefficient and even impossible means of evaluation. "Sitting solstices" could no longer be used as tests for advancement. Instead, "courses" of study developed, and marks were given. Modes of instruction also changed from forms of disputation to recitation and finally to written exams. In addition, nineteenth-century colleges in the United States relied heavily on textbooks. After all, scholars were not the sort of people who wanted to move from their "civilized" Europe to the wilderness of the new world (Connors, "Textbooks" 180). At first, the system required students to read the text and *recite* it back to the tutors. But soon, even this method became too time-consuming, and schools turned to written tests.

Increasing enrollments, then, promoted the rise in specialization of teachers and disciplines, leading eventually to the departmental system. Such a system of specialization led to fragmentation of the traditionally linked rhetorical arts of speaking (to speech departments), language study (to philology and linguistics), and reading or the interpretation of texts (to literature departments). Furthermore, while the great strength of rhetoric lies in its service across the disciplines, specialization cut off these arts from other fields. Writing for its own sake (or speaking or reading, for that matter) will inevitably weaken rhetorical theory.

Another reason for the decline of rhetorical theory and the shift from oratory to written discourse in schools and society was the rise of the belletristic movement. Increased recognition of the individual as the focus of society led to the development of the concept of genius. The expression of genius came to be associated with poetics, works concerned primarily with the aesthetic experience of the audience as distinct from the rhetorical experience, while rhetoric was associated with the old educational system that emphasized oratory in classical Greek and Latin.

A change in the perceived function of colleges themselves also occurred during the late nineteenth century.

Through the eighteenth and early nineteenth centuries, colleges devoted themselves to educating leaders of society: lawyers, political leaders, and clergy. However, as Western culture became increasingly secular and placed the individual at the psychological center of society, the function of a college education as preparation for leadership diminished. More and more, college came to be seen as a means by which the individual could advance socially (Halloran 261). And with the growth of the middle class and of interest in the sciences, demands increased for an expansion of the curriculum to include education in middle-class professions and in those same sciences. An increased emphasis on evaluating student achievements followed this change. Halloran writes:

> So long as the college served to provide leaders for the community, the issue of rigorous evaluation was not terribly crucial. If a man who was not particularly well qualified somehow got admitted to the baccalaureate degree, no real harm or injustice had been done, since the community . . . had its own means of judging the quality of men. But when higher education came to be understood as an opportunity for individual advancement, the degree became something more like a certificate of qualification, and the institution had to concern itself with 'quality control.' (262)

The 1870s, 1880s, and especially the 1890s became the setting for a series of battles among several different forces that led to the rise of what Daniel Fogarty and Richard Young have called "current-traditional rhetoric." Current-traditional rhetoric was less a theory of composition than a pedagogical system, and it dominates the teaching (though not the theory) of composition even today. It is in some ways an almost perfect doctrine of writing instruction for an educational system that desires easy evaluation. Berlin has noted that current-traditional rhetoric reduces to dogma the more mechanical and quantifiable features of eighteenth-century rhetorical theory and "makes them the sole concern of the writing teacher" (62). The main features of current-traditional rhetoric are the following:

1. An emphasis on the composed product rather than the composing process.
2. Belief that the discovery of the substance of rhetorical communication lies outside of rhetoric's province and the reduction of textbook discussions to the arrangement of the material and style of its presentation.
3. An absence of theoretical rationale accompanying the emphasis on style.
4. The analysis of discourse into words, sentences, and paragraphs.
5. The division of prose essay arrangement into three fundamental principles: unity, coherence, and emphasis.

6. The classification of discourse into four (sometimes five) modes: narration, description, exposition, argumentation, and sometimes persuasion. Connors, Kitzhaber, and others have noted the reductiveness and unreality of this classification (Connors, "Rise and Fall of Modes of Discourse" 453–54; Kitzhaber 220–21).
7. An emphasis on grammatical and mechanical correctness. Exercises and drills became popular pedagogical techniques in composition classes.

The belief developed in the late nineteenth century that instruction in grammar, spelling, and punctuation ought to be the job of secondary schools, not colleges and universities. One reason for the institution of the written Harvard entrance examinations in English (1873–1874) was to relegate more responsibility for these details to lower schools. By the early twentieth century, members of college-level English departments had begun to identify themselves less with writing instruction and more with the study of literature. Writing instruction, devoid of rhetorical theory, reduced to rules and formulas, was not considered to be part of higher education but remedial work, instruction that had to be done only because secondary schools had failed.

A series of reports out of Harvard in the 1890s supported this view and helped to create the perception of a nationwide "literacy crisis" around the turn of the century. The Harvard Reports, as they are called, were issued in 1892, 1895, and 1897. They complained that writing staffs were overworked; that the work these instructors did was "stupefying"; that it was looked upon as secondary to the primary work of teaching literature. In each case, the reports were right. Enrollments had continued to outrun trained teachers. At the University of Michigan in 1894–1895, for instance, a staff of four full-time and two part-time graduate assistants taught 1,198 students. The work of reading that many "themes" for mechanical correctness undoubtedly was "stupefying." But rather than question the complicity of colleges and universities in this situation, the reports faulted the lower schools. Indeed, only the use of greater numbers of graduate students, part-time instructors, and lower-rank instructors to teach composition would relieve this situation. But of course, relieving the numbers did little to change attitudes. Writing teachers during this period needed neither qualifications nor pedagogical training; in fact, they were usually trained in another discipline, most often literature. These attitudes toward composition exist even today in many English departments.

Given the variety of forces working against any kind of full rhetorical system and the pedagogical apparatus to teach it, it seems a wonder that any alternatives would be voiced. Yet such voices did emerge in the 1890s. Fred Newton Scott of Michigan and others opposed the Harvard entrance examination system; opposed the separation of reading, writing, and speaking; opposed the divorce of theory and practice; opposed the mechanistic view of composition; and argued for what James A. Berlin calls a "transactional rhetoric" (*Writing Instruction* 77–84; *Rhetoric and Reality* 35–50). For Scott, composition required a recognition of all aspects of the rhetorical situation: the writer, the audience, the message, and the context. And it required a recognition of the full rhetorical process, including the discovery of substance as well as stylistic expression. Unfortunately, Scott confronted forces that could not be overcome.

During the period 1900–1940, English departments further consolidated themselves as literature departments, and the current-traditional rhetoric remained dominant. However, the work of Scott was carried on by Gertrude Buck at Vassar and others well into the mid-twentieth century. Also, a system that Berlin refers to as "the rhetoric of Liberal Culture" grew out of the belletristic movement (*Rhetoric and Reality* 35). It was "elitist and aristocratic," suggesting that good writing cannot be taught, because it is the work of genius. The aim of writing instruction under this system was to encourage such genius in those students who exhibited it, and to provide "lessons in taste" for those who did not. Other expressionistic approaches to composition, some more democratic than others, developed out of the rhetoric of Liberal Culture. All had in common an emphasis on the personal and private nature of composing. Each encouraged the beliefs that writing cannot be taught, that the teachers should provide an environment for the expression of personal abilities, and most placed a great deal of emphasis on metaphor.

In addition to the dramatic effects of World War II on higher education in America in general and in the teaching of writing in particular, three major developments in the 1960s, 1970s, and 1980s have worked to displace the current-traditional system. First, the revival of classical rhetorical theory provided us with a knowledge of ancient rhetorical principles, some of which are still applicable today, such as the centrality to all rhetorical expression of invention (Connors, Ede, and Lunsford passim). In addition, it has reestablished a connection between theory and practice and has helped to provide composition with scholarly validity.

The rise in scholarly legitimacy for those working in rhetoric and composition—spurred on by the revival in classical rhetoric—has meant an improvement in the training of writing instructors and in the status of composition teaching and research in general. More and more graduate programs in rhetoric and composition nationwide appear every year. Also, writing-across-the-curriculum programs, which involve the training of teachers in other disciplines to teach writing and which thus reestablish a recognition of the interdisciplinary nature of composition, are becoming popular.

Furthermore, English departments are giving tenure more often to scholars and researchers in rhetoric and composition than they have in the past. The revival of classical rhetoric has helped to show administrators and colleagues the long tradition upon which we are building and has reestablished the importance of work in this field.

Another major development in the history of composition in the latter half of the twentieth century has been the increasing emphasis on the composing process as opposed to the composing product, the static text itself. As invention has reasserted its primacy in rhetorical theory, rhetoric is no longer looked upon as merely the stylistic vehicle for the substance of communication, but as including that substance, too.

The first discussions of "process" in composition occurred within the expressionistic rhetoric of the 1920s, while the first concern for process in a more socially based rhetorical setting seems to have appeared in the early 1950s. In 1953, Barriss Mills wrote an essay entitled "Writing as Process," in which he emphasized rhetorical purpose and context and the need for teaching revision (Berlin, *Rhetoric and Reality* 119). However, D. Gordon Rohman's essay "Pre-Writing: The Stage of Discovery in the Writing Process," published in 1965, seems to have begun the explosion of process-oriented research and writing in composition.

However, the ultimate source for our interest in process probably lies outside of the discipline. At about the same time as composition scholars, scholars in a variety of other disciplines also seemed to have begun viewing behavior as an on-going process, instead of a static, terminated product. In the "new physics," in existential philosophy, in humanistic education and psychology, and in many other fields, we witness an emphasis on the dynamic as well as static nature of physical and human existence, on becoming as well as being.

The consequences for writing instruction have been many. Some scholars have tried to chart stages in the writing process, but they have been countered by others who see the process as recursive and oscillating—that is, to view writing as proceeding less by stages than by activities, each activity available to the writer at any time. Writing is not described as being clean-cut and homogenous; instead, it is messy and multivaried. Also, scholars have come to see writing as having multiple purposes: no longer is it simply the vehicle for ideas, nor is its function simply that of communication; writing also acts as a way of discovering ideas and of forming opinions.

Finally, in the latter part of this century, our discipline has seen a rise in empirical research. Earlier, in the nineteenth and twentieth centuries, some writers in the field tried to apply scientific principles to descriptions of how composed products worked. But recent empirical research has been more experimental, attempting to describe and understand the process of composing, not the product. This rise in empirical research can be dated from the late 1950s and early 1960s. In *Research in Written Composition*, published in 1963, Richard Braddock, Richard Lloyd-Jones, and Lowell Schoer took their fellow researchers in composition to task:

> Not enough investigators are really informing themselves about the procedures and results of previous research before embarking on their own. Too few of them conduct pilot experiments and validate their measuring instruments before undertaking an investigation. . . . And far too few of those who have conducted an initial piece of research follow it with further exploration or replicate the investigations of others. (5)

These days, such criticisms can be leveled less and less against researchers in composition. Moreover, empirical research is slowly gaining validity within the still primarily humanistic English departments.

In the end, we need to recognize that the industry of composition is itself "in process." The history that I have outlined here represents an academic history, a *story* tied more to the teaching of composition than to the practice of it. Little work in composition outside of the academy has been done. Yet professional composing goes on every day and has gone on since the invention of writing.

Also, we have focused primarily upon the composing processes of white males. What we know about the black rhetorical tradition suggests the influence of a vigorous orality within the culture. The little that we know about women's use of rhetoric also suggests differences with the more publicized male practice. For one thing, feminine rhetoric appears to be less combative, more collaborative. The composing practices of other minorities also remain to be explored. And so, we need to qualify the history outlined here. Until very recently, the educational system that provided instruction in rhetoric and composition excluded more people than it included. The forces that shaped this white, male, mostly Anglo-Saxon tradition in America were probably not the same as those that shaped the other traditions of significant portions of our population. And while we need to understand as fully as we can the traditions of the dominant system, which is now beginning to embrace the formerly disenfranchised, we also need to understand the traditions of those who have been marginalized in the past. They, after all, represent the forces of change for the future.

WORKS CITED

Berlin, James A. *Rhetoric and Reality: Writing Instruction in American Colleges, 1900–1985.* Carbondale and Edwardsville, IL: Southern Illinois UP, 1987.

———. *Writing Instruction in Nineteenth-Century American Colleges.* Carbondale and Edwardsville, IL: Southern Illinois UP, 1984.

Braddock, Richard, Richard Lloyd-Jones, and Lowell Schoer. *Research in Written Composition.* Urbana, IL: NCTE, 1963.

Connors, Robert J. "The Rise and Fall of the Modes of Discourse." *College Composition and Communication* 32 (1981): 444–455.

———. "Textbooks and the Evolution of the Discipline. *College Composition and Communication* 37 (1986): 178–194.

———, Lisa S. Ede, and Andrea A. Lunsford. "The Revival of Rhetoric in America." *Essays on Classical Rhetoric and Modern Discourse.* Eds. Robert J. Connors, Lisa S. Ede, and Andrea A. Lunsford. Carbondale and Edwardsville, IL: Southern Illinois UP, 1984.

Fogarty, Daniel, S. J. *Roots for a New Rhetoric.* New York: Russell & Russell, 1959.

Guardini, Romano. *The End of the Modern World: A Search for Orientation.* Trans. Joseph Theman and Herbert Burke. Ed. Frederick D. Wilhelmsen. New York: Sheed & Ward, 1956.

Guthrie, Warren. "The Development of Rhetorical Theory in America." *Speech Monographs* 13 (1946): 14–22; 14 (1947): 38–54; 15 (1948): 61–71.

Halloran, S. Michael. "Rhetoric in the American College Curriculum: The Decline of Public Discourse." *PRE/TEXT* 3 (1982): 245–270.

Kitzhaber, Albert R. "Rhetoric in American Colleges, 1850–1900." Diss. U of Washington, 1953.

Rohman, D. Gordon. "Pre-Writing: The Stage of Discovery in the Writing Process." *College Composition and Communication* 16 (1965): 106–112.

Young, Richard E. "Paradigms and Problems: Needed Research in Rhetorical Invention." *Research on Composing: Points of Departure.* Eds. Charles R. Cooper and Lee Odell. Urbana, IL: NCTE, 1978.

Sample Syllabus for Fifteen-Week Semester

STRUCTURE OF THE COURSE

One of the best ways to learn to write is by writing, and for that reason students in this course will be asked to do a lot of inventing, drafting, and revising—that's what writing is. Sharing work with others, either in peer-response sessions, writing groups, or collaborative efforts, promotes learning about writing by widening the response writers get to their work. Finally, guidance from texts constitutes another important component of learning to write by answering questions you may have or suggesting ways of going about the business of writing. Because each of these three principles operates powerfully in the classroom, they form the basis of the course schedule outlined below. To provide practice writing and sharing those writings, often the class will be devoted to writing workshops. These writing workshops give students the chance to see how other students have handled writing assignments, to practice editing skills by helping other students edit their own work, and to draft essays. Many class days will involve a class discussion of a student essay that demonstrates how the writing being done might best be handled. In addition, many classes will open with a short writing assignment, freewrite, or writing log entry. Each week we will read sections from *The St. Martin's Handbook* that address issues about writing, guide us in our understanding of those issues, and suggest ways for us to broaden our knowledge and apply that knowledge to our writing.

WRITTEN ASSIGNMENTS

We will write five essays during the term. An "acceptable" draft of each essay must be turned in by the final due date for each essay. At any time during the term, I will assign a final grade to the draft that each student judges to be their final effort on each essay. At least one week before the end of the term, students must turn in four or five final drafts for final evaluation. Before the last day of classes, students must turn in the fifth essay for a final grade.

Since students can suspend final evaluation of their progress until the end of the semester, this grading system provides you with the opportunity to have your best work evaluated. (*Type* all final drafts.)

ATTENDANCE

Because much of each student's most important work will take place in class, attendance in class is mandatory. (Chronically late students will be warned once; after that, each late appearance will be counted as an absence.)

FINAL COURSE GRADES

Final course grades will be arrived at by combining grades for the five graded papers, class attendance, participation, and conferences with the teacher in the following manner:

—final, graded essays (4 × 15):	60%
—research essay (fourth essay)	20%
—attendance	10%
—conferences, writing logs	10%

Course Schedule

Week	Topics/Focus
1	Introduction: briefly outline the course; identify learning objectives from your perspective and ask the students to add some of their own; present guidelines for grading, plagiarism, late essays, attendance.
	Diagnostic writing sample.
	The writing process (Chapter 1, 2): rewrite diagnostic test to demonstrate drafting, learning through writing.

Assign the first essay: identify the task clearly, provide models of successful attempts, link the assignment to learning objectives, suggest ways for students to use the assignment to learn about something that interests them.

2   Invention techniques: mapping, brainstorming (Chapter 2); research as invention (Chapter 37). Apply invention methods to first assignment. Draft of first essay due; peer-response in class; teacher response: read for overall direction, scope, and suitability for your course and first assignment.

Revising and editing the draft (Chapter 3) Compare writing log entries.

3   Second draft of first essay due; peer-response in class; Crafting paragraphs (Chapter 5).

Confer with students individually either during office hours or classroom writing workshops. Identify specific error patterns you have noticed; conduct mini-lectures for students who share error patterns (the specific chapters you will need to refer to will emerge from the class' needs: see Chapters 6–16 and 27–36); for more guidance, see "Correctness and Patterns of Error in Writing").

4   First essay due.

Assign the second essay: identify the task clearly, provide models of successful attempts, link the assignment to learning objectives, suggest ways for students to use the assignment to learn about something that interests them. Repeat invention techniques used for the first essay; add Burke's dramatistic pentad Freewrite; repeat freewriting sessions and exchange freewrites to share ideas, approaches to the assignment.

5   Draft of the second essay due; peer-response in class, teacher response to focus and questions to promote further research or development. Creating effective prose (Chapter 17); Using coordinate and subordinate structures (Chapter 18).

Writing workshop and/or individual conferences. Second draft of second essay due.

6   Understanding diction (Chapter 24); Strengthening vocabulary (Chapter 26).

Confer with students individually either during office hours or classroom writing workshops. Identify specific error patterns you have noticed; conduct mini-lectures for students who share error patterns (the specific chapters you will need to refer to will emerge from the needs of the class: see Chapters 6–16 and 27–36).

7   Second essay due.

Assign the third essay: identify the task clearly, provide models of successful attempts, link the assignment to learning objectives, suggest ways for students to use the assignment to learn about something that interests them. Repeat invention techniques used for the second essay; add tagmemic heuristic or clustering. Understanding and using arguments (Chapter 4).

8   Draft of the third essay due; peer-response in class, teacher response to focus and questions to spur research or development.

Creating parallel sentence structures (Chapter 19); Creating varying sentence structures (Chapter 20).

Confer with students either individually in class or during office hours.

9   Identify specific error patterns you have noticed; conduct mini-lectures for students who share error patterns (the specific chapters you will need to refer to will emerge from the class' needs: see Chapters 6–16 and 27–36).

10   Third essay due.

Assign the fourth essay (a research essay: identify the task clearly, provide models of successful attempts, link the assignment to learning objectives, suggest ways for students to use the assignment to learn about something that interests them.

Becoming a researcher (Chapter 38); Conducting research (Chapter 39); Using dictionaries (Chapter 23).

11   Research file due: a list of all sources consulted so far; notes; photocopies of relevant readings; summaries; quotations.

	Evaluating and using source materials (Chapter 39); Organizing, drafting, and revising a research essay (Chapter 40).
12	Draft of research essay due; confer individually with students; devote class time to writing workshops.
	Establishing tone (Chapter 26); Creating memorable prose (Chapter 21).
13	Second draft of research essay due; peer-response in class.
	Documenting sources (Chapter 42).
14	Final draft of research essay due.
	Fifth assignment: rewrite or revise an essay from: 1) a course in your major, 2) a discipline that interests you, or 3) this course.
	Writing in the different disciplines (Chapter 42); Writing for non-academic audiences (Chapter 45).
	Due: a description of the conventions of your discipline; a description of the style of your field.
	Due: typed, final drafts of first four papers for final grading.
15	Draft of the fifth assignment due; peer-response in class, teacher response through individual conferences in class or during office hours; writing workshops in class.
	Final draft of fifth essay due.
	Course evaluations.

Sample Syllabus for Ten-Week Quarter

STRUCTURE OF THE COURSE

One of the best ways to learn to write is by writing, and for that reason students in this course will be asked to do a lot of inventing, drafting, and revising—that's what writing is. Sharing work with others, either in peer-response sessions, writing groups, or collaborative efforts, promotes learning about writing by widening the response writers get to their work. Finally, guidance from texts constitutes another important component of learning to write by answering questions you may have or suggesting ways of going about the business of writing. Because each of these three principles operates powerfully in the classroom, they form the basis of the course schedule outlined below. To provide practice writing and sharing those writings, often the class will be devoted to writing workshops. These writing workshops give students the chance to see how other students have handled writing assignments, to practice editing skills by helping other students edit their own work, and to draft essays. Many class days will involve a class discussion of a student essay that demonstrates how the writing being done might best be handled. In addition, many classes will open with a short writing assignment, freewrite, or writing log entry. Each week we will read sections from *The St. Martin's Handbook* that address issues about writing, guide us in our understanding of those issues, and suggest ways for us to broaden our knowledge and apply that knowledge to our writing.

WRITTEN ASSIGNMENTS

We will write four essays during the term. An "acceptable" draft of each essay must be turned in by the final due date for each essay. At any time during the term, I will assign a final grade to the draft that each student judges to be their final effort on each essay. At least one week before the end of the term, students must turn in three of four final drafts for final evaluation. Before the last day of classes, students must turn in the fourth essay for a final grade.

Since students can suspend final evaluation of their progress until the end of the semester, this grading system provides you with the opportunity to have your best work evaluated. (*Type* all final drafts.)

ATTENDANCE

Because much of each student's most important work will take place in class, attendance in class is mandatory. (Chronically late students will be warned once; after that, each late appearance will be counted as an absence.)

FINAL COURSE GRADES

Final course grades will be arrived at by combining grades for the four graded papers, class attendance, participation, and conferences with the teacher in the following manner:

—final, graded essays (4 × 20):   80%
—attendance   10%
—conferences, writing logs   10%

Course Schedule

Week	Topics/Focus
1	Introduction: briefly outline the course; identify learning objectives from your perspective and ask the students to add some of their own; present guidelines for grading, plagiarism, late essays, attendance.
	Diagnostic writing sample.
	The writing process (Chapter 1, 2): rewrite diagnostic test to demonstrate drafting, learning through writing.
	Assign the first essay: identify the task clearly, provide models of successful attempts, link the assignment to learning objectives, suggest ways for students to use the assignment to learn about something that interests them.
2	Invention techniques: mapping, brainstorming (Chapter 2); research as invention (Chapter 37).
	Apply invention methods to first assignment.
	Draft of first essay due; peer-response in class; teacher response: read for overall direction, scope, and suitability for your course and first assignment.
	Revising and editing the draft (Chapter 3).
	Compare writing log entries.
3	Second draft of first essay due; peer-response in class; Crafting paragraphs (Chapter 5).
	Confer with students individually either during office hours or classroom writing workshops.
	Identify specific error patterns you have noticed; conduct mini-lectures for students who share error patterns (the specific chapters you will need to refer to will emerge from the class' needs: see Chapters 6–16 and 27–36; for more guidance, see "Correctness and Patterns of Error in Writing").
4	First essay due.
	Assign the second essay: identify the task clearly, provide models of successful attempts, link the assignment to learning objectives, suggest ways for students to use the assignment to learn about something that interests them.
	Repeat invention techniques used for the first essay; add Burke's dramatistic pentad Free-write; repeat freewriting sessions and exchange freewrites to share ideas, approaches to the assignment.
5	Draft of the second essay due; peer-response in class, teacher response to focus and questions to promote further research or development.
	Creating effective prose (Chapter 17); Using coordinate and subordinate structures (Chapter 18).
	Writing workshop and/or individual conferences.
	Second draft of second essay due.

6 Understanding diction (Chapter 24); Strengthening vocabulary (Chapter 26).

Confer with students individually either during office hours or classroom writing workshops.

Identify specific error patterns you have noticed; conduct mini-lectures for students who share error patterns (the specific chapters you will need to refer to will emerge from the needs of the class' needs: see Chapters 6–16 and 27–36).

7 Second essay due.

Assign the third essay: identify the task clearly, provide models of successful attempts, link the assignment to learning objectives, suggest ways for students to use the assignment to learn about something that interests them.

Repeat invention techniques used for the second essay; add tagmemic heuristic or clustering.

Understanding and using arguments (Chapter 4).

8 Draft of the third essay due; peer-response in class, teacher response to focus and questions to spur research or development.

Creating parallel sentence structures (Chapter 19); Creating varying sentence structures (Chapter 20).

Confer with students either individually in class or during office hours.

Identify specific error patterns you have noticed; conduct mini-lectures for students who share error patterns (the specific chapters you will need to refer to will emerge from the class' needs: see Chapters 6–16 and 27–36).

9 Third essay due.

Assign the fourth essay: rewrite or revise an essay from: 1) a course in your major, 2) a discipline that interests you, or 3) this course.

Writing in the different disciplines (Chapter 42); Writing for non-academic audiences (Chapter 45).

Due: a description of the conventions of your discipline; a description of the style of your field.

Due: typed, final drafts of first three papers for final grading.

10 Draft of the fourth assignment due; peer-response in class, teacher response through individual conferences in class or during office hours; writing workshops in class.

Final draft of fourth essay due.

Course evaluations.

The
St. Martin's
HANDBOOK

Andrea Lunsford
Ohio State University

Robert Connors
University of New Hampshire

ST. MARTIN'S PRESS   New York

Senior Editor: Mark Gallaher
Developmental Editor: Marilyn Moller
Project Editor: Denise Quirk
Manuscript Editor: John Elliott
Editorial Assistant: Virginia Biggar
Production Supervisor: Julie Power
Text Design: Helen Granger/Levavi & Levavi, Inc.
Cover Design: Darby Downey

For information, write:
St. Martin's Press, Inc.
175 Fifth Avenue
New York, NY 10010

ISBN: 0-312-00264-5

Acknowledgments

The American Heritage Dictionary, Second College Edition. Copyright © 1985 by
Houghton Mifflin Company. Reprinted by permission.

J. Bland. "Spelling and Pronunciation—Hints for Foreigners," from a letter published
in London *Sunday Times*, January 3, 1965, from J. Bland. Cited by McKay and Thompson in "The Initial Teaching of Reading and Writing," *Program in Linguistics and
English Teaching*, paper 3, University College, London, and Longmans Green and Co.,
Ltd., London and Harlow, 1968, page 45.

James M. S. Careless, *Canada: A Story of Challenge*. Copyright © 1970 by St. Martin's
Press, Inc. Reprinted by permission of Macmillan of Canada, a division of Canada
Publishing Corporation.

"Chicken Soup: It Might Help Your Memory." From *Newsweek*, December 1, 1986.
Copyright © 1986, Newsweek, Inc. All rights reserved. Reprinted by permission.

E. E. Cummings, "Me up at does." Copyright © 1963 by Marion Morehouse Cummings, reprinted from *Complete Poems 1913–1962* by E. E. Cummings by permission
of Harcourt Brace Jovanovich, Inc.

Acknowledgments and copyrights are continued at the back of the book on
pages 758–59, which constitute an extension of the copyright page.

Preface

The story of *The St. Martin's Handbook* began in 1983. In the course of investigating the history of writing instruction, we came across some information about teaching composition that, though at first simply amusing, led us to a series of compelling questions. We discovered, for instance, that in the late nineteenth century, professors at Harvard perceived that their students had great difficulty distinguishing between the use of *shall* and *will*, and that in the 1930s, American students persistently misused *would* for the simple past. How quaint, we thought; look at how much student writers and their problems have changed.

We intuitively assumed that such changes must have taken place, but what exactly were they? This question took on greater significance as we focused our investigation on the history and development of composition textbooks. As part of that research, we found that the first edition of John C. Hodges's *Harbrace College Handbook* (1941) was based on an analysis of over 20,000 student papers written in the 1930s. So, we reasoned, that book reflected the writing problems of students of the time, problems that were decidedly different from how to use *shall* and *will*. How might the problems faced by our students, fifty years later, have changed?

With something of a shock, we realized that we didn't know. Further investigation showed us not only that Hodges's research seemed to be the last serious effort of that kind but that his handbook was still organized exactly as it had been in 1941. Since subsequent college handbooks had necessarily responded to that book, we realized with some surprise that the world of composition handbooks was still being tacitly guided by conceptions of error patterns that were almost a half century old.

We set out, then, to discover what patterns of error actually characterize student writing today, and which of these patterns seem most important to their instructors. To answer this question, we gathered a nationwide sample of over 20,000 student essays that had been marked by instructors and carefully analyzed a scientifically stratified sample of them, eventually identifying the twenty error patterns most characteristic of student writing today. As you might imagine, we got some provocative results.

Most intriguing to us is the fact that many of these errors relate in some way to visual memory—wrong words, wrong or missing verb endings, missing or misplaced possessive apostrophes, even the *its/it's* confusion—which suggests that students today may well be less familiar with the visible aspects of writing than students once were. Part of the effect of an oral, electronic culture seems to be, then, that students do not automatically bring with them the visual knowledge of writing conventions that text-wise writers possess and use effortlessly.

This problem of visualization was most pronounced in terms of spelling errors, which occur—by a factor of 300 percent—more frequently than any other error. Interestingly enough, the words students most often misspell are homonyms, words that sound alike but have different meanings and spellings. These findings support our other data linking error patterns to visual memory and suggest that the visual aspect of spelling is particularly important, that in a world of secondary orality we need to find ways to help students visualize their language.

Our research also revealed that many errors are governed not so much by hard and fast rule as by rhetorical decisions involving style, tone, and rhythm. Among others, such errors include the omission of a comma after an introductory element, inappropriate shift in verb tense, and misuse of commas with restrictive and nonrestrictive elements. This finding suggested to us that students need help writing prose that is not only mechanically correct but rhetorically effective as well. Doing so, we believe, demands that they view the tools of writing—grammar, punctuation, mechanics—as having rhetorical force and as being based on choices they must learn to make.

Armed with this information, we set out to create a textbook that would address the needs of students at the end of the twentieth century. The result is *The St. Martin's Handbook*. In many ways it is a traditional handbook, with all the requisite materials on the writing process, grammar, punctuation, mechanics, and research. In other respects, however, it charts new territory, extending writing instruction in features not found in any other handbook. Among its distinctive features are the following:

Special attention to the twenty most common errors. An introductory chapter entitled "Learning from Your Errors" offers practical guidelines for recognizing, understanding, and revising each of the top twenty errors that our research identified. This chapter also serves as an index, with cross-references to all the places in the book where students can find more help on each error. Especially helpful, we hope, will be step-by-step guidelines that show students how to check their own drafts for each error and then how to revise accordingly.

In presenting these errors, we have tried always to give a clear message about "correctness" *along with* realistic discussion of actual usage. Without oversimplification, our goal has been to help students know *what to do.* Most important, we present errors as opportunities for improving skills, as something to be examined in context and learned from rather than as blots to be eradicated. We ask students not simply to amass information about errors but to analyze the sources and consequences of those errors in their own writing—to build, if you will, a theory about how to improve their writing based on a close study of the errors that they make.

Attention to writing, not just to correctness. We feel strongly that students need practice in *writing*, not only in revising incorrect sentences. Like all composition handbooks, *The St. Martin's Handbook* provides guidance in checking and revising a draft for correctness; unlike most others, however, it also offers ample opportunity for student writing, in guided-writing and imitation exercises that get students to stretch their writing muscles, and in revising exercises that send them back into their own writing.

This attention to writing informs every chapter in the book, including those dealing with grammar and mechanics. In the chapter on adjectives and adverbs, for instance, we ask students to focus not only on how to use adjectives and adverbs correctly but also on the more compelling question of why and in what circumstances to use them at all. In the chapter on end punctuation, we provide rules for using periods, question marks, and exclamation points, and in addition, we ask students to try revising a piece of their own writing for sentence variety, using declarative, interrogatory, and exclamatory structures. In other words, we have tried to present grammar and mechanics as something to use for a writing purpose, not simply to use "correctly."

And because we believe that students learn best by reflecting on the rhetorical characteristics of what they have written, we show them how to keep a writing log—for recording their efforts at using grammatical structures, listing troublesome spelling words, jotting down noteworthy examples or images for future use. As a feature, the writing log is completely optional, but we recommend it as a means of helping students to reflect systematically on their own writing.

Systematic attention to reading. Because we see writing and reading as inextricably linked, we have included reading instruction throughout the text. Not only is there extensive guidance to help students read observantly and critically—whether evaluating a draft, an argument, a paragraph, or a source—but in addition, we present reading as one more tool that can help improve writing skills. Almost every chapter includes a special exercise asking students to "read with an eye for" some structure or element they are learning to use as writers—verbs, semicolons, hyphens, and so on. These exercises ask them to study passages from famous essays (and sometimes, poems) or from drafts of their own or other student work. In addition to the obvious benefits of studying expert use of basic rhetorical elements, such exercises will, we hope, help build students' visual knowledge of writing and writing conventions. Many of these exercises ask students then to try to imitate something in the passage—in other words, to step from their reading into writing.

Five chapters on the research process. Nowhere do students need more thorough instruction in how to move back and forth between reading and writing than in the writing they do based on sources. For this reason, *The St. Martin's Handbook* concentrates not simply on helping students produce a "research paper," but on how they might use research for many writing purposes. We show students how to approach all sources with a questioning eye, to assess source materials critically, not just to find them and use them. Like all handbooks, we give detailed instruction in quoting, paraphrasing, and summarizing; unlike others, however, we also show students how to discover patterns in the many discrete bits of data they find. With step-by-step guidelines in synthesizing data and drawing inferences, we help them to use their research in support of their own written argument.

Focus on student writing throughout. To illustrate the points made throughout this text, we have drawn most of our examples and exercises from the 20,000 essays gathered for our research. These are not handy-dandy examples manufactured by textbook authors but illustrations of conventions and error patterns as they really exist in student writing today. As such, these examples reflect the writing needs our students have as well as their interests. In addition, we have included seven full-length student essays.

A link with the most commonly studied essays. We have also drawn on examples from professional writing. And since we know that many of you use a handbook along with a reader, we have deliberately taken these from the essays most often included in composition readers—that is, from the essays your students are likely to be reading as they use this handbook. Many of these examples serve as models for imitation, as prompts for writing, or as occasion for readerly response. Such passages will of course serve as memorable examples; more important, however, they will provide the larger rhetorical context so often missing in most other handbooks. An index of authors and titles lists all the professional examples included in this book.

The greatest possible accessibility. As we worked on this book, we spoke with hundreds of colleagues about handbooks. Among the many concerns we found was one very common one—that a handbook must be accessible, that it has to be easy to get in and out of quickly. In then studying other handbooks, we noted that all put grammar, punctuation, and mechanics in easily accessible form, with many numbered headings, but that in no handbook were the rhetorical chapters as easy to use. Chapters on the writing process and on specific writing assignments were not set up to be dipped into quickly; they had to be read like chapters. In an attempt to make the rhetorical chapters in our handbook easier to use, we have deliberately added many more headings and put much of the information in list form. Many are in the form of questions, which we hope will guide students in making necessary rhetorical choices. Our goal here is for users of this book to be able to use it easily and quickly. Our greatest hope is that our readers will spend less time with our text and, as a result, have more time to contemplate their own.

Practical, helpful ancillary materials. Accompanying *The St. Martin's Handbook* are some companion materials we hope will facilitate its use: *The St. Martin's Workbook*, by Lex Runciman; an *Evaluation Manual* with diagnostic and competency tests and writing assignments, by Edward M. White; a *Guide to Teaching Writing*, by Robert Connors and Cheryl Glenn; transparency masters, prepared by

Roger C. Graves; and additional exercises on disk, available for IBM-compatible systems. Especially exciting, we think, is *The St. Martin's Hotline,* a complimentary "pop-up" reference system available for both IBM-compatible and MacIntosh systems. The handbook is available in both the student edition and an *Annotated Instructor's Edition,* prepared by Cheryl Glenn, Roger C. Graves, R. Gerald Nelms, and Dennis Quon, that includes practical and interesting information about using the handbook and about teaching writing.

Acknowledgments

We have been aided by an amazingly imaginative team. *The St. Martin's Handbook* has been a collaborative effort in the best and richest sense of the word. We are particularly indebted to Nancy Perry and Marilyn Moller of St. Martin's Press. From the beginning, Nancy supported both the research that underlies this book and our efforts to translate that research into a useful tool for instructors and students. Marilyn, whose efforts as developmental editor on this project have been above and beyond the call of any duty we have ever known, has earned our deep respect and gratitude. Jean Smith believed in this project, and has made the really extraordinary efforts made by St. Martin's on our behalf possible. Virginia Biggar, Kay Fleming, Alicia Mahaney, Susan Manning, Kim Richardson, Richard Steins, and Lynne Williams at St. Martin's all provided indispensable help at every stage. And Denise Quirk has worked so hard and on so many aspects of this project that we simply could not have gotten along without her. In addition, John Elliott, Marcia Muth, and Tyler Wasson provided editorial help on the original manuscripts that often emerged from their careful surgery transformed.

We are also more than grateful to the many instructors and students whose work we have depended on. First of all we wish to thank the many instructors who sent in essays:

Alabama: Rosemary M. Canfield, Troy State University; Charles R. Craig, Alabama State University; Stephen Glosecki, University of Alabama at Birmingham; Peggy Jolly, University of Alabama at Birmingham; Kris Lackey, Auburn University; Jane Latture, Jefferson State Junior College; Ronald F. Smith, University of North Alabama; *Arizona:* Delmar Kehl, Arizona State University; Vera Kielsky, Arizona State University; Lisa Miller, Phoenix College; Beth Stiefel, Northern Arizona University; *Arkansas:* Joyce Dempsey, Arkansas Technological University; *California:* Victoria Babcock, University of

California at Santa Barbara; Gwen Brewer, California State University at Northridge; Gary Brown, San Diego State University; Stanford Carlson, Grossmont College; Dennis Chaldecot, California State University at San Jose; Elena J. Cleef, University of California at Santa Barbara; Michael P. Collings, Pepperdine University; David Dickson, Sierra College; Antoinette Empringham, El Camino College; Diane Goodwin, College of San Mateo; Helen Gordon, Bakersfield College; W. Greenstein, Long Beach City College; Susan K. Hahn, University of California at Santa Barbara; Sherri Hallgren, University of California at Berkeley; Linda Humphrey, Citrus Community College; Malcolm Kiniry, University of California at Los Angeles; Michael Kramer, University of California at Davis; Robert E. Lend, University of California at Irvine; Arlene Lighthall, Miracosta College; Annette P. Lynch, Mount San Antonio College; Elizabeth Macey, Santa Ana College; Bruce McIver, University of California at Santa Barbara; David Madden, California State University at Sacramento; Charlotte Montandon, San Jose City College; Richard L. Moore, San Joaquin Delta College; Lawrence Parker, Mount San Antonio College; MeMe Riordan, City College of San Francisco; Ann Rothschild, University of California at Davis; Rodney Simard, California State College at Bakersfield; Mark Snowhite, Crafton Hills College; Cheryl Walker, Scripps College; Katherine Watson, Orange Coast College; Nancy Watts, Cuesta College; Jacqueline Webber, American River College; Leonard Weiss, College of Marin; *Colorado:* Edward A. Kearns, University of Northern Colorado; Jeane Luere, University of Northern Colorado; *Connecticut:* Srilekha Bell, University of New Haven; Gerald S. Coulter, Central Connecticut State University; Anne Greene, Wesleyan University; Lyda E. Lapalomara, South Connecticut State University; Mikail M. McIntosh, University of Connecticut; Mariann Russell, Sacred Heart University, David Sonstroem, University of Connecticut; *District of Columbia:* Judith Nembhard, Howard University; *Florida:* Sharon Cleland, Florida Junior College at Kent; Roger Drury, University of Florida; Dorothy P. Harris, Okaloosa-Walton Junior College; Lynn Hicks, Central Florida Community College; Mary Sue Koeppel, Florida Community College-South; Marcelle C. Lovett, University of North Florida; James F. O'Neil, Edison Community College; Hugh G. Paschal, Hillsborough Community College; April E. Riley, University of Florida; Steve Rubin, University of South Florida; Leora Schermerhorn, Seminole Community College; Gerald Schiffhorst, University of Central Florida; Jewell Sterling, Palm Beach Junior College; Carlos Valdes, University of Florida; *Georgia:* William Dodd, Augusta College; Tony Grooms, Macon Junior College; Patricia B. Handley, Macon Junior College; Donna Jones, Georgia Southern College; Marguerite P. Murphy, Georgia State University; Huey Owings, West Georgia College; Joseph J. Popson, Macon Junior College; John Presley, Augusta College; Lorie Roth, Armstrong State College; William R. Thurman, Georgia Southwestern College; *Idaho:* Okey Goode, Lewis-Clark State College; Richard Hannaford, University of Idaho; Gordon

Hinds, Boise State University; George Ives, North Idaho College; Scott Samuelson, Ricks College; *Illinois:* Steven Craig, Illinois State University; Marcia Gealy, Northwestern University; Edwina Jordan, Illinois Central College; Carolyn S. Kropp, Southern Illinois University; J. G. Lidaka, Northern Illinois University; Fred Robbins, Southern Illinois University; *Indiana:* Robert Habich, Ball State University; Jane Haynes, Ball State University; Stephen Heady, Indiana State University; Barry Kroll, Indiana University; John Lowe, Saint Mary's College; Rai Peterson, Ball State University; Mary C. Suttinger, Purdue University at Calumet; Keith Walsh, Indiana University; *Iowa:* Nancy K. Barry, University of Iowa; *Kansas:* Carol Ann Barnes, Kansas State University; James Bridson, University of Kansas; Donna Campbell, University of Kansas; Mary Grace Foret, Johnson County Community College; Patrick Giebler, Colby Community College; Myra Hinman, University of Kansas; Linda Hughes, Washburn University of Topeka; Beth Impson, University of Kansas; Linda Livingston, Dodge City Community College; Fred Terry, University of Kansas; Cheryl Hofstetter Towns, Colby Community College; Thomas Zelman, University of Kansas; *Kentucky:* George Cheatham, Eastern Kentucky University; Lou-Ann Crouther, Western Kentucky University; Katherine Fish, Cumberland College; *Louisiana:* Patricia Bates, Louisiana State University at Shreveport; Sara Burroughs, Northwestern State University of Louisiana; Robert H. Garner, Southern University in New Orleans; William Holditch, University of New Orleans; David H. Jackson, Centenary College; John Fleming McClelland, Northeast Louisiana University; Adelaide McGinnis, Delgado Community College; Mary Sue Ply, Southeastern Louisiana University; Ben Rushin, Delgado Community College; *Maine:* Alan Lindsay, University of Maine at Orono; *Maryland:* Jane Donawerth, University of Maryland; Jade Gorman, University of Maryland; Margaret Reid, Morgan State University; Margaret Wolfe, Anne Arundel Community College; *Massachusetts:* Priscilla Bellairs, Northern Essex Community College; Lila Chalpin, Massachusetts College of Art; James Dean, Tufts University; Patsy MacDonald, Northeastern University, Patricia Skarda, Smith College; *Michigan:* Alice Forer, University of Michigan at Flint; James C. Hines, Mott Community College; Geraldine Jacobs, Jackson Community College; Rowena Jones, Northern Michigan University; J. L. McDonald, University of Detroit; Robert Merkel, Monroe County Community College; Leslie Prast, Delta College; Kathleen Rout, Michigan State University; Maureen P. Taylor, Kalamazoo Valley Community College; *Minnesota:* Phyllis Ballata, Lakewood Community College; Gail Jardine, Rochester Community College; David L. Wee, Saint Olaf College; *Mississippi:* Faye Angelo, Hinds Junior College; De Lois Gatis, Northeast Mississippi Junior College; Tommy Ray, University of Mississippi; *Missouri:* Norma Bagnall, Missouri Western State College; Sally Fitzgerald, University of Missouri at St. Louis; Paul Jones, Northwest Missouri State University; Elizabeth Otten, Northeast Missouri State University; Pearl Saunders, St. Louis Community

College; David Slater, Northwest Missouri State University; *Montana:* Rachel Schaffer, Eastern Montana College; *Nebraska:* Jean Ferguson, University of Nebraska at Lincoln; Marge Holland, Wayne State College; *Nevada:* Terese Brychta, Truckee Meadows Community College; *New Hampshire:* W.C. Spengemann, Dartmouth College; *New Jersey:* Naomi Given, Middlesex County College; Harlan Hamilton, Jersey City State College; Albert Romano, Hudson County Community College; *New York:* Efrain Acevedo, Cornell University; Donna Allen, Erie Community College; Joyce Benson, Alfred University; Fred Blomgren, Monroe Community College; Diana Bloom, Mercy College; Ren Draya, Borough of Manhattan Community College, CUNY; Mary Erler, Fordham University; Richard Fabrizio, Pace University; W. Speed Hill, Lehman College, CUNY; Mary Anne Hutchinson, Utica College; Carol Kushner, Onondaga Community College; Carol Kusner, SUNY at Cortland; Morgan Jones, SUNY at New Paltz; Milton Levy, Kingsborough Community College, CUNY; Joyce Maggio, Suffolk County Community College; Carolyn McGrath, SUNY at Stony Brook; Rosa Lou Novi, SUNY at New Paltz; Astrid M. O'Brien, Fordham University at Lincoln Center; April Selly, College of St. Rose; Ilene Singh, College of Staten Island, CUNY; Karyn Sproles, SUNY at Buffalo; John Stinson, SUNY at Fredonia; Eve Maria Stwertka, SUNY at Farmingdale; Maeruth P. Wilson, SUNY at Buffalo; *North Carolina:* Mark Branson, Davidson County Community College; Jean Chase, Central Piedmont Community College; James Cuthbertson, Johnson C. Smith University; John Ebbs, East Carolina University; Terry J. Frazier, University of North Carolina at Charlotte; Kelly Griffith, University of North Carolina at Greensboro; Jay Jacoby, University of North Carolina at Charlotte; Rebecca W. Nail, Winston-Salem State University; Theresa Norman, Western Carolina University; Mary F. Stough, Davidson College; Mark Thomas, University of North Carolina; *Ohio:* Jutta Bendremer, University of Akron; Rosa I. Bhakuni, University of Akron; Leslie F. Chard, University of Cincinnati; Joyce R. Durham, University of Dayton; Bruce L. Edwards, Bowling Green State University; Jeffrey Hogeman, University of Cincinnati; Ann K. Jordan, University of Cincinnati, Clermont College; Barbara Langheim, University of Cincinnati; Christine H. Lavik, Lakeland Community College; Ulle Lewes, Ohio Wesleyan University; Nancy Kammer Peters, University of Cincinnati; William Pratt, Miami University; Deborah Roberts, University of Cincinnati; Janet Samuelson, University of Akron; Michael Shea, Miami University; Jacquie Skrzypiec, University of Akron; *Oklahoma:* Stanley Cameron, East Central University; Emily Dial-Driver, Rogers State University; Betty Gonul, East Central University; *Oregon:* Marna Broekhoff, University of Oregon; Warren Howe, Mountain Community College; John Miller, Umpqua Community College; Baxter Wilson, Portland State University; *Pennsylvania:* Ted Atkinson, Edinboro University of Pennsylvania; Rosemarie A. Battaglia, Kutztown University; William W. Betts, Indiana University of Pennsylvania; Terry P. Caesar, Clarion University of Pennsylvania; J. C. Condravy, Slippery Rock University; Elizabeth Curry, Slippery Rock University; Colleen Lamos, University of Pennsylvania; George Mower, Community College of Allegheny County; Gerald Siegel, York College of Pennsylvania; *Rhode Island:* David Hoch, Rhode Island College; Ira Schaeffer, Community College of Rhode Island; *South Carolina:* Ellen Arl, University of South Carolina at Sumter; Hallman B. Bryant, Clemson University; Bonnie Devet, University of South Carolina at Columbia; Larisa Garrison, Clemson University; Linda S. Schwartz, University of South Carolina-Coastal Carolina College; Sharon E. Spangler, Clemson University; Tom Waldrep, University of South Carolina at Columbia; Harriet S. Williams, University of South Carolina at Columbia; Laura Zaidman, University of South Carolina at Sumter; *South Dakota:* Ruth Foreman, South Dakota State University; John Taylor, South Dakota State University; *Tennessee:* Betty Hawkins, Volunteer State Community College; Charles H. Long, Memphis State University; Douglas Morris, David Lipscomb College; John Paine, Belmont College; Sue Palmer, Austin Peay State University; Stephen Prewitt, David Lipscomb College; David Worley, Lincoln Memorial University; Sally Young, University of Tennessee at Chattanooga; *Texas:* Bruce C. Autry, Lamar University; Suzanne Blaw, Richland College; Cleo Congrady, Alvin Community College; Barbara Craig, Del Mar College; Allen Billy Crider, Alvin Community College; Carl Fowler, Amarillo College; Charles Gongre, Lamar University; Perry E. Gragg, Angelo State University; Debra Hower, Texas A & M University; Glenda Hicks, Midland College; Henry Hutchings, Lamar University; Reba Kochersperger, North Harris County College; Joyce McEwing, Texas Southern University; Mary Jean Northcut, Richland College; Fred A. Rodewald, Stephen F. Austin State University; Vivian Rudisill, San Antonio College; Anne Sandel, Wharton County Junior College; Michael C. Sotterwhite, Texas Tech University; Lana White; West Texas State University; Terry Wiggs, Southwest Texas State University; Robert M. Wren, University of Houston; *Utah:* Kate Begnal, Utah State University; Kathryn Fitzgerald, University of Utah; Marne Isakson, Utah Technical College at Orem; Joyce Kinkead, Utah State University; Jan Ugan, Utah State University; *Vermont:* Francine Page, St. Michael's College; Cameron Thrull, University of Vermont; Arthur Tishman, University of Vermont; Rhoda Yerburgh, Vermont College; *Virginia:* Mary Balazs, Virginia Military Institute; Margaret Brandon, Thomas Nelson Community College; Elizabeth S. Byers, Virginia Polytechnic Institute and State University; John Lee, James Madison University; Stan Poole, University of Virginia; Michael Smith, Virginia Polytechnic Institute and State University; *Washington:* Debbie Kinerk, Tacoma Community College; Chris Kellett, University of Washington; Denis Thomas, Central Washington University; Jeff Wagnitz, Grays Harbor College; Carl Waluconis, Bellevue Community College; *West Virginia:* Stephen Warren, Fairmont State College; *Wisconsin:* Sue Beckham, University of Wisconsin at

Stout; James Plath, University of Wisconsin at Milwaukee; Jean P. Rumsey, University of Wisconsin at Stevens Point; Katherine White, University of Wisconsin at Stevens Point.

We also wish to thank the following colleagues who participated in focus groups held in the planning stages of this book: Joy Allameh, Eastern Kentucky University; Chris Burnham, New Mexico State University; Michael Cohen, Eastern Kentucky University; Don Richard Cox, University of Tennessee; Corrine Dale, Belmont College; Joyce Durham, University of Dayton; James David Earnest, Murray State University; Thomas L. Erskine, Salisbury State College; George D. Gopen, Duke University; Patricia H. Graves, Georgia State University; Edward Lotto, Lehigh University; Timothy P. Martin, Rutgers University; Mary Ellen Pitts, Memphis State University; Janet Samuelson, University of Akron; Barbara Sowders, Eastern Kentucky University. For their time and their many helpful suggestions we are grateful. Among our own students, Melissa Bloise, Laura Brannon, Leah Clendening, Amy Dierst, Elizabeth Lyon, Julie Slater, Colleen Starkey, and Tracy Vezdos all provided essays and other writing examples. Their good work is reflected in many, many pages of this book.

And we are especially appreciative of the many colleagues who painstakingly reviewed our manuscript and shared their thoughts on our efforts and on handbooks in general. Their incisive comments, queries, criticisms, and suggestions have improved this book immeasurably:

John Algeo, University of Georgia
Rise Axelrod, California State University at San Bernardino
David Bartholomae, University of Pittsburgh
Ray Brebach, Drexel University
Douglas Brent, University of Calgary
Monika Brown, Pembroke State University
Barbara Carson, University of Georgia
Charles Cooper, University of California at San Diego
Edward P. J. Corbett, Ohio State University
Cornelius Cronin, Louisiana State University
Carol David, Iowa State University
Angus Dunston, University of California at Santa Barbara
Joyce Durham, University of Dayton
Lisa Ede, Oregon State University
Thomas Gaston, Purdue University
Helen Gilbart, St. Petersburg Junior College

Jennifer Ginn, North Carolina State University at Raleigh
Patricia H. Graves, Georgia State University
Franklin Horowitz, Teachers College, Columbia University
Carl Klaus, University of Iowa
Edward Kline, University of Notre Dame
Janice Lauer, Purdue University
Edward Lotto, Lehigh University
David Mair, University of Oklahoma
Charles Meyer, University of Massachusetts at Boston
Michael Moran, University of Georgia
Patricia Murray, DePaul University
Lee Odell, Rensselaer Polytechnic Institute
MeMe Riordan, City College of San Francisco
Mike Rose, University of California at Los Angeles
Jane Stanhope, American University
Laura Stokes, University of California at Davis
William J. Vande Kopple, Calvin College
Harold Veeser, Wichita State University
Suellyn Winkle, Santa Fe Community College
Linda Woodson, University of Texas at San Antonio
Richard Zbaracki, Iowa State University

Finally, we are indebted to some special friends and colleagues: Charles Cooper, who provided invaluable advice about conducting the research; Mike Rose, who offered support and encouragement throughout; Douglas Brent, whose advice on research writing helped us immensely, Melinda Bako, Beverly Bruck, Sabina Foote, Heather Graves, Sue Lape, Jaime Mejia, Roxanne Mountford, Jon Olson, Dori Stratton, Kimberly Town, and Kelly Vezdos, who provided additional research, helped with assorted and sundry clerical tasks, and gave us smiles when we most needed them; the faculty and graduate students at Ohio State who helped us to organize and analyze the 3,000-paper sample—in particular, David Frantz, Murray Beja, and Michael Rupright; and, always, Lisa Ede, our critical reader and good friend extraordinaire.

We could go on and on and on, for we are fortunate (beyond our wildest dreams, as our mentor Ed Corbett would say) to be part of a true scholarly and academic community, one characterized by compassion, by commitment to students, by a celebration of learning. We are grateful to be among you.

Andrea Lunsford
Robert Connors

A Note to Students

Our goal in writing *The St. Martin's Handbook* has been to produce a book that will guide you to becoming competent and compelling writers, a book that you can use easily and efficiently throughout your college years.

We began work five years ago by examining a scientifically selected sample of more than 20,000 essays written by students from all areas of the country—students probably pretty much like you. We discovered the kinds of writing errors you are most likely to make and studied the twenty most common error patterns in detail. Throughout this book you will find guidance on those patterns. You will find help first of all in the chapter immediately following, one we call "Learning from Your Errors." This chapter will help you to analyze your own error patterns and especially to recognize, analyze, and overcome any of the twenty most common ones in your own writing.

Throughout this text, we ask that you look at errors in the context of your own writing, that you become accustomed to carefully analyzing your own prose. In almost every chapter, we will not only provide explanations and opportunity for practice, but also we will be asking you to apply the principles presented directly to your own writing. If you follow our directions, they will guide you in becoming a systematic self-critic—and a stronger writer. And since writing and reading in many ways go hand in hand, many chapters will also offer you a chance to read with an eye for various logical or stylistic or conventional aspects of writing, often in the work of some of the finest American and English writers. Sometimes you will be asked to try to imitate their sentences. As your writing improves, so will your reading.

Chapters 1–5 will guide you through the process of expository and argumentative essays—from your first choice of a topic to your final typed essay. Chapters 6–36 provide thorough discussion of writing conventions—grammar, punctuation, and mechanics. These chapters provide examples and practice to guide you in mastering such conventions and in learning to use them appropriately and effectively.

Next come chapters that will help you understand, carry out, and use research in your writing; examine the writing of your chosen discipline; and practice taking essay examinations or producing job application letters and résumés.

This book has been designed to make its information as easy as possible to find and use. You can find what you are looking for by consulting the table of contents, the subject index, or the index of authors and titles. Once you find the correct chapter, you can skim the many headings. If your instructor uses our codes in marking your essays, you can find the code symbols at the top of each page. Even the exercises can be "used" easily, for we include at the end of the book answers to many of them, to allow you to check your understanding as you work.

Because we assume you will be consulting this book regularly when you are revising your drafts, we wish to call to your attention the many sections designed to help you *check* various elements and structures. Especially notable are guidelines to assist you to check for—and revise—each of the twenty most common error patterns; to make these easy to find, we have marked them with a small red chevron:

For those who compose on a computer, we offer the complimentary *St. Martin's Hotline*, a "pop-up" reference system available for IBM-compatible and MacIntosh systems.

Finally, we'd like to call your attention to a small feature you might find valuable, a writing log. We urge you to keep a log as a repository of materials from and for your own writing—notable anecdotes, exemplary phrases, memorable images, troublesome words or structures. Procedures for keeping a log are described in 1c, and exercises throughout this text suggest materials to add to it. Keeping a log can help you to examine and contemplate your own writing.

We hope that this book will prove to be a useful reference. But in the long run, a book can be only a guide. You are the one who will put such guidance into practice, as you work to become a precise, a powerful, and a persuasive writer. Why not get started on achieving that goal right now?

Andrea Lunsford
Robert Connors

Contents

Part III
SENTENCES: MAKING CONVENTIONAL CHOICES   237

Learning from Your Errors

Many people who are not instructors or students tend to think of "correctness" in writing as an absolute. There are hard and fast "rules," they believe, and if all of those rules are followed, correct writing will result. Errors in writing result from not following these "rules," which are handed down from time immemorial and set out in grammar books and handbooks like this one. Learning to write, for these people, is learning the rules.

Instructors and students know different. They know that there are "rules," all right, but that the rules change all the time. "Is it okay to use *I* in essays for this class?" asks one student. "My high school teacher wouldn't let us." "Will more than one comma splice flunk an essay?" asks another. "Must I have three paragraphs on each page?" asks a third. These students know that rules clearly exist, but that they are part of a social transaction between writers and readers that is always shifting and thus needs constantly to be explored.

Research has shown how much that transaction has changed in the last century alone. Mechanical and grammatical questions that no longer concern us at all used to be perceived as extremely important. In the late nineteenth century, for instance, instructors at Harvard told us that the most serious writing problem their students had was an inability to distinguish between the proper uses of *shall* and *will*. Similarly, split infinitives seemed to many instructors of the 1950s a very serious problem, but ever since the starship *Enterprise* set out "to boldly go" where no one has gone before, split infinitives have wrinkled fewer brows.

These examples of shifting standards are not meant to suggest that there is no such thing as "correctness" in writing—only that correctness always depends on some context. Correctness is not so much a question of absolute right or wrong as a question of how a writer is perceived by an audience. As writers, we are all judged by the words we put on the page. We all want to be regarded as competent and careful, and formal errors in our writing work against that impression. As one very famous writing instructor put it, errors make unintentional demands on readers, drawing their attention to something from which they will gain no mental reward.* The world judges us by our mastery of the conventions we have agreed to use, and we all know it. As Robert Frost once said of poetry, trying to write without honoring the conventions and agreed-upon rules is like playing tennis without a net.

So fluency in writing means having something to say and saying it in the way most appropriate to a given audience and context. One assumption this book makes is that you already have important things to say and that as you learn more and more about the subjects you study in college, you will have more and more to say. A second assumption is that you want to master the conventions used in academic writing. Since you already know the vast majority of these conventions, the most efficient way to proceed is to focus on those conventions that are still unfamiliar or puzzling. Achieving this practical focus means identifying, analyzing, and overcoming *patterns of conventional error* in your writing.

Almost all writing problems follow a pattern. If you have ever gotten back an assignment covered with red marks, the task of figuring out how to solve all the problems no doubt seemed somewhat daunting. Each mark seemed to point to a separate error, and there were dozens of them. But if rather than considering each mark separately you try to fit them together into patterns, you will nearly always find one or two major kinds of errors. From, say, twenty different problems, you have cut your job down to only a few.

Make the effort, then, to take control of your own writing by seeking out your own patterns of error and learning from them. This task does not mean becoming obsessed with errors to the exclusion of everything else in your writing. A perfectly correct essay is, after all, a limited and limiting goal. You want to aim for a perfectly persuasive and enlightening essay—that also happens to be correct.

You should, in fact, *not* concern yourself with correctness at every stage of writing. Concentrating on errors during planning or drafting can inhibit you from writing freely. Instead, worry about errors

---

* Mina P. Shaughnessy, *Errors & Expectations* (New York: Oxford UP, 1977).

when you revise and edit. If your instructor comments on your early drafts, study them to identify patterns you follow.

Keep a record of your error patterns, perhaps in a writing log. If you find that you tend to leave off verb endings, for example, keep a list of the endings that have given you trouble; and check your drafts against that list as you proofread. Concentrate on one error pattern at a time. Dealing with errors systematically in this way is the best possible way of conquering them once and for all.

This handbook will help you take control of those writing conventions that give you trouble. Research conducted for this book has revealed much about the error patterns typical of college students today, and this chapter addresses those errors. Analysis of a scientifically determined sample taken from more than 20,000 freshman and sophomore essays from around the United States has shown which errors you are most likely to make—and which ones your instructor is most likely to mark. From this analysis comes some very interesting determinations about student writing, and especially about student errors.

First, spelling errors are by far the most common, by a factor of more than three to one. Because they are so plentiful, the words found to be most often misspelled are given in a separate list, which you can find in Chapter 22. Second, instructors do not always mark all errors; some error patterns clearly strike them as more serious than others. Whether your instructor comments on one of your writing problems in a particular assignment will depend on his or her judgment about how serious it is and what you should be dealing with at the time. Finally, not all errors are even seen as errors. In fact, some of the patterns identified in the research are considered errors by some instructors but stylistic options by others. This finding confirms the belief that "correctness" is really defined by a transaction between readers and writers. This book describes the nature of this transaction, noting those areas where agreement is widespread and others where it is not. You, of course, are a part of the transaction. As a writer, you will constantly need to consider the expectations of your readers and to make decisions about the appropriateness of certain writing conventions. For much of your college writing, your primary reader will be your instructor, and so if ever you are uncertain about whether something is appropriate (that is, correct), you should take the opportunity to discuss it with him or her.

Here, in order of occurrence, are the twenty most common error patterns among college students in the late 1980s.

XXXV

1. Missing comma after an introductory element
2. Vague pronoun reference
3. Missing comma in a compound sentence
4. Wrong word
5. Missing comma(s) with a nonrestrictive element
6. Wrong or missing verb ending
7. Wrong or missing preposition
8. Comma splice
9. Missing or misplaced possessive apostrophe
10. Unnecessary shift in tense
11. Unnecessary shift in pronoun
12. Sentence fragment
13. Wrong tense or verb form
14. Lack of agreement between subject and verb
15. Missing comma in a series
16. Lack of agreement between pronoun and antecedent
17. Unnecessary comma(s) with a restrictive element
18. Fused sentence
19. Dangling or misplaced modifier
20. *Its / it's* confusion

Statistically, these twenty are the errors most likely to cause you trouble. A brief explanation and examples of each one are given in this chapter, and each error pattern is cross-referenced to at least one place elsewhere in this book where you can find more detail or additional examples.

1. Missing comma after an introductory element

When a sentence opens with an introductory word, phrase, or clause, readers usually need a small pause between the introductory element and the main part of the sentence. Such a pause is most often signaled by a comma.

INTRODUCTORY WORD

Frankly, we were baffled by the committee's decision.

INTRODUCTORY PHRASE

In fact, the Philippines consist of more than eight thousand islands.

To tell the truth, I never have liked the Mets.

Because of its isolation in a rural area surrounded by mountains, Crawford Notch doesn't get many visitors.

INTRODUCTORY CLAUSE

Even though I provided detailed advice for revising, his draft became only worse.

Short introductory elements do not always need a comma. The test is whether the sentence can be easily understood without one. The following sentence, for example, would at first be misunderstood if it did not have a comma—readers would think the introductory phrase was *In German nouns*, rather than *In German*. The best advice is that you will rarely be wrong to add a comma after an introductory element.

In German, nouns are always capitalized.

➤ For guidelines on checking for commas after introductory elements, see page 425. For more on commas and introductory elements in general, see 6c, 15e, 20b, and 27a.

▌2. Vague pronoun reference

A pronoun like *he, she, it, they, this, that,* or *which* should refer clearly to a specific word (or words) elsewhere in the sentence or in a previous sentence. When readers cannot tell for sure who or what the pronoun refers to, the reference is said to be vague. There are two common kinds of vague pronoun reference. The first occurs when there is more than one word that the pronoun might refer to; the second, when the reference is to a word that is implied but not explicitly stated.

xxxvii

POSSIBLE REFERENCE TO MORE THAN ONE WORD

Before Mary Grace physically and verbally assaulted Mrs. Turpin, ~~she~~ *the latter*

was a judgmental woman who created her own ranking system of people

and used it to justify her self-proclaimed superiority.

Transmitting radio signals by satellite is a way of overcoming the problem

of scarce airwaves and limiting how ~~they~~ *the airwaves* are used.

REFERENCE IMPLIED BUT NOT STATED

The troopers burned an Indian camp as a result of the earlier attack.

This *destruction of the camp* ∧ was the cause of the war.

They believe that a zygote, an egg at the moment of fertilization, is as

deserving of protection as the born human being, but ~~it~~ *such an assertion* is totally un-

provable scientifically.

➤ For guidelines on checking for vague pronoun reference, see page
244. For more on pronoun reference, see Chapter 11.

▍ 3. Missing comma in a compound sentence

A compound sentence is made up of two (or more) parts that
could each function as an independent sentence. These parts may be
linked by either a semicolon or a coordinating conjunction (*and, but,
so, yet, nor, or, for*). When a conjunction is used, a comma should
usually be placed before it to indicate a pause between the two thoughts.

The words may sound simple, but "I do" mean a complex commitment

for life.

We wish dreamily upon a star and then we look down to see what we

have stepped in.

In *very* short sentences, this use of the comma is optional if the sentence can be easily understood without it. The following sentence, for example, would be misunderstood if it did not have a comma—readers would think at first that Meredith was wearing her feet. The best advice is to use the comma before the coordinating conjunction, since it will always be correct.

Meredith wore jeans and her feet were bare.

➤ For guidelines on checking for commas in compound sentences, see page 427. For further discussion and examples, see 6d1 and 27b.

▌ 4. Wrong word

"Wrong word" errors range from simple lack of proofreading, like using *should* for *would*, to mistakes in basic word meaning, like using *prevaricate* when you mean *procrastinate*, to mistakes in shades of meaning, like using *sedate* when you mean *sedentary*. Many errors marked "wrong word" are *homonyms*, words that are pronounced alike but spelled differently, like *their* and *there*.

A knowledge of computers is ~~inherent~~ *assumed* in this office.

Mark noticed the ~~stench~~ *fragrance* of roses as he entered the room.

Paradise Lost contains many ~~illusions~~ *allusions* to classical mythology.

➤ For guidelines on checking a draft for wrong words, see page 397. For additional, more detailed information about choosing the right word for your meaning, see 22a, 23c2, and 25b.

▌ 5. Missing comma(s) with a nonrestrictive element

A nonrestrictive element is a word, phrase, or clause that gives additional information about the preceding part of the sentence but does not restrict or limit the meaning of that part. A nonrestrictive element is not essential to the sentence; it can be deleted without changing the sentence's basic meaning. To indicate that it is not es-

xxxix

sential, it is always set off from the rest of the sentence with a comma before it and, if it is in the middle of the sentence, after it as well.

Marina‸who was the president of the club‸was first to speak.

Louis was forced to call a session of the Estates General‸which had not met for 175 years.

The bottom of the pond was covered with soft brown clay‸a natural base for a good swimming hole.

➤ For guidelines on checking for commas with nonrestrictive elements, see page 431. For additional explanation, see 27c.

▌ 6. Wrong or missing verb ending

The verb endings -s or (-es) and -ed (or -d) are important markers in standard edited English. It is easy to forget these endings in writing because they are not always pronounced clearly when spoken. In addition, some dialects do not use the -s ending in the same way as standard edited English.

Eliot ~~use~~ *uses* feline imagery throughout the poem.

I run̸ a mile every morning before breakfast.

The United States ~~drop~~ *dropped* two atomic bombs on Japan in 1945.

Nobody ~~imagine~~ *imagined* he would actually become president.

An -s (or -es) ending must be added to a present-tense verb whose subject is a singular noun; the personal pronouns *he, she,* or *it*; and most indefinite pronouns (such as *anyone, each, everybody, nobody, nothing, someone*). The ending is not added to a verb whose subject is a plural noun; the personal pronouns *I, you, we,* or *they*; and indefinite pronouns that have a plural meaning (such as *both or few*). The past-tense and past-participle forms of most verbs must end in -ed (or -d).

➤ For guidelines on checking for verb endings, see pages 189 and 192. For more on verb endings, see pages 187–190, 8b, 8c, and 9a.

▌ 7. Wrong or missing preposition

Many words in English are regularly used with a particular preposition to express a particular meaning; for example, we *agree to* a proposal, *agree with* another person, and *agree on* a price for something. Using the wrong preposition in such expressions is a common error. Because most prepositions are so short and are not stressed or pronounced clearly in speech, they are also often left out accidentally in writing.

The bus committee is trying to set a schedule that will meet the needs

of most people who rely ~~in~~ *on* public transportation.

Nixon compared the United States ~~with~~ *to* a "pitiful, helpless giant."

She received a dishonorable discharge for refusing to comply ~~to~~ *with* army

regulations.

In his moral blindness Gloucester is similar ~~with~~ *to* Lear.

Dennis found the shaving soap *in* the medicine cabinet.

➤ For guidelines on checking a draft for wrong or missing prepositions, see page 288. For additional information about choosing the correct preposition, see 6b6.

▌ 8. Comma splice

A comma splice occurs when two or more clauses that could each stand alone as a sentence are written with only a comma between them. Such clauses must be either clearly separated by a punctuation mark stronger than a comma—a period or semicolon—or clearly connected with a word like *and* or *although*, or else the ideas they state should be combined into one clause.

Westward migration had passed Wyoming by *;* even the discovery of gold

in nearby Montana failed to attract settlers.

I was strongly attracted to her *for* she had special qualities.

xli

Having
They ~~always had~~ roast beef for Thanksgiving, /~~this~~ was one of their family

traditions.

➤ For guidelines on checking for comma splices, see page 257. For additional information about ways to avoid or revise comma splices, see Chapter 13.

∎ 9. Missing or misplaced possessive apostrophe

To show that one thing belongs to another, either an apostrophe and an *-s* or an apostrophe alone is added to the word representing the thing that possesses the other. An apostrophe and *-s* are used for singular nouns (words that refer to one thing, such as *leader* or *Chicago*); for indefinite pronouns (words like *anybody, everyone, nobody, somebody*); and for plural nouns (words referring to more than one thing that do not end in *-s*, such as *men* and *women*. For plural nouns ending in *-s*, such as *creatures* or *fathers*, only the apostrophe is used.

child's
Over-ambitious parents can be very harmful to a ~~childs~~ well-being.
Yankees'
Ron Guidry has been one of the ~~Yankees~~ most electrifying pitchers.

➤ For guidelines on checking for possessive apostrophes, see page 458. For additional, more detailed information on use of the apostrophe to indicate possession, see page 175 and 30a.

∎ 10. Unnecessary shift in tense

An unnecessary shift in tense occurs when the verbs in a sentence or passage shift for no reason from one time period to another, such as from past to present or from present to future. Such tense shifts confuse the reader, who must guess which tense is the right one.

cries
Joy always laughs until she ~~cried~~ at that episode of *Dynasty*.
slipped fell
Lucy was watching the great blue heron take off when she ~~slips~~ and ~~falls~~

into the swamp.

Each team of detectives is assigned to three or four cases at a time. They ~~will~~ investigate only those leads that seem most promising.

The representative had begun his speech when a young man in blue jeans ran up to the podium. He ~~shaves~~ *shoved* a shaving-cream pie in the speaker's face.

➤ For guidelines on checking for unnecessary shifts in tense, see page 248. For more on shifting tenses, see 12a, and on using verb tenses in sequences, see 8g.

▌ 11. Unnecessary shift in pronoun

An unnecessary pronoun shift occurs when a writer who has been using one kind of pronoun to refer to someone or something shifts to another for no reason. The most common shift in pronoun is from *one* to *you* or *I*. This shift often results from an attempt at a more formal level of diction, which is hard to maintain when it is not completely natural.

When one first sees a painting by Georgia O'Keeffe, *one is* ~~you are~~ impressed by a sense of power and stillness.

If we had known about the ozone layer, *we* ~~you~~ could have banned aerosol sprays years ago.

➤ For guidelines on checking a draft for unnecessary pronoun shifts, see page 251. For additional information about shifts in pronouns, see 12d.

▌ 12. Sentence fragment

A sentence fragment is a part of a sentence that is written as if it were a whole sentence, with a capital letter at the beginning and a period, question mark, or exclamation point. A fragment lacks one or both of the two essential parts of a sentence, a subject and a complete verb; or else it begins with a subordinating word, which means that the idea it expresses depends for its meaning on another sentence.

LACKING SUBJECT

Marie Antoinette spent huge sums of money on herself and her favorites. *Her extravagance helped*
~~Helped~~ to bring on the French Revolution.

LACKING COMPLETE VERB

was
The old aluminum boat⌃sitting on its trailer.

BEGINNING WITH SUBORDINATING WORD

, *where*
We returned to the drugstore⌃ ~~Where~~ we waited for the rest of the gang.

➤ For guidelines on checking for sentence fragments, see page 266. For additional, more detailed information on sentence fragments, see Chapter 14.

▌ 13. Wrong tense or verb form

Errors that are marked as being the wrong tense or verb form include using a verb that does not indicate clearly that the action or condition it expresses is (or was or will be) completed—for example, using *walked* instead of *had walked* or *will go* instead of *will have gone*. In some dialects of English, the verbs *be* and *have* are used in ways that are not used by most other native speakers of the language; these uses may also be labeled as the wrong verb form. Finally, many errors of this kind occur with verbs whose basic forms for showing past time or a completed action or condition do not follow the regular pattern, like *begin, began, begun* and *break, broke, broken*. Errors may occur when a writer confuses the second and third forms or treats these verbs as if they followed the regular pattern—for example, using *beginned* instead of *began* or *have breaked* instead of *have broken*.

Ian was shocked to learn that Joe *had* died only the day before.

The poet *is* looking at a tree when she *has* a sudden inspiration.

Florence Griffith Joyner has *broken* many track records.

The Greeks *built* a wooden horse that the Trojans *took* into the city.

➤ For guidelines on checking verb tenses, see page 201. For additional, more detailed information about verb tenses and forms, see 6b1, Chapter 8, and 9a–9i.

▌ 14. Lack of agreement between subject and verb

A subject and verb must agree, or match. In many cases the verb must take a different form depending on whether the subject is singular (one) or plural (more than one): *The old <u>man is</u> angry and <u>stamps</u> into the house* but *The old <u>men are</u> angry and <u>stamp</u> into the house*. Lack of agreement between the subject and verb is often just a matter of leaving the *-s* ending off the verb out of carelessness and failure to proofread, or of following a dialect that does not use this ending (see Errors 6 and 13). Sometimes, however, it results from particular kinds of subjects of sentence constructions.

When other words come between subject and verb, a writer may mistake a noun nearest to the verb for the verb's real subject. In the following sentence, for example, the subject is the singular *part*, not the plural *goals*.

A central part of my life goals *has* been to go to law school.

Other problems can arise from subjects made up of two or more parts joined by *and* or *or*; subjects like *committee* or *jury*, which can take either singular or plural verb forms depending on whether they are treated as a unit or as a group of individuals; and subjects like *politics* and *measles*, which look plural but are singular in meaning.

My brother and his friend Larry commut*es* every day from Louisville.

The committee *were* taking all the responsibility themselves.

Politics *has* been defined as "the art of the possible."

xlv

Subjects that are pronouns cause problems for many writers. Most indefinite pronouns, like *each, either, neither,* or *one* take singular verb forms. The relative pronouns, *who, which,* or *that* take verbs that agree with the word the pronoun refers to.

coordinates
Each of the items in these designs ~~coordinate~~ with the others.

were
Johnson was one of the athletes who ~~was~~ disqualified.

Finally, some problems occur when writers make the verb agree with a word that follows or precedes it rather than with the grammatical subject. In the following sentences, for example, the subjects are *source* and *man.*

was
His only source of income ~~were~~ his parents.

stands
Behind the curtains ~~stand~~ an elderly man producing the wizard's effects.

➤ For guidelines on checking for subject-verb agreement, see page 219. For additional, more detailed information about subject-verb agreement, see pages 187–189 and 9a–9i.

▌15. Missing comma in a series

A series consists of three or more parallel words, phrases, or clauses that appear consecutively in a sentence. Traditionally, all the items in a series are separated by commas. Many newspapers and magazines do not use a comma before the *and* or *or* between the last two items, and some instructors do not require it. Check your instructor's preference, and be consistent in either using or omitting this comma.

Sharks eat mostly squid, shrimp, crabs, and other fish.

You must learn to talk to the earth, smell it, squeeze it in your hands.

➤ For guidelines on checking a draft for series commas, see page 434. For more on parallel structures in a series, see 19a, or on using commas in a series, see 27d.

xlvi

16. Lack of agreement between pronoun and antecedent

Most pronouns (words like *I, it, you, him, her, this, themselves, someone, who, which*) are used to restate another word (or words), so that that word does not have to be repeated. The word that the pronoun replaces or stands for is called its antecedent. Pronouns must agree with, or match, their antecedents in gender—for example, using *he* and *him* to replace *Abraham Lincoln* and *she* and *her* to replace *Queen Elizabeth*. They must also agree with their antecedents in referring to either one person or thing (singular) or more than one (plural)—for example, using *it* to replace *a book* and *they* and *them* to replace *fifteen books*.

Most people have few problems with pronoun-antecedent agreement except with certain kinds of antecedents. These include words like *each, either, neither*, and *one*, which are singular and take singular pronouns; antecedents made up of two or more parts joined by *or* or *nor*; and antecedents like *audience* or *team*, which can be either singular or plural depending on whether they are considered a single unit or a group of individuals.

Every one of the puppies thrived in ~~their~~ *its* new home.

Neither Jane nor Susan felt that ~~they~~ *she* had been treated fairly.

The team frequently changed ~~its~~ *their* positions to get varied experience.

The other main kind of antecedent that causes problems is a singular antecedent (such as *each* or *an employee*) that could be either male or female. Rather than use masculine pronouns (*he, him,* and so on) with such an antecedent, a traditional rule that excludes or ignores females, a writer should use *he or she, him or her,* and so on, or else rewrite the sentence to make the antecedent and pronoun plural or to eliminate the pronoun.

Every student must provide his *or her* own uniform.

~~Every~~ *All students* must provide ~~his~~ *their* own ~~uniform~~ *uniforms*.

Every student must provide ~~his own~~ *a* uniform.

xlvii

➤ For guidelines on checking for pronoun-antecedent agreement, see page 223. For additional, more detailed information about pronoun-antecedent agreement, see 9j–9m.

17. Unnecessary comma(s) with a restrictive element

A restrictive element is a word, phrase, or clause that restricts or limits the meaning of the preceding part of the sentence; it is essential to the meaning of what precedes it and cannot be left out without changing the sentence's basic meaning. Because of this close relationship, it is *not* set off from the rest of the sentence with a comma or commas.

An arrangement/for orchestra/was made by Ravel.

Several groups/ opposed to the use of animals for cosmetics testing/ picketed the laboratory.

People/who wanted to preserve wilderness areas/ opposed the plan to privatize national parks.

The vice-president succeeds/ if and when the president dies or becomes incapacitated.

Shakespeare's tragedy/*Othello*/deals with the dangers of jealousy.

In the last of the preceding examples, the appositive is essential to the meaning of the sentence because Shakespeare wrote more than one tragedy.

➤ For guidelines on checking for unnecessary commas with restrictive elements, see page 440. For additional, more detailed information about restrictive phrases and clauses, see 27c and 27i1.

xlviii

▌ 18. Fused sentence

Fused sentences (sometimes called run-on sentences) are created when two or more groups of words that could each be written as an independent sentence are written without any punctuation between them. Such groups of words must be either separated into two sentences, by using a period and a capital letter, or joined together in a way that shows their relationship, by either adding words and punctuation or by rewriting completely.

Klee's paintings seem simple, *but* they are very sophisticated.

The current was swift. *He* could not swim to shore.

She doubted the value of meditation; *nevertheless,* she decided to try it once.

➤ For guidelines on checking for fused sentences, see page 257. For more detailed information about ways to revise fused sentences, see Chapter 13.

▌ 19. Misplaced or dangling modifier

A misplaced modifier is a word, phrase, or clause that is not placed close enough to the word it describes or is related to. As a result, it seems to modify some other word, phrase, or clause, and readers can be confused or puzzled.

t They could see the eagles swooping and diving *w* with binoculars.

h He had decided he wanted to be a doctor *w* when he was ten years old.

s Slowly and precisely, I watched the teller count out the money.

The architect only wanted to use pine paneling for decoration.

r Rising over the trees, *T* the campers saw a bright red sun.

The woman bought the painting from the shop that depicted a Chicago street scene.

A dangling modifier is a word, phrase, or elliptical clause (a clause from which words have been left out) that is not clearly related to any other word in the sentence. The word that it modifies exists in the writer's mind, but not on paper in the sentence. Such a modifier is called "dangling" because it hangs precariously from the beginning or end of the sentence, attached to nothing very solid.

A doctor should check your eyes for glaucoma every year if ^*you are* over fifty.

Looking down the stretch of sandy beach, ^*one sees* people ~~are~~ lying face down trying to get a tan.

As a male college student, many people are surprised ~~at~~ *that I,* ~~any~~ support ~~for~~ the draft.
(a)   *M*

➤   For guidelines on checking for misplaced and dangling modifiers, see page 281. For additional, more detailed information on misplaced and dangling modifiers, see 15a and 15c.

▌ 20. *Its / It's* confusion

The word *its*, spelled without an apostrophe, is the possessive form of *it*, meaning "of it" or "belonging to it." The word *it's*, spelled with an apostrophe, is a shortened form of *it is* or *it has*. Even though an apostrophe often indicates a possessive form, in this case the possessive form is the one *without* the apostrophe.

The car is lying on its side in the ditch.

It's a white 1986 Buick.

It's been lying there for two days.

➤   For guidelines on checking *its* and *it's*, see page 459. For more on *its* and *it's*, see 22b and 30b.

1

PART ONE

The Writing Process

1. Understanding the Writing Process

A significant part of any college education involves reading and writing, two primary means of sharing knowledge. Of course, no one can complete college without doing an enormous amount of reading, and more and more people in education, business, and the professions now realize that the ability to write effectively is just as important as the ability to read well. In fact, research shows that writing encourages and enhances certain kinds of learning, and even that some kinds of complex thinking may be impossible without it. Writing, then, is not an artistic talent that only a lucky few possess, but an essential and powerful means of discovering what you know and of expressing that knowledge in communicating with others. As one author says:

> . . . writing is foremost a mode of thinking and, when it works well, an act of discovery. I write to find out what I believe, what seems logical and sensible to me, what notions, ideas, and views I can live with.
>
> —JOSEPH EPSTEIN

If you can read this text, you have the potential to be a writer of just the sort Epstein describes. There is nothing mysterious about the process of writing, and writers are not born with any special power. Writers simply explore observations and ideas on paper and care about the ways that their readers respond to their written words.

In order to write successfully, however, it helps to understand how the writing process works and how to develop a method that works for you. Charlotte W., for example, sits down at the typewriter a few hours before an essay is due and frantically pounds out a draft. Her essays often touch on interesting ideas, but they are so disorganized and full of grammatical errors that the effect of the ideas is lost. Peter

3

USEFUL READING

Lindemann, Erika. *A Rhetoric for Writing Teachers*. 2nd ed. New York: Oxford UP, 1987. A comprehensive and readable survey of the field of composition, especially for teachers of writing. Lindemann provides background material for the teaching of writing, including a history of rhetoric, a survey of linguistics, and a useful bibliography.

TEACHING PRACTICE

In your class are many students who know exactly what you expect of them: flawlessly executed, fully developed essays. They are sure that you write without anxiety, false starts, erasures, or dictionaries, for you are an English instructor. Unlike them, you put pen to paper and write effortlessly from start to finish. Therefore, you might want to start the term by asking your students how they think experienced writers work. Then discuss your writing process as well as theirs.

Your students will benefit from comparing their writing habits: what kind of paper they use, what kind of pen, how (and if) they gather their thoughts first, whether they add new information as they move through the writing assignment, if they prefer quiet or background noise, what time of day they do their best writing, how soon before the deadline they begin their assignments, and, most important, what kind of writing they do. In short, your students need to examine the process they use to produce a final draft.

By discussing your students' writing processes, you will help them accomplish three complementary goals: (1) They will listen and talk to one another, not just to their instructor, thereby fostering a classroom atmosphere that lends itself to collaborative and peer-group writing practices. (2) They will realize that you, too, have a unique writing process. (3) They will see that because writing is a recursive process consisting of planning, drafting, and revising, they can concentrate on one step at a time.

G. works terribly hard to put every comma in place and spell every word correctly, and his papers are letter-perfect—but rarely do they have anything to say. Although these writers put very different amounts and kinds of effort into their writing, neither is gaining much intellectual reward or academic credit. Looking carefully at the way they *go about* writing, at their processes of writing, should help them to see why they aren't writing effectively and to make the kinds of changes that will lead to better essays and greater rewards. Because the writing process is complex and directly related to the quality of the finished piece of writing, the next several chapters will focus on the various parts of that process.

1a. Recognizing the recursive parts of the writing process

The mental processes that actually accompany the writing process are tremendously complex. They are, moreover, so subtle and so lightning-fast that we are only now beginning to learn how they all interact. But we *do* know that writers always set and shift and reset a series of goals as they write. These goals range from those as large as "try to make the reader laugh here" or "explain that concept" to ones as small as "use a semicolon instead of a period here to make this section less choppy." Researchers often describe the process of writing as seamless and **recursive**, meaning that its goals or parts are constantly flowing into and influencing one another, without any clear break between them. The shifting set of goals may focus one moment on deciding how to organize a paragraph and the next moment on using knowledge gained from that decision to revise the wording of a sentence. Repetitive, erratic, and often messy, writing does not proceed in nice, neat steps: first an idea; then a plan; then an introduction, body, and conclusion. In fact, these "steps" often take place simultaneously, in a kind of spiraling sequence, with planning, drafting, and revising all taking place throughout the process of writing. A writer may get an idea for a conclusion while drafting the introduction, or may plan one paragraph while revising the previous one.

In any case, writers seldom pay conscious attention to these constantly shifting goals and recursive patterns. Ideally, writing can be like riding a bicycle; with practice the process becomes more and more automatic. As you become more practiced as a writer, more and more of the goal-juggling you do will become automatic. Like an experienced

(BACK)GROUNDING

In "Pre-writing: The Stage of Discovery in the Writing Process," D. Gordon Rohman challenged the field of composition studies by arguing that writing was a learnable process. He begins his essay, published in *College Composition and Communication* (CCC) (16 [1965]: 106–12), by positing the following:

> Writing is usefully described as a process, something which shows continuous change in time like growth in organic nature. Different things happen at different stages in the process of putting thoughts into words and words onto paper. In our Project English experiment, we divided the process at the point where the "writing idea" is ready for the words and the page: everything before that we called "Pre-Writing," everything after "Writing" and "Re-Writing."

For more information on the writing process, see the bibliography. It provides a selected listing of relevant books and articles. Abbreviations used are *CCC, College Composition and Communication; CE, College English; EJ, English Journal; EQ, English Quarterly; RTE, Research in the Teaching of English; WC, Written Communication.*

USEFUL READING

Perl, Sondra. "Understanding Composing." CCC 31 (Dec. 1980): 363–69. Rpt. *Rhetoric and Composition: A Sourcebook for Teachers and Writers.* 2nd ed. Ed. Richard L. Graves. Arguing that "throughout the process of writing, writers return to substrands of the overall process, or subroutines," Perl attempts to identify the features of this recursiveness, particularly the parts of the composition or the writing process to which writers return.

cyclist, you will be able to pay attention to the big things—oncoming traffic, the view, the route you're taking—without thinking too consciously about changing gears or moving your feet or stopping at red lights.

Instructors who study the ways writers work most effectively find it useful to think of the writing process as a series of recursive activities: **planning**, during which the writer finds information and prepares to write; **drafting**, during which the writer puts down on paper a version of the essay; and **revising**, during which the writer works with the draft to improve it. But these activities seldom, if ever, occur in a linear sequence, with one following another. Rather, writers move back and forth—planning, drafting, planning some more, revising, drafting, revising, planning a little more—until the writing is complete. Though the following sections discuss planning, drafting, and revising in that order, remember that in the process of writing these activities are always interwoven.

▌ 1. Planning

Effective writing does not just happen. Of course, you can merely sit down, dash something off, and call it writing, but writing worth reading usually starts with a nagging question or puzzle or idea that requires planning: thinking, investigating, organizing, and generally getting ready to write. While planning continues throughout the writing process, it is often the way a writer begins.

Depending on the writing task, planning can last a few minutes or several months. If you have to write a one-page essay in class about a member of your family, you will probably jot down a few notes, put them in order, and start writing very quickly. If, on the other hand, you have six weeks to prepare a fifteen-page paper on U.S.–Soviet relations, you will need to do some research and explore the topic thoroughly before deciding exactly what you want to say.

Planning includes everything you do as you prepare to draft: thinking about your purpose, exploring a topic, coming up with a working thesis, gathering materials, deciding how to appeal to your audience, and developing a strategy for organizing the writing. Your organizational plan may be a short list or a long, detailed outline accompanied by a tall stack of research cards. Whatever shape your planning takes, it will act as your guide as you draft your essay. Your planning and thesis may well shift as you draft, but just having them

---

USEFUL READING

Gebhardt, Richard. "Initial Plans and Spontaneous Composition: Toward a Comprehensive Theory of the Writing Process." *CE* 44 (Oct. 1982): 620–27. Gebhardt confronts the problem of choosing a composing-process model: the linear, stage-by-stage model, which emphasizes preplanning, or the recursive model, which allows for discovery during writing. He finds that some of the leading researchers in this seemingly diverse field share the same assumptions: that writers begin with a general sense of what they intend to say, but that these intentions do not prevent writers from making discoveries as they write (i.e., intentions evolve).

there will help you to keep on course, or at least to remember where you are headed. The process of planning is examined in detail in Chapter 2.

2. Drafting

Drafting is the central part of writing—the one element in the process that can never be skipped or avoided. As one student put it, drafting is "where the rubber meets the road," the time when you try your ideas out in writing.

Writing habits are, of course, as variable as writers. Some people can work on a draft only in complete silence; others need music playing. Some must be completely alone, while others work best in a crowded library. Some prefer to produce a draft in one long, sustained burst of energy; still others work more slowly, taking breaks after drafting each section.

As much as anything, drafting represents a process of exploration. The great British writer E. M. Forster once wrote, "How can I know what I think until I see what I say?" Indeed, some kinds of understanding come only from trying to express your ideas for others—in writing. No matter how thoroughly you explore your topic while planning, you will discover more about the topic while drafting your essay. Sometimes these new insights will cause you to turn back—to change your organizational plan, to bring in more information, to approach the subject from a new angle, or to rethink your appeal to your audience. Drafting, then, is *not* merely "putting your ideas down on paper." More often than not, drafting also involves coming up with new ideas or completely reshaping your concept of what you are trying to achieve in the essay. And since writing is indeed a recursive activity, this moving back and forth among planning, drafting, and revising is just what one would expect.

Some writers make drafting more difficult than it needs to be by trying to make their writing come out perfectly the first time. Agonizing over every sentence, word, and quotation mark can make drafting a lengthy, painful, and unsatisfying process. In fact, such agonizing often prevents effective writing. It is much more fruitful to view drafting as just that—the process of working out a *first draft*, which explores thoughts, expresses ideas, and tries out examples. The goal of drafting is not a final copy, or even a version good enough to show anyone else. Smooth sentences, the ideal word choice, and the right punctua-

WRITERS WRITING

As your class will soon realize, there are as many ways to write as there are writers. Jack Kerouac and James Joyce, for example, had absolutely antithetical writing habits: Kerouac wrote in a white heat whereas Joyce tinkered endlessly.

Kerouac is said to have arrived at his editor's office with a draft of *On the Road* typed uncorrected onto a continuous roll of paper, a draft he claimed to be divinely inspired and touched by the Holy Ghost. When his editor suggested that even a draft so inspired and so touched should be revised, Kerouac walked out of the office.

For seventeen years, Joyce worked at revising *Finnegans Wake*, mixing and blending, ordering and composing, choosing and discarding. Yet when his early drafts are compared with the printed version, we can see that most of his earliest concepts survived the revisions by becoming richer and more complex.

WRITERS ON WRITING

Writing and rewriting are a constant search for what it is one is saying.

—JOHN UPDIKE

I have never thought of myself as a good writer. Anyone who wants reassurance of that should read one of my first drafts. But I'm one of the world's great rewriters.

—JAMES A. MICHENER

The main thing I try to do is write as clearly as I can. Because I have the greatest respect for the reader, and if he's going to the trouble of reading what I've written—I'm a slow reader myself and I guess most people are—why, the least I can do is make it as easy as possible for him to find out what I'm trying to say, trying to get at. I rewrite a good deal to make it clear.

—E. B. WHITE

USEFUL READING

Emig, Janet. *The Web of Meaning: Essays on Writing, Teaching, Learning, and Thinking.* Eds. Dixie Goswami and Maureen Butler. Upper Montclair, NJ: Boynton/Cook, 1983. A collection of Emig's essays, including several chapters from *The Composing Processes of Twelfth Graders,* her pioneering case-study of students' composing habits. In these essays, Emig argues, among other things, that there is no one formula for teaching writing, that writing processes are typically recursive, and that writing "is as often a preconscious or unconscious roaming as it is a planned and conscious rendering of information and events" (141).

tion can come later; in your first draft, just try to express your thoughts clearly.

If your planning has been productive, the drafting stage may go almost as quickly as you can write. Maintaining momentum, without getting sidetracked by any one question or problem, is one of the most important skills a writer can develop. Problems may well crop up—questions to be answered, new areas to be explored—but these can be considered once the draft is finished. First you need to produce a draft. A thorough discussion of drafting appears in Chapter 2.

3. Revising

With your first draft, you have a version of your essay before you, and the rest of your work will be devoted to making sure it says what you want it to say. Doing so requires careful rereading and analysis of the draft with an eye toward establishing a systematic plan for revising.

Re-vision means literally "to see again." It means looking at a draft with a critical eye—seeing it anew and deciding if it accomplishes the goals you originally set out to accomplish. Some writers at first think revising is a matter of simply correcting misspellings, inserting commas, and typing up the result. Such tasks are important, but true revision is something more. It requires hard work, much harder and more demanding than fixing misspellings and commas, for it may mean eliminating whole sections, moving paragraphs, writing new sentences, doing additional research, or even choosing a new topic and starting all over again.

In fact, because it can be complex and quite extensive, revising more closely resembles drafting than it does editing or proofreading, the final steps of the writing process. With editing and proofreading, you make your essay ready for the world, which means it must meet those conventions of written form known as "correctness." Sentence structure, spelling, punctuation—all must meet conventional standards. Even editing, however, may lead you to reconsider a sentence, a paragraph, a transition, or an organizational pattern—and you may find yourself planning or drafting once again. Chapter 3 explores revising in some detail and provides a blueprint for successful revising and final editing.

In addition to your own analysis of the draft's strengths and weaknesses, you may want to get responses from other people. The analysis you do on your own is important, of course, because no one knows as

TEACHING PRACTICE

Early in the term, you may wish to show the class copies of your own work in progress so that your students can examine your writing process. If you write longhand, your students will be interested to see how you edit your manuscript. If you work at a typewriter, they can compare your first draft with subsequent versions. You may be one of those writers who cut and paste their typewritten drafts until the end. If you work on a word processor, your revisions may not be apparent, so bring in any versions that indicate changes (either substantive or cosmetic) that you made.

As the students look at your work, bring up the notion of "the rhetorical situation." Discuss your intended audience, your purpose for writing this piece; how you chose your topic or thesis, and any limitations imposed on you. Your students may want to know about particular problems (narrowing the subject, defining a thesis, finding the right words, procrastination) you faced and whether your final draft achieved its purpose.

USEFUL READING

Flower, Linda. "Writer-Based Prose: A Cognitive Basis for Problems in Writing." *CE* 41 (Sept. 1979): 19–37. Flower suggests that early drafts are frequently directed not to readers, but to the writer. A significant part of revision is the movement from writer-based to reader-based prose.

well as you what you are trying to say. Other readers, however, can be just as important in helping you to reexamine the thesis, the organization, the argument, the diction, the tone, the thoroughness with which the essay is developed.

All writing assumes a particular audience of readers—even if only the writers themselves. Revising can be made easier and more productive if you can actually make use of an audience, be it your friends, your classmates, or your instructor. Other people have a distance that is very difficult for writers to achieve; we are always attached to what we write, especially right after we have written it. Getting comments and criticisms from others is a way of seeing your work through new eyes, and it should be a part of every writer's process.

▌ 1b. Reading with an eye for writing

One good way to improve your writing is by paying close attention to what you read, taking tips from writers you especially admire. In the words of William Faulkner, "Read, read, read. Read everything—trash, classics, good and bad, and see how they do it." Throughout this handbook, we will be taking time to "see how they do it," examining the work of well-known writers to see what they do with the strategies and structures we ourselves will be practicing.

In addition, most chapters include exercises asking you to read a passage with an eye for some element in the writing—adjectives, subordination, whatever. These exercises should help you learn to use these elements in your own work—and might lead you to insights about how you can make your own writing more accurate and powerful.

FOR EXAMINING YOUR OWN READING PROCESS

The writer Anatole Broyard once cautioned readers about the perils of "just walking through" a book.* A good reader, he suggested, "stomps around" in a book—underlining passages, scribbling in the margin, noting any questions or comments.

How would you describe yourself as a reader—avid? hurried? meticulous? relaxed? what else? Do you annotate the text as you read, or are you careful never to write in a book? What role does reading play in your life as a student and as a writer?

---

* Anatole Broyard, "The Price of Reading Is Eternal Vigilance," *New York Times Book Review,* 10 Apr. 1988, pp. 11–12.

EXAMINING YOUR OWN WRITING   *wpr* 1c

1c. Examining your own writing

One of the best ways to improve your process of planning, drafting, and revising is to make the effort to analyze it from time to time. You can do this most systematically by keeping a **writing log**, a notebook in which you jot down your thoughts about a writing project while you are working on it or after you have completed it. Studying these notes will help you identify patterns of strength and weakness in your writing process, and sharing the writing log with your instructor or your classmates may yield some helpful advice on how you can write more efficiently and effectively.

Although you may not have thought very much about how you go about planning and producing an essay, you probably already have your own characteristic process of writing. Examining and understanding this process can help you make it work to your advantage. To get started on thinking about and evaluating your own writing process, answer the following questions. If you are keeping a writing log, you might record your answers as the first entry.

FOR EXAMINING YOUR OWN WRITING PROCESS

1. How do you typically go about preparing for a writing assignment? Describe the steps you take, including rereading the assignment, asking questions about it, talking to instructors or friends, jotting down ideas, gathering information, and so on. How far in advance of the due date do you usually begin working on the assignment?
2. When and where do your best ideas often come to you?
3. Where do you usually do your writing? Describe this place. Is it a good place to write? Why, or why not?
4. What materials do you typically use when writing? Pen or pencil and note pad, typewriter, word processor, something else?
5. Describe your typical drafting process. Do you finish a draft in one sitting, or do you prefer to take breaks? How many drafts do you usually go through before the final one? Why?
6. If you "get stuck" while writing, what do you usually do to get moving again?
7. How do you typically go about revising, and what does your revising include? What are the things you think about most as you revise?
8. What would you say is most efficient and effective about your writing process?
9. What is least efficient and effective about your writing process?
10. What specific steps could you take to improve your writing process?

9

TEACHING PRACTICE

Grading the students' writing logs may discourage them from analyzing their writing processes. The logs, however, can tell you what help your students need, and they may suggest strategies that will be useful to other members of the class.

An ungraded essay is a good way for you and your students to assess their current approach to composition. Assign the students to write a brief description of someone they knew well during childhood. Their essays should enable the reader to picture the person clearly and to understand how the writer felt about the subject. You may want to use this diagnostic essay as the basis for future assignments on the revision process.

After they have completed their essays, ask the students to answer the questions listed under FOR EXAMINING YOUR OWN WRITING PROCESS. Then read their writing logs to determine how they might improve their writing.

1. Could the student spend more time in preparation?
2. Is the essay aimed at a particular audience?
3. Is the purpose for writing evident?
4. Did the student do any revising at all? What kind(s)?
5. Do you and the student agree on the strengths of the essay?

Now is a good time to assure your students that you will help them improve their writing in specific ways, building on their strengths and concentrating on one problem at a time. Students should date their writing logs and keep them together in a notebook or folder so that they can monitor their progress.

WRITING TOGETHER

Divide the class in groups of three and ask the members of each group to discuss their writing processes, their writing practices, and their own answers to the above questions. Then have them work together to write a one- or two-page description on the findings of their group, first describing, then comparing and constrasting the writing strategies of each group member.

2. Planning and Drafting

Planning and drafting begin the moment a writer starts to think about a topic, question, or idea that will result in a piece of writing. And the process ends only after revising and editing, when the writer passes on the finished product for response by an instructor or some other intended audience. This chapter takes a close look at how planning and drafting work in practice.

▌ 2a. Deciding to write

Often the decision to write is made for you: you must take an essay examination at 10 A.M.; the editor of your newspaper sets a specific deadline; a professor announces that an essay will be due next Tuesday; your employer asks for a full report on a complex issue by the next management meeting. But even in such situations, consciously *deciding to write* is an important step to take. Here is why. Experienced writers report that making up their minds to begin a writing task represents a big step toward actually getting the job done. You can use this insight to your advantage, determining not to put off a writing assignment but to meet it head-on by consciously deciding to get to work on it.

Experienced writers also tell us that when a topic is not assigned but left open, the best way to choose one is literally to let the topic choose you. That is to say, those subjects that compel you—that puzzle, intrigue, or even irritate you—are likely to engage your interests and hence encourage your best writing. Even with assigned topics, you can often look for some aspect of the topic that is particularly compel-

10

USEFUL READING

Lindemann, Erika. *A Rhetoric for Writing Teachers*. 2nd ed. New York: Oxford UP, 1987. Chapter 6 provides a lengthy summary of various prewriting techniques.

TEACHING PRACTICE

Whether the stimulus for writing comes from outside the writer (as in a class assignment) or grows from the writer's own desire to put thoughts into words, the decision to write is a deliberate act of commitment.

When we commit ourselves to writing, we *prewrite* by assessing our writing (i.e., rhetorical) situation, asking ourselves questions such as the following. Who is my audience? What does the audience expect of me? What do I already know about this subject? What must I find out? How can I best arrange my information and ideas? How much time do I have? How long should the composition be?

Your students will soon understand the importance of prewriting to their success as writers. They will not only develop their own prewriting techniques but will come to depend upon them.

WRITERS ON WRITING

I am convinced that all writers are optimists whether they concede the point or not. . . . How otherwise could any human being sit down to a pile of blank sheets and decide to write. . . ?

—THOMAS COSTAIN

Writing is easy; all you do is sit staring at a blank sheet of paper until the drops of blood form on your forehead.

—GENE FOWLER

ling. Once you start to *wonder* about a topic, you are at the point of having something to write about.

This advice is not meant merely to encourage you to start early on any writing task. Rather, it suggests that you broaden your definition of writing to include your earliest thoughts on a topic and that you move deliberately from those early thoughts to begin writing. This conscious decision to begin working toward a draft represents an important though seldom discussed point in the writing process. And it is a decision that only you, the writer, can make.

▌ 2b. Understanding writing assignments

Most on-the-job writing addresses specific purposes, audiences, and topics: a group of chemists and biologists produces a report on food additives for the federal government; an editorial assistant composes a memo for an editor summarizing the problems in a new manuscript; a team of psychologists prepares scripts for videos intended to help large corporations deal with alcoholism among employees. These writers all have one thing in common: specific goals. They know exactly why and for whom they are writing.

College writing assignments, in contrast, may seem to appear out of the blue, with no specific purposes, audiences, or topics. In extreme cases, a college writing assignment may be only one word long, as in a theater examination that consisted of the single word "Tragedy!" At the opposite extreme come assignments in the form of fully developed cases, often favored in business, commerce, and engineering courses. Such cases are very specific: you could, for example, be asked to assume the role of a civil engineer who is to evaluate various proposals for constructing a bridge and report the results of your evaluation to your superiors.

In between the one-word assignment and the fully developed case lies a wide spectrum of assignments and topics. You may get assignments that specify purpose but not audience—to write an essay arguing for or against capital punishment, for example. Or you may be given an organizational pattern to use—to compare and contrast, for example—but no topic. Because each assignment is different, and because comprehending a topic is crucial to your success in responding to it, you should always make sure you understand the assignment as fully as possible. Consider the following questions as you analyze any assignment:

TEACHING PRACTICE
You might want to remind your students that almost all writers, even experienced ones, dread the blank page. Many authors say that the quickest way to face that challenge is to cover the blank page with writing, allowing anything to find its way onto the page.

Unlike experienced writers, students tend to spend little time prewriting. As soon as you make a writing assignment, encourage your students to respond immediately by jotting down their ideas or even fragments of ideas. You can use these responses as the basis for a discussion clarifying the requirements of the assignment. The students may want to keep a journal of their preliminary reactions to writing assignments.

WRITERS ON WRITING
To get started, I will accept anything that occurs to me.

—WILLIAM STAFFORD

How do I know what I think until I see what I say?

—E. M. FORSTER

USEFUL READING

Perl, Sondra. "The Composing Processes of Unskilled College Writers." *Research in the Teaching of English* 13 (1979): 317–36.

Pianko, Sharon. "A Description of the Composing Processes of College Freshman Writers." *Research in the Teaching of English* 13 (1979): 5–22.

In their case studies, both Perl and Pianko found that unlike accomplished writers, student writers spend very little time planning their compositions.

(BACK)GROUNDING

Most student writers will, initially, prefer to be assigned a topic. However, British researcher James Britton has shown that it is more difficult for inexperienced writers to accept an assigned topic than one they have chosen themselves. (*The Development of Writing Abilities* [11–18], London: Macmillan, 1975.)

In his study of language learning, James Moffett maintains that students can be both capable and committed writers if given a chance to express *who they are* instead of who educators want them to be. Moffett is convinced that when writers "write from the heart, they not only have something to say, something that interests others, but that they can better order their thoughts and can actualize their latent talents" (24). (*Coming on Center*, Montclair, NJ: Boynton/Cook, 1981.)

OPTIONAL EXERCISE

Ask your students to compile a list of subjects that interest them and to explore these topics in their writing logs. In this way they will have a ready store of writing topics. Once a topic has been selected, the others are available for future use.

WRITERS ON WRITING

Writing is a deliberate act; one has to make up one's mind to do it.

—JAMES BRITTON

- *What, exactly, does this assignment ask you to do?* Look for words like *analyze, classify, compare, contrast, describe, discuss, define, explain,* and *survey*. These are key terms, and you should be sure you understand what task they set. Remember that these words may differ in meaning among disciplines—*analyze* might mean one thing in literature and something rather different in biology.
- *What knowledge or information do you need to fulfill this assignment?* Do you need to do any research? See 2f and 2g for ways of assessing your own knowledge and gathering additional information.
- *How can you limit—or broaden—the topic or assignment to make it more interesting?* Is there any particular aspect of the topic in which you have special interest or knowledge? Be sure to check with your instructor if you wish to redefine the assignment in any way.
- *What are the assignment's specific requirements?* Consider length, format, organization, and deadline. Being sure of such things will help you not only to respond properly to the assignment but also to know the scope expected. Your instructor is not likely to expect library research for a paper due in twenty-four hours, for example. If no length is designated, you should ask for some guideline.
- *What is your purpose as a writer in this assignment?* Do you need to demonstrate knowledge of a certain body of material, or do you mainly need to show the ability to express certain ideas clearly? See 2c for a discussion of ways to assess purpose.
- *Who is the audience for this piece of writing?* Does the writing task tell you to *assume* a particular readership besides your instructor? See 2d for a discussion of ways to assess your audience.

Once you can answer these questions, you will have gone a good way toward exploring an assignment and making it one you can accomplish.

EXERCISE 2.1

The following assignment was given recently to an introductory psychology class: *Discuss in an essay the contributions of Jung and Freud to modern clinical psychology.* What would you need to know about the assignment in order to respond successfully? Using the set of questions in 2b, analyze this assignment.

2c. Deciding on purposes

The writing of college essays, reports, and other papers almost always involves dual or multiple purposes. On one level, you are writing to establish your credibility with your instructor, to demonstrate that you are a careful thinker and effective writer. Fulfilling this purpose means considering your instructor's expectations very carefully, a concern addressed in detail in 2d. But good college writing also accomplishes some other, more individual purpose that the writer has in mind. In fact, the best writing you do in college will be writing that in some way achieves a goal or goals of your own, that says as clearly and forcefully as possible what you think about a topic of importance to you, and what you have to say to readers about this topic. For example, if you are writing an essay about abortion, your purposes might be to share your knowledge of the topic with your readers, to persuade them to support or oppose legalized abortion, or even to clarify in your own mind the medical information about abortion or the moral debate over it. If you are writing a profile of your eccentric grandfather, you might be trying to amuse your readers at the same time that you are paying tribute to someone who was important to you.

In ancient Rome, the great orator Cicero noted that a good speech generally fulfilled one of three major purposes: to delight, to teach, or to move. Although the world has changed mightily in the two thousand years since Cicero, our purposes when we communicate with one another remain pretty much the same: we seek to *entertain* (delight), to *inform and explain* (teach), and to *persuade or convince* (move). Most of the writing you do in college will address one or some combination of these purposes, and it is thus important for you to be able to recognize the overriding purpose of any piece of writing. If, for example, an American history professor asks you to explain the web of causes that led up to the 1964 Civil Rights Act (primary purpose: to explain) and you respond by writing an impassioned plea for a new civil rights act (primary purpose: to persuade), you have misunderstood the purpose of the assignment.

For most college writing, you should think in terms of purposes rather than one single purpose. Specifically, you should consider **purpose** in terms of the *assignment*, in terms of the *instructor's expectations*, and in terms of *your own goals*.

The assignment

Is the primary purpose of the assignment to entertain, to explain, to persuade—or some other stated purpose? What does the primary purpose suggest about the best ways to achieve it? If you are unclear about the primary purpose, have you talked with your instructor or

13

WRITERS ON WRITING

To write is to write is to write is to write is to write is to write is to write.

—GERTRUDE STEIN

Without doubt, this business of writing is less difficult than burying people one knows, than lifting a piano, or than putting up with certain people. Come to think of it, sometimes it is also easier than examining one's conscience. It might also be mentioned that an advantage to writing is that one works alone.

There are worse jobs.

—ROLANDO HINOJOSA

TEACHING PRACTICE

What is the best page limit? Three to five pages. Most essays of fewer than three typed, double-spaced pages are inadequate in ways other than length. Three- to five-page papers demand development of a topic beyond simple description of a problem or a narration of an event, yet they are short enough to require significant narrowing of the topic.

What about deadlines? Consider assigning due-dates for drafts. A day or two after introducing invention strategies, assign an exploratory draft. A couple of days later, schedule conferences with your students to discuss their work. Within the next few days, have them bring their revisions—along with all their planning notes and earlier drafts—to class. Setting deadlines for drafts reinforces the importance of starting early.

WRITERS ON WRITING

I put things down on sheets of paper and stuff them in my pockets. When I have enough, I have a book.

—JOHN LENNON

other classmates about it? Are there any secondary purposes to keep in mind?

The instructor's expectations

What are the instructor's purposes in giving this assignment—to make sure you have read certain materials? to determine whether you understand certain materials? to evaluate your thinking and writing abilities? to determine whether you can evaluate certain materials critically? What can you include in your essay to fulfill these purposes?

Your own goals

What are your purposes in carrying out this assignment—to respond to the topic adequately and accurately? to meet the instructor's expectations? to learn as much as possible about a new topic? to communicate your ideas as clearly and forcefully as possible? What can you include in your essay in order to achieve these goals?

EXERCISE 2.2

Choose one of the following assignments and describe its various purposes. If your instructor allows, this exercise may be done in small-group discussions, with one group member taking notes and reporting to the rest of the class.

1. Compare two book-length biographies of Herman Melville.
2. Discuss the controversies surrounding the use of genetic engineering to change characteristics of unborn children.
3. Write about a person who has been important in your life, and describe why he or she has affected you strongly.
4. Support or attack the latest presidential request for military funding.
5. Analyze the use of headlines in a group of twenty advertisements.
6. Describe a favorite spot in your college town.

EXERCISE 2.3

Consider a writing assignment you are currently working on. What are its purposes, in terms of the assignment, the instructor, and you, the writer?

2d. Considering audiences

Although you may sometimes write only to yourself (as in diaries or personal journals, lists of things to do, and so on), most of your college writing will be addressed to others. An important part of your

---

OPTIONAL EXERCISE

Ask your students to jot down a few notes in response to one of the following topics:

1. Explain the public and private options available to pregnant teenagers or to dissatisfied married couples.
2. Imagine an alternative to age as the criterion for buying alcoholic beverages or to pregnancy as the criterion for parenthood.
3. Describe the most intense or fun-filled hour you spent last summer or last year.

Then talk about their reactions to the topic as a writing assignment. Is the assignment contextualized? Do they already have the necessary information? What wording cues will they follow? Who is their audience?

You may want to use class time to encourage discussion of these topics as practice for the next writing assignment.

TEACHING PRACTICE

A student's first response to the question of audience is usually to assume that the instructor is the audience as well as the evaluator of the essay. Help your students distinguish between the two by asking them to write a *general audience profile*. If, for example, their general topic is "part-time worker, full-time student," their audience profile might read something like this:

> My audience is seventeen- and eighteen-year-olds who are either attending or planning to attend college and who have experienced the dual obligations of work and school.

USEFUL READING

Booth, Wayne. "The Rhetorical Stance." CCC 14 (Oct. 1963): 139–45. A classic discussion of the hallmark of good writing: a conscious balance between subject, audience, and the writer's persona.

CONSIDERING AUDIENCES   *pln* 2d

writing process, therefore, involves thinking about your **audience**—who your readers are. Skilled writers consider their readers carefully; in fact, one of the characteristic traits of a mature writer is the ability to write for a variety of audiences, using language, style, and evidence all appropriate to particular readers.

The key word here is *appropriateness:* just as a funeral director would hardly greet a bereaved family with "Howdy, customers," neither would you be likely to sprinkle jokes through an analysis of child abuse written for a PTA group. Why not? Because such behavior would be wildly inappropriate in that context and because your good sense would lead you to consider the nature of your audience and to address them in an appropriate way.

For much of your college writing, an instructor may serve as the primary audience. You may, however, sometimes find yourself writing for others: lab reports addressed to your class, business proposals addressed to a hypothetical manager, or in one American history class, a letter to a seventeen-year-old living in the year 1775. Every writer can benefit from thinking carefully about who the audience is, what the audience already knows or thinks, and what the audience needs and expects to find out. The following questions will help you begin to think in such careful ways about the audience for your writing.

- *Who is your audience?* Your boss? Other college students? Scientists? People already sympathetic to your views? People unsympathetic to your views? Potential voters? The general public?
- *What do you need to be sensitive to in your audience's background?* Think in terms of level of education, geographical region, age, sex, occupation, cultural heritage, and special interests.
- *What does your audience value?* Think in terms of qualities such as brevity, originality, honesty, wit, thriftiness, and so on. What goals and aspirations do they have?
- *What is your audience's stance toward your topic?* What are they likely to know about the topic? What preconceived views might they have?
- *What is your relationship to the audience?* Is it student to instructor? friend to friend? subordinate to superior? superior to subordinate? citizen to community? anything else?

Thinking systematically about your audience will help you decide what sort of organizational plan to follow (which one would be easiest for a particular audience to understand, for example), what information to include or to exclude, and even what specific words to choose. If you

WRITING TOGETHER

If your students are working on an essay, have them exchange their drafts and write audience profiles of one another's topics. After they have returned the profiles and drafts, the students may need to redefine their original audience.

(BACK)GROUNDING

One of the first composition theorists and researchers to question what school writing *should* be was James Britton. In *The Development of Writing Abilities* (11–18) (London: Macmillan, 1975), he argued for the importance of audience awareness:

> [O]ne important dimension of development in writing ability is the growth of a sense of audience, the growth of the ability to make adjustments and choices in writing which take account of the audience for whom the writing is intended. This accommodation may be coarse or fine, highly calculated or totally intuitive, diffused through the text or explicit at particular points in it; but whatever the form of its realization, a highly developed sense of audience must be one of the marks of a competent mature writer. . . . (58)

TEACHING PRACTICE

Until now, many of your students have no doubt thought that their audience was always their instructor. By writing an *audience profile* for each paper, (see above), your students will begin to see that *they* control audience, not you. As they begin to visualize their audience, they can write directly to that audience instead of directly for you. It will also be easier for you to evaluate their work when they have defined their audience.

OPTIONAL EXERCISE

Often, letter-writing enables students to gear their information, tone, and diction to their intended audience. It is unlikely that they would describe campus activities to their parents in the same way they would to friends. A business letter will differ greatly from a love letter.

Ask your students to write a letter asking their parents for a short-term loan to cover an unanticipated expense. Afterwards, ask them to assess how well they know their audience. Now ask your students to answer their letters, this time taking the role of their parents. Students are often surprised to discover that writing in another voice—that is, paraphrasing the voice of their intended audience—gives an entirely new meaning to the concept of audience awareness.

WRITING TOGETHER

Ask your students to bring copies of campus newspapers to class. After they have spent a few minutes reading, ask them to pair up, choose a specific article, and write an audience profile for the article. The designation "college students," of course, is too vague. More precise descriptions might be "international students who need friends on Thanksgiving," "female students who must walk across campus at night," or "graduate students whose tuition waivers might be taxed."

are writing an article for a magazine for nurses about a new drug prescribed to prevent patients from developing infections from intravenous feeding tubes, you will not need to give much information about how such tubes work or to define many terms. But if you are writing about the same topic in a pamphlet given to patients when they check into the hospital, you will have to give a great deal of background information and define any technical terms or, better yet, use other words altogether. For writing intended to persuade, such as a newspaper column advocating a tax increase to pay for school construction, a writer in a community with many parents of young children might assume a fairly sympathetic audience and try to emphasize the benefits to the children that new schools would provide. In a community with many elderly people living on fixed incomes, on the other hand, a writer would anticipate resistance to higher taxes. Therefore, the column might express understanding of and sympathy with this point of view before arguing the case for building more schools; it might also emphasize the meeting space or recreational facilities new schools could provide for all of the community's citizens.

EXERCISE 2.4

In order to experiment with how considerations of appropriateness for a particular audience affect what you write, describe the last cultural or social event you especially enjoyed to three different audiences: first to your best friend, then to your parents, then to a group of high school students attending an open house at your college. Then describe the differences in content, organization, and wording that the differences in audience led you to make.

2e. Exploring a topic

The point is so simple that we often forget it: we write best about topics we know well. One of the most important parts of the entire writing process, therefore, is exploring your topic, surveying what you know about it and then determining what you need to find out.

You may already have a good system for exploring topics you wish to write about. If so, use it and share it with friends and members of your class. If you have no particular personal system, however, this chapter provides a brief description of strategies designed to help you explore a topic. These strategies can be very useful in getting you started in your thinking about a topic and in helping you determine what you already know—and indeed in helping you solve problems that crop up

USEFUL READING

Lauer, Janice M. "Issues in Rhetorical Invention." *Essays on Classical Rhetoric and Modern Discourse.* Eds. Robert J. Connors, Lisa S. Ede, and Andrea A. Lunsford. Carbondale, IL: Southern Illinois UP, 1984. 127–39. Various prewriting techniques imply various assumptions about the composing process. Lauer distinguishes prewriting methods according to such factors as "the genesis of writing, exploratory acts and their relationship to judgment, and the province of invention."

later in the writing of an essay. The strategies include brainstorming, freewriting, looping, and questioning.

▌1. Brainstorming

Used widely in business, industry, and engineering, **brainstorming** involves tossing out ideas—often with several other people—in order to find new or fresh ways to approach a topic. You can adapt brainstorming to writing, however, by quickly writing down everything that occurs to you about a topic. All you need is a pen or pencil and a blank sheet of paper. Give yourself a time limit—five minutes, perhaps—and write down in list form *every* word or phrase that comes into your mind about your topic. Just put down key words and phrases, not sentences. No one has to understand the list but you. Don't worry about whether something will be useful or not. Just get it *all* down. When the time is up, stop and read over your list. If anything else comes to you, add it to the list. Then reread, looking for repetitions and patterns in the list, for clusters of interesting ideas, or for one central idea. Brainstorming can work well alone, but it is particularly effective with a group of between three and five people. You may want to get together with several members of your class to brainstorm about one another's topics—and you may well be surprised at what good ideas can come from such spontaneous discussion.

▌2. Freewriting

Freewriting is a kind of structured brainstorming, a method of exploring a topic by writing about it—or whatever else it brings to mind—for a certain number of minutes *without stopping*. Set a time limit, begin by thinking about your topic, and then simply let your mind wander and write down everything that occurs to you—in complete sentences as much as possible.

Continue writing *without stopping* for your set length of time (ten minutes maximum to begin with). Don't stop for anything; if you can't think what to write next, you can write "I can't think of what to write next" over and over until something else occurs to you. Then stop and look at what you've written. You are sure to find much that is unusable, irrelevant, or nonsensical. But you may also find important insights and ideas that you didn't even know you had. Writing has a way of jogging loose ideas, and seeing a word or idea appear before you on paper will often trigger others.

17

USEFUL READING

Macrorie, Ken. *Telling Writing.* 2d ed. Rochelle Park, NJ: Hayden, 1970.

Elbow, Peter. *Writing without Teachers.* New York: Oxford UP, 1973. Both authors espouse the benefits of freewriting. According to them, the beauty of freewriting is its simplicity. It can be used by writers of any age, at any level of sophistication, at any point in the composing process; best of all, it is nonthreatening.

(BACK)GROUNDING

Classical rhetoric consisted of five canons: *dispositio* (arrangement), *elocutio* (style), *memoria* (memory), *pronunciatio* (delivery), and *inventio* (invention). Just as the classical orators appreciated the fluidity of these elements, modern writers realize that the ebb and flow of "prewriting," "writing," and "revising" aids in the composing process.

The process of discovery implied by the Latin *inventio* and the Greek *heuresis* (eureka!) parallel our modern concept of "prewriting," which is also called rhetorical "invention." Since "prewriting" is often used to refer both to "invention" and to "planning," your students might want to think of "invention" as discovering what to say about a topic; of "planning" as the choices of what, when, and how to say it; and of "prewriting" as the first stage in the writing process, when "invention" and "planning" most often occur.

WRITERS ON WRITING

I don't give a hoot what the writing's like. I write any sort of rubbish that will cover the main outlines of the story, then I can begin to see it.
—FRANK O'CONNOR

TEACHING PRACTICE

The brainstorming exercise works particularly well with groups of three to five students, but it generates even more energy when conducted with the entire class. Whether you or your students suggest the topic is not so important as getting started. Appoint two students to record ideas as they are suggested by the rest of the class. After about ten minutes, break the class into groups of four and ask each group to choose an idea and to develop a thesis from it.

(BACK)GROUNDING

James Moffett (*Teaching the Universe of Discourse*) and Janet Emig (*The Composing Processes of Twelfth Graders*) posit that freewriting not only increases verbal fluency but also provides a means for discovering ideas. In *Writing without Teachers*, Peter Elbow writes:

[t]he habit of compulsive, premature editing doesn't just make writing hard. It makes writing dead. Your voice is damped out by all the interruptions, changes, and hesitations between the consciousness and the page. (6)

Freewriting eliminates the beginning writer's most frustrating habit: focusing on correctness rather than content. During final drafting, your students will need to focus on correctness—but not until then.

TEACHING PRACTICE

Elbow suggests that students who sincerely want to improve their writing keep a freewriting diary:

> Just ten minutes a day. Not a complete account of your day; just a brief mind sample for each day. You don't have to think hard or prepare or be in the mood: without stopping, just write whatever words come out—whether or not you are thinking or in the mood. (9) ·

TEACHING PRACTICE

During freewriting and looping exercises, you may want to serve as a model for your students by writing along with them. Share your work with them, not as the expert-in-residence but as a fellow writer.

3. Looping

Looping is essentially a form of directed freewriting that narrows or focuses a topic in five-minute stages, or "loops." As in freewriting, you first write whatever comes to mind when you think of your topic, basically following the free flow of your thoughts. Then you follow a central thread of those thoughts wherever it leads you. Here is how to do looping:

1. With your topic in mind, spend five minutes freewriting *without stopping.* This is your first loop.
2. Stop and look back at what you have written. Find the strongest or most intriguing thought. This is your "center of gravity," which you should summarize in a single sentence; it will become the starting point of your next loop.
3. Starting with the summary sentence from your first loop, spend another five minutes freewriting. This second loop circles around the center of gravity in the first loop, just as the first loop circled around your topic. Look for a center of gravity within this second piece of freewriting, which will form the basis of a third loop.
4. Keep this process going until you have discovered a clear angle on your topic or have expressed something about it that you can pursue in a full-length essay.

4. Mapping

Mapping is a way of generating ideas using a visual scheme, or map. It is especially useful for finding relationships among the main parts of a broad topic. To create a planning map, start with a blank piece of paper, and write down your topic in the middle of the page. Circle it. Then write down the main parts of your topic; circle each one and connect it to the topic in the center. Next think of any ideas, details, examples, or facts relating to each main part; write them down, circle them, and attach each one to the main parts with a line.

Continue associating from each new circle until you can't think of any more details, creating a visual map of your topic. Some terms will generate outward and some will just come to a dead end, but you will end up with various information trails to follow and many useful connections among ideas. Mapping is an especially useful way of developing various subtopics in an essay. At the top of the facing page you can see a representation of a map.

USEFUL READING

Elbow, Peter. "The Loop Writing Process." *Writing with Power.* New York: Oxford UP, 1981. 59–77. Elbow offers a refinement of freewriting which he calls loop writing—"a way to get the best of both worlds: both control and creativity" (59).

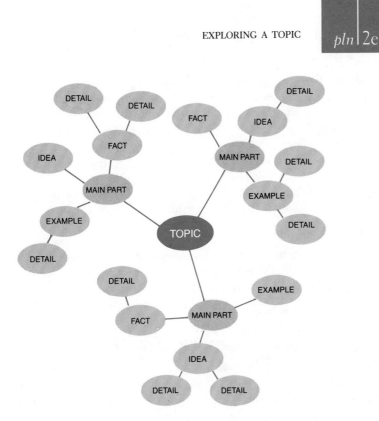

5. Questioning

The strategies presented thus far for exploring topics are all informal and based on freewheeling association of ideas. But there are more formal and structured ways of approaching topics that involve **asking**—and answering—particular **questions**. Such questions will help you probe a topic, look at it from varying perspectives, and generate ideas about it. The following are several widely used sets of questions designed to help you explore your topic. Of course, you can also make up your own questions to use.

Questions to describe a topic

Originally developed by Aristotle and refined by modern scholars, the following questions can help you explore any topic by carefully and systematically describing it.

1. *What is it?* What are its characteristics, dimensions, features, and parts? What does it look like?

19

(BACK)GROUNDING

The questions in this section are meant to prompt the writer's thinking and are based on various *heuristics* (prompts for thinking that involve questioning; various guides for investigation). Ultimately, all such heuristics derive from the *topoi*, the "topics" or "commonplaces" of classical rhetoric.

In *Classical Rhetoric for the Modern Student*, 2d ed. (New York: Oxford UP, 1971), Edward P. J. Corbett writes that the "topics constituted a method of probing one's subject in order to discover possible ways of developing that subject" (35). Special topics were those classes of argument appropriate to particular kinds of discourse: judicial, ceremonial, or political. Aristotle names the common topics, those that could be used for any occasion, as "definition," "comparison," "relationship," "testimony," and "circumstance."

Like the questioning strategies in this section, the *topoi* were a way to find something to say about a subject.

TEACHING PRACTICE

Before presenting these heuristics to your class, you may want to try them yourself. You will be better equipped to answer any questions about the procedures and to evaluate your students' work. Moreover, you can share your work with your students.

USEFUL READING

Corbett, Edward P. J. *Classical Rhetoric for the Modern Student*. 2d ed. New York: Oxford UP, 1971. This comprehensive text introduces both teacher and student to the theory and practice of classical rhetoric, including chapters on invention, arrangement, style, delivery, and memory.

Larson, Richard L. "Discovery through Questioning: A Plan for Teaching Rhetorical Invention." *CE* 30 (Nov. 1968): 126–34. According to Larson, a successful way to teach invention is to "help students see what is of interest and value in their experiences."

2. *What caused it?* What changes occurred to create your topic? How is it changing? How will it change? What part of a changing process is your topic? What may it lead to in the future?

3. *What is it like or unlike?* What features differentiate your topic from others? What analogies does your topic support?

4. *What is it part of?* What larger system is your topic a part of? How is your topic related to this larger system?

5. *What do people say about it?* What reaction does your topic arouse in people? What about the topic causes those reactions?

Questions to explain a topic

This is the well-known question set of *who, what, when, where, why,* and *how.* Widely used in news reporting, these questions are especially useful to help you explain a topic.

1. *Who* is doing it?
2. *What* is at issue?
3. *When* does it begin? When does it end?
4. *Where* is it taking place?
5. *Why* does it occur?
6. *How* is it done?

Questions to persuade

When your purpose is to persuade or convince, answering the following questions developed by the modern philosopher Stephen Toulmin can help you think analytically about your topic.

1. What CLAIM are you making about your topic?
2. What GOOD REASONS support your claim about the topic?
3. What UNDERLYING ASSUMPTIONS support the reasons for your claim?
4. What BACKUP EVIDENCE do you have or can you find to add further support to your claim?
5. What REFUTATIONS can be made against your claim?
6. In what ways is or should your claim be QUALIFIED?

Systematically using any of these strategies will be helpful, for doing so will get you thinking seriously about your topic—and putting those thoughts on paper. So don't be discouraged if your first attempts at looping or answering questions about a topic fail to produce timeless prose or revolutionary ideas. Be persistent, and these exploratory systems should begin to show results.

20

USEFUL READING

Toulmin, Stephen. *The Uses of Argument.* New York: Cambridge UP, 1964. The persuasiveness of our arguments ("claims") depends upon both the general principles ("warrants") that underlie our interpretations of data and the reasons we provide for them.

EXPLORING A TOPIC *pln* 2e

For an essay describing a favorite spot in her college town, Colleen Starkey, a student at the University of New Hampshire, began with brainstorming to explore a favorite spot, the bagel restaurant where she worked. Here are her brainstorming notes:

March 17th '83
Ports—since 7/85

May 1982—initial idea
Warren—full time
Ithaca—consultant
   from bagel bakery

Wkly shipments

per-day wholesale ave. 150 doz
   Durham 120 doz
   Ports.   50 doz

CR, P, Oat, onion,
Cart April—Oct

2 am—open
soups & quiches came later
bakery case

Horizontal mixer
Vertical mixer
Bagel machine

Boiled—1 min
550 degrees F—15 min
malt, salt, yeast, water

Brainstorming helped Colleen to get an idea of what she might have to say about the Bagelry. In order then to find out whether she really knew enough to write about the place, she decided to try describing it. She did this by writing out answers to the questions for describing shown above. Look at what she wrote:

1. What is the Bagelry? a restaurant that specializes in bagels, beverages, and sweets. small, contemporary, like a bakery, with a long counter. popular with students from UNH.

2. What caused the Bagelry? a couple from New York moved to Durham and realized there was a market for bagels here. already it has grown to two stores, the one in Durham and a branch in Portsmouth.

3. What is the Bagelry like or unlike? it's a little like a New York coffee shop, but because it's in Durham it's quite unlike a typical New York bagel shop—neater, less cluttered. I guess it's also basically similar to most bakeries that bake on the premises.

4. What is it part of? it's in a mall in downtown Durham. it's not far from a Burger King. but—and perhaps this is most important—it's part of everyday life for many students at UNH.

5. What do people say about the Bagelry? that it has great bagels. some say they'd have trouble getting through the morning without a wake-up bagel.

EXERCISE 2.5

Choose a topic that interests you, and explore it by using two of the strategies described in 2e. When you have generated some material, you might try comparing your results with those of other members of the class to see how effective or helpful each of the systems was. If you have trouble choosing a topic, use one of the working theses in Exercise 2.6.

TEACHING PRACTICE

To help your students develop working theses, you may wish to have them turn in written descriptions of their working theses with their subject ideas for each essay.

OPTIONAL EXERCISE

Thesis statements have two parts: a topic and a comment, the comment being the "so what?" of the thesis.

Work with your class to determine a possible "so what?" for the following general ideas:

1. Rock music lyrics promote sex and drugs.
2. Working mothers versus at-home mothers.
3. Living in a small town versus living in a big city.
4. Returning students bring their experiences to the classroom.
5. Joining a sorority or a fraternity—yes or no?
6. Living in the dorms versus living at home.

Articulating a "so what?" makes the topic not only more interesting and specific but also more manageable.

2f. Establishing a working thesis

A **thesis** states the main idea of your essay. Most kinds of college writing contain a thesis statement, often near the beginning of the essay, which functions as a promise to the readers—to let them know what will be discussed. Though you will probably not have a finished thesis when you begin to write, you should establish a tentative **working thesis** early on in your writing process. The word *working* is important here, as the working thesis may well be modified, clarified, or otherwise changed as you write. In spite of the fact that it will probably change, a working thesis is important for three main reasons: (1) it directs your thinking, research, and investigation and thus keeps you on track; (2) it helps you to focus on a particular point about the topic; (3) it provides concrete questions to ask about purpose and audience (helping you see, for example, what you must do to design a thesis for a particular audience).

A working thesis should have two parts: a topic part and a comment part. The **topic** part states the topic, while the **comment** part makes an important point about the topic. Here are some examples.

┌────── TOPIC ──────┐ ┌────── COMMENT ──────┐
Recent studies of depression suggest that it is much more closely

related to physiology than scientists had previously thought.

┌────── TOPIC ──────┐ ┌────── COMMENT ──────┐
The current American farm crisis can be traced to three major causes.

A successful working thesis has three characteristics. It should be potentially *interesting* to your intended audience. In its language, it should be as *specific* as possible; and it must limit and focus a topic enough to make it *manageable*. You can evaluate a working thesis by checking it against each of these criteria. For example:

ESTABLISHING A WORKING THESIS

Preliminary working thesis

The theory of "nuclear winter" is being debated around the globe.

INTEREST   The topic itself holds interest, but it seems to have no real comment attached to it. The thesis merely states a bare fact, and there seems no place to go from here except to more bare facts.

SPECIFICITY   The thesis is fairly clear, but not very specific. Who is debating the theory? What does it mean to these people? What are the larger implications of this debate? What does the writer think of the theory, or the debate?

MANAGEABILITY   The thesis is not manageable: it would require research in many countries and in many languages and would be beyond the capacities and time limits of most if not all students.

ASSESSMENT   The topic of this thesis is very general and needs to be narrowed by a workable comment before it will be useful. Right now the field of investigation is too large and vague. This preliminary thesis can be narrowed into the following working thesis:

Working thesis

Scientists from several different countries have challenged the "nuclear winter" theory and claimed that it is more propaganda than science.

Throughout this chapter and the next, we continue to follow the writing process of Colleen Starkey as she works her way through one writing assignment. For that essay, she produced the following preliminary working thesis:

    The Bagelry is a Durham restaurant popular with everyone.

When Colleen subjected this working thesis to the tests of interest, specificity, and manageability, she found that her thesis was manageable but was deficient in both interest and specificity. It contained only a statement of fact and did not make any real comment on the topic. After considering the problem, Colleen decided to show in what ways the Bagelry was unusual for a small New England college town. She then wrote the following working thesis:

    Set in the college town of Durham, New Hampshire, the
    Bagelry offers authentic bagels in an atmosphere much like
    the small coffee shops and cafés that line New York City
    streets.

EXERCISE 2.6

Choose one of the following preliminary working theses, and, after specifying an audience, evaluate the thesis in terms of interest, specificity, and manageability. Revise it as necessary to meet these criteria.

1. Drug abuse presents Americans with a big problem.
2. Abortion is a right.
3. Othello is a complex character whose greatest strength is, ironically, also his greatest weakness.
4. The Reagan Supreme Court decided many cases less conservatively than you might have expected.
5. White-collar crime poses greater danger to the economy than more obvious forms of street crime.

EXERCISE 2.7

Using the topic of the assignment you chose in Exercise 2.2, write a preliminary working thesis. Evaluate it in terms of interest, specificity, and manageability, and then revise it as necessary to create a satisfactory working thesis.

2g. Gathering information

Many of your writing assignments will call for some research. Your instructor may specify that you research your topic and cite your sources; or you may find that you do not know enough about your topic without doing some research. You may need to do research at various stages of the writing process—early on, to help you define your topic, or at a later point to find examples in support of your thesis—but usually you will want to consider what additional information you might need once you have defined a working thesis.

If you find it necessary to do research, you should probably begin with those resources closest to hand: your instructor, who can help you decide what kind of research to do, and your textbooks, which may include a bibliography or list of references. Basically, you can do two kinds of research: library research and field research.

Before going to the library you should try to think of general subject headings to check; then look in the card catalog, encyclopedias, periodical indexes, and bibliographies for specific materials. You may want to ask advice from a librarian. Consider field research: observation, interviews, or questionnaires. In Chapter 3, for instance, we will see how Colleen Starkey uses observation and interviews to find much good concrete detail for her essay about the bagel business.

24

WRITING TOGETHER

Exercise 2.7 can be extended to include peer responses. After your students have critiqued their own work, ask them to exchange their preliminary working theses and then evaluate them, using questions such as the following:

1. Does the thesis arouse your interest? What is the "so what?" of the thesis?
2. Is the thesis clear and specific? Can you make it more so?
3. Does the thesis seem manageable within the limits of time and length? Does the author promise to do too much? Can you help narrow the thesis?

The value of this additional exercise is greater perspective. What is patently obvious to the writer may not be so discernible to a reader, whose information is limited to the text.

WRITING TOGETHER

After dividing your class into several small groups, assign each group a different method of questioning (e.g., questions to describe, to explain, to persuade). Using one common subject, ask each group to explore it by answering their assigned questions. Discuss the results. Which method worked best for them? Which method was best suited for the particular subject?

Your students are apt to disagree about the most effective method for defining a thesis. Lead them to an understanding that each writer and each topic calls for a different method, and that there are a variety of ways to approach any given topic.

TEACHING PRACTICE

Many students—including juniors and seniors—have little experience with research projects or familiarity with a campus library. You might consider holding a class in the library and asking a reference librarian to describe the general resources of the library and to explain their location and usefulness.

USEFUL READING

Connors, Robert. "The Rise and Fall of the Modes of Discourse." CCC 32 (Dec. 1981): 444–55. Charts the history of the teaching of writing, especially the teaching of formal divisions of discourse.

Eckardt, Caroline D., and David H. Stewart. "Towards a Functional Taxonomy of Composition." CCC 30 (Dec. 1979): 338–42. Opposes the use of strategies as modes of discourse and argues, instead, for a new taxonomy of discourse that includes four basic purposes of writing: to clarify, to substantiate, to evaluate, and to recommend.

ORGANIZING INFORMATION   *pln* 2h

Detailed discussion of how to conduct both library and field research are given in Chapter 38. Once you determine you need to research your topic further, turn to that chapter for detailed guidelines.

2h. Organizing information

Exploring a topic and gathering information can provide essential data for an essay, but the data are *raw*—and not very helpful—until they are organized. Even as you are finding information, therefore, you should be thinking about how you will group or organize that information in your writing, how you will make your data accessible and persuasive to your readers.

At the simplest level, writers can group information in three ways: according to principles of **space** (*where* bits of information occur spatially); according to principles of **time** (*when* bits of information occur, usually chronologically); or according to principles of **logic** (*how* bits of information are related). The ways you group your information in an essay will ultimately depend on your topic, purpose, and audience.

1. Organizing information spatially

If the information you have gathered is *descriptive*, you may choose to organize it spatially (see 2e for questions that help you describe a topic). Using **spatial organization** allows the reader to "see" your information, to fix it in space. A report on the library's accessibility to students in wheelchairs, for example, might well group information spatially. In describing the spaces in the library that are most often used and evaluating their accessibility to a student in a wheelchair, the writer would most certainly present information spatially—one room or space or area at a time. In this case, the description of the student's progress through various library spaces might even be accompanied by a map. (See 5c for examples of information organized spatially.)

2. Organizing information chronologically

You are probably already very familiar with **chronological organization,** since it is the basic method used in stories, cookbooks, and instructions for assembling or using various products. All of these kinds of writing group information according to when it occurs in some process or sequence of events. Reports of laboratory studies and certain kinds of experiments also use chronological ordering of information.

(BACK)GROUNDING
The earliest rhetoricians spoke of the aims or purposes of rhetoric in primarily active terms: to inform, to move, to delight. Sometime during the eighteenth and nineteenth centuries, the focus shifted from active purpose to static form—exposition (to inform), argumentation (to move), description and narration (to delight). Later, such strategies as process, comparison and contrast, division, and classification were added to lists of methods of development, lists derived from the classical *topoi*.

In actual practice, no such thing as a purely descriptive essay or a comparison-and-contrast essay exists outside of the classroom. To teach these techniques as discourse structures is to confuse means with ends.

USEFUL READING

Kinneavy, James. "The Basic Aims of Discourse." *CCC* 20 (Dec. 1969): 297–304. A distilled version of Kinneavy's *Theory of Discourse,* in which he divides discourse into referential, persuasive, literary, and expressive, each emphasizing a particular element in the exchange between writer and audience about the subject of the discourse.

A student studying the availability of motorcycle parking in a campus lot ordered his information chronologically at least once in his proposal, to show the times when motorcycles entered and exited the parking lot and thus to identify peak periods of demand for parking spaces. This student chose to present this information in narrative (story) form, using chronological order to build tension as the minutes tick by and the lot gets more and more crowded, the drivers more and more frustrated. He could have altered the narrative order, however, and told his story backwards (using a kind of flashback technique). If you choose to use a narrative or story form for presenting information, you will probably use chronological order, but reversing that order—or starting "in the middle" and then going back to the beginning—can provide effective methods of organizing data as well.

Chronological order is especially useful in **explaining a process,** step by step by step. A biology report, for instance, might require describing a frog's process of circulation. An essay for an anthropology class might include an explanation of the rituals of initiation into the tribe in an Indian culture. If you decide to organize information about a process in chronological order, you can test whether your explanation is clear and precise by asking a fellow student to read the explanation and report how easy (or hard) it is to follow the steps of the process.

3. Organizing information logically

In much of the writing you do in college, you will find it appropriate to organize information according to some set of logical relationships. The most commonly used **logical patterns** include *illustration, definition, division/classification, comparison/contrast, cause-effect,* and *problem-solution.* (See 5c for examples of information organized logically.)

Illustrating points

Often much of the information you gather will serve as examples to **illustrate a point.** An essay discussing how one novelist influenced another might cite a number of examples from the second writer's books that echo themes, characters, or plots from the first writer's works. An appeal for donating money to the Red Cross might be organized around a series of examples of how such money will be used. If you use illustration in writing intended to persuade or convince, arrange the examples in order of increasing importance, for maximum effect.

WRITING TOGETHER
Ask your students to read and comment on one another's drafts, looking first at organizational patterns in individual paragraphs and then throughout the entire paper. Ask them to write, in the margin, the type of paragraph organization. Toward the end of class, call on several students to read paragraphs that illustrate different forms of organization. Some paragraphs may defy classification because of the ingenuity of the writer or the rough condition of the draft.

WRITERS WRITING
When the author and critic Joseph Epstein plans an essay, he uses a simple system that even a beginning writer can try. In a file folder, Epstein collects notes on everything he can think of that has any connection with the proposed subject of his essay: quotations, anecdotes, other books and articles on the same topic, stray ideas. On index cards and odd scraps of paper, he jots down whatever occurs to him as the days pass. If he thinks of an opening for his piece while shopping or driving around, he makes sure that this idea is added to the folder. When he finally sits down to write, he doesn't "sit down empty-handed—or, perhaps more precisely, empty-minded." He has a store of material to help him begin writing.

Defining terms

Many topics can be developed by **definition**: by saying what something is—and is not—and perhaps by identifying the characteristics that distinguish it from things that are similar or in the same general category. A magazine article about poverty in the United States, for example, would have to define very carefully what it meant by poverty—what level of personal income, household assets, or other measure defined a person, family, or household as poor. A student essay about Pentecostalism for a religion class might develop the topic by explaining what characteristics separate Pentecostalism from related religious movements, such as fundamentalism or evangelicalism.

Dividing and classifying

Division means breaking a single item into its parts; **classification** means grouping many separate items according to their similarities. Dividing a topic involves beginning with one object or idea and discussing each of its components separately. An essay about the recruiting policies of the United States military, for instance, might be organized by dividing the military into its different branches—army, air force, and so on—and then discussing how each branch recruits volunteers. Classifying involves putting items or pieces of information into categories. A writer discussing the student organizations on a college campus would probably call on classification as a way of organizing the information, classifying students' groups into service, academic, and social groups or into male, female, and mixed groups. If you have been reading histories of the eighteenth century in preparation for an essay on women's roles in that time, and you have accumulated dozens of pages of notes in the process, you could begin to organize this mass of undigested information by classifying it: information related to women's education, women's occupations, women's legal status, and so on.

Comparing and contrasting

Comparison focuses on the similarities between two things while **contrast** highlights their differences, but the two are often used together. Asked to read two chapters in an introductory philosophy text (one on Plato and the other on Aristotle), to analyze the information presented, and to write a brief response, a student might well use an organizational framework based on comparison and contrast. The student could then organize the response in one of two ways: by presenting all the information on Plato in one section and all on Aristotle in another *(block comparison)* or by alternating back and forth between Plato and Aristotle, looking at particular characteristics of each *(alternating comparison)*.

Analyzing causes and effects

Cause-effect analysis either examines why something happens or happened by looking at its causes or looks at a set of conditions and explains what effects result or are likely to result from them. A chemistry report on an experiment combining a mix of chemicals in several different ways, for instance, suggests moving from causes to effects. On the other hand, a newspaper article on the breakdown of authority in inner-city schools might well be organized by focusing on the effects of the breakdown and then tracing those effects back to their causes.

Considering problems and solutions

Moving from a **problem** or set of problems to a **solution** or solutions presents a natural and straightforward way of organizing certain kinds of information. The student studying motorcycle parking, in fact, decided to structure the overall organization of his data in just this way: he identified a problem (the need for more parking) and then offered two possible solutions to the problem. Many assignments in engineering, business, and economics call for a similar organizational strategy. One economics professor recently asked students to gather information on the latest slide in the stock market and to use that information to give advice to investors who lost money. The information students gathered first defined the problem the investors faced and then formed the basis for potential solutions.

EXERCISE 2.8

Using the topic you chose in Exercise 2.2, identify the most effective means of organizing your information. Write a brief paragraph explaining why you chose this particular method (or methods) of organization.

EXERCISE 2.9

Identify which method or methods of organization you would recommend for students who are writing on the following topics—and why.

1. The need for a new undergraduate library.
2. The autobiographical elements in Virginia Woolf's *To the Lighthouse.*
3. How to improve your writing.

WRITING OUT A ROUGH PLAN

4. Education to prevent the spread of AIDS.
5. The best places to study on campus.

2i. Writing out a rough plan

A writer who has carefully organized information is a writer who already has a rough plan for a draft, a plan that should then be written down. Our student who wrote about some possible solutions to the motorcycle parking problem on campus organized all his data and developed the following rough plan. Notice that his plan calls for several organizational strategies within an overall problem-solution framework:

INTRODUCTION

give background to problem (use *chronological order*)
give overview of problem (use *division*)
state purpose—to offer solutions

BODY

present proof of problem in detail (use *illustration*)
present two possible solutions (use *comparison*)

CONCLUSION

recommend that first solution be scrapped for reasons of (a) cost (b) space (c) relative disadvantages
recommend that second solution be adopted and summarize benefits of doing so

While an informal plan worked well for this writer, you may wish to prepare a more formal outline such as the one illustrated in Chapter 39. Whatever form your organizational plan takes, however, you may want or need to change it as you begin drafting. Writing has a way of stimulating thought, and you may find yourself getting new ideas in the process of drafting, ideas you could pursue effectively. Or you may find that you need to go back and reexamine some information or gather more information.

Colleen Starkey, whom we last saw exploring her topic and organizing the information she generated, worked with an informal outline. Outlining before writing is sometimes difficult, but Colleen was able to generate the following outline on the basis of her exploratory work for her essay on the Bagelry.

TEACHING PRACTICE

Any plan for a piece of writing can change. If you require an unchangeable, formal outline, your students may not be able to adhere to it. Instead, ask them to prepare a "writing plan," a backbone for the body of the paper. Then allow them to develop their papers as much by their drafting processes, which reveal form, as by their plan.

WRITERS ON WRITING

. . . content determines form, yet content is discovered only in form.

—DENISE LEVERTOV

In any work that is truly creative, the writer cannot be omniscient in advance about the effects that he or she proposes to produce. The suspense . . . is not just in the reader, but in the writer, who is intensely curious about what will happen.

—MARY MCCARTHY

(BACK)GROUNDING

Most professional writers do some kind of informal planning before drafting. The key word is, of course, *informal*. Rarely does a professional writer make elaborate outlines with letters and Roman and Arabic numerals. Such formal outlines assume that the writer knows everything (and in exact order) he or she needs to know before writing.

Most writers need to work through at least one rough draft before they can foresee their plan for organization or information. Outlining has benefits, however; your students can use it as a revision device or for analyzing their reading.

TEACHING PRACTICE

Even the most proficient pre-draft outliners need to know that outlines are not unalterable or absolute; they are merely guides. Outlines must conform to the paper—not the paper to the outline. Outlines, like the papers they help organize, must be revised.

If your students have trouble outlining or planning, suggest that they write each essay idea on a notecard. They can then easily rearrange their ideas and experiment with various orders. They will also learn that some ideas are expendable.

```
 I. Introduction
    set picture—atmosphere
    describe it as a bagelry straight from the metropolis
    of NYC
 II. Making bagels is their forte
    who—bakers
    what—all varieties (12)
    when—am and pm bake
    how—procedure—ingredients, baking time
    Business outside of store
III. Extra added specialties
    assorted sandwiches
    spreadables
    Bagel chips
    knishes
    pastries (6 layer—brownies, cakes)
    soups
 IV. A place for all to enjoy
    pleases tastes from plain to extravagant
    young to old
    NY'er to New Englander
    Health food nut to junk food junky
    meals and desserts
    Place to eat authentic . . . in NH
```

This informal outline shows elements of spatial order, description, process explanation, and illustration: she depicts the restaurant (spatial order and description); gives the procedure for making bagels (process explanation); and tells about the specialties of the house (illustration). On the basis of the above rough plan, Colleen began to draft her essay about the Bagelry.

EXERCISE 2.10

Write out a rough plan for an essay supporting the working thesis you developed in Exercise 2.7.

PRODUCING A DRAFT   *pln* 2j

▐ 2j. Producing a draft

Most of us are in some sense "producing a draft" the moment we begin thinking about a topic. One writer reports that his best ideas for opening essays almost always come to him in the shower, another that she "practices" writing versions of paragraphs or sentences in her head while driving to and from work. At some point, however, we commit our thoughts to paper, sitting down with pen, typewriter, or word processor to produce a draft.

No matter how good your planning, investigating, and organizing have been, chances are that you will want and need to alter some things as you draft. This fact of life leads to a first principle of successful drafting: be flexible. If you see that your rough plan is not working as you begin drafting do not hesitate to alter it. If some information now seems irrelevant, leave it out, even if you went to great lengths to obtain it. Through the entire drafting process, you may need to go back to some point you have already been through: you may learn that you need to do more research, or that your whole thesis must be reshaped, or that your topic is too broad and should be narrowed. The writing process is primarily a learning process, and you will continue planning, investigating, and organizing throughout the whole of that process. You may want to ask your instructor or a classmate to help you by reading drafts and telling you if your direction seems clear and effective.

Definite principles of drafting are hard to come by, because we actually know very little about how writers produce drafts. What we do know suggests that there may be almost as many ways to produce a successful draft as there are people to do it. Nevertheless, you can profit by learning as much as possible about what kind of situation is likely to help you produce your best writing. You can do so by considering a few simple questions: *Where* are you most comfortable and productive writing (in your room, in the library)? *When* are you most comfortable and productive writing (in the morning, late at night)? *Under what conditions* are you most comfortable and productive writing (with complete quiet, with "background" music, wearing jeans)? *What rituals* seem to help you produce good writing (exercising beforehand, sharpening pencils, cleaning up the room, scheduling breaks or treats)?

Once you have learned as much as you can about the atmosphere most conducive to your best writing, make every effort to do your drafting in that atmosphere. A few other practical tips about the drafting process may be helpful to you:

(BACK)GROUNDING

Remind your class that first drafts are never perfect. One of the many scholars and researchers who believe that first drafts are rarely directed toward an audience, Linda Flower has listed the features of what she calls "writer-based prose." According to Flower, this stage of writing is

1. Typically narrative or chronological in structure.
2. Usually filled with private terms that may not be meaningful to another reader.
3. Sometimes elliptical.
4. Filled with unclear referents and causal relations.
5. Frequently loaded with self-referents such as "I believe," "I feel," "in my opinion."

Flower views writer-based prose as a natural stage in the composing process, one that allows for discovery and growth and that should not be criticized because it is not yet "reader-based."

Often, proficient writers can skip the stage of writer-based prose and move directly to reader-based prose. These writers seem to internalize their writer-based drafts, unlike many beginning writers.

TEACHING PRACTICE

Keeping a writing log may help your students learn who they are as writers. Until now, most of the focus has been on subject, purpose, and audience. Now your students must begin to listen for their own voices in order to connect and build credibility with the reader.

The writing log journal also provides you with a record of your students' progress, showing how they have developed writing strategies and confidence in their ability to write. Such a record is a good resource for the instructor who needs to diagnose or treat a writer's specific problem.

WRITERS ON WRITING

The perfect place for a writer is within the hideous roar of the city, with men making a new road under the window in competition with a barrel organ. . . .

—HENRY VOLLAM MORTON

The habits of a lifetime when everything else had to come before writing are not easily broken.

—TILLIE OLSON

The ideal view for daily writing, hour on hour, is the black brick wall of a cold-storage warehouse. Failing this, a stretch of blue sky will do, cloudless if possible.

—EDNA FERBER

WRITERS WRITING

Ernest Hemingway was well known for quitting while he was ahead. Each day, he would stop writing after a few hours, even if he knew what would follow next. In this way, he was able to write every morning, as soon after the first light as possible.

WRITERS ON WRITING

Just get it down on paper, then we'll see what to do with it.

—MAXWELL PERKINS

Get black on white!

—GUY DE MAUPASSANT

I have written over—often several times—every word I have ever published. My pencils outlast their erasers.

—VLADIMIR NABOKOV

Asked how may drafts of a story he did, S. J. Perelman answered: "Thirty-seven. I once tried doing thirty-three, but something was lacking. . . . On another occasion, I tried forty-two versions, but the final effect was too lapidary—"

- *Have all your information close at hand and organized according to your organizational plan.* Having to stop to search for a piece of information can break your concentration or distract you in unhelpful ways.
- *Try to write in bursts of at least ten to twenty minutes.* Writing can provide its own momentum, and once you get going the task becomes easier.
- *Don't let small questions bog you down.* As you write, questions will come up that need to be answered, but unless they are major ones, make a tentative decision and move on.
- *Stop writing at a place where you know exactly what will come next.* Doing this will help you get started easily when you return to the draft.
- *Remember that a first draft need not be perfect.* In order to keep moving and get a draft done, you often must sacrifice some fine points of writing at this stage. Concentrate while drafting on getting your ideas across as clearly as possible. Don't worry about anything else, and don't stop writing.

Here is Colleen's first draft.

THE BAGELRY

It is a chilly fall morning. Many of the cars on 1
the road are covered with a thick crisp frost—a sure sign
that another cold New England winter is on its way. To
brighten this early morning and take the chill out of this
fall day, many will start the day off with a piping hot
cup of coffee and a fresh warm bagel straight from the
oven. Although set in the college town of Durham, NH,
the "Bagelry" offers authentic bagels in an atmosphere
much like the small coffee shops and cafes that line NY
city streets.

Making bagels is Warren and Elise Daniels' forte. 2
Having moved from Queens, NY, to the southeastern section
of NH they saw a market for the traditional bagel. Even
bakeries are a rarity in this area. With a store in Durham
and Portsmouth they must make hundreds of dozens of bagels

PRODUCING A DRAFT   *pln* 2j

to satisfy the needs of both stores. Along with providing
for their stores, they also sell bagels wholesale. Around
Durham they supply the university and off-campus living
areas—like the Greek houses. Deliveries are also made
as far north as Portland, ME, and as far south as
Manchester, NH.

A typical day at the Bagelry starts at 4 o'clock in 3
the morning. The first batch of bagels are prepared for
the morning bake. One hundred to one hundred and twenty
dozens of bagels are made for retail sales on the average.
Approximately seventy dozens of bagels will be prepared
for wholesale. All cooking and baking is performed at
the Durham location. The Portsmouth store calls in its
orders daily.

While most people are still sound asleep, the bakers 4
at the bagelry are busy making bagels before the sun rises.
One hundred pounds of flour is used at a time to make the
dough needed. Water and other ingredients are added.
The dough is prepared in a huge mixer (approx. 6 ft. x
6 ft. x 4 ft.). Once the dough reaches the proper consistency it is transferred to another contraption that
actually makes and shapes each individual bagel. It is
the bakers' job, at this point, to put the bagels in rows
on large flat boards. After all bagels have been put on
boards they are stacked on portable racks and covered with
cloth sheets to stand and rise. (The Baker knows the batch
has risen when an uncooked bagel, like those rising, has
begun to float in a pot of hot water on the stove.) After
the bagels have risen they are refrigerated until they
are baked. The first step in cooking the bagels is what
makes them authentic NY style. Unlike the frozen type
bagels one can buy in the supermarkets, these bagels are
boiled before they are baked. This is done to give a special
gloss to the outside of the bagel and a lighter—fluffier

consistency to the inside. After being boiled for approx. 5 mins., the bagels are placed on large baking boards and put into a four shelf oven set at 500 degrees F and baked for 15-20 mins. By seven a.m., the time the store opens, hundreds of fresh hot bagels are ready for the craving customer.

There are 12 varieties of bagels to choose from. 5 (If by chance your favorite is sold out when you arrive, never fear for there is an afternoon bake as well.) The types of bagels served range from the old stand-bys to one actually invented by the proprietors. As you walk into the Bagelry you can see all the bagels aligned, in wire baskets, in this order; Garlic, Onion, Wheat, Egg, Rye, Salt, Pumpernickel, Poppy, Oat, Sesame, Plain, and Cinnamon Raisin. While plain is the old safe stand-by, onion and cinnamon raisin seem to be the most popular. The oatmeal bagel was actually created by one of the owners Elise Daniels. This type has attracted a large following as well.

There are extra added specialties that the Bagelry 6 serves. Along with selling bagels by the dozens, one can get a bagel plain, toasted, with cream cheese or assorted spreadables, or even done up like a sandwich. Gallon tubs of cream cheese based spreads are prepared as needed. A variety of taste options are open to the customer. If you don't feel like cream cheese or butter, why not try veggie spread, garlic and herb spread, lox spread, walnut and raisin spread, cream cheese and chive spread, or olive spread. If the customer feels the need for something more substantial—there is a whole menu of assorted sandwiches that can be made on the bagel of your choice. These sand-wiches are combinations created by Elise Daniels that use a variety of meats, cheeses, spreads, and vegetables.

Also available to the customer are fresh baked 7

REFLECTING ON YOUR WRITING PROCESS

quiches, breads, cakes, knishes, brownies, and delicious
but fattening 6-layer bars. One can also indulge in hot
or cold soups with a side order of bagel chips. The problem
of thirst has not been forgotten nor neglected. At the
Bagelry there are hot and cold drinks, carbonated and non-
carbonated beverages as well as seasonal specials like
hot mulled cider or thirst quenching lemonade.

All in all, the Bagelry is a place for all to enjoy. 8
It pleases all tastes from plain to extravagant. One can
obtain any or all of the three meals consumed daily
(Breakfast, lunch and dinner foods are available). This
restaurant/bakery has fast, accommodating, pleasant
service. And it's the only one of its kind in this New
England area. If you ever have a craving for an authentic
NY bagel, the Bagelry is for you.

EXERCISE 2.11

Write a draft of an essay from the rough plan you worked on in Exercise 2.10.

▌ 2k. Reflecting on your writing process

Finishing a draft provides a good opportunity to sit back, relax, and reflect a bit on your drafting, and to make an entry in your writing log if you are keeping one (see 1b). With the experience of writing still fresh in your mind, you can note down what went well, what gave you problems and why, what you would like to change or improve. Here are the entries Colleen made in her writing log:

1. *How did you arrive at your topic?* One of our choices was to "describe a favorite spot in your college town." From that general topic, I started brainstorming. I brainstormed for about five minutes and came up with a list of spots I liked or had an interest in. The Bagelry seemed like a natural thing to write on because I work there, know its workings, and could research it easily and talk about it in detail.

2. *When did you first begin to think about the assignment?* When the essay was first assigned, I began to think of ways I could write about things. After I spoke with my instructor, I knew that a good, clear description of the place would be important.

3. *What kind of planning or investigating did you do?* I interviewed the bakers and the owners of the Bagelry and took notes of what they said. I then set up an outline before beginning to write. (I like to use outlines before I write. A lot of the other people in the class don't like outlines, I know, but I like them.)

4. *How long did it take to complete your draft (including time spent gathering information)?* Interviewing the owners and bakers took a few hours. I came up with the first draft in two days. I used Day 1 to organize and collect ideas. In my case, this meant coming up with a list of possible things to include in the paper and then working out an outline of the paper. On Day 2, I sat down and actually wrote out the first draft at one sitting. That took about two hours.

5. *Where did you write your draft? (Briefly describe the setting.)* I wrote my draft in my own room sitting at my desk. It is a quiet atmosphere and a comfortable setting for me.

6. *Who is the audience for this piece of writing?* At first the general public was my audience. I had no specific age group or category of people in mind. Now that I've talked to other friends and my instructor about this draft, I think of the audience more as the readers of *Granite State Profiles* or *New Hampshire Monthly*.

7. *What is your relationship to the audience?* Primarily that of an informant, telling them something they didn't know before. Also maybe that of an entertainer. I want them to enjoy reading the paper.

8. *What do you see as the major strengths of your draft?* If I succeed, it makes people want to go get bagels!

9. *What do you see as the major weaknesses of your draft?* As of right now, lack of quotations from owners and workers, and more vivid description of the inside of the store itself.

10. *What would you like to change about your drafting process?* Nothing . . . ? Honestly, I'd like to be able to work more quickly.

FOR EXAMINING YOUR OWN WRITING PROCESS

Using the preceding questions on the writing process or the questions in 1b, record the planning and drafting activities you went through as you prepared for and wrote the draft of your essay in Exercise 2.11. Make this an entry in your writing log if you are keeping one.

3. Revising and Editing

"There's only one person a writer should pay attention to," says author William Styron. "It's the reader. And that doesn't mean any compromise or sell-out. The writer must criticize his or her own work as a reader." Author Doris Lessing elaborates on what this writer/reader must do in the advice she always gives to beginning writers: "learn to trust your own judgment, learn inner independence, learn to trust that you will sort the good from the bad. . . ." These experienced writers know first-hand the power that self-criticism and self-confidence bring to the task of **revising**. If you have analyzed your own process of writing, you probably know whether you tend to revise extensively and when you tend to make any revisions. Perhaps you also know what kinds of revisions you typically make. And a careful look at any essay you have submitted to an instructor will reveal how well you edited the paper. You may, however, have thought of revising and editing as one and the same thing; after all, both involve changes in a draft. The distinction between the processes of revising and editing, however, is one that will be useful as you become a more powerful and efficient writer.

Revising involves reenvisioning your draft—taking a fresh look at how clearly your thesis is stated and how persuasively it is developed, how logical your organization is, how varied your sentences are, how appropriate and memorable your choice of words is. In each case, you will be rethinking your aims and methods in terms of your original purpose and audience and of all you have learned during work on the essay. Revising may call for changes both large and small. You may need to reshape sentences, rethink sections, gather more information to support a point, perhaps even do some further exploratory writing.

37

USEFUL READING

Murray, Donald. *Learning by Teaching*. Upper Montclair, NJ: Boynton/Cook, 1982. A collection of essays written by the former director of the freshman writing program at the University of New Hampshire. Of the several essays on revising, especially important is "Teaching the Motivating Force of Revision," in which Murray argues that revision, as a process of discovery, can actually become its own motivating force for students.

(BACK)GROUNDING

"I never have time to rewrite; I always wait until the night before."

"How can I improve my first draft when I don't know whether it's good?"

"I don't care about what I'm writing. I just want to get it over with."

"I'm such a bad writer that I hate to read my own writing."

"If I can't get it right the first time, I must be stupid."

Such typical attitudes toward revision support Erika Lindemann's claim that "[f]or most students, *rewriting* is a dirty word" (*A Rhetoric for Writing Teachers* 181). Students tend to view rewriting as an indication of failure, as punishment, or as simply a "filler" for classroom time. Because students have often been trained to outline carefully or to follow the format of a five-paragraph essay, revising means nothing more than making their words "prettier" or moving from handwriting to type or whiting-out misspelled words and mispunctuated sentences. In fact, many student writers are under the misapprehension that "real" writing is perfectly formed and flows onto the page at the touch of the Muse's hand. It is important for them to realize that almost all experienced writers revise their work repeatedly.

"Do you rewrite?" Frank O'Connor was asked.

"Endlessly, endlessly, endlessly." O'Connor went on to say that even after a book is published, "I usually rewrite again."

Your students must learn that their best writing can only occur after they take a series of sight-journeys back into the text. The poet Adrienne Rich calls this activity "re-entering" the text, re-vising (looking again) to see what new discoveries have been made by the writer.

TEACHING PRACTICE

Since students often confuse revising (making changes in content) with editing (correcting mechanical errors), you may wish to clarify the difference between these two steps. To reinforce this important distinction:

1. Try to observe the distinction yourself.
2. Try not to use both terms in the same phrase (e.g., "revising and editing").
3. Discuss revising and editing on separate days, as separate class topics.
4. Plan separate practice exercises for revising and editing.

OPTIONAL EXERCISE

During the first ten minutes of class, have your students review their drafts-in-progress. (To save time, you might ask them to concentrate on the two opening paragraphs.) Then have them put away their drafts and resume the class discussion on revision, or re-seeing. Toward the end of class, ask the students to revise the first two paragraphs again. What changes would they make? Students may see new places for revision that they were blind to before—in only half an hour, not the nine years Horace recommended.

TEACHING PRACTICE

Some students see revision as punishment for work not properly finished, when in fact the very unfinished status of early drafts provides motivation for growth and development through the reflective act of rewriting. Revision is the strongest motivation for improved student writing because it places the responsibility for improvement where it belongs: in the hands of the student writer.

Your students will want to know how long they should wait before doing their revisions. Because few first-year students produce a completed draft two days before the due date, overnight might be a practical cooling off period for both the piece and the writer.

Some writers find that if they set aside a manuscript too long, they cannot remember what they were trying to say. You may wish to ask your students to reread an essay they wrote last term or in high school and see if they can remember their purpose in writing it. Ask if they can discover any meaning in the piece that they hadn't noticed before.

Editing, on the other hand, involves fine-tuning your prose, attending to details of grammar, punctuation, and spelling. You might think of editing as the dress rehearsal for a written "performance"; as you edit, you work toward making your essay ready for public presentation. This chapter will explore the processes of revising and editing and provide you with a systematic plan for making the best use of these processes in your own writing.

3a. Getting distance before revising

The ancient Roman poet Horace advised aspiring writers to get distance from their work by putting it away for nine years. "Destroy whatever you haven't published," he wrote. "Once out, what you've said can't be stopped." If such advice seemed impractical to the Romans, it seems just about impossible to those writing in the late twentieth century. You have schedules to follow, deadlines to meet, examinations to take, graduation ceremonies to qualify for. Nevertheless, Horace's advice holds a germ of truth: the more time and distance you give yourself between the writing of a draft and its final revision, the more objectivity you will gain and the more options you will have as a writer. Even putting the draft away in a folder for a day or two will help clear your mind and give you some distance from your writing.

3b. Rereading your draft

If you give yourself—and your draft—a rest before revising, you will need to take time to review the draft by rereading it carefully for meaning, by recalling your purpose, and by considering your audience.

1. Rereading for meaning

Effective writers are almost always effective readers, particularly of their own writing. You can best begin revising, then, by finding a quiet and comfortable place to reread your draft carefully. For this reading, don't worry about small details. Instead, concentrate on your meaning and how clearly you have expressed it. If you see places where meaning seems unclear, note them in the margin.

2. Remembering your purpose

After rereading, quickly note the main purpose of the essay and decide whether it matches your original purpose. At this point, you may want to go back to your original assignment to see exactly what it

---

USEFUL READING

Garrison, Roger. "Revision—Seeing Again." In *How a Writer Works*. New York: Harper, 1981. 12–25. Another professional writer on the importance of revising. Garrison offers a detailed revision of a piece of his own writing. Students might benefit from reading this chapter.

GETTING CRITICAL RESPONSES TO YOUR DRAFT   *rev* 3c

asks you to do. If the assignment asks you to "prove" something, make sure you have done so. If you intended to propose a solution to a problem, make sure you have not simply analyzed the problem instead.

3. Considering your audience

Gaining some distance from your draft should help you think clearly about how appropriate the essay is for your audience. Is the language formal or informal enough for the audience? Will the audience be interested and be able to follow your discussion? What objections might the audience raise to the essay?

EXERCISE 3.1

Take twenty to thirty minutes to look critically at the draft you prepared in Exercise 2.11, rereading it carefully, checking how well the purpose is accomplished, and considering how appropriate the draft is for the audience. Then write a paragraph-length description of how you would go about revising it.

3c. Getting critical responses to your draft

Rereading and reviewing purpose and audience will allow you to take a good, critical look at your draft. In addition to your own critical response to your writing, however, you may want to get responses from friends, roommates, or classmates. Although you may trust your friends or classmates to do a thorough job for you, remember that they probably don't want to hurt your feelings by criticizing your writing. You can help by convincing them that constructive criticism is what you need, that trying to protect you by not mentioning problems does you no good.

But even honestly critical readers need to know where to focus their responses. In some cases, you may get exactly the advice you need by asking a quick, direct question: "What do you see as my thesis?" Be sure to pose questions that require more than yes/no answers. Ask readers to tell you in detail what they see, and then compare their reading to what you see. Merely asking "Is my thesis clear?" will not tell you nearly so much as "Would you paraphrase my thesis so I can see if it's clear?"

You may even want to provide a series of written questions for your readers. Following are some questions that might serve as guidelines for evaluating a draft. They can be used to respond to someone else's draft or to evaluate one of your own.

39

USEFUL READING

Brannon, Lil, Melinda Knight, and Vera Neverow-Turk. *Writers Writing.* Upper Montclair, NJ: Boynton/Cook, 1983. Arguing that writing and revising should not be considered two separate stages in the writing process, the authors provide examples of successive drafts by both student writers and professional writers.

Faigley, Lester, and Stephen Witte. "Analyzing Revision." *CE* 32 (1981): 400–14. The authors distinguish between surface revision (usually at the phrase or word level) and text-based revision (at the structural level).

TEACHING PRACTICE

Peer-responding, an increasingly popular method in many writing programs, helps students (1) learn to gauge their audience; (2) learn to accept and use constructive criticism; (3) practice analyzing written texts, including their own; and (4) acquire the vocabulary of composition.

Nevertheless, many students are reluctant to share their writing with one another. They may regard the instructor as the only one qualified to give advice or criticism; hence, time spent with peers is time wasted. Some students are embarrassed to show what they fear is poor writing to peers who will judge them personally. Moreover, they lack experience in offering constructive criticism. To help your students overcome these obstacles, you may want to try some of the following cooperative writing activities:

1. At the beginning of the term, have groups of students read and comment on one another's writing. You may wish to suggest a number of your own questions as well as those in the text to help them respond to what they read.

2. Your students may need help in learning how to respond to another's work—how to temper aggressiveness with tact, how to balance *what* has been said with *how* it has been said, both in terms of the writer's text and the reader's comments. In this way they will learn how to respond to drafts and how to trust and help one another, both vital aspects of a productive composition course.

3. Using an anonymous, imperfect model draft, provide at least one or two practice sessions before the class undertakes its first peer-responding session. During these preliminary discussions, check their responses and help students who have trouble offering comments.

4. To encourage group discussion, you may wish to share one of your preliminary drafts or examples of work in progress and have your students comment on it.

5. Remind your students that the goal of discussion is to improve, not merely approve, their writing.

6. To prevent cliques from forming, encourage each student to respond during group discussion.

7. After the first few responding sessions, you may want to collect and evaluate the responses. Doing so provides guidance and tells your students that you are serious about their ability to respond to written texts.

8. Ask your students to keep a record of peer responses to their work. Do certain problems recur? As they become increasingly aware of their writing profiles, your students will develop self-critical faculties which they can apply to their own writing. What they can do today in group discussion with peers, they will be able to do individually and by themselves in the future.

For additional peer-response questions, see Erika Lindemann, A *Rhetoric for Writing Teachers*, 181–200.

WRITERS ON WRITING

[W]riting is but a line that moves haltingly across the page, exposing as it goes all that the writer doesn't know. . . . Writing puts him on the line, and he doesn't want to be there.

—MINA SHAUGHNESSY

TEACHING PRACTICE

Having worked in groups, your students could have as many as four or five sets of responses to their writing. Lest they be overwhelmed by so many suggestions and questions, assure them that they need not heed all the advice, just weigh it. However, if several comments point in the same direction, the writer should take them seriously.

When students are faced with conflicting advice, they will naturally turn to you for the "right" answer. Because this is an impossible request, you will have to encourage them to reach their own decisions. Have them ask other students to respond to their particular problems. Ask about their original writing choices and about the potential effect of suggested changes. Using others' comments to make independent decisions should be a goal of every writer.

Questions for reviewing a draft

1. *Introduction:* What does the opening accomplish? How does it catch the reader's attention? How else might the essay begin? Can you suggest some better way of opening?

2. *Thesis:* Paraphrase the thesis of the essay in the form of a promise: "In this paper I will . . ." Does the draft fulfill the promise made by the thesis? Why, or why not?

3. *Supporting points:* List the main points made in the draft, in order of presentation. Then number them in order of interest to you, noting particularly parts that were *not* interesting to you or material that seemed unnecessary or added on for no reason. Review the main points one by one. Do any need to be explained more fully or less fully? Should any be eliminated? Are any confusing or boring to you? Do any make you want to know more?

4. *Organization:* What kind of overall organizational plan is used—spatial, chronological, or logical? Are the points presented in the most useful order? What, if anything, might be moved, deleted, or added? Can you suggest ways to make connections between paragraphs clearer and easier to follow?

5. *Paragraphs:* Which paragraphs are clearest and most interesting to read, and why? Which ones are well developed, and how are they developed? Which paragraphs need further development? What kinds of information seem to be missing?

6. *Sentences:* Number each sentence. Then reread the draft, and choose the three to five sentences you consider the most interesting or the best written—stylistically effective, entertaining, or memorable for some other reason. Then choose the three to five sentences you see as weakest, whether boring, bland, or simply uninspired. Are sentences varied in length, in structure, and in their openings?

7. *Words:* Mark words that are particularly effective—those that draw vivid pictures or provoke strong responses. Then mark words that are confusing or unclear. Do any words need to be defined? Are verbs active and vivid?

8. *Tone:* How does the writer come across in the draft—as serious, humorous, satiric, persuasive, passionately committed, highly objective? Mark specific places in the draft where the writer's voice comes through most clearly. Is the tone appropriate to the topic and the audience? Is the tone consistent throughout the essay? If not, is there a reason for varying the tone?

9. *Conclusion:* Does the essay conclude in a memorable way, or does it seem to end abruptly or trail off into vagueness? If you like the conclusion, tell why. How else might the essay end?

GETTING CRITICAL RESPONSES TO YOUR DRAFT   *rev* 3c

10. *Final thoughts:* What are the main strengths and weaknesses in the draft? What surprised you—and why? What was the single most important thing said?

Colleen Starkey, whose writing process we followed in Chapter 2, received the following responses from classmates to her draft. (Her draft appears in 2j.) Note that the first respondent followed the preceding list of questions very closely, answering almost every one in detail, while the other one gave much shorter and more generalized answers.

RESPONSE ONE

1. *Introduction:* Your introduction is good because it brings people to the scene. Maybe you should mention the Bagelry a little sooner to make sure that the readers know that you are going to talk about it all through the paper. It seems as if you are describing Durham. Another way of getting the reader's attention would be to start with the sights and smells inside the Bagelry—especially the aromas of the bagels and other goodies as they're baking. Or you could begin with the Danielses arriving in New Hampshire, seeing a market for bagels, and deciding to capitalize on it.

2. *Thesis:* "In this paper I will describe how/where a person can enjoy an authentic NY bagel in Durham, NH." Yes—fulfilled the thesis because you fully described the Bagelry.

3. *Supporting points:* (1) Danielses moving from NY; (2) size and scale of the Bagelry's operation; (3) how bagels are made; (4) varieties of bagels (5) bagel spreads and sandwiches; (6) other food and drinks. Interesting to me: how big the business is; how many different kinds of bagels are made; the variety of things the Bagelry sells. The Danielses might be interesting if they were developed more. Uninteresting to me: exactly how bagels are made. The point you could develop more perhaps is how the Bagelry is situated in such a small, quaint New England town and how it services it.

4. *Organization:* Overall organizational plan seems to be division— giving a sense of the scope of the business and how it got started and then discussing different aspects of how it operates and the products it sells. Order of points seems OK, but there are a few problems. Paragraph 3 starts out with the idea that work at the Bagelry begins early in the morning, but then you go on to other kinds of information before coming back to the early-morning idea at the beginning of the next paragraph. Also, in the conclusion you introduce an idea that hasn't been mentioned before—the Bagelry's "fast, pleasant, accommodating service." This idea needs to be either developed more or cut out. At the beginning of paragraph 2, you need

WRITING TOGETHER

Ideally, peer-responding sessions will be so effective, profitable, and stimulating that your students will initiate sessions outside the classroom. Realistically, however, they will probably hesitate to ask others who have no peer-responding experience or training. Therefore, you may want to provide them with several questions or statements for introducing a session:

1. "Would you mind telling me what you think of this?"
2. "The point I want to make in this paper is _____."
3. "How well did I succeed?"
4. "What do you think of my support?"
5. "I had trouble with this part. Does it make sense to you? What can I do to improve it?"

At least once during the term, have each of your students initiate a responding session with someone other than a classmate. Ask them to report on their success.

TEACHING PRACTICE

To make sure that your students are offering more than yes or no comments to the response questions, consider collecting and evaluating their responses. Reinforce specific responses that quote a word or phrase or that refer to a specific paragraph or line. Your interest will underscore the value of peer response.

OPTIONAL EXERCISE

In *How a Writer Works*, Roger Garrison provides additional suggestions for peer-response dialogue:

Your first resource is your own response to what you have read. How do you feel about it? Did it teach you anything?

Did it cause you to have a new awareness of the subject of the writing? Remember that what you read was written by someone who wanted to communicate with a reader—you.

Decide what the writer's main point was. Do you agree with it? What are your reasons for agreeing or disagreeing? Use *brief*, specific quotes from the writer's material to show what you are commenting about.

Try to characterize or summarize the subject of the writing. Then, as you discuss the piece and quote from it, your opinions have a clear base.

As you can see, these response prompts follow closely the writing process itself: first, the writer's *discovery*, then the significance of his or her discovery, then the enthusiasm generated by the discovery.

WRITERS ON WRITING

"No surprise for the writer, no surprise for the reader," writes Robert Frost. The only way to communicate effectively with a reader is through the sometimes painstaking but always rewarding process of writing, responding, and rewriting.

If your reader can't get your full meaning on a single reading—*and a single reading is all he owes you*—you must face up to the fact that you are still afflicted with residuals of mumbo jumbo.

—JOHN TRIMBLE

a clearer transition from the introduction—maybe mention the owners' move from New York right away.

5. *Paragraphs:* Even though I wasn't very interested in it, the paragraph on how bagels are made had a very clear chronological development that was easy to follow. Paragraph 2 needs more information about how the Danielses came to New Hampshire and opened the Bagelry and how it grew to its present size.

6. *Sentences:* I especially liked the second sentence of the introduction, the first sentence of paragraph 3 and the second and fourth sentences of paragraph 5. They all read smoothly and give interesting details. The other sentences in paragraph 3 seem weak—they just recite facts and statistics in a dull way, and it sounds as if the same sentence is being repeated again and again. Also, the first sentences of paragraphs 5 and 6 both start out with "There are" and don't arouse much interest. Except for paragraph 3, there's a good variety of length, structure, and openings.

7. *Words:* The words I thought were especially effective were *crisp* in the introduction, *contraption* and *gloss* in paragraph 4, and *delicious but fattening* and *indulge* in paragraph 7. I liked the word *craving* in the last sentence of the conclusion, but *the craving customer* sounds odd at the end of paragraph 4. I don't know what lox and knishes are. A couple of years ago I didn't even know what a bagel was—do you think most people in New Hampshire do?

8. *Tone:* The tone seemed objective, but at the same time you were trying to persuade people to like the Bagelry and its products. The persuasive tone comes through most in the sentences where you address the reader directly as *you*, especially the last sentence of the conclusion. The tone is consistent and I guess it's OK, even though sometimes it starts to sound like a commercial.

9. *Conclusion:* The conclusion is pretty good, but you should concentrate on the fact that the Bagelry is in a small town but is a "taste of NY."

10. *Final thoughts:* Strong points: It makes me want a bagel! There's a lot of colorful and mouthwatering detail. Weak points are just the listed information and description. Add more of your personality to it.

RESPONSE TWO

1. *Introduction:* The opening of this paper makes me hungry! I love the Bagelry! The lead draws me into the descriptive narrative on the Bagelry with sights, sounds, and taste sensations. It is great! Gives me a nice feel of NY and Durham.

2. *Thesis:* "In this paper I will describe how the Bagelry serves authentic NY bagels in a New England college town." You accomplished this nicely—but you also showed us how the Bagelry works.

3. *Supporting points:* The information on the whole was relatively new and informative to me. Good. Maybe you could pretend you were a bagel and write from that point of view. I would like to feel the culture and romance of bagels more. Even though I'm from a Jewish home, I can still remember what it was like to eat lox and cream cheese on a bagel for the first time. Your paper changes to a nearly scientific mode in its body. The intro. is great—description of cars, the smell of fresh dough, the warmth of the oven, and so on.

4. *Organization:* The paper organization is OK, I guess. I like the opening paragraphs best. Perhaps the paper would read better if the description were more involved and not so generalized—smells, taste-comparisons, textures, sights.

5. *Conclusion:* The essay concludes effectively. Perhaps you could let the reader know more about a NY delicatessen, Bagel Nosh, or bagelry. Colleen, perhaps you might consider playing up the role of the Bagelry in our small New England college town.

As these responses demonstrate, different readers react in very different ways to the same piece of writing. They do not always agree on what is strong or weak, effective or ineffective; they may not even agree on what the thesis is. In addition, you may find that you simply do not agree with their advice. As the author, the authority on what you want to say, you must decide what advice to follow and how best to do so. In examining responses to your writing, you can often proceed efficiently by looking first for areas of agreement ("everyone was confused by this sentence—I'd better review it") or strong disagreement ("one person said my conclusion was 'perfect' and someone else said it 'didn't conclude'—better look carefully at that paragraph again").

On the basis of broad areas of agreement in the responses she received, Colleen decided on the following changes: (1) to add more sensory details, since this description depends on appealing to the readers' senses; (2) to concentrate more on the Bagelry's location and its connection to New York, since the respondents like the idea of a "taste of NY"; and (3) to add more personal opinion in response to one reader's suggestion for "more personality."

Colleen also got some advice from her instructor. After noting that her topic seemed appropriate for readers of a local magazine, he suggested that she begin to consider the readers of such a magazine as her audience and that she add some quotations from the owners as well

WRITERS ON WRITING

I believe in miracles in every area of life *except* writing. Experience has shown me that there are no miracles in writing. The only thing that produces good writing is hard work.

—ISAAC BASHEVIS SINGER

WRITERS ON WRITING

. . . the only effect I ever had on Ernest [Hemingway] was to get him in a receptive mood and say let's cut everything that goes before this. Then the pieces got mislaid and he could never find the part that I said to cut out. And so he published it without that and later we agreed that it was a very wise cut. This is not literally true and I don't want it established as part of the Hemingway legend, but it's just about as far as one writer can go in helping another.

—F. SCOTT FITZGERALD

as some more information about the atmosphere of the restaurant. With these tips, Colleen saw that she needed to do more research on the Bagelry. She decided to interview the owners, bakers, and customers and to spend some time observing the restaurant, trying to see what made it so attractive to people in the area.

EXERCISE 3.2

Using the questions listed in 3c as a guide, analyze the draft you wrote in Exercise 2.11.

3d. Evaluating the thesis and its support

Once you have studied the responses to your essay and considered advice from all sources available to you, reread your essay once more, paying special attention to your thesis and its support. Check to make sure your thesis sentence contains a clear statement of the *topic* that the essay will discuss and a *comment* explaining what is particularly significant or noteworthy about the topic. As you continue to read, ask yourself how each sentence and paragraph relates to or supports the thesis. Such careful rereading can help to eliminate irrelevant sections or details or to identify sections needing further explanatory details or examples. If some points need more support, look back at your exploratory work and at suggestions from those who responded to your essay. If necessary, take time to gather more information and to do further exploration of ideas (see 2e).

EXERCISE 3.3

After rereading the draft you wrote in Exercise 2.11, evaluate the revised working thesis you produced in Exercise 2.7, and then evaluate its support in the draft. Identify points that need further support, and list those things you must do to provide that support.

3e. Analyzing organization

One good way to check the organization of a draft is by outlining it. You may have written an outline *before* the draft, but your organization may well have changed as you drafted. Drawing up an outline *after* the draft is finished allows you to evaluate the organizational plan as it actually exists in the draft. After numbering paragraphs in the

44

TEACHING PRACTICE

Writers must deal with focus or thesis problems right away. Inserting stronger transitions or adding supporting details won't help an unfocused essay. Is the writer still unsure of his or her focus or principal argument? Do some details detract from her main point? Whatever the reason for the problem, the writer needs to reread his or her rough draft to get a better feel for what to say or to freewrite until a reason for writing comes to mind. She or he may even want to start over.

People who do not understand their topic or have no purpose for writing on a particular subject do not and cannot write clearly. They have two choices: to stick to what they already know or to write in order to learn about the unknown.

WRITERS ON WRITING

H. L. Mencken earned much of his living and reputation by astutely judging the writings of other people. No one—not even the president of the United States—was exempt from his scrutiny. Here are some of Mencken's comments on President Warren G. Harding:

What is in the head infallibly oozes out of the nub of the pen. If it is sparkling Burgundy the writing is full of life and charm. If it is much the writing is much too. The late Dr. Harding . . . was a highly self-conscious stylist. He practiced prose composition assiduously, and was regarded by the pedagogues of Marion, Ohio, and vicinity as a very talented fellow. But when he sent a message to Congress it was so muddled in style that even the late Henry Cabot Lodge, a professional literary man, could not understand it. Why? Simply because Dr. Harding's thoughts, on the high and grave subjects he discussed were so muddled that he couldn't understand them himself. But on matters within his range of customary meditation he was clear and even charming, as all of us are. I once heard him address upon the ideals of the Elks. It was a topic close to his heart, and he had thought about it at length. . . . The result was an excellent speech—clear, logical, forceful, and with a touch of wild, romantic beauty. ("The Fringes of Lovely Letters," *Prejudices: Fifth Series*.)

ANALYZING ORGANIZATION   *rev* 3e

draft, read through each one, jotting down its main idea or topic in a sentence or phrase. Then examine your list, and ask yourself the following questions:

- What organizational strategies are used? spatial? chronological? logical? Are they used effectively?
- Do the main points clearly relate to the thesis and to one another?
- Can you identify any confusing leaps from point to point?
- Can you identify clear links between paragraphs and ideas? Do any others need to be added?
- Have any points been left out?
- Are any of the ones included irrelevant?

Colleen briefly outlined her draft in the following way:

1. Thesis: The Bagelry offers authentic NY-style bagels in an atmosphere much like that of the small shops that line NY streets.
2. Warren and Elise Daniels saw a market in SE NH for bagels and now have a two-store franchise that also makes wholesale deliveries in the area.
3. Typical day—average daily sales—all baking done at Durham.
4. Process of how bagels are made and cooked.
5. Variety of bagels offered.
6. Types of spreads and sandwiches available.
7. Baked goods, desserts, soups, beverages.
8. Conclusion: The Bagelry is fun for any and all!

Colleen's outline helped her to see some problems in the first three paragraphs. First of all, she saw that the link from paragraph 1 to paragraph 2 might be weak. In fact, the first sentence of paragraph 2, *Making bagels is Warren and Elise Daniels' forte*, comes as a bit of a surprise to the reader—the Danielses are not linked to anything in paragraph 1 except the word *bagels*. To strengthen the transition, Colleen decided to add a new sentence linking the Danielses clearly to the Bagelry and also reemphasizing the New York connection.

```
    . . . Although set in the college town of Durham,
NH, the "Bagelry" offers authentic bagels in an atmosphere
much like the small coffee shops and cafés that line NY
city streets.
```

OPTIONAL EXERCISES

Deducing a thesis:
An effective way to demonstrate topics and comments in thesis statements is to ask the students to bring prospective topics to class. Give them five to ten minutes to write at least one (but preferably more) thesis statement. Ask a volunteer to supply a thesis, and then, as a class, attempt to identify:

    –the topic
    –the comment
    –the terms that need more definition
    –possible subtopics for the paper.

Inducing a thesis:
After a student volunteers a topic, ask the class to brainstorm that topic, while you record student responses on the chalkboard. Give the class a few minutes to group some of the responses in any way that suggests a point of view or a comment about the subject of the brainstorming. What thesis statements can they devise for their groupings? Write their answers on the board, eliciting ways that each thesis incorporates certain groupings.

Outlining:
If your students need training in outlining, try creating a collaborative outline. After the class has read a particular essay, work together to produce an outline of the essay.

OPTIONAL EXERCISE

Ask your students to locate a story, an article, or a book they especially enjoyed. Either in class or as homework, have them analyze the organization of the piece by answering the following questions and citing examples:

1. Why do you suppose the author started here? Is there a flashback? a provocative question? a description?
2. Does the author "hook" you? If so, how?
3. At what point in the piece did you become interested and decide to go on?
4. How is the piece held together? Find appropriate transitional devices, repetion of key words, or repetitive sentence structures.
5. How does the author prepare you for the information in the middle and the end of the piece?
6. What would you like to ask the author?
7. Was the ending satisfying to you? predictable? surprising?
8. How does the author end the piece?
9. Look at the title. Does it seem appropriate to you now that you've finished the piece? Did it when you started? Can you improve upon it or provide an alternative?

> "This NY connection is no accident," said the Bagelry's
> ~~Making bagels is Warren and Elise Daniels' forte.~~
> owner, Warren Daniels.
> Having moved from Queens, NY, to the southeastern section
> , Warren and his wife, Elise,   in an area where
> of NH ~~they~~ saw a market for the traditional bagel. ~~E~~ven
>
> bakeries are a rarity~~, in this area.~~ . . .

In addition, Colleen sensed that there was a leap or gap between paragraphs 2 and 3. As she said, "Paragraph 2 introduces the Danielses—and then they disappear." She decided to add more information on them, including some quotations from an interview she decided to conduct, and several other new sentences.

EXERCISE 3.4

On the basis of Colleen's list of paragraph points, evaluate the organization of the rest of her first draft (in 2j). Begin by answering the questions given in 3e.

EXERCISE 3.5

In checking the rest of the paragraph transitions in Colleen's first draft, did you find any others that were weak or missing? If so, suggest at least two ways of strengthening or adding each one.

3f. Reconsidering the title, introduction, and conclusion

First and last impressions count. In fact, readers remember the first and last parts of sentences—and of essays—better than anything else. For this reason, it is wise to pay careful attention to three important elements in an essay—the title, the introduction, and the conclusion.

1. The title

A good **title** gives readers information, draws them into the essay, and even gives an indication of the writer's view of the topic. It is an important device for defining what the essay will be. Colleen's original title, "The Bagelry," was accurate enough but not vivid or particularly intriguing. Following a suggestion from a reader of her first draft, she changed it to "A Taste of New York City in Downtown Durham." This revision establishes the implied comparison between New York

---

TEACHING PRACTICE

"First impressions count," Emily Post wrote, speaking about one's manners and personal appearance. Similarly, the writer's introductory paragraph gives the reader a first impression of the writer. The following additional checks can help your students determine the effectiveness of their introductory paragraphs:

What tentative conclusions can you draw about the writer's personality from the introduction? Is the writer intelligent, well-informed, confident? Is the writer ill at ease or uncommitted to the topic?

Can you determine the intended audience from the first paragraph? Or does the introduction seem to be directed at no one in particular?

WRITERS ON WRITING

A good title should be like a good metaphor: it should intrigue without being too baffling or too obvious.

—E. B. WHITE

A title is the writer's stamp of approval on her or his work.

—SUE V. LAPE

and the small New England town and sets up expectations about just what the "taste of New York" might be.

❙ 2. The introduction

A good **introduction** accomplishes two important tasks: first, it draws readers into the essay, and second, it clearly states the topic and makes some comment on it. It contains, in other words, a strong lead, or a "hook," and often an explicit thesis as well. The most common kind of introduction opens with a general statement about the topic and then goes into more detail, leading up to a statement of the specific thesis at the end. A writer can also introduce an essay effectively with an *intriguing quotation,* an *anecdote,* a *question,* or a *strong opinion.* (See 5e for a fuller discussion and examples of various kinds of introductions.)

Colleen's original draft contained a fairly effective lead—a word picture of a fall morning in a small New England town, a picture her readers liked. But because it did not establish the connection between the Bagelry and New York as clearly as she wanted, she decided to add a sentence to do so: *Although bagels are not exactly a traditional New England breakfast, they have become a part of life for many people in southern New Hampshire.*

❙ 3. The conclusion

Like introductions, **conclusions** present special challenges to a writer. If a good introduction captures readers' attention, sets the scene, and signals what is to come, a good conclusion leaves readers satisfied that a full discussion has taken place. Often a conclusion will begin with a restatement of the thesis and then end with more general statements that grow out of it; this pattern reverses the common general-to-specific pattern of the introduction. Writers can also draw on a number of other ways to conclude effectively, including a *provocative question,* a *quotation,* a *vivid image,* a *call for action,* or a *warning.* If you look at the essay you are preparing now, you may find other means of concluding effectively. (See 5e for a fuller discussion and examples of various kinds of conclusions.)

Colleen signaled that she was drawing to a close—*all in all,*—then summed up the points she had made, and finally ended with an appeal to her readers: *If you ever have a craving . . . for an authentic NY bagel, the Bagelry is for you.* She felt that her conclusion was

TEACHING PRACTICE
Padded endings are common in student writing. Inexperienced writers may sense that the paper is finished, but lacking confidence in their own writing, may feel compelled to restate the thesis or summarize the entire essay.

WRITERS ON WRITING
When you're ready to stop, stop. If you have presented all the facts and made the point that you want to make, look for the nearest exit.
—WILLIAM ZINSSER

USEFUL READING

Williams, Joseph. *Style: Ten Lessons in Clarity and Grace.* 2d ed. Glenview, IL.: Scott, 1985. A brief, but practical book that offers explanations and practice in correcting stylistic errors at the word-, sentence-, and paragraph levels. Individual chapters deal with such problems as overuse of nominalization and passive voice, prose sprawl, and lack of coherence and emphasis.

sufficiently clear, but she decided that the last sentence lacked punch. To make the sentence more emphatic, she revised it thus: *So if ever you have a craving for an authentic New York bagel, the Bagelry can satisfy your desire.*

EXERCISE 3.6

Review Colleen's draft in 2j, and compose an alternative conclusion. Then write a paragraph commenting on the strengths and weaknesses of the conclusion she actually used.

3g. Examining paragraphs, sentences, words, and tone

In addition to the large-scale task of examining the logic, organization, and development of their essays, effective writers look closely at the smaller elements: paragraphs, sentences, and words. Many writers, in fact, look forward to this part of revising because its results can often be very dramatic. Turning a bland, forgettable sentence into a memorable one—or finding just exactly the right word to express a thought—can yield great satisfaction and confidence.

1. Examining paragraphs

Paragraphing serves the reader by visually breaking up long expanses of writing and by signaling a shift in topic or focus. Readers expect a paragraph to develop an idea or topic, a process that almost always demands several sentences or more (see 5a). The following guidelines can help you evaluate your paragraphs as you revise:

1. Look for the topic or main point of each paragraph, whether it is stated or merely implied. Then check to see that every sentence serves to expand or support the topic.
2. Check to see how each paragraph is organized—spatially, chronologically, or by some logical relationship such as cause-effect or comparison-contrast. Then determine whether the organization is appropriate to the topic of the paragraph and if it is used fully to develop the paragraph. (See 5c and 5d.)
3. Count the number of sentences in each paragraph, noting those that have only a few. Do these paragraphs sufficiently develop the topic of the paragraph?

In paragraph 3 of her draft, for instance, Colleen counted six sentences. And of these sentences, the last four really did very little to develop the

---

OPTIONAL EXERCISE

If your students are inexperienced writers, they may be unsure about where to break for paragraphs and may insist that you provide them a hard and fast rule. But of course you cannot. The most experienced writers—even English instructors—disagree about paragraphing. You can assure your students, though, that if each of their paragraphs concentrates on and develops one idea, they will be safe.

Like punctuation, paragraphing occurs only in the written language. Although it is not a feature that can be indicated in speech, perhaps your students can identify paragraph breaks when listening to speech. Read aloud the following passage from Garrison Keillor's *Lake Wobegon Days*, and ask your students to jot down the places Keillor might have divided his text into paragraphs:

What a target! She was seventeen, a girl with big hips, and bending over, she looked like the side of a barn.

I picked up a tomato so big it sat on the ground. It looked like it had sat there for a week. The underside was brown. Small white worms lived in it. It was very juicy. I had to handle it carefully to keep from spilling it on myself. I stood up and took aim, and went into the wind-up, when my mother at the kitchen window called my name in a sharp voice. I had to decide quickly. I decided.

A rotten Big Boy hitting the target is a memorable sound. Like a fat man doing a bellyflop, and followed by a whoop and a yell from the tomato. She came after me faster than I knew she could run, and I took off for the house, but she grabbed my shirt and was about to brain me when Mother yelled "Phyllis!" and my sister, who was a good person, obeyed and let go and burst into tears. I guess she knew that the pleasure of obedience is pretty thin compared to the pleasure of hearing a rotten tomato hit someone in the rear end.

topic introduced by the first sentence of the paragraph, the beginning of a typical day at the Bagelry. When she looked to paragraph 4, Colleen saw the topic of "a typical day" further developed there. She decided, therefore, to put the sentences relating to this topic into a single paragraph along with more information describing a typical early morning in the Bagelry; information that did not develop that topic was moved to other paragraphs. Her revision of these paragraphs is shown below.

A typical day at the Bagelry starts at 4 o'clock in the morning, when The first batch of bagels is prepared for the morning bake. ~~One hundred to one hundred and twenty dozens of bagels are made for retail sales on the average. Approximately seventy dozens of bagels will be prepared for wholesale. All cooking and baking is performed at the Durham location. The Portsmouth store calls in its orders daily.~~

While most people are still sound asleep, one of the five official bakers begins the task of preparing the dough. ~~at the bagelry are busy making bagels before the sun rises.~~
He starts with
One hundred pounds of flour, ~~is used at a time to make the dough needed. Water and other ingredients are added.~~

EXERCISE 3.7

Choose two other paragraphs in Colleen's draft in 2j, and evaluate them using the guidelines listed above. Write a brief paragraph in which you suggest ways to improve the development or organization of these paragraphs.

2. Examining sentences

Sentences are the soldiers of prose, ideally marching forward in an orderly and impressive way that keeps readers engaged and ready for more. As with life, variety is the spice of sentences. You can add variety to the life of your sentences by looking closely at their length, structure, and opening patterns.

Varying sentence length

Too many short sentences, especially one after another, can sound like a series of blasts on a car horn—or like an elementary school

TEACHING PRACTICE

It is important for students to hear their writing read aloud by someone other than themselves, by a reader who will respond authentically to the grammatical guides and punctuation cues actually supplied by the writer on the page.

OPTIONAL EXERCISE

For homework or as an in-class exercise, ask your students to examine a piece of their own writing. First, they should count the number of sentences in each paragraph, noting those with the most and the least number of sentences. Then, they should account for any variation and explain the effectiveness of the variation.

After looking at the number of sentences in paragraphs, the students should focus on the number of words in sentences. They should count the number of words in each sentence noting the sentences with the most and the least number of words. Can they account for any variation? Is the variation effective?

Their findings will sensitize them to the pace and rhythm of their prose and may help them to see which of their paragraphs is the best developed and which are the most and the least effective. See if they can tell why.

textbook—while a steady stream of long sentences may bore or confuse readers. Most writers aim for some variety of length, then, breaking up a series of fairly long sentences with a very brief one, for example. In looking at her conclusion, Colleen found all of its sentences roughly the same length: twelve, eight, twelve, seven, ten, fourteen, and sixteen words. In revising, she decided to join sentences one through four into one twenty-six-word sentence, with three briefer sentences remaining at the end. If you read the draft version and revised version aloud, you should be able to hear the difference in rhythm the greater variety of length makes. (See 20a for detailed guidelines for checking sentence length in your own writing.)

> All in all, the Bagelry is a place for ~~all~~ *everyone* to enjoy.
> ~~It pleases~~ *pleasing* all tastes from plain to extravagant. ~~One can~~
> ~~obtain any or~~ *at* all ~~of the three~~ meals ~~consumed daily~~
> (~~b~~Breakfast, lunch, and dinner ~~foods are available~~). This
> restaurant/bakery has fast, accommodating, pleasant
> service. And it's the only one of its kind in this New
> England area. *So* If you ever have a craving for an authentic
> NY bagel, the Bagelry ~~is for you~~.
>   *can satisfy your desire.*

Varying sentence structure

The simple sentence is the most common kind of sentence in modern English, but using all simple sentences can sound very dull. On the other hand, constant use of compound sentences may result in a singsong or repetitive rhythm, while long strings of complex sentences may sound, well, overly complex. The best rule is to strive to vary your sentences; see 20c2 for advice on ways to do so. Paragraph 3 of Colleen's draft could use some work on sentence variety, since all six of its sentences were simple. Colleen eventually decided that this paragraph should be completely revised and merged with paragraph 4, but she did revise sentences one and two to turn sentence two into a subordinate clause and hence create one complex sentence rather than two simple sentences. You can see the original two sentences along with her revision at the top of the facing page.

> A typical day at the Bagelry starts at 4 o'clock in
> the morning, when The first batch of bagels is prepared for
> what is known as
> the morning bake.

Varying sentence openings

If anyone has ever noted that your writing seemed "choppy," the cause of the problem probably lay in lack of variety in sentence openings. Most sentences in English follow subject-predicate order and hence open with the subject of an independent clause, as does the sentence you are now reading. But opening too many sentences in a row this way results in a jerky, abrupt, or "choppy" rhythm. You can vary sentence openings by beginning with a dependent clause, a phrase, or a subordinating conjunction. (See 20b for more information on ways of opening sentences.) Colleen's first paragraph suffered from a very jerky rhythm, probably because every one of its sentences opened with a subject. See how in the example that follows revising some of the openings improved the flow and made the entire paragraph easier to read.

> It is a chilly fall morning. Many of the cars on
> the road are covered with a thick crisp frost—a sure sign
> that another cold New England winter is on its way. Many
> will start the morning off with a piping hot cup of coffee
> and a fresh warm bagel straight from the oven to brighten
> this early morning and take the chill out of this fall
> though
> day. Bagels are not exactly a traditional New England
> breakfast, but they have become a part of life for many
> people in southern New Hampshire.

Checking for sentences with it is, there is, and there are

As you go over the sentences of your draft, look especially carefully at the ones beginning with *it is, there is,* or *there are.* In many cases, such as the first sentence of Colleen's draft (*It is a chilly fall morning*), which helps to create the setting for her essay, these phrases are perfectly good ways to start a sentence. But they can easily be overused or misused. You don't know what *it* means, for instance,

(BACK)GROUNDING

One of the most popular and influential texts of the Renaissance was Desiderius Erasmus's *De Copia* (*On Abundance*), aimed at helping schoolboys achieve variation, eloquence, abundance, and versatility in thinking and writing. After describing the various methods of achieving such richness in style, Erasmus demonstrates for his readers their application and in a *tour de force* shows 150 ways to say in Latin "Your letter has pleased me very much" and 200 ways to say "I shall remember you as long as I live."

unless the writer has already pointed out exactly what *it* stands for (see 11c). A more subtle problem with these openings, however, is that they may be used to avoid taking responsibility for a statement. Look at the following two sentences:

> It is necessary to raise student fees.

> The university must raise student fees.

The first sentence avoids responsibility by beginning with the weak *It is*—and fails to tell us *who says* it is necessary.

Many writers use *it is*, *there is*, and *there are* openings not to avoid responsibility but just because they are easy ways of getting a sentence going. But they are often unnecessary, and using them gives the important opening spot of a sentence to a vague, weak word (*it* or *there*) and the most overused verb in the English language (*be*). Usually a sentence will be much stronger if it is rewritten to begin another way. For example, *It is known that radon causes cancer* can be rewritten as *Radon is known to cause cancer.*

EXERCISE 3.8

Here are two sentences from Colleen's draft that open with *there are*. Find at least two ways to rewrite each one to eliminate the *there are* openings:

1. There are twelve varieties to choose from.
2. There are extra added specialties the Bagelry serves.

EXERCISE 3.9

Choose a paragraph of your own writing, and analyze it for variety of sentence length, sentence structure, and sentence openings. Then write a revised version of your paragraph.

3. Examining words

To an even greater extent than their paragraphs or sentences, writers' word choice, or diction, offers an opportunity for them to put their personal stamp on a piece of writing. As a result, writers often study their diction very carefully, making sure they get the most mileage out of each word. Because word choice is highly individual, general guidelines are hard to define. Nevertheless, the following questions should help you become aware of the kinds of words you most typically use.

OPTIONAL EXERCISE

After your students have written two versions of each of the "There are" sentences in the exercise, ask them to try their hand at Erasmus's model sentences and see how many variations they can achieve as a class. Have your class examine these sentences according to the questions on diction.

TEACHING PRACTICE

Student writers often overuse passive verbs because they lack confidence and do not want to be held accountable for what appears on the page. The results of this scribal side-stepping appear to have been written by a "ghost writer," or worse, by a machine. Encourage your students to take responsibility for their writing by being actively present in the text. Active verbs make for livelier reading.

After attending a football game, students might typically write:

> Their players were continually booed while our players were cheered. Or,

> The goal post was ripped out of the ground.

Their sentences would be livelier and more accurate if cast in the active voice:

> My buddies and I booed the opposing team's players incessantly, pausing only to cheer for our team. Or,

> My buddies and I celebrated the win by helping to rip the goal post out of the ground.

EXAMINING PARAGRAPHS, SENTENCES, WORDS, AND TONE   *rev* 3g

1. Are the nouns primarily abstract and general or concrete and specific? Too many abstract and general nouns can create boring prose. To say that you bought a new car is much less memorable or interesting than to say you bought a new convertible or a new Porsche. (See Chapter 25.)

2. Are there too many nouns in relation to the number of verbs? The *effect* of the *overuse* of *nouns* in *writing* is the *placing* of too much *strain* on the inadequate *number* of *verbs* and the resultant *prevention* of *movement* of the *thought*. In the preceding sentence, one tiny form of the verb *be* (*is*) has to drag along the entire weight of all those nouns. The result is a heavy, boring sentence.

3. How many verbs are forms of *be*? If *be* verbs account for any more than about a third of your total verbs, you are probably overusing them. (See Chapter 8.)

4. Are verbs *active* whenever possible? Passive verbs are harder to read and remember than active ones. *The student's question was answered* is not as easy to understand or remember as *Professor Corbett answered the student's question.* The first sentence calls attention to the act of answering, which is hard to visualize since apparently no one is around to do it—the question is simply there, being answered. The second sentence, however, points our attention to the concrete presence of a particular person answering the question. The passive voice has many uses (see Chapter 8), but in general your writing will be stronger, more lively and energetic, if you use active verbs.

4. Examining tone

Word choice is closely related to **tone,** the attitude toward the topic and the audience that the writer's language conveys. In examining the tone of your draft, you need to consider the nature of the topic, your own attitude toward it, and that of your intended audience. Check the use of slang, jargon, and emotional language and the level of formality to see whether they create the tone you want to achieve (humorous, serious, impassioned, and so on) and whether that tone is an appropriate one given your audience and topic. You may even discover from your tone that your own attitude toward the topic is different from what you originally thought. (See Chapter 26.)

EXERCISE 3.10

Turn to 2j; and read paragraphs 6 and 7 of Colleen's draft, and describe the tone you think she achieves. Does the tone seem appropriate to readers of a

WRITERS ON WRITING

If we had to say what writing is, we would define it essentially as an act of courage.

—CYNTHIA OZICK

WRITERS ON WRITING

No one can write decently who is distrustful of the reader's intelligence, or whose attitude is patronizing.

—E. B. WHITE

local magazine and to the topic she chose? What changes in wording would you recommend and why? Then revise the two paragraphs to create what you consider an appropriate tone.

3h. Editing

Because readers expect, even demand, a final copy that is clean and correct in every way, and because you want to put your very best foot forward in any formal writing you do, you need to make time for thorough and careful **editing**. You can make editing somewhat systematic by keeping a personal checklist of editing problems. All writers have personal trouble spots, problems that come up again and again in their writing. You may already be aware of some of your own trouble spots and will probably have others pointed out to you by instructors. Paying attention to the *patterns* of editing problems you find in your writing can help you overcome errors.

After identifying any typical trouble spots in your writing and getting advice on editing from this handbook, organize the information you have gathered in a systematic way. To begin, list all the errors or corrections marked on the last piece of writing you did. Then note the context of the sentence in which each error appeared. Finally, try to derive a guideline that will tell you what to look for to spot future errors of the same kind. You can broaden these guidelines as you begin to find patterns of errors, and you can then add to your system every time you write and edit a draft. Here is an example of such a checklist.

MARKED ERRORS	IN CONTEXT	LOOK FOR
wrong preposition	*to* for *on*	*to*
spelling	*to* for *too*	*to* before adjectives, adverbs
fragment	starts with *when*	sentences beginning with *when*
spelling	*a lot*	*alot*
missing comma	after *however*	sentences opening with *however*
missing apostrophe	*Michael's*	all names
missing apostrophe	*company's*	all possessive nouns
tense shift	*go* for *went*	use of present tense
fragment	starts with *while*	sentences beginning with *while*
spelling	*sacrifice*	*sacrafice*
comma	after *for example*	*for example*

TEACHING PRACTICE

Though only one stage in the writing process, the final step of editing and checking for surface-level errors is vital to the success of any composition. Many students' preoccupation with editing and with errors inhibits their writing process. You may wish to emphasize that editing is one of the last stages of writing, not a stage to worry about all the way through a piece.

Besides an editing chart, you may also want to supply your students with spelling charts to hand in with each of their assignments. A sheet of paper, folded in half, will do. On the left side of the paper, you write down any misspelled words as they appear in the students' paper. When the students hand in the next assignment, each should have corrected the spelling and noted why the word was misspelled (e.g., double consonants, unstressed syllables, transposed letters, mere typos).

By using this simple chart, students will record troublesome words and recurring problems. You'll have an alternative to circling the misspelled word and writing *sp* above it.

This writer has begun to isolate patterns, like her tendency to write sentence fragments beginning with subordinating conjunctions (*when* and *while*), her trouble with apostrophes in possessives (*company's* and *Michael's*), and her tendency to skip commas after introductory elements. Some sorts of errors, such as the use of wrong words or misspellings, may seem so unsystematic that you may not be able to identify patterns in an editing checklist. (If spelling presents a special problem for you, keeping a separate spelling checklist as explained in Chapter 22 can help, or you may have a program that checks spelling as part of a word processor package.) But keeping an editing checklist will gradually allow you to identify most of the error patterns that trouble you. And since keeping up your editing checklist takes only a few minutes for each piece of writing, doing so is well worth the time.

EXERCISE 3.11

Using several essays you have written, establish your own editing checklist based on the one on the facing page.

▌ 3i. Proofreading the final draft

As a writer, you need to make your final draft *errorless*. You can do so by taking time for one last, careful **proofreading,** which means reading to correct any typographical errors or other slips, such as inconsistencies in spelling and punctuation. To proofread most effectively, read through the copy *aloud*, making sure that punctuation marks are used correctly and consistently and that all sentences are complete and no words are left out. Then go through again, this time reading *backwards* so that you can focus on each individual word and its spelling. This final proofreading aims to make your written product letter-perfect, something you can be proud to put your name on.

You have already seen a number of the revisions Colleen made in her draft. Following is the edited and proofread version she turned in to her instructor. If you compare her final draft with her first draft, you will notice revisions of both the content and the writing. For example, she eliminated details about the Portsmouth store, about the bagel-making process (paragraph 4 was just too long), and about the beverages. As for the writing, she eliminated a shift between *you* and *one* and strengthened her wording. In the conclusion, for instance, she changed *extravagant* to *adventurous* (a term more appropriate to patrons of a bagel restaurant) and *has* to *boasts*, a more specific word.

TEACHING PRACTICE

Many students will cut out this final stage of the editing process because they were eager to finish, stayed up too late, or have lost interest in the writing. You may want to provide them a last-minute opportunity to proofread: before they hand in their papers, give them ten minutes of class time to proofread their final drafts; or ask them to trade papers and proofread one another's final drafts.

A Taste of New York City in Downtown Durham

It is a chilly fall morning. Many of the cars on the road are covered with a thick, crisp frost—a sure sign that another cold New England winter is on its way. To brighten this early morning and take the chill out of this fall day, many of the drivers and their passengers will start the morning off with a piping hot cup of coffee and a fresh, warm bagel straight from the oven. Although bagels are not exactly a traditional New England breakfast, they have become a normal part of life for many people in southern New Hampshire ever since the Bagelry opened its doors six years ago. Set in the college town of Durham, New Hampshire, the Bagelry offers authentic New York–style bagels in an atmosphere much like that of the small coffee shops and cafés that line the streets of New York.

"This New York connection is no accident," said the Bagelry's owner, Warren Daniels. Having moved from the New York City borough of Queens to the southeastern section of New Hampshire, Warren and his wife, Elise, saw a market for the traditional bagel in an area where even bakeries are a rarity. With help from a bagel consultant in Ithaca, New York, they set out to bring bagels to New Hampshire. Their dream became reality on March 17, 1983, the day the Bagelry opened its doors. It wasn't long before their business was booming—and they now supply the campus dining halls, the Memorial Union pub, the Greek houses, and most supermarkets in the area.

A typical day at the Bagelry starts at four o'clock in the morning, when the first batch of bagels is prepared for what is known as the morning bake. While most people are still sound asleep, one of the five official bakers begins the task of preparing the dough. The baker starts with one hundred pounds of flour. Other ingredients include yeast, malt, and salt, but no preservatives, sugar, or fat. In fact, bagels are actually less fattening than other kinds of bread.

All the ingredients are blended together in an enormous horizontal mixer. Once the dough reaches the proper consistency, it is transferred to another contraption—creatively labeled the Bagel Machine—that actually makes and shapes each individual bagel. This machine measures out three-ounce pieces of dough, forms them into rings, and pushes them down a large metal chute onto a canvas conveyor belt. At this point, the baker puts the bagels in rows on large flat boards. When all bagels have been put on boards, the boards are stacked on portable racks and covered with cloth sheaths to allow the bagels to rise.

The first step in cooking the bagels is what makes them authentic New York style. Unlike the frozen bagels for sale in supermarkets, these bagels are boiled before they are baked, a step that gives an attractive gloss to the outside and a lighter, fluffier consistency to the inside. After being boiled for approximately one minute, the bagels are baked at 550°F for fifteen to twenty minutes. At this time the aroma of hot, fresh baked goods fills the Bagelry. You can smell the yeast of dough rising and the strong tang of garlic and onion bagels.

The Bagelry offers twelve varieties of bagels to choose from, ranging from the old standbys to one actually invented by the proprietors. (If by chance your favorite is sold out when you arrive, try later in the day, for there is an afternoon bake as well.) As you walk into the Bagelry, you can see all the types aligned in wire baskets. First comes halitosis heaven, Garlic and Onion; for the more mellow palate, there are Wheat, Egg, and Plain. Rye, Pumpernickel, and Oat cater to the health-conscious customer, followed by Sesame, Poppyseed, and Salt. Cin—

namon Raisin brings up the rear and offers something on the sugary side for those with a sweet tooth. While Onion and Cinnamon Raisin seem to be the most popular, the oatmeal bagel, created by Elise Daniels, has attracted a large following as well. "I enjoy experimenting a lot with ideas at home," she said. "I'm constantly investigating new cookbooks and possible recipes."

Elise is largely responsible for the Bagelry's enticing menu, which includes many variations on the basic bagel. Along with bagels by the dozen, you can get a bagel toasted, with cream cheese or assorted spreadables, or even done up like a sandwich.

Also available are fresh baked knishes—another New York specialty, consisting of dough with meat, cheese, and other fillings—as well as various quiches, breads, cakes, brownies, and delicious but fattening six-layer bars. In addition, you can indulge in hot or cold soups with a side order of bagel chips.

But along with its large, assorted menu of tasty treats, the Bagelry has something more to offer—atmosphere. It is a quiet, serene shop that is well lighted and comfortably decorated, with bright white walls and a clean appearance. The Bagelry serves a large number of people, yet it offers quiet spaces to converse with friends or read without distraction. You can slip back to a far corner, bagel and coffee in hand, and settle down with a complimentary national or local paper—or you can sit under hanging plants in the front enjoying the comforts of the indoors while gazing at the outdoors.

The relaxed atmosphere is very welcoming to the frazzled business executive and the "always-on-the-go" college student. Quite often, area businesspeople will hold informal interviews at the Bagelry, and during finals time each semester, many students can be seen studying there. A majority of customers are regulars.

```
     All in all, the Bagelry is a place for everyone to
enjoy, pleasing all tastes from plain to adventurous, at
all meals—breakfast, lunch, and dinner. This restaurant/
bakery boasts fast, accommodating, pleasant service. And
it's the only one of its kind in this area of New England.
So if ever you have a craving for an authentic New York
bagel, the Bagelry can satisfy your desire.
```

3j. Using a word processor when revising and editing

If you have access to a word processor, you may want to take advantage of it as you revise, edit, and proofread. A word processor allows you to move sentences, paragraphs, and even whole sections of your essay around easily, so that you can experiment with various possibilities. You can also use a word processor to identify misspelled words and various other problems. (See Chapter 45 for a detailed discussion of how you can use a word processor as you write.)

EXERCISE 3.12

Using the guidelines presented in this chapter, revise, edit, and proofread the draft you wrote in Exercise 2.11.

FOR EXAMINING YOUR OWN WRITING PROCESS

While your revising, editing, and proofreading are still fresh in your mind, answer the following questions. Make your answers an entry in your writing log if you are keeping one.

1. How did you first begin revising?
2. What kinds of comments on or responses to your draft did you have? How helpful were they and why?
3. How long did the revising process take? How many drafts did you produce?
4. What kinds of changes did you tend to make—in organization, paragraph development, sentence structure, wording, adding or deleting information?
5. What worried you most as you were revising?
6. What pleased you most?
7. What would you most like to change about your process of revising, and how do you plan to go about doing so?

4. Understanding and Using Argument

(BACK)GROUNDING

Aristotle defined humans as "rational animals" imbued with ethical and emotional concerns, living during a time characterized by stable values, social cohesion, and a unified cultural ideal.

In *Rhetoric: Discovery and Change*, Young, Becker, and Pike argue that Aristotle's image of the "rational animal" directly influenced his rhetoric:

> Underlying the classical tradition is the notion that although [people] are often swayed by passions, their basic and distinguishing characteristic is their ability to reason. . . . [Thus for classical rhetoricians] logical argument . . . was the heart of persuasive discourse. (6)

Therefore, the authors argue, the emphasis of the classical tradition was on the logic (or rationale) underlying each argument.

However, contemporary rhetoricians view humankind as "symbol-using animals" who live in a fragmented world mediated by and through language. In *A Rhetoric of Motives*, Kenneth Burke refers to that society when he writes that "rhetoric is concerned with Babel after the Fall" (23) and goes on to substantiate the modern goal of rhetoric as "communication," differing from the traditional goal of combative or coercive "persuasion": "Wherever there is persuasion, there is rhetoric. And wherever there is 'meaning,' there is 'persuasion'" (127).

WRITERS ON WRITING

A writer who does not passionately believe in the perfectibility of man has no dedication to nor any membership in literature.

—ANONYMOUS

Some 2,400 years ago, Aristotle noted that we need to understand the art of language use (which he called rhetoric) in order to create meaning, to express meaning clearly, and to defend ourselves against others who would use language to manipulate us. Those needs are no less pressing today as we approach the twenty-first century than they were for Aristotle and the Greeks in the fourth century B.C. In fact, written language surrounds us more than ever before, and this language—advertisements, news stories, memos, reports—not only competes for our attention but argues for our agreement. Even supposedly abstract and uncontroversial subjects like mathematics depend to a large extent on successful **argument**: language whose purpose is to persuade. As two professors point out in a recent book, the common idea that mathematics represents an absolute, abstract level of truth is in fact a myth. "Mathematics in real life is a form of social interaction," the authors note, in which "proving" anything involves a mixture "of calculations and casual comments, of convincing argument and appeals to the imagination."* Since argument so pervades our lives, we need to understand and be able to use the strategies of effective argument. In this chapter, you will practice these "survival arts" of recognizing, understanding, and using written arguments.

---

*Phillip J. Davis and Reuben Hersh, *Descartes' Dream: The World According to Mathematics* (Boston: Houghton Mifflin, 1988).

USEFUL READING

Corbett, Edward P. J. *Classical Rhetoric for the Modern Student.* 2d ed. New York: Oxford UP, 1971. This text provides a thorough, cogent, and readable exposition of Aristotelian rhetoric and a brief history of rhetoric.

Ede, Lisa S. and Andrea A. Lunsford. "On Distinctions between Classical and Modern Rhetoric." *Essays on Classical Rhetoric and Modern Discourse.* Ed. Robert J. Connors, Lisa S. Ede, and Andrea A. Lunsford. Carbondale, IL: Southern Illinois P, 1984. 37–49.

RECOGNIZING ARGUMENT

4a. Recognizing argument

In a way, all language use is argumentative. Even when you greet someone warmly, you wish to convince the person that you are genuinely glad to see him or her, that you value the person's presence. In this sense we are immersed in argument the way we are immersed in air: advertisements argue that we should buy their products; clothing argues that we should admire or respect the people inside; our friends argue—through their actions, their language, even their personal style—that we should accept and value them. Even the apparently objective reporting of newspapers and television has strong argumentative overtones: by putting a particular story on the front page, for example, a paper "argues" that this subject is more important than others, or by using emotional language and focusing on certain details in reporting an event, a newscaster tries to persuade us to view the event in a particular way. What one reporter might call *public assistance,* for example, another might call *welfare,* and yet another, the *dole.* We could legitimately find an argumentative "edge," therefore, wherever we find meaning in language. This chapter will look at written arguments, and specifically at ways writers can provide convincing support for their assertions.

Of course, argument is not always necessary. If everyone can agree on the truth of a statement, no argument is needed. For instance, saying that personal ownership of computers in North America has increased in the last twenty years makes a factual statement that should not produce an argument. On the other hand, saying that computers pose dangers to mental health presents an arguable assertion that must be convincingly supported before being accepted.

In many important areas of our lives, widespread factual agreement seldom exists. Is nuclear power generation necessary? Should we take one job or another, live in one location or another, marry one person or another, or marry at all? Should our town increase taxes for schools? Should we risk job security by protesting a policy we feel to be unethical? Is a new building an architectural masterpiece or an eyesore? Is the use of pesticides threatening the lives of farm workers? Such arguable questions are often at the center of our lives, and in most instances they fall into that area where absolute knowledge or truth is simply unavailable. To acknowledge that we can seldom find *absolute* answers to moral, political, and artistic questions, however, is not to say that we cannot move toward agreement on such questions by thinking clearly about them. In fact, this is precisely the way most

61

USEFUL READING

Golden, James L., Goodwin F. Berquist, William E. Coleman. *The Rhetoric of Western Thought.* 3d ed. Dubuque, IA: Kendal/Hunt, 1983. Provides a fine diachronic overview of rhetoric and includes classic essays by modern rhetoricians Everett Lee Hunt, Lloyd Bitzer, Douglas Ehninger, Richard Weaver, Kenneth Burke, and Chaim Perelman.

(BACK)GROUNDING

In "The Rhetorical Situation," Lloyd Bitzer writes that rhetoric is necessary when something is waiting to be done, something that can be modified only through discourse (*Philosophy and Rhetoric* 1 [1968]: 1–14). Thus, a rhetorical situation is one that can be changed only through language. Situations calling for neither persuasion or communication are not rhetorical.

WRITERS ON WRITING

The art of writing has for backbone some fierce attachment to an idea.

—VIRGINIA WOOLF

TEACHING PRACTICE

Advertisers often deliberately blur the difference between facts and opinions; they stretch "facts" to strengthen their argument. For example, that "nine out of ten doctors recommend 'Blot-out' for headache relief" may be a fact, but this fact does not rule out the possibility that "ten out of ten" doctors may also recommend some other remedy: wearing sunglasses or a hat, reducing stress, lying down, taking aspirin.

To demonstrate the "objectivity" of "facts" in your class, reproduce two advertisements that use a logical proof like the above and discuss the way the "fact" is used to argue a position.

(BACK)GROUNDING

In *Modern Dogma and the Rhetoric of Assent,* Wayne Booth posits that good rhetoric is

the art of discovering good reasons, finding what really warrants assent because any reasonable person ought to be persuaded by what has been said. (xiv)

Although good reasons *ought* to guarantee assent, sometimes they do not, for each person finds a reason to believe or not. Sometimes, the reason is not a rational one. However, in *Classical Rhetoric for the Modern Student,* Edward P. J. Corbett echoes Aristotle, reminding us that

Rationality is man's essential characteristic. It is what makes man human and differentiates him from other animals. Ideally, reason should dominate all of man's thinking and actions, but actually, man is often influenced by prejudices and customs. To say that man often responds to irrational motives is not to say that he never listens to the voice of reason. We must have faith not only that man is capable of ordering his life by the dictates of reason but that most of the time he is disposed to do so. (50)

WRITERS ON WRITING

A writer's mind seems to be situated partly in the solar plexis and partly in the head.

—ETHEL WILSON

ANSWERS TO EXERCISE 4.1

The answers to this exercise will vary, depending on your students.

1. Arguable
2. Not arguable
3. Arguable
4. Not arguable
5. Arguable
6. Not arguable, unless students want to discuss boiling temperatures at different air pressures
7. Arguable
8. Arguable, depending on the acceptance of factual reports
9. Arguable
10. Arguable, although some studies continue to show correlations between reduced speed and lower accident rates. More readily verifiable is the correlation between speed limit and mortality rate.

human knowledge is gained: through the process of moving toward agreement on crucial issues.

In much of your work in college, you will be asked to participate in this process by taking a position and arguing for that position— whether to analyze a trend or explain a historical event or prove a mathematical equation. Such work will usually require you to make an arguable statement, to make a claim based on the statement, and finally to present *good reasons* in support of the claim.

The first step in the process of argument is to make a statement about a topic and then to check that the statement can, in fact, be argued. An arguable statement should have three characteristics:

- It should attempt to convince readers of something, change their minds about something, or urge them to do something.
- It should address a problem for which no easy solution exists or ask a question to which no absolute answers exist.
- It should present a position that readers could disagree with realistically.

EXERCISE 4.1

Using the three guidelines above, decide which of the following statements are arguable and which are not.

1. *Fatal Attraction* was the best movie of the 1980s.
2. The climate of the earth is gradually getting warmer.
3. The United States must drastically reduce military spending in order to balance the budget.
4. Shakespeare died in 1616.
5. Marlowe really wrote the plays of Shakespeare.
6. Water boils at 212 degrees Fahrenheit.
7. Van Gogh's paintings are the work of a madman.
8. The incidence of lung cancer has risen in the last ten years.
9. Abortion denies the fetus's inherent right to life.
10. The national 55-mile-per-hour speed limit was responsible for lower accident rates.

▌ 4b. Formulating an argumentative thesis

Once you have an arguable statement, you need to **make a claim** about the statement, one you will then work to persuade readers to accept. Your claim becomes the working thesis for your argument. For example, look at the following statement:

FORMULATING AN ARGUMENTATIVE THESIS

The use of pesticides endangers the lives of farm workers.

This statement is arguable—it aims to convince, it addresses an issue with no easily identifiable answer, and it can realistically be disagreed with. Although it does make a kind of claim—that pesticides threaten lives—the claim is just a factual statement about *what is*. To develop a claim that can become the working thesis for an argument, you usually need to direct this kind of statement toward some action; that is, your claim needs to move from *what is* to *what ought to be*:

STATEMENT ABOUT WHAT IS

Pesticides endanger the lives of farm workers.

CLAIM ABOUT WHAT OUGHT TO BE

Because pesticides endanger the lives of farm workers, their use should be banned.

This claim becomes your argumentative thesis. Like any working thesis, this one contains two elements, a topic (the statement about what is) and a comment (the claim about what ought to be). See 2f for more discussion of how to formulate a thesis.

TOPIC
Because pesticides endanger the lives of farm workers,
COMMENT
their use should be banned.

In some fields, such as literature or history, you will usually be making a claim that urges readers not to take action, but to interpret something in a certain way. In this case, the claim about what ought to be will usually be implied rather than stated directly. For example, a history essay that makes the claim that moral opposition to slavery was the major underlying cause of the Civil War is in effect arguing that readers should view the Civil War in this light rather than as a constitutional struggle over states' rights or an economic conflict between Northern industrialists and Southern planters. Or if you are asked on an art history examination to argue the claim that Van Gogh's paintings are the works of a madman, you are in effect trying to persuade your instructor that he or she ought to view Van Gogh's works as unconscious products of a disordered mind rather than the result of conscious rational decisions.

WRITERS ON WRITING

Failure to sharply define one's subject is the chief cause of fuzzy, disunified discourse. Vague beginnings invite chaotic endings. The audience for a discourse . . . can achieve no firmer grasp of the thesis than the writer or speaker . . . has.
—EDWARD P. J. CORBETT

An essay is only as good as its thesis.
—ANONYMOUS

OPTIONAL EXERCISE

Have your students test the following thesis statements for purpose, audience, position, and support: (1) My paper will deal with the issue of drug use by college athletes. My audience is made up of coaches and administrators, and I want to point out that it is their insistence on perfection and on winning at all costs that often causes athletes to turn to drugs to stimulate performance, to relieve stress, and to relax.

(2) In this essay, I will argue that this university discriminates against people who live off campus and who must drive to school. I know this is true because I am a commuter and can never find a parking spot. If there's a blizzard, the university doesn't close because students can walk to class. The university schedules two or three hours between classes for commuter students and then doesn't provide them with any place to go except the library, where you can't even get a coke.

How can these statements be improved?

ANSWERS TO EXERCISE 4.2 WILL VARY

ANSWERS TO EXERCISE 4.3 (WILL VARY)

1. The Arab-Israeli conflict can be managed but not solved.

The U.S. government should not attempt to solve the Arab-Israeli conflict because (1) it is essentially religious, not political; (2) neither side has a tradition of compromise; (3) both sides will accept nothing less than possession of the same territories.

2. Prison inmates retain basic human rights, including the right not to be tested for the AIDS virus.

Mandatory testing of prisoners for the AIDS virus is wrong because it would (1) infringe on their basic right to privacy; (2) and be tantamount to acknowledging that prisoners are sexually active and use drugs.

3. Free access to computers is an unrealistic goal.

Students should not have free access to computers because (1) the cost would be prohibitive; (2) they don't have equal access to other facilities such as study carrells, musical instruments, practice fields, and sports equipment.

4. The new federal student loan program is a step in the right direction.

A new federal student loan program should be created because (1) it ensures access to higher education for many more people; (2) it does not add substantially to the budget deficit because the funds will be repaid; and (3) its success may encourage the government to develop other useful programs.

5. Surrogate motherhood is another name for baby selling.

Women should not be allowed to act as surrogate mothers because (1) legalizing this practice justifies selling a human life; (2) a surrogate mother is not a factory but is in some sense "one" with the baby; and (3) the children of surrogates may be psychologically traumatized when they find out the truth about their birth.

EXERCISE 4.2

Using two arguable statements from Exercise 4.1 or two that you create, formulate two working argumentative theses, identifying the topic and the comment for each one.

EXERCISE 4.3

Formulate an arguable statement and create a working argumentative thesis for two of the following general topics.

1. the Arab-Israeli conflict
2. mandatory testing of prison inmates for the AIDS virus
3. free access to computers for all students on campus
4. a new federal student loan program
5. surrogate motherhood

4c. Formulating good reasons

In his *Rhetoric*, Aristotle discusses the various ways one can argue a point. Torture, he notes, makes for a very convincing argument, but not one that most responsible and reasonable people would resort to. A pointed gun is no substitute for good reasons, and today we still rely on the three types of good reasons named by Aristotle—those that establish credibility, those that appeal to logic, and those that appeal to emotion.

4d. Establishing credibility

To make your argument convincing, you must first gain the respect and trust of your readers, or **establish your credibility** with them. Your character is embodied in your words, and the way this character is perceived by others largely influences how credible you and your arguments will be. The ancient Greeks called this particular kind of character appeal *ethos* and valued it highly. The little boy who cried "Wolf!" when there really was no wolf approaching was very quickly mistrusted by his townspeople. His was essentially a problem of *ethos*: he lost credibility because he could not be trusted to tell the truth.

In general, writers can establish credibility in three ways: (1) by being knowledgeable about the topic at hand; (2) by establishing common ground with the audience, in the form of respect for their points of view and concern for their welfare; (3) by demonstrating fairness and

ESTABLISHING CREDIBILITY   *arg* +d

evenhandedness. Let us now look at each element of credibility more closely.

▌1. Demonstrating knowledge

A writer can establish credibility first by establishing his or her credentials. You can, for instance, show that you have some personal experience with the subject. In addition, showing that you have studied the subject, done research on it, and thought about it carefully can establish a confident tone. In doing so, your point is not to boast or show off; rather, you are assuring your audience that the position you hold is based on adequate knowledge and is systematically thought out.

To determine whether you can effectively present yourself as one knowledgeable enough to argue an issue, you might consider the following questions:

- Can you provide information from *several* sources to support your claim?
- What are the sources of your information?
- How reliable are your sources?
- Do any sources contradict each other? If so, can you account for or resolve the contradictions?
- If you have personal experience relating to the issue, is this experience directly applicable to your claim?

These questions will help you to probe your own stock of knowledge and assess your own credibility in making a claim, and they may help you to see what other work you need to do to establish your credibility. They may well tell you that you must do more research, check sources, try to resolve contradictions, refocus your working thesis, or even change your topic.

In demonstrating that you are knowledgeable, however, you must be careful not to sound high-handed or self-serving. Not only will you actually lose credibility by seeming to present a one-sided argument, but you will fail to establish common ground between yourself and your readers.

▌2. Establishing common ground

Many arguments between people or groups are doomed to end without resolution because the two sides occupy no common ground, no starting point of agreement. They are, to use an informal phrase,

USEFUL READING

Booth, Wayne C. *Modern Dogma and the Rhetoric of Assent.* Chicago: U of Chicago P, 1974. Booth argues for a Burkean form of rhetoric—one that seeks "assent" (i.e., Burke's "identification")—to counter the dogmatisms that have developed during this century.

(BACK)GROUNDING

According to Aristotle, *ethos* is established only at the time of the speech; the speech itself must create the ethical appeal. Thus a person wholly unknown to the audience could by words alone establish credibility.

Today, we often take *ethos* to be already established: as a nation, we have believed anything Walter Cronkite or Mike Wallace told us and little of what Richard Nixon or Rona Barrett told us. Jimmy Carter was considered an honest, knowledgeable, but naive president, while Ronald Reagan was widely thought to be calm, controlled, but often ill-informed.

Do actors-turned-politicians (e.g. Reagan, Eastwood, Temple, and Bono) have an advantage in establishing a credible *ethos*? How do they establish *ethos*? How do they demonstrate knowledge? From whom do we expect a demonstration of knowledge? of credibility?

We each measure credibility differently, according to our expectations. We are wary of the stereo salesclerk who claims to be an electronics engineer because we do not believe that a real engineer would work in this capacity. Yet if an engineer told us that she or he used to sell stereos, we would value her or his advice on compact-disc players. If we saw Albert Einstein walking down the street without socks and with his coat buttoned up wrong, we would accept him as a brilliant, absent-minded professor; yet, if we saw our dentist in the same disarray, we'd probably change dentists. We wouldn't want an absent-minded dentist working in our mouth.

TEACHING PRACTICE

Because they want to sound "scholarly" or "academic," student writers often resist using personal experiences in their essays, believing that such information is neither objective nor factual enough. But as an instructor, you know the importance of the writer's presence in the essay, for he or she is the "I" (the eye) who guides readers through the text, the person(a) whom readers must trust, the felt presence who is committed to a position.

(BACK)GROUNDING

Argumentation, persuasion, rhetoric—these terms may bring to mind images of hostility, manipulation, deception, and of overpowering, overmastering, outmaneuvering. In *A Rhetoric of Motives*, Kenneth Burke postulates that the image of persuasion should not be bellicose, but rather that

> a speaker persuades an audience by the use of stylistic identifications; his act of persuasion may be for the purpose of causing the audience to

identify itself with the speaker's interests; and the speaker draws on identification of interests to establish rapport between himself and his audience. (46)

Identification, Burke reminds us, occurs when people share some principle in common—that is, when they establish common ground. Persuasion should not begin with absolute confrontation and separation but with the establishment of common ground, from which differences can be worked out.

TEACHING PRACTICE

Your students will better understand the concept of "common ground" if you provide them with an opportunity to demonstrate how opposing parties can reach agreement. Divide the class into pairs of students who hold opposing views and ask each pair to establish a first principle of agreement, their common ground. Use frustrating situations the students experience as well as the following rhetorical situations:

–your roommate keeps an annoying schedule. (For example, if an earlybird and a night owl are roommates, they may keep antagonistic schedules. Yet when they discuss their unhappiness, both agree that they each need quiet for sleeping and studying and noise for relaxing. They have thus established common ground, a starting point for working out their differences.)
–your English teacher doesn't accept late papers.
–you'd like to borrow your mother's car.
–you show your parents your 2.0 average.
–you stay out past your curfew.
–you'd like permission (and money) to go to Florida during spring break.
–your roommate constantly borrows your belongings.
–you need help with child care or household duties.
–you are indeed 21, although you have no I.D. with you.

(BACK)GROUNDING

MOOR EEFFOC—that's coffee room backwards, when you look through the glass from the other side. Ask your students to try to see the point of view of the opposition. When they try to decipher "MOOR EEFFOC," they show their willingness to go over to the other side to get a better view of the rhetorical situation. They also demonstrate their sense of audience.

coming from completely different places. Such has often been the case, for example, in arms-control talks in which the beginning positions of the Soviet Union and the United States were so far apart that no resolution could ever be reached. The lack of common ground also dooms many arguments closer to our everyday lives. If you and your roommate cannot seem to agree on how often to clean the apartment, for instance, your difficulty may well be that your definition of a clean apartment conflicts radically with your roommate's. You may find, in fact, that you will not be able to resolve the issue until you can establish a common definition on which to base the argument. In this way, common ground provides a necessary starting point, one that can turn a futile quarrel into a constructive argument.

Common ground is just as important in written arguments as it is in diplomatic negotiations or personal disputes. Because topics and writers and audiences are so individual and varied, no foolproof or absolute guidelines exist for a writer to establish common ground with an audience. Following are some questions, however, that can help you to find common ground in presenting an argument:

- What are the differing perspectives on this issue?
- What are those aspects of the issue on which all sides agree?
- How can you express such areas of agreement clearly to all sides?
- How can you discover—and consider—opinions on this issue that differ from your own?

If you can establish common ground on an issue, you will have taken a giant step toward demonstrating good will toward your readers. We are inclined, after all, to listen with interest and attention to those we believe to have our best interests at heart. On the other hand, we are naturally suspicious of those who seem to want to further only their *own* interests.

3. Demonstrating fairness

In arguing a position, writers must demonstrate fairness toward opposing arguments. Audiences are more inclined to give credibility to writers they believe to be fairly considering and representing their opponents' views than to those who seem to be ignoring or distorting such views. We have all experienced unfair arguments: a co-worker loses his

USEFUL READING

Perelman, Chaim. "The Premises of Argumentation" in *The Realm of Rhetoric*. Notre Dame: U of Notre Dame P, 1982. 21–32. Discusses common ground, the starting point of agreement for any discourse.

ESTABLISHING CREDIBILITY   *arg* 4d

temper and blames you for a decision that was largely his idea, or a clever politician avoids a tough question at a news conference by giving an answer that ignores the questioner's point and then calling on someone else. Such tactics seem unfair, and to the extent that we recognize them we condemn them. It goes without saying, then, that to be an effective writer, you need to avoid such tactics and establish yourself as open-minded and evenhanded. Doing so often requires a genuine attempt to "walk a mile in the other person's shoes." Following are some questions that can help you discover ways of doing so:

- Can you show that you are taking into account all points of view? How?
- Can you demonstrate that you understand and sympathize with other points of view? How?
- What can you do to show that you have considered evidence carefully, even that which does not support your position?
- How can you demonstrate that you are open to other arguments, that you are not blindly advocating your claim?

4. Recognizing ethical fallacies

Some arguments focus not on establishing the credibility of the writer but on destroying the credibility of an opponent. In some cases such attacks are justified: if a nominee for the Supreme Court has acted in unethical ways in law school, for example, that information is a legitimate argument against the nominee's confirmation. Other times, however, someone may attack a person's character in order to avoid dealing with the issue at hand. Be extremely careful about attacking an opponent's credibility, for doing so without justification can harm your own credibility. Such unjustified attacks are called **ethical fallacies.** They take two main forms: *ad hominem* charges and guilt by association.

Ad hominem (Latin for "to the man") **charges** directly attack someone's character rather than focusing on the issue.

> Senator Kennedy has never fully explained his shameful complicity in the death of Mary Jo Kopechne, so he is not fit to pass judgment on a distinguished jurist like Judge Bork. [The Kopechne tragedy has no connection to Kennedy's judgment about Bork.]

TEACHING PRACTICE

Writers who rely on manufactured methods of persuasion—distorting evidence, misquoting, misrepresenting opposing views—do not trust their own position on an issue and may not be able to represent that position believably. Encourage your students to rely on the authentic strengths of their personal experience as well as the facts they have selected to support their position on an issue.

Ask the students to bring in ads that *do not* fairly represent a product, or an editorial or a letter to the editor that presents distorted evidence. What are the contexts for the examples? What specifically is slanted or unfair? Then ask the students (1) to write out their responses to the examples and (2) to rewrite the ad or example, according to fair standards. By doing such analyses, your students will sharpen their critical thinking, reading, and writing skills.

WRITERS ON WRITING

Writing . . . keeps me from believing everything I read.

—GLORIA STEINEM

Guilt by association attacks someone's credibility by linking that person with a person or activity the audience considers suspicious or untrustworthy.

> Senator Fleming does not deserve reelection; one of his staff assistants turned out to be involved with the Mafia. [Is there any evidence that the senator knew about the Mafia involvement?]

ANSWERS TO EXERCISE 4.4

The copywriters work to establish credibility by:

1. Demonstrating knowledge (of nuclear testing, toxic pollution).
2. Appealing to logical judgment (saving a life, preserving the environment).
3. Demonstrating fairness (putting knowledge and experience in the public domain).
4. Establishing common ground (we both care about the future of our planet. We'll both benefit from the organization's success).

EXERCISE 4.4

Study the following advertisement for Greenpeace, an environmental group, carefully, and then list the ways in which the copywriters demonstrate knowledge, establish common ground, and demonstrate fairness. Do you think they succeed or fail in establishing credibility?

HELP US MAKE WAVES!

You can help keep the world's most unusual fleet in action...

We go into action without force. Without violence. But we *do* make waves. We're Greenpeace.

From the North Atlantic to the South Pacific, on the Great Lakes or in the near-frozen bays of Antarctica, Greenpeace is fighting for a cleaner environment and a more peaceful earth. You've heard about our campaigns to intercept renegade whalers on the high seas... to confront the nuclear superpowers in their contaminated testing zones... to block the dumping of toxic wastes into our water.

Greenpeace fights to *save* life and preserve our environment. And now *you* can be part of our worldwide campaigns to stop the slaughter of whales, dolphins and other animals... to prevent the spread of toxic pollution... to halt further testing of nuclear weapons and rid the oceans of nuclear-armed warships... to protect wilderness and wildlife from industrial and military exploitation.

Dangerous work? Yes. But we're willing to face the risks.

Over the past 15 years, Greenpeace's nonviolent navy has taken on the U.S. Department of Defense, the Soviet Navy, the Norwegian Coast Guard and the Royal Canadian Mounted Police. Our flagship, the *Rainbow Warrior*, was blown up by French secret service operatives, killing a member of her crew. Our activists have been threatened, arrested and beaten. They've had explosive harpoons shot over their heads and barrels of radioactive waste dropped on their boats.

But tough challenges bring dramatic victories. As a result of just some of Greenpeace's campaigns: the International Whaling Commission voted to end all commercial whaling; 37 years of dumping radioactive waste into the Atlantic Ocean was stopped; the annual slaughter of harp seals in Canada is virtually over; the French ceased atmospheric testing of nuclear weapons.

You can help Greenpeace meet tomorrow's challenges — help win tomorrow's victories.

Greenpeace needs you.

Greenpeace depends on the financial support of thousands of citizens around the world — people like you who care about the future of our planet — to keep our fleet in action. Your tax-deductible contribution today will help pay for the supplies and equipment we must have to take on those who poison our seas and slaughter our marine life.

You benefit as well.

When you support Greenpeace, you'll have the satisfaction of knowing that every Greenpeace victory for the environment is a victory *you* have helped make possible. And, for your contribution of $15 or more, you will receive our colorful, informative magazine, *Greenpeace*, to keep you up to date on our worldwide actions to protect our planet. Make some waves today!

☐ **YES . . .** I want to help Greenpeace win more victories for our environment. Here's my contribution of:

☐ $15 ☐ $25 ☐ $35 ☐ $50 ☐ $100 ☐ Other $_____

Name _____

Address _____

City/state/zip _____

Your contribution to Greenpeace is tax-deductible.   G8C

Please make your check payable to Greenpeace, and send it with this coupon today to: *Greenpeace*, P.O. Box 3720, Washington, D.C. 20007.

A copy of our annual report is available upon request from Greenpeace or the New York Department of State, Office of Charities Registration, Albany, NY 12231.

APPEALING TO LOGIC

EXERCISE 4.5

Using a working argumentative thesis you drafted in Exercise 4.2 or 4.3, write a paragraph or two describing how you would go about establishing your credibility in arguing that thesis.

▌ 4e. Appealing to logic

While the character we present in writing always exerts a strong appeal (or lack of appeal) in an argument, our credibility alone cannot and should not carry the full burden of convincing a reader. Indeed, we are inclined to view the **logic of the argument**—the reasoning behind it—as more important than the character of the person presenting the case. In truth, the two are usually inseparable and thus of equal importance. Nevertheless, strong logical support characterizes most good arguments. This section will examine the most effective means of providing logical support for a written argument: examples and precedents, testimony and authority, and causes and effects.

▌ 1. Providing examples and precedents

Just as a picture can sometimes be worth a thousand words, so can a well-conceived **example** be extremely valuable in arguing a point. No one in recent years has used the example to greater effect than President Ronald Reagan, whose public statements often employed a homespun example from his childhood or even from one of his movies to drive home a point. This paragraph, in fact, has used Reagan as an example in making its point: that examples are one of the staples of everyday argument.

Examples are used most often to support generalizations or to bring abstractions to life. For instance, a *Newsweek* review of the movie *Star Trek* IV made the general statement that the movie contained "nutty throwaway lines that take a minute to sink in" and then illustrated the generalization with this example:

> When the crew, flying the Klingon warship they inherited . . . , land in Golden Gate Park, they fan out to different corners of the city. . . . Kirk's parting command, spoken like a PTA mother at the county fair: "Everybody remember where we parked."

The generalization would have meant little without the example to bring it to life.

ANSWERS TO EXERCISE 4.5 WILL VARY

TEACHING PRACTICE

Ask your students to look again at the misleading ads, editorials, or columns they brought to class, this time analyzing them for logical appeals. Often unfair text is based on emotional rather than logical or ethical appeals.

Examples can also help us understand abstractions. "Famine," for instance, may be difficult for us to think about in the abstract—but a graphic description of a drought-stricken community, its riverbed cracked dry, its people listless, emaciated, and with stomachs bloated by hunger, speaks directly to our understanding.

Precedents are particular kinds of examples taken from the past. The most common use of precedent occurs in law, where an attorney may argue a case by citing the precedent of past decisions. A judge may be asked to rule that a defendant was negligent, for example, because the Supreme Court upheld a ruling of negligence in an almost identical case ten years earlier.

Precedent appears, however, in everyday arguments as well. If you urge your best friend to work your shift for you on the basis that the last time she needed some time off you worked her shift, you are arguing on the basis of precedent. Or if as part of a report on campus safety, you back up your request for increased lighting in the library parking garage by pointing out that the university has increased lighting in four similar garages in the past year, you are again arguing on the basis of precedent.

In research-based writing, you usually must list your sources for examples and precedents that are not based on your own knowledge (see 40b).

2. Citing authority and testimony

Another way to support an argument logically is to cite **authority**. As young children we were easily swayed by authority; it was right to do something simply because our parents (the authorities) said so. In recent years the use of authority has figured prominently in the antismoking movement. Many older Americans will remember, for instance, the dramatic impact of the U.S. surgeon general's 1963 announcement that smoking is hazardous to health. Many people at the time quit smoking, largely convinced by the authority of the person offering the evidence. Authority has been used in a similar way in the more recent effort to control drug use and abuse in the United States.

Citing an authority is thus a time-honored strategy for building support for an argumentative claim. But as with other such strategies, citing authorities demands careful consideration. Following are some questions you might consider to be sure that you are using authorities effectively:

(BACK)GROUNDING

In 466 B.C., when a democracy was established in the ancient Greek colony of Syracuse, an art of rhetoric was first formulated by the Sicilian Corax, an art that was later transmitted to Greece by Corax's pupil Tisias. Rhetoric began as a practical art, a part of civic life in the democracy of Syracuse. An immediate consequence of the establishment of a democracy was a mass of litigation on claims to property, urged by democratic exiles who had been dispossessed. Their claims, going back many years, often required stating and arranging a complicated series of details. Without documents to prove ownership, the litigants were forced to rely on inferential reasoning; without lawyers to plead their cases, they were left to plead their own cases—hence the need for professional advice, and hence Corax's custom-designed art of rhetoric.

Throughout the classical period, Corax's art of inferential reasoning proved to be more persuasive than other forms of testimony. Today, however, jurors place a great deal of emphasis on testimony, while judges and attorneys are often still persuaded by inferential reasoning. In our writing, we expect both citations of authority and good reasoning.

APPEALING TO LOGIC

- Is the authority timely? (To argue that the United States should pursue a foreign policy because it is one supported by Thomas Jefferson will probably fail because Jefferson's times were so radically different from ours.)
- Is the authority qualified to judge the topic at hand? (To cite a biologist in an essay on linguistics is not likely to strengthen your argument.)
- Is the authority likely to be known and respected by readers? (To cite an unfamiliar authority without some identification would lessen the impact of the evidence given.)

Authorities are commonly cited in research-based writing (treated in Part Nine), which relies on the findings of other people. In addition, you can cite authorities in answering essay examination questions (treated in Chapter 43) or in an assignment that asks you to review the literature in any field (treated in Chapter 42).

   Testimony—the evidence an authority presents in support of a claim—is a feature of much contemporary argument. Most familiar are the testimonials found in advertisements—a television personality giving testimony for dog food, or a star athlete speaking for Wheaties. In fact, we are so inundated with the use of testimonials in television advertising that we may be inclined to think of them only in terms of *mis*use. But if the testimony is timely, accurate, representative, and provided by a respected authority, then it, like authority itself, can add powerful support to an argument. In an essay for a literature class, for example, you might argue that a new edition of a literary work will open up many new areas of interpretation. You could strengthen this argument by adding a quotation from the author's biographer noting that the new edition carries out the author's intentions much more closely than the previous edition did.

   In research-based writing you should list your sources for authority and testimony that are not based on your own knowledge (see 40b).

▌ 3. Establishing causes and effects

   Showing that one event is the cause—or the effect—of another can sometimes help to support an argument. (See Chapters 2 and 5 for a discussion and examples of developing a topic by cause-effect analysis.) To take an everyday example, suppose you are trying to explain, in a petition to change your grade in a course, why you were unable to take the final examination. In such a case you would most

TEACHING PRACTICE

Ask the nonsmokers in your class to identify themselves. What appeals dissuaded them from smoking? Logical—the statistics for lung cancer and heart disease. Medical—did the Surgeon General, a "spokesmodel" (actress, athlete), or a relative convince them not to smoke? Emotional—anti-smoking literature that pictures wrinkled, toothless smokers, and played on their vanity?

Student writers sometimes rely too heavily on authority figures because they doubt the power of their own strongly held opinions, opinions that might well influence their readers. Encourage your students to cite authorities to support—not substitute for—their own positions on an issue.

Often students overlook the testimony of ordinary people as a means of identifying with their readers; they don't realize that the testimony of someone with firsthand experience lends powerful credibility to an argument. Although television star Kirk Cameron tells audiences, "Just say no to drugs," his credibility is not as strong as the straight talk of an ordinary citizen with emphysema or lung cancer.

TEACHING PRACTICE

Remind your students about the overuse of authority; they want to weave their support into their papers, not create a hodgepodge of other people's ideas.

While you help your students consider the appropriateness and proportion of their use of authority, ask them to consider Nancy Reagan's authority. Do they pay any attention to her anti-drug campaign? Do your students rent cars, order flower arrangements, or buy recliners on the advice of the ex-pro football players who advertise them?

Some authorities, however, make a living as "experts": finance specialists testify before the courts, explaining the fine points of tax law, the legal use of money by financial institutions; art experts verify the authenticity of a work of art; county coroners account for unexplained or unexpected deaths.

TEACHING PRACTICE

Cause and effect relationships are often complex: what appears at first glance to be the obvious cause of an event turns out to be only a secondary influence, sometimes an influence that obscures the primary cause and effect relationship. For example, one student felt sure that her migraine headaches were brought on by stress, air pressure, and certain food allergies; only after several seizures was she convinced otherwise: she had a small brain tumor. Encourage your students to persevere in finding the real connections between events and their causes.

OPTIONAL EXERCISE

What might be the obvious and not-so-obvious connections in the following causes and events:

1. A large increase in church membership in recent years shows that people are becoming more religious.
2. Older women often fall and break their hips because they don't consume enough calcium.
3. Because of its elderly population, Florida is the best place to buy a gently used car.
4. The Challenger explosion was caused by faulty rubber seals.
5. He lost his sight because he is a diabetic.

WRITING TOGETHER

Have your students work in groups to devise a causal argument for either losing or establishing their reputation—morally, athetically, scholastically, aesthetically, ethically.

What causal argument can they set up for their grades in this class? last term?

naturally try to trace the **causes** of your failure to appear—the death of your grandmother followed by the theft of your car, perhaps—so that the committee reading the petition would change your grade. We tend not to think of such analysis as a form of argument, but in many ways it is: in identifying the causes of a situation, you are implicitly arguing that the **effect**—your not taking the examination—should be given new consideration.

Tracing causes often lays the groundwork for an argument, particularly if the effect of the causes is one we would like to change. Recent figures from the U.S. Department of Education, for example, indicate that the number of high school dropouts is rising. If we can identify and understand the causes of this increased dropout rate—for example, a decline in reading skills—we may be able to make an argument for policies aimed at reversing the trend by affecting the causes in some way—such as hiring more teachers to provide remedial reading instruction.

In college writing, you may often be asked to show causes and effects. In an environmental science class, for example, a student may argue that a national law regulating smokestack emissions from utility plants is needed because (1) acid rain on the East Coast originates from emissions at utility plants in the Midwest, (2) acid rain kills trees and other vegetation, (3) midwestern states have been prevented by utility lobbying from passing strict laws controlling emissions from such plants, and (4) unless checked, acid rain will destroy most eastern forests by 2020. In this case, the first point is that the emissions cause acid rain; the second, that acid rain causes destruction of eastern forests; and the third, that states have not acted to break the cause-effect relationship established by the first two points. The fourth point ties all of the previous points together to provide an overall argument from effect: "unless X, then Y."

In fact, a cause-effect relationship is often extremely difficult to establish. Scientists and politicians continue to disagree, for example, over the extent to which acid rain is responsible for the so-called dieback of many eastern forests. In spite of the difficulty, though, if we can show that X definitely causes Y, we will have a powerful argument at our disposal. That is why so much effort has gone into establishing a definite link between smoking and cancer and between certain dietary habits and heart disease; if the causal link can be established, it will argue most forcefully that we should alter our behavior in certain clear-cut ways.

APPEALING TO LOGIC   *arg* 4e

4. Using inductive and deductive reasoning

Traditionally, logical arguments are classified as using either inductive or deductive reasoning, which almost always work together. **Inductive reasoning,** most simply, is the process of making a generalization based on a number of specific instances: if you find you are ill on ten occasions after eating seafood, you will likely draw the inductive generalization that seafood makes you ill. It may not be an absolute certainty that the seafood was the culprit, but the *probability* lies in that direction. We all use such inductive reasoning for simple everyday discussions, but induction can be quite complex, as demonstrated by medical response to the sudden outbreak of an apparently new illness in the mid-1970s. This illness, later named Legionnaires' disease, resulted in many deaths. Medical researchers used a painstaking and time-consuming process of inductive elimination, examining every case in great detail to determine what the patients had in common, before they were able to generalize accurately about the cause of the disease.

Deductive reasoning, most simply, reaches a conclusion by assuming a general principle (known as a **major premise**) and then applying that principle to a specific case (the **minor premise**). In practice, this general principle is usually derived from induction. The inductive generalization "seafood makes me ill," for instance, could serve as the major premise for a deductive argument: "since all seafood makes me ill, the plate of it just put before me is certain to make me ill." The fictional detective Sherlock Holmes was famous for using deductive reasoning to solve his cases. Beginning, for instance, with the major premise "watchdogs always bark at strangers," Holmes applied that premise to the case of a stolen racehorse and reasoned that since the watchdog did not bark when the horse was stolen, the thief was not a stranger but someone the dog knew.

Deductive arguments like these have traditionally been analyzed as **syllogisms,** three-part statements containing a major premise, a minor premise, and a conclusion:

MAJOR PREMISE	All people die.
MINOR PREMISE	I am a person.
CONCLUSION	I will die.

Syllogisms may work for technical logical purposes, but rarely do they prove useful in the kind of arguments you are likely to write. They are

TEACHING PRACTICE

Most of us live our lives according to inductive generalizations: we are aware of the probability that we will miss the heavy traffic if we take a particular route to school each day, that going to bed at a certain time will guarantee our waking fresh in the morning, that we can stay in the hot sun only so long without getting burned, that we must eat and exercise a specific amount if we are to stay in shape, or that certain foods, animals, and plants provoke an allergic reaction in us.

Many such deductions stem from inductive reasoning: morning traffic is heavy; a late night makes for a slow morning; sun can burn the skin; too many calories make one fat; poison ivy causes a rash.

(BACK)GROUNDING

One of Aristotle's greatest contributions to rhetorical theory was the use of deductive as well as inductive logic: he used the enthymeme, whose essential difference from the syllogism in logic is not so much that one of the premises is left unstated as that the argument is based on premises that are probably true rather than absolutely true and that the opening premise is agreed on by speaker and audience. For Aristotle and for all of us since, the example has served as the rhetorical equivalent of logical induction. For Aristotle, the syllogism was a way to *examine*—not build—an argument.

WRITERS ON WRITING

Teach not the wife of thy bosom to hurl in whirling speech the crooked enthymeme.

—JUVENAL

simply too rigid and absolute to serve in arguments about questions that have no absolute answers, and they often lack any appeal to an audience. From Aristotle came a less rigid alternative, the **enthymeme,** which calls on the audience to supply the implied major premise. For example:

> This bridge is carrying twice as much traffic as it was built for, so we need to build a new bridge or restrict traffic on this one.

You can analyze this enthymeme by restating it in the form of two premises and a conclusion:

MAJOR PREMISE	Bridges should carry only the amount of traffic they were built for.
MINOR PREMISE	This bridge is carrying twice as much traffic as it was built for.
CONCLUSION	We need to build a new bridge or restrict traffic on this one.

Note that the major premise is one the writer can count on an audience agreeing to, or supplying: safety and common sense demand that bridges carry only the amount of traffic they are built for. By thus inspiring audience "participation," an enthymeme actually gets the audience to *contribute* to the argument.

Whether it is expressed as a syllogism or an enthymeme, however, a deductive conclusion is only as strong as the premises upon which it is based. The citizen who argues that "Edmunds is a crook who shouldn't be elected to public office" is arguing deductively, based on an implied major premise: "No crook should be elected to public office." In this case, most people would agree with this major premise. So the issue in this argument rests on the minor premise—that Edmunds is a crook. Only if that premise can be proven satisfactorily are we likely to accept the deductive conclusion that Edmunds shouldn't be elected to office.

While we may well agree with some unstated major premises (such as that no crook should be elected), at other times the unstated premise may be more problematic. The person who says, "Don't bother to ask for Jack's help with physics—he's a jock" is arguing deductively on the basis of an implied major premise: "jocks don't know anything about physics." In this case, careful listeners would demand proof of the unstated premise. Because bigoted or prejudiced statements often rest on this kind of reasoning, writers should be particularly alert to it.

USEFUL READING

D'Angelo, Frank. "Topoi, Paradigms, and Rhetorical Enthymemes." *Old-speak/Newspeak: Rhetorical Transformations.* Ed. Charles Kneupper. Arlington, VA.: Rhetoric Society of America, 1985. 217–26. A discussion of the relationships between these Aristotelian concepts, including the enthymeme.

APPEALING TO LOGIC

▌ 5. Recognizing logical fallacies

Logical fallacies are errors in reasoning. Though they cannot stand up to analysis, they are commonplace enough that they may be hard to spot as errors. Indeed, such reasoning can often convince uncritical audiences. Sharp readers will detect fallacious appeals, however—and may even reject an otherwise worthy argument that relies on them. Your time will be well spent, therefore, in learning to recognize—and to avoid—these fallacies. Common logical fallacies include begging the question, *post hoc*, non sequitur, either/or, hasty generalizations, and oversimplification.

Begging the question treats a question as if it has already been answered.

> The United States must defend democracy in Nicaragua by supporting the freedom fighters in their struggle with tyranny. [By calling the Nicaraguan rebels freedom fighters and the government a tyranny, this writer begs the question of whether U.S. aid to the rebels will actually help to defend democracy.]

The **post hoc fallacy,** from the Latin *post hoc ergo propter hoc,* which means "after this, therefore caused by this," assumes that just because Event B happened *after* Event A, it must have been *caused* by Event A.

> We should not rebuild the town docks because every time we do a big hurricane comes along and damages them. [Does the reconstruction cause hurricanes?]

A **non sequitur** (Latin for "it does not follow") attempts to tie together two or more logically unrelated ideas as if they *were* related.

> If we can send a spacecraft to Mars, then we can discover a cure for cancer. [These are both scientific goals, but do they have anything else in common? What does achieving one have to do with achieving the other?]

The **either/or fallacy** asserts that a complex situation can have only two possible outcomes, one of which is necessary or preferable.

> If we do not build the new aqueduct system this year, residents of the Tri-Cities area will be forced to move because of lack of water. [What is the evidence for this claim? Do no other alternatives exist?]

A **hasty generalization** bases a conclusion on too little evidence or on bad or misunderstood evidence.

I couldn't understand the lecture today, so I'm sure this course will be impossible. [How can the writer be so sure of this conclusion based on only *one* piece of evidence?]

Oversimplification of the relation between causes and effects is another fallacy based on careless reasoning.

If we prohibit the sale of alcohol, we will get rid of the problem of drunkenness. [This oversimplifies the relation between laws and human behavior.]

ANSWERS TO EXERCISE 4.6

1. Subjective feelings influence our pictures of reality.
2. Activities should not be considered illegal that are overtly or covertly approved of by the majority of Americans.
3. Whatever promotes the best interests of all concerned and violates no one's rights is morally acceptable.
4. A law that discriminates against adults of legal age should not be passed.
5. Only those who can talk can feel pain.

ANSWERS TO EXERCISE 4.7

1. (i) Purified lecithin may help aid memory.
   (ii) This soup has purified lecithin in it.
   (iii) This soup may help aid memory.
2. No: *may, could* are conditional.
3. Studies showing that lecithin improves memory in Alzheimer's patients; studies that show a similar improvement in people who do not have Alzheimer's.
4. Authority helps establish the illusion of causation: MIT and Harvard are so highly respected that if their professors show interest in this possibility, there must be a connection. The testimony of the Lipton spokesman establishes a link between research and marketing.
5. In family folklore, chicken noodle soup is thought to cure colds. Its effectiveness comes in that contemporary research has proved that Mother was right.
6. Begs the question of whether lecithin helps; *non sequitur*: just because chicken soup prevents colds doesn't mean that chicken soup with lecithin will do more and just because lecithin changes brain chemistry doesn't mean that the change will be discernable.

EXERCISE 4.6

The following sentences contain deductive arguments based on implied major premises. Identify each of the implied premises.

1. A dream is not an accurate picture of reality since it is heavily influenced by our subjective feelings.
2. In a recent national survey, a majority of Americans said they either smoke marijuana or do not care if others do; therefore, smoking marijuana should be legalized.
3. Active euthanasia is morally acceptable when it promotes the best interests of everyone concerned and violates no one's rights.
4. The law raising the drinking age to twenty-one should not be passed because it would unfairly discriminate against a group of people who are legally considered adults in all other respects.
5. Animals can't talk, so therefore they can't feel pain as humans do.

EXERCISE 4.7

The following brief article from *Newsweek* raises some provocative questions about causes and effects, and in doing so it uses example and authority. Read the article, and assess it in terms of the questions that follow.

Mom always told you chicken noodle soup could cure a cold. But could it prevent a disabling disease like Alzheimer's? That's what researchers are asking about a new chicken soup under development by Thomas J. Lipton Co. Inc. The still-to-be-named soup is enriched with purified lecithin, a nutrient undergoing testing as an Alzheimer's treatment. In accordance with Food and Drug Administration regulations, Lipton stops short of attaching medical claims to its new product. But the company may introduce it simply as "chicken soup with lecithin" sometime next year.

The soup is the brainchild of MIT Prof. Richard Wurtman and Harvard neurologist John Growden. Wurtman and Growden approached Lipton after discovering that purified lecithin could affect the chemistry of the brain. The purified lecithin, which is more concentrated than that sold in health-food stores, raises blood levels of choline, which, in turn, may aid memory.

Whether the new soup could benefit the general population is still unclear. But Wurtman and Growden are studying the product's effect on memory and fatigue. Says Lipton spokesman Larry Hicks, "The market may be much larger than we now know."

1. What is the cause-effect argument?
2. Is the link between cause and effect fully established?
3. What evidence would be required to establish that link more fully?
4. Does the use of authority or testimony help establish the link? Why, or why not?
5. What example is used in the introduction—and is it effective in illustrating the point?
6. Can you identify any logical fallacies?

EXERCISE 4.8

Analyze the advertisement in Exercise 4.4 for the use of examples and precedents; authority and testimony; causes and effects; induction and deduction; and logical fallacies.

EXERCISE 4.9

Using a working argumentative thesis that you created in Exercise 4.2 or 4.3, write a paragraph describing the logical appeals you would use to support the thesis.

▌ 4f. Appealing to emotion

Most successful arguments appeal to our hearts as well as to our minds. Good writers, therefore, supplement appeals to logic and reason with those designed to **enlist the emotional support** of their readers. This principle was vividly demonstrated a few years ago when Americans began hearing about a famine in Africa. Facts and figures (logical appeals) did indeed convince many Americans that the famine was both real and serious. What brought an outpouring of aid, however, were not the facts and figures but the arresting photographs of children, at once skeletal and bloated, dying of starvation. In this case, the emotional appeal of those photographs spoke more powerfully than did the logical statistics. Writers can gain similarly powerful effects through the use of description, concrete language, and figurative language.

ANSWERS TO EXERCISE 4.8 (WILL VARY)

The success of this advertisement is based on its use of deductive arguments supported with examples and precedents. Consider the following: "Greenpeace fights to *save* life and preserve the environment," followed by these examples: "to stop the slaughter of whales, dolphins, and other animals"; to prevent the spread of toxic pollution"; to halt further testing of nuclear weapons and rid the oceans of nuclear-armed warships"; "to protect wilderness and wildlife from industrial and military exploitation."

The advertisement declares that their activists are willing to face danger, supporting their claim with the following statements: they have "taken on the U.S. Department of Defense, the Soviet Navy, the Norwegian Coast Guard and the Royal Canadian Mounted Police." They go on to say that their flagship "was blown up" and that their activists have been killed, "threatened, arrested and beaten." "They've had explosive harpoons shot over their heads and barrels of radioactive waste dropped on their boats."

The only authority cited in the advertisement is the organization's unselfish and high-minded *ethos* and its appeals to their readers, "people like you who care about the future of our planet." In fact, the word *you* or *your* is used at least twelve times in the advertisement.

These activists argue from causes and effects (i.e. from a *non sequitur* argument) when they claim that only their efforts have resulted in ending all commercial whaling, radioactive waste dumping in the Atlantic Ocean, the annual slaughter of harp seals in Canada, and French testing of nuclear weapons.

The most obvious of the logical fallacies is the *either/or* fallacy: either you help us by sending money or we won't be able to keep our fleet in action and protect the environment for you.

ANSWERS TO EXERCISE 4.9 WILL VARY

TEACHING PRACTICE

Although they may deny it at first, many of your students read descriptions for their own sake. Even after they know the scores, for example, they read the play-by-play account of ball games. They read cookbook accounts of recipes for familiar dishes. After looking at a picture of a house or an apartment, they read on for its written description in the classified ads.

Discuss the reading of description with your students, asking them what kinds of appeals, pleasure, and information they get from the descriptions.

Ask your students about wheelchair accessibility on campus. What kind of additional information and explicit description could they expect if they took a wheelchair user to their library? Would the person have problems retrieving books from the stacks or simply getting into the stacks? Could he or she get by the entrance turnstile? Could he or she reach the circulation desk? What appeals would be implicit in such a description—ethical, emotional, rational.

1. Using description

Vivid **description** provides one of the most effective means of appealing to emotions. Travel articles and advertisements draw heavily on this principle: think of all the descriptions of sunny beaches that appear in newspapers during the dreary winter months. Description can work just as effectively in your written arguments. Using strong, descriptive details can bring a moving immediacy to any argument.

The student described in Chapter 2 who was at work on a proposal to make the library more accessible to students in wheelchairs had amassed plenty of facts and figures, including diagrams and maps, illustrating the problem. But her first draft seemed dry and lifeless in spite of all her information. She decided, therefore, to ask a friend who used a wheelchair to accompany her to the library—and she revised her proposal to open with a detailed description of that visit and the many frustrations her friend encountered.

2. Using concrete language

Concrete language stands at the heart of effective description and hence helps to build emotional appeal. The student urging improved wheelchair access to the library, for instance, could have said simply that her friend "had trouble entering the library." Such a general statement, however, has little impact; it does not appeal to readers' emotions or allow them to imagine themselves in a similar position. The revised version, full of concrete description, does so: *Maria inched her heavy wheelchair up the narrow, steep entrance ramp, her small arms straining to pull up the last twenty feet, her face pinched with the sheer effort of getting into Main Library.* (Concrete language is discussed in greater detail in 25c.)

3. Using figurative language

Figurative language, or figures of speech, can also help to paint a detailed and vivid picture. Figurative language does so by making striking comparisons between something you are writing about and something else that is easier for a reader to visualize, identify with, or understand. Figures of speech include metaphors, similes, and analogies (see 26b2). **Metaphors** compare two things directly: *Richard the Lion-Hearted; old age is the evening of life.* **Similes** make comparisons using *like* or *as: Richard is as brave as a lion; old age is like the evening of life.* **Analogies** are extended metaphors or similes that compare an

APPEALING TO EMOTION   *arg* |4f

unfamiliar concept or process to a more familiar one to help the reader understand the unfamiliar concept:

> The most instructive way I know to express this cosmic chronology is to imagine the fifteen-billion-year lifetime of the universe (or at least its present incarnation since the Big Bang) compressed into the span of a single year. Then every billion years of Earth history would correspond to about twenty-four days of our cosmic year, and one second of that year to 475 real revolutions of the Earth about the sun.
> —CARL SAGAN, "The Cosmic Calendar"

Metaphors, similes, and analogies can all make an abstract or otherwise difficult concept understandable in terms of more concrete, everyday experience. James Watson and Frances Crick, who won the Nobel Prize for their work on the structure of DNA, used the metaphor of a zipper to describe how two strands of molecules could separate during cell division. In the same way, a student arguing for a more streamlined course registration process may find good use for an analogy, saying that the current process makes students feel like laboratory rats in a maze. This analogy, which suggests manipulation, helpless victims, and a clinical coldness, creates a vivid description and hence adds emotional appeal to the argument. For an analogy to work effectively, however, it must be supported by additional evidence: the student would have to show that the current registration process has a number of similarities to a laboratory maze, such as uncaring officials overseeing the process and confused students wandering through complex bureaucratic channels and into dead ends.

▌ 4. Shaping your appeal to your audience

As with appeals to credibility and to logic, appealing to emotions is effective only insofar as it moves your particular audience. Of course, you must always evaluate such appeals, being sensitive to your audience. You can't predict absolutely any audience's emotional response, but you can consider your topic and assess its probable emotional effects.

A student arguing for increased lighting in campus parking garages, for instance, might consider the emotions such a discussion will potentially raise (fear of attackers, anger at being subjected to such danger, pity for victims of such attacks), decide which emotions would be most appropriately appealed to, and then look for descriptive and figurative language to carry out such an appeal.

OPTIONAL EXERCISES

Ask your students to extend the metaphor of registration being like a rat maze, alluding to instances of intermittent, positive, and negative reinforcement. Let them write in class.

Have students write at least one paragraph describing themselves through the image (verbal picture) of an animal they feel is most "like" their personality (e.g. tiger, German Shepherd, bear, Siamese cat, goldfish, nuthatch). Students should actually inhabit the skin of the animal they have chosen (e.g., "I galloped across the dark grass, sensing every rise and fall of the ground underneath my hooves, reading the earth like a map. Thus, I didn't stumble into a groundhog hole or trip over a stray piece of fence the storm had left behind, or lose the child who rested so lightly and with so much trust against my neck").

You can vary this exercise by asking your students to choose an animal they would most like to be, one that expresses qualities they do not have.

In a leaflet to be distributed on campus, for example, the student might describe the scene in a dimly lighted garage as a student parks her car and then has to walk to an exit alone through shadowy corridors and staircases. Parking in the garage might be compared to running the gauntlet in a fraternity hazing or venturing into a jungle with dangerous animals lurking behind every tree.

In a proposal to the university administration, on the other hand, the student might describe past attacks on students in campus parking garages and the negative publicity and criticism these provoked among students, parents, alumni, and other groups. For the administration, the student might compare the lighting in the garages to gambling, arguing that the university is taking a significant chance with the current lighting conditions and that increased lighting would lower the odds against future attacks.

▌ 5. Recognizing emotional fallacies

Appeals to the emotions of an audience constitute a valid and necessary part of argument. Unfair or overblown emotional appeals, however, attempt to overcome the reasonable judgment of readers. The most common kinds of these **emotional fallacies** include bandwagon appeal, flattery, in-crowd appeal, veiled threats, and false analogies.

Bandwagon appeal suggests that a great movement is under way and that the reader will be a fool or a traitor not to join it.

> Voters are flocking to candidate X by the millions, so you'd better cast your vote the right way. [Why should you jump on this bandwagon? Where is the evidence to support this claim?]

Flattery tries to persuade readers to do something by suggesting that they are thoughtful, intelligent, or perceptive enough to agree with the writer.

> We know you have the taste to recognize that an investment in an ArtForm ring will pay off in the future. [*How* will it pay off?]

In-crowd appeal, a special kind of flattery, invites readers to identify with an admired and select group.

> Thoughtful and progressive listeners find U2 the most consistently interesting band recording today. Join those in the know: subscribe to the U2 News. [Who are these listeners? Will subscribing put you "in the know"?]

(BACK)GROUNDING

People suspect the emotional appeal as being somehow unethical or undignified, as being a poor substitute for logical reasoning. They feel duped if they have succumbed to an emotional appeal, the kind of appeal that can be easily abused. In *Classical Rhetoric*, Edward P. J. Corbett writes:

> Emotional appeals play a vital part in the persuasive process; intellectual conviction is often not enough to move people's will to act. (107)

Since emotional appeals cannot be avoided, they ought to be reasonably made and relate logically to the action desired. An emotional appeal without a logical base is, perhaps, an unjustified appeal.

APPEALING TO EMOTION arg 4f

Veiled threats try to frighten readers into agreement by hinting that otherwise they will suffer adverse consequences.

> If Public Service Electric Company does not get an immediate 15 percent rate increase, its services to you, its customers, will be seriously affected. [What is the evidence for this claim? Is such an effect on services legal or likely?]

False analogies make misleading comparisons between two situations that are *not* alike in most or important respects.

> If the United States gets involved in a land war in the Middle East, it will turn out just like Vietnam. [Is there any point of analogy except that they are both wars?]

EXERCISE 4.10

Make a list of the common human emotions that might be attached to the following topics, and suggest appropriate ways to appeal to those emotions in a specific audience you choose to write for.

1. Prohibiting smoking on campus
2. Capital punishment
3. Nuclear power generation
4. Television evangelism
5. Competency testing for teachers

EXERCISE 4.11

The following brief essay argues that we have to improve our public lives. Read the essay carefully, underlining emotional appeals, including descriptive passages, concrete language, and figurative language.

OK, so the holidays are over. The yuletide fairy has come and gone, dropping 10 pounds of good cheer, five for each hip. The Christmas list is in the wastebasket and the New Year's resolutions are on the refrigerator door.

This year you're going to lower your cholesterol and raise your triceps, burn fat and cool off your credit cards, stop smoking and drink nothing but club soda laced with brewer's yeast. You're going into 1987 lean and mean.

Have you noticed anything funny about this annual passage yet? Have you noticed how the swing season from one year to the next mimics the universe? We go from a warm mood of expansion (and I'm not just talking waistlines) to a grim one of icy contraction. We go from giving to denying.

Most of us start out in December with a list of things to do for others and end up with a list of things to do to ourselves.

ANSWERS TO EXERCISE 4.10

1. Harmful to the environment and to smokers and nonsmokers as well; concern over basic human rights if banned.
2. Moral indignation as culpable citizen of a state that puts people to death; pity for condemned; gratification that criminals are punished within the full extent of the law; fear of being put to death.
3. Fear of radiation leakage; anger at the government for putting innocent citizens in danger; pride in technological achievement; distress at increased electricity bills to pay for new power plant.
4. Joy over the rebirth of overt religious conviction; distaste with the perceived abuse of emotional appeals and misuse of money; amusement by others' gullibility.
5. Fear of failure; belief that it is a waste of time, money, and energy; sympathy for the tested; belief in favorable consequences.

ANSWERS TO EXERCISE 4.11

NB: Paragraph 3—changing seasons (from summer to winter) is compared to changing temperaments from warm to icy.

Paragraphs 7, 8—we treat people as though they were objects, such as buildings or bridges. We don't give an inch.

Paragraph 11—connects with paragraphs 7, 8, 12 with reference to infrastructure.

Paragraphs 13, 14—civil interpersonal relationships develop like the shape of a weightlifter's body.

WRITERS ON WRITING

There are only three things, after all, that a [piece of writing] must reach: the eye, the ear, and what we may call the heart or mind. It is most important of all to reach the heart of the reader.

—ROBERT FROST

. . . [W]hen Einstein was looking for relativity, he did so because he had an emotional feeling that the universe has unity and sense. He believed this before he discovered the theory of relativity. It was a very strong feeling in him; then he discovered the theory of relativity which proved his feeling. . . . The point is not to get rid of those emotions but simply to know them for what they are.

—SUSAN GRIFFIN

I have no beef with self-criticism. I'll give at the office as well as at home to self-improvement. It's the self-centering that gets to me in January. The first month of the new year and we seem to retreat to a personal number one.

Check the national computer printout of New Year's resolutions and I'll wager that more than half of the top 10 have to do with our relationships with our bodies, ourselves. The second tier has to do with family and work. It is a rare list that includes the resolve to change our relationships with strangers. A rare list that mentions improvement in our public lives.

Blame it on the privatization of American life, blame it on the Manhattanization of city living, but increasingly we operate within our own inner concentric circles. We pay our public lives as little attention as we pay the tolltaker on the highway.

It isn't just the infrastructure of bridges and public housing that has deteriorated, it's the human infrastructure. The dozens of daily encounters between strangers who pass each other on the sidewalk, buy from each other in the stores and deal with each other crossing streets have indeed become lean and mean.

Most of us look away when we pass strangers. It is the exceptional person who stops to help the woman maneuvering her kids and groceries up the staircase. We rarely give up our place in line or on the subway. Locked into our automobiles, we prefer gridlock to giving way. Drivers who won't give each other an inch happily give each other the finger.

These daily encounters, when they are angry or alien, diminish our lives enormously. When they are pleasant, we feel buoyed. Yet when we sit at home and make resolutions, we think about what we can accomplish in private spaces: home, work. Too many have given up the belief that they control the public world.

I risk sounding like a greeting card or a bumper sticker—Have You Hugged Your Child Today?—but as individuals, we have enormous control over this human infrastructure. We can change the contour of a day, the mood of a moment, the way people feel.

The demolition and the reconstruction of public life is the result of personal decisions made every day: The decision to give up a seat on the bus. The decision to be patient or pleasant against all odds. The decision to let that jerk take a left-hand turn from the right-hand lane. Without rolling down the window and calling him a jerk.

It's the resolution to be a civil, social creature. Maybe even pick up a few pieces of someone else's litter.

This may be a peak period for the battle against the spread of a waistline and creeping cholesterol. But it is also within our willpower to fight the spread of urban rudeness and creeping hostility. Civility doesn't stop a nuclear holocaust and doesn't put a roof over the head of the homeless. But it makes a difference in the shape of a community, as surely as lifting weights can make a difference in the shape of a human torso. —ELLEN GOODMAN

EXERCISE 4.12

Read the following paragraph, and then write a paragraph evaluating its use of description and figurative language.

> Since 1973, all American women have been legally entitled to have abortions performed in hospitals by licensed physicians. Before they were legal, abortions were frequently performed by persons who bore more resemblance to butchers than they did to doctors. The all too common result was serious complications or death for the woman. If the 1973 Supreme Court decision is reversed, abortion will not end. Instead, women will again resort to illegal abortions, and there will be a return to the slaughterhouse. Since abortions are going to take place no matter what the law says, why not have them done safely and legally in hospitals instead of in basements, alleys, or dirty compartments in some killing shed? The decision to have an abortion is not an easy one to make, and I believe that a woman who makes it deserves to have her wish carried out in the very safest way possible. Critics of abortion stress the importance of the unborn child's life. At the very least, they should also take the woman's life and safety into consideration.

EXERCISE 4.13

Using a working argumentative thesis you formulated in Exercise 4.2 or 4.3, make a list of the emotional appeals most appropriate to your topic and audience. Then spend ten to fifteen minutes brainstorming, looking for descriptive and figurative language to carry out the appeals.

▌ 4g. Organizing an argument

Once you have assembled good reasons in support of an argumentative thesis, you must organize your material in order to present the argument convincingly. While there is no ideal or universally favored organizational framework for an argumentative essay, you may find the classical five-part system useful to try. This five-part pattern was often followed by ancient Greek and Roman orators. The speaker began with an *introduction*, which stated the thesis, then gave the *background* information. Next came the different *lines of argument*, and then the *refutation of opposing arguments*. A *conclusion* both summed up the argument and made an emotional appeal to the audience. You can adapt this format to written arguments as follows:

1. *Introduction*
gains readers' attention and interest
establishes your qualifications to write about your topic

**ANSWERS TO EXERCISE 4.12
WILL VARY**

**ANSWERS TO EXERCISE 4.13
WILL VARY**

TEACHING PRACTICE

Help clarify the five-part classical argument by providing the class with an essay that follows this format. The "My Turn" column in *Newsweek* or *On Campus* are good sources, as are the editorials in city and campus newspapers. Ask your students to analyze the essay, identifying the introduction, background, lines of argument, refutation, and conclusion. As you proceed through this exercise, use the board to outline the thesis statement as well as the five major headings.

You can extend this exercise by asking your students to find an essay on their own, that uses this form of argument and write a short commentary or outline.

USEFUL READING

Kneupper, Charles W. "Teaching Argument: An Introduction to the Toulmin Model." *CCC* 29 (1978): 237–41. An introduction to Toulmin logic.

Toulmin, Stephen. *The Uses of Argument.* New York: Cambridge UP, 1964. According to Toulmin, the persuasiveness of our arguments (i.e. "claims") depends upon both the general principles ("warrants") that underlie our interpretations of data and the reasons we provide for them.

WRITERS ON WRITING

There is a form to all things . . . [yet] . . . form is never more than a revelation of content.

—DENISE LEVERTOV

Content and form are in a state of dynamic interaction.

—DENISE LEVERTOV

WRITING TOGETHER

Divide the class in small groups, and ask your students to use the general topics in Exercise 4.10 to develop arguments. Have them speculate on what subtopics might be created to support these arguments, write out the working thesis, and then work to construct a set of rough notes for each argument.

They can come up with their own topics or use one of the following:

1. The smoking ban on airplanes
2. Two-career marriages
3. "Returning" students
4. Graduate students as teachers

TEACHING PRACTICE

To obtain backup evidence, your students will need to research, delve, question, and interview.

OPTIONAL EXERCISE

Choose one of the following statements and make notes regarding any personal experience you have that supports or refutes it. Then, using library sources, gather as much additional evidence as possible. Use this information and your notes on personal experiences to write a short essay arguing either for or against this statement.

1. Vegetarians have a lower incidence of heart attacks than meat-eaters.
2. College degrees mean higher incomes.
3. To succeed, college students must resort to various forms of dishonesty.
4. Students should graduate from college if only to be four years older and wiser when they join the job market.
5. Exercise relieves stress.
6. We are returning to the moral standards of the fifties.
7. AIDS is the worst disease the United States has ever known.
8. Student loans, grants, and scholarships are becoming scarce.

establishes common ground with readers
demonstrates fairness
states or implies your thesis
2. *Background*
present any necessary background information
3. *Lines of argument*
present good reasons (including logical and emotional appeals) in support of your thesis
generally present reasons in order of importance
demonstrate ways your argument is in readers' best interest
4. *Refutation of opposing arguments*
considers opposing points of view
notes both advantages and disadvantages of opposing views
5. *Conclusion*
summarizes the argument
elaborates on the implication of your thesis
makes clear what you want readers to think or do
makes a strong ethical or emotional appeal

Asked to write an argumentative essay addressed to fellow students about an issue of current interest on her campus, Ohio State University student Tracy Vezdos decided to write about the movement to put warning labels about "explicit lyrics" on record albums. Her thesis: *As a form of censorship, the labeling of record albums has no place in American society.* Following is Tracy's essay, which was written in 1987 and organized according to the five-part classical system. The parts are labeled in the margin. Notice that because the thesis is stated in a negative form, arguing *against* labeling, most of the essay is devoted to refuting the arguments in favor of labeling. Also notice that a source citation is given for a piece of information that Tracy considered specific enough to need it (see 40b).

```
           It's Only Rock 'n' Roll

    Devil worship, premarital sex, drugs,    INTRODUCTION
violence, suicide—can rock music really pro-
mote all these detriments to today's youth?
"Yes," says Tipper Gore of the Parents' Music
Resource Center (PMRC). "Absolutely not,"
responds the Musical Majority, a group formed
```

in opposition to PMRC's campaign to have warning labels placed on rock records. While parents are understandably concerned about rock
songs that seem to glorify promiscuous sex,
drugs, and other vices, this impression is
often misleading. In fact, song lyrics, like
other kinds of language, can invoke many varying interpretations. In recent years, Mark
Twain's most famous novel, The Adventures of
Huckleberry Finn, has been banned from literature courses in many high schools—including yours, perhaps—because of a single
word, nigger. If the persons advocating the
banning of this novel had bothered to read
the book carefully, they would have realized
Twain does not promote racism but denounces
it as ignorant and immoral. People of our age
know only too well how often things that teenagers like or do are misinterpreted by adults
and how any effort to control access to these
things only makes them more attractive. As
a form of censorship, the labeling of record
albums has no place in American society.

The PMRC campaign began in the mid-1980s   BACKGROUND
when Gore, the wife of Senator Albert Gore
of Tennessee, and a number of other wives of
prominent national politicians began lobbying
record companies and performers to label
records that the group considered too "explicit." In September 1985, the Senate Commerce Committee held hearings into the issue,
and soon afterward the twenty-two major record
companies that are members of the Recording
Industry Association of America accepted a

system of voluntary labels. The companies themselves decide which records need labels. If the recording artist agrees, the label <u>Explicit lyrics—parental advisory</u> will be placed on the album cover, or the lyrics will be printed there. (Tapes, which do not have enough room for the lyrics, include a label telling customers to look for the lyrics on the album.) Thus far, the effects of labeling are most obvious in smaller record stores: a decline in sales of labeled records and the refusal of some stores to carry them, for fear of being known as a "pornrock" store.

Do the record companies and artists who permit their albums to be labeled feel their freedom of expression will remain safe despite this first, major step toward censoring their material? Already, PMRC has moved on to the music television channel (MTV), where it wants to have editing done on what it deems explicitly sexual or violent videos. PMRC claims that it does not believe in government censorship. But the group's leaders are wives of prominent political figures who make decisions that affect the recording industry. With this kind of support, PMRC does not need to censor records directly because to avoid offending the politicians, the record companies will censor the artists, or artists will censor themselves. The result will be that no Americans —including those of us of college age—will be able to listen to certain songs that the PMRC considers too explicit for teenagers.

One of the many problems I have with PMRC

LINES OF
ARGUMENT

ORGANIZING AN ARGUMENT

involves its definition of the word <u>explicit</u>.
My dictionary defines <u>explicit</u> as "clearly
stated or expressed, with nothing implied;
definite." Almost any song could fall under
this broad definition. Surprisingly, the main
targets of PMRC are not heavy metal bands such
as Motley Crue and Black Sabbath, who adorn
their album covers with scantily dressed women
and sing rebellious, anti-authority songs.
Most of the artists with songs on the "Filthy
Fifteen," a list compiled by PMRC of the most
"harmful" songs of 1986, are mainstream performers such as Madonna, Bruce Springsteen,
and Cyndi Lauper. Madonna's "Papa, Don't
Preach," about a pregnant teenager who wants
to get married and keep her baby, had the PMRC
in an uproar. If these women would take the
time to examine the lyrics carefully, they
would realize the pregnant girl attempts to
gain her father's acceptance and guidance—not
to rebel against his authority. This case of
misinterpretation is not an isolated one. At
the Senate Commerce Committee hearings, John
Denver testified that his song "Rocky Mountain
High" had been banned from many radio stations
because station managers felt the tune advocated the use of drugs. The lyrics, however,
indicate that the "high" Denver feels comes
from the Colorado mountains, not marijuana.

The PMRC's concern about lyrics seems
unnecessary in any case. A survey of 266 junior
high and high school students that was reported
in <u>Newsweek</u> showed that the lyrics have very
little or no influence on teenagers who listen

REFUTATION
OF OPPOSING
ARGUMENTS

to them. In fact, 37 percent of the students couldn't even describe what their three favorite songs were about—they just liked them. As for Satanism, sex, drugs, and violence, only 7 percent of the 622 songs that were mentioned contained these elements, according to the students ("So Who Understands").

The PMRC admits that it finds only a small minority of rock lyrics offensive. But it argues that labeling of records with these lyrics is justified in order to give parents information about what their children are listening to and to discourage teenagers from buying—and being influenced by—records that seem to promote harmful and immoral activities. Many people can agree with these goals, and in some cases record labeling may help to accomplish them. But more often, labeling will probably increase teenagers' exposure to the very lyrics the PMRC considers harmful. We all know the thrill of sneaking into an R-rated movie or of looking up the bawdy parts of Chaucer's <u>Canterbury</u> <u>Tales</u> (those not printed in our literature textbooks). In the same way, an <u>Explicit</u> <u>lyrics</u> label will draw teenagers' attention and challenge their curiosity. Even if parents can prevent their children from buying a labeled record, the young people will be all the more eager—and likely—to listen to the album at a friend's. Instead of encouraging better communication and understanding between parents and children, labels will only result in more friction.

To find out how those of us who are

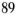

ORGANIZING AN ARGUMENT

slightly older feel about the issue, I took an informal survey of Ohio State students asking whether records should be labeled and why or why not. The majority said "No," on the grounds of freedom of speech. Surprisingly enough, a large minority favored labels as a guide for parents. One answer I received, however, completely dispels the parental guide argument: "We should make our children safe for ideas, not ideas safe for our children. . . . Only naive fools would say 'yes'— a record album should carry a warning about explicit material—and actually believe that the social control that they have imposed on themselves . . . will not grow."

I agree. Parents have an awesome re- **CONCLUSION** sponsibility in raising their children, and part of that responsibility includes monitoring the material their children are exposed to. Record companies and singers should not have to perform this service for the parents, and a group of politically influential people should not try to make them do so. Americans need to accept responsibility for what is wrong with our society and stop placing the blame on "outside forces" such as record albums. A serious and honest look into ourselves will reveal the true causes of the problems that face teenagers today. After all, as Mick Jagger proclaimed, "It's only rock 'n' roll."

References

So who understands rock lyrics, anyway. (1986, July). Newsweek, p. 71.

**ANSWERS TO EXERCISE 4.14
WILL VARY**

**ANSWERS TO EXERCISE 4.15
WILL VARY**

EXERCISE 4.14

Using the classical system, draft an argument in support of one of the theses you formulated in Exercises 4.2 or 4.3.

EXERCISE 4.15

Another useful system of argument was developed by the philosopher Stephen Toulmin. Essentially a modern elaboration of the system first put forth by Aristotle, the Toulmin system is presented in 2e as a way of generating material for an argumentative paper but might also be used for organizing such a paper, as follows:

1. State your claim or thesis.
2. Qualify your claim in any way necessary.
3. Present the good reasons you have to support your claim.
4. Discuss any underlying assumptions that support these reasons.
5. Give any evidence that might add support to your claim (facts, statistics, testimony, etc.).
6. Acknowledge and respond to any counterarguments readers might make.

Suppose you were writing an essay about smoking. Your claim might be that smoking should be banned. You could qualify your claim by suggesting that the ban be campuswide. As reasons in support of your claim you might say that smoking causes heart disease and lung cancer, and that nonsmokers are endangered by passive smoke. Your underlying assumptions would be that people are entitled to good health. As evidence you could cite statistics about lung and heart disease and perhaps quote the U.S. Surgeon General as an authority on the subject. One possible counterargument you could anticipate would be that smokers have rights too; you could respond by reminding readers that you are suggesting only a campuswide ban, and that they would be free to smoke *off* campus.

Use the Toulmin system to draft an argument in support of one of theses you formulated in Exercise 4.2 or 4.3. If you wish, you can write on the same topic you wrote on in Exercise 4.14.

▌ 4h. Analyzing an argument

Guidelines for organizing an argument can also be used to advantage in analyzing an argument to judge how effective it is. Tracy Vezdos used the classical system explained in 4g to analyze her essay

ANALYZING AN ARGUMENT

"It's Only Rock 'n' Roll." Here is her analysis, as she entered it in her writing log.

INTRODUCTION

- *What, specifically, have I done to gain the audience's attention and interest?* I've tried to use an eye-catching, controversial opening sentence—and an intriguing title that recalls a familiar phrase—I've tried to show why this argument is important to my readers by making it clear that record labeling is part of a much larger issue that affects all of us—censorship.
- *How have I established my qualifications to write about this topic?* I've used the precedent of *Huckleberry Finn.* I've shown that I am familiar with the arguments of PMRC and Musical Majority.
- *What have I done to establish common ground with readers?* My use of Twain (most people know him)—references to "yours" and "people of our age."
- *How have I shown fairness to opposing viewpoints?* I've said that parents are understandably concerned about the music their children are exposed to.
- *How have I made known my thesis? Is the thesis specific enough?* In the last sentence of the introductory paragraph—censorship is wrong in any form, including warning labels on albums.

BACKGROUND

- *What background have I presented?* I've given history, exact wording of labels, effects of labeling on sales.

LINES OF ARGUMENT

- *What good reasons have I presented to support my thesis?* I've explained how labeling is in fact a form of censorship by political forces.
- *How have I shown that my claim is in readers' best interest?* I've stressed that record labeling threatens their right as Americans to judge for themselves what they want to listen to.

REFUTATION OF OPPOSING ARGUMENTS

- *How have I dealt with opposing points of view and noted their advantages as well as disadvantages?* I've challenged the definition of *explicit*, pointed out the misinterpretation of lyrics, showed that teenagers don't pay attention to lyrics. I've said that labeling may achieve a useful purpose in some cases but is more likely to have the opposite effect.

UNDERSTANDING AND USING ARGUMENT

CONCLUSION

- *How have I summarized my argument?* I've used a striking quotation about censorship from my survey and then begun the concluding paragraph by expressing my agreement with it.

- *How have I elaborated on any implications of my claim?* I've pointed out that parents have a tremendous responsibility for their children that they shouldn't try to delegate to others.

- *What action have I called for from readers? What kind of ethical or emotional appeal have I ended with?* I've called for readers to look within themselves to find the causes of today's problems and to stop blaming record albums.

ANSWERS TO EXERCISE 4.16 (WILL VARY)

1. Claim: the reader can stop smuggling and stop extinction.
2. Grounds/Good Reasons: if the reader does not buy the smuggler's products, smuggling will no longer be profitable and will become extinct itself.
3. Underlying assumptions: the reader doesn't want the endangered species to become extinct; reader condemns smuggling; reader wants to help save endangered species.
4. Backup evidence: reader can dress in legally imported or exported clothes.
5. Refutation: since this ad is limited to the United States, it won't stop the problem in other countries.
6. Qualifications: legal purchases are permissible.

WRITERS ON WRITING

It is well to understand as early as possible in one's writing life that there is just one contribution which every one of us can make; we can give unto the common pool of experience some comprehension of the world as it looks to each of us.

—DOROTHEA BRANDE

EXERCISE 4.16

Try analyzing the argument implicit in this advertisement using the six categories in the Toulmin system (described in Exercise 4.15).

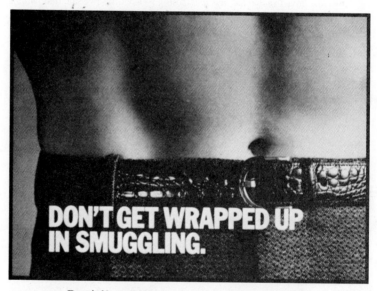

Don't buy exotic leather goods, furs, jewelry, plants or pets unless you're sure they're legal. Help save endangered species from smuggling and extinction. Send for our free Buyer Beware Guide.

TRAFFIC (U.S.A.)
1255 23rd Street, NW
Washington, DC 20037
800-634-4444

Prepared as a public service by Ogilvy & Mather. Photo by Mistretta.

ANALYZING AN ARGUMENT

READING WITH AN EYE FOR ARGUMENT

Return to Colleen Starkey's essay about the Bagelry in Chapter 3. Read it now as an implicit argument that people should eat there frequently. Analyze the essay, using the six Toulmin categories, focusing especially on the assumptions that underlie the claims about the Bagelry. Does the essay succeed as an argument? Why or why not?

FOR EXAMINING YOUR OWN WRITING

Using either the classical or the Toulmin guidelines, analyze the argument in an essay you've recently written or in the draft you wrote in Exercise 4.14. Decide what you need to do to revise your arguments, and write out a brief organizational plan.

5. Constructing Paragraphs

(BACK)GROUNDING
Earlymanuscriptsranwordstogether

Words were not considered individual entities, rather they formed the continuum of oral language. Later manuscripts, however, began to sacrifice precious paper by leaving space between the words and special marks in the margin. The space and special marks aided the reader, a public treasure who read aloud various texts. Often the marginalia were a series of alphabetized letters or pictorial signs that aided the copyist, the reader, and the memorizer alike in keeping their place. A favorite mark was the "paragraph" ("beside writing"), which was this mark: ¶, not a unit of discourse at all.

In fact, the paragraph as we know it today—with its qualities of consecutiveness and loose order or propositions—did not begin to emerge until the late seventeenth century and did not attain full codification until the eighteenth. And in the mid-nineteenth century, the first systematic formulation of paragraph theory appeared in Alexander Bain's *English Composition and Rhetoric* (1866).

Paragraphs are essential building blocks of writing, ones that every writer can come to understand and use to good effect. Paragraphs have existed for as long as people in the Western world have been writing. Long before the age of the printing press, sections of text were set off from one another by marks in the margin. In Greek, *para graphos* means "mark beside," and these marks looked like this: ¶. With the invention of movable type, printers had to fit lines of type into frames; because they could no longer use the margins easily, they began marking a paragraph by indenting its first line, as we still do today. The old name stuck, however, and so we call these units *paragraphs*.

Most simply, a **paragraph** is a group of sentences or a single sentence set off as a unit. Usually the sentences in a paragraph are related in some way because they all revolve around one main idea. When a new idea comes up, a new paragraph begins. Within this broad general guideline, however, paragraph structure is highly flexible, allowing writers to create many varied individual effects.

The hero of the Rex Stout mysteries, Nero Wolfe, once solved a case by identifying the paragraph structure of a particular writer/murderer. A person's style of paragraphing, Wolfe was later to claim, serves even more reliably than do fingerprints as a stamp of identity. Like Stout's character, you probably already have a characteristic way of paragraphing, although you may never have thought about it.

94

USEFUL READING

The Sentence and the Paragraph. Urbana: NCTE, 1963. An important collection comprising essays by Francis Christensen on the generative rhetoric of the sentence and the paragraph. Also includes Alton L. Becker's "A Tagmemic Approach to Paragraph Analysis" and a symposium on the paragraph by Francis Christensen, A. L. Becker, Paul C. Rodgers, Jr., Josephine Miles, and David H. Karrfalt.

CONSTRUCTING PARAGRAPHS

The following passage comprises a series of paragraphs, run together, from the opening of an essay on friendship by anthropologist Margaret Mead and Rhoda Metraux. Read this passage carefully, and decide how you would divide it into paragraphs.

(1) Few Americans stay put for a lifetime. (2) We move from town to city to suburb, from high school to college in a different state, from a job in one region to a better job somewhere else, from the home where we raise our children to the home where we plan to live in retirement. (3) With each move we are forever making new friends, who become part of our new life at that time. (4) For many of us the summer is a special time for forming new friendships. (5) Today millions of Americans vacation abroad, and they go not only to see new sights but also—in those places where they do not feel too strange—with the hope of meeting new people. (6) No one really expects a vacation trip to produce a close friend. (7) But surely the beginning of a friendship is possible? (8) Surely in every country people value friendship? (9) They do. (10) The difficulty when strangers from two countries meet is not a lack of appreciation of friendship, but different expectations about what constitutes friendship and how it comes into being. (11) In those European countries that Americans are most likely to visit, friendship is quite sharply distinguished from other more casual relations and is differently related to family life. (12) For a Frenchman, a German, or an Englishman friendship is usually more particularized and carries a heavier burden of commitment. (13) But as we use the word, *friend* can be applied to a wide range of relationships—to someone one has known for a few weeks in a new place, to a close business associate, to a childhood playmate, to a man or woman, to a trusted confidant. (14) There are real differences among these relations for Americans—a friendship may be superficial, casual, situational or deep and enduring. (15) But to a European, who sees only our surface behavior, the differences are not clear.

If you compare notes with others in your class, you will most likely find that you all chose similar paragraph breaks. Your instinctive sense about the shape and structure of paragraphs led you to that agreement. In fact, Mead and Metraux divided up their text in a fairly predictable manner. The first paragraph introduces the theme of the essay, friendship, by opening with a reference to the American tendency to move frequently and then relating this issue to the need for making friends. This first paragraph ends after sentence three. Paragraph two shifts the discussion of making friends to a specific time (summer) and place (travels abroad), ending with a question about other people's attitudes toward friendship ("Surely in every country people value friendship?").

(BACK)GROUNDING

In his "Structure and Form in Non-Narrative Prose," Richard Larson explains what he sees as the three categories of paragraph theory: (1) paragraphs as expanded sentences, governed by comparable syntactical forces; (2) as self-contained units of writing with their own unique principles; (3) and as parts of the overall discourse, informed by the strategies a writer chooses for the overall piece.

Larson concludes with a general theory of coherence in paragraphs: paragraphing is "part of a transaction between text and reader—between the reader's world and the writer's language" (72). Understanding the context for prose writing is essential for our understanding of how paragraphs work.

TEACHING PRACTICE

Ask your students to compare the length of paragraphs in their various texts: math, chemistry, history, English handbook, reader, school newspaper, etc. They might want to count the number of words and sentences per paragraph to measure accurately.

How can they account for the disparity in length? How does the density of information affect the length of the paragraph? How does the writer's expectation for the reader affect length? Under what circumstances might a short story, a chemistry text, a school newspaper be read? How does the context for the reading transaction affect length?

TEACHING PRACTICE

Students often have problems with paragraphing—with development and cohesion. And their problems are often diagnosed in various ways. For instance, George Goodin and Kyle Perkins argue that because students fail to subordinate effectively, their writing is replete with digressions and afterthoughts. Betty Bamberg argues that cohesion comes with the successful movement from "writer-based" to "reader-based" prose. "Writer-based" prose often consists of elliptical expressions, sentences that have meaning for the writer but that omit information necessary for the reader's understanding.

Successful prewriting may be the best cure for both of these paragraphing problems. By planning ahead what to say and how to say it, writers can better stay on course. Therefore, reaffirm the need for prewriting as you introduce paragraphing. Adequate prewriting will result in a more orderly text, one more easily paragraphed during drafting or revision.

The third paragraph opens by answering the question posed at the end of paragraph two, thus moving smoothly into a brief discussion of definitions and expectations for friendship in European countries Americans are likely to visit in their summer travels. The last paragraph in this passage begins with sentence thirteen, which shifts the discussion back from European ideas of friendship to American conceptions.

For special effect, Mead and Metraux might have divided this passage in a less expected way—for instance, by setting sentence nine off as a paragraph by itself. Doing this would have served to emphasize that statement, focusing readers' attention on it in a slightly startling way. But they did not do so. Paragraphs usually develop one main point and contain more than one sentence, and most writers follow these conventions unless they have a reason to do otherwise.

5a. Constructing unified, coherent, and well-developed paragraphs

This introduction should have convinced you that you know more about paragraphs than you may have thought. Let us look now at the specific elements that make up a well-written paragraph—one that makes a point in a way that is easy for readers to understand and follow. Consider the following paragraph by Eudora Welty:

> I never knew anyone who'd grown up in Jackson without being afraid of Mrs. Calloway, our librarian. She ran the Library absolutely by herself, from the desk where she sat with her back to the books and facing the stairs, her dragon eye on the front door, where who knew what kind of person might come in from the public? SILENCE in big black letters was on signs tacked up everywhere. She herself spoke in her normally commanding voice; every word could be heard all over the Library above a steady seething sound coming from her electric fan; it was the only fan in the Library and stood on her desk, turned directly onto her streaming face.   —EUDORA WELTY, *One Writer's Beginnings*

This paragraph begins with a general statement of the main idea: that everyone in Jackson feared Mrs. Calloway. All the other sentences then give specific details about why she inspired such fear. This example demonstrates the three qualities of a successful paragraph: **unity, coherence,** and **development**. It focuses on one main idea (unity); its parts are clearly related (coherence); and its main idea is supported with specifics (development).

USEFUL READING

Bamberg, Betty. "What Makes a Text Coherent?" *CE* 34 (Dec. 1983): 417–30.

Goodin, George, and Kyle Perkins. "Discourse Analysis and the Art of Coherence." *CE* 44 (Jan. 1982): 57–63.

5b. Making paragraphs unified: focusing on one main idea

To be readable and effective, paragraphs generally focus on one main idea. One good way to achieve such paragraph **unity** is to state the main idea clearly in one sentence and relate all the other sentences in the paragraph to that idea. The sentence that presents the main idea is called the **topic sentence.** Like the thesis for an entire essay, the topic sentence of a paragraph includes a topic and some comment on that topic (see 2f). In the above paragraph by Eudora Welty, the topic sentence opens the paragraph. Its topic is Mrs. Calloway; its comment is that everyone in Jackson was afraid of her.

1. Positioning a topic sentence

While a topic sentence usually appears at the beginning of a paragraph, it may appear anywhere in the paragraph—or it may not appear at all, but rather be implied.

At the beginning of a paragraph

It is a good idea to open with the topic sentence when you want readers to see your point immediately. Such a strategy can be particularly useful in essay examinations (Chapter 43), in memos (Chapter 44), or in argumentative essays (Chapter 4). The author of the following paragraph opens with a clear topic sentence on which subsequent sentences build:

> *Our friendship was the source of much happiness and many memories.* We danced and popped our fingers simultaneously to the soul tunes of the Jacksons and Stevie Wonder. We sweated together in the sweltering summer sun, trying to win the championship for our softball team. I recall the taste of pepperoni and sausage pizza as we discussed the highlights of our team's victory. Once we even became attracted to the same young man, but luckily we were able to share his friendship.

The topic sentence announces the main topic of the paragraph (friendship) and comments on it (as the source of happiness and memories). The next four sentences elaborate on the topic by giving specific examples and concrete physical description to show the reader how the happiness and memories were created.

USEFUL READING

Braddock, Richard. "The Frequency and Placement of Topic Sentences in Expository Prose." *Research in the Teaching of English* 8 (Winter 1974): 287–302. After analyzing the use of topic sentences by professional writers, Braddock concludes that topic sentences are used far less than textbooks claim. We should not deceive our students on the subject.

D'Angelo, Frank. "The Topic Sentence Revisited." *CE* 37 (Dec. 1986): 431–41. Citing work in psycholinguists, D'Angelo argues that the use of topic sentences improves readability, which justifies teaching them.

(BACK)GROUNDING

The notion that one sentence in every paragraph should announce the topic of that paragraph was derived from the fourth law of Alexander Bain's "seven laws" for creating paragraphs: "Indication of theme: The opening sentence, unless obviously preparatory, is expected to indicate the scope of the paragraph" (*English Composition and Rhetoric* 1866).

Since Bain, the "topic sentence" has remained controversial in composition theory. Although most compositionists agree with Bain that every paragraph should have a unifying theme or purpose, not all agree that it should be announced by a topic sentence. In his study of professional writers, Richard Braddock found that topic sentences are used far less than we have traditionally believed; his research calls into question the teaching of topic sentences. On the other hand, Frank D'Angelo argues that despite Braddock's findings, the use of topic sentences improves the readability of a paragraph; therefore, all writers—and especially beginning writers—should use topic sentences.

Beginning writers may want to heed D'Angelo's advice.

TEACHING PRACTICE

To help your students relate the topic sentence to subordinating or illustrative details, have them first identify the key words or phrases in the topic sentence:

friendship source
happiness memories

Then, they should look to see where those key words lead:

memories ⟶ dancing
               softball
               taste of pizza
               becoming attracted
                   to same young man

In this paragraph, the writer remembers four events that she shared with her friend. When your students include information that relates to some or all of the key words in the topic sentence, their paragraphs will have unity.

OPTIONAL EXERCISE

Turn to *any* essay in your reader. Read it to see if you find a topic sentence in each paragraph. (1) What is the placement of the topic sentence? (2) What are the key terms in that topic sentence? (3) How does the information in that paragraph relate to those key words?

At the end of a paragraph

When specific details lead up to a generalization, putting the topic sentence at the end of the paragraph makes good sense. In the following paragraph, the last sentence is a general statement that sums up and accounts for the specifics that have preceded it.

> During the visit, Dee takes the pictures, every one of them, including the one of the house that she used to live in and hate. She takes the churn top and dasher, both whittled out of a tree by one of Mama's uncles. She tries to take Grandma Dee's quilts. Mama and Maggie use these inherited items every day, not only appreciating their heritage but living it too. *Dee, on the other hand, wants these items only for decorative use, thus forsaking and ignoring their real heritage.*

In this instance, the concluding topic sentence brings the paragraph to its climax, explaining the significance of the things Dee takes.

At the beginning and end of a paragraph

Sometimes you will want to state a topic sentence at the beginning of the paragraph and then repeat it, usually in a slightly different form, at the end. Such an echo effect adds emphasis, pointing up the importance you attach to the idea. In the following paragraph, the writer begins with a topic sentence announcing a problem:

> *Many of the difficulties we experience in relationships are caused by the unrealistic expectations we have of each other.* Think about it. Women are expected to feel comfortable doing most of the sacrificing. They are supposed to stay fine, firm, and forever twenty-two, while doing double duty in the home and in the workplace. The burden on men is no easier. They should be tall, handsome, and able to wine and dine the woman. Many women go for the glitter and then expect these men to calm down once in a relationship and become faithful, sensitive, supportive, and loving. Let's face it. Both women and men have been unrealistic. *It's time we develop a new sensitivity toward each other and ask ourselves what it is we need from each other that is realistic and fair.*

The last sentence restates the topic sentence as a proposal for a solution to the problem. This repetition of the topic sentence is particularly appropriate, for the essay goes on to specify how the problem can be solved.

USEFUL READING

Markels, Robin Bell. *A New Perspective on Cohesion in Expository Paragraphs.* Carbondale, IL: Southern Illinois UP, 1984. Markels argues that cohesion is both syntactic and semantic. Adding to the recent research that has approached cohesion as a semantic phenomenon, Markels provides a methodology for specifying the necessary syntactic and semantic conditions for textual cohesion in paragraphs.

MAKING PARAGRAPHS UNIFIED

Implied but not stated in the paragraph

Occasionally, a topic will be so obvious or so clearly implied that no topic sentence is necessary at all. Here is an example of such a paragraph, from an essay about a car dealership:

> The Reedman newspaper advertisement invites customers to a hundred-and-fifty acre, one-stop car center that has a ten-million-dollar selection of cars—and then, adding the note of exclusivity that is considered necessary in advertising even the world's largest, it says, "Private Sale Now Going On." The premises on which the private sale is held look like the average citizen's vision of the supply depot at Cam Ranh Bay. Behind a series of showrooms on Route 1, just down the road from the Greenwood Dairies, the five thousand cars are lined up on acres and acres of asphalt—the neat rows interrupted by occasional watchtowers and the entire area surrounded by a heavy, iron, electronically monitored fence. On a busy Saturday, attendants direct streams of traffic in and out of the customers' parking lot. Hostesses with the dress and manner of airline stewardesses circulate in the showrooms offering to call a salesman for anybody who feels the need for one. Muzak, which reaches the most remote line of hardtops, is interrupted every two or three bars by calls for salesmen.   —CALVIN TRILLIN, "Working Out a Deal"

Here the implied topic sentence might be stated as *In spite of its pretense of being private and exclusive, Reedman's Car Dealership is huge, overwhelming, and impersonal.* But the writer does not have to state this information explicitly. We can gather it easily from the examples and specific details he provides: any place that brings to mind a "supply depot" with "acres and acres of asphalt," "hostesses" like "airline stewardesses," and "Muzak" can scarcely be regarded as private or exclusive.

EXERCISE 5.1

Choose an essay you have recently written, and identify the topic sentence of each paragraph, noting where in the paragraph each topic sentence appears and whether any is implied rather than stated. Would you now make any revisions in your topic sentences (including moving or adding them), and if so how would you revise, and why?

ǀ 2. Relating each sentence to the main idea

Whether the main idea of a paragraph appears in the topic sentence or is only implied, writing unified paragraphs demands that you

ANSWERS TO EXERCISE 5.1 WILL VARY

USEFUL READING

Rogers, Paul, Jr. "A Discourse-Centered Rhetoric of the Paragraph." CCC 17 (Feb. 1966): 2–11. Rogers does not believe that paragraphs are self-contained units; instead, they are stylistic choices determined by the overall purpose of the piece of writing.

make sure each sentence relates or contributes to the main idea. Look, for example, at the following paragraph, which opens an essay about black music.

> When I was a teenager, there were two distinct streams of popular music: one was black, and the other was white. The former could only be heard way at the end of the radio dial, while white music dominated everywhere else. This separation was a fact of life, the equivalent of blacks sitting in the back of the bus and "whites only" signs below the Mason-Dixon line. Satchmo might grin for days on "The Ed Sullivan Show" and certain historians hold forth *ad nauseam* on the black contribution to American music, but the truth was that our worlds rarely twined.
> —Marcia Gillespie,
> "They're Playing My Music, but Burying My Dreams"

The author announces her topic (two streams of popular music: black and white) in sentence one. Sentence two relates the topic to the respective positions of "black" and "white" music on the radio dial, and sentence three expands on this notion of musical separation by comparing it to the separate seats for blacks on buses or their exclusion from certain "public" places. The last sentence of this opening paragraph rephrases the topic sentence in a much more pointed way: though popular black music might appear regularly on television and people might write volumes about how much blacks have contributed to American music, the two worlds of black and white music remained separate. Each sentence clearly relates to the topic, and the paragraph as a whole is unified.

ANSWERS TO EXERCISE 5.2 (WILL VARY)

Since the mid-seventies, the economic condition of New York City has gone from "guarded" to "good." The years between 1969 and 1976 were especially grim. The city lost 600,000 jobs and ten major corporations; twenty office buildings in prime Manhattan areas were empty. The city was on the brink of bankruptcy. But since 1977, New York City has worked toward recovering its economic health. In the first year alone, it gained 9,000 jobs. Soon after, one million square feet of Manhattan office space was newly rented, and both AT&T and IBM built multimillion dollar buildings. Despite the increase in rents and prices for cooperative apartments, there is currently an apartment shortage in Manhattan and one-million dollar luxury penthouses are sold out.

EXERCISE 5.2

Following are some sentences adapted from a newspaper story about the economic prospects of New York City, which came very close to bankruptcy in the mid-1970s. Read the series of sentences carefully. Assuming that you are assigned to write a paragraph for an urban studies course on the economic health of New York City in the late 1970s, (1) compose a topic sentence for the paragraph, (2) decide where to position the topic sentence, and (3) use as many of the sentences as you need to create a unified paragraph. Omit any unnecessary sentences, and change wording if you need to.

1. New York lost 600,000 jobs between 1969 and 1976.
2. In 1975, twenty office buildings in prime Manhattan areas were empty.
3. Between 1970 and 1975, ten major corporations moved their headquarters from New York to the Sunbelt.

¶ 5b

4. In 1975, New York was on the brink of bankruptcy.
5. Between February 1977 and February 1978, New York gained 9,000 jobs.
6. Since January 1978, one million square feet of Manhattan office space have been newly rented.
7. AT&T has just built a $110 million headquarters in New York.
8. IBM has just built an $80 million building at 55th Street and Madison Avenue in New York.
9. Rents and prices for cooperative apartments have increased since 1977.
10. Even $1 million luxury penthouses are sold out.
11. There is currently an apartment shortage in Manhattan.
12. The president recently signed a bill authorizing $1.65 billion in federal loan guarantees for New York.

EXERCISE 5.3

The following two paragraphs lack unity. Identify the topic sentence of each one, and revise each paragraph by deleting any sentence unrelated to the topic.

1. Break dancing has produced unity among youngsters, a fact that is often overlooked. As break dancing spread across the United States, nearly every youngster became familiar with it. Many participated in learning the skill, and others just enjoyed watching their friends become "breakers." It is not at all strange to see break dancing groups with people of various races, creeds, and colors all working together in the synchronized steps of the dance routine. This diversity has characterized break dancing from its beginning. Blacks, Puerto Ricans, and other minority groups have played very important roles in the break dance phenomenon. Break dancing has now grown through publicity. Musical videos by top artists, including Lionel Ritchie and Herbie Hancock, feature break dancers. Special television programs have shown break dancing, and interviews have been conducted with those who have mastered the dance. All these factors have made break dancing more popular and exciting.

2. According to advertisers, one side of every woman's personality is sensual, knowing, experienced, worldly, unshockable, well-versed in the art of love: in short, a woman in every sense of the word. The opposing side is shy, sweet, trusting, innocent, untried: a maiden totally immersed in her own purity. Many argue that men possess a split personality, too. This is exactly how I feel as a woman: forever pushed, pulled, jostled, teased, and finally lured into treading a fine thread between blatant maturity and subtle innocence. No wonder so many women begin to feel like a Dr. Seuss "Push-me, Pull-me," the animal with two heads facing in opposite directions, each vying for its own desires and neither budging an inch.

ANSWERS TO EXERCISE 5.3 (WILL VARY)

1. Many factors have made break dancing popular and exciting. First of all, break dancing has produced unity among youngsters, a fact that is often overlooked. As break dancing spread across the United States, nearly every youngster became familiar with it. Many participated in learning the skill, and others just enjoyed watching their friends become "breakers." This diversified unity has characterized break dancing from its beginning. Break dancing has grown through publicity. Musical videos by top artists, including Lionel Ritchie and Herbie Hancock, and special television programs have featured break dancers, either dancing or talking about their new-found interest.

2. According to advertisers, all women possess a split personality. One side is sensual, knowing, experienced, worldly, unshockable, well-versed in the art of love: in short, a woman in every sense of the word. However, the opposite side is shy, sweet, trusting, innocent, untried—a maiden totally immersed in her own purity. No wonder we [women] begin to feel like a Hugh Lofting "Push-me, Pull-you," the animal with two heads facing in opposite directions, each vying for its own desires and neither budging an inch. That is exactly how I feel: forever pushed, pulled, jostled, teased, and finally lured into treading a fine thread between blatant maturity and subtle innocence.

ANSWERS TO EXERCISE 5.4
WILL VARY

ANSWERS TO EXERCISE 5.5
WILL VARY

(BACK)GROUNDING

Terminology used in the literature of paragraph theory can be confusing. For one thing, researchers often use the same terms (*unity, coherence, development*) to describe whole pieces of discourse as well as paragraphs. For instance, some textbooks and articles suggest that *coherence* and *cohesion* are separate features, while others take them to mean the same thing.

You may want to think of these three elements as separate entities: *unity* as a semantic concept, the paragraph's single topic; *coherence* as a stylistic concept, using various methods to interconnect the sentences of a paragraph; and *cohesion* as the whole-essay counterpart of *unity*.

EXERCISE 5.4

Choose one of the following topic sentences, and spend ten or fifteen minutes brainstorming, freewriting, looping, or mapping to gather ideas about the topic (see 2e). Then write a paragraph that includes the topic sentence, making sure that each of the other sentences relates to it. Assume that the paragraph will be part of a letter you are writing to a close friend.

1. I found out quickly that college life was not quite what I had expected.
2. Being part of the "in crowd" used to be of utmost importance to me.
3. My work experience has taught me several important lessons.
4. Until recently, I never appreciated my parents fully.
5. I expect my college education to do more than simply assure me of a job.

EXERCISE 5.5

Choose an essay you have written recently, and examine the second, third, and fourth paragraphs. Does each have a topic sentence or strongly imply one? Do all the other sentences in the paragraph focus on its main idea? Would you now revise any of these paragraphs—and if so, how?

5c. Making paragraphs coherent: fitting details together

A paragraph is **coherent** if its details fit together clearly in a way that readers can easily follow. For a paragraph to be unified, the sentences in it must relate to the same main idea; for it to be coherent, the sentences must relate to one another structurally. You can achieve paragraph coherence by organizing ideas, by repeating key terms or phrases, and by using parallel structures, pronouns, and transitions.

1. Organizing ideas

If you take every fourth sentence of an essay and arrange them together, one after another, in paragraph form, you will *not* end up with a paragraph. Why not? Because the sentences will have only a haphazard relationship to one another. Though they may well be connected to the same topic, the lack of any organizational relationship will result in incoherence. Clear organization of ideas goes a long way toward creating coherence, and the following discussion will review the most often used means of organizing a paragraph—spatial order, chronological order, and logical order. (See 2h for a discussion of organizing an entire essay.)

USEFUL READING

Halliday, M. A. K., and Rugaiya Hasan. *Cohesion in English*. London: Longman, 1976. A classification of cohesive ties in paragraphs and essays: reference, substitution, ellipsis, conjunction, and lexical ties.

Witte, Stephen P., and Lester Faigley. "Coherence, Cohesion, and Writing Quality." *CCC* 32 (May 1981): 189–204. Using an adjusted version of Halliday and Hasan's classifications, the authors conclude that cohesion is connected to our perceptions of how well the text fits to its context.

MAKING PARAGRAPHS COHERENT   ¶ 5c

Using spatial order

Paragraphs organized in **spatial order** take a "tour" of an object, person, or place, beginning at one point and moving, say, from near to far, left to right, north to south. Especially useful in **descriptive** paragraphs, spatial order allows a writer to direct readers' attention in an orderly way to various elements of something in physical space. A topic sentence is frequently unnecessary in a paragraph using spatial order, because the way the paragraph is organized will be obvious to the reader. Often, however, a topic sentence is used at the beginning of the paragraph to set the scene or tell the reader what is going to be described. Note the movement from ceiling to walls to floor in the following paragraph.

> The geology professor's voice began to fade into the background as my eyes wandered around the classroom in the old administration building. The water-stained ceiling was cracked and peeling, and the splitting wooden beams played host to a variety of lead pipes and coils. My eyes followed these pipes down the walls and around corners, until eventually I saw the electrical outlets. I thought it was strange that they were exposed, and not built in, until I realized that there was probably no electricity when the building had been built. Below the outlets the sunshine was falling in bright rays across the hardwood floor, and I noticed how smoothly it was worn. Time had certainly taken its toll on this building.

Using chronological order

Paragraphs organized in **chronological order** arrange a series of events according to time, putting earliest events first, followed in sequence by later events, one at a time. Chronological order is used frequently in **narrative** paragraphs, which basically tell a story. Rarely do they require a topic sentence, because the main idea is obvious in the action. The following paragraph uses careful chronology to tell a story and also to build suspense: we want to know what the last event in the sequence will be. The words expressing time help build this suspense: *all of a sudden, three months, a year later,* and so on.

> The experience of Lloyd S., an Oregon businessperson, is one of the most convincing cases for taking vitamins. For his first forty years, Lloyd was healthy and robust. He owned a thriving nursery and loved to hike, fish, and camp. All of a sudden, he started feeling fatigued. A loss of appetite and weight soon followed, and in three months he was

transformed from a ruddy, muscular man into a pallid, emaciated one. Lloyd had cancer of the pancreas. After he was given a prognosis of six months to live, his family and friends were devastated, but Lloyd was a fighter. When the conventional treatments of drugs and chemotherapy did not help, he turned to a holistic approach, which emphasized a change in diet and life style—and large doses of vitamins. After a series of blood tests to discover every possible nutritional deficiency, Lloyd was given concentrated vitamin and mineral supplements to ensure maximum cell efficiency and growth so that his body could attempt to heal itself. At the end of six months, Lloyd not only was alive but also showed improvement. A year later he was free of cancer and began the long battle to regain his original vitality. Coincidence? Perhaps. To Lloyd and me, however, his recovery became a powerful demonstration of how the world's most intricate machine, the human body, performs—if only we supply it with the needed nutrients.

Chronological order is also commonly used in **explaining a process.** Paragraphs that explain how something happens or how something is done proceed in chronological order: first one step, then the next, then the next. You are already very familiar with process as a means of organizing information. After all, every set of directions, every recipe, every user's manual presents a series of steps that make up a process someone wants to learn or to follow. Here is an example.

Before trying to play the flute, figure out how to put it together. The flute is divided into three parts: the mouthpiece, the main body, and the end piece. First remove the main body (the longest part) from the case, and set it down with the keys facing up and the openings away from you. Now, pick up the mouthpiece (the piece with one hole), and attach it to the hole at the far left end of the main body by gently twisting it from side to side, in a manner similar to jiggling a door knob. Repeat the same process in attaching the end piece to the other end of the main body, taking care not to twist or smash the keys. The keys on the end piece should be lined up with those on the main body.

In college writing, you will probably use process paragraphs less often to tell readers how to do something than to explain to them how a process occurs in general—for example, how a bill becomes law in the British Parliament or how aerosol sprays destroy the ozone layer of the atmosphere.

Using logical order

Paragraphs organized in **logical order** arrange details to reflect certain logical relationships. Explanations and examples of some of

OPTIONAL EXERCISE

Practice using a logical order by writing a paragraph describing your possessions—academic ⟷ personal; from home ⟷ from school; old ⟷ new; personal ⟷ public. You may want to sit on your bed and just look around your room as you write.

Did you start out or end up with a controlling idea? What is it? Do you have a topic sentence?

USEFUL READING

Backer, Alton. "A Tagmemic Approach to Paragraph Analysis." CCC 16 (1965): 237–42. Topic, restriction, and illustration (TRI) are the three elements that make up paragraphs.

MAKING PARAGRAPHS COHERENT ¶ 5c

these relationships—illustration, definition, division/classification, comparison/contrast, cause-effect, and problem-solution—are given in 5d. Two other logical patterns commonly used in paragraphs are *general-to-specific* and *specific-to-general*.

Paragraphs organized in a **general-to-specific** pattern usually open with a topic sentence presenting a general or abstract idea, followed by a number of more specific points designed to substantiate or prove or elaborate on the generalization. The following paragraph uses general-to-specific organization:

> We have surely all cheated at least one time in our lives. People cheat in dozens of ways, ranging from small-scale things like writing notes on their hands for tests to the monumental deception of having an affair. We cheat when we pass the speed limit. Powerful families and corporations cheat their way out of legal binds with the help of highly paid lawyers. Businesspeople record activities, such as dining out, as business-related so they will not have to pay for the expense personally. Dieters are always cheating, and if we really think about it, people cheat when they use makeup or fashion to cover up or disguise features they find unattractive. Even my grandmother cheats by taking short cuts in her prescribed daily walks.

GENERAL TOPIC

SPECIFICS

One common variation on the general-to-specific order moves from a statement of a general topic to a more **restricted topic** and finally to one or more specific details that illustrate the restricted topic. The following paragraph follows such an organizational plan:

> In 1941, war was at hand once again. Since World War I, the U.S. military had enjoyed its role as the symbol of a strong, proud nation. It was a time when "military" and "unity" went hand in hand, a time when soldiers sold products. From Lifesavers to Kodak and from government bonds to mimeograph machines, the soldier was used to give credibility to all kinds of products. One particularly compelling ad I found appeared in the December 15, 1941, issue of *Life* magazine. In it, the American Railroad Association proudly stated that it was "Backing Him Up." The "Him" was presented as a picture of a soldier—a proud soldier dressed for battle with his eyes uplifted, a soldier whose manner lifted him far above the average human. He was a god, or at least a king, and his gun was his scepter, the foxhole his throne. The world of

GENERAL TOPIC

RESTRICTION OF TOPIC

SPECIFIC DETAILS

1941 did not see violence in the gun, but security, and in his eyes it did not see death, but life.

Paragraphs can also follow a **specific-to-general** organization, first providing a series of specific examples or details and then tying them together with a general conclusion. The following paragraph uses a specific-to-general pattern:

> Many solutions have been proposed to the problem SPECIFIC
> of nuclear arms. One that has been gaining support calls DETAILS
> for a total and immediate freeze on the building, testing,
> and deployment of all new nuclear weapons by the United
> States and, if possible, the Soviet Union. A unilateral
> freeze would be effective only if we could trust the Soviets
> not to take advantage of the situation and build more and
> better weapons. History shows we cannot be certain of
> this outcome. A bilateral freeze cannot be verified by
> today's surveillance techniques, and even if agreed upon,
> it would leave the Soviets with a great advantage in nu-
> clear arms. If either plan were implemented at this time,
> the ability of the nuclear forces of the United States to
> act as a deterrent would be crippled. The answer is a
> build-down: an agreement to destroy several existing
> weapons for every new one that is built. We must first GENERAL
> equalize our arsenals through a build-down; only then TOPIC
> can a freeze and eventual reduction be possible.

ANSWERS TO EXERCISE 5.6
WILL VARY

EXERCISE 5.6

Choose one of the following topic sentences or create one of your own, and try writing two different paragraphs on the topic, using a different organizational pattern for each. Then explain, in writing, why you used the organizational patterns you did, which one seems most effective and coherent, and why.

1. I remember very clearly the first time I ever experienced great satisfaction.
2. Explaining _____ to my parents was the hardest thing I've ever done.
3. People who are extremely vain about their looks often go to ridiculous lengths to keep up their appearance.
4. My classes this term can, with understatement, be described as demanding.
5. Many people share one basic fear: public speaking.

2. Repeating key words and phrases

A major means of building coherence in paragraphs is through **repetition.** Weaving in repeated references to key words and phrases

MAKING PARAGRAPHS COHERENT ¶ 5c

not only links sentences but also alerts readers to the importance the words or phrases hold in the larger piece of writing. Notice how the repetition of the key words *textbooks*, *tuition*, *cost*, *pay*, and *army* helps hold the following paragraph together.

> "Thirty-nine fifty for one *textbook!* You've got to be kidding," I mumbled as I dragged myself slowly toward the checkout stand. I did not know how I was going to *pay* for *tuition*, housing, phone bills, and groceries if all my *textbooks cost* me that much. "I might as well join the *army*," I thought. At least it would *pay* my *tuition* and give me *army rations*. Right now, *army* chow sounded considerably better than boiled pages from a psychology text. I stood there full of resentment; I had no intention of spending all my hard-earned money on *textbooks*. Yet I had no choice. This was a book I had to have, whatever the *cost*.

Notice also that the cluster of terms related to money helps make the paragraph hang together: *pay, cost, pay, spending, hard-earned money, cost*. Such repetition helps us follow the logic of a paragraph and understand the point the writer is making.

EXERCISE 5.7

Read the following paragraph. Then identify the places where the author repeats key words and phrases, and explain how this strategy brings coherence to the paragraph.

> Nobody knows, of course, how many megatons would be exploded in a real nuclear war. There are some who think that a nuclear war can be "contained," bottled up before it runs away to involve many of the world's arsenals. But a number of detailed analyses, war games run by the U.S. Department of Defense and official Soviet pronouncements, all indicate that this containment may be too much to hope for: Once the bombs begin exploding, communications failures, disorganization, fear, the necessity of making in minutes decisions affecting the fates of millions and the immense psychological burden of knowing that your own loved ones may already have been destroyed are likely to result in a nuclear paroxysm. Many investigations, including a number of studies for the U.S. government, envision the explosion of 5000 to 10,000 megatons—the detonation of tens of thousands of nuclear weapons that now sit quietly, inconspicuously, in missile silos, submarines and long-range bombers, faithful servants, awaiting orders.   —CARL SAGAN, "The Nuclear Winter"

3. Using parallel structures

Parallel structures—structures that are grammatically similar—provide another effective way of bringing coherence to a paragraph.

(BACK)GROUNDING

Repetition of key words and phrases is an age-old technique for pulling together thematically related units; moreover, the rhythm of such verbal/visual echo effectively holds the audience's attention. We are all familiar with various repetitive devices:
single word

> Vanity of vanities, saith the preacher, vanity of vanities; all is vanity.
> —ECCLES. 1:1

syntactic structure

> The thoughts are but overflowings of the mind, and the tongue is but a servant of the thought.
> —PHILIP SIDNEY

> Blood hath bought blood, and
>   blows have answer'd blows;
> Strength match'd with strength,
>   and power confronted power.
> —KING JOHN

The most powerful device may be initial repetition, *anaphora*:

> [W]e shall defend our island, whatever the cost may be, we shall fight on the beaches, we shall fight on the landing grounds, we shall fight in the fields and in the streets, we shall fight in the hill; we shall never surrender.
> —WINSTON CHURCHILL

> Say that I was a drum major for justice. Say that I was a drum major for peace. That I was a drum major for righteousness. And all of the other shallow things will not matter.
> —MARTIN LUTHER KING, JR.

ANSWERS TO EXERCISE 5.7 (WILL VARY)
Repeated key words and phrases include:
*megatons; exploded; nuclear war
*nuclear war; contained
*containment
*bombs; exploding
*explosion of 5000 to 10,000 megatons; nuclear weapons; bombers

Parallel structures emphasize the connection between related ideas or events in different sentences, as in the following paragraph. (See Chapter 19 for further discussion of parallel structures.)

> William Faulkner's "Barn Burning" tells the story of a young boy trapped in a no-win situation. If he betrays his father, he loses his family. If he betrays justice, he becomes a fugitive. In trying to free himself from his trap, he does both.

In this paragraph, the writer skillfully uses the parallel structures *if he* X, *he* Y, in order to give the effect of a "no-win situation." At the end of the paragraph, we are prepared for the last sentence in the parallel sequence: *In doing* X, *he* Y. As readers, we feel pulled along by the force of the parallel structures in the paragraph.

EXERCISE 5.8

Read the following paragraph from an essay about wives, and identify every use of repetition and parallel structures. In a brief paragraph of your own, explain how their use helps build coherence in this paragraph.

> I would like to go back to school so that I can become economically independent, support myself, and, if need be, support those dependent upon me. I want a wife who will work and send me to school. And while I am going to school I want a wife to take care of my children. I want a wife to keep track of the children's doctor and dentist appointments. And to keep track of mine, too. I want a wife to make sure my children eat properly and are kept clean. I want a wife who will wash the children's clothes and keep them mended. I want a wife who is a good nuturant attendant to my children, who arranges for their schooling, makes sure that they have an adequate social life with their peers, takes them to the park, the zoo, etc. I want a wife who takes care of the children when they are sick, a wife who arranges to be around when the children need special care, because, of course, I cannot miss classes at school. My wife must arrange to lose time at work and not lose the job. It may mean a small cut in my wife's income from time to time, but I guess I can tolerate that. Needless to say, my wife will arrange and pay for the care of the children while my wife is working.   —JUDY SYFERS, "I Want a Wife"

4. Using pronouns

Writers also achieve coherence in a paragraph through the use of **pronouns**. Because pronouns usually refer back to nouns or other pronouns, they act as natural coherence devices, leading readers naturally from sentence to sentence. (See Chapter 11.) The following paragraph, from an essay on old age, uses pronouns effectively in linking

ANSWERS TO EXERCISE 5.8 (WILL VARY)

The repetitions and parallel structure are often intermingled:

*I would like; I can; I want; I am going; I want; I want; I want; I want; I want; I want; I cannot miss

*I want a wife; I want a wife; I want a wife; I want a wife; I want a wife; I want a wife; I want a wife

*support myself; support those dependent upon me

*go back to school; send me to school; going to school

*to take care of my children; to keep track of the children's doctor and dentist appointments; to keep track of mine; to make sure my children eat properly and are kept clean

*who will wash the children's clothes; who is a good nurturant attendant; who arranges for their schooling; who takes care of [sick] children; who arranges to be around

*makes sure that they have an adequate social life with their peers, takes them to the park

*my wife; my wife; my wife; my wife

OPTIONAL EXERCISE

"I Want a Wife" is a paragraph that begs for imitation. Useful starters could be:

1. I want an employer . . .
2. I want a boy/girlfriend . . .
3. I want a teacher . . .

MAKING PARAGRAPHS COHERENT   ¶5c

sentences to one another. Note how much slower and more awkward the paragraph would be if each pronoun were replaced with the noun it stands for. Also note that the writer uses the name when he first introduces each new artist—and then uses pronouns thereafter to refer to that person. (Italics added for emphasis.)

> For such [old] persons, every new infirmity is an enemy to be outwitted, an obstacle to be overcome by force of will. *They* enjoy each little victory over *themselves*, and sometimes *they* win a major success. Renoir was one of *them*. *He* continued painting, and magnificently, for years after *he* was crippled by arthritis; the brush had to be strapped to *his* arm. "You don't need your hand to paint," *he* said. Goya was another of the unvanquished. At 72 *he* retired as an official painter of the Spanish court and decided to work only for *himself*. *His* later years were those of the famous "black paintings" in which *he* let *his* imagination run (and also of the lithographs, then a new technique). At 78 *he* escaped a reign of terror in Spain by fleeing to Bordeaux. *He* was deaf and *his* eyes were failing; in order to work *he* had to wear several pairs of spectacles, one over another, and then use a magnifying glass; but *he* was producing splendid work in a totally new style. At 80 *he* drew an ancient man propped on two sticks, with a mass of white hair and beard hiding *his* face and with the inscription "*I* am still learning."
>
> —MALCOLM COWLEY, *The View from 80*

EXERCISE 5.9

Choose three paragraphs from an essay you have recently written, and analyze them for pronoun use. How do the pronouns bring coherence to the paragraphs? Is it clear what noun or pronoun each of the pronouns refers back to? Can you see ways of using pronouns to improve the coherence of these paragraphs?

5. Using transitional devices

Transitions are words and phrases that help bring coherence to a paragraph by signaling the exact relationships between sentences. In acting as signposts from one idea to the next, transitional expressions such as *after all*, *for example*, *indeed*, *so*, and *thus* help readers follow the progression of a paragraph. *Finally* indicates that a last point is at hand; *likewise*, that a similar point is about to be made, and so on. To get an idea of how important transitions are in directing readers, look at the following paragraph, from which all transitional devices have been removed:

ANSWERS TO EXERCISE 5.9 WILL VARY

TEACHING PRACTICE

Read aloud this selection from *Jane Eyre*. As you read, your students should jot down the transitional devices they hear.

> "My first aim will be to *clean down* . . . Moor House from chamber to cellar; my next to rub it up with beeswax, oil, and an indefinite number of cloths, till it glitters again; my third, to arrange every chair, table, bed, carpet with mathematical precision; afterwards I shall go near to ruin you in coals and peat to keep up good fires in every room; and lastly, the two days preceding that on which your sisters are expected will be devoted by Hannah and me to such a beating of eggs, sorting of currants, grating of spices, compounding of Christmas cakes, chopping up of materials for mince-pies, and solemnizing of other culinary rites, as words can convey but an inadequate notion of to the uninitiated like you. My purpose, in short, is to have all things in an absolutely perfect state of readiness for Diana and Mary before next Thursday; and my ambition is to give them a beau-ideal of a welcome when they come." (Chapter XXXIV)

OPTIONAL EXERCISE

Look through your textbooks for a paragraph using transitions, and bring in copies of the paragraph (with the transitions marked) or plan to read it aloud. Transitions often transport ideas through writing; so you should be able to describe the movement in their sample paragraph.

TEACHING PRACTICE

Sharp readers can detect use of faulty or "fake" transitions. One professor of English has made a hobby of collecting them in essays and offers this list of transitions with their real meanings "translated."

Transition	Translation
of course ⟶	Here comes a shaky assertion
with the exception of ⟶	Here is one of the many flaws in my argument
in conclusion ⟶	I can't think of anything else to say.

As effective writers, your students will want to make sure their transitions work for, not against, them.

In "The Fly," Katherine Mansfield tries to show us the "real" personality of "the boss" beneath his exterior. The fly helps her to portray this real self. The boss goes through a range of emotions and feelings. He expresses these feelings on a small but determined fly, whom the reader realizes he unconsciously relates to his son. The author basically splits up the story into three parts, with the boss's emotions and actions changing quite measurably. With old Woodifield, with himself, and with the fly, we see the boss's manipulativeness. Our understanding of him as a hard and cruel man grows.

We can, if we work at it, figure out the relationship of these ideas to one another, for this paragraph is essentially unified by one major idea. But the lack of transitions results in an abrupt, choppy rhythm that lurches from one idea to the next, dragging the confused reader behind. Look how much easier the paragraph is to read and understand when the transitional devices are added:

In "The Fly," Katherine Mansfield tries to show us the "real" personality of "the boss" beneath his exterior. The fly *in the story's title* helps her to portray this real self. *In the course of the story*, the boss goes through a range of emotions and feelings. *At the end*, he *finally* expresses these feelings on a small but determined fly, whom the reader realizes he unconsciously relates to his son. *To accomplish her goal*, the author basically splits up the story into three parts, with the boss's emotions and actions changing quite measurably *throughout*. *First* with old Woodifield, *then* with himself, and *last* with the fly, we see the boss's manipulativeness. *With each part*, our understanding of him as a hard and cruel man grows.

Note how the writer carefully leads us through the points of her paragraph. Most of the transitional devices here point to movement in time, helping us follow the chronology of the story being discussed: *in the course of the story; at the end; finally; throughout; first; then; last*.

It is important to note that transitions can only clarify connections between thoughts; they cannot create connections. As a writer, you must choose transitions that fit your meaning, and not expect a transition to *provide* meaning. If you open a sentence with *therefore*, for example, be sure that the thought expressed by the rest of the sentence really follows logically from the previous sentences.

The following list contains commonly used transitional devices, grouped by the functions they perform.

MAKING PARAGRAPHS COHERENT

TO SIGNAL SEQUENCE

again, also, and, and then, besides, finally, first . . . second . . . third, furthermore, last, moreover, next, still, too

TO SIGNAL TIME

after a bit, after a few days, after a while, afterward, as long as, as soon as, at last, at length, at that time, before, earlier, immediately, in the meantime, in the past, lately, later, meanwhile, now, presently, shortly, simultaneously, since, so far, soon, then, thereafter, until, when

TO SIGNAL COMPARISON

again, also, in the same way, likewise, once more, similarly

TO SIGNAL CONTRAST

although, but, despite, even though, however, in contrast, in spite of, instead, nevertheless, nonetheless, notwithstanding, on the contrary, on the one hand . . . on the other hand . . . , regardless, still, though, yet

TO SIGNAL EXAMPLES

after all, even, for example, for instance, indeed, in fact, of course, specifically, such as, the following example . . . , to illustrate

TO SIGNAL CAUSE AND EFFECT

accordingly, as a result, because, consequently, for this purpose, hence, so, then, therefore, thereupon, thus, to this end

TO SIGNAL PLACE

above, adjacent to, below, beyond, closer to, elsewhere, far, farther on, here, near, nearby, opposite to, there, to the left, to the right

TO SIGNAL CONCESSION

although it is true that, granted that, I admit that, it may appear that, naturally, of course

TO SIGNAL SUMMARY, REPETITION, OR CONCLUSION

all in all, as a result, as has been noted, as I have said, as we have seen, in any event, in conclusion, in other words, in short, on the whole, therefore, to conclude, to summarize, to sum up

For a discussion of using transitional devices to link separate paragraphs together, see 5f.

ANSWERS TO EXERCISE 5.10 (WILL VARY)

Transitional devices include:
like that of the various national style; also; Some years ago; Today; particularly; of course; For many years; for instance; but

ANSWERS TO EXERCISE 5.11

Here is the passage as published:
And in the next year the drought hit. My mother and father trudged from the well to the chickens, the well to the calf pasture, the well to the barn, and from the well to the garden. The sun came out hot and bright, endlessly, day after day. The crops shriveled and died. They harvested half the corn, and ground the other half, stalks and all, and fed it to the cattle as fodder. With the price at four cents a bushel for the harvested crop, they couldn't afford to haul it into town. They burned it in the furnace for fuel that winter.

ANSWERS TO EXERCISE 5.12 (WILL VARY)

(1) I must make, I must confess, I have been, I have almost; first; confessions/confess; white moderate, White Citizen's Counciler, white moderate; who is more devoted, who prefers, who constantly says, who paternalistically believes, who lives, who constantly advises; to "order" that to justice, a negative peace which is the absence of tension to a positive peace which is the presence of justice; I agree with you, but I cannot agree with; timetable, mythical concept of time, "more convenient season"; Shallow understanding from people of good will, absolute understanding from people of ill will; Lukewarm acceptance, outright rejection. (2) Back in 1972, Since that brief debut, Since 1972, In the last fifteen years; musician, guitar player, Jimmy Buffet, Buffet, Buffet; bell-bottom jeans, a T-shirt, and a cowboy hat; matured and mellowed; duplicated or even tried to match; has matured and mellowed, has become, has branched out; owns, publishes, sends; his sound, his unique Caribbean soul music sound, his own newspaper, his fan club, his new albums, his current tour; followers, fan, fan club, the Parrot Heads, them.

EXERCISE 5.10

Read the following paragraph, and identify all transitional devices. Then read the paragraph with these words or phrases left out, and briefly describe, in writing, the difference the transitional devices make.

The popularity of the various regional styles of American costume, like that of the various national styles, is also related to economic and political factors. Some years ago modes often originated in the Far West and the word "California" on a garment was thought to be an allurement. Today, with power and population growth shifting to the Southwestern oil-producing states, Wild West styles—particularly those of Texas—are in vogue. This fashion, of course, is not new. For many years men who have never been nearer to a cow than the local steakhouse have worn Western costume to signify that they are independent, tough and reliable. In a story by Flannery O'Connor, for instance, the sinister traveling salesman is described as wearing "a broad-brimmed stiff gray hat of the kind used by businessmen who would like to look like cowboys"—but, it is implied, seldom succeed in doing so.
–ALISON LURIE, *The Language of Clothes*

EXERCISE 5.11

The following sentences come from a paragraph of Donna Smith-Yackel's "My Mother Never Worked." They are shown in the following paragraph out of the original order. Rearrange the sentences so that the paragraph is once again coherent.

(1) The sun came out hot and bright, endlessly, day after day. (2) They harvested half the corn, and ground the other half, stalks and all, and fed it to the cattle as fodder. (3) And in the next year the drought hit. (4) They burned it in the furnace for fuel that winter. (5) My mother and father trudged from the well to the chickens, the well to the calf pasture, the well to the barn, and from the well to the garden. (6) The crops shriveled and died. (7) With the price at four cents a bushel for the harvested crop, they couldn't afford to haul it into town.   –DONNA SMITH-YACKEL, "My Mother Never Worked"

EXERCISE 5.12

For the following paragraphs, identify each of the devices—repetition of key words or phrases, parallel structures, pronouns, and transitional expressions—that make the paragraph coherent.

1.   I must make two honest confessions to you, my Christian and Jewish brothers. First, I must confess that over the past few years I have been gravely disappointed with the white moderate. I have almost reached the regrettable conclusion that the Negro's great stumbling block on his stride toward free-

dom is not the White Citizen's Counciler or the Ku Klux Klanner, but the white moderate, who is more devoted to "order" than to justice; who prefers a negative peace which is the absence of tension to a positive peace which is the presence of justice; who constantly says, "I agree with you in the goal you seek, but I cannot agree with your methods of direct action"; who paternalistically believes he can set the timetable for another man's freedom; who lives by a mythical concept of time and who constantly advises the Negro to wait for a "more convenient season." Shallow understanding from people of good will is more frustrating than absolute misunderstanding from people of ill will. Lukewarm acceptance is much more bewildering than outright rejection.

    –MARTIN LUTHER KING, JR., "Letter from Birmingham Jail"

2.   Back in 1972, an unknown musician got a much-needed break when *Playboy* magazine featured a brief article picturing a young, long-haired guitar player sporting bell-bottom jeans, a T-shirt, and a cowboy hat. Since that brief debut, Jimmy Buffet has matured and mellowed with age. But his sound, like that of Bruce Springsteen, has remained the same, much to the pleasure of his followers. Since 1972, Buffet has become a true original, and no one has duplicated or even tried to match his unique Caribbean soul music sound. In the last fifteen years, he has branched out into retail business. He owns several shops throughout Florida and the rest of the South that feature an array of goods that any Buffet fan cannot live without. He publishes his own newspaper, *The Coconut Telegraph*, which he sends to his fan club, the Parrot Heads, to keep them up to date on recent events such as releases of his new albums and reviews of his current tour.

▌ 5d. Developing paragraphs fully: providing details

In addition to being unified and coherent, a paragraph must hold readers' interest and explore its topic fully, using whatever details, evidence, and examples are necessary. Without such **development,** a paragraph may seem lifeless and abstract.

Most good essay writing does two things: it presents generalized ideas and explanations, and it backs up these generalities with specifics. This balance, the shifting between general and specific, is especially important at the paragraph level. If a paragraph contains nothing but specific details, with no explanation of how they should be viewed as a whole, readers may have trouble following the writer's meaning. If, on the other hand, a paragraph contains only abstract ideas and general statements, readers will soon become bored or will fail to be convinced by it. General statements or conclusions thus rest on specific, concrete

WRITING TOGETHER

Break into your groups and trade drafts of your current essays. As you read another's paper, draw arrows between or circles around key terms, ideas, pronouns. Mark transitional phrases with heavy underlining and parallelism with //*sm.* Simply stopping to analyze prose might help you better understand elements of unity and coherence.

WRITERS ON WRITING

Writing is like driving at night. You can see only as far as the headlights, but you can make the whole trip that way.

    —E. L. DOCTOROW

pieces of knowledge and sensory details. Well-developed paragraphs include examples and reasons that demonstrate such knowledge and details. Consider the following poorly developed paragraph:

> No such thing as "human nature" compels people to behave, think, or react in certain ways. Rather, from the time of our infancy to our death, we are constantly being taught by the society that surrounds us the customs, norms, and mores of our distinct culture. Everything in culture is learned, not genetically transmitted.

This paragraph is boring. Although its main idea is clear, and its sentences hold together, it fails to gain our interest, hold our attention, or convince us because it lacks any concrete illustrations. Now look at the paragraph in its original form:

> Imagine a child in Ecuador dancing to salsa music at a warm family gathering, while another child in the United States is decorating a Christmas tree with bright, shiny red ornaments. Both of these children are taking part in their country's cultures. It is not by instinct that one child knows how to dance to salsa music, nor is it by instinct that the other child knows how to decorate the tree. No such thing as "human nature" compels people to behave, think, or react in certain ways. Rather, from the time of our infancy to our death, we are constantly being taught by the society that surrounds us the customs, norms, and mores of our distinct culture. A majority of people feel that the evil in human beings is "human nature." However, the Tasaday, a "Stone Age" tribe who were discovered not long ago in the Philippines, do not even have equivalents in their language for the words *hatred, competition, acquisitiveness, aggression,* and *greed.* Such examples suggest that everything in culture is learned, not genetically transmitted.

Though both paragraphs argue the same point, only the second manages to come to life. It does so by bringing in specific details *from* life. We *want* to read this paragraph, for it appeals to our senses (a child dancing; bright, shiny red ornaments) and our curiosity (who are the Tasaday?).

Almost every paragraph can be improved by making sure that its general ideas rest on enough specific detail. You can, of course, add too many details, pushing examples at the reader when no more are needed. For every writer who has to chop back jungles of detail, however, there are five whose greatest task is to irrigate deserts of generality.

DEVELOPING PARAGRAPHS FULLY   ¶ 5d

EXERCISE 5.13

Rewrite the following undeveloped paragraphs by adding concrete supporting details, examples, and reasons to them.

1. *The introduction to an essay tentatively titled "A Week on $12.80"*

     Nothing is more frustrating to a college student than being dead broke. Not having money for enough food or for the rent, much less for entertainment, is not much fun. And of course debts for tuition and books keep piling up. No, being broke is not to be recommended.

2. *The introduction to a humorous essay contrasting cats and dogs*

     Have you threatened your cat lately? If not, why not? Why not get a *real* pet—a dog? Dogs, after all, are better pets. Cats, on the other hand, are a menace to the environment.

1. Using logical patterns of development

The **logical patterns** presented in 2h for organizing essays or sections of essays can also serve as a means of developing paragraphs. These patterns include illustrating, defining, classifying and dividing, comparing and contrasting, exploring causes and effects, and considering problems and solutions or questions and answers.

Illustrating a point

Illustrating a point is one of the most useful ways of developing the main idea of a paragraph. You can **illustrate a point** with examples or with reasons.

The following paragraphs use **concrete examples** to illustrate a point. The first offers one extended example, while the second offers a series of examples.

A SINGLE EXAMPLE

     The Indians made names for us children in their teasing way. Because our very busy mother kept my hair cut short, like my brothers', they called me Short Furred One, pointing to their hair and making the sign for short, the right hand with fingers pressed close together, held upward, back out, at the height intended. With me this was about two feet tall, the Indians laughing gently at my abashed face. I am told that I was given a pair of small moccasins that first time, to clear up my unhappiness at being picked out from the dusk behind the fire and my two unhappy shortcomings made conspicuous.

     –MARI SANDOZ, "The Go-Along Ones"

ANSWERS TO EXERCISE 5.13 (WILL VARY)

(1) Nothing is more frustrating to a college student than being dead broke. As though studying, doing written homework, taking exams, and performing lab experiments aren't enough, most students also have to worry about money. Not having money for enough food or for the rent, much less for entertainment, is not fun. Food and shelter are not comfort enough for the student who spends her days and nights in her schoolwork. She also needs to unwind, but going to the movies, out for pizza or beer, takes money. (2) Have you threatened your cat lately? If not, why not? Threaten your cat with another pet, a real pet, a better pet—a dog. While your cat lounges around the house, scattering its hair all over your favorite chair, ignoring all your requests to move, to eat, to go out, a dog will anticipate your every command. A dog will leap out of your chair when it sees you come, will lap up its food, and will scratch at the door when you reach for its leash. In addition to its good nature, a dog offers you loyalty and protection.

WRITING TOGETHER

Break into your groups to focus and expand the information in the two paragraphs in Exercise 5.13, revising them completely. Then, share your revisions and identify your topic sentences.

TEACHING PRACTICE

To help students become sensitive to perspective, ask them to assume distinct roles when deciding on perspective. They might imagine or recall, for example, a family reunion or a grandparents' fiftieth wedding anniversary, or a championship football game, and they will want to identify the individuals present. Have them describe the reunion or the anniversary from the grandmother's perspective, or from a nine-year-old's. The two perspectives are clearly different. They might want to describe the moments of the winning touchdown from a player's perspective, a cheerleader's, the high school principal's, or from the perspective of the losing team.

This activity shows students that while perspectives can be adopted, they are often determined by who we are in relation to the thing, event, or person being described.

SEVERAL EXAMPLES

There is a lot of energy at the Fair in Des Moines, but it is all peaceful. The double giant Ferris wheel circles, its swaying seats, a thousand men, women, and children walk all day and much of the night across the fairgrounds. Ponies pick up their feet in a slashing trot as if the ground burned them. Hard-rock music backgrounds the soft lowing of a Jersey cow in the cattle barn over her newborn calf, the color of a wild deer. Screaming speeches are made all around the world urging violence; here there are plenty of voices, but they are calling for you to throw baseballs at Kewpie dolls, to pitch nickels at a dish which won't hold them, to buy cotton candy, corn dogs, a paring knife that performs every useful act save mixing a martini.

–PAUL ENGLE, "The Iowa State Fair"

At times illustrating a point involves providing not examples but **good reasons** for believing the main idea of the paragraph to be true (see 4c). The following paragraph opens with a generalization in the topic sentence and then offers reasons to support the generalization:

But I did not want to shoot the elephant. I watched him beating his bunch of grass against his knees, with that preoccupied grandmotherly air that elephants have. It seemed to me that it would be murder to shoot him. At that age I was not squeamish about killing animals, but I had never shot an elephant and never wanted to. (Somehow it always seems worse to kill a large animal.) Besides, there was the beast's owner to be considered. Alive, the elephant was worth at least a hundred pounds; dead, he would only be worth the value of his tusks, five pounds, possibly. But I had got to act quickly. I turned to some experienced-looking Burmans who had been there when we arrived, and asked them how the elephant had been behaving. They all said the same thing: he took no notice of you if you left him alone, but he might charge if you went too close to him.   –GEORGE ORWELL, "Shooting an Elephant"

Defining

You will often have occasion to develop an entire paragraph by **defining** a word or concept. Some college courses, particularly ones that deal with difficult abstractions, require writing that often calls for this strategy. A philosophy exam, for instance, might require you to define words such as *truth* or *validity*. Often, however, you will find it necessary to combine definition with other methods of development. You may need to show examples or draw comparisons or divide a term you are defining into two parts. In the following paragraph, Tom Wolfe defines *pornoviolence*, a word he has coined, by contrasting it first with

DEVELOPING PARAGRAPHS FULLY ¶ 5d

"accumulated slayings and bone crushings" and then with violence seen from the point of view of "the hero."

> It is not the accumulated slayings and bone crushings that make [this TV show into] pornoviolence, however. What makes pornoviolence is that in almost every case the camera angle, therefore the viewer, is with the gun, the fist, the rock. The pornography of violence has no point of view in the old sense that novels do. You do not live the action through the hero's eyes. You live with the aggressor, whoever he may be. One moment you are the hero. The next you are the villain. No matter whose side you may be on consciously, you are in fact with the muscle, and it is you who disintegrate all comers, villains, lawmen, women, anybody. On the rare occasions in which the gun is emptied into the camera—i.e., into your face—the effect is so startling that the pornography of violence all but loses its fantasy charm. There are not nearly so many masochists as sadists among those little devils whispering into one's ears.   —TOM WOLFE, "Pornoviolence"

Dividing and classifying

Dividing breaks a single item into parts. **Classifying**, which is actually a form of dividing, groups many separate items according to their similarities. You could, for instance, develop a paragraph evaluating a history course by dividing the course into several segments—textbooks, lectures, assignments—and examining each one in turn. Or you could use classification in developing a paragraph giving an overview of history courses at your college, grouping the courses in a number of ways—by the time periods or geographic areas covered, by the kinds of assignments demanded, by the numbers of students enrolled, or by some other criterion. In the following paragraph, which introduces the American composer Aaron Copland's essay about how people listen to music, Copland explains the listening process by dividing it into three parts. The rest of the essay goes on to explain each of these parts in greater detail.

> We all listen to music according to our separate capacities. But, for the sake of analysis, the whole listening process may become clearer if we break it up into its component parts, so to speak. In a certain sense we all listen to music on three separate planes. For lack of a better terminology, one might name these: (1) the sensuous plane, (2) the expressive plane, (3) the sheerly musical plane. The only advantage to be gained from mechanically splitting up the listening process into these hypothetical planes is the clearer view to be had of the way in which we listen.   —AARON COPLAND, *What to Listen for in Music*

TEACHING PRACTICE

As a way of introducing the idea of classifying, consider asking the class to answer the following series of questions:

- What are your strengths and weaknesses as a writer?
- Is your writing process linear or recursive?
- How do you learn in this class: from writing? from taking notes? from reading and responding to your friends' work?
- What are your reasons for taking this course?

Use their answers to these questions to classify students into different groups. Not only does this exercise demonstrate classification, it also forces students to become aware of circumstances or context of this course. In *Teaching the Universe of Discourse*, James Moffett calls such awareness "meta-awareness," a consciousness of abstraction.

The students in your class must be aware of how to succeed as a writer and as a student if they are to improve. Meta-awareness is the knowledge of how to improve.

WRITING TOGETHER

In your groups, discuss the sharp contrast between the eleventh and twelfth grades, between high school and college, and between life with and without children. Take notes. Then write a short essay on one of the topics.

The following paragraph discusses dieters by classifying them as two types.

> Two types of people are seduced by fad diets. Those who have always been overweight turn to fad diets out of despair; they have tried everything, and yet nothing seems to work. The second group who succumb are those who appear perfectly healthy but are baited with slogans such as "look good, feel good." These slogans prompt self-questioning and insecurity—do I *really* look good and feel good?—and as a direct result, many of these people also fall prey to fad diets. With both types of people, however, the problems surrounding fad diets are numerous and dangerous. In fact, these diets provide neither intelligent nor effective answers to weight control.

Comparing and contrasting

You can develop some paragraphs easily and effectively by comparing and/or contrasting various aspects of the topic or by comparing and/or contrasting the topic to something else. **Comparing** things highlights their similarities; **contrasting,** their differences. Whether used alone or together, comparing and contrasting both act to bring the topic at hand more clearly into focus (we can better understand an unknown, for example, by comparing it to something we know well) or to help us evaluate the items compared and/or contrasted. You can structure comparison/contrast paragraphs in two basic ways: by first presenting all the information about one item, then presenting all the information about the other item (block method); or by alternating back and forth between the two items, focusing in turn on particular characteristics of each (alternating method). Mary Mebane uses the block method of comparing and contrasting to focus on two groups of job-seekers: the veterans and the rookies:

> You could tell the veterans from the rookies by the way they were dressed. The knowledgeable ones had their heads covered by kerchiefs, so that if they were hired, tobacco dust wouldn't get in their hair; they had on clean dresses that by now were faded and shapeless, so that if they were hired they wouldn't get tobacco dust and grime on their best clothes. Those who were trying for the first time had their hair freshly done and wore attractive dresses; they wanted to make a good impression. But the dresses couldn't be seen at the distance that many were standing from the employment office, and they were crumpled in the crush.
> —MARY MEBANE, "Summer Job"

TEACHING PRACTICE
Consumer Reports is one of the best sources of purposeful comparison/contrast writing; *Sports Illustrated*, of informational comparison/contrast writing. After your students have looked at examples from these sources, ask them to do their own comparison or contrast.

Often, students feel that they must attempt a lofty subject, "The Nonviolent Resistance Policies of Martin Luther King, Jr., and Mahatma Ghandi," for example. But they will meet with more success when they write about a familiar subject, and they practice decision-making comparison and contrast on a daily basis: why buy a particular brand of cosmetics; why wear one kind of sports shoes; why live on a certain part of campus; why date a "type" of person, etc. Encourage them to write a brief, purposeful comparison/contrast paper on a subject of their own choice.

DEVELOPING PARAGRAPHS FULLY

In the next paragraph, the student writer uses the alternating method of contrasting. Note how transitional expressions like *on the other hand* and *however* are very important in establishing the back and forth pattern and guiding readers from point to point.

> Unlike Martin Luther King, Malcolm X emphasized the use of violence in his movement and employed the biblical principle of "an eye for an eye and a tooth for a tooth." King, on the other hand, felt that blacks should use nonviolent civil disobedience and employed the theme "turning the other cheek," which Malcolm X rejected as "beggarly" and "feeble." The philosophy of Malcolm X was one of revenge, and too often it broke the unity of black Americans. More radical blacks supported him, while more rational and conservative ones supported King. King thought that blacks should transcend their humanity. Malcolm X thought they should embrace it and reserve their love for one another, regarding whites as "devils" and the "enemy." King's politics were those of a rainbow, but Malcolm X's rainbow was insistently one color—black. The distance between Martin Luther King's thinking and Malcolm X's was the distance between growing up in the seminary and growing up on the streets, between the American dream and the American reality of blacks.

EXERCISE 5.14

Outline the paragraph on Martin Luther King and Malcolm X, noting its alternating pattern. Then rewrite the paragraph using block organization: the first part of the paragraph devoted to King, the second to Malcolm X. Finally, write a brief paragraph analyzing which of the two paragraphs seems most coherent and easy to follow and why.

Exploring causes and effects

Certain topics will require you to consider the process of **cause and effect,** and you can often develop paragraphs by detailing the causes of something or the effects that something leads to. A geology study question, for instance, may lead you to write a paragraph describing the major causes of soil erosion in the Midwest—or the effects of such erosion. The following paragraph discusses the effects of television on the American family.

> Television's contribution to family life has been an equivocal one. For while it has, indeed, kept the members of the family from dispersing, it has not served to bring them *together*. By its domination of the time families spend together, it destroys the special quality that distinguishes

ANSWERS TO EXERCISE 5.14 WILL VARY

WRITING TOGETHER
Break into groups and work to enumerate and describe your most dominant, individual personality traits. Then, try to account for the causes of those traits, for who share certain traits, for the differences among you. Then, write a short essay, using one method of organization.

one family from another, a quality that depends to a great extent on what a family *does*, what special rituals, games, recurrent jokes, familiar songs, and shared activities it accumulates.   —MARIE WINN,
The Plug-in Drug: Television, Children, and the Family

Considering problems and solutions

As its name implies, paragraphs developed by the **problem-solution pattern** open with a statement of a problem, usually the topic sentence, and then offer a solution in the sentences that follow, as in this paragraph:

> All over the nation, textbook choice committees face   PROBLEM
> the same challenge: choosing textbooks that are factually accurate, of high intellectual quality, and acceptable to various "watchdog" committees. Such a choice is very difficult for nonspecialists. To aid these committees in   SOLUTION
> deciding what textbooks to adopt, I would like to see the formation of an academic journal devoted entirely to reviewing new texts. The most efficient way to accomplish this goal would probably be to have a journal covering each field of study, since it would be inefficient to review English and physics texts in the same journal. The new texts would be scrutinized carefully by scholars in the respective fields and would be judged for their intellectual quality. In this way, the textbook choice committees would have a guide to aid them in selecting texts that are of certified intellectual value.

Considering questions and answers

Like the problem-solution pattern, the **question-answer pattern** of development does just what its name suggests: the first sentence poses a question, and the rest of the paragraph provides the answer. Beginning with a question provides a means of getting readers' attention—and focusing that attention—as it does in the following paragraph from an essay on embarrassing slips of the tongue:

> Why then do we hoot at these mistakes? For one thing, it may be that we simply find conventional discourse so predictable and boring that any deviation comes as a delightful relief. In his deeply unfunny "Essay on Laughter" the philosopher Henri Bergson theorized that the act of laughter is caused by any interruption of normal human fluidity or momentum (a pie in the face, a mask, a pun). Slips of the tongue,

DEVELOPING PARAGRAPHS FULLY   ¶ 5d

therefore, are like slips on banana peels; we crave their occurrence if only to break the monotonies. The monotonies run to substance. When that announcer introduced Hoobert Heever, he may also have been saying that the nation had had enough of Herbert Hoover.
                    —ROGER ROSENBLATT, "Oops! How's That Again?"

Combining patterns

As you might expect, many paragraphs combine these methods of development. In the following paragraph the writer moves from a general topic (her record collection) to one specific part of it (blues) and then develops that topic through the use of classification (blues albums for the morning and for the evening), illustration (Robert Johnson, Ray Charles), and cause-effect (the blues cause a variety of effects on the listener).

> My album collection reached the 300 mark, so no matter what mood I'm in, I have a variety of pieces to choose from. In recent years I have found myself buying more and more blues albums. I don't know why, but I've simply been gobbling them up. I can listen to the blues in the morning when my head is still a little foggy, and the voices come through like lighthouses leading the way. Or I can listen to them after a long day and let that simplistic 12-bar rhythm put me to sleep. When I'm feeling bad, I put one of these albums on and sponge up all the raw emotion expressed on that vinyl. From there I can get back in the groove and progress in energy levels, from slow blues (Robert Johnson) to inspired blues (Ray Charles) to faster and upbeat blues (Taj Mahal). In this way the blues actually picks me up; it's like a catharsis of emotion.

EXERCISE 5.15

Identify the specific method of development used in each of the following paragraphs, and explain why you think each paragraph is or is not effectively developed using that method.

1.   Science, which is defined as the body of knowledge derived from observation and experimentation, is usually divided into two main branches. The first is the natural sciences, which study the physical and biological aspects of our world. The second is the social sciences, which study human behavior. The social sciences are further divided into five main fields: psychology, economics, political science, anthropology, and sociology. Psychology is the study of individual behavior. Economics studies the production, distribution, and consumption of goods, and political science concerns itself with principles and methods of government. Anthropology is usually defined as the study of traditional and primitive societies. The study of modern societies is called sociology.

ANSWERS TO EXERCISE 5.15
1. definition; division
2. specifics
3. comparison/contrast, illustration, specifics
4. illustration

OPTIONAL EXERCISE
Rewriting the paragraphs in Exercise 5.15 might be instructive. Here are weaknesses you may want to strengthen as you discuss and rewrite:

1. No discussion of natural sciences
2. Overall description is vague
3. No point of comparison—so what?
4. One-sided, no refutation

(BACK)GROUNDING

In "Paragraph Development in the Modern Age of Rhetoric," Richard A. Meade and W. Geiger Ellis surveyed kinds and frequency of paragraph development in a magazine, *Saturday Review*, a daily newspaper, *Richmond Times-Dispatch*, and a professional journal, *English Journal*. Meade and Ellis concluded that "writers generally use paragraphs which reflect development by additional *comment*, *reasons*, or *examples*, either separately or in combination." They also found such types of development to be linked with the writer's purpose: additional comment helps express opinions; examples help explain; reasons support arguments and persuasion—when these purposes are combined so are the methods of development.

ANSWERS TO EXERCISES 5.16–5.25 WILL VARY

2.   Beyond the alleys and up the road are rows of traditional-style town houses. Many of the town houses have been converted into specialty shops such as clothing boutiques, jewelry shops, hair salons, and gourmet food shops. Crowds browse up and down these shops; some people wear designer clothes. The clothes shops sell fashions that would seem to some people bizarre, and to others high fashion. The jewelry shops have everything from costume bangles to huge diamond rings. The hair salons give designer, punk, or traditional cuts.

3.   Other differences I saw between Florida and Germany were the scenery and the culture. Florida's scenery consisted of one-story houses and green lawns. Palm trees and occasional garbage could be seen along the road. In Germany, houses were weirdly shaped with small lawns, if any. Buildings were very close to the road, and very little garbage could be found on the streets. Driving in Germany could be hazardous as compared with driving in Florida, because in Germany there are not speed limits. Cultural differences, such as the time of day you eat and the food you eat, were apparent between Germany and Florida. Communications were obviously different, with the German language being spoken in Germany.

4.   According to Hollywood, the Indian was always the liar, the thief, the cold-blooded, ruthless killer with no compassion. For example, in many movies a wild band of Indians surround a helpless family and for absolutely no reason at all, slaughter the whole family. The Indians depicted by Hollywood also make sneak attacks on a sleeping town, killing the townspeople, and pillaging every inch of the town. In other films, the Indians rustle cattle and horses from farmers and, of course, slay the farmers. This picture of the "Old West" is one of the greatest fallacies of all time.

EXERCISE 5.16

Choose two of the following topics or two others that interest you, and brainstorm or freewrite about each one for ten minutes (see 2e). Then use the information you have produced to determine what method(s) of development would be most appropriate for each topic.

1. The pleasure a hobby has given you
2. U2's image and Mötley Crüe's image
3. An average Saturday morning
4. Why monopoly is an appropriate metaphor for the values of a capitalistic society
5. The best course you've ever taken

EXERCISE 5.17

Refer to the argument you drafted in Exercise 4.14, and study the ways you have developed each paragraph. For one of those paragraphs, write a brief

DEVELOPING PARAGRAPHS FULLY   ¶ 5d

evaluation of its development, including recommendations for expanding and/ or improving the development.

2. Determining paragraph length

While the paragraph has existed as a unit of writing for a long, long time, ideas about and expectations of paragraphs have changed over the years. If you look at Edward Gibbon's *Rise and Fall of the Roman Empire* (published in the late eighteenth century), for instance, you will see paragraphs longer than the ones you are used to. In general, both paragraphs and sentences have gotten shorter over the last two hundred years. Newspapers and magazines, with their narrow-column formats, are partially responsible for this shift in paragraph length, for they have accustomed readers to short lines and paragraphs. Though paragraph length must be determined to some degree by content, writers must also keep the expectations of readers firmly in mind.

Saying that the average paragraph has so many words or sentences is like saying the average family has 2.3 members and owns 1.8 cars. The information is so general that it means very little. Paragraphs should be long enough to develop an idea, create any particular effect the writer wishes to achieve (such as suspense, humor, or enthusiasm), and advance the piece of writing it is a part of. Fulfilling these aims will sometimes call for short paragraphs, sometimes for long ones.

For example, in an argumentative essay you may want to put all your lines of argument or all the evidence for your claim into one long paragraph to create the impression of a solid, overwhelmingly convincing thesis. In a narrative about an exciting event, on the other hand, a series of short paragraphs may help to create suspense, as the reader keeps reaching the end of a paragraph and rushing to the following one to find out what happened next. An important point to remember is that a new paragraph signals a pause or a break in thought for the reader. Just as timing can make a crucial difference in telling a joke, or a dramatic pause in telling a piece of news or gossip, so the pause signaled by a paragraph can raise readers' anticipation for what is to follow or give them a moment to "digest" mentally the material presented in the previous paragraph.

Notice how the following passage, the last three paragraphs of an essay on women and science, uses a very short paragraph as well as a fairly long one.

> Science is undeniably hard. Often, it can seem quite boring. It is unfortunately too often presented as laws to be memorized instead of

123

USEFUL READING

Christensen, Francis. "A Generative Rhetoric of the Paragraph." *CCC* 16 (Oct. 1965): 144–56. Exemplifies the view that paragraphs are determined by forces similar to those that determine sentences and explains the three principal kinds of paragraphs: coordinate, subordinate, and a mixture.

Larson, Richard. "Structure and Form in Non-Narrative Prose." *Ten Bibliographic Essays*. Ed. Gary Tate. Fort Worth: Texas Christian UP, 1987. 39–82. An exposition of his own paragraph theory as well as an overview of contemporary theory.

TEACHING PRACTICE

Modern stylist William Zinsser advises nonfiction writers to keep their paragraphs short. Visually, such paragraphs are more inviting because they have more white space around them. But he does not mean that all paragraphs should be the same short length.

Paragraph length should vary with purpose: long paragraphs often introduce a character, a setting, a situation, while short paragraphs add emphasis or move the reader through the text.

Ask your students to find a magazine article and a newspaper article that cover the same story. Newspaper articles are usually developed on the principle of the "inverted triangle"; thus, all of the important information (answers to the journalistic formula of "who? what? where? when? why? how?") comes at the very start of the story. Which medium has more consistent paragraph length? Is one story more in-depth? Does one have longer, more developed paragraphs, continue to introduce new information? Can your students account for the different styles and lengths of paragraphs?

OPTIONAL EXERCISE

Encourage your students to browse through their favorite nonacademic reading materials—newspapers, magazines, novels, nonfiction—looking for effective long and short paragraphs. They should bring their samples to class, either copies to be distributed or one copy to read aloud, and be prepared to explain the paragraphing conventions of this particular publication and of this particular author.

As a class, they'll want to answer the following questions:

1. What idea or topic does each paragraph develop?
2. What special effect(s) do they create, if any?
3. How do these effects move forward the main idea?

All writers tend to imitate the styles of their favorite authors, consciously and unconsciously. This exercise will heighten the students' awareness of paragraphing techniques—their own as well as their favorite authors'.

WRITERS WRITING

James Joyce produced a fourteen-page paragraph in *Ulysses*; John Barth ends *The End of the Road* with a one-word paragraph: "Terminal."

TEACHING PRACTICE

Ask your students to listen to "Ain't I a Woman?" (by Sojourner Truth [c. 1850]) and jot down the places they think Truth has broken or should break for paragraphs. Then discuss her paragraphing technique, noting especially the long second paragraph, which defines "woman," and the last one, which closes her talk.

Ain't I a Woman

Well, children where there is so much racket there must be something out of kilter. I think that 'twixt the negroes of the South and the women at the North, all talking about rights, the white men will be in a fix pretty soon. But what's all this here talking about?

That man over there says that women need to be helped into carriages, and lifted over ditches, and to have the best place everywhere. Nobody ever helps me into carriages, or over mud-puddles, or gives me any best place! Ain't I a woman? Look at me! Look at my arm! I have ploughed and planted, and gathered into barns, and no man could head me! And ain't I a woman? I could work as much and eat as much as a man—when I could get it—and bear the lash as well! And ain't I a woman? I have borne thirteen children, and seen them most all sold off to slavery, and when I cried out with my mother's grief, none but Jesus heard me! And ain't I a woman?

Then they talk about this thing in the head; what's this they call it? [Intellect, someone whispers.] That's it, honey. What's that got to do with women's rights or negro's rights? If my cup won't hold but a pint, and yours holds a quart, wouldn't you be mean not to let me have my little half-measure full?

Then that little man in black there, he says women can't have as much rights as men, 'cause Christ wasn't a woman! Where did your Christ come from? Where did your Christ come from? From God and a woman! Man had nothing to do with Him.

If the first woman God ever made was strong enough to turn the world upside down all alone, these women together ought to be able to turn it back, and get it right side up again! And now they is asking to do it, the men better let them.

Obliged to you for hearing me, and now old Sojourner ain't got nothing more to say.

mysteries to be explored. It is too often kept a secret that science, like art, takes a well developed esthetic sense. Women aren't the only ones who say, "I hate science." That's why everyone who goes into science needs a little help from friends. For the past ten years, I have been getting more than a little help from a friend who is a physicist. But my stepdaughter—who earned the highest grades ever recorded in her California high school on the math Scholastic Aptitude Test—flunked calculus in her first year at Harvard. When my friend the physicist heard about it, he said, "Harvard should be ashamed of itself." What he meant was that she needed that little extra encouragement that makes all the difference. Instead, she got that little extra discouragement that makes all the difference. "In the first place, all the math teachers are men," she explained. "In the second place, when I met a boy I liked and told him I was taking chemistry, he immediately said: 'Oh, you're one of those science types.' In the third place, it's just a kind of social thing. The math clubs are full of boys and you don't feel comfortable joining."

In other words, she was made to feel unnecessary, and out of place.

A few months ago, I accompanied a male colleague from the science museum where I sometimes work to a lunch of the history of science faculty at the University of California. I was the only woman there, and my presence for the most part was obviously and rudely ignored. I was so surprised and hurt by this that I made an extra effort to speak knowledgeably and well. At the end of the lunch, one of the professors turned to me in all seriousness and said: "Well, K. C., what do the women think of Carl Sagan?" I replied that I had no idea what "the women" thought about anything. But now I know what I should have said: I should have told him that his comment was unnecessary, injurious and out of place.   –K. C. COLE, "Women and Physics"

Cole uses the long paragraph to build up our frustrations as we learn about why science is so "hard" for her stepdaughter. The short, one-sentence paragraph then emphasizes the point made by the long paragraph, how out of place the stepdaughter was made to feel. With the final paragraph, the author turns the tables, ending with the assertion that it is really the male comment that is "out of place." As this example illustrates, paragraph length should be determined by the author's purpose, not by a set of hard and fast rules.

EXERCISE 5.18

The following passage introduces an essay describing an interview, and its author has chosen to write a series of very brief paragraphs. Read the passage carefully, considering the paragraph lengths and the effects they create. Then reparagraph the passage, making sure each paragraph is long enough to develop one main idea. Finally, explain your reasons for your changes.

An interview I found very interesting was one with a receptionist, Sharon A. Her job reveals quite a bit about herself and possibly others in her profession.

Sharon A. has developed a negative view of working with people. She does not enjoy her receptionist's job, but a college degree in art history did not seem to get her any further in the working world.

She first reveals that people have no respect for those in her field, especially those who are women. Receptionists are stereotyped as beautiful but dumb. It is not that Sharon does not have any bright ideas, but that others consider her function itself to have little meaning or importance.

Sharon's job deals mainly with the telephone, so the people she talks with at work, whom she cannot see, seem almost nonexistent to her. As a result, her conversations have become very abrupt.

This abruptness has carried over into her personal life, she reveals. Even if she sees the people with whom she is speaking, the conversations are brief. The constant threat of interruption also carries over from her professional to her personal life.

At work, the telephone must be answered the minute it rings, no matter what she is doing. She says this requirement makes her feel like a machine. Sharon seems to have become a little withdrawn, dreaming of a land with no phones, no interruptions.

EXERCISE 5.19

The following passage introduces an essay in which a student attempts to assess the "American dream" after reading an essay by Joan Didion, "Some Dreamers of the Golden Dream." The student uses a very long paragraph for her opening. Read this long paragraph, and decide whether or not it should be broken up into two or more paragraphs and where any new paragraphs should begin. Then explain your reasons for any changes you make and what effects are created by the new paragraphing.

When I think of the "American dream," I visualize a white and blue two-story Colonial house, complete with a two-car garage, white picket fence, happily married husband and wife, two children (one boy, one girl), a dog, and family vacations across the state in the Ford station wagon. I'm not really sure where I received my information on this subject; I have just learned through the years that this is the type of life I should strive for and look forward to. The traditional "American dream" is apparently changing, though. The white and blue two-story house is now a three-story mansion embedded in the cliffs of Malibu overlooking the Pacific Ocean; the happily married husband and wife have usually known the same happiness in three prior marriages; the

TEACHING PRACTICE

The rather cryptic passage in Exercise 5.18 about the office ladder could be much improved by specific details that elaborate or develop any of the several ideas introduced: office ladder, poor working environment, competition.

Ask your students to work either individually or in groups to focus and expand the information in these paragraphs, revising them completely. They will want to share their revisions and identify their topic sentences.

WRITERS ON WRITING

Too much noise deafens us; too much light dazzles us; too much distance or too much proximity impedes vision; too much length or too much brevity of discourse obscures it.

—BLAISE PASCAL

Then said I, Lord, how long?

—ISAIAH 6:11

OPTIONAL EXERCISE

Listen to the following paragraph, the first in "University Days" by James Thurber. (Listening is good practice for visualizing details and for holding information.) What is the "hook" of this paragraph? What are the supporting details? What is the closure?

I passed all the other courses that I took at my university, but I could never pass botany. This was because all botany students had to spend several hours a week in a laboratory looking through a microscope, and I could never see through a microscope. I never once saw a cell through a microscope. This used to enrage my instructor. He would wander around the laboratory pleased with the progress all the students were making in drawing the involved and, so I am told, interesting structure of flower cells, until he came to me. I would just be standing there. "I can't see anything," I would say. He would begin patiently enough, explaining how anybody can see through a microscope, but he would always end up in a fury, claiming that I could *too* see through a microscope but just pretended that I couldn't. "It takes away from the beauty of flowers anyway," I used to tell him. "We are not concerned with beauty in this course," he would say. "We are concerned solely with what I may call the *me-*

family vacations are now two weeks in Hawaii with the Mercedes station wagon waiting for them in the Los Angeles airport parking lot. This new and extreme version of the fairy tale is rapidly becoming everyone's new goal, according to Joan Didion's essay "Some Dreamers of the Golden Dream." Didion speaks of Southern California and states that people have derived their new ideal from newspapers and movies, not from reality. I find this statement very true to life, for most people do receive the majority of their ideas about how they should live from newspapers and movies. Therefore, if the movies present an image of gorgeous beachside mansions and expensive imported cars, then that is exactly what most people will strive for. This type of life style may not be right for every individual, though, and many people realize this fact too late. They spend their lives working and striving to become successful in society's eyes. Then, once they have reached their goal, they realize they are not truly happy, for they gained wealth and status for all the wrong reasons.

EXERCISE 5.20

Go through some of your favorite books, looking for two paragraphs—a very long one and a very short one—that impress you as particularly effective. What main idea does each develop? What effects does each create? How does each advance the piece of writing it is a part of?

EXERCISE 5.21

Examine the paragraph breaks in an essay you have written recently. Explain briefly in writing why you decided on each of the breaks. Would you change any of them now? If so, how and why?

▌ 5e. Composing special-purpose paragraphs

In addition to those that make up the main body of an essay, some paragraphs serve more specialized functions. These include opening paragraphs, concluding paragraphs, transitional paragraphs, and dialogue paragraphs.

▌ 1. Introducing an essay

Even a good essay may remain unread if it has a weak opening paragraph. In addition to announcing your topic (usually in a thesis statement), therefore, an introductory paragraph must engage the readers' interest and focus their attention on what is to come next. At their best, introductory paragraphs function as hors d'oeuvres, whetting the

COMPOSING SPECIAL-PURPOSE PARAGRAPHS

appetite for following courses, or as the title sequences in a film, carefully setting the scene and establishing themes the movie will explore. Because of the introduction's importance, writers often leave the *final* drafting of it until last, realizing that the focus of the introduction may change over the process of writing.

The most common kind of opening paragraph follows a general-to-specific pattern, ending with the thesis. In such an introduction, the writer opens with a general statement and then gets more and more specific, concluding with the most specific sentence in the paragraph—the thesis. The following paragraph illustrates such an opening:

> The United States has seen many changes in its **GENERAL** economy during the last hundred years. Among these **STATEMENT** changes is the organization of workers. Unions were **MOVE** formed in the late nineteenth and early twentieth cen- **TO** turies to battle against long work hours and bad working **SPECIFICITY** conditions. It was not uncommon then for a worker to be required to work twelve or more hours a day, six days a week, in hazardous and often deadly conditions. The workers organized against their employers and won their battles. Today, it is very uncommon to find such oppressive conditions in the workplace. Why, then, do unions still exist today? When we examine many of the labor **THESIS** battles of recent years, we find that unions exist mostly as bargaining units through which workers can gain higher wages—at any cost.

In this paragraph, the opening sentence introduces a general subject, changes in the U.S. economy; subsequent sentences focus more specifically on unionization; and the last sentence presents the thesis, which the rest of the essay will develop. Other ways of opening an essay include quotations, anecdotes, questions, or strong opinions.

Opening with a quotation

"Go back to hell where you came from, you old wart hog," says Mary Grace, an unattractive girl from a Massachusetts college, to Mrs. Ruby Turpin, a hypocritical Southern woman, in Flannery O'Connor's "Revelation." Mary Grace's words sting poor Mrs. Turpin, who is not used to taking criticism from anyone. Mary Grace's message is that Mrs. Turpin is not better than the people she thinks badly of, and her attack causes Mrs. Turpin to stop and scowl, in a moment of uncharacteristic self-doubt.

chanics of flars." "Well," I'd say, "I can't see anything." "Try it just once again," he'd say, and I would put my eye to the microscope and see nothing at all, except now and again a nebulous milky substance—a phenomenon of maladjustment. You were supposed to see a vivid, restless clockwork of sharply defined plant cells. "I see what looks like a lot of milk," I would tell him. This, he claimed, was the result of my not having adjusted the microscope properly, so he would readjust it for me, or rather, for himself. And I would look again and see milk.

WRITERS ON WRITING

Of a good beginning cometh a good end.
—JOHN HEYWOOD

What gets my interest is the sense that a writer is speaking honestly and fully of what he knows well.
—WENDELL BERRY

It is in the hard, hard rock-pile of seeking to win, hold, or deserve a reader's interest that the pleasant agony of writing comes in.
—JOHN MASON BROWN

TEACHING PRACTICE

As discussed in Chapter 2, lead "hooks" draw readers in and then quickly announce what they can expect from the essay. Ask your students to look for the "hook" of every selection in their anthology.

Opening with an anecdote

Imagine awakening to a thunderous roar that sounds like a herd of elephants and banshees, accompanied by an upheaval of your bed that dumps you on the floor. At first you think, "Earthquake!" Then, as you open your eyes and focus on two of the shiniest black boots you have ever seen, you remember where you are. You're in the Army now.

Opening with a question

Why is the American population terrified of turning to nuclear power as a future source of energy? People are misinformed, or not informed at all, about its benefits and safety. If Americans would take time to learn about what nuclear power offers, then their apprehension and fear might be transformed into hope.

Opening with a strong opinion

Exploitation in America is as common as the common cold. Since its beginning, this nation has thrived on economic exploitation, and the problem became especially widespread during the period from 1900 to 1920. During this time many children, as well as adults, were forced to work fourteen to fifteen hours a day for pennies. It did not take long for people to realize they were being exploited, but there was little they could do about it. Some people went on strike, but they accomplished little. Besides being taken advantage of economically, many people were also socially and sexually exploited. Both John Dos Passos's *Nineteen Nineteen* and E. L. Doctorow's *Ragtime* deal with people during this period exploiting one another economically, socially, and sexually. However, Dos Passos's treatment of this theme is pessimistic, while Doctorow's is optimistic.

EXERCISE 5.22

Refer once more to the argument you drafted in Exercise 4.14. Examine your introduction carefully, and then write an alternate introduction. Finally, write a paragraph evaluating which introduction is most effective and why.

2. Concluding an essay

A good conclusion wraps up an essay in a meaningful and memorable way. If a strong opening paragraph whets readers' appetite or arouses their curiosity, a strong concluding paragraph satisfies them that the job the essay set out to do is indeed completed, that their expectations have been met. In doing so, a strong conclusion reminds

OPTIONAL EXERCISE

Using the campus newspaper, find the lead and concluding paragraphs for several news stories. Discuss the effectiveness of each. Of special interest might be comparing the same story in both the local and campus newspaper.

COMPOSING SPECIAL-PURPOSE PARAGRAPHS

readers of the gist of the essay and leaves them feeling that they know a good deal more than when they began.

One of the most common strategies for concluding an essay makes use of the specific-to-general pattern, often beginning with a restatement of the thesis, and moving to several more general statements, almost in a reverse of the general-to-specific opening. The concluding paragraph of Bruce Catton's essay on Grant and Lee moves in such a way, opening with a final point of contrast, specifying it in several sentences, and then ending with a much more general statement:

> Lastly, and perhaps greatest of all, there was the ability, at the end, to turn quickly from war to peace once the fighting was over. Out of the way these two men behaved at Appomattox came the possibility of a peace of reconciliation. It was a possibility not wholly realized, in the years to come, but which did, in the end, help the two sections to become one nation again . . . after a war whose bitterness might have seemed to make such a reunion wholly impossible. No part of either man's life became him more than the part he played in this brief meeting in the McLean house at Appomattox. Their behavior there put all succeeding generations of Americans in their debt. Two great Americans, Grant and Lee—very different, yet under everything very much alike. Their encounter at Appomattox was one of the great moments of American history.
>
> –BRUCE CATTON, "Grant and Lee: A Study in Contrasts"

Other effective strategies for concluding an essay include questions, quotations, vivid images, calls for action, or warnings.

Concluding with a question

> All so-called "permanent" antifreeze is basically the same. It is made from a liquid known as ethylene glycol, which has two amazing properties: It has a lower freezing point than water, and a higher boiling point than water. It does not break down (lose its properties), nor will it boil away. And every permanent antifreeze starts with it as a base. Also, just about every antifreeze has now got antileak ingredients, as well as antirust and anticorrosion ingredients. Now, let's suppose that, in formulating the product, one of the companies comes up with a solution that is pink in color, as opposed to all the others, which are blue. Presto—an exclusivity claim. "Nothing else looks like it, nothing else performs like it." Or how about, "Look at ours, and look at anyone else's. You can see the difference our exclusive formula makes." Granted, I'm exaggerating. But did I prove a point?
>
> –PAUL STEVENS, "Weasel Words: God's Little Helpers"

WRITERS ON WRITING

Hold every moment sacred. Give each clarity and meaning, each the weight of thine awareness, each its true and due fulfillment.

—THOMAS MANN

Reading maketh a full man, conference a ready man, and writing an exact man.

—FRANCIS BACON

Concluding with a quotation

Despite the celebrity that accrued to her and the air of awesomeness with which she was surrounded in her later years, Miss Keller retained an unaffected personality, certain that her optimistic attitude toward life was justified. "I believe that all through these dark and silent years God has been using my life for a purpose I do not know," she said. "But one day I shall understand and then I will be satisfied."

—ALDEN WHITMAN, "Helen Keller: June 27, 1880–June 1, 1968"

Concluding with a vivid image

It is, in any case, finally you that I end up having to trust not to laugh, not to snicker. Even as you regard me in these lines, I try to imagine your face as you read. You who read "Aria," especially those of you with your theme-divining yellow felt pen poised in your hand, you for whom this essay is yet another "assignment," please do not forget that it is my life I am handing you in these pages—memories that are as personal for me as family photographs in an old cigar box.

—RICHARD RODRIGUEZ,
from a postscript to "Aria"

Concluding with a strong call for action

It is now almost 40 years since the invention of nuclear weapons. We have not yet experienced a global thermonuclear war—although on more than one occasion we have come tremulously close. I do not think our luck can hold forever. Men and machines are fallible, as recent events remind us. Fools and madmen do exist, and sometimes rise to power. Concentrating always on the near future, we have ignored the long-term consequences of our actions. We have placed our civilization and our species in jeopardy.

Fortunately, it is not yet too late. We can safeguard the planetary civilization and the human family if we so choose. There is no more important or more urgent issue. —CARL SAGAN, "The Nuclear Winter"

Concluding with a warning

Because propaganda is so effective, it is important to track it down and understand how it is used. We may eventually agree with what the propagandist says because all propaganda isn't necessarily bad; some advertising, for instance, urges us not to drive drunk, to have regular dental checkups, to contribute to the United Way. Even so, we must be aware that propaganda is being used. Otherwise, we will have consented to handing over our independence, our decision-making ability, and our brains.

—ANN McCLINTOCK, "Propaganda Techniques in Today's Advertising"

COMPOSING SPECIAL-PURPOSE PARAGRAPHS

The concluding paragraph provides the last opportunity for you to impress the message of an essay on your readers' minds and to create effects you desire. As such, it is well worth your time and effort.

EXERCISE 5.23

Choose an essay you have recently written, and examine the conclusion carefully. Then write at least one new conclusion for the essay, striving for the maximum effect on readers. Finally, describe and evaluate the techniques you used in your revision.

3. Using transitional paragraphs

On some occasions, you may need to call your readers' attention very powerfully to a major transition between ideas. To do so, consider using an entire short paragraph to signal that transition, as in the following example from an essay on "television addiction." The opening paragraphs of the essay characterize addiction in general, concluding with the paragraph about its destructive elements. The one-sentence paragraph that follows arrests our attention, announcing that these general characteristics will now be related to television viewing.

> Finally a serious addiction is distinguished from a harmless pursuit of pleasure by its distinctly destructive elements. A heroin addict, for instance, leads a damaged life: his increasing need for heroin in increasing doses prevents him from working, from maintaining relationships, from developing in human ways. Similarly an alcoholic's life is narrowed and dehumanized by his dependence on alcohol.
>
> Let us consider television viewing in the light of the conditions that define serious addictions. —MARIE WINN,
> *The Plug-in Drug: Television, Children, and the Family*

4. Using paragraphs to signal dialogue

Paragraphs of dialogue can bring added life to almost any sort of writing. The traditional way to set up dialogue in written form is simple: simply start a new paragraph each time the speaker changes, no matter how short each bit of conversation is. Here is an example:

> "Hey Clobberfoot, I bet you can't still ski all the way around the lake!" Chris shouted as I pushed across the overgrown lawn toward her.
> "Are you kidding?" I retorted cheerfully.
> "I'm willing to stake a banana split on it!" Chris added.

"You're on, you fool," I said, taking one last look over my shoulder. As we turned and headed down to the outlying boathouse, I heard a familiar seagull give me a squawk of encouragement as he flew by.

EXERCISE 5.24

Go through some of your favorite books, articles, or essays to find an opening or concluding paragraph that you consider particularly effective. Try to analyze what makes the paragraph so effective. Then, choosing a topic of great interest to you, try to write an opening or concluding paragraph imitating the paragraph you admire—the structure of its sentences, the pattern of its development, its use of particular devices such as quotations, questions, and so on. Then compare the two paragraphs, and decide how effective your own is.

5f. Linking paragraphs

The same methods that can be used to link sentences and create coherent paragraphs can be used to link paragraphs themselves together so that an essay as a whole flows smoothly and coherently. Some reference to the previous paragraph, either explicitly stated or merely implied, should occur in each paragraph after the introduction of an essay. As in linking sentences, you can create this reference by repeating or paraphrasing key words and terms and by using parallel structures, pronouns, and transitional expressions.

Repeating key words

. . . Thus, I learned that stealing and jealousy are wrong in my culture. Until I began to distinguish *acceptable* from unacceptable *behavior*, constant tension existed between my parents and me.

After I had learned *acceptable behavior*, the second step in my process of maturity was to balance my desires with my conscience in order to become a well-adjusted, acculturated individual. . . .

Using parallel structure

. . . Kennedy made an effort to assure non-Catholics that he would respect the separation of church and state, and most of them did not seem to hold his religion against him in deciding how to vote. Since his election, *the church to which a candidate belongs* has become less important in presidential politics.

The region from which a candidate comes remains an important factor. . . .

Using pronouns

Singer's tale is of a pathetic Polish Jew, Gimpel, who because of *his* strong faith believes everything *he* is told. At the beginning of the tale, we learn that Gimpel has had a gruesomely cruel life. *He* is an orphan, and all *his* life *he* has been teased and tormented for believing everything *he* hears.

Even the most ridiculous and far-fetched tales take *him* in. For example, when *he* is told that the messiah has come and *his* parents have risen from the dead, *he* goes out to search for *them*! In *his* seemingly foolish search, *he* is berated by the townsfolk.

Using other transitional devices

. . . While the Indian, in the character of Tonto, was more positively portrayed in "The Lone Ranger," such a portrayal was more the exception than the norm.

Moreover, despite this brief glimpse of an Indian as an ever-loyal sidekick, Tonto was never accorded the same stature as the man with the white horse and silver bullets. . . .

EXERCISE 5.25

Look at the essay you drafted in Exercise 2.11 or the argument you drafted in Exercise 4.14, and identify the ways your paragraphs are linked together. Identify each use of repetition, parallel structures, pronouns, and transitional expressions, and then evaluate how effectively you have joined paragraphs.

▌ 5g. Checking paragraphs

Here is a checklist you can use to evaluate—and to improve—your paragraphing:

1. What is the topic sentence of each paragraph, and is it stated or implied? Where in the paragraph does it fall? Should it come at some other point? Would any paragraph be improved by deleting or adding a topic sentence?

2. Which sentences, if any, do not relate in some way to the topic sentence? Is there any way to justify their inclusion?

3. What is the most general sentence in each paragraph? If not the topic sentence, should it remain or be omitted?

4. Is each paragraph organized in a way that is easy for readers to follow? By what means are sentences linked in each paragraph? Do any more

links need to be added? Do any of the transitional expressions try to create links that do not really exist between ideas?

5. How completely does each paragraph develop its topic sentence? What methods of development are used, and are they effective? What other methods might be used? Does the paragraph need more material?

6. How long is each paragraph? Are paragraphs varied in length? Does any paragraph seem too long or too short? Is there anything that might be given strong emphasis by a one-sentence paragraph?

7. By what means are the paragraphs linked together? Do any more links need to be added? Do any of the transitional expressions try to create links that do not really exist between ideas?

8. How does the introductory paragraph catch the interest of readers? How exactly does it open—with a quotation? an anecdote? a question? a strong statement? How else might it open?

9. How does the last paragraph draw the essay to a conclusion? What lasting impression will it leave with readers? How exactly does it close—with a question? a quotation? a vivid image? a warning or call for action? How else might this essay conclude?

READING WITH AN EYE FOR PARAGRAPHS

Think of a writer you admire, and read something she or he has written. Find one or two paragraphs that impress you in some way, and analyze them using the above questions. Try to decide what makes them effective as paragraphs.

FOR EXAMINING YOUR OWN PARAGRAPHS

Examine one or two paragraphs you have written, using the questions in 5g to evaluate their unity, coherence, and development. Identify the topic of each paragraph, the topic sentence (if one is explicitly stated), any methods of development, and any means used to create coherence. Decide whether or not each paragraph is successful as a paragraph, and explain your reasons. Finally, choose one paragraph and revise it.

PART TWO

Sentences: Making Grammatical Choices

6. Constructing Grammatical Sentences

When you hear the word *grammar*, the main subject of this chapter, you may think of any number of definitions: a way words are arranged into meaningful patterns ("Every language has a *grammar*"), the formal study of such patterns ("She is a well-known *grammarian*"); or a kind of linguistic good manners ("Oops—I'd better watch my *grammar!*"). In this chapter you will be concentrating on understanding the first of these definitions—grammar as the patterns into which words can be arranged to convey meanings.

Outside of school, you may not have thought very much about grammar. Indeed, you may agree in principle with the fifteenth-century Holy Roman Emperor Sigismund, who answered a question about his Latin grammar by saying, "I am the Roman emperor and am above grammar." In one sense, all native speakers of a language are, like Sigismund, "above" grammar. All speakers, that is, learn the grammar of their language naturally as they learn to speak. This intuitive grasp of grammar allows us to say, "The bright red cardinal surprised me," rather than "Cardinal bright the surprised me red"—without even thinking about it. This ability to make meaningful sentences comes, in fact, very early to each of us and accounts for the fact that young children often produce sophisticated sentences out of the blue, without having to study or "learn" a system by which to produce them.

But in another sense, none of us, including an emperor, is above grammar. As the sample sentence about the cardinal indicates, we are bound by certain patterns or "rules" in producing sentences. And breaking those "rules" moves a speaker from sense to nonsense, from being easily understood to being completely misunderstood.

137

USEFUL READING

Aitchison, Jean. *Language Change: Progress or Decay?* Suffolk, England: Fontana, 1981. See chapter one, "The Ever-Changing Wheel," 26–31.

Bartholomae, David. "The Study of Error." *CCC* 31 (October 1980): 253–69. He argues that learning formal written discourse amounts to learning a second language, and so English-as-a-Second-Language (ESL) techniques apply.

(BACK)GROUNDING

Although closely related, rhetoric and grammar have always maintained themselves as separate disciplines. Rhetoric, nearly as old as Greek culture itself, formed the basis of the *trivium*, the Greek educational system that also included grammar and dialectic (philosophical logic). For some 1700 years, from late antiquity to the Middle Ages, the *trivium* remained the centerpiece of education, keeping grammar allied with rhetoric. But today, grammar is more closely connected with other fields of language study—with linguistics, composition studies, speech communication, and stylistics—that make constant reference to grammatical terms. The relationship of grammar to composition studies has always been controversial: how to teach grammar in writing courses—indeed, whether to teach it at all—remains a topic much disputed. Few teachers have been brave enough to dispense entirely with instruction in grammar; most of us teach it without any conclusive evidence that teaching grammar in any way improves the writing of our students. In his impressive meta-analysis, *Research on Written Composition* (Urbana, IL: NCTE, 1986), George Hillocks reports that "[n]one of the studies reviewed . . . provides any support for teaching grammar as a means of improving composition skills" (138). In "The Uses—and Limits—of Grammar," Sara D'Eloia writes that

> the study of grammar has been shown to have rather negligible effects upon student writing. The results with traditional grammar are uniformly discouraging. . . . Wherever it has been seriously researched, the analytical study of grammar has failed to produce significant results in student writing across the board—whether the result sought was improvement in the control of errors, increased sentence length, or increased variety of sentence structure. . . . If there is one conclusion to be drawn which cuts across all the studies, it is this: the more time spent analyzing grammar as grammar, the less time spent writing; the less time spent writing, the less improvement in the written product.

Yet we continue to teach our students about grammar, perhaps because we feel that to be the most effective writers, they need to learn certain grammatical conventions. As William Irmscher writes, "The relation of grammar and writing is one of the enduring controversies of English studies. . . ." *Teaching Expository Writing* (New York: Holt, 1979. 16).

(BACK)GROUNDING

When students face grammar lessons, they often feel that their language has become suddenly foreign—that they don't know any grammar. Oh, but they do. They completely mastered the grammar of their native tongue long ago. They may be comforted to know that there is a difference between what they know about their language—their *competence*—and how they use their language—their linguistic *performance*. Unlike certain "speaking" animals, which can only imitate what they have heard before, your students know the rules for combining the elements of their native language—words, ideas, and sentences—and have the *competence* to say things that have never been said before and to create purposeful and meaningful discourse. If one of your students says, "Yesterday, I seen a horrible fight," you know exactly what she means. Her *competence* is perfect, though her *performance*—by the standards of Edited American English—may not be. She makes sense. But if she says, "A yesterday saw fight I horrible," you cannot understand her. The words themselves are correct, but not the grammar. Your student will be able to tell you that the second string of words is ungrammatical and that it doesn't make sense. Her *competence* with her language, her knowledge of grammar, gives her this ability. However, it is a matter of *performance* when she produces an "ungrammatical" sentence such as "Yesterday, I seen that we was almost out of gas."

Much of what we know about language—its grammar—is unconscious knowledge, and much of what we know about how the English language works, we know before we ever start school. Thus, when we teach grammatical conventions, we might want to keep in mind the following distinction: (1) *competence*—both our innate knowledge of grammar, enabling us to communicate and our learned awareness, enabling us to explain why certain sentences are unacceptable; *performance*—our production of both grammatical and "ungrammatical" utterances. When students understand these different grammars, they may become more tolerant of writing conventions and correctness, conventions that to them often seem artificial while their acceptance of them must be absolute.

If we learn the basic grammar of language as we learn to speak, then why bother to study it? In the first place, though all speakers know the *basic* grammatical "rules," these rules can generate a very broad range of sentences, some of which will be much more skillful and effective than others. As someone who uses written language, you want not simply to write, but to write skillfully and effectively, and understanding grammatical structures can help you do so.

Furthermore, within the basic "rules" of English grammar, wide latitude exists. Not everyone, for instance, grows up speaking with precisely the same set of grammatical principles. Knowledge of the differences can help you produce sentences that are not only grammatical but appropriate to a particular situation. The "rules" that allow you to say "Hey, man, this be one *fine* set of wheels" in one situation, for example, are not quite the same as those that lead you to say "Yes, sir, this car is completely acceptable" in another. If you understand grammar, you will not only understand both statements but know when and why to use one and when the other. Finally, because language is so closely related to thought, studying our language patterns, our grammar, can give us insight into our own ways of thinking. If in some important sense we *are* what we say (and write), then examining the principles through which we express our meanings can help us understand ourselves as well as others.

This chapter takes a look at what makes our language tick—those elements that allow us to produce meaningful sentences.

6a. Understanding the basic grammar of sentences

Put most simply, a **sentence** is a grammatically complete group of words that expresses a thought. To be grammatically complete, a group of words must contain two major structural components—a subject and a predicate. The **subject** identifies what the sentence is about, and the **predicate** asserts or asks something about the subject, or it tells the subject to do something.

SUBJECT	PREDICATE
We	shall overcome.
I	could have danced all night.
Life	is just a bowl of cherries.
(You)	Whistle a happy tune.
The rain in Spain	stays mainly on the plain.
Puff, the magic dragon,	lived by the sea.

USEFUL READING

Baugh, Albert C., and Thomas Cable. A *History of the English Language.* 3d ed. Englewood Cliffs: Prentice, 1978. A highly readable history of our language.

D'Eloia, Sarah. "The Uses—and Limits—of Grammar." *Journal of Basic Writing* 1 (Sp/Su 1977): 1–20. Rpt. in *A Sourcebook for Writing Teachers.* Eds. Gary Tate and Edward P. J. Corbett. New York: Oxford UP, 1981. 225–43. In addition to her insights into the relationship of grammar and writing, the author offers excellent classroom pedagogy.

RECOGNIZING THE PARTS OF SPEECH

Some very brief sentences have one-word subjects and predicates (for example, *Time passes*) or even a one-word predicate with an implied or "understood" subject (for example, *Stop!*). Most sentences, however, contain additional words that expand the basic subject and predicate. In the last of the examples above, for instance, the subject might have been simply *Puff*; the words *the magic dragon* merely say more about the subject. Similarly, the predicate of that sentence could grammatically be *lived*; the words *by the sea* expand the predicate by telling us where Puff lived. No matter how many words a sentence contains, however, it can always be divided into two basic parts—a subject and a predicate.

EXERCISE 6.1

The following sentences are taken from "A Hanging," an essay by George Orwell. Identify the subject and predicate in each sentence, underlining the subject once and the predicate twice.

Example
One prisoner had been brought out of his cell.

1. We set out for the gallows.
2. He was an army doctor, with a gray toothbrush moustache and a gruff voice.
3. The rest of us, magistrates and the like, followed behind.
4. The dog answered the sound with a whine.
5. The hangman, a gray-haired convict in the white uniform of the prison, was waiting beside his machine.

6b. Recognizing the parts of speech

If the basic parts of sentences are subjects and predicates, the central elements of subjects and predicates are nouns and verbs. For example:

┌─SUBJECT─┐ ┌─PREDICATE─┐
  NOUN   VERB
The little train rumbled over the tracks.*

Nouns and verbs are two of the eight **parts of speech**, one set of grammatical categories into which words may be classified. The other six parts of speech are pronouns, adjectives, adverbs, prepositions, con-

---

* From *The Little Engine That Could*, by Watty Piper, Platt & Munk (NY: Putnam, 1984).

USEFUL READING

Epes, Mary. "Tracing Errors to their Sources: A Study of the Encoding Processes of Adult Basic Writers." *Journal of Basic Writing* 4 (Sp 1985): 4–33. Epes makes a cogent argument for grammatical instruction that reflects Edited American English.

Finegan, Edward. *Attitudes Toward English Usage*. New York: Teachers College P, 1980. Charts the war between prescriptivists and descriptivists.

ANSWERS TO EXERCISE 6.1
1. *We* set out for the gallows.
2. *He* was an army doctor, with . . . a rough voice.
3. *The rest of us, magistrates and the like,* followed behind.
4. *The dog* answered the sound with a whine.
5. *The hangman, a gray-haired convict in the white uniform of the prison,* was waiting beside his machine.

TEACHING PRACTICE
Share the following poem with your students and ask them to identify the subject and predicate of each line and of the last two lines:

We'll begin with a box and the plural is boxes.
But the plural of ox should be oxen, not oxes.
The one fowl is a goose but two are called geese,
Yet the plural of moose should never be meese.
You may find a lone mouse or a whole set of mice,
Yet the plural of house is houses not hice.
If the plural of man is always called men,
Why shouldn't the plural of pan be called pen?
If I speak of a foot and you show me your feet,
And I give you a boot, would a pair be called beet?
If one is a tooth and whole set are teeth,
Why should not the plural of booth be called beeth?
Then one may be that, and three would be those,
Yet hat in the plural wouldn't be hose.
And the plural of cat is cats and not cose.
We speak of a brother and also of brethren,
But though we say Mother, we never say Methren.
Then the masculine pronouns are he, his, and him,
But imagine the feminine she, shis, and shim.
So English, I fancy, you all will agree,
Is the funniest language you ever did see.

Clear in the above poem are some of the inconsistencies of the English language, inconsistencies of plurality that have grown out of our long and colorful language history. Just as fashions inevitably change—more drastically and rapidly in some areas than others, over time, and because of foreign influence—so inevitably does English. Perhaps the most profound ramification of language change is the belief that in one region is spoken the standard language, while all the others use nonstandard.

Our society has agreed that one version of English—the version found in most printed materials and spoken in most public arenas—can be considered Edited American English, which is not quite the same as referring to it as the standard dialect.

(BACK)GROUNDING
Perhaps an outgrowth of Renaissance attitudes toward the use of "correct" or Ciceronian Latin, prescriptive attitudes toward English grammar devel-

oped in the eighteenth century and have dominated language study ever since. Prescriptive grammar holds that there are inherently correct and incorrect grammatical forms, while descriptive grammar holds that no language or variety of language (dialect) is superior to any other in a *linguistic* sense. For the descriptivist, no grammar is to be preferred except for *nonlinguistic* reasons.

In *Grammar and Good Taste: Reforming the American Language* (New Haven: Yale UP, 1982), Dennis E. Baron posits that the association of grammatical correctness with moral virtue and social prestige in the U.S. grew out of patriotic attempts during the post-Revolutionary period to distinguish American English from British English. He goes on to note that this association of grammar and morality fostered the anxiety over grammatical correctness that the public feels even today.

(BACK)GROUNDING

Perhaps the first Greek grammarian, Plato debated the theory of natural logic between thought and reality and the origin of language (*Cratylus*, 385 B.C.). He also examined the notions of truth and falsehood, asking whether grammatical structure can convey those notions. For example, the following sentences are perfectly grammatical—and false:

* The Ohio State University is moving its main campus to Brunswick, Maine.
* Ronald Reagan was once married to Bette Midler.
* Our male dog gave birth to kittens last night.

Although Plato concluded that judgments about grammatical correctness and truth should be made separate, the connection between correctness and morality has remained. Plato's most important contribution to grammar, however, was to develop sentence division into nominal and verbal components—*onoma* and *rheme*—which remained the primary grammatical distinction underlying syntactic analysis and word classification in all future linguistic description. Since Plato's time, all grammatical approaches divide sentences into two parts—subject and verb. Plato, then, invented the noun and the verb.

TEACHING PRACTICE

Discuss with your students the various native and second languages they speak and then talk with them about dialects. Dialects are often characterized by their deviation from the edited language or standard dialect in terms of accent, intonation, word choice, and meaning. In English, the choice of first-person singular pronoun often reflects a person's dialect:

* Me and Richie will take the aardvark for a walk.
* Between you and I, Richie should not be permitted to take the aardvark out alone after dark.

junctions, and interjections. Many English words can function as more than one part of speech. Take the word *book*, for instance: when you *book a plane flight*, it is a verb; when you *take a good book to the beach*, it is a noun; and when you *have book knowledge*, it is an adjective.

The system of categorizing words by part of speech comes to English from Latin, where it was first set forth by the Roman grammarian Donatus in the fourth century A.D. The differences between Latin and English are many, of course, and the parts of speech system is in certain ways not as precise for English as it is for Latin. Many grammarians argue that students of English grammar should focus less on the parts of speech and more on the parts of a sentence. Even so, the parts of speech remain an important part of our grammatical vocabulary, and all dictionaries use them to label their entries. In this chapter we will see how the various parts of speech are used in sentences.

1. Recognizing verbs

The word *verb* comes from the Latin *verbum*, which simply means "word." As this history indicates, **verbs** are among the most important words, for they move the meaning of sentences along by showing action (*glance, jump*), occurrence (*become, happen*), or a state of being (*be, live*).

Verbs change form to show *time*, *person*, and *number*.

TIME	we *work*, we *worked*
PERSON	I *work*, she *works*
NUMBER	one person *works*, two people *work*

See 9a for a discussion of how verbs change form to show person and number. **Auxiliary verbs** (also known as **helping verbs**) combine with other verbs (often called **main verbs**) to create *verb phrases*. Auxiliaries include the forms of *be, do,* and *have,* which are also used as main verbs, and the words *can, could, may, might, must, shall, should, will,* and *would*.

I *must get* some sleep tonight!

You *can find* Professor Kinder during his office hours.

Chapter 8 provides a complete discussion of the forms and functions of verbs.

USEFUL READING

Hartwell, Patrick. "Grammar, Grammars, and the Teaching of Grammar." *CE* 47 (Feb. 1985): 105–27. Definitions and purposes of the various grammars.

Kolln, Martha. "Closing the Books on Alchemy." *CCC* 32 (1981): 139–51. While no direct relation exists between grammar instruction and *writing* improvement, there are other important reasons for studying grammar—to analyze, to build shared vocabulary and conceptual frameworks.

EXERCISE 6.2

Identify and underline the verbs in each of the following sentences.

> *Example*
> Charlie <u>should do</u> fine in Saturday's tennis match.

1. His future does look bright.
2. The ice cream ran all over the table and the floor.
3. Over the next few days, I tapped about seventy maple trees.
4. One person can collect sap, a second might run the evaporator, and a third should finish the syrup.
5. A trip to Florida would be great.
6. On a crisp morning in early spring, a man walked alone through the forest.
7. The deer population rose drastically in the early twentieth century, after the disappearance of the cougar and the wolf.
8. The bookcase will extend from floor to ceiling.
9. One Saturday morning my mother, an orthopedic surgeon, took my brother and me to the hospital.
10. The dormitory kitchen smelled like old fish.

2. Recognizing nouns

The word *noun* comes from the Latin *nomen*, which means "name." That is what **nouns** do: they name things. Nouns can name persons (*aviator, chef*), places (*lake, library*), things (*truck, suitcase*), or concepts (*happiness, balance*). **Proper nouns** name specific persons, places, things, or concepts: *Tom, Iowa, General Mills, Buddhism*. Proper nouns are capitalized. (See 33b for an explanation of which nouns are considered proper nouns.) **Collective nouns** name groups: *team, flock, navy*. (See 9d for more information about collective nouns.)

Most nouns can be changed from **singular** (one) to **plural** (more than one) by adding *-s* or *-es: horse, horses; box, boxes*. Some nouns, however, have irregular plural forms: *woman, women: alumnus, alumni; mouse, mice*. (See 22e for more information about forming plurals.) **Mass nouns** cannot be made plural because they name something that cannot easily be counted: *dust, peace, tranquility*.

Nouns can also take a **possessive** form to show ownership. You form the possessive by adding *-'s* to a singular noun and just an apostrophe to a plural noun: *the horse's owner, the boys' department*. (See 30a for more information about forming possessives.)

141

USEFUL READING

Newman, Edwin. *A Civil Tongue*. New York: Warner, 1975. One of many entertaining popularizations of prescriptive grammar and usage.

Pyles, Thomas, and John Algeo. *The Origins and Development of the English Language*. 3d ed. New York: Harcourt, 1982. More systematic and textbook-like than Baugh, with more emphasis on American English.

ANSWERS TO EXERCISE 6.2

1. does look
2. ran, ran over (two-word verb)
3. tapped
4. can collect; might run; should finish
5. would be
6. walked
7. rose
8. will extend
9. took
10. smelled

TEACHING PRACTICE

Read aloud the following passage from Toni Morrison's *The Bluest Eye*, asking your students to record every main verb:

> Nuns go by as quiet as lust, and drunken men and sober eyes sing in the lobby of the Greek hotel. Rosemary Villanucci, our next-door friend who lives above her father's cafe, sits in a 1939 Buick eating bread and butter. She rolls down the window to tell my sister Frieda and me that we can't come in. We stare at her, wanting her bread, but more than that wanting to poke the arrogance out of her eyes and smash the pride of ownership that curls her chewing mouth. When she comes out of the car we will beat her up, make red marks on her white skin and she will cry and ask us do we want her to pull her pants down. We will say no. We don't know what we should feel or do if she does, but whenever she asks us, we know she is offering us something precious and that our own pride must be asserted by refusing to accept.

TEACHING PRACTICE

A verb is the key to a sentence: the starting point for any translation, the pivot of action, the movement. We tend to emphasize verbs in our teaching because so few writers use them effectively, and those that do, produce lively, often powerful, prose. We usually begin to learn a language, however, by building up our repertoire of nouns—in much the way multiply handicapped Helen Keller rose to a new level of consciousness when she learned her first word—a noun—with the help of Annie Sullivan. Read aloud the following exerpt from *The Story of My Life* in which Keller relates that magical event:

> We walked down the path to the well-house, attracted by the fragrance of the honeysuckle with which it was covered. Someone was drawing water and my teacher placed my hand under the spout. As the cool stream gushed over one hand, she spelled into the other the word *water*, first slowly then rapidly. I stood still, my whole atten-

tion fixed upon the motion of her fingers. Suddenly I felt a misty consciousness as of something forgotten—a thrill of returning thought; and somehow the mystery of language was revealed to me. I knew then that "w-a-t-e-r" meant the wonderful cool something that was flowing over my hand. That living word awakened my soul, gave it light, hope, joy, set it free! . . . I left the wellhouse eager to learn. Everything had a name, and each name gave birth to a new thought. As we returned to the house every object which I touched seemed to quiver with life. That was because I saw everything with the strange, new sight that had come to me. . . . [M]other, *father, sister, teacher* were . . . words that were to make the world blossom for me. . . .

ANSWERS TO EXERCISE 6.3

1. n-Nightlife; n-Georgetown; a-the; n-sun
2. n-plagiarism
3. n-all; n-Christmas; n-teeth
4. n-story; a-a; n-tale; n-theft; n-violation
5. a-the; n-row; n-people; a-a; n-man; n-hair; a-a; n-woman; n-jeans

Nouns are often preceded by one of the **articles** *a, an,* or *the: a rocket, an astronaut, the launch.* Articles are also known as **noun markers** or **determiners.**

EXERCISE 6.3

Identify the nouns, including possessive forms, and the articles in each of the following sentences. Underline the nouns once and the articles twice.

Example

The Puritans' hopes were dashed when Charles II was restored to the throne.

1. Nightlife begins in Georgetown even before the sun goes down.
2. Although plagiarism is dishonest and illegal, it does occur.
3. All I want for Christmas is my two front teeth.
4. Henderson's story is a tale of theft and violation.
5. In the front row sat two people, a man with slightly graying hair and a young woman in jeans.

3. Recognizing pronouns

Pronouns function as nouns in sentences and often take the place of specific nouns, serving as short forms so that we do not have to repeat a noun that has already been mentioned. A specific noun that a pronoun replaces or refers to is called the **antecedent** of the pronoun. (See Chapters 9 and 11 for more about pronouns and antecedents.) In the following example, the antecedent of the pronoun *it* is *bus.*

The *bus* was already late, but *it* stopped for Charlotte.

You are already familiar with pronouns; we could scarcely speak or write without them. (The preceding sentence, for instance, includes the pronouns *you, we,* and *them.*) You may not, however, be familiar with all the categories of pronouns, which include the following:

Personal pronouns refer to specific persons or things.

PERSONAL   I, you, he, she, it, we, they
PRONOUNS

After the scouts made camp, *they* ran along the beach.

Each personal pronoun has several different forms (for example, *I, me, my, mine*) depending on how it functions in a sentence. (See Chapter 7 for a discussion of these forms and how to use them.)

142

USEFUL READING

Shaughnessy, Mina P. *Errors & Expectations: A Guide for the Teacher of Basic Writing.* New York: Oxford UP, 1977. Since the publication of this book, every scholarly work on error has referred to it.

Williams, Joseph M. "The Phenomenology of Error." CCC 32 (May 1981): 152–68. Because we don't expect to find errors in professional writings, we tend not to notice them, yet we treat student essays just the opposite. Hence, we need to view errors as simply socially inappropriate, easily remedied behavior.

RECOGNIZING THE PARTS OF SPEECH   *gr* 6b

Reflexive pronouns refer back to the subject of the sentence or clause in which they appear. They end in *-self* or *-selves*.

REFLEXIVE PRONOUNS	myself, yourself, himself, herself, itself, oneself, ourselves, yourselves, themselves

The seals sunned *themselves* on the warm rocks.

Intensive pronouns have the same form as reflexive pronouns. They are used to emphasize their antecedents.

He decided to paint the apartment *himself.*

Indefinite pronouns do not refer to specific nouns, although they may refer to identifiable persons or things. They express the idea of "all," "some," "any," or "none." Indefinite pronouns are one of the largest categories of pronouns; the following list does not include all of them.

INDEFINITE PRONOUNS	all, anybody, both, each, everything, few, most, none, one, some, somebody

Somebody screamed when the lights went out.

Demonstrative pronouns identify or point to specific nouns.

DEMONSTRATIVE PRONOUNS	this, that, these, those

These are Peter's books.

Interrogative pronouns are used to ask questions.

INTERROGATIVE PRONOUNS	who, which, what

Who is teaching composition this term?

Relative pronouns introduce dependent clauses and "relate" the dependent clause to the rest of the sentence (see 6c4).

RELATIVE PRONOUNS	who, which, that, what, whoever, whichever, whatever

Margaret owns the car *that* is parked by the corner.

The interrogative pronoun *who* and the relative pronouns *who* and *whoever* have different forms depending on how they are used in a sentence. (See Chapter 7.)

Demonstrative pronouns, the possessive forms of personal pronouns, and some indefinite, interrogative, and relative pronouns can be used as adjectives. (See 6b4 for further discussion of pronouns used as adjectives.)

Reciprocal pronouns refer to the individual parts of a plural antecedent.

RECIPROCAL   each other, one another
PRONOUNS

The pirates began to quarrel with *one another* over their booty.

EXERCISE 6.4

Identify the pronouns and any antecedents in each of the following sentences, underlining the pronouns once and the antecedents twice.

> *Example*
> As identical <u>twins</u>, <u>they</u> really do understand <u>each other</u>.

1. She thanked everyone for helping.
2. The crowd that greeted the pope was the largest one I have ever seen.
3. Who knows better than Mark himself what he should do?
4. Celia chose to move from Bahia to New York, but still she considers herself more Brazilian than American.
5. People who are extremely fastidious often annoy those who are not.

4. Recognizing adjectives

Adjectives modify (limit the meaning of) nouns or pronouns, usually by describing, identifying, or quantifying those words.

> The *red* Corvette ran off the road. [describes]
>
> It was *red*. [describes]
>
> *That* Corvette needs to be repaired. [identifies]
>
> We saw *several* Corvettes race by. [quantifies]

Most adjectives, like *red* in the examples above, are used to describe. In addition to their basic form, most descriptive adjectives have other forms that are used to make comparisons: *small, smaller, smallest; foolish, more foolish, most foolish, less foolish, least foolish.*

> This year's attendance was *smaller* than last year's.
>
> This year's attendance was the *smallest* in ten years.

Many of the pronouns introduced in 6b3 can also be used as adjectives to identify or quantify.

ANSWERS TO EXERCISE 6.4

1. p-she; p-everyone
2. a-crowd; p-that; p-I
3. p-who; a-Mark; p-himself
4. a-Celie; p-she; p-herself
5. a-people; p-who; p-those; p-who

WRITERS ON WRITING

Who would succeed in the world should be wise in the use of pronouns. Utter the You twenty times, when you once utter the I.

—JOHN HAY

Those are my favorite dogs. [pronoun]

Those dogs should be on a leash. [adjective]

Kinds of pronouns that can be used as adjectives include personal (*her* idea), interrogative (*which* model should we buy?), relative (we're not sure *which* model we should buy), demonstrative (*this* book), and indefinite (*many* moons). Other kinds of adjectives that identify or quantify are articles (*a, an, the*) and numbers (*three, sixty-fifth, five thousand*).

Proper adjectives are adjectives that are formed from or related to proper nouns (*French, Emersonian*). Proper adjectives are capitalized. (See 33b for more information about proper adjectives.)

Chapter 10 provides a complete discussion of the forms and functions of adjectives.

5. Recognizing adverbs

Adverbs modify verbs, adjectives, other adverbs, or entire clauses. You can recognize many adverbs by their *-ly* ending, though some adverbs do not have such an ending (*always, never, very, well*) and some words that end in *-ly* are not adverbs but adjectives (*friendly, lovely*). Among the most common adverbs is *not*.

Virginia and Kim *recently* visited Santa Fe. [modifies the verb *visited*]

They had an *unexpectedly* exciting trip. [modifies the adjective *exciting*]

They *very* soon fell under the spell of New Mexico. [modifies the adverb *soon*]

Frankly, they would have liked to stay another month. [modifies the independent clause that makes up the rest of the sentence]

Adverbs often answer one of the following questions: *how? when? where? why? to what extent?* In the first example sentence above, for instance, *recently* answers the question *when?* In the third sentence, *very* answers the question *to what extent?*

Many adverbs, like many adjectives, have different forms that are used in making comparisons: *forcefully, more forcefully, most forcefully, less forcefully, least forcefully*.

The senator spoke *more forcefully* than her opponent.

Of all the candidates, she speaks the *most forcefully*.

Conjunctive adverbs modify an entire clause and express the connection in meaning between that clause and the preceding clause (or sentence). Examples of conjunctive adverbs include *however*, *furthermore*, *therefore*, and *likewise*. (See 6b7 for more information about conjunctive adverbs.)

The most movable of all parts of speech, adverbs can often be placed in different positions in a sentence without changing or disrupting the meaning of the sentence. Notice in the following examples how placement creates only slight differences in emphasis:

> *Quickly* Charles ran for the door.
>
> Charles *quickly* ran for the door.
>
> Charles ran for the door *quickly*.

Chapter 9 provides a complete discussion of the forms and functions of adverbs.

ANSWERS TO EXERCISE 6.5

1. *lucky*; *my*; **rarely**; **extremely**; *angry*
2. **anxiously**; *my*; *long*
3. *mysterious*; *our*; **hungrily**
4. *Twenty*; *Italian*; *strong*
5. *most*; *inspirational*; *three*
6. *Those*; **quite**; **happily**; *their*; *new*
7. **Never**; *small*
8. **more**; **pessimistically**; *his*
9. **Probably**; *biggest*; *federal*
10. *personal*; *political*; *relevant*; **not**

WRITING TOGETHER

Break into your groups and work to transform the following ordinary statements into powerful messages—expand them with adjectives and adverbs. Then, share your messages with the rest of the class.

1. Candidates travel across the nation.
2. The spider went up the waterspout.
3. A stir was audible in the hall.
4. Fifi gets angry.
5. The prisoner dozed off and was wakened.
6. The boy entered the line.

ANSWERS TO EXERCISE 6.6 (WILL VARY)

1. A multinational corporation can fire undependable workers.
2. The beautiful, athletic heroine marries charming, bookish prince.
3. In the pastoral painting a dirt road curves between the rolling hills.
4. Only the best students are using the vast library holdings for scholarly research.
5. Ardent feminists have staged impressive demonstrations against the obscenely violent movie.

EXERCISE 6.5

Identify the adjectives and adverbs in each of the following sentences, underlining the adjectives once and the adverbs twice. Remember that articles and some pronouns are used as adjectives.

> *Example*
>
> <u>Luckily</u>, <u>each</u> day brought <u>new</u> challenges.

1. You are lucky that your roommate rarely becomes extremely angry.
2. Anxiously, I took my place in the long line to register for classes.
3. The aromas from the pantry were rather mysterious, and our stomachs grumbled hungrily.
4. Twenty Italian flags snapped in the strong breeze.
5. Ms. Peters was the most inspirational of the three instructors.
6. Those people adjusted quite happily to their new situation.
7. Never did I expect to move to a small town in Texas.
8. After the election the president spoke more pessimistically about the future of the country.
9. The biggest factor in homelessness is a drop in federal aid for housing.
10. Some say that the personal life of a political candidate is not relevant.

EXERCISE 6.6

Expand each of the following sentences by adding appropriate adjectives and adverbs. Delete *the* if you need to.

Example

The veterinarians examined the patient.

Eventually, the *three young* veterinarians *thoroughly* examined the *nervous* patient.

1. A corporation can fire workers.
2. The heroine marries the prince.
3. In the painting a road curves between hills.
4. Students are using the library for research.
5. Feminists have staged demonstrations against the movie.

6. Recognizing prepositions

Prepositions are important structural words that express relationships—in space, time, or other senses—between nouns or pronouns and other words in a sentence.

We did not want to leave *during* the game.

Careful writers read their own pages *with* infinite care.

Drive *across* the bridge, go *down* the avenue *past* three stoplights, and then turn left *before* the Gulf station.

Here is a list of some common prepositions:

about	before	from	over
above	behind	in	past
across	beneath	inside	regarding
after	beside	into	since
against	between	like	through
along	beyond	near	toward
among	by	of	under
around	down	off	until
as	during	on	up
at	except	onto	with
below	for	out	without

In addition to the words on this list, some prepositions, called **compound prepositions**, are made up of more than one word: *according to, because of, by way of, due to, except for, in addition to, in front of, in place of, in spite of, instead of, next to, out of, with regard to.*

If you are ever in doubt about which preposition to use (for example, whether to write *agree to* or *agree with*), consult your dictionary. Your library may also have Frederich Wood's *English Prepositional Idioms*, a dictionary devoted entirely to prepositions.

(BACK)GROUNDING

Besides connecting nouns and pronouns to other words, prepositions also have important semantic dimensions, serving as the most important words in certain sentences:

Watch that crazed killer *behind* you.
Tie that artery *below* his ear.

Until the late Middle Ages, relationships among words were indicated by inflectional endings. But by 1300, when only the possessive (-'s) and plural (-s) endings remained, prepositions were used to signal relationships. Chaucer was the first to use the preposition *during* (c. 1385), while the *Piers Plowman* poet was the first to use the prepositions *concerning* and *except* (c. 1377).

A *prepositional phrase* is made of a preposition together with the noun or pronoun it connects to the rest of the sentence. For more information about prepositional phrases, see 6c3.

ANSWERS TO EXERCISE 6.7
1. of; through; on
2. through; across; into
3. past; at
4. from; beyond; toward
5. by; to; by; of

EXERCISE 6.7

Identify and underline the prepositions in each of the following sentences.

Example
In the dim interior of the hut crouched an old man.

1. A gust of wind blew through the window, upsetting the vase on the table.
2. He ran swiftly through the brush, across the beach, and into the sea.
3. A few minutes past noon the police arrived at the scene.
4. Far from sight, beyond the horizon, our ship heads toward the open sea.
5. The book, by Anne Morrow Lindbergh, describes the flight the Lindberghs made to the Orient by way of the Great Circle Route.

7. Recognizing conjunctions

Conjunctions connect other words or groups of words to one another. There are four kinds of conjunctions: coordinating conjunctions, correlative conjunctions, subordinating conjunctions, and conjunctive adverbs.

Coordinating conjunctions (*and, but, or, nor, for, so, yet*) join equivalent structures—two or more nouns, pronouns, verbs, adjectives, adverbs, prepositions, conjunctions, phrases, or clauses.

T. S. Eliot wrote poems *and* plays.

A strong *but* warm breeze blew across the desert.

Please print *or* type the information on the application form.

Her work demanded much time, *yet* she was able to join the team.

Nor, for, and *so* can connect independent clauses only.

He did not have much money, *nor* did he know how to get any.

The student glanced anxiously at the clock, *for* only twenty minutes remained in the exam period.

Ellen worked two shifts on Thursday, *so* she can take Friday off.

Correlative conjunctions (*both . . . and, either . . . or, just as . . . so, neither . . . nor, not only . . . but (also), whether . . . or*) also join equivalent words or word groups.

TEACHING PRACTICE
Attempting to learn conjunctions by their grammatical categories can be confusing. Some students may respond better when they are presented the following semantic categories of conjunctions (and transitional phrases):

1. **To express agreement between items**—and, also, likewise, both-and, similarly, not only-but also.
2. **To express additional items**—besides, furthermore, moreover, and, also (in addition)
3. **To express disagreement between items**—but yet, however, instead, anyway, nevertheless, still (in spite of that)
4. **To express alternative items**—or-nor, either-or, neither-nor
5. **To express causations**—for, so, since, because, therefore, thus
6. **To express various time relations**—when, often, before, while, as, until, finally, meanwhile, next, now, then
7. **To express certainty**—certainly, indeed, undoubtedly (to be certain, without a doubt)
8. **To express possibility or qualifications**—if, if-then, until, although, before, besides, unless, otherwise (on the other hand)
9. **To express parenthetically**—besides, incidentally
10. **To express specificity**—namely (that is to say)

Both W. H. Auden *and* William Carlos Williams wrote poems about Bruegel's *Fall of Icarus.*

Jeff *not only* applied for a summer job *but also* volunteered to work at the community center.

Subordinating conjunctions introduce adverb clauses and signal the relationship between the adverb clause and another clause, usually an independent clause. For instance, in the following sentence the subordinating conjunction *while* signals a time relationship, letting us know that the two events in the sentence happen simultaneously.

Sweat ran down my face *while* I frantically searched for my child.

Following are some of the most common subordinating conjunctions:

after	before	since	unless
although	even though	so that	until
as	if	than	when
as if	in order that	that	where
because	once	though	while

Unless sales improve dramatically, the company will soon be bankrupt.

My grandmother began traveling *after* she sold her house.

Conjunctive adverbs connect one independent clause (or sentence) to another. As their name suggests, conjunctive adverbs can be considered both adverbs and conjunctions because they modify the second clause in addition to expressing the connection in meaning between it and the preceding clause. Like many other adverbs and unlike other conjunctions, they can be moved to different positions in a clause without changing or disrupting the meaning of the clause. Look at the following sentences:

The cider tasted bitter; *however,* each of us drank a tall glass of it.

The cider tasted bitter; each of us, *however,* drank a tall glass of it.

The cider tasted bitter. Each of us drank a tall glass of it, *however.*

Commonly used conjunctive adverbs include the following:

also	furthermore	likewise
anyway	however	meanwhile
besides	incidentally	moreover
certainly	indeed	namely
finally	instead	nevertheless

next	similarly	therefore
now	still	thus
otherwise	then	undoubtedly

Independent clauses connected by a conjunctive adverb must be separated by a semicolon or a period, not just a comma (see 13c1).

> Carmen grabbed the ball and ran down the street; *consequently*, the stickball game came to an abrupt end.

> Some of these problems could occur at any company; many, *though*, could happen only here.

ANSWERS TO EXERCISE 6.8

1. sub-when; sub-as
2. conj-nevertheless
3. coor-for
4. coor-but
5. sub-because
6. corr-not only/but also
7. sub-after
8. sub-until
9. sub-although; sub-as if
10. corr-neither/nor; conj-therefore

TEACHING PRACTICE

To give your students practice in thinking about the relationships between words and ideas, you may want to present them a conjunction-less passage, asking them to insert the appropriate conjunctions. With the italicized conjunctions left out, present the following passage from Toni Morrison's *The Bluest Eye:*

> *If* my mother was in a singing mood, it wasn't so bad. She would sing about hard times, bad times, *and* somebody-done-gone-and-left-me times. *But* her voice was so sweet *and* her singing-eyes so melty I found myself longing for those hard times, yearning to be grown without "a thin di-i-ime to my name." I looked forward to the delicious time *when* "my man" would leave me, *when* I would "hate to see that evening sun go down . . ." 'cause *then* I would know "my man has left this town." Misery colored by the greens *and* blues in my mother's voice took all of the grief out of the words *and* left me with a conviction that pain was *not only* endurable, it was sweet.

EXERCISE 6.8

Identify and underline the coordinating, correlative, and subordinating conjunctions and the conjunctive adverbs in each of the following sentences.

> *Example*
> David used his sleeping bag <u>even though</u> the cabin was furnished with sheets <u>and</u> blankets.

1. When we arrived at the pond, we saw many children playing there.
2. Pokey is an outside cat; nevertheless, she greets me at the front door each night as I arrive home.
3. The colt walked calmly, for he seemed to know he would win the race.
4. The shops along the waterfront were open, but business was slow.
5. The Environmental Protection Agency was once forced to buy an entire town because dioxins had rendered it uninhabitable.
6. The office manager found imperfections not only in everything I did but also in the work every other employee did.
7. I did not know whether to laugh or to cry after I realized my mistake.
8. Exhausted men worked the pumps until their arms ached.
9. Although I live in a big city, my neighborhood has enough trees and raccoons to make me feel as if I live in the suburbs.
10. Neither Henry nor Rachel could understand the invitation; therefore, they did not respond to it.

▌ 8. Recognizing interjections

Interjections are words that express surprise or emotion: *oh, ouch, ah, hey*. Interjections often stand alone, as fragments, and even when they are included in a sentence, they are not related grammatically to the rest of the sentence. They are used mostly in speaking; in writing they are used mostly in dialogue.

"*Yeah! All right!*" The watching crowd hurled hats in the air and jumped up in joy.

We tiptoed cautiously through the dark basement until—*oh, no!*—we saw what lay under the pile of discarded clothing in the corner.

▌ 6c. Recognizing the parts of a sentence

While the parts of speech system helps us to understand the grammar of sentences, a sentence is not just made up of individual words. Every sentence has a grammatical pattern or structure, and the parts of speech are simply the categories of words used to create this structure.

Look again at the word *book*. In 6b we saw that *book* can function as various parts of speech—as a noun, an adjective, and a verb.

NOUN
A book is always a welcome gift.

ADJECTIVE
Henry has more book knowledge than wisdom.

VERB
May I book a flight to Fort Worth?

Notice that *book* has exactly the same form for each part of speech; it would be impossible to recognize its meaning outside the context of a particular sentence. In fact, even in a sentence a word that can be categorized as a certain part of speech can function in more than one way.

SUBJECT
This book looks great!

DIRECT OBJECT
I need a certain book.

Book acts as a noun in both of these sentences, yet in the first it serves as the subject of the verb *looks*, and in the second it serves as the direct object of the verb *need*. Knowing the word's part of speech tells only part of the story; we have to recognize the part it plays in the pattern or structure of the sentence.

Most English sentences follow one of five basic patterns: (1) subject/verb, (2) subject/verb/subject complement, (3) subject/verb/direct object, (4) subject/verb/indirect object/direct object, and (5) subject/verb/direct object/object complement. For example:

S   V
1. Babies cry.

S   V   SC
2. Babies seem fragile.

S   V   DO
3. Babies drink milk.

S   V   IO   DO
4. Babies give grandparents pleasure.

S   V   DO   OC
5. Parents consider babysitters essential.

This section examines the essential parts of a sentence—subjects, predicates, objects, complements, phrases, and clauses—and provides practice in using them to construct sentences of various kinds.

1. Recognizing subjects

As explained in 6a, almost every sentence has a stated subject, which identifies whom or what the sentence is about. The **simple subject** consists of one or more nouns or pronouns; the **complete subject** consists of the simple subject with all its modifiers. Depending on the kinds of modifiers, subjects can be as plain as one word or far more complex. The following examples show the complete subjects in italics, with the simple subjects labeled *ss*:

> ss
> *Baseball* is a summer game.
>
>   ss
> *Sailing over the fence, the ball* crashed through Mr. Wilson's window.
>
> ss
> *Stadiums with real grass* are hard to find these days.
>
> ss
> *Those who sit in the bleachers* have the most fun.

A **compound subject** contains two or more nouns or pronouns joined with a coordinating conjunction (*and, but, or*) or a correlative conjunction (*both . . . and, either . . . or, neither . . . nor, not only . . . but also*).

> *Mays and Mantle* destroyed pitchers.
>
> *Both he and Mantle* destroyed pitchers.

In imperative sentences, which express requests or commands, the subject *you* is implied but not stated.

(BACK)GROUNDING

In reaction to terms they deem static and purely formal labels, the Prague School linguists have tried to incorporate meaning into the sentence divisions of *subject* and *predicate*. Hence, the subject represents the "theme" of or "topic" of a sentence and the predicate comments on or enunciates that theme.

OPTIONAL EXERCISES

Identify the one complete sentence in each group (taken from D'Eloia's "The Uses—and Limits—of Grammar"):

1. for the child to sing sweetly
   the child's sweet song
   the sweetly singing child
   the child singing sweetly
   the child is singing sweetly
   that the child is singing sweetly
   whenever the child is singing sweetly

2. for the woman to smile knowingly
   the woman's knowing smile
   the knowingly smiling woman
   the woman smiling knowingly
   the woman was smiling knowingly
   that the woman was smiling knowingly
   because the woman was smiling knowingly
   so that the woman was smiling knowingly

RECOGNIZING THE PARTS OF A SENTENCE *gr* 6c

(*You*) Keep your eye on the ball.

In English sentences the simple subject usually comes before the predicate, or verb, but not always. Sometimes writers reverse this order for effect.

> Up to the plate stepped *Casey*.
>
> High were the *hopes* of Mudville fans.

In questions, the subject usually appears between the auxiliary verb and the main verb.

> Did *Casey* save the game?

In sentences beginning with *there* or *here* followed by a form of the verb *be* (*is, are, was, were, have been, will be,* and so on), the subject always follows the verb. *There* and *here* are never the subject.

> Here is the sad *ending* of the poem.
>
> There was no *joy* in Mudville.

EXERCISE 6.9

Identify the complete subject and the simple subject in each of the following sentences. Underline the complete subject once and the simple subject twice.

> *Example*
>
> A fresh, moist <u>breeze</u> kicked up at just the right time.

1. The novels of F. Scott Fitzgerald depict the Jazz Age.
2. A two-foot snowfall on April 13 was most unexpected.
3. Decisions about courses and majors should be the students'.
4. Anyone who lives in a glass house should never throw stones.
5. Some women worried about osteoporosis take calcium supplements.

2. Recognizing predicates

In addition to a subject, every sentence has a predicate which asserts or asks something about the subject or tells the subject to do something (as explained in 6a). The "hinge" or key word of most predicates is a verb. As we saw in 6b1, a verb can include auxiliary verbs (as in this sentence, where *can* is an auxiliary and *include* is the main verb). The **simple predicate** of a sentence is the main verb and any auxiliaries; the **complete predicate** also includes any modifiers of the verb and any objects or complements and their modifiers. In the

ANSWERS TO EXERCISE 6.9
1. *The* **novels** *of F. Scott Fitzgerald*
2. *A* **two-foot snowfall** *on April 13*
3. **Decisions** *about courses and majors*
4. **Anyone** *who lives in a glass house*
5. *Some* **women** *worried about osteoporosis*

following examples, the complete predicates are italicized and the simple predicates are labeled *sp:*

My roommate *seems wonderful.*

She *originally comes from* St. Paul, Minnesota.

Both of us *are planning to major in history.*

A **compound predicate** contains two or more verbs that have the same subject and are usually joined by a coordinating or correlative conjunction.

The student *shut the book, put it back on the shelf, and sighed.*

The Amish *neither drive cars nor use electricity.*

On the basis of how they function in predicates, verbs can be divided into three categories: linking, transitive, and intransitive.

Linking verbs

A **linking verb** links, or joins, the subject with a **subject complement,** a word or word group that identifies or describes the subject. If it identifies the subject, the complement is a noun or pronoun (and is sometimes called a **predicate noun**). If it describes the subject, the complement is an adjective (and is sometimes called a **predicate adjective**). In the following two sentences, for example, *an investment banker* is a predicate noun and *rich* is a predicate adjective:

Christine is an investment banker.

She is rich.

The forms of *be,* when used as main verbs rather than as auxiliary verbs, are linking verbs (like *are* in this sentence). Other verbs, such as *appear, become, feel, grow, look, make, seem, smell,* and *sound,* can also function as linking verbs, depending on the sense of the sentence.

Our mayor's famed contentiousness has become tedious.

His political rivals seem pleased.

Transitive and intransitive verbs

If a verb is not a linking verb, it is either transitive or intransitive. A **transitive verb** expresses action that is directed toward a noun or pronoun, called the **direct object** of the verb.

S┌────V────┐┌──DO──┐
I will analyze three poems.

A direct object answers the question *what?* or *whom?* about the transitive verb. In the preceding example sentence, the subject and verb alone do not express a complete thought: *what* will I analyze? The direct object completes the thought.

A direct object may be followed by an **object complement**, a word or words that identifies or describes the direct object.

S┌──V──┐┌───────DO───────┐┌──OC──┐
I consider Marianne Moore's poetry exquisite.

┌──────────S──────────┐┌─V─┐┌─DO─┐ ┌──OC──┐
Her poems and personality made Moore a celebrity.

A transitive verb may also be followed by an **indirect object,** which tells to whom or to what, or for whom or for what, the verb's action is done. You might say that the indirect object is the recipient of the direct object.

┌──────────S──────────┐┌─V─┐┌IO┐┌───────DO───────┐
Moore's poems about the Dodgers give me considerable pleasure.

┌─S─┐┌─V─┐┌───────IO───────┐┌──DO──┐
Brooklyn owes Marianne Moore something.

An **intransitive verb** expresses action that is not directed toward an object or is directed toward an object that is not mentioned. Therefore, an intransitive verb does not have a direct object.

┌────S────┐┌───V───┐
The Red Sox persevered.

┌────S────┐┌───V───┐
Their fans watched helplessly.

In the preceding sentences, the action of the verb *persevered* has no object (it makes no sense to ask *persevered what?* or *persevered whom?*), and the action of the verb *watched* is directed toward an object that is implied but not expressed.

Some verbs that express action can be only transitive or intransitive, but most such verbs can be used both ways, with or without a direct object.

```
    ┌──────────S──────────┐ ┌─V─┐ ┌──DO──┐
    The senator from Wyoming opened the hearings.
```

```
    ┌───S───┐ ┌─V─┐
    The door opened silently.
```

EXERCISE 6.10

Identify and underline the predicate in each of the following sentences. Then identify each verb as linking, transitive, or intransitive. Finally, identify all subject and object complements and all direct and indirect objects.

Example

```
    ┌───V───┐ ┌─DO─┐ ┌──OC──┐
    We considered city life unbearable.
```

1. California is dry in the summer.
2. The U.S. Constitution made us a nation.
3. The real victims become the taxpayers.
4. Hollywood shall rise again.
5. Advertisers promise uncritical consumers the world.

3. Recognizing and using phrases

A **phrase** is a group of words that lacks either a subject or a predicate or both. Phrases function in useful ways to add information to a sentence or shape it effectively. Look at the following sentence:

The new law will restrict smoking *in most public places.*

The basic subject and predicate of this sentence is simply *the new law will restrict smoking;* additional information is provided by the prepositional phrase *in most public places.* The phrase functions in the sentence as an adverb, telling *where* smoking will be restricted. This section will discuss the various kinds of phrases: noun, verb, prepositional, verbal, appositive, and absolute.

Noun phrases

Made up of a noun and all its modifiers, a **noun phrase** can function in a sentence as a subject, object, or complement.

```
    ┌────────SUBJECT────────┐
    Delicious, gooey peanut butter is surprisingly healthful.
```

ANSWERS TO EXERCISE 6.10

1. pred-is dry in the summer; lnkg-is; sc-dry
2. pred-made us a nation; trans-made; do-us; oc-nation
3. pred-become the taxpayers; lnkg-become; sc-taxpayers
4. pred-shall rise again; inr-shall rise
5. pred-promise uncritical consumers the world; trans-promise; io-consumers; do-world

RECOGNIZING THE PARTS OF A SENTENCE　　*gr* | 6c

   ┌─OBJECT─┐
Dieters prefer *green salad*.

   ┌─COMPLEMENT─┐
A tuna sandwich is *a popular lunch*.

Verb phrases

A main verb and its auxiliary verbs make up a **verb phrase,** which functions in a sentence in only one way: as a predicate.

Frank *had been depressed* for some time.

His problem *might have been caused* by tension between his parents.

Prepositional phrases

A **prepositional phrase** includes a preposition, a noun or pronoun called the **object of the preposition,** and any modifiers of the object. Prepositional phrases function as either adjectives or adverbs.

ADJECTIVE	Our house *in Maine* was a cabin.
ADVERB	*From Cadillac Mountain* you can clearly see the northern lights.

EXERCISE 6.11

Following are some sentences written by the sports columnist Red Smith. Identify and underline all the prepositional phrases. Then choose two of the sentences, and write sentences that imitate their structures.

> ### Example
> He glanced <u>about the room with a cocky, crooked grin</u>.
> The cat stalked around the yard in her quiet, arrogant way.

1. In those days the Yankees always won the pennant.
2. Fear wasn't in his vocabulary and pain had no meaning.
3. Coaching in Columbus is not quite like coaching in New Haven.
4. He stepped out of the dugout and faced the multitude, two fists and one cap uplifted.
5. The old champ looked fit, square of shoulder and springy of tread, his skin clear, his eyes bright behind the glittering glasses.

EXERCISE 6.12

Combine each of the following pairs of sentences into one sentence by making the second sentence into one or more prepositional phrases.

ANSWERS TO EXERCISE 6.11

1. In those days
2. in his vocabulary
3. in Columbus; in New Haven
4. of the dugout
5. of shoulder; of tread; behind the glittering glasses.

Imitations of these sentences will vary:

1. In those shoes, the young athlete always won the first-place medal.
2. Chocolate wasn't in her lunchbox and fruit had no value.
3. Surfing in St. Louis is not quite like surfing in Sydney.
4. She peeked out of the stretch limo and faced the throng, two fingers and one peace sign uplifted.
5. The old teacher looked worn, rounded of shoulder and mincing of tread, his skin sallow, his eyes rheumy behind the smeared glasses.

ANSWERS TO EXERCISE 6.12 (WILL VARY)

1. Socrates was condemned by a jury of his fellow citizens.
2. Without fear, Socrates faced death.
3. Aristophanes wrote a comedy about Socrates.
4. Except for a few of his followers, everyone thought Socrates was crazy.
5. Today Socrates is honored as the founder of Western philosophy.

Example

The Greeks won a tremendous victory. They were fighting the Persians. The Greeks won a tremendous victory *over the Persians.*

1. Socrates was condemned. His fellow citizens made up the jury that condemned him.
2. Socrates faced death. He had no fear.
3. The playwright Aristophanes wrote a comedy. Its subject was Socrates.
4. Everyone thought Socrates was crazy. Only a few followers disagreed.
5. Today Socrates is honored. He founded Western philosophy.

Verbal phrases

Verbals are verb forms that do not function as verbs in sentences. Instead, they function as nouns, adjectives, and adverbs. There are three kinds of verbals: participles, gerunds, and infinitives.

The **present participle** is the *-ing* form of a verb: *dreaming, being, seeing.* The **past participle** of most verbs ends in *-ed: dreamed, watched.* But some verbs have an irregular past participle: *been, seen, hidden, gone.* (See 8b for a list of irregular past participles.) Participles function as adjectives in sentences.

His kiss awakened the *dreaming* princess.

The cryptographers deciphered the *hidden* meaning in the message.

The **gerund** has the same form as the present participle but functions in sentences as a noun.

SUBJECT	*Writing* takes practice.
OBJECT	More than anything, Woody Hayes loved *winning.*

The **infinitive** is the *to* form of a verb: *to dream, to be, to see.* An infinitive can function in a sentence as a noun, adjective, or adverb.

NOUN	She wanted *to write.*
ADJECTIVE	They had no more time *to waste.*
ADVERB	The corporation was ready *to expand.*

A verbal can never stand alone as the verb of a sentence because it is a **nonfinite,** or "unfinished," **verb.** Take the present participle *barking,* for instance. *The terrier barking* is not a sentence; to make it a sentence you need to add one or more auxiliary verbs: *The terrier is barking* or

RECOGNIZING THE PARTS OF A SENTENCE   *gr* 6c

The terrier had been barking. The verb phrases *is barking* and *had been barking* are **finite verbs,** which do not need any other auxiliary to function as verbs in a sentence.

Verbal phrases are made up of a verbal and any modifiers, objects, or complements. Let us turn now to examine the forms and functions of the various kinds of verbal phrases.

Participial phrases

Participial phrases consist of a present participle or past participle with any modifiers, objects, or complements. Participial phrases always function as adjectives in sentences.

Thrilled with her performance, Mary Lou awaited the scores.

The old woman *standing self-righteously in the corner* is Mrs. Turpin.

Notice that many participial phrases may appear in different places in a sentence, as long as it is clear which word they modify (see Chapter 15). Decisions about where to place participial phrases must usually be made within the larger context of a piece of writing; the choice often depends on the rhythm or emphasis the writer wants to achieve.

Fearing that I would be left alone, I quickly followed the group.

I followed the group, *fearing that I would be left alone.*

Gerund phrases

Gerund phrases consist of a gerund with any modifiers, objects, or complements: *hoping for a victory, critical thinking.* In sentences, gerund phrases function as nouns—as a subject, a subject complement, a direct object, an indirect object, or an object of a preposition.

        ──────S──────

Opening my eyes to the problem was not easy.

               ──────SC──────

His downfall was *relying too much on his computer.*

                     ──────DO──────

They suddenly heard *a loud wailing from the sandbox.*

             ──────IO──────

The critics gave *Pavarotti's singing* their enthusiastic approval.

          ──OBJ OF PREP──

In addition to *being confused,* she was alone.

Infinitive phrases

Infinitive phrases consist of an infinitive with any modifiers, objects, or complements: *to be happy, to see a show tonight*. They can function as nouns, adjectives, or adverbs.

> NOUN/SC
> My goal is *to be a good citizen.*

> ADJECTIVE
> A party would be a good way *to end the semester.*

> ADVERB
> *To perfect a draft,* always proofread carefully.

Notice that infinitive phrases used as adverbs, like the last example above, may appear in different places in a sentence as long as it is clear which word they modify (see Chapter 15). For example, *To perfect a draft* could be moved to the end of its sentence. As with participial phrases, the placement should depend on the effect it creates within the larger context of the piece of writing.

EXERCISE 6.13

Identify each participial phrase, gerund phrase, and infinitive phrase in the following sentences, and specify which part of speech it functions as in the sentence.

Example

> PARTICIPIAL-ADJ
> Pacing the hall with impatience, I wished my friends would arrive.

1. Buying his first Corvette was the happiest moment in Ron's life.
2. After four years of careful saving, he got his car.
3. The solution was to warn Georgina: unless she worked to improve her behavior, she could not continue to attend our school.
4. Raised in Idaho, I spent plenty of time exploring nature.
5. Sitting by the window and listening to the wind blowing through the trees, I feel happy and lucky to be alive.

Absolute phrases

An **absolute phrase** consists of a noun or pronoun and a participle, together with any objects or modifiers. It modifies an entire sentence rather than a particular word. Absolutes may appear almost anywhere in a sentence and are always set off from the rest of the sentence with punctuation, usually commas. (See Chapter 27.)

ANSWERS TO EXERCISE 6.13

1. gerund-buying; n, subj
2. gerund-saving; n, object of prep
3. inf-to warn; n, subj compl; inf-to improve-adv; inf-to attend-do
4. part-raised; adj, modifying "I"
   part-exploring; adj, obj compl
5. part-Sitting, listening; adj, modifying I
   part-blowing; adj, obj compl; inf-to be-adv

TEACHING PRACTICE

Consider using sentence-combining techniques to reinforce the effective compression that can be achieved with absolute and appositive phrases. For instance, *I jumped into the car and took off, the tires screeching in protest* consists of at least three simpler sentences:

> I jumped; (I jumped) into the car
> I took off
> The tires were screeching in protest.

Write these sentences on the board and work with your students to delete repetitive elements to form a combined sentence with an absolute element.

You can do the same exercise to achieve an appositive phrase:

> Maya Angelou will appear on campus tonight
> Maya Angelou is a celebrated novelist and (Maya Angelous is a celebrated) essayist.

RECOGNIZING THE PARTS OF A SENTENCE

I jumped into the car and took off, *tires screeching in protest.*

My fears laid to rest, I climbed into the plane for my first solo flight.

Appositive phrases

A noun phrase that renames the noun or pronoun that immediately precedes it is called an **appositive phrase.**

Maya Angelou, *the celebrated writer,* will appear on campus tonight.

That's my sister, *the skinny kid in tights.*

EXERCISE 6.14

Read the following sentences, and identify and label all of the prepositional, verbal, absolute, and appositive phrases. Notice that one kind of phrase may appear within another kind.

Example

┌─ABSOLUTE─┐
His voice breaking, Ed thanked us for the award.

1. Approaching the rope, I suddenly fell into the icy pond.
2. To listen to Bruce Springsteen is sheer delight.
3. The figure outlined against the sky seemed unable to move.
4. Floating on my back, I ignored my practice requirements.
5. Jane stood still, her fingers clutching the fence.
6. Bobby, a sensitive child, was filled with a mixture of awe and excitement.
7. Shocked into silence, they kept their gaze fixed on the odd creature.
8. Basking in the sunlight, I had been lost somewhere in a reminiscence of golden birch trees.
9. Susan, the leader of the group, was reluctant to give up any authority.
10. His favorite form of recreation was taking a nap.

Using phrases to shape and expand sentences

Phrases provide valuable tools for shaping or expanding sentences. Not only do they bring in additional information, but they can help you to emphasize certain parts of a sentence and deemphasize others. In this way they help to distinguish the main idea of the sentence from the extra details. Look, for instance, at the following sentence:

Jupiter crashed through the tomato vines with the remains of a felt hat in his mouth.   —JOHN CHEEVER, "The Country Husband"

USEFUL READING

O'Hare, Frank. *Sentence-Combining: Improving Student Writing without Formal Grammar Instruction.* Urbana, IL: NCTE, 1973. Shows that practice in sentence combining leads to increased syntactic maturity, even in the absence of formal grammar training. See "Appendix A."

Williams, Joseph. *Style: Ten Lessons in Clarity and Grace.* 2d ed. Glenview, IL: Scott, 1985. Williams provides methods for both streamlining and enriching sentences.

ANSWERS TO EXERCISE 6.14

1. part-Approaching the rope; prep-into the icy pond
2. inf-To listen; prep-to Bruce Springsteen
3. part-outlined; prep-against the sky; inf-to move
4. part-Floating; prep-on my back
5. abso-her fingers clutching the fence
6. prep-of awe and excitement; app-a sensitive child
7. part-Shocked; prep-into silence; prep-on the odd creature
8. part-Basking; prep-in the sunlight; prep-in a reminiscence; prep-of golden birch trees
9. app-the leader; prep-of the group; inf-to give up
10. prep-of recreation; gerund-taking a nap

WRITERS WRITING

A skilled writer who delighted his audience, Sinclair Lewis used phrases to shape and expand his sentences. In *Elmer Gantry,* his credible and entertaining story of a successful evangelist, Lewis describes the preacher's new church with a beaut of a sentence, rhythmic and ironic:

It had Gothic windows, a carillon in the square stone tower, dozens of Sunday school rooms, a gymnasium, a social room with a stage and a motion-picture booth, an electric range in the kitchen, and over it all a revolving electric cross and a debt.

WRITERS ON WRITING

By being so long in the lowest forms [at Harrow] I gained an immense advantage over the clever boys . . . I got into my bones the essential structure of the ordinary British sentence—which is a noble thing.

—WINSTON CHURCHILL

Cheever might have expressed the ideas in this sentence in many other ways. For instance:

> Jupiter crashed through the tomato vines. He had the remains of a felt hat in his mouth.

> Crashing through the tomato vines, Jupiter held the remains of a felt hat in his mouth.

In the first possibility, turning some of the prepositional phrases into a second sentence separates the statement into two parts and thus weakens or at least changes the impact it has on readers—perhaps because we see the crash and the torn hat at a greater chronological distance from each other. In the second possibility, turning the verb of the original sentence into a participle puts greater emphasis on what was in the dog's mouth than on his crash through the vines and thus describes a slightly different scene.

As you write sentences, you should be alert to how you can use phrases to present your ideas and bits of information in particular ways. This consideration is especially important when you are revising. As you read over a draft, consider each sentence individually to see if phrases could help you add necessary detail, make your point clearer, or emphasize one idea instead of another.

Following are some examples of how some student writers used various kinds of phrases to shape and expand particular sentences.

NOUN PHRASE

That car will never win the race.

That battered, valveless, bent-up bone-shaker will never win the race.

PARTICIPIAL PHRASE

The subway was anything but inviting. It was covered with graffiti and packed with commuters.

Covered with graffiti and packed with commuters, the subway was anything but inviting.

ABSOLUTE PHRASE

The dictator's long period of absolute rule was over, and he stepped into his limousine.

His long period of absolute rule over, the dictator stepped into his limousine.

Positioning phrases

As noted earlier, many phrases can be placed either at the beginning, in the middle, or at the end of a sentence, as the following examples illustrate:

Calling on every ounce of energy, Jo sprinted toward the finish line.

Jo, *calling on every ounce of energy,* sprinted toward the finish line.

Jo sprinted toward the finish line, *calling on every ounce of energy.*

The phrase in these examples is a participial phrase that modifies *Jo*. While changing the placement of the phrase does not alter the basic meaning of the sentence, it does affect rhythm and emphasis, most notably in the third example by changing the important concluding words of the sentence.

Prepositional, infinitive, and absolute phrases can also occupy more than one sentence position. There are no absolute guidelines for placement, but always (1) check to see that the phrase clearly modifies any word it should modify (see Chapter 15), and (2) read the sentence in the context of the surrounding sentences to see which placement seems most effective (see 20b).

EXERCISE 6.15

Use prepositional, participial, infinitive, gerund, absolute, or appositive phrases to expand each of the following sentences.

Example

The apples dropped from the limb.

In response to my vigorous shake, the apples dropped from the limb.

1. Nancy jogged down Willow Street.
2. She looked healthy when he saw her the second time.
3. Richard had lost almost all of his hair.
4. The Sunday afternoon dragged.
5. The smell of burning leaves filled the air.
6. The candidates shook hands with the voters.
7. We were uncertain what to do.
8. Ben often thought regretfully about the past.
9. The sunshine made the day crystal clear.
10. They lived in a trailer.

EXERCISE 6.16

Use a participial, infinitive, gerund, absolute, or appositive phrase to combine each of the following pairs of sentences into one sentence.

ANSWERS TO EXERCISE 6.15 (WILL VARY)

1. Dressed in her brand new running shoes, Nancy jogged down Willow Street, hoping to cover more distance than she had yesterday, when she was running in worn-out sneakers.
2. After soaking up the sun and eating good food, she looked healthy when he saw her the second time.
3. Because he had taken such strong medication, Richard had lost almost all his hair.
4. The Sunday afternoon dragged to an absolute halt.
5. The smell of burning leaves filled the air, reminding us of long-past marshmallow and wiener roasts.
6. In addition to kissing babies, posing for pictures, and eating boiled chicken, the candidates shook hands with the voters.
7. Having thoughtlessly locked ourselves out while the bathtub filled with water, we were uncertain what to do.
8. A late bloomer, Ben often thought regretfully about the past.
9. The rain having passed through during the night, the sunshine made the day crystal-clear.
10. A young couple and their children, they lived in a trailer, crowded together like sardines.

ANSWERS TO EXERCISE 6.16 (WILL VARY)

1. An actor and comedian, David Klein performed a monologue at the club.
2. Waiting to go through customs, we clutched our passports.
3. To lift her spirits she bought a new dress.
4. To annoy his parents, Michael had his ear pierced.
5. Carrying their banners, the protesters headed down the street.

Example

He complained constantly. This habit irritated his co-workers.
His constant complaining irritated his co-workers.

1. David Klein performed a monologue at the club. He is an actor and comedian.
2. We waited to go through customs. Our passports were clutched in our hands.
3. She bought a new dress. This purchase lifted her spirits.
4. Michael had his ear pierced. He did this because it annoyed his parents.
5. The protesters were carrying their banners. They headed down the street.

 4. Recognizing and using clauses

A **clause** is a group of words containing a subject and a predicate. There are two kinds of clauses: independent and dependent. **Independent clauses** (also known as **main clauses**) can stand alone as complete sentences.

The window is open.

The batter swung at the ball.

Independent clauses may be joined with a coordinating conjunction and a comma. For more on joining independent clauses, see 6b7.

The window is open, *so* we'd better be quiet.

The batter swung at the ball, *and* the umpire called her out.

Like independent clauses, **dependent clauses** (also known as **subordinate clauses**) contain a subject and a predicate. They cannot stand alone as complete sentences, however, for they begin with a subordinating word—a subordinating conjunction (see 6b7) or a relative pronoun (see 6b3). The subordinating word connects the dependent clause to an independent clause. Each of the following sentences, for instance, consists of one brief independent clause.

The window is open.

The room feels cool.

You might choose to combine these two independent clauses with a comma and coordinating conjunction: *The window is open, and the room feels cool.* But you could also combine the two clauses by turning one into a dependent clause.

RECOGNIZING THE PARTS OF A SENTENCE   *gr* 6c

Because the window is open, the room feels cool.

In this combination the subordinating conjunction *because* transforms the independent clause *the window is open* into a dependent clause. In doing so, it indicates a causal relationship between the two clauses.

Dependent clauses function in sentences as nouns, adjectives, or adverbs.

Noun clauses

Noun clauses can function as subjects, direct objects, subject complements, or objects of prepositions. Thus they are always contained within another clause rather than simply attached to it, as adjective and adverb clauses are. They usually begin with a relative pronoun (*that, which, what, who, whom, whose, whatever, whoever, whomever, whichever*) or with *when, where, whether, why,* or *how.*

> ┌————————S————————┐
> That he had a college degree was important to her.

> ┌————————DO————————┐
> She asked where he went to college.

> ┌————————SC————————┐
> The real question was why she wanted to know.

> ┌————————OBJ OF PREP————————┐
> She was looking for whatever information she could get.

Notice that in each of these sentences the noun clause is an integral part of the independent clause that makes up the sentence; for example, in the second sentence the independent clause is not just *She asked* but *She asked where he went to college.*

Adjective clauses

Adjective clauses modify nouns and pronouns in another clause. Usually, they follow immediately after the words they modify. Most adjective clauses begin with the relative pronouns *who, whom, whose, that,* or *which.* Some begin with *when, where,* or *why.*

Zoe's decision, *which astonished everyone,* was to have a baby.

Aren't babies devious little creatures *who cry a great deal?*

All parents experience moments *when they feel that way.*

Sometimes the relative pronoun introducing an adjective clause may be deleted, as in the following example:

That is one book [that] I intend to read.

Adverb clauses

Adverb clauses modify verbs, adjectives, or other adverbs. They always begin with a subordinating conjunction (see 6b7). Like adverbs, they usually tell why, when, where, how, under what conditions, or to what extent.

We hiked *where there were few other hikers.*

My backpack felt heavier *than it ever had.*

I climbed as swiftly *as I could under the weight of my backpack.*

Like adverbs, adverb clauses can usually be placed in different positions in a sentence without affecting the meaning.

If you look up from the valley, you will see Half Dome.

You will see Half Dome *if you look up from the valley.*

ANSWERS TO EXERCISE 6.17

1. ind-The driver was driving a tan Pontiac; dep-who won the race; rel-who
2. dep-As a potential customer entered the store; sub conj-As; ind-Tony nervously attempted to retreat to the safety of the back room
3. ind-The names still haunt me; dep-they called my grandmother
4. dep-when she was deemed old enough to understand; sub conj-when; ind-she was told the truth; ind-she knew why; dep-her father had left home
5. ind-there were also great expanses of green lawns and quiet, trickling streams; dep-Though most of my grandfather's farm was wooded; sub conj-Though
6. ind-Mary and John decided to bake a chocolate cream pie; dep-which was Timothy's favorite; rel-which
7. ind-he became very excited; dep-When they asked him to accompany them; sub conj-When; dep-but he also felt some trepidation
8. ind-It was easier; dep-than she had expected
9. ind-Linda cleaned the brushes; dep-After she finished the painting
10. ind-I could see; dep-that he was very tired rel-that; dep-but I had to ask him a few questions

EXERCISE 6.17

Identify the independent and dependent clauses and any subordinating conjunctions and relative pronouns in each of the following sentences.

Example

┌————DEPENDENT CLAUSE————┐
If I were going on a really long hike, I would carry a lightweight stove.
[*If* is a subordinating conjunction.]

1. The driver who won the race was driving a tan Pontiac.
2. As a potential customer entered the store, Tony nervously attempted to retreat to the safety of the back room.
3. The names they called my grandmother still haunt me.
4. When she was deemed old enough to understand, she was told the truth, and she finally knew why her father had left home.
5. Though most of my grandfather's farm was wooded, there were also great expanses of green lawns and quiet, trickling streams.
6. Mary and John decided to bake a chocolate cream pie, which was Timothy's favorite.

RECOGNIZING THE PARTS OF A SENTENCE   *gr* 6c

7. When they asked him to accompany them, he became very excited, but he also felt some trepidation.
8. It was easier than she had expected.
9. After she finished the painting, Linda cleaned the brushes.
10. I could see that he was very tired, but I had to ask him a few questions.

Using clauses to shape and expand sentences

Like phrases, clauses are an important means of shaping sentences in particular ways or expanding sentences into more varied or interesting ones. For example, look at the following sentences, each of which consists of one independent clause expressing one idea:

Sarah's parents disliked her boyfriend. She was determined to marry him.

Now look at how clauses can be used to combine these ideas in one sentence.

1. Although her parents disliked her boyfriend, Sarah was determined to marry him.
2. Sarah's parents disliked her boyfriend, whom she was determined to marry.
3. Sarah's parents disliked her boyfriend, but she was determined to marry him.

In sentence 1, putting the information about the parents' dislike of the boyfriend into a dependent adverb clause gives less emphasis to that idea and more emphasis to the idea expressed in the subject and predicate—Sarah's determination to marry him. In sentence 2, on the other hand, the idea of Sarah's determination is deemphasized by being placed in a dependent adjective clause. Finally, in sentence 3, the two ideas are given equal emphasis by being expressed in two independent clauses connected by the coordinating conjunction *but*.

As you write sentences, and especially when you are revising a draft, pay attention to how you can use clauses to add details or emphasis to your ideas and information. Following are some examples of how student writers used various kinds of clauses to shape and expand particular sentences.

NOUN CLAUSE

Charles later learned the truth.

Charles later learned *what Vinnie had known for years.*

ADJECTIVE CLAUSE

Everything was swept away.

Everything *that he valued most in life* was swept away.

My childhood seemed entirely happy. I grew up on a large farm.

My childhood, *which was spent on a large farm*, seemed entirely happy.

ADVERB CLAUSE

Many young men opposed the war, and they burned their draft cards.

Because they opposed the war, many young men burned their draft cards.

For more information about using clauses to shape and expand sentences, see Chapters 17–20.

Positioning clauses

Like many phrases, most *adverb* clauses can be placed at the beginning, in the middle, or at the end of a sentence.

If nothing goes wrong, the furniture will be delivered tomorrow.

The furniture, *if nothing goes wrong*, will be delivered tomorrow.

The furniture will be delivered tomorrow *if nothing goes wrong*.

Changing the position of the adverb clause *if nothing goes wrong* does not affect the basic meaning of the sentence, but it affects the rhythm and the emphasis by highlighting or downplaying the possibility that something could go wrong. For more information about positioning clauses within sentences, see 15a and 20b.

EXERCISE 6.18

Expand each sentence below by adding at least one dependent clause.

Example
The books tumbled from the shelves.
As the earth continued to shake, the books tumbled from the shelves.

1. The Angolan army was exhausted.
2. George was worried about his real estate investments.
3. The new computer made a strange noise.
4. Rob always borrowed money from friends.
5. The streets were ringing with loud music.
6. We stood outside for an hour.
7. The history seminar begins tomorrow.
8. Erin won the translation contest.

168

ANSWERS TO EXERCISE 6.18 (WILL VARY)

1. The Angolan army, which had fought continuously for nearly a week, was exhausted.
2. George was worried about his real estate investments ever since the representatives of the nuclear power plant had come to town for a site inspection.
3. The new computer, which had been programmed by an employee who had long since left the company, made a strange noise.
4. Rob, who had an extensive collection of jazz records, always borrowed money from his friends.
5. The streets that the graduate students had overtaken were ringing with loud music, most of which was classical.
6. We, who remembered the Grateful Dead and wanted tickets for their next performance, stood outside for an hour.
7. The history seminar, which foregrounds the scientific achievements of women, begins tomorrow.
8. Because she was willing to stay home on weekends and study, Erin won the translation contest.
9. Before the drought hit, a river flowed through the forest.
10. The man, whose memorial plaque hangs in the lobby, was killed in that mill in 1867.

CLASSIFYING SENTENCES   *gr* 6d

9. A river flowed through the forest.
10. A man was killed in that mill in 1867.

EXERCISE 6.19

Following are some sentences from the letters of E. B. White. Read each one carefully, focusing on the phrases and clauses. Underline any dependent clauses once and any phrases twice. Finally, choose two sentences, and use them as a model to write sentences of your own, imitating White's structure phrase for phrase and clause for clause.

> *Example*
> I was born in 1899 and expect to live forever, searching for beauty and raising hell in general.
> Sarah was hired in May and plans to work all summer, living at home and saving money for law school.

1. You can see at a glance that Professor Strunk omitted needless words.
2. Either Macmillan takes Strunk and me in our bare skins, or I want out.
3. I regard the word *hopefully* as beyond recall.
4. Life in a zoo is just the ticket for some animals and birds.
5. I recall the pleasures and satisfactions of encountering a Perelman piece in a magazine.
6. The way to read Thoreau is to enjoy him—his enthusiasms, his acute perception.
7. When I start a book, I never know what my characters are going to do, and I accept no responsibility for their eccentric behavior.
8. No sensible writer sets out deliberately to develop a style, but all writers do have distinguishing qualities, and they become very evident when you read the words.
9. When I wrote "Death of a Pig," I was simply rendering an account of what actually happened on my place—to my pig, who died, and to me, who tended him in his last hours.
10. A good many of Charlotte's descendants still live in the barn, and when the warm days of spring arrive there will be lots of tiny spiders emerging into the world.

6d. Classifying sentences

Like words, sentences can be classified in several different ways: grammatically, functionally, or rhetorically. Grammatical classification groups sentences according to how many and what types of clauses they contain. Functional classification groups them according to whether they make a statement, ask a question, issue a command, or express an exclamation. Rhetorical classification groups them according to

169

USEFUL READING

Christensen, Francis. "A Generative Rhetoric of the Sentence." Rpt. in *Rhetoric and Composition*. Ed. Richard Graves. Upper Montclair, NY: Boynton/Cook, 1984. 110–18. The idea for expanding sentences by adding and manipulating modifying phrases derives largely from Francis Christensen, who maintained that students can achieve syntactic fluency by adding modifiers at the beginning, middle, and end of their sentences. He focuses on the cumulative sentence and demonstrates how writers can add final free modifiers to main clauses to expand sentences.

ANSWERS TO EXERCISE 6.19
(The entire sentences are of course independent clauses.)

1. ind cl-You can see at a glance; dep (rel) cl-that Professor Strunk omitted needless words; prep p-at a glance; n p-Professor Strunk; n p-a glance
2. ind cl-Macmillan takes Strunk and me in our bare skins; ind cl-I want out; prep p-in our bare skins; n p-our bare skins
3. ind cl-I regard the word *hopefully*; prep p-beyond recall; n p-the word
4. ind cl-Life in a zoo is just the ticket; prep p-in a zoo; n p-a zoo; n p-the ticket; prep p-for some animals and birds; n p-some animals and birds
5. ind cl-I recall the pleasures and satisfactions; prep p-of encountering a Perelman piece; prep p-in a magazine; n p-the pleasures and satisfactions; n p-a Perelman piece; n p-a magazine
6. ind cl-The way to read Thoreau is to enjoy him; inf p-to read Thoreau; inf p-to enjoy him; n p-his enthusiasms; n p-his acute perception
7. ind cl-I never know; dep (rel) cl-what my characters are going to do; n p-my characters; v p-are going; inf p-to do; ind cl-I accept no responsibility for their eccentric behavior; prep p-for their eccentric behavior; n p-their eccentric behavior
8. ind cl-No sensible writer sets out deliberately to develop a style; n p-no sensible writer; inf p-to develop; n p-a style; ind cl-all writers do have distinguishing qualities; v p-do have; n p-distinguishing qualities; ind cl-they become very evident; n p-very evident; dep cl-when you read the words; n p-the words
9. ind cl-I was simply rendering an account; v p-was rendering; n p-an account; dep cl-When I wrote "Death of a Pig"; prep p-of a Pig; prep p-of what actually happened; prep p-on my place; n p-my place; prep p-to my pig; n p-my pig; dep (rel) cl-who died; prep p-to me; dep (rel) cl-who tended him; prep p-in his last hours; n p-his last hours
10. ind cl-A good many of Charlotte's descendants still live in the barn; prep p-of Charlotte's descendants; v p-still live; prep p-in the barn; n p-Charlotte's descendants; n p-the barn; dep cl-when the warm days of spring arrive; n p-the warm days; prep p-of spring; ind cl-there will be lots of tiny spiders; n p-tiny spiders; part p-emerging into the world; n p-the world

where in the sentence the main idea is located. Understanding these methods of classification can help you analyze and assess your sentences as you write and revise.

1. Classifying sentences grammatically

Grammatically, sentences fall into one of the following types: *simple sentences, compound sentences, complex sentences,* and *compound-complex sentences.* You have already seen most of these types in the section on clauses.

Simple sentences

A **simple sentence** consists of one independent clause and no dependent clause. The subject or the predicate of the independent clause, or both, may be compound.

The trailer is surrounded by a wooden deck.

Both my roommate and I had left our keys in the room.

At the country club, the head pro and his assistant give lessons, run the golf shop, and try to keep the members content.

Compound sentences

A **compound sentence** consists of two or more independent clauses and no dependent clause. The clauses may be joined by a comma and a coordinating conjunction, by a comma and a correlative conjunction, or by a semicolon. (See Chapters 13, 18, 27, and 28).

Occasionally, a car goes up the dirt trail, and dust flies everywhere.

Not only are the adults unable to relax there, but their conflicting interests create even more tension among them.

George is obsessed with soccer; he eats, breathes, and lives the game.

Complex sentences

A **complex sentence** consists of one independent clause with at least one dependent clause.

┌───DEPENDENT CLAUSE───┐
Many people believe that anyone can earn a living.
┌───DEPENDENT CLAUSE───┐
Those who do not like to get dirty should not go camping.
┌───DEPENDENT CLAUSE───┐
As I awaited my interview, I sat with other nervous candidates.

OPTIONAL EXERCISE

Combine each group of the following sentences into a single sentence, transforming some sentences into phrases to expand and shape the basic sentence. Try to produce two versions of each combined sentence.

1. The house's paint is peeling.
   The house's roof is leaking.
   The house is a dump.
   The house will never sell.
   (ex) That paint-peeling, roof-leaking dump will never sell.
2. It was a crisp morning in early spring.
   A man walked through a forest.
   He was alone.
   The forest was newly budding.
   (ex) On a crisp morning in early spring, a man walked alone through a newly budding forest.
3. We climbed a tree.
   The tree stood in Jesse's backyard.
   We climbed all summer long.
   (ex) All summer long, we climbed the tree that stood in Jesse's backyard.
4. Only two people were in the library.
   A man with gray hair was slightly gray.
   A young woman was in the library.
   She wore jeans.
   (ex) Only two people, a man with slightly gray hair and a young woman in jeans, were in the library.
5. Mr. Preston suspected that his students planned to ridicule him.
   Mr. Preston refused to turn his back to his students in class.
   (ex) Suspecting that his students planned to ridicule him, Mr. Preston refused to turn his back to his students in class.
6. Anna played an elf in the Marysville Christmas parade.
   Anna had fun.
   It was cold.
   (ex) Although she was cold, playing an elf in the Marysville Christmas parade was fun for Anna.
7. New York City is a great place to visit.
   New York City is a prohibitively expensive place to live.
   (ex) Although living there is prohibitively expensive, New York City is a great place to visit.
8. Ellie was at the Easter egg hunt.
   Ellie found several eggs.
   The eggs were hidden.
   The eggs were underneath a tree.
   (ex) At the Easter egg hunt, Ellie found several eggs hidden underneath a tree.

CLASSIFYING SENTENCES   *gr* |6d|

Notice that when a dependent clause comes before the independent clause, as in the last example above, it is usually set off with a comma (see 27a).

Compound-complex sentences

A **compound-complex sentence** consists of two or more independent clauses and at least one dependent clause.

> ┌—IND CL—┐ ┌——IND CL——┐ ┌———DEP CL———┐
> We liked Joe, for he was a kind man who was nice to everyone.

> Sister Lucy tried her best to help Martin, but he was an undisciplined boy who drove many teachers to despair.

▌ 2. Classifying sentences functionally

In terms of function, sentences can be classified as **declarative** (making a statement), **interrogative** (asking a question), **imperative** (giving a command), or **exclamatory** (expressing strong feeling).

DECLARATIVE	Julian plays oboe for the Cleveland Orchestra.
INTERROGATIVE	Has he also performed with other orchestras?
IMPERATIVE	Get me a ticket for his next performance.
EXCLAMATORY	What a talented musician he is!

▌ 3. Classifying sentences rhetorically

In addition to permitting functional and grammatical classifications, some sentences can be classified rhetorically as either cumulative or periodic sentences. Such a classification is important because the two patterns create very different rhythms and emphases. Learning to identify them takes you well on the way toward incorporating such sentences in your own writing.

Cumulative sentences begin with the subject and predicate containing the main thought and then build on this foundation with a series of phrases or clauses. When they are constructed skillfully, cumulative sentences create a strong rhythm and make for easy, often exciting, reading. Look at the following examples (the second example includes two cumulative sentences):

> The old man sat, waiting, watching, never tiring of his self-appointed task of keeping track of all who passed, his hat pulled tightly over his forehead, hiding eyes that missed nothing.

USEFUL READING

Corbett, Edward P. J. *Classical Rhetoric for the Modern Student.* 2d ed. New York: Oxford UP, 1971. Chapter 4, "Style," provides several easy-to-use methods for analyzing prose, including a couple of telling sentence-level exercises.

TEACHING PRACTICE

Before your students turn in their papers, ask them to identify by type each of the sentences in their papers. (You may want to review with them the definitions and constructions of each sentence type.) Then, ask them to tally each type (simple, compound, complex, compound-complex, cumulative, periodic). The results should answer the following questions: What kinds of sentences do they use most often? Do they use all kinds of sentences or rely on just a couple? What effect does their choice of sentence structures have on their prose? Do they recognize or know how to construct all the sentence types? If any students express interest in doing so, you may want to give them an opportunity to revise these papers before they hand them in.

(BACK)GROUNDING

In a series of essays, Francis Christensen demonstrated a way to map sentences and paragraphs according to levels of generality and modification. According to Christensen, *periodic* sentences are those that delay or postpone announcing the general main clause until the very end, leading into the topic with supporting or modifying details. This kind of sentence forces a reader to hold the subject in mind until the very end and keeps syntactic tension high. In the hands of skilled writers, periodic sentences can keep readers alert for what is to come and make the main idea, when it finally does appear, all the more impressive.

Although structures using various degrees of periodicity can be very effective in challenging and interesting readers, they do not constitute the most frequently used pattern in modern English. Rather, the *cumulative* structure, which adds details after the main clause or announcement of the topic, is the more dominant. Christensen writes:

> The main clause, which may or may not have a sentence modifier before it, advances the discussion; but the additions move backwards, as in this clause, to modify the statement of the main clause or more often to explicate or exemplify it, so that the sentence has a flowing and ebbing movement, advancing to a new position and then pausing to consolidate it, leaping and lingering as the popular ballad does. ("A Generative Rhetoric of the Sentence," *CCC* XIV [1963]: 156)

Because the main clause is presented at or near the beginning of the sentence, cumulative structures do not require readers to hold the subject in suspense until the end. In one sense, then, these sentences may be easier to read than periodic ones, yet the skilful writer can position the most important piece of information at the end. But Christensen warns that "the cumulative sentence in unskilled hands is unsteady, allowing a writer to ramble on, adding modifier after modifer, until the reader is almost overwhelmed, because the writer's central idea is lost" (*Notes Toward a New Rhetoric* 1978).

Using exclusively periodic or cumulative sentences, of course, would be desperately monotonous. And so the best writers mingle structures—short and long, periodic and cumulative—though never forgetting that the most important ideas naturally deserve the most prominent positions. Our own students can easily test the structures of their own texts, relating purpose to structure, learning to balance their own prose with purposeful and effective movement between general and specific information.

ANSWERS TO EXERCISE 6.20

1. compound, interrogative
2. complex, declarative
3. simple, imperative
4. simple, declarative
5. compound, exclamatory
6. complex, declarative
7. simple, imperative
8. compound-complex, declarative
9. compound-complex, declarative
10. complex, declarative

I could still feel the way I'd moved with the horse, the ripple of muscle through both the striving bodies, uniting as one. I could still feel the irons round my feet, the calves of my legs gripping, the balance, the nearness to my head of the stretching brown neck, the mane blowing in my mouth, my hands on the reins.   –DICK FRANCIS

In contrast, **periodic sentences** save the subject and verb of the independent clause until the end, building toward them and making the reader wait for the full meaning or significance to emerge.

Pulling my tie off and flinging it haphazardly onto the sofa, stretching and sighing with the ease of homecoming, listening to the familiar silences of the place, I felt—as usual—the welcoming peace unlock the gritting tensions of my outside world.

Though we long for the easy answer, the simple solution, the quick rationalization, only the harsh truth shall set us free.

Although cumulative sentences are more common in most modern prose than are periodic sentences, the ability to construct both will give you stylistic options that will strengthen your writing. For more information on such sentence types, see 20c.

EXERCISE 6.20

Classify each of the following sentences as simple, compound, complex, or compound-complex. In addition, note any sentences that could be classified as cumulative or periodic or as imperative, interrogative, or exclamatory.

1. Should he admit his mistake, or should he keep quiet and hope to avoid discovery?
2. The screen door creaked and banged when she ran into the house.
3. Solve your problems yourself.
4. People go on safari to watch wild animals in their natural habitat.
5. What a risk they took, but what a prize they won!
6. Although I used to believe that love was all that I needed to make my marriage work, I now realize that my marriage failed not from a lack of love but rather from a lack of communication, honesty, and trust.
7. Keeping in mind the terrain, the weather, and the length of the hike, decide what you need to take.
8. Dreams are necessary, but they can be frustrating unless you have the means to attain them.

9. Anticipation grew as the band played, and the crowd went wild when the team ran onto the field.
10. Wandering in the stockroom, searching futilely for pairs of shoes that I would swear were not there and finally meekly asking my coworkers to help me find them, I wasted countless hours during my first week on the job.

EXERCISE 6.21

The following paragraph is adapted from "The Hard Kind of Patriotism," a speech once given by Adlai Stevenson. The sentences in the paragraph have been simplified greatly. Try revising the paragraph by using phrases and clauses to combine some of the sentences. You might find it necessary to add or drop words. There is no one "correct" way to revise the paragraph; the object of the exercise is simply to practice using the various structures presented in this chapter.

America is much more than an economic fact. It is much more than a geographical fact. It is a political fact. It is a moral fact. It is the first community in which men set out in principle to institutionalize freedom. It is the first community in which men set out to institutionalize responsible government. It is the first community in which they set out to institutionalize human equality. And we love it for this audacity! Jefferson and Lincoln saw in this vision "the last, best hope of man." How easy it is, contemplating this vision, to see in it "the last, best hope of man." To be a nation founded on an ideal in one sense makes our love of country a vital force. It is a more vital force than any instinctive pieties of blood. It is a more vital force than any instinctive pieties of soil.

READING WITH AN EYE FOR SENTENCES

The following sentences come from the openings of well-known works. Read each sentence carefully, and be prepared to identify the independent clauses and dependent clauses. Then choose one of the sentences, and write a sentence that imitates its structure clause for clause and phrase for phrase.

Example

She is an open and trusting child, unprepared for and unaccustomed to the ambushes of family life, and perhaps it is just as well that I can offer her little of that life.   —Joan Didion, "On Going Home"

Those were long and desperate years, filled with and burdened by the pain of multiple loss, yet now it is clear to me that they gave me strength for the future.

America is much more than an economic or geographical fact. It is a political and moral fact—the first community in which men set out in principle to institutionalize freedom, responsible government, and human equality. And we love it for this audacity! How easy it is, contemplating this vision, to see in it—as Jefferson or Lincoln saw in it—"The last, best hope of man." To be a nation founded on an ideal in one sense makes our love of country a more vital force than any instinctive pieties of blood and soil.

1. Most people who bother with the matter at all would admit that the English language is in a bad way, but it is generally assumed that we cannot by conscious action do anything about it.

    —GEORGE ORWELL, "Politics and the English Language"

2. We observe today not a victory of party but a celebration of freedom, symbolizing an end as well as a beginning, signifying renewal as well as change.

    —JOHN F. KENNEDY, Inaugural Address

3. Once in a long while, four times so far for me, my mother brings out the metal tube that holds her medical diploma.

    —MAXINE HONG KINGSTON, "Photographs of My Parents"

4. Moths that fly by day are not properly to be called moths; they do not excite that pleasant sense of dark autumn nights and ivy blossom which the commonest yellow underwing asleep in the shadow of the curtain never fails to rouse in us.   —VIRGINIA WOOLF, "The Death of the Moth"

5. When Ulysses S. Grant and Robert E. Lee met in the parlor of a modest house at Appomattox Court House, Virginia, on April 9, 1865, to work out the terms for the surrender of Lee's Army of Northern Virginia, a great chapter in American life came to a close, and a great new chapter began.

    —BRUCE CATTON, "Grant and Lee: A Study in Contrasts"

FOR EXAMINING YOUR OWN SENTENCES

Look at one or two paragraphs of an essay you have written recently, and classify the sentences grammatically (6d1) and rhetorically (6d3). Does your classification reveal that you vary the types of sentences you use, or do you tend to write primarily one type of sentence? If you find that you depend primarily on one type, revise the paragraphs to include other types—for example, if you write mainly simple sentences, try combining some of them to make compound or complex sentences. If you keep a writing log, you might record this work there.

7. Understanding Pronoun Case

The grammatical term *case* may be unfamiliar to you (since it comes, like many such terms, from Latin), but the concept it represents is one you will recognize immediately. Take a look, for example, at the first-person pronouns in the following excerpt from Judy Syfers's well-known essay about the advantages of having a wife.

> *I* want a wife who will care for *me* when *I* am sick and sympathize with *my* pain. . . . *I* want a wife who will keep *my* clothes clean, ironed, mended, replaced when need be, and who will see to it that *my* personal things are kept in their proper place. . . .
>
> —JUDY SYFERS, "I Want a Wife"

Most of us know intuitively when to use *I*, when to use *me*, and when to use *my*. Our choices reflect differences in **case,** the form a noun or pronoun takes to indicate its function in a sentence. The italicized words in the excerpt show the singular first-person pronoun in three different cases: the subjective case (*I*), the objective case (*me*), and the possessive case (*my*). As the example sentences demonstrate, pronouns functioning as subjects are in the subjective case; those functioning as objects are in the objective case; and those functioning as possessives are in the possessive case.

Nouns and indefinite pronouns have the same form whether they function as subjects or objects, but they have a separate possessive case. It is usually formed by adding 's to a singular noun or an indefinite pronoun (*the cat's meow, nobody's fool*) or an apostrophe to a plural noun (*the players' strike*). See Chapter 30 for additional discussion and examples of the possessive case of nouns and indefinite pronouns.

175

When a pronoun follows a pronoun's nature, a pronoun substitutes for a noun; the noun then becomes the pronoun's antecedent.

Thanks to the existence of pronouns, we are able to avoid such redundancy and write, instead:

> When a pronoun follows its nature, it substitutes for a noun that then becomes its antecedent.

The most highly inflected parts of speech in present-day English, pronouns are nearly as complex and informational as their Latinate counterparts. Compare:

> As Dennis delivered Dennis's inaugural address, Dennis nervously looked out into the freezing crowd only to see Dennis's mother smiling beatifically at Dennis.

> As *he* delivered *his* inaugural address, Dennis nervously looked out into the freezing crowd only to see *his* mother smiling beatifically at *him*.

Although *Dennis* is the antecedent of *he, his,* and *him,* the pronoun form changes. English pronouns are specific in terms of person, gender, and number. In fact, our pronouns often carry as much information as their antecedents. *I, you,* and *he* tell us about person: *I* and *we* are first person; *you* is second person; *he, she, it,* and *they* are third person. *He, she,* and *it* tell us about gender—masculine, feminine, and neuter—while *I, we, she,* and *they* tell us about number—singular or plural.

Sometimes called the nominative case, the subjective case is used in the subject of the verb, a predicate noun, and a word in direct address.

This chapter focuses on the following pronoun case forms:

SUBJECTIVE

I/we	you	he/she/it	they	who/whoever

OBJECTIVE

me/us	you	him/her/it	them	whom/whomever

POSSESSIVE

my	your	his/her/its	their	whose
mine	yours	his/hers/its	theirs	

▌ 7a. Using the subjective case

A pronoun should be in the **subjective case** when it is a subject of a clause, a subject complement, or an appositive renaming a subject or subject complement. (See 6b and 6c.)

SUBJECT OF AN INDEPENDENT CLAUSE

They could either fight or face certain death with the lions.

We felt that Betty was enthusiastic and wanted to learn the material.

My brother and *I* adored our grandparents.

Who wrote "Araby"?

SUBJECT OF A DEPENDENT CLAUSE

Before *they* could get to the front, the war ended.

Jason did not seem like the type of person *who* would plagiarize.

Our group appealed to *whoever* was willing to listen.

SUBJECT COMPLEMENT

Even though pronouns used as subject complements should, grammatically, be in the subjective case, Americans often use the objective case, especially in conversation: "Who's there? It's *me*." To many speakers of English, "it's me" sounds not only acceptable but preferable to "it's I." Nevertheless, you should use the subjective case for all formal writing.

The first person to see Monty after the awards was *she*.

The players invited for a second audition were Cheryl and *I*.

It is *he* who brings life and spirit to the class.

(BACK)GROUNDING

The pronoun *you* gives no information other than number—second person. Except for context, there is no way to tell if *you* is singular or plural, masculine or feminine. Such was not always the case. Until the thirteenth century, English used different forms of second-person pronouns: the *th*-forms, indicating singular (*thee, thy, thou*); and the *y*-forms, indicating plural (*ye, you, your*).

With the influence of the French language, the *th*-forms came to denote intimacy and were used with close friends, family, and children; the *y*-forms, to denote a measure of formality or respect and were used with everyone else. These two forms corresponded with the *tu* and *vous* forms of French.

TEACHING PRACTICE

If you have students who speak other languages, ask them to explain the pronoun system of those languages, in terms of person, number, and gender.

WRITERS ON WRITING

The best writing, both prose and poetry, as Shakespeare pre-eminently shows, makes use, with condensation and selection, of playful, impassioned, imaginative talk.

—SIDNEY COX

Madame, all our words from loose using have lost their edge.

—ERNEST HEMINGWAY

WRITERS ON WRITING

Words are all we have.

—SAMUEL BECKETT

USING THE OBJECTIVE CASE   *ca* 7b

If you find the subjective case for a subject complement stilted or awkward, try rewriting the sentence using the pronoun as the subject.

She was the first person to see Monty after the awards.

APPOSITIVE RENAMING A SUBJECT

Three students—Peter, Richard, and *she*—worked on the report.

APPOSITIVE RENAMING A SUBJECT COMPLEMENT

The finalists were two dark horses, Michael and *I*.

▌ 7b. Using the objective case

A pronoun should be in the **objective case** when it functions as a direct or indirect object (of a verb or verbal), a subject of an infinitive, an object of a preposition, or an appositive renaming an object. (See 6b3 and 6c3.)

OBJECT OF A VERB

The professor surprised *them* with a quiz. [direct object of *surprised*]

Martin Luther King, Jr., gave *us* hope. [indirect object of *gave*]

Reagan was a president *whom* conservative Americans adored. [direct object of *adored*]

OBJECT OF A VERBAL

The Parisians were wonderful about helping *me*, and I ended the year speaking fluently. [object of gerund]

Wishing *her* luck, the coach stepped back to watch the performance. [object of participle]

Leonard offered to show *him* around town. [object of infinitive]

SUBJECT OF AN INFINITIVE

The objective case is also used in sentences like the following, where the pronoun is preceded by a verb and followed by an infinitive. Even though the pronoun in such constructions is called the subject of the infinitive, it is in the objective case.

Writing helps *me* to know myself better.

The student campaigners convinced his wife and *him* to vote in favor of the school bond.

The trip led *us* to appreciate how much California owes to Mexico.

OBJECT OF A PREPOSITION

As Paul entered the room, a strange feeling came over *me*.

Alice planned a surprise party for *them*.

APPOSITIVE RENAMING AN OBJECT

We selected two managers, Joan and *her*, to attend the seminar.

7c. Using the possessive case

A pronoun should be in the **possessive case** when it shows possession or ownership. Notice that there are two forms of possessive pronouns: adjective forms, which are used before nouns or gerunds (*my, your, his, her, its, our, their, whose*), and noun forms, which take the place of a noun (*mine, yours, his, hers, its, ours, theirs, whose*). (See Chapter 30.)

ADJECTIVE FORMS

Many of Hitchcock's movies put viewers on the edge of *their* seats.

Whose life is it, anyway?

The sound of *his* hammering echoed through the corridor.

When a pronoun precedes a verb form ending in *-ing*, as in the preceding example, you need to decide whether the verb form is a gerund or a present participle to determine whether to use the possessive or the objective case of the pronoun. Gerunds always function as nouns, and if the verb form is a gerund, the pronoun modifies it and must be in the possessive case. Present participles function as adjectives, and if the verb form is a participle, it modifies the pronoun, which should be in the objective case.

Usually you can tell from the context of the sentence whether an *-ing* verb form is a gerund or a participle. In the example sentence, for instance, you can tell that *hammering* is a gerund and the pronoun should be *his* because it was the sound of *hammering*, not the sound of *him*, that was echoing through the corridor. In some sentences like this, however, you could use either an objective or a possessive pronoun, depending on the exact meaning you intend. Look at these two sentences:

I remember *his* singing.

I remember *him* singing.

USING THE POSSESSIVE CASE   *ca* 7*c*

In the first example, the memory is of *singing*, which is a gerund, modified by the possessive pronoun *his*. In the second example, the memory is of *him*, which functions as a direct object of *remember* and thus is in the objective case; *singing* is a present participle modifying *him*.

NOUN FORMS

The responsibility is *hers*.

"It's *mine!*" declared the child, clutching the golf club.

Whose did she borrow?

EXERCISE 7.1

The following passage comes from "University Days," James Thurber's classic essay about his years as a student at Ohio State University. Most of its pronouns have been removed. Put a correct pronoun in each blank, labeling each one as subjective, objective, or possessive case.

Another course that I didn't like, but somehow managed to pass, was economics. _____ went to that class straight from the botany class, which didn't help _____ to understand either subject. _____ used to get them mixed up. But not as mixed up as another student in _____ economics class who came there direct from a physics laboratory. _____ was a tackle on the football team, named Bolenciecwcz. At that time Ohio State University had one of the best football teams in the country, and Bolenciecwcz was one of _____ outstanding stars. In order to be eligible to play it was necessary for _____ to keep up in _____ studies, a very difficult matter, for while _____ was not dumber than an ox _____ was not any smarter. Most of _____ professors were lenient and helped _____ along. None gave _____ more hints in answering questions or asked _____ simpler ones than the economics professor, a thin, timid man named Bassum. One day when _____ were on the subject of transportation and distribution, it came Bolenciecwcz's turn to answer a question. "Name one means of transportation," the professor said to _____. No light came into the big tackle's eyes. "Just any means of transportation" said the professor. Bolenciecwcz sat staring at _____. "That is," pursued the professor, "any medium, agency, or method of going from one place to another." Bolenciecwcz had the look of a man _____ is being led into a trap. "You may choose among steam, horse-drawn, or electrically propelled vehicles," said the instructor. "I might suggest the one which _____ commonly take in making long journeys across land." There was a profound silence in which everybody stirred uneasily, including Bolenciecwcz and Mr. Bassum. Mr. Bassum abruptly broke this silence in an amazing manner. "Choo-choo-choo," _____ said, in a low voice, and turned instantly scarlet.

ANSWERS TO EXERCISE 7.1

Another course that I didn't like, but somehow managed to pass, was economics. I went to that class straight from the botany class, which didn't help me to understand either subject. I used to get them mixed up. But not as mixed up as another student in my economics class who came there direct from a physics laboratory. He was a tackle on the football team, named Bolenciecwcz. At that time Ohio State University had one of the best football teams in the country, and Bolenciecwcz was one of its outstanding stars. In order to be eligible to play it was necessary for him to keep up in his studies, a very difficult matter, for while he was not dumber than an ox he was not any smarter. Most of his professors were lenient and helped him along. None gave him more hints in answering questions or asked him simpler ones than the economics professor, a thin, timid man named Bassum. One day when we were on the subject of transportation and distribution, it came Bolenciecwcz's turn to answer a question. "Name one means of transportation," the professor said to him. No light came into the big tackle's eyes. "Just any means of transportation," said the professor, "any medium, agency, or method of going from one place to another." Bolenciecwcz had the look of a man who is being led into a trap. "You may choose among steam, horse-drawn, or electrically propelled vehicles," said the instructor. "I might suggest the one which we commonly take in making long journeys across land." There was a profound silence in which everybody stirred uneasily, including Bolenciecwcz and Mr. Bassum. Mr. Bassum abruptly broke this silence in an amazing manner. "Choo-choo-choo," he said, in a low voice, and turned instantly scarlet. He glanced appealingly around the room. All of us, of course, shared Mr. Bassum's desire that Bolenciecwcz should stay abreast of the class in economics, for the Illinois game, one of the hardest and most important of the season was just a week off. "Toot, toot, too-tooooooot!" some student with a deep voice moaned, and we all looked encouragingly at Bolenciecwcz. Somebody else gave a fine imitation of a locomotive letting off steam. Mr. Bassum himself rounded off the little show. "Ding, dong, ding, dong," he said, hopefully. Bolenciecwcz was staring at the floor now, trying to think, his great brow furrowed, his huge hands rubbing together, his face red.

WRITERS ON WRITING

A writer lives in awe of words for they can be cruel or kind, and they can change their meanings right in front of you. They pick up flavors and odors like butter in a refrigerator.

—JOHN STEINBECK

ANSWERS TO EXERCISE 7.2 (WILL VARY)

1. my, your, his, her, our, their
2. hers
3. our
4. his
5. Whose

WRITERS ON WRITING

You can be a little ungrammatical if you come from the right part of the country.

—ROBERT FROST

_____ glanced appealingly around the room. All of _____, of course, shared Mr. Bassum's desire that Bolenciecwcz should stay abreast of the class in economics, for the Illinois game, one of the hardest and most important of the season, was only a week off. "Toot, toot, too-toooooooot!" some student with a deep voice moaned, and _____ all looked encouragingly at Bolenciecwcz. Somebody else gave a fine imitation of a locomotive letting off steam. Mr. Bassum himself rounded off the little show. "Ding, dong, ding, dong," _____ said, hopefully. Bolenciecwcz was staring at the floor now, trying to think, _____ great brow furrowed, _____ huge hands rubbing together, _____ face red. —JAMES THURBER, "University Days"

EXERCISE 7.2

Insert a correct possessive pronoun in the blank in each sentence.

> _Example_
> My eyes ached after studying for ten hours.

1. Your parents must be pleased about _____ going back to college.
2. Kevin's dinner arrived after a thirty-minute wait, but she waited an hour for _____.
3. We all agreed to pool _____ knowledge in studying for the European history examination.
4. Even many supporters of Lincoln opposed _____ freeing the slaves.
5. _____ responsibility should it be to teach moral values?

7d. Using _who, whoever, whom,_ and _whomever_

One of the most common problems with pronoun case is deciding whether to use _who_ or _whom._ In speech and even in some informal writing, _whom_ has become a rarely used word. Even when traditional grammar requires _whom,_ many Americans use _who_ instead. Nevertheless, in formal written English, which includes most of the writing you do at college, the case of the pronoun should properly reflect its grammatical function. _Who_ and _whoever_ are the subjective case forms and should be used when the pronoun is a subject or subject complement. _Whom_ and _whomever_ are the objective case forms and should be used when the pronoun is a direct or indirect object or the object of a preposition.

Most writers find that two particular situations can lead to confusion with _who_ and _whom:_ when they begin a question and when they introduce a dependent clause. In a dependent clause, you may also have to choose between _whoever_ and _whomever._ (See 6c4.)

USING *WHO, WHOEVER, WHOM,* AND *WHOMEVER*   *ca* 7d

▌1. Beginning a question with *who* or *whom*

You can determine whether to use *who* or *whom* at the beginning of a question by answering the question using a personal pronoun. If the answer is in the subjective case, use *who*; if the answer is in the objective case, use *whom*.

> *Who* could best narrate such a story? *She* could best narrate such a story. [*She* is subjective; thus *who* is correct.]
>
> *Whom* did you visit? [I visited *them*. *Them* is objective; thus *whom* is correct.]
>
> *Whom* are you voting for? [I am voting for *her*. *Her* is objective; thus *whom* is correct.]

Notice that even if the *who/whom* clause is interrupted by the main subject and verb of the sentence—for example, *did you say* or *does she think*—answering the question using a personal pronoun will still tell you the right case to use.

> *Who* does he think can best narrate such a story? [He thinks *she* can best narrate such a story. *She* is subjective; thus *who* is correct.]

▌2. Beginning a dependent clause with *who, whoever, whom,* or *whomever*

The case of a pronoun in a dependent clause is determined by its function in the clause, no matter how that clause functions in the sentence. If the pronoun acts as a subject in the clause, use *who* or *whoever*. If the pronoun acts as an object, use *whom* or *whomever*. (See 6c4.)

> The new president was not *whom* she had expected. [*Whom* is the object of the verb *had expected* in the clause *whom she had expected*. Though the clause as a whole is the complement of the subject *president*, the pronoun should be in the objective case.]
>
> The waitress's work schedule changed from week to week, depending on *whoever* needed time off. [*Whoever* is the subject of the clause *whoever needed time off*. Though the clause as a whole is the object of the preposition *on*, the pronoun should be in the subjective case.]
>
> Richard feels like a knight *who* is headed for great adventure. [*Who* is the subject of the clause *who is headed for great adventure*.]
>
> *Whomever* the party suspected of disloyalty was executed. [*Whomever* is the object of the verb *suspected* in the clause *Whomever the party sus-*

WRITERS ON WRITING

The schoolmarm . . . continues the heroic task of trying to make her young charges grasp the difference between *who* and *whom*. Here, alas, the speechways of the American people seem to be again against her. The two forms of the pronoun are confused magnificently in the debates in Congress, and in most newspaper writing, and in ordinary discourse the great majority of Americans avoid *whom* diligently, as a word full of snares. When they employ it, it is often incorrectly, as in "*Whom* is your father?" and "*Whom* spoke to me?" Noah Webster, always the pragmatic reformer, denounced it as usually useless so long ago as 1783. Common sense, he argued, was on the side of "*Who* did he marry?" Today such a form as "*Whom* are you talking to?" would seem very affected to most Americans; they might write it, but they would never speak it. . . . A shadowy line often separates what is currently coming into sound usage from what is still regarded as barbarous.

—H. L. MENCKEN

When Jesus came into the coasts of Cesarea Philippi, he asked his disciples, saying, "*Whom* do men say that I, the Son of Man, am?"

—MATTHEW 16:13

pected of disloyalty. Though the clause as a whole is the subject of the sentence, the pronoun should be in the objective case.]

If you are not sure which case to use, try separating out the dependent clause from the rest of the sentence and looking at it in isolation. Rewrite the clause as a new sentence with a personal pronoun instead of *who(ever)* or *whom(ever)*. If the pronoun is in the subjective case, use *who* or *whoever* in the original clause; if it is in the objective case, use *whom* or *whomever*.

Anyone can hypnotize a person (*who/whom*) wants to be hypnotized. [Separate out the clause *who/whom wants to be hypnotized.* Substituting a personal pronoun gives you *he wants to be hypnotized. He* is subjective case; therefore: Anyone can hypnotize a person *who* wants to be hypnotized.]

The minister grimaced at (*whoever/whomever*) made any noise. [Separate out the clause *whoever/whomever made any noise.* Substituting a personal pronoun gives you *they made any noise. They* is subjective case; therefore: The minister grimaced at *whoever* made any noise.]

The minister smiled at (*whoever/whomever*) she greeted. [Separate out the clause *she greeted whoever/whomever.* Substituting a personal pronoun gives you *she greeted them. Them* is objective case; therefore: The minister smiled at *whomever* she greeted.]

If the dependent clause is interrupted by an expression such as *he thinks* or *she says,* delete the expression when you separate out the clause.

The minister grimaced at (whoever/whomever) she thought made any noise. [Separate out the clause *whoever/whomever made any noise,* deleting the interrupting expression *she thought.* Substituting a personal pronoun gives you *they made any noise. They* is subjective case; therefore: The minister grimaced at *whoever* she thought made any noise.]

ANSWERS TO EXERCISE 7.3

1. Who: subjective
2. whoever: subject of *faces*
3. whoever: subject of *sold*
4. whom: object of preposition, *with . . . whom we wanted*
5. whom: direct object

EXERCISE 7.3

Insert *who, whoever, whom,* or *whomever* correctly in the blank in each of the following sentences.

Example
She is someone <u>who</u> will go far.

1. _____ shall I say is calling?
2. _____ the voters choose faces an almost impossible challenge.
3. The manager promised to reward _____ sold the most cars.

USING THE CORRECT CASE IN APPOSITIVES

4. Professor Quiñones asked _____ we wanted to collaborate with.
5. _____ will the new tax law benefit most?

7e. Using the correct case in compound structures

Most problems with case of personal pronouns occur when the pronoun is part of a compound subject, complement, or object. Each part of a compound structure should be in the same case as it would if used alone: pronouns in compound subjects and subject complements should be in the subjective case; pronouns in compound objects should be in the objective case.

SUBJECTS

Mrs. Wentzel and *I* simply could not exist in the same classroom.

When *Zelda* and *he* were first married, they lived in New York.

SUBJECT COMPLEMENTS

The winners of the competition were *Renata* and *he*.

The next two speakers will be *Philip* and *she*.

OBJECTS OF VERBS

Smith College accepted *Andrea* and *me*. [direct object]

Rutgers University offered *Bob* and *her* a scholarship. [indirect object]

OBJECTS OF PREPOSITIONS

This morning saw yet another conflict between *my sister* and *me*.

My aunt put me in the room once shared by *my uncle* and *her*.

If you are unsure whether to use the subjective or the objective case in a compound structure, make each part of the compound into a separate sentence.

Come to the park with my roommate and (*I/me*). [Separating the compound structure gives you *come to the park with my roommate* and *come to the park with me*; thus: Come to the park with my roommate and *me*.]

7f. Using the correct case in appositives

The case of a pronoun that is part of an appositive is determined by the word that the appositive renames. If the word functions as a subject or subject complement, the pronoun should be in the subjective

WRITERS ON WRITING

The difference between the almost right word and the right word is really a large matter—'tis the difference between the lightning-bug and lightning.

—MARK TWAIN

case; if it functions as an object, the pronoun should be in the objective case.

> Three students—Victor, Sally, and *he*—were named Rhodes scholars. [*Students* is the subject of the sentence, so the pronoun in the appositive *Victor, Sally, and he* should be in the subjective case.]

> The poker game that night produced two big winners, my mother and *me*. [*Winners* is the direct object of the verb *produced*, so the pronoun in the appositive *my mother and me* should be in the objective case].

7g. Using the correct case in elliptical constructions

Elliptical constructions are those in which some words are understood but left out. In comparisons with *than* or *as*, we often leave words unsaid: *I see Elizabeth more often than* [*I see*] *her sister*. When sentences with such constructions end in a pronoun, the pronoun should be in the case it would be in if the construction were complete.

> His brother has always been more athletic than *he* [is].

In some constructions like this, the case of the pronoun depends on the meaning intended.

ELLIPTICAL	Willie likes Lily more than *she*.
COMPLETE	Willie likes Lily more than *she* [likes Lily].
ELLIPTICAL	Willie likes Lily more than *her*.
COMPLETE	Willie likes Lily more than [he likes] *her*.

As these examples demonstrate, use the subjective case if the pronoun is actually the subject of an omitted verb; use the objective case if it is an object of an omitted verb.

7h. Using *we* and *us* correctly before a noun

When the first-person plural pronoun is used with a noun, the case of the pronoun depends on the way the noun functions in the sentence. If the noun functions as a subject, the pronoun should be in the subjective case (*we*); if the noun functions as an object, the pronoun should be in the objective case (*us*).

> *We* fans never give up hope. [*Fans* is the subject.]

> The Orioles depend on *us* fans. [*Fans* is the object of a preposition.]

USING *WE* AND *US* CORRECTLY BEFORE A NOUN

If you are unsure about which case to use, recasting the sentence without the noun will give you the answer. Use whichever pronoun would be correct if the noun were omitted: *We never give up hope. The Orioles depend on us.*

EXERCISE 7.4

Choose the appropriate pronoun from the pair in parentheses in each of the following sentences.

Example

The fear of (*them*/*their*) taking advantage of him never entered his mind.

1. The relationship between (*they*/*them*) and their brother was often strained.
2. When I was young, I had a friend (*who*/*whom*) I idolized.
3. This love for children probably began because there were three children younger than (*I*/*me*) in my family.
4. The only candidates left in the race were (*he*/*him*) and Dukakis.
5. I am getting more and more interested in (*him*/*his*) accompanying me on the trip.
6. When Carol and (*she*/*her*) first met, they despised each other.
7. The two people closest to me, (*he*/*him*) and my mother, expected me to return home after graduation.
8. Soap operas appeal to (*whoever*/*whomever*) is interested in intrigue, suspense, joy, pain, grief, romance, infidelity, sex, or violence.
9. Later (*we*/*us*) "rejects" were taken to watch the taping of the show.
10. The only mother and father (*who*/*whom*) they know are the people (*who*/*whom*) raised them and took care of them.

EXERCISE 7.5

Edit each of the following sentences to correct errors in pronoun case. (Not all sentences contain errors.)

Example

Of the group, only her and I finished the race.
Of the group, only *she* and I finished the race.

1. The readers, her and me, agreed that the story was very suspenseful.
2. Just between you and I, this course is a disaster!
3. The people who Jay worked with were very cold and unsociable.
4. Who would have thought that twenty years later there would be a black presidential candidate.
5. Roderigo becomes involved in the plot without him knowing it.
6. Only him, a few cabinet members, and several military leaders were aware of the steady advance Japan was making toward Pearl Harbor.

ANSWERS TO EXERCISE 7.4

1. them
2. whom
3. I
4. he
5. his
6. she
7. he
8. whoever
9. we
10. whom, who

ANSWERS TO EXERCISE 7.5

1. her and me——→she and I
2. I——→me
3. who——→whom
4. correct
5. him——→his (or omit pronoun)
6. him——→he
7. correct
8. me——→I
9. correct
10. whomever——→whoever

WRITERS ON WRITING

Grammar is a piano I play by ear. All I know about grammar is its power.

—JOAN DIDION

Any fool can make a rule and every fool will mind it.

—HENRY DAVID THOREAU

7. All of the job candidates were far more experienced than I.
8. As out-of-towners, my buddy and me did not know too many people.
9. I never got to play that role in front of an audience, but I am one of the few performers who really did "break a leg."
10. Constance always lent money to whomever asked her for it.

READING WITH ATTENTION TO CASE

The poet E. E. Cummings often broke the standard rules of grammar and word order to create particular effects in his poetry. Read the following poem by Cummings, and note the function of each pronoun. Then rearrange the words of the poem so that they follow as closely as possible the normal order they would take in an ordinary sentence. How does pronoun case give you a clue to this arrangement?

Me up at does

out of the floor
quietly stare

a poisoned mouse

still who alive

is asking What
have i done that

you wouldn't have

FOR EXAMINING CASE IN YOUR OWN WRITING

Research shows that one of the most overused words in any language is the word for *I*. Whenever you write anything that includes your own opinions, you probably rely to some degree on first-person pronouns, singular and plural. Read over the excerpt from James Thurber's "University Days," in Exercise 7.1, and then write a paragraph or two about your own least favorite class. When you are finished, underline all the personal pronouns you used, and label each one for case. Do you find any patterns? If you find that you rely heavily on any one case—that half your sentences begin with *I*, for example— decide whether your writing seems at all monotonous as a result. If so, try revising, paying attention to pronoun case. See, in other words, whether revising some sentences to change *I* to *me* (or vice versa) brings greater variety to your writing. If you keep a writing log, you might enter your work into it, noting what you have learned about your use of pronoun case.

8. Using Verbs

When used skillfully, verbs can be called the heartbeat of prose, moving it along, enlivening it, carrying its action. Verbs are extremely flexible and can change form to mark grammatical agreement with the subject (see Chapter 9) or to indicate *tense*, *voice*, or *mood*.

CHANGE IN TENSE	The runner *skims* around the track. [present tense]
	The runner *skimmed* around the track. [past tense]
CHANGE IN VOICE	She *savors* every step. [active voice]
	Every step *is savored*. [passive voice]
CHANGE IN MOOD	She *is* completely content. [indicative]
	If she *were* not content, she *would* not *be* smiling. [subjunctive]

This chapter explores in detail the way verbs work, with attention to form, tense, voice, and mood.

VERB FORMS

Except for *be*, all English verbs have five forms.

BASE FORM	PAST TENSE	PAST PARTICIPLE	PRESENT PARTICIPLE	-S FORM
talk	talked	talked	talking	talks
adore	adored	adored	adoring	adores
jog	jogged	jogged	jogging	jogs

187

USEFUL READING

Aitchison, Jean. *Language Change: Progress or Decay*. Suffolk, England: Fontana, 1981. Written from a sociolinguist's perspective, this work explains the implementation, causes, and developmental features of language change. The entire discussion is accessible and straightforward; chapter 3 specifically discusses verb forms and the inherent causes of their change.

(BACK)GROUNDING

English verb forms are the most varied and flexible in all the modern languages: its six tenses can fall in the indicative, subjunctive, or imperative mood; its verbs can be in active or passive voice, in present, continuous, or emphatic form, in completed or progressive aspect. English verbs can stand alone or work together, or they can transform themselves into nouns and adjectives.

Such plasticity arose from Scandinavian, German, and French influences. In fact, Old English verbs were Germanic in nature: they distinguished between only two simple tenses, present and past, and signified all other information (number, person, gender, mood, voice) by inflectional endings. Old English verbs were more often strong than weak, or more often *irregular* than *regular*: strong verbs (sing, sang; bind, bound; choose, chosen) have the power to indicate tense by transforming their medial vowels, not by merely adding a feeble *-ed* inflectional ending (*kick, kicked, kicked*).

The Norman Invasion greatly influenced Middle English, infusing it with the vocabulary and grammar of the French- and Latin-speaking ruling class. One significant influence was the linguistic regularization of the verbs: more than half of the strong (irregular) verbs became weak (regular), using *-ed* inflectional endings rather than internal transformation to indicate tense. English was spoken chiefly by the lower classes, who were removed from the restraining influences of education and a literary standard. Naturally, many speakers wrongly applied the weak-verb pattern to some that should have been strong. This impulse to regularize verbs was checked by the rise of English on the social scale and the stabilizing effect of printing. Now, even the native-born English speaker must memorize the strong or irregular verb forms.

(BACK)GROUNDING

Fascinating are the verb-adverb combinations in modern English, which deliver the literal meaning of the verb and the adverb in combination:

bring about	cause
catch on	learn
give up	surrender
keep on	continue
put up with	endure
hold up	delay, exhibit, support
turn over	roll
check up (on)	inspect

Besides seeming less formal than their one-word counterparts, many of these verb phrases convey shades of meaning that could not be otherwise expressed. In addition, they are also used as nouns, as in a *checkup,* a *layoff,* and a *holdup,* testimony to the flexibility of our language. Some twenty verbs of this sort—among them, *back, break, come, go, hold, take,* and *work*—exist in over 155 combinations, with over 600 meanings.

The **base form** is the one listed in the dictionary. For all verbs except *be,* it is the form used to indicate action that takes place (or a condition that exists) in the present when the subject is a plural noun or the pronoun *I, you, we,* or *they.*

> In the ritual the women *go* into trances.

> The men *take* knives and *point* them at their chests.

The **past tense** indicates action that took place (or a condition that existed) in the past. The past tense of most verbs is formed by adding *-ed* or *-d* to the base form. Some verbs, however, have an irregular past tense form, as is explained in 8b. *Be* has two past-tense forms, *was* and *were.*

> The Globe *served* as the playhouse for many of Shakespeare's works.

> In 1613 it *caught* fire and *burned* to the ground.

The **past participle** usually has the same form as the past tense. As with the past tense, some verbs have irregular forms for the past participle (see 8b). The past participle cannot function alone as the predicate of a clause or sentence. To function as a predicate, it must be used with a form of the auxiliary verb *have* or *be.* In addition, the past participle can function as an adjective, modifying a noun or pronoun. (See 8e.)

> She *had accomplished* the impossible.

> The doctors *have asked* for my cooperation.

> No one *was injured* in the explosion.

> *Standardized* tests usually require *sharpened* pencils.

The **present participle** is constructed by adding *-ing* to the base form. Like the past participle, it cannot function alone as a predicate but must be used with one or more auxiliary verbs. A present participle used with the auxiliary *be* is called the progressive form of a verb and indicates continuing action. The present participle can also function as an adjective, like the past participle, or as a noun, called a gerund. (See 6c.)

> Several hundred students *are competing* in the race.

> He tried to comfort the *crying* child.

> Philosophy emphasizes the value of *thinking.*

USING VERBS

Except for *be* and *have*, the **-s form** consists of the base form plus *-s* or *-es*. This form indicates the present tense when the subject is third-person singular. All singular nouns, the pronouns *he, she,* and *it,* and many indefinite pronouns (such as *everyone,* or *someone*) are third-person singular.

> Life *demands* our participation.
>
> She usually *takes* the shortcut across campus.
>
> No one *believes* his story.

It is very important to note that the *-s* form occurs *only* in the third-person singular.

	SINGULAR	PLURAL
FIRST PERSON	I wish	we wish
SECOND PERSON	you wish	you wish
THIRD PERSON	he/she/it wishes	they wish
	Joe wishes	children wish
	someone wishes	

Some dialects of English use the base form instead of the *-s* form with a third-person singular subject. In addition, some people skip carelessly over the *-s* form in speech and then, as a result, often tend to forget the *-s* or *-es* in writing.

DIALECT	She *live* in a high-rise apartment.
ACADEMIC WRITING	She *lives* in a high-rise apartment.

The forms of *be* and *have* corresponding to the *-s* form of other verbs are *is* and *has.*

> The second stage of the ritual *is* the so-called liminal stage.
>
> A whale *has* lungs instead of gills.

➤ Checking for *-s* and *-es* endings

If you tend to leave off the *-s* and *-es* verb endings, you should check for them systematically when proofreading. Underline every verb, and then circle all those in the present tense. Find the subject for every verb you circle. If the subject is third-person singular (a singular noun; *he, she,* or *it;* or most indefinite pronouns), be sure the verb ends in *-s* or *-es.* If it is not third-person singular, the verb should not have an *-s* or *-es* ending.

TEACHING PRACTICE

Students who speak a dialect other than Edited American English need to master this form. Vocabulary may not be as much a problem as verb forms and inflectional endings. Because speakers of Black English Vernacular, Chinese, and Spanish, for example, often omit *s, ed, ing,* you may want to review the following chart with them:

I learn/am learning/learned
you learn/are learning/learned
s/he learns/is learning/learned

we learn/are learning/learned
you learn/are learning/learned
they learn/are learning/learned

Forms of be

Be has three different forms in the present tense and, as mentioned earlier, two forms in the past tense.

Present tense

	SINGULAR	PLURAL
FIRST PERSON	I *am*	we *are*
SECOND PERSON	you *are*	you *are*
THIRD PERSON	he/she/it *is*	they *are*
	Jane *is*	children *are*
	somebody *is*	some *are*

Past tense

	SINGULAR	PLURAL
FIRST PERSON	I *was*	we *were*
SECOND PERSON	you *were*	you *were*
THIRD PERSON	he/she/it *was*	they *were*
	Jane *was*	children *were*
	somebody *was*	some *were*

Although some dialects of English use the base form *be* in place of *am*, *is*, and *are* and the base form *have* in place of *has*, you should always use *am*, *is*, *are*, or *has* in college and other formal writing.

DIALECT	She *be* the oldest member of the family.
ACADEMIC WRITING	She *is* the oldest member of the family
DIALECT	She *have* ten great-grandchildren.
ACADEMIC WRITING	She *has* ten great-grandchildren.

▌ 8a. Using auxiliary verbs

Sometimes called helping verbs, **auxiliary verbs** are used with a base form, present participle, or past participle to create verb phrases. The base form or participle in a verb phrase is called the main verb. The most commonly used auxiliaries include forms of *have*, *be*, and *do*, which are used to indicate a completed action or condition (see 8c and 8d), to indicate the passive voice, to indicate a continuing action or condition, to add emphasis, to ask questions, and to make negative statements. *Will* and *shall* are auxiliaries used to show future time; unlike most auxiliaries, they never change form.

USING AUXILIARY VERBS   *vb* |8a

Dennis *has worked* late all month.

I *am working* hard.

She *has been warned* several times.

We *do respect* your viewpoint.

Do you *know* the answer?

He *does* not *like* wearing a tie.

They *will explain* the procedure.

Modal auxiliaries—*can, could, might, may, must, ought to, should, would*—show possibility, necessity, obligation, and so on.

> You *can see* three states from the top of the mountain. [possibility]
>
> I *must try* harder. [necessity]
>
> She *should visit* her parents more often. [obligation]

Although some dialects of English use the base form *be* as an auxiliary instead of *am, is,* or *are,* always use the standard forms in college and other formal writing.

DIALECT	They *be* working to earn money for tuition.
ACADEMIC WRITING	They *are* working to earn money for tuition.
DIALECT	I *be* scheduled to take biology next semester.
ACADEMIC WRITING	I *am* scheduled to take biology next semester.

In making a negative statement, some dialects use *don't* with a third-person singular subject. In formal writing, always use *doesn't* in such constructions.

DIALECT	The character *don't* seem true to life.
ACADEMIC WRITING	The character *doesn't* seem true to life.

Some dialects use the past participle or the present participle of a verb without an auxiliary verb as the predicate of a sentence. Many writers also leave out the auxiliary accidentally. In formal writing, a participle must have an auxiliary verb attached to it in order to function as a predicate. (See Chapter 14.)

DIALECT	They *working* to earn money for tuition.
ACADEMIC WRITING	They *are working* to earn money for tuition.
DIALECT	My roommate *gone* to her seminar.
ACADEMIC WRITING	My roommate *has gone* to her seminar.

TEACHING PRACTICE

To practice and highlight the use of modals and auxiliaries, ask the students to write an entry in their writing log about hopes and dreams, a stream-of-consciousness list of what could or should be, or what could, should, or might have been.

The exercise will work best if they write on several hopes rather than focusing on just one. (By focusing, they may shift tenses and stop using the modal auxiliaries that you will soon be calling to their attention.) Then, ask them to exchange their writing logs, read one another's entries, and mark the auxiliaries. Discuss their effective and their questionable uses of auxiliaries.

8b *vb*   USING VERBS

DIALECT	The porch needs fixed.
ACADEMIC WRITING	The porch needs to be fixed.

ANSWERS TO EXERCISE 8.1
(present tense)

1. begin———→begins
2. have———→has
3. correct
4. correct
5. relax———→relaxes
6. be———→is
7. suffers———→suffer
8. don't———→doesn't
9. is refunded
10. is running

EXERCISE 8.1

Edit the following sentences so that all verb forms are acceptable in formal written English. (Some of the sentences do not require any change.)

Example
Although Joe seem in control, his actions making me wonder.
Although Joe *seems* in control, his actions *make* me wonder.

1. When the dance begin, a man in costume appears.
2. The man have long fingernails and a mask.
3. All of the people in the village participate in the ceremony.
4. The doctor works two nights a week at a clinic.
5. A hot shower always relax me.
6. The thought of nuclear war be terrifying to most people.
7. New mothers often suffers from depression.
8. He don't know whether to try again or to give up.
9. The deposit refunded if the customer doesn't buy the equipment.
10. Mayor Burns running for reelection this fall.

TEACHING PRACTICE

Because everyone has a tendency to regularize, or generalize, the English language, even native speakers need to memorize the irregular verb forms. Until we incorporate those irregular forms of our language, we overgeneralize the regular forms. As children, we overgeneralize both the plural form (*dogs*, *mouses*, and *sheeps*) and the verb form (*hummed*, *runned*, *shaked*, and *catched*). You may want to review these verb paradigms with your students.

WRITERS WRITING

If a gentleman be to study any language, it ought to be that of his country.

—LOCKE

Aristocracy and exclusiveness tend to final overthrow, in language as well as in politics.

—W. D. WHITNEY

8b. Using regular and irregular verbs

A verb is **regular** when its past tense and past participle are formed by adding *-ed* or *-d* to the base form:

BASE FORM	PAST TENSE	PAST PARTICIPLE
love	loved	loved
honor	honored	honored
obey	obeyed	obeyed

The past tense and past participle of regular verbs sometimes cause difficulty for writers in spelling, because some of them double the final consonant or change final *y* to *i* before adding *-ed*. (See 22d.)

➤ **Checking for *-ed* or *-d* endings**

Some people skip over the *-ed* or *-d* endings in conversation and thus forget to include them in writing. If you tend to make this mistake, you should make a point of systematically checking for it when proofreading. Underline all the verbs, and then underline a second time any that are past tense or past participles. Check each of these for an *-ed*

USING REGULAR AND IRREGULAR VERBS   *vb* 8b

or *-d* ending. Unless the verb is irregular (see below), it should end in *-ed* or *-d*.

Irregular verbs

A verb is **irregular** when it does not follow the *-ed* or *-d* pattern. The past tense and past participle of irregular verbs are most often formed by changing an internal vowel: *begin, began, begun.* In some verbs like this, *-en* or *-n* is also added to the past participle: *break, broke, broken.* Other verbs change form more radically: *go, went, gone.* Still others do not change at all: *hurt, hurt, hurt.* If you are uncertain about the correct verb form, consult your dictionary, which lists any irregular past tense and past participle forms under the entry for the base form.

You probably know most irregular verb forms intuitively, but you may want to take the time now to memorize any that cause you difficulty. Here are some of the most common irregular verbs.

BASE FORM	PAST TENSE	PAST PARTICIPLE
arise	arose	arisen
be	was/were	been
bear	bore	borne/born
beat	beat	beaten
become	became	become
begin	began	begun
bite	bit	bitten
blow	blew	blown
break	broke	broken
bring	brought	brought
build	built	built
burn	burned/burnt	burned/burnt
burst	burst	burst
buy	bought	bought
catch	caught	caught
choose	chose	chosen
come	came	come
cost	cost	cost
cut	cut	cut
dig	dug	dug
dive	dived/dove	dived
do	did	done
draw	drew	drawn
drink	drank	drunk

WRITING TOGETHER

After the class has divided into groups, have the students compose two sentences for each of twelve verbs of either your own choosing or from the list on pp. 193–195. In one sentence they should use the past tense form; in the second they should use the past participle form.

These exercises will help your students recognize the comparative differences in usage and sense between the two forms. At the same time, the students will also develop an ear for which auxiliaries sound best with which past participles.

Let the students share their sentences with the rest of the class so they can see the range of possible combinations.

WRITERS WRITING

The world is satisfied with words; few care to dive beneath the surface.

—PASCAL

Words are the signs and symbols of things; and as in accounts, ciphers and symbols pass for real sums, so, in the course of human affairs, words and names pass for things themselves.

—ROBERT SOUTHEY

Words are things; and a small drop of ink, falling like dew upon a thought, produces that which makes thousand[s], perhaps millions, think.

—BYRON

TEACHING PRACTICE

For review, write the present tense of ten or twelve irregular verbs on the chalkboard and call on volunteers to provide the past tense and past participle forms.

Then have your students write entries in their logs, using only verbs from the list on pp. 193–195. Ask several of the students to read their work aloud, noting the irregular forms they have used properly.

WRITERS WRITING

Then, Brutus, I have much mistook your passion.

—JULIUS CAESAR

Have you chose this man?

—CORIOLANUS

When they are fretten with the gusts of heaven.

—MERCHANT OF VENICE

By today's standards, even Shakespeare himself sometimes chose the "incorrect" verb form.

TEACHING PRACTICE

Using a recent piece of writing, have your students identify the kinds of verbs they used: auxiliary, modal auxiliary, regular, and irregular. You might point out that most irregular verbs are Anglo-Saxon in origin and monosyllabic in nature, while the regular verbs are often Latinate and polysyllabic.

Ask the students to choose a portion of text and make all the verbs (except the verb *to be* and auxiliary verbs) monosyllabic, then recopy the same piece replacing all the verbs with polysyllabic ones of similar meaning. As they read to themselves or aloud, can they hear a difference in style and tone, simply from the change in verbs? Is one version stuffier? clearer? more academic? reader friendly?

WRITERS ON WRITING

When you doubt between words, use the plainest, the commonest, the most idiomatic. Eschew fine words as you would rouge; love simple ones as you would native roses on your cheek.

—JULIUS HARE

Were I mistress of fifty languages, I would think in the deep German, converse in the gay French, write in the copious English, sing in the majestic Spanish, deliver in the noble Greek, and make love in the soft Italian.

—ANNE-LOUISE-GERMAINE STAEL

drive	drove	driven
eat	ate	eaten
fall	fell	fallen
feel	felt	felt
fight	fought	fought
find	found	found
fly	flew	flown
forget	forgot	forgotten/forgot
freeze	froze	frozen
get	got	gotten/got
give	gave	given
go	went	gone
grow	grew	grown
hang[1]	hung	hung
have	had	had
hear	heard	heard
hide	hid	hidden
hit	hit	hit
keep	kept	kept
know	knew	known
lay	laid	laid
lead	led	led
leave	left	left
lend	lent	lent
let	let	let
lie (recline)[2]	lay	lain
lose	lost	lost
make	made	made
mean	meant	meant
meet	met	met
pay	paid	paid
prove	proved	proved/proven
put	put	put
read	read	read
ride	rode	ridden
ring	rang	rung
rise	rose	risen
run	ran	run
say	said	said
see	saw	seen

---

[1] *Hang* meaning "execute by hanging" is regular: *hang, hanged, hanged.*
[2] *Lie* meaning "tell a falsehood" is regular: *lie, lied, lied.*

send	sent	sent
set	set	set
shake	shook	shaken
shine (give light)[3]	shone	shone
shoot	shot	shot
show	showed	showed/shown
shrink	shrank	shrunk
sing	sang	sung
sink	sank	sunk
sit	sat	sat
sleep	slept	slept
speak	spoke	spoken
spend	spent	spent
spread	spread	spread
spring	sprang/sprung	sprung
stand	stood	stood
steal	stole	stolen
strike	struck	struck/stricken
swim	swam	swum
swing	swung	swung
take	took	taken
teach	taught	taught
tear	tore	torn
tell	told	told
think	thought	thought
throw	threw	thrown
wake	woke/waked	waked/woken/woke
wear	wore	worn
win	won	won
wind	wound	wound
write	wrote	written

[3] *Shine* meaning "polish" is regular: *shine, shined, shined.*

EXERCISE 8.2

Complete each of the following sentences by filling in each blank with the past tense or past participle of the verb listed in parentheses. Remember that a past participle cannot function by itself as a verb; for a past participle to fit in a blank, one or more auxiliary verbs must precede it.

Example
We had not <u>eaten</u> (eat) since lunch, yet we <u>felt</u> (feel) no hunger.

195

ANSWERS TO EXERCISE 8.2

1. been, written
2. come, found
3. began
4. lost/had lost; took/had taken
5. won/had won/would win; shot/had shot/would shoot
6. grew/have grown/could have grown
7. drew, set
8. met, taken
9. sank/was sinking; put/were putting; said/were saying
10. met, thought, known

After your students have completed this exercise, review their answers in class. Ask them why they chose certain forms. Indicators of appropriate forms were

–use of auxiliary, indicating past participle form (sentences 1, 2, 8)
–the tense of verb in other clauses, indicating tense of missing verb (sentences 2, 3, 4, 10)
–other indications of time in the sentence (sentence 5: past, indicated by "Saturdays"; sentence 6: past, semantically indicated)
–those sentences that require context of situation to determine form (sentences 7 and 9).

ANSWERS TO EXERCISE 8.3
1. correct
2. sang———→sung
3. beat———→beaten
4. went———→gone
5. freezed———→froze

(BACK)GROUNDING

Verbs that take an object are *transitive*, from the Latin *transire*, "pass over." Transitive verbs cannot express their meaning without passing over to a complement:

We *bounced* our *ball* in Waterford Gallery.
We *bounced* our *ideas* off one another.
We *bounced* the *pickpocket* out of the restaurant.

Intransitive, that is, "not passing over," verbs are capable of expressing themselves without a complement to complete their meaning:

Oz *has spoken.*
Jorge *slunk* past the mission.
Rosanne *blushed* at the attention.

Sometimes, transitive verbs take an indirect object as well as a direct object as in:

Christiana gave Alfred (i.o.) a black eye (d.o.).

Aurelia sent Kirsten (i.o.) a Christmas card (d.o.).

1. Clearly, this short story would not have _____(be) as effective if it had been _____(write) in the third-person.
2. Once she had _____(come) to this realization, she _____(find) that she was no longer afraid of change.
3. The process of hazing _____(begin) soon after fraternities were formed.
4. Hearnes _____(lose) control of the fight, and Hagler _____(take) advantage of this loss.
5. On the Saturdays before Geiberger and Langer _____(win) their respective tournaments, each had _____(shoot) a sixty-eight.
6. People think that we _____(grow) up together because we are practically inseparable.
7. I painfully _____(draw) ninety-five dollars from my wallet and _____(set) the money on the counter.
8. It would have been helpful if someone had _____(meet) me at the airport and had _____(take) me to the hotel.
9. As the boat _____(sink), the passengers _____(put) on their life preservers and _____(say) their prayers.
10. When I first _____(meet) her, I _____(think) that she was the most unpleasant person I had ever _____(know).

EXERCISE 8.3

Edit the following sentences to eliminate any inappropriate verb forms. (One of the sentences does not require any change.)

> *Example*
> She begin the examination on time.
> She *began* the examination on time.

1. Socrates drank the hemlock calmly and died a few hours later.
2. The band had sang its last song before the fight begun.
3. When the battle was over, the rebels had been beat badly.
4. By the mid-1970s New York had almost went bankrupt.
5. The lake freezed early this year.

▌ 8c. Using *lie* and *lay, sit* and *set, rise* and *raise*

Three pairs of verbs—*lie* and *lay, sit* and *set*, and *rise* and *raise*—cause problems for many writers because the two verbs in each pair have similar-sounding forms and somewhat related meanings. In each pair one of the verbs is transitive, meaning that it takes a direct object; the other is intransitive, meaning that it does not take an object. The best way to avoid confusing the two is to memorize their forms and meanings. All of these verbs except *raise* are irregular. Their forms are as follows:

196

USEFUL READING

Halliday, M. A. K. *System and Function in Language.* Gunther Kress, ed. London: Oxford UP, 1976. An enlightening, non-traditional grammarian's perspective on transitive verbs, their function and form. Known for both his collaborative work with Rugaiya Hasan on sentence cohesion and for his theory of systemic grammar, Halliday would regard the following as transitive: "the door slammed" and "he slammed the door (shut)." Chapter 11, a discussion of transitive and causative verbs, examines a pair of sentences analogous to those cited above.

USING *LIE* AND *LAY*, *SIT* AND *SET*, *RISE* AND *RAISE*

BASE FORM	PAST TENSE	PAST PARTICIPLE	PRESENT PARTICIPLE	-S FORM
lie	lay	lain	lying	lies
lay	laid	laid	laying	lays
sit	sat	sat	sitting	sits
set	set	set	setting	sets
rise	rose	risen	rising	rises
raise	raised	raised	raising	raises

Lie is intransitive and means "recline" or "be situated." *Lay* is transitive and means "put" or "place." This pair is especially confusing because *lay* is also the past-tense form of *lie*.

INTRANSITIVE   He *lay* on the floor unable to move.
TRANSITIVE   I *laid* the package on the counter.

Sit is intransitive and means "be seated." *Set* is transitive and usually means "put" or "place."

INTRANSITIVE   She *sat* in the rocking chair daydreaming.
TRANSITIVE   She *set* the package on the counter.

Rise is intransitive and means "get up" or "go up." *Raise* is transitive and means "lift" or "cause to go up."

INTRANSITIVE   He *rose* from the bed and left the room.
TRANSITIVE   He *raised* himself to a sitting position.
INTRANSITIVE   The price of coffee is *rising*.
TRANSITIVE   The store is *raising* the price of coffee.

EXERCISE 8.4

Choose the appropriate verb form from the pair in parentheses in each of the following sentences.

1. Sometimes she just (*lies/lays*) and stares at the ceiling.
2. I (*lay/laid*) my books down just as the telephone rang.
3. The doctor asked the patient to (*lie/lay*) on his side for an injection.
4. He used whatever was (*lying/laying*) around the house.
5. Doctors urge us to (*sit/set*) aside fad diets once and for all.
6. I (*sat/set*) back, closed my eyes, and began to meditate.
7. (*Sitting/Setting*) in the sun too long can lead to skin cancer.
8. The Federal Reserve Bank is planning to (*rise/raise*) interest rates.
9. When the temperature (*rises/raises*), the relative humidity usually declines.
10. We (*rose/raised*) every morning at six and went jogging.

197

USEFUL READING

Comrie, Bernard. *Aspect*. Cambridge, England: Cambridge UP, 1976. A study of *aspect*, which differs from tense in that it refers to the duration or continuation of an action in time, rather than its occurrence in relation to the present moment.

Williams, Joseph M. *Origins of the English Language: A Social and Linguistic History*. New York: Free Press, 1975. 265–74. Williams describes and traces the historical development of the two aspects: progressive ("He *was imitating* his mother") and perfect ("He *has fixed* the car").

These classifications, transitive and intransitive, vary from one sentence to another, depending on how a particular verb is used. A few words (*ignore*) are only transitive, while others (*shine, die*) are only intransitive.

Dictionaries label verbs as *v.t.* (transitive verb) or *v.i.* (intransitive verb), according to use.

TEACHING PRACTICE

Yet another pair of verbs that gives writers problems is *raise/rise*, perhaps because *raise* is the causative of *rise* (i.e., *to raise* means *to cause to rise*), with *raise* always taking an object. Also, *give rise to* is a roundabout way of saying *raise*: *Her resignation gave rise to (raised) questions about her personal life.* You may wish to review the principal parts of this troublesome pair.

I rise;   I rose;   I have risen
I raise;   I raised;   I have raised

OPTIONAL EXERCISE

For a quick review exercise, have your students fill each blank with a form of either *raise* or *rise*.

1. She suddenly (*rose*) up and spoke.
2. Yeast causes bread to (*rise*).
3. We all know to (*raise*) our hand before we speak in class.
4. Some say that Jesus (*raised*) Lazarus from the dead.

ANSWERS TO EXERCISE 8.4

1. lies
2. laid
3. lie
4. lying
5. set
6. sat
7. sitting
8. raise
9. rises
10. rose

HERE LIE I

Here lies the body of Ann Mann,
Who lived an old woman
And died an old Mann.

—ANONYMOUS

Here lies a man who was killed by lightning;
He died when his prospects seemed to be brightening.

—ANONYMOUS

(BACK)GROUNDING

The concept of tense can be especially confusing to those students who try to correlate it directly with actual time. Grammatical tense gives us the mechanical forms of verbs, forms that follow definite rules of construction, but it does not always represent actual time in past, present, or future.

For example, *present tense* can indicate an action or existence taking place in the present, past, or future:

–His feet hurt. (taking place right now—present)
–Water boils at 212°F. (a fact in the past, present, future)
–My roommate drinks iced tea every morning. (habitual action—past, present, future)
–We are having turkey for Thanksgiving. (intended future action)
–Kaoru leaves for Tokyo on the twenty-fifth. (intended future action)
–Gilda is to take office next week. (combined with infinitive—intended future action)
–Huckleberry Finn is a resourceful, sensitive boy. (historical present, giving vividness to a past event)
–I hear that Jaime spoke to the new students. (*hear* gives the past action a present connection)

VERB TENSES

Tenses are the forms of a verb that show when the action or condition expressed by the verb takes place or exists. We characteristically think of time in terms of present, past, and future, and the three *simple tenses* are the present tense, the past tense, and the future tense.

PRESENT TENSE	I jump
PAST TENSE	I jumped
FUTURE TENSE	I will jump

More complex aspects of time relationships, such as ongoing or completed actions or conditions, are expressed through *progressive*, *perfect*, and *perfect progressive forms* of the simple tenses. Such terminology sounds complicated in the abstract, but, in fact, you use all these forms in everyday speech. Here are all the tense forms of one verb, *ask*.

SIMPLE PRESENT	she *asks*
SIMPLE PAST	she *asked*
SIMPLE FUTURE	she *will ask*
PRESENT PERFECT	she *has asked*
PAST PERFECT	she *had asked*
FUTURE PERFECT	she *will have asked*
PRESENT PROGRESSIVE	she *is asking*
PAST PROGRESSIVE	she *was asking*
FUTURE PROGRESSIVE	she *will be asking*
PRESENT PERFECT PROGRESSIVE	she *has been asking*
PAST PERFECT PROGRESSIVE	she *had been asking*
FUTURE PERFECT PROGRESSIVE	she *will have been asking*

The simple tenses locate an action or condition only within the three basic time frames of present, past, and future. The perfect form of each tense expresses the idea of a *completed* action or condition in the present, past, or future, and the progressive form expresses the idea of a *continuing* action or condition. Finally, the perfect progressive form expresses the idea of an action or condition continuing up to a point of completion. The next section describes in greater detail how each of the forms of each tense is used.

USING THE PRESENT TENSE FORMS

vb 8d

8d. Using the present tense forms

The **simple present** indicates actions or conditions occurring at the time of speaking or writing, as well as those occurring habitually and those considered to be general truths or scientific facts. In addition, with appropriate expressions of time, the simple present can be used to indicate a scheduled event in the future.

> He now *lives* in San Diego.
>
> They *are* very angry about the decision.
>
> I *eat* breakfast every day at 8:00 A.M.
>
> Love *conquers* all.
>
> Water *freezes* at 0 degrees Celsius.
>
> The United States Constitution *guarantees* certain rights to all citizens.
>
> Residents of Greenland *endure* bitter cold for most of the year.
>
> Grandpa *arrives* tomorrow.

The simple present is also used in discussing literary and artistic works created in the past that exist in our experience as timeless. For example, a literary character such as Ishmael in *Moby Dick*, created by Herman Melville over a century ago, exists in our present time as well.

> Ishmael slowly *comes* to realize all that *is* at stake in the search for the white whale.

The **present progressive** indicates actions or conditions that are ongoing or continuous in the present.

> The children *are playing* in the back yard this afternoon.
>
> The defense attorney *is asking* for a retrial.

The present progressive is typically used to describe an action that is happening at the moment of speaking, in contrast to the simple present, which more often indicates habitual actions.

PRESENT PROGRESSIVE	You *are driving* too fast.
SIMPLE PRESENT	I always *drive* carefully.

With an appropriate expression of time, the present progressive can also be used to indicate a scheduled event in the future.

> We *are having* friends over for dinner tomorrow night.

The **present perfect** indicates actions or conditions begun in the past and either completed at some unspecified time in the past or continuing into the present.

> My father *has told* me many stories of his childhood.
>
> Uncontrolled logging *has destroyed* many tropical forests.
>
> Anti-abortion activists *have tried* to reverse the decision.

The **present perfect progressive** indicates that an ongoing action or condition begun in the past is very likely to continue into the present.

> For many years the United States and the Soviet Union *have been trying* to negotiate treaties to control nuclear arms.
>
> Since I *have been taking* vitamins regularly, I have had no colds.
>
> The company's management *has been fighting* an attempted takeover.

▌ 8e. Using the past tense forms

The **simple past** indicates actions or conditions that occurred at a specific time and do not extend into the present.

> She *felt* better as soon as her exams were over.
>
> Germany *invaded* Poland on September 1, 1939.
>
> We *moved* to this city only last year.

The **past progressive** indicates continuing actions or conditions in the past, often with specified limits.

> Lenin *was living* in exile in Zurich when the tsar was overthrown.
>
> By the 1970s many Americans *were buying* smaller cars.
>
> I *was visiting* a pecan orchard when I got a craving for a piece of pie.

The **past perfect** indicates actions or conditions that were completed by a specific time in the past or before some other past action or condition occurred.

> By the fourth century Christianity *had become* the state religion.
>
> She *had asked* the instructor for help before she turned to me.
>
> Homesteaders found that speculators *had* already *taken* the best land.

The **past perfect progressive** indicates continuous actions or conditions in the past that began before a specific time in the past or before some other past action or condition began.

They *had been living* beyond their means for years before they went bankrupt.

When they returned to Venice, the Polos *had been traveling* for almost twenty-five years.

Carter *had been planning* a naval career, but he returned to Plains to run the family business.

▌ 8f. Using the future tense forms

The **simple future** indicates actions or conditions that have yet to begin.

The exhibition *will come* to Washington in September.

I *shall graduate* the year after next.

Mortgage rates *will rise* if the money supply is restricted.

The **future progressive** indicates continuing actions or conditions in the future.

The loans *will be coming* due in the next two years.

A team of international observers *will be monitoring* the elections.

The **future perfect** indicates actions or conditions that will be completed by or before some specified time in the future.

They *will have exhausted* all their resources before the new year arrives.

In ten years the original investment *will have doubled*.

Finally, the **future perfect progressive** indicates continuing actions or conditions that will be completed by some specified time in the future.

By the time the session ends, the negotiators *will have been working* for ten hours without a break.

Hannah *will have been playing* the piano for five years this June.

➤ Checking verb tenses

Errors in verb tenses take several forms. Some are errors in verb form: writing *seen* for *saw*, for example, which is an instance of mixing up the participle and past tense forms. Others are errors in time: using the simple past (*Uncle Charlie arrived*) when meaning requires the present perfect (*Uncle Charlie has arrived*). Still others result from using

(BACK)GROUNDING

In the early seventeenth century, the rules of English usage were codified, according to the Latin model, by John Wallis, who prescribed that *shall* and *will* could not be considered synonymous. Simple future expectation was to be indicated by *shall* in first person and by *will* in second or third person:

I *shall* meet Jens in the morning, then we *shall* review his money-market account.

Although you *will* gasp when you see her tattoo, Delphine *will* be delighted that you noticed.

According to Wallis (and all prescriptivists since), determination, desire, willfulness, or promise on the part of the speaker is represented by just the opposite paradigm—*will* in the first person and *shall* in second or third person:

Tomorrow, I *will* return and defeat you.

Of course, we *will* go to the funeral, whatever the weather.

You *shall* remain in my will, no matter whom you marry.

Before they return to the Republic of China, Mei-mei is determined that both she and Sheng *shall* finish medical school and their internships.

Despite the three-hundred-year crusade to establish this distinction, most English speakers have successfully expressed futurity and determination without it.

WRITERS WRITING

It is seriously, my opinion, that every language must be servilely formed after the model of some one of the ancients, if we wish to give durability to our works.

—SAMUEL JOHNSON

TEACHING PRACTICE

Students claim that they never use the word *shall* in any locution, that *shall* is rare, hence "formal." Ask your students to think a minute about the use of *shall*. What examples can they offer? Which uses seem most natural to them? "*Shall* questions," which imply a certain amount of jointness, and "*shall* injunctions" are not so rare as the class might think. Consider the following examples:

–*Shall* I pick you up at six?
–What *shall* we drink? (first person—request)
–You *shall* not take the name of the Lord in vain.

–You *shall* regret your evil ways. (second person—moral injunction)

–The vendor *shall* maintain the equipment in good repair.

–The athlete *shall* maintain a 2.5 grade point average. (third person—legal or commercial usage; specifications or requirements)

–Who *shall* decide when doctors disagree? (third person—literary usage)

ANSWERS TO EXERCISE 8.5

1. expect—present; are expecting
2. have predicted/have been predicting—action begun in past continues
3. emigrated—completed action
4. arrived/has arrived—started in past, may continue today
5. will meet/will be meeting—future (continuing) action
6. rode/was riding—past action, completed
7. had fallen—in past, before other action
8. will have watched—future action, completed by a certain time
9. came—past action
10. rises—general truth

WRITERS ON WRITING

English usage is sometimes more than mere taste, judgment and education—sometimes it's sheer luck, like getting across a street.

—E. B. WHITE

ANSWERS TO EXERCISE 8.6 (WILL VARY)

I *was* eight years old; I *had* a cowboy hat; My playmates *were* my brothers; Their colors *were*; in the way we *were* dressed; On Saturday nights we all *went*; Westerns *were* her favorite kind; we *pretended* we *were* Tom Mix; we *chased*; then my parents *decided*; There *were* not "real" guns; They *shot* "BBs"; Because I *was* a girl; I *did* not *get* a gun; Instantly, I *was relegated*; Now there *appeared*; They *shot* and *shot*; I *tried* to keep up; One day while I *was* standing; I *felt* an incredible blow; I *looked* down.

dialect (*we be going*) in situations requiring standard edited English (*we are going*).

If you have trouble with verb tenses, the best thing you can do is to keep a log of your errors and then to look for patterns. Once you can identify specific problems, you can make a point of routinely proofreading for them.

EXERCISE 8.5

Complete each of the following sentences by filling in the blank with an appropriate form of the verb listed in parentheses. Since more than one form will sometimes be possible, be prepared to explain reasons for your choices.

1. In spite of the poor turnout in today's referendum, local officials _____(expect) the bond issue to pass.
2. Ever since the first nuclear power plants were built, opponents _____ (predict) disaster.
3. Thousands of Irish peasants _____(emigrate) to America after the potato famine of the 1840s.
4. The newspaper _____(arrive) late every day this week.
5. The committee _____(meet) again next week.
6. President Kennedy was shot while he _____(ride) in a limousine.
7. By eleven o'clock this morning, stock prices _____(fall) fifteen points.
8. By the time a child born today enters first grade, he or she _____ (watch) thousands of television commercials.
9. In "The Road Not Taken" the man _____(come) to a fork in the road.
10. The supply of a product _____(rise) when the demand is great.

EXERCISE 8.6

Verb tenses are essential for creating a sense of time. Read the following passage from an essay by Alice Walker, paying attention to the italicized verbs. Then reread the passage substituting forms of the simple past or past progressive for these verbs, and write a brief paragraph describing the difference in immediacy—and in emphasis—the substitutions make.

I *am* eight years old and a tomboy. I *have* a cowboy hat, cowboy boots, checkered shirt and pants, all red. My playmates *are* my brothers, two and four years older than I. Their colors *are* black and green, the only difference in the way we *are* dressed. On Saturday nights we all *go* to the picture show, even my mother; westerns *are* her favorite kind of movie. Back home, "on the ranch," we *pretend* we *are* Tom Mix, Hopalong Cassidy, Lash LaRue . . . ; we *chase* each other for hours rustling cattle, being outlaws, delivering damsels from distress. Then my parents *decide* to buy my brothers guns. These *are* not

USING VERB TENSES IN SEQUENCES *vb* 8g

"real" guns. They *shoot* "BBs." . . . Because I *am* a girl, I *do* not *get* a gun. Instantly, I *am relegated* to the position of Indian. Now there *appears* a great distance between us. They *shoot* and *shoot* at everything with their new guns. I *try* to keep up with my bow and arrows.

One day while I *am standing* on top of our makeshift "garage"—pieces of tin nailed across some poles—holding my bow and arrow and looking out toward the fields, I *feel* an incredible blow in my right eye. I *look* down just in time to see my brother lower his gun.

—ALICE WALKER, "Beauty: When the Other Dancer Is the Self"

▌ 8g. Using verb tenses in sequences

Because tense is crucial to our understanding of when actions or conditions occur and because time relationships can be very complex, careful and accurate use of tenses is important to clear writing. Even the simplest narrative describes actions that take place at different times; using particular tenses for particular actions allows readers to follow such time changes readily.

The relationship between the tense of the verb in the independent clause of a sentence and the tense of a verb in a dependent clause or a verbal is called the **sequence of tenses.** In general, the verb in a dependent clause may be in any tense form required for your meaning. The only limitation is that the relationship between the forms in the independent and dependent clauses make sense. For example, all of the following make sense and are acceptable grammatically:

He *lent* her the money because he *is* a generous man. [past/present]

He *lent* her the money because he *loved* her. [past/past]

He *lent* her the money because she *will invest* it wisely. [past/future]

Even though in general you can use almost any sequence of tenses, in a particular sentence the tense of the verb in the dependent clause may be limited by the meaning. For example, it makes no sense to say *He lent her the money because he will love her* or *He lent her the money because she had invested it wisely.*

Different forms of an infinitive are used to indicate the time relationship between the action expressed by the infinitive and that expressed by the verb in the predicate. The **present infinitive,** consisting of *to* plus the base form, indicates action occurring at the same time as or later than the action of the predicate verb.

203

TEACHING PRACTICE

The sequence-of-tense principle governs the relationship between the verbs in main and accompanying subordinate clauses.

Verbs in *natural sequence* indicate a natural, logical time relation between the actions they represent. In "Bob *believes* that you *are lying*," both actions take place simultaneously. Whereas, in "Celia *believes* that you *swiped* her candlesticks," the first verb reflects on a past-tense verb. And in "Tina *guarantees* that Ike *will sing* tonight," the first and second verbs represent present and future tenses, respectively and naturally.

Verbs in *attracted sequence* harmonize without regard to the actual time represented. Main verbs in *past-* and *past-perfect* tense followed by indirect discourse and clauses of purpose call for attracted sequence:

—Myra *said* that Rolf *was* fat and ugly. (He has not suddenly become slim and cute.)
—Myra *asked* if Rolf *was* smart. (He remains brilliant.)
—Adam *strangled* the serpent so that he *could live* without temptation. (purpose)
—Eve *entered* an assertiveness training course so she *could learn* to be forceful. (purpose)

A main verb in any other tense followed by a clause of purpose attracts the present tense:

—Helen *is joining* a health club so she *can get* in shape. (purpose)
—She *will enter* the Boston Marathon so she *can compete.*

Certain verbs (e.g., expect, suppose, thought, knew) and predicate adjectives (e.g., evident, certain, sure) also call for attracted sequence:

—We *expected/supposed/thought/knew* Chloe *would make* a scene.
—Fritz was *sure/certain* you *would plead* guilty.
—It was *evident* that Susan *was* pregnant.

USING VERBS

I *wanted to swim* in the ocean last summer. [The wanting and the swimming occurred at the same time in the past.]

I *expect to swim* in the ocean next summer. [The expecting is present; the swimming is in the future.]

The **perfect infinitive**, consisting of *to have* plus the past participle, indicates action occurring *before* the action of the predicate verb.

She *seems to have lost* her self-confidence. [The loss of self-confidence took place before the "seeming."]

He *was reported to have left* his fortune to his cat. [The leaving of the fortune took place before the reporting.]

Similarly, different kinds of participles are used to indicate the time relationship between the action expressed by the participle and that expressed by the verb in the predicate. The **present participle** indicates action occurring at the same time as that of the verb.

Seeking to relieve unemployment, Roosevelt *established* several public works programs. [Both the seeking and the establishment of the programs occurred simultaneously in the past.]

The **present perfect participle** indicates action occurring before that of the predicate verb. The present perfect participle consists of *having* plus the past participle: *having sent, having walked.*

Having won the election, he *is planning* his inauguration. [He began planning after he won the election.]

The **past participle** can indicate action occurring either before or at the same time as that of the predicate verb.

Flown by an expert pilot, the passengers *felt* completely secure. [The flying and the feeling were simultaneous.]

Flown to the front, the troops *joined* their hard-pressed comrades. [The flying occurred before the joining.]

EXERCISE 8.7

Edit each of the following sentences to create the appropriate sequence of tenses between the verb in the predicate and the participle or infinitive.

Example
He needs to send in his application before today.
He needs to *have sent* in his application before today.

VOICE   *vb* 8

1. When he was twenty-one, he wanted to have become a millionaire by the age of thirty.
2. Leaving England in December, the settlers arrived in Virginia in May.
3. They hoped to plant their garden by now.
4. Cutting off all contact with her parents, she did not know whom to ask for help.
5. Having sung in the shower, he did not hear the doorbell.

VOICE

Voice is the feature of transitive verbs that tells whether the subject is acting (*he questions us*) or being acted upon (*he is questioned*). When the subject is acting, the verb is in the **active voice;** when the subject is being acted upon, the verb is in the **passive voice.** The passive voice is formed, as in this sentence, by using the appropriate form of the auxiliary verb *be* followed by the past participle of the main verb.

	ACTIVE VOICE	PASSIVE VOICE
PRESENT	He *questions* us.	He *is questioned.*
PAST	He *questioned* us.	He *was questioned.*
FUTURE	He *will question* us.	He *will be questioned.*
PRESENT PERFECT	He *has questioned* us.	He *has been questioned.*
PAST PERFECT	He *had questioned* us.	He *had been questioned.*
FUTURE PERFECT	He *will have questioned* us.	He *will have been questioned.*

Most contemporary writers use the active voice as much as possible because it makes prose more *active*, more lively. To say that "the mail was opened" (passive voice) does not give the sense of action or immediacy that "Cheryl opened the mail" (active voice) does. In the passive construction, the mail is just there—being opened, by no one or nothing in particular. Even adding "by Cheryl" does not do much to enliven the passive version. When passive-voice verbs pile up in a writing passage, that passage will generally be harder to understand and remember. For instance, readers indicate they *remember* passages as being in the active voice even if the version they read used the passive voice.

The most problematic use of the passive voice occurs when writers seek to avoid taking responsibility for what they have written. A university president who announces that "it is recommended that fees

ANSWERS TO EXERCISE 8.7

1. When he was twenty-one, he wanted to become a millionaire by the age of thirty.
2. Having left England in December, the settlers arrived in Virginia in May.
3. They had hoped to plant their garden by now.
4. Having cut off all contact with her parents, she did not know whom to ask for help.
5. Singing in the shower, he did not hear the doorbell.

TEACHING PRACTICE

To increase your students' awareness of active and passive voice, read aloud the following recipe for banana-nut bread. As you read, the students should recast the recipe into the active voice:

> The oven should be set at 350°F. A 9 × 5 × 3-inch pan should be greased and floured. Two bananas are mashed. Then 1 c sugar, 3 T oil, and 1 egg are combined with the mashed bananas. These four ingredients are then beaten together in a large bowl. 2½ c flour, 1 t salt, 3½ t baking powder are sifted together. The dry ingredients are then added to the banana mixture. ½ c of nuts should be added. All these ingredients should be beaten on medium speed for ½ minute. The side and bottom of the bowl should be scraped continuously. The pan should be filled with the mixture. The mixture should be baked for 55–65 minutes or until a wooden pick inserted in center comes out clean.
>
> The bread should be removed from pan and should be cooled thoroughly before slicing.

USEFUL READING

Williams, Joseph M. *Style: Ten Lessons in Clarity and Grace.* Glenview, IL: Scott, 1981. For an advanced discussion of the stylistic virtues of active and passive voice, see pp. 8–32.

be raised substantially" skirts a number of pressing questions: recommended by whom? raised by whom?

In spite of such questionable uses, however, the passive voice can work to good advantage in some situations. Much scientific writing uses the passive voice effectively to highlight the object or phenomenon being studied rather than the person or persons doing the studying. Look at the following example, from an essay describing brain surgery:

> A curved incision was made behind the hairline so it would be concealed when the hair grew back. It extended almost from ear to ear. Plastic clips were applied to the cut edges of the scalp to arrest bleeding. The scalp was folded back to the level of the eyebrows. Incisions were made in the muscle of the right temple, and three sets of holes were drilled near the temple and the top of the head because the tumor had to be approached from directly in front. The drill, powered by nitrogen, was replaced with a fluted steel blade, and the holes were connected. The incised piece of skull was pried loose and held out of the way by a large sponge.   –ROY C. SELBY, JR., "A Delicate Operation"

Reporters often use the passive voice when they want to protect the confidentiality of their sources, as in the familiar phrase "It is reported that . . . ," or when the performer of an action is unknown or less important than the recipient of the action. When Tom Wicker submitted his article on the assassination of President Kennedy to the *New York Times*, he began this way:

> DALLAS, Nov. 22—President John Fitzgerald Kennedy was shot and killed by an assassin today.
>
> He died of a wound in the brain caused by a rifle bullet that was fired at him as he was riding through downtown Dallas in a motorcade.
>
> Vice President Lyndon Baines Johnson, who was riding in the third car behind Mr. Kennedy's, was sworn in as the 36th President of the United States 99 minutes after Mr. Kennedy's death.
>
> –TOM WICKER, *New York Times*

Wicker's article uses the passive voice with good reason: he wants the focus of the sentences on Kennedy, not on who killed him, and on Johnson, not on who swore him in.

Writers, then, must decide for themselves when the passive voice is appropriate and when it is not. If you find that you overuse the passive, you may want to practice shifting your sentences to active voice. To do so, convert the subject of the verb into a direct or indirect object, and make the performer of the action into the subject.

MOOD   *vb* 8

PASSIVE	The test administrator *was told* to give the student an electric shock each time a wrong answer *was given*.
ACTIVE	Researchers *told* the test administrator to give the student an electric shock each time he or she *gave* a wrong answer.
PASSIVE	I *was awakened* promptly at seven by the huge brown alarm clock.
ACTIVE	The huge brown alarm clock *awakened* me promptly at seven.

See 12c and 21b for further discussion of voice.

EXERCISE 8.8

Convert each of the following sentences from active to passive voice or from passive to active, and note the differences in emphasis and rhythm these changes make.

Example
Machiavelli advises the prince to gain the friendship of the people.
The prince *is advised* by Machiavelli to gain the friendship of the people.

1. Flannery O'Connor employs the images of both a boxcar and a swinging bridge to show the inconsistencies between Mrs. Turpin's classification of people and God's classification of people.
2. Huge pine trees were uprooted by the storm.
3. Marianne avoided such things as elevators, subways, and closets.
4. For months the baby kangaroo is protected, fed, and taught how to survive by its mother.
5. The lawns and rooftops of the neighborhood were covered with the first snow of winter.

EXERCISE 8.9

Look at several essays you have written recently or pieces of writing by others that you particularly like, and find five examples each of the active voice and the passive voice. Convert each of the examples to the other voice, and note the difference in emphasis and rhythm the changes make.

MOOD

The **mood** of a verb indicates the attitude of the speaker or writer toward what he or she is saying or writing. Different moods are used to express a fact or inquiry (indicative mood), a command or request

ANSWERS TO EXERCISE 8.8

1. To show the inconsistencies between Mrs. Turpin's classification of people and God's classification of people, images of both a boxcar and a swinging bridge are employed by Flannery O'Connor.
2. The storm uprooted huge pine trees.
3. Such things as elevators, subways, and closets were avoided by Marianne.
4. For months, the mother kangaroo protects, feeds, and teaches her baby to survive.
5. The first snow of winter covered the lawns and rooftops of the neighborhood.

WRITERS WRITING

If I feel physically as if the top of my head were taken off, I know that is poetry.
—EMILY DICKINSON

ANSWERS TO EXERCISE 8.9
WILL VARY

(imperative mood), or a wish, requirement, or condition contrary to fact (subjunctive mood).

INDICATIVE	I *ate* the plums
IMPERATIVE	*Eat* the plums.
SUBJUNCTIVE	If I *were to eat* the plums, I would be sick.

The most frequently used mood is the **indicative mood**, the one used for stating facts or opinions or asking questions.

> The Frisbees *soar* through the air.
>
> Carter *lost* the 1980 election.
>
> Where *are* you *going*?

The **imperative mood** is used for giving commands or making requests. It always uses the base form of the verb and almost always omits the subject, (*you*).

> *Look* at the girl with the orange spiked hair.
>
> *Take* the appropriate wrench, and *loosen* the plug counterclockwise.
>
> You *sit* down at once!
>
> *Help*!

The **subjunctive mood** expresses wishes, conditions that are contrary to fact, requests, or demands. It is used primarily in dependent clauses beginning with *that* or *if*.

▌ 8h. Using the subjunctive

The present tense of the subjunctive uses the base form of the verb. The past tense of the subjunctive is the same as the past tense of the indicative mood except for the verb *be*, which uses *were* for all subjects.

PRESENT

The professor demanded that she *arrive* as early as possible.

It is important that children *be* psychologically ready for a new sibling.

PAST

He spent money as if he *had* infinite credit.

If the store *were* better located, it would attract more customers.

OPTIONAL EXERCISE

In "What if Shakespeare Had a Sister," Virginia Woolf employs the subjunctive mood:

> [I]t is unthinkable that any women in Shakespeare's day *should have had* Shakespeare's genius. For genius like Shakespeare's is not born among laboring, uneducated, servile people. It was not born in England among the Saxons and the Britons. It is not born today among the working classes. How, then, *could* it *have been born* among women whose work began, . . . almost before they were out of the nursery, who were forced to it by their parents and held to it by all the power of law and custom? Yet genius of a sort *must have existed* among women as it *must have existed* among the working classes.

Discuss how Woolf's use of the subjunctive affects the tone and meaning of this passage. How does this mood help her make an ironic point? (By speculating on what could have been.)

USING THE SUBJUNCTIVE   *vb* 8h

Because the subjunctive can create a rather formal tone, many speakers today have a tendency to substitute the indicative in informal situations. Nevertheless, formal writing still requires the use of the subjunctive in the following kinds of dependent clauses:

INDICATIVE   If I *was* a better typist, I would type my own papers.
SUBJUNCTIVE   If I *were* a better typist, I would type my own papers.

1. Those expressing a wish

I wish I *were* with you right now.

He wished that his mother *were* not reluctant to quit smoking.

2. Those beginning with *if* and expressing a condition that does not exist

If the federal government *were* to ban the sale of tobacco, tobacco companies and distributors would suffer a great loss.

If no one *were allowed* to ignore the rules, language would cease to develop.

3. Those beginning with *as if* and *as though*

He cautiously started down the trail as if he *were walking* on thin ice.

During the 1920s Americans speculated in Florida real estate as though it *were* a risk-free investment.

4. Those beginning with *that* and expressing a demand, request, requirement, or suggestion

It is required that each fraternity *sponsor* three community service projects each semester.

Dad advised that neither of us *do* anything too hastily.

The job demands that the employee *be* in good physical condition.

EXERCISE 8.10

Revise any of the following sentences that do not use the appropriate subjunctive verb forms required in formal writing.

Example
I saw how carefully he moved, as if he was caring for an infant.
I saw how carefully he moved, as if he *were* caring for an infant.

ANSWERS TO EXERCISE 8.10

1. was———→were
2. was———→were
3. correct
4. was———→were
5. knows———→know

TEACHING PRACTICE

If the diversity of verbal forms (tense, voice, and mood) overwhelms your students, encourage them to appreciate how these forms help them convey their meaning accurately and flexibly. Assure them that what the forms are called is less important than how they are used for specific purposes. Whenever possible, point out and discuss how your students' purpose in writing dictates the choice of a particular verbal treatment.

WRITING TOGETHER

After the class has divided into small groups or pairs, have the students exchange recent essays or passages they have written. Can they identify the writer's use of tense, voice, and mood? Ask them to examine how the writer's purpose is related to these choices.

The same exercise can be conducted with published works. When considering voice, for example, your students might analyze the writer's intentions, the issue of authority and responsibility, the conventions followed in specific subjects and disciplines, and the nature of the subject itself and how that nature determines voice.

ANSWERS TO EXERCISE 8.11

'Twas; Did gyre . . . gimble; were; raths; Beware; bite; catch; Beware; shun; took; sought; rested; stood; stood; stood; came [whiffling is a participle]; burbled; went; left; went [galumphing is a participle]; hast . . . slain; come; chortled; 'Twas; Did gyre . . . gimble; were; raths.

1. Her stepsisters treated Cinderella as though she was a servant.
2. Hamlet wishes that he was not responsible for avenging his murdered father.
3. Freud recommended that an analyst use dreams as a means of studying the human personality.
4. If more money was available, the university would be able to offer more scholarships.
5. It is necessary that the manager knows how to do any job in the store.

EXERCISE 8.11

The poem below is a famous example of nonsense verse, one that plays games with words—and freely *invents* words. Read the poem out loud, and then underline all the verbs, whether actual English words (like *bite*) or made-up ones (like *outgrabe*).

> 'Twas brillig, and the slithy toves
>   Did gyre and gimble in the wabe;
> All mimsy were the borogoves,
>   And the mome raths outgrabe.
>
> "Beware the Jabberwock, my son!
>   The jaws that bite, the claws that catch!
> Beware the Jubjub bird, and shun
>   The frumious Bandersnatch!"
>
> He took his vorpal sword in hand;
>   Long time for manxome foe he sought—
> So rested he by the Tumtum tree,
>   And stood awhile in thought.
>
> And, as in uffish thought he stood,
>   The Jabberwock, with eyes of flame,
> Came whiffling through the tulgey wood,
>   And burbled as it came!
>
> One, two! One, two! And through and through
>   The vorpal blade went snicker-snack!
> He left it dead, and with its head
>   He went galumphing back.
>
> "And hast thou slain the Jabberwock?
>   Come to my arms, my beamish boy!
> O frabjous day! Callooh! Callay!"
>   He chortled in his joy.

USING THE SUBJUNCTIVE   *vb* 8h

> 'Twas brillig, and the slithy toves
>   Did gyre and gimble in the wabe;
> And mimsy were the borogoves,
>   And the mome raths outgrabe.
>   –LEWIS CARROLL, "Jabberwocky"

READING WITH AN EYE FOR VERBS

Read the following paragraph carefully, noting the way the author uses verbs to create a scene from his past. Especially note his one use of the present tense, which emphasizes the fact that he is recollecting a past experience. What different effects might this passage have if it were written all in the present tense?

> I came to suspect that I was setting about life in reverse: drawing the conclusions before experiencing the data. My eyes were opened by Bernard Berenson, whom my family knew quite well, and with whom I was staying at Vallombrosa. One day we took a tiny walk. I use that term because B.B., rug over immaculately tailored forearm, would creep along a few steps, halt, seize your elbow, swinging you around in front, and then say something. We were tottering along in this way when B.B. asked me, "What will you be doing next year?" "I may work on a doctorate in comp. lit.," I replied. His face clouded slightly. "What do you think of comp. lit.?" I inquired anxiously. He stopped, seized my elbow, swinging me around in front, and bayed hoarsely, "Comp. lit. is dead as cold mutton!" Since he always said he had gone astray in his own life in becoming an art "expert," he was glad to set young men straight.
>   –JOHN TRAIN, "For the Adventurous Few: How to Get Rich"

FOR EXAMINING VERBS IN YOUR OWN WRITING

Write a few paragraphs about a past event in your life—a visit, a ceremony, a job, anything you remember that you wish to write about. Describe it as a past event, using past-tense verbs. Then rewrite your description in the present tense, as if the event were taking place right now. Study the two versions, and write down any observations you can make about the effectiveness of each approach.

9. Maintaining Agreement

(BACK)GROUNDING

The English language, even in its earliest stages, is extremely redundant: such redundancy is a type of "agreement" in terms of person, number, gender, and tense. One needs only the most basic facility with language to leech meaning out of the following passage, written in modern English:

> The wolf stood in the pit, so hungry that he was crazy. He was really cursing the one who brought him there.

Look how much help we get with tense: *stood, was, was cursing*. We are provided with three times the information, the agreement, we need to know that this passage is in past tense. Now, look at the information telling us that there is only one wolf: *wolf* has no plural marker (-*s*); the *was* and *was cursing* are in the third-person-singular form, and the pronouns referring to the wolf are singular (*he* and *him*). We all know that *wolf* is masculine, for female wolves are *she-wolves*, but the English language tries hard to be fail-safe: not only are we given the word *wolf*, but all the pronouns referring to this wolf are masculine.

From the source of the above passage, *The Fox and the Wolf*, we can see the redundancy or agreement that even in A.D. 1200 wove a safety net for the reader:

> þe wolf in þe putte stod,
> A fingret so þat he ves wod.
> Inou he cursede þat þider him broute!
>
> (11. 257–59)

Here, we are given the same three clues, in verb forms that look vaguely familiar, that the passage is in past tense: *stod, ves, cursede*; and nearly the same information regarding the singleness of the wolf: *wolf* (without the single marker -*s*); the singular verb *ves*; and the three pronouns, *he, he,* and *him,* which also reinforce the gender of *wolf*.

In ordinary language, **agreement** refers to an accord or a correspondence between ideas or actions: you reach an *agreement* with your boss about salary; the United States and the Soviet Union negotiate an *agreement* about nuclear arms. This ordinary meaning of *agreement* covers its grammatical use as well. When subjects and verbs or pronouns and antecedents match each other in person, in number, and in gender, we say that they "agree." This chapter explores the conventions governing such agreement.

SUBJECT-VERB AGREEMENT

A verb must agree with its subject in number (singular or plural) and in person (first, second, or third).

> *Annie Dillard comes* from Pittsburgh. [third-person singular]
>
> *We* always *wear* rubber gloves in the lab. [first-person plural]
>
> *Whales are* mammals. [third-person plural]

In practice, only a very few subject-verb constructions cause confusion, so we will look at those constructions in greater detail.

9a. Making verbs agree with third-person singular subjects

English once used a complex system of word endings to reflect the person, number, and gender of the subject. Over the centuries, however, most such endings have disappeared from use. Today the

212

MAKING THE SUBJECT AND VERB AGREE   *agr* 9b

main kinds of subjects requiring a special verb form are third-person singular subjects: singular nouns and third-person singular pronouns. To make a present-tense verb agree with a third-person singular subject, we normally add *-s* or *-es* to the base form.

> A vegetarian diet *lowers* the risk of heart disease.

> He *wishes* to go to Europe next summer.

The only two verbs that do not follow this *-s* or *-es* pattern for third-person singular subjects in the present tense are *have* and *be*. *Have* changes to *has*; *be* has different forms for both the first and third persons and for both the present and past tense. (See 8b.)

Notice that although an *-s* or *-es* ending indicates a plural noun, the same kind of ending indicates a "singular" verb form. If the subject is a *plural* noun, the verb form does *not* take the *-s* or *-es*.

> A car *needs* regular maintenance.

> Cars *need* regular maintenance.

Some dialects of English do not use the *-s* or *-es* ending with a third-person singular subject, and many people forget to use it in writing because it is often not stressed or pronounced clearly in speech. Always use the ending, however, in any writing you do for college or a job. If you have trouble with this particular pattern of subject-verb agreement, you should proofread especially for it; see page 189.

9b. Making the subject and verb agree when separated by other words

When the simple subject of a sentence or clause is separated from the verb by other words, such as a prepositional phrase, be careful to make the verb agree with the subject and not with another noun that is closer to the verb.

> A *vase* of flowers *makes* a room attractive.

> Many *books* on the best-seller list *have* little literary value.

Many writers forget to maintain agreement when a plural noun falls between a singular subject and the verb, as in the first example above, or when a singular noun falls between a plural subject and the verb, as in the second example. In the first sentence, notice that the single subject is *vase*, not *flowers*, which is the object of the preposition *of*.

213

(BACK)GROUNDING

In *Errors & Expectations*, master diagnostician Mina Shaughnessy discusses agreement:

> The idea of agreement—that is, of certain words in sentences being formally linked to others so as to reinforce or repeat some kinds of meaning rather than others—is common to many languages. What is arbitrary in each language is what that language chooses to reinforce. Standard English, for example, is laced by forms that reinforce number . . . , a time frame . . . gender and person. (136)

One of the most common student errors, errors of agreement grew out of all the possibilities for agreement in our language. Shaughnessy saw such errors as "exercises in competence" and knew that students who have trouble with agreement need to become *habituated* in, need to develop an "ear" for the conventions of their language.

TEACHING PRACTICE

If your students speak languages in addition to English, ask them to explain the agreement necessary in those languages. Spanish, for example, extends agreement to the gender and number of adjectives; Black English Vernacular, French, and many other languages call for negative concord whereas English rejects it; Chinese languages do not use agreement, depending instead on word order to relate words in sentences.

USEFUL READING

Shaughnessy, Mina. *Errors & Expectations*. New York: Oxford UP, 1977. The best contribution to basic writing, a practical and philosophical guidebook. See especially Chapter 4, "Common Errors," and pp. 136–52, "Agreement"—concept, explanation, exercises.

WRITERS ON WRITING

In trying to explain how to write German correctly, how to achieve agreement, Mark Twain admonishes his readers to remember the gender of German nouns:

> In German, a young lady has no sex, while a turnip has. Think what overwrought reverence that shows for the turnip, and what callous disrespect for the girl. . . . A tree is male, its buds are female, its leaves are neuter; horses are sexless, dogs are male, cats are female—tomcats included, of course; a person's mouth, neck, bosom, elbows, fingers, nails, feet, and body are of the male sex, and his head is male or neuter according to the word selected to signify it, and *not* according to the sex of the individual who wears it—for in Germany all the women wear either male heads or sexless ones; a person's nose, lips, shoulders, breast, hands, and toes are of the female sex; and his hair, ears, eyes, chin, legs, knees, heart, and conscience haven't any sex at all. The inventor of the language probably got what he knew about a conscience from hearsay. . . .

ANSWERS TO EXERCISE 9.1

1. pains
2. am
3. characterize
4. supplies
5. stops
6. were
7. care
8. holds
9. writes
10. leaves

In the second sentence, the simple subject is *books*, not *list*, which is the object of the preposition *on*.

Also be careful when a simple subject is followed by a phrase beginning with *as well as*, *along with*, *together with*, *in addition to*, or a similar expression. Make the verb agree with the simple subject, not with a noun in the intervening phrase.

> The *president*, along with many senators, *opposes* the bill.

> A *passenger*, as well as the driver, *was injured* in the accident.

Some writers think it awkward to use a singular verb form when the complete subject, including the intervening phrase, expresses a plural idea. If a sentence like this strikes you as awkward, revise it by making the subject plural and using a plural verb form (see 9c).

> The president and many senators *oppose* the bill.

> The driver and a passenger *were injured* in the accident.

If you know that you have problems with subject-verb agreement when the simple subject and the verb are separated by other words, proofread each of your sentences to identify the simple subject and the verb. Then mentally delete the intervening words, if any, to make sure that the subject and verb agree in number and person.

EXERCISE 9.1

Underline the appropriate verb form in each of the following sentences.

> *Example*
>
> The benefits of family planning (*is/are*) not apparent to many peasants.

1. It (*pains/pain*) me to see so much misery in the world.
2. I, together with my sister, (*am/is/are*) planning a surprise party for him.
3. Walls of glass (*characterizes/characterize*) much modern architecture.
4. The system of sororities and fraternities (*supplies/supply*) much of the social life on college campuses.
5. The buck (*stops/stop*) here.
6. The soldiers, along with their commanding officer, (*was/were*) cited for bravery beyond the call of duty.
7. In many species the male, as well as the female, (*cares/care*) for the offspring.
8. He (*holds/hold*) a controlling interest in the company.
9. The author of those stories (*writes/write*) beautifully.
10. Current research on AIDS, in spite of the best efforts of hundreds of scientists, (*leaves/leave*) serious questions unanswered.

MAKING VERBS AGREE WITH COLLECTIVE-NOUN SUBJECTS

▌9c. Making verbs agree with compound subjects

Two or more subjects joined by *and* generally require a plural verb form.

> Tony and his friends *commute* every day from Louisville.
>
> Faith, hope, and charity *represent* virtues to most of us.

When subjects joined by *and* are considered a single unit or refer to a single person or thing, they take a singular verb form.

> Drinking and driving *remains* a major cause of highway fatalities.
>
> Bagels and cream cheese *is* Colleen's idea of a great breakfast.
>
> His closest friend and political ally *was* his brother.

If the word *each* or *every* precedes singular subjects joined by *and,* the verb form is singular.

> Each boy and girl *chooses* one gift to take home.
>
> Every city, town, and hamlet *has* a Main Street.

For compound subjects whose parts are joined by *or* or *nor,* the verb agrees in number and person with the part of the subject closest to the verb.

> Laws or convention *governs* most of our everyday decisions.
>
> Neither my roommate nor my parents *plan* to vote.
>
> Either Jean or you *were* at fault.
>
> Either you or I *am* wrong.

To avoid awkwardness with compound subjects made up of both singular and plural parts, place a plural part closest to the verb.

> AWKWARD   Either the pigs or the cow *tramples* down my rhubarb every year.
>
> REVISED   Either the cow or the pigs *trample* down my rhubarb every year.

▌9d. Making verbs agree with collective-noun subjects

Collective nouns, such as *family, team, audience, group, jury, crowd, band, class, flock,* and *committee,* are singular in form but refer to a group of individual persons or things. When used as subjects,

215

USEFUL READING

Follett, Wilson. *Modern American Usage.* New York: Hill, 1966. One among many available references, this selective guide discusses in detail matters of "usage and grammar, purism and pedantry" in American English. See pp. 140–42.

TEACHING PRACTICE

Traditionally, sentence diagramming has been the way students identified the subject and verb of a sentence. Although such close syntactical analysis will help *some* students determine subject-verb or pronoun-antecedent agreement, most of our students just don't have the technical command of grammar to diagram or parse a sentence.

To help your students develop their ear for agreement, ask them to bring in or create sentences that seem confusing. Then ask them to come up with ways of determining the information that separates the subject from the verb.

For example, try these sentences orally with your students:

1. To see so many people here *is/are* gratifying.
2. The problems with the house *is/are* overwhelming.
3. Every one of the details *was/were* perfect.
4. It *is/are* the fault of the citizens.
5. Pizza with pepperoni, mushrooms, and green peppers *is/are* delicious.

WRITERS ON WRITING

> Habit is habit, and not to be flung out of the window by any man, but coaxed downstairs a step at a time.
>
> —MARK TWAIN

TEACHING PRACTICE

Encourage your students to think critically about collective nouns as wholes or parts. Write this topic sentence on the board: "The jury disagree/disagrees on a number of details." Then ask your students to decide whether to treat *jury* as singular or plural, according to the following context:

> After examining both sides of the case for over seven hours, only one member thinks for certain that the defendant is "not guilty." Three other jurors, however, cannot decide at all. In view of this stand-off, the jury leader has no choice but to insist that the entire jury review the case and evidence yet one more time.

WRITING TOGETHER

Break the class into groups and edit the following sentences for subject-verb agreement. Note carefully the compound subjects and collective nouns.

1. Every week, Sharma, Julio, and Richard *attends*/*attend* a group total of fifty hours of school.
2. Crosby, Stills, Nash, and Young *was*/*were* one of the hottest groups in the early seventies.
3. Neither the president nor his administration *claims*/claim to know anything about arms shipment to the Middle East.
4. Mike and his friends *is*/*are* going to decorate your yard with crepe paper after the game.
5. The composition class *plan*/*plans* to celebrate Valentine's Day at the professor's house.
6. The professor or her assistant *is*/are always in the office.
7. The couple *vow*/vows to have and hold until death.

WRITERS ON WRITING

Always do right. This will gratify some people, and astonish the rest.

—MARK TWAIN

A powerful agent is the right word. Whenever we come upon one of those intensely right words in a book or a newspaper the resulting effect is physical as well as spiritual, and electrically prompt.

—MARK TWAIN

collective nouns can take either singular or plural verb forms, depending on the context. When they refer to a group as a single unit, they take a singular verb form.

> The team wearing red and black *controls* the ball.
>
> Waving banners frenetically, the crowd *screams* its support.

When they refer to the individual members of a collective, however, they take a plural verb form.

> The family of ducklings *scatter* when the cat approaches.
>
> The committee *have* not agreed on many points.

The meaning of a sentence as a whole is your guide to whether the collective noun refers to a unit or to the separate parts of a unit.

> After deliberating, the jury *reports* its verdict. [as a single unit]
>
> The jury still *disagree* on a number of counts. [as separate individuals]

9e. Making verbs agree with indefinite-pronoun subjects

Indefinite pronouns can pose difficulties with subject-verb agreement because they do not refer to specific persons or things, because some of them can be either singular or plural, and because some of them (*everybody, everyone, everything*) sound plural but are grammatically singular.

The following indefinite pronouns are singular in meaning and thus take singular verb forms:

another	everyone	nothing
anybody	everything	one
anyone	much	other
anything	neither	somebody
each	nobody	someone
either	no one	something

Of the two jobs, neither *holds* much appeal.

Each of the plays *depicts* a hero undone by a tragic flaw.

Indefinite pronouns that take plural verb forms include *both, few, many, others,* and *several.*

Though many *apply*, few *are* chosen.

Both *require* careful attention.

Several indefinite pronouns—*all, any, enough, more, most, none, some*—can be singular or plural, depending on the noun they refer to.

SINGULAR   All of the cake *was* eaten.

PLURAL   All of the candidates *promise* to improve the schools.

9f. Making verbs agree with relative-pronoun subjects

When the relative pronouns *who, which,* or *that* act as the subject of a dependent clause, the verb in the clause should agree in number with the antecedent of the pronoun.

> Fear is an ingredient that *goes* into creating stereotypes. [*That* refers to *ingredient*; hence the singular verb form *goes*.]

> Guilt, jealousy, and fear are ingredients that *go* into creating stereotypes. [*That* refers to *ingredients*; hence the plural verb form *go*.]

When the phrase *one of the* precedes the relative pronoun, you have to be especially careful to determine whether the pronoun refers to the word *one* or to another word. Look at the following sentence:

> Alex is one of the *employees* who always *work* overtime.

In this sentence a number of employees always work overtime, and Alex is among them. Thus *who* refers to *employees*, and the verb form is plural. Now look at the following sentence:

> Alex is the only *one* of the employees who always *works* overtime.

In this sentence only one employee always works overtime, and that employee is Alex. Thus *one* and not *employees* is the antecedent of *who,* and the verb form is singular.

9g. Making linking verbs agree with their subjects, not complements

A linking verb should agree with its subject, which precedes it, not with the subject complement, which follows it (see 6c2).

The signings of three key treaties *are* the topic of my talk. [The subject is *signings*.]

Nero Wolfe's passion *was* orchids. [The subject is *passion*.]

9h. Making verbs agree with subjects that are plural in form but singular in meaning

Some nouns that seem plural in form (such as *athletics*, *mathematics*, *measles*, *politics*, *statistics*) are usually singular in meaning and take singular verb forms.

Mathematics *is* not always an exact science.

Measles still *strikes* many Americans.

Some of these nouns may be either singular or plural.

Statistics *is* a course I really dread.

The statistics in that study *are* highly questionable.

In the first sentence above, *statistics* refers to a single course of study; hence it takes a singular verb form. In the second sentence, *statistics* refers to a number of individual figures; hence it takes a plural verb form.

When the subject is the title of a book, film, or other work of art, the verb form is singular even if the title is plural in form.

Sons and Lovers was left to the mercy of critics, many of whom did not fully comprehend it.

Similarly, a word referred to as a word requires a singular verb form even if the word itself is plural.

Scruples has always sounded funny to me.

Steroids is a little word that packs a big punch in the world of sports.

9i. Making verbs agree with subjects that follow them

In English, the subject usually precedes the verb, so check carefully for subject-verb agreement when this order is inverted, or reversed. Make the verb agree with the subject, not with a noun that happens to precede it. Writers often invert word order to ask questions or to emphasize the subject.

OPTIONAL EXERCISE

Edit the following sentences for subject-verb agreement:

1. The best thing about college *is*/are the vacations.
2. Panning up and down staircases *was*/were a frequent feature of Hitchcock's films.
3. In this context, the word *values* *is*/are vague.
4. *Henry James's Letters* provide/*provides* interesting and important, if sometimes ambiguous, information about the nineteenth-century author.
5. It *is*/are a melancholy object to those who *walk*/walks through this great town or *travel*/travels in the country, when they *see*/see in the streets, the road, and cabin doors, crowded with beggars of the female sex, followed by three, four, or six children, all in rags and importuning every passenger for an alms. These mothers, instead of being able to work for their honest livelihood, *is*/are forced to employ all their time in strolling to beg sustenance for their helpless infants, who, as they *grow*/grows up, either *turn*/turns thieves for want of work, or leaves/*leave* their dear country to fight for the Pretender of Spain, or *sell*/sells themselves to the Barbados. (Jonathan Swift, "A Modest Proposal.")

WRITERS ON WRITING

Nothing so needs reforming as other people's habits.

—MARK TWAIN

MAKING VERBS AND SUBJECTS THAT FOLLOW AGREE   *agr* 9i

Is a shark a vertebrate? [The subject is *shark*.]

Beside the tracks *stand* silos filled with grain. [The subject is *silos*.]

Another common inversion of subject-verb order occurs in sentences beginning with *there* followed by a form of *be* (*is, are, was, were*). *There* is never the subject in such constructions; usually it has no meaning and serves only as an introductory word, or expletive (see 21a1).

There *are* five basic positions in classical ballet. [The subject is *positions*.]

➤ Checking for subject-verb agreement

Underline each finite verb. Then identify the subject that corresponds to the verb. Read the two together to see if they sound right. For example, the sentence *The players on our side is sure to win* can be stripped down to a simple subject-verb *players is*. Bringing together the subject and verb in this way helps some writers to recognize agreement problems; here the verb should be *are*: *players are*. If, however, you find that you cannot trust your ear, you need to check each verb to see that it agrees with its subject.

EXERCISE 9.2

Revise any of the following sentences as necessary to establish subject-verb agreement. (Some of the sentences do not require any change.)

Example

Into the shadows dart the frightened raccoon.

Into the shadows *darts* the frightened raccoon.

1. Every check and money order cost 50 cents.
2. Talking and getting up from my seat was my crime.
3. If rhythm and blues is your kind of music, drive down Green Springs Highway to Mary Lou's.
4. His merry disposition and his recognized success in business make him popular in the community.
5. *The vapors* were a Victorian term for hypochondria.
6. Neither the lighting on the painting nor the wall it is hanging on display it well.
7. Child abuse is far more commonplace than anyone care to admit.
8. Most of the voters support a reduction in nuclear weapons.
9. Each of the players are dealt five cards to start the game.
10. Either his phony smile or his bragging seem to fool many people.

MAINTAINING AGREEMENT

WRITERS WRITING

I've got a sort of idea but I don't suppose it's a very good one.

—A. A. MILNE

11. The team needs time to learn to cooperate with one another.
12. Her grandmother is the only one of her relatives who still goes to church.
13. The situation is not entirely hopeless, for some do see the light.
14. *Our Tapes* were one of Fitzgerald's earlier titles for *Tender Is the Night*.
15. Sweden was one of the few European countries that was neutral in 1943.
16. Politics have been defined as the art of the possible.
17. The short-term effect of the company's expansion were lower dividends.
18. Mumps cause swelling of the salivary glands.
19. In the foreground is two women playing musical instruments and singing.
20. Dr. Pangloss believes that everything that happen is for the best.

PRONOUN-ANTECEDENT AGREEMENT

Most pronouns function in sentences as replacements for nouns or other pronouns, known as their antecedents. Like a verb with its subject, a pronoun must agree with its antecedent in person and number. In addition, a third-person singular pronoun must agree with its antecedent in *gender*—masculine, feminine, or neuter. (See 6a3.)

> Angry, *Mr. Blanchard* called in to say *he* was sick. [third-person singular, masculine]

> The *workers* elected a representative to voice *their* common complaints. [third-person plural]

As with subject-verb agreement, only a few kinds of pronoun-antecedent constructions cause problems in practice, so we will look at those constructions in greater detail.

9j. Making pronouns agree with compound antecedents

A compound antecedent whose parts are joined by *and* requires a plural pronoun.

> With great excitement, the children and I began *our* search for the perfect house.

> Keith, Molly, and Jane hid behind Dad's chair, and nobody saw *them*.

When a compound antecedent is preceded by *each* or *every*, however, it takes a singular pronoun.

> Every plant and animal has *its* own ecological niche.

A compound antecedent that refers to a single person or thing also takes a singular pronoun.

> The producer and director invested all of *her* savings in the film.

With a compound antecedent whose parts are joined by *or* or *nor*, the pronoun agrees with the nearest antecedent.

> Neither the players nor the owners will change *their* tactics.

> For us to win the meet, Marianne or Charlyce must win *her* next dive.

This kind of sentence, however, may be awkward if the parts of the antecedent are of different genders. Consider, for example, the following sentence:

> **AWKWARD**   For us to win the meet, Jim or Charlyce must win *her* next dive.

Such a sentence can be revised in a number of ways to eliminate the awkwardness.

> **REVISED**   For us to win the meet, Jim or Charlyce must win *his or her* next dive.

> **REVISED**   For us to win the meet, Jim must win *his* next dive, or Charlyce must win *hers*.

With compound antecedents containing both singular and plural parts, the sentence may sound awkward unless a plural part comes last.

> **AWKWARD**   Neither the Pointer Sisters nor Wayne Newton would disclose *his* income for 1985.

> **REVISED**   Neither Wayne Newton nor the Pointer Sisters would disclose *their* incomes for 1985.

9k. Making pronouns agree with collective-noun antecedents

When a collective-noun antecedent (*herd, team, committee, audience*, for example) refers to a single unit, it requires a singular pronoun.

> The audience fixed *its* attention on center stage.

> Finally, our team scored *its* first victory.

When such an antecedent refers to the individual parts of the unit, however, it requires a plural pronoun.

> The crew divided the loot among *themselves*.

> The director chose this cast because *they* had experience in the roles.

Remember that collective nouns referring to single units require not only singular pronouns but also singular verb forms. Collective nouns referring to separate individuals in a unit, on the other hand, require plural pronouns and plural verb forms.

> Each generation *has its* own slang. [*generation* as single unit]

> My generation *have* sold *their* souls for money. [*generation* as separate individuals]

9l. Making pronouns agree with indefinite-pronoun antecedents

A pronoun whose antecedent is an indefinite pronoun should agree with it in number. Indefinite pronouns may be always singular (as with *one*) or plural (as with *many*), or their number may depend on their context. (See 9e for a list.)

> One of the ballerinas lost *her* balance. [singular]

> Many in the audience jumped to *their* feet. [plural]

> All of the music was familiar to *its* listeners. [singular meaning for *all*]

> All of the principal dancers took *their* bows. [plural meaning for *all*]

9m. Avoiding sexism with pronouns

One somewhat complicated problem in pronoun-antecedent agreement involves a pronoun referring to a singular antecedent that may be either male or female. Look at the following passage:

> . . . the Country Club pool was small. One diving board, no spinning top. But its size only seemed to me to be a measure of its exclusiveness. *Whoever* had laid out plans for the Country Club was an entrepreneur with an eye for the one beautiful, rolling and wooded piece of land outside Ames. *He* must have known immediately that such an acreage had to be saved; *he* had a true aristocrat's instinct and converted it into a private preserve.   —SUSAN ALLEN TOTH, "Swimming Pools"

TEACHING PRACTICE

The adjectives *every* and *each* and the pronouns *everyone, no one, anyone, anybody* are generally regarded as singular, regardless of the sentence construction. These words cause difficulty for students, not so much because of their indefiniteness, but because of the agreement problem inherent in third-person-singular nouns and verbs: should agreement be reached in number or gender? The following examples are easy:

—*Every* dog in the kennel eats two meals a day.
—Although *no one* can figure out how Mr. Woskewicz manages to remember all twenty-seven birthdates, *every* grandchild receives a birthday gift without fail on the appropriate date.

In the following sentence, should you pair *every* with *his* and perpetuate sexist language? Or should you pair the singular *every* with the plural *their*, a practice that is falling into general usage?

—*Every* driver takes *his/her/its/their* lives into *his/her its/their* own hands. ???

Or should you recast the entire sentence into plural:
All drivers take *their* life into *their* own hands.

Current convention prefers the singular for *everybody* even when a contextual and common sense analysis shows that *everybody* refers to more than one person. Compare:

—On Saturday mornings, *everybody* meets at Shauna's place before heading to the ball diamond. Beth, Cindi, and Robert always show up first. Tim and Matt usually arrive last. It rarely fails: we always end up waiting for those two.

WRITERS ON WRITING

Every word almost was a sentence; every sentence a victory.

    —ST. VINCENT OF LERINS

For they wished to fill the winepress of eloquence not with the tendrils of mere words but with the rich grape juice of good sense.

    —ST. JEROME

AVOIDING SEXISM WITH PRONOUNS   *agr* | 9m

Notice that although the author apparently does not know who laid out the plans for the Country Club, she uses the pronoun *he* to refer to this person. In traditional English grammar, writers used masculine pronouns, known as the **generic he**, in such cases. In recent decades, however, many people have pointed out that such wording ignores or even excludes females—and thus should be avoided. There are several ways of avoiding the generic *he*. Consider, for example, the following sentence:

> Every citizen should know *his* rights under the law.

Now look at three ways to express the same idea without the *he*.

> 1. Every citizen should know *his or her* rights under the law.
> 2. All citizens should know *their* rights under the law.
> 3. Everyone should have some knowledge of basic legal rights.

As these examples show, you have three basic options: (1) using both masculine and feminine pronouns—*he or she, his or her,* and so forth; (2) revising into the plural; and (3) revising the sentence altogether. Keep in mind that overuse of *he or she* can be awkward.

When the antecedent is an indefinite pronoun (*anybody, both, each, few, neither, none, somebody,* see 6b3 for a more complete list), some people avoid the generic *he* by using a plural pronoun. For example:

> Everyone had *their* own theory about Marcia's resignation.

You will probably hear—and perhaps use—such sentences in conversation, but you should be careful about using them in writing. Although this usage is now gaining some acceptance, it is probably a good idea to talk to your instructor to see what he or she advises before using it in academic work. See 11c5 and 24b1 for more discussion of how to avoid sexist language.

➤ Checking for pronoun-antecedent agreement

Circle all pronouns, and then identify the antecedent of each one. Check to see that the pronoun agrees in person and number with its antecedent; if it does not, revise the pronoun accordingly. Look especially carefully at any compound antecedents (9j), indefinite-pronoun antecedents (9e and 9l), and collective-noun antecedents (9h) to see that the pronouns agree in both person and number.

WRITERS WRITING

Everybody to rest themselves take.
> —SHAKESPEARE

Everyone in the house were in their beds.
> —HENRY FIELDING

A person can't help their birth.
> —WILLIAM THACKERAY

It's enough to drive anyone out of their senses.
> —GEORGE BERNARD SHAW

Anybody is as their land and air is.
> —GERTRUDE STEIN

No man or woman can hesitate to give what they have.

> —WOODROW WILSON

9m agr   MAINTAINING AGREEMENT

ANSWERS TO EXERCISE 9.3 (WILL VARY)

Ask students to explain their revisions.

1. With tuition on the rise, students have to save money wherever they can.
2. Although roommates do not always get along, they can usually manage to tolerate each other temporarily.
3. Congress usually resists presidential attempts to encroach on what it considers congressional authority.
4. Both Tom and Teresa are willing to lend us a car.
5. If their own knowledge is all readers have to go by, how can they identify one source as more reliable than another?
6. Every house and apartment has its advantages and its drawbacks.
7. Neither the scouts nor their leader knew the way out of the forest.
8. Our team no longer wear their red and white uniforms.
9. To create positive impressions, candidates attempt to flood the media with favorable publicity about themselves.
10. Sometimes she turns on the bathroom fan and the infrared light and neglects to turn them off.

ANSWERS TO EXERCISE 9.4 (WILL VARY)

By this time, most of us have heard from one source or another that an excess of salt in our diets is damaging to our health. Why, then, do recent statistics indicate that Americans are consuming as much salt as ever? First of all, few of us are aware of how much salt we consume each day. Second, once we acquire a taste for salt, food begins to taste bland without it. Third, and perhaps most important, few of us realize what salt does to our bodies and why we should cut down on the excess. Americans have to shake the salt habit.

EXERCISE 9.3

Revise the following sentences as necessary to create pronoun-antecedent agreement and to eliminate the generic *he* and any awkward pronoun references. Some of the sentences can be revised in more than one way, and some of them do not require any change.

> *Example*
> Every graduate submitted his diploma card.
> Every graduate submitted *his or her* diploma card.

1. With tuition on the rise, a student has to save money wherever they can.
2. Everyone does not get along with his roommate, but the two can usually manage to tolerate each other temporarily.
3. Congress usually resists presidential attempts to encroach on what they consider their authority.
4. Either Tom or Teresa would be willing to lend us her car.
5. If his own knowledge is all the reader has to go by, how can he identify one source as more reliable than another?
6. Every house and apartment has their advantages and their drawbacks.
7. Neither the scouts nor their leader knew their way out of the forest.
8. Our team no longer wears their red and white uniforms.
9. To create a positive impression, a candidate attempts to flood the media with favorable publicity about themselves.
10. Sometimes she turns on the bathroom fan and the infrared light and neglects to turn it off.

EXERCISE 9.4

Revise the following paragraph to create subject-verb and pronoun-antecedent agreement and to eliminate the generic *he*.

By this time, most of us has heard from one source or another that an excess of salt in our diets are damaging to our health. Why, then, does recent statistics indicate that Americans are consuming as much salt as ever? First of all, few of us is aware of how much salt the average person consumes unnecessarily each day. Second, once we acquire a taste for salt, food begin to taste bland without it. Third, and perhaps most important, almost nobody realize what salt does to their bodies and why they should cut down on the excess. The American has to shake his salt habit.

READING WITH AN EYE FOR PRONOUNS

Following is the opening paragraph from *Democracy in America*, Alexis de Tocqueville's classic critique of American institutions and culture, which was first published in 1835. Read the paragraph with an eye for pronouns. Does the use of the masculine pronoun to refer to both men and women seem odd to you? Revise the paragraph to eliminate the use of masculine pronouns to refer to both men and women.

After the birth of a human being, his early years are obscurely spent in the toils or pleasures of childhood. As he grows up, the world receives him, when his manhood begins, and he enters into contact with his fellows. He is then studied for the first time, and it is imagined that the germ of the vices and the virtues of his maturer years is then formed. This, if I am not mistaken, is a great error. We must begin higher up; we must watch the infant in his mother's arms; we must see the first images which the external world casts upon the dark mirror of his mind, the first occurrences which he witnesses; we must hear the first words which awaken the sleeping powers of thought, and stand by his earliest efforts,—if we would understand the prejudices, the habits, and the passions which will rule his life. The entire man is, so to speak, to be seen in the cradle of the child.

—ALEXIS DE TOCQUEVILLE, *Democracy in America*

FOR EXAMINING YOUR OWN WRITING

In a paragraph or two, describe some "typical" person—a typical student at your school, a typical citizen in your hometown, a typical new parent, whatever. You might begin with the sentence "The typical _____ is. . . ." Then analyze your description for agreement—between subjects and verbs, of course, but especially between pronouns and their antecedents.

TEACHING PRACTICE

Ask students to look for other examples of writing that uses pronouns to refer to both men and women. Suggest that they look for both sexist and nonsexist examples, and have them bring their examples to class for discussion. You might want to read a few of them aloud and then to put one sexist example up on the board for the class to revise.

WRITERS ON WRITING

For me, writing is the only thing that passes the three tests of *metier* [a profession, a calling]: (1) when I'm doing it, I don't feel that I should be doing something else instead; (2) it produces a sense of accomplishment and, once in a while, pride; and (3) it's frightening.

—GLORIA STEINEM

10. Using Adjectives and Adverbs

(BACK)GROUNDING

In Early English, many adverbs were formed from adjectives by adding e: *bright*, the adjective, became *brighte*, the adverb. In time, the *e* was dropped, but the adverbial use was kept. Hence, from a false analogy, many adjectives (such as *excellent*) that could never form adverbs in *e*, were used as adverbs. Shakespeare freely used such a construction:

Which the false man does *easy*.
                              —*Macbeth* 2.3.143

Thou didst it *excellent*.
                    —*Taming of the Shrew* 1.1.89

Grow not *instant* old.
                              —*Hamlet* 1.5.94

'Tis *noble* spoken.
                    —*Antony and Cleopatra* 2.2.99

And he used both forms of the adverb side by side:

She was *new* lodged and *newly* deified.
                    —*Lover's Complaint* 84.

In function, adjectives and adverbs alike modify other parts of speech, and their differences in spelling and pronunciation have been conflated in that linguistic tendency toward regularization. Like that of Shakespeare's day, today's informal conversation often makes no distinction between an adjective and an adverb in constructions such as *Come quick!* and *The moon shines bright* that omit the *-ly*, adverb suffix. In their enthusiasm to be correct, some speakers even add the *-ly* suffix to words that function as adjectives, such as: *I feel badly that you've lost your job*. Since *feel* is a linking verb, the speaker should use the adjective *bad* rather than the adverb *badly*.

As words that describe other words, adjectives and adverbs add liveliness and color to the flat gray surface of writing, helping writers to *show* rather than just tell. Adjectives and adverbs allow us to show readers what we want them to see—to help them visualize objects, scenes, or even abstractions. See, for instance, how much Gretel Ehrlich relies on adjectives and adverbs in the following description of the cowboy.

In our *hellbent* earnestness to romanticize the cowboy we've *ironically* disesteemed his *true* character. . . . Instead of the *macho, trigger-happy* man our culture has *perversely* wanted him to be, the cowboy is *more apt* to be *convivial, quirky*, and *softhearted*. . . .
                    –GRETEL EHRLICH, "About Men"

Ehrlich could have said simply, "We have misrepresented the cowboy. He is not really so macho." But we would not be able to picture the cowboy and understand his image as we do in the passage above. Adjectives such as *convivial* and *soft-hearted* and adverbs such as *ironically* and *perversely* create a vivid image of the cowboy and evoke a definite impression of Ehrlich's own attitude about her subject.

Adjectives are particularly useful for conveying concrete and sensory details in physical descriptions. Look, for example, at the sensory adjectives Annie Dillard uses in describing a young copperhead snake.

Although it lay in a *loose* sprawl, all I saw at first was a *camouflage* pattern of *particolored* splotches confused by the *rushing* speckles of light

226

USEFUL READING

Lee, Donald W., ed. *English Language Reader: Introductory Essays and Exercises*. New York: Dodd, 1963. Essays on grammar, history of the language, dictionaries, and other language-related topics. The final section discusses the various definitions of *adjective*.

DISTINGUISHING ADJECTIVES FROM ADVERBS   *ad* 10a

in the weeds between us, and by the *deep twilight* dark of the quarry pond beyond the rock. Then suddenly the form of its head emerged from the confusion: *burnished brown, triangular, blunt* as a *stone* ax.
—ANNIE DILLARD, "The Copperhead and the Mosquito"

Adverbs can also make writing vivid or add emphasis to a point. In the following sentence, the qualifications provided by the adverbs carry the central idea:

After three years of torture, the man was found guilty—*legally, officially,* but *unjustly* found guilty.

The three adverbs build up to culminate in an accusation: the verdict is not a just one.

But if adjectives and adverbs can create many dramatic effects in writing, they can also "betray" a writer who uses them inappropriately. Like any other part of a sentence, they must follow certain rules and conventions. This chapter discusses some of these rules and conventions and common problems that writers have with adjectives and adverbs.

▌ 10a. Distinguishing adjectives from adverbs

Although adjectives and adverbs both modify other words, they each modify different parts of speech. **Adjectives** modify nouns and pronouns, answering the questions *which?, how many?,* and *what kind?* Many adjectives are formed by adding the suffixes *-able, -ful, -ish, -less* or *-y* to nouns and verbs.

Many customers wrote *angry* letters to *the* company.

His one comfortable chair is covered in *a colorful Spanish* fabric.

Participles and infinitives can also function as adjectives. (See 6c3.)

The *perplexed* clerk looked at me with a *questioning* expression.

Sandra could not decide which job *to take.*

Although adjectives usually precede the noun or pronoun they modify, they sometimes follow it instead. An adjective can also appear after a linking verb, as a subject complement that modifies the subject of the sentence or clause (see 6c2 and 10b).

(BACK)GROUNDING

In *Errors & Expectations,* Mina Shaughnessy describes the vocabulary features of three groups of writers (basic, intermediate, and advanced), including their use of adjectives and adverbs. Basic writers commonly use only a few, already-overused adverbs (*too, very, really, quite, hardly*) and just twenty-one or so adjectives. Intermediate writers, she claims, use *-ly* adverbs (*adequately, fluently,* for example) and adjectives more "informative" than *good, bad, important;* these include *hostile, honest, monstrous, impatient.* Shaughnessy encourages teachers to work with writers of all levels, building their academic vocabulary in three ways: learning about words, learning words, learning a sensitivity to words.

WRITERS ON WRITING

Those who are learning to compose and arrange their sentences with accuracy and order are learning, at the same time, to think with accuracy and order.

—HUGH BLAIR

USEFUL READING

Shaughnessy, Mina P. *Errors & Expectations.* New York: Oxford UP, 1977. Chapter 6, "Vocabulary."

Curmé, George O. *English Grammar.* New York: Harper, 1947. For a traditional grammarian's explanations and examples of the common kinds and forms of adjectives and adverbs.

(BACK)GROUNDING

In the third edition of *On Writing Well*, William Zinsser discusses the overuse of adjectives and adverbs, which he calls "clutter." He advises writers to "strip every sentence to its cleanest components:

> . . . Every word that serves no function, . . . [and] every adverb that carries the same meaning that's already in the verb, . . . weaken the strength of a sentence" (7).

Carefully chosen nouns and verbs reverberate with meaning, their connotative meaning. Those words rarely need modifiers: *friend* does not need *personal*; *moped* does not need *dejectedly*. Zinsser advises writers to either find the "right" nouns and verbs to start or use only those modifiers that actually do some work:

> "The judges were *impressed* by Miss Ohio, an *attractive* woman, wearing a *stylish* evening gown" pales in comparison to "The judges were *flabbergasted* by Miss Ohio, a *knock-out*, wearing a *drop-dead* evening gown."

WRITERS WRITING

Unhappy with the title of his manuscript, *Why People Are Poor*, John Kenneth Galbraith changed it. *The Opulent Society* was a big change from his first title—better, but still not right. That second title was a necessary wrong title, a big, necessary, wrong step that enabled him to take the little step toward the right title, his celebrated title, *The Affluent Society*.

ANSWERS TO EXERCISE 10.1

[a, an, the = articles; his = possessive pronoun; this/that = demonstrative pronouns]

serious⟶strutting; full⟶tail; usually⟶begins; after⟶begins; shortly⟶after; several⟶hours; late⟶afternoon; each⟶cock; favorite⟶station; every⟶day; some passing⟶hen; indifferent⟶anyone; peacock's ⟶display; telephone⟶lineman; raised ⟶tail; shimmering⟶arch; around⟶raised; clay-colored wing⟶feathers; touching ⟶feathers; forward/backward⟶will dance; curved⟶neck; parted⟶beak; glittering ⟶eyes; diligently⟶searching; searching ⟶goes about [*about* is a particle]; any ⟶bug; more⟶importance; unfurled⟶map; nearby⟶floats

Butler found the Victorian family *stifling*.

Chocolate is *irresistible* to Lee.

For information about when to capitalize adjectives, see 33b. For information about when to use commas between adjectives preceding a noun, see 27d.

Adverbs modify verbs, adjectives, and other adverbs; they answer the questions *how?*, *when?*, *where?*, or *to what extent?* Many adverbs are formed by adding *-ly* to adjectives.

> The bride smiled *nervously*. [modifies the verb *smiled*]
>
> She was *almost* ready. [modifies the adjective *ready*]
>
> The guests had arrived *rather* early. [modifies the adverb *early*]

Adverbs can also modify an entire clause.

> *Fortunately*, the rain had ended before the wedding.

Infinitives can function as adverbs. (See 6c3.)

> Her sister hoped *to catch* the bouquet. [modifies the verb *hoped*]

While adjectives usually are closely tied to the words they modify, adverbs that modify verbs or clauses can often move easily from one position in a sentence to another.

> Connor *gleefully* tore open his presents.
>
> Connor tore open his presents *gleefully*.
>
> *Gleefully*, Connor tore open his presents.

Since adjectives and adverbs both act as modifiers, often have similar forms, and can sometimes occupy the same positions in sentences, sometimes the only way of recognizing an adjective or an adverb is to identify its function in the sentence. Remember: adjectives modify *nouns* and *pronouns*, adverbs modify *verbs*, *adjectives*, and other *adverbs*.

EXERCISE 10.1

Read the following paragraph with an eye for the adjectives and adverbs. Identify each one, and determine which word each modifies.

> The peacock does most of his serious strutting in the spring and summer when he has a full tail to do it with. Usually he begins shortly after breakfast,

USEFUL READING

Christensen, Francis. "A Generative Rhetoric of the Sentence." Rpt. in *Rhetoric and Composition: A Sourcebook for Teacher*. Upper Montclair, NJ: Boynton, 1984. 110–18. The way to generate a mature and interesting prose style lies in the use of adjectives and adverbs, which enables students to express complicated thoughts in complicated ways.

struts for several hours, desists in the heat of the day, and begins again in the late afternoon. Each cock has a favorite station where he performs every day in the hope of attracting some passing hen; but if I have found anyone indifferent to the peacock's display, besides the telephone lineman, it is the peahen. She seldom casts an eye at it. The cock, his tail raised in a shimmering arch around him, will turn this way and that, and with his clay-colored wing feathers touching the ground, will dance forward and backward, his neck curved, his beak parted, his eyes glittering. Meanwhile the hen goes about her business, diligently searching the ground as if any bug in the grass were of more importance than the unfurled map of the universe which floats nearby.

—FLANNERY O'CONNOR, "The King of the Birds"

▌ 10b. Using adjectives after linking verbs

Be careful to use adjectives, not the corresponding -ly adverbs, after linking verbs. The most frequently used linking verbs are forms of *be*, but they also include sensory verbs such as *look, appear, seem, sound, feel, smell,* and *taste* and verbs of becoming such as *become, grow, prove,* and *turn.* (See 6c2). When they function as linking verbs, they are always followed by adjectives (or nouns). Most of these verbs, however, can also be used to express action. When they express action, they can be followed by adverbs.

> The dog looked *hungry.* [linking verb with adjective]
> The dog looked *hungrily* at the steak. [action verb with adverb]

▌ 10c. Using adverbs to modify verbs, adjectives, and adverbs

Be careful to use adverbs, not adjectives, to modify verbs, adjectives, and other adverbs.

> NOT   His writing style is *excessive* formal.
> BUT   His writing style is *excessively formal.*

Good and well, bad and badly

The modifiers *good, well, bad,* and *badly* cause problems for many writers because the distinctions between *good* and *well* and between *bad* and *badly* are often not observed in conversation and because *well* can function as either an adjective or an adverb. Be careful to use the appropriate word in formal writing.

Good and *bad* are adjectives, and can be used after a linking verb.

WRITING TOGETHER

The following sentence uses adjectives effectively to paint a picture of beauty in motion:

> *Tall, powerful, barefoot, graceful, soundless,* Missouri fever was like a *supple black* cat as she paraded serenely about the kitchen, the *casual* flow of *her* walk beautifully *sensuous* and *haughty.* (Truman Capote, *Other Voices, Other Rooms,* 1955)

Break into your groups and write imitations of Capote's sentence, using as the focus of your description either your own pet or a person you know. Compare sentences among your group and then select the most powerful one to share with the best sentences from the other groups.

By using Capote's sentence as a model, you'll be able to internalize his syntax while you experiment and discover the semantic possibilities of adjectives.

WRITERS ON WRITING

Originality is nothing but judicious imitation. The most original writers borrowed from one another. The instruction we find in books is like fire. We fetch it from our neighbors, kindle it at home, communicate it to others, and it becomes the property of all.

—VOLTAIRE

229

USEFUL READING

Curmé, George O. *English Grammar.* New York: Harper, 1947. 23. In traditional grammar, linking verbs are also known as *copulas* or copulative verbs, from the Latin verb *copulare,* "link, join together."

Fromkin, Victoria, and Robert Rodman. *An Introduction to Language.* 2d ed. New York: Holt, 1978. 264–67. The verb *be* is regularly deleted in Black English Vernacular (BEV). Fromkin and Rodman discuss the linguistic explanation of this and other features of BEV.

(BACK)GROUNDING

"I don't want to go to school this morning; I don't feel good, Mom."

"If you're well enough to stay up for 'Chiller Theatre,' you're well enough to go to school."

The use of *well* and *good* to describe physical health is confusing, especially since many English speakers consider the two words synonymous: "Don't you feel good?" "Don't you feel well?"

Used as an adjective, *well* expresses relief from sickness, while the adjective *good* expresses a more general sense of well-being. When *good* is used after such linking verbs as *be, feel, seem, smell, sound,* and *taste,* it qualifies the subject of the verb.

WRITERS WRITING

Laughter is the sensation of *feeling good* all over, and showing it principally in one spot.

—JOSH BILLINGS

ANSWERS TO EXERCISE 10.2

1. completely———→obsessed
2. negatively———→reacts
3. bad———→feel
4. really———→cold
5. often———→carefully; carefully———→is chosen
6. fully———→grown; well———→eating
7. badly———→wounded
8. surely———→have made
9. differently———→sounded
10. strictly———→brought

Do not use them to modify a verb, an adjective, or an adverb; use *well* or *badly* instead.

> Amanda looks *good* in black.
>
> He felt *bad* about missing his father's retirement party.

| NOT | He plays the trumpet *good* and the trombone not *bad.* |
| BUT | He plays the trumpet *well* and the trombone not *badly.* |

Badly is an adverb and can be used to modify a verb, an adjective, or another adverb. Do not use it after a linking verb; use *bad* instead.

> In her first recital, the soprano sang *badly.*

| NOT | The clams tasted *badly.* |
| BUT | The clams tasted *bad.* |

Well can be either an adjective (meaning "in good health") or an adverb.

| ADJECTIVE | After a week of rest Julio felt *well* again. |
| ADVERB | He cooks *well* enough to be a chef. |

Real and really

Be careful also to observe the distinction between *real* and *really.* In conversation and informal writing, the adjective *real* is often used in place of the adverb *really,* but in formal and academic writing, use the adverb form.

| INFORMAL | Most Americans were *real* shocked by the attack. |
| FORMAL | Most Americans were *really* shocked by the attack. |

EXERCISE 10.2

Revise each of the following sentences to maintain correct adverb and adjective use. Then identify each adjective or adverb that you have revised, and point out the word each modifies.

> *Example*
> Their shocking bad behavior annoyed us.
> Their *shockingly* bad behavior annoyed us.

1. Honest lawyers are not complete obsessed with status or money.
2. Although the hero reacts negative to her in this episode, in the next he proposes marriage!

USING COMPARATIVES AND SUPERLATIVES   *ad* | 10d

3. Hypochondriacs call a doctor whenever they feel badly.
4. Christmas Day was real cold, and it was raining heavy.
5. A politician's wardrobe is often careful chosen.
6. When fully grown, the silkworm stops eating good and spins its cocoon.
7. One soldier was wounded bad in the chest.
8. Computers have sure made a difference in Americans' lives.
9. On the new stereo, many of the records sounded differently.
10. They brought up their children very strict.

▌ 10d. Using comparatives and superlatives

In addition to their simple or positive form, many adjectives and adverbs have two other forms, the **comparative** and **superlative**, that are used for making comparisons.

POSITIVE	COMPARATIVE	SUPERLATIVE
large	larger	largest
early	earlier	earliest
careful	more careful	most careful
happily	more happily	most happily

Canada is *larger* than the United States

He promised to be *more careful* with his money.

They are the *most happily* married couple I know.

As these examples suggest, the comparative and superlative of most short (one-syllable and some two-syllable) adjectives are usually formed by adding the endings *-er* and *-est*. *More* and *most* are also used with short adjectives, however, and can sometimes create a more formal tone. The only ways to form the comparative and superlative of longer adjectives—three syllables or more—and of most adverbs is with *more* and *most*. If you are not sure whether an adjective or adverb has *-er* and *-est* forms, consult the dictionary entry for the simple form, where the *-er* and *-est* forms are usually listed if they exist.

▌ 1. Recognizing irregular forms

Some adjectives and adverbs have irregular comparative and superlative forms. Here is a list of them.

231

WRITERS WRITING

I feel good, like I knew that I would, Baby.
—JAMES BROWN

[Regarding Americanisms, *good*] is not only used as a general synonym for all adverbs connoting satisfaction, as in *to feel good, to be treated good, to sleep good,* but also as an adjectival reinforcement to adjectives, as in "I hit him *good* and hard" and "I am *good* and tired."
—H. L. MENCKEN

TEACHING PRACTICE

To sensitize your students to the positive, comparative, and superlative forms, give them example sentences. Ask your students to explain the context of those isolated sentences. Then, ask them to provide a context of at least five sentences.

Samples:
1. Gretchen was the more prepared runner.
2. Cher finally got her Oscar; she had the most votes.
3. Few Americans know who is more powerful: Nancy or Ron.

Context:
1. We were not surprised at the coach's decision to have Gretchen run the final stretch of the relay. Both Gretchen and Toni were fast runners, able to give the race a strong finish. But Gretchen had slightly better times in the 400-meter sprint than Toni. Also, Gretchen had trained harder than Toni, who had been sick just before the competition. The coach's decision was final. Gretchen was the more prepared runner.

Point out to your students all the elements and examples of comparison in this entire passage. Ask them to identify similar features in their own passages.

(BACK)GROUNDING

Not the product of a set of rules, the common irregular adjectives and adverbs originated from different Old English words. For example, *good* came from the Old English *god,* which is related to the German *gut.* Both words are derived from the Indo-European root *ghedh-,* "unite, join together, be suitable." *Better* and *best* come from the Old English *betera* and *betst,* both of which are derived from the Indo-European *bhad-,* "good."

Bad is not derived from the Old English word for bad or evil, *yfel.* Instead, it comes from the Old English *baedan,* "to compel, afflict." *Worse* and *worst* come from their Old English synonyms, *wiersa* and *wyrsta.*

TEACHING PRACTICE

Just like the irregular verb forms, the irregular forms of adjectives must be memorized by English speakers.

POSITIVE	COMPARATIVE	SUPERLATIVE
Adjectives		
good	better	best
well	better	best
bad	worse	worst
ill	worse	worst
little (quantity)	less	least
many	more	most
some	more	most
much	more	most
Adverbs		
well	better	best
ill	worse	worst
badly	worse	worst

2. Distinguishing between comparatives and superlatives

The comparative form of an adjective or adverb is used to compare two things. The superlative form is used to compare three or more things.

Rome is a much *older* city than New York.

Damascus is one of the *oldest* cities in the world.

In conversation, you will often hear the superlative form used even when only two things are being compared: *Of those two suits, the black one is the most becoming.* In academic or professional writing, however, be sure to use the comparative form: *Of those two suits, the black one is the more becoming.*

3. Checking for double comparatives and superlatives

Double comparatives and superlatives unnecessarily use both the *-er* or *-est* ending and *more* or *most*. When you edit an essay, check to make sure you have not used *more* or *most* before an adjective or adverb ending in *-er* or *-est*.

INCORRECT	Paris is the *most loveliest* city in the world.
REVISED	Paris is the *loveliest* city in the world.
INCORRECT	Rome lasted *more longer* than Carthage.
REVISED	Rome lasted *longer* than Carthage.

(BACK)GROUNDING

In *The American Language*, 4th ed., H. L. Mencken points out that some double comparatives may actually have a logic to their usage: "more better," for instance (463). One day we feel better than the day before; the next day, we feel completely well. Hence, we can report that we are "even better" or "still better" or, colloquially, "more better." The latter phrase may not be acceptable, but it is not illogical.

WRITERS ON WRITING

English usage is sometimes more than mere taste, judgment, and education—sometimes it's sheer luck, like getting across a street.

—E. B. WHITE

USING NOUNS AS MODIFIERS

4. Checking for incomplete comparisons

In speaking, we sometimes use incomplete comparisons—ones that specify only one of the things being compared—because the context makes the rest of the comparison clear. If, after comparing an essay of yours to a classmate's essay, you say "Yours is better," the context makes it clear that you mean "Yours is better *than mine.*" In writing, that context may not exist. So take time when editing to check for incomplete comparisons—and to complete them if they are unclear.

INCOMPLETE	The patients taking the drug appeared *healthier.*
COMPLETE	The patients taking the drug appeared *healthier than those receiving a placebo.*
INCOMPLETE	Many musicians consider Mozart *the greatest.*
COMPLETE	Many musicians consider Mozart *the greatest of all composers.*

EXERCISE 10.3

Choose three of the following numbered words, and write a brief passage that uses the simple, comparative, and superlative forms of each one.

Example
frisky   friskier   friskiest

George adopted a small, *frisky* puppy named Brutus. Quickly, Brutus became even *friskier,* chasing neighbors and jumping on children. He was at his *friskiest* the day Aunt Victoria came to visit.

1. loudly 2. well (adverb) 3. wholesome 4. some   5. little
6. rare   7. good   8. thirsty   9. heavily 10. sarcastically

10e. Using nouns as modifiers

Sometimes a noun can function as an adjective by modifying another noun, as in the following examples:

chicken soup	control center	atom bomb	law school
money supply	space station	day care	rye bread

In familiar terms such as those listed above, we have no trouble understanding the meaning. In fact, a phrase like *chicken soup* is the most succinct and direct way of expressing the idea of soup made from chicken. If noun modifiers pile up, however, they can obscure meaning and should thus be revised.

> **AWKWARD**   The 1964 New York Kitty Genovese murder story prompted a number of articles and television specials.
>
> **REVISED**   The 1964 story of Kitty Genovese's murder in New York prompted a number of articles and television specials.

Here the string of nouns is broken up by turning one (*Kitty Genovese*) into a possessive and two (*murder* and *New York*) into objects of prepositions.

EXERCISE 10.4

Revise each of the following sentences to use modifiers correctly, clearly, and effectively. Many of the sentences can be revised in more than one way.

> *Example·*
>
> The mayor is sponsoring a housing project finance plan approval bill.
>
> The mayor is sponsoring a bill to approve a financial plan for the housing project.

1. In the Macbeths' marriage, Lady Macbeth is presented as the most ambitious of the two.
2. The article argued that walking is more healthier than jogging.
3. St. Francis made Assisi one of the famousest towns in Italy.
4. Most of the elderly are women because women tend to live longer.
5. Minneapolis is the largest of the Twin Cities.
6. A University of Arizona Lunar and Planetary Laboratory research scientist agrees that mining asteroids may well prove economically important.
7. My graduation day will be the most happiest day of my life.
8. The student cafeteria is operated by a college food service system chain.
9. Japanese cars captured much of the American market because American consumers found they were more reliable.
10. I think *Oedipus Rex* is a successfuler play than *The Sandbox*.

EXERCISE 10.5

Read the following passage, from which most adjectives and adverbs have been removed. Fill the blanks with adjectives or adverbs that seem effective and appropriate to you. Then compare your version with those of other students and with the original version printed in your instructor's copy of this text.

What Elvis demanded for his travels was a flying hotel suite. The forward cabin is a very plushy, _____ _____ club room, furnished with

ANSWERS TO EXERCISE 10.4 (WILL VARY)

1. Of the Macbeths, Lady Macbeth is presented as the more ambitious.
2. According to the article, walking is more healthful [not healthy] than jogging.
3. St. Francis made Assisi one of the most famous towns in Italy.
4. Women tend to live longer than men; hence, more of the elderly are women.
5. Minneapolis is the larger of the Twin Cities.
6. A research scientist from the Lunar and Planetary Laboratory, University of Arizona, argues that mining asteroids may well prove economically important.
7. My graduation day will be the happiest day of my life.
8. The student cafeteria is operated by a college food service, part of a chain.
9. Because Americans found they were more reliable, Japanese cars captured much of the American car market.
10. *Oedipus Rex* is a more successful play than *The Sandbox*.

ANSWERS TO EXERCISE 10.5 (WILL VARY)

What Elvis demanded for his travels was a flying hotel suite. The forward cabin is a very plushy, oddly effeminate club room, furnished with two long curving bench sofas covered with fat cushions of crushed velour, one aquamarine, the other chocolate brown. The plush aqua carpet catches the light from the arched ceiling, which is padded with canary yellow vinyl.

USING NOUNS AS MODIFIERS   *ad* |10e

_____ _____ _____ _____ sofas covered with _____ cushions of _____ velour, one _____, the other _____ _____. The _____ _____ carpet catches the light from the _____ ceiling, which is padded with _____ _____ vinyl.   –ALBERT GOLDMAN, "Graceland"

READING WITH AN EYE FOR ADJECTIVES AND ADVERBS

Find some examples of adjectives and adverbs that you consider noteworthy. You might look anywhere—in essays, short stories, newspaper editorials, your own journal. Copy down five examples, and comment in writing on why they impress you as so effective. What do they add to the larger piece of writing? What would be lost if they were removed?

FOR EXAMINING THE ADJECTIVES AND ADVERBS IN YOUR OWN WRITING

Think of something you can observe or examine closely, and take a few minutes to study it. In a paragraph or two, describe your subject for someone who has never seen it. Identify all the adjectives and adverbs in your description, and list two possible synonyms for each one. Would changing any of these modifiers strengthen your description? Are there any places where you could make it more specific or vivid by adding an adjective or adverb? Do you see any adjectives or adverbs that are not really necessary or that do not create exactly the image you intend? Revise the description with such considerations in mind.

TEACHING PRACTICE

Have students bring their examples to class, and put them up on the board. Ask for comments about what the adjectives and adverbs add in each case. Ask students to suggest synonyms that might be substituted, and consider the effectiveness of the different versions. Try removing the adjectives and adverbs altogether, and consider the result. Finally, ask students which version they prefer, and why.

OPTIONAL EXERCISE

Unpack the compound-noun phrases in the sentences below and rewrite them. You may have to invent agents of the action. Answers will vary.

1. Last year's West Indian nuclear power plant proposal lost considerable support when Eastern congressional supporters refused to go along with pro–South Africa Reagan administration aid requests tacked on to the bill.
2. Car seatbelt enforcement guidelines are Eldridge subcommittee responsibility.
3. Tabled university affirmative action procedures are the fault of Albert administration foot-dragging.
4. The loss of aforementioned financial stability in regard to company policy claims reimbursement is due to sales personnel communications failure and stock market decline.
5. Successful pluralistic literature analysis procedures require correct attitude flexibility.

PART THREE

Sentences: Making Conventional Choices

11. Maintaining Clear Pronoun Reference

In writing, one of your key responsibilities to your readers is making sure that any pronouns refer clearly to their antecedents. Clear pronoun reference oils the wheels of good prose, helping avoid unnecessary repetition and moving a passage along easily, as in the following paragraph:

> *He* was crude, certainly, my Uncle Jake; *he* was coarse, of course; gross, it goes without saying; uncouth, beyond question. But was *he* vulgar? I don't think *he* was. For one thing, *he* was good-hearted, and it somehow seems wrong to call anyone vulgar who is good-hearted. But more to the point, I don't think that if you had accused *him* of being vulgar, *he* would have known what the devil you were talking about. To be vulgar requires at least a modicum of pretension, and this Uncle Jake sorely lacked.   —JOSEPH EPSTEIN, "What is Vulgar?"

If you read the paragraph again, repeating *Uncle Jake* in place of every *he* and *him*, you can see for yourself how useful these pronouns can be. Now look what happens if another uncle is added to the story:

> *He* was crude, certainly, my Uncle Jake, and my Uncle Alfred was sloppy; *he* was coarse, of course. . . .

In this instance, the reference for the first *he* is clear, because it is followed by *Uncle Jake*. But what about the second *he*—does it refer to Uncle Jake, or to Uncle Alfred?

This chapter will alert you to ways of avoiding such problems in your own writing by maintaining clear pronoun reference.

239

(BACK)GROUNDING

The necessity for clear pronoun reference originates in the distance between speaker/writer and her or his audience: The greater the physical, intellectual, or knowledge distance between them, the greater the need for clear pronoun references. Two speakers immersed in conversation can be somewhat ambiguous about their pronoun references because they are speaking in an immediate context. They can rely more on their physical signals and close proximity than on their actual syntax. Each listener has opportunities to interrupt and question anything that seems unclear, or to look perplexed.

But the audience of a public speech and the reader of written discourse have little chance to interrupt or question the speaker or author. The rules of etiquette and the varying degrees of formality produce this distance and its demand for clarity of references. Members of an audience rarely interrupt a speaker to ask a question. Readers rarely telephone authors to clarify their pronoun references.

A piece of oratory or writing often creates its own context that clarifies potentially confusing pronoun references. Take, for example, the last sentence of the above paragraph: *Readers rarely telephone authors to clarify their pronoun references*. Taken out of context, *their* could confuse us, but we know that only authors create pronoun references—a fact made clear in the context.

Even those pronoun references that cannot be misjudged can be clear, but awkward: *The management wanted to dump the computer because it was old*. Clearly, the computer—not management—is old, but the sentence remains awkward, and funny. Writers who want to be neither unclear, awkward (nor funny) must pay careful attention to pronoun antecedents.

TEACHING PRACTICE

Because many students have been told never to use "first person *I*" in their papers, they frequently alternate between *I* and *you* within a single piece of writing:

> *I* went to the fair and couldn't find any of my friends. So *I* was really bored. *You* know how boring it is when *you* want to be with *your* friends, but *you* can't find them, and *you* don't see anyone *you* know to ride the ferris wheel with. So *I* went to the beer garden, ordered a beer, sat down, and waited to see if *I* would see anybody *I* know.

To help make students aware of their shifts in pronoun, ask them to circle all their uses of *I* and *you* in one of their essays. Then, ask them to exchange essays and let their partner help them find appropriate alternatives to the constant shift.

TEACHING PRACTICE

As the handbook illustrates, the use of quotation marks clarifies who said what to whom. However, you may want to warn your students not to revise paraphrases into direct quotations without making sure that the quotation is exact, and intact.

WRITERS ON WRITING

quotation: The act of repeating erroneously the words of another.

—AMBROSE BIERCE

11a. Matching pronouns to their appropriate antecedents

If more than one possible antecedent for a personal pronoun appears in a sentence or passage, a pronoun must refer unambiguously to only *one* of them.

AMBIGUOUS The meeting between Bowman and Sonny makes *him* compare *his* own unsatisfying domestic life with one that is emotionally secure and involved.

CLEAR The meeting between Bowman and Sonny makes *Bowman* compare *his* own unsatisfying domestic life with one that is emotionally secure and involved.

CLEAR Meeting Sonny makes *Bowman* compare *his* own unsatisfying domestic life with one that is emotionally secure and involved.

CLEAR After meeting Sonny, whose domestic life is emotionally secure and involved, *Bowman* finds *his* own domestic life unsatisfying.

In the ambiguous sentence, readers cannot tell whether Bowman or Sonny is the antecedent of *him* and *his*. All three revisions make the reference clear. The first does so by replacing a pronoun (*him*) with a noun (*Bowman*), but it requires repeating the noun. The second alternative eliminates one of the pronouns, and the third recasts the sentence altogether.

If you are reporting what someone else said, check carefully for clear pronoun reference. In the sentence *Karen told Ellen she should be ready soon*, readers cannot be sure which of the two people should be ready because *she* does not clearly relate to one or the other. Such a sentence can be revised by quoting directly to make clear who is saying what, or it can be reworded to eliminate the ambiguity.

> Karen told Ellen to be ready soon.
> Karen told Ellen, "I should be ready soon."
> Karen told Ellen, "You should be ready soon."

11b. Keeping pronouns and antecedents close together

If a pronoun is too far from its antecedent, readers will have trouble making the connection between the two. Maintaining clear

KEEPING PRONOUNS AND ANTECEDENTS TOGETHER

reference calls for keeping pronouns and their antecedents in close proximity.

CONFUSING   The right-to-life coalition believes that a zygote, an egg at the moment of fertilization, is as deserving of protection as is the born human being, and thus that abortion is as much murder as is the killing of a child. The coalition's focus is on what *it* will become, a conscious being with reasoning power, a sense of self, and the capacity to communicate, as much as on what *it* is now.

CLEAR   The right-to-life coalition believes that a *zygote*, an egg at the moment of fertilization, is as deserving of protection as is the born human being, and thus that abortion is as much murder as is the killing of a child. The coalition's focus is on what *the zygote* will become, a conscious being with reasoning power, a sense of self, and the capacity to communicate, as much as on what *it* is now.

EXERCISE 11.1

Revise each of the following items to clarify pronoun reference. All of the items can be revised in more than one way. If a pronoun refers ambiguously to more than one possible antecedent, revise the sentence in at least two different ways, reflecting each possible meaning.

Example
While Melinda was away, Sheila found the ring she had lost.
While Melinda was away, the ring she had lost was found by Sheila.
Sheila found Melinda's lost ring while Melinda was away.
Sheila found her lost ring while Melinda was away.

1. Anna smiled at her mother as she opened the birthday package.
2. Lear divides his kingdom between the two older daughters, Goneril and Regan, whose extravagant professions of love are more flattering than the simple affection of the youngest daughter, Cordelia. The consequences of this error in judgment soon become apparent, as they prove neither grateful nor kind to him.
3. In many cases of child abuse, especially when the parents totally ignore their children, they eventually become criminals.
4. New England helped to shape many aspects of American culture, including education, religion, and government. As New Englanders moved west, they carried its institutions with them.
5. Leroy went to the races with George because he was feeling lonely.

ANSWERS TO EXERCISE 11.1 (WILL VARY)

1. As Anna opened her birthday gift, she smiled at her mother. As her mother opened her birthday gift, Anna smiled at her.
2. Lear divides his kingdom between the two older daughters, Goneril and Regan, whose extravagant professions of love are more flattering than the simple affection of the youngest daughter, Cordelia. The consequences of this error in judgment soon become apparent, as the older daughters prove neither grateful nor kind to him.
3. Abused children, especially those totally ignored by their parents, often become criminals. Child abusers, especially those who totally ignore their children, often become criminals.
4. New England helped to shape many aspects of American culture, including education, religion, and government. As New Englanders moved west, they carried their institutions with them.
5. Feeling lonely, Leroy went to the stock-car races with George. Because George was feeling lonely, Leroy went to the stock-car races with him.
6. Jimmy told Allen that his own mother was ill. Jimmy told Allen that Allen's mother was ill.
7. Ms. Callahan felt relieved after she hired Patricia for the job. Patricia felt relieved after Ms. Callahan hired her for the job.
8. When drug therapy is combined with psychotherapy, the patients relate better and are more responsive to their therapists, and they are less vulnerable to what disturbs them.
9. Not long after the company set up the subsidiary, the subsidiary (the company) went bankrupt.
10. If guns cause crimes, outlaw guns.

6. Jimmie told Allen that his mother was ill.
7. After Ms. Callahan hired Patricia for the job, she felt relieved.
8. When drug therapy is combined with psychotherapy, the patients relate better to their therapists, are less vulnerable to what disturbs them, and are more responsive to them.
9. Not long after the company set up the subsidiary, it went bankrupt.
10. If guns cause crimes, outlaw them.

(BACK)GROUNDING

In *Linguistics for Students of Literature*, Elizabeth Traugott and Mary Louise Pratt explain pronoun reference in terms of *deixis*, the process of anchoring in the "spatio-temporal perspective of the speaker." More explicitly, *deixis* allows us to understand a communicative act as an interaction among the universe of discourse. Each communicative act, then—be it speaking, writing, listening, reading, or even watching and observing—involves an interaction among (1) the writer/speaker; (2) the reader/listener; (3) the written, spoken, or visual text; and (4) the referent of that text—the four components of the universe of discourse.

We tend to rely on *deictic* pronouns because we have a clear, context-bound sense of their reference. Confusion occurs only when our audience (readers or listeners) don't share our vantage point, or when they cannot or do not reconstruct the position or perspective of the speaker or hearer.

> *You* did so *do it*.
> *I did* nothing *of the sort*.
> *She* saw *you* leave *there*.
> *That* is *what she* thinks *she* saw, but *she didn't*.
> Well, *I'm* not standing for any more of *this treatment*.

The italicized words exemplify *deixis*, for they make sense in a reliable or reconstructable context. (Why not ask your students to use *deixis* to create a context for the above exchange?)

When we are asked to clarify *this* in the second example (11c1), we can say—with little difficulty—that *this* refers to *creating rhetoric*. The issue of pronoun reference is one of clarity and effective communication. Writers, who are rarely present or available to clarify any confusion, must write so that their readers do not have to second-guess them.

11c. Recognizing troublesome pronoun references

Matching a pronoun to one specific antecedent and keeping pronouns and antecedents close together will take you a long way toward establishing clear pronoun reference. A few pronouns, however, cause particular problems for writers. The sections that follow provide practice in checking to see that these pronouns are used clearly and properly.

1. Checking for vague and ambiguous use of *it, this, that,* and *which*

Writers are often tempted to use *it, this, that,* or *which* as a kind of shortcut, a quick and easy way of referring to something mentioned earlier. But such shortcuts can often cause confusion. Make sure that these pronouns refer clearly to a specific antecedent.

VAGUE	The Engineering Society sponsored a charity drive last week, and students responded enthusiastically. *It* really surprised us. [What does *it* refer to—the fact that the Engineering Society sponsored a charity drive, that students responded enthusiastically, or perhaps both?]
CLEAR	The Engineering Society sponsored a charity drive last week, and students responded enthusiastically. *The response* really surprised us.
VAGUE	The art of rhetoric was created in the ancient world in response to the economic and political need for a fair method of property redistribution. Corax devised the first known system for *this*. [For what, exactly—creating rhetoric? redistributing property?]
CLEAR	Rhetoric was created in the ancient world out of the economic and political need for a fair method of property redistribution. Corax devised the first *such method* known.

USEFUL READING

Traugott, Elizabeth, and Mary Louise Pratt. *Linguistics for Students of Literature.* New York: Harcourt, 1980.

RECOGNIZING TROUBLESOME PRONOUN REFERENCE

AMBIGUOUS	I am taking a course in Romantic poetry, *which* has been the bane of my existence. [What does *which* refer to—the course or the poetry?]
CLEAR	I am taking a course in Romantic poetry, *a kind of literature* that has been the bane of my existence.
CLEAR	I am taking a course in Romantic poetry, *a class* that has been the bane of my existence.

If *that* or *which* opens a clause that refers to a specific noun, put *that* or *which* directly after the noun, if possible.

AMBIGUOUS	We worked all night on the float for the Rose Parade *that* our club was going to sponsor. [Does *that* refer to the float or the Rose Parade?]
CLEAR	We worked all night on the float *that* our club was going to sponsor for the Rose Parade.

2. Checking for appropriate use of *who, which,* and *that*

Be careful to use the relative pronouns *who, which,* and *that* appropriately. *Who* refers primarily to people or to animals with names. *Which* refers to animals or to things, and *that* refers to animals, things, and anonymous persons or people treated collectively. (See 27c for information about the use of commas with clauses beginning with *who, which,* and *that*.)

Stephen Jay Gould, *who* has won many awards for his writing about science, teaches at Harvard.

The whale, *which* has only one baby a year, is subject to extinction because it does not reproduce quickly.

People *that* support animal rights oppose laboratory experimentation with animals.

People *who* support animal rights oppose laboratory experimentation with animals.

3. Checking for indefinite use of *you* and *they*

In conversation, we frequently use *you* and *they* in an indefinite sense, as in such expressions as *you never know* and *on television they said*. In college and professional writing, however, such constructions are inappropriately informal and often unnecessarily wordy. Be careful

---

USEFUL READING

Francis, W. Nelson, and Henry Kucera. *Frequency Analysis of English Usage.* Boston: Houghton, 1982.

Williams, Joseph M. *Style: Ten Lessons in Clarity and Grace.* 2d ed. Glenview: Scott, 1985. See p. 136 on summative modifiers, illustrated by the following: "I am taking a course in Romantic poetry, a kind of literature which has been. . . ."

(BACK)GROUNDING

In their *Frequency Analysis of English Usage,* W. Nelson Francis and Henry Kucera studied the frequency with which words appear in standard edited English. Pronouns are among the most frequently used words, as the following chart indicates:

Word	Rank
he	7
it	11
they	13
I	15
we	23
she	24
you	30
who	35

The authors also note that personal, reflexive, singular pronouns (*myself, herself, himself*) occur much more frequently in imaginative prose than in informative prose. Conversely, plural forms of these reflexive, personal pronouns (*ourselves, themselves*) occur much more frequently in informative prose than in imaginative prose (544). While Francis and Kucera offer no explanation for this relationship, pronoun use seems to indicate that imaginative prose tends to focus on individuals, while transactional or informative prose tends to focus on groups of people.

OPTIONAL EXERCISES

Read each paragraph aloud, and have your students answer the question that follows.

After we lost our first intramural game, a couple of us agreed that we needed more practice. We needed to work on our inner fielding and our batting before playing our next game. Sherry said she'd find out when we could have diamond time for a practice or two. Tom said he would find out when our next game would be. Robin said she'd phone everyone about this.

To what does *this* refer?

Every Friday night, we meet at someone's place for supper. Everyone brings something to eat. Tom brings salad; Anna brings dessert; Theresa always brings something to drink, because she doesn't have time to cook. I usually prepare spaghetti, lasagna, or a casserole of some sort. Sari provides the entertainment. *It's* something I look forward to every week.

To what does *it* refer?

TEACHING PRACTICE

The indefinite use of *you*, used frequently in spoken English, can be vague or confusing in writing.

Spoken English: Professor Corbett always warns you not to be late for class. (To whom does *you* refer?)

Revised: Professor Corbett always warns me not to be late for class. (The warning goes to the *speaker*.)

Or: Professor Corbett always warns students not to be late for class. (The warning is to all students in the class.)

Although the use of *you* in the Professor Corbett example may not seem confusing or vague, this usage does involve questions beyond matters of formality:

To whom does *you* refer?

1. The writer wishes to directly address readers, using *you* as a speech-act device; it recognizes that readers will be present whom the writer wishes to engage and bring into the discourse.
2. It is a stylistic device involving the second-person plural as a general pronoun, called the second-person plural indefinite or general. The writer is not referring to anyone in particular, only to a potential audience.
3. Similar to #2. Professor Corbett warns people not to be late for class. *People* in general, but with some restrictions: those people who are taking or planning to take a class with him.

to use *you* only to mean "you, the reader," and *they* only to refer to a clear antecedent.

INAPPROPRIATE	Television commercials try to make *you* buy without thinking.
REVISED	Television commercials try to make *viewers* buy without thinking.
INAPPROPRIATE	In France *they* allow dogs in most restaurants.
REVISED	Most restaurants in France allow dogs.

4. Checking to see that antecedents are nouns or pronouns, not adjectives or possessives

In conversation, a pronoun often refers to an antecedent that is an adjective or the possessive form of a noun. In writing, an antecedent must always be a noun or pronoun in the subjective case.

INAPPROPRIATE	In Welty's story, *she* characterizes Bowman as a man unaware of his own isolation.
REVISED	In her story, Welty characterizes Bowman as a man unaware of his own isolation.
REVISED	In Welty's story, Bowman is characterized as a man unaware of his own isolation.

5. Checking for sexist pronoun usage

Remember to avoid using masculine pronouns to refer to antecedents that include or may include both males and females. For example, the sentence *Every attorney values his client's testimony* implies that only men are attorneys. Such a sentence can be revised in several ways: by eliminating the pronoun, by using both masculine and feminine pronouns, or by shifting to the plural. A more complete discussion of nonsexist pronoun usage can be found in 9m.

Every attorney values *a* client's testimony.

Every attorney values *his or her* client's testimony.

All attorneys value *their* clients' testimonies.

➤ Checking for vague pronoun reference

Circle all pronouns, and draw an arrow from each one to its antecedent. Look especially at *this, that, which,* and *it* to be sure you

RECOGNIZING TROUBLESOME PRONOUN REFERENCE

can relate them to a specific word in the same sentence. If you cannot find an antecedent in the sentence, revise by replacing the pronoun with a noun or by supplying an antecedent to which the pronoun clearly refers. Next look to see if the pronoun could relate to more than one antecedent. If so, revise by replacing the pronoun with the appropriate noun or by rewriting the sentence so that the pronoun can refer to only one possible antecedent.

EXERCISE 11.2

Revise the following sentences to establish clear and appropriate pronoun reference, and to eliminate any sexist pronoun usage. Most of the sentences can be revised in more than one way.

> *Example*
> It says in the newspaper to expect rain today.
> The newspaper says to expect rain today.

1. On the turnpike they charge very high prices for gasoline.
2. In Texas, you often hear about the influence of big oil corporations on political candidates.
3. They said on the radio that somebody had won the lottery.
4. A friend of mine recently had a conversation with a Vietnam veteran that changed his view of the war.
5. She dropped off a friend which had gone to the party with her.
6. Not only was the chair delivered three weeks late, but the store told me this was normal.
7. I take care not to get too bundled up in the winter because it will be too hot when you are indoors.
8. The company had a policy prohibiting smoking, which many employees resented.
9. I called as soon as the catalog arrived, but they were already sold out of the leather moccasins.
10. Every doctor can count on making his fortune within ten years of graduation.

READING WITH ATTENTION TO PRONOUN REFERENCE

The following poem depends on its title to supply the antecedent for the pronouns that follow and that knit the poem together. Read the poem out loud, and then provide its one-word title. How did you know what the title should be? Then try writing a poem of your own (perhaps three or four verses) like this one, using pronouns and other words to give "clues" to your title.

ANSWERS TO EXERCISE 11.2 (WILL VARY)

1. Gas stations on the turnpike have very high prices.
2. Texans often hear about the influence of big oil corporations on their political candidates.
3. The lottery winner was announced on the radio.
4. After having a conversation with a Vietnam veteran, my friend saw the war differently.
5. She dropped off her friend who had gone to the party with her.
6. The chair was delivered three weeks late, which, according to the store management, is a normal practice.
7. I take care not to get too bundled up in the winter because I get too hot when I go indoors.
8. Many employees resented the company's no-smoking policy. (the no-smoking policy of the company)
9. As soon as their catalog arrived, I called the company, but they were already sold out of the leather moccasins.
10. Doctors can count on making their fortune within ten years of graduation.

WRITERS ON WRITING

Long afterward, Oedipus, old and blinded, walked the roads. He smelled a familiar smell. It was the Sphinx. Oedipus said, "I want to ask one question. Why didn't I recognize my mother?" "You gave the wrong answer," said the Sphinx. "But that was what made everything possible," said Oedipus. "No," she said. "When I asked, What walks on four legs in the morning, two at noon, and three in the evening, you answered, Man. You didn't say anything about woman." "When you say Man," said Oedipus, "you include women too. Everyone knows that." She said, "That's what you think."

—MURIEL RUKEYSER

TEACHING PRACTICE

Students will have fun finding the clues that identify *pitcher* as the title word/antecedent in Francis's poem. With a little encouragement, they may surprise themselves by producing some fine four-line "mystery title" poems of their own. Ask them to duplicate their poems and bring them to class; then have them work together to follow any clues to identify the missing titles.

TEACHING PRACTICE

Use some of these descriptive paragraphs for class discussion, asking students to identify antecedents for each pronoun. Unclear or ambiguous references can be edited by the group as a whole.

His art is eccentricity, his aim
How not to hit the mark he seems to aim at,

His passion how to avoid the obvious,
His technique how to vary the avoidance.

The others throw to be comprehended. He
Throws to be a moment misunderstood.

Yet not too much. Not too errant, arrant, wild,
But every seeming aberration willed.

Not to, yet still, still to communicate
Making the batter understand too late.

—Robert Francis

FOR EXAMINING PRONOUN REFERENCE IN YOUR OWN WRITING

Write a paragraph or two describing two favorite aunts—or two people or animals of the same sex. Then analyze your use of pronouns. Have you used any pronouns that do not refer clearly and directly to the correct antecedent? Any whose antecedents could be ambiguous? Using the guidelines shown in this chapter, revise as necessary.

12. Recognizing Shifts

A **shift** in writing is, most simply, an abrupt change of some sort that results in inconsistency. Consider, for example, the very famous opening lines of *The Adventures of Huckleberry Finn:*

> You don't know about me without you have read a book by the name of *The Adventures of Tom Sawyer;* but that ain't no matter. That book was made by Mr. Mark Twain, and he told the truth, mainly. There was things which he stretched, but mainly he told the truth.

Now replace the last sentence with this one: *On occasion Mr. Twain has been known to utter falsehoods; nevertheless, he did in this instance show proper respect for factuality.* As readers, we would be jolted and no doubt confused by such a shift in tone, from exaggerated informality to almost straightlaced formality.

Such a shift, because it is so blatant, is hard to miss. This chapter will help you to recognize shifts that are a bit more subtle and will offer strategies for revising to eliminate them. These include shifts in the tense, mood, and voice of verbs; in the person and number of pronouns; from direct to indirect discourse; and in tone and diction. If you have had such shifts pointed out in your writing, take the time to make checking for and revising shifts a regular part of your writing process.

12a. Recognizing shifts in tense

If the verbs in a sentence or passage refer to actions occurring at different times, they may require different tenses: *Mac started the kennel because he had always loved dogs.* Be careful, however, not to

247

USEFUL READING

Halsted, Isabella. "Putting Error in Its Place." *Journal of Basic Writing* 1 (Spring 1975): 72–86. Rpt. in *The Writing Teacher's Sourcebook*. Eds. Gary Tate and Edward P. J. Corbett. New York: Oxford, 1981. 244–56.

(BACK)GROUNDING

The greater the writer's fixation on error, the greater the difficulty that writer will have writing. The more the instructor focuses on error, the more the student will worry about error. In *The Concept of the Mind* (1949), British philosopher Gilbert Ryle wrote that "errors are exercises in competence." And this new concept of error as "portals to discovery" became the mainstay of Mina Shaughnessy's study of basic writing (1977). By 1981, Isabella Halsted was writing that errors are "*not* Sin, not Crime punishable by F." Errors are simply mistakes that we are all capable of, given the wrong circumstances: lack of sleep, deadline pressure, unfamiliarity with formal English. Halsted posits as right her own attitude toward error:

> Like soot on the pane, Error is something that gets in the way of the clear vision. . . . Error on all levels is distracting, annoying, obstructive. Error is inexcusable ultimately, yes, [but] not because it is Wrong *per se.* . . . In plain pragmatic terms, the absence of Error is useful; but when our students take pains to avoid it—by writing short sentences, by sticking to one tense, by writing as little as possible—I doubt very much that they do so in order to better communicate with a reader, but rather to play safe, to avoid the red marks.

Errors in shift are relatively minor: they rarely obstruct communication; usually they amount to only stumbling blocks. Shaughnessy says, for example, that pronoun shifts "usually go unnoticed by the writer until someone points them out" (113), for the writer usually believes she or he has written the sentence correctly.

TEACHING PRACTICE

One way to approach errors like those described in this chapter is to have your students read about them, do exercises, and attempt to find them in their own work. Or you can wait until the error appears, then ask the student to read the erroneous sentence(s) aloud. In "The Study of Error," David Bartholomae suggests that students will often orally correct written errors without noticing the correction. Not only does the reading-aloud technique reveal their competence but it also allows you a dramatic way to reveal the error to them.

change tenses unnecessarily or in a way that does not make sense. Look, for instance, at this sentence: *Clarissa* <u>*yowled*</u> *until her owner* <u>*looks up*</u>. The shift in tenses from past to present confuses readers, who are left to guess which tense is the correct one.

INCONSISTENT	A very few countries *produce* most of the world's illegal drugs, but drug addiction *affected* many more countries.
REVISED	A very few countries *produce* most of the world's illegal drugs, but drug addiction *affects* many more countries.
INCONSISTENT	Some people never really *settle* down to a profession. In fact, such people *have found* jobs only when they *needed* food or shelter.
REVISED	Some people never really *settle* down to a profession. In fact, such people *find* jobs only when they *need* food or shelter.

See Chapter 8 for a complete discussion of verb tense.

➤ Checking for unnecessary shifts in tense

Because we deliberately—and necessarily— shift back and forth among tenses all the time, it can be difficult to spot tense shifts that are not logically consistent. If you have problems with shifts, try circling all the verbs in a draft and then checking carefully any shifts from one tense to another, *both within a sentence and between sentences*. Any time a shift occurs, check to be sure that it is logically consistent. You might even find it helpful to chart out verbs in timeline fashion.

ANSWERS TO EXERCISE 12.1 (WILL VARY)

1. The day is hot, stifling, and typical of July, a day when no one willingly *ventures* out onto the burning asphalt.
2. Then, suddenly, the big day *arrived*. The children were still a bit sleepy, for their anticipation had kept them awake.
3. The importance of music to society is evident throughout the entire magazine. A good example *is* the first advertisement.
4. A cloud of snow powder rose as skis and poles *flew* in every direction.
5. After fitness became popular in the 1970s, all of a sudden there *were* fewer and fewer fleshy Americans parked in front of their television sets.

EXERCISE 12.1

Revise any of the following sentences in which you find unnecessary shifts in verb tense. Most of the sentences can be revised in more than one way.

Example
The local newspaper covers campus events, but it did not appeal to many student readers.

The local newspaper *covers* campus events, but it *does not appeal* to many student readers.

1. The day is hot, stifling, and typical of July, a day when no one willingly ventured out onto the burning asphalt.

USEFUL READING

Bartholomae, David. "The Study of Error." Rpt. in *Rhetoric and Composition: A Sourcebook for Teachers and Writers*. Ed. Richard L. Graves. Upper Montclair, NJ: Boynton, 1984. 311–27.

2. Then, suddenly, the big day arrives. The children were still a bit sleepy, for their anticipation had kept them awake.
3. The importance of music to society is evident throughout the entire magazine. A good example was the first advertisement.
4. A cloud of snow powder rose as skis and poles fly in every direction.
5. After fitness became popular in the 1970s, all of a sudden there are fewer and fewer fleshy Americans parked in front of their television sets.

▋ 12b. Recognizing shifts in mood

Be careful not to shift from one mood to another without reason. The mood of a verb can be indicative (He *closes* the door), imperative (*Close* the door), or subjunctive (If the door *were closed*, . . .). (See Chapter 8 for a discussion of mood.)

INCONSISTENT	*Keep* your eye on the ball, and you *should bend* your knees. [shift from imperative to indicative]
REVISED	*Keep* your eye on the ball, and *bend* your knees.
INCONSISTENT	The counselor asked that Rhonda *tutor* the Laotian children in English and that she *teaches* them some American games as well. [shift from subjunctive to indicative]
REVISED	The counselor asked that Rhonda *tutor* the Laotian children in English and that she *teach* them some American games as well.

EXERCISE 12.2

Revise the following sentences to eliminate any unnecessary shifts in mood.

Example
Walk over to the field house, and then you should get in line.
Walk over to the field house, and then get in line.

1. Place a test strip on the subject area; you should expose the test strip to light and develop it for two and a half minutes.
2. I think it is better that Grandfather die painlessly, bravely, and with dignity than that he continues to live in terrible physical pain.
3. Whether women be homemakers or are business executives, they deserve respect.
4. The consultant recommended that the candidates tell more jokes and that they smile more during their speeches.
5. Say no to drugs, and you should consider alcohol a drug, too!

USEFUL READING

Curmé, George O. *English Grammar*. New York: Harper, 1947. 54–55. He defines moods as "the changes in the form of the verb to show the various ways in which the action of state [of the verb] is thought of by the speaker" (54).

(BACK)GROUNDING

The label *mood* is related to the Latin *modus*, meaning "measure, moderation, manner." Used always in reference to Greek and Latin, not until the sixteenth century was *mood* used to describe English.

TEACHING PRACTICE

Help your students identify mood by using the following passages from Martin Luther King, Jr.'s "I Have a Dream."

Indicative: used in making a statement of fact.

It is obvious today that America has defaulted on this promissory note insofar as her citizens of color are concerned. Instead of honoring this sacred obligation, America has given the Negro people a bad check; a check which has come back marked "insufficient funds." But we refuse to believe that the bank of justice is bankrupt. We refuse to believe that there are insufficient funds in the great vaults of opportunity of this nation. So we have come to cash this check—a check that will give us upon demand the riches of freedom and the security of justice.

Imperative: expresses a command or an entreaty.

Go back to Mississippi, go back to Alabama, go back to South Carolina, go back to Georgia, go back to Louisiana, go back to the slums and ghettos of our northern cities, knowing that somehow this situation can and will be changed. Let us not wallow in the valley of despair.

Subjunctive: makes a conditional statement, expresses a wish, or indicates doubt and uncertainty.

I have a dream that one day every valley shall be exalted, every hill and mountain shall be made low, the rough places will be made plain, and the crooked places will be made straight, and the glory of the Lord shall be revealed, and all flesh shall see it together.

ANSWERS TO EXERCISE 12.2 (WILL VARY)

1. Place a test strip on the subject area; then *expose* the test strip to light and develop it for two and a half minutes.
2. I think it better that Grandfather die painlessly, bravely, and with dignity than that he *continue* to live in terrible pain.
3. Whether women *are* homemakers or are business executives, they deserve respect.
4. The consultant recommended that the candidates tell more jokes and *smile* more during their speeches.
5. Say no to drugs, and *consider* alcohol a drug, too!

TEACHING PRACTICE

Depending on the context, either the imperative mood or subjunctive mood can be acceptable. To explain the difference, ask your students to imagine this scenario for sentence 1 in Exercise 12.2:

> After you develop your own pictures, you are to explain the procedure to the rest of your photography class. But your pictures are all black, so your instructor has asked you to review the procedure. While you explain your procedures, she makes suggestions: "You should turn off the light first, and then you should carefully remove a piece of print paper, etc."

(BACK)GROUNDING

Voice comes from the Latin *vox*, meaning "voice" or "sound." In 1382, John Wyclif became the first to use *voice* as a grammatical label in English.

WRITERS ON WRITING

Language is the archives of history. . . . Language is fossil poetry.

—RALPH WALDO EMERSON

Every vital development in language is a development of feeling as well.

—T. S. ELIOT

ANSWERS TO EXERCISE 12.3 (WILL VARY)

1. I call it smooth, but my parents *see* it as sneaky and devious.
2. No change
3. When someone says "roommate" to a high school senior bound for college, that senior *conjures up* thoughts of no privacy and potential fights.
4. The first thing *we see* as we start down the slope is a large green banner.
5. The physician moves the knee around to observe the connections of the cartilage and ligaments, and *injects* a fluid into the joint.

12c. Recognizing shifts in voice

Do not shift unnecessarily between the active voice (She <u>sold</u> the furniture) and the passive voice (The furniture <u>was sold</u>). Sometimes a shift in voice is perfectly justified. In the sentence I <u>am known</u> for being unpredictable and adventurous, but I <u>consider</u> myself a practical person, the shift from passive (am known) to active (consider) allows the writer to keep the emphasis on the subject I. Making both verbs active (People <u>know</u> me as an unpredictable and adventurous person, but I <u>consider</u> myself a practical person) changes the focus of the sentence. Often, however, shifts in voice merely confuse readers. (See Chapter 8.)

INCONSISTENT	After we finished decorating the house, it was photographed by us.
REVISED	After we finished decorating the house, we photographed it.
INCONSISTENT	Four youngsters approached him, and he was asked to buy a raffle ticket.
REVISED	Four youngsters approached him and asked him to buy a raffle ticket.

EXERCISE 12.3

Revise each of the following sentences that contains an unnecessary shift in voice. One of the sentences does not require any change.

> *Example*
> Although she enjoys rock music, jazz is preferred by her.
> Although she enjoys rock music, she prefers jazz.

1. I call it smooth, but it is seen as sneaky and devious by my parents.
2. Once these shells housed creatures; now they are crushed by the waves.
3. When someone says "roommate" to a high school senior bound for college, thoughts of no privacy and potential fights are conjured up.
4. The first thing that is seen as we start down the slope is a large green banner.
5. The physician moves the knee around to observe the connections of the cartilage and ligaments, and a fluid is injected into the joint.

12d. Recognizing shifts in person and number

Do not shift unnecessarily between first person (*I, we*), second person (*you*), and third person (*he, she, it, one,* or *they*) or between singular and plural. Such shifts in person and number create confusion.

RECOGNIZING SHIFTS IN PERSON AND NUMBER

INCONSISTENT	*One* can do well in college if *you* budget *your* time carefully.
REVISED	*One* can do well in college if *one* budgets *one's* time carefully.
REVISED	*You* can do well in college if *you* budget *your* time carefully.
INCONSISTENT	*Nurses* are paid much less than doctors, even though *a nurse* has the primary responsibility for daily care of patients.
REVISED	*Nurses* are paid much less than doctors, even though *nurses* have the primary responsibility for daily care of patients.

Many shifts in number are actually problems with pronoun-antecedent agreement (see 9j–9m).

INCONSISTENT	I have difficulty seeing another *person's* position, especially if *their* opinion contradicts mine.
REVISED	I have difficulty seeing another *person's* position, especially if *his or her* opinion contradicts mine.
REVISED	I have difficulty seeing other *people's* positions, especially if *their* opinions contradict mine.

➤ **Checking for unnecessary shifts in pronoun**

To check a draft for illogical pronoun shifts, try circling all the pronouns and then drawing a line from pronoun to pronoun watching for shifts. Look especially at the pronouns *I*, *you*, and *one* to see that you don't shift among them interchangeably. If you do have problems with pronoun shifts, keep a list of your mistakes, see if they fall into any predictable patterns, and then to proofread especially for them.

EXERCISE 12.4

Revise each of the following sentences to eliminate any unnecessary shifts in person or number. Some of the sentences can be revised in more than one way. Be prepared to explain your answers.

Example

When a person goes to college, you face many new situations.

When a person goes to college, he or she faces many new situations.

When you go to college, you face many new situations.

When people go to college, they face many new situations.

USEFUL READING

Iser, Wolfgang. *The Act of Reading: A Theory of Aesthetic Response.* Baltimore: Johns Hopkins, 1978. Chapter 3, on speech-act theory (especially pp. 54–62).

Shaughnessy, Mina P. *Errors & Expectations: A Guide for the Teacher of Basic Writing.* New York: Oxford UP, 1977. Chapter 4, "Common Errors," pp. 113–14.

WRITERS ON WRITING

Unlearned, he knew no schoolman's subtle art,
No language but the language of the heart.
—ALEXANDER POPE

But, for the unquiet heart and brain
A use in measured language lies;
The sad mechanic exercise,
Like dull narcotics numbing pain.
—ALFRED LORD TENNYSON

WRITING TOGETHER

To illustrate how shifts in person (and in tense) can be used effectively, read aloud Martin Luther King, Jr.'s "I Have a Dream." Make a special point of focusing on paragraphs 7, 8, and 11–18, discussing King's rhetorical purpose.

(BACK)GROUNDING

To complement these exercises on pronoun shift, consult Wolfgang Iser. His explanation of the "pragmatic nature of nature" includes basic discussion of factors that determine successful communication. To understand how effective writing and reading occur involves "establishing a relationship between text and reader" (54–55). Writers establish this relationship by recognizing that linguistic utterances take on meaning in the context of the reader and text.

(BACK)GROUNDING

Mina P. Shaughnessy suggests that problems in pronoun shifts go beyond the writer's "unstable sense of the writer-audience relationship, with the shift to 'you' signifying a more direct sense of audience" (113). She identifies three additional general sources of pronoun-shift errors: (1) students' tendency "to reduce complexity without impairing communication"; (2) the problem of remembering which pronouns have been used; and (3) learning the differences among descriptive, narrative, and analytic writing.

Moving from the first two to analytic writing requires learning when and how to use pronouns such as *they* or *one* or *person*.

ANSWERS TO EXERCISE 12.4 (WILL VARY)

1. Suddenly, we heard an explosion of wings off to our right, and *we* could see a hundred or more ducks lifting off the water.
2. Workers with computer skills were in great demand, and a programmer could almost name *his or her* salary.
3. I liked the sense of individualism, the crowd yelling for *me*, and the feeling I was in command.
4. New parents often find it hard to adjust to having a baby around; *they* can't just get up and go someplace.
5. *People need* to feel that they are respected by others to perform well in a leadership position.

TEACHING PRACTICE

Indirect discourse is often preceded by the word *that*, and both pronouns and verb tenses are often different from those used in direct discourse. Generally, if the introducing verb is past, it doesn't affect the verb in a direct quotation (direct discourse). However, an introducing verb in past tense will ordinarily shift the verbs in indirect discourse one step back into the past:

Direct discourse: *The president said, "I have no knowledge of those events."*

Indirect discourse: *The president said that he had no knowledge of those events.*

When questions appear in direct discourse, they are followed by a question mark (*The instructor confronted us, asking "What do you think you are doing?"*). When reported in indirect discourse, questions often include *who, if, why, whether, what,* or *how*—and they omit the question mark (*The instructor confronted us, asking whether we knew what we were doing.*).

1. Suddenly we heard an explosion of wings off to our right, and you could see a hundred or more ducks lifting off the water.
2. Workers with computer skills were in great demand, and a programmer could almost name their salary.
3. I liked the sense of individualism, the crowd yelling for you, and the feeling that I was in command.
4. New parents often find it hard to adjust to having a baby around; you can't just get up and go someplace.
5. A person needs to feel that they are respected by others to perform well in a leadership position.

12e. Recognizing shifts between direct and indirect discourse

When you quote someone's exact words, setting them off in quotation marks, you are using **direct discourse**. On the other hand, when you summarize or report what someone has said (rather than quote the exact words), you are using **indirect discourse**.

DIRECT	Ambrose Bierce defined *love* as "a temporary insanity curable by marriage."
INDIRECT	Ambrose Bierce said that love is a temporary form of madness that can be cured by marriage.

Do not shift between direct and indirect discourse in the same sentence. Use *either* direct or indirect discourse throughout.

INCONSISTENT	Chief Seattle *said* that one nation *followed* another like the waves of the sea and therefore "regret is useless."
REVISED	Chief Seattle said that "nation follows nation, like the waves of the sea" and that therefore "regret is useless."
REVISED	Chief Seattle said that one nation followed another like the waves of the sea and that therefore feeling sad was useless.

EXERCISE 12.5

Revise each of the following sentences to eliminate the shifts between direct and indirect discourse by putting the direct discourse into indirect form.

Example

Nathaniel Hawthorne once stated that there was nothing he preferred to "my own solitude."

Nathaniel Hawthorne once stated that there was nothing he preferred to his own solitude.

1. Loren Eiseley feels an urge to join the birds in their soundless flight, but in the end he knows that he cannot, and "I was, after all, only a man."
2. According to the article, the ozone layer is rapidly dwindling, and "we are endangering the lives of future generations."
3. The instructor told us, "Please read the next two stories before the next class" and that she might give us a quiz on them.
4. Oscar Wilde wrote that books cannot be divided into moral and immoral categories, and "books are either well-written or badly written."
5. Richard Rodriguez acknowledged that intimacy was not created by a language; "it is created by intimates."

▋ 12f. Recognizing shifts in tone and diction

Tone in writing refers to the way the writer's attitude toward the topic and/or audience comes across to the audience. (See 3g4.) Tone is closely related to **diction**, or word choice—not only the choice of individual words, but the overall level of formality, technicality, or other effects created by the individual words. Within a sentence, a paragraph, or an entire piece of writing, be careful not to change your tone or level of diction unless you have a reason for doing so. (See Chapters 25 and 26 for a complete discussion of diction and tone.)

Tone

When they are used for emphasis or humor, shifts in tone can be effective. Mark Twain was a master of such shifts. In the following passage, he presents a mock graduation address, "Advice to Youth," beginning with a serious tone and then shifting at the beginning of the second paragraph to characteristic humor:

> Being told I would be expected to talk here, I inquired what sort of a talk I ought to make. They said it should be something suitable to youth—something didactic, instructive, or something in the nature of good advice. Very well. I have a few things in my mind which I have often longed to say for the instruction of the young; for it is in one's tender early years that such things will best take root and be most enduring and most valuable. First, then, I will say to you, my young friends—and I say it beseechingly, urgingly—

253

ANSWERS TO EXERCISE 12.5 (WILL VARY)

1. Loren Eiseley feels an urge to join the birds in their soundless flight, but in the end he knows that he cannot, *and that he is only a man.*
2. According to the article, the ozone layer is rapidly dwindling, *and the lives of future generations are endangered.*
3. The instructor told us *to read the next two stories before next class* and that she might give us a quiz on them.
4. Oscar Wilde wrote that books cannot be divided into moral and immoral categories, *and that books are either written well or badly.*
5. Richard Rodriguez acknowledged that intimacy was not created by a language *but was created by intimates.*

(BACK)GROUNDING

Tone denotes the way a writer's attitude toward a subject or audience comes across to an audience. Just as tone of voice in speaking may be irritating, harsh, or soothing, the tone of a piece of writing may be humorous, bitter, ironic, patronizing, passionate, or angry. Tone affects the attitude of readers just as tone affects listeners. A word like *terrific*, for example, can suggest something wonderful, frustration, or sarcasm depending on the speaker's tone.

WRITING TOGETHER

Read the following passage from Jessica Mitford's "Beyond the Formaldehyde Curtain" to your class, and then ask them to write a short paragraph describing the tone and including specific references. Then ask students with differing opinions about the tone to read the passage aloud, demonstrating the tone they think suits the words. The drama begins to unfold with the arrival of the corpse at the mortuary.

> Alas, poor Yorick! How surprised he would be to see how his counterpart of today is whisked off to a funeral parlor and is in short order sprayed, sliced, pierced, pickled, trussed, trimmed, creamed, waxed, painted, rouged and neatly dressed—transformed from a common corpse into a Beautiful Memory Picture. This process is known in the trade as embalming and restorative art.

USEFUL READING

Shaughnessy, Mina P. *Errors & Expectations: A Guide for the Teacher of Basic Writing.* New York: Oxford UP, 1977. See pp. 36–37 on punctuation problems with quoted material.

TEACHING PRACTICE

To illustrate shifts in tone, you may want to provide your class with copies of both Lincoln's "Gettysburg Address" and Mencken's "Gettysburg Address in Vulgate." To highlight the change in tone, read them aloud. Then ask the class to identify the phrases and words Mencken uses in place of Lincoln's terms. Discuss how the connotations of words control the "meaning" of a piece of writing.

To give your students additional practice in identifying tone, you may want to break them into five to seven groups, asking each group to describe the characteristics of one Gettysburg Address. You can use Lincoln's version, Mencken's, as well as the five versions taken from *Preface to Critical Reading*, 6th ed., by Richard D. Altick and Andrea A. Lunsford (NY: Holt, 1984. pp. 104–7).

WRITERS WRITING

[F]or the first time in the semester, he wrote steadily, two full pages. "I cannot put it down on paper," he wrote. "Sam," I said afterwards, "you just did."

"What do you do when you sit down to write?" I ask Diane, who is biting the end of her ballpoint, unable to start. "Well, first I figure out what you want me to say, then I try to say it."

—ISABELLA HALSTED

(BACK)GROUNDING

Shifts in tone and diction can be justified; much humor is based on just such shifts. In the following excerpt from Woody Allen's "Spring Bulletin," the diction shifts from formal, sometimes technical, language to much less formal, colloquial language, and finally, to slang.

Economic Theory: A systematic application and critical evaluation of the basic analytic concepts of economic theory, with an emphasis on money and why it's good. Fixed coefficient production functions, cost and supply curves, and non-convexity comprise the first semester, with the second semester concentrating on spending, making change, and keeping a neat wallet. The Federal Reserve System is analyzed, and advanced students are coached in the proper method of filling out a deposit slip. Other topics include: Inflation and Depression—how to dress for each. Loans, interest, welching.

Always obey your parents, when they are present. This is the best policy in the long run, because if you don't they will make you. Most parents think they know better than you do, and you can generally make more by humoring that superstition than you can by acting on your own better judgment.   —MARK TWAIN, "Advice to Youth"

Twain opens with a flowery, slightly pompous tone with references to the "instruction of the young" and "one's tender early years." With the adverbs *beseechingly*, *urgingly*, he seems about to launch into a stereotypically high-flown "leaders of tomorrow" commencement speech. Abruptly, however, he overturns readers' expectations in the second paragraph, to deliver his subversive advice in brisk, plain language. The only "formal" phrase in this paragraph, *humoring that superstition*, only highlights and contributes to the informal comic tone.

Unintended shifts in tone, on the other hand, confuse readers and leave them wondering what the writer's real attitude is. In the following passage, notice how the tone shifts in the last sentence:

The question of child care forces a society to make profound decisions about its economic values. Can most families with young children actually live adequately on only one salary? If some conservatives had their way, June Cleaver would still be stuck in the kitchen baking cookies for the Beaver and waiting for Ward to bring home the bacon, except that with only one income the Cleavers would be lucky to afford hot dogs.

The first two sentences of this passage set a serious, formal tone, discussing child care in fairly general, abstract terms, but in the third sentence the writer shifts suddenly to a sarcastic attack based on references to television characters. Readers cannot tell whether the writer is presenting a serious analysis of the child-care issue or a passionate argument about a hotly debated topic. See how the passage was revised to make the tone consistent.

The question of child care forces a society to make profound decisions about its economic values. Can most families with young children actually live adequately on only one salary? Some conservatives believe that women with young children should not work outside the home, but many are forced to do so for financial reasons.

Diction

Like shifts in tone, inappropriate shifts in level of diction can confuse readers. In general, diction may be classified as technical (*Araucaria araucama* instead of *monkey puzzle tree*), informal or col-

RECOGNIZING SHIFTS IN TONE AND DICTION   *sh* 12f

loquial (*Give me a ring if there's anything I can do*), formal, (*Please inform me if I can be of further assistance*), or slang (*He used to be a real jock, but now he's a couch potato*). In the following sentences, the diction shifts from formal to highly informal, giving an odd, disjointed feeling to the passage:

INCONSISTENT   The law enabled illegal aliens who had entered the United States before 1982 and resided there continuously to obtain legal status and citizenship. But folks who'd hopped a plane for home since the beginning of 1982 were up the creek.

REVISED   The law enabled illegal aliens who had entered the United States before 1982 and resided there continuously to obtain legal status and citizenship. But aliens who had left the United States since the beginning of 1982 were not eligible.

READING WITH AN EYE FOR SHIFTS

Read the following passages carefully, noting any shifts in tone and diction. Then revise them for consistency.

1. Lately, I have been bugged because there are not enough cashiers on each shift. We cashiers attempt to ring the customer's orders through quickly and efficiently, but sometimes we make a few mistakes, and the customers get mad that we are messing up their bills. Some people are very mean and sarcastic toward us, and, of course, we cannot protest. Repressing my feelings is the most frustrating thing about this job. The customers complain about high prices, too, something over which we have no control. In short, it is difficult to work in such a high-pressure atmosphere. Cashiering is a hard job; we deserve more respect than we normally get.

2. In *The Great Gatsby*, the rich and poor alike can harbor malevolence. For instance, Myrtle Wilson is unkind to her husband primarily because he is poor. To Myrtle, the rich are better people, so she becomes a rich man's mistress. Her lover, Tom Buchanan, is filthy rich, but he smacks the living daylights out of Myrtle. Hey, there must be a message here!

FOR EXAMINING YOUR OWN WRITING FOR SHIFTS

Think of a well-known person you admire and find an article about that person. Then write a paragraph or two about him or her making a point of using direct quotations and of reporting in your own words statements made by that person. Using the guidelines in 12e, check your writing for any inappropriate shifts between direct and indirect discourse, and revise as necessary.

TEACHING PRACTICE

Read these passages together in class, asking students to identify inappropriate shifts. You should be able to build from their responses to a discussion of *appropriateness* and *consistency*, asking them to specify what is inappropriate or inconsistent about each shift.

13. Identifying Comma Splices and Fused Sentences

(BACK)GROUNDING

In their attempts to recapture the "stream of consciousness," both James Joyce and William Faulkner experimented freely with comma splices and fused sentences. "Molly's Soliloquy" in Joyce's *Ulysses* is one of the most famous of these attempts:

> why cant you kiss a man without going and marrying him first you sometimes love to wildly when you feel that way so nice all over you you cant help yourself I wish some man or other would take me sometime when hes there and kiss me in his arms theres nothing like a kiss long and hot down to your soul almost paralyses you[.]

Joyce deliberately used comma splices and fused sentences—for purpose and effect. But when student writers use them, they usually do so unknowingly. When they combine two independent clauses without appropriately signaling the combination, they produce a *comma splice* (often called a *comma fault*) or a *fused sentence* (often called a *run-on sentence*). And student writers often defend their *comma splices* in terms of their closely connected ideas or logical progression:

> Anna came in from the tennis court absolutely famished, she opened the freezer, took out the chocolate mocha ice cream, and dug in.

But because it indicates how the two independent clauses are to be separated, the *comma splice* above is easier to read than the following *fused sentence:*

> Anna came into her room to find her cat prancing around on her dresser her jewelry box was lying sideways on the floor her jewelry all sprawled out.

Although these sentence-level "errors" often indicate closely connected ideas, they just as often reflect hurried writing or typing and little or no proofreading.

The terms *comma splice* and *fused sentence* grow out of metaphors based on the words *splice* and *fuse*. In grammatical terms, a **comma splice** occurs when two independent clauses are joined with only a comma; a **fused sentence,** when two independent clauses are joined with no punctuation or connecting word between them.

SPLICE	It was already spring, the tulips were in bloom.
FUSED	It was already spring the tulips were in bloom.

Comma splices and fused sentences can be problematical, for though both are considered "errors," we see them frequently in literary and journalistic writing. Like many other structures we commonly identify as "errors," each can be used to powerful effect.

E. M. Forster, for instance, is known as a careful and correct stylist, yet he often deviates from the "correct" to create special effects. Look, for example, at the following passage from his essay about the 1937 Paris Exhibition:

> . . . For the Soviet Pavilion . . . is trying . . . to dodge money and to wipe away the film of coins and notes which keeps forming on the human retina. One of the evils of money is that it tempts us to look at it rather than at the things that it buys. They are dimmed because of the metal and the paper through which we receive them. That is the fundamental deceitfulness of riches, which kept worrying Christ. That is the treachery of the purse, the wallet and the bank-balance, even from the capitalist point of view. *They were invented as a convenience to the flesh, they have become a chain for the spirit.*
>
> —E. M. FORSTER, "The Last Parade"

256

IDENTIFYING COMMA SPLICES AND FUSED SENTENCES

Forster uses a comma splice in the last sentence to emphasize parallel ideas; any conjunction, even *and*, would change the causal relationship he wishes to show. The effect is to stop us in our tracks as readers—because the grammar is unexpected, it attracts just the attention that Forster wants for his statement.

In your college writing, you will seldom if ever wish to focus attention on sentences in this particular way. In fact, doing so will almost always be identified not as a means of creating emphasis or special effect but as an error. This chapter aims to help you learn to recognize comma splices and fused sentences in your own writing and provides five methods of revising to eliminate them.

> ### Checking for comma splices and fused sentences

Go through your draft, underlining every independent clause. Then go through again looking for places where independent clauses fall one after the other. Look at what comes between any two independent clauses. If you find only a comma (without any other word), you have identified a comma splice. If you find nothing at all between the two clauses, you have identified a fused sentence. In either case, you can revise according to any one of the five methods described in this chapter.

Five methods of eliminating comma splices and fused sentences

13a. Revise by separating the clauses into two sentences
13b. Revise by linking the clauses with a semicolon
13c. Revise by linking the clauses with a comma and a coordinating conjunction
13d. Revise by recasting the two clauses as *one* independent clause
13e. Revise by recasting one of the independent clauses as a dependent clause

As a writer, you must decide which method to use in revising—or avoiding—comma splices and fused sentences. The choice requires looking at the sentences before and after the ones you are revising, to see how a particular method will affect the rhythm of the passage, and perhaps reading the passage aloud to see how the revision will sound. You will have an opportunity to practice such decision-making in exercises in this chapter.

(BACK)GROUNDING

Parataxis—Greek for "placing side by side." Paratactic clauses, phrases, or sentences are arranged independently (a coordinate, rather than a subordinate, construction), often without the customary connectives. In the following passage from *A Farewell to Arms*, Ernest Hemingway leaves the causal connections up to the reader:

> There were wet dead leaves on the road from the rows of bare trees and men were working on the road, tamping stone in the ruts from piles of crushed stone along the side of the road between the trees.

Although many beginning writers use parataxis, few use it with Hemingway's skill. Hence, their prose, which balances overtly equal relationships, often elicits simple, spliced, or fused sentences.

Hypotaxis—Greek for subjection. Hypotactic prose makes clear the dependent or subordinate relationships. In H. L. Mencken's "Travail," he makes clear causal and logical relationships:

> It is no wonder that schoolboys so often turn for stimulus from their teachers to their fellows. The fact, I believe, is largely to blame for the juvenile lawlessness that prevails in America, for it is the relatively daring and lawless boys who stand out from the mass, and so attract their weaker brethren. . . . On the female side they have the instincts of duennas, and on the male side they seldom rise above the levels of scoutmasters and Y.M.C.A. secretaries.

Students who write in paratactic style (and who are writing comma splices and fused sentences) are often thinking in hypotactic style. Ask them to think, to make their connections, aloud.

TEACHING PRACTICE

As important as sentence pattern (syntax) is word choice (semantics). In his or her mind and experience, the writer may understand the relationship between two sentences, but the reader may have to struggle to determine the writer's meaning:

> I was strongly attracted to her. She had qualities that are very rare in a woman of my age.

In this example, it's likely the writer wants to say that he was attracted to her, because (or for) she had qualities that are rare in a woman the writer's age (enthusiasm and daring, perhaps?). *Because* and *for* indicate the positive causal connection between the two clauses. If the woman were hard-of-hearing and cranky, she would also have rare qualities, so the writer would connect the two sentences with *however* or *nonetheless*.

Writers must be careful to use the sentence patterns and the connectors that accurately transfer their intended meaning to their readers. The following spliced sentence results from the writer knowing—but not making clear—that the two clauses are causally related:

> Turn on the water sprinklers, I have the kids.

In her mind, this writer has supplied the (missing) logical connection or the context that could provide any of the following meanings:

1. Since I'm holding the kids, they won't get wet.
2. We've been waiting for the kids to get here so they could run through the sprinklers.
3. Now the kids cannot get in the way of the sprinklers or fool around with them.

TEACHING PRACTICE

Review the *revised* example given in 13b:

> Emma gives Harriet advice about marriage proposals. She soon regrets having done so.

The two sentences may seem overly abrupt and terse. To avoid this effect, anticipate using the coordinate conjunction *and*.

In the following sentences, the connection between them is causal:

> This photograph is not at all realistic. It uses grotesque dream-like images to convey its message.

The reason the writer gives for the photograph's not being realistic is that it uses *grotesque dream-like images to convey its message*. In other words, *This photograph is not at all realistic <u>because</u> it uses grotesque dream-like images.*

▌ 13a. Separating the clauses into two sentences

The simplest way to revise comma splices or fused sentences is to separate them into two sentences.

COMMA SPLICE	Emma encourages Harriet to reject a proposal from a young farmer and to expect one from Mr. Elton, her interference soon leads to embarrassment.
FUSED SENTENCE	Emma encourages Harriet to reject a proposal from a young farmer and to expect one from Mr. Elton her interference soon leads to embarrassment.
REVISED	Emma encourages Harriet to reject a proposal from a young farmer and to expect one from Mr. Elton. Her interference soon leads to embarrassment.

Although this method may be the simplest, it is not always the most appropriate. In the preceding example, choosing to divide the two independent clauses into two separate sentences makes good sentence sense: the combined sentences contain twenty-four words, and dividing them into two sentences of eighteen and six words adds emphasis to the last six words by putting them in a sentence of their own. If the two spliced or fused clauses are very short, however, dividing them into two separate sentences may not succeed so well.

COMMA SPLICE	Emma gives Harriet advice about marriage proposals, she soon regrets having done so.
FUSED SENTENCE	Emma gives Harriet advice about marriage proposals she soon regrets having done so.
REVISED	Emma gives Harriet advice about marriage proposals. She soon regrets having done so.

Here the two short sentences in a row, both opening with the subject, sound abrupt and overly terse, and some other method of revision would probably be preferable. (See Chapter 20.)

▌ 13b. Linking the clauses with a semicolon

If the ideas in the two independent clauses in a comma splice or fused sentence are closely related and you want to give them equal emphasis, link them with a semicolon.

COMMA SPLICE	This photograph is not at all realistic, it uses dreamlike images to convey its message.

USEFUL READING

Weathers, Winston. "Grammars of Style: New Options in Composition." *Freshman English News* 4 (Winter 1976): 1–4. Rpt. in *Rhetoric and Composition: A Sourcebook for Teachers and Writers.* Ed. Richard L. Graves. Upper Montclair, NJ: Boynton, 1984. 133–47.

LINKING THE CLAUSES

| FUSED SENTENCE | This photograph is not at all realistic it uses dreamlike images to convey its message. |
| REVISED | This photograph is not at all realistic; it uses dreamlike images to convey its message. |

In the preceding example, the second independent clause elaborates on and gives a reason for the statement in the first independent clause: it offers evidence that the photograph is not at all realistic. Because the two independent clauses are closely related and of equal importance, linking them with a semicolon represents a sound choice.

13c. Linking the clauses with a comma and a coordinating conjunction

For comma splices and fused sentences in which the two clauses are fairly closely related and equally important, another alternative for revision is to use a comma and a coordinating conjunction: *and*, *but*, *or*, *nor*, *for*, *so*, or *yet*. Using a coordinating conjunction helps to indicate what kind of link exists between the ideas in the two clauses. For instance, *but* and *yet* signal opposition or contrast (*I am strong*, *but she is stronger*); *for* and *so* signal cause-effect relationships (*The cabin was bitterly cold*, *so we built a fire*).

COMMA SPLICE	Windows were opened to the warm night air, furnaces were turned off for the season.
FUSED SENTENCE	Windows were opened to the warm night air furnaces were turned off for the season.
REVISED	Windows were opened to the warm night air, *and* furnaces were turned off for the season.

In the preceding example, two acts simply occur in conjunction with each other; thus *and* is an appropriate conjunction to link the two clauses.

See 18a for more information about using coordinating conjunctions to write more varied and interesting sentences.

1. Distinguishing between coordinating conjunctions and conjunctive adverbs or transitional phrases

The seven coordinating conjunctions can be used with a comma alone to link independent clauses. Do not confuse them with conjunctive adverbs (words like *however*, *therefore*, *moreover*, *then*, *also*) or

WRITING TOGETHER

Ask students to adapt two paragraphs from their readers or to compose two paragraphs, inserting three comma splices or fused sentences. After giving you the original, correct copy, they should trade modified texts among themselves, breaking into groups of three or five. Keep time to see which group can revise their paragraphs the fastest. Encourage them to check one another's work and to trade papers. When all the groups have finished, they should check their work with your corrected copies.

TEACHING PRACTICE

If you provide your students with practices for differentiating among conjunctions, about the meanings of their fused sentences, and about the contexts of their passages, then they will be better able to write effective, meaningful, and correct sentences. Supply them with the following fused sentences and ask them to make revisions:

The apple cider was steaming hot, we sipped it eagerly, it took the chill out of us.

They will likely come up with revisions like these:

1. Because/Although/Even though the apple cider was steaming hot, we sipped it eagerly. It took the chill out of us.
2. The apple cider was steaming hot. Even so, we sipped it eagerly because it took the chill out of us.
3. The apple cider was steaming hot, but/yet/and we sipped it eagerly for it took the chill out of us.

Each of these combinations results from and indicates a particular meaning connection.

Give the students the following sentences and ask them to explain their revision choices, carefully accounting for the context of each revision:

The clock struck 2:00 A.M. We continued talking.

Perhaps their contexts will include friends who needed to catch up on the news or fear of falling asleep during a no-sleep marathon.

with transitional phrases *(in fact, in contrast, in addition)*. (See 6b7.) Such words and phrases, even if preceded by a comma, are not enough to link independent clauses grammatically; they must be used with a semicolon, a period, or a coordinating conjunction. In fact, the inappropriate use of conjunctive adverbs and transitional phrases is responsible for many comma splices and fused sentences.

COMMA SPLICE	Most Third World countries have very high birthrates, therefore most of their citizens are young.
FUSED SENTENCE	Most Third World countries have very high birthrates therefore most of their citizens are young.
REVISED	Most Third World countries have very high birthrates. Therefore, most of their citizens are young.
REVISED	Most Third World countries have very high birthrates; therefore, most of their citizens are young.
REVISED	Most Third World countries have very high birthrates; most of their citizens, therefore, are young.
REVISED	Most Third World countries have very high birthrates, and therefore, most of their citizens are young.

As you can see from the preceding example, any of the three methods discussed thus far in this chapter can be used to revise a comma splice or fused sentence that uses a conjunctive adverb or transitional phrase inappropriately. The context of the passage can help you decide which method to choose. Notice that conjunctive adverbs and transitional phrases, unlike coordinating conjunctions, can appear in positions other than between independent clauses. These words and expressions are usually set off from the rest of the clause by commas (see 27a).

13d. Recasting the two clauses as a single independent clause

Sometimes two independent clauses that are spliced or fused together can be reduced to a single independent clause that gets the point across in fewer words.

COMMA SPLICE	High school and college prepare students for later life, they do so in slightly different ways.
FUSED SENTENCE	High school and college prepare students for later life they do so in slightly different ways.
REVISED	High school and college prepare students for later life in slightly different ways.

The revision deletes *they do so*, three words that simply repeat what has been said in the first independent clause. Deleting these three words reduces the sentence to a single independent clause that is more direct and succinct than the original version. (See 17b for more information about ways to avoid needless repetition.)

13e. Recasting one of the independent clauses as a dependent clause

Another option for revising two spliced or fused independent clauses is to convert one of them to a dependent clause. This method is most appropriate when the meaning or effect of one clause is dependent on the other or when one is less important than the other.

COMMA SPLICE	Herman Melville is regarded as one of America's foremost novelists, he died in obscurity.
FUSED SENTENCE	Herman Melville is regarded as one of America's foremost novelists he died in obscurity.
REVISED	*Although* Herman Melville is regarded as one of America's foremost novelists, he died in obscurity.

In the preceding example, the first clause stands in contrast to the second one: in contrast to Melville's importance today (he is held in high esteem) are the circumstances of his death (obscurity and poverty). In the revision, the writer chose to emphasize the second clause and to make the first one into a dependent clause by adding the subordinating conjunction *although*. (For a review of subordinating conjunctions, see 6b7.)

COMMA SPLICE	The Arts and Crafts movement called for simplicity, it reacted against Victorian clutter.
FUSED SENTENCE	The Arts and Crafts movement called for simplicity it reacted against Victorian clutter.
REVISED	The Arts and Crafts movement, *which reacted against Victorian clutter*, called for simplicity.

In this example, both clauses discuss related aspects of the Arts and Crafts movement. In the revision, the writer chose to emphasize the first clause, the one describing what the movement advocated, and to make the second clause, the one describing what it reacted against, into a dependent clause by adding the relative pronoun *which*. (For a review of relative pronouns, see 6b3.)

Notice that dependent clauses must often be set off from the rest of the sentence with commas. For information about the use of commas with dependent clauses, see Chapter 27.

See 18a2 and 18b2 for more information about using dependent clauses to write more varied and effective sentences.

ANSWERS TO EXERCISE 13.1 (WILL VARY)

1. I was sitting on a log bridge when the sun sank lower in the sky.
2. Film-makers today have no choice; therefore, they must use complicated electronic equipment.
3. I cannot find answers to certain questions, but these are the ones that stick in my mind.
4. My mother taught me to read, but my grandmother taught me to *love* to read.
5. *David Copperfield* was originally written as a serial, so it is ideally constructed for television adaptation.

EXERCISE 13.1

Revise each of the following sentences to correct any comma splices or fused sentences in *two* of the five methods presented in this chapter. Use each of the methods at least once.

> *Example*
> I had misgivings about the marriage, I did not attend the ceremony.
> I had misgivings about the marriage, *so* I did not attend the ceremony.
> *Because* I had misgivings about the marriage, I did not attend the ceremony.

1. I was sitting on a log bridge, the sun sank lower in the sky.
2. Film-makers today have no choice they must use complicated electronic equipment.
3. I cannot find answers to certain questions, these are the ones that stick in my mind.
4. My mother taught me to read my grandmother taught me to *love* to read.
5. *David Copperfield* was originally written as a serial it is ideally constructed for television adaptation.

ANSWERS TO EXERCISE 13.2 (WILL VARY)

1. Lincoln called for troops to fight the confederacy; as a result, four more southern states seceded.
2. The mother eagle called twice *before* the young eagle finally answered.
3. Jim grew beautiful tulips, *but* he had less luck with strawberries.
4. *After* the Soviet Union expelled Solzhenitsyn in 1974, he eventually settled in Vermont.
5. *As* the music lifted her spirits, she stopped sighing and began singing.

EXERCISE 13.2

Combine each of the following pairs of sentences into one sentence, using one of the five methods presented in this chapter for revising comma splices and fused sentences. Use each method at least once. In some sentences, you may have to add, delete, or change words.

> *Example*
> The rain subsided.
> The players returned to the field.
> The rain subsided, *and* the players returned to the field.
> *As soon as* the rain subsided, the players returned to the field.

1. Lincoln called for troops to fight the Confederacy.
   Four more southern states seceded as a result.
2. The mother eagle called twice.
   The young eagle finally answered.

RECASTING ONE CLAUSE AS A DEPENDENT CLAUSE

3. Jim grew beautiful tulips.
   He had less success with strawberries.
4. The Soviet Union expelled Solzhenitsyn in 1974.
   He eventually settled in Vermont.
5. The music lifted her spirits.
   She stopped sighing and began singing.

EXERCISE 13.3

ANSWERS TO EXERCISE 13.3
WILL VARY

Revise the following paragraph, eliminating all comma splices by using a period or a semicolon. Then revise the paragraph again, this time using any of the other methods presented in this chapter. Comment on the two paragraphs you have written. What differences in rhythm do you detect? Which version do you prefer, and why?

My sister Mary decided to paint her house last summer, consequently, she had to buy some paint. She wanted inexpensive paint, at the same time, it had to go on easily and cover well, that combination was unrealistic to start with. She was sure that she would have no trouble doing the work all herself, however, she had never done exterior painting before, she did not even own a ladder. She was a complete beginner, on the other hand, she was a hard worker and was willing to learn. She got her husband, Dan, to take a week off from work, likewise she let her two teenage sons take three days off from school to help. Mary went out and bought the "dark green" paint for $6.99 a gallon, it must have been mostly water, in fact, you could almost see through it when it was opened. Mary and Dan and the boys put one coat of this paint on the house, as a result, their white house turned a streaky light green. Dan and the boys rebelled, declaring they would not work any more with this cheap paint. Mary was forced to go out and buy all new good-quality paint, even so, the house did not really get painted until September.

EXERCISE 13.4

ANSWERS TO EXERCISE 13.4
WILL VARY

Revise the following paragraph, eliminating the comma splices and fused sentences by using any of the methods discussed in this chapter. Then revise the paragraph again, this time eliminating each comma splice and fused sentence by a *different* method. Decide which paragraph is most effective and why. Finally, compare the revision you prefer with the revisions of several other students, and discuss the ways in which the versions differ in meaning.

Gardening can be very satisfying, it is also hard work people who just see the pretty flowers may not realize this. My mother spends long hours every spring tilling up the soil, she moves many wheelbarrow-loads of disgusting cow manure and chicken droppings, in fact, the whole early part of gardening is

WRITING TOGETHER

Consider reading aloud the following passage by Gertrude Stein for your class to analyze. Ask your students to read the passage and then write a short paragraph describing the effects Stein achieves with her comma splices. As a class, share your insights in a discussion. Then ask your students to rewrite the passage to achieve different effects, such as short, choppy sentences or a stream-of-consciousness narration.

Think of all the detective stories everybody reads. The kind of crime is the same, and the idea of the story is very often the same, take for example a man like Wallace, he always has the same theme, take a man like Fletcher he always has the same theme, take any American ones, they too always have the scene, the same scene, the kind of invention that is necessary to make a general scene is very limited in everybody's experience, every time one of the hundreds of times a newspaper man makes fun of my writing and of my repetition he always has the same theme, always having the same theme, that is, if you like, repetition, that is if you like repeating that is the same thing, but once started expressing this thing, expressing any thing there can be no repetition because the essence of that expression is insistence, and if you insist you must each time use emphasis and if you use emphasis it is not possible while anybody is alive that they should use exactly the same emphasis.

TEACHING PRACTICE

Ask students to read the Cameron passage aloud, first as she has written it and then with the series of commas in the last sentence changed to periods. Then ask them to describe the difference in sound and rhythm between the two versions.

nauseating. The whole garden area has to be rototilled every year, this process is not much like the advertisements showing people walking quietly behind the Rototiller, on the contrary, my father has to fight that machine every inch of the way, sweating so much he looks like Hulk Hogan after a hard bout. Then the planting all must be done by hand, my back aches, my hands get raw, my skin gets sunburned. All my clothes get filthy whenever I go near that garden my mother always asks me to help, though. When harvest time comes the effort is *almost* worth it, however, there are always all those extra zucchinis I have to try to give away at school everybody else is trying to give away zucchinis, too. We also have tomatoes, squash, beans, and lettuce, there is always more than we need and we feel bad wasting it wouldn't you like this nice five-pound bag of cucumbers?

READING WITH AN EYE FOR PROSE STYLE

Comma splices and fused sentences are sometimes used to create special effects. In the following passage, see how Anne Cameron uses comma splices to create momentum and build to a climax:

Golden eagles sit in every tree and watch us watch them watch us, although there are bird experts who will tell you in all seriousness that there are NO golden eagles here. Bald eagles are common, ospreys abound, we have herons and mergansers and kingfishers, we have logging with percherons and belgians, we have park land and nature trails, we have enough oddballs, weirdos, and loons to satisfy anybody.

In the second sentence, six independent clauses are spliced together with commas. The effect: a rush of details, from the rather oddball birds to the oddball people, and finally to the *loons*, a word that can apply to either birds or people.

Look through some stories or essays to find some comma splices and fused sentences. Copy down one or two, including enough of the surrounding text to show context, and comment in writing on the effect they create.

FOR EXAMINING YOUR OWN WRITING
FOR COMMA SPLICES AND FUSED SENTENCES

Go through the last two or three essays you have written, checking for comma splices and fused sentences. If you find any, revise them using one of the methods discussed in this chapter. Comment in writing on your chosen methods.

14. Recognizing Sentence Fragments

Sentence fragments are groups of words punctuated as sentences but lacking some element grammatically necessary to a sentence, usually either a subject or a finite verb. We see them sometimes in literary works, used to add dramatic emphasis, to speed up rhythm, or to create realistic dialogue. Notice the effect that is achieved with a sentence fragment in the following example:

> The history of England is the history of the male line, not of the female. Of our fathers we know always some fact, some distinction. They were soldiers or they were sailors; they filled that office or they made that law. But of our mothers, our grandmothers, our great-grandmothers, what remains? *Nothing but a tradition.* One was beautiful; one was red-haired; one was kissed by a Queen. We know nothing of them except their names and the dates of their marriages and the number of children they bore.   —VIRGINIA WOOLF, "Women and Literature"

Nothing but a tradition. This fragment brings drama to Woolf's statement, arresting readers' attention in a way that a complete sentence would not. Notice how it gives added emphasis to the word *nothing*, and thus to Woolf's point.

Sentence fragments pose potential problems for you as a student writer, however, for although you will read them in literature, hear them in conversation, and see them everywhere in advertising, they are usually considered "errors" in most academic prose. This chapter will provide you with practice at recognizing and revising sentence fragments.

265

USEFUL READING

Kline, Charles R., Jr., and W. Dean Memering. "Formal Fragments: The English Minor Sentence." *Research in the Teaching of English* 11 (Fall 1977): 97–110. Rpt. in *Rhetoric and Composition: A Sourcebook for Teachers and Writers.* Ed. Richard L. Graves. Upper Montclair, NJ: Boynton, 1984. 148–61.

(BACK)GROUNDING

Many instructors have no problem with sentence fragments: they simply ban them outright. Until students learn to use all kinds of sentences effectively, that approach may be the safest. However, certain students will discover in their reading and their writing just how effectively fragments can be used. Even how powerfully. Ultimately, then, teachers must deal with those sentence fragments that frequently appear in formal and academic prose. In their research, Charles R. Kline, Jr., and W. Dean Memering quote fragments from a number of "formal" writings:

1. "They then determined the number of these unrelated words and the sequence of words. 'The more words recalled, the less memory used to store the sentence. The fewer words recalled, the more memory used to store the sentence.'" (Noam Chomsky, "Language and Mind")

2. "Emily Dickinson's poems . . . are more authentically in the metaphysical tradition than Emerson's are. Not, however, that many of his values were hers also—especially where they concerned the integrity of the mind and the sufficiency of inner resources." (F. O. Matthiesen, *American Renaissance*)

3. "We hold these truths to be self-evident, that all men are created equal, that they are endowed by their Creator with certain unalienable Rights, that among these are Life, Liberty, and the pursuit of Happiness. That to secure these rights, Governments are instituted among Men, deriving their just Powers from the consent of the governed." (Thomas Jefferson, The Declaration of Independence)

What distinguishes these "professional" fragments from those of our students? Often nothing. Were teachers not so attuned to locating "errors" in student papers, they might find some fragments acceptable on rhetorical or stylistic grounds. Unacceptable fragments are those that (1) lack a close relationship to other sentences; (2) create noncontinuous thought; or (3) confuse the reader.

TEACHING PRACTICE

As minor rhetorical devices, sentence fragments should not be overused lest they lose their effect. But, first of all, students need to be able to recognize unacceptable sentence fragments, those discontinuous ones that confuse the reader. Introduce the ineffective fragment to them by speaking to them in fragments: "Today. Chapter 14. Frequently used. Understand?" Naturally, your students won't know what you mean and will try to get more information from you. Write what you said on the board. Eventually, your students will tell you that your statements are incomplete. Then, drop your mask and announce that they've just given you the definition of "sentence fragment." Ask them to complete your statements. Once they demonstrate their ability to recognize and revise unacceptable fragments, introduce the concept of acceptable "nonsentences." On the board, write this famous quote of Mark Twain: "Man is the only animal that blushes. Or needs to." Ask your students to "correct" this fragment, no doubt an easy task for them: "Man is the only animal that blushes or needs to." Some of your students may be bothered by this revision and may suggest other forms of punctuation in an attempt to recapture the emphasis lost in the revision, while others may be content. You may want to ask what is wrong with the original. Is it confusing? Does the second part connect with the preceding sentence? Were they bothered or confused when they first read it?

From here, you can explain the difference between acceptable and unacceptable fragments: (1) the criteria of clarity and continuity; (2) fragments of any kind should be used rarely; (3) acceptable fragments do not validate those that should be corrected.

➢ Checking for sentence fragments

If you have a tendency to write fragments, you should check for them in every piece of writing that you do. A group of words must meet the following three criteria to be a complete sentence. If it does not meet all three, it is a fragment and must be revised.

1. It must have a subject.
2. It must have a finite verb, not just a verbal (see 6c3).
3. Unless it is a question, it must have at least one clause that does *not* begin with a subordinating word—a subordinating conjunction, a relative pronoun, or the words *when, where, why, how,* and *whether.*

Two Methods of Eliminating Fragments

In general, a fragment can be revised by combining it with an independent clause or by turning it into an independent clause.

FRAGMENT	The beaver dam holding back the shallow pond.
REVISED	I was startled at the sight of the beaver dam holding back the shallow pond. [combined with independent clause *I was startled*]
REVISED	The beaver dam was holding back the shallow pond. [turned into independent clause by adding *was* to participle *holding,* making verb finite]
FRAGMENT	Barely seven inches long, with nothing but a barrel, a handle, and a trigger.
REVISED	He was holding a gun barely seven inches long, with nothing but a barrel, a handle, and a trigger.
REVISED	It was barely seven inches long, with nothing but a barrel, a handle, and a trigger.

14a. Revising phrase fragments

Phrases, groups of words lacking either a subject, a finite verb, or both, appear frequently as fragments. Most common are verbal phrases, prepositional phrases, noun phrases, and appositive phrases.

Verbal-phrase fragments

A verbal phrase includes a gerund, an infinitive, a present participle, or a past participle, together with any objects or modifiers (see 6c3). To revise, combine them with an independent clause or turn them into two separate sentences.

REVISING PHRASE FRAGMENTS   *fr* 14a

FRAGMENT   Vivian stayed out of school for three months after Julia was born. *To recuperate and to take care of her.*

REVISED   Vivian stayed out of school for three months after Julia was born to recuperate and to take care of her. [combined with independent clause]

REVISED   Vivian stayed out of school for three months after Julia was born. She did so to recuperate and to take care of her. [turned into complete sentence]

Prepositional-phrase fragments

A prepositional phrase consists of a preposition, its object, and any modifiers of the object (see 6c3). Like verbal-phrase fragments, prepositional-phrase fragments contain neither subjects nor finite verbs. Usually you can best revise them by simply joining them to the independent clause containing the word they modify.

FRAGMENT   Several civic groups are sponsoring public debates. *With discussions afterward.*

REVISED   Several civic groups are sponsoring public debates with discussions afterward.

Noun-phrase fragments

A noun phrase consists of a noun together with any adjectives, phrases, or clauses that modify it (see 6c3). Noun-phrase fragments contain a subject but no finite verb, and they frequently appear before fragments containing a verb but no subject. You can best revise such fragments by combining them into one sentence containing both a subject *and* a verb.

FRAGMENTS   *His editorial making a plea for better facilities for severely handicapped children. Pointed out that these facilities are always located in poor areas.*

REVISED   In his editorial making a plea for better facilities for severely handicapped children, he pointed out that these facilities are always located in poor areas.

REVISED   His editorial making a plea for better facilities for severely handicapped children pointed out that these facilities are always located in poor areas.

Appositive-phrase fragments

An appositive phrase is a noun phrase that renames or describes another noun (see 6c3). You can revise appositive-phrase fragments by

267

USEFUL READING

Fowler, H. W. A *Dictionary of Modern English Usage.* Rev. and ed. Sir Ernest Gowers. Oxford: Oxford UP, 1965. See the entry under "sentence," page 546.

(BACK)GROUNDING

What is a sentence? In A *Dictionary of Modern English Usage,* H. W. Fowler claims that modern writers "show greater freedom than was once customary" and that the word *sentence* has "broken the bounds" once set for it (546). He lists some ten definitions for *sentence,* the first seven, "popular"; the eighth and ninth, grammatical; and the tenth, a combination of the two:

1. A group of words followed by a pause and revealing an intelligible purpose.
2. A group of words which makes sense.
3. A combination of words which is complete as expressing a thought.
4. A collection of words of such kind and arranged in such manner as to make complete sense.
5. A meaningful group of words that is grammatically independent.
6. A complete and independent unit of communication, the completeness and independence being shown by its capability of standing alone. i.e., of being uttered by itself.
7. A group of words, or in some cases a single word, which makes a statement, or a command (or expression of wish), or a question or an exclamation.
8. A number of words making a complete grammatical structure.
9. A combination of words that contains at least one subject and one predicate.
10. A set of words complete in itself, having either expressed or understood in it a subject or question or command or exclamation; if its subject or predicate or verb (or more) is understood, it is an elliptical sentence.

WRITERS ON WRITING

A writer is not someone who expresses his thoughts, his passion or his imagination in sentences but someone who thinks sentences. A Sentence-Thinker.

—ROLAND BARTHES

TEACHING PRACTICE

To help your students develop that sense of "completeness/incompleteness" necessary to understanding fragments, apply the following steps:

1. Write one of the following fragments on the board: "Putting the steak on when the coals are cold." "Going running without a proper warm-up and stretching session."
2. Ask your students for the information that will give completeness to the fragment.
3. What are their revisions of the fragment?
4. Write the other fragment on the board.
5. Add the following list of tag questions: Is what? Was what? Does what? Did what?

6. Ask your students to apply these questions to the fragment. (They can use any verb and interrogative pronoun whatsoever.)

7. If they find—and they will—that any of these tags apply, then they can be fairly sure that they're dealing with a fragment. If they answer the question as they apply it to the fragment, they'll have little trouble completing their fragments.

This revision tactic helps students formulate and complete all kinds of fragments, especially those with no explicit or available (con)text.

WRITERS ON WRITING

I do an enormous amount of rewriting. And when I finally let go, when I know it's complete and as it should be, is when I see a production of it that satisfies me.

—TENNESSEE WILLIAMS

ANSWERS TO EXERCISE 14.1 (WILL VARY)

1. Small, long-veined, fuzzy green leaves add to the appeal of this newly developed variety of carrot.

2. Americans yearn to live with gusto.

3. The region's dry, sandy soil is blown into strange formations by the ever-present wind.

4. The climbers had two choices—to go over a four-hundred-foot cliff or to turn back—but they decided to make the attempt.

5. Connie picked up the cat and started playing with it. It scratched her neck with its sharp little claws.

6. Westerners objected in particular to a law that limited traffic speed to fifty-five miles per hour.

7. I must have looked ridiculous struggling to carry a portfolio, art box, illustration boards, and drawing pads.

8. Offering good pay, good working conditions, and the best equipment money can buy, organized crime has been able to attract graduates just as big business has.

9. The captain sent some men up onto the remaining rigging and ordered the rest to arm themselves.

10. Wollstonecraft believed in universal public education and in education that forms the heart and strengthens the body.

joining them to the independent clause containing the noun to which the appositive phrase refers.

FRAGMENT	One of our nation's most cherished dreams seems to be in danger. *The dream of a good education for every child.*
REVISED	One of our nation's most cherished dreams, the dream of a good education for every child, seems to be in danger.
REVISED	One of our nation's dreams seems to be in danger: the dream of a good education for every child. [In this revision, the use of the colon creates greater emphasis.]

14b. Revising compound-predicate fragments

A compound predicate consists of two or more verbs, along with their modifiers and objects, that have the same subject (see 6c2). Compound-predicate fragments occur when one of these verbs is punctuated as a separate sentence without a subject. These fragments usually begin with the conjunction that connects the parts of the compound. You can revise them by attaching them to the independent clause that contains the rest of the predicate.

| FRAGMENT | The miser put some of the money in the bank. *But hid most of it under his mattress.* |
| REVISED | The miser put some of the money in the bank but hid most of it under his mattress. |

EXERCISE 14.1

Revise each of the following items to eliminate any sentence fragments, either by combining fragments with independent clauses or by rewriting them as separate sentences.

Example

Zoe looked close to tears. Standing in the door with her head bowed.

Standing in the door with her head bowed, Zoe looked close to tears.

Zoe, standing in the door with her head bowed, looked close to tears.

Zoe looked close to tears. She was standing in the door with her head bowed.

1. Small, long-veined, fuzzy green leaves. Add to the appeal of this newly developed variety of carrot.

268

USEFUL READING

Elbow Peter. *Writing without Teachers.* New York: Oxford UP, 1973. 30–31. Elbow views sentence fragments as part of a writer's repertoire rather than a flaw to be expunged.

REVISING DEPENDENT-CLAUSE FRAGMENTS

2. Living with gusto. That is what many Americans yearn for.
3. The region has dry, sandy soil. Blown into strange formations by the ever-present wind.
4. The climbers had two choices. To go over a four-hundred-foot cliff or to turn back. They decided to make the attempt.
5. Connie picked up the cat and started playing with it. It scratched her neck. With its sharp little claws.
6. Westerners objected to one law in particular. The law that limited traffic speed to fifty-five miles an hour.
7. Trying to carry a portfolio, art box, illustration boards, and drawing pads. I must have looked ridiculous.
8. Organized crime has been able to attract graduates just as big business has. With good pay, good working conditions, and the best equipment money can buy.
9. The captain sent some crew members up onto the remaining rigging. And ordered the rest to arm themselves.
10. Wollstonecraft believed in universal public education. Also, in education that forms the heart and strengthens the body.

▌ 14c. Revising dependent-clause fragments

Unlike phrases, dependent clauses contain both a subject and a finite verb. Because they *depend* upon an independent clause to complete their meaning, however, they cannot stand alone as grammatically complete sentences (see 6c4). Such clauses usually begin with a subordinating conjunction—such as *after, even though, if*—or a relative pronoun—such as *who, which, that*. (See 6b3 and 6b7 for lists of relative pronouns and subordinating conjunctions.) You can usually revise dependent clause fragments by either combining the dependent clause with the independent clause that precedes or follows it, or by deleting the subordinating word to create an independent clause.

FRAGMENT	*If a woman chooses the traditional role of mother and homemaker.* She may fear the loss of her own identity.
REVISED	If a woman chooses the traditional role of mother and homemaker, she may fear the loss of her own identity.
FRAGMENT	The plane landed at Heathrow. *Which is one of the world's largest airports.*
REVISED	The plane landed at Heathrow, which is one of the world's largest airports.

269

OPTIONAL EXERCISE

Complete the following sentence fragments in two ways: first, make each of them into a complete sentence, using verbs and interrogative pronouns as your prompt; then, create a context for each of the fragments, a preceding sentence that allows them to remain just as they are.

1. Teaching sleepy students is.
2. To finish my degree.
3. Remained comatose for three months.
4. With the rest of the world.
5. His mother constantly nagging him.
6. First the Senate and then the House.
7. After my 8:00 A.M. class.
8. Which made me furious.
9. Because we all need money.

TEACHING PRACTICE

After providing a list of definitions for each entry, many unabridged dictionaries provide excellent, full-sentence examples of each meaning. For the dictionary entries that follow (or others that you find more interesting or entertaining), ask students to provide sentences that illustrate each definition.

buckeye 1. any of various trees of the horse-chestnut family with large, spiny capsules enclosing shiny brown seeds. 2. the seed of such a tree. 3. a native or inhabitant of Ohio, called the *Buckeye State*.

handbook 1. a compact reference on some subject; manual of facts or instructions. 2. same as guidebook. 3. a book in which bets are recorded, as on horse races.

strut vt. 1. to provide with a strut or brace. 2. to make display of; show off.

(From Webster's *New World Dictionary*.)

FRAGMENT	Injuries in automobile accidents occur in two ways. *When an occupant is hurt by something inside the car, or when an occupant is thrown from the car.*
REVISED	Injuries in automobile accidents occur in two ways: when an occupant is hurt by something inside the car, or when an occupant is thrown from the car.
REVISED	Injuries in automobile accidents occur in two ways. An occupant is hurt by something inside the car, or when an occupant is thrown from the car.

ANSWERS TO EXERCISE 14.2 (WILL VARY)

1. Almost all of my former colleagues have quit because they were bored.
2. The researchers saw few, if any, teachers threaten students with bodily harm. Occasionally, though, they saw a teacher *resist* striking a student.
3. Although my friend fell in and got his jeans wet, the canoe trip was a success.
4. She scooped up the fur jacket which had been thrown into a heap on the dirt floor.
5. Many people take offense at Joe's thoughtless remarks.

ANSWERS TO EXERCISE 14.3 (WILL VARY)

1. *subordinate-clause fragment:* When Rick was in the fifth grade, his parents often left him with his sister.
2. *verbal-phrase fragment:* The protagonist came to a decision to leave his family and go to London.
3. *main verb missing:* Throughout time, people have experienced fear, one of the basic emotions.
4. *subordinate-clause fragment:* Many senators from the West opposed the bill because of its restrictions on mining and oil drilling.
5. *relative pronoun fragment:* Buying a computer will help me organize my finances and my calendar.
6. *appositive fragment:* Forster stopped writing novels after *A Passage to India*, one of the greatest novels of the twentieth century.
7. *gerund-phrase fragment:* Because this battery never runs out of water, it eliminates the possibility of ruined clothing from battery acid.
8. *compound-predicate fragment:* I loved Toni Morrison's *Beloved* and thought she deserved the Pulitzer prize.
9. *dependent relative-clause fragment:* The president appointed five members to draw up a set of bylaws.
10. *subordinate-clause fragment:* Because the younger generation often rejects the ways of its elders, one might say that rebellion is normal.

EXERCISE 14.2

Revise each of the following items to eliminate any fragments, either by combining them with independent clauses or by making them into separate complete sentences.

Example

Miss Marple heard doors slamming and angry voices shouting. Before she heard the shot.

Miss Marple heard doors slamming and angry voices shouting before she heard the shot.

1. Almost all of my former colleagues have quit. Because they were bored.
2. The researchers saw few, if any, teachers threaten students with bodily harm. Though occasionally they saw a teacher *resist* striking a student.
3. Although my friend fell in and got his jeans wet. The canoe trip was a success.
4. She scooped up the fur jacket. Which had been thrown into a heap on the dirt floor.
5. Many people take offense at Joe. Whose remarks are often thoughtless.

EXERCISE 14.3

Identify all of the sentence fragments in the following items, and explain why each is grammatically incomplete. Then revise each one in at least two ways.

Example

Controlling my temper. That has been one of my goals this year.

Controlling my temper has been one of my goals this year.

One of my goals this year has been controlling my temper.

1. When Rick was in the fifth grade. His parents often left him with his sister.
2. The protagonist comes to a decision. To leave his family and go to London.

REVISING DEPENDENT-CLAUSE FRAGMENTS

3. Fear, one of the basic emotions people have experienced throughout time.
4. Many senators from the West opposed the bill. Because of its restrictions on mining and oil drilling.
5. I plan to buy a computer. Which will help me organize my finances and my calendar.
6. Forster stopped writing novels after *A Passage to India*. One of the greatest novels of the twentieth century.
7. This battery never runs out of water. Eliminating the possibility of ruined clothing from battery acid.
8. I loved Toni Morrison's *Beloved*. And thought she deserved the Pulitzer Prize.
9. The president appointed five members. Who drew up a set of bylaws.
10. One might say that rebellion is normal. Because the younger generation often rejects the ways of its elders.

READING WITH AN EYE FOR FRAGMENTS

Each of the following paragraphs includes a sentence fragment. Read each paragraph, identify the fragment, and then decide to what effect each writer wished to achieve by using a fragment rather than a complete sentence.

I was looking through binoculars at a pair of whistling swans. Whistling swans! It is impossible to say how excited I was to see whistling swans in Daleville, Virginia. The two were a pair, mated for life, migrating north and west from the Atlantic coast to the high arctic. They had paused to feed at Daleville Pond. I had flushed them, and now they were flying and circling the pond. I crouched in the reeds so they would not be afraid to come back to the water.   —ANNIE DILLARD, "Lenses"

Now one can hear the warning rumble begin: if everyone is allowed to take drugs everyone will and the GNP will decrease, the Commies will stop us from making everyone free, and we shall end up a race of zombies, passively murmuring "groovy" to one another. Alarming thought. Yet it seems most unlikely that any reasonably sane person will become a drug addict if he knows in advance what addiction is going to be like.   —GORE VIDAL, "Drugs"

FOR EXAMINING YOUR OWN WRITING FOR FRAGMENTS

Read through several essays you have written to see whether they include any sentence fragments. Check each group of words punctuated as a sentence to be sure that it contains the three elements listed at the beginning of this chapter: (1) a subject, (2) a finite verb, and (3) unless the sentence is a question, at least one clause that does not begin with a subordinating word. If you find any groups of words that lack any of these elements, revise them to form complete sentences.

271

WRITING TOGETHER

In dialogue, the speaker and hearer can supply the information that gives the fragment complete sense. Ask your students to read the Hemingway dialogue, making each fragment a complete sentence:

Why are you going away?
I'm going away because it's *better for you* and *better for me.*
When are you going?
I'm going as *soon as I can.*
Where are you going?
I'm going to *San Sebastian.*

Then ask them to create their own *fragmented dialogue* to distribute among their classmates. Someone else should transform all the fragments into complete sentences.

You might want to use the following dialogue from Andrew Ward's "They Also Wait Who Stand and Serve Themselves":

"Hey, buddy, flick the switch."
"Right. Thanks."
"The switch. Flick the switch.
[Pause.] What the hell's the matter with you? All you gotta do is flick the switch."
"I couldn't find the switch."
"Well, what do you call this?"
"A lever."
"Christ. All right, it's set. Now you can serve yourself."

If your students have any trouble creating a context for this dialogue, you can provide them with the following information: a man is trying to figure out how to serve himself gas, and the "attendant" is giving him directions over a microphone. Finally, the "attendant" comes out to demonstrate how to flick the switch.

TEACHING PRACTICE

Ask students to bring to class any essays in which they find fragments. Choose several fragments, and put them on the board for class discussion. Ask students to identify the missing element and then to decide on the *best* means of revision. Compare the student fragments with those in the Dillard and Vidal passages, reading each one with some surrounding text for context. Ask students if they can see a difference in the way the fragments are used in the professional writers' work.

15. Recognizing Misplaced, Disruptive, and Dangling Modifiers

(BACK)GROUNDING

Although formally related, misplaced, disruptive, and dangling modifiers affect the reader differently. Misplaced and disruptive modifiers often lead to confusing or garbled sentences. Dangling modifiers leave the reader guessing to which word or phrase the modifier belongs.

For most of us, clarity is an unchallenged ideal. Indeed, when assembling a new barbeque grill, we want clear, utterly unambiguous instructions. Many advertisements, however, deliberately conflate the product being advertised with another desirable image. For example, an advertisement for a television uses the caption "PLAY TIME," suggesting vigorous physical activity, while purveying the passive watching of a playing television program. In this case, the advertising is deliberately ambiguous, merging both meanings of "PLAY TIME." And the reader has little trouble understanding and synthesizing the ambiguity.

TEACHING PRACTICE

In our students' writing, we often trip across ambiguous words, phrases, or clauses. We resolve many of these by simply referring to the context of the passage. If, for example, we read *She read to the child in the chair*, we may already have information telling us that both *she* and *the child* were sitting in the chair or that only *the child* sitting in the chair was lucky enough to be read to. Without such contextual information, such a sentence would need to be improved, unless, of course, ambiguity enriched the passage, or—more importantly—the student writer had more important overall writing improvements to make.

Adjectives, adverbs, and the various kinds of phrases and clauses used as adjectives and adverbs enrich writing by making it more concrete, vivid, and memorable. As a writer, you want to take full advantage of them. To be effective, however, these **modifiers** must be carefully placed and must refer clearly to another word or words in the sentence. If modifiers seem to modify words they are not meant to, if they disrupt the continuity of a grammatical structure or of the sentence as a whole, or if they are not clearly attached to any other word in the sentence, the results can be ambiguous, confusing, or even nonsensical.

We see examples of modifiers with these problems even in the work of many professional writers, for they are among the most difficult things to spot when editing. James Thurber was perhaps being somewhat defensive in poking fun at one of the most common problems of this kind:

> Where to use *only* in a sentence is a moot question, one of the mootest questions in all rhetoric. The purist will say the expression "He only died last week" is incorrect, and that it should be "He died only last week." The purist's contention is that the first sentence, if carried out to a natural conclusion, would give us something like this: "He only died last week; he didn't do anything else; that's all he did." It isn't a natural conclusion, however, because nobody would say that. . . . The best way is often to omit *only* and use some other expression. Thus . . . one could say: "It was no longer ago than last Thursday that George L. Wodolgoffing became an angel."
>
> —JAMES THURBER, "Ladies and Gentlemen's Guide to Modern English Usage"

272

USEFUL READING

Williams, Joseph M. *Style: Ten Lessons in Clarity and Grace*, 2nd ed. Glenview, IL: Scott, 1985. See pp. 145–48, "Some Problems with Modifiers," where Williams discusses dangling and misplaced modifiers.

Unfortunately, modifiers often cause greater confusion than in Thurber's example, nor is his revision the kind a writer can often use. This chapter will examine three types of problem modifiers—misplaced, disruptive, and dangling—and ways of revising them that do not depend on the assistance of angels.

▮ 15a. Revising misplaced modifiers

Misplaced modifiers are words, phrases, and clauses that cause ambiguity or confusion because they are not placed close enough to the words they modify or because they could modify the words either before or after them.

▮ 1. Misplaced words and phrases

In the sentence *Softly I could hear the tumbleweeds rustling in the wind*, the adverb *softly* seems to modify *could hear*. Yet the writer obviously meant it to modify *rustling*. Such confusion can be avoided by placing a modifier close to the word or words it really refers to.

> I could hear the tumbleweeds *softly* rustling in the wind.

> I could hear the tumbleweeds rustling *softly* in the wind.

Be especially careful with the placement of **limiting modifiers** like *almost, even, hardly, just, merely, nearly, only, scarcely,* and *simply*. In general, these modifiers should be placed right before the words they modify, because putting them in other positions may produce not just ambiguity but a completely different meaning. Consider the following set of sentences:

AMBIGUOUS	The court only hears civil cases on Tuesday.
CLEAR	The court hears *only* civil cases on Tuesday.
CLEAR	The court hears civil cases *only* on Tuesday.

In the first sentence, placing *only* before the verb makes the meaning ambiguous. Does the writer mean that civil cases are the only kind of cases heard on Tuesdays, or that those are the only days on which civil cases are heard? The second and third sentences each express one of these meanings clearly.

Phrases also should ordinarily be placed close to the words they modify. The most common type of phrase modifier, the prepositional phrase, usually appears right after the word it modifies. In the following

273

TEACHING PRACTICE

Although it is most clear to place a modifier either directly before or after the words it modifies, there are exceptions. For example, another possibility for the sample sentence could be: *I could hear the tumbleweeds rustling in the wind softly*. Sometimes, the writer's *emphasis* or *sense of rhythm* or *intention* determines the syntactic placement of the modifier in a sentence.

(BACK)GROUNDING

In *A Dictionary of Contemporary American Usage* (NY: Random, 1957), Bergen and Cornelia Evans give the following advice about *only*: In most cases *only* is a sentence adverb and qualifies the entire statement. When used in this way its natural position is before the verb, as in *but now I only hear its melancholy, long, withdrawing roar*. This word order is standard literary English and should be followed unless there is a very good reason for placing *only* somewhere else in the sentence. . . . Only may be placed later. But when it is, it puts special emphasis on a subordinate part of the sentence, and this is often undesirable.

The Evanses use for their example a sentence (stanzas 3, 4) from Matthew Arnold's "Dover Beach":

> The sea of faith
> Was once, too, at the full, and round
>   earth's shore
> Lay like the folds of a bright girdle
>   furled;
> But now I only hear
> Its melancholy, long, withdrawing roar,
> Retreating, to the breath
> Of the night wind down the vast edges
>   drear
> And naked shingles of the world.

The Evanses go on to say that

> at the moment there is nothing in the world for [Arnold] except this melancholy sound. It does not say he only hears and does not see. And if *only* is placed after *hear* to avoid this imaginary ambiguity, *roar* is given undue importance. We may be left feeling that he heard the roar but not the other sounds that went with it. . . . Like other negative adverbs, *only* must be placed ahead of its natural position if it is to be made emphatic. (338)

(BACK)GROUNDING

Misplaced modifiers usually lead to confusion, but sometimes, they lead to amusing double entendres as well. Consider, for example, the following AP description of England's Prince Andrew as "the son of Queen Elizabeth and a Royal Navy helicopter pilot." Whether deliberate (for effect) or inadvertent, these little beauties crop up from time to time. Several months later, the AP reported that Princess Anne was the daughter of Queen Elizabeth and a noted equestrian performer. A Florida newspaper reported that "The 37-year-old daughter of Queen Elizabeth II and her horse finished fourth in the National Hunt at Hereford."

WRITING TOGETHER

Consider sharing the following paragraph from Margaret Mead's "One Vote for This Age of Anxiety." Ask your students to revise it, moving modifiers around to make the sentences more effective. Finally, ask two or three students to read their versions aloud; note and discuss the various choices each student makes.

> When critics wish to repudiate the world in which we live today, one of their familiar ways of doing it is to castigate modern man because anxiety is his chief problem. This, they say, in W. H. Auden's phrase, is the age of anxiety. This is what we have arrived at with all our vaunted progress, our great technological advances, our great wealth—everyone goes about with a burden of anxiety so enormous that, in the end, our stomachs and our arteries and our skins express the tension under which we live. Americans who have lived in Europe come back to comment on our favorite farewell which, instead of the old goodbye (God be with you), is now "Take it easy," each American admonishing the other not to break down from the tension and strain of modern life.

TEACHING PRACTICE

Transformational grammar identifies the placement of this prepositional modifier as an example of the transformation "relative clause reduction." In the sentence *The protestors were running in the administration building from the police* the "surface structure" version could mean that the protesters were running from *the police in the administration building*. The "deep structure" probably carries the following information: *The protesters were running from the police, who were in the administration building.*

WRITERS ON WRITING

> The average editor cannot escape feeling that telling a writer to do something is almost the same thing as performing it himself.
>
> —HEYWOOD CAMPBELL BROUN

sentences, note how misplaced prepositional phrases cause confusion.

MISPLACED	The runners stood ignoring the crowd in their lanes. [This sentence implies that the crowd were in the lanes.]
REVISED	The runners *stood in their lanes* ignoring the crowd.
MISPLACED	She will be teaching a seminar this term on voodoo at Skyline College. [Surely the voodoo was not at the college.]
REVISED	She will be teaching *a seminar on voodoo* this term at Skyline College.

Participial phrases usually appear right before or right after the words they modify. In the following sentences, notice how misplacing these phrases can lead to confusion.

MISPLACED	The host pointed out the moose head to the guests mounted on the wall. [This sentence implies that the guests were mounted on the wall.]
REVISED	The host pointed out the *moose head mounted on the wall* to the guests.
REVISED	The host pointed out to the guests the *moose head mounted on the wall.*
MISPLACED	Billowing from every window, we saw clouds of smoke. [People cannot billow from windows.]
REVISED	We saw *clouds of smoke billowing from every window.*

EXERCISE 15.1

Revise each of the following sentences by moving any misplaced modifying words and phrases so that they clearly modify the words they are intended to.

> *Example*
> The blue law only allowed food and medicine to be sold on Sundays.
> The blue law allowed *only food and medicine* to be sold on Sundays.

1. Slick and professional, the audience applauded the comedian's routine.
2. Enthusiastically, I heard my friends talk about their great weekends while I tried to finish my assignment.
3. The city almost spent $2 million on the new stadium that opened last year.
4. On the day in question, the patient was not normally able to breathe.
5. The reporter barely submitted his story ahead of deadline.
6. He sat very quietly rolling his eyes in his chair.
7. I went through the process of taxiing and taking off in my mind.

USEFUL READING

Broderick, John P. *Modern English Linguistics: A Structural and Transformational Grammar*. New York: Harper, 1975. 156–66.

REVISING MISPLACED MODIFIERS   *mm* 15a

8. Vernon made an agreement to pay back the loan with his father.
9. The bank offered flood insurance to the homeowners underwritten by the federal government.
10. Revolving out of control, the maintenance worker shut down the turbine.

2. Misplaced clauses

While you have more flexibility in the placement of dependent clauses than of modifying words and phrases, you should still try whenever possible to place them close to whatever you wish them to modify. If you do not, unintended meanings can result.

MISPLACED	The man carrying a baby *who was quoting Cicero* startled us. [Surely the baby wasn't quoting Cicero.]
REVISED	The *man who was quoting Cicero* and carrying a baby startled us.
MISPLACED	Nixon told reporters that he planned to get out of politics after he lost the 1962 gubernatorial race. [The sentence implies that Nixon planned to lose the race.]
REVISED	*After he lost the 1962 gubernatorial race,* Nixon told reporters that he planned to get out of politics.

EXERCISE 15.2

Revise each of the following sentences by moving any misplaced modifying clauses so that they clearly modify the words they are intended to.

Example

The book was missing from the library that we needed to finish our research.

The *book that we needed to finish our research* was missing from the library.

1. Illegal aliens are often exploited by employers who are afraid of being deported.
2. I was glad to know that the money would stay in my pocket that I had made for the night.
3. Elderly people and students live in the neighborhood surrounding the university, which is full of identical tract houses.
4. His doctor recommended a new examination for heart disease, which is painless.
5. She knew that the investment would pay off in a dramatic way before she decided to buy the stock.

ANSWERS TO EXERCISE 15.1 (WILL VARY)

1. The audience applauded the comedian's slick and professional routine.
2. I heard my friends talk enthusiastically about their great weekends while I tried to finish my assignment.
3. The city spent almost $2 million on the new stadium that opened last year.
4. On the day in question, the patient was not able to breathe normally.
5. The reporter submitted his story barely ahead of the deadline.
6. He sat in his chair very quietly, rolling his eyes.
7. In my mind, I went through the process of taxiing and taking off.
8. Vernon made an agreement with his father to pay the loan back.
9. The bank offered flood insurance underwritten by the federal government to the homeowners.
10. The maintenance worker shut down the turbine that was revolving out of control.

ANSWERS TO EXERCISE 15.2 (WILL VARY)

1. Illegal aliens, afraid of being deported, are often exploited by employers.
2. I was glad to know that the money I had made for the night would stay in my pocket.
3. Elderly people and students live in the neighborhood full of identical tract houses which surrounds the university.
4. His doctor recommended a new, painless examination for heart disease.
5. Before she decided to buy the stock, she knew the investment would pay off dramatically.

3. Squinting modifiers

If a modifier could refer to either the word(s) before it or the word(s) after it, it is called a **squinting modifier**. For example:

SQUINTING   Students who practice writing *often* will improve their grades.

The modifier *often* might describe either *practice* or *will improve*. That is, the sentence might have either of the following meanings:

REVISED   Students who *often practice* writing will improve their grades.

REVISED   Students who practice writing will *often improve* their grades.

If a sentence could be read more than one way because of your placement of a modifying word, phrase, or clause, move the modifier to a position where it clearly relates to only a single term.

EXERCISE 15.3

Revise each of the following sentences in at least two ways by moving the squinting modifier so that it unambiguously modifies either the word(s) before it or the word(s) after it.

> *Example*
> The course we hoped would challenge us severely depressed us.
> The course we hoped would *severely challenge us* depressed us.
> The course we hoped would challenge us *depressed us severely*.

1. He remembered vividly enjoying the sound of Mrs. McIntosh singing while cleaning her house.
2. The mayor promised during her first term she would not raise taxes.
3. People who can hear normally have trouble imagining what life is like for a deaf person.
4. Doctors can now restore limbs that have been severed partially to functioning condition.
5. The speaker said when he finished his talk he would answer questions.

15b. Revising disruptive modifiers

Whereas misplaced modifiers confuse readers by appearing to modify the wrong word(s), **disruptive modifiers** cause problems because they interrupt the connections between parts of a grammatical structure

ANSWERS TO EXERCISE 15.3 (WILL VARY)

1. He vividly remembered enjoying the sound of Mrs. McIntosh singing while cleaning her house. He remembered enjoying vividly Mrs. McIntosh singing while cleaning her house.
2. The mayor promised that during her first term she would not raise taxes. During her first term, the mayor promised that she would not raise taxes.
3. People with normal hearing have trouble imagining what life is like for a deaf person. Most people normally have trouble imagining what life is like for a deaf person.
4. Doctors can now restore limbs that have been partially severed to functioning condition. Doctors can now restore limbs that have been severed to partially functioning condition.
5. The speaker said he would answer questions when he finished his talk. When he finished his talk, the speaker said he would answer questions.

TEACHING PRACTICE

You may want to share the following "made-up examples" of dangling, misplaced, and disruptive modifiers with your students:

1. Pregnant and on the way to the hospital, a traffic cop told Mrs. Rogers to pull over.
2. Retrieving the duck, Kevin knew he could become a trainer.
3. I ate a hamburger wearing my tuxedo.
4. Soft and mushy, Albert baked a banana cake.
5. Big and noisy, Tom ran for his life away from the street gang.
6. Hanging from the telephone pole, Sally could not retrieve her kite.

REVISING DISRUPTIVE MODIFIERS   *dm* | 15b

or a sentence, making it hard for readers to follow the progress of the thought. Be careful not to place modifiers in such a way that they disrupt the normal grammatical flow of a sentence.

1. Modifiers splitting an infinitive

In general, do not split an infinitive by placing a modifier between the *to* and the verb. Doing so makes it hard for readers to recognize that the two go together.

> DISRUPTIVE   Hitler expected the British to fairly quickly surrender.
>
> REVISED   Hitler expected the British *to surrender* fairly quickly.

In some cases, however, a modifier sounds awkward in any position other than between the parts of the infinitive.

> She hopes this year *to* almost exactly *equal* her last year's income.

To avoid a split infinitive, it may be best to reword the sentence to eliminate the infinitive altogether.

> She hopes that this year she will earn almost exactly as much as she did last year.

2. Modifiers between the parts of a verb phrase

A verb phrase consists of a main verb together with one or more auxiliary verbs: *had studied, will be moving* (see 6c3). Modifiers consisting of one or even two or three adverbs can often appear between parts of a verb phrase without causing awkwardness: *He <u>had</u> very seldom actually <u>fired</u> a gun in the line of duty.* In general, however, do not interrupt a verb phrase with modifiers that are phrases or clauses.

> DISRUPTIVE   Vegetables will, if they are cooked too long, lose most of their nutritional value.
>
> REVISED   Vegetables *will lose* most of their nutritional value if they are cooked too long.
>
> REVISED   If they are cooked too long, vegetables *will lose* most of their nutritional value.

3. Modifiers between a subject and verb

Adjective phrases and clauses often appear between a subject and verb: *The <u>books</u> that the librarians had decided were no longer useful <u>were discarded</u>.* In general, however, do not use an adverb clause or

277

phrase in this position, because it disrupts the natural progression from subject to verb that readers expect.

DISRUPTIVE	The books, because the librarians had decided they were no longer useful, were discarded.
REVISED	The *books were discarded* because the librarians had decided they were no longer useful.
REVISED	Because the librarians had decided the books were no longer useful, *they were discarded.*

4. Modifiers between a verb and an object or subject complement

In general, do not place an adverb phrase or clause between a verb and a direct object or subject complement, because readers expect the object or complement to follow directly after the verb.

DISRUPTIVE	He bought with his first paycheck a secondhand car.
REVISED	He *bought a secondhand car* with his first paycheck.
REVISED	With his first paycheck he *bought a secondhand car.*

EXERCISE 15.4

Revise each of the following sentences by moving the disruptive modifier so that the sentence reads smoothly.

Example

Rock festivals became during the 1960s a form of political protest.

During the 1960s, rock festivals became a form of political protest.

1. Eastern North America was, when the first Europeans arrived, covered in forest.
2. The exhibit, because it had been heavily publicized, attracted large audiences.
3. The Soviet skaters were expected to easily take the gold medal.
4. Bookstores sold, in the first week after publication, fifty thousand copies.
5. The singer had because of illness canceled her concert.

15c. Revising dangling modifiers

Dangling modifiers are words (usually adverbs), phrases (prepositional or participial), and elliptical clauses (clauses from which a word or words have been left out) that modify nothing in particular in the rest of a sentence. They often seem to modify something that is suggested or implied but does not exist grammatically in the sentence.

ANSWERS TO EXERCISE 15.4 (WILL VARY)

1. Eastern North America was covered in forest when the first Europeans arrived.
2. The exhibit attracted large audiences because it had been heavily publicized.
3. The Soviet skaters were expected to take the gold medal easily.
4. Bookstores sold fifty thousand copies in the first week after publication.
5. Because of illness, the singer canceled her concert.

REVISING DANGLING MODIFIERS   *dm* 15c

Such modifiers are called dangling because they hang loosely from the rest of the sentence, attached to no specific element. They frequently appear at the beginnings or ends of sentences.

To revise dangling modifiers, you can change the subject of the main clause so that the modifier clearly refers to it, or you can change the dangling modifier itself into a phrase or a nonelliptical clause that clearly modifies an existing part of the sentence.

1. Dangling words and phrases

DANGLING	Satisfactorily, Martin was confined to the dugout for a week. [There is no indication of who found the confinement satisfactory.]
REVISED	*To the umpires' satisfaction*, Martin was confined to the dugout for a week.
DANGLING	Raised in the suburbs, a built-in swimming pool and a two-car garage seem rather basic. [*Raised in the suburbs* does not refer specifically to anything in the sentence, though it seems to refer to a person or persons who are not mentioned.]
REVISED	*Raised in the suburbs*, I consider a built-in swimming pool and a two-car garage rather basic.
REVISED	*Because I was raised in the suburbs*, a built-in swimming pool and a two-car garage seem rather basic.
REVISED	*To those raised in the suburbs*, a built-in swimming pool and a two-car garage seem rather basic.
DANGLING	As a young boy, his grandmother told stories of her years as a country schoolteacher. [His grandmother was never a young boy.]
REVISED	*As a young boy, he* heard his grandmother tell stories of her years as a country schoolteacher.
REVISED	*When he was a young boy*, his grandmother told stories of her years as a country schoolteacher.
DANGLING	In thumbing through the magazine, my eyes automatically noticed the perfume ads. [Eyes cannot thumb through magazines.]
REVISED	*In thumbing through the magazine*, I automatically noticed the perfume ads.
REVISED	*As I was thumbing through the magazine*, my eyes automatically noticed the perfume ads.

(BACK)GROUNDING

We have not always been so strict about enforcing the incorrectness of dangling modifiers in the past. In *Modern American Usage* (New York: Hill, 1966, 117), Wilson Follett points out that in the eighteenth century, any modifier was acceptable as long as it referred to a noun either present or implied in the sentence. Follett quotes from the *Old Farmer's Almanac:*

> Sheridan was once staying at the house of an elderly maiden lady who wanted more of his company than he was willing to give. Proposing, one day, to take a stroll with him, he excused himself on account of the badness of the weather.

Follett tells us that "it was the maiden lady that did the proposing; she is present only in the preceding sentence, and not only in a very subordinate construction. But the passage does not violate the canons of Sheridan's generation or the next." He goes on to explain that after around 1880, such constructions began to be cited as errors, as they are today. Nevertheless, experienced adult writers continue to use, and to get by with using such constructions. Although "dangling" remains the most common label for these constructions, Follett believes it to be a misnomer, indicating an attachment that is not really there, and would have us use, instead, words such as *adrift, unanchored, unmoored, unlinked, floating, disconnected, loose,* or *unattached.*

WRITERS ON WRITING

When I stepped from hard manual work to writing, I just stepped from one kind of hard work to another.

—SEAN O'CASEY

I opened [Mencken's] *A Book Of Prefaces* and began to read. I was jarred and shocked by the style, the clear, clean, sweeping sentences. Why did he write like that? And how did one write like that? I pictured the man as a raging demon, slashing with his pen, consumed with hate, denouncing everything American, extolling everything European or German, laughing at the weaknesses of people, mocking God, authority. What was this?

—RICHARD WRIGHT

ANSWERS TO EXERCISE 15.5 (WILL VARY)

1. Statistics on gun ownership show that more American women are taking up arms.
2. Given the sharp increase in the crime rate, many women feel that their safety is being threatened.
3. Women own twelve million guns to protect themselves.
4. Women go to shooting ranges and gun clubs to train to use weapons.
5. The vast majority of women do not buy guns for sporting purposes.

(BACK)GROUNDING

Cornelia and Bergen Evans tell us that the rule against the dangling modifier must sometimes be broken. In *A Dictionary of Contemporary American Usage* (New York: Random, 1957. 354–55), they discuss two types of participial phrases that are exceptions. First of all, some participles are often used independently either as prepositions or conjunctions: *concerning, regarding, providing, owing to, excepting,* and *failing.* Frequently, an unattached participle is meant to apply indefinitely to anyone or everyone, as in "Facing north, there is a large mountain on the right" and "Looking at the subject dispassionately, what evidence is there?" Constructed any other way, these idiomatic statements would seem unnatural and cumbersome.

The Evanses go on to say that there is no need to twist a sentence out of its natural form in order to make the subject of the participle also the subject of the verb. Good writers do not hesitate to violate the rule: "Lying in my bed, everything seemed so different"; "Taking up, by the merest chance, a finely bound book, it proved to be . . ."; "Thus loaded, our progress was slower"; "Bred up from boyhood in the Custom House, it was his proper field of activity." In the sentence "Having eaten our lunch, the bus went on to Chicago," the participle is not dangling; it is firmly attached to "bus." Therefore, the rule about a dangling modifier should say that a participial phrase having the force of an adverb of time, manner, or circumstance should never be attached to a noun element in the sentence. Disregarding *this* rule is a grammatical blunder. And, the Evanses add, such a mistake usually occurs with *having* and *past participle.* The "dangling modifier" problem is extremely rare in another form, occurring most often in made-up examples.

EXERCISE 15.5

Revise each of the following sentences to correct the dangling words or phrases.

Example

Having spent the last six summers on my grandparents' farm, my return was expected this summer.

Having spent the last six summers on my grandparents' farm, *I was expected* to return this summer.

1. Looking at the statistics on gun ownership, more American women are taking up arms.
2. Given the sharp increase in the crime rate, their safety seems threatened.
3. To protect themselves, twelve million guns are owned.
4. Training in the use of weapons is achieved by going to shooting ranges and gun clubs.
5. Based on surveys, the vast majority of women buying guns are not doing so for sporting reasons.

2. Dangling elliptical clauses

DANGLING	Where still seen, tourists find these aging flower children a picturesque spectacle. [Is it the tourists who are still seen?]
REVISED	*Where these aging flower children are still seen,* tourists find them a picturesque spectacle.
REVISED	Tourists find *these aging flower children, where still seen,* a picturesque spectacle.
DANGLING	Although a reserved and private man, everyone who met him seemed to like him. [The elliptical clause cannot refer to *everyone.*]
REVISED	*Although he was a reserved and private man,* everyone who met him seemed to like him.
REVISED	*Although a reserved and private man, he* seemed to be liked by everyone who met him.

EXERCISE 15.6

Revise each of the following sentences to correct any dangling elliptical clauses.

Example

While cycling through southern France, the music on my Sony Walkman entertained me.

While cycling through southern France, I was entertained by the music on my Sony Walkman.

REVISING DANGLING MODIFIERS   *dm* | 15c

1. However unhappy, my part-time job is something I have to put up with.
2. While attending a performance at Ford's Theater, Booth shot Lincoln.
3. A waiter's job can become very stressful when faced with a busy restaurant full of hungry people.
4. Dreams are somewhat like a jigsaw puzzle; if put together in the correct order, organization and coherence become obvious.
5. No matter how costly, my family insists on a college education.

➤ Checking for misplaced or dangling modifiers

Check each sentence for modifiers. Draw an arrow from each modifier to the word it modifies. If they are far removed from each other, try to move them closer together. Then check again, to see if the modifier could possibly refer to any other words in the sentence. If so, move the modifier so that it clearly refers to only one word. If you cannot find a word to which the modifier relates, you have a dangling modifier. Revise the sentence so that it has a clear referent for the modifier, or revise the modifier itself as a complete cause.

EXERCISE 15.7

Revise the following passage to eliminate any misplaced, disruptive, or dangling modifiers.

One day last December, before going to class, a blizzard forced the administration to, for the first time anyone could remember, announce that all classes would be until further notice suspended. After leaving the dorm, the first thing that we noticed was the silence. The snow that had been falling all night steadily covered the ground. Being the last day of the semester, we weren't very worried about classes, so we "arranged," with another dormitory, a snowball fight. While building up a stock of good snowballs near Lord Hall, our jackets began to get oppressively warm. Eventually, we peeled down to shirt sleeves, ready for a fight. The central lawn became the battleground for the great Stoke-Lord Snowball Fight, where the Stoke Hall people finally set up their forts. Our piles of snowballs almost reached the tops of our forts, which were well-packed and handy to be picked up and thrown. At last both sides were ready, and the first snowball flew through the air from the "Stoke stack." The bombardment was for a while fierce and deadly. I learned that when throwing a snowball, the standing position is very risky, getting a hard one in the mouth. Finally, having almost thrown all of our snowballs, the Stoke charge was met and resisted. The timing was measured with great accuracy, being sure not to countercharge until we saw that Stoke was low on snowballs. Then we all ran toward the enemy carrying three or four snowballs each and routed them.

ANSWERS TO EXERCISE 15.6 (WILL VARY)

1. However unhappy I am with my part-time job, I have to put up with it.
2. While attending a performance at Ford's Theatre, Lincoln was shot by John Wilkes Booth.
3. When a waiter is faced with a busy restaurant full of hungry people, the job becomes stressful.
4. Dreams are somewhat like a jigsaw puzzle: when put together in the correct order, both dreams and puzzles have organization and coherence.
5. No matter how costly a college education may be, my family insists on it.

ANSWERS TO EXERCISE 15.7 WILL VARY

OPTIONAL EXERCISE

Revise each of the following sentences to eliminate the dangler (1) by providing a subject that tells who or what is being modified; (2) by rewording. One sentence is correct.

1. Diving into the lake, Bev's head struck the raft.
2. To be considered for a teaching job, your references must be top-notch.
3. Listening to the album, we forgot our worries.
4. Found guilty, the judge dismissed him.
5. At the age of two, my dad took me and my mom with him to Texas.
6. While writing his exam, Jerry's computer broke down.
7. When out of town, the vice-chair covers for the chair.

READING WITH ATTENTION TO LIMITING MODIFIERS

E. B. White was a master of precise wording, choosing—and positioning—his words with great care. Read the following sentences by White, paying attention to the limiting modifiers italicized in each one. Identify which word or words each one modifies, and then consider what would happen if the modifier were placed somewhere else in the sentence.

1. When we got back for a swim before lunch, the lake was exactly where we had left it, the same number of inches from the dock, and there was *only* the merest suggestion of a breeze.   –"Once More to the Lake"
2. Most of the time she *simply* rode in a standing position, well aft on the beast, her hands hanging easily at her sides, her head erect, her straw-colored ponytail lightly brushing her shoulders, the blood of exertion showing faintly through the tan of her skin.   –"The Ring of Time"
3. *Even* our new shoes seemed to be working out all right and weren't hurting much.   –"Twins"
4. It was, among other things, the sort of railroad you would occasionally ride *just* for the hell of it, a higher existence into which you would escape unconsciously and without hesitation.   –"Progress and Change"

FOR EXAMINING MODIFIERS IN YOUR OWN WRITING

Choose two pages of a draft you have written recently, and examine them for clear and effective modification. Can you identify any misplaced, disruptive, or dangling modifiers? Using the guidelines in this chapter, revise as need be.

16. Maintaining Consistent and Complete Grammatical Structures

About fifteen years ago, a writing instructor who had studied thousands of student essays came to a simple but profound conclusion about many of the sentences in them: though at first glance the sentences seemed incoherent or nonsensical, they actually fell into certain patterns. They could be better characterized, the instructor decided, either as (1) unsuccessful attempts to combine sentence structures that did not fit together grammatically or sensibly or as (2) sentences missing some element necessary to complete meaning. In fact, many writers who produce garbled sentences do so in an attempt to use and master complex and sophisticated structures. What look like "errors," then, may be stepping stones on a writer's way to greater stylistic maturity. This chapter will provide practice in recognizing such mixed or incomplete structures and, more important, in revising or building on them.

▌ 16a. Making grammatical patterns consistent

Mixed construction results from beginning a sentence with one grammatical pattern and then switching to another one. In informal speech, we are all familiar with the kind of "sentence" that starts out one way and ends another, as in the following example:

> MIXED   The fact that I get up at 5 A.M. every day, which explains why I'm always tired in the evenings.

The speaker starts out with a subject (*fact*) followed by a dependent clause (*that I get up at 5 A.M. every day*). This structure should lead into a predicate to complete the independent clause begun by *The fact*,

283

USEFUL READING

D'Eloia, Sarah. "The Uses—and Limits—of Grammar." Rpt. in *The Writing Teacher's Sourcebook*. Eds. Gary Tate and Edward P. J. Corbett. New York: Oxford UP, 1981. 225–43.

Krishna, Valerie. "The Syntax of Error." *Journal of Basic Writing* 1 (Spring 1975): 43–9. Rpt. in *Rhetoric and Composition: A Sourcebook for Teachers and Writers*. Ed. Richard L. Graves. Upper Montclair, NJ: Boynton/Cook, 1984. 128–32.

(BACK)GROUNDING

In "The Uses—and Limits—of Grammar," Sarah D'Eloia explains "syntactically tangled sentences" as inconsistent and incomplete sentences that confuse the reader and that cannot be rhetorically justified in normal prose. She goes on to say:

> Tangles increase with abstract topics because the student must perceive, consolidate, and clarify the complex relations between the observable facts and his conclusions. Thus the more perceptive and far-reaching a student's insights, the more difficulty he will have parcelling them out into sentences that properly order and relate them; the more inexperienced the student is as a writer, the less he will know how to start and, if off on the wrong foot, how to start over again. (228)

Thus, these garbled sentences are the results of experiments in "logical and grammatical subordination, differential relation, and equivalence" (228), which students write for several reasons: (1) not knowing the "right" word or syntactic structure, the student may turn to the familiar (but inappropriate); (2) the student tries to juggle a number of subordinations at once; (3) unsure of the choice, the student may allow the alternatives to "contaminate" his or her decision; (4) the student lacks the academic self-confidence necessary to produce syntactically complex structures; (5) the student is unaware of the benefits that come with revision. Unfortunately, some of the most outgoing and sociable students lack confidence in academic situations: they do not believe their knowledge or opinions warrant development; their syntax is often tentative and qualifying. Worse, many of these students believe that "real" writers get it right the first time. When Mina Shaughnessy's students saw the messy pages of Richard Wright's *Native Son*, they concluded that Wright was not a good writer—he made too many mistakes.

TEACHING PRACTICE

We want our students to produce clear and consistent texts, yet we ask them to appreciate texts—canonized essays and stories—that often do not incorporate those same qualities. The distinctive syntactic styles of professional writers, however, lend themselves to analysis of purpose and effect. Critically acclaimed writer Toni Cade Bambara, for instance, frequently uses sentence structures that fall short of our classroom standards. Ask your students to listen for purpose and effect as you read aloud the following passage from Bambara's "My Man Bovanne," a story of a woman and a blind man at a benefit dance, who slow dance in such a way that her adult children are offended:

> But right away Joe Lee come up on us and frown for dancin so close to the man. My own son who knows what kind of warm I am about; and don't grown men all call me long distance and in the middle of the night for a little Mama comfort? But he frown. Which ain't right since Bovanne can't see and defend himself. Just a nice old man who fixes toasters and busted irons . . . and changes the lock on my door when my men friends get messy. Nice man. Which is not why they invited him. Grass roots you see. Me and Sister Taylor and the woman who does heads at Mamies and the man from the barber shop, we all there on account of we grass roots. And I ain't never been souther than Brooklyn Battery and no more country than the window box on my fire escape. And just yesterday my kids tellin me to take them countrified rags off my head and be cool. And now can't get Black enough to suit 'em. So everybody passin sayin My Man Bovanne. . . . And him standin there with a smile ready case someone do speak he want to be ready. So that's how come I pull him on the dance floor and we dance. . . .

WRITING TOGETHER

Ask your students to review the passage from "My Man Bovanne" according to standard edited English. After writing out their revisions, they can share them with the class. Did they improve Bambara's text? interfere with it? What were the specific effects of their revisions? Do some students have background knowledge and experience that make the original passage understandable and especially meaningful to them?

WRITERS ON WRITING

If I had to give a young writer some advice, I would say to write about something that has happened to him.

—GABRIEL GARCÍA MARQUEZ

but instead the speaker shifts to another dependent clause (*which explains why I'm always tired in the evenings*). Thus the independent clause is never completed, and what results is a fragment. In writing, this fragment could be revised into a complete sentence in at least two ways:

REVISED   The fact that I get up at 5 A.M. every day explains why I'm always tired in the evenings. [Deleting *which* changes the second dependent clause into a predicate.]

REVISED   I get up at 5 A.M. every day, which explains why I'm always so tired in the evenings. [Deleting *The fact that* makes the first dependent clause into an independent clause.]

Although most listeners would have little difficulty in following the speaker's intended meaning, failure to maintain consistent grammatical patterns often leads to confusion, especially in writing. Recognizing and revising mixed sentences call for very careful proofreading, and especially for noting the relationship between subject and predicate or between clauses. Here are some other examples of mixed sentences:

MIXED   Before the world as we know it was created, the universe was only chaos existed—a mass of nothing. [*Only chaos* must function in two different ways: as the subject complement of *universe* and as the subject of *existed*.]

REVISED   Before the world as we know it was created, the universe was only chaos—a mass of nothing. [Deleting *existed* leaves *only chaos* as a subject complement only.]

REVISED   Before the world as we know it was created, only chaos existed—a mass of nothing. [Deleting *was* leaves *only chaos* as a subject only.]

MIXED   Because hope was the only thing left when Pandora finally closed up the mythical box explains why we never lose hope no matter how bad life gets. [The adverb clause beginning with *Because* is followed not by an independent clause but by a predicate beginning with *explains*, which lacks a subject.]

REVISED   Because hope was the only thing left when Pandora finally closed up the mythical box, we never lose hope no matter how bad life gets. [Deleting *explains why* changes the original predicate into an independent clause to which the adverb clause can be attached.]

16b. Matching subjects and predicates

Another kind of mixed sentence occurs when a subject and predicate do not fit together grammatically or do not make sense together. Such a mismatch, sometimes called **faulty predication**, often appears in sentences with the verb *be*, in which the subject complement that follows the verb does not grammatically or sensibly rename the subject. In many cases, faulty predication results from using forms of *be* in sentences in which another verb would be stronger and more appropriate.

FAULTY   A characteristic that I admire is a person who is generous.

This sentence says that a person is a kind of characteristic. To make its subject and predicate consistent, you could change either the subject or the complement to make them both refer to either persons or characteristics, or you could rewrite the sentence to change the verb.

REVISED   A *characteristic* that I admire is *generosity*.

REVISED   A *kind of person* that I admire is *one who is generous*.

REVISED   I *admire* a person who is generous.

The verb *be* also leads to faulty predication when it is used before an adverb clause opening with *when* or *where*.

FAULTY   A stereotype is when someone characterizes a group unfairly.

Although you will often hear constructions like this in conversation, an adverb clause cannot function as a subject complement in academic or other formal writing. To revise this sentence, you can change the complement to a noun that will grammatically match the subject *stereotype*, or you can rewrite the sentence to change the verb.

REVISED   A *stereotype* is an unfair *characterization* of a group.

REVISED   A stereotype characterizes a group unfairly.

REVISED   *When someone characterizes a group unfairly*, he or she *creates* a stereotype.

Using *the reason (that)* . . . *is because* construction, which causes inconsistency between the subject and the subject complement, is another form of faulty predication.

(BACK)GROUNDING

The mismatch of the linking verb *be* and clauses opening with *when* or *because* is often termed "faulty predication." Linking verbs of course link a subject with a subjective complement, which renames or modifies the subject: *Sports courtesy is maturity in fast action. Sports courtesy is important to team players.* When a student uses *when* after *is*, he or she introduces an adverbial element, which no longer renames or modifies the subject, but modifies the verb: *Sports courtesy is when players treat one another with fairness and consideration.* In *Words and Ways of American English*, Thomas Pyles posits that faulty predication is an error of usage rather than a grammatical error and is, according to many handbooks, a violation of consistency. And Pyles provides us with the violations of H. G. Wells and John Ruskin:

> The real reason I am out of place here is because I like men. (Wells, *Ann Veronica*)

> The false, unnatural, and destructive system is when the bad workman is allowed to offer. . . . (Ruskin, *Unto This Last*)

Pyles goes on to write: "Wells and Ruskin, it is obvious, would not be able to do well in Freshman English in most American universities, assuming that they could get through high school" (New York: Random, 1952. 278).

(BACK)GROUNDING

One of the best explanations of *reason . . . because* can be found in Wilson Follett's *Modern English Usage* (New York: Hill, 1966, 275). Follett tells us that when we make *reason* the subject of a sentence, we tend to substitute *because* for *that*. Such a switch "besides being a breach of idiom, is an obvious redundancy: *because = for the reason that*." Hence, *the reason is because* paraphrases as *the reason is for the reason that*. Compare:

> The reason I am overweight is because I constantly crave and eat sweets.
> The reason I am overweight is for the reason that I constantly crave and eat sweets.

Revised:

> Because I constantly crave and eat sweets, I am overweight.
> The reason I am overweight is that I constantly crave and eat sweets.

FAULTY	The reason I like to play soccer is because it provides aerobic exercise.
REVISED	I like to play soccer *because* it provides aerobic exercise. [Deleting *the reason (that)* leaves an independent clause to which the *because* clause can be attached.]
REVISED	*The reason* I like to play soccer *is that* it provides aerobic exercise. [Changing *because* to *that* makes the adverb clause into a noun clause that can function as a subject complement.]

Faulty predication also occurs with verbs other than *be*, as the following examples illustrate:

FAULTY	The rules of the corporation expect employees to be properly dressed. [*Rules* cannot expect anything.]
REVISED	As its rules state, the corporation expects employees to be properly dressed.
REVISED	The rules of the corporation require that employees be properly dressed.
FAULTY	The popularity of underground comics began to appear in many stores throughout the country. [*Popularity* cannot appear in stores.]
REVISED	The popularity of underground comics began to be obvious to owners of many stores throughout the country.
REVISED	Increasing numbers of underground comics began to appear in many stores throughout the country.

EXERCISE 16.1

Revise each of the following sentences in two ways to make its structures consistent in grammar and meaning.

Example
The fact that our room was cold that night we put an electric space heater between our beds.

Because our room was cold that night, we put an electric space heater between our beds.

The fact that our room was cold that night led us to put an electric space heater between our beds.

1. My interest in a political career would satisfy my desire for public service.
2. To find out if you need braces, you dentist will usually tell you.
3. The reason air pollution standards should not be relaxed is because many people would suffer.

TEACHING PRACTICE
You may want to indicate to your students that the mismatch in the following sentence is equally one of word choice and meaning:

The rules of the corporation expect employees to be properly dressed.

As the handbook points out, rules cannot expect anything; corrections to this sentence depend on semantics or meaning. In our society we have chosen to give corporations "life," which is why a corporation can be said to expect something.

ANSWERS TO EXERCISE 16.1 (WILL VARY)
1. My interest in a political career would also satisfy my desire for a public service career. My interest in politics would also satisfy my interest in public service.
2. Your dentist will usually tell you if you need braces. To find out if you need braces, ask your dentist.
3. Many people would suffer if air pollution standards were relaxed. The reason air pollution standards should not be relaxed is that many people would suffer.
4. By not prosecuting white-collar crime as vigorously as we prosecute violent crime, we encourage white-collar criminals to ignore the law. We must prosecute white-collar crime as vigorously as violent crime unless we want to encourage white-collar criminals to ignore the law.
5. Although she looks twenty-one, she is only eighteen. She looks like a twenty-one-year-old, but she is only eighteen.
6. People in love want to make each other happy. Love is often characterized by two people who want to make each other happy.
7. Hawthorne's short stories are drawn from his life experiences. Hawthorne draws on his life experiences to create his short stories.
8. Oedipus has the "shock of recognition" when he suddenly realizes that he has killed his father and married his mother. The "shock of recognition"

CHECKING FOR MISSING OR MISUSED WORDS   *inc* 16d

4. By not prosecuting white-collar crime as vigorously as violent crime encourages white-collar criminals to think they can ignore the law.
5. Her age is a bit deceiving, with looks of a twenty-one-year-old but a true age of only eighteen.
6. Love is when two people want to make each other happy.
7. Hawthorne's short stories are experiences drawn from his own life.
8. When Oedipus suddenly realizes he has killed his father and married his mother causes a "shock of recognition."
9. One controversial element of the curriculum has been colleges with a required course in Western culture.
10. The European discovery of Australia became a penal colony for Britain.

comes when Oedipus suddenly realizes that he has killed his father and married his mother.
9. One controversial element of college curriculums has been a required course in Western culture. Required college courses in Western culture cause controversy.
10. Europeans discovered Australia, but the British made it into a penal colony. Although it was a European discovery, Australia became a British penal colony.

16c. Using elliptical structures carefully

Sometimes writers can avoid repetition and gain emphasis by using **elliptical structures,** in which they omit certain words or phrases in compound structures, as the following sentences demonstrate (omitted words are in brackets):

We are wiser in mind but [we are] weaker in body.

A person without an education, or [without] the desire for one, is an unlucky person indeed.

His hair was red, his skin [was] fair, and his body [was] underweight.

These sentences are clear and effective because the omitted words match those in the other part of the compound.

In the following sentence, however, the omitted verb does not match the one that occurs in the first part of the compound, and so the sentence is incomplete. Therefore, the sentence must be revised to include both verbs.

INCOMPLETE   His skills are underdeveloped, and his performance only average.

REVISED   His skills *are* underdeveloped, and his performance *is* only average.

16d. Checking for missing or misused words

In the rush of composing, when the brain almost always runs ahead of the hand, writers sometimes accidentally leave out words, especially short ones like articles, pronouns, and prepositions. The best way to catch such inadvertent omissions is to proofread carefully, read-

287

USEFUL READING

Curmé, George O. *English Grammar.* New York: Harper, 1947. For a list of different kinds of ellipsis, i.e., the stylistic and syntactic omission of key words and phrases.

(BACK)GROUNDING

Elliptical structures omit certain *understood* words. For instance, when your students ask you when you plan to pass back their papers and you answer "Tomorrow," you have left out the understood words, "I will pass back your papers." And when you say to them, "If in doubt about the comments I've made on your papers, please see me," you've left out the understood information: "If *you are* in doubt." One student may say to another, "You'll" probably get an A, but I won't (get an A).

Although dependent on context, elliptical structures are the most convenient way to avoid repetition while providing conciseness and movement in speech and writing.

Closely related, the *elliptical* clause differs from the *abridged* clause in that the elliptical clause implies a finite (or sentence-ready) verb, while the abridged clause never expresses a finite verb:

No one was there but I (*was* there). (An elliptical clause using the finite verb, *was.*)

There was nothing left for me to do *but to* withdraw. (An abridged clause, using no finite verb.)

WRITERS WRITING

In composing, as a general rule, run your pen through every other word you have written; you have no idea what vigor it will give your style.
—SYDNEY SMITH

TEACHING PRACTICE

To better acquaint yourself with the concept of ellipsis, you may want to turn to Curmé's *English Grammar,* which provides a list of different kinds of ellipses—the stylistic and syntactic omission of key words and phrases. Curmé explains the following kinds of omissions:

clauses of comparison

That teacher cares for her students as a mother (cares for) her children.

conditional sentences

She could easily win the contest (if she tried).

clauses of exception

Nobody knew her except/but I (knew her).

imperatives

Heads, eyes front. (Turn your heads and eyes to the front.)

independent propositions—suppression of the verb

He cooks better than you *do* (better than you cook).

ing each sentence slowly—and aloud. If a word or phrase is missing, you are very likely to hear its omission.

INCOMPLETE	A good transportation system makes easier for people move from one place to another.
REVISED	A good transportation system makes *it* easier for people *to* move from one place to another.
INCOMPLETE	Finally, it is impossible to ignore fact that women were not able to participate fully political activities.
REVISED	Finally, it is impossible to ignore *the* fact that women were not able to participate fully *in* political activities.

Especially in speaking, we often omit *that* when it introduces a noun clause following a verb: *Yesterday, I realized [that] I was hopelessly behind in my work.* In this instance, omitting *that* does not obscure meaning. If any possible confusion could arise, however, be sure to include the *that* in writing.

| UNCLEAR | I noticed many motorcycles from the 1940s had become classics. [Readers at first assume *many motorcycles* is the object of *noticed* rather than the subject of the subordinate clause.] |
| REVISED | I noticed *that* many motorcycles from the 1940s had become classics. |

 Checking for wrong prepositions

Circle the prepositions in a draft, and then read aloud any sentences in which they appear. Are you unsure about any of them? If so, check a dictionary to see that you've used them properly. (The *Oxford Advanced Learners* dictionary has especially good coverage of prepositions.) Keep a list of any that you misuse, with the sentences in which you used them incorrectly. Check carefully for them in your drafts.

16e. Checking comparisons for completeness, consistency, and clarity

As you revise and proofread your writing, check comparative structures closely, remembering that when you compare two or more things, the comparison must be *complete*, *logically consistent*, and

TEACHING PRACTICE

"Incomplete" comparisons are common in spoken discourse. In fact, *A person who drives drunk is more dangerous*, and *My two sisters are so different* will probably make sense to most of your students; context will supply the missing information, or your students will effortlessly fill in the missing information. Ask your students if they can create a context for the three incomplete comparisons on p. 289.

WRITERS WRITING

He can compress the most words into the smallest ideas of any man I ever met.

—ABRAHAM LINCOLN

CHECKING COMPARISONS FOR COMPLETENESS   *inc* 16e

clear. (See Chapter 10 for further discussion of comparative and superlative forms of adjectives and adverbs.)

Complete comparisons

INCOMPLETE	A person who drives drunk is more dangerous. [More dangerous than what?]
REVISED	A person who drives drunk is more dangerous *than one who drives carelessly.*
INCOMPLETE	My two sisters are so different. [So different that what?]
REVISED	My two sisters are so different *that they can hardly communicate with each other.*

Logically consistent comparisons

ILLOGICAL	Woodberry's biography is better researched than Fields. [This sentence compares *biography*, a book, to *Fields*, a person.]
REVISED	Woodberry's biography is better researched than *the one by* Fields.
REVISED	Woodberry's biography is better researched than *Fields's is.*

Clear comparisons

UNCLEAR	Ted always felt more affection for his brother than his sister. [Did Ted feel more affection for his brother than his sister did or more affection for his brother than he felt for his sister?]
REVISED	Ted always felt more affection for his brother than *he did for* his sister.
REVISED	Ted always felt more affection for his brother than his sister *did.*

EXERCISE 16.2

Revise each of the following sentences to eliminate any inappropriate elliptical constructions; to make comparisons complete, logically consistent, and clear; and to supply any other omitted words that are necessary for meaning.

Example
Most of the candidates are bright, and one brilliant.
Most of the candidates are bright, and one is brilliant.

WRITING TOGETHER
Consider sharing the following passage with your students. Ask them to change the point-of-view from first person to third person; that change will require them to make explicit and complete the utterances that Elizabeth and Miss Kilman make to themselves. Then ask your students to exchange rewritten versions to discover what each viewed as the unspoken words.

Elizabeth said she had forgotten her gloves. That was because Miss Kilman and her mother hated each other. She could not bear to see them together. She ran upstairs to find her gloves.

But Miss Kilman did not hate Mrs. Dalloway. Turning her large gooseberry-coloured eyes upon Clarissa [Dalloway], observing her small pink face, her delicate body, her air of freshness and fashion, Miss Kilman felt, Fool! Simpleton! You who have known neither sorrow nor pleasure; who have trifled your life away! And there rose in her an overmastering desire to overcome her; to unmask her. But it was not the body; it was the soul and its mockery that she wished to subdue; make feel her mastery. If only she could make her weep; could ruin her; her; humiliate her; bring her to her knees crying, You are right! But this was God's will, not Miss Kilman's. It was to be a religious victory. So she glared; so she glowered. (Virginia Woolf, *Mrs. Dalloway*)

ANSWERS TO EXERCISE 16.2 (WILL VARY)

1. My new stepmother makes my father happier than the last one did.
2. Argentina and Uruguay were originally colonized by Spain, and Brazil was colonized by Portugal.
3. Because they are still uncomfortable with young men, Jasmine and Donna get along together better on a double date than they do when they go out separately.
4. During the football strike, fans were angrier at the players than they were at the management.
5. Most young people think their parents are old and out of touch.
6. The picture made me think about whether Baby M's life would be more difficult than any other children's lives.
7. Taking a driving test was a nerve-wracking experience.
8. Nonsmokers and marijuana smokers have different personalities.
9. The driver did not see the light turn red.
10. One way to develop a topic for an essay is to jot down whatever comes to mind on a sheet of paper.

TEACHING PRACTICE

If students identify problem sentences in their own essays, they can profit by working in small groups to revise the passages, the writer explaining what he or she *meant* to say and the group working out various ways to convey that meaning.

1. My new stepmother makes my father happier.
2. Argentina and Uruguay were originally colonized by Spain, and Brazil by Portugal.
3. Jasmine and Donna get along together better on a double date.
4. During the strike, fans were angrier at the players than the owners.
5. Most young people think their parents are so old and out of touch.
6. The picture made me think about whether Baby M's life would be more difficult than many other children.
7. Taking a driving test was the most nerve-wracking experience.
8. The personalities of marijuana smokers are very different from nonsmokers.
9. The driver never saw the light had turned red.
10. One way to develop a topic for essay is to jot down on a sheet paper whatever comes to mind.

FOR EXAMINING YOUR OWN WRITING FOR MIXED OR INCOMPLETE STRUCTURES

Read over three or four paragraphs from a draft or completed essay you have written recently, checking for any mixed sentences, and incomplete or missing structures. Revise the paragraphs to correct any problems you find.

PART FOUR

Sentences: Making Stylistic Choices

17. Constructing Effective Sentences

The philosopher, critic, and poet Kenneth Burke defines *form* in writing as "the arousal and fulfillment of desire." Odd as this definition may seem at first, it suggests an excellent test for effective prose. Substituting the more mundane *expectations* for Burke's deliberately provocative *desire* illustrates the test more clearly. An **effective sentence** is one that creates or appeals to certain expectations and then either fulfills those expectations or—as is sometimes the case—startles or amuses or alarms readers by *not* fulfilling them. Look at the following sentence:

> I sometimes think of the reader as a cat, endlessly fastidious, capable, by turns, of mordant indifference and riveted attention, luxurious, recumbent, and ever poised.
>
> –Patricia Hampl, "Memory and Imagination"

This sentence fulfills expectations by following up on the image of the reader as cat with cat imagery ("endlessly fastidious," "luxurious"), thus linking the picture of the reader with one of a cat. In addition, the sentence is structured so as to pull its readers along, saving its most powerful image for the end, closing with the image of the catlike reader, "ever poised."

The writer of the following sentence, on the other hand, surprises readers by *breaking* expectations:

> He was a tall, dark, and handsome creep.

In this sentence, the writer plays on readers' expectations with the

293

USEFUL READING

Burke, Kenneth. "Lexicon Rhetoricae." *Counter-Statement*. 1931. Berkeley: U of California P, 1968. 123–83. Burke explores the appeal to the reader of various categories of forms.

Lanham, Richard. *Style: An Anti-Textbook*. New Haven: Yale UP, 1977. Lanham argues for the teaching of style, not of clarity. He writes that "instruction in composition builds on a single premise—clarity—and that premise is false."

(BACK)GROUNDING

In "Lexicon Rhetoricae" Kenneth Burke defines form as the "arousal and fulfillment of desires" (124). Burke goes on to describe the five types of verbal form, each with its own unique appeal:

1. *syllogistic progressive form*, whereby the reader is advanced (by the text) step by step in cause-and-effect fashion, as in a mystery story
2. *qualitative progressive form*, whereby the reader connects one quality to an earlier quality; the reader recognizes the rightness of one event to follow another, as in the death of Juliet after Romeo
3. *repetitive form*, which involves the restatement of a theme with new details, as in the exemplifications of size discrepancy in *Gulliver's Travels*
4. *conventional form*, whose appeal is that of form *per se*, as in a sestina, a sonnet, an invocation
5. *minor form*, which involves the natural appeal of the various figures of speech, such as metaphor, simile, synecdoche.

Any form at whatever level of discourse, from the phrase and the sentence to the paragraph and the entire work may take any of these forms. Any writer may purposely suggest fulfillment of any of these formal appeals and then surprise the reader—by denying it.

WRITERS ON WRITING

[Dr.] Johnson's esthetic judgements are almost invariably subtle, or solid, or bold, they always have some good quality to recommend them except one: they are never right.

—LYTTON STRACHEY

OPTIONAL EXERCISE

Read the following sentences, winners of the annual Bulwer-Lytton Fiction Contest for most wretched opening sentence, to your class. Start your discussion by asking the following questions: How do these sentences relate to Burke's theory of form? Do they arouse expectation or desires? Do they fulfill the reader's expectations? Do they follow one or more of the types? Do they subvert the form, allowing for an element of surprise?

> The evilly gibbous moon shed its leering light upon the moor and the running figure of Ronald Brownley who—with hands clutching the forbidden amulet and ears filled with the hellish ululations of thousands of bounding, spectral hounds—realized that it had been he, and he alone, who had cast the horribly portentous deciding vote against the town's leash law.
>
> —JOSETTE ROZANSKI

> Like an expensive sports car, fine-tuned and well-built, Portia was sleek, shapely and gorgeous, her red jumpsuit molding her body, which was as warm as the seat covers in July, her hair as dark as new tires, her eyes flashing like bright hubcaps, and her lips as dewy as the beads of fresh rain on the hood; she was a woman driven—fueled by a single accelerant—and she needed a man, a man who wouldn't shift from his views, a man to steer her along the right road: a man like Alf Romeo.
>
> —RACHEL SHEELEY

TEACHING PRACTICE

When discussing the principle of emphasizing information, you might ask your students to follow the age-old principle of "given-new": start out the sentence with understood information to give the reader a toe hold; then, introduce the new information. Joseph Williams uses the chart below to show how sentence position is linked to rhetorical emphasis.

| Previous (start————————end) Next | | |
| Sentence | | Sentence |

Topic		Stress
old/less important		new/more important
subject	verb	object
agent	action	goal

(*Style: Ten Lessons in Clarity and Grace*. 2d ed. Glenview, IL.: Scott, 1985. 65)

loaded words *tall*, *dark*, and *handsome*—only to undercut those expectations with the final *creep*.

You may want to try using such an element of surprise as one way to create effective sentences. The rest of this chapter, however, will focus on two basic devices writers use to create effective sentences by fulfilling rather than breaking expectations: *emphasis* and *conciseness*.

▌ 17a. Emphasizing main ideas

Effective sentences put the spotlight on main ideas, thus letting readers know which elements of the sentence are most important. We call this spotlighting of significant words and ideas **emphasis.** Careful control of the emphasis in each sentence will make your writing both easier and more enjoyable to read. This section focuses on the ways you can emphasize main ideas by putting them in opening and closing positions and by arranging them in climactic order.

▌ 1. Using opening and closing positions for emphasis

When you read a sentence, what are you most likely to remember? Other things being equal, you remember the end. This is the part of the sentence that should move the writing forward by providing new information, as it does in the following example:

> To protect her skin, *she took plenty of sun-block lotion.*

A less emphatic but still important position in a sentence is the opening, which hooks up the new sentence with what has come before.

> When Rosita went to the beach, she was anxious not to get a sunburn. *To protect her skin*, she took plenty of sun-block lotion.

In this example, *to protect her skin* connects the new sentence to *anxious not to get a sunburn* in the sentence before. The second sentence would lose emphasis if the key words, *plenty of sun-block lotion*, were buried in the middle, as in the following version:

> To protect her skin, *she took plenty of sun-block lotion*, and she also planned to stay under a beach umbrella most of the time.

Placing relatively unimportant information in the memorable closing position of a sentence undercuts proper emphasis or gives more em-

USEFUL READING

Coe, Richard. *Toward a Grammar of Passages*. Carbondale, IL: Southern Illinois UP, 1988. Coe has developed a two-dimensional, graphic matrix for the analysis of logical semantic relations among sentences.

Markels, Robin Bell. *A New Perspective on Cohesion in Expository Paragraphs*. Carbondale, IL: Southern Illinois UP, 1984. Investigating paragraph cohesion from a perspective that focuses both on semantics and structural (syntactic) cohesiveness, Markels offers useful alternative backgrounding to the grammatical concept of unity.

phasis to the closing words than you may intend:

> She contributed $500,000 to the campaign last month.

Revised to gain emphasis, the sentence reads:

> Last month she contributed $500,000 to the campaign.

To emphasize the amount of the contribution even more, the sentence could be reworded this way:

> Last month she gave the campaign committee $500,000.

2. Using climactic order

Presenting ideas in **climactic order** means sequencing them in order of increasing importance, power, or drama: building to climax. The following sentences show climactic order at work:

> Dissidents risk social rejection, forced relocation, long imprisonment, and almost certain death.

> The primary danger of the television screen lies not so much in the behavior it produces—although there is danger there—as in the behavior it prevents: the talks, the games, the family festivities and arguments through which much of the child's learning takes place and through which his character is formed.   —MARIE WINN,
> *The Plug-in Drug: Television, Children, and the Family*

Each of the preceding examples derives much of its power from the sequencing of its details. If the first sentence concluded with "long imprisonment" rather than "almost certain death," it would not make such an emphatic statement; similarly, the second example saves its most dramatic item for last, making its point forcefully. The following sentence includes a series that fails to achieve strong emphasis by not sequencing verbs in order of increasing power:

| UNEMPHATIC | Soap operas assault our eyes, damage our brain cells, and offend our ears. |
| REVISED | Soap operas offend our ears, assault our eyes, and damage our brain cells. |

3. Checking for emphatic sentences

As you revise a draft, make sure that each sentence emphasizes the ideas you *want* emphasized. First, identify the word or words you

TEACHING PRACTICE

You may want to discuss Burke's theory of form with your students, asking them for examples of each type. Not all their examples will come from books or stories; some may come from movies, television programs, or music videos, compelling examples that will help the entire class better understand.

WRITING TOGETHER

To demonstrate climactic order, ask your class to suggest a topic (such as the qualities of a good friend, a good car, a popular campus restaurant). Brainstorm the topic, creating a list of associations on the board. Then, ask each student to write a thesis statement for an essay describing the topic, using the pattern described in Chapter 4. Ask students to read their statements and comment on possible reasons for ordering their subtopics the way they did. You may want to take this opportunity to point out that climactic order reflects the relative importance the writer attaches to ideas.

OPTIONAL EXERCISE

Ask students to imitate the climactic form of the handbook example: *Television soap operas offend our ears, assault our eyes, and kill our brain cells.* Then after reading aloud the following sentences and examining their climactic order, ask them to write imitations.

1. I have in my own life a precious friend, a woman of 65 who has lived very hard, who is wise, who listens well, who has been where I am and can help me understand it; and who represents not only an ultimate ideal mother to me but also the person I'd like to be when I grow up. (Judith Viorst)
2. To assign unanswered letters their proper weight, to free us from the expectations of others, to give us back to ourselves—here lies the great, the singular power of self-respect. (Joan Didion)
3. She loved the flat, she loved her life, she loved Herbie. (Dorothy Parker)
4. I came, I saw, I conquered. (Julius Caesar)

USEFUL READING

Williams, Joseph M. *Style: Ten Lessons in Clarity and Grace.* 2d ed. Glenview, IL.: Scott, 1985. In Lesson Three, "The Grammar of Emphasis," Williams demonstrates ways of shifting emphasis to the end of sentences (57–62), and in Lesson Seven, "Managing Long Sentences," Williams discusses how grammatical connections (particularly subject-verb-complement patterns) contribute to smooth prose (see 140–45).

TEACHING PRACTICE

The handbook presents two of the most important and common ways of emphasizing main points or ideas in prose: opening or ending position; climactic order. Consider discussing the following additional ways to pursue emphasis.

1. Repeat key words or phrases: The old pornography was the fantasy of easy sexual delights in a world where sex was kept unavailable. The new pornography is the fantasy of easy triumph in a world where status competition has become so complicated and frustrating. (Tom Wolfe, "Pornoviolence")
2. Deliberately choose a word that breaks the level of formality: But Dick and Perry, Capote's killers, are only a couple of Low Rent bums. (Tom Wolfe, "Pornoviolence")
3. Insert a deliberate sentence fragment: If Mr. Jones has died of jaundice, the embalming fluid will very likely turn him green. Does this deter the embalmer? Not if he has intestinal fortitude. (Jessica Mitford, "Behind the Formaldehyde Curtain")
4. Use parallel constructions: Masking pastes and cosmetics are heavily laid on, burial garments and casket interiors are color-correlated with particular care, and Jones is displayed beneath rose-colored lights. (Jessica Mitford, "Behind the Formaldehyde Curtain")

want to receive special emphasis, and underline them. If those words are buried in the middle of the sentence or blurred in some way, revise the sentence to change their position, remembering that the end position is generally most emphatic.

Next, note any sentences that include a series of three or more words, phrases, or clauses. Check to see whether the items in the series could be arranged in climactic order and, if so, whether they are. If they could be but are not, decide whether the sentence would be stronger with climactic order, and rearrange if necessary.

Notice how the sentence below can be revised using these two steps:

> For a whole complex of claimed "reasons," we in the Student Senate have for years been saddled with the burdens, which we're tired of, of low budgets, no real legislative power, and a depressing room to meet in.

The main point the writer wants to emphasize, that the Student Senate is tired of being saddled with poor conditions and no power, is obscured by unemphatic placement in the middle of the sentence. A revision of it might look like this:

> We in the Student Senate are tired of being saddled, whatever the claimed "reasons," with low budgets, no real legislative power, and a depressing room to meet in.

Next, we have to look for climactic order. The items in the series at the end of the sentence do not seem to be arranged in any particular order, even though they could be. In climactic order, the meeting room is least important and the lack of power most important. So the final revision might read:

> We in the Student Senate are tired of being saddled, whatever the claimed "reasons," with a depressing room to meet in, low budgets, and no real legislative power.

EXERCISE 17.1

Revise each of the following sentences to highlight what you take to be the main or most important ideas.

Example

Tobacco companies continue to fight the antismoking campaign—through the highest courts of the land, through congressional lobbying, through local advertising.

BEING CONCISE   *es* 17b

Tobacco companies continue to fight the antismoking campaign—through local advertising, through congressional lobbying, through the highest courts of the land.

1. All seagoing vessels, whether outrigger canoes, giant aircraft carriers, or run-of-the-mill cargo ships, must be designed according to certain specifications.
2. Also notable is the image of chrysanthemums throughout the story.
3. I feel that living in the dorm was easier to adjust to than living in my condominium.
4. The presence of the Indian in these movies always conjures up destructive stereotypes of bloodthirsty war parties, horse thieves, and drunkenness.
5. Victorian women were warned that if they smoked, they would become sterile, grow a moustache, die young, contract tuberculosis, or have trouble breathing.

▌ 17b. Being concise

In general, effective sentences are as **concise** as possible. There are exceptions: on some occasions, writers want—or need—to hammer home a point or create a certain effect by using what in other situations might look like unnecessary redundancy, or repetition. In *The Elements of Style*, E. B. White uses such repetition to good effect when he says, "There is no satisfactory explanation of style, no infallible guide to good writing, . . . no key that unlocks the door, no inflexible rule by which the young writer may shape his [or her] course." So as White's advice both suggests and illustrates, every writer must decide individually when "redundancy" is worthwhile and when it is not. More often than not, however, making a point in the fewest possible words is a hallmark of effective prose. Look at the following sentence:

> It is not a mistake—nor is it incorrect—to say that the characteristics of repetition, redundancy, and saying the same thing over and over again that typify most or much or at least a great deal of writing in the modern world of today should be eliminated or done away with by every means available to the person or persons who teach these writers.

Why write that when you could instead write the following?

> Instructors should use all means of decreasing redundancy in their students' writing.

This example demonstrates how radical a change can be wrought by snipping away at the underbrush of *unnecessary* words and phrases in a sentence. Doing so involves several kinds of changes: deleting un-

297

ANSWERS TO EXERCISE 17.1 (WILL VARY)

1. All sea-going vessels must be designed according to certain specifications, whether they are outrigger canoes, giant aircraft carriers, or run-of-the-mill cargo ships.
2. Also notable throughout the story is the image of chrysanthemums.
3. I feel that adjusting to dorm life is easier than adjusting to condo life.
4. Movie Indians always conjure up destructive stereotypes of drunkenness, horse thieves, and bloodthirsty war parties.
5. Victorian women were warned that smoking would cause them to have trouble breathing, grow a mustache, contract tuberculosis, become sterile, and die young.

WRITING TOGETHER

To demonstrate that being concise may not always be preferable, discuss with your class the opening paragraph of Charles Dickens's *A Tale of Two Cities* followed by a revision by the computer program *Workbench*. Read both versions aloud, and then get the class to decide which makes a more effective opening for the novel.

> It was the best of times, it was the worst of times, it was the age of wisdom, it was the age of foolishness, it was the epoch of belief, it was the epoch of incredulity, it was the season of Light, it was the season of Darkness, it was the spring of hope, it was the winter of despair, we had everything before us, we had nothing before us, we were all going direct to Heaven, we were all going direct the other way—in short, the period was so far like the present period, that some of its noisiest authorities insisted on being received, for good or for evil, in the superlative degree of comparison only.
>
> —CHARLES DICKENS

> The times were the best and worst, wise and foolish. The era was one of belief and disbelief, light and darkness, hope and despair. Before us lay everything and nothing. We were all going direct to heaven or straight to hell. The period was so much like today that its loudest critics could describe it only in superlatives.
>
> —WORKBENCH

WRITERS ON WRITING

> Seeing the sincere affection of the mind cannot be expressed by the mouth and that no art can unfold the entire love of the heart, I am earnestly to beseech you not to measure the firmness of my faith by the fewness of my words.
>
> —JOHN LYLY

necessarily redundant words, deleting or replacing "buzzwords," replacing wordy phrases with one-word equivalents, and simplifying grammatical structures.

1. Deleting unnecessarily redundant words

Some of the most common unnecessary words are parts of redundant phrases, in which only one word of the phrase is necessary to the meaning. Such phrases include *few in number, large in size, combine together, continue on, continue to remain, repeat again, red in color,* and *free gift.* Redundancy can also result from unnecessary repetition of information that can be found elsewhere in the sentence.

REDUNDANT	*Physical aerobic exercise* is her hobby.
REVISED	*Aerobic exercise* is her hobby.
REDUNDANT	Delia sold houses at a *large 600-home* development.
REVISED	Delia sold houses at a *600-home* development.
REDUNDANT	*"Contemporary* antiques" *made recently* have been showing up more and more at auctions.
REVISED	*"Contemporary* antiques" have been showing up more and more at auctions.
REVISED	"Antiques" *made recently* have been showing up more and more at auctions.

2. Deleting or replacing buzzwords

In addition to unnecessarily redundant words, you should note another class of unnecessary words, called **buzzwords** because, while they *sound* as if they mean something, they are only "vibrating" or "buzzing" without contributing any real meaning. Common buzzword nouns include the following: *angle, area, point, aspect, case, nature, character, element, factor, field, sort, kind, situation, scope, type, thing,* and so on. The other important class of buzzwords consists of adjectives and adverbs used as all-purpose modifiers: *absolutely, definitely, really, very, quite, literally, great, awfully, fine, weird, major, central, important,* and so on. Taken together, buzzwords can build up whole sentences that say almost nothing at all:

The scope of this thing, the importance of this field, is so absolutely vital that I get really overwhelmed at the significance of the situation.

BEING CONCISE   *es* 17b

Because buzzwords tend to make your writing dull as well as wordy, use them very sparingly. When you cannot simply delete them, take the time to think of a more specific term that says exactly what you mean.

WORDY	I found that *the area of encyclopedia sales* did not offer the *sort of thing* I was looking for *in the marketing field.*
REVISED	I found that *encyclopedia sales* did not offer the *varied marketing experience* I was looking for.
WORDY	She found the apartment *quite nice in most ways,* and although she was nervous about *the situation of living alone* the friendly neighbors were *the major factor in her decision* to stay.
REVISED	She found the apartment *bright and spacious,* and although she was nervous about *living alone,* the friendly neighbors *made her decide* to stay.

3. Replacing wordy phrases

Writers sometimes fall back on wordy, stereotyped phrases, as they do on buzzwords, rather than taking time to think of a single word that will convey meaning more forcefully. Usually, such roundabout "filler" expressions only clutter up a page and put up barriers to comprehension. Here are some of the most common filler phrases and their more concise counterparts.

at the present time	now/today
at that point in time	then
in the event that	if
it is believed by many	many believe
form a consensus of opinion	agree
exhibit a tendency to	tend to
informs as to the fact that	tell

WORDY	I see no reason at this point in time why we should not rely, as has often been the case in the past, on the good offices of the mayor.
REVISED	We should rely now, as we have in the past, on the help of the mayor.

Sometimes writers resort to this kind of wordiness because they think it sounds more formal, more official. Such might have been the case in what has come to be a classic story about the dangers of wordiness.

TEACHING PRACTICE

Deciding when wordiness is effective and when it merely clutters up the page depends foremost upon the audience: first, who is reading the writing? What amount of explanation and background information does this audience need? A second factor that affects wordiness is the writer's voice or persona: to what degree does the writer want to use words to create an image of a writer as compassionate and understanding, for example, or as efficient and terse? A third factor is the writer's purpose: is the purpose to communicate as clearly and concisely as possible, or is the purpose to mollify a disgruntled customer?

On some occasions, roundabout expressions may be useful:

1. We have no competent leadership *today.* (Did we have it yesterday?)
2. We have no competent leadership *now.* (Did the competent leaders just resign?)
3. We have no competent leadership *at the present time.*

In this instance, *at the present time* is a useful phrase because it indicates that the writer is referring to a more extended period than *today.* As with stereotyped phrases, writers must decide when wordiness is effective and when it merely clutters up the page.

A plumber wrote to the Federal Bureau of Standards that he had found hydrochloric acid did a fine job of clearing out his clogged drains.

The Bureau answered: "The effectiveness and efficiency of hydrochloric acid is indisputable, but the corrosive or detrimental residue is incompatible with metallic permanence."

The plumber replied he was delighted the Bureau agreed with him.

Then the Bureau wrote: "We cannot and must not assume responsibility or admit to culpability in event of the production of toxic and noxious residue with hydrochloric acid and, therefore, recommend you use an alternate or secondary procedure."

Again the plumber responded that he was delighted that the Bureau agreed.

At last the Bureau wrote, with admirable unity, emphasis, and concision, a reply that spoke volumes to the plumber: "Don't use hydrochloric acid. It eats the hell out of the pipes."

Jargon, including corporate, bureaucratic, academic, and scientific jargon, is often the cause of wordiness. Examples of jargon include: *facilitate, viable, ambulate*.

4. Simplifying grammatical structures

Using the simplest grammatical structures possible to express your meaning will tighten and strengthen your sentences considerably. In the following sentence, for example, notice how conciseness results from reducing an adjective clause to an appositive phrase, deleting a grammatically unnecessary *to be*, and reducing an adverb phrase to a one-word adverb.

WORDY	Kennedy, *who was only the second Roman Catholic to be nominated for the presidency by a major party*, had to handle the religion issue *in a delicate manner*.
REVISED	Kennedy, *only the second Roman Catholic nominated for the presidency by a major party*, had to handle the religion issue *delicately*.

In the following example, reducing an adverb clause to an elliptical form and combining two sentences by using a compound predicate produces one concise sentence.

WORDY	When she was questioned about her previous job, she seemed nervous. She also tried to change the subject.
REVISED	When questioned about her previous job, she seemed nervous and tried to change the subject.

OPTIONAL EXERCISE

Read the following paragraph from Amanda Cross's *In the Last Analysis* aloud (the heroine, Kate Fansler, is mapping out her mystery-solving plan), and then ask your students to revise it using the simplest grammatical structures.

She felt, nonetheless, as she stood indecisively in the hall, like a knight who has set off to slay the dragon but has neglected to ask in what part of the world the dragon may be found. It was all very well to decide upon action, but what action, after all, was she to take? As was her habit, she extracted notebook and pen and began to make a list: see Janet Harrison's room, and talk to people who knew her in dormitory; find out about ten and twelve o'clock patients; find out who person in picture Janet Harrison had was (lists always had a devastating effect on Kate's syntax).

BEING CONCISE

Other ways to achieve conciseness by simplifying grammatical structures include using strong verbs and nouns, avoiding expletive constructions (those beginning with *there* or *it* followed by a form of *be*), and using the active rather than the passive voice. All of these methods are discussed in detail in Chapter 21.

5. Checking for conciseness

When you revise a draft, work on making each sentence as concise and powerful as possible. To do so, underline any unnecessarily redundant words or buzzwords that you can find. Then go back over each sentence, seeking out stereotyped phrases and other official-sounding but unnecessarily wordy language. Finally, look for grammatical structures that could be simplified. When you have identified the words and phrases that do not add directly to your meaning, rephrase or delete them until you have tightened up each sentence. In the following sentence, note how the writer has trimmed unnecessary words and phrases to produce a much shorter but a much more pithy and effective sentence:

> Her constant and continual use of the vulgar expressions with obscene meanings indicated to her pre-elementary supervisory group that she was rather deficient in terms of her ability to interact in an efficient manner with peers in her potential interaction group.

> Her constant use of "four-letter words" told the day-care workers that she might have trouble getting along with other four-year-olds.

EXERCISE 17.2

Revise each of the following sentences to make it clear and concise by eliminating unnecessary words and phrases.

Example
Let me fill you in on the main points of the overall picture here.
Let me summarize.

1. At the present time, many different forms of hazing occur, such as various forms of physical abuse and also mental abuse.
2. A prime example, it seems to me, was the seizure of American hostages by Iranian radicals, which resulted in the death of eight Marines who died as a result of a disastrous rescue attempt.
3. One of the major problems that is faced at this point in time is that there is world hunger.

ANSWERS TO EXERCISE 17.2 (WILL VARY)

1. Many forms of hazing occur, such as physical and mental abuse.
2. A prime example was the rescue attempt of the American hostages in Iran that resulted in the death of eight Marines.
3. World hunger is a major problem.
4. I put on ten pounds immediately after I stopped exercising.
5. Even children who are scolded often persist in performing the forbidden act.
6. To check the engine, listen for rattling or pinging noises.
7. Rarely do skiers get perfect snow for skiing: deep and powdery.
8. Randall exposes the injustices that confront American blacks.
9. Human beings are social animals: despite adequate food and water, an isolated person would eventually die of loneliness. However, the forced constant companionship of two people would also be unhealthy.
10. Waitressing for six hours, followed by mopping and sweeping half a restaurant, can lead to exhaustion.

4. After I stopped the practice of exercising regularly, I became ten pounds heavier in weight in a relatively short amount of time.

5. It frequently happens that a child can be scolded a numerous amount of times for doing something wrong, and he or she will persist in performing the forbidden act.

6. The way in which one goes about checking the engine is to listen for rattling or pinging noises.

7. A situation of quality, deep-powder snow symbolizes a goal that is not easily attainable by skiers and that they can achieve only in rare cases.

8. It is Randall's approach that exposes the injustices with which the black American is confronted.

9. Humans are very socially oriented beings; this statement is substantiated by the fact that a person left completely alone in a room with adequate food and water would eventually die from the lack of social interaction. However, the opposite end of the social interaction concept relates to the idea that the case of two people forced to be together all of the time is not healthy either.

10. Sweeping and mopping half a restaurant after running around waitressing for five or six hours is enough to give occasion for an exhaustive collapse.

ANSWERS TO EXERCISE 17.3 WILL VARY

EXERCISE 17.3

Read over Colleen Starkey's essay in 3i, paying attention to the sentences. Then choose a paragraph, and evaluate its sentences in terms of emphasis and conciseness. Try to find a paragraph that you think might be made more emphatic or more concise, and revise accordingly.

TEACHING PRACTICE

Ask students to bring their imitation sentences to class. Duplicate some or all of them, read them aloud, and use them to stimulate class discussion of and appreciation for powerfully constructed sentences. You might also wish to ask students to match the imitations to the models, clause for clause, phrase for phrase, as a means of identifying structural elements in sentences.

READING WITH AN EYE FOR SENTENCE STYLE

Here are some sentences from "Memory and Imagination," Patricia Hampl's essay about memoir writing. (You will recognize the example sentence from the opening of this chapter.) Each sentence makes a powerfully emphatic statement. Read each one, and decide how Hampl achieves such uncommonly strong emphasis. Then choose one to use as a model for writing a sentence of your own.

Example

I sometimes think of the reader as a cat, endlessly fastidious, capable, by turns, of mordant indifference and riveted attention, luxurious, recumbent, and ever poised.

I sometimes think of television as a shrew, incessantly noisy, demanding attention at all times to its advertising and mindless programming, insistently shrill, forever heckling.

BEING CONCISE

1. We wish to talk to each other about life and death, about love, despair, loss, and innocence.
2. The heart, the guardian of intuition with its secret, often fearful intentions, is the boss.
3. I am forced to admit that memoir is not a matter of transcription, that memory itself is not a warehouse of finished stories, not a static gallery of framed pictures.

FOR EXAMINING SENTENCE EFFECTIVENESS IN YOUR OWN WRITING

Study two or three paragraphs you have written recently to determine how emphatic and effectively concise each sentence is. Using the suggestions in this chapter, revise your paragraphs, making each sentence as emphatic and concise as possible.

18. Creating Coordinate and Subordinate Structures

(BACK)GROUNDING

Current pedagogical theory values clarity and conciseness. Yet, composition researchers tell us that complex sentences indicate a writer's syntactic maturity. Are we sending our students mixed messages, then? No. The two concepts are not necessarily contradictory: Beginning writers often use clarity and conciseness to make meaning; more mature writers can use those same qualities to grace their more complex sentence structures.

The notion that subordination and complex sentence structures indicate sophistication of thought and language ability, or maturity in the writer, needs some qualification, if only historical. In Old and Middle English, subordination was not expected, nor was it used to measure a writer's skill. In *Classical Rhetoric for the Modern Student*, 2nd ed., Edward P. J. Corbett tells us that "the history of the prose style of most Western languages reveals a gradual evolution from a paratactic syntax—stringing together a series of coordinate structures without conjunctions—to the most sophisticated of sentence patterns, subordination" (441).

Creating effective sentences calls on a writer to act as a conductor, directing the arrangement and flow of verbal passages just as the conductor of an orchestra does with musical passages. Such effective orchestration very often involves creating sentences that use *coordinate* and *subordinate* structures. **Coordinate structures** give essentially equal importance to two or more words, phrases, or clauses, often linking them together with coordinating conjunctions like *and* or *but*. In the following sentence, linking the two clauses with *but* gives them equal significance:

> Freud's theories cannot be proved by laboratory experiment, but their "rightness" can be sensed in myths and legends.

Subordinate structures create different levels of significance, stressing some ideas by expressing them in independent clauses or in key nouns or verbs and subordinating others by putting them into dependent clauses, phrases, or single words. In the following sentence, beginning the first clause with *although* subordinates the idea in that clause to the one in the second clause.

> Although Freud's theories cannot be proved by laboratory experiment, their "rightness" can be sensed in myths and legends.

Learning to use different kinds of coordinate and subordinate structures will increase your sentence repertoire and allow you to write varied, interesting, and effective sentences. Look, for instance, at the following sentences:

> Kit went through the new part of the library to the old.
> He walked around for a while.

304

USEFUL READING

Bennett, James R., ed. *Prose Style: A Historical Approach Through Studies.* San Francisco: Chandler, 1971. Excerpts Samuel Workman's book on the rise of greater sentence complexity as well as a number of other works, arranged chronologically.

Then he went to the periodical section.
He started looking at the *Times* on microfilm.

We could choose to combine these sentences in several ways:

Using coordination

Kit went through the new part of the library to the old, and he walked around for a while; then he went to the periodical section and started looking at the *Times* on microfilm.

Using subordination

After going through the new part of the library to the old and walking around for a while, Kit went to the periodical section, where he started looking at the *Times* on microfilm.

Of course, these sentences could be combined in a number of other ways as well, but these two will serve to illustrate how coordinate structures differ from subordinate structures. In the example that uses coordination, the four actions of going through the new part of the library to the old, walking around, going to the periodical section, and looking at the *Times* are all given the same emphasis or importance by being placed in three independent clauses, the last of which has a compound predicate. The second combination gives a different emphasis to the sentence, suggesting that Kit's destination, the periodical section, is most important. The action of his going there is expressed in an independent clause, whereas the other three actions are given less emphasis by being placed in a prepositional phrase (with compound gerund-phrase objects) and a dependent clause.

In addition to indicating emphasis, coordination and subordination can be used to create special, sometimes dramatic effects in writing. As a writer, you must often decide whether to use coordination, subordination, both, or neither, depending on which structure provides the emphasis and effect you want to achieve. This chapter will furnish you with some guidelines for using these structures appropriately.

18a. Using coordination to relate equal ideas

What can you say about the following passage?

It was my birthday today, and I took cupcakes to school, and I wore a birthday crown, and we ate cupcakes, and we sang "Happy Birthday," and I sat in the middle, and I'm six years old.

305

USEFUL READING

Traugott, Lee Elizabeth Closs, and Mary Louise Pratt. *Linguistics for Students of Literature.* New York: Harcourt, 1980. 154–55. See the discussion on the "recursive property of language" for a transformational-linguistics perspective on coordination and subordination. Traugott and Pratt call subordination and coordination "linguistic creativity," that is, the ability to create complex sentences out of simple sentences by applying the generative principles of "recursiveness."

(BACK)GROUNDING

In *Teaching English Grammar* (New York: Appleton, 1957), Robert C. Pooley cites passages from the King James Version (KJV) of the Bible as examples of the predominance of coordination over subordination in earlier English, not knowing that that particular translation reflects the sentence structure of the original Hebrew, not English. John B. Gabel and Charles B. Wheeler tell us that "in general [Hebrew] lacks our great variety of words that indicate logical connections between clauses and phrases. In Hebrew narrative, sentence units tend to string out one after another in boxcar fashion and to be hooked together by means of a single, all-purpose connective that is usually translated 'and' in the KJV" (*The Bible As Literature: An Introduction*, New York: Oxford UP, 1986). For example, Genesis 19: 1–3 repeats that connective seventeen times in Hebrew; in the KJV, it appears as "and" sixteen of those times.

(1) And there came two angels to Sodom at even; and Lot sat in the gate of Sodom: and Lot seeing *them* rose up to meet them; and he bowed himself with his face toward the ground; (2) And he said, Behold now, my lords, turn in, I pray you, into your servant's house, and tarry all night, and wash your feet, and ye shall rise up early, and go on your ways. And they said, Nay; but we will abide in the street all night. (3) And he pressed upon them greatly; and they turned in unto him, and entered into his house; and he made them a feast, and did bake unleavened bread, and they did eat.

TEACHING PRACTICE

Students tend to have little problem understanding coordination, dependent as they usually are upon a few all-purpose connectors like *and* or *but*. Since some students overuse coordination, you may want to emphasize their striking a balance among coordinated, subordinated, and simple constructions. A variety of sentence patterns should be a writer's goal, unless the writer desires the rhetorical effect achieved by the predominance of one kind of construction. (See 18b.)

TEACHING PRACTICE

In *Style: Ten Lessons in Clarity and Grace*, Joseph Williams cites another problem connected with co-ordination: "lost connections" (134–35). When the grammatical coordination of a sentence becomes too long, the reader cannot follow its internal connections. He uses the following sentence as an example: "Every teacher ought to remind himself daily that his students are vulnerable people, insecure and uncertain about those everyday, ego-bruising moments that adults no longer concern themselves with, **and that they do not understand that one day they** will become as confident and as secure as the adults that bruise them." According to Williams, placement of that boldface clause is troublesome because it is not close enough to its source of coordination. And he offers two possible revisions: repetition of a key phrase or starting a new sentence. "Every teacher ought to *remind* himself daily that his students are vulnerable people, . . . and *to remind himself* that his students do not understand. . . . (or) . . . adults no longer concern themselves with. Teachers should remind themselves that their students do not understand." (134)

WRITING TOGETHER

As a class, identify the coordinate elements of the following passage, taken from Mark Twain's "Jim Smiley and His Jumping Frog." What is their effect? Ask your students to rewrite the passage, using subordination to create a different effect—from the point of view, perhaps, of the Society for the Prevention of Cruelty to Animals.

> *And* [Smiley] had a little small bull-pup, that to look at him you'd think he warn't worth a cent, *but* to set around and look ornery, *and* lay for a chance to steal something. *But* as soon as money was set up on him he was a different dog—his jaw'd begin to stick out like the for'castle of a steamboat, *and* his teeth would uncover, *and* shine savage like the furnaces. *And* a dog might tackle him, *and* bully-rag him, *and* bite him, *and* throw him over his shoulder two or three times, *and* Andrew Jackson—which was the name of the pup—Andrew Jackson would let on but what he was satisfied, *and* hadn't expected nothing else— *and* the bets being doubled *and* doubled on the other side all the time, till the money was all up— *and* then all of a sudden he would grab that other dog just by the joint of his hind legs *and* freeze to it—not chaw, you understand, *but* only just grip *and* hang on till they throwed up the sponge, if it was a year.

We realize early on that the writer is a child—or someone writing from a child's point of view. Because the passage mentions cupcakes and school and a crown, we make this assumption even before we find out, in the last clause, that the writer is six years old. But the *style* of this passage, as well as its content, helps identify the writer. We get a clue from the seven short independent clauses strung together like beads with the coordinating conjunction *and*, a style typical of young writers who are learning to sequence events in a story. Note that aside from the clue "I'm six years old" at the very end of the sentence (generally an emphatic spot), we are given no grammatical signals to tell us how these clauses rank in importance. Were the cupcakes most significant to the writer? the birthday crown? We cannot tell, because the coordinate structure makes all the clauses grammatical equals.

Not all coordination must sound like "Run, Spot, run," however. When used well, coordinate structures relate separate but equal elements, making clear the emphasis given to different ideas. The precise relationship is stated in the element that links the ideas, usually a coordinating conjunction (*and, but, for, nor, or, so, yet*) or a semicolon. The following sentences by N. Scott Momaday all use coordination, but note that the precise relationship between clauses differs in each sentence as expressed in the connecting element:

> They acquired horses, *and* their ancient nomadic spirit was suddenly free of the ground.

> There is perfect freedom in the mountains, *but* it belongs to the eagle and the elk, the badger and the bear.

> No longer were they slaves to the simple necessity of survival; they were a lordly and dangerous society of fighters and thieves, hunters and priests of the sun.   –N. SCOTT MOMADAY, "The Way to Rainy Mountain"

1. Using coordination for special effect

Coordination can also be used to create special effects. Note the way in which coordination creates a particular effect in a passage by Carl Sandburg describing the reaction of the American people to Abraham Lincoln's assassination:

> Men tried to talk about it and the words failed and they came back to silence.
> To say nothing was best.
> Lincoln was dead.
> Was there anything more to say?

USEFUL READING

Lanham, Richard A. *Analyzing Prose.* New York: Scribner's, 1983. Lanham attacks the dominant theory of prose style, which values clarity, brevity, and sincerity. Instead, Lanham calls for use of a variety of different styles, depending upon the desired rhetorical effects.

Williams, Joseph M. *Style: Ten Lessons in Clarity and Grace.* 2nd ed. Glenview, IL: Scott, 1981. Chapter 4 offers advice for the control of "sprawling" sentences, the result of a main clause connected to too many subordinate clauses.

USING COORDINATION

Yes, they would go through the motions of grief and they would take part in a national funeral and a ceremony of humiliation and abasement and tears.

But words were no help.

Lincoln was dead.   –CARL SANDBURG, *The War Years*

Together with the other short simple sentences, the coordinate clauses, phrases, and words in sentences 1 and 5 create a very definite effect: everything in the passage is grammatically equal, flattened out by the pain and shock of the death. In this way, the sentence structure and grammar mirror the dazed state of the populace. The short sentences and clauses are almost like sobs and illustrate the thought of sentence 1, that "the words failed." Here coordination is used to create a very powerful effect.

The formal name for the conspicuous use of conjunctions to join words, phrases, or clauses is **polysyndeton**, from Greek *poly* ("many") *syndeton* ("connectives.") Following are some additional examples:

Satan pursues his way. And swims, or sinks, or wades, or creeps, or flies.   –MILTON, *Paradise Lost*

Here the use of coordination piles up images of movement, giving the impression that Satan can use *any* kind of movement and cannot be stopped.

He [the writer] must teach himself that the basest of all things is to be afraid; and, teaching himself that, forget it forever, leaving no room in his workshop for anything but the old verities and truths of the heart, the old universal truths lacking which any story is ephemeral and doomed—*love and honor and pity and pride and compassion and sacrifice*.   –WILLIAM FAULKNER, Nobel Prize Acceptance Speech

Here the repetition of the coordinating conjunction *and* creates a solemn rhythm, almost like the tolling of a bell.

Are you familiar with Motel 8? It's a chain of cheesy cheap motels across the South—twenty dollars a night gets you peeling beaverboard walls *and* thin pink blankets. There's no phone in the room, *but* a TV set that's always tuned to the Nashville Channel, *and* an air conditioner that's always got a screw or three loose *and* vibrates like a 747 on takeoff. You see piles of emptied cigarette butts in the parking lot, *and* always cigarette burns on the table, *and* more cigarette burns on the carpet, *and* a poorly repaired hole in the wall where some redneck put his fist through it in anger at his pregnant sixteen-year-old wife who didn't wanna go out to the Ponderosa.

WRITERS ON WRITING
Most of the basic material a writer works with is acquired before the age of fifteen.

—WILLA CATHER

TEACHING PRACTICE
Before you read the following paragraph from Don Marquis' "The Old Soak's History of the World" to the class, ask them to listen for coordinating and subordinating elements. Ask them, too, to listen for the elements of spoken language that are in this passage. Your students will be surprised at their facility for differentiating between spoken and written discourse. Is there a tendency to use coordinate elements in spoken discourse and subordinate, in written?

One difference of the old days in the early times of the world whose history I am going to write is that they didn't have no glass bottles, they kept it in jugs and skins which they was bladders I guess like they keep oil and putty in nowadays and they drunk it right out of the jug. Well, I have drunk cider that a way, and oncet I run onto a gang of Scandinavians building a barn and them fellows was drinking equival parts of sweet cider and straight alkohawl mixed right out of a jug and Oh boy! what a head ache you can get out of that stuff.

WRITERS ON WRITING
However great a [person's] natural talent may be, the art of writing cannot be learned all at once.

—JEAN JACQUES ROUSSEAU

Here the use of *and* and *but* results in a catalogue of colorful, if somewhat unsavory, detail. By stringing together images in this way, the author presents them in a kind of heap, which contributes to the overall impression of the Motel 8.

2. Revising for more effective coordination

As you revise, consider the relative importance of the different ideas within each sentence. How many coordinate structures can you identify in the draft? If you find few, see whether any ideas or elements should be linked in some way. If you find that you depend primarily on coordination rather than subordination to link ideas, does the draft sound jerky or unnatural? Should any of the coordinate structures be deleted or changed to subordinate ones?

You can answer this last question by taking the following steps. Underline all of the coordinating conjunctions (*and, but, for, nor, or, so, yet*) or semicolons. Now look on either side of each conjunction, and ask yourself two questions. First, does the conjunction link words, phrases, or clauses that really need to be related? Second, are the words, phrases, or clauses linked by the conjunction *equally important* ideas? If the answer to either of these questions is no, revise the sentence to eliminate the coordinate structure or to substitute a subordinate one. Notice how the following passage can be analyzed and revised.

> Part of the problem is that spring semester is a heavy semester for me, <u>and</u> I have five courses, <u>but</u> part of the problem is that I just promised too much to too many people, <u>so</u> I have to do a lot of other library work too. In addition, I had to begin wearing that back brace, <u>and</u> it's making my skin sore, <u>and</u> each night I have to come home <u>and</u> take it off, <u>and</u> that takes time, <u>or</u> I have to go out to the library.

This passage depends too heavily on coordination, which obscures the ways in which the ideas in the sentences relate to one another. Rewritten, with more subordinate structures and with the first sentence separated into two sentences with the coordinating conjunction *but* replaced by the conjunctive adverb *though*, the passage reads more clearly.

> Part of the problem is that spring semester is a heavy semester for me, with five courses. Part of the problem, though, is that I just promised too much to too many people, so I have to do a lot of other work, especially in the library at night. In addition, I had to begin wearing that back brace, which makes my skin sore, and when I come home each night, I have to spend time taking it off.

Consider sharing the following excerpt from William Gass's *Habitations of the Word* to demonstrate how the coordinating conjunction *and* can be used for special effect:

'Ands'

are most essential for excess. They are perfect if you want to make big piles or imply an endless addition. One "and" may make a tidy pair, closing a couple like a lock: *War and Peace*, ham and eggs, *Pride and Prejudice*. Add another, however, and the third "and" will begin to alter the earlier ones the same miraculous way the squashed and flattened condition designated by "mashed" is lent the fully contrasting sense of "heaped" simply by putting it near the word "potato." No one is any better at this energetic mounding than the Dickens of *Dombey*. Here is part of a long passage describing the ruination of a neighborhood by some new-laid railroad tracks. It implies he is not telling us the half of it:

There were frowzy fields, and cow-houses, and dunghills, and dust-heaps, and ditches, and gardens, and summerhouses, and carpet-beating grounds, at the very door of the railway. Little tumuli of oyster shells in the oyster season, and of lobster shells in the lobster season, and of broken crockery and faded cabbage in all seasons, encroached upon its high places. Posts, and rails, and old cautions to trespassers, and backs of mean houses, and patches of wretched vegetation, stared it out of countenance.

USING COORDINATION   *co* 18a

If you think you are using too many coordinating conjunctions in your own writing, turn to 18b for advice about using subordination.

In addition to checking for excessive and insufficient coordination, check to see that the relationship between coordinated elements of a sentence is clear and makes sense. Look at the following sentence:

> Watching television is a good way to spend some leisure time and makes viewers apathetic.

The relationship of the ideas here is confusing. What does being a good way to spend leisure time have to do with making viewers apathetic? This sentence might be revised in either of the following ways:

> Watching television is a good way to spend some leisure time, but excessive watching makes viewers apathetic and indifferent to their real lives.

> Although watching television is a good way to spend some leisure time, excessive watching makes viewers apathetic and indifferent to their real lives.

Notice that the revisions not only signal a contrast by using *but* or *although* but also add information to explain *apathetic*.

EXERCISE 18.1

Many of the ideas in the following passage are related in ways that are not made clear. Revise the passage by using coordinate structures, where appropriate, to clarify the relationships between equally important ideas.

> We came to the Friday Candlelight Dinner. We had a wonderful meal. We got a tour from Bud that we both found quite moving. We came away with very good memories of Quaker Village. We came away with very good memories of the people we had met there, all of whom seemed to go out of their way to be pleasant. On Monday, a Visa slip came for me in the mail. It indicated that I would be charged $48.00 despite my cancellation of two of the reservations. I called to ask if this bill was a mistake. I engaged in a conversation with Sophie that was deeply disturbing. She told me then that the Candlelight Dinner had a 48-hour cancellation policy. She told me that both Dori and I had been charged the full $48.00 for the dinner. She refused to consider any argument. I argued that I had never been told about the policy. I said that if I had known about it, I could have brought two other friends on Friday. That way the meals would not have been wasted. I was told repeatedly that this was the policy. I was told that I should have known the policy. I was told that she had been too busy to tell me the policy when I called Thursday to cancel the reservations. It was, to tell the truth, like a scene from Kafka.

ANSWERS TO EXERCISE 18.1 WILL VARY

(BACK)GROUNDING

Exercise 18.1 is a variation on *sentence combining*, an application of transformational-generative grammar, based on the hypothesis that humans transform sentences intuitively by adding to, deleting from, and rearranging kernel sentences. Sentence-combining exercises should never be graded, for they allow students a risk-free way to practice generating a variety of syntactic structures. These exercises can be given as homework or as writing log entries.

USEFUL READING

Ong, Walter J., S. J. *Orality and Literacy*. London: Methuen, 1982. 37. In chapter 3, "Some Psychodynamics of Orality," Ong discusses the additive rather than subordinative nature of oral discourse.

Winterowd, Ross. "The Grammar of Coherence." *CE* 31 (1970): 328–35. Transformational grammar does not fully explain the coherence of units of discourse. Seven transitional relations account for coherence: coordinate expressed (*and*); obversive (*but*); causative (*for*); conclusive (*so*); alternative (*or*); inclusive (the colon); and sequential (*first . . . second*).

ANSWERS TO EXERCISE 18.2 (WILL VARY)

The bull riding arena was fairly crowded, but this made no impression on me, for I had made a decision. It was now time to prove myself, and I was scared. I walked to the entry window, and I laid my money on the counter. The clerk held up a Stetson hat filled with slips of paper. I reached in and picked one. The slip held the number of the bull I was to ride, so I headed towards the stock corral.

WRITERS ON WRITING

I was a boy with too many words on my mind and no one to trust.

—RICHARD RODRIGUEZ

(BACK)GROUNDING

In *Errors & Expectations*, Mina P. Shaughnessy describes subordination in terms of the demands it makes upon the student writer:

If the dependent unit comes first in the sentence, the writer must suspend the independent unit in his mind while he qualifies it (as with introductory adverbial phrases and clauses). If the dependent unit comes between the subject and predicate of the base sentence (as with a relative clause after the subject), the writer must hold the main subject in his mind while he writes out the subject and predicate of the qualifying clause, and then he must return to the predicate of the base sentence. These operations require a memory for written words and grammatical structures that the inexperienced writer may not have. He hears what he says easily enough, but he does not as easily recall what he has written once his hand has moved on to another part of the sentence, and like the experienced writer, he is not in the habit of reviewing what he has written but instead moves headlong, as a speaker might, toward the open line, often forgetting the constraints he has set for himself a few words back.

Students react to these demands in different ways, of course. Some will shy away from the complexity and rely as much as possible on simple and compound structures. Others, motivated by a perceived need to write academic-sounding discourse, will produce what Shaughnessy calls "ruptured" or garbled sentences. Shaughnessy offers several options for the teacher: drills and grammatical explanations, sentence-combining exercises, and other types of exercises. But she concludes that the most improvement may occur when the student commits herself to communicating with her reader, despite "the exasperating literalism of the medium" (89).

EXERCISE 18.2

Using the principles of coordination to signal equal importance or to create special emphasis, combine and revise the following twelve short sentences into several longer and more effective ones. Add or delete words if you need to.

The bull-riding arena was fairly crowded.
The crowd made no impression on me.
I had made a decision.
It was now time to prove myself.
I was scared.
I walked to the entry window.
I laid my money on the counter.
The clerk held up a Stetson hat filled with slips of paper.
I reached in.
I picked one.
The slip held the number of the bull I was to ride.
I headed toward the stock corral.

18b. Using subordination to distinguish main ideas

Subordination provides the means of distinguishing major points from minor points or bringing in supporting context or details. If, for instance, you put your main idea in an independent clause, you might then put any lesser ideas in dependent clauses, phrases, or even single words. Look, for instance, at the following sentence by Maya Angelou, which shows the subordinated point in italics:

Mrs. Viola Cullinan was a plump woman *who lived in a three-bedroom house somewhere behind the post office.*

—MAYA ANGELOU, "My Name is Margaret"

In this sentence, the dependent clause adds information about Mrs. Cullinan. While the information is important, it is grammatically subordinate to the independent clause, which carries the main idea: *Mrs. Viola Cullinan was a plump woman.*

Notice that the choice of what to subordinate rests with the writer and depends on the intended meaning. Angelou might have given the same basic information differently: *Mrs. Viola Cullinan, a plump woman, lived in a three-bedroom house somewhere behind the post office.* Subordinating the information about Mrs. Cullinan's size to that about her house would have resulted in a slightly different meaning, of

310

USEFUL READING

O'Hare, Frank. *Sentence Combining: Improving Student Writing without Formal Grammar Instruction.* Urbana, IL: NCTE, 1973. O'Hare studied sentence combining in seventh-grade classes. Especially notable about his study is the absence of any formal grammar instruction. His book provides a full explanation of sentence combining and sample lessons.

Shaughnessy, Mina P. *Errors & Expectations: A Guide for the Teacher of Basic Writing.* New York: Oxford UP, 1977.

USING SUBORDINATION   *sub* 18b

course. As a writer, you must think carefully about where you want your emphasis to be and subordinate accordingly.

Besides adding information, subordination also helps establish logical relationships among the facts in a sentence. These relationships are often specified by the subordinating conjunctions introducing many dependent clauses—words such as *after*, *because*, or *so* (see 6b7 for a complete list). Look, for example, at two more sentences from Maya Angelou, shown with the subordinate clauses italicized and the subordinating conjunctions underlined.

> I left the front door wide open <u>so</u> *all the neighbors could hear.* She usually rested her smile until late afternoon <u>when</u> *her women friends dropped in and Miss Glory, the cook, served them cold drinks on the closed-in porch.*
> —MAYA ANGELOU, "My Name is Margaret"

Subordination can be used to combine short sentences in ways that signal logical relationships. For example:

SEPARATE SENTENCES

Todd tried to explain the frying process.

I was mesmerized by the blast of heat.

The heat billowed from the vat of grease.

COMBINED SENTENCE

While Todd tried to explain the frying process, I was mesmerized by the blast of heat *that* billowed from the vat of grease.

Depending on what grammatical structures you use to subordinate, you can call attention to a less important element of a sentence in various ways, as the following series demonstrates:

The Parks Council report was persuasively written. It contained five typed pages. [no subordination]

The Parks Council report, *which contained five typed pages*, was persuasively written. [clause]

The Parks Council report, *containing five typed pages*, was persuasively written. [participial phrase]

The *five-page* Parks Council report was persuasively written. [single-word modifier]

The Parks Council report, *five typed pages*, was persuasively written. [appositive]

(BACK)GROUNDING

Traditionally, teachers have assumed that grammar reflected logical thinking—that use of subordination should include subordinate ideas, with the most important ideas going in the main clause, and that coordination juxtaposed two ideas of equal rank. Linguists, however, hold that grammar is not necessarily logical. In "Coordination (Faulty) and Subordination (Upside Down)," James Sledd writes that "the traditional theory of clauses is simply untenable" (CCC 7 [1956]: 181–87). Subordinate ideas can and often do show up in main clauses, and main ideas can appear in subordinate clauses, as indicated in the opening sentences of this (Back)grounding.

WRITERS ON WRITING

Writers, real writers, I thought, lived in New York or Paris; they smoked on the back jackets of library books, their chores done.
—RICHARD RODRIGUEZ

ANSWERS TO EXERCISE 18.3 (WILL VARY)

1. When I entered the hospital room, I was shocked by the tubes and life-support machines everywhere.
2. When Entwhistle and Townshend met singer and guitarist Roger Daltrey, they formed a group called the High Numbers.
3. After my boss poured gravel into the seventy-foot-long ditch we had dug, I leveled the gravel with a shovel.
4. *Working*, an important book by Studs Terkel, examines the situation of the American worker.
5. The snow-capped mountains, green pastures, and deep, fish-filled lakes make the park a beautiful and ideal spot to spend spring break.

WRITERS ON WRITING

The secret of popular writing is never to put more on a given page than the common reader can lap off it with no strain *whatsoever* on his habitually slack attention.

—EZRA POUND

ANSWERS TO EXERCISE 18.4 WILL VARY

EXERCISE 18.3

Combine each of the following sets of sentences into one sentence that uses subordination to signal the relationships among ideas.

> *Example*
> I was looking over my books.
> I noticed that *Burr* was missing.
> This book is a favorite of my roommate's.
>
> While I was looking over my books, I noticed that *Burr*, one of my roommate's favorite books, was missing.

1. I entered the hospital room.
   I was shocked.
   Tubes and life-support machines filled the room.
2. Entwistle and Townshend met Roger Daltrey.
   Roger Daltrey played guitar and sang.
   They formed a group called the High Numbers.
3. We had dug a seventy-foot ditch.
   My boss would pour gravel into the ditch.
   I would level the gravel with a shovel.
4. *Working* was written by Studs Terkel.
   It is an important book.
   It examines the situation of the American worker.
5. The scenery in there is beautiful.
   The mountains have caps of snow.
   The lakes are deep and full of fish.
   The pastures are green.
   It is an ideal spot to spend spring break.

EXERCISE 18.4

Revise the following paragraph, subordinating the less important ideas to the more important where appropriate.

I stayed with my friend Louise. She owns a huge mangy wolf. It is actually a seven-eighths wolf cross. The poor creature is allergic to everything. It looks like a shabby, moth-eaten exhibit of a stuffed wolf in a third-rate museum. Louise and Bill feed it rice and raw potatoes. It slavers all over everything. It snaps up the pieces of potato. It never goes out of the house. It sleeps on the beds. They are covered with animal hair. It makes no sounds. It just looks at you with those sunken, wild eyes. It is not dangerous or ferocious. It is just completely miserable. This animal should never have been born. It's trying to tell you that with every twitch.

USING SUBORDINATION

sub 18b

1. Using subordination for special effect

Carefully used subordination can create powerful effects. Some particularly fine examples come from Martin Luther King, Jr. In the following passage he piles up dependent clauses to gain emphasis for his main statement, given in the independent clause. This emphasis is heightened by the repetition of the subordinating conjunction *when* to suggest forcefully, "why we find it difficult to wait."

> Perhaps it is easy for those who have never felt the stinging darts of segregation to say, "Wait." But *when* you have seen vicious mobs lynch your mothers and fathers at will and drown your sisters and brothers at whim; *when* you have seen hate-filled policemen curse, kick, and even kill your black brothers and sisters; . . . *when* you have to concoct an answer for a five-year-old son who is asking: "Daddy, why do white people treat colored people so mean?"; *when* you take a cross-country drive and find it necessary to sleep night after night in the uncomfortable corners of your automobile because no motel will accept you; . . . *when* your first name becomes "nigger," your middle name becomes "boy" (however old you are) and your last name becomes "John," and your wife and mother are never given the respected title "Mrs."; . . . *when* you are forever fighting a degenerating sense of "nobodiness"—then you will understand why we find it difficult to wait.
>
> –Martin Luther King, Jr., "Letter from Birmingham Jail"

Look now at a student example that uses subordination in a similar way:

> *Though* dogs are messy and hard to train, *though* they chew up my shoes and give me the blues, *though* they howl like wolves but jump at their own shadows, *though* they eat me out of house and home—still, I love them all.

A dependent clause can also be used to create an ironic effect if it somehow undercuts the independent clause. Probably no American writer was better at using this technique than Mark Twain. In a tongue-in-cheek commencement address, Twain once opened a paragraph with this sentence (which you can see in context in 12f as an example of a shift in tone):

> Always obey your parents, *when they are present*.
>
> –Mark Twain, "Advice to Youth"

In undercutting the parental authority asserted in the independent

WRITERS ON WRITING

I have had a lot of fun with the American language; it has fascinating idioms, is constantly creative, very much like the English of Shakespeare's time, its slang and argot are wonderful.

—RAYMOND CHANDLER

WRITERS WRITING

Although he maintains he has nothing to say in an empty and meaningless world, author-dramatist Samuel Beckett has just published (1988) a new work in France. The ten-page book, titled *L'Image*, consists of a single 1,200-word sentence.

WRITERS ON WRITING

A thing well said will be wit in all languages.

—JOHN DRYDEN

WRITING TOGETHER

The dominant prose form in late Anglo-Saxon England was the sermon. The most impressive surviving sermon of the age, a blast warning at once horrifying in its detail and arresting in its complete conviction, is Wulfstan's *Sermo Lupi ad Anglos* (*The Sermon of the Wolf to the English* [c. A.D. 1002]). Consider the syntax of the following passage for its use of coordinate sentences. Read it aloud. Then, ask your students to revise it, using subordination wherever possible. Ask them to read aloud their revisions. What are the audible differences between the original and the revisions?

> Understand . . . completely that the devil has deceived his people too much, and that there has been little faith among men, though they speak fair words, and too many crimes have gone unchecked in the land. And there were never many men who considered what steps should be taken as earnestly as one ought to do, but each day one added evil to evil and committed crime and much injustice altogether too widely throughout all this nation. And also we have for that reason endured many injuries and insults, and if we shall look for any remedy then we must deserve better of God than we have done hitherto. Because with great deservings we have earned the miseries which lie upon us, and with very great deservings we must obtain the remedy at the hands of God if henceforth things shall become better.

clause, this dependent clause creates irony—and makes us laugh. Now look at a student writer's use of the same technique:

> Never eat fattening foods—*unless you are hungry*.

2. Revising for more effective subordination

When you are revising a draft, it is a good idea to give some attention to the way you use subordination, especially if you tend to use too many short sentences or coordinate structures. Begin by figuring out which of your ideas are most important. Take a page of your draft, and underline the main ideas. You may find it useful to underline major ideas twice, lesser ones once. If the ideas marked as *most* important do not appear in independent clauses, revise the page so that they do. Subordinate the less important ideas by putting them in dependent clauses or phrases. If ideas are of equal importance, turn back to 18a2 for advice.

Study the following passage from an essay about Edgar Allan Poe's "William Wilson," a strange tale about a young man who meets his double. Notice how the paragraph can be revised in order to connect and order its ideas more effectively.

> In the following years at the academy, <u>the two William Wilsons shared a bizarre relationship.</u> <u>The second Wilson established himself as equal to the first.</u> He was equal both in the classroom and on the playground. The first Wilson was used to feeling superior to his schoolmates, so <u>he was quite disturbed at the thought of having an equal.</u> He was especially disturbed that this equal had the same name and birthdate.

This passage depends heavily on simple sentences and use of simple coordination. Underlining the most important ideas gives the writer an idea of what might be subordinated to them, and the revision changes three of the less important ideas into prepositional phrases, an adjective clause, and an appositive phrase (shown here in italics).

> In the following years at the academy, the two William Wilsons shared a bizarre relationship. The second Wilson established himself as equal to the first, *both in the classroom and on the playground*. The first Wilson, *who was used to feeling superior to his schoolmates*, was quite disturbed at the thought of having an equal, *especially one with the same name and birthdate*.

In addition to checking for places where subordination might be more effective than coordination or separate sentences, you need to

---

USEFUL READING

Witte, Stephen P. "Topical Structure and Revision: An Exploratory Study." *CCC* 34 (1983): 313–41. For an in-depth look at one method of identifying topics in paragraphs.

make sure that you have not used subordination inappropriately. **Excessive subordination** occurs when too many subordinating structures, usually dependent clauses, are strung together, so that readers have trouble keeping track of the main idea expressed in the independent clause. Look, for example, at the following sentence:

> Philip II sent the Spanish Armada to conquer England, which was ruled by Elizabeth, who had executed Mary because she was plotting to overthrow Elizabeth, who was a Protestant, whereas Mary and Philip were Roman Catholics.

The long string of subordinate clauses at the end of this sentence makes the relationship of the ideas very hard to follow and also makes it hard for readers to remember the idea in the independent clause at the beginning. Notice how changing one of the dependent clauses to the independent clause of a new sentence and reducing two others to appositive phrases makes the relationship of ideas clearer:

> Philip II sent the Spanish Armada to conquer England, which was ruled by Elizabeth. She had executed Mary, a Roman Catholic like Philip, because Mary was plotting to overthrow Elizabeth, a Protestant.

READING WITH AN EYE FOR COORDINATION AND SUBORDINATION

Turn to the first draft of "The Bagelry," in 2j. Read it over with special attention to the use of coordination and subordination. Do you notice any patterns—is there some of each? more of one than the other? Analyze one paragraph, identifying the coordinate and subordinate phrases and clauses. Do they make their points with clear emphasis? If not, revise the paragraphs following the advice given in 18a2 and 18b2.

FOR EXAMINING SUBORDINATION IN YOUR OWN WRITING

Choose two paragraphs from one of your current drafts, and analyze them for use of subordination. How many dependent clauses do you find? How do they function in the sentences—as nouns, adjectives, or adverbs? Are the ideas in the dependent clauses those that *should* be subordinate to the ones in the independent clauses? On the basis of this analysis, revise the passage to use subordination effectively.

OPTIONAL EXERCISE

Ask your students to describe the sentences in the following passage adapted from Stephen Leacock's "How to Live to Be 200." Then ask them to try restructuring the short passage from Leacock using coordinate and subordinate sentence patterns. Finally, discuss the effect(s) of their revisions.

> What is their effect? They are ridden by the Health Mania. They make themselves a nuisance. They get up at impossible hours. They go out in silly little suits and run Marathon heats before breakfast. They chase around barefoot to get the dew on their feet. They hunt for ozone. They bother about pepsin. They won't eat meat because it has too much nitrogen. They won't eat fruit because it hasn't any. They prefer albumen and starch and nitrogen to huckleberry pie and doughnuts. They won't drink water out of a tap. They won't eat sardines out of a can. They won't use oysters out of a pail. They won't drink milk out of a glass. They are afraid of alcohol in any shape. Yes, sir, afraid. "Cowards."

TEACHING PRACTICE

Ask students to use this analysis as the basis for a brief report to you on (1) what they have learned about their own use of subordination and coordination, and (2) what plans or goals they have for using the two syntactic structures more effectively.

19. Creating and Maintaining Parallel Structures

(BACK)GROUNDING

All successful rhetoricians recognize the power of parallel structures. The rhetorician Gorgias (c. 420 B.C.) was noted for his use of parallelism and antithesis. In his encomium (formal expression of enthusiastic praise) to Helen, he declares:

> Speech is a powerful lord which by means of the finest and most invisible body effects the divinest words: it can stop fear and banish grief and create joy and nurture piety.

By our contemporary standards, Gorgias's style is considered artificial and contrived—partially because of what we perceive as excessive parallelism.

In spite of our modern tendency to dislike excessive ornamentation of any kind, the appeal of parallel structures may be inherent in human existence, or so argues Richard L. Graves in "Symmetrical Form and the Rhetoric of the Sentence." Graves notes that symmetry is everywhere—from our own physiology and self-expression to our art and architecture. Kenneth Burke, too, suggests that the concept of symmetry may be one of "the innate forms of the mind," along with comparison/contrast and repetition ("The Poetic Process," *Counter-Statement*, 1931, Berkeley: U of California P, 1968, 46). And Susanne Langer found symmetry to be fundamental to art. "Symmetrical form," she writes, expresses "our deepest vital feeling" (*Mind: An Essay on Human Feeling*, Vol. 1, Baltimore: Johns Hopkins UP, 1967, 125).

Parallel grammatical structures form many of our most familiar phrases: *sink or swim, live and let live, shape up or ship out*. These clichés demonstrate **parallelism,** expressing parallel elements in the same grammatical form. But parallelism goes far beyond such clichés, and, in fact, characterizes some of the most elegant passages in our language. Look, for example, at how E. B. White uses parallel structures to describe the enchantment of watching a bareback circus rider practicing her act:

> The enchantment grew *not out of something that happened* or was performed *but out of something that seemed* to go round and around and around with the girl, attending her, a steady gleam in the shape of a circle—a ring *of ambition, of happiness, of youth*.
>
> –E. B. WHITE, "The Ring of Time"

This description uses the power of parallelism to create its special rhythms. Just as the young woman goes "round and around and around," balanced easily on her horse, so the sentence circles rhythmically too, balanced by a series of parallel phrases and clauses. Read the sentence aloud, and you will hear the effect of those parallel structures, rocking gently back and forth much as does the horse in the ring.

This chapter will provide you the opportunity to practice parallelism and help you to create pleasing rhythmic effects in your own writing.

316

USEFUL READING

Graves, Richard L. "Symmetrical Form and the Rhetoric of the Sentence." *Classical Rhetoric and Modern Discourse.* Eds. Robert J. Connors, Lisa S. Ede, and Andrea A. Lunsford. Carbondale IL: Southern Illinois UP, 1984. 170–78. Graves identifies four major categories of parallelism: the repetition of key words; the use of opposite words (antithesis); repetition of grammatical elements; and various combinations of the above three categories.

USING PARALLEL STRUCTURES IN A SERIES

▌ 19a. Using parallel structures in a series

All items in a series should be in parallel form—all nouns, all prepositional phrases, all adverb clauses, and so on. Parallel structure makes the series clear and easy to follow, bringing both grace and coherence.

> The quarterhorse *skipped*, *pranced*, and absolutely *sashayed* onto the track. [verbs]

> Three subjects guaranteed to cause a fight are *politics*, *religion*, and *money*. [nouns]

> A cloud *of critics*, *of compilers*, *of commentators*, darkened the face of learning, and the decline *of genius* was soon followed by the corruption *of taste*. [prepositional phrases]
> —EDWARD GIBBON, *The Decline and Fall of the Roman Empire*

> As more and more antismoking laws are passed, we see legions of potential nonsmokers *munching Nicorette*, *gnawing peppermints*, *chewing pencils*, *knitting sweaters*, or *practicing self-hypnotism*. [participial phrases]

> *Pushing a pen or pencil*, *pounding a typewriter*, or *manipulating a word processor* just does not appeal to me. [gerund phrases]

When parallel elements are *not* presented in parallel grammatical form, the result can be awkward and even difficult to follow.

> NONPARALLEL   The duties of the job included baby-sitting, house-cleaning, and the preparation of the meals.

> PARALLEL   The duties of the job included *baby-sitting*, *house-cleaning*, and *preparing the meals*.

Lists

Items in a list should also be parallel in structure. Note the lack of parallelism in the following list:

> Please observe the following regulations when using the library coffee service:
>
> 1. Coffee *to be made* only by library staff.
> 2. Coffee service *to be closed* at 4 P.M.
> 3. Doughnuts *to be kept* in cabinet.
> 4. No faculty members *should handle* coffee materials.

The fourth item on the list is not parallel with the others because

TEACHING PRACTICE

Joseph Williams, echoing tradition, writes that "a common rule of rhetoric and grammar is that we can coordinate elements only of the same grammatical structure: clause and clause, predicate and predicate, prepositional phrase and prepositional phrase" (*Style: Ten Lessons in Clarity and Grace*, 2d ed, Glenview, IL: Scott, 1985. 132). Yet Williams concedes that the rule is often broken, on the grounds that clarity—not grammatical structure—measure the success or failure of parallel structures. Parallelism involves more than initially meets the eye. For instance, instead of looking at *She is tall, tanned, and very handsome* as a set of parallel adjectives, why not regard it as a combination of three separate but parallel sentences: She is tall. She is tanned. She is very handsome. In combining these sentences, the writer suppresses the repeated subject-verb cluster *She is*, expecting the reader to provide it mentally. When students see the source of parallel structures, they become more sensitive to their own parallel constructions.

USEFUL READING

Lindemann, Erika. *A Rhetoric for Writing Teachers*. 2d ed. New York: Oxford UP, 1987. Chapter 9 deals with teaching sentences. Especially useful is the discussion of sentence combining, backgrounding for understanding syntactic parallelism, repetition, and reduction.

O'Hare, Frank. *Sentencecraft*. Columbus, OH: Ginn, 1974. Excellent sentence-combining exercises.

Read, Herbert. *English Prose Style*. London: Bell, 1963. Chapter 4, a reprint of Read's 1928 book, discusses sentence balance and prose rhythm.

it contains a finite verb rather than an infinitive, and thus is a full sentence, not a phrase. Rewritten to maintain parallelism, this item could read:

4. Coffee materials *not to be handled* by faculty members.

A formal outline should also be parallel in form (see 39b3.)

EXERCISE 19.1

Using two of the example sentences above as models to imitate, write two sentences of your own that include a series of parallel phrases.

▌ 19b. Using parallel structures with pairs

One common use of parallel structures occurs in the pairing of two ideas. If the ideas in a pair are parallel in thought, they should be parallel in grammatical structure. Parallel structures are especially appropriate when two ideas are being compared or contrasted.

> History became popular, and historians became alarmed.
> —WILL DURANT

> It's easier to drive a new pickup truck than an old luxury car.

When two clauses in a sentence express compared or contrasted ideas in exactly or almost exactly parallel structures, they produce a **balanced sentence,** one with two parts that "mirror" each other. Balanced sentences create an especially forceful impression.

> Mankind must put an end to war, or war will put an end to mankind.
> —JOHN F. KENNEDY

> There is much in your book that is original and valuable—but what is original is not valuable, and what is valuable is not original.
> —SAMUEL JOHNSON

With coordinating conjunctions

In general, use the same grammatical structure on both sides of any of the coordinating conjunctions—*and, but, or, nor, for, so.* (See 6b7 for more information about coordinating conjunctions). The more nearly parallel the two structures are, the stronger the connection of ideas will be.

> The group performed *whenever anyone would listen* and *wherever anyone would pay.*

ANSWERS TO EXERCISE 19.1 WILL VARY

TEACHING PRACTICE

The following examples of parallel structures can be used to supplement those in the text:

Why is second base so important? Because when an easy grounder or a high pop-up is hit to that position, and you kick it away, or misjudge it and let it bounce on your head, the whole team gets demoralized. The shortstop comes over and says, Too bad the school bus didn't clip you this morning. The first baseman slaps his leg and laughs. The pitcher gives you the finger in front of everybody. (Laurence Sheehan. "How to Play Second Base.")

The dog has got more fun out of Man than Man has got out of the dog, for the clearly demonstrable reason that Man is the more laughable of the two animals. The dog has long been bemused by the singular activities and the curious practices of men, cocking his head inquiringly to one side, intently watching and listening to the strangest goings-on in the world. He has seen men sing together and fight one another in the same evening. He has watched them go to bed when it is time to get up, and get up when it is time to go to bed. He has observed them destroying the soil in vast areas, and nurturing it in small patches. He has stood by while men built strong and solid houses for rest and quiet, and then filled them with lights and bells and machinery. His sensitive nose, which can detect what's cooking in the next township, has caught at one and the same time the bewildering smells of the hospital and the munitions factory. He has seen men raise up great cities to heaven and then blow them to hell. (James Thurber. "A Dog's Eye View of Man.")

USING PARALLEL STRUCTURES WITH PAIRS   //|19b

When elements connected by a coordinating conjunction are not parallel in form, the relationship of the elements can be hard to see.

NONPARALLEL	Medical surveys suggest that Americans *are dieting more* but *still consume too much fat.*
REVISED	Medical surveys suggest that Americans *are dieting more* but *are still consuming too much fat.*

With correlative conjunctions

Use the same structure after both parts of a *correlative conjunction—either . . . or; both . . . and; neither . . . nor; not only . . . but also.* (See 6b7 for more information about correlative conjunctions.)

Native Son depicts a world where blacks have neither *decent housing* nor *secure family lives.*

NONPARALLEL	I wanted not only *to go away to school* but also *to New England.*
REVISED	I wanted not only *to go away to school* but also *to live in New England.*

EXERCISE 19.2

Complete the following sentences, using parallel words or phrases in each case.

Example

The best teacher is one who <u>loves learning</u>, <u>respects students</u>, and <u>demands the best</u>.

1. _____, _____, and _____, for tomorrow we die.
2. My favorite pastimes include _____, _____, and _____.
3. We must either _____ or _____.
4. I want not only _____ but also _____.
5. The ideal parent will be _____, _____, and _____.

EXERCISE 19.3

Revise the following sentences to eliminate any errors in parallel structure.

Example

Roger has studied archery, forestry, and how to treat wild animals.
Roger has studied *archery*, *forestry*, and the *treatment of wild animals.*

1. I remember the sticky, humid afternoons with the air as heavy as a mother's suitcase, my body dripping with sweat, how my sandy mouth yearned for an ice-cold glass of water.

USEFUL READING

Corbett, Edward P. J. *Classical Rhetoric for the Modern Student.* 2d ed. New York: Oxford UP, 1971. See pp. 526–62 for a discussion of some of the more common figures of speech.

Woodson, Linda. *A Handbook of Modern Rhetorical Terms.* Urbana, IL: NCTE, 1979. A sourcebook for teachers listing some of the most common figures of speech and nearly all other rhetorical terms.

OPTIONAL EXERCISE

Consider the following passage from John F. Kennedy's Inaugural Address. Read it aloud, and ask students to try to identify the parallel structures.

Let the word go forth from this time and place, to friend and foe alike, that the torch has been passed to a new generation of Americans—born in this century, tempered by war, disciplined by a hard and bitter peace, proud of our ancient heritage—and unwilling to witness or permit the slow undoing of those human rights to which this nation has always been committed, and to which we are committed today at home and around the world.

What is the aural effect of the parallelism? Help your students break down each sentence into its root sentences, so they can see how beautifully those sentences were combined.

ANSWERS TO EXERCISE 19.2 (WILL VARY)

1. Live, drink, and be merry, for tomorrow we die.
2. My favorite pastimes include reading, exercising, and talking with friends.
3. We must either walk quickly or drive slowly to the fairgrounds.
4. I want not only hot fudge but also whipped cream.
5. The ideal parent will be patient, wise, and mature.

TEACHING PRACTICE

The following sentence exemplifies *chiasmus*, the device in which the elements of a first clause, phrase, or sentence are inverted in the second clause, phrase, or sentence.

Humankind must put an end to war, or war will put an end to humankind.

Used sparingly, this rhetorical flourish is effective. When such rhetorical/poetic techniques are taught, they are introduced as style and are related to the teaching of schemes and tropes, so popular in classical rhetoric. Other famous examples of chiasmus include the following:

Ask not what your country can do for you, but what you can do for your country.

—JOHN F. KENNEDY

Let us never negotiate out of fear. But never let us fear to negotiate.

—JOHN F. KENNEDY

ANSWERS TO EXERCISE 19.3 (WILL VARY)

1. I remember the sticky, humid afternoons with the air as heavy as a mother's suitcase, my body dripping with sweat, my sandy mouth yearning for an ice-cold glass of water.

2. Most readers begin reading with an implicit faith that the text will be coherent and that the writer will convey meaning clearly.

3. It was a question of either reducing their staff or somehow finding new customers for their baked potatoes.

4. Needing a new pair of shoes and not being able to afford them is enough to make anybody sensitive.

5. I'll never forget the good times we had—the skiing, the swimming, and especially the windsurfing.

6. Too many students came to college to have fun, to find a husband or wife, or to put off having to go to work.

7. We can improve the cafeteria by doing several things: making less noise, returning the trays, and cleaning the tables.

8. Her job was to show new products, to help Mr. Greer with sales, and to participate in advertising.

9. The Greek system provides an incentive for academic success; it also contributes to the development of leadership skills.

10. Stress can result in low self-esteem, total frustration, sleeplessness, nervousness, or eventually suicide.

2. Most readers begin reading with an implicit faith in the coherence of the text and that the writer will convey meaning clearly.

3. It was a question of either reducing their staff, or they had to somehow find new customers for their baked potatoes.

4. To need a new pair of shoes and not being able to afford them is enough to make anybody sensitive.

5. I'll never forget the good times we had—skiing, the swims, and especially that you taught me how to handle a windsurfer.

6. Too many students come to college only for fun, to find a husband or wife, or for putting off having to go to work.

7. We can improve the cafeteria by doing several things: less noise, not leaving trays around, and we should leave the tables clean.

8. Her job was to show new products, help Mr. Greer with sales, and an opportunity was given to be part of advertising.

9. The Greek system not only provides the individual with an incentive for striving toward academic success but also it contributes to the development of leadership skills.

10. Stress can result in low self-esteem, total frustration, inability to sleep, nervous breakdown, or eventually resulting in suicide.

19c. Including all necessary words in parallel constructions

In addition to making parallel elements grammatically similar, be careful to include any other necessary words—prepositions, relative pronouns, and so on.

NONPARALLEL	We considered moving to a small town in the Southwest or a suburb of San Francisco.
PARALLEL	We considered moving *to a small town in the Southwest* or *to a suburb of San Francisco.*
NONPARALLEL	High on our list was Mill Valley, located in Marin County and which is only a half-hour from San Francisco.
PARALLEL	High on our list was Mill Valley, *which is located in Marin County* and *which is only a half-hour from San Francisco.*

19d. Using parallel structures for emphasis and special effect

Parallel structures can help a writer emphasize the most important ideas in a sentence. Look at the following sentence:

USING PARALLEL STRUCTURES FOR EMPHASIS

> The dancers wore costumes that were exquisitely perfect in every detail, and they filed onto the stage with their arms akimbo and their toes pointed.

The meaning of this sentence is clear, but what seems to be the most important idea, the exquisitely perfect costumes, is buried in a dependent clause in the middle of the sentence. This idea can be emphasized by making it the last in a series of parallel absolute phrases arranged in climactic order:

> The dancers filed onto the stage, arms akimbo, toes pointed, costumes exquisitely perfect in every detail.

See 17a for more information about emphasis within a sentence.

Besides emphasizing main ideas, parallel structures can create a number of different stylistic effects. One of these is orderliness, a sense of steady or building rhythm, as in the following sentence:

> Most police work is concerned with scared people who have been bitten by dogs, frantic people whose children have run away from home, old people who have no one to talk to, and impatient people whose first response to any situation is to "call the cops."

Note here how the repetition of the parallel phrases *scared people* . . . , *frantic people* . . . , *old people* . . . , *impatient people* builds a rhythm or beat that leads us to expect more of the same. Parallel elements thus work to create and fulfill reader expectations.

> At work, he may have time to gulp down a cup of coffee if the dining halls are running smoothly, if all the workers show up, and if the boss is not asking questions.

This sentence creates an impression of somewhat desperate activity as it piles up the three parallel *if* clauses.

EXERCISE 19.4

Underline the parallel structures in the following passage. Then use the passage as a model to imitate in creating a passage that uses parallelism in a similar way. You might begin such a passage with "But love is not all . . ." or "But youth is not all . . ." or even "But getting a degree is not all. . . ."

> But life is not all eloquence and adulation: life is wiping the baby's bum; it is a bad case of croup; it is quarrels with one's spouse; it is disappointment, distraction, indignities by the dozen; it is the death of friends, wife, son, and

TEACHING PRACTICE

Songwriters, like poets and other professional users of language, become exceptionally aware of the effects of parallelism (and of many other stylistic devices). In "Getting Better," from the *Sgt. Pepper's Lonely Hearts Club Band*, Paul McCartney and John Lennon use parallel structures to great effect:

> I used to get mad at my school
> The teachers who taught me weren't cool
> You're holding me down
> turning me round
> filling me up with your rules.

In fact, a look at the songs from any generation will provide you with examples of parallelism. You might consider sending your students out to find examples of various types of parallelism. Encourage them to look in essays, novels, poems, songs, jingles, advertisements, lectures—in short, encourage them to look and listen.

WRITERS ON WRITING

> Any writer overwhelmingly honest about pleasing himself is almost sure to please others.
> —MARIANNE MOORE

ANSWERS TO EXERCISE 19.4

life is; life is; it is; it is; it is; disappointment; distraction; indignities by the dozen; it is; friends; wife; son; brothers; it is; alien evenings; cold stairwells; frosty sheets; lack of love; as oratory needs silence; and revolution peace

Imitation passages will vary.

brothers, carried off like fluff in the wind; it is alien evenings, cold stairwells, frosty sheets, lack of love; for what does the great spirit need that touches the body but the touch of the body, as oratory needs silence, and revolution peace? We are nourished by our absences and opposites; contraries quench our thirst.

–WILLIAM GASS, "Emerson and the Essay"

ANSWERS TO EXERCISE 19.5 (WILL VARY)

1. I will always remember how the girls dressed in green plaid skirts and the boys in green plaid ties.
2. There are three ways to apply Ninhydrin to the area to be examined: by brushing, spraying, or dipping.
3. No longer are women required to play supporting roles behind their male leads nor to play the emptyheaded, superficial debutante.
4. There are two types of wallflowers: the male nerd and the female skeeve.
5. Kris was off to the big university and sorority life; Stacy to attend the community college and life at home.

EXERCISE 19.5

Revise the following sentences to make effective use of parallel clauses. Change or add words if need be.

> *Example*
> Where we eat, how we eat, what we eat, and what are our reasons for eating—these are major questions for many yuppies.
> *Where we eat, how we eat, what we eat*, and *why we eat*—these are major questions for many yuppies.

1. I will always remember how the girls dressed in green plaid skirts and the boys wearing green plaid ties.
2. There are three ways to apply Ninhydrin to the area to be examined: it may be applied with a brush; it may be sprayed on with a spray gun; or you can dip the object in the solution.
3. No longer are women required to play supporting roles behind their male leads; they do not have to play empty-headed debutantes whose only attributes are superficial, either.
4. There are two types of wallflowers: the male wallflower is known as the nerd, and the female, who is known as the skeeve.
5. Kris was off to the big university and sorority life; Stacy, on the other hand, was remaining at home and attending the local community college.

TEACHING PRACTICE

Ask students to bring their imitations *and* their revisions of their own paragraphs to class for discussion. Then divide the imitations and revisions into groups of five and ask students to work in groups to choose the one or two *most effective* uses of parallelism and to be prepared to report the reasons for their decisions to the rest of the class.

READING WITH AN EYE FOR PARALLELISM

The following paragraph about a bareback rider practicing her circus act is laden with parallelism. (You will recognize the second sentence as the example used to open this chapter.) Read the paragraph, and identify all the parallel structures. Consider what effect they create on you as a reader, and try to decide why the author chose to put his ideas in such overtly parallel form. Try imitating the penultimate sentence, the one beginning *In a week or two*.

The richness of the scene was in its plainness, its natural condition—of horse, of ring, of girl, even to the girl's bare feet that gripped the bare back of her proud and ridiculous mount. The enchantment grew not out of anything that happened or was performed but out of something that seemed to go round and around and around with the girl, attending her, a steady gleam in the shape of a circle—a ring of ambition, of happiness, of youth. (And the positive pleasures of equilibrium under difficulties.) In a week or two, all would be changed, all (or almost all) lost: the girl would wear makeup, the horse would wear gold, the ring would be painted, the bark would be clean for the feet of the horse, the girl's feet would be clean for the slippers that she'd wear. All, all would be lost.   —E. B. WHITE, "The Ring of Time"

FOR EXAMINING PARALLELISM IN YOUR OWN WRITING

Choose four or five paragraphs from a draft you have recently written. Read through them carefully, noting any series of words, phrases, or clauses. Determine whether these series are in parallel form, and if not, revise them for parallelism. Then reread the paragraphs, looking for places where parallel structures would add emphasis or clarity to your writing, and revise those places to use such structures.

20. Varying Sentence Structures

(BACK)GROUNDING

Gifted writer, journalist, and literary, social, and political critic, H. L. Mencken rarely limited his reviews to content: He enjoyed immensely writing reviews of style as well. In 1921, Mencken wrote a column on former newspaper reporter Warren G. Harding, making clear that not even the president of the United States was safe from his iconoclastic sensibilities. Using the simplest of sentences and sustained repetition, Mencken writes a powerful and memorable review of Harding's style:

> He writes the worst English that I have ever encountered. It reminds me of a string of wet sponges; it reminds me of tattered washing on the line; it reminds me of stale bean soup, of college yells, of dogs barking idiotically through endless nights. It is so bad that a sort of grandeur creeps into it. It drags itself out of the dark abyss of pish, and crawls insanely up to the topmost pinnacle of posh. It is rumble and bumble. It is flap and doodle. It is balder and dash.

Row upon row of trees identical in size and shape may appeal at some level to our sense of orderliness, but in spite of that appeal they soon become very boring. Constant unanimity in anything, in fact, soon gets tiresome; perhaps variety *is* the spice of life. Certainly that is true in sentence structures, where sameness can result in dull, listless prose. The truth of this maxim was illustrated anew not long ago in a college classroom discussion of one student's essay. The group had worked on the essay for most of an hour, correcting errors, reorganizing paragraphs, clarifying the major points. Finally, one person said, "Okay, okay—but it's still BORING." All of the others, including the author, agreed. But they were stuck. The group could not come up with any new ideas and was about ready to give up when one student exclaimed, "I've got it! Look at these sentences. They all look about the same length!"

And they were. In fact, impossible as it may sound, every sentence in the essay was between twenty-two and twenty-five words long. Once the group realized this fact, they could begin to work again, carving some of the sentences into very short ones and combining others to create new rhythms. Through this revision, the essay took on new life as its boring sameness faded away.

This chapter will examine how to use the traditional foes of boring sentences—variety in lengths, in openings, and in grammatical, functional, and rhetorical patterns.

324

VARYING SENTENCE LENGTHS

20a. Varying sentence lengths

The situation described in the introduction above illustrates perfectly the need for varying sentence length. Doing so not only makes prose more readable and interesting but also creates a pleasing rhythmic effect, what some students have called "flow." Once you begin to pay attention to sentence length, varying it for specific effects can be very satisfying.

Deciding how and when to vary and balance sentence length is not always easy, however. How short is too short? How long is too long? Is there a "just right" length for a particular sentence or idea? These questions are difficult to answer because the answers depend on, among other things, the writer's purpose, intended audience, and topic. A children's story, for instance, may call for mostly short sentences, while an article on nuclear disarmament in *The Atlantic* may call for considerably longer ones. In other words, in different situations, either very long or very short sentences can be effective.

1. Using short sentences

Very short sentences can often pack a powerful punch. Study the following famous short sentences, and see if you agree that each owes much of its power to its brevity; more words would detract.

Nice guys finish last.

Crime doesn't pay.

Let them eat cake.

War is hell.

The following passage from a speech by Chief Sitting Bull illustrates how effective a series of short sentences and other short structures can be:

What treaty that the whites have kept has the red man broken? Not one. What treaty that the white men ever made with us have they kept? Not one. When I was a boy the Sioux owned the world; the sun rose and set on their land; they sent ten thousand men to battle. Where are the warriors today? Who slew them? Where are our lands? Who owns them?
—SITTING BULL, *Touch the Earth*

Notice how Sitting Bull's short questions, clauses, and fragments build a rhythm that gives power to his indictment of the white world. Re-

USEFUL READING

Corbett, Edward P. J. *Classical Rhetoric for the Modern Student.* 2d ed. New York: Oxford UP, 1971. 456–58. An analysis of sentence structure.

Larson, Richard. "Back to the Board." *CCC* 29 (1978): 292–94. A further explanation of his composing technique.

Lindemann, Erika. *A Rhetoric for Writing Teachers.* 2d ed. New York: Oxford UP, 1987. 133–39. A historical survey of sentence-combining research, from Hunt and O'Hare to Daiker and Morenberg.

TEACHING PRACTICE

Several techniques have been developed to help teach students to vary sentence structures, with sentence combining being perhaps the most well known and thoroughly studied. A lesser-known technique is Richard Larson's strategy of writing an essay on the board over several days, correcting and talking about the stylistic choices he makes as he writes. A third way to draw students' attention to varying sentence structures is Edward P. J. Corbett's method of stylistic analysis.

Whatever method you may choose, remember that stylistic choices about sentence structures depend upon the larger context of each individual sentence, the intended audience, and the purpose for writing.

TEACHING PRACTICE

If your students are interested in the source of these aphorisms, you may want to direct them to *Brewer's Dictionary of Phrase and Fable* (rev. by Ivor H. Evans, New York: Harper, 1981). If they write a short report on one or two of their favorite one-liners, they will come away with an appreciation for succinctness. Students might be interested to know, for example, that the expression "I nailed him" comes from the Bible: "I will fashion him as a nail in a sure place" (Isaiah 22.23).

TEACHING PRACTICE

Consider selecting passages such as the following from "Pornoviolence" to use as prose models for your students to analyze and imitate. Perhaps your students will connect the style with the meaning and see how Tom Wolfe deliberately uses short sentences to emphasize how insipid, violent, and predictable television has become.

The television networks have schooled us in the view from Oswald's rifle and made it seem a normal pastime. The TV viewpoint is nearly always that of the man who is going to strike. The last time I watched *Gunsmoke*, which was not known as a very violent Western in TV terms, the action went like this: The Wellington agents and the stagecoach driver pull guns on the badlands gang leader's daughter and Kitty, the heart-of-gold saloonkeeper, and kidnap them. Then the badlands gang shoots two Wellington agents. Then they tie up five more and talk about shooting them. Then they desist because they might not be able to get a hotel room in the next town if the word got around. Then one badlands gang gunslinger attempts to rape Kitty while the gang leader's younger daughter looks on. Then Kitty resists, so he slugs her one in the jaw. Then the gang leader slugs him. Then Kitty throws hot stew in a gang member's face and hits him over the back of the head with a revolver. Then he knocks her down with a rock. Then the gang sticks up a bank. Here comes the marshall, Matt Dillon. He shoots a gang member and breaks it up. Then the gang leader shoots the guy who was guarding his daughter and the woman. Then the marshall shoots the gang leader. The final exploding bullet signals The End.

WRITING TOGETHER

Read aloud the following paragraph from Mary Shelley's *Frankenstein*, announcing the final punctuation of each sentence. Ask your students to recast the information in the passage into a series of long sentences. Then, have them recast it into a string of short sentences. How do they compare? Reading the revisions aloud will help them "see" the difference.

As I said this I suddenly beheld the figure of a man, at some distance, advancing towards me with superhuman speed. He bounded over the crevices in the ice, among which I had walked with caution; his stature, also, as he approached, seemed to exceed that of man. I was troubled; a mist came over my eyes, and I felt a faintness seize me; but I was quickly restored by the cold gale of the mountains. I perceived, as the shape came nearer (sight tremendous and abhorred!) that it was the wretch whom I had created. I trembled with rage and horror, resolving to wait his approach and then close with him in mortal combat. He approached; his countenance bespoke bitter anguish, combined with disdain and malignity, while its unearthly ugliness rendered it almost too horrible for human eyes. But I scarcely observed this; rage and hatred had at first deprived me of utterance, and I recovered only to overwhelm him with words expressive of furious detestation and contempt.

WRITERS ON WRITING

All those clauses, appositions, amplifications, qualifications, asides, God knows what else, hanging inside the poor old skeleton of one sentence like some kind of Spanish moss.

—TOM WOLFE

peated short sentences, if used with awareness of their effect, can go far beyond "See Spot run" into rhythmic beat and cadenced dignity.

2. Using long sentences

In contrast to short sentences, long sentences are particularly useful for presenting a set of complex, interlocking ideas or for building up momentum. The following paragraph shows how a series of long sentences can be used effectively in this way:

Femininity pleases men because it makes them appear more masculine by contrast; and, in truth, conferring an extra portion of unearned gender distinction on men, an unchallenged space in which to breathe freely and feel stronger, wiser, more competent, is femininity's special gift. One could say that masculinity is often an effort to please women, but masculinity is known to please by displays of mastery and competence while femininity pleases by suggesting that these concerns, except in small matters, are beyond its intent. Whimsy, unpredictability and patterns of thinking and behavior that are dominated by emotion, such as tearful expressions of sentiment and fear, are thought to be feminine precisely because they lie outside the established route to success.

—SUSAN BROWNMILLER, *Femininity*

Notice that each of the three long sentences encapsulates the complex relationships between femininity and masculinity, and between women and men, that Brownmiller is seeking to explore. Short sentences would not work as effectively here because they would not adequately reflect the complexity of the ideas being presented.

3. Alternating short and long sentences

Although series of short and long sentences can both be effective in individual situations, frequent alternation in sentence length characterizes much memorable writing. After one or more long sentences that express complex ideas or images, the pith of a short sentence can be refreshing and arresting. Similarly, a long sentence that follows a series of short ones can serve as a climax or summation that relaxes the tension or fulfills the expectation created by the series, giving readers a sense of completion. Notice the difference between these two passages, one of which contains sentences of fairly uniform length and the other of which varies sentence length.

VARYING SENTENCE LENGTHS   *var* 20a

UNIFORM LENGTHS

The house is a fixer-upper, of course. For the past two days, I've been fixing things. It seems like the past two decades. I've been crawling about in the basement, which is dirt-floored, trying to learn to fix copper plumbing. The people renting the house last winter froze and burst the pipes. As a result, I have to put in all new stuff, learning as I go. With five-foot headroom, it's a real joy to be playing with torch and hot solder down there. I climb around oozing soilpipes from another era. I crouch Quasimodo-like, measuring, cutting, crouching, slouching, until my back is permanently bent. I have been picking spiders out of my beard, and my clothes are indescribable.

VARIED LENGTHS

The house is a fixer-upper, of course, and so for the past two days (it seems like the past two decades), I've been fixing things, crawling about in the basement—dirt-floored, naturally—trying to learn to fix copper plumbing. What a nightmare! The people renting the house last winter froze and burst the pipes, and so I have to put in all new stuff. I'm learning as I go. With five-foot headroom, it's a real joy to be playing with torch and hot solder down there, climbing around oozing soilpipes from another era, crouching Quasimodo-like, measuring, cutting, crouching, slouching. My back is permanently bent. My beard is full of spiders. My clothes are indescribable.

See the next section (20a4) for an analysis of this passage.

4. Checking for varied sentence lengths

As you revise a draft, begin by looking at the lengths of your sentences. If they do not seem to vary enough in length, begin revising them so that they do. Do not, however, change sentence lengths arbitrarily. Rather, balance them so they most effectively convey your meaning. Think about the ideas you want to emphasize, and try to arrange your sentence lengths in a way that emphasizes them. For example, if two or more short sentences in a row express closely related ideas, ask yourself if you could make the relationship between these ideas clearer or more precise by using coordination or subordination to combine them into a single, longer sentence. (See Chapter 18 for more information about coordination and subordination.) You may discover, on the other hand, that a long sentence contains two or three important ideas that would be more emphatic if each was expressed in a short sentence of its own.

WRITING TOGETHER

Consider the following paragraph from "Champion of the World" by Maya Angelou that includes both long and short sentences used effectively. After your class has identified the variety of sentences according to length and type, ask them to write an imitation of these paragraphs on a topic of their own, such as sports, childbirth, winning an award, or attending a concert. Finally, get your students to exchange papers with at least three or four other students.

> Champion of the world. A Black boy. Some Black mother's son. He was the strongest man in the world. People drank Coca-Colas like ambrosia and ate candy bars like Christmas. Some of the men went behind the Store and poured white lightning in their soft-drink bottles, and a few of the bigger boys followed them. Those who were not chased away came back blowing their breath in front of themselves like proud smokers.
>
> It would take an hour or more before the people would leave the Store and head for home. Those who lived too far had made arrangements to stay in town. It wouldn't do for a Black man and his family to be caught on a lonely country road on a night when Joe Louis had proved that we were the strongest people in the world.

WRITERS ON WRITING

All my books literally come to me in the form of a sentence, an original sentence which contains the entire book.

—RAYMOND FEDERMAN

Look back at the passage in 20a3 to see how this kind of revision can bring life to prose that suffers from overly uniform sentence lengths. In the second version, the writer uses coordination and subordination to combine the first four sentences of the first version into one long sentence that connects the main ideas of *a fixer-upper*, doing the fixing, and crawling about the basement. After this long sentence, he then adds a very short exclamatory sentence that both sums up the ideas in the first sentence and points ahead to the rest of the passage. Next, he combines two closely related ideas, about burst pipes and the installation of new ones, into one sentence of medium length, changing the participial phrase *learning as I go* into a separate short sentence. The next three sentences of the original version, all dealing with the ordeal of working in the basement, are combined into one long sentence. Finally, a dependent clause and the two short clauses of a compound sentence are separated into three short, parallel sentences (see Chapter 19), which give a blunt, hammering effect to the writer's expression of his complaints.

ANSWERS TO EXERCISE 20.1 (WILL VARY)

To play bridge, you need to have the proper materials, the correct number of people, and a knowledge of card ranking. Besides the four players—North, South, East, and West—you need a full deck of playing cards (minus the jokers), a score pad, and a pen or pencil. Partnerships, an important part of the game, are usually decided by cards drawn from a shuffled deck. The two players who draw the highest cards are partners, and they sit across from each other. The person who draws the highest card during partnership is the first dealer. The dealer, starting clockwise with the person on the left, deals each person one facedown card at a time until all four players have thirteen cards apiece. After the deal, the players sort their cards by suit, usually alternating black and red. Then they arrange their cards in ranking order, from the highest, the ace, to the lowest, the deuce. The five highest cards, the ace, king, queen, jack, and ten, are referred to as honors.

EXERCISE 20.1

Following is a paragraph that can be improved by varying sentence length. Read the paragraph aloud to get a sense of how it sounds. Then revise it, creating some short emphatic sentences and combining other sentences to create more effective long sentences. Add words or change punctuation as you need to.

Before beginning to play bridge, it is necessary to have the proper materials, the correct number of people, and a knowledge of the rank of suits and cards. The necessary materials include a full deck of playing cards (minus the jokers) and a score pad, along with a pen or pencil. Bridge is played by four people divided into two partnerships, which are usually decided by drawing cards from a shuffled deck. The two players who draw the highest cards and the two who draw the lowest are partners, and the partners sit across from each other. The person who draws the highest card during partnership is the first dealer. Starting with the person on his or her left and going clockwise, the dealer deals each person one card at a time, face down. The deal continues until all four players have thirteen cards apiece. After the deal, the players sort their cards by suit, usually alternating black and red suits. The players then arrange the cards in ranking order from the highest, the ace, to the lowest, the deuce. The five highest cards, the ace, king, queen, jack, and ten, are referred to as honors. There is one suit that has great power and outranks every other one, the trump suit, which is designated at the start of the game.

VARYING SENTENCE OPENINGS   *var* 20b

▌ 20b. Varying sentence openings

In making prose readable and interesting, beginning sentences in different ways is just as important as making them of different lengths. For instance, when each sentence begins with the subject of an independent clause, a passage may seem to lurch or jerk along:

> *The way* football and basketball are played is as interesting as the players. *Football* is a game of precision. *Each play* is diagrammed to accomplish a certain goal. A *coach* designs the plays like an engineer would design a bridge. *Basketball* is a game of availability. A *basketball game* looks like a track meet. *The team* that drops of exhaustion first loses. *Basketball players* are also often compared to artists. *The players' moves and slam dunks* are their masterpieces.

Varying sentence openings can prevent this jerky effect. This section will focus on three ways of varying openings—transitional expressions; prepositional, verbal, and absolute phrases; and dependent clauses.

▌ 1. Using transitional expressions

Note the ways in which opening transitions bring variety and clarity to this passage:

> In order to be alert Friday morning in New York, I planned to take the shuttle from Washington Thursday night. *On Thursday morning* it began to snow in Washington and to snow even harder in New York. *By mid-afternoon* I decided not to risk the shuttle and caught a train to New York. *Seven hours later* the train completed its three-hour trip. I arrived at Penn Station to find a city shut down by the worst blizzard since 1947.   –Linda Ellerbee, *"And So It Goes"*

Here the transitional words establish chronology and help carry us along smoothly through the paragraph. Other groups of transitional expressions that establish a sequence include *on the one hand . . . on the other hand* and *on the left . . . straight ahead . . . on the right.*

Single-word transitional expressions that can be used to vary sentence openings include these:

ADVERBS	suddenly, fortunately, surprisingly
COORDINATING CONJUNCTIONS	and, but, or, nor, for, so, yet
CONJUNCTIVE ADVERBS	however, nevertheless, therefore, hence

TEACHING PRACTICE

Some students have considerable trouble punctuating dependent clauses, especially introductory dependent clauses. They often turn them into sentence fragments by separating them from the main clause with a period. Outlined below is one possible method for helping students overcome this problem:

I worked all summer at the car dealership. Although I really wanted to go to baseball camp.

1. You may want to point out the problem in meaning for the reader—the false or due expectation (Coming after a period, the *Although I really wanted* clause makes us think that another sentence is coming.)
2. Then, ask students to supply an alternative, relying on their competence to provide a solution. (They may want to erase the period and make the *A* of *Although* a lowercase letter. Or then may add more information to the *Although* clause: *Although I really wanted to go to baseball camp, I needed to earn money not spend it.*
3. You can use this opportunity to suggest other alternatives that clarify or reiterate the meaning conveyed by the kernel sentence ([1] *Although I really wanted to go to baseball camp, I worked all summer at the car dealership.* [2] *I worked all summer at the car dealership although I really wanted to go to baseball camp instead.* [3] *I worked all summer at the car dealership. Although I really wanted to go to baseball camp, I needed to earn money not spend it.*)

TEACHING PRACTICE

Consider sharing with your students the following passage from Richard Rodriguez's "Aria: A Memoir of a Bilingual Childhood." Point out to them the ways Rodriguez varies his sentence openers, including his use of dependent clauses.

Three months passed. Five. A half year. Unsmiling, ever watchful, my teachers noted my silence. They began to connect my behavior with the slow progress my brother and sisters were making. Until, one Saturday morning, three nuns arrived at the house to talk to our parents. Stiffly they sat on the blue living-room sofa. From the doorway of another room, spying on the visitors, I noticed the incongruity, the clash of two worlds, the faces and voices of school intruding upon the familiar setting of home. I overheard one voice gently wondering, "Do your children speak only Spanish at home, Mrs. Rodriguez?" While another voice added, "That Richard especially seems so timid and shy."

Be careful to check that any such sentence opening suits the occasion and signals the appropriate chronological, spatial, or logical relationship with the preceding sentence. (See 5c5 for a discussion and list of transitional expressions.)

2. Using phrases

Prepositional, verbal, and absolute phrases can also provide variety in sentence openers.

Prepositional phrases

At each desk, a computer printout gives the necessary data.

From a few scraps of wood in the Middle Ages to a precisely carved, electrified instrument in the 1980s, the guitar has gone through uncounted changes.

Verbal phrases

Dressed in denim jeans and a dark-blue chamois shirt, a young woman appeared at the door.

To qualify for flight training, one must be in good physical condition and pass a written test.

Absolute phrases

Our hopes for snow shattered, we started home.

Baton raised in a salute, the maestro readied the orchestra.

3. Using dependent clauses

Dependent clauses are another way to open a sentence.

While the boss sat on his tractor, I was down in a ditch pounding in stakes and leveling out the bottom.

Who she is is difficult to explain.

4. Checking for varied sentence openings

As you revise, especially if you think your writing may be choppy, look carefully at your sentence openings. Underline the subject of each sentence. If most of your sentences begin with the subject, revise some of them by opening with transitional expressions, phrases, or dependent clauses.

VARYING SENTENCE TYPES   var|20c

Look at the following passage, which uses only subject openings, and then see how varying the sentence openings makes the passage easier to read.

FIRST DRAFT

<u>Most marathon runners</u> find that running with another person is helpful. <u>They</u> must not be afraid to pass this person, though, in order to run as well as possible. <u>Runners</u> must realize furthermore that even if they do not win the race, they achieve a victory by pushing their bodies to finish.

REVISED

Most marathon runners find that running with another person is helpful. In order to run as well as possible, though, *they* must not be afraid to pass this person. Furthermore, *runners* must realize that even if they do not win the race, they achieve victory by pushing their bodies to finish.

EXERCISE 20.2

Go back to the paragraph comparing football and basketball in 20b. Using transitional expressions, phrases, and/or dependent clauses, revise the paragraph to vary its sentence openings and thus to make the passage smoother and more coherent.

▌ 20c. Varying sentence types

In addition to using different lengths and openings, you can help to vary your sentence structures by using different *types* of sentences. Sentences can be classified in three different ways: grammatically, functionally, and rhetorically (see 6d).

Grammatical types

Grammatically, sentences fall into four categories—**simple, compound, complex,** and **compound-complex**—based on the number of independent and dependent clauses they contain. Varying your sentences among these grammatical types will go a long way toward creating readable, effective prose. (See 6d1 for an explanation and examples of each type.)

Functional types

Functional types of sentences include **declarative** (making a statement), **interrogative** (asking a question), **imperative** (giving a command), and **exclamatory** (expressing strong feeling). (See 6d2.) Most

**ANSWERS TO EXERCISE 20.2
WILL VARY**

TEACHING PRACTICE

Point out to your students that varying sentences among grammatical types helps create readable, effective prose.

Simple: Later, Susan arrived.

Compound: People tried to reassure me, but they could not understand my fear.

Complex: While we walked over to the picnic, we talked about the problem of being roommates.

Compound-Complex: I told her about the courses I enjoyed most, and she told me about her current reading, including *The Sheep Look Up*.

sentences in essays are declarative, but occasionally you may want to include a command, a question, or even an exclamation of some kind if such sentence types are appropriate for your purpose. Note how they are used in these examples:

> Coal-burning plants undoubtedly harm the environment in various ways; among others, they contribute to acid rain. *But consider the alternatives.*

> We kept pressing on into the park. *And why? Why would sixteen middle-aged people try to backpack thirty-seven miles?* At this point, I was not at all sure.

> *Divorcés! They were everywhere!* Sometimes he felt like a new member of an enormous club, the Divorcés of America, that he had never before even heard of.

Rhetorical types

Two rhetorical sentence types, periodic and cumulative, spotlight sentence endings and beginnings and can be especially helpful in achieving sentence variety. Although not all sentences can be classified as cumulative or periodic, they can create strong effects when used in appropriate situations.

Periodic sentences postpone the main idea (usually in an independent clause) until the very end of the sentence. Effectively written periodic sentences are especially useful for building tension or building toward a climactic or surprise ending. At their best, they keep us alert by forcing us to hold information in a kind of "suspended animation" until the end. (See 6d3 for more discussion.)

> Early one morning, under the arc of a lamp, carefully, silently, in smock and leather gloves, old Doctor Manza grafted a cat's head onto a chicken's trunk.   –DYLAN THOMAS

> Few more obvious, natural, apparent, ostensible, plain, intelligent, literal, and downright objects exist on this earth than a boiled potato.
> –MARY ELLEN CHASE

> Even though large tracts of Europe and many old and famous states have fallen or may fall into the grasp of the Gestapo and all the odious apparatus of Nazi rule, we shall not flag or fail.   –WINSTON CHURCHILL

Note in each example how the writer holds back the main idea, thus using the end of the sentence to shock, surprise, or inspire.

Look at the following sentence and its revision to see how periodic order can provide emphasis.

OPTIONAL EXERCISE

Using the periodic sentences in the handbook as models, ask your students to write periodic sentences of their own. To do this well, they will need to break sentences down into grammatical units and recombine these units, placing the main clause at the end of the new sentence.

WRITERS WRITING

In "Why I Write," Joan Didion states that upon admitting to herself that she did not belong in the "world of ideas," the undergraduate English program at Berkeley, she discovered who she really was: a writer.

> By which I mean not a "good" writer or a "bad" writer but simply a writer, a person whose most absorbed and passionate hours are spent arranging words on pieces of paper. Had my credentials been in order I would never have become a writer. Had I been blessed with even limited access to my own mind there would have been no reason to write. I write entirely to find out what I'm thinking, what I'm looking at, what I see and what it means. What I want and what I fear. . . . *What is going on in these pictures in my mind?*

VARYING SENTENCE TYPES   *var* 20c

The nations of the world have no alternative but coexistence because another world war would be unwinnable and because total destruction would certainly occur.

PERIODIC

Because another world war would be unwinnable and because total destruction would certainly occur, the nations of the world have no alternative but coexistence.

Nothing is wrong with the first sentence, which conveys the information clearly. But to put greater emphasis on the idea in the independent clause of the sentence—no alternative but coexistence—the writer chose to revise using the periodic pattern.

Cumulative sentences, which begin with an independent clause and then add details in phrases and other clauses, are the dominant rhetorical pattern today, far more common than periodic sentences. They are useful when you want to provide both immediate understanding of the main idea and a great deal of supporting detail. Note how the writers of the following sentences use the cumulative pattern not only to add important detail to the independent clause but also to end with a strong word or image:

> From boyhood to manhood, I have remembered him in a single image— seated, asleep on the sofa, his head thrown back in a hideous corpselike grin, the evening newspaper spread out before him.
> —RICHARD RODRIGUEZ, "My Parents"

> Four steps past the turnstiles everybody is already backed up haunch to paunch for the climb up the ramp and the stairs to the surface, a great funnel of flesh, wool, felt, leather, rubber and steaming alumicrom, with the blood squeezing through everybody's old sclerotic arteries in hopped-up spurts from too much coffee and the effort of surfacing from the subway at the rush hour.   —TOM WOLFE

EXERCISE 20.3

Revise the following sentences into periodic form.

1. The members of the crew team entered the shell house one by one, tired and weary, at four o'clock on a cold, damp morning in Seattle, Washington.
2. I became the best salesperson in our store once I mastered the problems that I had encountered at the beginning and once I had become thoroughly familiar with the stock.

ANSWERS TO EXERCISE 20.3 (WILL VARY)

1. At four o'clock on a cold, damp morning in Seattle, Washington, one by one, tired and weary, the members of the crew team entered the shell house.
2. Once I mastered the problems that I had encountered at the beginning and once I had become thoroughly familiar with the stock, I became the best salesperson in our store.

WRITING TOGETHER

Consider using Edward P. J. Corbett's system from *Classical Rhetoric for the Modern Student* for studying the grammatical types of sentences that students use. First, make sure that your students can name and distinguish between different kinds of grammatical sentences. Next, consider using the chart below to ask them to compare their own writing to a professional example of the same type, or perhaps to that of another student in the class. Finally, discuss the results as a class. You might also want to copy and distribute examples from your class of writing that differs widely in number of simple sentences or number of compound-complex sentences.

Total number of sentences in essay:

Total number of simple sentences:
Percentage of simple sentences:

Total number of compound sentences:
Percentage of compound sentences:

Total number of complex sentences:
Percentage of complex sentences:

Total number of compound-complex sentences:
Percentage of compound-complex sentences:

Write down the sequence of grammatical types in two or three consecutive paragraphs.

WRITING TOGETHER

Have students work in pairs or in groups of three, and choose a topic of interest to all the members and then write passages of at least twenty-five short sentences (shorter than twelve words). After trading passages with another group or pair, ask each group to combine some of the twenty-five sentences into longer sentences, while retaining some short sentences for emphasis.

Naturally, each group will combine sentences differently, so you might want to make an opportunity to explain their choices and reasons for combining some sentences while keeping others short.

WRITERS ON WRITING

Don't think and then write it down. Think on paper.

—HARRY KEMELMAN

1. Checking for varied sentence types

As you revise, check to see that you have varied your sentence types sufficiently. Begin by noting the grammatical types you have used, marking each of your sentences as simple, compound, complex, or compound-complex. If any one or two patterns overwhelmingly predominate, combine, divide, and otherwise revise sentences until you have a wide range of types in your draft.

Next, note any sentences that are commands, questions, or exclamations. Decide whether these sentences are appropriate in context, and if not, delete or revise them.

To check for rhetorical sentence types, underline the independent clause(s) in each sentence. If a sentence opens with an independent clause and then builds with a series of modifying details, label it cumulative. If a sentence opens with a series of subordinating clauses or phrases and holds the independent clause "in suspense" until the end, label it periodic. (Many sentences will be neither.) Now consider whether each type is being used as effectively as possible. For each periodic sentence, see if you have used suspense to best advantage and built up to a climax. For each cumulative sentence, see if you have established your main point at the beginning and if the information in the rest of the sentence develops this point clearly and grammatically.

Finally, look at the balance of all sentence types. If your writing is like most people's, you will have few periodic sentences; few imperative, interrogative, or exclamatory sentences; and few compound-complex sentences. Be aware of this information as you revise, but do not revise arbitrarily to include more of a specific type. Revise only when the content calls for it—if, for instance, a sentence contains a surprise, a periodic structure will help emphasize that surprise.

Study how the sentences in the following passage are identified and then revised:

FIRST DRAFT

The purpose of speech is most often to persuade. [simple] It is seldom to generate understanding or to stimulate thoughtful response. [simple] Speeches on television take advantage of this fact. [simple] A televised speech gives viewers the time only to receive information, to respond emotionally to it, to "feel" it. [simple/cumulative] Viewers can simply enjoy or deplore its impact. [simple] Unlike a televised speech, a written speech can be read, reread, and analyzed. [simple] The reader can thoroughly process and analyze it. [simple] For this reason, I prefer to read

VARYING SENTENCE TYPES

and study a speech, not watch and instantly swallow it. [simple] This preference is limited to speeches that may be of great importance to me. [simple]

REVISED

The purpose of speech is most often not to generate understanding or to stimulate thoughtful response; rather, its purpose is merely to persuade. [compound] A televised speech takes advantage of this merely persuasive purpose by giving viewers time only to receive information, to respond emotionally to it, to "feel" or simply enjoy or deplore it. [simple/cumulative] Unlike a televised speech, a written speech can be read and reread, thoroughly analyzed and processed. [simple/periodic] For this reason, I prefer to read and study, not watch and instantly "swallow," any speech that may be of great importance to me. [complex]

EXERCISE 20.4

Following is an introductory paragraph from an essay. Analyze the paragraph carefully, noting for each sentence, the length, the kind of opening, and the grammatical and rhetorical type. Then revise the paragraph to add variety in sentence lengths, sentence openings, and sentence types.

When we arrived at the accident scene, I could tell that the injuries were not minor. I walked up to the car nearest me to check the injuries of the people inside. I looked through the driver's window and saw the woman's body entangled in the steering wheel. I told dispatch, via two-way radio, to send medics "code red, lights and siren." I then went to see how the passenger in the car was. The passenger appeared to be in shock and had a broken leg. The officer walked over and checked the other vehicle. The driver of the other vehicle was drunk and had received no injuries at all.

READING WITH AN EYE FOR SENTENCE VARIETY

Read the following paragraph, paying careful attention to the way the author varies its sentences—in length, opening, and types (grammatical, functional, and rhetorical).

I was never much of an athlete, but I was once a member of a team. Indeed, I was its star, and we were champions. I belonged to a squad of speed readers, although I was never awarded a letter for it. Still, we took on the top teams in our territory, and read as rapidly as possible every time we were challenged to a match, hoping to finish in front of our opponents: that tow-headed punk from Canton, the tomato-cheeked girl from Marietta, or that silent pair of sisters, all spectacles and squints, who looked tough as German script, and who hailed from Shaker Heights, Ohio, a region noted for its swift,

ANSWERS TO EXERCISE 20.4 (WILL VARY)

When we arrived at the accident scene, I could tell that the injuries were not minor. (CX; 16 words; adverb clause) I walked up to the car nearest me to check the injuries of the people inside. (S; 16 words; subject) I looked through the driver's window and saw the lady's body entangled in the steering wheel. (S; 16 words; subject) I told dispatch, via two-way radio, to send medics "code red, lights and siren." (S; 14 words; subject) I then went to see how the passenger in the car was. (S; 12 words; subject) The passenger appeared to be in shock and had a broken leg. (S; 12 words; subject) The officer walked over and checked the other vehicle. (S; 9 words; subject) The driver of the other vehicle was drunk and had received no injuries at all. (S; 15 words; subject)

OPTIONAL EXERCISE

To extend exercise 20.4, read aloud the following paragraph and ask your students to analyze and revise it according to the instructions for exercise 20.4.

The bell rang, and I ran to my locker to put my books up. I hurried to get out of the parking lot before the gang of kids got out of the building. I had to hurry that day because my football game started in three hours. I lived approximately five minutes from the school, so it was a short ride. I ran into the house and began looking for my football uniform. I crammed everything into my equipment bag. Then I ran to my car and returned to school.

20c *var*   VARYING SENTENCE STRUCTURES

TEACHING PRACTICE

Be sure to read this passage aloud, so that students can practice *listening* to variation in length, opening, and sentence types. You might want to use this reading exercise as a springboard into writing, asking students to write a paragraph describing their own membership in some team and aiming for excellent use of variation throughout.

TEACHING PRACTICE

Ask students to make an entry in their writing logs (or to write a brief paragraph to you) reporting on their findings and explaining a plan for incorporating greater variety into their own prose.

mean raveners of text. We called ourselves "The Speeders." Of course. Everybody did. There were the Sharon Speeders, the Steubenville Speeders, the Sperryville Speeders, and the Niles Nouns. The Niles Nouns never won. How could they—with that name. Nouns are always at rest.

—WILLIAM GASS, "On Reading to Oneself"

FOR EXAMINING SENTENCE VARIETY IN YOUR OWN WRITING

Choose several paragraphs of an essay you have recently written, and examine them very carefully for variety of sentence structure. For each sentence, note the length, the kind of opening, and the grammatical, functional, and rhetorical type. Then revise the paragraphs to achieve as wide a range of variation as possible in these qualities. Read the original and revised versions aloud, noting the differences in rhythm and impact.

21. Creating Memorable Prose

How many times have you read something so striking that you wanted immediately to share it with a friend? And how many times have you remembered the exact words of something you have read or heard? All of us recognize, and can even quote, certain passages from literature or history—the opening of A *Tale of Two Cities*, perhaps, or passages from "I Have a Dream." As students of writing, we would profit by taking the time to examine some of the elements that make pieces such as these so memorable. Consider, for instance, some lines from one of the most quoted speeches of recent times, John F. Kennedy's Inaugural Address:

> Let every nation know, whether it wishes us well or ill, that we shall   1
> pay any price, bear any burden, meet any hardship, support any friend,
> oppose any foe to assure the survival and the success of liberty.
>
> In your hands, my fellow citizens, more than mine, will rest the final   2
> success or failure of our course.
>
> And so, my fellow Americans, ask not what your country can do for   3
> you; ask what you can do for your country.
>   —JOHN F. KENNEDY, Inaugural Address

What strategies did Kennedy use to make these lines so very memorable? First would be his use of *repetition:* in sentence 1, the repetition of short verb phrases, each with the word *any*, creates a powerful, hammerlike rhythm. Second might be his use of *inverted word order:* saving the subject until the end of sentence 2 adds dramatic emphasis

337

USEFUL READING

Highet, Gilbert. "Ciceronianism and Anti-Ciceronianism." *Prose Style: A Historical Approach through Studies*. San Francisco: Chandler, 1971. 53–62. Highet provides a discussion of the plain style versus embellished style debate, focusing on Cicero's influence and participation.

Lanham, Richard A. *Analyzing Prose*. New York: Scribner's, 1983. Lanham provides a full system for stylistic analyses.

(BACK)GROUNDING

"Creating Memorable Prose" has not been a stylistic goal for every philosopher of rhetoric throughout history. In fact as far back as Plato, we can find the debate over whether discourse should be "memorable" or not. We can phrase the basic issue this way: Should a writer's style be distinctive and conspicuous, or should it be so plain as to be transparent?

Inherent in Plato's attack on rhetoric as a craft that may be used to obscure truth is the notion that the rhetorician manipulates the audience through the use of stylistic devices. In Rome, several hundred centuries later, rhetoricians debated over whether "Asiatic" style—ornate, highly mannered, emotional, and associated with the famous Roman orator and rhetorician Cicero—was to be preferred over "Attic" style with its "virtues" of brevity, simplicity, and sincerity. In the early seventeenth century, with the rise of science, some philosophers and rhetoricians, among them Francis Bacon, reacted strongly against the "Ciceronianism" of past discourse. They preferred the simple, utilitarian style of scientific discourse. Thomas Sprat in his *History of the Royal Society* (1667) calls for the banishment of eloquence. He said that society ought "to reject all amplifications, digressions, and swellings of style" and "to return back to the primitive purity and shortness, when men deliver'd so many things in an equal number of words" (qtd. in Corbett, *Classical Rhetoric for the Modern Student*, 616). Even today, the debate continues, though in less extreme forms. Of the ten "lessons" in Joseph M. Williams' *Style: Ten Lessons in Clarity and Grace*, seven are concerned primarily with achieving clarity, especially by controlling long sentences. Only one deals with embellishment per se. On the other hand, Richard A. Lanham in *Analyzing Prose* argues against a strict adoption of what he calls the "C-B-S" (clarity, brevity, sincerity) style.

to his statement. Third would be his use of *antithesis*, seen in sentence 3 in the two parallel clauses that accentuate the contrast of self and country. Finally, Kennedy's reliance on *strong verbs* and the *active voice* results in prose that is lively and thus memorable.

Each of these strategies and devices can be used to good effect by all writers. This chapter will examine each one and offer practice to help you use them in your work, to make your writing not only worth reading—but worth remembering.

▌21a. Choosing strong verbs

The greatest writers in any language are those with a genius for choosing the precise words that will arrest and hold a reader's attention. In your own writing, you can help to gain this attention by using precise nouns and adjectives instead of vague, catchall "buzzwords" (see 17b2). Perhaps even more important, however, you can use strong, precise verbs instead of weak, catchall verbs and instead of nouns.

▌1. Using strong, precise verbs

Verbs serve as the real workhorses of our language. Take a look, for instance, at the strong, precise verbs in the following passage:

> A fire engine, out for a trial spin, *roared* past Emerson's house, hot with readiness for public duty. Over the barn roofs the martens *dipped* and *chittered*. A swarthy daughter of an asparagus grower, in culottes, shirt, and bandanna, *pedalled* past on her bicycle.
>
> –E. B. WHITE, "Walden"

Instead of the italicized verbs, White could have used more general verbs such as *drove, flew, called,* and *rode*. But the more precise verbs are stronger because they give readers vivid sensory impressions of the actions they express. In White's verbs, readers can hear the roar of the fire engine, see the martens swooping downward and hear them chirping shrilly, and feel the girl pushing on the pedals of her bicycle.

Some of the most common verbs in English—especially *be, do,* and *have*—carry little or no sense of specific action, and many writers tend to overuse them in a situation where a more precise verb would be clearer and more effective. Look at how the following sentences are strengthened by replacing forms of *be, do,* and *have* with more precise verbs:

CHOOSING STRONG VERBS

WEAK   Constant viewing of rock videos *is* harmful to children's emotional development.

REVISED   Constant viewing of rock videos *stunts* and *distorts* children's emotional development.

WEAK   In front of the hotel, an artist would *do* your portrait on a framed sheet of glass.

REVISED   In front of the hotel, an artist would *etch* your portrait on a framed sheet of glass.

WEAK   We *had* basic training at Fort Ord.

REVISED   We *sweated* through basic training at Fort Ord.

The verb *be* is essential to writing; indeed, it appears in some of the most memorable English prose, such as the opening of the Gospel According to St. John:

> In the beginning was the Word, and the Word was with God, and the Word was God.

As the three examples above illustrate, however, forms of *be* can often be replaced by verbs that express action. As a general rule of thumb, if forms of *be* (*is, are, was, were, has been,* and so on) account for more than about a third of the verbs in a piece of writing, the writing may well seem static and flat.

Expletives

One potentially weak verb construction to watch out for is the **expletive,** which begins with *there* or *it* followed by a form of *be.* Expletives can be effective ways of introducing something with extra emphasis, but too many writers tend to overuse them, resulting in sentences that needlessly bury action in a noun, verbal, or dependent clause. Notice how the following sentences are strengthened by deleting the expletive:

WEAK   *There are* many people who fear success because they believe they do not deserve it.

REVISED   Many people *fear* success because they believe they do not deserve it.

WEAK   *It is* necessary for a presidential candidate today to perform well on television.

REVISED   A presidential candidate today *must perform* well on television.

339

USEFUL READING

Havelock, Eric A. "The Character and Content of the Code." Rpt. in *The Literate Revolution in Speech and Its Cultural Consequences* (Princeton: Princeton UP, 1982). 140–144. Havelock identifies the characteristics of memorable oral speech: parataxis, echoes, correspondences and symmetries, foreshadowing, and repetition.

TEACHING PRACTICE

Consider structuring your discussions of how to achieve memorable prose around a reading of George Orwell's "Politics and the English Language." In this essay, Orwell discusses what he considers to be the "mental vices" of modern prose: dying metaphors, pretentious diction, meaningless words, and euphemisms. Orwell also has a list of rules that could provoke discussion:

1. Never use a metaphor, simile or other figure of speech which you are used to seeing in print.
2. Never use a long word where a short one will do.
3. If it is possible to cut a word out, always cut it out.
4. Never use a passive voice where you can use an active.
5. Never use a foreign phrase, a scientific word or a jargon word if you can think of an everyday English equivalent.
6. Break any of these rules sooner than say anything outright barbarous.

You might ask your students to imagine instances where these rules might not apply. For example, both this handbook and Orwell advise against using the passive voice; however, many of the headlines in daily newspapers are cast in the passive. Is this appropriate? Discussions of these rules or similar ones should lead students to examine what they write more closely and help them form their own theories of style and the appropriate occasions for various styles of writing.

(BACK)GROUNDING

Expletive structures can be used effectively for emphasis, especially if you want to highlight what immediately follows the weak beginning. For instance, consider the sentence *It was Alice Roosevelt Longworth who said of Thomas E. Dewey, "He looks like the little man on the wedding cake."*

WRITING TOGETHER

Ask students to bring a section of a newspaper to class. Direct their attention to the headlines, and ask them to make a list of the headlines that they think are most effective. Divide the class into small groups of three to five, and ask them to read their lists of headlines and identify strong verbs and nouns. Next, ask students to rewrite the headlines with weak verbs and nouns. Finally, ask one member of each group to read the following: (1) a few of the headlines that the group felt used strong verbs and nouns, and (2) some of the weak headlines and the group's revisions of those weak headlines.

ANSWERS TO EXERCISE 21.1 (WILL VARY)

1. Fanatic groups threaten the American people.
2. I work for two brothers who own a hardware store.
3. Two hundred students might work as extras in a movie to be shot on our campus.
4. The sweater feels soft and warm.
5. In some places, tests determine if children get into kindergarten.

ANSWERS TO EXERCISE 21.2 (WILL VARY)

Not all the verbs in this passage necessarily must be changed. Here is a sample revision:

Dating is a socially acceptable form of getting to know members of the opposite sex. On a date, a couple ought to have fun. But I haven't had a fun date recently. In fact, my last two dates ended in fiascos. Although complete opposites, Steve and Dave were both duds.

(BACK)GROUNDING

In *Style: Ten Lessons in Clarity and Grace* (18), Joseph Williams offers four cases of useful nominalization:

1. Nominalizations can be subjects referring to previous sentences: *These arguments* all depend on a single unproven claim.
2. Nominalizations can name what would be the objects of their verbs: I do not understand *her meaning.*
3. *The fact that* typically can be reduced to a more succinct nominalization: *My denial* [replacing *the fact that I denied*] his accusations impressed the jury.
4. Some nominalizations serve as a conventional shorthand, having well established already: *Taxation* without *representation* was not the central concern of the American *Revolution.*

EXERCISE 21.1

Revise the following sentences, replacing any weak verbs—especially forms of *be, do,* and *have*—with stronger and more specific verbs.

> *Example*
>
> It is argued by many that doctors do unnecessary tests to make more money.
>
> Many argue that doctors *order* unnecessary tests to collect more money.

1. Fanatic groups are a threat to the American people.
2. I have a job with two brothers who have a hardware store.
3. There is an opportunity for two hundred students to be extras in a movie to be shot on our campus.
4. The sweater is soft and warm.
5. In some places, children have tests to get into kindergarten.

EXERCISE 21.2

Revise the sentences in the following paragraph, replacing weak verbs (and particularly forms of *be*) with stronger and more specific verbs.

Dating is a socially acceptable form of getting to know members of the opposite sex. On a date, a couple is supposed to have fun. This outcome has not been the case with me lately. My last two dates were fiascos. Steve was one extreme, and Dave was another. As far as personalities were concerned, they were both duds.

2. Changing nouns to verbs

Much modern writing tends to express action by using nouns that are formed from verbs, a process called **nominalization.** Although nominalization can help make prose clearer and more concise—for example, using *abolition* instead of *the process of abolishing*—it can also produce the opposite effect, making a sentence unnecessarily wordy and hard to read. Nominalization reduces the *active* quality of a sentence, burying the action in an abstract noun and forcing the writer to use weak, generalized verbs and too many prepositional phrases. Too often, writers use nominalizations not to make a complex process easier to talk about but to make an idea *sound* more complex and abstract than it really is. Bureaucratic writing especially tends to use excessive nominalization in this way.

You can decide when to use a nominalized form and when to use the verb from which it derives by asking one question: which is

CHOOSING STRONG VERBS   *pr* 21a

most readily understandable? Take a look at the following sentence, for example:

> The firm is now engaged in an assessment of its procedures for the development of new products.

This sentence scarcely impresses itself on our memories, and it sounds pretentious and stuffy as well. In contrast, note the more easily understood and forceful version:

> The firm is now assessing its procedures for developing new products.

3. Checking your verbs and nouns

To revise a draft for stronger verbs, first circle all the verbs, and look to see whether you are relying too much on *be, do,* and *have.* If so, try to substitute more specific verbs whenever possible. Next, circle every noun whose meaning could be expressed by a verb. Try rewriting the sentence using the verb instead of the noun, adjusting any words necessary to keep the meaning you intended. Finally, underline all expletives, omitting any that are not used to create special emphasis. Study how the following passage is revised:

WEAK

Last February, when I made the determination to buy a house, I opened a separate checking (and savings) account in order to give attention more easily to my household expenses. (There is a credit union policy that for every checking account there must be a matching savings account: thus the dormant savings account.) This new checking account was where the deposit of the inheritance from my grandmother occurred along with any other accumulation of money from outside sources.

REVISED

Last February, when I determined to buy a house, I opened a separate checking (and savings) account to deal more easily with household expenses. (Credit union policy demands a matching savings account for every checking account; thus the dormant savings account.) Into this new checking account I deposited the inheritance from my grandmother, along with any other money I accumulated from outside sources.

EXERCISE 21.3

Revise the following paragraph to eliminate weak verbs and unnecessary nominalizations and expletives.

(BACK)GROUNDING

Joseph Williams also lists five common patterns of abstract nominalization and how to revise them (15–17):

1. When the nominalization is the subject of an empty verb, change the nominalization to a verb and find a new subject: "Our *intention* is" becomes "We *intend.*"
2. When the nominalization follows an empty verb, change the nominalization to a verb that can replace the empty verb; "The committee has no *expectation*" becomes "The committee does not *expect.*"
3. When the nominalization follows a *there is* or *there are*, change the nominalization to a verb that replaces the *is* or *are* and find a subject: "There is a *need* for further *study*" becomes "The staff *must study.*"
4. When a nominalization in a subject is linked to another nominalization in the predicate by a verb or a phrase that expresses some kind of logical connection such as cause and effect, condition and consequence, revise as follows: (a) Change both abstractions to verbs, (b) find the subject of those verbs, and (c) link the new clauses with a word that expresses the logical connection: "the group's failure was the result of its chairman's resignation" becomes "the group failed because its chairman resigned."
5. When you have two nominalizations in a row, turn at least the first into a verb. Then either leave the second as it is or turn it into a verb in a clause beginning with *how* or *why:* "There was first a *review* of the evolution of the medial dorsal fin" becomes "First, she *reviewed* the *evolution* of the medial dorsal fin."

ANSWERS TO EXERCISE 21.3 WILL VARY

(BACK)GROUNDING

Both active and passive voices are natural to English speakers. When people are asked to recall a passage or sentence, they will regularly remember the verb as active even when it was passive in the original. Yet, occasions do occur when the passive is more natural and memorable. For instance, when relating something that happened to ourselves, we use the passive voice as often as the active:

> I was bruised by the fall.
> The fall bruised me.

Otto Jespersen notes in *Essentials of English Grammar,* "As a rule the person or thing that is the centre of interest at the moment is made the subject of the sentence, and therefore the verb is in some cases put in the active, in others in the passive" (120).

As a rule of thumb, Joseph Williams, in *Style: Ten Lessons in Clarity and Grace,* suggests avoiding all "unnecessary" passive constructions (21). That is, when an active construction says exactly what the passive construction says and works as effectively (often more so), then the student ought to use the active voice. In choosing between active and passive, Williams says we ought to ask ourselves two questions. "First, must your audience know who is performing the action? Second, are you able to maintain a logical consistency in the subjects of your sentences?" (22). If the writer finds she is shifting from one subject to another from sentence to sentence in a passage, then she ought to try revising these sentences in the active voice.

The writing instructor needs to be aware that there are contexts in which the passive voice is expected and may even be preferred. A reporter protecting his or her source will write, "It is reported that. . . ." In such cases, the reader must be the final judge. However, in some academic settings, passive voice is not just expected; it is commanded by the conventions of the discipline. In scientific writing, for example, the writer is expected to remain objective; the third-person reflects that objectivity better than the first-person. Williams calls the voice used in such situations "the institutional passive" (23).

There has long been resistance to the proposition that the effectiveness of methods and teachers must be measured in terms of the results secured. Those responsible for evaluating teachers have exalted procedures in teaching and have seldom examined the products, that is, the efficiency of the teacher as indicated by what his or her pupils can do following instruction. However, we are beginning to see an increasing number of bold proposals founded on the assumption that the American public has expectations of results from schooling. As public support of education increases, there will be greater insistence on judging a teacher in the light of his or her ability to enhance the learning of pupils.

▌ 21b. Choosing between active and passive voice

In addition to choosing strong, precise verbs, you can help to make your prose memorable by varying those verbs appropriately between active and passive voice. Look at the following paragraph:

> A young man might go into military flight training believing that he was entering some sort of technical school in which he was simply going to acquire a certain set of skills. Instead, he found himself all at once enclosed in a fraternity. And in this fraternity, even though it was military, men were not rated by their outward rank as ensigns, lieutenants, commanders, or whatever. No, herein the world was divided into those who had it and those who did not. This quality, this *it,* was never named, however, nor was it talked about in any way.
> –TOM WOLFE, *The Right Stuff*

In this paragraph, Wolfe introduces the indefinable quality that he has made the title of his book. Notice that in the first sentence, the focus is on someone, a hypothetical young man, *doing* things: going into flight training, entering a school, acquiring skills. All of the verbs are in the active voice.

In the second sentence, the verb is still active. But notice that because the subject and object are the same person, because the subject of the verb *found* also receives the action of the verb, the sentence almost has the *feel* of being in the passive voice, as if the verb were *was enclosed.* And in the independent clauses of the last three sentences, the focus clearly shifts to things *being done* (or not done): men not being rated, the world being divided, and a quality never being named or talked about. The persons doing these things are unimportant or unknown; in fact, like the quality itself, they are never named, and the verbs are in the passive voice. Notice, however, that Wolfe returns

---

USEFUL READING

Jespersen, Otto. *Essentials of English Grammar.* University, AL: U of Alabama P, 1964. In this work, originally published in 1933, Jespersen synthesizes the principles that inform his seven-volume *Modern English Grammar.* Although often dismissed as a "traditional" grammarian, Jespersen shows great insight and has had a substantial influence on later linguistic theory. The work can be a useful reference book.

CREATING SPECIAL EFFECTS

pr 21c

to the active voice when he again wants to emphasize the persons doing something: *those who had it and those who did not.*

To make your writing memorable, try to use the active voice whenever possible. Because the passive focuses attention away from the performer of an action and because it is usually wordier than the active, excessive use of it makes for dull and difficult reading.

But as the Wolfe paragraph indicates, the passive can be used very effectively in certain situations: when the performer is unknown, unwilling to be identified, or less important than the recipient of the action. In the last sentence, for example, Wolfe could have written *No one ever named this quality, this* it, *however, nor did anyone talk about it in any way.* By using the passive voice, however, he focuses attention on the quality itself rather than on the persons who do not name or talk about it; in fact, by not mentioning them, he heightens the sense of a mysterious quality that cannot be defined.

See Chapter 8 for further discussion of voice.

EXERCISE 21.4

Look at the following sentences, in which some of the verbs are active and some passive. Then rewrite each sentence in the other voice, and decide which version you find preferable and why.

> **Example**
> You are hereby relieved of your duties by me.
> I hereby relieve you of your duties.

1. In Gower's research, it was found that pythons often dwell in trees and live near rivers.
2. They started shooting pool, and before Marie knew it, she owed the kid ten dollars.
3. When I was eight, my father's crazy dreams uprooted our family from Florida to California.
4. For me, living in a dorm was more easily adjusted to than living in an apartment.
5. The image of native Americans has been totally distorted by Hollywood in most of its films about the West.

▌ 21c. Creating special effects

Contemporary movies often live or die, succeed or fail, on the basis of their special effects. In the same way, special effects, like repe-

ANSWERS TO EXERCISE 21.4 (WILL VARY)

1. In his research, Gower found that pythons often dwell in trees and live near rivers.

   The active construction is preferable. It gives Gower the responsibility and recognition he deserves.
2. They started shooting pool, and before Marie knew it, ten dollars was owed to the kid.

   Preference depends somewhat upon the context. The passive voice is unclear about who owes the kid ten dollars. Is Marie alone? Are she and the kid the "they" of the sentence, or is someone else involved? The active is clearer but might be incorrect, if others besides Marie owe the kid money.
3. When I was eight, our family was uprooted from Florida to California by my father's crazy dreams.

   The active is preferred, since the passive doesn't add anything to the text.
4. I adjusted more easily to living in a dorm than to living in an apartment.

   Again, the active is preferred, since the passive adds nothing.
5. Westerns totally distort the image of native Americans.

   Again, much depends on context. Which is to be emphasized: native Americans? or Westerns?

(BACK)GROUNDING

Linguistic special effects are not unlike the special effects produced for films; they can be spectacular and obvious or quiet and subtle; they ought to be meaningful, not simply ornamental. Of course, the choices of special effects—which to use, when to use them, whether to use them at all—depend upon the overall rhetorical effects sought. The style of James Joyce probably is not appropriate for a business report. Students need to recognize that different writing situations involve different reader expectations. Special effects may make for livelier prose, but not always more appropriate prose.

OPTIONAL EXERCISE

The difference between effective and ineffective repetition can be difficult to pinpoint and is sometimes even a matter of taste. Ask students to consider the following passage. Is the writer's use of repetition effective? Italics are added for emphasis.

> My thesis is that such a search demands total involvement and maximum awareness, but that man is encapsulated. *By encapsulated I mean* claiming to have the whole truth when one has only part of it. *By encapsulated I mean* looking at life partially and proceeding to make statements concerning the whole of life. And *by encapsulated I mean* living partially because one's daily activities are based on a world-view or philosophy of life which is meager next to the larger meaning of existence. Thus, this book focuses its attention on the dilemma of contemporary specialism in work. *I mean*, in other words, the outlook that only certain views are correct and that only certain people have the proper background to have these views. *I mean* the narrowing down of vocational tasks brought on by the industrial revolution and resulting in twenty different "experts" making a shoe rather than one master shoemaker. *I mean* the situation in which a person dares not comment "outside his field" and feels he must take a course in electrical engineering before replacing a light bulb. *I mean* those policies which are promulgated as supra-national but are, in fact, nationalistic in intent. *I mean*, in short, the fragmentary ethos of the 20th century. (Joseph R. Royce, *The Encapsulated Man*)

On answer would be that although the writer has used parallel structures, what is being repeated is unnecessary information. After the first few times saying "I mean," readers understand; the rest is overkill.

ANSWERS TO EXERCISE 21.5 WILL VARY

tition, antithesis, and inversion can animate your prose and often make it much more memorable.

1. Using repetition

Carefully used, repetition of sounds, words, phrases, or other grammatical constructions serves as a powerful stylistic device. Orators in particular have long known its power. Here is a famous use of repetition, from one of Sir Winston Churchill's addresses to the British people during World War II:

> We shall not flag or fail, we shall go on to the end. We shall fight in France, we shall fight on the seas and oceans, we shall fight with growing confidence and growing strength in the air, we shall defend our island, whatever the cost may be; we shall fight on the beaches, . . . we shall fight in the fields and in the streets, . . . we shall never surrender.
> —WINSTON CHURCHILL

In this passage, the constant hammering *we shall*, accompanied by the repetition of *f* sounds (*flag, fail, fight, France, confidence, defend, fields*) had the effect of strengthening British resolve.

Though we may not be prime ministers, we can use repetition to equally good effect. Here are some examples by students.

> So my dream date turned into a nightmare. Where was the quiet, considerate, caring guy I thought I had met? In his place appeared this jerk. He strutted, he postured, he preened—and then he bragged, he bellowed, he practically brayed—just like the donkey he so much reminded me of.

> Pepperoni and sausage, mushrooms and olives, onions and anchovies, peppers and tomatoes, and cheese and cheese and cheese: we ate it all. We ate, and ate, and ate, and ate. And when we couldn't possibly eat another bite, . . . then we ate some more.

Be careful, however, to use repetition only for a deliberate purpose. See 17b for a discussion of how unnecessary repetition can lead to wordiness.

EXERCISE 21.5

Go through the examples above, identifying all of the uses of repetition. Then, using one example as a model, write a passage of your own that uses repetition effectively.

USEFUL READING

Tufte, Virginia. *Grammar as Style*. New York: Holt, 1971. Tufte discusses the stylistic consequences of various grammatical elements, including passive voice, repetition, antithesis, inversion, and elliptical constructions. Her emphasis is on how writers use grammar to create memorable prose and not as much on how writers can avoid problems with grammar.

CREATING SPECIAL EFFECTS   pr 21c

2. Using antithesis

Another special effect that can contribute to memorable writing is **antithesis,** the use of parallel structures to highlight contrast or opposition. Like other uses of parallelism (see Chapter 19), antithesis provides a pleasing rhythm that calls readers' attention to the contrast, often in a startling or amusing way. For example:

> Love is an ideal thing, marriage a real thing.

> The congregation didn't think much of the new preacher, and what the new preacher thought of the congregation she didn't wish to say.

> It is a sin to believe evil of others—but it is not a mistake.
>   –H. L. MENCKEN

You can often use antithesis effectively when you are developing a paragraph by the alternating method of comparison and contrast (see 2h3 and 5d). By using parallel form to express the differences between two things or ideas or between two aspects of the same thing or idea, antithesis helps to clarify the points of contrast in a way that is easy for readers to follow and remember. Look at the following sentences from a paragraph contrasting the situation of ROTC on American campuses during the Vietnam War and in the late 1980s; each sentence is an example of antithesis:

> Yesterday's officers admired and emulated Pershing and Patton; today's cadets admire and emulate Lee Iacocca or Bunker Hunt. The management of money and materials, not the command of combat troops, is of the most interest to many of them.

EXERCISE 21.6

Using one of the examples of antithesis above, create a sentence of your own that uses antithesis. Then consider whether the antithesis makes the sentence more memorable or effective. You might begin by thinking of pairs of opposites you could build on: hope-despair, good-evil, spring-fall, fire-ice. Or you might begin with a *topic* you want to write an antithesis about: success, greed, generosity, pet peeves, and so on.

3. Using inverted word order

Inversion, or altering the usual word order of a sentence, can make for memorable writing by creating surprise or putting emphasis on a particular word or phrase. The word order in English is usually

(BACK)GROUNDING
Antithesis was included as a figure of speech by classical rhetoricians. The anonymous author of *Rhetorica ad Alexandrum* notes that the antithesis can be either strictly a matter of style or strictly a matter of content or a matter of both.

(BACK)GROUNDING
Use of antithesis carried through multiple sentences in modern prose is unusual. Typically, we find antithesis as short, sharp contrasts. Here's an example:

> Shallow understanding from people of good will is more frustrating than absolute misunderstanding from people of ill will. Lukewarm acceptance is much more bewildering than outright rejection. (Martin Luther King, Jr., "Letter from Birmingham Jail")

ANSWERS TO EXERCISE 21.6 WILL VARY

(BACK)GROUNDING

Readers come to sentences with certain expectations, conditioned by familiarity to recognize typical patterns of language. For English speakers, one of these patterns is the subject-verb-object structure of the basic declarative sentence. Expectations change when we read a question or an imperative; we expect inversions then. But inversions in declarative sentences surprise us, and that surprise can be used to good effect.

As with any special effect, some inversions are less ornamental than others. Look at this Truman Capote sentence from *The Glass Harp*:

> Dolly she called Dollyheart, but Verena she called That One,

This sentence is much clearer in its inverted form than if structured conventionally:

> She called Dolly Dollyheart, but she called Verena That One.

A good rule of thumb in using inversion is the test of emphasis. Placement within a sentence alters the emphasis that a word gets. Here is a sentence from Mary McCarthy's *Cast a Cold Eye*:

> Gone are the potted plants, the Christmas cheeses, the toys for the children that were regularly issued by the old Francis Cleary.

Note the drastic change in emphasis when we restructure the sentence into its conventional form:

> The potted plants, the Christmas cheeses, the toys for the children that were regularly issued by the old Francis Cleary are gone.

ANSWERS TO EXERCISE 21.7 WILL VARY

subject–verb–object/complement (if any). Inversion refers to any change in that order, such as putting the verb before the subject or putting the object or complement before the subject and verb. Look at the following example:

NORMAL   Two dead birds plummeted out of the tree.

INVERTED   Out of the tree plummeted two dead birds.

The inverted word order of the second version makes for a more dramatic sentence by putting the emphasis on *two dead birds* at the end of the sentence.

As with any unusual sentence pattern, inverted word order should be used sparingly. But as the following examples illustrate, inversion can indeed create special effects:

> Into this grey lake plopped the thought, I know this man, don't I?
> –DORIS LESSING

> In a hole in the ground there lived a hobbit.   –J. R. R. TOLKIEN

> The bulk of her estate she left to the SPCA.

> Good-looking he was not; wealthy he was not; but brilliant—he was.

> Vietnam passed and with its passing came a new era for ROTC.

EXERCISE 21.7

After studying the examples of inversion above, look at an essay you have recently written, and find a sentence that might be more effective with inverted word order. Experiment with the word order, reading the results aloud and comparing differences in effect.

READING WITH AN EYE FOR MEMORABLE PROSE

Think of something in either your past or your current reading that sticks in your mind as particularly memorable. Then find that piece of writing, and reread it to identify what structures, techniques, and special effects make the passage so memorable.

FOR CREATING MEMORABLE PROSE OF YOUR OWN

The last five chapters have presented many elements that mark effective prose. One excellent—and amusing—way to practice these elements lies in a special kind of imitation. Choose a writer you very much admire—Virginia Woolf, Chaucer, Shakespeare, Alice Walker, Stephen King, Erma Bombeck—or any

CREATING SPECIAL EFFECTS   *pr* 21c

writer whose style you find unique. Then reread this writer's work, getting a "feel" for the rhythms, the structures, the special effects of the prose. Make a list of the elements that contribute to his or her distinctive style. Then choose a well-known story, and retell it in the style of your chosen author.

Following is the opening of a version of "The Three Little Pigs" written by one freshman as he imagined Edgar Allan Poe might have done. You can, if you wish, read one or two of Poe's stories and try finishing this version of "The Three Little Pigs."

It began as a mere infatuation. I admired them from afar, with a longing which only a wolf may know. Soon, these feelings turned to torment. Were I even to set eyes upon their porcine forms, the bowels of my soul raged, as if goaded by some festering poison. As the chilling winds of November howled, my gullet yearned for them. I soon feasted only upon an earnest and consuming desire for the moment of their decease.

FOR CREATING WRETCHED PROSE

Prose can be memorable for reasons quite different from those presented in this chapter. The Bulwer-Lytton Competition, known less formally as the "Wretched Writing" contest, challenges writers to produce an opening sentence to a novel, one that will celebrate the possibilities of "deliberate wretchedness" without hurting anyone's feelings. Writing strikingly bad opening sentences is great fun—and can be a true challenge. Here are a few finalists in a recent competition:

1. It was the eve of the yearly whale-slaughtering festival, thought Mamook as her horny fingers relentlessly pushed the whalebone needle through the sole of the mukluk; and suddenly, unaccountably, uncontrollably, she began to blubber.
2. Shirley doubted that her alien escort, composed as he was of vegetable matter, seaweed, and a thick coating of swampy muck, would be a suitable date for the Intergalactic kegger, but he turned out to be a real fungi.
3. When the last of the afterglow faded and the air was still, Josh liked to sit in the porch swing, in the dark, and test his night vision by spitting through the banisters.

Think of an idea for a story, and then write an opening sentence. Try to make it a "wonderfully bad" sentence. And why not enter it in the contest? Just send it to The Bulwer-Lytton Competition, c/o Professor Scott Rice, San Jose State University, San Jose, CA 95192.

TEACHING PRACTICE

Students can produce remarkably effective and amusing imitations. Have them complete the "Three Little Pigs" or create completely new imitations of their own, and ask them to bring in several representative pieces by the author being imitated. Then ask students to identify the *precise* characteristics that are being imitated. How, for instance, do we *know* that the passage here imitates Poe?

PART FIVE

Selecting Effective Words

22. Mastering Spelling

The historical evolution of the English language from the tongue of Germanic tribes to a hybrid of Germanic, Scandinavian, and Norman French, with a multitude of other languages represented as well, makes English spelling a complex system. For example, English includes at least twelve different ways of representing the *sh* sound: *shoe, sugar, ocean, issue, nation, schist, pshaw, suspicion, conscious, nauseous, mansion,* and *fuchsia*. As everyone who has ever struggled to remember—or to find—a correct spelling knows, this complexity can lead to much frustration, and in fact, some have called for "spelling liberation." When a judge in Dickens's *Pickwick Papers* asks Sam Weller how to spell a particular word, for instance, Weller insists, "That depends entirely upon the taste and fancy of the speller, my Lord." Closer to home, President Andrew Jackson once exclaimed in exasperation. "It's a damn poor mind that can think of only one way to spell a word!"

In spite of this tradition of complaint, modern linguists have demonstrated that English spelling is much more regular than is commonly thought and that this regularity relates not only to sound-letter connections but also to our stored visual memory of related words. We know that *president* is not spelled "presadent," for example, because we recognize its relation to *preside*.

The good news, then, is simply this: careful attention to your own spelling patterns and attention to some fairly straightforward guidelines of English spelling can lead you to master spelling. This chapter will introduce you to these guidelines and help you begin your analysis.

(BACK)GROUNDING

In their research for this handbook, Lunsford and Connors found in their national survey of freshman essays that spelling errors were the most common mistakes made by student writers. These findings suggest that error-free spelling cannot—and should not—be overlooked by writing instructors.

The public unfortunately believes that the majority of students are bad spellers, but in fact, the results of recent research contradict this notion. For instance, Karl Taylor and Ede Kidder conclude that generally, spelling errors decline from the first through the eighth grades. Only the "wrong words" category, primarily homonyms, increases ("The Development of Spelling Skills from First Grade through Eighth Grade." *Written Communication* 5 [April 1988]: 222–244). Their conclusion corroborates that of the authors, who found that the most frequent spelling errors involved problems with homonyms. As with other writing errors, spelling errors tend to fall into patterns which, once discovered, can be corrected.

351

USEFUL READING

Taylor, Karl K. and Ede B. Kidder. "The Development of Spelling Skills from First Grade through Eighth Grade." *Written Communication* 5 (1988): 222–244. The authors provide a clear description of a significant study on spelling and their findings and the implications of the study. The major conclusion is that while the total number of errors increase from the first through fourth grades, that same total number gradually decreases after the fourth grade.

(BACK)GROUNDING

In 1066, England was invaded for a fourth time. The Normans from France were led by William the Conqueror, and they overran the island in just a year. They declared their language, Norman French, to be the official language, and for the next 200 years or so, business, education, and government were all done in French. Literature was written in either French or Latin. English was considered barbaric. However, the government could not—and didn't even bother to try to—control the language of the masses. Therefore, English continued to be spoken by most people in their daily lives.

As with the Norse invasion earlier, the Normans influenced the lexicon of the English language but little else. In *The Origins and Development of the English Language*, Thomas Pyles and John Algeo point out that French spelling conventions were borrowed along with French vocabulary.

Pyles and Algeo note, "Some of the apparent innovations in Middle English spelling were, in fact, a return to earlier conventions" (139). For instance, *th* was reintroduced. "Other new spellings were true innovations" (139); *g* entered English orthography for the first time.

The Normans were finally exiled from France entirely, and French was spoken less and less. English began to reappear in education, in business affairs, and in government documents. By the fifteenth century, English had once again been taken up by imaginative writers. Chaucer's *The Canterbury Tales* was written in English.

22a. Mastering the most commonly misspelled words

A study of the spelling errors in the three thousand freshman essays that were used in the research for this book revealed a fairly small number of persistently misspelled words. A list of the fifty most common misspellings appears below. You may want to look over it carefully and compare it with words you have trouble spelling correctly (see 22f for ways to establish your own spelling inventory).

1. their/there/they're
2. too/to
3. a lot
4. noticeable
5. received/e/es
6. lose
7. you're/your
8. an/and
9. develop/s
10. definitely
11. than/then
12. believe/d/s
13. occurred
14. affect/s
15. cannot
16. separate
17. success
18. through
19. until
20. where
21. successful/ly
22. truly
23. argument/s
24. experience/s
25. environment
26. exercise/s/ing
27. necessary
28. sense
29. therefore
30. accept/ed
31. heroes
32. professor
33. whether
34. without
35. business/es
36. dependent
37. every day
38. may be
39. occasion/s
40. occurrences
41. woman
42. all right
43. apparent/ly
44. categories
45. final/ly
46. immediate/ely
47. roommate/s
48. against
49. before
50. beginning

EXERCISE 22.1

Choose the correct spelling from the pair of words in the parentheses in each of the sentences below. After checking your answers, compare your misspellings with the list of fifty words most frequently misspelled. Enter the words you misspelled in your spelling log.

1. (*Their/There/They're*) going to put (*their/there/they're*) new stereo system over (*their/there/they're*) in the corner.
2. My little brother wants (*to/too*) go swimming (*to/too*).
3. The (*begining/beginning*) of spring term is (*a lot/alot*) earlier this year than last.
4. The rise in temperature isn't (*noticable/noticeable*) (*until/untill*) the humidity rises.

5. The accident (*occured/occurred*) (*before/befour*) I could step aside.
6. We couldn't (*beleive/believe*) the national champions were expected to (*loose/lose*) the playoffs.
7. In making your major life decisions, (*your/you're*) (*definately/definitely*) on (*your/you're*) own.
8. Nothing (*affects/effects*) (*success/sucess*) more (*than/then*) self-confidence or (*its/it's*) absence.
9. We (*received/recieved*) our notice (*threw/through*) the mail.
10. The group hopes to (*develop/develope*) a (*trully/truly*) (*succesful/successful*) fast-food franchise.
11. We (*can not/cannot*) easily (*separate/seperate*) fact and opinion.
12. Please tell me (*wear/where*) (*an/and*) when we should meet.
13. Our (*argumants/arguments*) (*against/aginst*) continuing to pollute the (*enviroment/environment*) fell on deaf ears.
14. Local (*businesses/businesses*) are (*dependant/dependent*) on a strong tourist trade.
15. (*Heroes/Heros*) are (*necesary/necessary*) to every culture's mythology.
16. Our first (*experiance/experience*) with aerobic (*exercise/exercize*) left us tired.
17. The (*professor/profesor*) agreed to (*accept/except*) our essays on Friday.
18. Our top speaker qualified for three (*catagories/categories*) in the (*final/finel*) competition.
19. The two (*roomates/roommates*) would be lost (*without/witout*) each other.
20. We intend to celebrate the (*ocasion/occasion*) (*weather/whether*) or not the (*weather/whether*) cooperates.
21. The plane to Chicago (*may be/maybe*) late; (*therefore/therfore*), we don't need to leave for the airport (*imediately/immediately*).
22. A (*woman's/women's*) place is now wherever she wants it to be.
23. Police report (*occurences/ocurrences*) of more and more burglaries (*every day/everyday*).
24. (*Its/It's*) not (*all right/alright*) to forego common (*since/sense*).
25. (*Aparently/Apparently*), the shipment of books never arrived.

■ 22b. Recognizing homonyms

Of the words most often misspelled by college students, the largest number are **homonyms**—words that sound alike but have different spellings and meanings. English has many homonyms, but a relatively small number of them—eight pairs or trios—cause student writers frequent trouble. If you tend to confuse any of these words, now is a good time to stop and study them, looking for some twist of memory to help you remember the differences.

ANSWERS TO EXERCISE 22.1

1. They're; their; there
2. to; too
3. beginning; a lot
4. noticeable; until
5. occurred; before
6. believe; lose
7. you're; definitely; your
8. affects; success; than; its
9. received; through
10. develop; truly; successful
11. cannot; separate
12. where; and
13. arguments; against; environment
14. businesses; dependent
15. Heroes; necessary
16. experience; exercise
17. professor; accept
18. categories; final
19. roommates; without
20. occasion; whether; weather
21. may be; therefore; immediately
22. woman's
23. occurrences; every day
24. It's; all right; sense
25. Apparently

(BACK)GROUNDING

William and Mary Morris (*Harper Dictionary of Contemporary Usage*, New York: Harper, 1975, 309) make an interesting distinction between homographs, homonyms, and homophones. *Homographs* are words spelled alike but pronounced differently (e.g., *tears* we shed and *tears* in a cloth). *Homonyms* are words spelled alike and pronounced alike (e.g., *bear* the animal, and *bear* meaning to carry). *Homophones* are words spelled differently but pronounced alike (*peace* and *piece*). Normally, we just refer to all three under the label of homonym.

USEFUL READING

Pyles, Thomas, and John Algeo. *The Origins and Development of the English Language.* 3rd ed. New York: Harcourt, 1982. The third edition of this history of the language contains a good deal of information on spelling.

WRITERS ON WRITING

As their language evolves, children use longer, more complicated [syntactic] structures and more sophisticated vocabulary. As they begin to use less familiar words and to employ different structures, they make errors of all types from comma splices to misspellings. Error, then, is a sign of growth.

—KARL K. TAYLOR AND EDE B. KIDDER

(BACK)GROUNDING

Never in the history of the English language was spelling more uniform than today. Spelling during the Middle Ages and early Renaissance was very relaxed. No prescriptions existed for spelling uniformity—not even within the same text. Orthographic conventions "were used with a nonchalance that is hardly imaginable in the era of the printing press" (Pyles and Algeo 142). A person might even spell his or her own name in different ways. Shakespeare, for instance, was spelled *Shakespeare*, *Shakespear*, and *Shake-spear*, and the "correct" spelling is still being argued.

Of course, most writers spelled words more or less consistently and people communicated with one another without a lot of confusion. It is difficult to tell whether some spelling inconsistencies were products of the writers themselves or of the printers taking advantage of instability in spelling in order to easily "justify" a line. In spite of all the variety, Baugh and Cable tell us that "by 1550 a nucleus of common [spelling] practice" existed. In fact, the sixteenth century marked a distinct change in attitude toward spelling. Changing cultural values marked this period, and in their search for stability, scholars focused on stabilizing English spelling.

Throughout the sixteenth and seventeenth centuries, numerous attempts to standardize (and, in many cases, reform) spelling were made. The earliest one, *An A. B. C. for Children*, appeared sometime before 1558. Most of these attempts tried to develop an alphabet that corresponded to pronunciation.

The most important of these treatises is *Elementarie* (1582) by Richard Mulcaster. Mulcaster saw the futility of trying for an exact, scientific correspondence between spelling and pronunciation. Whether Mulcaster's work really influenced the stability of spelling or simply reflected that stability as it developed naturally is impossible to say, but English spelling did develop along the lines he called for.

their [possessive form of *they*]
there [in that place]
they're [contraction of *they are*]

to [in the direction of]
too [in addition; excessive]
two [number between one and three]

your [possessive form of *you*]
you're [contraction of *you are*]

affect [to have an influence]
effect [noun: result]
     [verb: to cause to happen]

weather [climatic conditions]
whether [if]

accept [to take or receive]
except [to leave out]

who's [contraction of *who is* or *who has*]
whose [possessive form of *who*]

its [possessive form of *it*]
it's [contraction of *it is* or *it has*]

For your easy reference, here is a list of other homonyms and of other words that are frequently confused because they sound *nearly* alike:

Homonyms and frequently confused words

advice [suggestion]
advise [to suggest (to)]

allude [to refer]
elude [to avoid or escape]

allusion [reference]
illusion [false idea or appearance]

altar [sacred platform or table]
alter [to change]

are [form of *be*]
our [belonging to us]

bare [uncovered]
bear [animal; to carry or endure]

board [piece of lumber]
bored [uninterested]

brake [device for stopping]
break [to fragment]

buy [to purchase]
by [near; beside; through]

capital [principal city]
capitol [legislative building]

cite [to refer to]
sight [seeing; something seen]
site [location]

coarse [rough or crude]
course [plan of study; path]

complement [something that
    completes; to make complete]
compliment [praise; to praise]

USEFUL READING

Baugh, Albert C., and Thomas Cable. A *History of the English Language*. 3rd ed. Englewood Cliffs, NJ: Prentice, 1978. The authors cover the whole history of the language, including excellent sections on spelling.

RECOGNIZING HOMONYMS

conscience [feeling of right and wrong]

conscious [mentally aware]

council [leadership group]
counsel [advice; to advise]

dairy [source of milk]
diary [journal]

desert [dry area; to abandon]
dessert [sweet course of a meal]

device [something planned or invented]
devise [to plan or invent]

die [to expire]
dye [color; to color]

elicit [to draw forth]
illicit [illegal]

eminent [distinguished]
immanent [inherent]
imminent [expected in the immediate future]

fair [just or right; light in complexion; exposition]
fare [price of transportation; to go through an experience]

forth [forward; out into view]
fourth [between third and fifth]

gorilla [ape]
guerrilla [irregular soldier]

hear [to perceive with the ears]
here [in this place]

heard [past tense of *hear*]
herd [group of animals]

hoarse [sounding rough or harsh]
horse [animal]

know [to understand]
no [opposite of *yes*]

lead [a metal; to go before]
led [past tense of *lead*]

loose [not tight; not confined]
lose [to misplace; to fail to win]

meat [flesh used as food]
meet [to encounter]

passed [went by; received a passing grade]
past [beyond; events that have already occurred]

patience [quality of being patient]
patients [persons under medical care]

peace [absence of war]
piece [part]

personal [private or individual]
personnel [employees]

plain [simple, not fancy; flat land]
plane [airplane; tool; flat surface]

presence [condition of being]
presents [gifts; gives]

principal [most important; head of a school]
principle [fundamental truth]

rain [precipitation]
rein [strap to control a horse]
reign [period of rule]

right [correct; opposite of left]
rite [ceremony]
write [to produce words on a surface]

road [street or highway]
rode [past tense of *ride*]

scene [setting; view]
seen [past participle of *see*]

sense [feeling; intelligence]
since [from the time that; because]

stationary [unmoving]
stationery [writing paper]

TEACHING PRACTICE

The findings of recent research have important implications for spelling instruction and suggest that traditional methods of such instruction do not suffice.

Traditionally, instructors have marked orthographical errors and told students to look up misspelled words in the dictionary. But Mina Shaughnessy claims that just pointing out misspellings without helping students to understand them and how to revise for them sends the message that such misspellings cannot be revised, that the student is a " 'born' misspeller" (*Errors & Expectations*, New York: Oxford UP, 1977, 175). If the student continues to spell as she hears without regard to semantic connections, she will continue to misspell.

Also, traditional spelling instruction has taken the form of drills, unrelated to the student's other writing. But spelling instruction is not an end in itself. As Taylor and Kidder point out, "Learning how to spell will not necessarily improve reading or speaking, but it is essential for writing and is reinforced when practiced in real writing situations" (237). Spelling has been generally self-taught. Spelling drills are of little value, unless students use the words themselves in their own writing.

In addition, Dorothy Thompson argues that short periods of spelling instruction are more effective than longer periods ("Spelling's Day in the Sun," *Instructor* 85 [1976]: 16). Ann Dobie suggests no more than fifteen or twenty minutes per class time.

Consider the following practice for each student's final draft:

1. Circle all misspelled words in the paper.
2. Ask the student to correct the misspelling herself.
3. Ask the student to bring in two other related words and identify the shared core.

than [as compared with]
then [at that time; therefore]

threw [past tense of *throw*]
thorough [complete]
through [in one side of and out
   the other; by means of]

waist [part of the body]
waste [to squander]

weak [feeble]
week [seven days]

wear [to put onto the body]
were [past tense of *be*]
where [in what place]

which [what; that]
witch [woman with supernatural
   power]

ANSWERS TO EXERCISE 22.2

If *you're* looking for summer fun, *accept* the friendly *advice* of thousands of happy adventurers: spend three *weeks* kayaking *through* the inside passage *to* Alaska. For ten years, Outings, Inc. has *led* groups of novice kayakers *past* some of the most breathtaking scenery in North America. *Their* goal is simple: to give participants the time of *their* lives. As one of last year's adventurers said, "It's a trip I will remember vividly, one that *affected* me powerfully."

WRITERS ON WRITING

Fortunately both my wife and my mother-in-law seem to love digging up mistakes in spelling, punctuation, etc. I can hear them in the next room laughing at me.

—SHERWOOD ANDERSON

EXERCISE 22.2

Choose the appropriate word in parentheses to fill each blank in the following paragraph.

If _____ (*your/you're*) looking for summer fun, _____ (*accept/ except*) the friendly _____ (*advice/advise*) of thousands of happy adventurers: spend three _____ (*weaks/weeks*) kayaking _____ (*threw/thorough/ through*) the inside passage _____ (*to/too/two*) Alaska. For ten years, Outings, Inc., has _____ (*lead/led*) groups of novice kayakers _____ (*passed/ past*) some of the most breathtaking scenery in North America. _____ (*Their/There/They're*) goal is simple: to give participants the time of _____ (*their/there/they're*) lives. As one of last year's adventurers said, " _____ (*Its/ It's*) a trip I will remember vividly, one that _____ (*affected/effected*) me powerfully."

1. Recognizing words with more than one form

One special group of homonyms appearing in the list of words most often misspelled by college writers are words written sometimes as one word and other times as two words. The correct spelling depends on the meaning. Note the differences illustrated here:

Of course, they did not wear *everyday* clothes *every day* of the year.

Ideally, children *always* love their parents—in *all ways*.

By the time we were *all ready* for the game to begin, the coach's patience was *already* exhausted.

We *may be* on time for the meeting, or *maybe* we won't!

Nobody was surprised when the police announced that they had found *no body* at the scene of the crime.

The study of three thousand freshman essays mentioned in the introduction to this chapter revealed three particularly troublesome words

LINKING SPELLING AND PRONUNCIATION   *sp* 22c

that are often written in the wrong form. Two of them are always written as two words: *a lot* and *all right*. The third is written as one word: *cannot*. If you tend to misspell these words, take time now to commit the correct spelling to memory.

2. Recognizing American, British, and Canadian spellings

Spelling varies slightly among English-speaking countries. What is considered "correct" in Britain or Canada may be considered "incorrect" in the United States, and vice versa. Following is a list of some words that are spelled differently in American and British English. If you have trouble remembering the American spellings of words like these—whether, for example, a verb ends in *-ise* or *-ize*—always consult a dictionary.

AMERICAN	BRITISH AND CANADIAN
center	centre
check	cheque
color	colour
criticize	criticise
judgment	judgement

22c. Linking spelling and pronunciation

Even for words without homonyms, pronunciation often leads spellers astray. Pronunciation can vary considerably from one region of the United States to another, many words have letters that are not pronounced in any region, and the informality of spoken English allows us to slur or blur other letters or syllables. The best way to link spelling and pronunciation is to learn to "pronounce" words mentally as they look, every letter and syllable included (so that, for example, you hear the *b* at the end of *crumb*) and to enunciate them slowly and clearly when you are trying to spell them.

1. Noting unpronounced letters or syllables

Learning to "see" words with unpronounced letters or syllables will help you remember to spell them correctly. Here are some of the most frequently misspelled words of this kind, with their unpronounced letters or syllables italicized:

357

USEFUL READING

Chomsky, Carol. "Reading, Writing, and Phonology." *Harvard Education Review* 40 (May 1970): 287–309. Chomsky argues that despite many people's belief that English spelling is related to English pronunciation, spelling corresponds more to underlying lexical meaning. She also provides some practical advice for teaching spelling.

(BACK)GROUNDING

The most influential individual in the history of American spelling was Noah Webster. We know him from the series of dictionaries that take his name—some based on the one he published in 1828. But before that, he published a speller, a grammar, and a reader. The speller sold over eighty million copies in his lifetime.

Webster's influence took two forms. He worked hard to standardize the language in many respects, not the least of which being in its spelling. Also, he sought to and, in many ways, succeeded in, "Americanizing" English in the United States. Webster excised the *u* from many words spelled in Britain with the *-our* ending: *colour, favour, labour,* and so on. He was responsible for the American practice of using *-er* rather than *-re* to end many words: *theater, center, sepulcher,* and so on. The use of *-se* in place of *-ce* is also attributable to Webster: *defense, offense,* and so on. And Webster recommended dropping the final *k* in words like *almanack, musick,* and *publick.*

(BACK)GROUNDING

One of the most controversial areas in the study of spelling remains the relationship of orthography (the written representation of the lexicon or vocabulary) to pronunciation. The Roman alphabet cannot phonetically represent the English language; for instance, the alphabet possesses only five vowel symbols, while the language has eleven, not including diphthongs and [r] modifications. Some language reformers call for refashioning spelling to conform to pronunciation. Yet good, practical reasons exist for differentiating the lexical and phonetic aspects of language.

Wilson Follett (*Modern American Usage: A Guide,* New York: Hill and Wang, 1966, 310) noted that pronunciations differ with dialects. Therefore, choosing the phonetic representation of words as a measure for spelling becomes a political decision as much as anything else.

William J. Stevens ("Obstacles to Spelling Reform," *The English Journal* 54 [1965]: 85–90) cites the problem of homonyms being spelled alike under the above reform. We could not differentiate between *to, too,* and *two.*

More importantly, Carol Chomsky ("Reading, Writing, and Phonology," *Harvard Education Review* 40 [May 1970]: 287–309) argues that spelling corresponds less to surface features of the language (i.e., pronunciation) than to the underlying meanings of words. Spelling, she claims, retains lexical connections between words, connections that might be lost in pronunciation shifts. For instance, *nation* retains its semantic affiliation with *nationality* through their sharing of the same semantic core, represented orthographically as *nation* despite a different pronunciation of that core. On the other hand, such a connection does not exist between *nation* and *notion*. They share a common ending but not a semantic core. While variations in pronunciation, instigated by phonological rules such as the shifts in phonological stress with the addition of suffixes, may occur, semantic connections are retained through the spelling of the two words.

(BACK)GROUNDING

Thomas Pyles and John Algeo (*The Origins and Development of the English Language*, 3rd ed., New York: Harcourt, 1982, 171) describe several situations where spelling has influenced pronunciation, rather than the opposite. Learned scribes of the Renaissance tended to be conservative men who preferred archaic spellings. Under the influence of Classical Latin, they reinserted *h* into the spelling of many words. "During the Renaissance *h* was inserted after *t* in a number of foreign words—for instance, *throne*, from Old French *trone*." In French, many of these *h*'s are silent, but in English, many came to be pronounced.

(BACK)GROUNDING

The dream of a universal language that could unite the world linguistically, culturally, and ultimately, politically goes back at least to the seventeenth century. The most well-known "universal language" is Esperanto, invented in 1887 by a Russian physician, Ludwig Zamenhof. Esperanto has gained some success, because it looks European. Other artificial languages include Volapuk, which appeared a few years before Esperanto; Mundo Lingue (1889); Idiom Neutral (1902); Occidental (1925); Novial (1928); Mondial (1943); and Interlingua (1951). None has succeeded in attracting many adherents.

can*di*date	foreign	pro*b*ably
condem*n*	govern*m*ent	quan*ti*ty
di*ff*erent	inte*r*est	resta*u*rant
drasti*cal*ly	lib*r*ary	*sep*arate (adjective)
envi*r*onment	ma*rr*iage	su*r*prise
Feb*r*uary	mu*sc*le	Wed*nes*day

2. Noting unstressed vowels

In English words, *a*, *i*, and *e* can often sound alike if they are in syllables that are not stressed. Hearing the word *definite*, for instance, gives us few clues as to whether the vowels in the second and third syllables should be *i*'s or *a*'s. In this case, remembering how the related word *finite* looks or sounds helps us know that the *i*'s are correct. If you are puzzled about how to spell a word containing unstressed vowels, first try to think of a related word that would give you a clue to the correct spelling. Then check your dictionary.

22d. Taking advantage of spelling rules

Fortunately, English spelling does follow some general rules that can be of enormous help to writers. This section focuses on those rules closely related to commonly misspelled words.

1. Remembering "i before e"

Most of you probably memorized the "*i* before *e*" rule long ago. Here is a slightly expanded version:

> *I* before *e* except after *c*
> or when pronounced *ay*
> as in *neighbor* or *weigh*
> or in *weird* exceptions like *either*
> and *species*.

i BEFORE *e*

ach*ie*ve	exper*ie*nce	p*ie*ce
bel*ie*ve	fr*ie*nd	rel*ie*ve
br*ie*f	f*ie*ld	th*ie*f
ch*ie*f		

EXCEPT AFTER *c*

c*ei*ling	dec*ei*ve	perc*ei*ve
conc*ei*ve	rec*ei*ve	

USEFUL READING

Dobie, Ann B. "Orthographical Theory and Practice, Or How to Teach Spelling." *Journal of Basic Writing* 5 (1986): 41–48.

Anderson, Kristen F. "Using a Spelling Survey to Develop Basic Writers' Linguistic Awareness: A Response to Ann B. Dobie." *Journal of Basic Writing* 6 (1987): 72–78.

Dobie, Ann B. "Orthography Revisited: A Response to Kristen Anderson." *Journal of Basic Writing* (1988): 82–83.

TAKING ADVANTAGE OF SPELLING RULES   *sp* 22d

OR WHEN PRONOUNCED "AY"

n*ei*ghbor   w*ei*gh   *ei*ghth

OR IN WEIRD EXCEPTIONS

either	seize	species
weird	foreign	ancient
neither	height	conscience
leisure	caffeine	science

EXERCISE 22.3

Insert either *ei* or *ie* in the blank in each of the following words.

1. sl—gh
2. consc—nce
3. anc—nt
4. l—sure
5. p—rce
6. caff—ne
7. ch—f
8. rec—ve
9. ach—ve
10. h—ress

2. Adding prefixes

Prefixes are verbal elements placed at the beginnings of words to add to or qualify their meaning. The prefix *re-*, for example, adds repetition to the meaning of a word: *reappear* means "appear again." (See 24c for more information about prefixes.) Prefixes do not change the spelling of the words they are added to, even when the last letter of the prefix and the first letter of the word it is added to are the same. In such cases, keep both letters:

dis- + service = disservice
over- + rate = overrate

Some prefixes require the use of hyphens. For a discussion of such usage, see 36b. If you are in doubt about whether to hyphenate a word beginning with a prefix, always check your dictionary.

3. Adding suffixes

Suffixes are verbal elements placed at the *ends* of words in order to form related words. For example, we can build on the basic word *short* to get the following words:

short*age*   short*en*   short*er*   short*ly*   short*ness*

This section will provide guidance to spelling words with suffixes.

ANSWERS TO EXERCISE 22.3

1. sleigh
2. conscience
3. ancient
4. leisure
5. pierce
6. caffeine
7. chief
8. receive
9. achieve
10. heiress

WRITERS WRITING

William Morris, one of the editors of *Harper Dictionary of Contemporary Usage* (New York: Harper, 1975, 571) asked a group of 172 schoolteachers to spell his list of the most frequently misspelled words in print: *accommodate, affidavit, diphtheria, embarrass, harass, inoculate, precede, supersede,* and *siege.* Only three got perfect scores.

WRITING TOGETHER

The difference between a typographical error and a genuine spelling error is the difference between knowledge and ignorance. We all commit "typos," but they indicate nothing more than our imperfect humanity, and they are easily corrected during proofreading. Genuine spelling errors are, of course, a different story. However, the reader has no way to distinguish between the two. Therefore, proofreading becomes a vitally important activity for the writer. Many "spelling" errors are actually errors of proof-reading—or the lack thereof. To encourage students to proofread more carefully, you might consider the following practice:

Before taking up the final draft of the first paper, divide the class into groups of two or three. Have them exchange papers and check for words that they think might be misspelled. On a separate sheet of paper they should note the page number and para-graph number, the misspelled word, and what they believe is the correct spelling of that word. After the papers have been returned to the authors, allow them time to go through their papers and make the cor-rections. They should be aware that there is no guar-antee that their proofreaders are correct 100 percent of the time. The writers themselves must make the rhetorical choice about the spelling. Along with the paper, the separate sheet with the proofreader's notes on the spelling should be handed in. When grading this first paper, don't count off for any corrected spelling but do record the originally misspelled words pointed out by the proofreader.

Do the same thing for the next paper, except that this time count off one-quarter point for every time the student misspells the same words corrected in the first paper. Take off another one-quarter point for each time these same words must be corrected on each subsequent paper.

Dropping the final e

For words ending in an unpronounced *e* (*receive, lose, definite*), you must decide whether or not to drop the *e* when adding a suffix. In general, if the suffix starts with a vowel, *drop* the *e*.

explore + -ation = exploration
imagine + -able = imaginable
future + -ism = futurism
exercise + -ing = exercising
continue + -ous = continuous
productive + -ity = productivity

EXCEPTIONS

- To distinguish homonyms or potentially confusing words
    dye + -ing = dyeing (not *dying*)
    singe + -ing = singeing (not *singing*)

- To clarify pronunciation
    be + -ing = being (not *bing*)
    shoe + -ing = shoeing (not *shoing*)

- To keep the sound of *c* or *g* soft
    notice + -able = noticeable
    marriage + -able = marriageable
    salvage + -able = salvageable
    courage + -ous = courageous
    peace + -able = peaceable

Keeping the final e

If the suffix starts with a consonant, *keep* the *e*.

force + -ful = forceful
excite + -ment = excitement
state + -ly = stately
same + -ness = sameness

EXCEPTIONS

acknowledge + -ment = acknowledgment
argue + -ment = argument
judge + -ment = judgment
true + ly = truly
whole + -ly = wholly
nine + -th = ninth

TAKING ADVANTAGE OF SPELLING RULES

EXERCISE 22.4

Combine each of the following words and suffixes, dropping the unpronounced *e* when necessary.

1. future + -ism
2. whole + -ly
3. argue + -ment
4. lone + -ly
5. malice + -ious
6. dye + -ing
7. hope + -ful
8. continue + -ous
9. exercise + -ing
10. outrage + -ous

Using -ally

Use *-ally* if the base word ends in *ic*.

drastic + -ally = drastically
basic + -ally = basically
characteristic + -ally = characteristically
dramatic + -ally = dramatically

Using -ly

Use *-ly* if the base word does not end in *ic*.

apparent + -ly = apparently
certain + -ly = certainly
conscious + -ly = consciously
quick + -ly = quickly
supposed + -ly = supposedly

EXCEPTION

public + -ly = publicly

EXERCISE 22.5

Insert either *-ally* or *-ly* in the blank in each of the following words.

1. tragic _____
2. fatal _____
3. realistic _____
4. final _____
5. apparent _____

Using -cede, -ceed, *and* -sede

The suffixes *-cede, -ceed,* and *-sede* are especially easy to master because almost all words ending in the sound pronounced "seed" use the spelling *-cede*. Use *-sede* with only one word: supersede. Use *-ceed*

WRITING TOGETHER

One reason that spelling drills don't work, of course, is that they are boring, existing out of context as they do. However, if you can create an interesting context for spelling drills, then they may have some effect.

Consider a spelling competition for your class, similar to a spelling bee. One problem with a spelling bee is that it spotlights individuals and can thereby diminish the self-esteem of poor spellers. Therefore, consider creating teams of three or four students, each with at least one good speller.

Take five or ten minutes each class period for a competition. Choose two teams to play in each period. You say a word, and each team must decide upon its spelling and write it out on a three-by-five card. Each team then reveals its answer at the same time. Each correct answer gets a point. The first to get five points wins. If after five words, the teams are tied, play "sudden-death rounds."

An alternative way to play the game is to name the teams in advance and have them collect a list of ten or fifteen words to give their opponent to spell.

with only three words: exceed, proceed, succeed. Use *-cede* with all other words ending in the "seed" sound:

accede	intercede	recede
concede	precede	secede

Words ending in consonant and y

For words ending in *y*, you must sometimes change the *y* to *i* when you add a suffix. In general, if the *y* is preceded by a consonant, *change* the *y*.

bounty + -ful = bountiful
try + -ed = tried
silly + -er = sillier
breezy + -ness = breeziness
busy + -ily = busily

EXCEPTIONS

- Keep the *y* before the suffix *-ing*.

  dry + -ing = drying
  liquefy + -ing = liquefying
  carry + -ing = carrying

- Keep the *y* in some one-syllable base words.

  shy + -er = shyer
  dry + -ly = dryly
  wry + -ness = wryness

- Keep the *y* if the base word is a proper name.

  Kennedy + -esque = Kennedyesque

Words ending in vowel and y

If the *y* is preceded by a vowel, keep the *y*.

joy + -ous = joyous
play + -ful = playful
employ + -ment = employment
buoy + -ed = buoyed

EXCEPTIONS

day + ly = daily
gay + ly = gaily

TAKING ADVANTAGE OF SPELLING RULES

sp 22d

EXERCISE 22.6

Combine each of the following words and suffixes, changing the final *y* to *i* when necessary.

1. lonely + -er
2. carry + -ing
3. defy + -ance
4. study + -s
5. supply + -ed
6. duty + -ful
7. likely + -hood
8. obey + -ed
9. rainy + -est
10. coy + -ly

Doubling the final consonant

When a word ends in a consonant, the consonant is sometimes doubled when a suffix is added. If the word ends in consonant-vowel-consonant, the suffix begins with a vowel, and the word contains only one syllable or ends in an accented syllable, double the final consonant.

stop + -ing = stopping
slap + -ed = slapped
hot + -est = hottest
run + -er = runner
begin + -ing = beginning
occur + -ence = occurrence
refer + -ing = referring

DO NOT DOUBLE THE CONSONANT

- If it is preceded by more than one vowel or by another consonant

  bait + -ing = baiting
  sleep + -ing = sleeping
  fight + -er = fighter
  start + -ed = started

- If the suffix begins with a consonant

  ship + -ment = shipment
  fit + -ness = fitness

- If the word is not accented on the last syllable

  benefit + -ing = benefiting
  fasten + -er = fastener

- If the accent shifts from the last to the first syllable when the suffix is added.

  infer + -ence = inference
  prefer + -ence = preference

ANSWERS TO EXERCISE 22.6

1. lonelier
2. carrying
3. defiance
4. studies
5. supplied
6. dutiful
7. likelihood
8. obeyed
9. rainiest
10. coyly

TEACHING PRACTICE

Although spelling can be very important in the creation of *ethos* for the writer, too much emphasis on spelling in the classroom might eventually paralyze some writers. It is important to emphasize to your students that spelling correction is a late-draft revision activity rather than an early-draft revision activity. Writers should not be concerned with spelling during early drafts that they know will be revised; they should get down on paper their ideas and the organization of those ideas before they need to be concerned with spelling. However, if a student writer finds himself or herself bothered by the fact that he or she knows some of the words are misspelled, between writing drafts, he or she should go through the text of the last draft, marking with a differently colored check mark, all the words the spelling of which he or she is unsure about. Then, before the next draft the writer can look them up and write them out on a separate sheet of paper that he or she can refer to during the writing of the next draft.

If the last letter of the word and the first letter of the suffix are the same, keep both letters:

mortal + -ly = mortally
room + -mate = roommate
rotten + -ness = rottenness
usual + -ly = usually

EXERCISE 22.7

Combine each of the following words and suffixes, doubling the final consonant when necessary.

1. occur + -ed
2. fast + -est
3. skip + -er
4. refer + -ence
5. commit + -ment

6. regret + -able
7. submit + -ed
8. drastic + -ally
9. benefit + -ed
10. weep + -ing

ANSWERS TO EXERCISE 22.7

1. occurred
2. fastest
3. skipper
4. reference
5. commitment
6. regrettable
7. submitted
8. drastically
9. benefitted
10. weeping

WRITERS ON WRITING

It's good style to use simple spelling whenever you have a choice. . . . But don't use spellings that may annoy some readers, like *nite, tho, thru.*
    —RUDOLF FLESCH

▌ 22e. Making words plural

Making singular nouns into plurals calls for using several different spelling guidelines.

Adding -s

For most words, add -*s*.

pencil, pencils   computer, computers

Adding -es

For words ending in *s*, *ch*, *sh*, *x*, or *z*, add -*es*.

Jones, Joneses   church, churches
bus, buses   flash, flashes
fox, foxes   buzz, buzzes

For words ending in *o*, add -*es* if the *o* is preceded by a consonant.

potato, potatoes   hero, heroes   veto, vetoes

EXCEPTIONS

memo, memos   piano, pianos
pro, pros   solo, solos

■ Add -*s* if the *o* is preceded by a vowel.

rodeo, rodeos   patio, patios
zoo, zoos   curio, curios

MAKING WORDS PLURAL

Words ending in f *or* fe

For some words ending in *f* or *fe*, change *f* to *v* and add *-s* or *-es*.

calf, calves	shelf, shelves
half, halves	elf, elves
self, selves	leaf, leaves
life, lives	hoof, hooves
wife, wives	knife, knives

Words ending in y

For words ending in *y*, change *y* to *i* and add *-es* if the *y* is preceded by a consonant.

theory, theories	huckleberry, huckleberries
eighty, eighties	sky, skies

EXCEPTIONS

- Proper names
  Henry, Henrys

- Keep the *y* and add *-s* if the *y* is preceded by a vowel.

guy, guys	attorney, attorneys
delay, delays	alloy, alloys

Irregular plurals

For irregular plurals and nouns that have the same form in the singular and plural, memorize those you do not already know.

man, men	bacterium, bacteria	deer, deer
woman, women	locus, loci	sheep, sheep
child, children	alga, algae	moose, moose
foot, feet	basis, bases	series, series
tooth, teeth	phenomenon, phenomena	species, species

Compound words

For compound nouns written as one word, make the last part of the compound plural.

briefcase, briefcases	bookshelf, bookshelves
mailbox, mailboxes	grandchild, grandchildren

For compound nouns written as separate words or hyphenated, make the most important part of the compound plural.

brother-in-law, brothers-in-law
lieutenant governor, lieutenant
    governors

sergeant major, sergeants major
leap year, leap years
bus stop, bus stops

ANSWERS TO EXERCISE 22.8

1. tomatoes
2. hooves
3. volunteers
4. babies
5. dishes
6. stepchildren
7. turkeys
8. miles per hour
9. radios
10. phenomena
11. spoofs
12. beaches
13. yourselves
14. golf clubs
15. roses

OPTIONAL EXERCISE

Ask students who compose or type their papers on computer, in addition to using the spell checker feature on their word-processing program, to use the *search* feature to check for homonym problems.

Instruct them to choose the homonyms and frequently confused words that they are unsure about (see the list on pp. 354–356). Search for these in a draft, using the *search* feature. When the *search* stops at each instance of the word they are concerned about, they should double-check their use of it with the explanations from this handbook and with a dictionary.

EXERCISE 22.8

Form the plural of each of the following words.

1. tomato
2. hoof
3. volunteer
4. baby
5. dish

6. stepchild
7. turkey
8. mile per hour
9. radio
10. phenomenon

11. spoof
12. beach
13. yourself
14. golf club
15. rose

▌ 22f. Taking a personal spelling inventory

This chapter has surveyed general spelling rules and guidelines. You need now to tailor this advice to your own spelling patterns and problems. Doing so means becoming a detective of your own writing, looking for clues in as large and varied a sample of your prose as you have time to examine.

▌ 1. Identifying troublesome words and patterns

You can begin your inventory by looking through several essays you have written and making a list of every word misspelled. Whenever possible, identify the guideline in this chapter that deals with the misspellings. Here is the beginning of one student's personal spelling inventory:

WORD	MISSPELLING	GUIDELINE
their	there	homonyms
receiving	recieving	"*i* before *e*"
hastiest	hastyest	suffix with final *y*
beginning	begining	double consonants
affect	effect	homonyms
sharing	shareing	unpronounced final *e*
environment	enviroment	unpronounced letters
theories	theorys	plural for words ending in *y*
successful	succesful	double consonants
dissatisfied	disatisfied	prefix

TAKING A PERSONAL SPELLING INVENTORY

2. Using a spell checker

If you write on a word processor and have some essays in draft or if you have some of your writing that has not been marked for spelling, you can use the *spell checker* on most word processing programs to identify misspelled words and add them to your personal spelling inventory. Those who use this feature frequently, however, know that it provides only limited help. It will not, for instance, pick up homonym problems—*you're* may be the wrong spelling in the context of the essay, but the spell checker will recognize it only as a correct possible spelling. (See Chapter 45 for more information on using spell checkers when revising and editing a draft.)

3. Annotating your dictionary

For mastering particularly troublesome words, author John Irving recommends making a mark and listing the date whenever you look up a word in the dictionary. If you follow this advice, you will be able to identify words you are looking up frequently—and take steps to learn the correct spelling once and for all. You may also find that some or most of these words follow a similar pattern. This discovery can then become part of your personal spelling inventory.

4. Building on memory cues

Before the advent of printing, not to mention photocopying machines, people learned to train their memories extensively. You can learn to use memory cues, or **mnemonic devices** (named for the Greek goddess of memory, Mnemosyne), in mastering words whose spelling tends to trip you up. Here are some memory cues one student devised to go along with her personal spelling inventory:

WORD	MISSPELLING	CUE
environment	enviroment	There's *iron* in our environment.
all right	alright	I wouldn't write *alwrong*, would I?
a lot	alot	I wouldn't write *alittle*, would I?
government	goverment	Government should serve those it *governs*.
separate	seperate	*Separate* rates two *a*'s.
definitely	definately	There are a *finite* number of ways to spell *definitely*.

ANSWERS TO EXERCISE 22.9

For me the *ideal occupation* would be an *arrangement* in which I could play with a band for six months and tour the other six months of the year. I wouldn't want to teach music because I would *probably* have to teach in a school, where many students are forced to take music by *their parents*. When children are forced to do something, *it's likely* that they won't enjoy it. If I were able to both tour *and* teach, however, I would be happy.

I'm *really* glad that I've gotten involved in music; it looks as if I'm destined to be a *professional* musician. *Surely* I don't know what else I could do; I *doubt* I'd be a good *administrator* or *business* executive or lawyer. And the idea of being a doctor or *dentist* and probing around people's *bodies* or looking at teeth that have huge, *rotting* cavities isn't appealing to me. The more I think about it, the *happier* I am with my music. I *definitely* plan to pursue that career.

The misspellings in this passage can be attributed to three causes:

1. The writer's reliance upon pronunciation as a guide for spelling, thus leading to leaving out unpronounced consonants and vowels and to additions and substitutions of wrong letters as in *ideel, ocupation, arangement, probly, parrents, likly, an, realy, profesional, surly, dout, administrater, bussiness, denist,* and *definately.*
2. The writer's difficulty distinguishing homonyms as in *there* and *its.*
3. The writer's unfamiliarity of rules governing addition of suffixes to words ending in *y* as in *bodys* and *happyer.*

EXERCISE 22.9

Read the following passage from a brief student essay, noting and correcting each misspelling. Whenever possible, classify the misspelling under one of the guidelines presented in this chapter. Then draw up three or four tips you could give this particular student on how to improve spelling.

   For me, the ideel ocupation would be an arangement in which I could play with a band for six months and tour the other six months of the year. I wouldn't want to teach music because I would probly have to teach in a school, where many students are forced to take music by there parrents. When children are forced to do something, its likly that they won't enjoy it. If I were able to both tour an teach, however, I would be happy.

   I'm realy glad that I've gotten involved in music; it looks as if I'm destined to be a profesional musician. Surly I don't know what else I could do; I dout I'd be a good administrater or bussiness executive or lawyer. And the idea of being a doctor or denist and probing around people's bodies or looking at teeth that have huge, roting cavities isn't appealing to me. The more I think about it, the happyer I am with my music. I definately plan to pursue that career.

READING FOR SPELLING

Readers store the visual memory of words in their minds and can often spell them correctly by "seeing" them. You can make use of this fact by attending to the spelling of new or unfamiliar words as you read, making a conscious mental "note" of how the word looks correctly spelled. Many writers, in fact, jot down new words as they read and later concentrate on learning the meaning—and spelling—of them.

   Once you start paying attention to spelling as you read, you will probably marvel at how well you generally spell. That is the whole point of the following humorous poem, entitled "Spelling and Pronunciation—Hints for Foreigners."

> I take it you already know
> Of tough and bough and cough and dough?
> Others may stumble but not you,
> On hiccough, thorough, laugh and through
> Well done! And now you wish, perhaps,
> To learn of less familiar traps?
>
> Beware of heard, a dreadful word
> That looks like beard and sounds like bird,
> And dead: it's said like bed, not bead—
> For goodness' sake don't call it "deed"!
> Watch out for meat and great and threat
> (They rhyme with suite and straight and debt.)

TAKING A PERSONAL SPELLING INVENTORY

A moth is not a moth in mother
Nor both in bother, broth in brother,
And here is not a match for there
Nor dear and fear for bear and pear,
And then there's does and rose and lose—
Just look them up—and goose and choose,
And cork and work and card and ward,
And font and front and word and sword,
And do and go and thwart and cart—
Come, come, I've hardly made a start!
A dreadful language? Man alive,
I'd mastered it when I was five.

FOR EXAMINING YOUR OWN SPELLING

If you are keeping a writing log, devote a section of it to a personal spelling inventory. Choose a sample of your recent writing, and identify every misspelling. If you have any drafts in a word processor, use a spell checker, and ask an instructor or several friends who are good spellers to help you. Then, following the format presented in 22f1, enter the word, your misspelling, and the guideline or pattern that relates to it. For persistent misspellings, create a memory cue (see 22f4), and enter it in the log along with the correct spelling of the word.

TEACHING PRACTICE
Ask students to work together to create memory cues that they all can use.

23. Using Dictionaries

(BACK)GROUNDING

The dictionary, as we know it, is comparatively modern. To the medieval scholar, a dictionary was a collection of "dictions" or phrases put together for the use of pupils studying Latin—the social elite. The earliest dictionaries in English (Robert Cawdray's *A Table Alphabetical* of 1604 is the first) consisted of *hard words*. Through the seventeenth and eighteenth centuries, dictionaries steadily increased in size as lexicographers gradually moved toward the principle of including all words, not just hard words, in dictionaries. By the time Samuel Johnson composed his dictionary, Johnson could assume that he had to include all words in his dictionary; Johnson's contribution was his systematic inclusion of illustrative quotations to demonstrate proper usage. Noah Webster's *An American Dictionary of the English Language* built on Johnson's use of quotations by including selections from the Founding Fathers of the Republic and by insisting on American spellings. In 1961 *Webster's Third International Dictionary of the English Language* caused an outcry because the editors decided to let usage determine correctness rather than impose an external authority. In contrast to the prescriptive dictionaries of Johnson and Webster, most modern dictionaries tend to describe how words are actually used.

In the opening scene of Rex Stout's *Gambit*, master sleuth Nero Wolfe is "in the middle of a fit," solemnly tearing the pages out of a large volume and dropping them into a fire. What is the book that Wolfe finds "subversive and intolerably offensive"? It is a dictionary—specifically, the third edition of *Webster's New International Dictionary*. Guilty of thousands of "crimes" and threatening the very "integrity of the English language," this dictionary must be destroyed, Wolfe declares, down to its very fine binding.

You may not have thought of dictionaries as the cause of violent controversy, but very often they have been. Such controversy usually relates to a tension between two basic and competing aims for dictionaries. One aim is to fix a standard of the language, so that users of it can know once and for all what is "right" and what is "wrong." Before the advent of the printing press, English spelling in particular was far from fixed, and with good reason; few people had occasion to write words down. Even later, the author we designate as Shakespeare is known to have spelled his own name in several different ways. By the eighteenth century, however, writers such as Alexander Pope urged a codification of the language, which they felt had reached perfection. Enter Samuel Johnson, whose *English Dictionary* (1755) established an authoritative right and wrong for a long time.

The second and competing aim of an English dictionary was articulated forcefully about one hundred years after Johnson: to record a full inventory of the language as it is used, without trying to prescribe

370

USEFUL READING

Baugh, Albert C., and Thomas Cable. A *History of the English Language*. 3rd ed. Englewood Cliffs, NJ: Prentice, 1978. See items 170, "Dictionaries of Hard Words," 197, "Johnson's Dictionary," and 246, "Noah Webster and an American Language."

Johnson, Samuel. "Preface to a Dictionary of the English Language." Rpt. in Bertrand H. Bronson, *Samuel Johnson: Rasselas, Poems, and Selected Prose*, 3rd ed. New York: Holt, 1971, pp. 234–260. Johnson describes his goals, the problems he encountered, and the limitations of the work.

EXPLORING THE DICTIONARY   *di* 23a

"right" and "wrong." What enraged Wolfe was its focus on this second aim rather than the first. These dual aims persist in our dictionaries today and may in fact influence your choice of which dictionary to use on which occasion. This chapter will map the territory covered by dictionaries and provide you with a means of choosing the dictionaries you want to work with.

▌ 23a. Exploring the dictionary

A good dictionary packs a surprising amount of information into a relatively small space, including much more than the correct spelling. Take a look, for instance, at this entry in *Webster's New World Dictionary*, Third College Edition:

In fact, a dictionary entry may contain a dozen or more kinds of information about a word, the most common of which are listed below. The first six normally appear in all entries, the others only where they are necessary or relevant.

1. *Spelling,* including alternate spellings if they exist
2. *Word division,* with bars and/or dots separating syllables and showing where a word may be divided at the end of a line
3. *Pronunciation,* including alternate pronunciations
4. *Grammatical functions and irregular forms,* including plurals of nouns, principal parts of verbs, and comparative and superlative forms of adjectives and adverbs
5. *Etymology,* the languages and words that the word comes from
6. *Meanings,* in order of either development or frequency of use
7. *Examples* of the word in the context of a phrase or sentence
8. *Usage labels and notes* (see explanation below)
9. *Field labels,* indicating that a word has a specialized meaning in a particular field of knowledge or activity
10. *Synonyms* and *antonyms*

371

WRITERS ON WRITING
Wrestling with words gave me my moments of greatest meaning.

—RICHARD WRIGHT

USEFUL READING

Markwardt, Albert H. "Dictionaries and the English Language." Rpt. in *Introductory Readings on Language.* Ed. Wallace L. Anderson and Norman Stageberg. New York: Holt, 1970, pp. 114–128. This article details two traditions in the lexicography of the English language: as prescriptive (Samuel Johnson) and as descriptive (*Oxford English Dictionary* and *Webster's Third New International Dictionary*).

11. *Related* words and their grammatical functions

12. *Idioms*, phrases in which the word appears and their meanings

Usage labeling and notes

For some words, many dictionaries include a kind of usage labeling, intended to let readers know that some or all meanings of the word are not considered appropriate in certain contexts. You can generally find such labels identified at the beginning of the dictionary. Here are some of the labels the *Webster's New World* uses.

1. *Archaic:* rarely used today except in specialized contexts

2. *Obsolete:* no longer used

3. *Colloquial:* characteristic of conversation and informal writing

4. *Slang:* extremely informal

5. *Dialect:* used mostly in a particular geographical or linguistic area, often one that is specified, such as Scotland and New England

In addition to labels, dictionaries sometimes include notes discussing usage in greater detail. In the *Webster's New World* entry for *unique*, notice that the third meaning includes a note that using the word with this meaning is "common" but is "still objected to by some."

ANSWERS TO EXERCISE 23.1 (WILL VARY)

It might be interesting to have students bring their answers to class and then to put them on the board for comparison.

ANSWERS TO EXERCISE 23.2

1. rhetoric: from ME *rethorike* < L *rhetorica* < Gr *rhetor*, orator < *eirein*, to speak

2. student: from ME < L *studere*, to study

3. curry: from Tamil *kari*, sauce

4. whine: from ME *whinen* < Indo-European *kwein*, to whiz, hiss, whistle

5. apple: from ME *appel* < OE *aeppel*, fruit, apple, eyeball, anything round

6. sex: from ME < L *sexus* < *secare*, to cut

7. okra: a word of West African origin

8. tortilla: from Sp, diminutive of *torta*, cake

9. cinema: from Fr *cinematographe* < Gr *kinema*, motion + *graphein*, to write

10. video: from L, I see < *videre*, to see

EXERCISE 23.1

Look up the spelling, syllable division, and pronunciation of the following words in your dictionary. Note any variants in spelling and/or pronunciation.

1. process (noun)	5. whippet	8. hurrah
2. heinous	6. crayfish	9. greasy
3. exigency	7. macabre	10. theater
4. schedule		

EXERCISE 23.2

Look up the etymology of the following words in your dictionary.

1. rhetoric	5. apple	8. tortilla
2. student	6. sex	9. cinema
3. curry (noun)	7. okra	10. video
4. whine		

EXERCISE 23.3

Use your dictionary to find synonyms (and antonyms) for the following words.

USEFUL READING

Matthews, Mitford M. "The Freshman and His Dictionary." Rpt. in William H. Roberts and Gregoire Turgeon, *About Language.* Boston: Houghton, 1986. Mathews describes three categories of information freshmen need to know about dictionaries: 1) that unabridged dictionaries are treasure-houses of knowledge, 2) that they give overviews of the relationships among Indo-European languages, and 3) that they also provide quick and useful information about spelling, pronunciation, and meanings.

DISTINGUISHING AMONG DICTIONARIES

1. coerce
2. prevaricate
3. parameter
4. odious
5. awesome

▌ 23b. Distinguishing among dictionaries

Since the time of Samuel Johnson's 1755 dictionary and Noah Webster's *American Dictionary of the English Language* (1828), the number and kinds of English-language dictionaries have multiplied many times over. You may in fact own several dictionaries and have easy access to many more. While they all share the name *dictionary*, these numerous volumes differ considerably from one another. You may most often use an easily portable paperback dictionary, but you should be familiar with larger abridged and unabridged dictionaries as well.

▌ 1. Abridged dictionaries

Abridged or "abbreviated" **dictionaries** are the type most often used by college writers. Though they are not as complete as unabridged dictionaries, they are more affordable and more portable than their larger cousins. Among the most helpful abridged dictionaries are *Webster's New World Dictionary* and *The American Heritage Dictionary*.

Webster's New World Dictionary of the American Language, 3rd College Edition. New York: Simon, 1988. This abridged dictionary lists all of its more than 170,000 entries in alphabetical order; within individual entries, meanings are listed chronologically as they entered the language. Geographical and biographical names are included among the regular entries, and more than 800 drawings are provided.

The American Heritage Dictionary. 2nd College Edition. Boston: Houghton, 1982. The more than 200,000 listings in this dictionary are augmented by 5,000 new scientific and technical terms and 3,000 new photographs supplementing the many photographs, drawings, and maps in the first edition. The *American Heritage* lists meanings in the order of most to least common. Notes on usage are extensive. Introductory essays provide a context for the usage notes in the form of a debate on the issue. Sections on biographical and geographical names, also liberally illustrated, follow the dictionary of general vocabulary, as does a section on abbreviations and a list of the addresses for four-year colleges and universities.

373

USEFUL READING

The Encyclopaedia Britannica. 1911 ed. The dictionary entry in this edition describes the history of dictionaries in great detail and includes a list of dictionaries that have been written in English. See also the entry in the 1975 edition for a more current discussion.

ANSWERS TO EXERCISE 23.3 WILL VARY

Synonyms for *odious*, for instance, might include *disgusting*, *ghastly*, *hideous*, or *unpleasant*; antonyms might include *attractive*, *exquisite*, *fair*, or *picturesque*. You might wish to have students bring their answers to class and then to compare them by using each one in a sentence.

TEACHING PRACTICE

To extend the ways students use dictionaries, devise assignments that require students to use a dictionary to complete the assignment. One such assignment might be an extended definition of a term (for example, *wife*), either of your own or of the students' choice. To define the term fully, you might require that students include all uses of the term, from formal to slang. You might also require that students examine how the term has changed over time (for example, *guy*), or you might require students to examine how the meaning of a certain word changes from country to country and region to region (*grill* and *barbeque*). The various requirements demand that students examine a variety of sources, but these requirements also allow students to examine the sources with more purpose and freedom, particularly if the students choose the term to define.

WRITING TOGETHER

Break the class into small groups, and either assign a word to each group or allow the group to pick a word they find interesting. Each person in the group should investigate the definition and usage of the word in one of the following dictionaries, usage books, or thesauruses. The group is responsible for presenting as rich a definition as possible for the word they research. The "product" of the research can take the form of a written report, but an oral presentation is often more valuable and interesting, particularly if the words the students choose contain surprises for them.

Here is a list of potential sources (not including the ones listed in the handbook):

Brewer's Dictionary of Phrase and Fable: Centenary Edition. New York: Harper, 1981.

Chapman, Robert L. *New Dictionary of American Slang*. New York: Harper, 1986.

Hall, John R. *A Concise Anglo-Saxon Dictionary*. Toronto: U of Toronto P, 1984.

Matthews, Mitford M. *A Dictionary of Americanisms on Historical Principles.* Chicago, 1951.

Partridge, Eric. *A Dictionary of Slang and Unconventional English.* 8th ed. New York: Macmillan, 1985.

Wentworth, Harold. *American Dialect Dictionary.* New York, 1944.

Wentworth, Harold, and Stuart B. Flexner. *Dictionary of American Slang.* 2nd ed. New York: Crowell, 1975.

(BACK)GROUNDING

In late 1989, Oxford University plans to publish a new edition of the *Oxford English Dictionary* (*OED*) that will integrate the entries in the four supplements into the main volumes, thus making the *OED* easier to use. And in 1990, Oxford will begin a total revision of the dictionary, a project that should take its team of editors well into the twenty-first century. Eventually, the *OED* should be available electronically. Already scholars can consult an extremely flexible *OED* database system that is capable of very sophisticated analysis. This system can tell a researcher, for instance, every location in the entire *OED* where the word *authorship* appears. This system can tell a researcher that Shakespeare is the most quoted author in the *OED*. And the system can give a copy of the 32,868 quotations that appear in entries throughout the dictionary. The advent of electronic dictionaries undoubtedly will make the vast amount of information packed in them much more readily available to their users.

OPTIONAL EXERCISE

Ask your students to copy the definitions of a word of their choice from three unabridged dictionaries: the *Oxford English Dictionary*, *Webster's Third New International Dictionary of the English Language*, and *The Random House Dictionary of the English Language*. If you assign a word, make sure that the definitions include enough material for the length of assignment you expect. If the students choose their own words, take care to emphasize that they need to choose a word with enough information listed about that word. Assign a short essay (250-500 words) that describes the changes in meaning their word has undergone. Ask students to append copies of the dictionary definitions to eliminate the need for extensive citations and to help build a file of words and definitions.

Here is the *American Heritage* entry for *unique*. Notice that instead of the third meaning listed in the *Webster's New World* entry, it provides a note discussing the Usage Panel's opinion of this usage.

> **u·nique** (yōō-nēk′) *adj.* **1.** Being the only one of its kind; sole. **2.** Being without an equal or equivalent; unparalleled. [Fr. < Lat. *unicus,* sole < *unus,* one.] —**u·nique′ly** *adv.* —**u·nique′ness** *n.*
>
>   **Usage:** Traditional grammarians are uncompromising in the insistence that *unique* is an "absolute" term—either something is unique or it isn't—so that it does not allow qualification of degree. The vast majority of the Usage Panel finds unacceptable such uses as are found in the advertising claim *"Omaha's most unique restaurant is now even more unique,"* whose author might have avoided the scorn of the grammarians if he had used instead a word like *unusual* or *remarkable.* Like other absolute words such as *chief* and *unanimous,* however, *unique* can be modified by words like *almost* and *nearly.*

2. Unabridged dictionaries

Unabridged, or "unabbreviated," **dictionaries** are the royalty of their species—the most complete, richly detailed,* and thoroughly presented dictionaries of English. Whereas good abridged dictionaries may include 200,000 items, unabridged dictionaries far more than double that figure. Because they are large and often multivolume—and hence expensive, you may not own an unabridged dictionary, but you will want and need to consult one on occasion in your library. Among the leading unabridged dictionaries are the *Oxford English Dictionary* and *Webster's Third New International Dictionary of the English Language.*

The Oxford English Dictionary. 13 volumes and 4 supplements. New York: Oxford UP, 1933, 1972, 1976. The grandparent of unabridged dictionaries in English, *The Oxford English Dictionary* (known as the *OED*) began in Britain in the nineteenth century as an attempt to give a full history of each English word, recording its entry into the language and illustrating the development of its various meanings with dated quotations in chronological order. Volunteers all over the world contributed quotations to the editors at Oxford University, and the dictionary was published piecemeal over a period of more than forty years. The *OED* lists more than half a million words and is unparalleled in its historical account of changes in word meanings and spellings. The *OED* is also available now at an affordable price in a large two-volume version, featuring photographically reduced pages that can be read with the magnifying glass that accompanies this edition.

Here is the *OED*'s entry for *unique*. Notice that in addition to

USEFUL READING

McCrum, Robert, William Cran, and Robert MacNeil. *The Story of English.* New York: Penguin, 1987. For discussions of Johnson's dictionary, see pages 130–136; for a discussion of Noah Webster's dictionary, see pages 240–244.

the meanings given in the two abridged dictionaries, it lists several obsolete and specialized meanings for *unique* as an adjective; it also includes meanings and examples for *unique* as a noun, a use that is apparently too rare to find space in the abridged dictionaries. Compared with these, the *OED* also provides more detailed etymological information and uses a different system of phonetic symbols for pronunciation. Finally, notice that the related forms *uniquely* and *uniqueness* are not included because they have their own entries.

Unique (yǔnīˑk), *a.* and *sb.* Also 7 unick(e, 7–8 unio. [a. F. *unique* (+ *unic* masc.), ad. L. *únic-us* (whence also Sp., Pg., It. *unico*) single, sole, alone of its kind, f. *únus* one. In early use also directly ad. L. *únicus*, and stressed on the first syllable.]

Regarded by Todd (1818) as 'an affected and useless term of modern times'.

A. *adj.* **1.** Of which there is only one; one and no other; single, sole, solitary.

1602 DOLMAN *La Primaud. Fr. Acad.* (1618) III. 639 Engendring one eternitie, and by an alone vnique action never disturbed, his linage full of understanding. *c* 1645 HOWELL *Lett.* II. xliv, He hath lost..his unic Son in the very flower of his age. 1677 GALE *Crt. Gentiles* IV. I. ii. 53 Divines, who make..right Reason the unic Criterion or Rule of moral Vertue. 1818 TODD, *Unique, adj.,..sole;..without another of the same kind known to exist.* 1861 PALEY *Æschylus, Prometh.* (ed. 2) 39 The student will notice the unique example of στιχομυθία. 1873 HAMERTON *Intell. Life* III. iii. 87 A man ..who made Latin scholarship his unique intellectual purpose. 1882 FARRAR *Early Chr.* II. 476 St. John instantly leaves the subject..to which he has made this unique and passing allusion.

2. That is or forms the only one of its kind; having no like or equal; standing alone in comparison with others, freq. by reason of superior excellence; unequalled, unparalleled, unrivalled.

In this sense readopted from French at the end of the 18th c. and regarded as a foreign word down to the middle of the 19th, from which date it has been in very common use, with a tendency to take the wider meaning of 'uncommon, unusual, remarkable'.

The usage in the comparative and superlative, and with advs. as *absolutely, most, quite, thoroughly, totally,* etc., has been objected to as tautological.

1618 W. BARCLAY *Well at King-horne* A vij, This is a soueraigne and vnicke remedie for that disease in Women. 1794 R. J. SULIVAN *View Nat.* I. 3 A concentrated, and an unique aggregation of almost all the wonders of the natural world. 1809 R. K. PORTER *Trav. Sk. Russia & Sweden* (1813) I. xxv. 285 As it was thoroughly *unique*, I cannot forbear presenting you with so singular a curiosity. 1842 J. P. COLLIER *Armin's Nest Ninn.* Introd., A relic..not only *unique* in itself, but unprecedented in its kind. 1866 LIDDON *Bamp. Lect.* v. (1867) 368 [Christ's] relationship to the Father..is absolutely unique. 1871 B. TAYLOR *Faust* (1875) II. ii. i. 84 A thing so totally unique that collectors would go far to seek. 1885 *Harper's Mag.* April 703/1 When these summer guests found themselves defrauded of their uniquest recreations.

b. Of persons.

1808 FOSTER *Contrib. Eclectic Rev.* (1844) I. 233 [Sir T. More] is a person so *unique* in the records of statesmen, that [etc.]. 1871 BLACKIE *Four Phases* 15 Such a unique mortal.. no man can describe. 1885 MABEL COLLINS *Prettiest Woman* xi, He believed this woman whom he loved to be unique.

c. *absol.* with *the:* (see quots.).

1767 *Phil. Trans.* LVIII. 26 All these are examples of the *unique;* that is, of quantities in a state that is..exclusive of all others. 1849 C. BRONTE *Shirley* xxiii, She felt that Rose Yorke was a peculiar child—one of the unique.

†3. Formed or consisting of one or a single thing. *Obs.—¹*

a 1631 DONNE *Lett.* (1651) 163 A Mathematique point, which is the most indivisible and unique thing which art can present.

B. *sb.* **1.** A thing of which there is only one example, copy, or specimen; esp., in early use, a coin or medal of this class.

1714 R. THORESBY *Diary* 23 June, My Lord showed me some unics and other valuable curiosities. 1730 A. GORDON *Maffei's Amphith.* 47 It ..may be an Unic, for what we know as yet. 1774 *Gentl. Mag.* XLIV. 8 A coin, which I have reason to think is a Unic. 1826 DISRAELI *V. Grey* II. viii, Mr. Vivian Grey had promised his Lordship, who was a collector of medals, an unique which had never yet been heard of. 1872 O. W. HOLMES *Poet Breakf-t.* iii. 89 A unique, sir, and there is a pleasure in exclusive possession.

† b. Something of which only one is possessed by a person or persons. *Obs. rare.*

1783 H. WALPOLE *Let. to C'tess Upper Ossory* 20 June, Lady Pembroke having lent them a servant besides their own unique. 1806 SURR *Winter in Lond.* III. 170 This Belcher girdle was not old; but being an *unique,* it had been..constantly in use.

2. A thing, fact, or circumstance which by reason of exceptional or special qualities stands alone and is without equal or parallel in its kind.

1768 *Phil. Trans.* LVIII. 215 When I presented this map to the Academy..it was looked upon as an Unique. 1781 *Gentl. Mag.* LI. 280/2 The dedication [of a volume of Sermons] being an *unique* in its kind. 1794 PALEY *Evid.* II. ix. iii. ad fin., The propagation of Christianity..is an *unique* in the history of the species. 1835 *Tait's Mag* II. 651 It is.. an *unique* in English biography. 1838 DE QUINCEY *Lamb* Wks. 1858 IX. 156 Of Lamb's writings..some were so memorably beautiful as to be uniques in their class. 1844 *N. Brit. Rev.* I. 124 A conflict, that stands out from all shadow of parallelism—a wild originality—a terrible unique.

b. A person of this class.

1758 *Case of Authors Stated* 14 He presumes, that he, this *Unic,* must therefore appear in the same stupendous Magnitude to every body else. 1782 COWPER *Let.* Nov., Wks. (1876) 121 He is a man much to my taste, and quite an unique in this country. 1802 MRS. E. PARSONS *Myst. Visit* IV. 145, I trust that he though very good, is not an unique. 1813 *Examiner* 22 Feb. 122/2 Those..charms of manner, which constitute an *unique.* 1866 ALGER *Solit. Nat. & Man* II. 65 The peculiar endowment in which he so far surpasses others as to be an insulated unique.

But it wasn't the living room I needed: it was the writing room, which now comes back to me with its metal table, its stack of white paper that did not diminish between my visits. I would try my hand at poems; I would also construct elaborate multiple-choice tests. "A child is an artist when, seeing a tree at dusk, she (a) climbs it (b) sketches it (c) goes home and describes it in her notebook." And another (possibly imagined) one: "A child is an artist when, visiting her relatives, she (a) goes down the street to play (b) talks with her family and becomes part of them (c) goes into the back room to write."

—JANET STERNBURG

WRITERS WRITING

The following quotation illustrates a contemporary use of *unique* as comparative [general manager Jerry West speaking about Kareem Abdul-Jabbar's successful free-throw attempts in game six of the National Basketball Association championship series]:

> "You must understand Kareem Abdul-Jabbar is a very special person. He wouldn't have accomplished what he has without being so unique."

WRITING TOGETHER

Ask your students to bring their dictionaries to class. Read some of the following Ambrose Bierce definitions from *The Devil's Dictionary* to them. Then ask your students to find the correct use of the term that Bierce satirizes. Finally, ask your students to write their own satiric definitions.

Here are some examples from Bierce:

corporation, n. An ingenious device for obtaining individual profit without individual responsibility.

edible, adj. Good to eat, and wholesome to digest, as a worm to a toad, a toad to a snake, a snake to a pig, a pig to a man, and man to a worm.

impiety, n. Your irreverence toward my deity.

lawyer, n. One skilled in circumvention of the law.

Occident, n. The part of the world lying west (or east) of the Orient. It is largely inhabited by Christians, a powerful sub-tribe of the Hypocrites, whose principle industries are murder and cheating, which they are pleased to call "war" and "commerce." These, also, are the principle industries of the Orient.

positive, adj. Mistaken at the top of one's voice.

radicalism, n. The conservatism of tomorrow injected into the affairs of today.

WRITING TOGETHER

Ask students to write down any words or expressions from their past assignments that they felt did not express the ideas they had in mind. Then ask them to exchange these words and attempt to find words for others who were stuck; of course, they may not find the word the other person was searching for, but they may come up with a synonym that will help the writer find the right word. In the process of exchanging words, students will broaden their vocabularies.

ANSWERS TO EXERCISE 23.4
(WILL VARY)

Webster's Third New International Dictionary of the English Language. Springfield, MA: Merriam, 1986. Containing more entries than any dictionary besides the *OED*—more than 450,000 in all, this one-volume work stirred considerable controversy at its publication because of its tendency, as mentioned in the introduction to this chapter, to *describe* rather than to *prescribe* usage. In all, the editors collected 6,165,000 examples of recorded usage, on which they drew for their Usage Notes. *Webster's Third* lists meanings in order of their entry into the language and quotes from over 14,000 different authors to provide illustrations of words in context.

Here are the *Webster's Third* entries for *unique* as an adjective and as a noun. Notice that the adjective entry simply lists the meaning "unusual, notable" and examples of the use of *most unique*, without discussing the controversy over this usage. In addition, notice that at the end of the entry, the notation **syn** refers the reader to the entries for *single* and *strange*, where the shades of meaning that distinguish *unique* from its synonyms are explained. The phonetic symbols differ slightly from those in either the *OED* or the abridged dictionaries.

¹unique \yü'nēk, 's,s\ *adj, sometimes* -ER/-EST [F, fr. L *unicus* sole, single, unique, fr. *unus* one + *-icus* -ic — more at ONE] **1 a :** being the only one **:** SOLE ⟨earning money whose ~ object could be nothing but Cyril's welfare —Arnold Bennett⟩ ⟨has thus preserved the original and often ~ records —G.B. Parks⟩ ⟨you are a miracle, a wonder, a mystery . . . one single ~ and inimitable living thing —J.C.Powys⟩ **b** *of a book* **:** known to exist in no other copy **2 :** being without a like or equal **:** single in kind or excellence **:** UNEQUALED ⟨they stand alone, ~, objects of supreme interest —A.B.Osborne⟩ ⟨as historian he knows that events, like persons, are ~ —J.M. Barzun⟩ ⟨remains singularly himself, a ~ lyrist of the first water —I.L.Salomon⟩ ⟨an almost ~ experience —Havelock Ellis⟩ ⟨tendencies present in our contemporary world which make our own times somewhat ~ —M.B.Smith⟩ ⟨story of his life is considerably more ~ than most autobiographies —Dorothy C. Fisher⟩ ⟨the more we study him, the less ~ he seems —Harry Levin⟩ — sometimes used with *to* ⟨the problem of what to do with surplus women is by no means ~ to our own society — Ralph Linton⟩ or *with* ⟨by no means ~ with the song sparrow —*Nature Mag.*⟩ **3 :** UNUSUAL, NOTABLE ⟨possessed ~ ability in the raising of funds —C.F.Thwing⟩ ⟨the wife of a career diplomat has a ~ opportunity to observe the world political scene —Ray Pierre⟩ ⟨a frankness ~ in literature —David Daiches⟩ ⟨~ peace and privacy —R.W.Hatch⟩ ⟨cheap, nourishing, and a ~ dining experience —T.H.Fielding⟩ ⟨the most ~ characteristic of that environment —R.A.Billington⟩ ⟨she's the most ~ person I ever met —Arthur Miller⟩ ⟨the most ~ theater in town —*advt*⟩ **4 :** capable of being performed in only one way ⟨the factorization of a number into its prime factors is ~⟩ **syn** see SINGLE, STRANGE
²unique \"\ *n* -s **:** something (as a specimen, thing, circumstance, or person) that is unique **:** the only one of its kind ⟨mistaking the ~ for the typical —W.J.Reilly⟩ ⟨the zest of the collector for possession of a ~ —Roy Bedichek⟩ ⟨a display of glass, including undercoated ~s —*Danish Foreign Office Jour.*⟩ ⟨the phoenix, the ~ of birds —Thomas De Quincey⟩

EXERCISE 23.4

Compare two of the entries on *unique* in this chapter for their advice on how to use the word correctly. Then write a paragraph in which you summarize their major differences of opinion.

EXERCISE 23.5

Look up the following words in at least one abridged and one unabridged dictionary, and compare the entries. Record any differences or disagreements you find, and bring this record to class for discussion.

1. dogmatism
2. alienate
3. discriminate
4. hopefully
5. humanism

EXERCISE 23.6

Look up one of the following words in the *OED*, and write a paragraph describing any changes in meaning it has undergone since its entry into English.

1. lie (verb)	6. humor (noun)
2. cheerful	7. quaint
3. machine	8. honest
4. ornament (noun)	9. testify
5. vulgar	10. romance

▌ 23c. Consulting specialized dictionaries

The dictionaries you have just surveyed will provide you with an enormous amount of information. Sometimes, however, you will need to turn to additional sources for more specialized information. Such sources are available in dictionaries of usage, of synonyms, of slang, and of particular subjects (such as philosophy, mathematics, and biography).

▌ 1. Dictionaries of usage

As the entries for *unique* in 23a and 23b demonstrate, dictionaries sometimes are unable to provide agreed-upon answers to questions of usage. More often than not, questions of usage are not reducible to any simple, easy right or wrong; most of them are very complex and relate not only to linguistic concerns but to social, educational, economic, and regional matters as well. In cases where usage is disputed or where you feel unsure of your own usage, you may wish to consult

377

ANSWERS TO EXERCISE 23.5 (WILL VARY)

1. The *OED* lists a 16th century definition of *dogmatism* as the preaching of new doctrine; as positive assertion of opinion, and as a way of thinking based on principles that have not been tested by reflection.

   Webster's New World Dictionary gives both the idea of asserting opinion as well as the notion that this opinion usually occurs without reference to evidence.

2. The *OED* lists to make strange or turn away from, to transfer ownership, and to change or alter something.

   Webster's New World Dictionary adds two slightly different meanings: to cause to be withdrawn from society, and to transfer affection.

3. The *OED* defines *discriminate* as to make or constitute a difference, to distinguish with the mind or intellect, and to make a distinction.

   Webster's New World Dictionary also includes the notion of discernment or observing distinctions and adds the idea of showing partiality or prejudice.

4. The *OED* defines *hopefully* as an adverb: "In a hopeful manner; with a feeling of hope; with ground for hope, promisingly."

   Webster's New World Dictionary lists both adverb and adjective uses but notes that the adjectival use is "regarded by some as loose usage, but widely current."

5. The *OED* defines *humanism* as belief in the mere humanity of Christ, the quality of being human, a system of thought concerned with merely human interests, and the Renaissance study of Greek and Roman culture.

   Webster's New World Dictionary describes the philosophical basis of modern *humanism* in detail: "a modern, nontheistic, rationalist movement that holds that man is capable of self-fulfillment, ethical conduct, etc. without the recourse to supernaturalism."

ANSWERS TO EXERCISE 23.6 WILL VARY

USEFUL READING

Schweik, Robert, and Dieter Riesner. *Reference Sources in English and American Literature: An Annotated Bibliography*. New York: Norton, 1977. See section "XXII. Dictionaries," pages 208–220, for a list of dictionaries for special uses.

OPTIONAL EXERCISE

Consider using an excerpt of Susan Brownmiller's book, *Femininity*, as an example of an extended definition of that term. Read the excerpt to your students, and ask them to work in small groups to identify each statement or partial definition that Brownmiller uses to build her complex definition and support her thesis. Then ask your students to use an invention technique, such as brainstorming or clustering, to find a word that they could define at length (perhaps *masculinity* might be a good place to start). Finally, ask each student to write a short extended definition. This exercise could be extended by asking students to define a word using other texts, such as magazine advertisements, as sources and support for their extended definitions.

The following statements all appear in *Femininity* and help to define Brownmiller's use of *femininity*:

"Femininity, in essence, is a romantic sentiment, a nostalgic tradition of imposed limitations" (215).

"Femininity functions as an effective antidote to the unrelieved seriousness, the pressure of making one's way in a harsh, difficult world" (217).

"Femininity operates as a value system of niceness, a code of thoughtfulness and sensitivity that in modern society is sadly in short supply" (218).

ANSWERS TO EXERCISE 23.7 (WILL VARY)

These three dictionaries of usage differ in the degree to which they condemn qualifying or comparing "uniqueness." Fowler is most adamant that one cannot compare degrees of uniqueness and stipulates clearly the adverbs that one can and cannot use with *unique*. Bryant acknowledges briefly the quarrel, but implies that since words like *unique* are compared freely, this usage has become acceptable. The Evanses's note that popular usage defines *unique* as meaning both "in a class by itself" and "remarkable" and cites usage by "outstanding writers and educators" as proof that the debate has become irrelevant. Over time the unacceptable has become acceptable.

a specialized dictionary of usage. The most widely used such work, although it is much more about British than about American usage, is H. W. Fowler's *Dictionary of Modern English Usage*, which was published in 1926 and revised by Sir Ernest Gowers in 1965. Here is Fowler's discussion of *unique*.

> **unique.** A watertight definition or paraphrase of the word, securing it against confusion with all synonyms that might be suggested, is difficult to frame. In the first place, it is applicable only to what is in some respect the sole existing specimen, the precise like of which may be sought in vain. That gives a clean line of division between it and the many adjectives for which it is often ignorantly substituted—*remarkable, exceptional, fabulous, rare, marvellous*, and the like. In the qualities represented by those epithets there are degrees; but uniqueness is a matter of yes or no only; no unique thing is more or less unique than another unique thing, as a rare thing may be rarer or less rare than another rare thing. The adverbs that *u.* can tolerate are e.g. *quite, almost, nearly, really, surely, perhaps, absolutely*, or *in some respects*; and it is nonsense to call anything *more, most, very, somewhat, rather*, or *comparatively u.* Such nonsense, however, is often written:
>
> *What made Laker's achievement* all the more unique was. . . . / *I am now at one of* the most unique *writers' colonies imaginable.* / *I have just come across the production of a boy aged seven which is, in my experience, somewhat unique.* / *Sir, I venture to send you a copy of* a rather unique *inscription on a tombstone.* / *A* very unique *child, thought I.*
> But, secondly, there is another set of synonyms—*sole, single, peculiar to*, etc.—from which *u.* is divided not by a clear difference of meaning, but by an idiomatic limitation (in English though not in French) of the contexts to which it is suited. It will be admitted that we improve the two following sentences if we change *u.* in the first into *sole*, and in the second into *peculiar: In the always delicate and difficult domain of diplomatic relations the Foreign Minister must be* the unique *medium of communication with foreign Powers.* / *He relates Christianity to other religions, and notes what is* unique *to the former and what is common to all of them. Unique* so used is a GALLICISM.

EXERCISE 23.7

Look up *unique* in Bergen Evans and Cornelia Evans's *A Dictionary of Contemporary American Usage* and in Margaret M. Bryant's *Current American Usage*. Compare their entries with the one printed above from Fowler. Then write a brief description of how these three works agree and disagree on the usage of *unique*.

2. Dictionaries of synonyms

All writers are sometimes stuck for just the right word, and at such times, a dictionary of synonyms or a thesaurus is a friend indeed. These works follow each entry with a list of words whose meanings are similar to the meaning of the entry. A useful source for students is *Webster's Dictionary of Synonyms*, which includes the following entry for *unique*:

CONSULTING SPECIALIZED DICTIONARIES

di|23c

unique 1 **single, sole, lone, solitary, separate, particular*
   Ana *only, alone
   2 *singular, *strange, peculiar, eccentric, erratic, odd, queer, quaint, outlandish, curious*
   Ana *exceptional: uncommon, rare, *infrequent

The entry indicates, by way of asterisks, that further information on synonyms for *unique* may be found by looking up several other words (the abbreviation *Ana.* marks analogous words). Checking these entries carefully should help you decide which, if any, of these synonyms would be appropriate in a particular sentence.

A **thesaurus,** which comes from a word meaning "treasure" or "storehouse," provides lists of antonyms as well as synonyms for many words. Two are particularly helpful: *Webster's Collegiate Thesaurus* and *The New Roget's Thesaurus of the English Language in Dictionary Form.*

Remember, however, to use dictionaries of synonyms and thesauruses very carefully, because very rarely in English are two words so close in meaning that they can be used interchangeably in radically different contexts. As Mark Twain put it, the difference between the right word and the almost-right word is the difference between lightning and the lightning bug.

EXERCISE 23.8

Look up the entry *strange* in *Webster's New Dictionary of Synonyms.* Read it carefully, and then write a brief summary of what the entry has to say about the relationship of *unique* to *strange.* Then look up *strange* in *The New Roget's Thesaurus,* and compare that entry with the one in *Webster's.*

| 3. Dictionaries of etymology, regional English, and slang

On some occasions, you may want or need to find out all you can about the origins of a word, to find out about a term used only in one area of the country, or to see whether a term is considered to be slang or not. The following specialized dictionaries can help out:

> *The Oxford Dictionary of English Etymology,* ed. C. T. Onions. New York: Oxford UP, 1966.
>
> *Dictionary of American Regional English,* ed. Frederic G. Cassidy. Cambridge, MA: The Belknap Press of Harvard UP, 1985.
>
> *Dictionary of American Slang,* 2nd supplemented edition, ed. Harold Wentworth and Stuart Berg Flexner. New York: Crowell, 1978.

USEFUL READING

Daly, Mary, and Jane Caputi. *Webster's First New Intergalactic Wickedary of the English Language.* Boston: Beacon, 1987. The authors define a wickedary as "a dictionary for wicked women." This is a feminist deconstruction of language and of the form of dictionaries.

OPTIONAL EXERCISE

Ask your students to bring their dictionaries to class, and them have them identify the various usage labels their dictionary employs. *Webster's New World Dictionary* uses the following labels: colloquial, slang, obsolete, archaic, poetic, dialect, and British/Canadian/Scottish or other nationality. For each usage label, ask students to find as many words as they can that illustrate what this label means. After students have found some illustrations, get them to read their words, definitions, and usages to the class.

ANSWER TO EXERCISE 23.8 (WILL VARY)

Webster's reports that *unique* means "strange," but with the added notions of "singularly strange" or "one of a kind." *Roget's* defines it similarly but adds one additional sense, "peculiar but not exclusively original."

ANSWERS TO ANSWERS 23.9
WILL VARY

EXERCISE 23.9

Look up the following words in several specialized dictionaries, and find out as much as you can about their meanings, origins, and uses.

1. wazoo
2. tip
3. scam
4. jazz
5. whammy

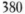 **4. Subject dictionaries**

Special subject dictionaries can help us understand specialized or technical vocabulary and provide a rough map of any field. Such dictionaries exist for music, classical literature, biography, mathematics, philosophy, geography, religion, and many other fields. Suppose, for instance, that you find the word *unique* used in a math textbook in a way that puzzles you. Check a source such as the *Mathematics Dictionary*, 4th edition (eds. Glen James and Robert C. James. New York: Van Nostrand Reinhold Co., 1976). There you will find the following entry:

> **U·NIQUE′,** *adj.* Leading to one and only one result; consisting of one, and only one. The product of two integers is unique; the square root of an integer is not unless the integer is 0.
>
> **unique factorization.** See DOMAIN—integral domain, FUNDAMENTAL—fundamental theorem of arithmetic, IRREDUCIBLE—irreducible polynomial.

You will find more on special subject dictionaries in Chapter 39.

READING WITH ATTENTION TO WORDS

In his autobiography, Malcolm X says that he taught himself to write by reading and copying the dictionary. Certainly you can teach yourself to be a better writer by reading with very careful attention to the way other writers use words you are not very familiar with. Choose a writer whose work you admire, and read that author's work for at least thirty minutes, noting down six or seven words that you would not ordinarily have thought to use in such a situation. Do a little dictionary investigative work on these words, and bring your results to class for discussion.

CONSULTING SPECIALIZED DICTIONARIES

FOR EXAMINING SOME WORDS IN YOUR OWN WRITING

Look back through the last several essays or drafts of essays you have written, looking for two or three words you have used that interest you but that you know very little about. Then look up those words in at least one abridged and one unabridged dictionary and in any specialized dictionary that might give you further information. On the basis of what you have learned, check the way you have used these words in your essays. How accurately and appropriately have you used them? What synonyms could you have appropriately substituted?

24. Enriching Vocabulary

(BACK)GROUNDING

Studying how the English colonists in the New World confronted many new places, plants, animals, and experiences reveals how speakers of English have always developed new words. The colonists provided new names for new things in four ways:

1. By borrowing directly from another language, usually one of the native American languages. Native Americans spoke 350 different languages. The largest number of loan words came from the Algonquin languages. *Wigwam* is an example.
2. By translating foreign words and phrases into English. Again, the sources were usually native American. An example is *war path*.
3. By using an English word to serve as a label for something new. *Corn* and *robin* refer to different objects in England than they do in America.
4. By coining a new word entirely, although such coinages were rare. The *Bobwhite* and the *Whip-porwill* received names meant as imitations of the sounds they made. And *backwoods* is another early American coinage.

Using words to mean something different from their original meanings is another way of introducing "new" vocabulary. Students provide many new words that our language assimilates. For instance, the authors of *The Story of English* cite the assimilation of *Valspeak* (supposedly begun in the San Fernando Valley, north of Los Angeles, California) and *Preppy talk* by many young people. In *Valspeak*, *awesome* means "very good," *max* means "maximum," and *grody* means "unspeakably awful." In *Preppy talk*, *rude* means "in bad taste," *dork* means "an outsider," and *poo* (from *shampoo*) means "champagne."

Language continues to change. The process of adapting language to fit current needs never stops. Your students and their coinages are best seen as part of this process.

In one of the great heroic tales in English literature, *Beowulf* faces a series of difficult challenges. In the face of them, he calls not for weapons or for superhuman strength. Instead he says, quite simply, "I will unlock my word-hoard." Beowulf regards his "word-hoard," his vocabulary or language, as his greatest strength. Indeed, throughout the history of the West, the connection between language and creative power has been very close. In the Bible, for instance, how does God create the world? By calling it into existence through *naming* it.

Vocabulary comes from a Latin term for "name" (*vocabulum*), which in turn comes from the Latin verb for "call." Thus, our vocabulary "calls forth" or names things in our worlds. This connection between vocabulary and calling into being is what led a famous philosopher to declare that "the limits of my language are the limits of my world." You can recognize what the philosopher means easily enough by remembering a time in your life when you learned the name of something new. Before that time, this thing did not exist for you; yet curiously enough, once you know its name, you begin to recognize it all around you. Such is the power of vocabulary in enriching not only your personal language but our lives as well.

24a. Extending your vocabulary

If you grew up speaking English, your English vocabulary is already extensive. At its largest, it includes all those words whose meanings you either recognize or can deduce from context. This, your

382

Baugh, Albert C., and Thomas Cable. *A History of the English Language*. 3d ed. Englewood Cliffs, NJ: Prentice-Hall, 1978. See item 9, "Cosmopolitan Vocabulary" (pp. 9–10).

McCrum, Robert, William Cran and Robert MacNeil. *The Story of English*. New York: Penguin, 1987. See the epilogue, "Next Year's Words" (pp. 343–351), for a discussion of vocabulary.

CHARTING THE HISTORY OF ENGLISH   *voc* | 24b

processing vocabulary, allows you to interpret the meanings of many passages whose words you might not actively use yourself. Your **producing vocabulary** is more limited, comprising those words you actually use in writing and/or speaking.

Part of what it means to mature intellectually is to broaden your mental horizons by learning how to name more things more accurately, to increase your own word-hoard. Doing so involves consciously strengthening the bridges between your processing vocabulary and your producing vocabulary by beginning to use in your own speaking and writing more of the words you recognize and can interpret in context. To accomplish this goal, you must become an investigative reporter of your own language and the language of others.

▍ 24b. Charting the history of English

Try to imagine a world without language. In fact, you probably cannot do so, for language is perhaps the most ancient heritage of the human race. Because language brings us together and indeed allows us to name and structure our experience of the world, it is well worth understanding how this heritage originated and has changed over the centuries. Knowing at least a little about the relationship of English to German, Norse, Latin, Greek, and French can guide you as you seek to learn more about any particular modern English word.

English has always been a hybrid language, what Daniel Defoe called "your Roman-Saxon-Danish-Norman English." Where did this hybrid come from, and how did it evolve? English, like one-third of all languages in the world, descends from Indo-European, a language spoken by a group of seminomadic peoples who almost certainly had domestic animals, worked leather, wove wool, and planted some crops. Where they lived is the subject of great controversy, though their home must have been in some part of north-central Europe. Scholars began to argue for Indo-European, the language of these people, as a "common source" and to try to identify its features when they noted more and more striking resemblances between words in a number of languages:

English	Latin	French	Greek	German	Dutch	Swedish	Danish
three	*tres*	*trois*	*treis*	*drei*	*drie*	*tre*	*tre*

Eventually, a version of Indo-European was brought to Britain by the Germanic invasions following 449. This early language, called Anglo-

(BACK)GROUNDING

The distinction between *processing* and *producing* vocabularies parallels Noam Chomsky's distinction between competence (every speaker's intuitive knowledge of the basic workings of her language—what Ferdinand De Saussure called *la langue*) and performance (day-to-day language use together with competence—what De Saussure called *la parole*). Here the distinction between producing (speaking or writing the language) and processing (recognizing or deriving meaning) reflects the theories of De Saussure and Chomsky while it explains the difficulties students may have moving from an education that asks them to be primarily readers (processors) rather than writers (producers).

The graphic below may help you and your students understand the distinction between producing and processing vocabularies and how the kinds of vocabularies relate to each other.

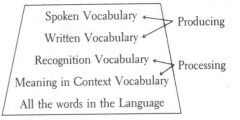

(BACK)GROUNDING

One of the ways linguists have tried to determine the origin of the Indo-European language is by looking for groups of words that might suggest the kinds of experiences that these people had. For example, there were no words in Indo-European for *elephant*, *rhinoceros*, or *camel*, but there were words for *snow*, *beaver*, and *eagle*. Albert C. Baugh and Thomas Cable conclude their discussion of this issue in *A History of the English Language* by stating that "most of the present locations can be accommodated in the district east of the Germanic area stretching from central Europe to the steppes of southern Russia" (39).

USEFUL READING

Heath, Shirley Brice. *Ways With Words*. Cambridge: Cambridge University Press, 1983. See ch. 9, "Learners as Ethnographers," for more information about students as "investigative reporters."

Herndon, Jeanne H. *A Survey of Modern Grammars*. New York: Holt, 1976. See pages 146–147 for a discussion of competence and performance, *la langue* and *la parole*.

WRITING TOGETHER

Old or middle English may look very remote to your students on paper, but if you read a middle English text aloud to them, they will be surprised at how much they can pick up. Provide your students with a copy of one of Chaucer's *Canterbury Tales*, and read part of it to them. Ask them to underline any words they cannot understand, and as a class, attempt to define these words. The following is a section from the Wife of Bath's tale:

> Lo, here the wyse kind, dan Salomon
> I towe he hadd wyves mo than oon.
> As wolde God it level ful were to me
> To be refressed half so ofte as he!
> Which yifte of God hadde he for alle his wyvis!
> No man hath switch, that in this world alyve is.

(BACK)GROUNDING

English owes its hybrid nature to the various invasions of Britain—that is, to the fact that the earliest native peoples and their language, the Celts, and the later dominant peoples, the three Germanic tribes (the Jutes, the Angles, and the Saxons) intermixed with each other and other peoples invading the country. The Romans, who ruled Britain for almost 400 years, contributed *castra*, the Latin word meaning "camp." It is evident in the names of such places as *Lancaster* and *Winchester*. Also, Latin words were brought over to Britain by the German invaders, whose language had borrowed them previously: *win* ("wine"), *ancor* ("anchor"), *weall* ("wall"). The Anglo-Saxons gave us the earliest ancestors of many modern English words, such as *hus* ("house"), *wulf* ("wolf"), and *faeder* ("father"). They also gave the island its permanent name, *Englaland* ("England"), the "land of the Angles." The Danes, who invaded Britain in the ninth century, added words like *skull*, *sky*, *band*, *egg*, *want*, and *low*. And they gave us our personal pronouns for the third person, *they*, *their*, and *them*. A tremendous number of new English words and new spellings originated with the Norman Invasion in 1066. Words like *service*, *castle*, *chancellor*, *army*, and *literature* all came from Norman French originally.

Renaissance scholars deliberately borrowed many Greek and Latin words. Also, many Greek and Latin prefixes, suffixes, and roots of words were borrowed and combined with other borrowings to form whole new words.

Saxon or Old English, was further influenced by Latin and Greek when Christianity was reintroduced into England beginning in 597, was later shaped by the Viking invasions beginning in the late 700s (the Danes feature prominently in *Beowulf*), and was transformed after the Norman Conquest (1066) by French.

While the English vernacular continued to evolve in the centuries after the Conquest, however, Latin and French remained the languages of the learned—of the church and court. (Indeed, lectures at Oxford University were delivered in Latin well into the nineteenth century.) It was Chaucer, through his decision in the late 1300s to write *The Canterbury Tales* not in Latin or French but in the earthy language of the people, who helped establish English as the political, legal, and literary language of Britain. And with the advent of printing in the mid-1400s, that language became more accessible and more standardized.

One brief example will give you an idea of how much English had evolved up to this time. Here are three versions of a Biblical passage:

ANGLO-SAXON GOSPELS, AROUND 1000 A.D.

And eft hē ongan hī æt þǣre sǣ lǣran. And him wæs mycel męnegu tō gegaderod, swā þæt hē on scip ēode, and on bǣre sǣ wæs; and eall sēo męnegu ymbe þē sǣ wæs on lande.

WYCLIFFE BIBLE, ABOUT 1380

And eft Jhesus bigan to teche at the see; and myche puple was gaderid to hym, so that he wente in to a boot, and sat in the see, and al the puple was aboute the see on the loond.

KING JAMES VERSION, 1611

And he began again to teach by the seaside: and there was gathered unto him a great multitude, so that he entered into a ship, and sat in the sea: and the whole multitude was by the sea on the land.

Note that in the Old English text, only a few words—*and*, *he*, *him*, *waes*, *lande*, *sae*—look familiar. By the time of Chaucer, however, many words are recognizable. And by the time of the Renaissance, the language is easily readable by us.

In the last four hundred years, as the extension of British, and later American, political and cultural influence has made English the second most widely spoken language in the world, continued borrow-

USEFUL READING

Alexander, Henry. "English: Its Origin and Relation to Other Languages." Rpt. in *Introductory Readings on Language*. Eds. Wallace L. Anderson and Norman C. Stageberg. New York: Holt, 1970 (pp. 57–67). This is a concise description of the relationships among the Indo-European languages.

Baugh, Albert C., and Thomas Cable. A *History of the English Language*. 3d ed. Englewood Cliffs, NJ: Prentice-Hall, 1978. See item 28, "The Home of the Indo-European Family" (35–39).

ings from many languages have given it the world's largest vocabulary. Modern English, then, is a composite language, a plant growing luxuriously in the soil of multiple sources.

▌ 24c. Recognizing word roots

As its name suggests, a **root** is a word from which other words grow, usually through the addition of prefixes or suffixes. From the Latin roots *-dic-* or *-dict-* ("speak"), for instance, grows a whole range of words in English: *contradict, dictate, dictator, diction, edict, predict, dictaphone,* and others. From the Greek root *-chrono-* ("time") come our words *chronology, chronometer, synchronize,* and so on.

Here are some other Latin (marked L) and Greek (marked G) roots. Recognizing them will help you recognize networks of words in the language.

ROOT	MEANING	EXAMPLES
-audi- (L)	to hear	audience, audio, auditorium
-bene- (L)	good, well	benevolent, benefit, benefactor
-bio- (G)	life	biography, biosphere, biopsy
-duc(t)- (L)	to lead or to make	ductile, reduce, reproduce
-gen- (G)	race, kind	genealogy, gene
-geo- (G)	earth	geography, geometry
-graph- (G)	to write	graphic, photography, pictograph
-jur-, -jus- (L)	law	justice, jurisdiction
-log(o)- (G)	word, thought	biology, logical, logocentric
-luc- (L)	light	lucid, translucent
-manu- (L)	hand	manufacture, manual, manipulate
-mit-, -mis- (L)	to send	permit, transmission, intermittent
-path- (G)	feel, suffer	empathy, pathetic
-phil- (G)	love	philosopher, bibliophile
-photo- (G)	light	photography, telephoto
-port- (L)	to carry	transport, portable
-psych- (G)	soul	psychology, psychopath
-scrib-, -script- (L)	to write	inscribe, manuscript, descriptive
-sent-, -sens- (L)	to feel	sensation, resent

(BACK)GROUNDING

English continues to be a very democratic language, borrowing from almost every language it comes in contact with. From Spanish, we have *canyon, cafeteria,* and *taco.* From German, we borrowed *protein* and *bratwurst.* From Italian, we have *malaria,* but also *pasta* and *studio.* From Slavic, we have *robot* and *vampire.* From Arabic, we adopted *genie, candy, safari,* and *assassin* (originally meaning "hashish-eater"). From Hebrew, we borrowed *amen, Sabbath,* and *Satan.* From Yiddish, we borrowed *kosher* and *matzo.* From Persian, we got *spinach, lilac,* and *bazaar.* From Sanskrit, we have *swastika* and *yoga.* From Hindustani, we got *dungaree, pajamas, jungle,* and *loot.* From Chinese, we adopted *tea* and *ketchup.* From Japanese, we borrowed *zen* and *karate.*

TEACHING PRACTICE

In *Classical Rhetoric for the Modern Student,* Edward P. J. Corbett notes that Samuel Johnson and Oliver Goldsmith identified themselves in their writing by habitual stylistic choices, such as diction (440). Johnson's is described as "philosophical, polysyllabic, Latinate;" Goldsmith's as "concrete, familiar, colloquial."

Consider using examples of writing, either from these authors or from legalese and rock lyrics, to point out how vocabulary can restrict or free writers.

USEFUL READING

Mencken, H. L. *The American Language.* New York: Knopf, 1937. See "The Expanding Vocabulary" (140–150), "The Making of New Nouns" (168–191), and "American Slang" (555–589).

Pyles, Thomas. *Words and Ways of American English.* New York: Random House, 1952. See chapters 1, 2, 7, and 8 for discussions of how American speech adapts and adopts words from other languages and dialects.

-tele- (G)	far away	telegraph, telepathy
-tend- (L)	to stretch	extend, tendency
-terr- (L)	earth	inter, territorial
-therm- (G)	heat	thermonuclear, thermostat
-vac- (L)	empty	vacuole, evacuation
-vid-, -vis- (L)	to see	video, envision, visit

ANSWERS TO EXERCISE 24.1 WILL VARY

OPTIONAL EXERCISE

Consider asking your students to read and record inventive uses of vocabulary. To get them started, read some of Tom Wolfe's prose, such as "Porno-violence" (the title coins a new word), "Hugh Hefner" (in which he coins the word *statusphere*), or "Las Vegas (What!) Las Vegas (Can't Hear You! Too Noisy) Las Vegas!!" (in which Wolfe names the signs on the strip: "Boomerang Modern, Palette Curvilinear, Flash Gordon Ming Alert Spiral, McDonald's Hamburger Parabola, Mint Casino Elliptical, Miami Beach Kidney"). Paul Fussell's "Notes on Class" uses the following terms to identify his classifications of society into groups: "Top Out-of-Sight; Upper [class]; Upper Middle;/Middle; High-Proletarian; Mid-Proletarian; Low-Proletarian;/Destitute; Bottom Out-of-Sight," and a floating class "Class X."

After students have had time to read (either in class with a copy of one of the essays or as homework with texts of their own), have them present their findings to the class by describing the word, the word's definition, and reading sentences where the word is used in context.

WRITERS ON WRITING

Oh! it gives me the hydrostatics to such a degree. I thought she had persisted from corresponding with him; but, behold, this very day I have interceded another letter from the fellow.

—MRS. MALAPROP
IN RICHARD SHERIDAN'S *THE RIVALS*

EXERCISE 24.1

Using the list of roots above, try to figure out the meaning of each of the following words. Write a potential definition for each one, and then compare your dictionary's definition to yours.

1. terrestrial
2. scriptorium
3. geothermal
4. lucent
5. beneficent
6. audiology
7. vacuous
8. pathogenic
9. juridical
10. graphology

▌ 24d. Recognizing prefixes and suffixes

Originally individual words themselves, prefixes and suffixes are groups of letters added to words or to word roots to create new words. These word additions account for much of the flexibility of English, often allowing dozens of words to be built on one root.

▌ 1. Prefixes

Prefix appropriately demonstrates its own meaning: it is made up of a prefix (-*pre*-) and a root (-*fix*-) and means literally "fasten before." Fastened to the beginnings of words or roots, prefixes modify and extend meanings. Recognizing common prefixes can often help you decipher the meaning of otherwise unfamiliar words.

Prefixes of negation or opposition

PREFIX	MEANING	EXAMPLES
a-, an-	without, not	ahistorical, anemia
anti-	against	antibody, antiphonal
contra-	against	contravene, contramand
de-	from, take away from	demerit, declaw
dis-	apart, away	disappear, discharge
il-, im-, in-, ir-	not	illegal, immature, indistinct, irreverent

mal-	wrong	malevolent, malpractice
mis-	wrong, bad	misapply, misanthrope
non-	not	nonentity, nonsense
un-	not	unbreakable, unable

Prefixes of quantity

PREFIX	MEANING	EXAMPLES
bi-	two	bipolar, bilateral
milli-	thousand	millimeter, milligram
mono-	one, single	monotone, monologue
omni-	all	omniscient, omnipotent
semi-	half	semicolon, semiconductor
tri-	three	tripod, trimester
uni-	one	unitary, univocal

Prefixes of time and space

PREFIX	MEANING	EXAMPLES
ante-	before	antedate, antebellum
circum-	around	circumlocution, circumnavigate
co-, col-, com-, con-, cor-	with	coequal, collaborate, commiserate, contact, correspond
e-, ex-	out of	emit, extort, expunge
hyper-	over, more than	hypersonic, hypersensitive
hypo-	under, less than	hypodermic, hypoglycemia
inter-	between	intervene, international
mega-	enlarge, large	megalomania, megaphone
micro-	tiny	micrometer, microscopic
neo-	recent	neologism, neophyte
post-	after	postwar, postscript
pre-	before	previous, prepublication
pro-	before, onward	project, propel
re-	again, back	review, recreate
sub-	under, beneath	subhuman, submarine
super-	over, above	supercargo, superimpose
syn-	at the same time	synonym, synchronize
trans-	across, over	transport, transition

WRITERS WRITING

For Joan Didion, writing is an exploration, a way of answering questions, of finding out rather than simply recording and filling out a plot she has figured in her head. Didion wrote two lines that appear in her novel, *A Book of Common Prayer*— "I knew why Charlotte went to the airport even if Victor did not" and "I knew about airports"— before she knew who Victor was, before she knew why Charlotte was in the airport, and before she knew who the narrator was. Didion comments about this experience, "Let me tell you one thing about why writers write: had I known the answer to any of these questions I would never have needed to write a novel."

OPTIONAL EXERCISE

Present the following Old English words to your class (without definitions) and ask them to suggest modern cognates.

1. cyng = king
2. deor = animal; deer
3. dohtor = daughter
4. feond = friend
5. faeder = father
6. for-giefen = forgiven
7. god-spell = gospel
8. iren = iron
9. sawol = soul
10. turf = turf

USEFUL READING

Whitelock, Dorothy. *Sweet's Anglo-Saxon Reader in Prose and Verse*. Oxford: Oxford UP, 1967. The Old English/modern English dictionary at the back is a good source of more cognates for the optional exercise above.

24d voc   ENRICHING VOCABULARY

ANSWERS TO EXERCISE 24.2 (WILL VARY)

1. remit: send again or send back; to release from the guilt or penalty of, to refrain from, to desist from an activity.
2. subterranean: beneath earth; of or relating to under the surface of the earth.
3. translucent: across or over light; permitting the passage of light, clear or transparent.
4. monograph: to write one or a single writing; a learned treatise on a small area of learning.
5. distend: to stretch apart or away; extend, to enlarge from internal pressure.
6. superscript: to write over or above; a distinguishing symbol written immediately above or above and to the right of another character.
7. deport: to carry from; to carry away, to send out of the country by legal deportation, to behave or comport oneself.
8. neologism: recent word or thought; a word, usage, or expression that is often disapproved because of its newness or barbarousness.
9. inaudible: to hear not; not capable of being heard.
10. apathetic: without feeling or not suffering; having or showing little or no feeling or emotion, having or showing little or no interest or concern.

OPTIONAL EXERCISE

Ask students to choose a language to investigate: the language of rock music, the language of parents, the language of doctors. As part of their investigation, ask students to draw up a "vocabulary" complete with definitions, examples, and pronunciations for the language they choose. When the assignments are due, make sure students share their work. A compendium of the language of freshmen could include words like *chill* (short for *chill out*, which means to cool it or calm down) and *yo* (a glottal vibration meant to indicate "Yes, you have my attention").

EXERCISE 24.2

Using the list of prefixes above and the list of roots in 24c, try to figure out the meaning of each of the following words. Write a potential definition for each one, and then compare your dictionary's definition to yours.

1. remit
2. subterranean
3. translucent
4. monograph
5. distend
6. superscript
7. deport
8. neologism
9. inaudible
10. apathetic

2. Suffixes

Attached to the ends of words and word roots, **suffixes** modify and extend meanings, many times by altering the grammatical function or part of speech of the original word. Suffixes can, for example, turn the verb *create* into a noun, an adjective, or an adverb.

VERB	create
NOUNS	crea*tor*/crea*tion*/crea*tivity*/crea*ture*
ADJECTIVE	crea*tive*
ADVERB	crea*tively*

Noun suffixes

SUFFIX	MEANING	EXAMPLES
-acy	state or quality	democracy, privacy
-al	act of	rebuttal, refusal
-ance, -ence	state or quality of	maintenance, eminence
-dom	place or state of being	freedom, thralldom
-er, -or	one who	trainer, investor
-ism	doctrine or belief characteristic of	liberalism, Taoism
-ist	one who	organist, physicist
-ity	quality of	veracity, opacity
-ment	condition of	payment, argument
-ness	state of being	watchfulness, cleanliness
-ship	position held	professorship, fellowship
-sion, -tion	state of being or action	digression, transition

Verb suffixes

SUFFIX	MEANING	EXAMPLES
-ate	cause to be	concentrate, regulate
-en	cause to be or become	enliven, blacken

| -ify, -fy | make or cause to be | unify, terrify, amplify |
| -ize | cause to become | magnetize, civilize |

Adjective suffixes

SUFFIX	MEANING	EXAMPLES
-able, -ible	capable of being	assumable, edible
-al	pertaining to	regional, political
-esque	reminiscent of	picturesque, statuesque
-ful	having a notable quality	colorful, sorrowful
-ic	pertaining to	poetic, mythic
-ish	having the quality of	prudish, clownish
-ious, -ous	of or characterized by	famous, nutritious
-ive	having the nature of	festive, creative, massive
-less	without	endless, senseless

EXERCISE 24.3

Using the list of suffixes above, figure out the meaning of each of the following words. (Use your dictionary if necessary.) Then choose two of the words, and use each one in a sentence.

1. contemplative
2. fanciful
3. impairment
4. liquefy
5. barrenness
6. defiance
7. defiantly
8. redden
9. standardize
10. satirist

24e. Building a word-hoard

Making good use of prefixes or suffixes will increase the power of your vocabulary, but other methods will be even more helpful in creating a word-hoard that is a match for Beowulf's. These methods include analyzing word contexts, becoming an active reader, and becoming a collector of words.

1. Analyzing word contexts

If you have ever run into a person you knew but simply could not place—until you remembered the place where you normally saw the person (at the grocery store, say, or the bank), you know firsthand the importance of context in helping you identify people and things. The same principle holds true for words. So if a word is at first unfa-

WRITERS ON WRITING

WORDS . . . are the wildest, freest, most irresponsible, most unteachable of all things. Of course, you can catch them and place them in alphabetical order in dictionaries. But words do not live in dictionaries; they live in the mind . . . all we can say about them, as we peer at them over the edge of that deep, dark and only fitfully illuminated cavern in which they live—the mind—all we can say about them is that they seem to like people to think and to feel before they use them, but to think and to feel not about them, but about something different.

—VIRGINIA WOOLF

Words are with us everywhere. In our erotic secrecies, in our sleep. We're often no more aware of them than our own spit, although we use them oftener than legs. So of course in the customary shallow unconscious sense, we comprehend the curse, the prayer, and the whoop.

—WILLIAM H. GASS

OPTIONAL EXERCISE

To demonstrate how vocabulary creates an *ethos* or persona for the writer, read the following paragraph from Frederick C. Crews's *The Pooh Perplex* aloud to your class. Ask the class to characterize the persona. Then, ask the class to re-write the paragraph to construct a different persona.

> Today I want to tell you guys about a terrific book that you all ought to read for the final exam, if you haven't already. It's very, very big in the English tradition, and has lots of really key things in it. It's called *Winnie-the-Pooh*, and it was written by Al Milne, an English "chap" who took quite a liking to me after the War. He was a real character, but I don't want to go into that—no, no, fellas, really—I've got to give you the scoop on his lit. Let's stick right on the beam today, not like Wednesday when you got me off on those Italian babes I met in the Occupation. We've got to put this bird against the context of his age, you know what I mean?—we've got to get with his world-picture so we can shoot some balanced historical perspective into this *Winnie-the-Pooh*.

miliar to you, look carefully at its context, paying attention to all the clues that context can give; often you will be able to deduce the meaning.

For instance, if the word *accouterments* is unfamiliar in the sentence *We stopped at a camping supply store to pick up last-minute accouterments*, you can figure out its meaning from its context: *the camping supply store* and *last-minute* suggest strongly that *equipment* or some similar word fits the bill. And that is what *accouterments* means.

Sometimes, as in the following sentences, the context will include examples or definitions of unfamiliar words:

> In grammars of the late medieval period, figures of speech were organized into *schemes*—figures having to do with word choice—and *tropes*—figures having to do with sentence construction.

> The troop leader quickly removed all *incendiary* materials—matches, gas lanterns, and firecrackers.

Sometimes, however, deciphering the meaning of a word calls on your greatest detective powers. The following example, for instance, demands very careful attention to context:

> Interpretive frameworks at their most radical become reflexive, arguing that the observer's own understanding of any phenomenon must arise through a complex interaction between the process of observing and the characteristics of the thing being observed.

This is not an easy sentence to read, because much of the diction is general and abstract. *Interpretive frameworks* suggests structures that interpret information or data. *Radical* interpretive frameworks is more problematic. Although *radical* refers back to Latin *radix* ("root"), the usual meaning of *radical* today is "extreme." So the most extreme forms of interpretive frameworks become reflexive. What might that mean? A reflex is a response, like the knee-jerk reflex, so *reflexive* probably has to do with response. The sentence structure tells us that *become reflexive* here means that an observer's understanding arises through an interaction between observing and what is observed. Perhaps that interaction is the response that *reflexive* seems to refer to. Our provisional understanding of this sentence, then, might be paraphrased as "extreme forms of interpretation depend on an interaction of observer and observed." When you encounter such passages, your best strategy is to continue reading, looking for additional contextual clues to meaning.

BUILDING A WORD-HOARD   *voc* 24e

EXERCISE 24.4

Identify the contextual clues that help you understand any unfamiliar words in the following sentences. Then write paraphrases of three of the sentences.

1. Before Prohibition, the criminal fringe in the United States had been a self-effacing, scattered class with little popular support.
2. I felt ambivalent. I was angry with Sylvia, but I understood why she behaved so audaciously in asking for a raise after three days on the job.
3. The community's reaction to the preternatural creature in Mary Shelley's *Frankenstein* shows that people are often more monstrous than a monster.
4. My fifth-grade teacher was the epitome of what I wanted to be, and I began to imitate him scrupulously.
5. Aristarchus showed that the sun is larger than the earth and proposed a heliocentric model of the solar system. During the second century A.D., however, Ptolemy challenged this theory with his geocentric model, which came to dominate astronomical thought for the next 1,400 years.

ANSWERS TO EXERCISE 24.4 WILL VARY

2. Becoming an active reader

As processors of information, we can read words alone, or we can read meanings. To read meanings means filling in blanks, making connections, leaping ahead, asking questions, taking mental notes. Active readers flex their mental muscles while reading; they exercise their own understanding and thereby stretch to greater knowledge. Out of such activity great word-hoards are born. Here are some tips for building your vocabulary through active reading:

- Make a habit of paraphrasing or summarizing unfamiliar words or phrases. Then check the dictionary to see how accurate your paraphrase is.
- Practice naming the opposites of words. If you see *abbreviation*, for instance, try supplying its opposite—*enlargement, elaboration*, etc.
- Challenge authors by trying to come up with a better word or words than the ones they used.
- Read aloud to yourself from time to time, noting any words whose pronunciation you are unsure of. Check them out in the dictionary.

3. Becoming a collector of words

Collecting words is an important part of reading actively. Pay close attention to words, choosing those you like best and taking them home as part of your producing vocabulary. You are already a collector of words in one sense: you probably add words to your vocabulary on

WRITING TOGETHER

Discuss Gerard Manley Hopkins's "Pied Beauty" (reprinted below), and divide the class into groups of four to six. Ask students to generate a list of words used in this poem and to define as many of the words as they can; encourage students to attempt to define words they do not recognize from context or by constructing a group "interpretive framework" (brainstorming to suggest possible meanings that can be judged against the context the poem provides).

Glory be to god for dappled things—
    For skies of couple-colour as a brinded cow;
        For rose-moles all in stipple upon trout that
            swim;
Fresh-firecoal chestnut-falls; finches' wings;
    Landscape plotted and pieced—fold, fallow, and
        plough;
        And all trades, their gear and tackle and trim.

All things counter, original, spare, strange;
    Whatever is fickle, freckled (who knows how?)
        With swift, slow; sweet, sour; adazzle, dim;
He fathers-forth whose beauty is past change:
    Praise him.

OPTIONAL EXERCISE

Ask students to read Jessica Mitford's "Behind the Formaldehyde Curtain," and construct a list of the vocabulary that Mitford imports from the undertaker's profession. Then ask them to define these terms.

TEACHING PRACTICE

Students can build word power by trying to think of words to substitute for the italicized ones in the passages in the reading exercise. You can use these potential substitutes (*erased*, say, for *eradicated*) to reflect on nuances of connotation and on why a writer may have chosen one particular word over another.

a fairly regular basis. All you need to do now is make that activity more conscientious and systematic. Begin by choosing a writer you admire and reading for as long as it takes to identify several words you like but would not use in speaking or writing. Your collection has started. Now analyze these words for what you like about them—for pronunciation, meaning, and usage. Next, try the words out on your friends and instructors. And then just continue to build your collection.

READING WITH ATTENTION TO VOCABULARY

Read each of the following passages, paying particular attention to the italicized words. See if you can determine the meaning of any words that are not part of your processing vocabulary by using the clues suggested in this chapter—context, prefixes, roots, suffixes. Check your understanding by then looking up each word in the dictionary.

1. Now, I doubt that the imagination can be suppressed. If you truly *eradicated* it in a child, he would grow up to be an eggplant. Like all our evil *propensities*, the imagination will win out.
    —URSULA LeGUIN, "Why Are Americans Afraid of Dragons?"
2. I am enjoying a *reprieve* of warm sun in a season of rain and *impending* frost. Around me today is the wine of the garden's final ripening.
    —LIANE ELLISON NORMAN,
        "Pedestrian Students and High-Flying Squirrels"
3. But this is the *hiatus* between harvests; the oppressive lull before the bust of monsoon rains; the season of flies and dust, heat and disease, *querulous* voices and frayed tempers—and the season of want.
    —PEGGY AND PIERRE STREIT, "A Well in India"
4. I now firmly believe that when it comes to *instilling* in others—and in myself—the virtues of the Christmas spirit, there is no better way than as Santa Claus. How else could I so easily set aside my *inhibitions* . . . and become a *mirthful*, winking, ho-ho-ho-ing, joking, hugging, *exuberant* man?   —MARK L. DEMBERT, "Being Santa"
5. I think it is agreed by all parties, that this *prodigious* number of children in the arms, or on the backs, or at the heels of their mothers . . . is in the present *deplorable* state of the kingdom, a very great additional *grievance*. . . .   —JONATHAN SWIFT, "A Modest Proposal"

FOR EXAMINING VOCABULARY IN YOUR OWN WRITING

Read over a piece of writing you are working on or have recently completed. Underline any words you think could be improved on, and then come up with several possible substitutes. Bring them and your piece of writing to class for discussion.

25. Analyzing and Using Diction

In writing of someone you work with, you might choose one or more of the following words: *accomplice, ally, associate, buddy, cohort, collaborator, colleague, comrade, co-worker, mate, partner, sidekick.* The choice you make is a matter of **diction,** which derives from the Latin word for "say" and means literally how you say or express something. Good diction, or choosing words well, involves many issues discussed elsewhere in this book, such as being concise (see 17b), using parallel structures (see Chapter 19), choosing strong, precise verbs (see 21a), using dictionaries (see Chapter 23), strengthening vocabulary (see Chapter 24), and establishing tone (see Chapter 26). This chapter will give you some guidance about three other aspects of good diction: using language appropriate to the writer's purpose, topic, and audience; choosing words with the right denotations and connotations; and balancing general and abstract words with specific and concrete ones.

25a. Choosing appropriate language

Musing on the many possible ways to describe a face, Ford Maddox Ford says,

> That a face resembles a Dutch clock has been said too often; to say that it resembles a ham is inexact and conveys nothing; to say that it has the mournfulness of an old smashed-in meat tin, cast away on a waste building lot, would be smart—but too much of that sort of thing would become a nuisance. —FORD MADDOX FORD, *Joseph Conrad*

393

USEFUL READING

Weaver, Richard M. "Ultimate Terms in Contemporary Rhetoric" in *Language is Sermonic: Richard M. Weaver on the Nature of Rhetoric.* Ed. Richard L. Johannesen, et al. Baton Rouge: Louisiana State U P, 1970. See pp. 87–112, a discussion of the power of value-associated terms.

(BACK)GROUNDING

In the essay "Ultimate Terms in Contemporary Rhetoric," Richard M. Weaver offers a forceful argument for the careful study of word choice. Weaver distinguishes two kinds of connotative words: "God terms" and "devil terms." God terms strike in the reader extremely favorable chords. Words such as *progress, science, efficient,* and, not surprisingly, *American* carry a high degree of positive value. Devil terms, on the other hand, carry the greatest degree of negative connotation in American culture, for example: *Un-American activities, Communist,* and *prejudice.* Weaver argues that, because of the attitudes and values associated with certain terms, we must choose our words carefully and responsibly to be sure we express our exact meaning.

WRITERS ON WRITING

Every writer must be aware that whether he or she uses written language to communicate carelessly, or with premeditated precision, the reader will be affected to some degree by what is on the page. Denise Levertov, although she is here talking about poetry, nevertheless captures the nature of the transmission of energy that occurs between writer and reader, whether he or she intends it or not.

> The poem has an effect of some kind whether the poet wills it or not. It has kinetic force, it sets in motion . . . elements in the reader that otherwise would be stagnate. And that movement, that coming into play of the otherwise dormant or stagnate element, however small, cannot be without importance if one conceives of the human being as one in which all parts are connected. . . .
>
> —DENISE LEVERTOV

TEACHING PRACTICE

Transformational grammar might help explain this dialectal feature of the Appalachian Valley regions of the United States. *The car needs washed* is a reduced version of *The car needs to be washed*, carrying a meaning similar to that of *The car needs washing*.

WRITERS ON WRITING

Sometimes beginning writers have difficulty in facing the responsibility they must bear for the weight of the words they choose in communicating with their readers. Yet it is a responsibility they must learn to bear, for as William Stafford has said: "Writing is one of the great, free, human activities."

WRITERS ON WRITING

[Slang] . . . at once a sign and a cause of mental atrophy.

—OLIVER WENDELL HOLMES

Ford here implies a major point about diction: effective word choice can be made only on the basis of what is appropriate to the writer's purpose, to the topic, and to the audience. Specifically, he is saying that making appropriate word choices requires a writer to take into account a number of considerations. For instance, many terms vary from one region to another: the hard round object in the center of a cherry might be described as a stone, a pit, a pip, or a seed, depending on where the writer comes from. *Cherry pip* and *cherry stone* are examples of **regionalisms,** words or expressions peculiar to only one region or part of the country. Regionalisms form one aspect of **dialects,** forms of a language that are distinctive to a particular region or social or ethnic group. In addition to distinctive words and expressions, dialects usually include distinctive pronunciations and grammatical constructions.

If you have never heard the phrase *cherry pip* used before, that particular choice of words will sound odd and perhaps puzzling to you. In other cases, especially in writing, a phrase or construction perfectly understandable and acceptable to users of one dialect will sound not only odd or puzzling but wrong to others. The verb constructions in *the car needs washed* or *the grass be dried up*, for example, would look wrong to most Americans who read them in a book or magazine, even though in certain American dialects these are standard ways of speaking. Knowing what features of your dialect do not "match" those of many other Americans can help you decide how to make appropriate diction choices.

In addition to considerations of region or dialect, a writer must also be alert to the level of formality, or register, that is appropriate for a particular topic and audience. Doing so requires that the writer recognize slang and colloquial language.

Slang is extremely informal language that is often confined to a relatively small group of people and usually becomes obsolete rather quickly. In the 1980s, examples of slang that gained fairly wide use included *yuppie, sleaze,* and *number-crunching*.

Colloquial language, such as *a lot, in a bind,* or *snooze,* is less informal, more widely used, and longer-lasting. Like regional and dialectical words and constructions, slang and colloquial language can expose a writer to the risk of not being understood or of sounding wrong. If you are writing for a general audience about arms-control negotiations, for example, and you use the term *nukes* to refer to nuclear missiles, some readers may not know what you mean, and others may

USEFUL READING

Johnson, Nancy Ainsworth. *Current Topics in Language: Introductory Readings.* Cambridge, Mass.: Winthrop, 1976. Part 2 of this edition contains numerous informative selections on dialect and geographical region, social factors, ethnic background, and cognition.

Williams, Joseph M. *Origins of the English Language: A Social and Linguistic History.* New York: Macmillan, 1975. See pp. 204–207, a discussion of slang as a source of change in word meaning. Williams cites interesting historical instances of slang.

be distracted or irritated by what they see as a frivolous reference to a deadly serious subject.

For most of the college writing you do, meeting the challenge of appropriateness means choosing words that will be most clear and most understandable to a wide range of educated readers. Edited American English (sometimes referred to as EAE) ordinarily fulfills this goal because it is *shared* by most writers throughout the country. In general, edited American English does not use regionalisms, dialect, slang, or colloquial language except deliberately for a special purpose. So if you find instances of these in your writing, examine them very closely. Most often, they will be *inappropriate* for college writing; in Ford Maddox Ford's words, "too much of that sort of thing" is not "smart."

25b. Denotation and connotation

Think of a stone tossed into a pool, and imagine the ripples spreading out from it, circle by circle. Or think of a note struck clear and clean, and the multiple vibrations that echo from it. In such images you can capture the distinction between **denotation,** the general meaning of a word, and **connotation,** the ripples, vibrations, associations that accompany the word. As a writer, you want to choose words that are both denotatively and connotatively appropriate.

Words with similar denotations may have connotations that vary widely. The words *maxim, epigram, proverb, saw, saying,* and *motto,* for instance, all carry roughly the same denotation. Because of their different connotations, however, *proverb* would be the appropriate word to use in reference to a saying from the Bible; *saw* in reference to the kind of wisdom handed down to us anonymously; *epigram* in reference to something written by Oscar Wilde. *Dirt* and *soil* have roughly the same denotative meaning, and their connotations are close enough to allow us to use them interchangeably in most cases. *Pushy* and *assertive* also have much the same denotative meaning, but in this case their connotations suggest different attitudes on the part of the speaker or writer, one neutral or positive, the other negative.

Mistakes in denotation are bound to occur as we try out new words. A person who writes "The party managed to diverge my thoughts from the hard work ahead" is confusing *divert* and *diverge* but is on the way to learning to use both. To avoid mistakes in denotation, pay careful attention to the way words are used in context, and check your dictionary whenever you are unsure of meaning.

OPTIONAL EXERCISE
To help students learn more about how the connotative impact of words often involves associational or emotional responses, ask groups of two to compile for class discussion a list of words according to their denotation and connotation. This exercise will help students see how words have an effect beyond their dictionary level of meaning.

USEFUL READING

Altick, Richard D., and Andrea A. Lunsford. *Preface to Critical Reading.* 6th ed. New York: Holt, 1984. Chapter 1 discusses the uses of connotation in advertising, political persuasion, and literature.

WRITERS ON WRITING

The mixture of vagueness and sheer incompetence is the most marked characteristic of modern English prose, and especially of any political writing. As soon as certain topics are raised, the concreteness melts into the abstract and no one seems to think of turns of speech that are not hackneyed: Prose consists less and less of *words* chosen for the sake of their meaning, and more and more of *phrases* tacked together like the sections of a prefabricated hen-house.

WRITERS ON WRITING

To write simply is as difficult as to be good.
—W. SOMERSET MAUGHAM

Although words with the wrong connotations for your intended meaning may not be as obvious as those with wrong denotations, take equal care to avoid them. Good writers and readers are sensitive to the power of connotation for a number of reasons. In the first place, we do not want to be misunderstood: calling someone *skinny* rather than *slender,* for instance, might be taken as an insult or joke when such a meaning was unintended. And because connotation plays an important part in the language of politics and advertising (to name only the two most obvious fields), being alert to connotation and its power can help us read and listen more critically. Look, for instance, at the differences in connotation among the following three statements:

> Antiapartheid activists built a symbolic shanty on the green this morning to protest the university's refusal to sell its investments in companies doing business in South Africa.

> A gang of left-wing agitators threw up an eyesore right on the green this morning to try to stampede the university into politicizing its investment policy.

> Supporters of human rights in South Africa challenged the university's investment in racism by erecting a protest shanty in the heart of the campus this morning.

As this example demonstrates, positive and negative connotations can shift meaning significantly. Take note of such powerful uses of connotation in the writing of others; even more important, examine the connotative power of your own writing, and try to use connotation to help make your meanings clear and effective.

Many words carry fairly general connotations, evoking similar associational responses in most listeners or readers. But connotations can be personal or distinctive to a particular audience as well. If you ever got violently ill right after eating some particular dish as a child, you know the power of personal connotation. The mere mention of, say, peanut butter cookies carries powerful negative connotations.

The power of connotations to a particular audience was well illustrated by the meeting between Michael Dukakis and Jesse Jackson at the 1988 Democratic National Convention. Jackson was offended that Dukakis, who had clinched the party's presidential nomination, had asserted his leadership by describing himself as "the quarterback on this team," a phrase that reminded blacks of the stereotype that they were not intelligent enough to play quarterback on football teams. For his part, Dukakis was upset by Jackson's having told the new voters he

DENOTATION AND CONNOTATION   *d* 25b

had brought into the party that they were being used to "carry bales of cotton" up to "the big house," because the connotations of this language suggested to blacks that Dukakis was like a white plantation owner profiting from the labor of black slaves. Whenever you write for a particular audience, try to be aware of the connotations your language will hold for that group of people.

➤ **Checking for wrong words**

"Wrong word" errors take so many different forms that it is very difficult to name any foolproof methods of checking for them. If you often find yourself using the "wrong word," however, it will probably be well worth your time to go through each draft looking carefully at every word you are not absolutely sure of. Check each one in a dictionary to see that you're using it properly. Next, look for homonyms, words that sound like other words (such as *to, too,* and *two*). Using the information in 22b, make sure you are using the correct form. If you have persistent problems with wrong words, ask someone to read your drafts. Keep a list of any words you use incorrectly, including example sentences showing the way you've misused them. Make a point of proofreading carefully for them.

EXERCISE 25.1

For each of the following sentences, choose the word in parentheses whose denotative meaning makes sense in the context of the sentence. Use a dictionary if necessary.

1. She always listened (*apprehensively/attentively*) to the lecture and took excellent notes.
2. Going swimming on a hot day can be a (*rapturous/ravenous*) experience.
3. Please take good care of this antique photo album; it's very (*fractious/fragile*).
4. The instructor congratulated Bev for improving her backhand (*dramatically/ drastically*) since the last lesson.
5. Benjamin Franklin advised readers of *Poor Richard's Almanac* to be (*feudal/ frugal*) and industrious.

EXERCISE 25.2

The contractor who advertises "We don't build *houses,* we build *homes*" counts on the positive connotations of *home* to boost sales. *New* and *improved* apparently have such powerful connotations that advertisers rely on them regularly.

ANSWERS TO EXERCISE 25.1

1. attentively
2. rapturous
3. fragile
4. dramatically
5. frugal

ANSWERS TO EXERCISE 25.2 WILL VARY

Look through a magazine you read frequently, and find three or four especially effective uses of connotation—either negative or positive—in advertisements. Bring these advertisements to class for discussion.

EXERCISE 25.3

Study the italicized words in each of the following passages, and decide what each word's connotations contribute to your understanding of the passage. Think of a synonym for each word, and see if you can decide what difference your word would make to the effect of the passage.

1. The Burmans were already *racing* past me across the mud. It was obvious that the elephant would never *rise* again, but he was not dead. He was breathing very rhythmically with long *rattling gasps*, his great *mound* of a side painfully rising and falling.
   —GEORGE ORWELL, "Shooting an Elephant"
2. If boxing is a sport, it is the most *tragic* of all sports because, more than any human activity, it *consumes* the very excellence it *displays*: Its very *drama* is this consumption. —JOYCE CAROL OATES, "On Boxing"
3. We caught two bass, *hauling* them in *briskly* as though they were mackerel, pulling them over the side of the boat in a *businesslike* manner without any landing net, and stunning them with a *blow* on the back of the head.
   —E. B. WHITE, "Once More to the Lake"
4. The air *held* a *keenness* that made her nose *twitch*. The harvesting of the corn and cotton, peanuts and squash, made each day a golden *surprise* that caused excited little *tremors* to *run* up her jaw.
   —ALICE WALKER, "The Flowers"
5. The Kiowas are a summer people; they *abide* the cold and keep to themselves; but when the season *turns* and the land becomes warm and *vital*, they cannot *hold still*; . . .
   —N. SCOTT MOMADAY, "The Way to Rainy Mountain"

25c. Balancing general and specific diction

Good writers move their prose along and help readers follow the meaning by balancing **general words**—those that refer to groups or classes of things—with **specific words**—those that refer to individual things. One kind of general words, **abstractions,** are words or phrases that refer to qualities or ideas, things we cannot perceive through our five senses. Specific words are often **concrete words;** they name things we can see, hear, touch, taste, or smell. Most often, we cannot draw a clear-cut line between general or abstract words on the one hand and specific or concrete ones on the other. Instead, most words and phrases fall somewhere on a continuum between these two extremes:

ANSWERS TO EXERCISE 25.3 (WILL VARY)

1. *Racing*—charging, tearing, marching: these alternatives each connote a different context and set of circumstances, giving the reader a different impression of the Burmans' action. *Charging* suggests an attack, whereas *racing* gives the impression of the Burmans competing against one another and the author *me* to arrive at a destination. *Marching* suggests regimented, ordered, or determined movement, and *tearing* a frenzied, excited, wild, or uncontrolled pace. *rise*—stand; *rhythmically*—evenly, smoothly; *rattling*—heaving, pulsing; *mound*—mountain, hump; *painfully*—stingingly, throbbingly.
2. *tragic*—distressing, alarming, disturbing; *consumes*—defeats, feeds on, erodes; *displays*—champions, thrives on, builds up, promotes; *drama*—excitement, tension, vitality; *expend*—commit; *greatest*—most challenging; *immediately*—instantly; *plunge*—dive; *incomprehensible*—unanticipated
3. *hauling*—drawing; *briskly*—quickly; *businesslike*—efficient, effortless; *blow*—club, smack
4. *lightly*—carelessly; *held*—breathed; *keenness*—coolness, crispness; *twitch*—perk up; *surprise*—adventure, enterprise; *tremors*—chills; *run*—jet
5. *abide*—tolerate; *turns*—changes; *vital*—alive; *hold still*—contain their energy

BALANCING GENERAL AND SPECIFIC DICTION

GENERAL	LESS GENERAL	SPECIFIC	MORE SPECIFIC
book	dictionary	unabridged dictionary	my 1988 edition of *Webster's Dictionary*
furniture	bed	antique bed	1840 curly maple bedstead of my grandmother's

ABSTRACT	LESS ABSTRACT	CONCRETE	MORE CONCRETE
culture	art	painting	Van Gogh's *Starry Night*
winter	cold weather	icicles	fifteen-inch icicle hanging from the eaves of the dormitory

Because passages that contain mostly general terms or abstractions demand that readers supply most of the specific examples or concrete details, such writing is often hard to read. Taken to extremes, it is dull or boring. But writing that is full of specifics can also be tedious and hard to follow if the main point is not made clearly or is lost amid a flood of extraneous details. Strong writing must usually both provide readers with a general idea or "big picture" and tie that idea down with specific examples or concrete details.

In the following passage, for instance, the author might have simply made a main general statement—*their breakfast was always liberal and good*—or simply described the breakfast in detail. Instead, he does both.

> There would be a brisk fire crackling in the hearth, the old smoke-gold of morning and the smell of fog, the crisp cheerful voices of the people and their ruddy competent morning look, and the cheerful smells of breakfast, which was always liberal and good, the best meal that they had: kidneys and ham and eggs and sausages and toast and marmalade and tea. —THOMAS WOLFE, *Of Time and the River*

Here are two student writers balancing general statements with illustrative specific details.

GENERAL   My neighbor is a nuisance.

SPECIFIC   My next-door neighbor is a nuisance, poking and prying into my life, constantly watching me as I enter and leave my house, complaining about the noise when I am having a good time, and telling my parents whenever she sees me kissing my date.

WRITING TOGETHER

Moving from general to specific language often involves describing something so that it can be seen, heard, felt, experienced.

1. We had a good time.
2. We were bored and had nothing to do.
3. Their tiredness showed.
4. We weren't content to just sit there, frustrated, impatient, and annoyed.

Divide the class into groups, and ask them to expand each of these brief sentences into a paragraph. Ask them to work on showing the reader "the good time" or the frustration and annoyance. Suggest questions such as the following to help them develop the sentences into concrete descriptions. For example, to develop *We had a good time*, you might have them ask:

What were you doing?
With whom?
How did you do it?
What did it involve?

You can also ask them to apply the same questions to *Their tiredness showed*.

WRITERS ON WRITING

We have too many high sounding words, and too few actions that correspond with them.

—ABIGAIL ADAMS

WRITERS ON WRITING

I never write *metropolis* for seven cents because I can get the same price for *city*. I never write *policeman* because I can get the same money for *cop*.

—MARK TWAIN

WRITERS ON WRITING

Why shouldn't we quarrel about a word? What is the good of words if they aren't important enough to quarrel over? Why do we choose one word more than another if there isn't any difference between them?

—G. K. CHESTERTON

GENERAL   Central Texas has an unusual climate.

SPECIFIC   Few places in the United States display the wild climatic variations of central Texas: at one moment, the sky may be clear blue and the air balmy; at another, a racing flash flood may drown the landscape and threaten people's lives.

ANSWERS TO EXERCISE 25.4 WILL VARY

ANSWERS TO EXERCISE 25.5 (WILL VARY)

1. The entryway of the building looked like a garbage dump; paper was littered about, all kinds of bottles lay shattered, and rotting cantelope and chicken parts gave off an unbearable odor.
2. Cooing, singing, twittering—the early morning beckoning of birds outside my window make it a treat to get up.
3. The feast at mom's on Sunday was delicious as usual: roast chicken, garlic and sage stuffing, sweet garden peas, gallons of gravy, and half a fresh-baked apple pie each.
4. The valet stepped cautiously yet excitedly toward my Porsche.
5. Erin raced up to, then retreated from, then charged again, finally wetting her chubby toes in the surf.

EXERCISE 25.4

Choose two of the following abstract terms, and write a sentence for each one that provides concrete illustration of the term: *fear, joy, inspiration, boredom, contentment, exhaustion*.

EXERCISE 25.5

Rewrite each of the following sentences to make them more specific and concrete.

1. The entryway of the building was dirty.
2. The sounds at dawn are memorable.
3. Sunday dinner was good.
4. The attendant came toward my car.
5. The child played on the beach.

READING WITH AN EYE FOR DICTION

The following passage is from Joan Didion's essay "In Bed." Read it carefully, and identify the balance of abstract and concrete and of general and specific diction.

Migraine is something more than the fancy of a neurotic imagination. It is an essentially hereditary complex of symptoms, the most frequently noted but by no means the most unpleasant of which is a vascular headache of blinding severity, suffered by a surprising number of women, a fair number of men (Thomas Jefferson had migraine, and so did Ulysses S. Grant, the day he accepted Lee's surrender), and by some unfortunate children as young as two years old. (I had my first when I was eight. It came on during a fire drill at the Columbia School in Colorado Springs, Colorado. I was taken first home and then to the infirmary at Peterson Field, where my father was stationed. The Air Corps doctor prescribed an enema.) Almost anything can trigger a specific attack of migraine: stress, allergy, fatigue, an abrupt change in barometric pressure, a contretemps over a parking ticket. A flashing light. A fire drill. One inherits, of course, only the predisposition. In other words I spent

BALANCING GENERAL AND SPECIFIC DICTION

yesterday in bed with a headache not merely because of my bad attitudes, unpleasant tempers and wrongthink, but because both my grandmothers had migraine, my father has migraine and my mother has migraine.

–JOAN DIDION, "In Bed"

FOR EXAMINING DICTION IN YOUR OWN WRITING

Write a paragraph or two describing one of your friends. Then analyze what you have written, and identify the concrete and abstract language you used. Decide whether you have achieved the proper balance between the two, and if not, revise accordingly.

TEACHING PRACTICE

Ask students to bring their descriptions to class, choose several to duplicate or put on an overhead, and then ask the class as a whole to differentiate concrete from abstract language. Ask which words seem most effective and memorable, and why.

26. Establishing Tone

(BACK)GROUNDING

The word *tone* comes into our language from the Latin *tonus*, which means "sound." It has traditionally been used to describe music (*tonal quality*) and speech (*tone of voice*). In addition, tone can refer to social style (*the cultured tone of the gathering*), to color (*tones of red*), and to physiology (*healthy muscle tone*). In all its uses, however, tone suggests something about the overall quality—what this chapter calls the *dominant impression*—of a piece of writing.

Anyone who has spent any time with a child knows firsthand the truth of what linguists tell us: regardless of the words actually used, children sense immediately whether a parent is sad, angry, delighted, or alarmed. They get this important information from the tone of voice with which the words are spoken, a tone that creates a strong overall impression. So it is with the **tone** of a piece of writing: it creates an overall or **dominant impression**—perhaps humorous, outraged, friendly, skeptical. Tone, then, is the atmosphere of a piece of writing. Just as you can distinguish the atmosphere created by "The Star-Spangled Banner," "I've Been Working on the Railroad," and a heavy-metal rock song, so can you distinguish among tones in writing. And like the blend of musical notes and lyrics in a song, the tone of any piece of writing results from a blend of several factors: the writer's purpose, the writer's relationship to the audience, and the writer's relationship to the topic. This chapter explores each of these factors.

26a. Considering purpose and audience

The key to establishing an *effective* tone, to creating the impression that you *want* to create, is to consider carefully what tone is most appropriate to your purpose, audience, and topic. Your choice of tone should always reflect the reason that you are writing and the particular readers you want to address: you say something one way to entertain or inform close friends, another way to explain to parents, and yet

402

USEFUL READING

Corbett, Edward P. J. *Classical Rhetoric for the Modern Student*. 2nd ed. New York: Oxford UP, 1971. Corbett's discussion of ethical and emotional appeals provides a sound rationale for the importance of tone.

another way to persuade an audience you do not know well. For instance, you might say the following to friends:

> I had to pull an incomplete in psych because I was barfing with that stomach flu all finals week and couldn't book it at all.

That same thought might be expressed to parents as:

> I had to take an incomplete in psychology because I had the stomach flu that was going around and couldn't study because I was throwing up all night before the final exam.

And to a committee that is evaluating you for a scholarship, you might explain (probably in writing):

> I was forced to request an incomplete in my Psychology 102 course because I had been violently ill with an intestinal virus for three days before the final examination (doctor's letter is enclosed) and was therefore unable to study.

What are the differences between these versions? Diction is the most obvious difference, but if you look more closely, you will see that each version reveals definite judgments about purpose, audience, and context, or how much the audience already knows. Consider how strange your friends would think you if you spoke to them in the language you might use to the scholarship committee. Your distant, formal tone, created by giving such full background, would confuse them. Similarly, if you wrote to the scholarship committee in the words you would use with friends, the committee would be equally confused. They would probably think either that you were trying to be funny at a serious time or that you did not know how to address people outside your personal circle. In either case, you would be less likely to achieve your purpose in writing—to persuade the committee to give you the scholarship.

As this example indicates, the better you know the audience, the less context or background information you must specify. (Note that the three examples get progressively longer as the speaker must supply more and more context.) Your friends know you well, know about incompletes, know about finals week, know about the flu. They know your context, and thus you can use slang and informal terms that are short and telegraphic. Your parents do not know as much of your context. You must be slightly more formal with them (they have always hated the word *barf*) in addition to explaining more of the situation. For the committee, you must be even more formal, supplying a detailed

(BACK)GROUNDING

In "On the Sublime," Longinus wrote that composition is "a special melody of words . . . carrying moreover, by the very commixture and multiplicity of its own sounds, the passion which is present to the speaker into the souls of the bystanders, and bringing them into partnership. . . . Composition [must] at once soothe us as we hear and also dispose to stateliness, and high mood, and sublimity" (Chapter XXXIX). For Longinus, the proper tone for orators who wanted to reach the sublime was dignified but spirited. Longinus' limited prescription of tone contrasts with I. A. Richards's more familiar literary definition of tone as the attitude an author takes to his subject and audience. Kenneth Burke examines the idea of an author's tone or attitude rhetorically; he regards "tonalities" as more persuasive than reasoned arguments because "they imply a tone of voice, and this is a tone of voice proper to a certain kind of conclusion" (*A Rhetoric of Motives* 98). For Burke, the tone a writer establishes at the beginning of a text implies conclusions, conclusions that suggest themselves from the start and not just the end of a text. Tone therefore sets the mood of the entire discourse.

explanation that will show them your seriousness. This implicit knowledge about your purpose and audience leads you to create a different tone for each version.

▌ 26b. Appealing to your audience

Like a pair of shoes, tone needs to "fit" an audience, striking just the right note, creating just the right impression, making just the right appeal. To make judgments about tone and audience, ask yourself these questions:

1. Of all the people whom I want to read this piece of writing, who is least well known to me?
2. What is my relationship with that person? What attitudes and word choices does that person expect from me?
3. What attitudes or word choices might offend or disturb that person?
4. What kind of response do I want to evoke from that person? What dominant impression do I want to create?

The answers to these questions can guide word choice as you seek the proper tone for any piece of writing. The reason for considering the potential reader *least* well known to you is that you must shape your tone to appeal to this person, who is least likely to identify with you or accept what you say just because you are the one saying it. For this person, you must make more arguments, supply more context, and use more formal language than would be necessary for people who knew you better.

Philosopher of language Kenneth Burke notes that we use language as a primary means of identifying with other people. The example in 26a, for instance, showed how you could use different language to appeal to friends, parents, and a scholarship committee and lead each of these groups to identify with you and your situation. Tone is crucial to such identification. Audiences are less likely, for instance, to identify with a writer whose tone is abusive or malicious, and much more likely to identify with and respond to the appeal of a writer whose tone is friendly and respectful. How can you make sure that your tone wins your audience's empathy? Because audiences, purposes, and topics for writing vary so widely, few absolute guidelines exist. Two rules of thumb, however, should serve you well: (1) use language that is respectful and courteous to your audience, and (2) use figurative lan-

APPEALING TO YOUR AUDIENCE   *t* 26b

guage, to help the audience understand your message as clearly and dramatically as possible. (See 4d and 4f.)

1. Remembering the "golden rule"

As young children, most of us learned to "do to others what you would have done to you." To that lesson, we could add "say to others what you would have said to you." Language has power. It can praise, delight, inspire. It can also hurt, maim, destroy. Language that insults or offends any group of readers—such as racial, religious, ethnic, sexual, or age-related stereotyping—breaks the golden rule of language use, destroying identification and harming the writer's credibility. By avoiding such language, you can help establish the appropriate tone of respect for and courtesy toward your audience.

In many instances, doing so is simple enough: we can safely assume, for instance, that no readers respond well to a slur on their race or to a form of address like "you complacent slobs," and that such language use will reflect not on the audience but on the writer or speaker. But other cases are more subtle and may well call for some investigation. One student found, for example, that a group he had been referring to as *senior citizens* were irritated by that label. In another instance, a writer discovered that the native people of Alaska wished to be referred to as Eskimos, while those in British Columbia preferred to be called Inuit. Before using a term referring to a group of people, be sure that members of that group approve of it.

Using nonsexist language

Growing awareness of and sensitivity to sexism have done much to demonstrate how powerfully and often invisibly elements of language affect the ways we think and behave. We now know, for instance, that many young women at one time failed to consider careers in medicine or engineering at least partially because our language always referred to a hypothetical doctor or engineer as *he*. Sexist language, those words and phrases that stereotype members of one sex, can be corrected readily enough. We can substitute terms such as *mail carrier* and *police officer* for *mailman* and *policeman*, we can avoid using phrases that call unnecessary attention to gender (such as *coed*, *woman engineer*, or *male secretary*), and we can use personal and professional titles on an equal basis for both men and women (Mr. Hinojosa and Ms. Walker or Hinojosa and Walker instead of Hinojosa and Ms. Walker).

WRITERS ON WRITING

Probably it is better to put off using words as long as possible and get one's meaning as clear as one can through pictures or sensations. Afterwards, one can choose—not simply *accept*—the phrases that will best cover the meaning, and then switch round and decide what impression one's words are likely to make on another person.

—GEORGE ORWELL

ANSWERS TO EXERCISE 26.1

Language that might be considered sexist includes:

–over all men: over all people, over all folks
–to be a steamboatman: to work on a steamboat, to crew a steamboat
–to be a cabin-boy: to be a cabin assistant, to be a cabin aid (Note that "cabin-person" sounds forced.) Trust your ear and good judgment when you revise for non-sexist words.
–my old comrades: my old companions
–in his hand, because he was particularly conspicuous: in his or her hand, because he or she was; in their hands, because they were. . . .

By far the most problematic of sexist terms for writers is the traditional use of *man, mankind,* and the masculine pronouns to refer to all humanity or to people who could be either male or female, as in "all men are mortal" or "a lawyer must pass his bar exam before he can begin to practice." Because such usage ignores half the human race, it does not help build identification between the writer and those this usage excludes. Here are some alternatives to such usage:

1. Use plural forms:

    Lawyers must pass *their* bar exams before beginning to practice.

2. Use *he or she, him or her,* and so on:

    A lawyer must pass *his or her* bar exam before beginning to practice.

3. Eliminate the pronouns:

    A lawyer must pass the bar exam before beginning to practice.

4. Use *humanity, humans, people,* and *humankind*:

    All people are mortal.

For further discussion of nonsexist pronoun use, see 9m and 11c5.

EXERCISE 26.1

The following paragraph is from Mark Twain's *Old Times on the Mississippi*. Read it carefully, noting any language we today might consider sexist. Then do your best to substitute nonsexist words or phrases.

My father was a justice of the peace, and I suppose he possessed the power of life and death over all men and could hang anybody that offended him. This was distinction enough for me as a general thing; but the desire to be a steamboatman kept intruding, nevertheless. I first wanted to be a cabin-boy, so that I could come out with a white apron on and shake a table-cloth over the side, where all my old comrades could see me; later I thought I would rather be the deck-hand who stood on the end of the state-plank with the coil of rope in his hand, because he was particularly conspicuous. But these were only daydreams—they were too heavenly to be contemplated as real possibilities. —MARK TWAIN, *Old Times on the Mississippi*

 2. **Using figurative language**

A second good way to create a tone that will appeal to an audience and allow them to "identify" with the writer is by using figurative language, or figures of speech. Such language paints pictures in our minds, allows us to "see" a point and hence understand more readily and clearly. Economists trying to explain the magnitude of the federal deficit use figurative language when they tell us how many times hundred-thousand-dollar bills would have to circle the globe to equal it; scientists describing the way genetic data are transmitted use figurative language when they liken the data to a messenger that carries bits of information from one generation of cells to another. Far from being a mere "decoration" of writing, figurative language plays a crucial role in helping us follow the writer's meaning, quickly and easily. Particularly helpful in building an appealing tone are figures that compare one thing to another—similes, metaphors, and analogies. Other figures include personification, hyperbole, litotes, irony, and allusion.

Similes

Similes make explicit the comparison between two things by using the terms *like, as,* or *as if:*

> Buttresses flew like angels' wings against the exteriors.
> —BARBARA TUCHMAN, "Mankind's Better Moments"

> The comb felt as if it was raking my skin off.
> —MALCOLM X, "My First Conk"

> The migraine acted as a circuit breaker, and the fuses have emerged intact. —JOAN DIDION, "In Bed"

Metaphors

Metaphors are *implicit comparisons,* omitting the *like, as,* or *as if* of similes.

> Black women are called, in the folklore that so aptly identifies one's status in society, "the mule of the world," because we have been handed the burdens that everyone else—everyone else—refused to carry.
> —ALICE WALKER, *In Search of Our Mothers' Gardens*

> Lee was tidewater Virginia, and in his backyard were family, culture, and tradition.
> —BRUCE CATTON, "Grant and Lee: A Study in Contrasts"

Analogies

Analogies compare similar features of two dissimilar things and are often extended to several sentences or paragraphs in length. The following sentence, for example, uses an analogy to help us understand the rapid growth of the computer industry:

USEFUL READING

Lakoff, George, and Mark Johnson. *Metaphors We Live By.* Chicago: U of Chicago P, 1980. An extensive discussion of the wide-ranging influence of metaphor on our perceptions, thoughts, and actions.

TEACHING PRACTICE

To show your students that the use of figurative language occurs in our everyday reading and writing, encourage them to look at magazines, articles, and books that they read outside the classroom in their leisure time. Roger Angell's collection of essays on baseball, published in the *New Yorker* between 1983 and 1987, contain wonderful examples of simile, for example, in popular literature and journalism. Joel Conarroe, in a review in the *New York Times Book Review,* praises Angell and his collection *Season Ticket: A Baseball Companion:* "This is a meticulous writer with an eye for the telling simile, the domestic image that can bring an observation vividly to life." Conarroe mentions Angell's description of *a slumping team* going through September *like an ember in a snowbank* and Steve Carlton's three-quarter-speed slider which *drops out of the strike zone like a mouse behind the sink.*

WRITERS ON WRITING

Every writer acts as a landlord to an unforgiving editor who squats in some upper story of his head and sends rejection slips to nearly all the writer's phrases. I have sent my editor on a long vacation. I hope he's happy. In the meantime, I'm free to write reams of unpublishable sentences.

—JONATHAN RABAN

> If the aircraft industry had evolved as spectacularly as the computer industry over the past twenty-five years, a Boeing 767 would cost five hundred dollars today, and it would circle the globe in twenty minutes on five gallons of fuel.

The analogy in the next passage helps us "see" an abstract point.

> Our lives are plays, and we are the actors playing the parts. The scenes are set, and each of us takes on a role—followers, leaders, manipulators. Manipulators, who coax and coerce people into doing what the manipulators want, are often the playwrights in our lives.

Before you use an analogy, though, make sure that the two things you are comparing have enough points of similarity so that the comparison is justified and will convince readers. For further discussion of analogies, see 4f3.

Clichés and mixed metaphors

Just as effective use of figurative language can create the tone or impression that the writer wants to create, so *ineffective* figures of speech can create the *wrong* impression by boring, irritating, or unintentionally amusing readers. Among the most common kinds of ineffective figurative language are clichés and mixed metaphors.

Cliché comes from the French word for "stereotype," a metal plate cast from a page of type and used, before photographic printing processes, to produce multiple copies of a book or page without having to reset the type. So a **cliché** in language is an expression stamped out in duplicate to avoid the trouble of "resetting" the thought. Many clichés, like *busy as a bee* or *youth is the springtime of life*, are similes or metaphors.

By definition, we use clichés all the time, especially in speech, and many serve us quite usefully as familiar shorthand for familiar ideas. But as a writer you should use them with caution, for good reason: if your audience recognizes that you are using stereotyped, paint-by-the-numbers language, they are likely to conclude that what you are saying is not very new or interesting—or perhaps even true. The person who tells you that you look "pretty as a picture" uses a clichéd simile that may well sound false or insincere. Compare it with a more original compliment a grandmother once paid to her grandchildren: "You all look as pretty as brand-new red shoes."

How can you check for clichés? While one person's trite phrase may be completely new to another, one rule of thumb will serve you

WRITERS ON WRITING
Cliches are *the last word* in bad writing, and it's *a crying shame* to see all you *bright young things* spoiling your *deathless prose* with phrases *as old as the hills*. You must *keep your nose to the grindstone*, because the *sweet smell of success* only comes to those who *march to the tune of a different drummer*.

—JANET BURROWAY

OPTIONAL EXERCISE
Divide the class into groups of three, and ask each group to compose five examples of mixed metaphors. Have them exchange with another group for revision and explain their revisions.

WRITERS ON WRITING
One ought to write only when one leaves a piece of one's flesh in the inkpot each time one dips one's pen.

—LEO TOLSTOY

APPEALING TO YOUR AUDIENCE

well: if you can predict exactly what the upcoming word(s) in a phrase will be, it stands a very good chance of being a cliché.

Mixed metaphors are comparisons that are not consistent. Instead of creating a clear and dominant impression, they confuse the reader by pulling against one another, often in unintentionally funny ways, as in the announcement by a government official that "we must not drag our dirty linen through the eye of the public."

Here is a mixed metaphor revised for consistency.

MIXED   The lectures were like brilliant comets streaking through the night sky, drenching the listeners with a blizzard of insight.

REVISED   The lectures were like brilliant comets streaking through the night sky, dazzling listeners with flashes of insight.

Personification

Personification gives human qualities to animals, inanimate objects, or ideas, making them more vivid or understandable.

[Television] . . . stays in one corner of the room like a horrible electronic gossip.   —JONATHAN MILLER

In the meanwhile there came along a single red ant on the hillside of this valley, evidently full of excitement, who had either dispatched his foe, or had not yet taken part in the battle; . . . whose mother had charged him to return with his shield or upon it.
                                  —HENRY DAVID THOREAU, "The Battle of the Ants"

Hyperbole

Hyperbole, or **overstatement,** deliberately exaggerates to create special emphasis or a humorous tone.

Under certain emotional circumstances, I can stand the spasms of a rich violin, but the concert piece and all wind instruments bore me in small doses and flay me in large doses.   —VLADIMIR NABOKOV

What a travesty of truth are those TV commercials in which we watch a family falling over themselves to reach the fast-food restaurant before they drown in their own drool!   —MAX WYMAN

Litotes

Like hyperbole, **litotes** (or **understatement**) depends on a gap between statement and fact. But while hyperbole is loud and noisy,

WRITERS ON WRITING

And so it goes . . . a cent's worth of information wrapped in a bale of polysyllables . . . It is . . . a sort of progressive intellectual diabetes, a leprosy of the horse sense. Words were flung upon words until all recollection that there must be meaning in them, a ground and excuse for them, was lost. One wanders in a labyrinth of nouns, adjectives, verbs, pronouns, adverbs, prepositions, conjunctions, and particles, verbs, pronouns, adverbs, prepositions, conjunctions, and particles, most of them swollen and nearly all of them unable to walk.

—MARK TWAIN

litotes turns the volume down to a whisper. Understatement can help create a very solemn tone, as it does when one of the characters in Stephen Crane's *The Open Boat*, faced with imminent death, remarks that if he drowns, it "will be a shame"—or when the hero of Ernest Hemingway's *A Farewell to Arms*, having lost his wife and baby in childbirth, quietly "left the hospital and walked back to the hotel in the rain." It can also create humor and other tones. In their first article on DNA, Watson and Crick were reporting that they had discovered what they felt was the secret of life. Yet they carefully closed the article with understatement, creating a tone of quiet confidence: "It has not escaped our notice that the specific pairing we have postulated immediately suggests a possible copying mechanism for the genetic material."

Irony

Irony, language that suggests a meaning that contrasts with or undercuts the literal meaning of the words, can result in a lighthearted, spoofing tone or a serious and bitter one. In probably the most famous piece of sustained irony in English literature, Jonathan Swift's "A Modest Proposal," Swift solemnly recommends the sale and consumption of children, a proposal intended to reveal the poverty and inhuman conditions in Ireland that were condoned by its British rulers at the time. The following "definition" of *writing principles* provides an example of more lighthearted irony.

> Write hurriedly, preferably when tired. Have no plans; write down items as they occur to you. . . . Hand in your manuscript the moment it is finished.   —AMBROSE BIERCE

Irony can work well to gain an audience's attention and set a definite tone, but only if the audience can be expected to recognize and appreciate the irony. (See 3ld for a discussion of ways you can use quotation marks to convey irony.)

Allusion

Allusions, indirect references to cultural works, people, or events, can bring an entire world of associations to the minds of readers who recognize them. If, for instance, you tell a friend in a letter that you have to return to your herculean task of writing a research essay, you are expecting that your reader will understand, by your allusion to the

APPEALING TO YOUR AUDIENCE

Labors of Hercules in classical mythology, how big a job you think the essay is. If you choose to title an essay on the antiapartheid movement in the 1980s "A Terrible Beauty is Born," your allusion to William Butler Yeats's poem about the Irish Rebellion of 1916 will give readers the idea that you see important parallels between the two struggles.

You can draw allusions from history, from literature, from the Bible, from common wisdom, or from current events. Many current popular songs are full of allusions. Remember, however, that allusions work to create effective tone only if your audience recognizes them.

EXERCISE 26.2

Evaluate the effectiveness of similes, metaphors, and analogies in the following sentences, and revise any that are mixed or clichés.

1. These children were brought up to eat, drink, and sleep tennis.
2. In presenting his alibi, the defendant chose the alley he was going to bowl on—and the jury wouldn't swallow it.
3. The president's economic plan is about as useful as rearranging the deck chairs on the *Titanic*.
4. The narrative was heavy as lead—it just flowed on and on and on.
5. For as long as I can remember, my mother has been the backbone for my father's convictions.

EXERCISE 26.3

Here are some metaphorical definitions of slang. Decide which one you like best—and why, and then create your own metaphorical definition of slang or of some other abstraction.

> [Slang] is always strong. . . . Cut these words and they would bleed; they are vascular and alive; they walk and run.
> —RALPH WALDO EMERSON

> Slang is the speech of him who rolls the literary garbage carts on their way to the dump.　—AMBROSE BIERCE

> Slang is language that takes off its coat, spits on its hands, and gets to work.　—CARL SANDBURG

> Slang: words with their shoes off.　—PATRICK HARTWELL

EXERCISE 26.4

Identify the similes and metaphors in the following passages, and decide how each contributes to your understanding of the passage it appears in.

ANSWERS TO EXERCISE 26.2 WILL VARY

ANSWERS TO EXERCISE 26.3 WILL VARY

ANSWERS TO EXERCISE 26.4 (WILL VARY)

1. –come apart and rise up (metaphor): this metaphor gives the image of the bridge as an animate thing, living and active

    –like giant black jaws taking a bite of sky (simile): likening the bridge to a huge animal or insect, this simile suggests the disturbing awesomeness of the bridge

2. –destroys his victims with flashes of lightning (metaphor)

    –roasted her victims over a fire (metaphor): both of these metaphors suggest the powerful effect that Pope's and Austen's words could have on the targets of their criticism or attacks; Pope's words were flashes of lightning, Austen's words made her victims feel as though they were being roasted over a fire

3. –seedy cronies (metaphor): this image emphasizes the writer's perception of the father's undesirable or shabby companions

    –seedy cronies . . . as if anchored in a houseboat (simile): emphasizes the writer's impression of these companions of the father as they hung around the garage and driveway

4. –deep and soft like water moving in a cavern (simile): this simile compares the sound of her voice to water in a cavern

5. –lounging (metaphor): compares the horse in pasture to people relaxing

    –cuddling up (metaphor): emphasizes the pleasure the writer has reading mysteries

    –top priority (metaphor): the reading is an activity of official importance

ANSWERS TO EXERCISE 26.5 WILL VARY

1. Most often we walked on the banks of the Cuyahoga River to see the drawbridge come apart and rise up, like giant black jaws taking a bite of sky. –SALLY CARRIGHAR, "The Blast Furnace"
2. Where a satirist like Pope destroys his victims with flashes of lightning, . . . Jane Austen often roasted her victims over a fire so slow and nicely judged that the thick-skinned feel no discomfort on their behalf but only a gentle tickling. –WILLIAM GOLDING, *A Moving Target*
3. At the very beginning, when my father's old touring car . . . still remained in our garage, Myers had certain seedy cronies whom he took riding in it or who simply sat in it in our driveway, as if anchored in a houseboat. . . .
   –MARY MCCARTHY "Uncle Myers"
4. I was watching everyone else and didn't see the waitress standing quietly by. Her voice was deep and soft like water moving in a cavern.
   –WILLIAM LEAST HEAT MOON, "In the Land of 'Coke-Cola' "
5. My horse, when he is in his stall or lounging about the pasture, has the same relationship to pain that I have when cuddling up with a good murder mystery—comfort and convenience have top priority.
   –VICKI HEARNE, "Horses in Partnership with Time"

EXERCISE 26.5

Read through a magazine, an essay, a story, or some reading you have been assigned and find some examples of personification, hyperbole, litotes, irony, and allusion. Bring these examples to class for discussion.

▌ 26c. Using the appropriate register

On the basis of the writer's relationship to the topic and the audience, we can distinguish four general levels of diction, or **registers**, that constitute one of the major elements of tone. In order of increasing distance from the writer, these levels are *familiar*, *informal*, *formal*, and *ceremonial*. While the formal register is the one most often appropriate and useful for college writing, you should be able to recognize and use other registers as well.

▌ 1. Familiar register

Familiar register represents a very close relationship between writer and topic and between writer and audience—it is the language you probably use to talk to yourself or to those you are closest to. It is the register found in diaries, journals, and personal letters; writers sometimes use it in essays, stories, plays, and novels to create a sense of intimacy between themselves and readers or between characters.

Among the characteristics of familiar register are the frequent use of the first person (*I*) and first names, a lack of explicitly stated context (because the audience does not need it), and the use of sentence fragments, contractions, slang, colloquial language, regionalisms, dialect, and other grammatical constructions that disregard the "rules."

You will seldom, if ever, be called on to write in familiar register in college writing. You should, however, learn to recognize it as a reader. The following example is a letter from the English writer Virginia Stephen responding to a marriage proposal from her future husband, Leonard Woolf:

> My dear Leonard,
>
> I am rushing for a train so I can only send a line in answer. There isn't anything really for me to say, except that I should like to go on as before; and that you should leave me free, and that I should be honest. As to faults, I expect mine are just as bad—less noble perhaps. But of course they are not really the question. I have decided to keep this completely secret, except for Vanessa; and I have made her promise not to tell Clive. I told Adrian that you had come up about a job which was promised you. So keep this up if he asks.
>
> I am very sorry to be the cause of so much rush and worry. I am just off to Firle.
>
> > Yrs.
> >
> > VS

Notice that Stephen assumes Woolf will know what her "line" is "in answer" to, what "this" is, and who Vanessa, Clive, and Adrian are. She uses a contraction (*isn't*) and abbreviations (*Yrs.*, her initials), as well as the colloquial expression *keep this up* to mean "pretend that this story is true." Because she was a professional writer living in a different time and a different culture, your familiar register is probably less formal than hers, but you can see that she is writing to a very intimate audience (of one) on a very intimate topic.

2. Informal register

Informal register assumes a fairly close but not extremely close relationship or familiarity between the writer and the audience and topic. It may use colloquial language, slang, and regionalisms or dialect (see 25a), as well as contractions and other grammatical constructions that are not considered appropriate in more formal writing. The language of most conversation and of much popular media, it is often found in short stories and novels as well, especially in dialogue. Some of your college classes, particularly if you take journalism, communications, or creative writing, may call on you to use informal register. Here is an example.

> If I went through anguish in botany and economics—for different reasons—gymnasium work was even worse. I don't even like to think about it. They wouldn't let you play games or join the exercises with your glasses on and I couldn't see with mine off. I bumped into professors, horizontal bars, agricultural students, and swinging iron rings. Not being able to see, I could take it but I couldn't dish it out.
>
> —JAMES THURBER, "University Days"

Thurber is obviously closely involved with his topic, although the involvement is not as close as that of Virginia Stephen with Leonard Woolf's marriage proposal; Thurber is looking back at his college gymnasium work from the distance of years. Nor is he as intimately related to his audience, but his use of contractions (*don't, wouldn't, couldn't*) and the indefinite *They* and *you* create an informal tone of easy familiarity. Notice that in the last sentence he amuses the audience—a purpose for which informal register is often used—by coming up with a twist on a clichéd slang expression.

3. Formal register

Formal register is the language found in most academic, business, and professional writing and in serious nonfiction books and magazine articles. Because most of the writing you will do in college and probably throughout your life should be in formal register, study carefully the following list of its characteristics:

1. Emotional distance between the writer and the audience: your stance should be friendly and courteous but not chummy or intimate.
2. Emotional distance between the writer and the topic: though you may know the topic very well and have strong feelings about it, your stance toward it should be as objective as possible.
3. No colloquial language, slang, regionalisms, and dialects.
4. Careful attention to the conventions of edited American English, the grammatical "rules" like those presented in this book.
5. Attention to the logical relationships among words and ideas: phrases and sentences should be carefully structured, not just tossed out.

Here is an example of formal register.

> "A people who mean to be their own governors," James Madison wrote, "must arm themselves with the power knowledge gives. A popular government without popular information or the means of acquiring it, is but a prologue to a farce or a tragedy, or perhaps both."
>
> Tragedy looms larger than farce in the United States today. Illiterate citizens seldom vote. Those who do are forced to cast a vote of questionable worth. They cannot make informed decisions based on serious print information. Sometimes they can be alerted to their interests by aggressive voter education. More frequently, they vote for a face, a smile, or a style, not for a mind or character or body of beliefs.
>
> —JONATHAN KOZOL, "The Human Cost of an Illiterate Society"

Notice that Kozol opens with an appeal to authority, citing the fourth United States president who, in very strong and serious terms, warns against the effect of a populace without knowledge. Kozol repeats the key terms of Madison's warning, _tragedy_ and _farce_, in the next sentence, and goes on to develop one tragic aspect of illiteracy. His brief, straightforward sentences state the facts objectively, building up to the parallel structures of the last sentence, which contrasts voting for "a smile" with voting for "character." Though Kozol knows a great deal about his subject and feels strongly that illiteracy is a national tragedy, his tone throughout is restrained.

4. Ceremonial register

For some solemn occasions, speakers or writers move beyond formal language to **ceremonial register**, the language of ceremony or ritual. You can recognize ceremonial register by its very careful attention to rhythm or cadence, to the sound of words, and to building toward a climax, a powerful dominant impression. If you are ever asked to make a statement at a funeral, to present a very important award, or to address a group on a very important occasion, you may want to use ceremonial register. Here is a famous example.

> With malice toward none, with charity for all, with firmness in the right as God gives us to see the right, let us finish the work we are in, to bind up the nation's wounds, to care for him who shall have borne the battle, and for his widow and his orphans, to do all which may achieve and cherish a just and lasting peace among ourselves and with all nations.
>
> —ABRAHAM LINCOLN, Second Inaugural Address

Notice how this conclusion to a speech delivered just before the end of the Civil War uses antithesis (in the opening phrases), parallelism (*to bind . . . to care . . . to do*), alliteration, and a lofty metaphor (*bind up the nation's wounds*) to build to a stirring climax.

5. Register in technical writing

One special kind of language frequently found in formal register is the technical discourse used in particular fields that have created special vocabularies or given common words special meaning. Business people talk about *greenmail* and *upside movement*, biologists about *nucleotides* and *immunodestruction*, and baseball fans about *fielder's choices* and *suicide bunts*. Such terms are understood by other specialists, but they can be very confusing to those outside the field. You need, then, to judge any use of technical language very carefully, making sure that your intended audience will understand your terms and replacing or defining those that they will not. Technical language can be divided into two overlapping categories: jargon and neologisms.

Neologisms

New words that have not yet found their way into dictionaries, **neologisms** can be very helpful to writers, especially in the sciences and applied disciplines, where new things and concepts appear every day and need names. Terms like *byte*, *thermosiphon*, *deconstruct*, and *neutrino*, for example, could not be easily replaced except by a much longer and more complex explanation. Some neologisms, however, do not meet a real need. Words like *deaccess* and *prioritization* could be easily replaced by existing words or phrases that general readers would understand.

Jargon

Jargon is the special vocabulary of a trade or profession, enabling members to speak and write concisely to one another. Thus, jargon should be reserved as much as possible for a specific technical audience. Here is an example of jargon used inappropriately in writing addressed to general readers:

> JARGON   The VDT's were down at the newspaper office last week, so we had to do the page makeup on dummies and use a wheel to crop the pictures.

Notice that the following revision eliminates some of the jargon terms and defines others:

USEFUL READING

Williams, Joseph M. *Origins of the English Language: A Social and Linguistic History*. New York: Macmillan, 1975. A brief discussion of the linguistic, psychological, and cultural reasons for jargon and euphemism.

TEACHING PRACTICE

Inform your students that dictionaries of "new terms" are readily available. For example, *The Random House Dictionary of New Information Technology* (1982).

REVISED The video display terminals were not working at the newspaper office last week, so we had to arrange the type for each page on a large cardboard sheet and use a wheel, a kind of circular slide rule, to figure out the size and shape of the pictures.

▌6. Pompous language, euphemisms, and doublespeak

In addition to avoiding inappropriate use of technical language, be alert to three other kinds of language sometimes found in formal register that can make for ineffective tone: pompous language, euphemisms, and doublespeak.

Pompous language is unnecessarily formal for the purpose, audience, or topic. Hence it often gives writing an insincere or unintentionally humorous tone, making the writer's idea seem less significant or believable rather than more so.

POMPOUS Pursuant to the recent memorandum issued August 9, 1979, because of petroleum supply exigencies, it is incumbent upon us all to endeavor to make maximal utilization of telephonic communication in lieu of personal visitation.

REVISED As of August 9, 1979, shortages of petroleum require us to try to use the telephone as much as possible rather than make personal visits.

Euphemisms are terms designed to make an unpleasant idea more attractive or acceptable. *Your position is being eliminated* seeks to soften the blow of being fired or laid off; the British call this *being declared redundant*, while Canadians refer to *being made surplus*. Other euphemisms include *pass on* for *die* and *sanitation engineer* for *garbage collector*.

While euphemisms can appeal to an audience by showing that the writer is considering their feelings, they can also sound pompous or suggest a wishy-washy, timid, or evasive attitude. Moreover, when they are used to protect the speaker or writer rather than the audience, they cross the line into doublespeak. Therefore, use euphemisms with great care.

The name given by George Orwell to the language of Big Brother in his novel *1984*, **doublespeak** is the use of language to hide or distort the truth in the interest of the speaker or writer. The extensive use of such language by public officials led the National Council of Teachers

---

USEFUL READING

Orwell, George. "Politics and the English Language." *Shooting an Elephant and other Essays*. New York: Harcourt, 1974. A discussion of appropriate verbs and nouns, pretentious diction, and meaningless words.

of English to form a committee to alert citizens to such verbal sleight of hand and to promote honesty and clarity in public language use. The committee publishes a *Doublespeak Newsletter* and each year presents an award for the best example of honesty in public discourse and a series of awards for the worst doublespeakers. One year such an award went to a military official who said to reporters: "You always write it's bombing, bombing, bombing. It's not bombing! It's air support!"

As you read and listen to public discourse, watch especially for doublespeak. And why not "nominate" the worst example you find for a Doublespeak Award? To do so, send your example, including the place and date of its publication or broadcast, to the Committee on Public Doublespeak, NCTE, Urbana, Illinois 61801.

ANSWERS TO EXERCISE 26.6 (WILL VARY)

1. Desdemona's attitude is that of a submissive victim; she just lies down and dies, accepting her death as inevitable.
2. All candidates strive for the same results: they strive to discredit the opposition, and to persuade the majority of voters that they are qualified for the position.
3. Sometimes, instead of dismissing an incompetent teacher, school officials will transfer the person to another school in order to avoid the problems involved in a dismissal.
4. The more angry she became over his actions, the more he rebelled and continued doing what he pleased.
5. My family lived in Trinidad for the first ten years of my life, and we experienced a great deal, but when we came to America, the experiences were entirely different.

EXERCISE 26.6

Revise each of the following sentences to use formal register consistently.

Example

I can be all enthused about writing, but as soon as I sit down to write, my mind immediately goes out to lunch.

I can be excited about writing, but as soon as I sit down to write, my mind immediately goes blank.

1. Desdemona's attitude is that of a wimp; she just lies down and dies, accepting her death as inevitable.
2. All candidates strive for the same results: you try to make the other guy look gross and to persuade the majority of voters that you're okay for the job.
3. Sometimes, instead of firing an incompetent teacher, school officials will transfer the person to another school in order to avoid the hassles involved in a dismissal.
4. The more she flipped out about his actions, the more he rebelled and continued doing what he pleased.
5. My family lived in Trinidad for the first ten years of my life, and we went through a lot, but when we came to America, we thought we had it made.

EXERCISE 26.7

Try to identify the meanings of the following doublespeak terms.

Example

therapeutic misadventure
doctor's mistake

USING THE APPROPRIATE REGISTER

1. radiation enhancement device
2. mutual assured destruction
3. incomplete success
4. pacification
5. arbitrary deprivation of life

READING WITH AWARENESS OF TONE

Read the following brief poem, and then identify its tone. Then identify the specific words and phrases that help create that tone.

What happens to a dream deferred?

Does it dry up
Like a raisin in the sun?
Or fester like a sore—
And then run?
Does it stink like rotten meat?
Or crust and sugar over—
Like a syrupy sweet?

Maybe it just sags
Like a heavy load.

Or does it explode?
—Langston Hughes, "Harlem"

FOR EXAMINING THE TONE OF YOUR OWN WRITING

Write a paragraph about something you might want to do at school—change your major, spend your junior year abroad, take a semester off, or something else. Use familiar register, assuming your audience to be someone close—parents, spouse, good friend. Then rewrite your paragraph to address your academic adviser, using formal register. Finally, analyze each paragraph to identify the elements that create familiar or formal register.

ANSWERS TO EXERCISE 26.7 (WILL VARY)

1. atom bomb or nuclear power plant
2. total annihilation
3. failure
4. to make peace
5. senseless killing

TEACHING PRACTICE

Students may profit by working in small groups, first reading the poem aloud a couple of times and then brainstorming together for the best way to describe the tone. Ask groups to report back to the class as a whole, and discuss any differences in the way they have described tone.

WRITERS ON WRITING

Re-vision is the act of looking back, of seeing with fresh eyes, of entering an old text from a new critical direction.

—ADRIENNE RICH

PART SIX

Understanding
Punctuation Conventions

27. Using Commas

The word *comma* comes from the Greek *komma*, meaning "cut" or "segment." A clause, for example, is a segment of a sentence, and it is often set off with a comma. In English, the comma is the most frequently used punctuation mark, serving to separate words and word groups.

While the familiar comma appears everywhere in modern writing, reducing this particular punctuation mark to hard and fast rules is very difficult, for several reasons. First, the comma can play a number of different roles in a sentence, making general rules hard to come by. More important, many decisions about commas relate to matters of purpose, rhythm, and style. As a result, comma conventions can and do differ from one English-speaking country to another, even from one professional writer to another.

In the essay "In Praise of the Humble Comma," Pico Iyer likens a comma to a flashing yellow light that asks the reader to slow down.* You can see what he means by reading through the following sentences, first with the commas and then without.

> The hangman, a gray-haired convict in the white uniform of the prison, was waiting beside his machine.
>
> And then, when the noose was fixed, the prisoner began crying out to his god.
>
> The prisoner had vanished, and the rope was twisting on itself.
>
> "Well, that's all for this morning, thank God."
>
> —George Orwell, "A Hanging"

---

* *Time*, 13 June 1988.

423

USEFUL READING

Ong, Walter J. "Historical Backgrounds of Elizabethan and Jacobean Punctuation Theory." *PMLA* 59 (1944): 349–360. Despite the title, both the history of punctuation and renaissance attitudes are treated equally.

Robertson, Joseph. *An Essay on Punctuation.* London: J. Walter, 1785. See chapter one for a discussion of the history of punctuation.

(BACK)GROUNDING

Writers began punctuating their work as early as the third century B.C. They used three marks: the *distinctio* or *positura* (our period), the *media distinctio* (our semicolon, colon, and sometimes our comma), and the *subdistinctio* (our comma). In these early times, punctuation could appear above the line (period), halfway between the top and bottom of letters (comma), or on the line (colon). At this stage in the history of literacy, oral discourse was preeminent; it comes as no surprise, then, that these marks signalled places for the speaker to breath. In "Historical Backgrounds of Elizabethan and Jacobean Punctuation Theory," Walter J. Ong notes that

> "these grammarians [Dositheus, Cassiodorus, and the author of *Excerpta Donatiani*] *never* refer to the position of a punctuation mark in terms of grammatical structure. For the most part, they are content to indicate where a *distinctio* may (not where it must or must not) occur, and if one wishes to breath oftener than would be usual, there is no objection, apparently, to inserting the marks 'ex abundanti.'" (351)

The concept of punctuation as breathing marks continued through the sixteenth and seventeenth centuries. In *An Essay on Punctuation* (1785), grammarian Joseph Robertson defines commas both in structural terms and as an aid to reading (18–19). Today, most handbooks define the proper uses of commas in grammatical terms, although this chapter does note the stylistic uses of commas (for rhythm, emphasis, and clarity).

You can, no doubt, *hear* the need for the commas in each of these sentences. In fact, however, each comma is governed not just by sound, but by *sentence structure*. For this reason, commas count in your writing. In fact, the study of student writing undertaken as part of the research for this book reveals that five of the twenty most common errors involve the comma. Getting full control of comma usage in your own writing thus presents a special challenge to you, one that involves not only learning some rules but practicing the use of commas in writing and concentrating on the stylistic decisions you must learn to make as a writer. This chapter presents an opportunity for you to accomplish both these goals.

27a. Using commas after introductory elements

A comma usually follows an introductory word, expression, phrase, or clause. Introductory elements that are followed by commas include adverbs (see 6b5); conjunctive adverbs (see 6b7); transitional expressions (see 5c5); participles, infinitives, and prepositional, participial, infinitive, and absolute phrases (see 6c3); and adverb clauses (see 6c4).

> *Slowly,* she became conscious of her predicament. [adverb]
>
> *Nevertheless,* the hours of a typist are flexible. [conjunctive adverb]
>
> *In fact,* only you can decide. [transitional expression]
>
> *Frustrated,* he wondered whether he should change careers. [participle]
>
> *In Fitzgerald's novel,* the color green takes on great symbolic qualities. [prepositional phrase]
>
> *Sporting a pair of specially made running shoes,* Jamie prepared for the race. [participial phrase]
>
> *To win the contest,* Paul needed luck. [infinitive phrase]
>
> *Pens poised in anticipation,* the students waited for the test to be distributed. [absolute phrase]
>
> *Since her mind was not receiving enough stimulation,* she had to resort to her imagination. [adverb clause]

For certain kinds of introductory elements—adverbs, infinitives, prepositional and infinitive phrases, and adverb clauses—some writers omit the comma if the element is short and does not seem to require a pause after it. Try to use your ear to decide if a comma is needed in such cases; if in doubt, put in the comma.

AFTER INTRODUCTORY ELEMENTS

At the racetrack Henry lost nearly his entire paycheck.

If the introductory element is followed by inverted word order, with the verb preceding the subject, do not use a comma.

From directly behind my seat came huge clouds of cigar smoke.

➤ Checking for commas after introductory elements

To check for commas after introductory elements, place a check mark next to every sentence that opens directly with the subject, with no introductory word, phrase, or clause. Then look carefully at each sentence not checked to decide if it needs a comma after the opening element.

First, look for sentences that open with adverbs, conjunctive adverbs like *however* or *therefore*, or transitional expressions like *in fact*, *for example*, or *in the first place*. Read the sentence aloud to see if a pause after the opening word or phrase indicates a need for a comma. Conjunctive adverbs and transitional expressions almost always need a comma after them; for other adverbs, listen carefully to see whether a comma sounds right or would break up the rhythm of the sentence unnecessarily.

Next, look for sentences that begin with participial phrases or absolute phrases. Use a comma after these phrases.

Then look for sentences beginning with participles, infinitives, infinitive phrases, and prepositional phrases. Read the sentence aloud to judge the need for a comma after these elements. In general, use a comma if the sentence opens with a sequence of two or more prepositional phrases.

At this point, look at all the sentences you have revised so far. In any of them, is the introductory element immediately followed by the verb? If so, do not use a comma after the element.

Finally, look for sentences opening with adverb clauses, those beginning with subordinating conjunctions like *although*, *because*, *unless*, and *when*. (See 6b7 for a list of subordinating conjunctions.) Read the sentence aloud to judge the need for a comma; in general, use one unless the adverb clause is very short.

EXERCISE 27.1

Place a comma after the introductory element in any of the following sentences where the comma is needed. Some of the sentences do not require a comma.

425

WRITERS ON WRITING

Popping in a comma can be like slipping on the necklace that gives an outfit quiet elegance, or like catching the sound of running water that complements, as it completes, the silence of a Japanese landscape.

—PICO IYER

WRITERS ON WRITING

To say that no two persons punctuate exactly alike would no doubt be an exaggeration, but most people would probably agree that punctuation is a matter not only of rules but of personal taste. . . . I should define punctuation as being governed two-thirds by rule and one-third by personal taste.

—G. V. CAREY

USEFUL READING

Period Styles: A History of Punctuation. New York: The Herb Lubalin Study Center of Design and Typography in The Cooper Union for the Advancement of Science and Art, 1988. See the first essay, "Period Styles: A Punctuated History."

ANSWERS TO EXERCISE 27.1

1. In one of his most famous poems,
2. Unfortunately,
3. Unable to make such a decision alone,
4. If you follow instructions carefully,
5. Therefore,
6. No comma needed
7. Their bags packed,
8. No comma needed
9. Like all other disciplines,
10. Founded by Alexander the Great,

WRITERS ON WRITING

A world that has only periods is a world without inflections. It is a world without shade. It has a music without sharps and flats. It is a martial music. It has a jackboot rhythm. Words cannot bend and curve. A comma, by comparison, catches the gentle drift of the mind in thought, turning in on itself and back on itself, reversing, redoubling and returning along the course of its own sweet river music while the semicolon brings clauses and thoughts together with all the silent discretion of a hostess arranging guests around her dinner table.

—PICO IYER

WRITERS ON WRITING

The commas are the most useful and usable of all the stops. It is highly important to put them in place as you go along. If you try to come back after doing a paragraph and stick them in the various spots that tempt you you will discover that they tend to swarm like minnows into all sorts of crevices whose existence you hadn't realized and before you know it the whole long sentence becomes immobilized and lashed up squirming in commas. Better to use them sparingly, and with affection, precisely when the need for each one arises, nicely, by itself.

—LEWIS THOMAS

1. In one of his most famous poems Frost asks why people need walls.
2. Unfortunately the door to the kennel had been left open.
3. Unable to make such a decision alone I asked my brother for help.
4. If you follow instructions carefully you will be able to install your radio.
5. Therefore answering the seemingly simple question is very difficult.
6. With the fifth century came the fall of the Roman Empire.
7. Their bags packed they waited for the taxi to the airport.
8. To become an Olympic competitor an athlete must train for years.
9. Like all other disciplines psychology draws general principles from specific observations.
10. Founded by Alexander the Great Alexandria became a great center of learning.

27b. Using commas in compound sentences

A comma usually precedes a coordinating conjunction (*and, but, or, for, nor, so,* or *yet*) that joins two independent clauses in a compound sentence.

> The title may sound important, but *administrative clerk* is only a euphemism for *photocopier.*
>
> The climbers will reach the summit today, or they must turn back.
>
> The show started at last, and the crowd grew quiet.
>
> I was often bullied in grade school, for I was the smallest in my class.

You may want to use a semicolon rather than a comma when the clauses are long and complex or contain other punctuation.

> Since baseball time is measured only in outs, all you have to do is succeed utterly; keep hitting, keep the rally alive, and you have defeated time.   –ROGER ANGELL, *The Summer Game*

If the clauses are very brief, on the other hand, you can often omit the comma before *and* or *or.*

> She saw her chance and she took it.

Always use the comma if there is any chance the sentence will be misread without it.

| CONFUSING | The game ended in victory and pandemonium erupted on the court. |
| REVISED | The game ended in victory, and pandemonium erupted on the court. |

IN COMPOUND SENTENCES

Be careful not to use *only* a comma between independent clauses; doing so is considered a serious grammatical error, called a comma splice. Either use a coordinating conjunction after the comma, or use a semicolon. (See Chapter 13 for further discussion of comma splices.)

COMMA SPLICE	Do not thank "luck" for your new job, give yourself the credit you deserve.
REVISED	Do not thank "luck" for your new job, *but* give yourself the credit you deserve.
REVISED	Do not thank "luck" for your new job; give yourself the credit you deserve.

➤ Checking for commas in compound sentences

To check a draft for commas in compound sentences, first circle every coordinating conjunction: *and, but, or, nor, for, so, yet.* Then look at each sentence in which you found such a conjunction, and examine the words before it. Could they function as a complete sentence, with a subject and predicate? Now look at the words following the conjunction. Could they function as a sentence? If the answer to both of these questions is yes, the two groups of words are two independent clauses joined with a coordinating conjunction: a compound sentence. Check to see that the conjunction is preceded (*not* followed) by a comma.

EXERCISE 27.2

Use a comma and a coordinating conjunction (*and, but, or, for, nor, so,* or *yet*) to combine each of the following pairs of sentences into one sentence. Delete or rearrange words if necessary.

Example
I had finished studying for the test. I went to bed.
I had finished studying for the test, so I went to bed.

1. Max Weber was not in favor of a classless society. It would lead to the expansion of the power of the state over the individual.
2. Immigrants came to the United States with high hopes. Their illusions were often shattered.
3. It felt good to be home. I had the odd feeling of being an outsider.
4. A basic quality of leather is stretchability. It takes on the shape of a foot.
5. Babies never have to feed themselves. They are not punished for misbehaving, either.

ANSWERS TO EXERCISE 27.2 (WILL VARY)

1. Max Weber was not in favor of a classless society, *for* it would lead to the expansion of the power of the state over the individual.
2. Immigrants came to the United States with high hopes, *but* their illusions were often shattered.
3. It felt good to be home, *yet* I had the odd feeling of being an outsider.
4. A basic quality of leather is stretchability, *so* it takes on the shape of a foot.
5. Babies never have to feed themselves, *nor* are they punished for misbehaving.

27c. Using commas to set off nonrestrictive elements

Nonrestrictive elements of a sentence—clauses, phrases, and appositives that do not limit or "restrict" the meaning of the words they modify or refer to—are set off from the rest of the sentence with commas. **Restrictive** elements *do* limit meaning and are *not* set off with commas. Look at the following examples:

RESTRICTIVE	Drivers *who have been convicted of drunken driving* should lose their licenses.
NONRESTRICTIVE	The two drivers involved in the accident, *who have been convicted of drunken driving*, should lose their licenses.

In the first sentence, the clause *who have been convicted of drunken driving* is essential to the meaning of the sentence because it limits the word it modifies, *Drivers*, to only those drivers who have been convicted of drunken driving. Therefore, it is not set off by commas. In the second sentence, the same clause is not essential to the meaning because it does not limit what it modifies, *The two drivers involved in the accident*, but merely provides additional information about these drivers. Therefore, it *is* set off with commas.

Notice how using or not using commas to set off such an element can change the meaning of a sentence:

The bus drivers *rejecting the management offer* remained on strike.

The bus drivers, *rejecting the management offer*, remained on strike.

In the first sentence, not using commas to set off the participial phrase *rejecting the management offer* makes the phrase restrictive, limiting the meaning of *The bus drivers*. This sentence says that only some of the total group of bus drivers, the ones who rejected the offer, remained on strike, implying that other drivers went back to work. In the second sentence, using the commas around the participial phrase makes it nonrestrictive, implying that *The bus drivers* refers to all of the drivers and that all of them remained on strike.

To decide whether a sentence element is restrictive or nonrestrictive, mentally delete the element, and then decide whether the deletion changes the meaning of the rest of the sentence or makes it unclear. If it does, the element is probably restrictive and should not be set off with commas; if it does not, the element is probably nonrestrictive and requires commas.

USEFUL READING

Williams, Joseph M. *Style: Ten Lessons in Style and Grace.* Glenview, IL: Scott, 1985. See pages 206–207 where Williams groups nonrestrictive modifiers under the heading loose or nonspecifying commentary.

TO SET OFF NONRESTRICTIVE ELEMENTS

Sentence elements that may be nonrestrictive and require commas to set them off include adjective and adverb clauses; participial, infinitive, and prepositional phrases; and appositive phrases.

1. Using commas with adjective and adverb clauses

Adjective clauses begin with *who, whom, whose, which, that, when, where,* or *why*. (See 6c4.) Adverb clauses begin with subordinating conjunctions like *because, although,* or *before*. (See 6b7 and 6c4.) Adverb clauses are usually essential to the meaning of the sentence; do not set them off with commas unless they precede the independent clause (see 27a) or begin with *although, even though, while, whereas,* or another conjunction expressing the idea of contrast.

NONRESTRICTIVE CLAUSES

The Indians, *who range in color from mocha to Dentyne,* are generally under five feet tall. [The central statement of this sentence is that the Indians are under five feet tall; the information about their color simply provides additional information and therefore should be set off with commas.]   –JOHN UPDIKE, "Venezuela for Visitors"

I borrowed books from the rental library of Shakespeare and Company, *which was the library and bookstore of Sylvia Beach at 12 rue de l'Odeon.* [The adjective clause gives additional information not necessary to complete the meaning of the independent clause and therefore is set off with a comma.]   –ERNEST HEMINGWAY, *A Movable Feast*

The park soon became a popular gathering place, *although some nearby residents complained about the noise.* [The adverb clause expresses the idea of contrast; therefore it is set off with a comma.]

RESTRICTIVE CLAUSES

I grew up in a house *where the only regular guests were my relations.* [The information in the adjective clause is essential to the meaning of the sentence and therefore should not be set off with commas.]
  –RICHARD RODRIGUEZ, "Aria: A Memoir of a Bilingual Childhood"

The claim *that men like seriously to battle one another to some sort of finish* is a myth. [The adjective clause beginning with *that* is necessary to the meaning of the sentence because it explains *which* claim is a myth.]   –JOHN MCMURTRY, "Kill 'Em! Crush 'Em! Eat 'Em Raw!"

An adjective clause that begins with *that* is always restrictive and is not set off with commas. An adjective clause beginning with *which* may be either restrictive or nonrestrictive; however, some writers prefer to use *which* only for nonrestrictive clauses.

2. Using commas with participial, infinitive, and prepositional phrases

Participial phrases may be either restrictive or nonrestrictive. Infinitive and prepositional phrases are usually restrictive but sometimes are not essential to the meaning of a sentence and are therefore set off with commas.

NONRESTRICTIVE PHRASES

Stephanie, amazed, stared at the strange vehicle. [The participle does not limit the meaning of *Stephanie*.]

The "synfuels" program, *launched at the height of the energy crisis*, languished with the drop in fuel prices. [The participial phrase does not limit the meaning of *the "synfuels" program* or change the central meaning of the sentence.]

Her long-term goal, *to become a child psychologist*, would require great financial discipline. [The infinitive phrase does not limit the meaning of *Her long-term goal*.]

Howard Hughes, *despite his billions*, lived a tortured life. [The prepositional phrase does not limit the meaning of *Howard Hughes*.]

RESTRICTIVE PHRASES

A penny *saved* is a penny *earned*. [Without the participles, the sentence has a very different meaning.]

Wood *cut from living trees* does not burn as well as dead wood. [The participial phrase is essential to the meaning.]

His ability *to make decisions quickly* made him a valuable employee. [The infinitive phrase restricts the meaning of *ability*.]

The wire *for the antenna* is the last one to be connected. [The prepositional phrase restricts the meaning of *wire*.]

3. Using commas with appositive phrases

An appositive phrase is a noun or noun substitute, together with its modifiers, that renames the noun immediately preceding it. When the appositive phrase is not essential to identify the noun it follows, it is set off with commas.

NONRESTRICTIVE APPOSITIVES

Ms. Baker, *my high school chemistry teacher*, inspired my love of science. [Ms. Baker's name identifies her; the appositive simply provides extra information.]

Beethoven's opera, *Fidelio*, includes the famous "Prisoners' Chorus." [*Fidelio* is nonrestrictive because Beethoven wrote only one opera, so the name is not essential.]

RESTRICTIVE APPOSITIVES

The editorial cartoonist *Thomas Nast* helped to bring about the downfall of the Tweed Ring in New York City. [The appositive identifies *The editorial cartoonist* as a specific cartoonist.]

Mozart's opera *The Marriage of Figaro* was considered revolutionary in the eighteenth century. [The appositive is restrictive because Mozart wrote more than one opera.]

➤ **Checking for commas with nonrestrictive elements**

To check a draft for commas with nonrestrictive elements, first find and underline all the dependent clauses. Then put a check mark beside each adjective clause beginning with *which, who, whom, whose, when,* or *where.* For each clause, ask yourself if the clause *identifies* the noun or pronoun it modifies by answering the question "which?" or "what kind of?" about it. If it does not answer one of these questions but merely provides "extra" information about the noun or pronoun, it is nonrestrictive. Check to see that there is a comma before it (if it falls at the end of the sentence) or before and after it (if it falls in the middle of a sentence).

Now look at the underlined clauses that are not checked to see if any of them begin with *although, while, whereas,* or another conjunction expressing the idea of contrast. If such clauses are not set off with commas, add them.

Next, find and put parentheses around all the participial phrases and around all the infinitive and prepositional phrases that follow a noun or pronoun. Draw an arrow from each phrase to the word it modifies. If a participial or infinitive phrase modifies a noun or pronoun other than the one just before it, it is nonrestrictive; make sure it is set off with commas. If a participial, infinitive, or prepositional phrase does modify the noun or pronoun immediately preceding it, ask yourself if the phrase *identifies* the noun or pronoun by answering the question "which?" or "what kind of?" If it does not answer one of these

431

questions but merely provides "extra" information about the noun or pronoun, it is nonrestrictive; make sure it is set off with commas. (Most of the infinitive and prepositional phrases will be restrictive and should not be set off.)

Finally, find and circle all the appositives and appositive phrases. Ask yourself if each appositive or phrase is essential to identify the noun or pronoun it refers to. If it is not, if it merely provides "extra" information about the noun or pronoun, it is nonrestrictive; make sure it is set off with commas.

EXERCISE 27.3

Identify the restrictive and the nonrestrictive elements in these sentences.

1. One of the great mystery writers, John D. MacDonald, died in 1987.
2. She who laughs last laughs best.
3. Neil Armstrong, who first walked on the moon, is a national hero.
4. Salmon smoked over an alder wood fire has a unique flavor.
5. Bill Reid, a highly respected practitioner of Haida Indian art, is creating a sculpture for the Mall in Washington, D.C.

EXERCISE 27.4

Use commas to set off nonrestrictive clauses, phrases, and appositives in any of the following sentences that contain such elements. Some of the sentences do not contain nonrestrictive elements.

1. Anyone who is fourteen years old faces strong peer pressure every day.
2. Embalming is a technique that preserves a cadaver for viewing.
3. I would feel right at home in the city dump which bears a striking resemblance to my bedroom.
4. The first one is the power wire which is usually red; the second is the ground wire which is usually black.
5. Most noteworthy is Aristarchus who showed that the sun is larger than the earth and proposed a heliocentric model for the solar system.
6. The Zunis an ancient tribe dwelling in New Mexico have a highly integrated culture.
7. Sociology which encompasses most of the other social sciences is the study of human social behavior.
8. An important nineteenth-century sociologist was Karl Marx who believed that his role as a social thinker was to change the world.
9. About two-thirds of the Swiss speak a German dialect while most of the rest speak French.
10. Britain and France agreed to come to each other's aid if one of them was attacked.

ANSWERS TO EXERCISE 27.3

1. *John D. MacDonald* is a nonrestrictive appositive because mentioning MacDonald is not essential to the meaning of the sentence. The appositive specifies *who* the great mystery writer is, but the noun phrase *one of the great modern mystery writers* is sufficient by itself.
2. *who laughs last* is a restrictive clause because only the *she* who has the last laugh can laugh best. The person who laughs first or second doesn't laugh best. Laughing best is restricted to the person who laughs last.
3. *who first walked on the moon* is a nonrestrictive clause because it provides additional, not essential, information.
4. *smoked over an alder wood fire* is a restrictive appositive phrase because the meaning of the sentence is not complete without it. Only salmon that is smoked over an alder wood fire can have *a unique flavor.*
5. *a highly respected practitioner of Haida Indian art* is a nonrestrictive appositive phrase because it provides nonessential information. Naming Bill Reid is sufficient.

ANSWERS TO EXERCISE 27.4

1. No commas needed
2. No comma needed
3. . . . the city dump, which bears. . . .
4. . . . power wire, which is usually red; . . . the ground wire, which is usually black.
5. . . . Aristarchus, who showed . . .
6. The Zunis, an ancient tribe dwelling in New Mexico,
7. Sociology, which encompasses most of the other social sciences, is
8. . . . was Karl Marx, who believed that his role as a social thinker . . .
9. a German dialect, while most. . . .
10. aid, if one of them . . .

▌ 27d. Using commas to separate items in a series

A comma is used after each item in a series of three or more words, phrases, or clauses.

> I bumped into professors, horizontal bars, agricultural students, and swinging iron rings. —JAMES THURBER, "University Days"

> He has plundered our seas, ravaged our coasts, burnt our towns, and destroyed the lives of our people.
> —THOMAS JEFFERSON, Declaration of Independence

You may often see a series with no comma after the next-to-last item, particularly in newspaper writing, as in *The day was cold, dark and dreary*. Occasionally, however, omitting the comma can cause confusion, and you will never be wrong to include it.

When the items in a series are long and complex or when they contain commas of their own, use semicolons rather than commas to separate them (see 28b).

Coordinate adjectives, those that relate equally to the noun they modify, should be separated by commas. In the sentence *They are sincere, inquisitive, talented researchers*, the three adjectives are coordinate: they each modify *researchers* and are therefore separated by commas. Here are some other examples of coordinate adjectives.

> The *long, twisting, muddy* road led to a shack in the woods.

> His *bizarre, outrageous* sense of humor endeared him to his friends.

In a sentence like *The cracked bathroom mirror reflected his face*, however, *cracked* and *bathroom* are not coordinate because *bathroom mirror* is the equivalent of a single word, which is modified by *cracked*. Hence they are *not* separated by commas.

> Byron carried an *elegant pocket* watch.
> *Outdated black nylon furniture* sat in dusty silence on the porch.

You can determine whether adjectives are coordinate by inserting the conjunction *and* between them. If the sentence makes sense with the *and*, the adjectives are coordinate and should be separated by commas.

> They are sincere *and* talented *and* inquisitive researchers. [The sentence makes sense with the inserted *and*'s, so the adjectives *sincere, talented,* and *inquisitive* should be separated by commas.]

> Byron carried an elegant *and* pocket watch. [In this instance, the sentence does not make sense with the *and*, so, the adjectives *elegant* and *pocket* should not be separated by a comma.]

433

WRITERS ON WRITING

Punctuation has long been considered the stronghold of inflexible and prescriptive rules. This tradition is unfortunate. To a great degree, punctuation is variable, flexible, and even imaginative.

—WILLIAM D. DRAKE

➤ Checking for commas in a series

To check a draft for commas in a series, circle every *and* and *or* in the draft. Then look at each one to see if it joins only two words, phrases, or clauses, or if it comes at the end of a series of three or more. Next, look through the draft for any series that do not use an *and* or *or*. If you find any series, check to see that each item except the last is followed by a comma; if not, add the necessary commas. Do *not* add a comma before the first item in the series or after the last item.

ANSWERS TO EXERCISE 27.5

1. They found employment in truck driving, farming, and mining.
2. The social sciences include economics, psychology, political science, anthropology, and sociology.
3. Members plant, tend, and harvest corn.
4. The daddy-long-legs's orange body resembled a colored dot amidst eight black legs.
5. A prestigious car, a large house, and membership in an exclusive club are taken as the signs of success.
6. Superficial observation does not provide accurate insight into people's lives—how they feel, what they believe in, how they respond to others.
7. What is impossible today may become reality: traveling to other planets, colonizing the moon, maybe even reaching out to distant galaxies.
8. I timidly offered to help a loud, overbearing, lavishly dressed customer.
9. No comma needed
10. These Cosell clones insist on calling every play, judging every move, and telling everyone within earshot exactly what is wrong with the team.

TEACHING PRACTICE

To develop your students' skills with commas in a series, consider extending their work from the exercises in the book to exercises that require students to write long sentences with multiple modifiers. Francis Christensen's analysis of cumulative sentences in "A Generative Rhetoric of the Sentence" contains some good models for students to imitate, including this one by William Faulkner: "Calico-coated, small-bodied, with delicate legs and pink faces in which their mismatched eyes rolled wild and subdued, they huddled, gaudy motionless and alert, wild as deer, deadly as rattlesnakes, quiet as doves."

EXERCISE 27.5

Revise each of the following sentences that require commas to set off words, phrases, or clauses in a series. Some of the sentences do not require commas.

1. They found employment in truck driving farming and mining.
2. The social sciences include economics psychology political science anthropology and sociology.
3. Members plant tend and harvest corn.
4. The daddy-long-legs's orange body resembled a colored dot amidst eight black legs.
5. A prestigious car a large house and membership in an exclusive club are taken as signs of success.
6. Superficial observation does not provide accurate insight into people's lives—how they feel what they believe in how they respond to others.
7. What is impossible today may soon become reality: traveling to other planets colonizing the moon maybe even reaching out to distant galaxies.
8. I timidly offered to help a loud overbearing lavishly dressed customer.
9. Ellen is an accomplished free-lance writer.
10. These Cosell clones insist on calling every play judging every move and telling everyone within earshot exactly what is wrong with the team.

27e. Using commas to set off parenthetical and transitional expressions, contrasting elements, interjections, direct address, and tag questions

Use commas to set off parenthetical and transitional expressions, elements expressing a contrast with what precedes them, mild interjections, words directly addressing readers, and tag questions.

Parenthetical and transitional expressions

Parenthetical expressions are relatively unimportant comments by the writer or pieces of supplementary information. Transitional expres-

USEFUL READING

Christensen, Francis. "A Generative Rhetoric of the Sentence." Rpt. in *Rhetoric and Composition*, ed. Richard Graves, Upper Montclair, NJ: Boynton/Cook, 1984, pp. 110–118. The examples referred to above are on pages 113–116.

sions include conjunctive adverbs like *however* and *furthermore* (see 6b7) and other words and phrases used to express connections between clauses, sentences, or paragraphs. (For a full list, see 5c5.)

Some studies, *incidentally*, have shown that chocolate, *of all things*, helps to prevent tooth decay.

Ceiling fans are, *moreover*, less expensive than air conditioners.

Many people do not realize that ozone is produced by dry cleaning, *for example*.

Contrasting elements

On official business it was she, *not my father*, one would usually hear on the phone or in stores. . . .
—RICHARD RODRIGUEZ, "Aria: A Memoir of a Bilingual Childhood"

The story is narrated objectively at first, *subjectively toward the end*.

Interjections

My God, who wouldn't want a wife?
—JUDY SYFERS, "I Want a Wife"

We had hiked for, *say*, seven miles before stopping to rest.

Stronger interjections are followed by exclamation points (see 29c).

Direct address

Ah, *swinging generation*, what new delights await?
—TOM WOLFE, "Pornoviolence"

My friends, I must say to you that we have not made a single gain in civil rights without determined legal and nonviolent pressure.
—MARTIN LUTHER KING, JR., "Letter from Birmingham Jail"

Tag questions

Tag questions "echo" the statement preceding them.

The homeless are our fellow citizens, *are they not?*

Seattle is not the capital of Washington, *is it?*

EXERCISE 27.6

Revise each of the following sentences, using commas to set off parenthetical and transitional expressions, contrasting elements, interjections, words used in direct address, and tag questions.

OPTIONAL EXERCISE

Consider sharing the following paragraph with your students, asking them to identify the grammatical reasons for Mark Twain's commas. Then ask your students to rewrite some or all of the passage, combining sentences or eliminating commas by shortening sentences. Finally, discuss Twain's stylistic reasons for punctuating this passage (suspense; create a feeling of the story happening in the present through short sentences). What effects have your students achieved by punctuating the passage differently?

"The bull started up, and got along well for about ten feet, then slipped and slid back. I breathed easier. He tried it again—got a little higher—slipped again. But he came at it once more, and this time he was careful. He got gradually higher and higher, and my spirits went down more and more. Up he came—an inch at a time—with his eyes hot, and his tongue hanging out. Higher and higher—hitched his foot over the stump of a limb, and looked up, as much as to say, 'You are my meat, friend.' Up again—higher and higher, and getting more excited the higher he got. He was within ten feet of me! I took a long breath—and then said I, 'It is now or never.' I had the coil of the lariat all ready; I paid it out slowly, till it hung right over his head; all of a sudden I let go of the slack, and the slip noose fell fairly round his neck! Quicker than lightning I out with the allen and let him have it in the face, It was an awful roar, and must have scared the bull out of his senses. When the smoke cleared away, there he was, dangling in the air, twenty foot from the ground, and going out of one convulsion into another faster than you could count! I didn't stop to count, anyhow—I shinned down the tree and shot for home." (Mark Twain, *Roughing It*.).

ANSWERS TO EXERCISE 27.6

1. One must consider the society as a whole, not its individual components, to understand a particular culture.
2. The West, in fact, has become solidly Republican in presidential elections.
3. Her friends did not know about her illness, did they?
4. Fictions about race, not the facts, influence human relations.
5. We found, therefore, that we had more tomatoes than we could use.
6. No comma needed
7. Oh, I do not know how to do anything but farm.
8. And now, customers, follow along as I demonstrate the latest in video discs.
9. Regional accents have shown few signs of weakening, surprisingly enough.
10. This is imported pâté, not chopped liver.

WRITERS ON WRITING

Occasionally a student discovers that novelists and poets often do not abide by the "rules" of punctuation. Naturally, he wonders why he cannot do the same. Usually he is told that he must first master the rules before earning the right to break them. This answer places the issue on an authoritarian basis which seldom appeals. There is actually a much better reason for mastering the "rules." A study of imaginative uses of punctuation will show that departures from conventional usage are careful and deliberate, and often make no sense unless one takes standard punctuation as a reference point.

—WILLIAM D. DRAKE

1. One must consider the society as a whole not its individual components to understand a particular culture.
2. The West in fact has become solidly Republican in presidential elections.
3. Her friends did not know about her illness did they?
4. Fictions about race not the facts influence human relations.
5. We found therefore that we had more tomatoes than we could use.
6. We must act quickly to stop this threat to our health and safety.
7. Oh I do not know how to do anything but farm.
8. And now customers follow along as I demonstrate the latest in video discs.
9. Regional accents have shown few signs of weakening surprisingly enough.
10. This is imported pâté not chopped liver.

27f. Using commas in dates, addresses, titles, and numbers

Commas are used according to established rules within dates, addresses and place names, and numbers. Commas are also used to separate personal and professional titles from the name preceding them.

Dates

For dates, use a comma between the day of the week and the month, between the day of the month and the year, and between the year and the rest of the sentence, if any.

Reagan was elected president on *Tuesday, November 7, 1980,* and was inaugurated on *January 20, 1981.*

Do not use a comma with dates in inverted order or with dates consisting only of the month and the year.

16 January 1987

Thousands of Cubans stormed the American embassy in Havana in *May 1980* and asked for asylum in the United States.

Addresses and place names

In addresses and place names, use a comma after each part, including the state if no ZIP code is given. In addresses that include the ZIP code, do not use a comma either before or after it.

Forward my mail to The Department of English, Ohio State University, Columbus, Ohio 43210 until further notice.

Miami, Florida, is now a bilingual city because about half its population is Cuban.

USEFUL READING

Drake, William D. *The Way to Punctuate.* Scranton: Chandler, 1971. See Part 3, "Punctuating Imaginative Writing," for a discussion of the nuances of punctuating fiction.

WITH QUOTATIONS

Titles

Use commas to set off a title such as *Jr.*, *M.D.*, and so on from the name preceding it and from the rest of the sentence.

> James Siddens, *Ph.D.*, recently joined the faculty as the new dean of the School of Arts and Sciences.

> Martin Luther King, *Jr.*, was one of this century's greatest orators.

Numbers

In numbers of five digits or more, use a comma between each group of three digits, starting from the right.

> Give me *10,000* reasons, and then I'll change my mind.

Do not use a comma within street numbers or ZIP codes.

> My parents live at *11311* Wimberly Drive, Richmond, Virginia 23233.

The comma is optional within numbers of four digits, except for years, where it is never used.

> The college has an enrollment of *1,789* (or *1789*) this semester.

> The French Revolution began in 1789.

EXERCISE 27.7

Revise each of the following sentences, using commas appropriately with dates, addresses and place names, titles, and numbers.

1. People were cultivating crops before 10000 B.C.
2. Ithaca New York has a population of about 20000.
3. The ship was hit by two torpedoes on May 7 1915 and sank in less than half an hour.
4. The Modern Language Association headquarters recently moved to 10 Astor Place New York New York 10003.
5. The nameplate on the office door read *Donald Good R.N.* and looked quite impressive.

ANSWERS TO EXERCISE 27.7

1. People were cultivating crops before 10,000 B.C.
2. Ithaca, New York, has a population of about 20,000.
3. The ship was hit by two torpedoes on May 7, 1915, and sank in less than half an hour.
4. The Modern Language Association headquarters recently moved to 10 Astor Place, New York, New York 10003.
5. The nameplate on the office door read *Donald Good*, *R.N.*, and looked quite impressive.

▌ 27g. Using commas with quotations

Commas are used to set off quotations from words used to introduce or explain the quotations. A comma following a quotation goes *inside* the closing quotation mark.

> "No one becomes depraved all at once," wrote Juvenal.

> A German proverb warns, "Go to law for a sheep, and lose your cow."
>
> "Nothing has really happened," said Virginia Woolf, "until it has been recorded."

When a quotation followed by explanatory words is a question or an exclamation, do not use a comma after the question mark or exclamation point.

> "What's a thousand dollars?" asks Groucho Marx in *Coconuts*. "Mere chicken feed. A poultry matter."
>
> "Out, damned spot!" cries Lady Macbeth.

Do not use a comma when a quotation is introduced by *that* or when the rest of the sentence includes more than the words used to introduce or explain the quotation.

> The writer of Ecclesiastes concludes that "all is vanity."
>
> People who say "Have a nice day" irritate me.

Do not use a comma before an indirect quotation, one that does not use the speaker's exact words.

> Patrick Henry declared that he wanted either liberty or death.
>
> Virginia Woolf said that a woman needs money and her own room in order to write fiction.

ANSWERS TO EXERCISE 27.8
1. No change
2. No change
3. No change
4. "Neat people are lazier and meaner than sloppy people," according to Suzanne Britt.
5. No change

EXERCISE 27.8

Insert a comma in each of the following sentences that requires one. Some of the sentences do not need an additional comma.

1. "The public be damned!" William Henry Vanderbilt was reported to have said. "I'm working for my stockholders."
2. Joseph Epstein admits, "I prefer not to be thought vulgar in any wise."
3. Paul Fussell argues that "if the dirty little secret used to be sex, now it's the facts about social class."
4. "Neat people are lazier and meaner than sloppy people" according to Suzanne Britt.
5. "Who shall decide when doctors disagree?" asked Alexander Pope.

▌ 27h. Using commas to facilitate understanding

Sometimes a comma, though not required, can make a sentence much easier to read or understand.

TO FACILITATE UNDERSTANDING

CONFUSING	The members of the dance troupe strutted in in matching tuxedos and top hats.
REVISED	The members of the dance troupe strutted in, in matching tuxedos and top hats.
CONFUSING	Still liquids are necessary to sustain life.
REVISED	Still, liquids are necessary to sustain life.

EXERCISE 27.9

Revise the following paragraph by inserting commas where necessary. Be prepared to explain why you added each comma.

As the most recent show confirmed the audience at a Jimmy Buffet concert compares to no other. Dressed from head to toe in outlandish tropical prints and sunglasses the Parrot Heads danced rocked rolled juked and jived through the duration of the concert. At one point a fan pitched a giant blow-up Godzilla onto the stage and Buffet gently took the monster in his arms and danced the two-step. Beach balls flew around the amphitheater as people called for margaritas margaritas and more margaritas to the sounds of "Margaritaville." Never ceasing were the dancing and conga lines that wove serpent-like through the crowd of 20000. Even when the band had cleared the stage and the dust had settled the greedy crowd wanted more. After two hours of prime performance they would not be denied an encore. Buffet rising to the occasion returned for one last number. The audience had come to hear a Buffet connoisseur's extravaganza which was exactly what they got.

EXERCISE 27.10

In the following passage, Richard Wright tells about his discovery of books and his subsequent self-education. Read the passage aloud, listening for Wright's use of commas. Then read it again, mentally deleting the commas and noting how their absence affects meaning and rhythm. Finally, choose two of the sentences to use as a model for imitation, creating a similar pair of sentences of your own.

I ran across many words whose meanings I did not know, and I either looked them up in a dictionary or, before I had a chance to do that, encountered the word in a context that made its meaning clear. But what strange world was this? I concluded the book with the conviction that I had somehow overlooked something terribly important in life. I had once tried to write, had once reveled in feeling, had let my crude imagination roam, but the impulse to dream had been slowly beaten out of me by experience. Now it surged up again and I hungered for books, new ways of looking and seeing. It was not a

ANSWERS TO EXERCISE 27.9 (WILL VARY)

As the most recent show confirmed, the audience at a Jimmy Buffet concert compares to no other. Dressed from head to toe in outlandish tropical prints and sunglasses, the Parrot Heads danced, rocked, rolled, juked, and jived through the duration of the concert. At one point, a fan pitched a giant blow-up Godzilla onto the stage, and Mr. Buffet gently took the monster up his arms and danced the two-step. Beach balls flew around the ampitheatre, as people called for margaritas, margaritas, and more margaritas to the sounds of "Margaritaville." Never ceasing were the dancing and conga lines that wove serpent-like through the crowd. Even when the band had cleared the stage and the dust had settled, the greedy crowd wanted more. After two hours of prime performance, they would not be denied an encore. Buffet, rising to the occasion, returned for one last number. The audience had come to hear a Buffet connoisseur's extravaganza, which was exactly what they got.

ANSWERS TO EXERCISE 27.10 WILL VARY

matter of believing or disbelieving what I read, but of feeling something new, of being affected by something that made the look of the world different.

–RICHARD WRIGHT, "The Library Card"

27i. Checking for unnecessary commas

Just like insufficient use, excessive use of commas can spoil what may otherwise be a fine sentence or passage. This section will help you avoid using commas unnecessarily.

1. Omitting commas around restrictive phrases and clauses

Do not use commas to set off restrictive elements, which limit or restrict the meaning of the words they modify or refer to (see 27c).

UNNECESSARY	I don't let my children watch TV shows, that are violent.
REVISED	I don't let my children watch TV shows that are violent. [restrictive adjective clause]
UNNECESSARY	The decision, to stop the flow of irrigation water, is long overdue.
REVISED	The decision to stop the flow of irrigation water is long overdue. [restrictive infinitive phrase]
UNNECESSARY	My only defense, against my allergies, is to stay indoors.
REVISED	My only defense against my allergies is to stay indoors. [restrictive prepositional phrase]
UNNECESSARY	The actor, James Earl Jones, will speak on campus this fall.
REVISED	The actor James Earl Jones will speak on campus this fall. [restrictive appositive phrase]

➤ **Checking for unnecessary commas with restrictive elements**

To check a draft for unnecessary commas with restrictive elements, first underline all the dependent clauses. Then put a check mark beside each adjective clause, and look to see what word introduces it. If a clause is introduced by *that*, it is restrictive; if you have set it off with commas, remove them. If it is introduced by another word, such as *which, who,*

WRITERS ON WRITING

The most important fact about a comma is that there are places where it must not be used. That is, there are places where a comma alters the meaning of a statement. Max Beerbohm was being witty when he used a comma in writing about *Frank Harris, and many good writers.*

—BERGEN EVANS AND CORNELIA EVANS

The comma, the most ubiquitous and flexible, not to say slippery, of all stops, is the least susceptible to hard and fast rules.

—G. V. CAREY

OPTIONAL EXERCISE

Consider reading aloud the following paragraph. Ask your students to identify the nonrestrictive elements in it (shown in italics here):

This single stick, *which you now behold ingloriously lying in that neglected corner,* I once knew in a flourishing state in a forest: it was full of sap, full of leaves, and full of boughs; but now, in vain does the busy art of man pretend to vie with nature, by tying that withered bundle of twigs to its sapless trunk; it is now, *at best,* but the reverse of what it was, *a tree turned upside down, the branches on the earth, and the root in the air;* it is now handled by every dirty wench, condemned to do her drudgery, and, *by a capricious kind of fate,* destined to make other things clean, and be nasty itself; at length, *worn to the stumps in the service of the maids,* it is thrown out of doors, or condemned to the last use, *of kindling a fire.* When I beheld this, I sighed, and said within myself, *Surely man is a Broomstick!* Nature sent him into the world strong and lusty, in a thriving condition, wearing his own hair on his head, *the proper branches of this reasoning vegetable,* until the axe of intemperance has lopped off his green boughs, and left him a withered trunk (Jonathan Swift, "A Meditation Upon a Broomstick").

or *when*, ask yourself if the clause *identifies* the noun or pronoun it modifies by answering the question "which?" or "what kind of?" If so, it is restrictive and should not be set off with commas.

Now look at the underlined clauses that are not checked. Put an X beside each adverb clause, and look to see what subordinating conjunction introduces it. Unless the clause is introduced by *although*, *while*, *whereas*, or another conjunction expressing the idea of contrast, it is probably restrictive and should not be set off with commas.

Next, find and put parentheses around all the participial, infinitive, and prepositional phrases that immediately follow a noun or pronoun. Draw an arrow from each phrase to the word it modifies. If a phrase modifies the noun or pronoun immediately preceding it, decide if it *identifies* the noun or pronoun by answering the question "which?" or "what kind of?" If so, it is restrictive and should not be set off with commas. (Most prepositional phrases are restrictive.)

Finally, circle all the appositives and appositive phrases. Decide if each appositive or phrase is essential to identify the noun or pronoun it refers to. If so, it is restrictive and should not be set off with commas.

2. Omitting commas between subjects and verbs, verbs and objects or complements, and prepositions and objects

Do not use a comma between a subject and its verb, a verb and its object or complement, or a preposition and its object. This general rule holds true even if the subject, object, or complement is a long phrase or clause.

UNNECESSARY	*Watching movies on my* VCR *late at night*, has become an important way for me to relax. [comma between subject and verb]
REVISED	Watching movies on my VCR late at night has become an important way for me to relax.
UNNECESSARY	Parents *must decide, how much TV their children may watch*. [comma between verb and object]
REVISED	Parents must decide how much TV their children may watch.
UNNECESSARY	The winner *of, the trophy* stepped forward. [comma between preposition and object]
REVISED	The winner of the trophy stepped forward.

TEACHING PRACTICE

Consider using sentence-combining exercises to help students practice when to use commas. As Erika Lindemann comments, "Sentence-combining exercises not only illustrate how punctuation organizes sentence elements for a reader but also how to solve punctuation problems which for years have limited a student's range of syntactic options" (A *Rhetoric for Writing Teachers* 135). To help make the purpose of the sentence combining clear to your students, start off with "signaled" exercises, which ask for a particular combination and supply the grammatical element needed to combine the sentences:

Erin gathered the blocks.
~~She~~ took careful aim. (,)
~~She~~ flung handful after handful at her little brother. (, and)
~~She~~ finally relented. (before -ing)

Erin gathered the blocks, took careful aim, and flung handful after handful at her little brother before finally relenting.

WRITERS WRITING

For Morley Callaghan, watching the ways words collide with each other is a constant source of fascination. At an early age he was taken by Keats's lines "Charm'd magic casements, opening on the foam / Of perilous seas, in fairy lands forlorn" [from "Ode to a Nightingale"]. But Callaghan doesn't think much of these lines now: "Sure, it sounds great, it rolls off the tongue, but it just, really, creates a blur, a blob." Because words are so fickle, and writing is not easy, Callaghan revises as a way of getting started again: "I write all over what I've done, between the lines, everywhere, and by the time I've got a pile of stuff the spirit picks up and then it becomes an impulse to just go upstairs [to write]."

3. Omitting commas in compound constructions

Do not use a comma before or after coordinating conjunctions joining the two parts of a compound construction.

UNNECESSARY	*Defense spending, and economic deregulation* were the Reagan administration's goals. [compound subject]
REVISED	Defense spending and economic deregulation were the Reagan administration's goals.
UNNECESSARY	Mark Twain *trained as a printer and, worked as a steamboat pilot.* [compound predicate]
REVISED	Mark Twain trained as a printer and worked as a steamboat pilot.

4. Omitting commas before the first item or after the last item in a series

Do not use a comma before the first item or after the last item in a series, unless another rule requires a comma.

UNNECESSARY	Our government's first priority is to ensure, *freedom of speech and press, the right to assemble peacefully, and the right to petition the government for redress of grievances.*
REVISED	Our government's first priority is to ensure freedom of speech and press, the right to assemble peacefully, and the right to petition the government for redress of grievances.
UNNECESSARY	The swimmer took slow, powerful, strokes.
REVISED	The swimmer took slow, powerful strokes.

EXERCISE 27.11

Revise each of the following sentences that contains unnecessary commas.

1. There are four types of nonverbal communication: kinesic, haptic, proxemic, and dormant, communication.
2. Observers watch, and interpret facial expressions and gestures.
3. There was nothing to do, after we ate, but go to bed, so we all crawled into our sleeping bags.
4. Our supper that evening, consisted of, stale bologna sandwiches, soggy cookies, and leftover trail mix.

442

USEFUL READING

Lindemann, Erika. A *Rhetoric for Writing Teachers.* 2nd ed. New York: Oxford UP, 1987.

Shaughnessy, Mina P. *Errors & Expectations: A Guide for the Teacher of Basic Writing.* New York: Oxford UP, 1977. See Chap. 2, "Handwriting and Punctuation," particularly pages 18–24 for a discussion of how basic writers use commas and periods.

CHECKING FOR UNNECESSARY COMMAS

5. The ability to use language, to express ourselves, is a unique human trait.
6. As we sat around the campfire, we felt boredom, and disappointment.
7. Movies, such as *Jaws* and *E.T.*, depend heavily on special effects.
8. The photographer, Edward Curtis, is known for his depiction of the West.
9. We all took panicked, hasty, looks at our notebooks.
10. Driving a car, and talking on the car phone at the same time demand care.

READING WITH AN EYE FOR COMMAS

The following poem by Robert Frost uses commas to create rhythm and guide readers. Read the poem aloud, listening especially to the effect of the commas at the end of lines one and five. Then read it again as if those commas were omitted, noting the difference. What is the effect of Frost's decision *not* to use a comma at the end of line three?

> Some say the world will end in fire,
> Some say in ice.
> From what I've tasted of desire
> I hold with those who favor fire.
> But if it had to perish twice,
> I think I know enough of hate
> To say that for destruction ice
> Is also great
> And would suffice.
>   —ROBERT FROST, "Fire and Ice"

FOR EXAMINING COMMAS IN YOUR OWN WRITING

Study the way Alice Walker uses commas in the following description of a scene from her childhood. Write a paragraph about some scene from your life, perhaps beginning as she has: "It is a _____ day in _____." Try imitating the structure of her second sentence, using commas as she does. Then examine your own use of commas: read your paragraph aloud, listening for the rhythm of your description.

> It is a bright summer day in 1947. My father, a fat, funny man with beautiful eyes and a subversive wit, is trying to decide which of his eight children he will take with him to the county fair. My mother, of course, will not go. She is knocked out from getting most of us ready: I hold my neck stiff against the pressure of her knuckles as she hastily completes the braiding and then beribboning of my hair. . . . Whirling happily in my starchy frock, showing off my biscuit-polished patent-leather shoes and lavender socks, tossing my head in a way that makes my ribbons bounce, I stand, hands on hips, before my father. "Take me, Daddy," I say with assurance; "I'm the prettiest!"
> —ALICE WALKER, *In Search of Our Mothers' Gardens*

ANSWERS TO EXERCISE 27.11

1. There are four types of non-verbal communication: kinesic, haptic, proxemic, and dormant communication.
2. Observers watch and interpret facial expressions and gestures.
3. There was nothing to do after we ate but go to bed, so we all crawled into our sleeping bags.
4. Our supper that evening consisted of stale bologna sandwiches, soggy cookies, and leftover trail mix.
5. The ability of use language to express ourselves is a unique human trait.
6. As we sat around the campfire, we felt boredom and disappointment.
7. Movies such as *Jaws* and *E.T.* depend on special effects.
8. The photographer Edward Curtis is known for his depiction of the West.
9. We all took panicked, hasty looks at our notebooks.
10. Driving a car and talking on the car phone at the same time demand great care.

TEACHING PRACTICE

Write the poem on the board, and read it aloud. Then try changing its comma structure—perhaps by ending line 4 with a comma instead of a period, or by adding commas in line 7 after *that* and *destruction*. Read the poem aloud each way, and ask students to describe the different effects. Finally, ask them to decide which one they prefer, and why.

28. Using Semicolons

(BACK)GROUNDING

The Greeks used a punctuation symbol like the semicolon as their question mark. The semicolon as we know it today was introduced in the seventh century. During the eighth century, an inverted semicolon was used to indicate a vocal pause halfway between the comma and the semicolon. By the fifteenth century, however, the inverted semicolon had fallen out of favor. It no longer exists today.

WRITERS ON WRITING

Punctuation contributes to art as well as to correctness, to style as well as to styling. Make it work for you, not just to develop prose that is "clear enough"—not just to prevent confusion—but to help you express yourself, or your characters express themselves. Don't lean on it; don't shy away from it; just *use* it—and in doing so, let it help you convey nuances too subtle for words alone to convey; let it help you evoke effects so delicate that talk would shatter them. And remember that if you frequently use more marks than usual—or fewer than usual—you will call attention to your craft, with the results possibly seeming artful rather than artistic, posturing rather than expressive. Nor do I for a moment suggest that punctuation can, or should, be charged with sole responsibility for effectiveness; descriptive detail, diction, sentence length, sentence rhythm, paragraph structure, timing—these and other elements of style can and must share the load.

—ROBERT M. PIERSON

In classical Greek, groups of words comparable to what we call sentences were set off and called *colons*. A semicolon, therefore, is literally half of a colon, or half of a sentence divided by the punctuation mark we call a **semicolon**. Lewis Thomas demonstrates effective use of the semicolon as he defines it, noting that

> The semicolon tells you that there is still some question about the preceding full sentence; something needs to be added. . . . It is almost always a greater pleasure to come across a semicolon than a period. The period tells you that is that; if you didn't get all the meaning you wanted or expected, you got all the writer intended to parcel out and now you have to move along. But with a semicolon there you get a pleasant little feeling of expectancy; there is more to come; read on; it will get clearer.
>
> —LEWIS THOMAS, "Notes on Punctuation"

As Thomas suggests, semicolons have the effect of creating a pause stronger than that of a comma but not as strong as the full pause of a period. Their primary uses are to link coordinate independent clauses and to separate items in a series.

28a. Using semicolons to link independent clauses

You can join independent clauses in several ways: with a comma and a coordinating conjunction (see 27b), with a colon (see 32d), with a dash (see 32c), or with a semicolon. Semicolons provide writers with subtle ways of signaling closely related clauses: the second clause often

444

restates an idea expressed in the first, as it does in the first sentence of the Lewis Thomas passage above, or it sometimes exemplifies or presents a contrast to the first. As a writer, you must choose when and where to use semicolons to signal such relationships. Note, for instance, the way semicolons are used in the following examples:

> Shakespeare wrote for the Medium of his day; if Shakespeare were alive now, he'd be writing *My Fair Lady.*
> —RANDALL JARRELL, "A Sad Heart at the Supermarket"

> The power of science for good and evil has troubled other minds than ours. We are not fumbling here with a new dilemma; our subject and our fears are as old as the tool-making civilizations.
> —JACOB BRONOWSKI, "The Creative Mind"

In the first sentence, Jarrell uses a semicolon to lead to a clause that exemplifies the statement made in the first clause. He might have joined the two clauses with the coordinating conjunction *and*, but such a link would be somewhat misleading, for *and* tells readers to expect more information, not an example. He might also have used a period to separate the two clauses into two sentences, but then the two ideas would not be so clearly linked. In the second example, the semicolon links two contrasting clauses; the logical connection between the two clauses is far more subtle and more immediate than it would be had Bronowski instead used the coordinating conjunction *for*.

The sentences above are compound sentences containing only two independent clauses, but semicolons can also join independent clauses in compound-complex sentences and in compound sentences containing more than two independent clauses.

> The Good Souls will, doubtless, gain their reward in Heaven; on this earth, certainly, theirs is what is technically known as a rough deal.
> On Mother's Day, Good Souls conscientiously wear carnations; on St. Patrick's Day, they faithfully don boutonnieres of shamrocks; on Columbus Day, they carefully pin on miniature Italian flags.
> —DOROTHY PARKER, "Good Souls"

A semicolon can also be used to link independent clauses joined by conjunctive adverbs like *therefore*, *however*, and *indeed* or transitional expressions like *in fact*, *in addition*, or *for example*. (See 6b7 and 5c5 for lists of conjunctive adverbs and transitional expressions.)

> The West German economy recovered quickly from the devastation of World War II; indeed, the recovery was labeled the "economic miracle."

TEACHING PRACTICE

Mina P. Shaughnessy notes that semicolons are rarely used by beginning writers, who typically read little and so are unfamiliar with the form. Their errors result from ignorance. They sometimes "strain the resources of the comma" to cover situations requiring other marks, including semicolons. Thus, comma splices may result (23, 33–34).

The opposite problem can occur once students have been introduced to semicolons—that is, they may begin to overuse them (Shaughnessy 34). Part of the problem is the power of the semicolon itself. Shaughnessy notes that "as its form suggests, it has the linking power of a comma and the terminating authority of a period. Given the difficulties of the unpracticed writer with both linking and sustaining sentences, the semicolon must appear as something of a bargain" (34). Punctuation marks produce different psychological effects—on the writer as well as the reader. If the writer resists putting an end to sentences, because she fears having to start another, the instructor may see an overuse of semicolons.

In a sense, the writer must get a feel for when to use semicolons to link ideas. Shaughnessy goes on to note that use of the semicolon, unlike the period and the comma, for instance, depends on the situation, on the relationships of ideas as much as on conventional formal requirements. George Summey, Jr., states that the semicolon is "the most clearly specialized balancing and coordinating mark" and is "not a general-purpose mark like the comma (*American Punctuation*, New York: Ronald P, 1949. 97).

USEFUL READING

Shaughnessy, Mina P. *Errors & Expectations: A Guide for the Teacher of Basic Writing.* New York: Oxford UP, 1977. In her section on punctuation, Shaughnessy argues that, like other errors of beginning writers, punctuation errors are not random and are not indications of laziness or stupidity. Rather, they generally reflect the student's development of an incorrect punctuation system; in effect, they exist by design. Shaughnessy states, "There are styles to being wrong" (40).

28a ;   USING SEMICOLONS

Note that conjunctive adverbs can change position in a sentence:

> Fine diamonds are colorless; some, however, have a yellowish color.

> Fine diamonds are colorless; some have a yellowish color, however.

If two independent clauses joined by a coordinating conjunction contain commas, use a semicolon instead of a comma before the conjunction. The semicolon makes such a sentence easier to read.

> Every year, whether the Republican or the Democratic Party is in office, more and more power drains away from the individual to feed vast reservoirs in far-off places; and we have less and less say about the shape of events which shape our future.
> –WILLIAM F. BUCKLEY, JR., "Why Don't We Complain?"

ANSWERS TO EXERCISE 28.1

1. If you are preoccupied, your game will suffer; an opportunity for a relaxing afternoon will turn into a frustrating experience.
2. City life offers many advantages; however, in many ways, life in a small town is much more pleasant.
3. *Newspeak* greatly reduced people's vocabulary; they could no longer understand philosophical and scientific works.
4. Physical education forms an important part of many university programs; nevertheless, few students and professors clearly recognize its value.
5. Physical education provides students with exercise; moreover, games and sports provide a chance for them to mingle outside the classroom.
6. Voltaire was concerned about the political implications of his skepticism; he warned his friends not to discuss atheism in front of the servants.
7. Kerosene, solar power, and electricity are popular sources of energy for heating homes in New England; the most popular, however, is wood.
8. My high school was excessively competitive; virtually everyone went on to college, many to the top schools in the nation.
9. Pittsburgh was once notorious for its smoke and grime; today, its skies and streets are cleaner than those of many other American cities.
10. Propaganda is defined as the spread of ideas to further a cause; therefore, propaganda and advertisement are synonymous terms.

EXERCISE 28.1

Revise each of the following sentences by adding a semicolon to link independent clauses.

Example
The exam begins in two hours please be on time.
The exam begins in two hours; please be on time.

1. If you are preoccupied, your game will suffer an opportunity for a relaxing afternoon will turn into a frustrating experience.
2. City life offers many advantages, however, in many ways, life in a small town is much more pleasant.
3. *Newspeak* greatly reduced people's vocabulary they could no longer understand philosophical and scientific works.
4. Physical education forms an important part of a university's program nevertheless, few students and professors clearly recognize its value.
5. Physical education provides students with exercise moreover, games and sports provide a chance for them to mingle outside of the classroom.
6. Voltaire was concerned about the political implications of his skepticism he warned his friends not to discuss atheism in front of the servants.
7. Kerosene, solar power, and electricity are popular sources of energy for heating homes in New England the most popular, however, is wood.
8. My high school was excessively competitive virtually everyone went on to college, many to the top schools in the nation.
9. Pittsburgh was once notorious for its smoke and grime today its skies and streets are cleaner than those of many other American cities.
10. Propaganda is defined as the spread of ideas to further a cause therefore, propaganda and advertisement are synonymous terms.

28b. Using semicolons to separate items in a series

Ordinarily, commas separate items in a series (see 27d). But when the items themselves contain commas or other punctuation, using semicolons will make the sentence clearer and easier to read.

> Anthropology encompasses archaeology, the study of ancient civilizations through artifacts; linguistics, the study of the structure and development of language; and cultural anthropology, which examines the life styles of various peoples, especially those in small, nonindustrialized societies.

> I recognized the film as a political document, expressing the worst sentiments of America in the cold war: its hero, a tough military man who wants only to destroy the enemy utterly; its villain, a naively liberal scientist who wants to learn more about it; the carrot and its flying saucer, a certain surrogate for the red menace; the film's famous last words—a newsman's impassioned plea to "watch the skies"—an invitation to extended fear and jingoism.
>
> —Stephen Jay Gould, *Ever Since Darwin*

Note that a semicolon never introduces a series (see 28d).

EXERCISE 28.2

Using one of the example sentences in 28a or 28b as a model, write a sentence of your own that uses semicolons to separate items in a complex series.

28c. Checking for overused semicolons

If semicolons are used too often, they distract readers in the same way unnecessary repetition does, by calling attention to themselves instead of to what the writer is saying. In addition, sentence upon sentence punctuated with semicolons will sound monotonous and jerky.

OVERUSED	Like many people in public life, he spoke with confidence; perhaps he even spoke with arrogance; yet I noted a certain anxiety; it touched and puzzled me; he seemed too eager to demonstrate his control of a situation and his command of the necessary data.
REVISED	Like many people in public life, he spoke with confidence, perhaps even with arrogance; yet I noted a certain anxiety that touched and puzzled me. He seemed too eager to demonstrate his control of a situation and his command of the necessary data.

(BACK)GROUNDING

Bergen and Cornelia Evans claim that the semicolon is more appropriate for formal writing. "If a writer wishes to use an informal narrative style he should avoid semicolons as much as possible" (A *Dictionary of Contemporary American Usage*. New York: Random, 1957. 440).

However, George Summey, Jr. argues against thinking of the semicolon as "a stiff and formal mark that ought to be seldom used." He writes, "It is actually used by good current writers today and might well be used oftener if our writers would take the trouble to drop some of their *and's* and *but's* and use patterns that take semicolon and no conjunction." The problem is not with the semicolon, Summey says, but with the "awkward patterns" and "stiff wording" with which it has been associated (98).

William and Mary Morris suggest that one reason for the lack of use of the semicolon is "the trend toward short, trenchant sentences" in journalism (*Harper Dictionary of Contemporary Usage*. New York: Harper, 1975. 547). But in fact, the absence of the semicolon in less formal writing is changing. Still, the tendency to use the semicolon remains a stylistic choice. Some writers like Annie Dillard, whose *Pilgrim at Tinker Creek* is definitely not a formal piece, seem somewhat fond of the semicolon, while other writers, like John McPhee, seem to rarely use it. Donald Barthelme's short story "Sentence" (*City Life*. New York: Farrar, 1970. 107–114) consists of one long sentence (or actually of a part of one sentence). While it includes numerous instances of dashes, parentheses, quotation marks, question marks, exclamation points, and commas, it has only one semicolon. The reason might be that the semicolon seems too close to being end punctuation, and the story is meant to give us the feeling of continuousness and endlessness. Only the period appears less; it doesn't appear at all.

ANSWERS TO EXERCISE 28.2 WILL VARY

USEFUL READING

Summey, George, Jr. *American Punctuation*. New York: Ronald P, 1949. This work remains the most balanced and reasonable approach to punctuation.

ANSWERS TO EXERCISE 28.3 WILL VARY

(BACK)GROUNDING

One can imagine writers getting away with never using semicolons, except perhaps the rare use with a series of items. From this perspective, the semicolon becomes more a stylistic device than a grammatical one, which is not something you can say about the period, for instance. Clearly, then, the choice of a semicolon over another punctuation mark is often a rhetorical choice.

Summey offers these flexible guidelines for when to choose the semicolon:

What mark should be used in a given case—comma or semicolon, semicolon or period—will depend only in part on the length of the groups. Circumstances that may make the semicolon preferable to the comma are length and complexity of the groups, the absence of a connective, or a shift of grammatical subject. And any of these same circumstances may make the period better than the semicolon. Each case must be settled by the writer according to the immediate situation. The more important a group is in its context, the more reason for preferring semicolon to comma or period to semicolon" (99).

WRITERS ON WRITING

That learned men are well known to disagree on this subject of punctuation is in itself a proof, that the knowledge of it, in theory and practice, is of some importance. I myself have learned by experience, that, if ideas that are difficult to understand are properly separated, they become clearer; and that, on the other hand, through defective punctuation, many passages are confused and distorted to such a degree, that sometimes they can with difficulty be understood, or even not be understood at all.

—ALDUS MANUTIUS

EXERCISE 28.3

Revise the following passage, substituting other punctuation for some of the semicolons. Add or delete words if necessary.

Remember when the neighborhood kids played football out in the vacant lot; they were there every Saturday, having a good time. Whatever happened to just playing for a good time? Now, uniformed coaches yell at young players to win; they put more and more pressure on them; and parents join in the chant of win, win, win; in fact, if the child is not a winner, he or she must be—that's right—a loser. The young athlete is constantly told that winning is everything; what used to be fun is now just like a job; play to win, the adults say, or do not play at all.

28d. Checking for misused semicolons

A comma, not a semicolon, should separate an independent clause from a dependent clause or a phrase.

MISUSED   For centuries, the Plains Indians maintained their way of life; which included hunting, fishing, and gathering wild berries.

REVISED   For centuries, the Plains Indians maintained their way of life, which included hunting, fishing, and gathering wild berries.

A colon, not a semicolon, should introduce a series.

MISUSED   The tour includes visits to the following art museums; the Prado, in Madrid; the Louvre, in Paris; and the Rijksmuseum, in Amsterdam.

REVISED   The tour includes visits to the following art museums: the Prado, in Madrid; the Louvre, in Paris; and the Rijksmuseum, in Amsterdam.

EXERCISE 28.4

Revise each of the following sentences to correct the misuse of semicolons.

Example
The new system would encourage high school students to take more academic courses; thus strengthening college preparation.
The new system would encourage high school students to take more academic courses, thus strengthening college preparation.

448

1. The comparison Osborne makes between the two wages is based primarily on three factors; the amount of time dedicated to work, the degree of responsibility, and the traditions attached to the jobs.
2. If the North had followed up its victory at Gettysburg more vigorously; the Civil War might have ended sooner.
3. The time seemed to fly; which was surprising because I was not having any fun whatsoever.
4. Our uniforms were unbelievably dingy; stained from being splattered with food and often torn here and there.
5. Verbal scores have decreased more than fifty-four points; while math scores have decreased more than thirty-six.

▌28e. Using semicolons with quotation marks

Ordinarily, a semicolon goes *outside* closing quotation marks.

Jackson's most famous story is "The Lottery"; it is a horrifying allegory about the power of tradition and the search for scapegoats.

EXERCISE 28.5

In the reading you are currently doing, find two passages that use semicolons particularly effectively. Then choose those two passages or two of the following ones, and use them as models for sentences of your own.

1. An evening with [composer Richard Wagner] was an evening spent in listening to a monologue. Sometimes he was brilliant; sometimes he was maddeningly tiresome. But whether he was brilliant or dull, he had one topic of conversation: himself.   —DEEMS TAYLOR, "The Monster"
2. The real question, however, it appears to me, is not whether poor people will adopt the middle-class mentality once they are well fed; rather, it is whether they will ever be well fed enough to be able to choose whatever mentality they think will suit them.
    —ALICE WALKER, "The Civil Rights Movement: What Good Was It?"
3. Baseball, football, basketball—these quintessentially American pastimes are recognizably sports because they involve play: They are games. One *plays* football; one doesn't *play* boxing.   —JOYCE CAROL OATES, "On Boxing"

READING WITH AN EYE FOR SEMICOLONS

In the following paragraph, Annie Dillard describes a solar eclipse in elaborate detail, using semicolons to separate each part of her description. Read the paragraph with attention to the use of semicolons. What different effect would

ANSWERS TO EXERCISE 28.4

1. The comparison Osborne makes between the two wages is based primarily on three factors: the amount of time dedicated to work; the degree of responsibility; and the traditions attached to the jobs.
2. If the North had followed up its victory at Gettysburg more vigorously, the Civil War might have ended sooner.
3. The time seemed to fly, which was surprising because I was not having any fun whatsoever.
4. Our uniforms were unbelievably dingy, stained from being constantly splattered with food and often torn here and there.
5. Verbal scores have decreased more than fifty-four points, while math scores have decreased more than thirty-six.

ANSWERS TO EXERCISE 28.5 WILL VARY

the paragraph have if Dillard had used periods instead of semicolons? Imagine also if she had used commas and coordinating conjunctions. What is the effect of all the semicolons?

> You see the wide world swaddled in darkness; you see a vast breadth of hilly land, and an enormous, distant, blackened valley; you see towns' lights, a river's path, and blurred portions of your hat and scarf; you see your husband's face looking like an early black-and-white film; and you see a sprawl of black sky and blue sky together, with unfamiliar stars in it, some barely visible bands of cloud, and over there, a small white ring. The ring is as small as one goose in a flock of migrating geese—if you happen to notice a flock of migrating geese. It is one 360th part of the visible sky. The sun we see is less than half the diameter of a dime held at arm's length.
>
> —ANNIE DILLARD, "Solar Eclipse"

TEACHING PRACTICE

Ask students to bring their descriptions to class and read them aloud. Then ask the class to respond to what they have heard. Can they "hear" the semicolons? Do they "hear" them in the places the author intended them to be? What suggestions for revision can they make?

FOR EXAMINING SEMICOLONS IN YOUR OWN WRITING

Think of something you might take five or ten minutes to observe—a football game, a brewing storm, an ant awkwardly carrying a crumb—and write a paragraph describing your observations point by point and using semicolons to separate each point, as Annie Dillard does in the paragraph above. When you have finished, look at the way you used semicolons. Are there places where a period or a comma and a coordinating conjunction would better serve your meaning? Revise appropriately.

29. Using End Punctuation

Ending a sentence with a well-chosen period, question mark, or exclamation point allows your readers a certain satisfaction: they have reached the end of one unit of thought and can pause and take a mental breath before moving on to the next one. As a writer, you are most often guided by meaning in your choice of end·punctuation. Sometimes, however, you can use end punctuation for special effect. Look, for instance, at the way end punctuation guides readers in the following three sentences:

Am I tired.

Am I tired?

Am I tired!

In these brief examples, the end punctuation tells us how to read each sentence: the first one as a dry, matter-of-fact statement; the second as a puzzled or perhaps ironic query; the last as a note of exasperation. This chapter will explain how you can use these three kinds of end punctuation.

29a. Using periods

Use a period to close sentences that make statements or give mild commands.

> All I know about grammar is its infinite power.
> —JOAN DIDION, "Why I Write"

> Never use a foreign phrase, a scientific word or a jargon word if you can think of an everyday English equivalent.
> —GEORGE ORWELL, "Politics and the English Language"

451

USEFUL READING

Shaughnessy, Mina P. *Errors & Expectations: A Guide for the Teacher of Basic Writing.* New York: Oxford UP, 1977. Chapter 2, "Handwriting and Punctuation," focuses on end punctuation.

TEACHING PRACTICE

In order to use end punctuation of any kind, the student must first have a sense of what a sentence is. As Mina P. Shaughnessy points out, end punctuation requires "a familiarity with the sentence as a grammatical unity and with the process whereby simple sentences are enlarged so as to include various types of subordinate structures" (27). Beginning writers will have been producing sentences orally for a long time before they come to produce them in writing, but writing is an abstract operation, not a natural operation like speaking. We speak, producing whole thoughts in subjects and predicates, without reflection; writing requires a great deal of reflecting on what we are doing. Thus, you may want to review sentence production (Chapter 6: Constructing Grammatical Sentences) as you introduce end punctuation. Ideally, your students should study both simultaneously. Shaughnessy writes, "Thus although punctuation is often set off in the *mechanics* section of handbooks and English courses, it should not be isolated in this way from the dynamics of composition, for the process whereby writers *mark* sentences is related to the process whereby they *make* them" (28).

You may also encounter "a psychological resistance to the period" (Shaughnessy 18). The period imposes an end to the thought that the student may have had difficulty in beginning. The period tells the writer that he or she must begin again, a task that the inexperienced writer may find fearful.

Also, students sometimes become overly concerned with end punctuation. Shaughnessy believes that such concern suggests a perception of the sentence as a whole unit that ought not to be divided or modified in any way. Students sometimes become very defensive when instructors ask them to change sentences, even the end punctuation of sentences. "What one senses through such punctuation is a caution about losing control of the sentence by allowing it to become too long" (Shaughnessy 28).

(BACK)GROUNDING

Greek and Latin observed no punctuation at all until about the ninth century A.D. The first period, called *periodos*, was introduced circa 260 B.C. by a librarian in Alexandria named Aristophanes. His punctuation system can be viewed as a forerunner of our own, but generally speaking, his system was ignored. Aristophanes' *periodos* was a dot set high on the line, while a dot set at the bottom of a line was called the *colon*. By the seventeenth century, the modern system had established itself, and the period had sunk to the bottom of the line, and the colon had become something else.

WRITERS ON WRITING

For many beginning writers, the need to mark off sentences inhibits the progress of their thoughts. In speech, they can produce sentences as easily and unconsciously as they can walk; in writing, they must stop to deliberate over what is and what is not a sentence.

—MINA SHAUGHNESSY

ANSWERS TO EXERCISE 29.1

1. Please attend the meeting on Tuesday at 10 A.M. in the Board Room.
2. Cicero was murdered in 43 B.C.
3. "What's the matter, Darryl?" I asked.
4. In April 1981, NBC interviewed Dr. Spock.
5. A national voluntary effort sponsored by the A.M.A. could help contain hospital costs.

A period also closes indirect questions, which report rather than ask questions.

> I asked how old the child was.
>
> We all wonder who will win the election.
>
> Many parents ask if autism is an inherited disorder.

Periods are also used with most abbreviations:

Mr.	A.M./a.m.	B.C.	Dr.	D.D.S.
Ms.	P.M./p.m.	A.D.	Ph.D.	R.N.
Mrs.	Jr.	ibid.	M.D.	M. Ed.

Some abbreviations do not require periods. Among them are the two-capital-letter abbreviations of state names used with ZIP codes, such as *FL* and *TN* (though note that the traditional abbreviations of state names such as *Fla.* or *Tenn.* do call for periods); abbreviations of familiar businesses, organizations, and government agencies (*NBC*, *YWCA*, *CIA*); and groups of initials that are pronounced as words (*NASA*, *MADD*, *UNICEF*).

If you are not sure whether a particular abbreviation should include periods, check the term in a dictionary. (See Chapter 34 for more information about abbreviations.)

EXERCISE 29.1

Revise each of the following sentences, inserting periods in appropriate places.

> *Example*
> Ms Maria Jordan received both a PhD in chemistry and an MEd
> Ms. Maria Jordan received both a Ph.D. in chemistry and an M.Ed.

1. Please attend the meeting on Tuesday at 10 AM in the Board Room
2. Cicero was murdered in 43 BC
3. "What's the matter, Darryl?" I asked
4. In April 1981, NBC interviewed Dr Spock
5. A national voluntary effort by the AMA could help contain hospital costs

29b. Using question marks

A question mark closes sentences that ask direct questions.

If women's professional sports can thrive in Europe, why not in the United States?

USEFUL READING

Thomas, Lewis. "Notes on Punctuation." *New England Journal of Medicine* 296 (1977): 1103–1105. This witty personal essay is remarkable for its erudition—perhaps more so, because it is written by a medical researcher (turned essayist) and published originally in a medical journal.

USING QUESTION MARKS   ? 29b

How can we admit that the agreeable past, which we thought was permanent and inviolable, has slipped away like a Mississippi steamboat?
—EVAN CONNELL, "The Palace of Moorish Kings"

Question marks do not close *indirect* questions, which report rather than ask questions. Indirect questions close with a period (see 29a).

Do not use a comma or a period after a question mark that ends a direct quotation.

"What do I do now?" my mind kept repeating.

My mind kept repeating, "What do I do now?"

Polite requests phrased as questions can be followed by periods rather than question marks.

Would you please close the door.

Question marks appear between questions in a series even when the questions do not form separate sentences:

I often confronted a dilemma: should I go to practice? finish my homework? spend time with my friends?

A question mark in parentheses can be used to indicate that a writer is unsure about a date, figure, or word.

The house has a total of 5,000 square feet (?).

Quintilian died in A.D. 95 (?).

The meeting is on Oleonga (?) Street.

EXERCISE 29.2

Revise each of the following sentences, adding question marks and substituting them for other punctuation where appropriate. One of the sentences does not require any question marks.

> *Example*
> She asked the travel agent, "What is the air fare to Greece."
> She asked the travel agent, "What is the air fare to Greece?"

1. Social scientists face difficult questions: should they use their knowledge to shape and guide society, merely describe human behavior, try to do both.
2. Are people with so many possessions really happy.
3. "Can I play this" asked Manuel.
4. I looked at him and asked what his point was.
5. "Were you lying about our friendship" I yelled at her.

(BACK)GROUNDING

The question mark appeared in the eighth century. Lewis Thomas, in his "Notes on Punctuation," claims the question mark is not, "strictly speaking," a stop, but rather an "indicator of tone." Yet question marks also indicate grammatical meaning, too. A sentence like *Joseph danced the boogaloo* may be either declarative or interrogative, depending on the context:

> Joseph danced the boogaloo.
> Joseph danced the boogaloo?

In Spanish, an upside down question mark precedes the interrogative sentence and a rightside up question mark follows it, thus warning the reader ahead of time of both phonological and grammatical meaning. In Arabic, the question mark is placed only at the beginning of an interrogative. (On the other hand, the Chinese did not have a question mark until it began to be transliterated into a Roman alphabet.)

John Wilson, in *The Elements of Punctuation*, published in 1856, describes the dual function of the question mark, along with the exclamation point, parenthesis, and dash:

> They are rhetorical, so far as they help to exhibit the force and intensity of a style which is rhetorical in its structure; but they are also grammatical, because they often serve to indicate, in connection with other marks, the nature, construction, and sense of the passages in which they occur (92).

ANSWERS TO EXERCISE 29.2

1. Social scientists face difficult questions: should they use their knowledge to shape and guide society? merely describe human behavior? try to do both?
2. Are people with so many possessions really happy?
3. "Can I play this?" asked Manuel.
4. Correct, indirect question.
5. "Were you lying about our friendship?" I yelled at her.

USEFUL READING

Wilson, John. *The Elements of Punctuation.* Boston: Crosby, Nichols, and Co., 1856. Despite its age, this book remains a sound discussion of punctuation.

(BACK)GROUNDING

The exclamation point was rarely used before the Renaissance. It differs fundamentally from the other two end punctuation marks. While the period and the question mark function grammatically (as well as "rhetorically"—that is, phonologically—in the case of the question mark), the exclamation point functions almost entirely to indicate a change in voice. While it does mark the end of a sentence, it does not do so always, and in every such case, it could be replaced with a period or question mark.

WRITERS ON WRITING

The exclamation point has been variously called the note of admiration, the shriek of surprise, the astonisher or paralyzer, the period that blew its top.

—GEORGE SUMMEY, JR.

(BACK)GROUNDING

Attitudes toward the exclamation point have ranged from disgust, as Lewis Thomas expresses, to simple tolerance. Rarely has anyone exclaimed the praises of the exclamation point. At best, commentators describe it neutrally, as did the author of A *Treatise of Stops, Points, or Pauses* in 1680, calling it "a Note of Admiration, wondering, or crying out" (6). Typically, we encounter descriptions like that of George Summey, Jr., who notes that, at the time he was writing (1949), typewriters did not possess exclamation point keys. Instead, the mark was made by striking a period, backspacing, and then striking an apostrophe. Summey calls this procedure "more trouble than the mark is likely to be worth" (90).

ANSWERS TO EXERCISE 29.3 (WILL VARY)

1. This university is so large, so varied, that attempting to tell someone everything about it would take three years.
2. I screamed at Jamie, "You rat! You tricked me!"
3. "This time, we're starting early!" she shouted.
4. Get away from that window right now!
5. Oh no! A flash flood warning!

ANSWERS TO EXERCISE 29.4 WILL VARY

29c. Using exclamation points

Exclamation points close sentences that show surprise or strong emotion: emphatic statements, interjections, and emphatic commands.

Look out!

Help!

In those few moments of geologic time will be the story of all that has happened since we became a nation. And what a story it will be!
—JAMES RETTIE, "But a Watch in the Night"

Use exclamation points very sparingly because they can distract your readers by suggesting an exaggerated sense of urgency. Do not, for instance, use exclamation points with mild interjections or to suggest sarcasm or criticism. In general, try to create emphasis through diction (see Chapter 25) and sentence structure (see 17a) rather than exclamation points.

Do not use a comma or a period after an exclamation mark that ends a direct quotation.

"We shall next be told," exclaims Seneca, "that the first shoemaker was a philosopher!"   —THOMAS BABINGTON MACAULAY, "Francis Bacon"

EXERCISE 29.3

Revise each of the following sentences, adding exclamation points and substituting them for other punctuation where appropriate and removing any unnecessary exclamation points and other punctuation.

Example
Look out. The tide is coming in fast.
Look out! The tide is coming in fast!

1. This university is so large, so varied, that attempting to tell someone everything about it would take three years!
2. I screamed at Jamie, "You rat. You tricked me."
3. "This time we're starting early!," she shouted.
4. Get away from that window right now.
5. Oh, no. A flash flood warning.

EXERCISE 29.4

Turn to the passage by Tom Wolfe that opens Chapter 32. Read it over, and you will see that Wolfe has punctuated it as one very long sentence. Revise

USEFUL READING

Summey, George, Jr. *American Punctuation*. New York: Ronald, 1949. Summey provides generally sound and provocative discussions of all elements of punctuation.

the sentence by breaking it into several shorter sentences. Try using periods, question marks, and exclamation points to achieve the same rhythm that Wolfe has. Change the wording as you need to (probably, you will not need to change much).

READING WITH AN EYE FOR END PUNCTUATION

Read the following passage and consider the author's use of end punctuation. Then read it again, and experiment with changing some of the end punctuation. What would be the effect of deleting the exclamation point from the quote by Cicero? What would be the effect of changing Cicero's question to a statement?

> To be admired and praised, especially by the young, is an autumnal pleasure enjoyed by the lucky ones (who are not always the most deserving). "What is more charming," Cicero observes in his famous essay *De Senectute*, "than an old age surrounded by the enthusiasm of youth! . . . Attentions which seem trivial and conventional are marks of honor—the morning call, being sought after, precedence, having people rise for you, being escorted to and from the forum. . . . What pleasures of the body can be compared to the prerogatives of influence?" But there are also pleasures of the body, or the mind, that are enjoyed by a greater number of older persons.
>
> –MALCOLM COWLEY, *The View from 80*

FOR EXAMINING END PUNCTUATION IN YOUR OWN WRITING

Look through an essay you have written recently, noting end punctuation carefully. How many of your sentences end with periods? How many with question marks? Have you used any exclamation points, and if so, are they actually called for? Then read through the essay again, seeing if you can find any sentences that might be better phrased as questions. If you find that all or almost all of your sentences end with periods, see if changing one or more to questions or exclamations proves effective. If you keep a writing log, you might copy some of this work into it for future study.

30. Using Apostrophes

(BACK)GROUNDING

One of the difficulties in teaching students to use apostrophes is tied to the differences between speaking and writing. Most of our students are very capable at spoken English, but often not very familiar with the conventions of written English. The apostrophe is an example of this situation. Our students will often omit apostrophes because they do not hear them in oral discourse. Though we can make the argument that indeed we *do* hear punctuation (intonation, rhythm, pauses, and breathing) the student whose eye and ear is not trained in turning spoken discourse into written will have difficulty remembering to insert apostrophes. To illustrate, it is easy to see that students would not necessarily see anything missing or problematic in contractions and possessive words such as *isnt, cant, peoples, radios,* or *heros.* (Note also that learning the use of the apostrophe involves learning the difference between the plural and the possessive forms of words, for example, *hero's* and *heros.*

As a mark of the possessive case, the punctuation mark we call the apostrophe has an unusual history. In Old English, the endings of nouns changed depending on their grammatical function—a noun used as a subject, for example, had a different ending from the same noun used as a direct object. By the fourteenth century, Middle English had dropped most of this complicated system except for possessive and plural endings: *Haroldes* (or *Haroldis* or *Haroldys*) *sword* was still used to mean "the sword of Harold." Then, in the sixteenth century, scholars concluded that the ending *-es* and its variant forms were actually contractions of *his.* Believing that *Haroldes sword* meant "Harold his sword," they began using an apostrophe instead of the *e: Harold's sword.*

Even though this theory was later discredited, the possessive ending retained the apostrophe because it was a useful way to distinguish between possessive and plural forms in writing. Today, we use the apostrophe primarily to signal possessive case, contractions and other omissions of words and letters, and certain plural forms. This chapter presents the conventions governing its use.

▌ 30a. Using apostrophes to signal possessive case

The possessive case denotes ownership or possession of one thing by another (see Chapter 7). The apostrophe is used to form the possessive case of nouns and indefinite pronouns—*Francine's mink coat, nobody's fault.*

456

USEFUL READING

Summey, George, Jr. *American Punctuation.* New York: Ronald, 1949. See pp. 149–50 for a brief statement on the history of the apostrophe as a sign of the possessive, of omissions, and of the plural.

TO SIGNAL POSSESSIVE CASE ｜'｜30a

1. Forming the possessive case of singular nouns and indefinite pronouns

Add an apostrophe and -s to form the possessive of most singular nouns and indefinite pronouns, including those singular nouns that end in -s.

His *coach's* advice helped Sydney win the class.

John Wayne's first westerns are considered classics.

The reading list included *Keats's* poem.

Anyone's guess is as good as mine.

Apostrophes are *not* used with the possessive forms of *personal* pronouns: *yours, his, hers, its, ours, theirs.*

2. Forming the possessive case of plural nouns

For plural nouns not ending in -s, add an apostrophe and -s as with singular nouns.

The *women's* caucus will include representatives from thirty cities.

The *children's* first Christmas was spent in Wales.

For plural nouns ending in -s, add only the apostrophe.

The *clowns'* costumes were bright green and orange.

Fifty dollars' worth of groceries filled only two shopping bags.

3. Forming the possessive case of compound words

For compound words, make the last word in the group possessive.

The *secretary of state's* speech was televised.

Her *daughters-in-law's* birthdays both fall in July.

His *in-laws'* disapproval dampened his enthusiasm for the new house.

4. Forming the possessive case with two or more nouns

To signal individual possession by two or more owners, make each noun possessive.

There are great differences between *John Wayne's* and *Henry Fonda's* westerns. [Wayne and Fonda appeared in different westerns.]

457

(BACK)GROUNDING

Things and abstractions cannot *possess* any other item, of course, and so, such common indications of possession as *television's The Cosby Show* and *Missouri's governor* are technically incorrect. We can restate such phrases in the same way we can restate phrases involving genuine possession: *The Cosby Show of television, the governor of Missouri, the letters and poems of Emily Dickinson.* However, the *of* in the first two cases is not indicative of true possession in the same way as the *of* in the third case. The *of* in *the governor of Missouri* simply defines *governor* in the same way that the *of* in a phrase like *a loss of breath* defines the loss involved.

Yet we might well wonder why we can restate the first three examples as possessives but not the last. The reason may involve personification. We can think of Missouri as a personification of all its citizens. We can think of television as a human corporate entity that can then possess a particular show. The same would go for the following possessives:

Ohio State's new football coach
the association's registration fee
the oil cartel's embargo

However, such reasoning does not explain the following uses of possessive case for non-human things:

the breath's loss
the book's cover
meal's end

TEACHING PRACTICE

Although there is some disagreement over adding just an apostrophe rather than an apostrophe and -s to singular nouns ending in -s, the most authoritative sources on usage recommend using an apostrophe and an -s with all singular nouns, including those words ending with -s. Here are some examples.

Nogales's hot and dry summers
Cass's research into the squash melon
the *princess's* last visit

USEFUL READING

Gowers, Sir Ernest. *The Complete Plain Words.* London: Her Majesty's Stationery Office, 1973. See p. 172 for a discussion of guidelines for using apostrophes.

To signal joint possession, make only the last noun possessive.

Rogers and Astaire's first film together was *Flying Down to Rio*.

➤ **Checking for possessive apostrophes**

To check for possessive apostrophes, circle all the nouns that end in -*s*. Then look at the circled nouns, and put a check mark beside each one that shows ownership or possession. Make sure that each of these nouns has an apostrophe in the right place, either before or after the -*s*. Next underline all the indefinite pronouns (someone, nobody— see 6b3 for a more complete list); any that end in -*s* should have an apostrophe before the -*s*.

ANSWERS TO EXERCISE 30.1

1. Grammar is *everybody's* favorite subject.
2. *CBS's* acquisition of the guitar company disappointed some musicians.
3. I was having a good time at *P.J.'s*, but my friends wanted to go to *Sunny's*.
4. *Carol and Jim's* income dropped drastically after Jim quit his job.
5. Parents often question their *children's* choice of friends.
6. Many smokers disregard the *surgeon general's* warnings.
7. The restaurant management took a percentage of *everyone's* tips.
8. The *governors'* attitude changed after the convention.
9. This is the strangest dog I've ever seen; she has a *beagle's* ears, and a *St. Bernard's* nose and feet.
10. My *friend's* and my *brother's* cars have the same kind of stereo systems.

EXERCISE 30.1

Complete each of the following sentences by inserting 's or an apostrophe alone to form the possessive case of the italicized words.

1. Grammar is *everybody* favorite subject.
2. *CBS* acquisition of the guitar company disappointed some musicians.
3. I was having a good time at *P.J.*, but my friends wanted to go to *Sunny*.
4. *Carol and Jim* income dropped drastically after Jim quit his job.
5. Parents often question their *children* choice of friends.
6. Many smokers disregard the *surgeon general* warnings.
7. The restaurant management took a percentage of *everyone* tips.
8. The *governors* attitudes changed after the convention.
9. This is the strangest dog I've ever seen; she has a *beagle* ears, and a *St. Bernard* nose and feet.
10. *My friend and my brother* cars have the same kind of stereo system.

30b. Using apostrophes to signal contractions and other omissions

Contractions are combinations of two words that are formed by leaving out certain letters, which are indicated by apostrophes. Note the use of the apostrophe in the following commonly contracted forms:

it is	it's	would not	wouldn't
was not	wasn't	do not	don't
I am	I'm	does not	doesn't
he is, he has	he's	will not	won't
you will	you'll	let us	let's
I would	I'd	who is, who has	who's
he would	he'd	cannot	can't

TO SIGNAL CONTRACTIONS AND OTHER OMISSIONS ' 30b

Contractions are common in conversation and informal writing. Most academic work, however, calls for greater formality. Check with your instructor about the appropriateness of contractions in your college writing.

Do not confuse the possessive pronoun *its* with the contraction *it's*. *Its* is the possessive form of *it*. *It's* is a contraction for *it is*.

> This disease is unusual; *its* symptoms vary from person to person.

> *It's* a difficult disease to diagnose.

(See 22b for other commonly confused pairs of possessive pronouns and contractions—*their/they're*, *whose/who's*, and *your/you're*.)

An apostrophe is also used to signal omission of letters or numbers in other common phrases:

ten of the clock	rock and roll	class of 1989
ten o'clock	rock 'n' roll	class of '89

In addition, writers can use an apostrophe to signal omitted letters in approximating the sound of spoken English or some specific dialect of spoken English. Note the way Mark Twain uses the apostrophe to form contractions in the following passage, in which Huckleberry Finn tells Jim about King Henry the Eighth:

> S'pose people left money laying around where he was—what did he do? He collared it. S'pose he contracted to do a thing, and you paid him, and didn't set down there and see that he done it—what did he do? He always done the other thing. S'pose he opened his mouth—what then? If he didn't shut it up powerful quick he'd lose a lie every time. That's the king of a bug Henry was; and if we'd 'a' had him along 'stead of our Kings he'd 'a' fooled that town a heap worse than ours done.
> –MARK TWAIN, *The Adventures of Huckleberry Finn*

➤ Checking for misuse of *its* and *it's*

To check a draft for misuse of *its* and *it's*, first circle each *its* in the draft. Check to see that it shows possession; if not, add an apostrophe before the *-s*. Then underline each *it's*. Check to see that it means "it is"; if not, remove the apostrophe.

EXERCISE 30.2

Go through the Twain passage in 30b, writing out the full form in place of each contraction. Then read the two versions aloud, and note how much more the one with contractions sounds like spoken English.

459

USEFUL READING

Flesch, Rudolf. *The ABC of Style: A Guide to Plain English*. New York: Harper, 1964. See pp. 29–30, which encourage the use of contractions in writing.

(BACK)GROUNDING

Typically, contractions are less formal forms than the words written out in full. The use of contractions in more formal settings is still considered controversial. While most commentators encourage the use of contractions, writers are probably wise to limit their use in any formal writing, including letters of application, business letters, legal documents, and papers for college courses. Yet even in more formal contexts, contractions sometimes cannot be avoided. Spelling out some contractions results in artificiality: *let us* instead of *let's*; *is it not* instead of *isn't it*. The rhetorical considerations of purpose, content, context, and audience should always guide the writer's use of contractions.

ANSWER TO EXERCISE 30.2

Suppose (S'pose) people left money laying around where he was—what did he do? He collared it. *Suppose* (S'pose) he contracted to do a thing, and you paid him, and *did not* (didn't) set down there and see that he done it—what did he do? He always done the other thing. *Suppose* (S'pose) he opened his mouth—what then? If he *did not* (didn't) shut it up powerful quick *he would* (he'd) lose a lie every time. *That is* (That's) the kind of a bug Henry was; and if *we would* (we'd) *have* ('a') had him along *instead* ('stead) of our Kings *he would* (he'd) *have* ('a') fooled that town a heap worse than ours done.

TEACHING PRACTICE

Refer your students to William Zinsser's essay, "College Pressures." Note that Zinsser does not use apostrophes to indicate the plural of numbers and letters. In particular, see paragraph 16, where he writes "in the late 1960s," and paragraph 19, where he writes "as for Cs." Ask your students to decide for themselves which form, with or without the apostrophe, they prefer. But they need to recognize that in formal writing, they need to follow the rules for use of the apostrophe.

30c. Using apostrophes to form the plural of numbers, letters, symbols, and words used as terms

An apostrophe and *-s* are used to form the plural of numbers, letters, symbols, and words referred to as terms.

> Several Cessna *150*'s sat on the ground.
>
> The gymnasts need marks of *8*'s and *9*'s to qualify for the finals.
>
> Ideally, all swimmers should know the *ABC*'s of lifesaving.
>
> The computer prints *e*'s whenever there is an error in the program.
>
> I marked special passages with a series of three ***'s.
>
> The five *Shakespeare*'s in the essay were spelled five different ways.

Note that numbers, letters, and words referred to as terms are usually italicized; but the plural ending is not, as in the examples above.

The plural of years can be written with or without the apostrophe (*1990's* or *1990s*). Whichever style you follow, be consistent.

ANSWERS TO EXERCISE 30.3

1. There was a big revival at my Auntie *Reed's* church.
2. That night I was escorted to the front row and placed on the *mourner's* bench with all the other young sinners. . . .
3. Finally Westly said to me: . . . "*Let's* get up and be saved."
4. Then I was left all alone on the *mourner's* bench.
5. That night, . . . I cried, in bed alone, and *couldn't* stop.

EXERCISE 30.3

The following sentences, from which all apostrophes have been deleted, appear in Langston Hughes's "Salvation." Insert apostrophes where appropriate in each sentence.

> *Example*
> "Sister Reed, what is this childs name?"
> "Sister Reed, what is this child's name?"

1. There was a big revival at my Auntie Reeds church.
2. That night I was escorted to the front row and placed on the mourners bench with all the other young sinners. . . .
3. Finally Westly said to me: . . . "Lets get up and be saved."
4. Then I was left all alone on the mourners bench.
5. That night, . . . I cried, in bed alone, and couldnt stop.

READING WITH AN EYE FOR APOSTROPHES

In "Danny Deever," Rudyard Kipling uses apostrophes to mark contractions and omitted letters. Both help create a sense of informal spoken English in late nineteenth century Britain. Read the following stanza aloud, listening for

USEFUL READING

Evans, Bergen, and Cornelia Evans. A *Dictionary of Contemporary American Usage*. New York: Random, 1957. A brief discussion of the apostrophe and its usage.

the rhythm of the language. To get a sense of how apostrophes help to create this rhythm, you might try reading the poem with the missing letters filled in.

> "What's that so black agin the sun?" said Files-on-Parade.
> "It's Danny fightin' 'ard for life," the Color-Sergeant said.
> "What's that that whimpers over'ead?" said Files-on-Parade.
> "It's Danny's soul that's passin' now," the Color-Sergeant said.
>   For they're done with Danny Deever, you can 'ear the quickstep play,
>   The Regiment's in column, an' they're marchin' us away;
>   Ho! the young recruits are shakin', an' they'll want their beer today,
>   After hangin' Danny Deever in the mornin'!
>   –RUDYARD KIPLING, "Danny Deever"

FOR EXAMINING YOUR OWN USE OF APOSTROPHES

As a tool for presenting contractions and omitted letters, apostrophes play a larger role in informal writing than in formal writing. One thing that many students need to learn is to write with few or no contractions, a task that requires some effort because we all use contractions in conversation. To get an idea of the difference between spoken and written language, try transcribing a "paragraph" or so of your own spoken words. Make a point of using apostrophes whenever you use a contraction or otherwise omit a letter. Look over your paragraph to see how many apostrophes you used, and then revise the piece to make it more formal, eliminating all or most apostrophes.

TEACHING PRACTICE

Ask students to practice reading this passage aloud, first with all the contractions written out and omitted letters restored and then as Kipling wrote it. Ask them then to work together to describe the difference, considering, for example, which version sounds more like speech and which version sounds more formal.

31. Using Quotation Marks

(BACK)GROUNDING

Before the seventeenth century, there was no regulated punctuation mark to indicate quotations. In ancient Greek texts, the *paragraphos* (a short horizontal line used to divide texts into units) was used to indicate changes in dialogue. Quotations and direct speech were simply introduced with phrases like *he said*, without any punctuation. To indicate its importance, double commas were placed before a sentence: ,,*The time to act is now.* The double comma was later used to enclose quotations. In the early seventeenth century, printers first began to edge both margins of quoted material with double commas.

(BACK)GROUNDING

In Great Britain, the label for *quotation marks* is *inverted commas*, recalling the origin of the marks in the seventeenth century. However, Wilson Follett points out that, although either expression is acceptable, *inverted commas* is an inaccurate label:

> The opening signs (" and ') consist of commas both inverted and reversed; the closing signs (" and ') are neither inverted nor reversed, but merely superior—i.e. above the line. (*Modern American Usage.* New York: Hill, 1966, 186)

WRITERS ON WRITING

Few common things are more difficult than to find the right word, and many people are too lazy to try. This form of indolence sometimes betrays itself by a copious use of inverted commas.

—SIR ERNEST GOWERS

"By necessity, by proclivity,—and by delight, we all quote," wrote Ralph Waldo Emerson. Quotation marks, which tell readers that certain words were spoken or written by someone other than the writer, have been a convention of written English since before the time of the printing press. As printing techniques evolved and became standardized, quotation marks came to signal not only direct quotations but also certain titles, definitions, and words used ironically or invented by the writer. This chapter presents the conventions governing their use.

31a. Using quotation marks to signal direct quotation

In written American English, double quotation marks signal a direct quotation.

> "Imagery," Laurence Perrine states, "may be defined as the representation through language of sense experience."

> He smiled and said, "Son, this is one incident that I will never forget."

Single quotation marks enclose a quotation within a quotation. Open and close the passage you are quoting with double quotation marks, and change any quotation marks that appear *within* the quotation to single quotation marks.

> In "The Uses of the Blues," James Baldwin says that "The title 'The Uses of the Blues' does not refer to music; I don't know anything about music."

USEFUL READING

Shaughnessy, Mina P. *Errors & Expectations: A Guide for the Teacher of Basic Writing.* New York: Oxford UP, 1977. See Chapter 2, an insightful discussion of punctuation. In particular, Shaughnessy claims that basic writers rarely use quotation marks.

TO SIGNAL DIRECT QUOTATION " " 31a

Do not use quotation marks for *indirect* discourse, which does not quote the speaker's or writer's exact words.

The father smiled and said that he would never forget the incident.

▍1. Quoting longer passages

If the passage you wish to quote exceeds four typewritten or hand-written lines, set it off from the rest of the text by starting it on a new line and indenting it ten spaces from the left margin. Double-space above and below the quotation, and double-space the quotation itself. This format, known as **block quotation,** does not require quotation marks.

Jean Shepherd identifies the Van People, who he says

> tend to be heavily bearded, dedicated lifetime subscribers to *Rolling Stone*, compulsive consumers of granola. . . . The Van People are fond of plastering their equipment with such goodies as: Danger—I Brake for Animals (apparently on the assumption that the mean old Others are endlessly and maliciously bashing their cars into goats, pigs, elderly St. Bernards, draft horses, mud turtles, and other lowly creatures with which we share this planet). . . .
> —JEAN SHEPHERD, "The Van Culture and the Camper Crowd"

▍2. Quoting poetry

The same general rules apply to quoting poetry as to quoting prose. If the quotation is brief (fewer than four lines), include it within your text, enclosed in double quotation marks. Separate the lines of the poem with slashes, each preceded and followed by a space.

> In one of his best-known poems, Robert Frost remarks, "Two roads diverged in a yellow wood, and I— / I took the one less traveled by / And that has made all the difference."

If the poetic quotation is longer, set it off from the text with double spacing, and indent each line ten spaces from the left margin.

> The duke in Robert Browning's "My Last Duchess" is clearly a jealous, vain person, whose arrogance is illustrated through his statement:
>
> > She thanked men—good! but thanked
> > Somehow—I know not how—as if she ranked
> > My gift of a nine-hundred-years-old name
> > With anybody's gift.

(BACK)GROUNDING

Lewis Thomas offers the following advice for using quotation marks: (1) quote exact words; (2) do not string together thoughts which the author did not intend to be connected; (3) do not use quotation marks to qualify ideas that you would like to disown; (4) do not put them around clichés to avoid your responsibility in using them.

(BACK)GROUNDING

As a general rule, a writer can decide whether or not to use a comma or a colon before a quotation by reading aloud the sentence or passage containing the quotation. If the quotation follows smoothly from the text that precedes it, no comma or colon is necessary. For instance, the quotation in the following sentence needs no comma or colon:

> Mannes argues that television commercials "contribute to the diminution of human worth and the fragmenting of our psyches."

However, if the quotation is not a natural part of the clause or phrase that introduces it, then it should be set off with a comma or colon, as in the following sentence:

> When Ralph Waldo Emerson was asked to take part in directly promoting abolition, he said: "I have my own spirits in prison—spirits in deeper prisons—whom no man visits if I do not."

USEFUL READING

Summey, George, Jr. *American Punctuation.* New York: Ronald, 1949. See Chapter 9, which discusses quotations from a number of helpful perspectives, including rhetorical considerations, when to omit quotations, and how to interrupt and resume quotations.

Thomas, Lewis. "Notes on Punctuation." *New England Journal of Medicine* 296 (1977): 1103–1105.

When you quote poetry, take care to follow the indentation, spacing, capitalization, punctuation, and other features of the original passage.

EXERCISE 31.1

Use quotation marks to enclose direct quotations in the following passage:

After the speaker of the sonnet becomes so depressed that he despises himself, he happens to think of his lover, and his mood suddenly changes. In this transitional section, Shakespeare's main device is the imagery in lines 11 and 12: Like to the lark at break of day arising / From sullen earth, sings hymns at heaven's gate. The image of a lark rising from the earth suggests freedom, joy, and rapture. In addition, the phrase at break of day arising / From sullen earth suggests rebirth or a new beginning.

▎31b. Using quotation marks to signal dialogue

When you write dialogue or quote a conversation, enclose the words of each speaker in quotation marks, and mark each shift in speaker by beginning a new paragraph, no matter how brief the quoted remark may be.

"But I can see you're bound to come," said his father. "Only we ain't going to catch us no fish, because there ain't no water left to catch 'em in."

"The river!"

"All but dry."

"You been many times already?"

"Son, this is my first time this year."

—EUDORA WELTY, "Ladies in Spring"

Beginning a new paragraph with each change in speaker helps readers follow the dialogue. In the example above, we know when the father is speaking and when the son is speaking without the author's having to repeat "said his father" and so on.

▎31c. Using quotation marks to signal titles and definitions

Quotation marks are used to enclose the titles of short poems, short stories, articles, essays, songs, sections of books, and episodes of television and radio programs.

ANSWER TO EXERCISE 31.1

After the speaker of the sonnet becomes so depressed that he despises himself, he happens to think of his lover, and his mood suddenly changes. In this transitional section, Shakespeare's main device is the imagery in lines 11 and 12: "Like to the lark at break of day arising / From sullen earth, sings hymns at heaven's gate." The image of a lark rising from the earth suggests freedom, joy, and rapture. In addition, the phrase "at break of day arising / From sullen earth" suggests rebirth or a new beginning.

WRITING TOGETHER

Divide the class into groups of three. Using one of the following sentences as an opener, have two of each group take on the roles involved and produce a dialogue. The third person of the group records the dialogue, and together afterwards, they decide on how it should be punctuated.

1. One roommate asks the other, "What should we do tonight?"
2. One sibling says to the other, "Oh no you don't."
3. As I turned the corner, I heard someone say "Stop right there."

USEFUL READING

Gowers, Sir Ernest. *The Complete Plain Words*. Rev. ed. Ed. Sir Bruce Fraser. London: Her Majesty's Stationery Office, 1973. Though he aims to correct and prescribe, Gowers argues sensibly on matters of quotations (as well as other marks of punctuation).

TO SIGNAL IRONY AND COINAGES

Matthew Arnold moves from calmness to sadness in "Dover Beach." [poem]

Woodberry uses "The Devil in Manuscript" to show that Hawthorne's writing reflects his life. [short story]

In "Don't Pay the Language No Mind, Honey," William Grieder uses informal language effectively. [essay]

A recent *Newsweek* article on Pablo Picasso is entitled "Portrait of a Raging Bull." [article]

To distract the children, we began singing "She'll Be Coming 'Round the Mountain" and "The Green Grass Grows All Around." [songs]

Throughout the chapter "Chamber Under the Eaves," Turner implies that Hawthorne's life during this period was one of complete dedication and solitude. [section of book]

In tonight's episode, "Murder Most Foul," Jessica matches wits with a psychopath. [television episode]

Use italics rather than quotation marks for the titles of longer works, such as books and magazines (see 35a).

Definitions of words or phrases are sometimes set off with quotation marks:

The French phrase *idée fixe* means literally "fixed idea."

Oxymoronic means "self-contradictory."

31d. Using quotation marks to signal irony and coinages

One way of showing readers that you are using a word or a phrase ironically is to enclose it in quotation marks.

During that rehearsal, I really was "lucky" enough to break a leg. [The quotation marks around the word *lucky* suggest ironically that the narrator was anything but lucky.]

Quotation marks are also used to enclose words or phrases coined by the writer.

Your whole first paragraph or first page may have to be guillotined in any case after your piece is finished: it is a kind of "forebirth." [The word *forebirth* was coined by the writer.]

—JACQUES BARZUN, "A Writer's Discipline"

TEACHING PRACTICE

In the essay "The Little Store," Eudora Welty uses quotation marks to indicate words having a special emphasis. Ask your students to explain why Welty has enclosed the following phrases in quotation marks:

"The Little Store": the quotation marks indicate that this is a special title or name, just as the narrator herself tells us that "our store had its name."

"played out": the use of quotation marks signals the narrator's awareness that her use of *played out* is idiomatic and that its meaning in this *special* case may not be familiar to all readers.

ANSWERS TO EXERCISE 31.2

1. "Daddy," a poem by Sylvia Plath, describes a young woman's attitude toward her father.
2. In Flannery O'Connor's short story "Revelation," colors symbolize passion, violence, sadness, and even "God."
3. "The little that is known about gorillas certainly makes you want to know a great deal more," writes Alan Moorehead in an essay called "A Most Forgiving Ape."
4. The "fun" of surgery begins before the operation ever takes place.
5. I will evaluate an article entitled "The Graying of the Campuses."
6. "Big Bill," the first section of Dos Passos's *U.S.A.*, opens with a birth.
7. Tolkein refers to this sudden, joyous turn as a "eucatastrophe," a word he invented to mean the consolation of the happy ending.
8. Pink Floyd's song "Time" depicts the growth of technology and its impact on society.
9. My dictionary defines *isolation* as "the quality or state of being alone."
10. This review will examine a TV episode entitled "48 Hours on Gang Street."

TEACHING PRACTICE

H. D. F. Kitto's "The Polis" is an excellent example of the variety of uses of quotation marks. Have your students go through this essay, and identify the various uses. For example, Kitto uses quotation marks to indicate *translations* ("Polis" which translates into "city-state," but really means "a structure that can be called an advanced or a degenerate form of tribalism"); *direct quotations* ("So we read in Thucydides, 'Epidamnus is a polis on the right as you sail into the Ionian gulf.' "); *definitions* ("But the phrase 'avoids the polis' tells us nothing about his domicile; it means that he took no part in public life—"); and terms bearing *special emphasis* ("The word therefore now means 'people' in actual distinction from 'state.' ").

EXERCISE 31.2

Revise each of the following sentences, using quotation marks appropriately to signal titles, definitions, irony, or coinages.

1. Daddy, a poem by Sylvia Plath, describes a young woman's attitude toward her father.
2. In Flannery O'Connor's short story Revelation, colors symbolize passion, violence, sadness, and even God.
3. The little that is known about gorillas certainly makes you want to know a great deal more, writes Alan Moorehead in an essay called A Most Forgiving Ape.
4. The fun of surgery begins before the operation ever takes place.
5. I will evaluate an article entitled The Graying of the Campuses.
6. Big Bill, the first section of Dos Passos's U.S.A., opens with a birth.
7. Tolkien refers to this sudden, joyous turn as a eucatastrophe, a word he invented to mean the consolation of the happy ending.
8. Pink Floyd's song Time depicts the impact of technology on society.
9. My dictionary defines *isolation* as the quality or state of being alone.
10. This review will examine a TV episode entitled 48 Hours on Gang Street.

■ 31e. Checking for misused quotation marks

Use quotation marks only when there is a reason for them; do not use them just to emphasize particular words or phrases, as in the following sentence:

MISUSED   "Some of the boys," not including Travis, of course, would take "stingers" off wasps and bees and then put the insects "down" others' shirts.

REVISED   Some of the boys, not including Travis, of course, would take stingers off wasps and bees and then put the insects down others' shirts.

Do not use quotation marks around slang or colloquial language that you think is inappropriate for formal register (see 26c3); they create the impression that you are apologizing for using such language. In general, try to express your idea in formal language. If you have a good reason to use a slang or colloquial term, use it without quotation marks.

MISUSED   After their twenty-mile hike, the campers were "wiped out" and ready to "hit the sack."

REVISED   After their twenty-mile hike, the campers were exhausted and ready to go to bed.

WITH OTHER PUNCTUATION 31f

Even though you enclose many titles in quotation marks to refer to them in writing, do not use them with the titles of your own essays.

EXERCISE 31.3

According to Lewis Thomas, "The most objectionable misuse of quotation marks, but one which illustrates the dangers of misuse in ordinary prose, is seen in advertising." What is the effect of the quotation marks in the following advertisements?

> On a movie marquee: Coming "Attractions"
>
> At a supermarket: "Fresh" Asparagus

31f. Using quotation marks with other punctuation

1. Periods and commas go inside quotation marks.

"Marriage has many pains," wrote Samuel Johnson, "but celibacy has no pleasures."

2. Colons and semicolons go outside quotation marks.

Everything is dark, and "a visionary light settles in her eyes"; this vision, this light, is her salvation.

I felt only one emotion after finishing "Eveline": pity.

3. Question marks, exclamation points, and dashes go inside quotation marks if they are part of the quotation.

PART OF QUOTATION

Gently shake the injured person while asking, "Are you all right?"

"Jump!" one of the firefighters shouted.

"Watch out—watch out for—" Jessica began nervously.

NOT PART OF QUOTATION

Is Hawthorne expressing his subconscious thoughts in "My Kinsman, Major Molineaux"?

What a shame that Scott Joplin did not live to see the popularity of his "Maple Leaf Rag"!

"Break a leg"—that phrase is supposed to bring good luck to a performer.

ANSWER TO EXERCISE 31.3

These quotation marks tend to strike the observer as odd and unnecessary. They may even suggest unintended irony: "Coming 'Attractions' " that are not really attractive; " 'Fresh' Asparagus" that is not really fresh.

WRITING TOGETHER

Divide the class into groups of three, and ask each group to compose a one- or two-page passage that includes as many of the following as possible: direct quotations, quotations within quotations, dialogue, titles, definitions, and special emphasis words or phrases. Then ask the group to remove the quotation marks and exchange the passage with another group for revision.

WRITERS ON WRITING

Sir Ernest Gowers offers this advice on the overuse of quotation marks to indicate the irregular use of terms: "If the word is the right one, do not be ashamed of it: if it is the wrong one, do not use it."

| 4. Footnote numbers go outside quotation marks.

Tragedy is defined by Aristotle as "an imitation of an action that is serious and of a certain magnitude."[1]

For more information on footnotes and for examples of quotation marks used with bibliographical references, see Chapter 41.

ANSWERS TO EXERCISE 31.4 (WILL VARY)

1. The grandmother in O'Connor's story shows she is still misguided when she says, "You've got good blood! I know you wouldn't shoot a lady!"
2. What is Hawthorne telling the readers in "Rappaccini's Daughter"?
3. You could hear the elation in her voice when she said, "We did it."
4. This "typical American" is Ruby Turpin, who in the course of the story receives a message that brings about a change in her life.
5. Being overweight is a big problem because excess weight is hard to lose and can be dangerous to a person's health.
6. One of Jackson's least-known stories is "Janice"; this story, like many of her others, leaves the reader shocked.
7. Macbeth murders Duncan to gain the throne for himself.
8. In his article, "How the Freeze Movement Was Born," Michael Kazin states that a freeze's "bilateral nature nullifies fears of a Soviet advantage."[1]
9. "Know thyself"—this is the quest of the main characters in both Ibsen's *Peer Gynt* and Lewis's *Till We Have Faces.*
10. One thought flashed through my mind as I finished *In Search of Our Mothers' Garden:* "I want to read more of this writer's work."

EXERCISE 31.4

Revise each of the following sentences, deleting quotation marks used inappropriately, moving those placed incorrectly, and using more formal language in place of slang expressions in quotation marks.

Example

In Herman Melville's "Bartleby the Scrivener", Bartleby states time and again, "I would prefer not to".

In Herman Melville's "Bartleby the Scrivener," Bartleby states time and again, "I would prefer not to."

1. The grandmother in O'Connor's story shows she is still misguided when she says, "You've got good blood! I know you wouldn't shoot a lady"!
2. What is Hawthorne telling the readers in "Rappaccini's Daughter?"
3. You could hear the elation in her voice when she said, "We did it".
4. This "typical American" is Ruby Turpin, who in the course of the story receives a "message" that brings about a "change" in her life.
5. Being overweight is a "big" problem because "excess" weight is hard to lose and can be dangerous to a person's health.
6. One of Jackson's least-known stories is "Janice;" this story, like many of her others, leaves the reader shocked.
7. Macbeth "bumps off" Duncan to gain the throne for himself.
8. In his article "How the Freeze Movement Was Born", Michael Kazin states that a freeze's "bilateral nature nullifies fears of a Soviet advantage[1]."
9. "Know thyself—" this is the quest of the main characters in both Ibsen's *Peer Gynt* and Lewis's *Till We Have Faces.*
10. One thought flashed through my mind as I finished "*In Search of Our Mothers' Gardens:*" I want to read more of this writer's work.

READING WITH AN EYE FOR QUOTATION MARKS

Read the following passage from an essay by Joan Didion about the painter Georgia O'Keeffe, paying particular attention to the use of quotation marks. What effect is created by Didion's use of quotation marks around the words *Hardness, crustiness,* and *crusty?* How do the quotations by O'Keeffe help to support Didion's description of her?

"Hardness" has not been in our century a quality much admired in women, nor in the past twenty years has it even been in official favor for men. When hardness surfaces in the very old we tend to transform it into "crustiness" or eccentricity, some tonic pepperiness to be indulged at a distance. On the evidence of her work and what she has said about it, Georgia O'Keeffe is neither "crusty" nor eccentric. She is simply hard, a straight shooter, a woman clean of received wisdom and open to what she sees. This is a woman who could early on dismiss most of her contemporaries as "dreamy," and would later single out one she liked as "a very poor painter." (And then add, apparently by way of softening the judgment: "I guess he wasn't a painter at all. He had no courage and I believe that to create one's own world in any of the arts takes courage.") This is a woman who in 1939 could advise her admirers that they were missing her point, that their appreciation of her famous flowers was merely sentimental. "When I paint a red hill," she observed coolly in the catalogue for an exhibition that year, "you say it is too bad that I don't always paint flowers. A flower touches almost everyone's heart. A red hill doesn't touch everyone's heart."   —JOAN DIDION, "Georgia O'Keeffe"

FOR USING QUOTATION MARKS IN YOUR OWN WRITING

Choose a topic that is currently of interest to students on your campus, and interview one of your friends about it for ten or fifteen minutes. On the basis of your notes from the interview, write two or three paragraphs about your friend's views on the topic, using as many direct quotations as possible. Then look at what you have written to see how closely you followed the conventions for quotation marks that have been explained in this chapter.

TEACHING PRACTICE

Ask students to bring their interviews to class. Then ask them to work in pairs, trading interviews and reading them with special attention to use of quotation marks. Are they used accurately throughout? Are any uses of quotation marks confusing or unclear? What suggestions could they give each other for revision?

32. Using Other Punctuation Marks

(BACK)GROUNDING

Parentheses, brackets, dashes, and slashes developed well after the technology of the written word first appeared, but the colon was one of the first punctuation marks used. Since most discourse was oral rather than written, punctuation evolved to mark places where speakers paused or breathed rather than grammatical units. The first system of punctuation, created by Aristophanes in the second century B.C., used only three marks: the period, colon, and comma. Six centuries later, St. Jerome (A.D. 400) punctuated his translation of the Vulgate Bible using a rhetorical system of colons and commas to mark breathing points. The elocutionary nature of punctuation developed further during the tenth to thirteenth centuries with the addition of marks to denote places where the speakers should raise their voices (the *punctus elevatus*, *punctus interrogativus*, and *punctus circumflexus*) and confirmed the use of the colon as a breathing stop, particularly between verses of the Psalms. However, over time, written discourse becoming less connected to oral discourse, especially after the invention of printing, punctuation began to take on more rhetorical or grammatical functions. Parentheses, brackets, dashes, and slashes function primarily to indicate grammatical divisions. Parentheses began to appear around 1500, and dashes by 1700, but the slash (also called a virgule or solidus) has been with us a little longer. Virgules first appeared in the thirteenth and fourteenth centuries as a form of light stop; after about 1450 the virgule, which was originally placed high, began to appear on the base line and developed a curve. Today we know this mark as a comma.

Parentheses, brackets, dashes, colons, slashes, and ellipses are marks that allow writers to punctuate sentences so that readers can best understand their meaning. Following is a sentence that demonstrates the use of all these punctuation marks.

> Likewise, "hassling"—mock dogfighting—was strictly forbidden, and so naturally young fighter jocks could hardly wait to go up in, say, a pair of F-100s and start the duel by making a pass at each other at 800 miles an hour, the winner being the pilot who could slip in behind the other one and get locked in on his [never *her* or *his or her!*] tail ("wax his tail"), and it was not uncommon for some eager jock to try too tight an outside turn and have his engine flame out, whereupon, unable to restart it, he has to eject . . . and he shakes his fist at the victor as he floats down by parachute and his million-dollar aircraft goes *kaboom!* on the palmetto grass or the desert floor, and he starts thinking about how he can get together with the other guy back at the base in time for the two of them to get their stories straight before the investigation: "I don't know what happened, sir. I was pulling up after a target run, and it just flamed out on me."   —TOM WOLFE, *The Right Stuff*

Here Wolfe uses dashes, parentheses, ellipses, slashes, and colons to create rhythm and build momentum in a very long (178-word) sentence that starts with a definition of *hassling* set off by dashes and builds to the pilot's less-than-truthful "story" after the colon: "I don't know what happened, sir." The editorial comment inserted in brackets calls attention to the fact that the "right stuff" is, in the world Wolfe describes, always male. This chapter will guide you in deciding when you can

470

USEFUL READING

The New Encyclopaedia Britannica Macropaedia. Vol. 15. Chicago: Encyclopaedia Britannica, 1975. See the entry under "punctuation," pp. 274–277, for a discussion of the history of punctuation.

Fowler, H. W. A *Dictionary of Modern English Usage.* 2nd ed. Rev. and ed. Sir Ernest Gowers. New York: Oxford UP, 1965. See the entry "stops," pp. 586–592, for a concise description of the uses of each major punctuation mark.

USING PARENTHESES

use these marks of punctuation to signal relationships among sentence parts, to create particular rhythms, and to help readers follow your thoughts.

▌ 32a. Using parentheses

Parentheses can be used to add information that is of minor or secondary importance—information that clarifies, comments on, or illustrates what precedes it. Parentheses are also used around numbers or letters that precede items in a list.

Adding information

Once a star of the Green Bay Packers, Jerry Kramer is an oil and energy executive whose transition from sports to business was made smoother by several best-selling books (*Instant Replay* and more recently *Distant Replay*) about his old team.

Normal children do not confuse reality and fantasy—they confuse them much less often than we adults do (as a certain great fantasist pointed out in a story called "The Emperor's New Clothes").
    —URSULA LEGUIN, "Why Are Americans Afraid of Dragons?"

Boxing is a purely masculine world. (Though there are female boxers—the most famous is the black champion Lady Tyger Trimiar with her shaved head and tiger-striped attire—women's role in the sport is extremely marginal.)   —JOYCE CAROL OATES, "On Boxing"

As the second and third examples above demonstrate, a period may be placed either inside or outside a closing parenthesis, depending on whether the material inside the parentheses is a complete sentence. A comma, on the other hand, is always placed *outside* a closing parenthesis (and never before an opening one).

Gene Tunney's single defeat in an eleven-year career was to a flamboyant and dangerous fighter named Harry Greb ("The Human Windmill"), who seems to have been, judging from boxing literature, the dirtiest fighter in history.   —JOYCE CAROL OATES, "On Boxing"

If the material in parentheses is a question or an exclamation, use a question mark or exclamation mark inside the closing parenthesis.

Our laughing (so deep was the pleasure!) became screaming.
    —RICHARD RODRIGUEZ, "Aria: A Memoir of a Bilingual Childhood"

TEACHING PRACTICE

The term *parentheses* derives from the classical Greek figure of speech *parenthesis*, which denotes the act of inserting a verbal unit (a word, phrase, or sentence) into a position that interrupts the sentence flow. Such material can be punctuated with dashes or commas as well as with parentheses.

The Chicago Manual of Style draws the following distinction between when writers should choose to use parentheses rather than commas or dashes:

Parentheses, like commas or dashes, may be used to set off amplifying, explanatory, or digressive elements. If such parenthetical elements retain a close logical relationship to the rest of the sentence, commas should be used. If the logical relationship is more remote, dashes or parentheses should be used. (153)

WRITERS ON WRITING

A parenthesis is a convenient device, but a writer indulges his own convenience at the expense of his readers' if his parenthesis is so long that a reader, when he comes to the end of it, has little chance of remembering where he was when it began.

—H. W. FOWLER

The created world is but a small parenthesis in eternity.

—SIR THOMAS BROWNE

for life's not a paragraph
and death i think is no parenthesis.

—E. E. CUMMINGS

USEFUL READING

The Chicago Manual of Style. 13th ed. Chicago: U of Chicago P, 1982. See Chapter Five, "Punctuation," which discuss colons, dashes, parentheses, brackets, and hyphens.

Evans, Bergen, and Cornelia Evans. A *Dictionary of Contemporary Usage.* New York: Random, 1957. For a concise list of the uses of colons, see "colon," p. 100.

WRITERS ON WRITING

A long, long time ago, in another century—1951, in fact—when you, dear younger readers, were most likely still in your nuclear-family playpen (where, if female, you cuddled a rag-baby to your potential titties, or, if male, let down virile drool over your plastic bulldozer), The Famous Critic [Lionel Trilling] told me never, never to use a parenthesis in the very first sentence.

—CYNTHIA OZICK

As a writer, you can punctuate supplemental information in three ways: with commas, with parentheses, or with dashes. The distinction is partially one of how interruptive the information is and partially one of personal style. In general, use commas when the material is least interruptive (see 27c and f), parentheses when it is more interruptive, and dashes when it is the most interruptive (see 32c). One other consideration is whether the material to be added ends in an exclamation point or question mark (as does the preceding Rodriguez example); if so, you can use *only* parentheses or dashes.

Use parentheses judiciously, because they break up the flow of a sentence or passage, forcing readers to hold the original train of thought in their minds while considering a secondary one. To decide whether to use parentheses, read the sentence or passage aloud, or have someone read it aloud to you. Decide whether the parentheses make it harder to follow; if so, try to revise to eliminate them.

Enclosing numbers or letters in a list

Five distinct styles can be distinguished: (1) Old New England, (2) Deep South, (3) Middle American, (4) Wild West and (5) Far West or Californian.   –ALISON LURIE, *The Language of Clothes*

We then settled down, coming to rest on the presumption that: (a) someone connected with the management of the theatre must soon notice the blur and make the connection; or (b) that someone seated near the rear of the house would make the complaint in behalf of those of us up front; or (c) that—any minute now—the entire house would explode into catcalls and foot stamping, calling dramatic attention to the irksome distortion.

–WILLIAM F. BUCKLEY, JR., "Why Don't We Complain?"

(BACK)GROUNDING

Brackets have a purely rhetorical or grammatical function. They are notoriously modern-looking, too, and they rarely show up outside of formal, usually academic, discourse. For that matter, they are rare in any writing. They occur much more often in mathematical formulas then they do in discourse.

▌ 32b. Using brackets

Brackets are used to set off parenthetical elements in material within parentheses and to set off explanatory words or comments inserted into a quotation. If your typewriter does not include keys for brackets, draw them in by hand.

Setting off material within parentheses

Eventually the investigation had to examine the major agencies (including the previously sacrosanct National Security Agency [NSA]) that were conducting covert operations.

USING BRACKETS [ ]32b

Adding material to quotations

In the following sentence, the bracketed word replaces the word *he* in the original quotation.

> Turner writes, "[Hawthorne] is known as Oberon and has shown himself closely akin to the Oberon in 'The Devil in Manuscript.' "

In the following sentence, the bracketed material explains what the *that* in the quotation refers to.

> In defending his station's inferior children's programs, a network executive states, "If we were to do that [supply quality programs in the afternoon, one of the demands of ACT], a lot of people might say: 'How dare they lock the kids up for another two and a half hours.' "
> –MARIE WINN, *The Plug-In Drug: Television, Children, and the Family*

In the quotation in the following sentence, the artist Gauguin's name is misspelled. The bracketed word *sic*, which means "thus," tells readers that the person being quoted made the mistake—not the writer.

> One admirer wrote, "She was the most striking woman I'd ever seen— a sort of wonderful combination of Mia Farrow and one of Gaugin's [sic] Polynesian nymphs."

EXERCISE 32.1

Revise the following sentences, using parentheses and brackets correctly.

> *Example*
> She was in fourth grade or was it third? when she decided to become a writer.
> She was in fourth grade (or was it third?) when she decided to become a writer.

1. One incident of cruelty was brought to public attention by the Animal Liberation Front ALF.
2. During my research, I found that a flat-rate income tax a single-rate tax with no deductions has its problems.
3. Nixon mentions his family early in the speech, saying he "would have preferred to carry it the presidency through to the finish whatever the personal agony it would have involved."
4. Many researchers used the Massachusetts Multiphasic Personal Inventory the MMPI for hypnotizability studies.
5. Some of the alternatives suggested include 1 tissue cultures, 2 mechanical models, 3 *in vitro* techniques, and 4 mathematical and electrical models.

WRITERS ON WRITING

Brackets need not detain us long; their use is almost self-evident and should need but little illustration. They introduce into a context something that has a bearing upon it in a purely subordinate way, and their effect is to keep the words that they enclose "out of the light," as it were, so that the words that precede and follow them may run on with the least possible interruption.

—G. V. CAREY

ANSWERS TO EXERCISE 32.1

1. One incident of cruelty was brought to public attention by the Animal Liberation Front (ALF).
2. During my research, I found that a flat-rate income tax (a single-rate tax rate with no deductions) has its problems.
3. Nixon mentions his family early in the speech, saying he "would have preferred to carry it [the presidency] through to the finish, whatever the personal agony it would have involved."
4. Many researchers used the Massachusetts Multiphasic Personal Inventory (MMPI) for hypnotizability studies.
5. Some of the alternatives suggested include (1) tissue cultures, (2) mechanical models, (3) *in vitro* techniques and (4) mathematical and electrical models.

(BACK)GROUNDING

There are actually different kinds of dashes: *em* dashes, 2- and 3-*em* dashes and *en* dashes. When writers refer to *the dash*, they mean the most common kind of dash, the *em* dash (in typing, the *em* dash is represented as two hyphens with no space before or after). *Em* dashes usually indicate sudden breaks in the normal word order of a sentence and changes in thought or tone.

Two em dashes indicate letters have been left out in a word, such as in the following lines from John Dryden's satire of Thomas Shadwell in "Mac-Flecknoe":

"Much Heywood, Shirly, Ogleby there lay,
But loads of Sh—— almost choakt the way,"

Three em dashes indicate where a word has been left out altogether, as in the following line from Jonathan Swift's "On Poetry: A Rhapsody":

O, what Indignity and Shame
To prostitute the Muse's Name,
By flatt'ring————whom Heaven design'd
The Plague and Scourges of Mankind.

The *en* dash is a printer's convention used in published works to signal consecutive numbers (23–33) or dates (1988–1989) and to join compound adjectives if one element of the compound adjective is already hyphenated: *post–Carter administration procedure*. In typewritten material, a hyphen serves these purposes.

WRITERS ON WRITING

The dash is a handy device, informal and essentially playful, telling you that you're about to take off on a different tack but still in some way connected to the present course—only you have to remember that the dash is there, and either put in a second dash at the end of the notion to let the reader know that he's back on course, or else end the sentence, as here, with a period.

—LEWIS THOMAS

32c. Using dashes

Pairs of dashes allow you to interrupt the normal word order of a sentence to insert additional explanation or information. Compared with parentheses or commas, dashes bring special emphasis to the added material.

Interrupting the normal word order

The pleasures of reading itself—who doesn't remember?—were like those of Christmas cake, a sweet devouring.

–EUDORA WELTY, "A Sweet Devouring"

Emphasizing parenthetical or explanatory elements

Mr. Angell is addicted to dashes and parentheses—small pauses or digressions in a narrative like those moments when the umpire dusts off home plate or a pitcher rubs up a new ball—that serve to slow an already deliberate movement almost to a standstill.

–JOEL CONARROE, *New York Times Book Review*

Single dashes are used to mark a sudden shift in tone, to introduce a summary or explanation of what has come before, or to indicate hesitation in speech.

Emphasizing a sudden change in tone

Under democracy, one party always devotes its chief efforts to trying to prove that the other is unfit to rule—and both commonly succeed and are right. –H. L. MENCKEN, "Minority Report"

If you are truly serious about preparing your child for the future, don't teach him to subtract—teach him to deduct.

–FRAN LEBOWITZ, "Parental Guidance"

Introducing a summary or explanation

In walking, the average adult person employs a motor mechanism that weighs about eighty pounds—sixty pounds of muscle and twenty pounds of bone. –EDWARD WAY TEALE

Indicating hesitation or awkwardness in speech

As the officer approached his car, the driver stammered, "What—what have I done?"

The difference between a single dash and a colon is a subtle one. In general, dashes are much less formal than colons. In fact, you should use dashes sparingly, if at all, in most of your college writing.

EXERCISE 32.2

Punctuate the following sentences with dashes where appropriate.

Example

He is quick, violent, and mean they don't call him "Dirty Harry" for nothing but appealing nonetheless.

He is quick, violent, and mean—they don't call him "Dirty Harry" for nothing—but appealing nonetheless.

1. Union Carbide's plant in Bhopal, India, sprang a leak a leak that killed over 2,500 people and injured 150,000 more.
2. Even if smoking is harmful and there is no real proof of this assertion it is unjust to outlaw smoking while other harmful substances remain legal.
3. I recall thinking to myself, "I'm going I'm going to oh, I don't know!"
4. Many people would have ignored the children's taunts but not Ace.
5. On the morning of April 30, 1975, the remaining American military personnel in South Vietnam the eleven Marines who guarded the American embassy were finally evacuated.

32d. Using colons

Colons are used to introduce a sentence that is an explanation, example, or appositive of what precedes it; to introduce a series, list, or quotation; and to separate elements such as hours, minutes, and seconds; biblical chapter numbers; titles and subtitles; and parts of bibliographical references.

Introducing an explanation, example, or appositive

And we are all on our own when it comes to keeping those lines open to ourselves: your notebook will never help me, nor mine you.
—JOAN DIDION, "On Keeping a Notebook"

The men may also wear the getup known as Sun Belt Cool: a pale beige suit, open collared shirt (often in a darker shade than the suit), cream-colored loafers and aviator sunglasses.
—ALISON LURIE, *The Language of Clothes*

Introducing a series, list, or quotation

As the name implies, this stretch of the river was in fact so easy and gentle that the trip could be and was made by all sorts of amateurs: by Boy Scouts, Camp Fire Girls, stenographers, school teachers, students, little old ladies in inner tubes.
—EDWARD ABBEY, "The Damnation of a Canyon"

ANSWERS TO EXERCISE 32.2

1. Union Carbide's plant in Bhopal, India, sprang a leak—a leak that killed over 2,500 people and injured 150,000 more.
2. Even if smoking is harmful—and there is no real proof of this assertion—it is unjust to outlaw smoking while other harmful substances remain legal.
3. I recall thinking to myself—"I'm going—I'm going to—oh, I don't know!"
4. Many people would have ignored the children's taunts—but not Ace.
5. On the morning of April 30, 1975, the remaining military personnel in South Vietnam—the eleven Marines who guarded the American embassy—were finally evacuated.

(BACK)GROUNDING

In Greek, the word *colon* denoted a unit of prose with certain rhythmical qualities, linking it to oral delivery. But today, colons function primarily to indicate a kind of grammatical equality or identification between the material located on one side of it and that on the other side of it. One of the benefits of the colon is the leisure it allows the writer to explain without having to write full sentences.

OPTIONAL EXERCISE

Present these sentences to the class to rewrite without using colons. Note that they may have to divide them into multiple sentences.

1. Here is a case in point: the material on this side of the colon is a full sentence.
2. In order to change a tire, you need the following: an inflated spare tire, a lug wrench, and something to pry the hub caps loose.

WRITERS WRITING

For Jack Kerouac, periods, commas, and colons are false and timid, used by people who write artificial, conscious art. Kerouac advocates *"no revisions"* while in the act of writing, although he does note that changes can be made in the act of *"inserting."* Kerouac's point here is similar to Peter Elbow's in *Writing without Teachers:* defeat writer's block by suppressing the urge to edit while composing. Kerouac uses the metaphor of the jazz musician:

> No periods separating sentence-structures already arbitrarily riddled by false colons and timid usually needless commas—but the vigorous space dash separating rhetorical breathing (as jazz musician drawing breath between outblown phrases)—"measured pauses which are the essentials of speech"—"divisions of the *sounds* we hear"—"time and how to note it down." [the quotations are taken from William Carlos Williams]

We began a series of workshops on nonviolence, and we repeatedly asked ourselves: "Are you able to accept blows without retaliation?"
    –MARTIN LUTHER KING, JR., "Letter from Birmingham Jail"

Separating elements according to standard use

HOURS, MINUTES, AND SECONDS

4:59 P.M.
2:15:06

BIBLICAL CHAPTERS AND VERSES

Deuteronomy 17:2–7

I Chronicles 3:3–5

TITLES AND SUBTITLES

"Grant and Lee: A Study in Contrasts"

Nuclear War: The Facts of Our Survival

PARTS OF BIBLIOGRAPHICAL REFERENCES

New York: St. Martin's Press [The colon separates the place of publication from the publisher.]

Newsweek, November 5, 1978: 53 [The colon separates the year from the page number.]

Checking for incorrect colons

Except when it is used to separate the standard elements discussed in the preceding section, a colon should be used only at the end of an independent clause.

Do not put a colon between verb and object or complement, or between preposition and object. Avoid putting colons after such expressions as *such as, especially,* or *including.*

MISUSED	Some of these effects include: reddening of the eyes, an increase in heartbeat, dryness of the mouth, and irritation of the throat.
REVISED	Some of these effects include reddening of the eyes, an increase in heartbeat, dryness of the mouth, and irritation of the throat.
MISUSED	The artificial heart can cause complications, especially: blood clots, brain seizures, and strokes.
REVISED	The artificial heart can cause complications, especially blood clots, brain seizures, and strokes.

MISUSED	Every year, in the name of science, thousands of animals are exposed to: severe pain, physical and behavioral stress, extreme heat and cold, electric shock, starvation, and mutilation.
REVISED	Every year, in the name of science, thousands of animals are exposed to severe pain, physical and behavioral stress, extreme heat and cold, electric shock, starvation, and mutilation.
MISUSED	In poetry, additional power may come from devices such as: simile, metaphor, and alliteration.
REVISED	In poetry, additional power may come from devices such as simile, metaphor, and alliteration.

EXERCISE 32.3

Insert a colon in each of the following items that needs one. Some of the items do not require a colon, and one requires two colons.

Example
Canada A Story of Challenge is required reading for the course.
Canada: A Story of Challenge is required reading for the course.

1. The sonnet's structure is effective in revealing the speaker's message love has changed his life and ended his depression.
2. Another example is taken from Psalm 139 16.
3. Nixon claims that throughout the Watergate investigation he believed it was his duty to stay on as president "to make every possible effort to complete the term of office to which you elected me."
4. Layton, Ed. *Martin Luther King The Peaceful Warrior.* 3rd ed. Englewood Cliffs, NJ Prentice-Hall, 1968.
5. Education can alleviate problems such as poverty, poor health, and the energy shortage.
6. Gandhi urged four things tell the truth even in business, adopt more sanitary habits, abolish caste and religious divisions, and learn English.
7. Some of the improvements included the establishment of after-school recreation programs and a consumer cooperative, the opening or expansion of health clinics, and changes in the content of school curricula.
8. *Signs of Trouble and Erosion A Report on Education in America* was submitted to Congress and the president in January 1984.
9. Even more important was what money represented success and prestige.
10. The article in *Time* reported that at 418 p.m. the surgeon, Dr. William DeVries, leaned over the heavily sedated man and said, "Everything went well—perfectly."

ANSWERS TO EXERCISE 32.3

1. The sonnet's structure is effective in revealing the speaker's message: love has changed his life and ended his depression.
2. Another example is taken from Psalm 139: 16.
3. Nixon claims that throughout the Watergate investigation he believed it was his duty to stay on as president: "to make every possible effort to complete the term of office to which you elected me."
4. Layton, Ed. *Martin Luther King: The Peaceful Warrior,* 3rd ed. Englewood Cliffs, NJ: Prentice, 1968.
5. Education can alleviate problems such as poverty, poor health, and the energy shortage.
6. Ghandi urged four things: tell the truth, even in business, adopt more sanitary habits, abolish caste and religious divisions, and learn English.
7. Some of the improvements included the establishment of after-school recreation programs and a consumer cooperative, the opening or expansion of health clinics, and changes in the content of school curricula.
8. *Signs of Trouble and Erosion: A Report on Education in America* was submitted to Congress and the president in January 1984.
9. Even more important was what money represented: success and prestige.
10. The article in *Time* reported that at 4:18 p.m. the surgeon, Dr. William DeVries, leaned over the heavily sedated man and said, "Everything went well—perfectly."

OPTIONAL EXERCISE

Consider reading aloud the following passage by William Caxton (1422–1491). Caxton uses slashes heavily; ask your class to modernize the punctuation of this passage by suggesting marks that could replace the slashes.

And also my lorde abbot of westmynster ded do shewe me late certayn euydences wryton in olde englysshe for to reduce it in to our englysshe nowvsid / And certaynly it was wreton in suche wyse that it was more lyke to duche than englysshe I coude not reduce ne brynge it to be vnderstonden / And certaynly our language now vsed varyeth ferre from that which was vsed and spoken when I was borne / For we englysshe men / ben borne vnder the domynacyon of the mone. whiche is neuer stedfaste / but euer wauerynge / wexynge one season / and waneth & dycreaseth another season / And that comyn englysshe that is spoken in one shyre varyeth from a nother.

(BACK)GROUNDING

Ellipses are also purely rhetorical or grammatical in function. They derive from the classical Greek scheme *ellipsis*, which refers to the omission of a word or of words from a text. Classical rhetoricians had in mind a conscious omission that would be implied by the context:

And he to England shall along with you.

—*HAMLET*

So let the class invent its own assignments. If it wants more sophistication, fine.

—PETER ELBOW

▌ 32e. Using slashes

Slashes are used to mark line divisions in poetry quoted within text (see 31a2), to separate two alternative terms, and to separate the parts of fractions. When used to separate lines of poetry, the slash should be surrounded by space.

Marking line divisions in poetry

In "Sonnet 29," the persona states, "For thy sweet love rememb'red such wealth brings, / That then I scorn to change my state with kings."

Separating alternatives

"I'm not the typical wife/girlfriend of a baseball player—those women you see on TV with their hair done up and their Rose Bowl Parade wave to the crowds."   –ROGER ANGELL, "In the Country"

Separating parts of fractions

Over the last thirty years, the average yield of American farms increased by only 2½ percent.

▌ 32f. Using ellipses

Ellipses are three equally spaced dots used to indicate that something has been omitted from a quoted passage. They can also be used to signal hesitation, in the same way that a dash can (see 32c).

Indicating omissions

Just as you should be very careful to use quotation marks around any material that you quote directly from a source, so you should use an ellipsis to indicate that you have left out part of a quotation that appears to be a complete sentence. Look at the following example:

ORIGINAL TEXT

The quasi-official division of the population into three economic classes called high-, middle-, and low-income groups rather misses the point, because as a class indicator the amount of money is not as important as the source.   –PAUL FUSSELL, "Notes on Class"

WITH ELLIPSES

As Paul Fussell argues, "The quasi-official division of the population into three economic classes . . . rather misses the point. . . ."

USING ELLIPSES

In this example, the ellipses are used to indicate two different omissions—one in the middle of the sentence and one at the end of the sentence. When you omit the last part of a quoted sentence, add a period before the ellipsis—for a total of four dots. Be sure a complete sentence comes before and after the four points. If your quotation ends with a source documentation (such as a page number, a name, or a title), follow these steps:

1. Use three ellipsis points but no period after the quotation.
2. Add the closing quotation mark, closed up to the third ellipsis point.
3. Add the source documentation in parentheses.
4. Use a period to indicate the end of the sentence.

Hawthorne writes, "My friend, whom I shall call Oberon—it was a name of fancy and friendship between him and me . . ." (575).

Indicating a pause or hesitation

What you get is . . . the view from Oswald's rifle.
—Tom Wolfe, "Pornoviolence"

Because of her creativity with her flowers, even my memories of poverty are seen through a screen of blooms—sunflowers, petunias, roses, dahlias, forsythia, spirea, delphiniums, verbena . . . and on and on.
—Alice Walker, *In Search of Our Mothers' Gardens*

EXERCISE 32.4

Complete the following sentence, incorporating only those *parts* of the passage that you need to make a complete grammatical sentence. Use ellipsis points to indicate what you have omitted.

In Mortimer Adler's *How to Read a Book*, he says that . . .

If we consider men and women generally, and apart from their professions or occupations, there is only one situation I can think of in which they almost pull themselves up by their bootstraps, making an effort to read better than they usually do. When they are in love and are reading a love letter, they read for all they are worth. They read every word three ways; they read between the lines and in the margins; they read the whole in terms of the parts, and each part in terms of the whole; they grow sensitive to context and ambiguity, to insinuation and implication; they perceive the color of words, the odor of phrases, and the weight of sentences. They may even take the punctuation into account. Then, if never before or after, they read.
—Mortimer Adler, *How to Read a Book*

ANSWER TO EXERCISE 32.4 (WILL VARY)

In Mortimer Adler's *How to Read a Book*, he says that " . . . there is only one situation . . . in which they [men and women] . . . [make] an effort to read better than they usually do. When they are in love and are reading a love letter, they read for all they are worth. They read every word three ways; they read between the lines and in the margins; they read the whole in terms of the parts, and each part in terms of the whole; they grow sensitive to context and ambiguity, to insinuation and implication; they perceive the color of words, the odor of phrases, and the weight of sentences. They may even take the punctuation into account. Then, if never before or after, they read."

ANSWERS TO EXERCISE 32.5 WILL VARY

(BACK)GROUNDING

Emily Dickinson published very few poems during her lifetime. But privately, she bound her manuscripts into packets or "fascicles," folded sheets of paper sewn together by hand, which gives the impression of being little "books," meant to be read by others. Yet her capitalization and punctuation were very unconventional. Especially curious is her use of dashes as an almost universal punctuation mark, sometimes occurring in places that break up sentences into ungrammatical units.

Until the middle of this century, editors always normalized her mechanics. In 1950, Edith Perry Stamm proposed a theory to explain Dickinson's dashes. She claims that Dickinson's system of dashes indicated various spoken intonations. Most experts discount Stamm's theory, because it seems likely that if Dickinson had wanted to indicate intonation, she would have made her marks clearer to distinguish. On the other hand, she apparently took great care to arrange her poems in a certain order in her fascicles, sometimes rearranging them as she produced new poems. Did she really believe posterity would appreciate her poetry? (If so, why leave it hidden in her desk drawer?) Or were her little "books" simply part of a fantasy life of recognition that included publication and, perhaps, oral readings of her poetry, guided by her system of dashes?

EXERCISE 32.5

The following sentences use the punctuation marks presented in this chapter very effectively. Read the sentences carefully; then choose one, and use it as a model for writing a sentence of your own, making sure to use the punctuation marks in the same way in your sentence.

1. The dad was—how can you put this gracefully?—a real blimp, a wide load, and the white polyester stretch-pants only emphasized the cargo.
   —GARRISON KEILLOR, "Happy to Be Here"

2. I took exercise daily (as I still do), did not smoke (and still don't), and though excessively fond of wine, seldom drank spirits, not much liking the taste of them.   —JAN MORRIS, "To Everest"

3. Not only are the distinctions we draw between male nature and female nature largely arbitrary and often pure superstition: they are completely beside the point.   —BRIGID BROPHY, "Women"

4. One day a man would be ascending the pyramid at a terrific clip, and the next—bingo!—he would reach his own limits in the most unexpected way.
   —TOM WOLFE, The Right Stuff

5. A few traditions, thank heaven, remain fixed in the summer state of things—the June collapse of the Giants, Gaylord Perry throwing (or not throwing) spitballs, Hank Aaron hitting homers, and the commissioner . . . well, commissioning.   —ROGER ANGELL, Five Seasons

READING WITH AN EYE FOR PUNCTUATION

Although Emily Dickinson's poems are characteristically punctuated with dashes, the first editor of her work systematically eliminated them. Here is a brief Dickinson poem—with her original dashes restored. Read it twice, first ignoring the dashes and then using them to guide your reading. What effect does the final dash have? Finally, try composing a four-line poem that uses dashes to guide reading and meaning.

> Much Madness is divinest Sense—
> To a discerning Eye—
> Much Sense—the starkest Madness—
> 'Tis the Majority
> In this, as All, prevail—
> Assent—and you are sane—
> Demur—you're straightway dangerous—
> And handled with a Chain—
> —EMILY DICKINSON

USING ELLIPSES ...32f

FOR EXAMINING PUNCTUATION IN YOUR OWN WRITING

Look through a draft you have recently written or are working on, and check your use of parentheses, brackets, dashes, colons, slashes, and ellipses. Have you followed the conventions presented in this chapter? If not, revise accordingly. Then read through the draft again, looking especially at all the parentheses and dashes. Are there too many? Check the material in parentheses to see if it could use more emphasis and thus be set off instead with dashes. Then check any material in dashes to see if it could do with less emphasis and thus be punctuated with commas or parentheses. If you keep a writing log, enter some examples of this work in your log.

OPTIONAL EXERCISE

Ask students to read some other poems with dashes and to study the effects they bring to the poem. They might even try repunctuating the poem, replacing dashes with colons or parentheses, for instance, to appreciate the difference. You could refer them to Langston Hughes's "Harlem" on page 419; other poems with dashes you might suggest include:

"Birches" and "Mending Wall" by Robert Frost
"The Love Song of J. Alfred Prufrock" by T. S. Eliot
"The Ruined Maid" by Thomas Hardy
"Daddy" by Sylvia Plath

PART SEVEN

Understanding
Mechanical Conventions

33. Using Capitals

AT ONE TIME, ALL LETTERS WERE WRITTEN AS CAPITALS, LIKE THIS. By the time that movable type was invented, a new system had evolved, and printers used a capital letter only for the first letter of any word they felt was particularly important. Today, the conventions of capitalization are fairly well standardized. This chapter presents those conventions.

33a. Using capitals for the first word of a sentence or of a line of poetry

Capitalize the first word of a sentence.

Family photos bring great pleasure.

May I take your picture?

Smile, and say cheese!

If you are quoting a full sentence, set off that sentence, too, with an initial capital letter.

Everyone was asking the question, "What will I do after I graduate?"

Capitalization of a sentence following a colon is optional.

Gould cites the work of Darwin: The [or the] theory of natural selection incorporates the principle of evolutionary ties between all animals.

A sentence that is set off within another sentence by dashes or parentheses should not be capitalized. Note, however, that a sentence within parentheses that stands by itself *is* capitalized.

(BACK)GROUNDING

Originally, a large letter usually marked the beginning of a sentence, and that letter could be either upper- or lowercase (it was simply larger). The *Codex Alexandrinus* (a fifth century copy of the Bible) is one of the first documents that uses large letters to mark off each sentence. A full lowercase set of characters existed as early as A.D. 510, and the mixing of lowercase and uppercase characters developed from this date. By the time printing became established (in the mid-1500s), capital letters always signaled the start of a sentence (as in the Gutenberg Bible), but they were also liberally scattered throughout manuscripts at the printer's discretion. Even the terms *uppercase* and *lowercase* derive from drawers (or cases) that held each font in a printing shop. By the seventeenth century, the use of capital letters had become somewhat standardized (used at the beginning of sentences and for proper names and titles). The *Encyclopaedia Britannica* (1975) notes that standardizing the usage of uppercase and lowercase letters was a crucial development:

> Three of the most important components [of a system of punctuation] are the space left blank between words; the indentation of the first line of a new paragraph; and the uppercase, or capital, letter written at the beginning of a sentence and at the beginning of a proper name or a title.

Today, we take blank (or white) space and paragraph indentation for granted. However, our elaborate conventions for the use of capital letters take more time and effort for students to recognize and adhere to.

485

USEFUL READING

The New Encyclopaedia Britannica Macropaedia. Vol. 15. Chicago: Encyclopaedia Britannica, 1975. See the entry under "punctuation," pp. 274–277.

Thompson, Sir Edward Maunde. *An Introduction to Greek and Latin Paleography*. Oxford: Clarendon, 1912. See Chapter Five for a discussion of punctuation and the facsimiles of Greek and Latin writing throughout.

(BACK)GROUNDING

The use of capitals may seem simply conventional, but the conventions involved have rhetorical functions. George Summey, Jr., lists three general functions of capitalization:

1. "As an aid to clearness." (Capitalizing proper nouns to distinguish them from common nouns and capitalizing the first letter of a sentence aid the *logos* of the writer's work.)
2. "For courtesy or reverence." (Capitalizing names and titles aid the writer's *ethos*.)
3. "For emphasis." (Although generally out of fashion nowadays, capitalizing words such as *Nature* can possibly aid a writer's *logos* or *pathos*.)

Also, despite general agreement on most of the conventions of capitalization, exceptions do exist. For instance, some newspapers, such as the *Milwaukee Journal*, do not capitalize common nouns or adjectives that form parts of proper names. They print *the Thames river*, *Central park*, and *Ohio State university*.

(BACK)GROUNDING

One newspaper style sheet (*The Canadian Press Style Book*) distinguishes between capitalization conventions for proper titles presently held and proper titles that are no longer held. For example, former baseball commissioner Bowie Kuhn doesn't get a capital, but present baseball Commissioner A. Bartlett Giametti does. The same style sheet also points out that capitalization sometimes depends on meaning: *Central Park* is in New York, but a *central park* may designate any park that is easy to get to. The decision to capitalize depends on whether the writer means to designate any park or a specific park.

OPTIONAL EXERCISE

Consider encouraging your students to act as researchers by asking them to bring to class examples of how capitalization rules are used and abused. Direct them to print advertisements, labels on bottles and cans, and billboards for examples, and ask them to determine what they feel are appropriate and inappropriate uses (when capitals *should* be used), and effective and ineffective uses (when capitals help focus attention). Try to direct attention to the context of language use: what may be appropriate in an advertisement may be inappropriate in a formal paper for your class.

Those assigned to transports were not humiliated like washouts—*somebody* had to fly those planes—nevertheless, they, too, had been *left behind* for lack of the right stuff.

It *heaved*, it moved up and down underneath his feet, it pitched up, it pitched down, it rolled to port (this great beast *rolled!*) and it rolled to starboard, as the ship moved into the wind and, therefore, into the waves, and the wind kept sweeping across, sixty feet up in the air out in the open sea, and there were no railings whatsoever.

Or a man could go for a routine physical one fine day, feeling like a million dollars, and be grounded for *fallen arches*. It happened!—just like that! (And try raising them.)

–TOM WOLFE, The Right Stuff

The first word of each line in a poem is also usually capitalized.

> Loveliest of trees, the cherry now
> Is hung with bloom along the bough,
> And stands about the woodland ride
> Wearing white for Eastertide.
> –A. E. HOUSMAN, "Loveliest of Trees"

Some poets do *not* capitalize each line, however. When citing lines from a poem that has unconventional capitalization, copy them exactly as they appear in their original form.

> What was our hurry? Sunday afternoon
> beckoned with radioed ballgames, soft ice cream,
> furtive trips into the country, naps
> for the elderly, daydreams for the young,
> while blind growth steamed to the horizon of hills,
> the Lord ignoring His own injunction to rest.
> –JOHN UPDIKE, "Leaving Church Early"

33b. Using capitals for proper nouns and proper adjectives

Capitalize **proper nouns** (those naming specific persons, places, and things) and **proper adjectives** formed from them. In general, do not capitalize **common nouns** (those naming general classes of people, places, and things) unless they start a sentence. When used as part of a proper noun, however, many common nouns are capitalized.

USEFUL READING

Summey, George, Jr. *Modern Punctuation*. New York: Oxford UP, 1919. pp. 164–166. The author provides a coherent and balanced view of capitalization.

Period Styles: A History of Punctuation. New York: The Herb Lubalin Study Center of Design and Typography in the Cooper Union for the Advancement of Science and Art, 1988. See the first essay, "Period Styles: A Punctuated History."

FOR PROPER NOUNS AND PROPER ADJECTIVES

PROPER	COMMON
Alfred Hitchcock, Hitchcockian	a director, directorial
Brazil, Brazilian	a nation
Golden Gate Bridge	a bridge

Following are some categories of words that are commonly capitalized:

NAMES OF INDIVIDUALS

Martin Luther King, Jr.	Eleanor Roosevelt
Bette Davis	Willie Mays
X. J. Kennedy	Toni Morrison
Aristotelian logic	Petrarchan sonnet form

NAMES OF GEOGRAPHICAL AREAS

Asia	Pacific Ocean
Nepal	Painted Desert
St. Louis	Sugarloaf Mountain
the Dead Sea	Michigan Avenue

STRUCTURES AND MONUMENTS

Flatiron Building	Lincoln Memorial
Golden Gate Bridge	Coit Tower

SHIPS, TRAINS, AIRCRAFT, AND SPACECRAFT

S.S. *Titanic*	Broadway Limited
Spirit of St. Louis	*Pioneer II*

INSTITUTIONS AND ORGANIZATIONS

Library of Congress	Kiwanis Club
University of Oklahoma	United Auto Workers
Skyline High School	Democratic Party

HISTORICAL EVENTS, ERAS, AND CALENDAR ITEMS

Shays' Rebellion	Saturday
the Great Depression	July
Reformation	Memorial Day

(BACK)GROUNDING

The eighteenth century saw a movement to reduce all capitals to lowercase letters. In a letter to his son, dated April 13, 1752, Lord Chesterfield denounced the fashion:

> It offends my eyes to see *rome, france, caesar, henry the fourth,* etc. begin with small letters; and I do not conceive that there can be any reason for doing it half so strong as the reason of long usage to the contrary. This is an affectation of Voltaire.

However, in the first draft of the Declaration of Independence, Thomas Jefferson did not capitalize words that usually received capitalization in the eighteenth century, including *nature, creator,* and even *god.*

TEACHING PRACTICE

The rule concerning capitalizing common nouns may seem simple enough; they are not capitalized except when they form part of a title with proper nouns. However, this exception requires students to distinguish three concepts (titles, common nouns, and proper nouns) and to reverse the standard rule in order to correctly apply the exception. If students have trouble with this rule, make sure that they understand the following:

1. A proper noun signifies a specific person, animal, or thing.
2. A common noun names one of a group or class of things.
3. A title is a name formed by compounding common and proper nouns.

Consider stepping students through the stages outlined above: name a class of things (*river*), and then name a specific member of that group (*Mississippi River*). After a couple of repetitions, ask students to suggest examples and work through them with you.

TEACHING PRACTICE

We might ask our students what the effect of capitalizing a word is: to draw attention to it, to give the term respectability or power, or to recognize the term as a term. The capital letter draws attention to the term and gives it a kind of identity. Point out to your students that capitalization rules, as with most rules of convention, contain within them statements about their culture, and to some extent reflect the culture of the people who observe these rules.

OPTIONAL EXERCISE

Consider distributing examples of prose from an eighteenth century text and a modernized version of the same text. Focus your students' attention on the way uppercase and lowercase letters are used, and discuss the confusion or distractions that arise from texts that do not use capital letters consistently. Jonathan Swift's commonly anthologized "A Modest Proposal" will get discussion started.

RELIGIONS AND RELIGIOUS SUBJECTS

Buddhism, Buddhists	Allah
Catholicism, Catholics	Jesus Christ
Hinduism, Hindus	God
Islam, Moslems or Muslims	the Bible
Judaism, Jews	the Koran

RACES, NATIONALITIES, AND LANGUAGES

Afro-American	Portuguese
Chicano	Chinese
Slavic	Japanese
Arab	Latin

TRADE NAMES

Reeboks	Huggies
Xerox	Levi's
Chanel	Land's End

1. Using capitals for titles of individuals

Capitalize titles used before a proper name, but not those used alone or following a proper name.

Justice O'Connor	Sandra Day O'Connor, the justice
Senator Paul Simon	Paul Simon, the senator
Professor Lisa Ede	Lisa Ede, the professor
Doctor Edward Davies	Edward Davies, the doctor

When they are used without a name attached, most titles are not capitalized. The only exceptions are titles of some very powerful officials—for example, many writers capitalize the word *President* when it refers to the President of the United States.

2. Using capitals for specific academic institutions and courses

Capitalize specific schools, departments, or courses, but not the common nouns or names of general subject areas.

University of California (*but* a California university)
History Department (*but* a history major)
Political Science 10 (*but* political science for nonmajors)

USEFUL READING

Fowler, H. W. *A Dictionary of Modern English Usage*. 2nd ed. Rev. and ed. Sir Ernest Gowers. New York: Oxford UP, 1965. See the entry "capitals," pp. 73–75, for guidelines regarding words that have both restricted and more common meanings (*state* denotes a condition, while *State* signifies the government).

CHECKING FOR UNNECESSARY CAPITALS   cap 33e

33c. Using capitals for titles of works

Capitalize most words in titles of books, articles, stories, essays, plays, poems, documents, films, paintings, and musical compositions. Articles (*a*, *an*, *the*), prepositions, conjunctions, and the *to* of an infinitive are not capitalized unless they are the first or last words in a title or subtitle.

Gone with the Wind	"Fire and Ice"
"Revelation"	Magna Carta
"Shooting an Elephant"	*Dirty Harry*
Our Town	*The Magic Flute*

Remember to capitalize the titles of your own compositions.

33d. Using capitals for the pronoun *I* and the interjection *O*

Always capitalize the pronoun *I* and the interjection *O*. Be careful, however, to distinguish between the interjection *O* and *oh*. *O* is an older form that is usually used for direct address in ceremonial register (see 26c4). It is always capitalized, whereas *oh* is not unless it begins a sentence.

I took her advice, and oh, how I regretted it!

Grant us peace, O Lord.

33e. Checking for unnecessary capitals

1. With compass directions, unless the word designates a specific geographic place

John Muir headed west, filled with the need to explore. The nation was at that time divided into three competing economic sections: the Northeast, the South, and the West.

2. With family relationships, unless the word is used as part of the name or as a substitute for the name

My nieces, Jamie and Marianne, both live in blue jeans.

We all agreed that Father had every right to be grumpy.

The train on which Uncle Charlie arrived spewed out thick black smoke, foreshadowing a disastrous visit.

TEACHING PRACTICE

The Chicago Manual of Style advises writers to "Lowercase articles, coordinate conjunctions, and prepositions, regardless of length, unless they are the first or last words of the title or subtitle" (187). The handbook follows this advice. We recognize and discuss with our students that rules for capitalization (as well as punctuation and mechanics in general) are conventions, agreements between readers and writers. These rules may differ from publisher to publisher, between English and psychology, and from instructor to instructor. Students need to know the conventions they are asked to write in. To work from a position of strength, students should become familiar with the basic rules that have achieved the consensus in Edited American English (the rules summarized in the handbook), and then find out how those rules differ in other disciplines or from one instructor to another.

USEFUL READING

The Chicago Manual of Style. 13th ed. Chicago: U of Chicago P, 1982. See Chapter Seven, "Names and Terms," for a discussion of when to use capital letters; section 7.123 comments on articles in titles.

(BACK)GROUNDING

According to *The Chicago Manual of Style*, acronyms, such as AIDS, are usually capitalized and set without periods between the letters. Scientific terms are not capitalized unless a proper name forms part of the term: *Boyle's law* gets a capital, but *the general theory of relativity* does not. Chemical elements are capitalized when represented by a symbol (*Au*), but not when they are written out (*uranium*).

ANSWERS TO EXERCISE 33.1

1. The town in the South where I was raised had a Civil War monument in the center of Main Street.
2. Eating at a restaurant, whether it be a fast-food, Chinese, or Italian place, is always a treat.
3. His car skidded right into the rear of a Plymouth van.
4. The Council of Trent was convened to draw up the Catholic response to the Protestant Reformation.
5. In the *Odyssey*, three members of Odysseus's crew go ashore and lose their memories by eating the lotus plant.
6. I wondered if my new Lee jeans were faded enough and if I could possibly scuff up my new Nikes just a little more before I arrived for spring term.
7. In a speech accepting an award for the musical score for the film *The High and the Mighty*, Dimitri Tiomkin began by thanking Beethoven, Brahms, Wagner, and Strauss.
8. In this essay I will be citing the works of Vladimir Nabokov, in particular his novels *Pnin* and *Lolita* and his story "The Vane Sisters."
9. The battle of Lexington and Concord was fought in April 1775.
10. Few music lovers can resist the music of George Gershwin. (*Rhapsody in Blue* and *Porgy and Bess* are two personal favorites.)

ANSWERS TO EXERCISE 33.2 WILL VARY

3. With medical and scientific terms, except for proper nouns that are part of the term

scarlet fever   deoxyribonucleic acid
Kaposi's sarcoma   Wassermann test
insectivore   homo sapiens

EXERCISE 33.1

Capitalize words as needed in the following sentences.

> *Example*
>
> t. s. eliot, who wrote *the waste land*, worked as an editor at faber and faber.
>
> T. S. Eliot, who wrote *The Waste Land*, worked as an editor at Faber and Faber.

1. the town in the south where i was raised had a civil war monument in the center of main street.
2. eating at a restaurant, whether it be a fast-food, chinese, or italian place, is always a treat.
3. his car skidded right into the rear end of a plymouth van.
4. the council of trent was convened to draw up the catholic response to the protestant reformation.
5. in the *odyssey*, three members of odysseus's crew go ashore and lose their memories by eating the lotus plant.
6. i wondered if my new lee jeans were faded enough and if i could possibly scuff up my new nikes just a little more before i arrived for spring term.
7. in a speech accepting an award for the musical score for the film the high and the mighty, dimitri tiomkin began by thanking beethoven, brahms, wagner, and strauss.
8. in this essay i will be citing the works of vladimir nabokov, in particular his novels *pnin* and *lolita* and his story "the vane sisters."
9. the battle of lexington and concord was fought in april 1775.
10. few music lovers can resist the music of george gershwin. (*rhapsody in blue* and *porgy and bess* are two personal favorites.)

EXERCISE 33.2

Turn to page 186, and read the poem by E. E. Cummings. Pay particular attention to his use of capitalization: how does it help you to understand the poem?

CHECKING FOR UNNECESSARY CAPITALS   cap 33e

READING WITH AN EYE FOR CAPITALIZATION

The following poem uses capitalization in an unconventional way. Read it over a few times, at least once aloud. What effect does the capitalization have on your understanding and recitation of the poem? Why do you think the poet chose to use capitals as she did?

> A little Madness in the Spring
> Is wholesome even for the King,
> But God be with the Clown—
> Who ponders this tremendous scene—
> This whole Experiment of Green—
> As if it were his own!
> —EMILY DICKINSON

FOR EXAMINING YOUR OWN USE OF CAPITAL LETTERS

Read over something you have written recently with an eye for capitalization. Have you capitalized all proper nouns and adjectives? Have you used capitals properly with dashes and parentheses? Have you capitalized sentences following colons, and if so, have you done so consistently? If you keep a writing log, enter notes and examples of any problems you have with capital letters.

34. Using Abbreviations and Numbers

(BACK)GROUNDING

The controversy over whether to abbreviate or spell out a word can become heated. On the one hand, commentators William and Mary Morris take the conservative approach: "Generally speaking, *abbreviations* are to be avoided in formal writing . . ." (2). On the other hand, commentators like Rudolf Flesch take a different view: "It's a superstition that abbreviations shouldn't be used in serious writing and that it's good style to spell everything out. Nonsense: use abbreviations whenever they are customary and won't attract the attention of the reader" (3).

Flesch's statement points to an important aspect of abbreviation usage: choosing whether to use abbreviations or spell out the words is a rhetorical decision. As the authors of *Words into Type* note, "An abbreviation that can be used in certain branches of writing might be poor form in others" (100). For instance, *vs.* for *versus* is acceptable in legal writing, but not in most other formal writing. The writer must once again recognize and evaluate her or his audience.

One important rule of thumb, however, does apply across all disciplines: when in doubt, spell it out.

In his essays and by the example of his life, Henry David Thoreau urged us to "simplify, simplify." Two of the tools that help us as writers to reach that goal are abbreviations and numerals. Both serve to speed up prose and thus to allow readers to process information most efficiently. As with other elements, there are certain conventions for using abbreviations and numerals, especially in formal or academic work. This chapter will explain these conventions to help you as a writer use abbreviations and numbers appropriately and correctly.*

ABBREVIATIONS

▮ 34a. Abbreviating personal and professional titles

When they are used before or after a name, most personal and professional titles and academic degrees are regularly abbreviated, even in academic writing.

Ms. Gloria Steinem	St. Matthew
Mr. Richard Guenette	Paul Irvin, M.D.
Dr. Nancy Carlman	Jamie Barlow Kayes, Ph.D.

---

*For rules on using abbreviations and numbers in a particular discipline, you might ask your instructor what style manual you should consult. In general, the *MLA Handbook for Writers of Research Papers* is usually followed in the humanities; the *Publication Manual of the American Psychological Association*, in the social sciences; and the *CBE Style Manual*, in the natural sciences.

492

USEFUL READING

Flesch, Rudolf. *The ABC of Style: A Guide to Plain English*. New York: Harper, 1964. This alphabetically arranged book provides entertaining, if sometimes idiosyncratic, discussions of many aspects of style, including abbreviations and numbers.

Morris, William and Mary. *Harper Dictionary of Contemporary Usage*. New York: Harper, 1975. This usage guide differs somewhat from others by relying on a panel of writers to discuss problems of usage.

Less common titles, including religious, military, academic, and government titles, may be abbreviated when they appear before a full name. If they appear before only a surname, the title should be spelled out. In academic writing, such titles should always be spelled out.

Rev. Jesse Jackson	the Reverend Jesse Jackson
Col. Oliver Wickham	Colonel Wickham
Prof. Linda Johnson	Professor Johnson
Sen. Nancy Kassebaum	Senator Kassebaum

Never abbreviate personal or professional titles used alone.

MISUSED   She was a rigorous *prof.*, and we worked hard.

REVISED   She was a rigorous *professor*, and we worked hard.

Use either a title or an academic degree, but not both.

MISUSED   Dr. James Dillon, Ph.D.

REVISED   Dr. James Dillon

REVISED   James Dillon, Ph.D.

▌ 34b. Using abbreviations with numerals

The following abbreviations are always acceptable, as long as they are used with numerals.

399 B.C. ("before Christ"; follows the date)

A.D. 49 (*anno Domini*, Latin for "year of our Lord"; precedes the date)

11:15 A.M. (*ante meridiem*, Latin for "before noon")

9:00 P.M. (*post meridiem*, Latin for "after noon")

2700 r.p.m. (revolutions per minute)

212°F (Fahrenheit scale)

24°C (Centigrade or Celsius scale)

Abbreviations for some units of measurement (*km, cc, lb., qts.*) are frequently used in scientific and technical writing—but again, only with a numeral (see 34d).

▌ 34c. Using acronyms and initial abbreviations

Abbreviations that can be pronounced as words are called **acronyms**: NOW, for example, is the acronym for the National Organi-

WRITERS ON WRITING

Life, they [abbreviations] say, is short and the pace is quick; brevity, therefore, is not only the soul of wit, but the essence of business capacity as well. This trait of the American character is discernible in every department of the national life and thought. . . .

—JOHN S. FARMER

WRITERS WRITING

Most of us don't always remember that while B.C. follows a date, A.D. precedes it. Even columnist and conservative grammarian William Safire admits an infamous mistake regarding the use of A.D. As a speechwriter at the White House, he approved of the wording of the plaque left on the moon by the first American astronauts to land there. It reads, "July 1969, A.D." Safire expresses the wish that "some descendant of mine will take a sharp stylus on some weekend rocket to the moon and, while awaiting a transfer rocket to Mars, will draw a little arrow placing it in front of the word *July*. This will show that human beings in the early days of space were grammatically fallible; that mankind . . . is forever editing, and that a little precision is a dangerous thing."

USEFUL READING

Skillin, Marjorie E., et. al. *Words into Type*. 3rd ed. Englewood Cliffs, NJ: Prentice, 1974. A sound usage and style guide.

(BACK)GROUNDING

Writers have always used abbreviations whether on stone, paper, or computer screens. SPQR, *Senatus Populusque Romanus*, the insignia of Rome, was the most famous abbreviation of antiquity. For the several centuries preceding our own the use of abbreviations declined, but since World War II, we have experienced a veritable flood of abbreviated words, especially in technical writing—and more especially in the United States.

H. L. Mencken, in *The American Language*, notes "the general American liking for short cuts in speech," of which the tendency to abbreviate is an example. We abbreviate much more than other cultures. Just looking at the way some companies and products are spelled will indicate the extent to which people in the United States like to abbreviate:

EZ for *easy* as in EZ Sleep Motel and E-Z-Go Golf Cart
X for *extra* as in X-cel Optical Co.
Hi for *high* as in Hi-Lo Oil Co.

Also, our abbreviations, taking the general meaning of that word, involve much more than this chapter suggests. *Laser, radar, scuba, snafu,* and *sonar* are among the acronyms that are now integral parts of the English lexicon. Abbreviations as well as acronyms can become pronounceable words themselves. Abbreviating has become an important way of coining new words: *ad* for *advertisement; auto* for *automobile; bra* for *brassiere; exam* for *examination; lab* for *laboratory; phone* for *telephone; photo* for *photograph.*

zation of Women. **Initial abbreviations** are those which are pronounced, quite literally, as separate initials: ETS for Educational Testing Service, for instance. Many of the most common abbreviations of these types come from business, government, and science: NASA, PBS, DNA, GE, UNICEF, AIDS, SAT.

As long as you can be sure your readers will understand them, you can use such abbreviations in much of your college writing. You have to use them carefully and according to convention, however. If you are using a term only once or twice in a paper, you should spell it out, but when you need to use a term repeatedly, abbreviating it will serve as a convenience for you and your readers alike.

If you need to use an abbreviation your readers may not know, you can do so as long as you first "define" it for them. Spell out the full term at the first use, and give the abbreviation in parentheses. After that, you can use the abbreviation by itself.

> The Comprehensive Test Ban (CTB) Treaty was first proposed in the 1950s. For those nations signing it, the CTB would bring to a halt all nuclear weapons testing.

▌ 34d. Checking for inappropriate abbreviations

Abbreviations exist to facilitate reading and writing, but they are not appropriate in all writing contexts. The following guidelines will help you to use some common abbreviations in the writing you do for your college courses.

Company names

It is acceptable to use such abbreviations as *Inc., Co.,* and *Corp.* and the ampersand symbol (&) if they are part of a company's official name. You should not, however, use these abbreviated forms in most other contexts.

> One company—Sears, Roebuck & Co.—had sales of over $27 billion and a net income of just over $650 million in 1981 alone.

Reference information

Though it is conventional to abbreviate such words as *chapter* (ch.) or *page* (p.) in endnotes or source citations, it is not acceptable to do so in the body of your essay.

USEFUL READING

Mencken, H. L. *The American Language.* New York: Knopf, 1937. The author provides a readable discussion of abbreviations.

INAPPROPRIATE	In his preface to the 1851 *ed.* of *Twice-Told Tales*, Hawthorne states that the stories are not autobiographical.
REVISED	In his preface to the 1851 *edition* of *Twice-Told Tales*, Hawthorne states that the stories are not autobiographical.

Latin abbreviations

In general, avoid the following abbreviations except when citing sources or making parenthetical remarks.

c.f.	compare *(confer)*
e.g.	for example *(exempli gratia)*
et al.	and others *(et alii)*
etc.	and so forth *(et cetera)*
i.e.	that is *(id est)*
N.B.	note well *(nota bene)*

INAPPROPRIATE	Many firms now have policies to help working parents—e.g., flexible hours, maternity leave, day care.
REVISED	Many firms now have policies to help working parents—*for example*, flexible hours, maternity leave, day care.

Geographical places

Place names can be abbreviated in informal correspondence or in reference notes, but they should always be written out within sentences.

INAPPROPRIATE	Tired of life in the East, we set off for Cloverdale, *Calif.*
REVISED	Tired of life in the East, we set off for Cloverdale, *California.*

One common exception is *U.S.*, which is acceptable used as an adjective, though not as a noun.

UNACCEPTABLE	As an exchange student, I spent a summer in the *U.S.*
ACCEPTABLE	The *U.S. delegation* negotiated the treaty with success.

(BACK)GROUNDING

Two Latin abbreviations, *e.g.* and *i.e.*, can easily be confused, although their meanings are rarely interchangeable. *E.g.* means "for example" (from the Latin *exempli gratia*). It introduces an instance or examples of that to which it relates. *I.e.* means "that is" (from the Latin *id est*). It introduces a repetition in different words, a restatement or amplification of ideas that just precede it. Wilson Follett suggests that "a good way to make the distinction firm after it is learned is to think of *here are (is)* for *e.g.* and *I mean* for *i.e.*" (44).

USEFUL READING

Follett, Wilson. *Modern American Usage: A Guide.* Ed. Jacques Barzun, et al. New York: Hill, 1966. Another alphabetically arranged usage guide.

Symbols

Symbols such as ¢ @ # % + and = should not be used in the body of a paper, though they are commonly used in graphs and tables. One common exception is the dollar sign ($), which is acceptable to use with figures.

INAPPROPRIATE	Less than *50%* of those who applied were accepted.
REVISED	Less than *50 percent* of those who applied were accepted.

Units of Measurement

Except for scientific and technical writing, most units of measurement should not be abbreviated in the body of a paper.

INAPPROPRIATE	The ball sailed 400 *ft.* over the leftfield fence.
REVISED	The ball sailed 400 *feet* over the leftfield fence.

ANSWERS TO EXERCISE 34.1

1. We breathed a sigh of relief when we met the doctor, a young woman with a very confident manner.
2. An MX missile is 71 feet long, 92 inches around, and weighs 190,000 pounds.
3. Even AT&T has lowered its long distance rates by 6 percent this year.
4. In 1955 the Reverend Martin Luther King, Jr., was elected president of the Montgomery Improvement Association.
5. Levi Strauss is one company that has long offered childcare to its workers.
6. Like black-and-white television, the five-cent candy bar is a relic of the past.
7. Founded in 1966, the National Organization of Women fights discrimination against women.
8. The Public Broadcasting System is promoting more and better programs in the arts throughout the country, not just in Los Angeles and New York City.
9. After less than a year of attendance, Edgar Allan Poe withdrew from the University of Virginia and joined the United States army.
10. Dostoevsky was influenced by many European writers—for example, Dickens, Stendhal, and Balzac.

EXERCISE 34.1

Revise each of the following sentences to eliminate any abbreviations that would be inappropriate in academic writing.

Example

Ishi's story began in Oroville, Calif., in the early 1900s.

Ishi's story began in Oroville, California, in the early 1900s.

1. We breathed a sigh of relief when we met the dr., a young woman with a very confident manner.
2. An MX missile is 71 ft. long, 92 in. around, and weighs 190,000 lbs.
3. Even AT&T has lowered its long-distance rates by 6% this year.
4. In 1955 the Rev. Martin Luther King, Jr., was elected president of the Montgomery Improvement Assoc.
5. Levi Strauss is one co. that has long offered childcare to its workers.
6. Like black-and-white TV, the 5¢ candy bar is a relic of the past.
7. Founded in 1966, NOW fights discrimination against women.
8. PBS is promoting more and better programs in the arts throughout the country, not just in L.A. and N.Y.C.
9. After less than a yr. of attendance, Edgar Allan Poe withdrew from the U. of VA and joined the U.S. army.
10. Dostoevsky was influenced by many European writers—e.g., Dickens, Stendhal, and Balzac.

NUMBERS

▌ 34e. Spelling out numbers of one or two words

If a number can be written as one or two words, spell it out.

The victim's screams were heard by *thirty-eight* people, none of whom called the police.

Six days later, police arrested the assailant.

▌ 34f. Using figures for numbers longer than two words

Numbers that cannot be written in one or two words should be stated in figures.

Did you know that a baseball is wrapped in 174 yards of blue-gray wool yarn and is held together by 216 red stitches?

If one of several numbers in the same sentence needs to be expressed in figures, they all should be expressed that way.

INCONSISTENT	A complete audio system can range in cost from one hundred dollars to $2,500; however, a reliable system can be purchased for approximately five hundred dollars.
CONSISTENT	A complete audio system can range in cost from $100 to $2,500; however, a reliable system can be purchased for approximately $500.

▌ 34g. Spelling out numbers that begin sentences

When a sentence begins with a number, spell out the number or rewrite the sentence.

INAPPROPRIATE	277,000 hours, or 119 years, of CIA labor cost taxpayers $16 million.
HARD TO READ	Two hundred seventy-seven thousand hours, or one hundred nineteen years of CIA labor, cost taxpayers $16 million.
REVISED	Taxpayers spend $16 million for 277,000 hours, or 119 years, of CIA labor.

TEACHING PRACTICE

You might be asked to specify relatedness as a factor in deciding whether to use a numeral or spell out the number. *The Chicago Manual of Style* states:

> Numbers applicable to the same category should be treated alike within the same context, whether paragraph or series of paragraphs; do not use figures for some and spell out others (234).

Below is an example.

> The English Department has 75 graduate students in six major areas: 29 in literature; 25 in rhetoric and composition; 8 in literary theory; 6 in linguistics; 4 in folklore; and 3 in film.

In the sentence above, all the numerals relate to student population. However, the spelled-out number (*six*) relates to *major areas*. Therefore, the writer is permitted to spell out numbers and use numerals in the same sentence. The key factor in deciding whether to spell it out or not is rhetorical: which way would cause less confusion? Spelling out the one number that is unrelated to the seven other numbers distinguishes it so that the reader will not confuse it with the others.

USEFUL READING

The Chicago Manual of Style. 13th ed. Chicago: U of Chicago P, 1982. One of the best, most complete style manuals on the market.

(BACK)GROUNDING

A couple of significant differences exist between the British and Continental European expression of numbers and that of speakers in the United States. Continental writers use a comma instead of a decimal point; the older British practice is to use a raised dot as a decimal point. Also in Britain, a billion is equal to a million million, but in the United States, a billion is equal to a thousand million. Finally, Britain and the United States use different conventions for abbreviating dates, yet the results can look alike. For instance, 7/4/89 in the United States indicates July (the seventh month) 4 (the fourth day of the month), 1989 (the year). But in Britain, 7/4/89 means April 7, 1989 (the seventh day of the fourth month of 1989).

Other systems also exist. Continental Europeans use a lowercase roman numeral for the month, thus indicating July 4, 1989 as *4. vii. 89.* The U.S. military has two systems, that of the army and that of the navy, *4 Jul 89* and *4 JUL 89,* respectively. And finally, computer operators have developed their own system, so that July 4, 1989 becomes *1989-07-04.*

WRITERS ON WRITING

Douglas R. Hofstadter, in *Metamagical Themas: Questing for the Essence of Mind and Pattern,* presents the following humorous look at the use of large numbers:

> The renowned cosmologist Professor Bignumska, lecturing on the future of the universe, had just stated that in about a billion years, according to her calculations, the earth would fall into the sun in a fiery death. In the back of the auditorium a tremulous voice piped up: "Excuse me, Professor, but h-h-how long did you say it would be?" Professor Bignumska calmy replied, "About a billion years." A sigh of relief was heard. "Whew! For a minute there, I thought you'd said a *million* years."

■ 34h. Using figures according to convention

ADDRESSES

23 Main Street; 175 Fifth Avenue, New York, NY 10010

DATES

September 17, 1951, 411 B.C., 1865
Spell out dates that do not include the year: *June sixth.*
Spell out decades and centuries: *the fifties, the twentieth century.*

DECIMALS, FRACTIONS, AND PERCENTAGES

65.34, 8½, 77% (or 77 percent)

DIVISIONS OF BOOKS AND PLAYS

Volume 5, Pages 81–85 (*not* 81–5)
Act III, Scene ii (or Act 3, Scene 2), lines 3–9

SPECIFIC AMOUNTS OF MONEY

$7,348, $1.46 trillion
Spell out dollars or cents of two or three words: *fifty cents.*

SCORES AND STATISTICS

an 8–3 Red Sox victory, a verbal score of 650
average age of 22, a mean of 53, a ratio of 3 to 1

TIME OF DAY

6:00 A.M., 5:45 P.M., eight o'clock
Without A.M. or P.M., spell out time: *five in the morning.*
With the word *o'clock,* spell out time: *four o'clock,* not *4 o'clock.*

EXERCISE 34.2

Revise the numbers in the following sentences as necessary for correctness and consistency. If a sentence is correct, circle its number.

Example
The art of rhetoric began, in Sicily, in the 5th century B.C.
The art of rhetoric began, in Sicily, in the *fifth century* B.C.

1. 307 miles long and eighty-two miles wide, the island offered little.
2. Some call it the handbook for the 90s.
3. You can travel around the city for only 65 cents.

4. I am writing in response to a letter submitted to the *Times-Picayune* on December ninth, 1984 by George F. Lundy.
5. The Department of Health and Human Services has received 1,633 calls and has investigated forty-three incidents.
6. Educational broadcasting is at present available to seventy-two percent of the population.
7. Walker signed a three-year, $4.5 million contract.
8. In the thirty-five through 44 age group, the risk is estimated to be about 1 in 2,500.
9. Frankly, we consider 25 cents enough for a five-year-old.
10. The ancient amulet measured one and one-eighth by two and two-fifths inches.

EXERCISE 34.3

Revise the following passage adapted from an essay by Jean Shepherd ("Hairy Gertz and the Forty-Seven Crappies") to make its treatment of abbreviations and numbers correct and consistent.

And in the middle of the lake, several yds. away, are over 17,000 fishermen, in wooden rowboats rented at a buck and a ½ an hr. It is 2 A.M. The temp is 175, with humidity to match. And the smell of decayed toads, the dumps at the far end of the lake, and an occasional soupcon of Std. Oil, whose refinery is a couple of mi. away, is enough to put hair on the back of a mud turtle. 17 thousand guys clumped together in the middle fishing for the known 64 crappies in that lake. . . . Each boat contains a minimum of 9 guys and 14 cases of beer. And once in a while, in the darkness, is heard the sound of a guy falling over backward into the slime: SSSSGLUNK!

FOR EXAMINING YOUR OWN USE OF ABBREVIATIONS AND NUMBERS

Look over an essay or two that you have written, noting all the places where you use abbreviations and numbers. Check your usage for both correctness and consistency. If you discover anything you have done wrong, make a note of it (in your writing log, if you are keeping one) so that you will do it correctly the next time.

ANSWERS TO EXERCISE 34.2 (WILL VARY)

1. Three hundred and seven miles long and eighty-two miles wide, the island offered little.
2. Some call it the handbook for the nineties.
3. You can travel around the city for only sixty-five cents.
4. I am writing in response to a letter submitted to the *Times-Picayune* on December 9, 1984, by George F. Lundy.
5. This sentence could be left as is, or *forty-three* could be expressed as a numeral (43), depending on whether the writer perceived *incidents* as the same thing as *calls*.
6. Educational broadcasting is at present available to 72 percent of the population.
7. Correct
8. In the thirty-five through forty-four age group, the risk is estimated to be about 1 in 2,500.
9. Frankly, we consider twenty-five cents enough for a five-year-old.
10. The ancient amulet measured 1⅛ by 2⅖ inches.

ANSWERS TO EXERCISE 34.3

Here is the passage as published.

And in the middle of the lake, several *yards* away, are over *17,000* fishermen, in wooden rowboats rented at a buck and a *half* an hour. It is 2 A.M. The *temperature* is *175*, with humidity to match. And the smell of decayed toads, the dumps at the far end of the lake, and an occasional soupçon of *Standard Oil*, whose refinery is a couple of *miles* away, is enough to put hair on the back of a mud turtle. *Seventeen thousand* guys clumped together in the middle fishing for the known *sixty-four* crappies in that lake. . . . Each boat contains a minimum of *nine* guys and *fourteen* cases of beer. And once in a while, in the darkness, is heard the sound of a guy falling over backward into the slime: SSSSGLUNK!

35. Using Italics

(BACK)GROUNDING

Italic is one of the three families of types that have dominated Western typography since before the invention of printing. The other two are *roman* and *black letter* (also referred to as Old English or Gothic but not to be confused with newer Gothic typefaces). Black letter type is used today almost exclusively for decoration. Roman is the name for the kind of type that is used predominantly in printing in the West today. Italic falls in between, having both technical uses (to indicate titles, etc.) and rhetorical uses (to indicate emphasis). Each of the three major types has its origins in calligraphy.

Black letter type developed out of decorative handwriting usually associated with Germany and England. Roman letters developed first as capitals—in Rome, of course. Italic letters were based on the cursive writing used by chancery scribes in Italy to speed up their work.

The preferred type of the earliest printers was black letter. However, the first printers in Italy, Konrad Sweynheim and Arnold Pannartz, found it inappropriate for the Humanist movement that was sweeping fifteenth-century Italy. They searched calligraphic history for a more "Humanistic" type and developed what they called "Antiqua." In time, Antiqua became what we know of as "roman." For many years, black letter continued to be used for non-Humanist texts, ecclesiastical writings, and legal works.

The first printer to use italic type was Aldus Manutius, who worked in Venice in the late fifteenth century. His type designer, Francesco Griffo of Bologna, modeled his italic design on the cursive letters used in the papal chanceries of the time. Italic type first appeared in a series of Latin pocketbook-size texts, aimed at the new audience of Renaissance readers who had the Humanist love for Latin writers. The series succeeded immediately. The first volume, the "Aldine Virgil," appeared in 1501.

After the invention of printing, most type-carvers produced type that printed letters with the vertical strokes straight up and down, as in this sentence; today such type is called *roman*. Early Italian type designers, however, came to specialize in a slanted type, *like this*, known today as *italic*. Italics are used to set off words and phrases for special consideration or emphasis. As with other formal devices in writing, italic usage is governed by conventions, which this chapter presents.

If you have a fairly sophisticated word processor and printer, you may be able to print italic type. Otherwise, you can indicate italics by underlining the words you wish to treat in that way.

35a. Using italics for titles

In general, italics are used to signal the titles of long or complete works; shorter works or sections of works are set off with quotation marks. Use italics for the following kinds of works:

BOOKS

A Tale of Two Cities
Personal Memoirs of U. S. Grant

CHOREOGRAPHIC WORKS

Martha Graham's *Frontier*
Agnes De Mille's *Rodeo*

FILMS

Psycho
Black Orpheus

500

USEFUL READING

"Printing, Typography, and Photoengraving." *The New Encyclopaedia Britannica: Macropaedia.* 1987. This article provides a brief history and discussion of the nature of typography.

FOR TITLES   *it* 35a

JOURNALS

New England Journal of Medicine
Daedalus

LONG MUSICAL WORKS

Bach's *The Well-Tempered Clavier*
The Grateful Dead's *American Beauty*

LONG POEMS

The Odyssey
Hiawatha

MAGAZINES

Newsweek
the *New Yorker*

NEWSPAPERS

the *New York Times*
the *Cleveland Plain Dealer*

PAMPHLETS

Thomas Paine's *Common Sense*

PAINTINGS AND SCULPTURE

Picasso's *Three Musicians*
O'Keeffe's *Black Iris*

PLAYS

Long Day's Journey into Night
She Stoops to Conquer

TELEVISION AND RADIO PROGRAMS

The David Letterman Show
All Things Considered

A couple of exceptions are worth noting. Sacred books, such as the Bible or the Koran; and public documents, such as the Constitution or the Magna Carta, should *not* be italicized. Notice also with magazines and newspapers that an initial *the* is neither italicized nor capitalized, even if it is part of the official name.

(BACK)GROUNDING

William Caxton introduced printing into England in 1474, using a striking black letter type. His assistant, Wynkyn de Worde, to whom he turned over his business, used the first italic type in England in 1524. Richard Pinson, a Norman, introduced roman type into England in 1518. Pinson issued more than four hundred works during his forty or so years of printing.

French printers led the way in establishing the dominance of roman type. In 1540, Claude Garamond, the first commercial typefounder, designed and cut a roman type, referred to as the "Garamond type." It quickly displaced most of the other types used in Europe. However, in 1692, Louis XIV ordered the creation of a commission whose job it was to design a new type based on "scientific principles." Such a type was developed, but the man hired to cut the type, Philippe Grandjean, instead used the commission's designs as models for his own new designs. His type, known as *Romain du Roi*, immediately took over as the preferred type.

In 1734, William Caslon introduced a refined version of the Garamond type. It has become what we think of as the traditional roman type. The Caslon type won wide acceptance and was introduced into the American colonies by Benjamin Franklin. The official copies of the Declaration of Independence are printed in Caslon's roman type.

(BACK)GROUNDING

Whether or not to italicize initial articles when indicating book titles can be tricky. As the authors of *Words into Type* note, "Strictly speaking, an initial article should be italicized if it is part of the official title; but the fact is often difficult to verify. . . ." (140).

501

USEFUL READING

Gaskell, Philip. *New Introduction to Bibliography*. Oxford: Clarendon, 1972.
 Gaskell provides a full discussion of not only typography but also all other aspects of book production, including composition, paper, imposition, and presswork.

TEACHING PRACTICE

Newspapers provide an inexpensive, always available source of writing from which students can model much of their own discourse. However, in some cases, a newspaper may not be a good resource for models of italics usage. Traditionally, they have used quotation marks in place of italics. Today, many major newspapers, including the *New York Times*, the *Washington Post*, the *Chicago Tribune*, and the *Los Angeles Times*, italicize their headlines. They use a number of different typefaces in order to produce variety, especially on front pages which are full of different news stories. However, they continue to use quotation marks to indicate any titles, including those of books, plays, and magazines, despite style manuals that say these titles ought to be italicized.

35b. Using italics for words, letters, and numbers referred to as words

Italicize words, letters, or numbers referred to as words.

> Words like *romantic, plastic, values, human, dead, sentimental, natural, vitality,* as used in art criticism, are strictly meaningless, in the sense that they not only do not point to any discoverable object, but are hardly ever expected to do so by the reader.
> —George Orwell, "Politics and the English Language"

> The first four orbitals are represented by the letters *s, p, d,* and *f,* in lieu of numerical values.

> On the back of his jersey was the famous *24.*

Italics are also sometimes used to signal a word that is being defined.

> Learning to play the flute depends mostly on *embouchure*—the way in which the lips are positioned over the mouthpiece.

35c. Using italics for foreign words and phrases

Italicize words and phrases from other languages unless they are so frequently used by English speakers that they have come to be considered a part of English. The French word "bourgeois" or the Italian "pasta," for instance, do not need to be italicized. If you are in doubt about whether or not to italicize a particular word, most dictionaries offer guidelines.

> At last one of the phantom sleighs gliding along the street would come to a stop, and with gawky haste Mr. Burness in his fox-furred *shapka* would make for our door.
> —Vladimir Nabokov, *Speak, Memory*

> One cannot overestimate the usefulness of *Schlag* and *Zug*.
> —Mark Twain, "The Awful German Language"

Note, in addition, that Latin genus and species names are always signaled by italics.

> The caterpillars of *Hapalia*, when attacked by the wasp *Apanteles machaeralis*, drop suddenly from their leaves and suspend themselves in air by a silken thread.
> —Stephen Jay Gould, "Nonmoral Nature"

FOR SPECIAL EMPHASIS

35d. Using italics for the names of vehicles

Italicize names of specific aircraft, spacecraft, ships, and trains. Do not italicize types and classes, such as "Learjet," "space shuttle," "airbus," or "Bonanza."

AIRCRAFT AND SPACECRAFT

Spirit of St. Louis
Pioneer VII

SHIPS

the *Santa Maria*
U.S.S. *Missouri*

TRAINS

The *Orient Express*
The *Montrealer*

35e. Using italics for special emphasis

Just as vocal stress can add emphasis in spoken language, so italics can help create emphasis in writing.

> *Now* is the time to make real the promises of democracy.
> —MARTIN LUTHER KING, JR., "I Have a Dream"

> Gil's homer pulled the cork, and now there arose from all over the park a full, furious, happy shout of "Let's go, *Mets!* Let's go, *Mets!*" There were wild cries of encouragement before every pitch, boos for every called strike. . . . The fans' hopes, of course, *were* insane.
> —ROGER ANGELL, *The Summer Game*

> I am one of those unambitious lawyers who never address a jury, or in any way draw down public applause; but, in the cool tranquillity of a snug retreat, do a snug business among rich men's bonds, and mortgages, and title-deeds. All who know me, consider me an eminently *safe* man.
> —HERMAN MELVILLE, "Bartleby, the Scrivener"

Although italic emphasis is useful on occasion, especially in informal writing, it is best to use it sparingly. It is usually better to create emphasis with sentence structure and word choice.

TEACHING PRACTICE
Providing your students with models can help them to see both how italics are used and how use of italics for emphasis is a rhetorical decision, thus varying from writer to writer.

Consider having your class read *extensively* (for more than just a few paragraphs) in the work of a writer or writers who use italics regularly. Ask your students to consider whether the writer overuses italics.

(BACK)GROUNDING
Writers may want to emphasize with italics parts of a work for a variety of different reasons. Fowler suggests several:

1. To emphasize the main point of the phrase or clause or sentence.
2. To stress a contrast with reader expectations (and, of course, reveal the writer's awareness of the contrast).
3. To stress a contrast with another word, phrase, etc., within proximity (with both words, phrases, etc., usually italicized).
4. To suggest a stress upon a word or phrase, if it were read aloud.
5. To suggest that that which is being emphasized deserves more consideration or "thinking over" than the reader would normally give it. As Fowler says, "They pull up the reader and tell him not to read on, or he will miss some peculiarity in the italicized word. The particular point he is to notice is left to his own discernment . . ." (313).

Whether or not to use italics for emphasis is still being debated and probably will continue to be debated as long as some writers feel the need for that special emphasis. Fowler calls it "a primitive way of soliciting attention" (313). Yet, as *The Chicago Manual of Style* states, "Writers have probably always felt the need for devices to give special expression . . ." (140).

USEFUL READING

The Chicago Manual of Style. 13th ed. Chicago: U of Chicago P, 1982. *The Chicago Manual* provides full guidance in the use of italics.

Fowler, H. W. *A Dictionary of Modern English Usage*. 2nd ed. Rev. and ed. Sir Ernest Gowers. New York: Oxford UP, 1965. Fowler is conservative and traditional, but his conservatism is balanced and to the point.

ANSWERS TO EXERCISE 35.1

1. Hawthorne's story "My Kinsman, Major Molineux" bears a striking resemblance to Shakespeare's play *A Midsummer Night's Dream*.
2. When people think about the word *business*, they may associate it with people and companies that care about nothing but making money.
3. Georgetown offers a great blend of cultures and styles, a potpourri of people.
4. The word *veterinary* comes from the Latin *veterinarius*, meaning "of beasts of burden."
5. Niko Tinbergen's essay "The Bee-Hunters of Hulshorst" is a diary of the experiments performed by the author on *Philanthus triangulum Fabr*, the bee-killer wasp.
6. Flying the *Glamorous Glennis*, a plane named for his wife, Chuck Yeager was the first pilot to fly faster than the speed of sound.
7. The *Washington Post* provides extensive coverage of Congress.
8. *The Waste Land* is a long and difficult but ultimately rewarding poem.
9. If you have seen only a reproduction of Picasso's *Guernica*, you can scarcely imagine the impact the original painting makes.
10. My grandparents remember the sinking of the *Titanic*.

OPTIONAL EXERCISE

Find examples of writers who use italics for emphasis. Consider the ease with which you are able to spot the italics in different typographies. Now, evaluate the writer's use of italics in each instance of it: are italics warranted or appropriate in each case? Does the writer overuse the device?

EXERCISE 35.1

In each of the following sentences, underline any words that should be italicized and circle any italicized words that should not be.

> *Example*
> Those who can take it consider Dirty Harry a first-rate film.
> Those who can take it consider *Dirty Harry* a first-rate film.

1. Hawthorne's story *My Kinsman, Major Molineux* bears a striking resemblance to Shakespeare's play A Midsummer Night's Dream.
2. When people think about the word business, they may associate it with people and companies that care about nothing but making money.
3. Georgetown offers a great blend of cultures and styles, a *potpourri* of people.
4. The word *veterinary* comes from the Latin *veterinarius*, meaning *of beasts of burden*.
5. Niko Tinbergen's essay *The Bee-Hunters of Hulshorst* is a diary of the experiments performed by the author on *Philanthus triangulum Fabr*, the *bee-killer wasp*.
6. Flying the Glamorous Glennis, a plane named for his wife, Chuck Yeager was the first pilot to fly faster than the speed of sound.
7. The Washington Post provides extensive coverage of Congress.
8. The Waste Land is a long and difficult but ultimately rewarding poem.
9. If you have seen only a reproduction of Picasso's Guernica, you can scarcely imagine the impact the original painting makes.
10. My grandparents remember the sinking of the Titanic.

READING WITH AN EYE FOR ITALICS

The following passage about a graduate English seminar uses italics in several different ways—for emphasis, for a foreign phrase, and for a title. Read the passage carefully, particularly noting the effects created by the italics. How would it differ without any italic emphasis? What other words or phrases might Ozick have chosen to emphasize?

To get into this seminar, you had to submit to a grilling wherein you renounced all former allegiance to the then-current literary religion, New Criticism, which considered that only the text existed, not the world. I passed the interview by lying—cunningly, and against my real convictions. I said that probably the world *did* exist—and walked triumphantly into the seminar room.

There were four big tables arranged in a square, with everyone's feet sticking out into the open middle of the square. You could tell who was nervous, and how much, by watching the pairs of feet twist around each other.

The Great Man presided awesomely from the high bar of the square. His head was a majestic granite-gray, like a centurion in command; he *looked* famous. His clean shoes twitched only slightly, and only when he was angry.

It turned out he was angry at me a lot of the time. He was angry because he thought me a disrupter, a rioter, a provocateur, and a fool; also crazy. And this was twenty years ago, before these things were *de rigueur* in the universities. Everything was very quiet in those days: there were only the Cold War and Korea and Joe McCarthy and the Old Old Nixon, and the only revolutionaries around were in Henry James's *The Princess Casamassima*.

—Cynthia Ozick, "We Are the Crazy Lady"

FOR EXAMINING ITALICS IN YOUR OWN WRITING

Write a paragraph or two describing the most eccentric person you know. Make a point to italicize some words for special emphasis. Read your passage aloud to see what effect the italics bring. Consider italicizing any other words you wish to emphasize. Now explain each use of italics, stating in words the reason for the special attention. If you find yourself unable to give a reason, ask yourself whether the word should in fact be italicized at all. Then revise the passage to eliminate *all but one* use of italics. Try revising sentences and choosing more precise words to convey emphasis without italics. Compare the various versions, and decide which one is the most effective. Can you make any conclusions about using italics for emphasis? If you keep a writing log, add to it any thoughts, with examples from this exercise. In addition, you might keep your eye open for italics in your reading and copy down in your log any examples that impress you.

36. Using Hyphens

(BACK)GROUNDING

Early Greek grammarians placed a short line under a compound to indicate that it was not to be read as two words. This sign did not appear within the line because paper was scarce. Its scarcity was one reason why Greek and Early Latin manuscripts were usually written until around the ninth century with no space between words. And even after spacing had been introduced, it was still haphazard at best. Greek manuscripts never perfectly divided text into words, and it was only in the eleventh century that hyphens began appearing in Latin manuscripts. But, as A. C. Partridge points out, use of the hyphen really does not become systematic until the twelfth century, although then it "sometimes is also repeated at the beginning of the next line" (58). By the sixteenth century hyphens were commonplace and used for the same purposes that we use them today, although they appeared in manuscripts doubled, like an equal sign (=) and slanted.

WRITERS ON WRITING

Hooray for the hyphen! Or, rather, Hoo-ray!

—GEORGE PLIMPTON

The "merest" hyphen is a small horizontal line used to divide words at the end of a line and to link words or word parts (such as *hand-me-down* or *bye-bye*). As such, it serves purposes both mechanical and rhetorical. Its mechanical ones are fairly straightforward, with simple rules that tell us when and where to divide a word at the end of a line. The rhetorical ones, however, are somewhat more complicated, for though they are governed in some cases by rules, they are, in other cases, defined by the needs of readers. Stewart Beach points out the rhetorical usefulness of a hyphen nicely in his comments about one experience he recalled having as a reader:

> I came across a word I thought was a series of typos for *collaborators*. Reading it again, I realized the word was *colaborers*. But a hyphen would have [prevented] all the confusion.   —STEWART BEACH

Indeed, had the word included a hyphen—*co-laborers*—its meaning would have been instantly clear. Sometimes the dictionary will tell you when to hyphenate a word. Other times, you will be putting together words in ways not listed in a dictionary, and you will have to decide whether or not to add a hyphen. This chapter will help you with the decisions and the rules that go along with using hyphens.

36a. Using hyphens to divide words at the end of a line

Hyphens are used at the end of a line to break a word that will be completed on the next line. It is best not to have to divide words in

---

USEFUL READING

Partridge, A. C. *Orthography in Shakespeare and Elizabethan Drama*. Lincoln: U of Nebraska P, 1964. For a concise and informative discussion of how the major punctuation marks evolved, see Appendix VIII, "The Historical Development of Punctuation Marks."

Thompson, Sir Edward Maunde. *An Introduction to Greek and Latin Paleography*. Oxford: Clarendon Press, 1912. See Chapter Five for a discussion of punctuation and the facsimiles of Greek and Latin writing throughout.

this way, but sometimes you must. When you do, the main thing to remember is to break words between syllables. The word *metaphor*, for instance, is made up of three syllables (*met-a-phor*), and you could break it after either the *t* or the *a*. All dictionaries show syllable breaks, and so the best advice for dividing words correctly is simply to look them up. In addition, you should follow certain other conventions, including the following:

- *Never divide one-syllable words*, even relatively long words such as *draught* or *through*.
- *Divide compound words only between the parts*. Words such as *head-ache* or *mother-in-law* should be broken between their parts (*head-ache*) or at their hyphens (*mother-in-law*).
- *Divide words with prefixes or suffixes between the parts*. The word *disappearance*, then, might be broken after its prefix (*dis-appearance*) or before its suffix (*disappear-ance*). Prefixed words that include hyphens, such as *self-righteous*, should be divided at the hyphen.
- *Never divide abbreviations, contractions, or figures*. Though such "words" as *NASA*, *didn't*, and *250* do have audible syllables, it is not permissible to divide them in writing.
- *Leave at least two letters when dividing a word*. Words such as *acorn* (*a-corn*) or *scratchy* (*scratch-y*), therefore, cannot be divided at all, and a word such as *Americana* (*A-mer-i-can-a*) can be broken only after the *r* or the *i*.

EXERCISE 36.1

Divide each of the following words into syllables, first referring to your dictionary. Then indicate with a hyphen the places where you might break each word at the end of a line. Indicate any words that cannot be divided into syllables or broken at the end of a line.

1. passable
2. retract
3. scoffed
4. military
5. antechamber

6. other-centered
7. haven't
8. dimming
9. anonymous
10. attitude

ANSWERS TO EXERCISE 36.1

1. pass*able; pass-able
2. re*tract; re-tract
3. scoffed; do not break one-syllable words
4. mil*i*tar*y; mili-tary
5. an*te*cham*ber; ante-chamber
6. oth*er*cen*tered; other-centered
7. have*n't; do not break contractions
8. dim*ming; dim-ming
9. a*non*y*mous; anon-ymous, anony-mous
10. at*ti*tude; atti-tude

▌ **36b. Using hyphens with compound words**

Compound words are words such as *rowboat* or *up-to-date* that are made up of more than one word. Compound words are written as one word, as separate words, or with hyphens.

507

USEFUL READING

Teall, Edward N. *Meet Mr. Hyphen and Put Him in His Place*. New York: Funk & Wagnalls, 1937. See Chapter One for a short history of hyphens.

Webb, Robert A. *The Washington Post Deskbook on Style*. New York: McGraw, 1978. See the entry under "hyphens" for rules and illustrative examples.

ONE WORD	*grandmother, textbook, extraterrestrial*
SEPARATE WORDS	*high school, parking meter, floppy disk*
WITH HYPHENS	*city-state, great-grandmother, ex-husband*

It is difficult, maybe even impossible, to know when a particular compound word is one word, separate words, or hyphenated. Even compounds that begin with the same word are even treated every which way—*blueberry, blue-collar,* and *blue cheese,* for instance. In general, then, you should always consult the dictionary to know how to spell compounds. There are, in addition, some conventions that can guide you in using hyphens with compound words.

1. Hyphenating compound modifiers

Often you will use compound modifiers that are not listed in a dictionary. The guiding principle then is to hyphenate most compound adjectives that precede a noun but not to hyphenate ones that follow a noun.

> a *hard-nosed* boss, a *two-to-one* decision
>
> My boss is extremely *hard nosed.*
>
> The decision against the plan was *two to one.*

In general, the reason for hyphenating such compound modifiers is to facilitate reading. Notice, for example, how the hyphen affects your understanding of the following two sentences.

> The designers used potted palms as *living room* dividers.
>
> The designers used potted palms as *living-room* dividers.

In the first sentence, the word *living* seems to modify *room dividers;* in the second, the hyphen makes clear that it is part of a compound adjective. Compound adjectives that are commonly used and thus likely to be easily understood by your readers, however, do not always need to be hyphenated—*income tax reform* or *first class mail* would never be misunderstood, for example.

Two more instances of compound modifiers that are never hyphenated include those with an adverb ending in *-ly* and those with comparative or superlative forms.

> a *radically different* approach
>
> *more extensive* coverage, the *most stimulating* group

508

USEFUL READING

Dawson, Giles E., and Laetitia Kennedy-Skipton. *Elizabethan Handwriting 1500–1650.* Chichester: Phillimore, 1981. Part four of the introduction (13–21) discusses the mechanics of writing during this time, including punctuation.

Fowler, H. W. *A Dictionary of Modern English Usage.* Rev. and ed. Sir Ernest Gowers. New York: Oxford UP, 1965. The entry under hyphens describes how compound words are formed with hyphens and how hyphens drop from these compounds to form one word.

WITH PREFIXES AND SUFFIXES

A series of compound words in a sentence that share the same base word can be shortened by the use of suspended hyphens.

> I taught *two-, three-,* and *four-year-olds.*

▌ 2. Hyphenating specially coined compounds

You may sometimes coin your own original compounds, usually for descriptive reasons. Such **coined compounds** should always be hyphenated.

> Unfortunately, nature is very much a *now-you-see-it, now-you-don't* affair.   —ANNIE DILLARD, "Sight into Insight"

> The . . . problem with a *no-first-use* policy is that it might paradoxically increase the chances of nuclear war.
> —CHARLES KRAUTHAMMER, "In Defense of Deterrence"

▌ 3. Hyphenating fractions and compound numbers

To write out fractions, use a hyphen to join the numerator and denominator.

> one-seventh
> seven-sixteenths

Use hyphens to spell out whole numbers from twenty-one to ninety-nine, both when they stand alone and when they are part of larger numbers. (Note that such larger numbers can usually be written as numerals.)

> thirty-seven
> three hundred fifty-four thousand

▌ 36c. Using hyphens with prefixes and suffixes

Most words with prefixes or suffixes are written as one word, without hyphens: *antiwar, misinform, understated.* Only in the following cases do you need a hyphen with prefixed or suffixed words:

CAPITALIZED BASE WORDS

post-Civil War, pro-Democrat, un-American

FIGURES

pre-1960, post-1945

OPTIONAL EXERCISE

Consider the following excerpt from *Beowulf.* Read it aloud to the class, and then ask them to suggest synonyms for the compounded terms. Finally, read both the translation below and the version with their synonyms, and attempt to describe the difference in tone that results.

> There was stone paving on the path that brought
> the war-band on its way. The war-coats shone
> and the links of hard hand-locked iron
> sang in their harness as they stepped along
> in their gear of grim aspect, going to the hall.
> Sea-wearied, they then set against the wall
> their broad shields of special temper,
> and bowed to bench, battle-shirts clinking,
> the war-dress of warriors. The weapons of the
>   seamen
> stood in the spear-rack, stacked together,
> an ash-wood grey-tipped. These iron-shirted men
> were handsomely armed.

WRITING TOGETHER

Consider reading Paul Fussell's "Notes on Class" with your class and focusing on the way he uses hyphenated compounds to name social classes. Because the topic of the essay—class divisions in society—is "a dirty little secret," no names exist to designate the distinctions Fussell wishes to make:

> Top Out-of-sight
> Upper Class
> Upper-Middle-Class
> Middle Class
> High-Proletarian
> Mid-Proletarian
> Low-Proletarian
> Destitute
> Bottom Out-of-Sight

Fussell also uses hyphens to create compound words to express his ideas: *pseudo-genteel, shape-change, quasi-official,* and *dark-suited first-generation aspirants.*

WITH ALL-, EX-, SELF-, AND -ELECT

all-state, ex-husband, self-possessed, mayor-elect

Note, however, that *selfish* is written without a hyphen because *self* acts as a root, not a prefix.

BEFORE COMPOUND WORDS

pre-high school, pro-civil rights

TO AVOID CONFUSION WITH HOMONYMS

Re-cover means to "cover again"; the hyphen distinguishes it from *recover* meaning "get well."

ANSWERS TO EXERCISE 36.2

1. Correct
2. pre-World War II
3. two- and four-cylinder motorcycles
4. Correct
5. a come-up-and-see-me-sometime gaze
6. self-important
7. president-elect
8. seven hundred thirty-three
9. a hard-working farmer
10. Correct

EXERCISE 36.2

Using the dictionary as a reference, insert hyphens as needed in the following terms. Circle the number of any term that is correct as it stands.

1. deionization
2. pre World War II
3. two and four-cylinder motorcycles
4. happily married couple
5. a come up and see me sometime gaze
6. self important
7. president elect
8. seven hundred thirty three
9. a hard working farmer
10. a politician who is quick witted

EXERCISE 36.3

Insert any necessary hyphens, delete any unnecessary ones, and correct any incorrect word divisions in the following sentences. Use your dictionary if necessary. Some of the sentences do not require any change.

1. Stress can lead to hypertension and ulcers.
2. McKuen began to write as an escape from his on the move life, which included various odd jobs ranging from ditchdigging to cookiecutting.
3. The carpenter asked for a two pound bag of three quarter inch nails.
4. Suicide among teen-agers has tripled in the past thirty five years, making it the third leading cause of death among fifteen to twentyfour year olds.
5. We encouraged him to be more open minded and to temper his dogmatic views.
6. Since the use of PCB's has been out-lawed, environmentalists feel somewhat encouraged.

WITH PREFIXES AND SUFFIXES

7. One of Mikhail Baryshnikov's favorite dancers is none other than Fred A-staire.
8. The government declared an all-out war on poverty and homelessness.
9. The antiAmerican rally attracted large crowds.
10. The beautifully-written essay earned high praise.

READING WITH AN EYE FOR HYPHENATION

The following paragraph about semi-professional baseball uses many hyphens. Read it carefully, and note how the hyphens make the paragraph easier to read. Why is it necessary to hyphenate *junior-college* in the last sentence?

All semi-pro leagues, it should be understood, are self-sustaining, and have no farm affiliation or other connection with the twenty-six major-league clubs, or with the seventeen leagues and hundred and fifty-two teams (ranging from Rookie League at the lowest level, to Class A and Summer Class A, up to the AAA designation at the highest) that make up the National Association— the minors, that is. There is no central body of semi-pro teams, and semi-pro players are not included among the six hundred and fifty major-leaguers, the twenty-five hundred-odd minor-leaguers, plus all the managers, coaches, presidents, commissioners, front-office people, and scouts, who, taken together, constitute the great tent called organized ball. (A much diminished tent, at that; back in 1949, the minors included fifty-nine leagues, about four hundred and forty-eight teams, and perhaps ten thousand players.) Also outside the tent, but perhaps within its shade, are five college leagues, ranging across the country from Cape Cod to Alaska, where the most promising freshman, sophomore, and junior-college ballplayers may compete against each other in the summertime without losing their amateur status. . . .

–ROGER ANGELL, "In the Country"

FOR EXAMINING HYPHENATION IN YOUR OWN WRITING

Look carefully at an essay or assignment you are working on, particularly noting your use of hyphens. Have you broken words at the ends of lines correctly? Have you followed the conventions governing use of hyphens in compound words, with prefixes and suffixes, with fractions and numbers? If you find you are misusing hyphens or are unclear about how to use them in certain situations, check those instances against the advice in this chapter. If you are keeping a writing log, make an entry in it about anything with hyphens that confused you.

ANSWERS TO EXERCISE 36.3

1. Correct
2. McKuen began to write as an escape from his on-the-move life, which included various odd jobs ranging from ditch-digging to cookie-cutting.
3. The carpenter asked for a two-pound bag of three-quarter-inch nails.
4. Suicide among teenagers has tripled in the past thirty-five years, making it the third-leading cause of death among fifteen to twenty-four-year-olds.
5. We encouraged him to be more open-minded and to temper his dogmatic views.
6. Since the use of PCB's has been outlawed, environmentalists feel somewhat encouraged.
7. One of Mikhail Baryshnikov's favorite dancers is Fred Astaire.
8. Correct
9. The anti-American rally attracted large crowds.
10. The beautifully written essay earned high praise

TEACHING PRACTICE

Ask students to bring examples of their own use of hyphens in writing to class for discussion, using these examples as a way to talk about using hyphens effectively and correctly.

PART EIGHT

Doing Research and Using Sources

37. Becoming a Researcher

The English word *research* derives not only from the French *chercher*, which means to "search," but from the Late Latin *circare*, which means to "circle around, explore." **Research,** then, is a means of critical inquiry, of circling carefully around and around a subject, a process that the editors of the famous eleventh edition of the *Encyclopaedia Britannica* identify as all "investigations . . . based on sources of knowledge." Without research, they go on, "no authoritative words could have been written, no scientific discoveries or inventions made, no theories of any value propounded." Nor could many personal or work-related decisions be made. Consider the following situations:

> Your employer tells you that the company needs a new intercom system and asks you to recommend the best system for the money.
>
> You have an opportunity to visit Tokyo, but you can stay only one week. You want to plan that week.
>
> Some friends tell you that a song you admire is dedicated to the "disappeared." You determine to find out all you can about the song and the dedication.
>
> Your introduction to sociology professor asks you to write an essay on the clothing styles characteristic of young teenagers. You decide to visit a local junior high school.
>
> You are part of a task force charged with charting the responses of consumers to a product's new packaging.

As these situations illustrate, much, if not most, work relies on research: we find something out, and then we report on it. Some professions rely heavily on research—news reporting, police detection, and law, for example. In fact, this process of investigating sources and drawing conclusions based on what we find pervades our personal lives as well

(BACK)GROUNDING

The fifteenth edition of the *New Encyclopaedia Britannica (NEB)* (1987) attributes the dominance of human beings on earth to the "innate ability to communicate and to store, retrieve, and use knowledge so that each generation does not have to relearn the lessons of the past in order to act effectively in the present." The *NEB* also points out that this ability for passing on information from generation to generation has transformed human beings into the composite beneficiaries of the ideas and experiences of our ancestors.

Research is the activity that enables us to process, create, and communicate knowledge. But research goes beyond simply gathering data and passing it on. In its most beneficial sense, research is the process of investigating information or data for a purpose: to make decisions about our lives, to understand our world; or to create or advance understanding. Research then is the use of information in "decision making" that depends on specific situations, times, and needs. Far from being restricted to work on a college "research essay," research informs much of what we do throughout our lives.

USEFUL READING

Langer, Judith A. "Learning through Writing: Study Skills in the Content Areas." *Journal of Reading* 29 (1986): 400–406. Langer reports that writing essays encourages content learning more effectively than taking notes and answering questions.

TEACHING PRACTICE

To show your students that they do indeed know how to do research, ask your students to give you advice and help in deciding on your purchase of a stereo system, or a bicycle; or have them help you decide whether to live on the north side of campus or the south side. You might ask them to help you draw up a list of things you would need to find out in deciding whether to accept job offers in the Pacific Northwest, on the East Coast, or in the Midwest.

In each of these cases, having your students work together brainstorming questions and generating information and criteria that will help you decide shows them that they already have ways of researching. They'll ask questions. They'll rely on their own experiences. They'll consult other people or other sources, such as consumer magazines or encyclopedias. By investigating your choices and reporting their findings back to you, they'll help you make your choice. These activities will help reinforce the fact that all research is purposeful.

WRITERS ON WRITING

I doubt if there is much to choose here between science and the arts: the imagination is not much more free, and not much less free, in one than in the other. All great scientists have used their imagination freely, and let it ride them to outrageous conclusions without crying "Halt!"
—JACOB BRONOWSKI

WRITERS ON WRITING

Essays do, in a way, resemble scientific writing: they report experiments in thought.
—LEWIS THOMAS

as our work. This chapter rests on that assumption. From this basic assumption come five important premises:

1. *You already know how to do research.* It is impossible to live in our consumer-oriented culture without knowing how to find out about things *and* how to act on such information. You act as a researcher whenever you investigate a product—whether a videotape, a cosmetic, a computer, or a car—by reading up on its reliability, discussing its features with your friends, or checking several stores to see what is in stock, how much it costs, and what it can do. You conducted research when you chose a college—and then when you studied the catalog, consulted your adviser, and talked with other students to plan your academic program.

You may not be able to name all the procedures of conducting research and presenting it in writing, but you do already possess many essential research skills. You know how to combine experience, observation, and new information when you try to solve a problem, answer a question, make a decision, or analyze a situation. You know how to seek out pieces of information, evaluate their usefulness, fit them all together, and then use them to make an "educated guess." Such basic research methods are not just academic requirements but important skills for working and living. You do—and will—use these skills whenever you make reasoned choices or whenever you discover and share knowledge with others. And these are the very skills you will build on as you become more familiar with academic research.

2. *Presenting your research in writing draws you into the conversation surrounding any area of inquiry.* Good research, in fact, makes you into a genuine expert. If you approach your research with serious intent, you may gradually become someone who knows more than anyone else on campus about Joseph McCarthy's political affiliations, or Wordsworth's "Lucy poems," or new uses of metal hybrids, or Jackie Robinson's place in sports history. You will be truly knowledgeable, and you will be able to add your knowledge to the conversation of educated people that goes on all about you, not only in college but in the media, in community groups, and in the workplace.

3. *Research is always driven by a purpose.* Whether for common everyday needs or for formal academic inquiry, researchers seek out facts and opinions for a reason—wanting to make a discovery; hoping to answer a question, solve a problem, or prove something; wishing to

BECOMING A RESEARCHER   *res* 37

teach or to correct an error or to advocate a position. Research is not an end in itself. Instead it is a process or method, used in many situations and fields, for systematically discovering, testing, and sharing new ideas.

4. *Your purpose influences the research you do, which in turn refines your purpose.* When you begin any research, it is impossible to know exactly what you will find out. You begin with a question you want to answer or a general idea that you want to probe or illustrate or prove. As research discovery leads to discovery, your initial idea may come into sharper focus and become stronger and more detailed—or it could fail to take useful shape and even be replaced by some other idea. Only after you have done a fair amount of searching, re-searching, and writing will you know whether your initial idea should remain the focus of your research.

5. *Although research typically begins with a problem or question and moves toward a solution or answer, it is almost always a recursive rather than a linear process.* In other words, research rarely progresses in a neat line from start to finish. Doing research might be likened to following an upward spiral, winding round and round but steadily progressing toward the top. You begin with an idea that may or may not be concrete, explorable, or supportable. Then you follow the spiral through some background research and perhaps some writing. Your initial investigation may lead you to start all over again—or to modify your idea and then to spiral further upward to more specific sources. This additional research sharpens your idea even more, leading you to more and more specific sources. As you read and investigate the topic, your initial ideas get focused and modified (and occasionally completely disproved) by what you find. The spiral sometimes causes you to circle past familiar materials; occasionally seeing them from a different perspective helps you to ask different and more sophisticated questions. Writing is an important part of this investigative spiral, for it forces you to sharpen your ideas and perhaps to turn back to your sources for more information. Wherever the spiral of research takes you, however, your overriding goal remains the same: to develop a strong critical understanding of the information you are gathering.

One student's experience illustrates how ideas can change and develop during the research process. Assigned to write an essay on a topic of current interest to him, this student began by puzzling over whether modern rock guitar styles could be traced to the electric guitar

(BACK)GROUNDING

Regardless of the field of study, researching, writing, and learning are interconnected. James Britton's distinction between *expressive* and *transactional* writing helps to explain this interconnection. We write in order to learn; that is, we think on paper, using writing to process information and to probe ideas. This function of writing, a form of self-expression and exploration, Britton calls *expressive*; it serves the writer; it enables him or her to learn and understand information. We also write to communicate learning. We use language to inform, to persuade, or to help someone else understand. This function Britton calls *transactional* to emphasize the exchange or transmission of information for an audience's learning purposes.

USEFUL READING

Britton, James, et al. *The Development of Writing Abilities, 11–18.* London: Macmillan Education P, 1975. A model of writing development whose key feature is the continuum that connects expressive writing and transactional, that connects "self-expression" and writing intended for others.

Emig, Janet. "Writing as a Mode of Learning." *College Composition and Communication* 28 (1977): 122–28. Emig's view of writing as a means of learning informs the interconnection among researching, writing, and learning.

TEACHING PRACTICE

After students have read the description of the student's research into guitar styles, take time in class and ask them to think of an occasion when a question has puzzled or challenged them. Ask them to jot down ideas about the kind of research they could do to help answer their questions. Then take one or two examples of such questions from the class, put them on the board, and lead the class in a brainstorming session on what kind of research would best help answer these questions.

WRITERS ON WRITING

The most frequent evasive tactic for the would-be writer is to say, "But before I have anything to say, I must get *experience*." . . . But experience isn't something you go and *get*—it's a gift, and the only requisite for receiving it is that you be open to it. A closed soul can have the most immense adventures, go through a civil war or a trip to the moon, and have nothing to show for all that "experience;" whereas the open soul can do wonders with nothing.

—URSULA L. LE GUIN

styles developed in Chicago in the 1940s by urban blues groups. This beginning was a good one; the student liked the subject and already knew something about it. Starting with background sources about modern rock guitarists like Eric Clapton and Pete Townshend, he found repeated references to Muddy Waters, B. B. King, Albert King, and other Chicago blues singers. He listened to a number of records and found repeated riffs (musical phrases) and clear derivations. So far, so good. Based on the information he found about his subject and his understanding of the records themselves, he began to make notes toward an essay.

This student's research might have ended at the point of drafting, but it did not. In several sources on the Chicago electric blues tradition, he found references to "country blues" and Southern "race records" as influences on the Chicago artists. He was not sure what these terms meant but wanted to find out. As he continued his research, the writer learned of a more complex and far older blues tradition than he had known existed. He discovered that blues music harks back to nineteenth-century slave songs and chants, that the country blues was nearly always played on a single acoustic guitar, and that the well-documented history of country blues guitar styles was easily traced back to the 1920s.

This new information called out for investigation. He felt that his early conjecture about the influence of the Chicago blues singers still held true, but clearly the story was older and the traditions much deeper than he had imagined. He decided to get more books about Southern and country blues musicians of the 1920s and 1930s in order to learn all he could about the guitar styles of musicians like Robert Johnson, Leadbelly, John Hurt, and Lightnin' Hopkins. In addition, he began to consider the differences between electric and acoustic instruments. Finally, he looked for records still available by some of the very early country blues musicians. To his amazement, the writer heard on these very early records some of the exact guitar riffs and techniques he so admired by contemporary guitarists. Thus, this writer arrived at this point of his research with a stronger and deeper idea for development, a far better grasp of musical history, and more and better research sources. And he had accumulated enough information and evidence to begin crafting a fine essay.

Research for writing

For college work, much of the research you will do will be for writing projects—to find evidence for a proposal, to discover anecdotes

USING BOTH PRIMARY AND SECONDARY SOURCES   *res* 37a

for an autobiographical essay, to investigate a subject for a term paper. The results of your research—your discoveries, your evidence, your conclusions, your new ideas—may be only one small part of an essay. You might, for example, need to do minimal research to supply background details about a topic or evidence for an argument. On the other hand, your research may be reported in a full-scale "research essay," devoted entirely to the results of your investigation. Chapters 37–41 provide guidelines to help you with any research done for the purpose of writing—from defining a topic to discovering and evaluating evidence to arguing a thesis and documenting your sources.

▌ 37a. Using both primary and secondary sources

Samuel Johnson once remarked that "knowledge is of two kinds: we know a subject ourselves, or we know where we can find information upon it." Johnson has summed up, in this sentence, the distinction between primary sources—firsthand knowledge—and secondary sources—knowledge available from the work of others.

Primary sources represent the basic sources of raw information. Primary sources you produce include laboratory experiments you conduct, notes you take in the field, and surveys or interviews you conduct. Also considered primary sources are objects or art works you examine, literary works you read, and performances you attend. Other primary sources include diaries, letters, firsthand accounts of events by eyewitnesses, contemporary news reports, historical documents, or raw data from experiments conducted by others.

Secondary sources consist of oral and written accounts of phenomena produced by others. Secondary sources include reports and analyses by scholars, experts, and researchers of other people's laboratory work, field experiences, surveys, and so forth. Secondary sources also include various sorts of critical writing.

Sometimes, what constitutes a primary or secondary source depends on your purpose or your field of study. A critic's evaluation of a painting, for instance, serves as a secondary work if you are writing an essay on that painting, but as a primary work if you are conducting a study of that critic's writings.

Most research writing depends on both primary and secondary sources. The primary sources ground the project in facts from firsthand accounts and your own discoveries, while the secondary sources provide background for your investigation and support for your conclusions.

TEACHING PRACTICE

Have your students list the sources of the information they found to help you decide on the stereo system to buy. They will probably mention their own experiences or their family's experience with a reliable or unreliable system. They will probably mention consumer guides. They'll also likely mention popular stereo magazines or newspaper and television advertisements. Have them classify these sources as either primary or secondary and explain their classifications. For example, their own experience is a primary source. The fact that they have owned a particular system for many years and that they have recommended it to relatives and friends who've had trouble-free experiences is a form of raw data. If they mention an article in *Stereo Review* that speaks praisingly of their system, the magazine is a secondary source.

37b res   BECOMING A RESEARCHER

Literary research, for instance, is very likely to combine primary and secondary sources: your major primary source is the text of the work you are examining, and secondary sources are biographies, analyses of the text, and other works of criticism.

Some projects may require no primary sources at all, such as a background survey or a review of the literature on a given topic. Secondary sources, on the other hand, are necessary for most research projects; even a report of a laboratory experiment is ordinarily prefaced by a discussion of what other researchers have done previously. Research very often builds on secondary sources in this way: you read to find out what is known or not known about a problem; you formulate a question based on what needs to be found out; then you devise a research method to answer that question. The research process, in fact, calls for active reading and writing throughout. As you read sources, you write out questions, summaries, notes, and so on. These in turn lead you back to more reading.

37b. Understanding and choosing a research topic

Sometimes a research topic may choose you: it so fascinates or compels you that you simply *must* explore it, or an assignment you are working on—a proposal for a business class or a personal essay for a journalism class—may call for some research. Other times, a specific research topic is assigned. Even in these cases, however, you will probably have some leeway in tailoring the assigned topic to your interests. In doing so, you want to follow your own curiosity, to conduct research that will enlighten you or answer a question that intrigues or puzzles you. Accomplishing this goal, however, calls for careful thinking on your part: you want to end up pursuing a topic that is not only interesting and challenging to you but manageable as well.

1. Analyzing an assigned topic

In college writing, most research responds to a writing assignment. You can begin your research, then, by paying very close attention to the exact wording of that assignment. If the assignment is handed out to you, study it, and keep it for future reference. If it is written on the chalkboard or if your instructor reads it aloud, copy it carefully, word for word. Consider any requirements for the essay's essential purpose, research scope, audience, length, and deadline.

UNDERSTANDING AND CHOOSING A RESEARCH TOPIC

Identifying the purpose

Read through the assignment for **cue words,** those like *describe, survey, analyze, explain, classify, compare,* or *contrast,* that describe the logical pattern the instructor expects the essay to follow. What do words like these mean in the context of this particular research assignment? For instance, in a biology class, *analyze* means "to break down into parts"; in a literature class, *analyze* means "to interpret." What do these meanings suggest about the purpose(s) of the assignment?

Gauging the scope

Next consider any information about the kind of research you will need to do. Does the assignment specify anything about the use of library sources, about how many sources you can or should use? Does the instructor require that you use a minimum number of sources of different sorts? (For example, your instructor may require that you consult a mix of books, periodicals, and interviews so that you gain experience with each kind of source.) If your assignment includes such requirements, plan your research accordingly.

Identifying the audience

Find out if your assignment specifies an audience other than the instructor. Then spend some time considering what this audience and your instructor will expect you to provide in a discussion of your topic. Make some preliminary notes based on these considerations, answering the following questions:

- Who will be interested in the information you gather, and why?
- What will they want to know?
- What will they already know?
- What response do you want to elicit from them?
- What assumptions might they hold about your topic?
- What information will you need to present in order to convince them?
- What will your instructor expect in a strong essay on this topic?

Noting the length

Does your assignment specify or limit the number of pages in the final essay? The amount of research and writing time you must budget for a five- to seven-page essay differs markedly from that needed for one of fifteen to twenty pages.

WRITERS ON WRITING

To imagine is the characteristic act, not of the poet's mind, or the painter's, or the scientist's, but of the mind of man [and woman].

—JACOB BRONOWSKI

TEACHING PRACTICE

Identifying the audience will likely pose problems for your students. Answering the questions in the text will help them understand that they must consider the audience when deciding on word choice, tone, strategy, and presentation.

Point out that one of their responsibilities as researchers and writers is to make information available and understandable to a variety of audiences. To do so involves making choices about language and development that depend on their analysis of the purpose of the research, the scope of the project or topic, the specific audience, and so on. For example, the physiologist presenting material on limb regeneration should judge how much he or she needs to explain the significance of *blastema* and the relevant aspects of it to the research on the basis of purpose, audience, and scope. Clearly, colleagues in the writer's field, unlike a general audience, will not require a preliminary basic working definition of the term *blastema.* On the other hand, this physiologist would need to define this term and others particular to the field if the essay were written for an audience made up of readers outside the field.

WRITERS ON WRITING

Even when we write, alone in a room to an absent audience, there are occasions when we are struggling to figure something out and need to push aside awareness of those absent readers.

—PETER ELBOW

Working toward the deadline

What is your deadline for the completed project? Are any preliminary materials—a working bibliography, a research thesis, an outline, or a first draft—due before this date? Answering these questions will help you to construct a reasonable timetable for completing your work.

2. Choosing your own topic

If your assignment does not specify a topic, you can best begin articulating one by considering what subjects puzzle you, challenge you, engage your curiosity in some way. Ask yourself the following questions:

- What subjects do you know something about?
- What subjects might you like to become an "expert" on?
- What subjects evoke a strong reaction from you—intense curiosity, puzzlement, or skepticism?
- Are there any subjects others have investigated and written about that you would like to look into?

In addition, skim through your textbooks or class notes, looking for subjects that catch your interest. Or browse through current magazines, journals, or standard reference works, again looking for some topic or question that intrigues you. You may find the techniques presented in 2e for exploring a topic—brainstorming, freewriting, looping, mapping, or questioning—useful for discovering one.

Getting response to your topic

As soon as you can, draft several sentences that describe the topic (or topics) you have come up with; then try to get some response—from your instructor and perhaps from friends or classmates. Ask them to consider the following questions:

- What do you think of this approach to the topic?
- Is the topic manageable?
- Can you suggest any other angles?
- Can you suggest any good sources of information on this topic?
- Would you be interested in reading about this topic?
- Can you suggest any approach that might be more provocative?

Make sure you understand any specifications about purpose, scope, audience, length, and deadline (see 37b1).

▌ 37c. Narrowing and focusing a topic

Any topic you choose to research must be manageable—must suit the purpose, scope, audience, length, and time limits for your final writing purpose. Making a topic manageable often requires "narrowing" it, but narrowing is not always sufficient in itself. "World War II" may be too general a topic, but the "Battle of Midway" will probably not be any easier to manage. Rather than simply narrowing a broad subject to a smaller one, then, it may be more useful to *focus* on a specific aspect, on a particular slant, looking for a governing question to guide your research.

Asking a research question and developing a hypothesis

The result of this focusing process is a **research question,** a query or problem or issue that can be answered or solved or considered through research data. The research question may be tentatively answered by a **hypothesis,** a statement of what you anticipate your research might show. Thus you can begin your research by trying to answer this question, eventually trying to prove, disprove, or illustrate your hypothesis. (If the research question you pose has an obvious answer or if it requires technical knowledge beyond your grasp, go back to the drawing board to refocus your question.)

Like a working thesis (see 2f), a hypothesis must be not only manageable, but interesting and specific. In addition, it must be argumentative, a debatable proposition that can be proved or disproved by research evidence (see 4b). For example, a statement like this one cannot be disproved: "Roy Cohn was an assistant to Senator Joseph McCarthy during the 1950s." No one would argue against this fact, and its statement is not a hypothesis. On the other hand, this statement is debatable: "Roy Cohn's political views and assiduous but biased research while he was an assistant to Senator Joseph McCarthy during the 1950s were responsible for the larger part of McCarthy's anti-Communist witch hunts." Such a statement would have to be proved or disproved; thus, it is a hypothesis.

In most cases, you will want to explore your topic by doing background reading and making notes before you can formulate a research question or develop a hypothesis. In moving from a general topic of interest to a useful hypothesis, you progress from subject to issue to research question and eventually to hypothesis. In other words, from a large field of knowledge or interest, you narrow down to one single

TEACHING PRACTICE

One way of working toward a manageable topic or question is to have students brainstorm together on a topic. After students have explored a topic using some of the techniques presented in 2e, have them individually explain their interest in a topic, briefly giving some background or other information on it. Open the discussion up to the class, encouraging them to ask questions and to respond to the topic.

By fielding the class's questions and responses, students develop a sense of the possible directions their topics can have. This informal class brainstorming session helps them identify perspectives on the topic that interest others. Limit each session to fifteen minutes, five minutes for the student to present his or her topic, ten minutes for the class to respond and ask questions. At the end of the fifteen minutes, have each student freewrite for ten to fifteen minutes (1) suggestions for focusing, narrowing, or phrasing the research question, (2) a statement on his or her own interest in or possible approach to the topic, or (3) remarks on matters of purpose, audience, scope, or length.

To make the most of the activity, have at least four individual sessions, with no more than two presented in any one given class. Then break up the class into groups of four or five to work through this activity. The small group activity gives the entire class practice at working out possible topics.

manageable issue within the field. You then raise a question about that issue and put forward a possible answer, your hypothesis. Throughout this process, you will profit by *writing*, by trying to articulate your thoughts as clearly as possible. The following examples outline two students' movement from general subject to hypothesis:

SUBJECT	World War II
ISSUE	technological innovations in World War II
RESEARCH QUESTION	Did technological innovations in World War II make a significant difference to the Allies?
HYPOTHESIS	Superior technological innovations in a number of areas allowed the Allies to gain a decisive advantage in World War II.

SUBJECT	Shelley's poetry
ISSUE	my responses to the poem "The Sensitive Plant"
RESEARCH QUESTION	What accounts for the fact that I seem to read this poem in two conflicting ways?
HYPOTHESIS	Shelley's "The Sensitive Plant" resists easy reading or set interpretation in surprising ways.

Each of these student writers focuses on an issue about which a research question can be asked. The hypothesis that tentatively answers each question is precise enough to be supported or challenged by a manageable amount of research.

37d. Investigating what you know about your topic

Once you have narrowed and focused a topic, you need to marshal everything you already know about it. In practice, this step calls for what computer scientists call a "data dump": you try to "dump" all your immediate thoughts about the topic onto paper. Here are some useful methods for getting all your knowledge down on paper.

Brainstorming

Take five minutes to list everything you can think of concerning your hypothesis. Put down everything you know or wonder about your topic. You may find it helpful to work with one or two other students, using one another as sounding boards.

MOVING FROM HYPOTHESIS TO WORKING THESIS   *res* 37e

Freewriting in favor of your hypothesis

For five minutes, write without stopping about every reason that you believe your hypothesis is true. Put down everything you can think of. As in any freewriting (see 2e2), do not stop writing for any reason; simply go on writing for the full five minutes. No one will see this writing; its purpose is simply to provoke you to recall and write down what you already know and think about a topic.

Freewriting against your hypothesis

For five minutes, write down every argument you can think of that someone opposed to your hypothesis would make. Simply attack your hypothesis in every way you can, even in ways that might seem improbable.

Freewriting on your audience

Write for five minutes about your audience, including your instructor. Write about what they need or want to know in order to accept your hypothesis. What do they currently believe about your topic? What sorts of evidence will convince them to believe your hypothesis? What sorts of sources will they respect?

Tapping your memory for sources

List, in the form of short notes, everything you can remember about *where* you learned about the topic you are writing on: books, magazines, courses, conversations, television. Much of what you know may seem to you "common knowledge," but remember that common knowledge comes from somewhere. The places where you learned things can serve as starting points for investigation.

▌ 37e. Moving from hypothesis to working thesis

If you begin research with a research question and a hypothesis, your next goal is a working thesis. In between, as your research proceeds, your question is likely to be refined and your hypothesis is likely to go through some significant changes. Only after you have tested it, sharpened it, supported it, and explored it through your reading and writing does the hypothesis become a working thesis.

The hypotheses illustrated in 37c, for instance, might be focused further, or even completely changed, once research begins. The first

WRITERS WRITING

Description is a matter of observation, of paying attention to the world outside yourself. It is not "so hard," according to Annie Dillard, "if you mind your active verbs, keep ticking off as many sense impressions as you can, and omit feelings."

WRITERS ON WRITING

I was brought up to try to see what was wrong, and right it. Since I am a writer, writing is how I right it. I was brought up to look at things that are out of joint, out of balance, and to try to bring them into balance. And as a writer that's what I do.

—ALICE WALKER

writer might be able to discover very little on air force innovations but so much on naval technology and innovation during World War II that she decides to stick to that focus. The second writer might find in his research a critical reading of the Shelley poem that resolves his conflicting readings. In consequence, he would have to change the whole thrust of his discussion.

In doing research, you may find that a whole line of inquiry is unproductive, that a journal you need to complete an argument is not available, or that your hypothesis is simply wrong and must be discarded completely. In each case, the process of research pushes you to know more and more about your hypothesis, to make it more focused and precise. Such learning is what research is all about: in pursuing a research question and refining it into a hypothesis and eventually into a working thesis, you are teaching yourself how to become an expert. You are, in short, becoming a researcher.

READING ABOUT RESEARCH

In the following passage, astronomer Carl Sagan describes the excitement of the kind of research in which he is engaged, research that makes you "*really* think" and consequently "experience a kind of exhilaration." Read Sagan's description carefully. Have you done any research that fits his description? Try to think of one or two topics that you would really like to know more about or questions to which you have always wanted to know the answers. What kind of research would allow you to experience "exhilaration?"

. . . the main trick of [doing research in] science is to *really* think of something: the shape of clouds and their occasional sharp bottom edges at the same altitude everywhere in the sky; the formation of a dewdrop on a leaf; the origin of a name or a word—Shakespeare, say, or "philanthropic"; the reason for human social customs—the incest taboo, for example; how it is that a lens in sunlight can make paper burn; how a "walking stick" got to look so much like a twig; why the Moon seems to follow us as we walk; what prevents us from digging a hole down to the center of the Earth; what the definition is of "down" on a spherical Earth; how it is possible for the body to convert yesterday's lunch into today's muscle and sinew; or how far is up—does the universe go on forever, or if it does not, is there any meaning to the question of what lies on the other side? Some of these questions are pretty easy. Others, especially the last, are mysteries to which no one even today knows the answer. They are natural questions to ask. Every culture has posed such questions in one way or another. Almost always the proposed answers are in the nature of "Just So Stories," attempted explanations divorced from experiment, or even from careful comparative observations.

But the scientific cast of mind examines the world critically as if many alternative worlds might exist, as if other things might be here which are not. Then we are forced to ask why what we see is present and not something else. Why are the Sun and the Moon and the planets spheres? Why not pyramids, or cubes, or dodecahedra? Why not irregular, jumbly shapes? Why so symmetrical, worlds? If you spend any time spinning hypotheses, checking to see whether they make sense, whether they conform to what else we know, thinking of tests you can pose to substantiate or deflate your hypotheses, you will find yourself doing science. And as you come to practice this habit of thought more and more you will get better and better at it. To penetrate into the heart of the thing—even a little thing, a blade of grass, as Walt Whitman said—is to experience a kind of exhilaration that, it may be, only human beings of all the beings on this planet can feel. We are an intelligent species and the use of our intelligence quite properly gives us pleasure. In this respect the brain is like a muscle. When we think well, we feel good. Understanding is a kind of ecstasy.

—CARL SAGAN, *Broca's Brain*

FOR EXAMINING YOUR OWN WRITING

If you have done research for an essay before, now is a good time to go back and evaluate the work you did both as a researcher and as a writer in light of the principles developed in this chapter. What was the purpose of that research? What kinds of sources did you use? Did you have any audience other than your instructor? How was your topic focused? What were you most pleased with about your research, and about your essay? What were you least pleased with? What advice would you give yourself if you were to revise that essay?

38. Conducting Research

(BACK)GROUNDING

According to Charles Bazerman, "gathering convincing data is not easy." The method that a researcher uses greatly determines the evidence that supports the research, the conclusions the researcher is able to draw, and ultimately whether the research influences others to accept its claims. In other words, the way a researcher explores and produces data will affect how an audience responds to the research. Will it be believable? Is it accurate? reasonable and reliable? thorough? careful? appropriate? significant?

Bazerman advises researchers that "method is so central to the understanding and evaluation of the final written product that in many disciplines a writer is obliged to describe as part of the statement the method used to produce and analyze the data. In this way, many articles contain stories of how they were made" (331).

To appreciate the importance of choosing the methods appropriate to different research projects, researchers need to know that methods vary across disciplines and within them, and that they often change with time. For example, in linguistics, many sociolinguists believe that understanding the way words change in meaning is most accurately explained by observing the way words are used in different social contexts. Historical linguists, on the other hand, prefer to explain meaning changes in terms of the historical origins of words and language groups.

Once you have a topic or research question or hypothesis, how do you go about conducting research on it? That question was recently faced by an enterprising pair of writers with a passion for ice cream, who wanted to write an article for a local magazine on the best ice cream in Pittsburgh. Their guiding research questions (who has the best ice cream, and what makes it the best?) led them first to the library, where they did background reading on the history of ice cream and on how it is made. Then they went into the field, systematically tasting ice cream all over the city and interviewing ice cream makers. In preparing their article, these writers carried out the two basic kinds of research—*field* and *library* research.

38a. Collecting data in the field

For many research projects, you will need to collect data "in the field"—whether that field is an ice cream parlor, your own home, a laboratory, or the corner grocery store. When you gather information in the field, you are the primary reporter. You must discover where you can find relevant information, decide on the best ways to gather it, and find the best people to inform you about it. As a field researcher, you will become a detective not only of books and journals, but of the world. Three useful techniques for field research include observing, interviewing, and surveying.

1. Observing

Much professional writing depends on careful direct observation: a doctor's diagnostic notes, a reporter's news article, a social worker's case study. Observing can also provide rich information for your research writing. Sometimes called naturalistic research, **observation**

528

USEFUL READING

Bazerman, Charles. *The Informed Writer: Using Sources in the Disciplines.* 2d ed. Boston: Houghton, 1985. See Chapters 11–15 for an extensive, in-depth discussion of the ways different disciplines gather data for research. Bazerman describes the various methods of data gathering in the social and natural sciences, the historical, the experimental, and in the humanities and theoretical disciplines.

COLLECTING DATA IN THE FIELD   *res* 38a

calls on you to look at phenomena without trying to alter them in any way, keeping yourself out of the picture as much as possible. You can observe anything in this way, from the use of bicycle paths on campus to the kinds of products advertised during Saturday morning television shows to the growth of chicks in an agriculture lab.

Careful observation can supply support for a hypothesis or working thesis. For example, one student decided to write a proposal to try to persuade the traffic and parking division of his college to provide more motorcycle parking space in his dormitory parking lot. Because he wanted to show the need for such space, he set aside an eight-hour period to sit in the lot, recording the number of cars and motorcycles unable to find space. When he found that the ratio of motorcycles to cars was roughly three to one, direct observation paved the way for his request by helping to demonstrate a need.

Observation is also useful for finding out what people are actually doing as opposed to what they think or say they are doing. A reference librarian may believe he answers ten questions every five minutes and may report that to you in an interview, but observation may show you that he actually averages only seven questions every five minutes. The head of the dining commons may believe that most students eat two eggs for breakfast, but observation of people eating may reveal that most of them throw away at least one egg.

Preparing for observation

Before you go out into the field to observe, decide exactly what you are trying to find out and try to anticipate what you are likely to see. Are you going to observe an action repeated by many people (such as pedestrians crossing a street) or a sequence of actions (such as a medical procedure)? Are you observing a situation that might produce many different reactions—a child crying in a grocery store, for example? Try to decide exactly what you want to record and how to do so. In the grocery store, for instance, decide whether to observe the crying child, his or her parents, other shoppers, or store employees, and what you want to note—what they say, or what they do.

A checklist for conducting observation

- Determine the purpose of the observation, and review your research question and hypothesis to see that they relate.
- Set a definite period of time for the observation.
- If necessary, make an appointment.

WRITERS ON WRITING

The first commandment of writing is "Live!" The second is like unto it: "Pay attention!" I don't mean that you have to live high or fast or deep or wise or broad. And I certainly don't mean you have to suck out all the marrow of whatever you do, whether it's picking the lint off the navy-blue suit you'll be wearing to Cousin Ione's funeral or popping an Aunt Jemimah frozen waffle into the toaster. . . . The ominous question put to me by my students on all occasions of possible accountability is "Will this count?" My answer is rock bottom and hard: "Everything counts."

—SUZANNE BRITT

TEACHING PRACTICE

Though you will often assign research to be carried out individually, you might ask students to work as a team or group on a project. As one possibility, ask students to work in research teams to gather information for a report on the condition, the level of use, and any needed changes of the bike paths on campus. Allow a week or so for them to organize their efforts and to decide what kind of observations, interviews, and other data gathering they will need to do. Then ask them to write together a brief summary of how they have proceeded, noting problems they have encountered, and projecting ways to solve them.

Encourage your students to benefit from their colleagues' feedback, input, contributions, responses, and constructive criticism when they are, for example, working out an observation schedule. Or encourage them to brainstorm in groups, for example, to generate the most purposeful, specific questions for a survey.

USEFUL READING

McCartney, Robert. "The Cumulative Research Paper." *Teaching English in the Two-Year College* 12 (1985): 198–202. This article provides a model for allowing students to research in depth on one topic through several assignments.

- Develop a system for recording information. (The student studying motorcycle parking, for instance, used lined paper with three vertical columns to tabulate cars, motorcycles, and times).
- Take materials for keeping notes.
- Consider using a camera, tape recorder, or videocassette recorder.
- Assume the role of reporter, using the questions in 2e5 (*who, what, when, where, why,* and *how*) to note down what you see and hear.

2. Interviewing

Sometimes you will need information that is best sought by **interviewing,** or asking direct questions, of other people. If you can talk with an expert, in person or on the telephone, you might get information you could not get through any other kind of research. In addition to getting "expert opinion," you might ask for first-hand accounts, for biographical information, or for suggestions of other places to look or people to consult.

Finding people to interview

How do you go about identifying people to interview? Check first to see whether your research thus far names any people you might contact directly. Next, try to think of people who might be helpful—take a few minutes to brainstorm for names. In addition to authorities on your topic, consider people in your community who might be knowledgeable—lawyers, librarians, local government officials, alumni of your college.

Once you identify people you would like to talk with, either write or telephone to see whether an interview might be arranged. (See 44b for a discussion of letters of inquiry.)

Composing questions

To prepare useful questions, you need to know your topic well and to know a fair amount about your interviewee. Try to learn as much as you can about his or her experience and opinions. You will probably want to ask several kinds of questions. **Factual questions** ask for specific answers, ones that do not invite expansion or opinion.

> How many firebases was your unit posted to during your tour of duty in Vietnam?
>
> What flavors of ice cream does your company produce?
>
> How many people contributed to this year's United Way campaign?

COLLECTING DATA IN THE FIELD   *res* 38a

In contrast, **open-ended questions** ask the interviewee to think out loud, to go in directions that interest him or her, and to give additional details or anecdotes.

> How would you characterize the atmosphere of the Watergate hearings?

> How does public acceptance of modern art today compare with the situation forty years ago? How would you account for the change?

> How do you feel now about your decision to go to Canada in 1968 rather than be drafted?

Avoid questions that may (1) insult the interviewee—"Why was the city sued so frequently for police brutality during your term as chief of police?" (2) invite the interviewee to ramble on—"What do you think of youth today?" (3) elicit short yes/no answers—"Should the Indian Point reactor be closed down?" Instead, ask the interviewee to support an answer in some way—"Why should the Indian Point reactor be closed down?"

A checklist for planning an interview

- Determine your exact purpose, and check it with your research question and hypothesis to be sure they all relate.
- Set the interview up well in advance, specifying the amount of time it will take and asking permission to tape if you wish to do so.
- Prepare a written list of questions you can use to structure the interview. Brainstorming or freewriting techniques can help you to come up with questions (see 2e).
- If possible, try out your questions on one or two people to determine how clear and precise they are and how long answers will take. Revise and edit the questions as need be.
- Prepare a final copy of your questions, leaving plenty of space for notes after each one.
- Check out all equipment beforehand—pens, tape recorder, and so on. Record the subject, date, time, and place of interview at the beginning of all tapes.
- Take several pencils or pens and a notebook.

Conducting an interview

Be prompt, and dress appropriately. If you bring a tape recorder, ask the interviewee again for permission to record your conversation. Even if you use a recorder, bring a notebook with your questions, and write down the answers and any other notes you wish to make. Do not

WRITERS ON WRITING

A person observing the occurrence of certain facts and phenomena asks, naturally enough, what process, what kind of operation known to occur in Nature applied to the particular case, will unravel and explain the mystery? Hence you have the scientific hypothesis; and its value will be proportionate to the care and completeness with which its basis has been tested and verified. It is in these matters as in the commonest affairs of practical life: the guess of the fool will be folly, while the guess of the wise man will contain wisdom. In all cases, you see that the value of the result depends on the patience and faithfulness with which the investigator applies to his hypothesis every possible kind of verification.

—THOMAS HUXLEY

OPTIONAL EXERCISE

Ask students to choose a professor in a field of study that interests them, and interview that person about the research he or she tends to do. Encourage them to draw up a list of questions they would like answered about the kind of research questions asked in that field, the most typical methods of answering them, and the kinds of sources most often used. After the interview, have students summarize in two or three paragraphs what they have learned.

feel bound to the exact structure of your prepared questions, as long as the interview proceeds in a direction that seems fruitful. Be flexible. Note the time, and be careful not to take up more time than you said you would. End the interview with a thank you—and follow up with a letter thanking the person for taking the time to meet with you. (See 44e for a discussion of follow-up letters.)

3. Surveying opinion

One kind of large-scale interviewing surveys a number of people about an issue and provides one means of determining public opinion.

Surveys can take the form of interviews (see 38a2), but more often they depend on **questionnaires.** For an introductory language course, for instance, one student decided to investigate the variety of terms used to refer to grandparents. To gather this information, she prepared a simple questionnaire and distributed it to the members of five sections of the linguistics class she was taking.

The student investigating campus parking for motorcycles surveyed his dormitory's residents, asking how many owned motorcycles and how many of them had difficulty finding parking spaces. Though he sent questionnaires to everyone in the dorm, such extensive surveying is often unwieldy and even unnecessary. What you need is a representative sample of people, enough so that your survey accurately reflects opinion within the group you are discussing.

Preparing a questionnaire

To be effective, a questionnaire asks questions that will elicit the information necessary to accomplish your purpose. Questions should be clear and easy to understand and should be designed so that you will be able to analyze the answers easily. For example, questions that ask respondents to say yes or no or to rank something on a five-point scale of most to least desirable are easy to tabulate.

A checklist for designing a questionnaire

1. Write out your purpose, and review your research question and hypothesis to determine the kinds of questions to ask.
2. Determine the audience for your questionnaire, and figure out how you will reach them.
3. Using brainstorming, freewriting, or another strategy from 2e, draft some potential questions.
4. Check each question to see that it calls for short, specific answers.

EXPLORING LIBRARY RESOURCES   *res* | 38b

5. Test the questions on three or four people—including your instructor, if possible. Note which questions are hard to answer and why, and how much time the answers require.

6. Revise the questions as necessary to make them clear and specific.

7. Be sure to state a deadline as well as a place for returning the form.

8. Consider adding a question that asks for any other comments.

9. Type the questionnaire so that it is easy to follow, leaving adequate space for all answers.

10. Proofread your questionnaire.

▌ 38b. Exploring library resources

The library is one of a researcher's best friends, for answering a research question and exploring and testing a hypothesis most often begin there. Libraries provide two necessary kinds of information: general background, which will give you an overview of your topic and place your research question in context, and particular support, which helps answer your research question and develop your hypothesis.

▌ 1. Beginning your library research

Start by reviewing your research question, hypothesis, and knowledge you already have about your topic (see 37e). Where did that knowledge come from? Do you own any books about your topic? Have you recently read any magazine articles about it? Do your textbooks help? This is the place to begin a working bibliography, your list of possible sources, jotting down whatever sources you can think of.

When you have exhausted your own resources, turn to acquaintances who may be able to point you in useful directions. If, for instance, you are writing about computers, and a student down the hall knows everything about computers, go and talk to her. What books does she recommend? Does she have any computer magazines? How can she help get you going? Call that biology major you met last weekend, and ask her about genetic engineering. Take notes on what she says. Look up the teaching assistant you had for chemistry lab, and ask him for a reading list on radioisotope decay. If your library offers an orientation tour, go along and ask about sources on your topic.

Finally, talk to your instructor. Even if you are researching a topic you yourself selected, your instructor may be able to suggest where to begin looking for sources.

Choosing note-taking materials

Many researchers like to gather and organize information on index cards because they are easy to carry, and can be easily rearranged and grouped. Others prefer to use a tablet or notebook. Whichever form you choose, using it systematically will later help you to locate data and can serve as the basis for endnotes or a list of sources.

Identifying key words

Looking through card catalogs, databases, or indexes can be accelerated if you have identified **key words** to look for—synonyms for your topic, broader terms that would include it, or appropriate subtopics. Information on ice cream, for instance, might appear under the heading of frozen desserts, dairy products, or sherbet.

Choosing sources

Where to start? You may decide to begin with an overview, looking first, for example, at an encyclopedia. This strategy may be especially useful if you need a better focus on a research question or want to check for basic bibliographies. On the other hand, you may already have ideas about where to begin. Before you plunge in, however, ask yourself a few questions.

- *How current do your sources need to be?* If you must investigate the "cutting edge" of a field, you will want to check current periodicals (rather than books, which take longer to reach publication). On the other hand, if you want broader, more detailed coverage and background information, you will look more to books.
- *How much time do you have to spend?* If you have only two weeks to do your research, you will want to be selective about how broadly you cast your net. In fact, you probably will need to discipline yourself to move quickly along a fairly narrow research track. If you have several months, however, you can follow a broader course, perhaps even consulting materials beyond those available in your library.
- *How many sources should you consult?* You can expect to look over many more sources than you actually end up using. Your best guideline is to make sure you have enough sources to support your hypothesis or to prove your point.

Consulting the library staff

Your most valuable source at the library is the highly trained staff, especially the reference librarians. To get the most helpful advice,

(BACK)GROUNDING

When the inventions of writing and paper enabled people to accumulate information, efforts were put into keeping and presenting the new written information. Constructed in about 600 B.C., the royal library at Nineveh, capital of the Assyrian empire, may have been among the world's first great libraries. Historians and archeologists believe that it contained tens of thousands of works on the arts, sciences, and religion. Its grand achievement of cataloguing all contemporary knowledge made it the early ancestor of today's huge information systems and scientific data bases.

you should pose *specific* questions. "Where can I find information about computers?" will not give a librarian much specific information to go on, but "Where can I find information on the history of computers?" should help the librarian to lead you more directly to the sources you need. The more precise your question, the more useful an answer you will get.

If you find yourself unable to ask clear and precise questions, you probably need to do some general background research into your topic. Then work again on narrowing and focusing, defining a clearer issue, asking a more specific research question, and finding a sharper hypothesis. On your second trip, you will be ready to ask more specific questions and to find appropriate sources. (See 37c for more information on asking a research question and formulating a hypothesis.)

2. Selecting reference books

Your library's reference collection includes two broad types of **reference materials**: those that are general in scope and those that deal with specific disciplines (music, zoology, political science, and so on). Guides to reference books can help you identify sources that suit your purpose. Your research question can then help you choose the best references to use. Among the types most often consulted are encyclopedias, biographical dictionaries, almanacs, and periodical indexes.

Guides to reference books

Whether your interest is in nuclear physics, baseball history, or agricultural economics, you can probably find it in one of the two guides to reference books listed below. These guides group reference books by fields, including specialized bibliographies—lists of books and articles about a particular issue or discipline. Because these guides list other reference books—not actual sources—a few minutes with them can be a shortcut to the books that match your interests and purposes.

> *Guide to Reference Books*, 10th ed., 1986. Edited by Eugene P. Sheehy, this large book is usually just called "Sheehy." It supplies annotated lists of general reference works and specialized bibliographies. Sheehy is divided into five sections: General Reference; Humanities; Social and Behavioral Sciences; History and Area Studies; and Science, Technology, and Medicine. Each of these sections is further subdivided into areas and then into special approaches. Full bibliographic information, including the Library of Congress call number, is provided for each entry.

WRITERS ON WRITING

But the intellect which has been disciplined to the perfection of its powers, which knows, and thinks while it knows, which has learned to leaven the dense mass of facts and events with the elastic force of reason, such an intellect cannot be partial, cannot be exclusive, cannot be impetuous, cannot be at a loss, cannot but be patient, collected, and majestically calm, because it discerns the end in every beginning, the origin in every end, the law in every interruption, the limit in each delay; because it ever knows where it stands, and how its path lies from one point to another.

—JOHN HENRY NEWMAN

WRITERS ON WRITING

If you make a person understand something, you make that person happy—you communicate joy.

—CARL SAGAN

WRITERS ON WRITING

It is often when we dare to write beyond the edges of our own discipline, when we cross the border into another realm, perhaps not quite so familiar, that the real surprises occur. Astronomer/writer Carl Sagan delights in living on the edge. "Such insights as I've been able to achieve have been at the borders of the sciences, where different disciplines overlap. That's where the excitement is and where I want to be."

Walford's Guide to Reference Material, 4th ed., 1980–1987. "Walford" consists of three volumes: Volume 1—Science and Technology; Volume 2—Social and Historical Sciences, Philosophy, and Religion; and Volume 3—Generalia, Language and Literature, the Arts.

Encyclopedias

For general background on a subject, **encyclopedias** are a good place to begin. Though some encyclopedias do provide in-depth information, more often they serve as a place to start, not as a major source of information.

GENERAL ENCYCLOPEDIAS

Collier's Encyclopedia, 24 volumes. *Collier's* presents many topics and illustrations chosen to meet the needs of current student research.

Encyclopaedia Britannica, 15th ed., 32 volumes. The *Britannica* has a two-part structure; the *Micropaedia*, which contains general knowledge and short entries; and the *Macropaedia*, which contains longer entries that treat selected important subjects in depth. For fine essays on subjects in the classics and humanities, see if your library has the famous eleventh edition of the *Britannica*, published in 1911 and considered by many to be the most thoughtful and scholarly encyclopedia ever produced.

Encyclopedia Americana, 30 volumes. The *Americana* pays particular attention to American public figures, institutions, and places.

Encyclopedia Canadiana, 10 volumes. The *Canadiana* coverage of Canadian people, places, and institutions is more comprehensive than that of any other work.

SPECIALIZED ENCYCLOPEDIAS

Compared with general encyclopedias, **specialized encyclopedias** usually provide more detailed articles by authorities in the field as well as more extensive bibliographies for beginning research. These volumes are often located in the reference area or reading room for the particular discipline. Here are just a few examples.

Encyclopedia of Anthropology
Encyclopedia of Banking and Finance
Encyclopedia of Bioethics
Encyclopedia of Chemistry
Encyclopedia of Computer Science and Technology
Encyclopedia of Crime and Justice

EXPLORING LIBRARY RESOURCES

Encyclopedia of Earth Sciences
Encyclopedia of Economics
Encyclopedia of Education
Encyclopedia of Educational Research
Encyclopedia of Management
Encyclopedia of Philosophy
Encyclopedia of Physical Education, Fitness and Sports
Encyclopedia of Physics
Encyclopedia of Psychology
Encyclopedia of Religion and Ethics
Encyclopedia of Social Work
Encyclopedia of the Biological Sciences
Encyclopedia of World Art
International Encyclopedia of the Social Sciences
McGraw-Hill Encyclopedia of Environmental Science
McGraw-Hill Encyclopedia of Science and Technology
McGraw-Hill Encyclopedia of World Drama
New Illustrated Encyclopedia of World History

Biographical dictionaries and indexes

The lives and historical settings of famous people are the topics of **biographical dictionaries** and **indexes.** Before you use these sources, consider whether you need a volume covering people who are living or people who are dead. If the latter, decide if you want a current volume covering deceased people or an older volume covering living people that was published during the person's lifetime. Here are a few examples of biographical reference works; many others, particularly volumes specialized by geographic area or field, are available.

> *Biography Index*, 1946–. This quarterly index lists biographical material found in current books and over 1,500 periodicals.
>
> *Current Biography*, 1940–. This monthly publication carries informative articles on men and women in current events. It includes photographs and useful short bibliographies.
>
> *Dictionary of American Biography*, 1928–1937 plus supplements. Usually called the DAB, these volumes contain biographies of over 15,000 deceased Americans from all phases of public life since colonial days. The entries include bibliographies of sources.

WRITERS ON WRITING

Whether writer or scientist, it is important for every one of us to take responsibility for what we create. Arnold Toynbee writes: "To discover the existence of the atom and to go on to discover how to split it has been the *chef d'oeuvre* of Western science and technology. I do not love Western science for having made these deadly inventions; but I have just enough faith in Western man's political commonsense to expect that he will not liquidate himself."

WRITERS ON WRITING

When I [Anna Brito] recall what a mess we were in at times, I realize all over again that things don't work out—the "mistakes"—are integral to the whole process. You can't tell that a road will end in a cul-de-sac until you've gone down it, and someone must go down it so that other scientists will know that it is a cul-de-sac. The reason why science is so absorbing and exciting is that every new fact may be important, and so every new day may be important. As you go through the process, there is no way you can tell beforehand which fact, or which day, is going to be the golden one.

—JUNE GOODFIELD

WRITERS ON WRITING

The making of meaning is the work of the active mind, of what used to be called the imagination—that power to create, to discover, to respond to forms of all kinds.

—ANN BERTHOFF

WRITERS ON WRITING

You can deliberately force your mind through channels of deductions and associations in search of a solution to some problem and before long you have dug mental furrows for yourself and find yourself circling round and round the same limited pathways. . . . On the other hand, if you let go, then the thinking process comes under automatic involuntary control and is more apt to take new pathways and make erratic associations you would not think of consciously. The solution will come while you *think* you are not thinking.

—ISAAC ASIMOV

Dictionary of National Biography, 1882–1900 plus supplements. The DNB covers deceased notables from Great Britain and its colonies (excluding the postcolonial United States).

Who's Who in America, 1899–. Published every other year, this is the standard biographical reference for information about famous living Americans. Notable Americans no longer living are included in *Who Was Who in America*, covering from 1607 to the present. Similar specialized reference works include *Who's Who of American Women, Who's Who in Government,* and so on.

Who's Who, 1849–. Published annually, this reference supplies brief biographical listings for well-known living British people. *Who Was Who,* with volumes covering about a decade each, lists British notables who died between 1897 and the present.

International Who's Who, 1935–. Published annually, this source contains biographies of persons of international status.

Sources for current events and statistics

Almanacs, yearbooks, and other sources provide information on current events and **statistical data.** In addition to the following works, each of the general encyclopedias listed earlier in this section publishes an annual yearbook surveying events and developments of the preceding year in various fields.

Editorial Research Reports. Each of the weekly reports in this series consists of a twenty-page survey of a current issue and includes a current bibliography. The reports for each six months are gathered and published in hardcover volumes.

Facts on File. This weekly publication summarizes and indexes facts about current events, making topical information easy to find.

Statistical Abstract of the United States. This annual publication of the Bureau of the Census presents government data on population, business, commerce, industry, immigration, and other subjects.

World Almanac and Book of Facts. This annual publication presents data and statistics on business, education, sports, government, population, and many other topics. It covers institutional names and addresses and reviews important public events of the year.

Information Please Almanac. This annual publication includes many charts, facts, and lists as well as short summaries of the year's events and accomplishments in various fields.

Statesman's Year-Book. This source contains facts and helpful current statistics about agriculture, government, population, development, religion, and other topics in different countries of the world.

EXPLORING LIBRARY RESOURCES

res 38b

Periodical indexes

Periodical indexes provide guides to articles published in periodicals—journals, magazines, or newspapers. Each index chooses a group of periodicals to analyze and usually identifies them at the beginning of the volume. A general index for periodicals lists articles from current general-interest magazines, a newspaper index lists articles from a particular newspaper or selection of papers, and a specialized index covers articles in the scholarly journals of a particular discipline. These indexes will be among your most useful reference books for current articles and information.

GENERAL INDEXES

Readers' Guide to Periodical Literature. A good place to begin for any topic of general or popular interest is the *Readers' Guide,* which indexes articles from over 170 magazines. It is particularly helpful if you need to investigate social trends, popular scientific questions, and contemporary political issues. The *Readers' Guide* appears semi-monthly, with quarterly and annual cumulations. Entries are arranged by author and subject, with cross-references leading to related topics. Here is a typical *Readers' Guide* entry, covering entries under the subject heading *Divorce.*

> **DIVORCE**
> > See also
> > Children of divorced parents
> > Custody of children
> > Palimony
> > Support (Domestic relations)
> Johnson Products president hit with divorce petition after 37-year marriage. il pors *Jet* 74:32-3 My 23 '88
> Judgment call [Barnstable County (Mass.) Judge S. Lewis charged with favoring women in divorce proceedings] C. Colbath. il *Ms.* 16:81 Ap '88
> Mum's the word as Di's mom's marriage to a wallpaper heir comes unglued after 19 years [F. Shand Kydd] B. Johnson. il pors *People Weekly* 29:107+ Je 20 '88
> > **Statistics**
> Divorce insurance: have a son [effect of sons on marital stability; study by S. Philip Morgan] M. Adessa. *Psychology Today* 22:14-15 My '88
> Labor and love lost [relationship between hours worked and divorce rate for women; study by Julia Heath] V. Bozzi. *Psychology Today* 22:16 Ap '88
> > **Kenya**
> Divorce of two women tests Kenyan system. *Jet* 74:36 Je 13 '88
> > **United States**
> > See Divorce

The New York Times Index. Now extending back to 1851, this index appears twice a month, is accumulated yearly, and lists, by subject, every article that has appeared in the *Times.* For most articles of any length, short summaries are given as well.

Book Review Digest. This index contains excerpts from reviews of books along with information for locating the full reviews in popular and scholarly periodicals. Published yearly, this is the place to look for critical reviews and commentary on a book. When looking for reviews of a book, be sure to check for not only the year of the book's publication but also the next year.

Some libraries own **microfilm indexes** that cover many of the same entries as the printed indexes listed above. Microfilm are strips of film showing reduced pages of information. Each microfilm index covers only a limited period of time, usually several years, but for the recent past they are very efficient. Microfilm run on motorized projection machines that make the task of searching fast and easy. Ask the librarian for help in locating the microfilm and in running the machine. Here are three popular microfilm indexes.

Magazine Index. This index, updated monthly, analyzes four hundred general-interest magazines.

National Newspaper Index. This index, appearing monthly, covers the *New York Times,* the *Los Angeles Times,* the *Washington Post,* the *Wall Street Journal,* and the *Christian Science Monitor.*

Business Index. This index covers more than eight hundred business publications.

Special indexes and abstracts

Many disciplines have **specialized indexes** to help researchers find information in great depth. In general, such indexes list journal articles in periodicals but may include other publications as well. (Check the beginning of the volume for an explanation of what it includes.) Those with **abstracts** also briefly summarize entries, thus supplying more than a title to help you judge an item's potential usefulness. Here is a list of specialized indexes.

America: History and Life
Applied Science and Technology Index
Art Index
Biological Abstracts
Biological and Agricultural Index
Business Periodicals Index
Chemical Abstracts
Communications Abstracts
Computer Literature Index

EXPLORING LIBRARY RESOURCES

Cumulative Index to Nursing and Allied Health Literature
Current Index to Journals in Education
Dissertation Abstracts International
Ecology Abstracts
Education Index
Essay and General Literature Index
General Science Index
Historical Abstracts
Humanities Index
Index Medicus
Index to Government Periodicals
Index to Legal Periodicals
MLA International Bibliography
Music Index
Philosopher's Index
Physical Education Index
Physics Abstracts
Psychological Abstracts
Public Affairs Information Service (PAIS)
Science Abstracts
Social Sciences Index
Sociological Abstracts

❚ 3. Using the card catalog or circulation computer

A library's **card catalog** lists all the library's available materials, or holdings. Many libraries are gradually transferring the holdings in their card catalogs to **circulation computer** systems, which allow patrons to use public terminals to ask the computer to search for material on a topic. Most libraries with circulation computers, however, maintain card catalogs as well.

Finding author, title, and subject cards

In card catalogs, separate cards are prepared for each item—one headed by the author, one by the title, and others by subject. Thus you can look up a book by the last name of the author, by the first main word in the title, or by the subject of the book. Here are examples of author, title, and subject cards.

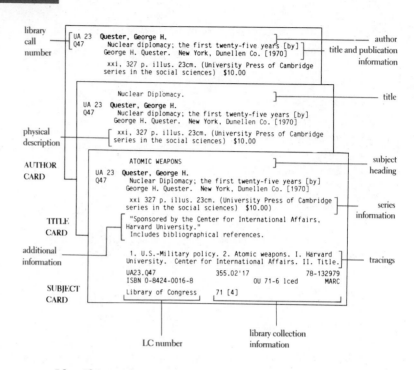

Identifying subjects

The card catalog provides an important source, but searching only subject cards is likely to be inefficient. Subjects are usually identified and arranged according to the system presented in *Library of Congress Subject Headings*. This large reference book may be kept at the reference desk or near the catalog so that you can check the exact wording of subject headings of interest to you.

Problems arise when the Library of Congress heading does not match your particular needs or when it is so broad that it lists hundreds of books, only a few of which will be helpful to you. If you were doing research on nuclear power plants, for instance, and looked up the Library of Congress heading "Nuclear Energy," you would find many books about nuclear weapons that had nothing to do with the nuclear generation of energy. For this reason, you need to screen subject entries carefully. In addition, use other leads—bibliographies, reference books, periodical indexes, notes in other publications, and so on—to identify potentially useful authors and titles. Though demanding more background work from you, such leads are likely to be much more specific and helpful.

EXPLORING LIBRARY RESOURCES   *res* 38b

Using the call numbers

Besides identifying a book's author, title, subject, and publication information, each catalog card also lists a **call number**—the book's identification number. For these numbers, most academic libraries now use the Library of Congress System, which begins call numbers with letters of the alphabet. Some libraries, however, still use the older Dewey Decimal System with all numerals, while others combine both systems. Once you have written down the complete call number, look for a library map or shelving plan to tell you which section or floor houses your book. When you find the area where your book is shelved, take the time to browse through the books shelved around it. Very often you will find the immediate area a more important treasure trove than any bibliography or index.

If your book is not on the shelf, ask about it at the circulation desk. You may be able to find out if someone has checked it out and if it is due soon. Very often a library will recall a book when another patron needs it. Allow for the time required for the library to notify the patron to return the book and then to notify you that it is available. Your deadline will determine whether it is realistic to request a recall.

4. Searching computerized databases

Although libraries differ in type and extent of computerization, more and more college libraries are subscribing to **databases,** highly specialized electronic indexes listing thousands of books and articles by authors, titles, and key words describing subjects. Currently, databases are available in the sciences, the social sciences, and the humanities. To use a database service, you provide a list of authors, titles, or key terms, and the computer searches the database for all references to them and then prints out a list of every reference in the database.

To use most databases, you will need the help of a librarian. Usually you must pay a fee for access time, so you will probably want to discuss with the librarian the available services, your needs, and the cost before deciding to consult an electronic database.

Selecting key words

Sometimes the key words for which you will ask a database to search its memory will be authors or titles, but more often they will be subject headings. Choose key words carefully, making them as precise as possible. The key word *brain*, for example, would yield many bibliographic items, probably thousands, but your task would be no easier

TEACHING PRACTICE
Ask students to brainstorm together on the best key words on the following topics: AIDS, computer viruses, white-collar crime.

as a result, and your bill might be tremendous. Using key words such as *neurological disorders* or *neural networks* would be much more helpful and cheaper. Often the most useful items you can give a librarian helping you are one or two good sources you have already found on your topic. The librarian can then determine some key words.

Reading a printout

After your search has been run, you will receive a printout of the results. As the following example printout demonstrates, each entry includes the author, title, publication information, subject, and index.

```
Subjects covered
----------------
Neural nets
Computer research

1   (GENERAL SCIENCE INDEX)
Bower, Bruce
Neural networks set sights on visual processing in brain
Science News 133:149 Mr 5  '88

Subjects covered
----------------
Neural network computers
Brain/Localization of function

2   (GENERAL SCIENCE INDEX)
Zipser, David; Anderson, Richard A.
A back-propagation programmed network that simulates
response properties of a subset of posterior
parietal neurons
Nature 331: 679-84 F 25  '88

Subjects covered
----------------
Neuran network computers
Brain/Innervation

3   (GENERAL SCIENCE INDEX)
Anderson, Alun
Neural networks: learning from a computer cat
Nature 331: 657-9 F 25  '88

Subjects covered
----------------
Neural network computers
Brain/Innervation

4   (GENERAL SCIENCE INDEX)
Farnat, Nabil H.
Optical associative memories: first step
toward neuromorphic optical data processing
Physics Today 41:S62-S63 Ja '88
```

39. Evaluating and Using Source Materials

All research builds on the astute, judicious, and sometimes inspired use of sources—that research work done by others. As Isaac Newton noted, those researchers who see the farthest do so because they "stand on the shoulders of giants." And while researchers cannot always count on a giant's shoulders to stand on, the quality of their insights is often directly related to how well they have understood and used the source materials—the shoulders—they have relied on. As a reader, you will want to make the most of your sources, using the insights you have gained from them in creating powerful prose of your own. This chapter will guide you in considering your use of sources in research.

39a. Choosing sources

Experienced researchers know that all sources are not created equally useful, that some are infinitely more helpful or provocative than others. One of your goals, therefore, is to learn to recognize which sources will be most helpful, which ones will allow you to see the farthest.

The following sections will provide some guidance to help you decide when to delve more deeply into a work and when to set it aside. Not all sources you examine will prove useful to you, so you need to learn how to judge, in Francis Bacon's words, which are to be tasted, which swallowed, and which chewed and digested.

1. Assessing the usefulness of a source

Several characteristics of a book or article can help you assess its usefulness.

(BACK)GROUNDING

In ordinary language, we say we have received information when *what we know* has changed. The bigger the change in what we know, the more information we have received. Information, like energy, does work. But whereas energy does physical work, information does logical work. While this view that increased information changes what we know is largely true, it's intellectually disastrous to accept blindly and unquestioningly our information sources. A judicious, practiced researcher learns that not everything she or he reads in journals, magazines, or scholarly books is true simply because it appears in publication. The truly inquisitive researcher understands that no source is totally beyond dispute.

545

USEFUL READING

Bronowski, Jacob. "The Creative Mind." Chapter 1 of *Science and Human Values*. New York: Simon, 1965. A provocative essay on (1) the role of the creative mind in scientific activity, (2) the nature of truth in science and social life, and (3) the connection between human values and science.

Date of original publication

The more recent the source, the more up-to-date you can generally expect its information to be. Recent sources are often more useful than older sources, especially in the sciences, which change so quickly. Be cautious, however, about judging a source only by age. Some older sources in any field are still the most authoritative works of the discipline. Thus, age must be balanced with other factors such as the quality or current acceptance of the material.

Level of specialization

Determine quickly whether a source provides a general overview or whether it is specialized in a way that is useful to you. General sources read easily and may be helpful as you begin your research, but they often lack the authority or up-to-dateness of the more specialized sources you may need later. Extremely specialized works, on the other hand, may be too technical to be read or understood easily.

Relevance to your topic

The most helpful sources are those most closely related to your research area. Look beyond the title to the subtitle, preface, introduction, and table of contents to determine just how directly a particular source addresses your topic.

Cross-referencing

Note those sources that are cited again and again in your reading. The more a source is referred to in other works, the more you can assume it to be a standard work whose content and approach are widely respected.

2. Looking through a source

Researchers can often pick up a book or article, look it over quickly, and decide within a few minutes whether it merits more careful study. Here are some elements to check for in looking over a source to help you use it most efficiently.

- *Title and subtitle.* If you are investigating coeducation in the nineteenth century and find a book called *Women in Education*, the subtitle *The Challenge of the 1970s* will tell you that you probably do not need to examine the book.

CHOOSING SOURCES *res* 39a

- *Abstract*. Abstracts are concise summaries of articles or books. They routinely precede articles in some journals and are included in certain periodical or bibliographic guides. The purpose of an abstract is to help readers decide whether to read the entire work, so if you run across a source that includes one, you should read it.
- *Table of contents*. Part and chapter titles can often give you a good idea of what a book contains, so turning directly to the table of contents is an efficient first step. Try to determine whether the chapter topics seem *specific* enough to be useful to you.
- *Preface or foreword*. Very often the preliminary pages of a book specify in detail the writer's purposes, range of interests, intended audience, topic restrictions, research limitations, and thesis. If the book contains either a preface or a foreword, check to see whether either summarizes what is to come.
- *Conclusion*. Some books and articles end with a summary of the contents and a statement of significance that could help you decide how appropriate that source is for your project.
- *Index*. A good index is like a cutaway drawing of the book's contents. Turn right away to the back of the book and check the index for words and topics key to your project. Then see whether they seem to have much importance in the book. Are the listings for your key terms many or few?
- *Bibliography and/or footnotes*. Lists of references on a subject, usually at the end of a book or article, show how carefully a writer has investigated the subject. In addition, they may help you find other sources for your study.

3. Skimming

If your investigation suggests that a source is potentially useful, take time to skim through it. Skimming a source can tell you a great deal about its approach and tone. Just by quickly reading over a few pages—or even a few sentences—of several parts of a source, you can get an idea of whether or not the book or article will be truly useful for your purposes. Look at the subheadings and at the first sentences of paragraphs. Then check the index for one of your key terms, turn to two or three pages listed, and skim them with the following questions in mind:

- Does this source cover material you need?
- What is the author's perspective—as advocate, critic?

TEACHING PRACTICE

Reading through sources with one's research question in mind is the ideal way of reading with focused efficiency. However, students do not always have a research question in mind when they start. If a student hasn't formalized one, encourage him or her to look through the table of contents for a perspective or subheading on the general topic. Before he or she begins to skim through, the writer might ask himself or herself a question about the topic based on the table of contents subheadings.

For example, a student is working on a research project that helps her to understand the connection between philosophy and science. Since this is obviously a huge topic with virtually unlimited possibilities, she should find out what others have said about this connection, one possibility being Charles S. Pierce, considered by some to be among America's most original philosophers and logicians. The student suspects that a book by Richard Tursman, *Pierce's Theory of Scientific Discovery: A System of Logic Conceived as Semiotic* (1987), may be too specialized. She looks at it anyway because the table of contents lists two sections on critical logic. It inspires her to ask the question "what's the connection between critical logic and science?" As it turns out, Tursman is too specialized. Nonetheless, she now has a question that she continues to apply to her reading. Though this process may seem inefficient, it is a necessary part of the discovery of the available sources on a subject.

USEFUL READING

Quantic, Diane. "Insights into the Research Process from Student Logs." *Journal of Teaching Writing* 5 (1986): 211–225. This article discusses writing blocks related to research papers and suggests strategies to overcome these blocks.

- How does this perspective relate to your own?
- Are there facts, examples, research data, or expert opinions that you can use as evidence?

ANSWERS TO EXERCISE 39.1 WILL VARY

EXERCISE 39.1

Work in the library for an hour or so, using the techniques explained in 39a to evaluate several possible sources for a topic you are considering. Choose two sources and assess them carefully, entering your comments in your writing log if you are keeping one. Note the sources you examined, what you looked for, what specific elements helped you decide whether or not the sources would be useful, what use you expect to make of the sources, and how long you spent evaluating them. Finally, summarize where the research seems to be headed and what you now most need to do.

39b. Reading sources

Research calls for active, aggressive reading. "Active" readers take up conversation with the books they read, responding to the text with questions and comments. The more attentively you read, and the more you respond to what you read, the better your research will be. This section will guide you through some steps that will help you to become an active, questioning reader.

1. Building a working bibliography

One of the most basic requirements of reading for research is the creation of a working bibliography—a list of books, articles, and other sources that seem likely to address your research question. The emphasis here is on *working*—for this list will continue to evolve as you go along. Your working bibliography will include materials that may end up *not* being useful—one path will lead to another, and you will probably go in a few directions before you can know the one that's right. Keeping a working bibliography can help you to chart your course—and from this bibliography will evolve the list of works you finally use and cite in the essay.

As you use periodical indexes, the card catalog, or the circulation computer, make a bibliography card or notebook entry for each source you expect to be useful. At this stage, you need not be too selective; if you think you *might* use the source, make up an entry. As long as you have a bibliography entry for it, a source is easy to find a second time if you need to.

READING SOURCES   *res* 39b

Some researchers prefer to use cards for bibliography entries because they can easily be arranged and rearranged—alphabetically for your list of sources, or by subtopic for the content of your essay. Other researchers prefer to keep bibliography entries in a notebook. Whichever format you choose, bibliography entries must contain all of the information necessary to produce your final list of sources—author, title, publisher's name and location, year of publication—plus the library call numbers of books or journals, in case you need to retrieve them. When you look at the actual source, be sure to check the accuracy of your entry by consulting the title and copyright pages of a book and the table of contents and first page of an article in a magazine or journal. Here are examples of bibliography cards or notebook entries for a book and a magazine article.

```
Pn 1992.3
u 5G57
1983

      Gitlin, Todd. Inside Prime Time.
      New York: Pantheon, 1983.
```

```
   Swertlow, Frank. "Hollywood's
   Cocaine Connection." TV Guide 28
   Feb., 1981: 6-12.
```

WRITERS ON WRITING

Scientific papers are not devoid of human touches if you know the code, if you know where to find the various clues. In the introduction you can pick up the writer's position in relation to his [or her] question; you can pick up his [her] individual judgment in the method he, or she, has chosen; and in the way the results are presented, you pick up the quality of mind; finally, you again pick up the quality of mind in the discussion sections at the end of the paper, when the writer looks at his [or her] own particular problems and places them in perspective—in their relation to the problems and ideas currently in circulation.

—JUNE GOODFIELD

WRITERS ON WRITING

The most difficult portion of any inquiry is its initiation.

—F. S. C. NORTHROP

After I have chosen a topic, the easiest thing for me to do is to write about how I really feel about it.

—LINNEA SAUKKO

WRITERS ON WRITING

As a writer you are free. You are about the freest person that ever was . . . but, absolute freedom is absolute responsibility. The writer's job, as I see it, is to tell the truth. The writer's truth—nobody else's.

—URSULA K. LE GUIN

The entries shown above follow the Modern Language Association (MLA) style, the system for citing sources most widely used in English courses, but different disciplines use other systems (see Chapter 41). Writing the entries on the cards in the exact form you will use in your final bibliography will save you considerable time.

ANSWERS TO EXERCISE 39.2 WILL VARY

EXERCISE 39.2

If you have been making a working bibliography during your current research, take time now to check your entries for accuracy and fullness of information. If you have not yet made any entries, do so now for the sources you evaluated in Exercise 39.1, following the appropriate citation style.

2. Reading your sources with a critical eye

Researchers read with a strong sense of purpose: how does this source relate to my research goals? does it support my ideas, develop them further, or challenge them? Reading with a purpose calls for examining your sources with an astute, critical eye. Because of time constraints and the wealth of material available on most topics, you probably will not have time to read completely through all of your potential material. Thus, reading with a critical eye can make your research process more efficient; and the following considerations can guide your critical reading:

Reading with your research question in mind

A very good way of focusing your attention on the information most necessary to your research is to read with your research question in mind. Use the index and the table of contents to zero in on the parts of books that will help you answer your research question. Consider the following questions as you read:

- How does this material address your research question?
- In what ways does it provide support for your hypothesis?
- How might particular quotations help support your thesis?
- Does the source include counterarguments to your hypothesis that you will need to answer? What are they? What answers can you provide?

Identifying the author's perspective and tone

Every author holds opinions that affect his or her discussion of an issue, which you as a reader must try to recognize and understand.

Even the most seemingly factual report, like an encyclopedia article, is necessarily filled with implicit, often unstated, judgments. Read with an eye for the author's overall **perspective**—is he or she an advocate, in favor of something, or a critic, at odds with it?—as well as to seek out facts. In addition, identify the author's **tone**, or attitude toward both issues and audience. Is it cautious, angry, flippant, serious, impassioned? (For more on tone, see Chapter 26.) Alertness to perspective and tone will help you fully understand a source and, as a result, better decide how (or whether) to use it. The following questions can help you to read for perspective and tone:

- What is the author's perspective?
- What has persuaded the author to take this perspective? Does the author have a particular orientation toward the subject area?
- In what ways do you share the author's perspective?
- In what ways do you question or differ with the author's perspective?
- What is the author's tone? What words express this tone?

Assessing the author's argument and evidence

Every piece of writing has what may be called an argument, a position it takes. Even a report of scientific data implicitly "argues" that we should accept it as reliably gathered and reported. As you read, then, try to identify the author's argument, for it is his or her main point. Then try to decide *why* the author holds this view. Considering the following questions as you read can help you to recognize—and assess—the points being argued in your sources:

- What is the author's main point?
- How much and what kind of evidence supports that point?
- How persuasive do you find the evidence?
- Can you offer any counterarguments or refutations to the evidence?
- Can you detect any questionable logic or fallacious thinking? (See 4e.)

Questioning your sources

Because all sources make an explicit or implicit argument, they often disagree with one another. Disagreements among sources arise sometimes from different factual understandings, sometimes from different perspectives—ways of looking at things. For instance, if an authoritative source says that the chances of a nuclear power plant melting down are 1 in 100,000, two different commentators could interpret that statistic very differently. A critic of nuclear power could argue that nuclear accidents are so terrible that this chance is too much to take, while a supporter of nuclear power could argue that such a small chance is essentially no chance at all.

The point is that all knowledge must be interpreted subjectively, by people. As a result, a writer may well tell the truth and nothing but the truth; but he or she can never tell the *whole* truth because people are not all-knowing. Thus you must build your own informed opinion, your own truth, by seeking out and assessing many viewpoints as you read. Not all disputes can be solved by appealing to "neutral facts" because there *are* no neutral facts in the world of meanings. You must examine all sources critically, using them not as unquestioned authorities but as contributions to your own interpretation.

▌ 39c. Taking notes

Once you have decided a source might be useful to you, you will want to take notes on what you read. Note-taking requires reading carefully and purposefully, approaching a source with some general questions in mind. What do you expect the source to say about the subject? What will the source help you to demonstrate or prove? What part of your research is the source most relevant to? What else do you need to know?

Notes may be recorded either on index cards or in a notebook. Many writers like cards because they can be arranged in the order in which the notes are to be used in the essay. If you use cards, try to put only one piece of information or quotation on each one, so you can move it easily if necessary.

Because the bibliography entry (see 39b1) for a source fully identifies it, writing the author's last name and a key word from the title at the beginning or end of each note is usually enough to identify it for you. Then your note-taking can begin. Record the exact page reference for the note. If the note refers to more than one page, indicate the page breaks so that if you decide to use only part of the note in your essay, you will know which page to cite.

As you complete each note, read it over carefully. Recheck quotations, statistics, and specific facts for accuracy. Avoid abbreviations that may be confusing, especially in quotations, which should use the exact wording, spelling, and punctuation of the original.

TAKING NOTES

Most of your notes will take the form of direct quotation, para-phrase, summary, or key terms. These forms can be combined; for example, you may want to summarize a passage but to quote one particular phrase or sentence from the same passage. In addition, you can photocopy material that you do not have time to take handwritten notes on.

Quoting

Quoting involves noting down direct quotations, a source's *exact words*. As a general rule, use direct quotations when the quotation is so memorable or expresses a point so perfectly that you cannot improve or shorten it without destroying the meaning you need. Because they represent a source's words exactly, direct quotations give special weight to their author's opinion. Quotations from those directly involved in an issue (crime victims, political leaders) are effective in social science essays; quotations from primary sources (literary works, eyewitness ac-counts) are especially important in humanities essays.

In any research essay, however, quotations from reliable and re-spected authorities can help establish your credibility as a researcher and thus increase your audience's confidence in your research and your conclusions. In addition, well-chosen quotations can broaden the appeal of your final essay by drawing on emotion as well as logic, appealing both to the reader's mind and heart. A student writing a research essay on the ethical issues involved in bullfighting, for ex-ample, might introduce an argument demonstrating that bullfighting is not a real sport by quoting Ernest Hemingway's striking comment that "the formal bull-fight is a tragedy, not a sport, and the bull is certain to be killed." (See 4e and 4f for more on logical and emotional appeals.)

In beginning research on traditional distinctions between *mind* and *brain*, a student writer came across the following sentences. The first could easily be paraphrased; the second, however, seemed partic-ularly memorable, so the student recorded it exactly.

ORIGINAL SOURCE

Mind is nothing more than a term we employ to describe some of the functions of the brain.

And further brain research isn't going to define further the matter of "mind" any more than turning over all the turf in Ireland is likely to turn up a colony of leprechauns.   —RICHARD RESNICK, *The Brain*

Copy direct quotations *carefully*, with every punctuation mark, capital letter, and spelling exactly as in the original. Be sure, as the student does in the sample card below, to use brackets to introduce any words of your own and ellipses to show where you have cut material from a long quotation (see 32b and 32f). Of course, you will need to transfer the brackets or ellipses directly into your paper if you use the quotation. Here is the student's note card for the second sentence above. Notice that he uses both brackets and ellipses.

Resnick, <u>The Brain</u>, p. 343

"And [more] brain research isn't going to
define.., 'mind' any more than turning over
all the turf in Ireland is likely to turn up
a colony of leprechauns."

ANSWERS TO EXERCISE 39.3 WILL VARY

(BACK)GROUNDING

Paraphrasing is a skill that has twofold value. It helps us to communicate. But it also helps us do something else that isn't always readily apparent to students: it helps us in our learning. Because a paraphrase requires us to put someone else's meaning into our own words, we have to understand the meaning of the original. If we have trouble with the paraphrase, our difficulty likely indicates that we don't have an adequate grasp of the original passage. The measure of how well we understand what we've read is the paraphrase (or the summary). This claim is based on the thinking that we don't understand what we read as well as we think we do unless we can express that understanding with our own words. In expressing our understanding we are involved in a process of learning.

EXERCISE 39.3

Select one or two striking or especially authoritative quotations from a source listed in the working bibliography you created in Exercise 39.2, and enter them on note cards or in a notebook. Explain briefly why you consider each quotation noteworthy—why, in other words, you would quote rather than paraphrase or summarize.

Paraphrasing

A **paraphrase** accurately and thoroughly states all the relevant information from a passage *in your own words*. Paraphrase passages whose full meaning you want to include in your note.

ORIGINAL	Mind is nothing more than a term we employ to describe some of the functions of the brain.
PARAPHRASE	The term *mind* often simply denotes some of the brain's activities. (Resnick, 343)

TAKING NOTES   *res* 39c

If the paraphrase read "Mind and brain are the same thing," the para-phrase would have been less than accurate and thorough; if it read "*Mind* is nothing more than a word for some of the functions of the brain," it would risk the danger of plagiarizing by relying too much on the original author's own words.

Here is a longer example and a student's paraphrase as noted on a card.

ORIGINAL SOURCE

Certainly the site of the Popham colony was not the best choice. A few miles upriver from the mouth of the Kennebec, the site was on an open bluff which may have looked splendid in August and September when they landed, but during winter it was exposed to bitter weather and biting winds. This caused suffering, and the colonists later com-plained that winter was their downfall. Indeed, that winter of 1607 was a severe one, even in England. But if the weather had been terribly bad, the colony could have moved farther up the Kennebec, which they explored as far as Augusta, or to the sheltered islands in Muscongus Bay, which Weymouth had suggested. The site near the mouth of the Ken-nebec, however, offered a good location for trading with the Indians and good fishing grounds.

The prime reason for failure lay not with the weather or sickness or site, but with the character of the colonists and their leaders. They were not of the right stuff. They failed to form themselves into an ef-fective, pioneering community.

—BILL CALDWELL, *The Islands of Maine*

Caldwell, <u>Islands of Maine</u>, pp. 56–57

Situated on an open bluff above the mouth of the Kennebec, the Popham colony of 1607 was established in August and September but was then exposed to harsh weather during the bitter winter of that year. Nevertheless, the colonists chose to stay there because the river made fishing and trading with the local Indians possible. When the colony failed, the colonists blamed the harsh winter, but in reality they had poor leaders and were themselves poorly chosen. As a result, they never became a cohesive group.

TEACHING PRACTICE

Points to emphasize in discussing paraphrasing:

Retain the points of the original. Do not simply sub-stitute single words or phrases. Often a synonym will not convey the same sense as the original, although the thesaurus lists them as synonymous. According to the *Roget's Thesaurus*, the following list offers sub-stitutes for *exact* (adjective):

> accurate, precise, nice (RIGHT); specific, defi-nite, unequivocal (BOUNDARY); literal, verbal, verbatim (MEANING).

Ask your students to discuss which of the synonyms can be inserted in place of *exact* in the following sentences:

> Although we insisted she'd made a mistake, the metermaid maintained she'd recorded the *exact* reading on the meter.

> I wonder why many people who study or speak additional languages think that *exact* translations from one language to another are impossible.

A paraphrase does not have to have the same number of words as the original passage—the paraphrase should be at least 80 percent the original length. If it totals fewer words than 80 percent of the original, the writer has likely left out minor information or details. If the paraphrase totals more than 135 per-cent, the paraphrase may be repeating or overstating points. Excessive length may indicate rambling, or inserting information not from the original, such as the writer's critical or evaluative comments.

TEACHING PRACTICE

As invaluable pedagogical practice, have students paraphrase (and summarize) their reading assignments on a regular basis. Whenever students paraphrase (or summarize), have them compare versions and explain similarities and differences. Collaborating on a second version will help them appreciate not simply where their troubles lie but also the learning effectiveness of collaboratively talking out, working out, and writing out material they are studying.

ANSWERS TO EXERCISE 39.4 WILL VARY

TEACHING PRACTICE

Like the paraphrase, the summary is a useful learning as well as communicating skill. Summaries give students practice identifying and coordinating the main points of a passage. Although summaries don't have to be written in students' own words, insisting that students rephrase in their own words the main points of an original passage will help them better understand what they are reading. This practice of rephrasing summarized (and paraphrased) information will also help them work source material into their research projects more easily. For this reason, discourage them from simply pulling out phrases, sentences, or chunks of the original, then merely stringing them together.

A CHECKLIST FOR PARAPHRASING

- Include all relevant information from the original.
- State the meaning completely in your own words; if you want to include an especially memorable phrase or sentence from the original passage, enclose it in quotation marks.
- Omit your own comments, elaborations, or reactions.
- Make sure to record the original source of the paraphrase.
- Recheck the paraphrase for accuracy and thoroughness.

EXERCISE 39.4

Choose an important passage from one of the sources you listed in the working bibliography in Exercise 39.2, and paraphrase it following the guidelines above.

Summarizing

A **summary** is a significantly shortened version of a passage, a section, or even a whole chapter or work that captures the main ideas *in your own words*. A good summary conveys the heart of a source with just enough information to record the main points. If you must include any of the original wording, put it in quotation marks. A summary card of the passage about the Popham colony that was paraphrased above might look like this:

> Caldwell, Islands of Maine, pp. 56-57
>
> The Popham colony of 1607 failed because of a poor site subject to harsh winter weather, poor leadership, and the poor character of company members, who were never able to work together as a group.

The length of a summary depends on how long the original is and how much information you will need to use. Your goal is to keep the summary as brief as possible, capturing only the gist of the passage. As

TAKING NOTES

a general rule, aim for no more than two sentences of summary for a paragraph. If you must summarize a book, pay particular attention to the preface or introduction, which often states the book's main ideas.

EXERCISE 39.5

Choose a section from a source you listed in the working bibliography in Exercise 39.2, and write a summary of it, emphasizing the main ideas in your own words.

Taking key-term notes

Taking key-term notes is a technique many researchers use. As their name suggests, such notes consist of significant terms jotted down as you read along. They may include names, dates, short statements, or quotations—anything that can jog your memory or be used in drafting the essay. Key-term notes on the passage about the Popham colony that was paraphrased and summarized above might look like this:

> Caldwell, <u>Islands of Maine</u>, pp. 56-57
>
> Popham colony 1607-failed at mouth of Kennebec
> poor site on bluff - col. blamed winter
> stayed because could trade and fish
> poor leadership & poor character

Key-term notes are useful in condensing an article or a source to a "nutshell" of information. But you must be sure that they are complete enough so you can remember what they mean and how they fit together. Be sure to include the author and title, and note the page numbers of the passage to which the key terms refer. Be careful about using abbreviations in key-term notes. In this case, the writer probably would recognize *col.* as *colonists*. Had the writer used *co.*, however, remembering whether the abbreviation meant *company*, *colony*, *companions*, or some other word might have been difficult.

ANSWERS TO EXERCISE 39.5 WILL VARY

TEACHING PRACTICE
Some students will tend to pick only one- or two-term key words, while others will pick phrases or clauses, essentially the core of a passage. Since the importance of key words is that they enable a reader to cluster the terms into some meaningful essential form of the original, more is better.

ANSWERS TO EXERCISE 39.6
WILL VARY

EXERCISE 39.6

Review the key-term notes on the passage about the Popham colony, and answer the following questions.

1. What points would you add to the notes?
2. What points would you leave out of the notes?

Then create a few key-term notes from the source that you summarized in Exercise 39.5. Then, ask yourself these questions: Do the notes provide enough information to bring back the original passage? What could you do to make these notes more useful?

Photocopying source material

Nearly all libraries are equipped with photocopying machines, and as a researcher you can use them to photocopy pages or even whole articles or chapters. If you photocopy materials, make sure to write out on the photocopy all the source information you will need to cite in your bibliography (see 39b1). (And check to make sure that page numbers are clearly legible on copies.)

39d. Interpreting sources

Your task as a reader is to identify and understand sources and sets of data as completely as possible. As a writer, your aim must be to present data and sources *to other readers* so that they can most readily understand the point you are making. Doing so calls for careful thinking on your part, as you work to interpret sources.

Turning data into information

Computer scientists sometimes distinguish between **data**—bits of facts or strings of statements—and **information**—the meaning attached to the data. As a researcher, you will gather a great deal of data, probably more than you need or can use. But those data become information only when their meaning is made clear. You may have gathered two dozen facts about a particular city's finances, for example, but together they form a rather random list of facts. Turning them into information calls for pointing out their significance or meaning—that, for instance, the city is on the brink of bankruptcy.

Synthesizing data and drawing inferences

You can begin turning data into information by **synthesizing**—grouping similar pieces of data together; looking for patterns or trends, identifying the gist, or main point, of the data. Most often, finding the gist of a source or set of data will call for drawing **inferences**—conclusions that are not explicitly stated but that follow logically from the data given. For example, you may have data indicating severe drought in every Midwestern state. Other data report very low levels of crop production in those states. From these data, you draw the inference that farmers in the Midwest face financial crisis. As a researcher, you have turned data into information.

Recording your thoughts and ideas

Perhaps the most exciting part of research occurs when the materials you are reading spark something in your mind and new ideas take hold. As you read, your mind is busy processing all the materials you are discovering with those you have previously discovered, seeking connections and similarities, making distinctions, synthesizing in the ways discussed above. As you work, ideas will occur to you that will become part of your position or argument. *Don't let them get away.* Jot down the ideas that come to you as you read, perhaps in a special section of your writing log if you are keeping one. Do not worry about whether the idea is true or right or even useful—just get it down and think about it later. Some ideas may be thrown away because they do not suit the final shape your essay takes, but others will likely *provide* that final shape.

Disagreements among sources can provide particularly fruitful areas to consider and may provoke you to new insights all your own. Consequently, you need to pay close attention to the arguments put forth by all your sources—those you agree with as well as those you disagree with. Jot down your thoughts as you read—agreements, questions, comments, reactions.

EXERCISE 39.7

Following are two passages about the War of 1812, the first from an American encyclopedia and the second from a Canadian history book. Read each one carefully, and then answer the following questions, noting any differences in the two accounts.

1. What motivated the War Hawks?
2. Who attacked whom at the beginning of the Battle of Tippecanoe?
3. What did the War of 1812 mean in British, American, and Canadian history?
4. Why did the Treaty of Ghent end up restoring the prewar boundaries?

ANSWERS TO EXERCISE 39.7

Part 1

From *The World Book Encyclopedia*

1. A desire for territorial expansion that was resisted by the Indians with the suspected aid of the British.
2. The Indians attacked some Americans.
3. The invasion of Canada. The American reaction to the trade and territorial interference of the British. The rise of manufacturing in the United States.
4. The Treaty of Ghent restored everyone's lands because the American victories forced the British to drop their demands for certain territory on the northern frontier and for the establishment of a large permanent Indian reservation. The British had no bargaining power.

From *Canada: A Story of Challenge*

1. To acquire Canada, already invaded by American settlers.
2. Americans attacked the Indians.
3. In Canadian history, it meant a land war, a struggle against American invasion. The war was vitally more important for Canada than for Britain and much more dangerous for Canada than for the United States. It meant the survival of British North America, the fostering of anti-American attitudes and Canadian nationalism.
4. According to Careless, the Treaty of Ghent restored everyone's original lands because Britain wanted to direct her attention to the Napoleonic revival rather than expend it on land disputes.

Part 2

1. The perspective is one that appears to favor the American side of the conflict.
2. The events are evaluated from the perspective of American interest.
3. For example, we are told that the reasons for the war include British interference in U.S. naval trade and that an important result of the War was the rapid rise of manufacturing in the United States.
4. This source takes its view because it is written for an American audience, likely by an American. The interpretation isn't necessarily inaccurate or misleading, but rather one that focuses on the events from an American perspective.

Then, answer these questions about *both* passages.

1. What is the perspective, tone, and argument of each passage?
2. How does each passage make clear its point of view?
3. Can you find at least one example in each passage that seems to show how the author's point of view accounts for or affects the interpretation of events?
4. Why do you think each passage takes the view it does?
5. How would you, as a researcher, evaluate and use these sources?

Compare your analysis with those of other students in your class, and be prepared for a full class discussion.

From the *World Book Encyclopedia*

War of 1812

The War of 1812 was in many ways the strangest war in United States history. It could well be named the War of Faulty Communication. Two days before war was declared, the British Government had stated that it would repeal the laws which were the chief excuse for fighting. If there had been telegraphic communication with Europe, the war might well have been avoided. Speedy communication would also have prevented the greatest battle of the war, which was fought at New Orleans fifteen days after a treaty of peace had been signed.

It is strange also that the war for freedom of the seas began with the invasion of Canada, and that the treaty of peace which ended the war settled none of the issues over which it had supposedly been fought.

The chief United States complaint against the British was interference with shipping. But New England, the great shipping section of the United States, bitterly opposed the idea of going to war. The demand for war came chiefly from the West and South, although these sections were not really hurt by British naval policy.

When we add that both sides claimed victory in the War of 1812, it becomes clear that the whole struggle was a confused mass of contradictions. These must be explained and cleared up before we can understand why the democratic United States sided with Napoleon I, the French dictator, in a struggle for world power. . . .

The War Hawks. A group of young men known as "War Hawks" dominated Congress during this period. Henry Clay of Kentucky and John C. Calhoun of South Carolina were the outstanding leaders of the group. Clay was then Speaker of the House of Representatives. Like Clay and Calhoun, most of the War Hawks came from western and southern states, where many of the people were in favor of going to war with Great Britain.

The people of New England generally opposed going to war, because war with Great Britain would wipe out entirely the New England shipping trade which had already been heavily damaged. Another reason New England opposed war was because many New Englanders sympathized with Great Britain in its struggle against the dictator Napoleon.

Many historians believe that a leading motive of the War Hawks was a desire for expansion. The people of the Northwest were meeting armed resistance in their attempt to take more land from the Indians, and they believed that the Indians had considerable British support. An American army was attacked by Indians at the Battle of Tippecanoe in the Wabash Valley in November, 1811, and British guns were found on the battlefield. The Westerners, therefore, were anxious to drive the British out of Canada. Southerners looked longingly at Florida, which belonged to Great Britain's ally, Spain. The South had also suffered a serious loss of markets. But the deciding motive for war seems to have been a strong desire for more territory.

Progress of the war

Declaration of war. On June 1, 1812, President Madison asked Congress to declare war against Great Britain. He gave as his reasons the impressment of United States seamen and the interference with United States trade. He charged also that the British had stirred up Indian warfare in the Northwest. Congress declared war on June 18, 1812. Two days earlier, the British Foreign Minister had announced that the Orders in Council would be repealed, but word of this announcement did not reach America until after the war had begun.

Because President Madison asked for the declaration of war, many Federalists blamed him for the conflict, calling it "Mr. Madison's war." But it was more the War Hawks' war than it was Madison's. . . .

Treaty of Ghent. The British public was tired of war and especially of war taxes. The British Government therefore proposed discussing terms. Commissioners of the two countries met at Ghent, Belgium, in August, 1814.

The British at first insisted that the United States should give up certain territory on the northern frontier, and set up a large permanent Indian reservation in the Northwest. But American victories in the summer and fall of 1814 led the British to drop these demands. A treaty was finally signed on December 24, 1814, in Ghent, Belgium. By its terms, all land which had been captured by either party was to be given up. Everything was to be exactly as it was before the war, and commissions from both of the countries were to settle any disputed points about boundaries. Nothing whatever was said in the treaty about impressments, blockades, or the British Orders in Council, which supposedly had caused the war. The treaty was formally ratified on February 17, 1815.

1. A Canadian perspective coupled with a sympathy for British loyalism.
2. Careless admits that his perspective is influenced by his intention to depict the War of 1812 as it affected Canada.
3. "This anti-American spirit was still a narrow basis on which to build a Canadian nationalism." Careless concludes that the 1812 War wasn't an extreme price to pay for the survival of British North America.
4. Canadian nationalism of the author.
5. It's apparent that each piece is biased. I would trust those facts that both agree on. For example, both agree that the leading motive for the war was American expansion. I'd watch for differences between the reasons either source gives for an event. For example, *WBE* says the Indians attacked the Americans, Careless the reverse. I'd consult other sources for additional explanation.

Results of the war

One important result of the War of 1812 was the rapid rise of manufacturing in the United States. During the war, United States citizens were unable to import goods from Great Britain, and had to begin making many articles for themselves. The war also increased national patriotism, and helped to unite the United States into one nation.

The war settled none of the issues over which the United States had fought. But most of these issues faded out during the following years. In the long period of peace after 1815, the British had no occasion to make use of impressments or blockades. Indian troubles in the Northwest were practically ended by the death of the chief Tecumseh and by the British surrender of Detroit and other posts. The United States occupied part of Florida during the war, and was soon able to buy the rest of it from Spain.

One indirect result of the War of 1812 was the later election to the Presidency of Andrew Jackson and of William Henry Harrison. Both of these men won military fame which had much to do with their elections. Another indirect result was the decline of Federalist power. New England leaders, most of them Federalists, met secretly in Hartford, Conn., to study amendments to the Constitution. Their opponents charged that they had plotted treason, and the Federalists never recovered. . . .

Chief battles of the war

The War of 1812 was not an all-out struggle on either side. For the British, the war was just an annoying part of their struggle with Napoleon. For many Americans, it was an unjustified attempt to gratify the expansionist ambitions of the South and West.

From *Canada: A Story of Challenge*

Danger on the western border

From the Treaty of Versailles in 1783 until the outbreak of a second war with the United States in 1812, the western border of young Canada was never secure. Trouble arose in the lands south of the Great Lakes; in the Ohio country which had been officially granted to the United States in 1783, but which had remained tied to the St Lawrence fur trade. The final consequence was open war. The trouble began almost with the signing of peace in 1783, when Britain quickly came to regret the ready surrender of so much of the West, and sought at least to delay its transfer to the United States.

The chief reasons for delay arose from the fur traders and the Indians who were still the masters of the unsettled Ohio West. The Canadian fur merchants of the St Lawrence drew most of their trade from

INTERPRETING SOURCES

that country, and they asked that the transfer be postponed for two years until they could adjust their business to this heavy loss. The Indians supplied the major reason, however. They declared that they had been ignored in the Treaty of Versailles and that Britain had handed over their lands, which they had never ceded, to the United States. There was danger that if the West was transferred and opened to American settlement the Indians would, in revenge, attack the thinly held and almost unprotected British settlements in Upper Canada.

Taking advantage of vague wording in the peace treaty, therefore, the British held on to the military and trading posts in the West below the Lakes, giving as their reason the failure of the Americans to carry out the term of the treaty that called for the restoration of Loyalist property. It was a sound reason, but not the chief one for failing to transfer the West.

This situation dragged on into the 1790's, while the Americans feared that the British were arousing the Indians against them, and the British feared that the Indians would become aroused. Dorchester, as governor, darkly expected a new war with the United States, and had some hope of building an Indian state in the Ohio country that would stand between the Americans and the Upper Canadian frontier and help to protect the latter. The Americans, meanwhile, were pressing forward from the region south of the Ohio, and sending forces against the Indians in order to break their hold on the western country. In 1794 one of these expeditions completely defeated the tribes at the battle of Fallen Timbers, and hope of an Indian 'buffer state' collapsed. The tribes ceded their lands to the United States. . . .

The rapidly advancing western states of the American union made good use of the growing warlike spirit in the republic. They held that the place to punish Britain was in Canada. Filled with the forceful confidence and expansive drive of the frontier they wanted to add Canada to the American union: a Canada which American frontier settlement had already invaded. Was not Upper Canada by now practically an American state? The 'war hawks' of the American West clamoured for an easy conquest. Their chance seemed to arrive in 1811.

In that year the western Indians, being steadily pushed back by advancing American settlement, attempted a last stand. Led by the chief Tecumseh, they formed a league to resist further inroads. The Americans saw this as the threat of a new Pontiac uprising, of savage Indian raids on the frontier. They attacked the Indians, and by their victory at the battle of Tippecanoe, destroyed Tecumseh's league. Yet the American West was not satisfied. It was fully convinced that the British had been behind the Indians, although the Canadian government had actually sought to keep the Indian league at peace. It seemed that the West would only be safe when the British had been driven out of Canada. The war hawks cried for blood, the American frontier wanted new lands to conquer, and the American East was newly aroused by fresh skirmishes over the right of search. The United States declared war in June, 1812, and set out to capture Canada.

The second struggle with the Americans

The War of 1812 in British history is only a side-show, not altogether successful, during the huge and victorious contest with Napoleon. In United States history it is a second war of independence, chiefly against the weight of British sea-power. In Canadian history it is above all a land war, a second struggle against American invasion. All these pictures are partly true; and in studying the Canadian version one must bear in mind that it portrays only the War of 1812 as it affected Canada. Yet for Canada the war was vitally important; far more important than it was for Britain, and much more dangerous than it was for the United States. . . .

Thus the war ended late in 1814 in a stalemate, which was probably a good thing for future peace.

It was not completely a stalemate. Britain still held the West and some of the Maine coast, and the British naval blockade was strangling American commerce. But in the peace negotiations the Americans made clear their readiness to go on fighting rather than yield territory. Faced with a revival of Napoleon's power in Europe at that very moment, Britain did not press the point. As a result the Treaty of Ghent of 1814 simply stopped the fighting, restored the pre-war boundaries, and said little about the problems that had caused the conflict.

Nevertheless in the next few years many of these problems disappeared. The question of the right of search ended with the Napoleonic Wars, and vanished in the long years of peace after 1815. The Indian problem declined as American settlement filled in the old West; the tribes had been too weakened by the war to offer any further resistance. The American war-hawks had found Canada no willing mouthful, and the United States was turning away to expand in a new direction, towards the south. . . .

The War of 1812 thus tended to bring British North America together and strengthened the bond with Britain. Any common feelings among the colonists, however, were largely directed against the United States. This anti-American spirit was still a narrow basis on which to build a Canadian nationalism. Anti-Americanism was particularly evident in Upper Canada. Further American settlement was largely prevented there, and American settlers already in the province were in danger of persecution—the Loyalists' case in reverse—if their declarations of British sentiments were not loud enough. Nevertheless, on the

AVOIDING PLAGIARISM AND CREDITING YOUR SOURCES

whole these reactions to the strain of the War of 1812 were understandable; and not an extreme price to pay for the survival of British North America.   —J.M.S. CARELESS

EXERCISE 39.8

Identify two sources in the research you considered in Exercise 39.1 that hold different perspectives. Then analyze these sources, using the guidelines in 39b2 for doing so. How can you synthesize the information given from the different perspectives? What inferences can you draw from these sources?

▌ 39e. Avoiding plagiarism and crediting your sources

"There is," in the words of Ecclesiastes, "no new thing under the sun." In a way, the biblical saying is true of research as well as of life in general: whatever research we do is influenced and affected by everything we have already read and experienced. Our written research acts as part of a larger conversation, and it reflects and depends on that larger context for much of its meaning. If you try, for instance, to trace the origins of every idea you have had just *today*, you will quickly see the extent to which we are all indebted to others as the sources of information.

Given every writer's dependence on a vast network of sources, giving full credit to those sources presents a challenge. Nevertheless, crediting sources as fully as possible is important for several reasons. First, acknowledging your sources helps you critically examine your own research and thinking. How timely and reliable are those sources? Have you used them accurately? Second, crediting sources helps readers by placing your research into a *context* of other thinking and research; it shows in what ways your research is part of a larger conversation and lets readers know where *they* can find more information on a topic. Finally, crediting your sources allows you to thank those whose work you have built on and thus to avoid plagiarism.

Crediting sources fully and generously, then, provides a means of establishing your *ethos*, or credibility, as a researcher (see 4d for further discussion of *ethos*.) Failure to credit sources breaks trust both with the research "conversation" and with readers; as a sign of dishonesty, it can easily destroy the credibility of both researcher and research.

ANSWERS TO EXERCISE 39.8 WILL VARY

(BACK)GROUNDING

In a lecture called "Why Is Plagiarism Wrong?" given at DePauw University on November 11, 1987, Barry M. Kroll outlined the five different strategies instructors take to discourage plagiarism. The most traditional—and apparently least effective—approach involves *prohibitions*. The instructor simply tells students, typically in moralistic terms, that plagiarism is wrong. Kroll warns us, "Virtually all college students already 'know' that plagiarism is a prohibited act. But despite that knowledge, a significant number of students do not appear to take the prohibition seriously enough to be dissuaded from plagiarizing in their college papers" (2).

The second approach involves *prevention*, an attempt to make it difficult to plagiarize. Some strategies of this approach include assigning different textbooks and paper topics from term to term and not using books for which *Cliff's Notes* exist. Unfortunately, this approach does little to teach the student not to plagiarize.

Some instructors and institutions try to deter students from plagiarizing by establishing *penalties* for those caught plagiarizing. This approach gains effectiveness when supported by the institution. However, it turns instructors into police, and most instructors dislike such a role. Such a role tends to undermine instructor-student rapport.

Other instructors and institutions reject the notion that without penalties cheating would increase. Their remedy for plagiarism is to provide students with *practice* in using source material. This perspective assumes that most plagiarism is caused by unfamiliarity with the conventions of citation, sloppiness and neglect, and insufficient practice with citing sources. Unfortunately, we have ample evidence that students often do plagiarize intentionally. The cases of copying sections from *Cliff's Notes* are indicators that plagiarism is much more complicated than this approach suggests.

The fifth approach to plagiarism—and the one that Kroll recommends—consists of teaching the *principles* behind society's attitudes toward plagiarism. In a separate study of how freshmen actually view plagiarism, Kroll discovered that students understood what it was and took it seriously, and that they could explain the wrongness of plagiarism with reference to three principles: fairness to authors; responsibility to one's education; and ownership of ideas. The latter two principles, Kroll argues, are inadequate, and the first incomplete. Kroll found no reference by students to the idea that plagiarism is wrong because it is deception. Yet, Kroll recommends that principle as being the best argument against plagiarism. Such deception is morally unacceptable and is detrimental to the institution, to the community, and to the character of the individual. Moreover, this principle is the basis for the other approaches: "For unless our students understand the reasons that plagiarism is wrong and destructive, they are likely to see our prohibitions as outmoded, to see the practices of careful documentation as merely tedious exercises, and to see the penalties for plagiarism as irrationally punitive" (9).

In the final analysis, plagiarism can be both personally and rhetorically devastating. Whatever the personal consequences, plagiarism inevitably undermines the writer's *ethos*. The writer who plagiarizes loses all authority, and thus persuasion becomes an impossibility.

1. Avoiding plagiarism

Plagiarism is the use of someone else's words as your own without crediting the original writer for those words. As a careful and credible researcher, you want to give full credit to sources both in parenthetical citations and bibliographic entries (see Chapter 41). Doing so for every single idea you build upon is an impossible task, however. In practical terms, where do you draw the line?

Materials not requiring credit

Common knowledge. If most readers like yourself would be likely to know something, you need not cite it. You do not need to credit a source for a statement that Ronald Reagan was elected to his first term as president in 1980, for example. If, on the other hand, you give the exact number of popular votes Reagan received in the 1980 election, you should cite the source for that figure.

Facts available in a wide variety of sources. If a number of encyclopedias, almanacs, or textbooks include the information, you need not cite a specific source. For instance, you would not need to cite a source for the fact that the Japanese bombing of Pearl Harbor on December 7, 1941, destroyed most of the base except for the oil tanks and submarines. You would, however, need to credit a source that argued that the failure of the bombing to destroy the submarines meant that Japan was destined to lose the Pacific War.

Your own findings from field research. If you conduct field research—observation, interviews, surveys—and produce results, simply announce those results as your own.

2. Crediting your sources

For material that does not fall under these three headings, credit sources as fully as possible, using quotation marks and citing the source parenthetically or in an endnote and listing it in a list of sources (see Chapter 41).

Materials requiring credit

Direct quotations. Whenever you use another person's words directly, credit the source. (If two quotations from the same source appear close together and separate parenthetical citations would sound awkward, use only one, placed *after* the second quotation.) Even if you

USEFUL READING

Kroll, Barry M. "How College Freshmen View Plagiarism." *Written Communication* 5 (1988): 203–21. One-hundred and fifty college freshmen wrote their explanations of why plagiarism is wrong, rated five standard explanations, and responded to statements about the seriousness and possible consequences of plagiarism.

AVOIDING PLAGIARISM AND CREDITING YOUR SOURCES

are quoting in the middle of a paraphrase whose source you intend to acknowledge, set off in quotes and *separately* acknowledge the direct use of the author's words.

Assertions that are arguable or facts that are not widely known. If your readers would be unlikely to know a fact, or if an author presents an assertion that may or may not be true, cite the source. To claim, for instance, that Israel has built atomic weapons, you would need to cite the source of your claim, because Israel has denied doing so.

Judgments, opinions, and claims of others. Whenever you summarize or paraphrase anyone else's opinion, give the source for that summary or paraphrase. Even though the wording may be completely your own, you need to give credit for the idea.

Statistics, charts, tables, and graphs from any source. Credit all graphic material, even if you yourself create the graph from data in another source.

Information or help provided by friends, instructors, or others. A conference with an instructor may give you just the idea you need to clinch an argument. Give credit. Friends may help you conduct surveys, refine questionnaires, or think through a major problem. Credit them, too.

READING WITH AN EYE FOR PERSPECTIVE AND TONE

The following paragraphs come from the opening of an essay about nuclear war published in *Parade*. Read the paragraphs carefully, paying close attention to the tone the author creates and to the perspective he takes on his subject. In one or two sentences, describe the author's tone and perspective. What elements in the paragraphs signal the tone? Imagine that you ran across this essay in research for an essay about nuclear armaments. How would the tone and perspective in this source be useful to you? How, on the other hand, might it prove troublesome?

Except for fools and madmen, everyone knows that nuclear war would be an unprecedented human catastrophe. A more or less typical strategic warhead has a yield of 2 megatons, the explosive equivalent of 2 million tons of TNT. But 2 million tons of TNT is about the same as all the bombs exploded in World War II—a single bomb with the explosive power of the entire Second World War but compressed into a few seconds of time and an area 30 or 40 miles across. . . .

In a 2-megaton explosion over a fairly large city, buildings would be vaporized, people reduced to atoms and shadows, outlying structures blown down like matchsticks and raging fires ignited. And if the bomb were exploded on the ground, an enormous crater, like those that can be seen through a telescope on the surface of the Moon, would be all that remained where midtown once had been. There are now more than 50,000 nuclear weapons, more than 13,000 megatons of yield, deployed in the arsenals of the United States and the Soviet Union—enough to obliterate a million Hiroshimas.

—CARL SAGAN, "Nuclear War and Climatic Catastrophe: A Nuclear Winter"

FOR EXAMINING YOUR OWN PARAPHRASES AND SUMMARIES

Choose a section consisting of two or three paragraphs from one of the passages in Exercise 39.7 on the War of 1812, and write a paraphase of it, following the author's content but using your own words. Reread your paraphrase, and analyze it using the guidelines for paraphrasing listed on page 556. Then try summarizing the same section. Reread your summary, and check to see how well you followed the suggestions for summarizing given on page 556.

40. Organizing, Drafting, and Revising a Research Essay

A nineteenth-century author once remarked that "In research the horizon recedes as we advance. . . . And research is always incomplete." Indeed, we might slightly alter a line from Samuel Johnson and say that a person who is tired of research is tired of living. For in many ways, the process of living constantly demands research. But while you may continue to pursue a research question for a long time, there comes a time to draw the strands of research together and to articulate your conclusions in writing. This chapter will help you at that point.

The processes of research and writing are intimately linked. While you are conducting research, you will also be coming up with ideas, considering organizational possibilities, and recognizing connections among your materials, making notes and perhaps attempting partial drafts as you work. From among these thoughts, you will eventually choose the final form in which to cast your own conclusions.

Probably, you will do most of your final organizing and drafting when your research is largely complete and you have most of the facts, citations, quotations, and other data you think you need. For most college research essays, the process of drafting a final version should begin at least two weeks before the deadline, in order to allow for response to the draft, for further research, and for revision.

40a. Refining your plans

Throughout your research, you have been generating notes that answer your research question and reflect on your hypothesis. Your growing understanding of the subject, in turn, has no doubt led you to gather other information, which may have altered your original

(BACK)GROUNDING

In 1948–1949, Claude E. Shannon, an American electrical engineer, published a model depicting the way information is transmitted and processed. An American mathematician, Warren Weaver, elaborated on Shannon's model to produce the Shannon-Weaver Information Theory. This first scientific model of a modern communication system greatly affected many disciplines, including linguistics, communications, data processing, and library science. The basic model consists of six elements:

1. An information source
2. An encoder
3. A message
4. A channel (over which information is transmitted)
5. A decoder, and
6. A receiver

Shannon added another element to the model—entropy, or noise, which he defines as any outside influence (audible or visual static, for example) which interferes with the quality of communication and distorts the meaning of the message. The clearest example of the Shannon-Weaver theory is the telephone system. The theory can also describe more complex communication processes such as the way an artist's work affects the audience.

569

question. This somewhat circular process, which may best be described as a research spiral, is at the heart of all research-based writing.

You should by now have a fair number of notes containing facts, opinions, paraphrases, summaries, quotations, and citations of all kinds. You probably also have thoughts about the connections among the many pieces of information you found. And you should have some sense of whether your hypothesis has been proved and can serve as the thesis of an essay. At this point, you should reconsider your purpose, your audience, and your thesis.

▌ 1. Reconsidering purpose, audience, and thesis

Given what you now know about your research question, consider questions such as the following:

1. Are you addressing an audience other than your instructor?
2. How much about your research question does your audience know already? How much background will they need to be told?
3. What sorts of supporting information are they likely to find convincing—examples? precedents? quotations from authorities? (See 4e.)
4. What tone will most appeal to them? Should you present yourself as a colleague, an expert, or a student? How can you establish some common ground with them and show fair consideration of their points of view? (See 4d.)
5. What is your central purpose? What other purposes, if any, do you have?
6. What is your thesis trying to establish? How likely is your audience to accept it?

▌ 2. Developing an explicit thesis

A useful means of relating your purpose, thesis, and audience before you begin a full draft is to write out an **explicit thesis statement** specifying a number of elements about your essay in advance. Such a statement forces you to articulate all your major lines of argument and to see how well those arguments carry out your purpose and appeal to your audience. At the drafting stage, your explicit thesis statement might take the following form:

> In this essay, I plan to (explain, argue, demonstrate, analyze, and so on)
> for an audience of _____
> that _____

TEACHING PRACTICE

To help your students appreciate the value of these questions, point out that they help students:

1. Identify their intended audience.
2. Judge whether to define basic terms (special language or terminology) or to take for granted that their audience already has a basic familiarity with the subject or field. For example, they wouldn't have to define the concept *regeneration* for an audience of senior-level students working in molecular genetics. Nor would they have to define a term such as *apartheid* for senior-level political science students. But in a paper examining economic disparity in South Africa that they are writing for a composition class, they might want to define and explain the term fully.
3. Evaluate the sources they will use and how to use them. If the audience is not a specialized one, students will want not to assume that a simple mention of some researcher's claims will give an audience sufficient understanding. If the source involves an advanced level of understanding, and the audience is not a professor or some other well-informed, advanced audience, then sources will have to be carefully explained.
4. Decide on how to present themselves; to identify their relationship to the audience; and to judge how they want to appear to the audience.
5. Consider further how they see their subject. What are they trying to prove? What are they trying to explain? What is their purpose in relation to their potential audience?
6. Reconsider their thesis with the audience in mind. Is their thesis new to the audience? A restatement? A reexamination of something they already assume or accept?

USEFUL READING

Jeske, Jeff. "Borrowing from the Sciences: A Model for the Freshman Research Paper." *The Writing Instructor* 6 (Winter 1987): 62–67. A helpful four-part model for writing the research essay that encourages students to reflect on the research process itself while they are producing a research project.

because or if (1) _____ , (2) _____ ,
(3) _____ .

3. Testing your thesis

Writing out an explicit thesis will many times confirm the research you have been doing and support your hypothesis. Sometimes, however, it may reveal that your hypothesis is not valid, is unsupportable, or is insufficiently focused. In such cases, you must then rethink your original research question, perhaps do further research, and work toward a revised hypothesis and eventually a revised thesis. To test and probe your explicit thesis statement at this point, consider the following list of questions:

1. How can you state the topic of your thesis or your comment about the topic more precisely or more clearly? (See 2f for more information about topic and comment.)

2. In what ways will your thesis interest and appeal to your audience? What can you do to make that interest grow? (See 4f.)

3. How could the wording of your thesis be more specific? Could you use more concrete nouns (see 25c) or stronger verbs (see 21a)? Should you add qualifying adjectives or adverbs (see Chapter 10)?

4. Is your thesis going to be manageable, given your limits of time and knowledge? What might you do to make it more manageable?

5. What research evidence do you have to support each aspect of your thesis? What additional evidence do you need?

The goal of such questions is to push your thinking about your research as far as you can, exercising your mental muscles and leading you to a richer, more complete understanding of your subject.

40b. Organizing information

In discussing her own process of writing, Marie Winn talks about the challenge of transforming the tangle of ideas and information "into an orderly and logical sequence on a blank piece of paper." This is the task of organization, of grouping information effectively. Experienced writers differ considerably in the ways they go about this task, and you will want to experiment until you find an organizational method that works well for you. This section will review two common planning strategies—clustering and outlining. Before examining these strategies,

(BACK)GROUNDING

In A *Theory of Discourse*, a study of rhetoric and discourse theory, James Kinneavy points out that the communication triangle corresponds essentially to Shannon and Weaver's information theory scheme. However, the triangle has been the basis of the study of rhetorical theory since Aristotle made these components the foundation for his study of rhetoric: speaker/encoder, audience/decoder, speech/message. In fact, this foundation has dominated rhetorical theory for twenty-three centuries. Many other fields interested in language, knowledge, communication, and discourse now regard this structure as basic to understanding themselves. These include literary theory and criticism, communications, and linguistics. This model of communication should be applied to our understanding of the purpose of research, which is to give information and understanding to an audience.

WRITING TOGETHER

To make fuller use of the thesis statement form, call on a student to present his or her statement on the board. Open the class up to respond to the statement. To get things started ask the writer to clarify or define terms or vague points. Ask the student why he or she has picked the subject. In other words, open the class up to a brainstorming session in which the writer is required to answer the class's questions and make clearer the thesis and purpose and outline. In fielding the class's responses, the writer will likely clarify in his or her own mind the project. The writer will see where his or her difficulties lie, where his or her command of the subject is lacking, or where he or she will need to elaborate. The writer may find that the project is too large or may find a way of refining the thesis.

Once you have demonstrated this activity for the whole class, break them up into groups of four or five and have them work on each other's thesis statements.

USEFUL READING

Dinitz, Susan, and Jean Kiedaisch. "The Research Paper: Teaching Students to Be Members of the Academic Community." *Exercise Exchange* 31 (1986): 8–10. The authors suggest that rhetorical concerns—purpose and voice—should be primary concerns for research papers.

however, you should consider whether or not your course discipline has a conventional research-writing format that you will need to follow.

1. Considering conventional formats

In many disciplines, essays tend to follow certain conventional patterns. These formats may be fairly consistent, as in laboratory reports and certain research reports in the natural or social sciences, or fairly loose, as in the great range of historical surveys, literature reviews, arguments, and interpretations common in the humanities. An instructor may, in fact, specify the format expected in your final essay or, less formally, advise you to include certain features without requiring a specific structure. On the other hand, your instructor may simply tell you to shape your research essay as you would any other essay (see 2h) or argument (see 4g). The following formats are intended as rough guides that may serve to get you started thinking about organizational patterns. Your purpose and audience and the kind and number of your materials will be of paramount importance in the final organizational pattern you develop.

Surveying literature

In many disciplines you will have occasion to write a **literature survey,** which orients a reader to some of the significant work that has been done in the field or on your topic. Sometimes called a **review of the literature** or **bibliographic essay,** a literature survey serves as a guide to the major resources in a field or supplies an update or an overview of work done on a particular issue. It may be a section within an essay or an essay in itself. A literature survey may not build on an argumentative hypothesis, but it is interpretive in that the writer provides a perspective on the works discussed. This evaluation is explicit in the running commentary on the works discussed and implicit in the act of selecting what to cover in the survey. A literature survey often includes an *introduction*, a *division section* that explains the method of selection and previews the topics to be covered, a *discussion* of the works surveyed, a concluding *commentary*, and a *list of works cited*.

Reporting research

Experimental or field research is often another conventional report format, which usually includes eight standard sections: an *abstract*,

(BACK)GROUNDING

A literature survey helps students validate the focus and purpose of their research projects by giving students a sense of what has been said on a subject, what continues to be of interest, and what needs to be examined further.

Furthermore, the survey is a valuable study guide that will be a useful record to subsequent researchers as well as to the original researcher. In general, the literature survey serves the purpose of indicating the major perspectives or "currents of thought" on a subject. What are the major perspectives, attitudes, schools of thought, or sides on subjects such as nuclear energy (or acid rain, the role of NATO in Europe, the responsibility of industrial nations in Third World economic development, the creative abilities of Prince or Philip Glass, the musical career of Yoko Ono, or the early paintings of Klee or Kandinsky)? An obvious example showing the need to identify the "currents of thought" on a subject is nuclear energy. While it may be ideally the power resource of the immediate future, the safety hazards are an ongoing concern.

USEFUL READING

Bazerman, Charles. *The Informed Writer: Using Sources in the Disciplines.* 2nd ed. Boston: Houghton, 1985. See pp. 293–300 for a brief discussion and example of literature reviews.

ORGANIZING INFORMATION res 40b

which sums up the study's hypothesis, methods, findings, and conclusions; an *introduction*, which poses the question behind the research and proposes the hypothesis to be tested; a *survey of previous work*, which reviews background studies and discusses how they affect the current hypothesis; a discussion of *materials and methods*, which reports exactly what was done and how it was done; *results*, which summarize findings that relate to the hypothesis; *discussion*, which highlights the significance of the results; *conclusion*, which answers, tentatively, the question posed at the beginning of the study and suggests areas for further research; and a *list of references*.

Interpreting sources

In the humanities and sometimes in the sciences as well, you may have cause to follow a conventional format for essays that interpret sources. Such an essay typically includes the following sections, though not necessarily in this order: an *introduction*, explaining the specific question and its importance; *background of previous work*, surveying some of the literature and perhaps identifying controversies or errors; a *statement of purpose or thesis*; an *exploration of the thesis*, supporting it and introducing additional information; a *conclusion*, pointing out any ramifications or complications; and a *list of works cited*.

2. Clustering

During your research, you have been taking notes and keeping lists of ideas. To organize these materials using a clustering strategy, examine them for connections, finding what might be presented with what, which notes will be more useful and which less useful, which ideas lend support to the thesis and which should be put aside. Brainstorm about your research question one last time, and add the resulting notes to your other materials, looking to see if they fit with any of the materials you already have.

If you have been keeping notes on cards, you can arrange the cards in clusters, putting the ones with your main topics in the center and arranging any related cards around them. If you have been taking notes in a notebook, identify your major topics and write them on a blank piece of paper with a circle around each one. Then "cluster" related supporting ideas, quotations, key words, and so forth around them, as shown in the following diagram:

WRITERS ON WRITING

If philosophy is the study of beginnings, how is it to be taught without patient fresh starts? In the realm of the mind, to begin is to know one has the right to begin again.

—GASTON BACHELARD

Whatever else learning may be, it is clearly a disposition to form structures.

—GORDON ALLPORT

WRITERS ON WRITING

Then there is the business of surprise. I never know what is coming next. The phrase that sounds in the head changes when it appears on the page. Then I start probing it with a pen, finding new meanings. Sometimes I burst out laughing at what is happening as I twist and turn sentences. Strange business, all in all. One never gets to the end of it.

—GORE VIDAL

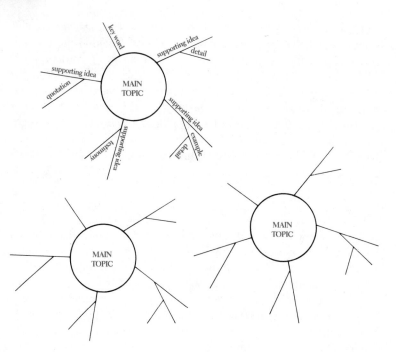

Clustering will help you to identify your major ideas and to see whether you have covered all the necessary areas. It will help you see whether you have too many ideas to manage—or whether you need to do more research in some area. Most important, it will allow you to see how the many small pieces of your research fit together and result in the larger structure of a complete essay.

3. Outlining

Writers use outlines in various ways. Some move from clustering into drafting and then outline the draft to study its tentative structure. Others prefer to use material generated in clustering to develop a working outline, listing the major points in a tentative order with support for each major point. Such a working outline may see you through the rest of the process, or you may decide to revise it as you go along. Still other writers prefer to plot out their organization early on and do so in a formal outline.

TEACHING PRACTICE

The point can't be overemphasized: a full formal outline is devilishly hard to write before your students have actually produced at least a revised draft. A working outline is all that students should expect to produce. It can tentatively guide or reflect their planning. Assure your students that an outline is flexible. It mainly serves as a rough plan that enables them to start writing and organizing information. It is subject to revision once they've started writing. This advice rests on the thinking that not until writers put something down on paper can they really judge and plan the appropriateness of the content and format to purpose and audience.

USEFUL READING

Rico, Gabriele L. *Writing the Natural Way.* Los Angeles: Tarcher, 1983. The foremost proponent of the value of clustering in writing, Rico defines clustering as a "nonlinear brainstorming process akin to free association." See Chapter 2, "Clustering: Doorway to Your Design Mind."

ORGANIZING INFORMATION   *res* 40b

A formal outline is a double-edged sword. On the one hand, it allows you to see before drafting exactly how all the main parts of your essay will fit together—how your ideas relate, how abstract your ideas are, what the overall structure of your argument will be. On the other hand, most people find a full formal outline devilishly hard to write before they have considered their material in some less formal way. That is why you may decide to make a rough outline *before* a formal outline.

Most formal outlines follow a conventional format of numbered and lettered headings and subheadings using Roman numerals, capital letters, Arabic numbers, and lower-case letters to show the levels of importance of the various ideas and their relationships. Each new level is indented to show its subordination to the preceding level. Following is a model of a typical formal outline:

Thesis statement

  I. First main topic
    A. First subordinate idea
      1. First supporting idea
      2. Second supporting idea
      3. Third supporting idea
    B. Second subordinate idea
      1. First supporting idea
      2. Second supporting idea

  II. Second main topic
    A. First subordinate idea
      1. First supporting idea
      2. Second supporting idea
    B. Second subordinate idea
      1. First supporting idea
      2. Second supporting idea
        a. First supporting detail
        b. Second supporting detail

Each level contains at least two parts, so there is no A without a B, no 1 without a 2. Comparable items are placed on the same level—all capital letters, for instance, or all Arabic numbers. Each level develops the idea before it—1 and 2 under A, for example, include the points that develop, explain, or demonstrate. Headings are stated in parallel form—either all sentences, or all topics that are grammatically parallel.

WRITERS ON WRITING

Outlines work for some writers, not for others, as Joseph Epstein points out: "I am not opposed to outlines in logic or on principle but by temperament. . . . I have discovered that there is no way I can know what will be in the second paragraph of something I write until I have written the first paragraph. My first paragraph may contain a phrase or end on a point I hadn't anticipated, and this phrase or point may send me off into an entirely unexpected direction in my second paragraph."

WRITERS ON WRITING

"How do you become a writer? You write!"
—URSULA K. LE GUIN

Formal outlining requires logical thought and careful evaluation of your ideas, which is precisely why it is a valuable effort. Charting out such an outline allows a writer to see the skeleton of an essay, making sure that all the "bones" are in the right and logical places, that all the relationships make sense. A full-sentence outline will make those relationships most clear, so if you want to give your organization the most rigorous test of its structure, try working it into a full-sentence outline. If the logical relationships seem fully established to you, a topic outline will provide the necessary test of coherence. Remember, however, that an outline is at best a means to an end, not an end in itself. New ideas will almost surely occur as you write, and you should not feel bound to the ideas on your outline. Though an outline serves, on one level, as a plan for your essay, it can also serve to stimulate altogether new thoughts and plans, ones you should feel free to consider and pursue.

Here is a typical topic outline for a literary research essay:

Thesis: F. Scott Fitzgerald helped create the image of the Jazz Age, with all its frivolity and irresponsibility, but at the same time he exposed the corruption and moral decay that were as much a part of the era as were the pursuit of money, youth, and idealized romance.

I. The corruption and tragedy of wealth
   A. *The Great Gatsby*
      1. Ostentatiousness and display
      2. The corruption of Jay Gatz's innocence
      3. The carelessness of Daisy
   B. "The Rich Boy"
      1. Ruin by money
      2. Lack of any moral responsibility
   C. *The Beautiful and the Damned*
      1. Anthony and Gloria's refusal to live without wealth
      2. Total purposelessness
      3. The fight for inheritance
         a. Moral failure
         b. Emotional exhaustion
      4. Hollowness of the material victory

II. The vain attempts to recapture youth and beauty
   A. *The Beautiful and the Damned*
      1. A world for the young
      2. Anthony and Gloria's deterioration with age
      3. Youthful beauty the basis of Gloria's entire personality

B. "Babylon Revisited"
        1. Search for the meaning of youth
        2. Charlie's failure to overcome the mistakes of youth
           a. Aged and alone
           b. Lost and regretful
    C. *The Great Gatsby*
        1. Gatsby's failure to recognize the destructiveness of time
        2. His search for the love of his youth
        3. "Vision without youth"
III. The illusory idealization of romance
    A. *The Great Gatsby*
        1. Gatsby's romantic vision of Daisy
        2. Daisy's coldness
        3. The tragic outcome
    B. "Winter Dreams"
        1. Dexter's infatuation with Judy
        2. His sacrifices and disappointments
        3. Judy's ultimate decay

40c. Drafting your essay

At the point when you are ready to draft your essay, set yourself a deadline and structure all your tasks with that deadline in mind. Gather your notes, clustered or outlined materials, quotations, any sources you may need to consult. Most writers find that some sustained work (perhaps two or three hours) at this point pays off. Begin drafting where you feel most confident. If you have a good idea for an introduction, begin there. If you are not sure exactly what you want to do in the introduction but do know how you want to approach some particular point, begin with that and return to the introduction later. The most important thing is to get started.

The drafting process itself varies considerably among researchers, and much about the way you draft will be up to you. Some writers try to make the first draft as perfect as possible, working meticulously paragraph by paragraph. Others draft as fast as they can, getting all their material down in whatever form and smoothing it out later. Some follow an outline from start to finish; others draft sections separately and arrange them later. Your writing process is your own, and no one else can tell you what works best for you. A few tips, however, may help:

- Draft your material on one point at a time. You may want to plan to draft in several short sessions.
- Don't let yourself get bogged down at this point with individual details. Jot down in the margin notes about any problems or unresolved matters to return to later so that you don't get sidetracked now. Your main objective is to get your draft on paper; later you can revise, fill in the gaps, and refine the details.
- Use any clustering or outlining as a springboard to help you know where and how to start.
- End each writing session by deciding what comes next and making some notes to help you get started when you turn to that topic.

1. Drafting your introduction

The introduction to a research essay plays a special role, for it must set the context for what is to come. Like any introduction, it should draw readers into the essay, but also it needs to provide them with any background they will need to understand the discussion. You can find general advice on writing introductions in 3f2 and 5e1, but some specific things you should consider in drafting an introduction for a research essay include the following:

- It is often effective to *open with a question*, especially your research question. Then you might explain what you will do to answer the question and *end with your hypothesis or thesis* (in essence, the answer to the question).
- Because in your essay you will be bringing together several distinct points from various sources, you will probably want to *forecast your main points*, to help readers get their bearings.
- You will want to *establish your own credibility* as a research writer by showing your experience and demonstrating what you have done to become an expert on your topic.
- In general, you may *not* want to open with a quotation—though it can be a good attention-getter, it is probably not a good idea to give any one source such prominence. In a research essay, you may want to quote several sources to support your ideas; opening with a quotation from one source may give the impression that you will be presenting that writer's ideas rather than using them in support of your own.

2. Drafting your conclusion

A good conclusion to a research essay helps readers to know what they have learned. Its job is not to persuade (the body of your essay should already have done that), but it *can* leave the reader with a memorable phrase or example that will in fact contribute to the overall effectiveness of your argument. General advice on writing conclusions can be found in 3f3 and 5e2, but following are some specific strategies especially appropriate for research essays.

- A specific-to-general pattern is frequently appropriate, opening with a restatement of your thesis and then expanding to some more general conclusion to remind readers of the significance of your discussion.
- If you have covered several main points, you may want to restate them in your conclusion.
- Try to end with something that will have lasting impact—a provocative question, a vivid image, a call for action, a warning—and that will give readers an idea of what they should think or do.
- Tailor your conclusion to the needs of your readers, both in terms of the information you include and the tone and style of your final appeal.

40d. Incorporating source materials

Once you are at the point of drafting your essay, a new task awaits: how to weave your source materials into your own writing. The challenge is to use your sources yet to remain the author of your paper—to quote, paraphrase, and summarize other voices while at the same time remaining the single dominant voice in your essay. The decision you will often face in using source material is *how* to do so—whether to use a direct quotation, to paraphrase, or to summarize.

1. Using direct quotations

What are the characteristics of a good quotation? They can be boiled down to two: a good quotation should be either necessary or memorable.

Your essay must be your own work, and you should depend on other people's words as little as possible, limiting quotations to those *necessary* to your argument. You can demonstrate that you know the authoritative sources with summary and paraphrase, for instance, but you may want to quote a source if he or she has said something so effectively that the words cannot be paraphrased without altering meaning. Quoting someone's words exactly is also a way of bringing that person into the "conversation" of your discussion, thus linking you to the larger dialogue in the field. Finally, quoting an authority on your subject contributes to your own credibility as a writer.

In addition, you will find some quotations during your research that are so memorable that you may use them largely for effect; to *delight* your audience as much as to inform them.

You can incorporate quotations into your discussion in two ways—by enclosing them in quotation marks within your text or by setting them off as a block. The choice depends on the length of the quotation.

Enclosing brief quotations within your text

Quotations of no more than four lines (MLA style) or no more than forty words (APA style) should be worked into your text, set off only by quotation marks. For example:

> In Chillingworth, Hawthorne shows both good and evil, creating "about as queer a combination as the world has ever witnessed" (Turner 200).

> Technology has become our number one priority. The amount of information continues to grow, making obsolescence a problem for everyone. This pace of change has "magnified the difference between the scientist-technologist and the layperson." Technology is now "specialized, professionalized, and institutionalized" (Pytlik, Lauda, and Johnson 6).

Notice that both of the preceding examples mention the sources of the quotations only in the parenthetical references. Often, however, you will want to mention your source directly, especially when he or she is an authority on your subject. If you introduce quotations in this way you need not repeat the author's name in the parenthetical citation.

> In Russia, however, the men who took control had hardly any experience in military or administrative fields at all. As Edward Crankshaw explained, "They were a disciplined set of revolutionary conspirators who had spent most of their adult lives in exile in Russia or abroad" (44).

Setting off long quotations

Set off long quotations: in MLA style, longer than four lines; in APA style, longer than forty words. Begin such a quotation on a new line, and indent each line of the quotation ten spaces (MLA) or five spaces (APA) from the left margin. This indentation sets off the quotation clearly so that quotation marks are unnecessary. Long quotations must always be introduced in some explanatory way:

INCORPORATING SOURCE MATERIALS

A good seating arrangement can prevent problems; however, the technique that Woolfolk calls "withitness" works even better in maintaining effective discipline.

> Withitness is the ability to communicate to students that you are aware of what is happening in the classroom, that you "don't miss anything." With-it teachers seem to have "eyes in the back of their heads." They avoid becoming too absorbed with a few students, since this allows the rest of the class to wander. (359)

This technique works, however, only if students actually believe that their teacher will know everything that goes on.

In general, you should avoid using many long quotations.

Integrating quotations in your text

Quotations have to be carefully integrated into your text so that they link smoothly and clearly with the surrounding sentences. As a writer, you must provide enough explanation so that your readers can follow your meaning. Look, for instance, at the following:

> In *Death of a Salesman*, Willy Loman dreams the wrong dreams and idealizes the wrong ideals. "He has lived on his smile and on his hopes, survived from sale to sale, been sustained by the illusion that he has countless friends in his territory, that everything will be all right. . . ." (Brown 97).

It is possible to figure out the connection between quotation and text, but see how the following revisions make the link far easier to recognize. Note also the slightly awkward shift in verb tenses from text to quotation, which is smoothed out in the revisions.

> In *Death of a Salesman*, Willy Loman dreams the wrong dreams and idealizes the wrong ideals. His misguided perceptions are well captured by Brown: "He has lived on his smile and on his hopes, survived from sale to sale, been sustained by the illusion that he has countless friends in his territory, that everything will be all right. . . ." (97).

> In *Death of a Salesman*, Willy Loman dreams the wrong dreams and idealizes the wrong ideals, living "on his smile and on his hopes . . . sustained by the illusion . . . that everything will be all right. . . ." (Brown 97).

Indicating changes with brackets and ellipses

Sometimes, for the sake of clarity or length, you will wish to alter a direct quotation in some way—to make a verb tense fit smoothly in your text, to replace a pronoun with a noun, to eliminate unnecessary detail. Enclose any changed or added words with brackets, and indicate any deletions with three ellipsis points.

> A farmer, Jane Lee, spoke to the Nuclear Regulatory Commission about the occurrences. "There is something wrong in the [Three Mile Island] area. It is happening within nature itself," she said, referring to human miscarriages, stillbirths, and birth defects in farm animals ("Legacy" 33).

> Economist John Kenneth Galbraith has pointed out that "large corporations cannot afford to compete with one another. Their survival is predicated upon . . . market segmentation. In a truly competitive market someone loses. . . . American big business has finally learned that everybody has to protect everybody else's investment" (Key 17).

Be especially careful that any changes you make in a quotation do not alter its essential meaning. In addition, use these marks sparingly, for too many brackets and ellipsis points make for difficult reading. (For more information on brackets and ellipses, see 32b and 32f.)

2. Using paraphrases and summaries

When you want to cite ideas from sources but have no need to quote their exact words, you will use paraphrases or summaries. You may find various occasions for paraphrasing or summarizing, but in general these forms will be most necessary for providing background information, presenting facts that may not be commonly known, and explaining various positions on your topic. However frequently you need them, you must work paraphrases and summaries into your essay in a way that both reads smoothly and identifies your sources clearly.

Incorporating paraphrases and summaries

At times, you may choose to introduce a paraphrase or summary with an introduction noting the author of the information (*Professor Karlinsky notes that . . .*). Using the author's name in this way helps to lend authority to the information. Sometimes, in fact, you will want to highlight the source even more prominently. Notice how the writer in the following example focuses on one authority, first introducing him by name and then both quoting and paraphrasing from his work:

> Robert Ornstein, whose book I read during my research on brain lateralization, said he got "vague ideas" over a period of time, ideas that eventually led to the writing of his book. These ideas came from the

TEACHING PRACTICE
The importance of paraphrasing cannot be overestimated. Make sure to point out to students that:

1. Often a paraphrase may seem to make sense to the writer but that it may not to a reader because of the writer's familiarity with the original passage and because the paraphrase is in his or her choice of language.
2. There are at least two purposes of paraphrasing, one to help the writer himself or herself understand, and another to present the information to another person to understand.
3. Much research involves paraphrasing or explaining ideas in their own words.
4. Having others respond to their writing helps them learn how to judge and use language for different audiences, different in their levels of understanding and expertise with a subject.

INCORPORATING SOURCE MATERIALS

right side of the brain; by acknowledging them as valid messages, Ornstein says he was able to use them to his advantage in his work (68).

In the following example, on the other hand, the writer focuses more on the information paraphrased, using no introductory tag and identifying the authors only parenthetically:

> Three areas of established differences in cognitive abilities are recognized by the majority of researchers: verbal ability, mathematical ability, and spatial ability (Block 517). As shown by current research, a specific cognitive sex difference exists in verbal ability; in general, females are superior to males in this area starting in early childhood (Weitz 99).

Regardless of the method you use to introduce information, indicating the sources of paraphrases and summaries is important. Failure to cite sources for materials that are not in quotation marks but that you could not have arrived at originally, even unintentionally, constitutes plagiarism. Make certain that you record the sources of general background information as well as specific quotations, facts, viewpoints, and so forth. If your notes are incomplete or your source is unclear, relocate the original to clarify the information. If you are unable to do so, you would be wiser to leave out the material than to risk plagiarism (see Chapters 39 and 41 for further discussion on crediting sources).

▌ 3. Checking for excessive citations

Exactly how much you should cite sources in your essay has to depend on your purpose, your audience, and the section of your essay. In general, however, your essay should not give the impression of being a patchwork of quotations, paraphrases, and summaries from other people. If it does, you will have merely accumulated data; you won't have actually presented information (see 39b2). You need an authorial voice, a perspective that represents you as the author. If you are over-quoting and over-citing, your own voice will disappear. The following discussion illustrates this problem:

> The United States is one of the countries with the most rapid population growth. In fact, rapid population increase has been a "prominent feature of American life since before the founding of the republic" (Day 31). In the past, the cause of the high rate of population growth was the combination of large-scale immigration and a high birthrate. As Day notes, "Two facts stand out in the demographic history of the United

WRITING TOGETHER

Ask students to work in pairs and select an article from a major journal in a field of interest to them. Have them identify each occurrence of paraphrase, summary, or quotation and the function that each serves. These may include:

> To provide background information
> To define terms
> To provide a position for rebuttal
> To explain quoted material
> To illustrate a point
> To show disagreements among sources
> To cite authorities and, hence, to reinforce claims or statements
> To state a point more precisely, powerfully, or accurately than with a paraphrased version

Once the group has identified the functions, have them exchange their article with another group. Have them repeat the exercise, and then compare versions and findings.

WRITING TOGETHER

Divide the class into groups of six, and present them with these instructions: choose a short passage of about 100 words from a text, an essay, or an article for paraphrasing. Each member of the group should first individually restate the original in his or her own words. Keep in mind that the paraphrase requires a writer to include all major and supporting details. Once you have produced your paraphrase, break into three groups of two, and working together, co-write a paraphrase of the original excerpt. Then discuss the similarities or differences of the three versions. Try to explain them, especially the differences, focusing on the following guiding questions:

1. Working in pairs, did you disagree over terms and their meaning in the original passage?
2. Was it easy to agree on synonyms or on paraphrases of ideas and concepts?
3. Did you agree on the information to include? to leave out?
4. How similar are the three coauthored versions? Why, or why not?
5. What does trying to agree on a paraphrase tell you about how different people read and interpret a passage? About how they choose to rephrase it?

States: first, the single position as a receiver of immigrants; second, our high rate of growth from natural increase" (31).

Nevertheless, American population density is not as high as in most European countries. Day points out that the Netherlands, with a density of 906 persons per square mile, is more crowded than even the most densely populated American states (33).

Most readers would think that the source, Day, was much too prominent here. If this passage were a background discussion or a literature survey, with each source being different, such a large number of citations might be acceptable. But all these citations are from the same source, and readers are likely to conclude that the source is primary and the author only secondary.

▌ 40e. Reviewing your draft

As with most kinds of writing, taking a break after drafting a research essay is important. Get away from the draft, and try to put it out of your mind. Stay away from it for as long as you can, so that when you reread it you can bring a fresh eye to the task.

When you return to the draft, read it straight through without stopping. Then, read it again slowly, reconsidering three things: purpose, audience, and thesis. You might find that outlining your draft helps you to analyze it at this point (see 40b3).

- From your reading of your draft, what do you now see as its *purpose?* How does this compare with your original purpose? How does it do what your assignment requires?
- What *audience* does your essay address?
- What is your *thesis?* Is it clearly stated?

Answer these three questions as best you can, since they are the starting point for revision. Next, you need a closer reading of your essay. At this point, you might benefit from the comments of other readers. Consider asking friends or classmates to read your draft and respond to the following questions. You can also use these questions yourself as you analyze your own essay in greater detail.

Questions for reviewing the draft of a research essay

1. *Introduction:* How does the opening of the essay gain readers' attention? How does it suggest what readers will learn from the essay?

(Does it forecast the main points?) Does it provide any background information readers may need? How else might the essay begin?

2. *Thesis:* Paraphrase the thesis of the essay in the form of a promise: "This essay will . . ." Does the essay fulfill this promise? Does it express a stand on the topic? How might the thesis be qualified or made more pointed?

3. *Main points:* List the main points made in the essay. Arrange and number these points in the order of their interest to you. Which are most interesting? least interesting? Do any seem extraneous? Which seem incompletely or excessively developed? Does the overall development seem clear and balanced?

4. *Organization:* What is the essay's basic organization? How is this plan made clear to readers? Does the organization seem to work? What, if anything, would you move, cut out, or add?

5. *Supporting information:* Does the essay marshal sufficient support for its case? What kind of support does it offer—examples, precedents, quotations from experts? statistics? Which research materials does it use most convincingly? Which seem less effective? Do any points need more support? What attention is shown to arguments *against* the thesis? Should there be more? Do you accept the essay's argument?

6. *Author's Voice:* Does the writer's own perspective control the tone of the essay, or do the sources cited seem more dominant? What makes the writer's view clear? What sections, if any, are dominated by the sources? How has the writer established his or her credibility on the subject?

7. *Source materials:* Consider the source citations one by one. Is each one smoothly integrated into the text? Can you easily see its connection to the text around it? Are any quotations less than quotable—that is, might they be as well paraphrased? Are any longer than need be? Is any one source relied on too much?

8. *Conclusion:* How does the essay end? What does it tell you to think or do? Does it summarize the essay's main points—and if not, should it do so? How else might it end?

9. *Paragraphs, sentences, and words:* Which paragraphs and sentences seem especially effective? Identify any that you consider strong, and then do the same with those you find weak. Look at the individual words—do any need to be defined? Are any too abstract or vague? Identify any words you find especially vivid.

10. *Final thoughts:* What are the essay's strongest points? What are its weaknesses? What kind of revision does the essay need most? What revision advice would you anticipate an instructor might give?

You may also get helpful advice if you ask questions specific to your essay. Whether you are doubtful about including or omitting discussion of a particular point, unsure about whether to use a certain quotation, or anxious about the impact of an example, ask readers specifically what they think you should do. (For more information on getting critical responses to a draft, see 3c.)

40f. Revising and editing your draft

Using any responses you have gathered and your own analysis of your draft, turn now to your final revision. It is advisable, at this stage, to work in several steps:

Considering any reviews

Have readers identified any problems you need to solve? If so, do they make any specific suggestions about ways you might or must revise your essay? Have they identified any strengths that might suggest ways of revising your essay—for example, if they showed great interest in a particular point but no interest at all in another point, perhaps you might expand the first and delete the second.

Reconsidering your original purpose and audience

From the above analysis, do you feel confident that you have achieved your purpose? If not, what is missing? Have you made your strongest possible appeal to your readers? How have you established common ground with them? How have you satisfied any special needs they may have?

Gathering any additional material

If you need to strengthen treatment of any points, go back to your notes to see if you have the necessary materials. If not, consider whether you need to do any more research. If you failed to consider adequately any opposing viewpoints, for instance, you may need to go back to the library to find material.

Deciding on any changes you need to make

Figure out everything you have to do to perfect your draft, and write it out. With your deadline firmly in mind, plan your revision.

WRITERS ON WRITING

I am strongly in favor of intelligent, even fastidious revision, which is, or certainly should be, an art in itself. . . .

—JOYCE CAROL OATES

WRITERS ON WRITING

I rewrite so much that the first chapter of a book sometimes may be rewritten forty or fifty times. . . . It's this way, see—when a writer first starts out, he gets a big kick from the stuff he does, and the reader doesn't get any; then, after a while, the writer gets a little kick and the reader gets a little kick; and finally, if the writer's any good, he doesn't get any kick at all and the reader gets everything.

—ERNEST HEMINGWAY

WRITERS ON WRITING

I love spending an hour or two with a dictionary and a thesaurus looking for a more nearly perfect word. Or taking my pen and ruthlessly pruning all the unnecessary adjectives, or fooling around with the rhythm of a sentence or a paragraph by changing a verb into a participle or making any number of little changes that a magazine editor I work with calls "mouse milking."

—MARIE WINN

REVISING AND EDITING YOUR DRAFT

Rewriting your draft

Do the major work first—changes in content, added examples or citations, paragraph-level concerns. Then turn to sentence-level work, and finally to individual words. Revise for clarity and to sharpen the dominant impression of the essay as a whole. For this part of your work, follow the guidelines on pages 48-53, which will help you examine your paragraphs, sentences, words, and tone.

Reconsidering your introduction and conclusion

In light of your re-evaluation and revision of your draft, reread these very important parts to see that they still serve their purpose. Does anything need refocusing? Do you need to forecast your main points in the introduction or to summarize them in the conclusion? Check to be sure that your introduction captures readers' attention and that your conclusion helps them see the significance of your argument.

Checking your documentation

Are all sources documented, and have you followed the appropriate style consistently? Check Chapter 41 for complete MLA and APA guidelines.

Editing your draft

Now is the time to attend to any problems in grammar, usage, spelling, punctuation, and mechanics. Check for any patterns you have identified as problems in your own writing. It may be fruitful as well to check for the twenty most common errors, listed on page xxxvi, and to consult the editing checklist in 3h. At this point, look very closely at details, checking any spelling, wording, or phrasing about which you are in doubt. You are fine-tuning here, polishing your essay.

Choosing a title

If you have not done so thus far, choose a title, crafting one that is specific enough to let your readers know about your research question and engaging enough to make them want to read *your* answer to it. Following are some examples of working titles that were changed to make them more specific and engaging:

WORKING TITLE	Nuclear Power [too general]
REVISED	Nuclear Power and the Menace to the Seacoast

40f|res   DRAFTING AND REVISING A RESEARCH ESSAY

WORKING TITLE	Testing Minoxidil [too general, uninformative]
REVISED	Minoxidil: A Cure for Baldness or Corporate Snake-Oil?
WORKING TITLE	Don't Lose Your Head—or Your Hand [uninformative]
REVISED	Hard Justice: Law Enforcement in Iran

Preparing your final copy

Your final rough draft may end up looking very rough indeed, filled with cross-outs, additions in the margins, circles, and arrows. So your next task is to create a final, carefully typed, painstakingly prepared clean copy. This is the version of the paper that you will submit, the one that will represent all your work and effort. For information on preparing a final manuscript, see Chapter 46.

Proofreading your final copy

Proofreading is a time for celebration. At this point, you are making your research essay watertight, your very best effort. Many writers look forward to this final reading, often taking time to read through once backwards in order to catch every word-level typographical error. So after proofreading, congratulate yourself and savor the rewards of a job well done. You have produced a solid piece of research, clearly written and cogently argued. You have become a researcher.

READING WITH AN EYE FOR RESEARCH

The following research essays were written by students, the first for a composition class, the second for a psychology class. Read these essays carefully, and study the marginal annotations. Compare your research essay to these, noting differences in approach, style, format, and use of sources.

STUDENT ESSAY—MLA STYLE   40

½" from top
Bloise 1   Pages numbered with writer's name

1" from top

Heading in place of title page

Melissa Bloise
Professor Connors
English 401
4 May 1988

The Strategic Defense Initiative:
Too Good to Be True

Title centered

Paragraphs indented five spaces

      Proposed by President Reagan in 1983 and originally estimated to cost $26 billion, the Strategic Defense Initiative (SDI) has been touted as a system that will render nuclear weapons impotent and thus free the world of the fear of nuclear annihilation, lead to overall arms reduction, and stimulate the economy by producing technological innovations useful in the private sector. If even one of these outcomes were likely, the SDI project would deserve our careful consideration. Unfortunately, however, it not only will not lead to any of these desirable goals but will in fact produce precisely the opposite effects from those claimed by its proponents.

Abbreviation introduced

Main points of argument presented

Thesis stated

Common ground established by acknowledging desirability of goals

      At its most effective, in fact, SDI will provide an imperfect defense against only one form of nuclear attack, long-range missiles that travel through space. Weapons that do not penetrate the upper atmosphere will, in

First main point of argument (ineffectiveness) introduced

TEACHING PRACTICE

After reading the introduction, direct your students to p. 570 and use the six questions under "Reconsidering purpose, audience, and thesis" as a basis for discussing how Melissa Bloise establishes her rhetorical stance.

TEACHING PRACTICE

Note that Melissa Bloise does not use a question to introduce her research question, but she does forecast her main arguments and establishes her credibility by including specific information, such as costs ($26 billion).

TEACHING PRACTICE

Refer students to the discussion of direct quotations on pp. 579–81 and then ask them to examine the use of direct quotations in this paragraph. What in these quotations is particularly necessary and/or memorable?

TEACHING PRACTICE

Consider directing students' attention to the outline model on p. 575. Then ask them to make an outline for this essay and use it to evaluate the organizational structure of the essay.

Bloise 2

essence, fly "under SDI" and will not be deterred by the system. At best, therefore, SDI will "provide a leaky roof on a house with no walls" (Center for Defense Information [CDI], "Star Wars" 2).

Partial quotation integrated into Bloise's sentence

Even many of those committed to the development of SDI acknowledge the low probability of achieving the level of technical development that is needed for a truly effective system. Lieutenant General James A. Abrahamson, director of the SDI Office, refuses to predict the number of enemy warheads that would be able to penetrate SDI defenses. Fred Hoffman, who chairs one of the Pentagon's SDI study teams, notes that the "likelihood" of the system's being able to protect "the bulk of our population" is small. In addition, the Congressional Office of Technology Assessment reports that "the prospect [of] . . . a perfect or near-perfect defense . . . is so remote that it should not serve as the basis of public expectations or national policy about ballistic missile defense" (qtd. in CDI, "Star Wars" 2).

Short title used to identify one of several references by the same author

Brackets and ellipses used to indicate changes in quotation

Authorities cited

Indirect source noted with qtd. in

Despite its questionable effectiveness, many SDI proponents claim that the system would at least lead to a reduction in the number

Second point of argument (arms reduction) introduced with transition

STUDENT ESSAY—MLA STYLE   40

Bloise   3

of nuclear weapons that the United States and
the Soviet Union would need to maintain. By
researching and deploying SDI, however, the
United States would nullify the Antiballistic
Missile (ABM) Treaty of 1972, thus allowing
for a buildup of both offensive and defensive
arms by both the United States and the Soviet
Union. And Gorbachev has specifically stated
that if the United States proceeds with SDI,
the Soviet Union will increase both the number
and sophistication of its offensive nuclear
weapons (CDI, "Unravelling" 4).

> Cause-effect
> relationship
> between SDI
> and arms
> buildup
> explained

Gerard Smith, chief U.S. negotiator for
the ABM Treaty, described it in August 1986
as "an essential component of the effort to
keep the arms race from going completely out
of control" (CDI, "Unravelling" 5). Similarly, former secretary of defense Harold
Brown has said, "To the extent that the U.S.
is committed to SDI, I think arms control is
not going to be feasible. Indeed, I think
existing agreements will either erode or be
abandoned." Agreeing with Brown are Soviet
expert George Kennan and former secretaries
of defense Robert McNamara and James Schles-
inger, who all believe that SDI and arms control
are mutually exclusive (CDI, "Pentagon" 4).

> Authorities
> cited for link
> between SDI
> and arms race

TEACHING PRACTICE

Reread the section on "Integrating quotations in your text" (p. 581) and then discuss how Melissa Bloise integrates the quotations from Gerard Smith and Harold Brown into the syntax of her own sentences. You might also ask students to speculate on answers to this question: Why does Melissa *not* quote from the three sources she cites near the end of the paragraph?

TEACHING PRACTICE

The long paragraph on this page contains many facts but only two references. Your students may be puzzled at the seeming lack of references here. Refer them to "Checking for excessive citations" (pp. 583–84) and point out that too many references could obscure the argument Melissa Bloise wants readers to focus on.

Bloise 4

Fueling a new arms buildup without providing adequate protection from the consequences of the old one, SDI would hardly, as its proponents insist, make nuclear weapons obsolete and free us of the fear of a "nuclear winter." Nevertheless, we are being asked to pay dearly for this supposed security shield. Official Reagan administration figures now project research and development costs at $40 billion through 1991, with another $30 billion projected to be spent by 1993. These costs are minuscule compared with projected production and deployment costs. According to a Johns Hopkins University study, a "comprehensive defense" system deployed by 2005 could cost $770 billion (CDI, "Unravelling" 5), and a study conducted for Senators J. Bennett Johnston, Lawton Chiles, and William Proxmire shows that annual maintenance and modernization expenses alone would exceed $200 billion and that total costs could perhaps reach several trillion dollars (Proxmire). According to the House Armed Services Committee, every dollar spent for military research and development creates an additional ten dollars in future defense spending (Shapiro 32). Since at least $70 billion would be spent on SDI research by only 1993, these

Transitional sentence summing up first two points of argument

No source citation needed for information available in several sources

Authorities cited for costs of SDI

Third main point of argument (cost-effectiveness) introduced

No page citation needed for one page article

Bloise   5

estimates of total costs do not seem far-
fetched. In comparison, the development of
the B-1 bomber and production of one hundred
planes cost only $28 billion; the Trident
submarine development program and the purchase
of seventeen submarines each equipped with
twenty-four nuclear missiles totaled only $67
billion (CDI, "Star Wars" 4). Clearly, SDI
would ultimately cost hundreds of billions
of dollars that could be used in much more
cost-effective ways.

Nor would SDI be likely to prove a boon
to our economy in other ways. Proponents of
the system have often made the claim that SDI
research will produce many spinoff technologies, technologies that will profit the commercial sector. While a few SDI technologies
may have commercial applications, that probability does not warrant the continuation of
the SDI project.

At present, the United States is losing
ground to foreign competitors in just those
industries, such as electronics and aerospace,
in which military research is overwhelmingly
concentrated (CDI, "Military" 1). If significant commercial applications of military
research were occurring, we would expect these
areas to have gained ground instead of losing

Comparison
used in
argument that
SDI is not
cost-effective

Next point of
argument
(economic
drawbacks)
introduced

Limited merit
granted to
opposing
argument
(spinoff
technologies
from military
research)

Appeals to
logic:
refutation of
claimed
cause-effect
relationship

TEACHING PRACTICE

After reading this paragraph of the essay, point out Melissa's use of paraphrase and summary. Refer students to "Incorporating paraphrases and summaries" (pp. 582–83), noting the method of citing sources here.

Bloise 6

it. In addition, if spinoffs were common, one would expect successful military contractors to be successful in the civilian sector as well. Instead, dual markets, military and civilian, have developed in the airplane industry and others. The reason is that much of military research is devoted to trying to produce equipment with very particular specifications, such as a refrigerator that can withstand an airplane crash and operate in an unpressurized cabin. Equipment with such rugged and specific performance requirements is too costly and "overdesigned" to have any cost-effective application to the commercial sector of the economy (CDI, "Military" 6).

Finally, the chance of commercial spinoffs is minimal because military research concentrates on the development of weapon prototypes rather than on general technology (CDI, "Military" 2). Far from aiding the civilian sector, in fact, military research actually reduces the amount of civilian research being conducted, a reduction that further hurts our economy. Simon Ramo, former president of TRW, an economic forecasting firm, confirms the adverse economic effects of much military spending, saying,

between military research and spinoffs

Example of military research cited

Authority cited for argument that military spending retards economic growth

STUDENT ESSAY—MLA STYLE

Bloise 7

Block →
**quotation
indented ten
spaces**

> In the past thirty years, had the
> total dollars we spent on military
> R & D been expended instead in
> those areas of science and tech-
> nology promising the most economic
> progress, we probably would be
> today where we are going to find
> ourselves arriving technologically
> in the year 2000 (qtd. in CDI,
> "Military" 6).

**Quotation of
more than
four lines set
off**

Thus far, over one thousand applications
from American universities have been submitted
to SDI headquarters in search of some of the
$600 million available for university research
on SDI. Many academics worry that important
nonmilitary research will be neglected as a
result of the intense concentration by the
nation's top scientific talent on the SDI
project. As Marvin Goldberger, president of
the California Institute of Technology, says,
"The infusion of such a large amount of money
can distort activities within the university.
It can draw people into research areas they
might not otherwise pursue" (Sanger 135).

**Authority
cited for
argument that
SDI will hurt
civilian
research**

Even in the event that SDI research does
produce some spinoff technologies, many seriously doubt that the Pentagon would allow the

**Refutation of
opposing
position that
had been
granted
limited merit**

TEACHING PRACTICE
Point out the formal features of long quotations, such as rules for indentation, and then reread "Setting off long quotations" (pp. 580–81) with the class, noting that long quotations must be introduced in some clear and explanatory way.

Bloise 8

private sector to develop them. U.S. university researchers anticipate that key elements of their SDI projects will become classified. If this occurs, they will be unable to publish their results or discuss possible applications with colleagues (Sanger 134). As early as 1985, the Pentagon began halting the flow of information by restricting access to civilian engineering meetings where unclassified research into SDI was being presented (Marlin and Nimroody). Recently, the military has become even more concerned about the flow of technological information and has imposed tighter restrictions both domestically and internationally, thus further reducing commercial possibilities.

Chronology of restrictions on information explained

Finally, the SDI program damages our economy by allowing a substantial amount of funding to go to other countries. Since the project's conception, a steady flow of international defense contractors has visited the SDI headquarters. In the first six months of 1985 alone, at least seven countries sent delegations expressing interest in participating in SDI development. Foreign companies view SDI as a great source of research funds, and rightly so: up to one-third of funds for the project could be spent abroad (Griffiths,

Last point of argument (American economic interests) introduced

TEACHING PRACTICE

This would be an appropriate time to ask students to complete and review the outline they have been making of this essay. Their review should serve two purposes for you: to make sure each student has identified the major points and to generate discussion over different interpretations of what the main points are.

Bloise 9

Taggiasco, Peterson, and Miller 68). The U.S. government, in fact, has been actively seeking foreign company involvement. Abrahamson, Defense Secretary Caspar Weinberger, and Vice-President George Bush have encouraged European participation. In addition to private companies, European universities are climbing on the bandwagon; some are submitting bids at the SDI office's request. In 1986, SDI planned to spend $50 million at foreign educational institutions (Griffiths, Taggiasco, Peterson, and Miller 72). While SDI spending is far from an effective way to spur our economy, spending the money within our borders at least may provide some benefit. By dispersing the funds abroad, we are using U.S. tax revenue to aid other economies.

> Clearly, SDI will not significantly increase the safety of our society from the threat of nuclear annihilation, and in fact, it may well increase our peril. The possibility of greater danger rather than the purported safety should be sufficient to deter a reasoned society from pursuing such a path without thoroughly and reasonably considering questions of secondary benefits. But even the arguments regarding the secondary benefits

Figurative language used to clarify idea of enthusiastic foreign participation

Major arguments (military and economic) restated in conclusion

TEACHING PRACTICE
Ask students to apply the four strategies listed on p. 579 under "Drafting your conclusion" to the conclusion of this essay.

Bloise 10

ostensibly to be gained from SDI are fallacious. Rather than stimulate and strengthen
our economy, SDI would place the United States
in an even weaker economic position in the
world. Development of SDI would reduce research and development in vitally needed
civilian areas while strengthening the econ-
omies of the major economic rivals of the United
States. More important societal issues will
be relegated to a lower priority, with almost
every sector of our society feeling both direct
and indirect negative effects of the cost of
this weapons system. That is assuming, of
course, that there will be anyone left to feel.

Appeal to
emotions in
conclusion

Bloise 11

Works Cited

First line of
each entry flush
with left margin

Center for Defense Information. "Military
      Research and the Economy: Burden or Bene-
      fit?" The Defense Monitor 14.1 (1985):
      1–8.

Subsequent
lines indented
five spaces

---."The Pentagon Prepares For Nuclear War:
      The 1988 Budget." The Defense Monitor
      16.4 (1987): 1–8.

Three
hyphens used
to indicate
additional
works by the
same author

---."Star Wars: Vision and Reality." The
      Defense Monitor 15.2 (1986): 1–8.

---."The Unravelling of Nuclear Arms Trea-
      ties: Another Step Toward Nuclear War."
      The Defense Monitor 16.1 (1987): 1–8.

Griffiths, Dave, Ronald Taggiasco, Thane Pe-
      terson, and Frederic A. Miller. "The
      Selling of Star Wars to Businesses
      Abroad." Business Week 15 July 1985: 68.

Marlin, Alice Tepper, and Rosy Nimroody.
      "'Star Wars' Benefits Are an Illusion
      With Mirrors." New York Times 14 Nov.
      1986: A34.

Proxmire, William. "When You Talk About 'Star
      Wars' You're Talking Trillions." Chris-
      tian Science Monitor 19 May 1986: 16.

Sanger, David E. "Campuses' Role in Arms De-
      bated as 'Star Wars' Funds are Sought."
      New York Times 22 July 1985: A1+.

Shapiro, Robert J. "A Frightening New Numbers
      Game." U.S. News & World Report 28 Sept.
      1987: 32–33.

Title centered

Entries listed
in
alphabetical
order by
author

TEACHING PRACTICE

Direct students' attention to Chapter 41 for explanations of how Melissa Bloise documented her
sources.

A Content Analysis of Letters
to the Editor
Leah Clendening

Title and
author
centered

Content Analysis 1

Short title
and page
number

TEACHING PRACTICE
Refer students to the discussion of introductions on p. 578. Then ask them to evaluate the effectiveness of this introduction to an essay in the social sciences. How does it differ from Melissa Bloise's introduction to her essay on p. 589?

Paragraphs indented five spaces

Would people from a large community be more interested in local or national issues? In order to answer this question, I conducted a content analysis of 624 letters to the editor in two newspapers to discover if community size affected the subjects of the letters. One newspaper was from a city with a population of over 500,000, while the second was from a city of about 15,000. Issues for both newspapers were read for the same three months and were compared. Results show a significant difference between the subjects of letters and the community size from which they originated.

Passive voice used to focus on the research rather than the researcher

Problem

Research indicates that the average person who writes letters to a newspaper is a conservative, well-adjusted, white American male who is usually middle-aged or older and a long-term resident of his community (Singletary & Cowling, 1979). One study has concluded that 71.4% of the letters printed were written by people who wished to inform or persuade by writing their letters. Most of the remainder, 27.0%, wished only to use the letter as a means of self-expression; another 1.6% wished to arouse readers to action (Lemert & Larkin, 1979).

Headings centered

Previous work surveyed

TEACHING PRACTICE

Ask students to compare the organizational format of this essay to the one by Melissa Bloise and to the one by Julie Slater on pp. 657–662. What similarities and differences can they identify?

Content Analysis 2

But what are the major concerns of these letter writers? Are they more concerned about events in their local communities, or about national issues? And does the size of the community have some influence on what its members write letters about? These questions led to the following hypothesis: people living in a small community (with a population of about 15,000) tend to be concerned more with local than with national issues. People living in a large community (with a population over 500,000) show more concern for national than for local issues.

Research question stated

Hypotheses stated

Method

Newspapers

The two newspapers that served as data sources, the Mount Vernon News and the Cleveland Plain Dealer, were chosen for convenience and availability. Cleveland has a population of 573,822 and a weekly distribution of the Plain Dealer of 482,564. Mount Vernon has a population of 14,380 and a weekly distribution of the Mount Vernon News of 10,936 (1985 IMS/Ayer Directory, 1985). Each newspaper's letters were read for the months of October 1986, December 1986, and February 1987. Sunday issues were not taken into account.

Subjects of study identified

Short title used to identify source with no author

STUDENT ESSAY—APA STYLE   40

Content Analysis 3

A category sheet of possible subjects for the letters to the editor was adapted from the coding sheet of Donohew's study on Medicare (Budd, Thorp, & Donohew, 1967, p. 41). One column recorded national issues, and a second local issues. The sheet was constructed with a space for the newspaper's abbreviation, the date, and the letter number(s). The <u>Mount Vernon News</u> was given the abbreviation MVN, and the <u>Cleveland Plain Dealer</u> the abbreviation CPD.

<u>Procedure</u>

After the category sheet was finished and approved, observation began. The newspapers were read and marked for content in a library setting. Each newspaper was skimmed until the Opinion page or the People's Forum section (depending on which newspaper was being observed) was found. Each letter was read and then classified on the category sheet that had been titled with the proper abbreviations, date, and letter number. As observation progressed, constraints of time demanded a change from filling out a separate sheet for each letter to recording each day's letters on the same category sheet. The space left for recording the letter number was used to record the total number of letters for each

Materials described

Page noted for specific source

Steps in carrying out research explained

TEACHING PRACTICE

Consider providing students with several letters to the editor of your local newspaper and ask them to follow the procedures described in this paragraph of the essay. Use their experiences to generate discussion on how effectively this paragraph is organized and on how well they were able to replicate the procedure.

TEACHING PRACTICE

As a focus for discussion of these "Results," ask students to reread "Reconsidering purpose, audience, and thesis" (p. 570). What audience is Leah Clendening addressing? How likely is it that this audience will be convinced by the results of the Chi square test?

Content Analysis 4

particular day. After all observation was finished, the counts for each of the newspapers were totaled for each month and overall.

Results

Over the 3-month period, 60 letters were read from the <u>Mount Vernon News</u>. Fifty-three of these pertained to local issues while seven pertained to national issues. A Chi Square test with an adjustment for continuity was used on these data to find if there was a statistically significant difference between concern with local and national issues. Results showed an overwhelming difference between issues, even at the .01 probability level. A graph was also constructed to show the number of national issues and local issues for each month for the MVN.

Results from first newspaper analyzed statistically

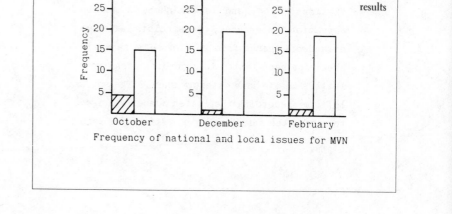

Figure 1.

Frequency of national and local issues for MVN

Graph used to show results

STUDENT ESSAY—APA STYLE

Content Analysis 5

From a total of 564 letters read from the <u>Cleveland</u> <u>Plain</u> <u>Dealer</u>, 248 pertained to local issues and 316 pertained to national issues. A Chi Square test with an adjustment for continuity was also used on these data and once again, showed statistically a significant difference. A graph was also constructed to show the frequency of national and local issues for each month for the CPD.

Results from second newspaper analyzed statistically

Figure 2. **Graph used to show results**

Frequency of national and local issues for CPD

TEACHING PRACTICE

Consider doing a bit of research of your own on how best to present information in graphic form. Most technical writing textbooks include a section on graphs and tables. See, for example, *Technical Writing: Principles and Forms*, pp. 151–185.

USEFUL READING

Andrews, Deborah, and Margaret Blickle. *Technical Writing: Principles and Forms.* 2d. ed. New York: Macmillan, 1982.

TEACHING PRACTICE

The discussion here functions as a conclusion. Ask students to use the strategies on p. 579 under "Drafting your conclusion" as a means of evaluating this section of the essay.

Content Analysis 6

One interesting side note is that 21.6% of the letters from the Cleveland Plain Dealer stated grievances or appreciation of some local happenings or people while 36% of the letters from the Mount Vernon News were about grievances or appreciation. These findings differ considerably from those of Lister, who found that only 5% of letters to the editor were of this particular type (Lister, 1985).

Discussion

The findings of this study generally supported the hypothesis, especially in the smaller community where letters concentrated overwhelmingly on local issues. Perhaps residents of such a community do not see themselves as strongly affected by governmental decisions and national happenings. For the larger community, the findings were not quite as clear; current studies do not suggest any apparent reason for this discrepancy, but perhaps further study may reveal the causes.

If more time had been permitted, an entire year's newspapers could have been categorized, thus yielding more accurate information. In addition, a second reader would have eliminated bias on the part of a single reader. It was found as the study progressed that a

Findings counter to previous research noted

Results interpreted

Biases and possible improvements in the study listed

Content Analysis 7

few categories could have been added, such
as religion and local and state elections:
the lack of these categories, however, did
not severely affect the study. Another bias
that would be difficult to account for is
editorial bias: one study found that only 68%
of the letters received by editors were published (Renfro, 1979). The only way to eliminate this bias would be to read all the letters
received by editors instead of only those that
were printed.

The study raises some interesting questions that further study would probably help
to answer. Does gender or age seem to influence
whether people are interested in local or
national issues? What is the causal relationship between residents of small towns and
their greater interest in local affairs? Are
the writers local people? Future studies may
be able to answer such questions by building
on the basic information provided here.

Larger
questions
noted in
conclusion

TEACHING PRACTICE

Direct students to Chapter 41 for explanations of how Leah Clendening documented her sources.

Content Analysis 8

References

Budd, R. W., Thorp, K., & Donohew, L. (1967). Content analysis of communications. New York: Macmillan.

Lemert, J. B., & Larkin, J. P. (1979). Some reasons why mobilizing information fails to be in letters to the editor. Journalism Quarterly, 56, 504–512.

Lister, L. (1985). An analysis of letters to the editor. Social Work, 30, 77–78.

The 1985 IMS/Ayer Directory of Publications (117th ed.). (1985). Fort Washington, PA: IMS Press.

Renfro, P. C. (1979). Bias in selection of letters to the editor. Journalism Quarterly, 56, 822–826.

Singletary, M. W., & Cowling, M. (1979). Letters to the editor of the non–daily press. Journalism Quarterly, 56, 165–168.

First line of each entry flush with left margin

Subsequent lines indented three spaces

Title centered on new page

Entries listed in alphabetical order by author

Last names always first; only initials used for first and middle names

41. Documenting Sources

Adam was the only man who, when he said a good thing, knew that nobody had said it before him.   —MARK TWAIN

Adam, in other words, had the luxury of not having to document his sources, but no writer since Adam has been able to make that claim. In your writing, full and accurate documentation is important because it helps build your credibility as a writer and researcher by giving credit to those people whose works influenced your own ideas.

Documentation styles vary among disciplines, with one format favored in the humanities, for instance, another in the social sciences, and another in engineering, but they all require the same basic information. Thus you will want to use the conventions of documentation appropriate to a particular course and field. Correct use of punctuation and format are central to consistency, demonstrate that you have taken pains to follow the conventions of your discipline, and protect you from plagiarizing because of omitted source information (see 39e).

The widely used citation styles presented here have in common two central objectives: to let your readers know what sources you used in your writing; and to help them find the sources, should they wish to. To accomplish these objectives, each style uses specific citations in the text that indicate that source information is being used and corresponding entries in the list of sources cited following the text of the essay that give all the information readers need to find a source.

The **Modern Language Association (MLA) style** is widely used in literature and languages as well as other fields. Revised in 1984, MLA style calls for noting brief references to sources in parentheses in the text of an essay and appending an alphabetical list of sources, called *Works Cited*, at the end. Used in many journals in the field of psychology, the **American Psychological Association (APA) style** is widely followed throughout the social sciences. Like MLA style, APA paren-

(BACK)GROUNDING
Writers document their sources for four reasons.

1. Careful documentation relieves the writer of any indictment of plagiarism, and gives credit for words or ideas to the original writer or speaker.
2. Documentation lends the writer authority as a researcher. It says to the reader, "I am honest and open to anyone wishing to retrace the steps in my research." Documentation is an important element in the *ethos* of the writer presenting research. Undocumented (plagiarized) sources—or sources imprecisely documented, even if only slightly—suggest that this writer is careless or even dishonest.
3. Documentation is a courtesy to later writers on the subject who may want to use some of the material. Documentation provides them with directions for finding it.
4. Documentation allows others to follow up on a writer's research in order to test its validity. Not only should writers tolerate such a procedure; they should welcome it. To have others look so carefully at one's work implies that such work is important.

WRITERS ON WRITING
When a thing has been said and well said, have no scruple; take it and copy it. Give references? Why should you? Either your readers know where you have taken the passage and the precaution is needless, or they do not know and you humiliate them.

—ANATOLE FRANCE

Plagiarists are always suspicious of being stolen from.

—SAMUEL TAYLOR COLERIDGE

(BACK)GROUNDING

While MLA and APA styles of documentation are widely used in the humanities and social sciences, other disciplines typically use other styles. The following style manuals provide documentation styles for other disciplines.

Geology: *Suggestions to Authors of the Reports of the United States Geological Survey.* 6th ed. Washington: GPO, 1978.

Law: *A Uniform System of Citation.* 14th ed. Cambridge, MA: Harvard Law Rev. Assn., 1986.

Linguistics: *LSA Bulletin,* Dec. issue, annually.

Mathematics: *A Manual for Authors of Mathematical Papers.* 7th ed. Providence: Amer. Math. Soc., 1980.

Medicine: International Steering Committee of Medical Editors. "Uniform Requirements for Manuscripts Submitted to Biomedical Journals." *Annals of Internal Medicine* 90 (Jan. 1979): 95–99.

Huth, Edward J. *Medical Style and Format: An International Manual for Authors, Editors, and Publishers.* Philadelphia: ISI P, 1987.

(BACK)GROUNDING

Several other style manuals are used across the disciplines. Frequently, in fact, journals in varied disciplines will specify use of one of these style manuals, including their documentation styles, over the style manuals usually recommended.

The Chicago Manual of Style. 13th ed. Chicago: U of Chicago P, 1982.

Ostermann, Georg F. von. *Manual of Foreign Languages: For the Use of Librarians, Bibliographers, Research Workers, Editors, Translators, and Printers.* 4th ed. NY: Central, 1952.

For information on other style manuals, see John Bruce Howell, *Style Manuals of the English-Speaking World.* Phoenix: Oryx, 1983.

thetical citations within the text direct readers to a list of sources. In APA style, this list is titled *References.* Various versions of the **number style,** whose parenthetical citations identify each work by a number assigned to it in the list of sources (usually titled *Literature Cited*) document work in many scientific papers and journals. Finally, history and some other humanities disciplines still prefer the traditional **note-and-bibliography (Old MLA) style.** This style uses note numbers in the text, keyed to a numerical list of *Notes;* an alphabetically arranged *Bibliography* lists the same sources at the end. Examples of documentation forms, parenthetical citations, and note forms in each of these styles appear in this chapter.

41a. Modern Language Association style

The MLA style uses parenthetical citations of sources within the text and a list of these sources at the end of the text. This section discusses the basic format for MLA style and shows examples of the bibliographic forms and parenthetical citations for various kinds of source materials. For further reference, consult:

MLA Handbook for Writers of Research Papers. 3rd ed. New York: Mod. Lang. Assoc., 1988.

1. MLA format for the list of works cited

The *Works Cited* list generally includes only those works actually cited in the paper. (If your instructor asks that you list everything you have read as background, call the list *Works Consulted* instead.)

Arrange this list alphabetically by authors' last names. If your list includes sources for which no author is known, alphabetize them according to their titles. If a title begins with *A, An,* or *The,* use its next word to determine its alphabetical placement.

Start your *Works Cited* list on a separate page, with *Works Cited* neither underlined nor in quotation marks, and centered on the page one inch from the top. Quadruple space and start your list. Begin typing the first line of each entry at the left margin, but indent each of the next lines within the entry five spaces so that the author's last names will stand out for easy reference. Double-space each line in the entire list, whether it begins or continues an entry.

Each entry includes the author's name, the title (and any subtitle), and the publication information. List the author's last name first,

MODERN LANGUAGE ASSOCIATION STYLE   *doc* 41a

followed by a comma and the author's first name and any middle initial, with a period. Follow each period in the entry with two spaces.

Underline the titles (and any subtitles) of books and periodicals; put titles (and any subtitles) of articles, short fiction, and poems in quotation marks. Capitalize all major words in the title and subtitle. If a work has a subtitle, place a colon after the main title, one space, and then add the subtitle. Follow the title or subtitle with a period.

The publication information for a book lists the city where the publisher is located (and state or country if your reader is unfamiliar with the city), followed by a colon and one space, a shortened version of the publisher's name (*St. Martin's* for *St. Martin's Press, Inc.*, or *Oxford UP* for *Oxford University Press*), a comma, and the date of publication. For an article in a periodical, you do not need to list the place of publication but simply the name of the periodical in which the article appears, the volume or issue number, the year of publication in parentheses, a colon, one space, and the inclusive page numbers of the article. End the entry with a period.

Consult the various example entries presented in this section for information on where in an entry you should place supplementary information. Here are examples of basic book and periodical entries.

```
                    two spaces                    one space after colon
        author, last name first      title, underlined              subtitle
doublespace →  Secord, James A. Controversy in Victorian Geology: The Cambrian-
indent 5 spaces →   Silurian Dispute. Princeton: Princeton UP, 1986.   publisher's
                                                                       city and name
```

```
                         article title,              periodical title,
                         in quotation marks           underlined
        author, last name first
doublespace →  Ficaro, Barbara. "Canterbury's First Dean." Sixteenth Century
indent 5 spaces →   Journal 18 (1987): 343-346.
                         |        |            |
                     volume   date, in     page numbers
                     number   parentheses
```

Books and pamphlets

The examples below show how to treat the various parts of information in book and pamphlet entries.

A book written by one author

```
De Vries, Peter. Peckham's Marbles. New York: Putnam's,
     1986.
```

(BACK)GROUNDING

The practice of documenting sources developed out of the larger movement toward bibliography and documentation that has become one of the great contributions of the twentieth century. Documentation arose out of the increase of information and the gradual growth of information systems.

In ancient times, information storage and retrieval was accomplished for the most part by individuals mnemonically and by societies through rituals. With the rise of literacy came the desire to classify information systematically in the form of writing. Libraries are the most familiar information systems. The first libraries were built simply to preserve but not make available their information. That intention really did not begin to change until the late nineteenth century.

Of course, there were earlier attempts at systematic classification of information, but only at a local level. In the second century A.D., the Greek physician Galen compiled a catalog of his works. In A.D. 731 or 732, Bede the Venerable provided a bibliography in his *Ecclesiastical History of the English People.* The most ambitious bibliography was produced in the sixteenth century by the Swiss scientist Conrad Gesner, who compiled a twenty-volume bibliography of world literature.

The invention of the printing press and the great increase in the desire for knowledge during the Renaissance helped to increase the flow of information via books and the need and desire for some way to classify such information in order to make it more readily available. Many different and individualized systems of classification and organization of information developed until, in the late nineteenth century, American librarian Melvil Dewey invented the Dewey Decimal System of Classification, which libraries quickly adopted.

(BACK)GROUNDING

Another important development in the history of documentation was the change during the late Middle Ages and Renaissance in the notion of authorship. Medieval authors did not view their work as necessarily theirs alone; there was little sense of knowledge as somehow owned or its origins as deserving acknowledgement. However, as the world progressed into modern times, authorship became more personalized; writers began to think in terms of original ideas and to believe that they had a right to be acknowledged as the author of such ideas.

The form of such acknowledgement, whether it is MLA style or APA style or any of the many other documentation styles, derives from bibliographical description. Such description is meant to record various characteristics of each book thereby revealing the uniqueness of each. Citation of a source is not nearly as detailed as a true bibliographical description, which records physical qualities of each book as well as author, title, place of publication, and so on.

A book written by two or three authors

List the first author last name first; then list the other author or authors in regular order, with commas between the names.

McNeill, John T, and Helena M. Gamer. <u>Medieval Handbooks of Penance</u>. New York: Octagon, 1965.

A book written by more than three authors

Name the first author listed on the book's title page, follow it with a comma, and then add the abbreviation *et al.* ("and others").

Britton, James, et al. <u>The Development of Writing Abilities (11–18)</u>. London: Macmillan Education, 1975.

A book written by a group

Use the name of a group or organization listed on the title page as the author in place of individual authors.

Carnegie Corporation on Higher Education. <u>The Academic System in American Society</u>. New York: McGraw, 1974.

A book prepared by an editor

If a work was prepared by an editor, list this person as you would an author and add a comma and the abbreviation *ed.* (for *editor*).

Parker, Dorothy, ed. <u>Essays on Modern American Drama</u>. Toronto: U of Toronto P, 1987.

If a book has both an author and an editor, your entry should show whose work you cite. If you cite the author's work, name the author first. Then add the editor's name, with the abbreviation *Ed.*, after the title. If you cite the editor's work, such as the variations in the edition or the commentary, name the editor first, followed by *ed.* After the title, add the author's name, introduced with *By*.

A book prepared by a translator

When a book has an author and a translator, your entry should show whose work you cite. If you cite the author's work—the text itself—begin with the author's name. After the title, introduce the translator's name with *Trans.* (for *translator*).

MODERN LANGUAGE ASSOCIATION STYLE

Jansson, Sven B. F. The Runes of Sweden. Trans. Peter
    G. Foote. Stockholm: Norstedt Forlag, 1962.

A second work by the same author

If you cite more than one work by a particular author, arrange
the entries alphabetically by title. After the first entry, begin with three
hyphens followed by a period instead of the author's name.

Lasswell, Harold D. The Analysis of Political Behaviour:
    An Empirical Approach. New York: Oxford UP, 1948.
---. The Future of Political Science. American Political
    Science Association Series. New York: Atherton,
    1963.

A republication

If you cite a modern edition of an older book, a paperback edition, or other republication, add the original publication date, with a
period, right after the title. Then give the publication details for the
edition you used.

Scott, Walter. Kenilworth. 1821. New York: Dodd, 1956.

A particular edition

If a book is identified on its title page as a particular edition, add
this information, in abbreviated form, after the title.

Kelly, Alfred H., Winfred A. Harbison, and Herman Belz.
    The American Constitution: Its Origins and Devel-
    opment. 6th ed. New York: Norton, 1983.

A work in two or more volumes

If a work has more than one volume, note the number of volumes
in the complete work before the publication information, if you used
more than one volume. If the volumes were published over several
years, give the inclusive dates.

Braudel, Fernand. The Mediterranean and the Mediterranean
    World in the Age of Philip II. Trans. Siân Reynolds.
    2 vols. New York: Harper, 1972–73.

If you used only one volume, cite only that volume before the publication information; then give the number of volumes at the end of the entry. (Then, because the volume is specified, your text citation needs only the page number.)

> Stevenson, Ian. <u>Cases of the Reincarnation Type</u>. Vol.
>   3. Charlottesville: UP of Virginia, 1980. 4 vols.

A book that is part of a series

If a book is part of a series (as noted on the title page or the page before), add the series name and any number after the title.

> Bloom, Harold, ed. <u>Ralph Waldo Emerson</u>. Modern Critical
>   Views. New York: Chelsea, 1985.

An item in an anthology or collection

If you cite a selection in an anthology, name the author of the selection. Then list the selection's title, set off by quotation marks (or by underlining if the selection first appeared as a book), the anthology's title, underlined, and the name of any editor. Finally, note the inclusive pages of the selection, followed by a period.

> Didion, Joan. "Why I Write." <u>The Writer on Her Work</u>.
>   Ed. Janet Sternburg. New York: Norton, 1980. 3-16.

An article in an encyclopedia

List the author of the article, often identified by initials corresponding to full names in a list of contributors. If no author is identified, begin with the title. For a well-known encyclopedia, just note any edition number and date. If the encyclopedia entries are arranged in alphabetical order, no volume or page numbers are needed.

> "Traquair, Sir John Stewart." <u>Encyclopaedia Britannica</u>.
>   11th ed. 1909.

A preface, introduction, foreword, or afterword

List the author of the item, then its title, set off only by an initial capital letter, and a period. After the title of the work in which the item appears, introduce the name of the author of the complete work with *By*. (If the same person wrote both, just the last name is needed here.) List the item's page numbers at the end of the entry.

```
Schlesinger, Arthur M., Jr. Introduction. Pioneer Women:
     Voices from the Kansas Frontier. By Joanna L. Strat-
     ton. New York: Simon, 1981. 11-15.
```

A government document

List government documents as you would books, beginning with the author, if identified, and giving the name of the government agency after the title. If no author is given, first list the government and then the department or agency.

```
New Hampshire. Dept. of Transportation. Right of Way
     Salinity Reports, Hillsborough County, 1985. Con-
     cord: New Hampshire Dept. of Transportation, 1986.
```

An unpublished dissertation

Set off the title of an unpublished dissertation with quotation marks. Add the identification *Diss.*, the name of the school at which the study was done, a comma, and the date.

```
Kitzhaber, Albert R. "Rhetoric in American Colleges 1850-
     1900." Diss. U of Washington, 1953.
```

Periodicals

Use the examples below as a guide to the main variations in journal, magazine, and other periodical entries. (See p. 611 for a sample periodical entry.)

An article in a scholarly periodical that numbers pages consecutively within a volume

If a periodical continues page numbering from one issue to the next within the annual volume, follow the title of the publication with the volume number in arabic numerals.

```
Norris, Margot. "Narration under a Blindfold: Reading
     Joyce's 'Clay.'" PMLA 102 (1987): 206-215.
```

An article in a scholarly periodical that numbers pages separately within each issue

If a periodical numbers pages in each issue separately, include the volume number and the issue number, separated by a period.

```
Loffy, John.  "The Politics at Modernism's Funeral."
     Canadian Journal of Political and Social Theory 6.3
     (1987): 89-96.
```

An article in a monthly or weekly periodical

For a monthly or bimonthly periodical, abbreviate the month (except May, June, or July), and put the date after the periodical's title.

```
Said, Edward.  "Through Gringo Eyes."  Harper's Apr. 1988:
     70-72.
```

For a weekly or biweekly periodical, note the day, the month, the year.

```
Holden, Ted.  "Campbell's Taste of the Japanese Market
     is Mm-Mm Good."  Business Week 28 Mar. 1988: 42.
```

An article in a newspaper

List the author, article title, and then the newspaper's title (dropping any initial A, An, or The) as it appears on the front page. Follow it with the city or place in square brackets if this information is not part of the title. Give the exact date of the issue, followed by a colon and the page number. If the page number does not include the section (such as B4 or C1), follow the date with a comma, the section (with *sec.*) followed by a colon, and the page number.

```
Sharpe, Lora.  "A Quilters' Tribute."  Boston Globe 25
     Mar. 1988, sec. 2: 47.
```

An editorial or letter in a periodical

Identify an editorial or letter by adding the word *Editorial* or *Letter* after the title.

```
Magee, Doug.  "Soldier's Home."  Editorial.  Nation 26
     Mar. 1988: 400-401.
Stewart, Francis.  Letter.  Economist 19-25 Mar. 1988: 4.
```

A review in a periodical

Give the author's name, if identified, and the title, if the review has one. If not, begin the entry with the phrase *Rev. of* (with just a capital *R*) and the name of the work being reviewed. After this title, add a comma, *by*, and the work's author.

```
Block, J. H. "Debatable Conclusions about Sex Differ-
      ences." Rev. of The Psychology of Sex Differences,
      by E. E. Maccoby and C. N. Jacklin. Contemporary
      Psychology Aug. 1976: 517-522.
```

An article whose author is not identified

Begin with the article title, dropping any initial *A*, *An*, or *The* and place it in alphabetical order. The article below begins on page 20 and continues on pages 23 and 24. To show that the pages are not consecutive, note only the first page number followed by a plus sign.

```
"The Odds of March." Time 15 Apr. 1985: 20+.
```

Other sources

The examples below show how to treat the main types of entries for other sources of information.

An interview

List first the person who has been interviewed. Then list the title, if the interview has one, in quotation marks (or underlined if it is the complete work). If it does not have a title, use the word *Interview*. If the interview comes from a source, identify the source. If you were the interviewer, identify the type as *Telephone Interview* or *Personal Interview*, and note the date.

```
Schorr, Daniel. Interview. Weekend Edition. Natl. Public
      Radio. WEVO, Concord. 26 Mar. 1988.
Berkson, Larry. Personal Interview. 16 May 1989.
```

A letter

If you cite a published letter, enter it like a selection from a book. Note the letter's date and any number used in the source after the title of the letter.

```
Frost, Robert. "Letter to Editor of the Independent." 28
      Mar. 1894. Selected Letters of Robert Frost. Ed.
      Lawrance Thompson. New York: Holt, 1964. 19.
```

TEACHING PRACTICE

If your students conducted interviews as part of their work in 38a2, ask them to write up the proper citations for those interviews and bring them to class to share.

Follow the form below if you cite a letter sent to you.

```
Diaz, Gloria. Letter to the author. 12 Feb. 1989.
```

A computer software program

List the writer of the program if identified. Then add the title of the software, underlined, followed by the words *Computer software*. Next identify the company that distributes the software, and the date. Note the computer type, memory required, operating system, format, and any other details.

```
Nota Bene. Vers. 3.0. Computer software. Dragonfly Soft-
    ware, 1988. MS-DOS 2.0, 512 KB, disk.
```

A film or videotape

For a film, a videotape, or a slide program, include the film's title, underlined; director; the company distributing the film; and the date. Other contributors, such as writers or actors, may follow the director's name. If you are interested in one person's work, such as the director's, list that person's name first.

```
The Night of the Hunter. Dir. Charles Laughton. With Robert
    Mitchum, Shelley Winters, and Lillian Gish. United
    Artists, 1955.
```

A television or radio program

Begin the entry with the title of the program, underlined. Add other details (such as narrator, director, writer, and principal actors) after the title as necessary. Then identify the network, the local station and city, and the date. If you are interested in the work of a particular person, begin the entry with that person's name. If you cite a particular episode, begin with the episode's title in quotation marks.

```
Hill Street Blues. Writ. Michael Kozoll and Stephen Bochco.
    With Daniel J. Travanti, Joe Spano, and Charles Haid.
    NBC. WNBC, New York. 15 Jan. 1981.
```

A recording

Your research interest determines whether the name of the composer, artist, or conductor precedes the title of the album or tape, which is underlined, or the name of the composition recorded, which is not underlined. Then add the names of any other pertinent people. End with the name of the manufacturer, the catalog number, and the date, all separated by commas.

```
Vega, Suzanne. Solitude Standing. A & M, SP 3156, 1987.
Grieg, Edvard. Concerto in A-minor, op. 16. Perf. Van
     Cliburn. Cond. Eugene Ormandy. Philadelphia Orch.
     RCA, Red Seal LSC 3065, 1969.
```

An artistic work

List the artist, and then give the work's title, underlined. Add the name of the museum or other location, and identify the city.

```
Munch, Edvard. The Cry. Museum of Fine Arts, Boston.
```

A performance

List the title or the name of someone involved if that person's work is your particular interest. Add other appropriate details (such as the composer, writer, director). Then identify where and when the performance took place.

```
Frankie and Johnny in the Clair de Lune. By Terrence
     McNally. Dir. Paul Benedict. Westside Arts Theater,
     New York. 18 Jan. 1988.
```

2. MLA format for parenthetical citations

MLA style uses parenthetical citations in the text following each quotation, paraphrase, summary, or reference to a source. Each citation, made up of the author's last name or key words from the title, and the page reference, refers to an entry in the *Works Cited* list at the end of the essay. The name or key words allow the reader to locate the entry with complete publication information for the source. The page reference allows readers to find the exact material in the source itself. Place the citation, in parentheses, at the end of a sentence or at a logical break in its syntax. Place any punctuation marks—periods, commas, semicolons, or whatever—*after* the closing parenthesis. If your citation refers to a direct quotation, place the citation *after* the closing quotation mark, and *before* any punctuation mark. For longer quotations typed as a block with no quotation marks, place the citation two spaces after the period of the last sentence of the quotation. The parenthetical citation should fit smoothly into your text, interrupting your discussion as little as possible. With this aim in mind, MLA style allows for variations in citing references.

Author and page format

After a quotation, paraphrase, or summary of an author's work, add the author's last name and the page number of the source in parentheses. Note that you do not need a comma to separate the author's name and the page number.

> In places de Beauvoir "sees Marxists as believing in subjectivity as much as existentialists do" (Whitmarsh 63).

Author named in text

The shorter your parenthetical references are, the easier your essay will be to read. Therefore, you can name the author in your text, then include only a page number as the citation.

> As Mueller and Rodgers have shown, television holds the potential for distorting and manipulating consumers as free-willed decision makers (370).

If you refer to a whole work rather than a specific passage, or to a one-page article, include the reference in the text without any page numbers or parentheses.

> Virginia Woolf's interpretation of Hardy's tragic vision is very different from Lawrence's.

Author of more than one reference

If you cite more than one work by an author in your *Works Cited* list, signal which work you mean by adding a comma and a short form of the title after the author's name.

> Through Grendel, a "pointless, ridiculous monster, crouched in the shadows, stinking of dead men, murdered children, and martyred cows" (Gardner, <u>Grendel</u> 2), readers are presented with their own silliness.

MODERN LANGUAGE ASSOCIATION STYLE   *doc* 41a

Long quotation

If you use a long quotation (five lines or more), type it as a block indented ten spaces from the left margin, and do not use quotation marks. Skip two spaces *after* the last punctuation mark, and add the parenthetical reference.

> In similar fashion, the beginning of <u>Being</u> <u>and</u> <u>Time</u> also
> raises this problem:
>
>> The question of the meaning of Being must be
>> <u>formulated</u>. If it is a fundamental question,
>> or indeed <u>the</u> fundamental question, it must be
>> made transparent and in an appropriate way.
>> We must therefore explain briefly what belongs
>> to any question whatsoever, so that from this
>> standpoint the question of Being can be made
>> visible as a <u>very</u> <u>special</u> one with its own
>> distinctive character. (Heidigger 24)

More than one author

If you cite a work with two or three authors, list each author's last name in the order used on the title page.

> "Opinion leaders" influence other people in an organi-
> zation because they are respected, not because they hold
> high positions (Gortner, Mahler, and Nicholson 175).

For a work with four authors or more, use only the last name of the first author, followed by *et al.*

> As the Schools Council study showed in the 1960s, children
> will learn to write if they are allowed to choose their
> own subjects (Britton et al. 37–42).

Title without identified author

Use a short version of titles with no identified author. Use quotation marks or underlining as you would in the *Works Cited* list.

> "Hype," by one analysis, is "an artificially engendered
> atmosphere of hysteria" ("Today's Marketplace" 51).

TEACHING PRACTICE

You may wish to refer students back to the discussion in Chapter 40 of quotations and how to open long ones. If they are having difficulty with long quotations, use some class time to examine one or two long quotations in the context of a student's essay, checking not only for correct citations but also for appropriate introductions to them.

Indirect sources for quotations

Use the abbreviation *qtd. in* to indicate that you are quoting from an indirect source—that is, someone else's report of a conversation, statement, interview, letter, or whatever.

> As Arthur Miller says, "When somebody is destroyed every-
> body finally contributes to it, but in Willy's case, [the
> end product] would be virtually the same" (qtd. in Martin
> and Meyer 375).

Source with a volume number

If you cite a work with several volumes, note the volume number and the page number, with a colon between the two, after the author.

> Modernist writers prized experimentation and gradually
> even sought to blur the line between poetry and prose
> (Foerster et al. 3: 150).

If you list only one volume of the work in your *Works Cited*, you need only include the page number after the author.

Literary works

To help a reader find a reference to a literary work available in many editions, cite the page number from the edition you used and include such information as part or chapter in a novel (175; ch. 10), the lines in a poem (33; 22-23). If you cite a play, you need only give the act, scene, and line numbers.

> As <u>Macbeth</u> begins, the witches greet Banquo as "Lesser
> than Macbeth, and greater" (1.3.65).

3. MLA format for explanatory notes

MLA style allows explanatory footnotes for commentary on sources or observations that would not fit readily into the text but are needed for clarification or further explanation. The notes, numbered consecutively, are identified by superscript numbers in the text. The full notes may appear as endnotes (typed in a list headed *Notes* after the text but before the *Works Cited*), or as footnotes at the bottom of the page (typed four lines below the last line of text). (See 41d2 for more information on note forms in MLA style.)

AMERICAN PSYCHOLOGICAL ASSOCIATION STYLE   *doc* 41b

Superscript number in text

Stewart seems to emphasize the existence of social con-
tracts in Hawthorne's life so that the audience will accept
a different Hawthorne, one more attuned to modern times
than the figure in Woodberry.³

Endnote or footnote

³Woodberry does, however, show that Hawthorne <u>was</u>
often an unsociable individual. He emphasizes the se-
clusion of Hawthorne's mother, who separated herself from
her family after the death of her husband, often even taking
meals alone (Woodberry 28). Woodberry seems to imply that
Mrs. Hawthorne's isolation rubbed off onto her son.

41b. American Psychological Association style

The APA style cites sources parenthetically in the text and then
lists these references at the end of the paper. This section discusses the
basic format for APA style and shows examples of the bibliographic
forms and parenthetical citations for various kinds of sources. For further reference, consult the following:

Publication Manual of the American Psychological Association. 3rd ed.
Washington: Amer. Psych. Assoc., 1983.

1. APA format for references

In APA style, the list of sources, labeled *References*, appears after
the body of your essay but before any appendices explaining your research procedures or results. (If your instructor asks you to list sources
read as background as well as those you cite specifically, label your list
Bibliography.)

Organize your list alphabetically by authors' last names. If a work
has no identified author or editor, list it alphabetically by its title (excluding A, An, or The). If you cite more than one work by the same
author, list the works chronologically under the author's last name.

Start your *References* list on a separate page, with the word *References* (neither underlined nor in quotation marks) centered at the top
of the page. Double-space, and begin your list. Begin typing the first

line of each entry at the left margin; indent the next lines in that entry three spaces. Double-space the entire list.

Each entry includes the author's name, the publication date, the title (and any subtitle), and the publication information, each followed by a period and two spaces. List the author's name with the last name first, a comma, and just the initials of the author's first and middle names. For more than one author, list the others in reverse order as well, with the names separated by a comma and an ampersand (&). Follow the author's name with the date of publication, in parentheses.

Underline titles of books and periodicals, but do not underline nor put in quotation marks the titles of articles. For book and article titles, capitalize only the first word of the title and any subtitle and any proper nouns. For periodical titles, capitalize all major words.

The publication information for a book includes the city where the publisher is located (and the state or country, if your readers are unfamiliar with the city), followed by a colon and one space, and the publisher's name. Like MLA style, APA style calls for a shortened version of the publisher's name, but calls for the names of university presses to be spelled out. In general, just drop any *Inc.*, *Corp.*, or *Publishers*. For an article in a periodical, the publication information includes the title of the periodical in which the article appears, a comma, the volume number (underlined), a comma, and the inclusive page numbers. The entry ends with a period.

Consult the various example entries presented in this section for information on where in an entry you should place supplementary information—particularly for publication information needed for different kinds of periodicals. Here are examples of basic book and periodical entries.

AMERICAN PSYCHOLOGICAL ASSOCIATION STYLE

Books and pamphlets

A book written by one author

Coon, D. (1980). <u>Introduction to psychology: Exploration and application</u>. New York: West Publishing.

A book written by two or more authors

Newcombe, F., & Ratcliffe, G. (1978). <u>Defining females --The nature of women in society</u>. New York: Wiley.

A book written by a group

Institute of Financial Education. (1983). <u>Income property lending</u>. Homewood, IL: Dow Jones-Irwin.

A book prepared by an editor

Solomon, A. P. (Ed.). (1980). <u>The prospective city</u>. Cambridge, MA: MIT Press.

A second work by the same author

Macrorie, K. (1968). <u>Writing to be read</u>. New York: Hayden.
Macrorie, K. (1970). <u>Uptaught</u>. Rochelle Park: Hayden.

An item in an anthology or collection

Taylor, R. C. R. (1982). The politics of prevention. In P. Conrad & R. Kern (Eds.), <u>The sociology of health and illness</u> (pp. 471-483). New York: St. Martin's.

A government document

U.S. Bureau of the Census. (1984). <u>Statistical abstract of the United States: 1985</u> (105th ed.). Washington, DC: U.S. Government Printing Office.

Periodicals

An article in a scholarly periodical that numbers pages consecutively within a volume

Shuy, R. (1981). A holistic view of language. <u>Research in the Teaching of English</u>, <u>15</u>, 101-111.

An article in a scholarly periodical that numbers pages separately within each issue

Maienza, J. G. (1986). The superintendency: Characteristics of access for men and women. <u>Educational Administration Quarterly</u>, <u>22</u>(4), 59–79.

An article in a monthly or weekly periodical

Seymour, J. (1988, May 31). Preventing data loss disasters. <u>PC Magazine</u>, pp. 92–96.

An article in a newspaper

Browne, M. W. (1988, April 26). Lasers for the battlefield raise concern for eyesight. <u>The New York Times</u>, pp. C1, C8.

A letter to a periodical

Burney, P. S. (1985, May). Cryptographic message sending [Letter to the editor]. <u>Byte: The Small Systems Journal</u>, p. 14.

An article whose author is not identified

What sort of person reads creative computing? (1985, August). <u>Creative Computing</u>, pp. 8, 10.

Other sources

An interview

Kort, M. (1988, February). Ms. conversation [Interview with Martina Navratilova & Billie Jean King]. <u>Ms.</u>, pp. 58–62.

A computer software program

<u>SuperCalc3 Release 2.1</u> (1985). [Computer program]. San Jose, CA: Computer Associates, Micro Products Division.

AMERICAN PSYCHOLOGICAL ASSOCIATION STYLE   *doc* 41b

2. APA format for parenthetical citations

APA parenthetical citations identify each quotation, paraphrase, summary, or reference in your text. These citations generally include the author's last name, the date of publication, and the page number if it is a specific citation. The author's last name is the key to the corresponding full-information entry in the alphabetically arranged *References* list. The year distinguishes one work from another by the same author, and the page reference identifies the exact location of the cited material in the original source. In general, place citations at the end of a sentence or at a logical break in syntax, after the closing quotation mark of a direct quotation, with any punctuation mark *after* the closing parenthesis. For long quotations typed as a block, place the citation two spaces after the period of the last sentence of the quotation. All APA citations follow the same general form, but below are some of the ways to treat variations in form.

Author and date format

The two basic items in a citation are the author's name and the publication date, separated by a comma. Researchers in fields that use the APA style often cite a whole experiment or study rather than quote heavily from specific pages. As a result, APA style citations may refer to whole works without page numbers.

> It takes a 900% increase in profit to offset a 90% decrease
> so that the company can return to the same profit level
> as before (Meigs, 1981).

Author, date, and page format

If you need to specify the page, add a comma following the date, and use the abbreviation *p.* for *page*.

> Parents play an important role in building their children's
> self-esteem because "children value themselves to the
> degree that they have been valued" (Briggs, 1970, p. 14).

Author named in text

If you name the author in your text, you need only cite the date in parentheses, immediately after the author's name.

> Key (1983) showed how the placement of women in print
> advertisements was subliminally important.

You can refer to the author and date of the study in your text and eliminate the citation.

> As Mueller and Rodgers demonstrated in 1980, television holds the potential for distorting and manipulating consumers as free-willed decision makers.

Author of more than one reference

When you refer to more than one work by an author in the same citation, use the author's last name and include the dates of all works cited. If you cite two or more works by the same author published in the same year, include the lowercase letter you assigned to each of these works in your *References* list.

> Several other essays continued this exploration of female heroes in science fiction (Russ, 1972a, 1972b).

Long quotation

Type long quotations (more than forty words), as a block indented five spaces from the left margin, and do not use quotation marks. *After* the final punctuation in the quotation, skip two spaces, and add the parenthetical citation.

> Unhealthy cafeteria lunches, full of salt and fat, result from more than just children's love of fast food:
>
> > As mandated by the Child Nutrition Act of 1946, the school lunch program must not only satisfy the nutritional needs of children, but also assist the agriculture industry as an effective farm support program. In 1986, this mandate meant that U.S. schools received more than $1 billion in government-donated agricultural commodities. (Montgomery, 1988, p. 28)

More than one author

If a work was written by two authors, use both names in all citations. Join the names with an ampersand (&) in parenthetical references, but spell out *and* when you name the authors in the text itself.

> While positioning is a successful method for handling students, group focus will also help prevent many problems. "Group focus is the ability to keep as many students as

```
possible involved in appropriate class activities" (Wool-
folk & McCune-Nicolich, 1984, p. 360).
```

If a work was written by three to five people, list all their names in the first citation. In any other citations of the same source, just use the first author's last name plus *et al.* (for "and others"): (Bradley et al., 1979). Only if a work was written by six or more people should you use the first author's name and *et al.* from the first citation onward.

Title without identified author

When the author is not identified, use the first few words of the title in the citation.

```
The school profiles for the county substantiate this trend
(Guide to Secondary Schools, 1983).
```

Indirect sources

Use *cited in* to show when you are using information taken from an indirect source.

```
The entire procedure was replicated with similar results
in Hermosa's study (cited in Poster, 1986).
```

3. APA content footnotes

APA style allows content footnotes for information you wish to include to expand or supplement your text, marked in the text by superscript numbers in consecutive order. The footnotes are listed on a separate page after the last page of your text, under the heading *Footnotes*, centered at the top of the page. Double-space all entries. Indent the first line of each footnote five spaces, but begin subsequent lines at the left margin. Ask your instructor or consult the APA manual for more specific typing requirements for footnotes.

Superscript in text

```
The age of the children involved was an important factor
in the selection of items for the questionnaire.[1]
```

Footnote

```
[1]The advice of Marjorie Youngston Forman and William
Cole of the Child Study Team provided great assistance
in identifying appropriate items.
```

▌41c. Number style

In the number style, which is used in many of the natural sciences, parenthetical citations in the text are numbers that correspond to entries in a final list of sources, often called *Literature Cited*. Variations in the number style exist from discipline to discipline, so be sure to ask your instructor which style you should follow. Some common style manuals are the following:

CBE Style Manual. 5th ed. Bethesda: Council of Biology Editors, 1983.

Handbook for Authors of Papers in American Chemical Society Publications. Washington, DC: American Chemical Society, 1978.

Style Manual for Guidance in Preparation of Papers. 3rd ed. New York: American Institute of Physics, 1978.

For essays using the number style, your list of sources includes only works you actually cite in the essay. The list is arranged either alphabetically by authors' last names, with each entry assigned a number in sequence, or by chronological sequence according to the order in which you cited your sources in the text.

References in the text are identified by a number in parentheses following any quotation, paraphrase, summary, or reference to a source. The numbers refer readers to the corresponding entry in the *Literature Cited* list. If your citation refers to a specific page, include the page number after the entry number with a comma and the abbreviation *p*. Here is sample text reference and corresponding *Literature Cited* entry.

Text reference

```
First of all, the doctor is in the autonomous position
of having a monopoly on the applied uses of medical sci-
entific knowledge, as argued in Freidson (1).
```

Literature Cited entry

```
     1. Freidson, E. Profession of Medicine, Dodd-Mead,
New York, 1972.
```

▌41d. Note-and-bibliography style

The **note-and-bibliography style** was the standard format preferred by Modern Language Association (MLA) until 1984 (and thus is sometimes referred to as **Old MLA style**). This style is still used in many fields, particularly in the humanities. In this style, references in the text are noted with superscript numbers that correspond to footnotes or endnotes, which contain full publication information. Sources consulted are also listed in an alphabetically arranged list at the end of an essay, called a *Bibliography*. You may not be called upon to follow this style for essays of your own, but you will want to be familiar with it and understand its conventions because you are likely to see this style in many of the sources you consult during your research. If you need further information, consult *The MLA Handbook for Writers of Research Papers*, 3rd edition.

1. Note-and-bibliography format for the bibliography

The format for entries in the *Bibliography* is the same as the current MLA format for entries in the *Works Cited* list (see 41a1). The *Bibliography* appears on a separate page at the end of the essay, after the list of *Notes* (see 41d2).

2. Note-and-bibliograpy format for notes

The note-and-bibliography style uses superscript numbers ([1]) to mark citations in the text of an essay. Citations are numbered sequentially throughout the essay and correspond to notes that contain complete publication information about the sources cited.

In the text, the superscript number for each note is placed near the cited material, at the end of a quotation, a sentence, or a clause or phrase. The number is typed after any punctuation, with no space between the preceding letter or punctuation mark and the number.

```
As Glueck says, "Most addicts have had dealings with some
type of crime before they became acquainted with nar-
cotics."5
```

Notes can be footnotes (typed at the bottom of the page on which the citation appears in the text) or endnotes (typed on a separate page at the end of the essay, before the *Bibliography*). Footnotes are typed four lines below the last line of text on a page, double-spaced between notes but single-spaced within entries. Endnotes are typed on a separate page with *Notes* (neither underlined nor in quotation marks) centered at the top of the page. Endnotes are double-spaced both between and within entries. The format of individual footnotes and endnotes is the same.

The first line of a note is indented five spaces and begins with the superscript number. All remaining lines of the entry are typed flush with the left margin. Before typing your final list of notes, doublecheck that the number of each note matches the correct citation in the text.

Notes follow a rigidly prescribed form, and differ slightly from bibliographic entries: the author's name is listed in normal order, all parts of the entry are separated by commas (instead of periods) and one space, and the publication information is placed in parentheses. The first time you refer to a source in a note you must include all information about it. In subsequent notes, you can list a short form of reference, usually the author's name and the page number. Examples of common variations in entries for different kinds of sources are shown in this section. Corresponding bibliographic entries for these examples appear in 41a1.

Books and pamphlets

A book written by one author

^{1}Peter De Vries, <u>Peckham's Marbles</u> (New York: Putnam's, 1986) 25.

A book by more than one author

^{2}John T. McNeill and Helena M. Gamer, <u>Medieval Handbooks of Penance</u> (New York: Octagon, 1965) 139.

A book written by a group

^{3}Carnegie Corporation on Higher Education, <u>The Academic System in American Society</u> (New York: McGraw, 1974) 56.

A book prepared by an editor

^{4}Dorothy Parker, ed., <u>Essays on Modern American Drama</u> (Toronto: U of Toronto P, 1987) xviii–xxiv.

A book prepared by a translator

^{5}Sven B. F. Jansson, <u>The Runes of Sweden</u>, trans. Peter G. Foote (Stockholm: Norstedt Forlag, 1962) 38.

NOTE-AND-BIBLIOGRAPHY STYLE

A republication

    ⁶Walter Scott, <u>Kenilworth</u> (1821; New York: Dodd, 1956) 85–86.

A particular edition

    ⁷Alfred A. Kelly, Winifred A. Harbison, and Herman Belz, <u>The American Constitution: Its Origins and Development</u>, 6th ed. (New York: Norton, 1983) 187.

A work in two or more volumes

    ⁸Fernand Braudel, <u>The Mediterranean and the Mediterranean World in the Age of Philip II</u>, trans. Siân Reynolds, vol. 1 (New York: Harper, 1972–73) 345.

An item in an anthology or collection

    ⁹Joan Didion, "Why I Write," <u>The Writer on Her Work</u>, ed. Janet Sternburg (New York: Norton, 1980) 5.

An article in an encyclopedia

    ¹⁰"Traquair, Sir John Stewart," <u>Encyclopaedia Britannica</u>, 11th ed.

Periodicals

An article in a scholarly periodical that numbers pages consecutively within a volume

    ¹¹Margot Norris, "Narration under a Blindfold: Reading Joyce's 'Clay'," <u>PMLA</u> 102 (1987): 206.

An article in a scholarly periodical that numbers pages separately within each issue

    ¹²John Loffy, "The Politics at Modernism's Funeral," <u>Canadian Journal of Political and Social Theory</u> 6.3 (1987): 88.

An article in a monthly or weekly periodical

    ¹³Edward Said, "Through Gringo Eyes," <u>Harper's</u> Apr. 1988: 71.

An article in a newspaper

¹⁴Lora Sharpe, "A Quilters' Tribute," <u>Boston Globe</u> 25 Mar. 1987: 47

An editorial in a periodical

¹⁵Doug Magee, "Soldier's Home," editorial, <u>Nation</u> 26 Mar. 1988: 401.

A review in a periodical

¹⁶J. H. Block, "Debatable Conclusions about Sex Differences," rev. of <u>The Psychology of Sex Differences</u>, by E. E. Maccoby and C. N. Jacklin, <u>Contemporary Psychology</u> Aug. 1976: 517.

An article whose author is not identified

¹⁷"The Odds of March," <u>Time</u> 15 Apr. 1985: 20+.

Other sources
An interview

¹⁸Daniel Schorr, interview, Weekend Edition, Natl. Public Radio, WEVO, Concord, NH, 26 Mar. 1988.

¹⁹Larry Berkson, personal interview, 16 May 1988.

A letter

²¹Robert Frost, "Letter to the Editor of the <u>Independent</u>," 28 Mar. 1894, <u>Selected Letters of Robert Frost</u>, ed. Lawrance Thompson (New York: Holt, 1964) 19.

A speech or lecture

²²Virginia F. Stern, "Sir Stephen Powle as Adventurer in the Virginia Company of London," Seminar on the Renaissance, Columbia University, New York, 15 Oct. 1985.

A computer software program

²³<u>Nota Bene</u>, vers. 3.0., computer software, Dragonfly Software, 1988 (MS-DOS 2.0, 512 KB, disk).

A film or videotape

²⁴<u>The</u> <u>Night</u> <u>of</u> <u>the</u> <u>Hunter</u>, dir. Charles Laughton, with Robert Mitchum, Shelley Winters, and Lillian Gish, United Artists, 1955.

A television or radio program

²⁴<u>Hill</u> <u>Street</u> <u>Blues</u>, writ., Michael Kozoll and Stephen Bochco, with Daniel J. Travanti, Joe Spano, and Charles Haid, NBC, WNBC, New York, 15 Jan. 1981.

A performance

²⁵<u>Frankie</u> <u>and</u> <u>Johnny</u> <u>in</u> <u>the</u> <u>Clair</u> <u>de</u> <u>Lune</u>, by Terrence McNally, dir. Paul Benedict, Westside Arts Theater, New York, 18 Jan. 1988.

Subsequent notes to the same source

After you have given the full information for a source in a note, you can use shortened form, usually the author's name and the page number, in subsequent notes. If you use two works by the same author, add a comma and a short version of the title after the author's name so that a reader will know which source you are citing.

²⁶De Vries 82.

²⁷De Vries, <u>Peckham's</u> 37.

If you need to cite a particular source repeatedly, such as one literary work, mention in your first reference that subsequent references to the work will be found in the text. Then, for subsequent references, simply note the page, line, or act, scene, and line numbers in parentheses after your quotations or references.

¹Kenneth Roberts, <u>Lydia</u> <u>Bailey</u> (New York: Doubleday, 1947) 14. All subsequent references to this work will appear in the text.

▌ 41e. Using common abbreviations

Many research essays and scholarly works use abbreviations, most of them Latin. The use of such abbreviations has been somewhat discouraged today, but you may come across them in sources you consult.

In your own papers, you should use only those abbreviations that are part of your citation style—unless your instructor specifies that you use others. Here is a list of the most commonly used abbreviations.

anon.	anonymous
bk., bks.	book, books
c., ca.	around a given date (*circa*)
cf.	compare (*confer*)
ch., chs.	chapter, chapters
col., cols.	column, columns
ed., eds.	edition(s) or editor(s)
e.g.	for example (*exempli gratia*)
et al.	and others (*et alii*)
etc.	and so on (*et cetera*)
ff.	and the following pages
ibid.	in the same place (*ibidem*)
i.e.	that is (*id est*)
illus.	illustrated by or illustrations
l., ll.	line, lines
loc. cit.	in the same place cited (*loc citato*)
ms., mss.	manuscript, manuscripts
n., nn.	note, notes
n.d.	no publication date
no.	number
n.p.	no place or no publisher
n. pag.	no pagination
op. cit.	in the work cited (*opere citato*)
p., pp.	page, pages
passim	throughout the whole work
q.v.	which see (*quod vide*)
rev.	revision, revised by, review
rpt.	reprint, reprinted
sec.	section
supp., supps.	supplement, supplements
trans.	translated by, translator
viz.	namely or that is (*videlicet*)

PART NINE

Academic Writing

42. Writing in Different Disciplines

How is writing used in various professions? A recent survey asked that question of two hundred members of professional organizations serving the following seven groups: chemists, psychologists, technical writers, city planners and managers, engineers, business executives, and teachers of language and literature. As you might guess, the great majority (98 percent) report that writing is very important to doing their jobs well. More surprising is just how *much* time these professionals devote to writing—an average of 46 percent of their working hours. Other surprises emerged in comparing results by profession; for instance, engineers report spending more time writing than do English teachers. But overall, this survey confirmed that good writing plays an important role in almost every profession, and in some it is crucial to success. As one MBA wrote, "Those who advance quickly in my company are those who write and speak well."

This chapter will lead you to think about the different ways writing works in various disciplines. You may begin to get a sense of such differences as you prepare essays or other written assignments for various other courses. Certainly by the time you choose a major, you should be ready to familiarize yourself with the expectations, vocabularies, styles, methods of proof, and conventional formats used in your field.

This chapter will alert you to ways of analyzing and understanding the writing conventions of any discipline. Only insofar as you can reach such an understanding can you hope not only to use but to assess and perhaps even influence those conventions.

(BACK)GROUNDING

The belief that writing should be the concern of the entire school community underlies this chapter on writing in the disciplines. According to Art Young and Toby Fulwiler, composition researchers and theorists such as James Britton, Janet Emig, James Kinneavy, James Moffett, and Mina Shaughnessy have all variously suggested that student writing will not improve until students see writing at the center of their academic experience. They will learn to value it and practice it when it is incorporated usefully into the daily process of learning in all disciplines. Writing across the curriculum programs work toward these goals. Over the last ten years, dozens of these programs have emerged in American colleges and universities. Individual programs may differ in scope and practice, but all of them aim to improve student writing by showing faculty from across the disciplines how to use writing regularly and thoughtfully in their classrooms.

639

USEFUL READING

Young, Art, and Toby Fulwiler. *Writing across the Disciplines: Research into Practice.* Upper Montclair, N.J.: Boynton, 1986. An informative collection of research on writing across the discipline programs from four perspectives: purpose, evaluation, writing and learning connections, politics and the effectiveness of these programs.

ANSWERS TO EXERCISE 42.1 WILL VARY

EXERCISE 42.1

Consider how the following topics might be approached in the specified disciplines or fields. What issues might each field see? What approach might each take? How might each investigate and write about the topic?

1. First-grade reading abilities—as seen by reading teachers, librarians, ophthalmologists (eye doctors), or reading-test designers
2. Soccer—as seen by sports physicians, psychologists, recreation department directors, or historians
3. Ancient Egyptian mythology—as seen by comparative literature specialists, anthropologists, archaeologists, or art historians
4. A sunken ship—as seen by engineers, marine biologists, economists, or journalists

42a. Analyzing academic assignments and expectations

Assignments vary widely from course to course and even from professor to professor. You may be asked to prepare one-sentence answers to study questions in history or physics, detailed laboratory reports in biology, case studies in psychology or sociology, or even film scripts in a visual media course. Thus the directions this section offers can only be general, based on experience and on discussions with professors in many disciplines. The best advice is really very simple: make sure you are in control of the assignment rather than the assignment's being in control of you. To take control, you need to understand the assignment fully and to understand what professors in the particular discipline expect in an effective response to the assignment.

When you receive an assignment in *any* discipline, your first job is to make sure you understand what that assignment is asking you to do. Some assignments may be as vague as "Write a five-page essay on one aspect of the Civil War." Others, like this psychology assignment, will be fairly specific: "For your first research assignment, you are to collect, summarize, and interpret data drawn from a sample of letters to the editor published in two newspapers, one in a small rural community, and one in an urban community, over a period of three months. Organize your research report into four sections: problem, methods, results, and discussion." (See the end of Chapter 40 for one student's essay in response to this assignment.) In any case, you must take charge of analyzing the assignment. Answering the following questions can help you to do so.

USEFUL READING

Shamoon, Linda K., and Robert A. Schwegler. "Sociologists Reading Student Texts: Expectations and Perceptions." *The Writing Instructor* 7 (Winter 88): 71–81. Examines the expectations and perceptions that instructors have of their students' writing. A group of sociology instructors are asked two questions: (1) to what extent are instructor expectations and perceptions discipline specific; (2) what features of good expository writing do college instructors look for—thesis statements? topic sentences? paragraph coherence?

ANALYZING ACADEMIC ASSIGNMENTS

dis 42a

Questions for analyzing an assignment

1. *What is the assignment asking you to do?* Are you to summarize, explain, evaluate, interpret, illustrate, define? If the assignment asks you to do more than one of these things, does it specify the order in which you are to do them? (Note that the psychology assignment above does specify the activities to be carried out and the general topics to be covered in the report.)

2. *Do you need to ask for clarification of any terms?* Students responding to the psychology assignment might well ask the instructor, for instance, to discuss the meaning of "collect" or "interpret" and perhaps to give examples. Or they might want further clarification of the term "urban community" or the size of a suitable "sample."

3. *What do you need to know or find out to do the assignment?* Students doing the psychology assignment need to develop a procedure—a way to analyze or categorize the letters to the editor. Furthermore, they need to know how to carry out simple statistical analyses of the data.

4. *Do you understand the professor's expectations regarding background reading and preparation, method of organization and development, and format and length?* The psychology assignment mentions no background reading, but in this field an adequate statement of a problem usually requires setting that problem in the context of other research. A student might well ask how extensive this part of the report is to be.

5. *Can you find an example of an effective response to a similar assignment?* If you can, or if the instructor will provide one, you can analyze its parts and use it as a model for developing your own response. One psychology student, when asked to describe what constituted a "good" essay in that discipline, said "Well, for the first two assignments I basically summarized the relevant research data as clearly and briefly as I could and then pointed out weaknesses in the research and implications of it. Since I got A's on both papers I decided I must be doing something right." And indeed she was. By trial and error, she had fixed on an approach to the assignments, a method of organization, and a format that fit into what was accepted as "good" writing in her psychology courses.

EXERCISE 42.2

Here is an assignment from a communications course. Read it carefully, and then use the list of five questions in 42a to analyze the assignment.

Assignment: Distribute a questionnaire to twenty people (ten male, ten female) asking these four questions: (1) What do you expect to say and do when you

WRITERS ON WRITING

Writing is an action, a different action from talking. The only conceivable reason for engaging in writing is to make something relatively permanent which one might otherwise forget. That would seem to imply that one thinks there is some value in the thing not to be forgotten.

—JOHN GARDNER

ANSWERS TO EXERCISE 42.2 WILL VARY

USEFUL READING

Larsen, Richard L. "Selected Bibliography of Scholarship on Composition and Rhetoric, 1986." *CCC* 38 (1987): 319–36. See "Writing in Non-Academic Settings" for an annotated guide to further reading.

Bean, John C., Dean Drenk, and F. D. Lee. "Microtheme Strategies for Cognitive Skills." *New Directions for Teaching and Learning: Teaching Writing in the Disciplines.* Ed. C. W. Griffin. San Francisco: Jossey-Bass, 1982. The authors describe how to use a series of short assignments to improve thinking and writing skills.

meet a stranger? (2) What don't you expect to say and do when you meet a stranger? (3) What do you expect to say and do when you meet a very close friend? (4) What don't you expect to say and do when you meet a very close friend? When you have collected your twenty questionnaires, read through your results and answer the following questions:

1. What, if any, descriptions were common to all respondents' answers?
2. What similarities and differences were found between the male and female responses?
3. What similarities and differences were found between the responses to the stranger and to the very close friend situations?
4. What factors (such as environment, time, status, gender, and so on) do you feel have an impact on these responses? How do the factors affect the responses?
5. Discuss your findings, using concepts and theories explained in your text.

▋ 42b. Understanding disciplinary vocabularies

A modern rhetorician describes the way people become active participants in the "conversation of humankind" in the following way. Imagine, he says, that you enter a crowded room in which everyone is talking and gesturing animatedly. You know no one there and cannot catch much of what is being said. Slowly you move from group to group listening, and finally you take a chance and interject a brief statement into the conversation. Others listen to you and respond. Thus, slowly but surely, do you come to *participate* in, rather than to observe, the conversation.

Entering into an academic discipline or a profession is much like entering into such a conversation. At first you feel like an outsider, and you do not catch much of what you hear or read. You may be experiencing this situation right now. Indeed, everyone experiences the same thing when entering a brand-new field. To the new and uninitiated computer owner, the bits and bytes and macros and sidekicks and modem capabilities and other technical terms seem overwhelming. Trying to enter the new "conversation" takes time and careful attention. Eventually, however, the vocabulary becomes familiar, and participating in the conversation seems easy and natural.

▋ 1. Joining the conversation in a discipline

Of course, this chapter cannot introduce you to the vocabulary of every field, nor would it be helpful to do so. The point is that *you*

(BACK)GROUNDING

Since special vocabulary and their definitions are crucial to studying and working in a field, it will be helpful to know the various kinds of parenthetic constructions. Their general function is to provide further information. The means by which they do so include:

Defining: Bernard loves moussaka, a delicious Greek casserole made basically from potatoes, eggplant, ground lamb, and a light bechamel custard.

Expanding: He's a true patriot; he's someone who loves his country, shows the utmost loyalty to her, and always defends her, no matter what.

Qualifying: I'd like you to meet my Big Sister, who I think you will like because she knows how to have fun, yet is responsible, too.

Specifying: She admits that, of course, she is a woman. But unlike you, she is not white, nor a wealthy self-employed professional, but rather a single mother, working two jobs while raising three children.

UNDERSTANDING DISCIPLINARY VOCABULARIES

must make the effort to enter into the conversation, and that again means taking charge of the situation. To get started, one of the first things you need to do is to study the vocabulary.

Determine how much of what you are hearing and reading depends on specialized or technical vocabulary. Try highlighting key terms in your reading or your notes to help you distinguish the specialized vocabulary of the field from the larger discussion. If you find little specialized vocabulary, try to master the new terms quickly by reading your textbook carefully, by asking questions of the instructor and other students, and by looking up a few key words or phrases.

If you find a great deal of specialized vocabulary, however, you may want to familiarize yourself with it somewhat methodically. Any of the following procedures may prove helpful:

- Keep a reading log, listing unfamiliar or confusing words *in context*. To locate definitions or explanations, review past reading or check the terms in your textbook's glossary or index.

- Review your class notes each day after class. Underline important terms, review their definitions, and identify anything that is unclear. Use your textbook or ask questions to clarify anything confusing before the class moves on to a new topic.

- Check to see if your textbook has a glossary of terms or sets off definitions in italics or boldface type. If so, study pertinent sections carefully to master the terms.

- Try to start using or working with key concepts. Even if they are not yet entirely clear to you, working with them will help you to formulate questions that will help you come to understand them. For example, in a statistics class, try to work out (in words) how to do an analysis of covariance, step by step, even if you are not sure you could come up with your own precise definition of the term. Or in a biology class, try charting the circulation of the blood even if you do not understand the whole process.

- Find the standard dictionaries or handbooks of terms for your field. Students beginning the study of literature, for instance, can turn to several guides such as *A Dictionary of Literary, Dramatic, and Cinematic Terms*. Those entering the discipline of sociology may refer to the *Dictionary of the Social Sciences*, while students beginning statistical analysis may turn to *Statistics Without Tears*. Ask your instructor or a librarian for help finding the standard references in your field.

Whatever your techniques for learning a field's specialized vocabulary, begin to use the new terms whenever you can—in class, in discussion

WRITING TOGETHER

Ask students to work in groups of three. Each student should bring to class two copies of a short passage of approximately 100 words taken from an article, an essay, or a textbook in a field with which he or she is familiar. Have students give a copy to each of their partners and ask them to list terms, phrases, or concepts that seem to involve specialized or highly technical language. Ask them to define and explain these terms. Have students retrieve their articles and their partners' lists, check their efforts, and then in discussion, clarify the terms for them. Discuss their confusion or lack of it.

This exercise gives students familiar with a particular field practice explaining basic terms to an audience unfamiliar with that field. For example, the term *blastema* is basic knowledge to students in molecular genetics, as is *Cyrillic alphabet* to Slavic language majors. *Morpheme* is a basic concept to linguistics students, as is *hypotenuse* to geometry students. Thus, this exercise serves two purposes:

1. It helps students develop an awareness of how to adapt their language and explanations to audiences with different degrees of expertise or familiarity with a field's vocabulary.
2. It also allows students to test their own understanding of terms and concepts. One way we determine how well we ourselves understand these is to explain them to someone else.

WRITERS ON WRITING

What is it that brings about such an intimate connection between language and thinking? Is there no thinking without the use of language, namely in concepts and concept-combinations for which words need not necessarily come to mind? Has not everyone of us struggled for words although the connection between "things" was already clear?

—ALBERT EINSTEIN

WRITERS ON WRITING

Whenever I write an essay, I go first to my journals. I write in 9 × 6 spiral notebooks, nothing fancy, and though they're not an exact daily record of everything I think, I do note down thoughts worth keeping as well as dreams, snatches of conversation, events that somehow feel larger than they look, i.e. that which seems to have a metaphorical value.

—GRETEL EHRLICH

with instructors and other students, and in your assignments. This ability to *use* what you learn in speaking and writing is crucial to your full understanding of and participation in the discipline.

2. Writing about literary texts

One example of a special vocabulary is the language of literary analysis, which is used in the fields of English and American literature, literature in other languages, and comparative literature. To analyze literary works and narratives that tell a story, you need to understand the following key terms:

character—the people in the story, who have different motivations and who may act, react, and change accordingly during the course of the story

plot—the events selected by the writer to reveal the conflicts among or within the characters, often arranged in chronological order but sometimes including flashbacks to past events

dialogue—the conversation among characters, which can show how they interact and suggest why they act as they do

setting—the scene of the story, including the time, physical location, and social situation

point of view—the perspective from which the story is told, whether presented by a narrator outside the story, or through the eyes of a character speaking in first or third person

style—the writer's choice of words and sentence structures

figurative language—the use of metaphor, simile, personification, and other figures of speech that enrich description (see 4f3 and 26b2)

imagery—the perceptions and observations created by descriptions and figures of speech that appeal to the senses

symbolism—the use of one thing to represent or suggest other things or ideas

rhythm—the beat or pattern of stresses in a line of poetry, including traditional metrical patterns or the movement of free verse

persona—the perspective and personality through which the events or emotions of the work are presented

tone—the writer's attitude toward the topic, conveyed through specific word choices and structures (see Chapter 26)

Looking for the features identified in the special vocabulary of literary study is one way to begin training yourself to read, to interpret, and criticize literary works—to join the conversation of English studies.

TEACHING PRACTICE
This list is of course only brief. If your students will be writing essays about literary texts, introduce them to at least one handbook of literary terms, such as the *Handbook to Literature*.

WRITING TOGETHER
Divide the class into groups of no more than three students who are working in the same major field or some fairly closely related field. Ask each group to compile a glossary of twenty key terms that are essential to a field or that overlap related fields. Have students alphabetize the terms and give a definition and explanation of each.

USEFUL READING
Homan, C. Hugh. *Handbook to Literature*. 4th ed. Indianapolis: Bobbs, 1980.

UNDERSTANDING DISCIPLINARY VOCABULARIES

EXERCISE 42.3

Here are the opening paragraphs of *General Chemistry*, a textbook by John B. Russell. Read through the passage, and then analyze it by answering the questions that follow the passage about the special vocabulary in the passage:

At one time it was easy to define chemistry. The traditional definition goes something like this: Chemistry is the study of the nature, properties, and composition of matter, and how these undergo changes. That served as a perfectly adequate definition as late as the 1930s, when natural science (the systematic knowledge of nature) seemed quite clearly divisible into the physical and biological sciences, with the former being comprised of physics, chemistry, geology, and astronomy and the latter consisting of botany and zoology. This classification is still used, but the emergence of important fields of study such as oceanography, paleobotany, meteorology, and biochemistry, for example, have made it increasingly clear that the dividing lines between the sciences are no longer at all sharp. Chemistry, for instance, now overlaps so much with geology (thus we have *geochemistry*), astronomy (*astrochemistry*), and physics (*physical chemistry*) that it is probably impossible to devise a really good modern definition of chemistry, except, perhaps, to fall back on the operational definition: chemistry is what chemists do. (And what chemists do is what this book is all about!). . .

To make a very long story short, copper and bronze gave way to iron and steel, the latter being an iron-carbon alloy. Metals were very important in early civilization and the practice of metallurgy provided a wealth of chemical information. Egyptians, for example, learned how to obtain many different metals from their ores, and according to some experts the word *chemistry* is derived from an ancient word *khemeia*, which may refer to the Egyptians' name for their own country, *Kham*. However, some experts believe *chemistry* came from the Greek word *chyma*, which means "to melt or cast a metal." . . .

It was not until around 600 B.C. that the beginnings of chemical theory emerged. Thales, a Greek philosopher, proposed that all chemical change was merely a change in the aspect of one fundamental material or *element*. Later, Empedocles, who lived about 450 B.C. proposed that there were four elements: earth, air, fire, and water. . . .

1. What terms are defined? Highlight or circle each one, and underline each definition.
2. What techniques or methods are used to point out or emphasize key terms? Note an example of each.
3. What techniques or methods are used to present definitions of key terms? Note an example of each.
4. How many different ways is *chemistry* defined? What is the function or purpose of each definition?

645

ANSWERS TO EXERCISE 42.3 (WILL VARY)

The term defined is in boldface. The definition is italicized. Techniques used to define the term appear in brackets.

Chemistry *is the study of the nature, properties, and composition of matter, and how these undergo changes.* [definition in a declarative sentence]

natural science *(the systematic knowledge of nature)* [parenthetical definition]

physical sciences, *comprised of physics, chemistry, geology, and astronomy* [definition by listing subgroups]

biological sciences, *consisting of botany and zoology* [definition by listing subgroups]

chemistry *is what chemists do.* [definition by declarative sentence]

khemeia, *which may refer to the Egyptians' name for their own country,* Kham [definition by etymology]

chyma, *which means "to melt or cast a metal"* [definition by etymology]

element, *fundamental material* [definition by renaming]

Terms that seem important are sometimes italicized; all are defined.

WRITERS ON WRITING

A truly great intellect, and recognized to be such by the common opinion of mankind, such as the intellect of Aristotle, or of St. Thomas, or of Newton, or of Goethe . . . is one which takes a connected view of old and new, past and present, far and near, and which has an insight into the influence of all these one on another; without which there is no whole, and no centre. It possesses the knowledge, not only of things, but also of their mutual and true relations; knowledge, not merely considered acquirement but as philosophy.

—JOHN HENRY NEWMAN

WRITERS ON WRITING

Language . . . is an organ—the supreme organ of the mind's self-ordering growth.

—JOSEPHINE MILES

5. Which terms seem most important? Why do you think so?
6. After reading the passage, which of the special vocabulary here is clear to you, and which needs further definition?

▌ 42c. Identifying the style of a discipline

Getting familiar with technical vocabulary is one important way of initiating yourself into a discipline or field of study. Another method is to identify stylistic features of the writing in that field. You will begin to assimilate these features automatically if you take time simply to immerse yourself in reading and thinking about the field. To speed up this process, however, study some representative pieces of writing in the field. Consider them with the following questions in mind:

- In general, how long are the sentences? How long are the paragraphs?
- Are verbs generally active or passive—and why? Do active or passive verbs seem to be part of a characteristic manner of speaking used by writers and researchers in the field?
- How would you describe the overall *tone* of the writing? Is it very formal, somewhat formal, informal?
- Do the writers use first person (*I*) or prefer terms such as *one* or *the investigator*? What is the effect of this stylistic choice?
- Does the writing use visual elements such as graphs, tables, charts, or maps? How are these integrated into the text?
- What bibliographical styles (such as MLA, APA, note, or number style) are used? (See Chapter 41 for illustrations of several styles.)

Of course, writings within a single discipline may have different purposes and different styles. Although a research report is likely to follow a conventional form, a published speech greeting specialists at a convention may well be less formal and more personal no matter what the field. Furthermore, answering questions such as those above will not guarantee that you can produce a piece of writing similar to the one you are analyzing. Nevertheless, looking carefully at writing in the field brings you one step closer not only to producing similar writing but to producing more effective writing as well.

ANSWERS TO EXERCISE 42.4 (WILL VARY)

1. Varied sentences, long paragraphs—indicating sustained or complex thoughts.
2. Use of mainly passive voice, to eliminate the presence of the writer/researcher.
3. Informative, relatively formal tone; passive voice gives an impression of objective presentation of information.
4. Writers avoid referring to themselves. The absence of *I* or *we* has a stylistic effect similar to that created by the passive voice: objective, neutral presentation of facts and information.

EXERCISE 42.4

The following passage comes from the opening of *The Social Construction of Reality*, by sociologists Peter L. Berger and Thomas Luckmann. Read the passage carefully and answer the questions that follow it.

646

IDENTIFYING THE STYLE OF A DISCIPLINE   dis|42c

The term "sociology of knowledge" (*Wissenssoziologie*) was coined by Max Scheler. The time was the 1920s, the place was Germany, and Scheler was a philosopher. These three facts are quite important for an understanding of the genesis and further development of the new discipline. The sociology of knowledge originated in a particular situation of German intellectual history and in a philosophical context. While the new discipline was subsequently introduced into the sociological context proper, particularly in the English-speaking world, it continued to be marked by the problems of the particular intellectual situation from which it arose. As a result the sociology of knowledge remained a peripheral concern among sociologists at large, who did not share the particular problems that troubled German thinkers in the 1920s. This was especially true of American sociologists, who have in the main looked upon the discipline as a marginal specialty with a persistent European flavor. More importantly, however, the continuing linkage of the sociology of knowledge with its original constellation of problems has been a theoretical weakness even where there has been an interest in the discipline. To wit, the sociology of knowledge has been looked upon, by its protagonists and by the more or less indifferent sociological public at large, as a sort of sociological gloss on the history of ideas. This has resulted in considerable myopia regarding the potential theoretical significance of the sociology of knowledge.

There have been different definitions of the nature and scope of the sociology of knowledge. Indeed, it might almost be said that the history of the subdiscipline thus far has been the history of its various definitions. Nevertheless, there has been general agreement to the effect that the sociology of knowledge is concerned with the relationship between human thought and the social context within which it arises. It may thus be said that the sociology of knowledge constitutes the sociological focus of a much more general problem, that of the existential determination (*Seinsgebundenheit*) of thought as such. Although here the social factor is concentrated upon, the theoretical difficulties are similar to those that have arisen when other factors (such as the historical, the psychological or the biological) have been proposed as determinative of human thought. In all these cases the general problem has been the extent to which thought reflects or is independent of the proposed determinative factors. . . .

Neither the general problem nor its narrower focus is new. An awareness of the social foundations of values and world views can be found in antiquity. At least as far back as the Enlightenment this awareness crystallized into a major theme of modern Western thought. It would thus be possible to make a good case for a number of "genealogies" for the central problem of the sociology of knowledge. It may even be said that the problem is contained *in nuce* in Pascal's famous statement that what is truth on one side of the Pyrenees is error on the other. Yet the immediate intellectual antecedents of the sociology of knowledge are three developments in nineteenth-century German thought—the Marxian, the Nietzschean, and the historicist.

TEACHING PRACTICE
This passage is fairly easy to read, and so students should be able to spot the use of passive verbs and discuss their appropriateness and to identify the overall tone as formal and academic. You might ask them to identify sentences that seem difficult to understand and then discuss the reasons for that difficulty. Does it lie in vocabulary, in syntax, in ideas?

1. How long are the sentences and paragraphs?
2. Are the verbs mainly active or passive?
3. What is the overall tone?
4. Do the writers refer to themselves? In what way? What effect do such references have on tone?

42d. Understanding the use of evidence in different disciplines

"Good reasons" form the core of any writing that argues a point, for they provide the *evidence* for the argument. Chapter 4 explains how to formulate good reasons. However, what is acceptable and persuasive evidence in one discipline may be more or less so in another. Observable, quantifiable data may constitute the very best evidence in, say, experimental psychology, but the same kind of data may be less appropriate—or even impossible to come by—in a historical study. As you grow familiar with any area of study, you will gather a sense of just what it takes to prove a point in that field. You can speed up this process or make it more efficient, however, by doing some investigating and questioning of your own. As you read your textbook and other assigned materials, make a point of noticing the use of evidence. The following questions are designed to help you to do so:

- How do writers in the field use precedent and authority? What or who counts as an authority in this field? How are the credentials of an authority established?
- What use is made of empirical data (things that can be observed and measured)? What kinds of data are used? How are such data gathered and presented?
- How are statistics used? How is numerical information used and presented? Are tables, charts, or graphs common? How much weight do they seem to carry?
- How is logical reasoning used? How are definition, cause and effect, analogies, and examples used in this discipline?
- How does the field use primary and secondary sources? What are the primary materials—the firsthand sources of information—in this field? What are the secondary materials—the sources of information derived from others? How is each type of source likely to be presented?

In addition to carrying out your own informal investigation of the evidence used in your discipline, you may well want to raise this issue

USING CONVENTIONAL PATTERNS AND FORMATS

in class. Ask your instructor how you can best go about making a case in that field.

EXERCISE 42.5

Do some reading in books and journals associated with your prospective major or a discipline of particular interest to you, using the questions above to study the use of evidence in that discipline. If you are keeping a writing log, make an entry in it summarizing what you have learned.

42e. Using conventional patterns and formats

You can gather all the evidence in the world and still fail to produce effective writing in your discipline if you do not know the field's conventions, the generally accepted format for organizing and presenting evidence. Again, these formats vary widely from discipline to discipline and sometimes from instructor to instructor, but patterns do emerge. In fact, disciplines may share similar conventions for similar types of studies. The typical laboratory report, for instance, follows a fairly standard organizational framework whether it is in botany, chemistry, or parasitology. A case study in sociology or education or anthropology likewise follows a typical organizational plan. And many disciplines share a conventional format for problem-solution reports: statement of problem, background for the problem's formulation, review of the literature on the subject, findings and possible solution, conclusions, and recommendations.

Your job in any discipline is to discover its conventional formats and organizing principles so that you can practice using them. This task is easy enough to begin. Ask your instructor to recommend some excellent examples of the kind of writing you will do in the course. Then analyze these examples in terms of format and organization. You might also look at major scholarly journals in your field, checking to see what types of formats seem most common and how each is organized. Study these examples, keeping in mind these questions about organization and format:

- What types of essays or reports are common in this field? What is the purpose of each type?
- What can a reader expect to find in each type of essay or report? What does each type assume about its readers?

ANSWERS TO EXERCISE 42.5 WILL VARY

- How is a particular type of essay or report organized? What are its main parts? Are they labeled with conventional headings? What logic underlies this sequence of parts?
- How does a particular type of essay or report show the connections among ideas? What assumptions of the discipline does it take for granted? What points does its organization emphasize?

The following sections illustrate three general patterns common in research essays—surveying literature, reporting experimental or field research, and interpreting sources.

1. Surveying literature in the social sciences

An introductory psychology class was given the assignment to write a brief literature review related to one aspect of child development, summarizing three journal articles addressing the topic, and drawing some conclusions based on their findings. Following are the notes one student made analyzing first the assignment and then the vocabulary, style, evidence, and organizational pattern appropriate for the field of psychology. These notes correspond to the appropriate questions for analysis presented in 42a–42e.

ANALYZING THE ASSIGNMENT AND THE EXPECTATIONS

1. Assignment says to summarize three journal articles. Then, evaluate and interpret their findings.
2. "Literature review" is defined in the assignment.
3. The articles I plan to review each focus on a particular study, so I need to be able to see the strengths and weaknesses of each study. (I also must be able to understand their use of statistics to be able to evaluate the data and then must be able to draw conclusions based upon this evaluation.)
4. No specific format is specified.
5. By examining previous responses to similar assignments, I can determine an acceptable format—will ask professor for some.

ANALYZING THE SPECIALIZED VOCABULARY

1. Articles will have technical vocabulary from psychology and statistics.
2. I will need to know terms such as *variables, inter-rater agreement,* and so on to understanding reading.
3. Terms showing reliability of research need to be mentioned in my summary.

USING CONVENTIONAL PATTERNS AND FORMATS

ANALYZING THE STYLE

1. Sentences and paragraphs tend to be short.

2. Many passive verbs are used, especially in the sections presenting data (resembles newspaper style).

3. Overall tone is very formal (although can be slightly less so in the introduction).

4. First person is used very little.

5. Visual elements are used when necessary to clarify the findings. They are first mentioned in text (i.e., *see Table 1*) and then table follows (i.e., at end of paragraph).

6. Professor says journals use APA style; must check out exactly what this means.

ANALYZING THE USE OF EVIDENCE

1. Psychology relies heavily on previous related findings. Credentials are often based upon data alone. Statistically significant findings are very important.

2. Experimental data are very important. Experiments are devised to control for all variables other than the one being manipulated. (If extraneous variables are not controlled, the data will probably be rejected as worthless.)

3. Statistics are very important—results must be within the 0.05 level of significance (only a 5 percent possibility that the results were caused by chance). Probabilities must be presented with results, but tables and graphs are used as necessary.

4. Cause-to-effect logic is very important. Frequently, generalizations are made concerning the "real" world, based upon current research findings.

5. All three articles report on primary research.

ANALYZING CONVENTIONAL PATTERNS

1. In a literature survey, the three articles can be discussed in separate sections. Label each one with a heading. Change to new section for each article discussed, and introduction to each.

2. Arrange articles in chronological order.

3. Summarize each article and include quotations as appropriate to make my main points clear.

4. End with my conclusions about what articles show and about what may happen in the future.

After browsing through her textbook and thinking about the assignment, the student decided to focus on child abuse. A trip to the library turned up many articles on this subject, and she chose three. She summarized the three articles, worked through a draft, and analyzed it, following revision guidelines (see Chapter 3). Here is the final version of her essay, a literature survey reviewing three articles and drawing conclusions about what they show and mean.

Early Detection of Child Abuse*

There is no simple one-word answer to the question of what causes child abuse. The abuse of children results from a complex interaction among parent, child, and environmental factors. This complexity does not necessarily mean, however, that potential victims and abusers cannot be identified before serious damage is done. Researchers have examined methods of detecting potential or actual child abuse.

Prediction of Child Abuse: Interviews

In a study by Altemeier, O'Connor, Vietze, Sandler, and Sherrod (1984), 1,400 women between nine and forty weeks pregnant were interviewed to test their abusive tendencies. Four researchers were present (with an interrater agreement of 90 percent or better). The Maternal History Interview included questions about the mother's own childhood, self-image, support from others, parenting philosophy, attitudes toward pregnancy, and health-related problems (including substance abuse). Maternal and paternal stresses during the preceding year were measured with a modified Life Stress Inventory. Any information not included in the standard interview but felt by the researchers to make the mother a high risk for abuse of her child—for example, being overtly untruthful—was also recorded. When the infants were twenty-one to forty-eight months old, the Juvenile Court and the Department

---

* by Laura Brannon

TEACHING PRACTICE
Ask students to examine the introduction of this essay and determine what function it plays. How could they improve it?

TEACHING PRACTICE
Note that Laura follows the directions she identified in her analysis of the conventional pattern for a literature survey: each article is labeled and discussed separately.

USING CONVENTIONAL PATTERNS AND FORMATS

of Human Services were checked for reports of their abuse or neglect.

Although the interview predicted abuse (p < .0001), its ability to predict decreased with time; for example, although "six of seven families reported for abuse within the first nine months following the interview were high risk, . . . after 24 months only one of seven had been assigned to this group" (Altemeier, et. al., p. 395). The researchers point out some shortcomings of their study, particularly the high rate of false positives. (Only 6 percent of the high-risk population was reported for abuse, 22 percent if failure to thrive and neglect were included.) Although many incidents of abuse may go unreported (which could account for some of the false positives), this false-positive percentage should be reduced. Also, it would be preferable if the role of subjective judgments in the method for prediction could be reduced as well.

Toward Improving Child Abuse Prediction

A later study by Murphy, Orkow, and Nicola (1985) was less dependent on subjective judgments. In this study, 587 women between three and six months pregnant were interviewed using the Family Stress Checklist. This checklist has ten factors: parent beaten or deprived as a child; parent with record of criminal activity or mental illness; parent suspected of abuse in the past; parent with low self-esteem, social isolation, or depression; parent with multiple crises or stresses; parent with violent temper outbursts; parent with rigid, unrealistic expectations of child's behavior; parent's harsh punishment of a previous child; child difficult and/or provocative or perceived to be by parents; and child unwanted or at risk of poor bonding. Each item is scored as either no risk (0), risk (5), or high risk (10); consequently, an individual's score can range from 0 to 100.

TEACHING PRACTICE

Ask students to discuss the kinds of evidence presented in these three articles. Empirical data are obviously valued a great deal. Students might profit by brainstorming about what other kinds of evidence might be appropriate—or *not* appropriate—for such an article.

TEACHING PRACTICE

Ask students to identify vocabulary terms that are unfamiliar or confusing to them. Are they the kinds of words that would be in general use in psychology?

Scores of 40 or above represent high risk; 7 percent of the tested mothers were in this range. Although all of the items were somewhat more common among the high-risk group, the following factors were almost totally absent from the low-scoring population and increased as total scores increased: criminal activity, serious mental illness, suspicions of past abuse, violent temper outbursts, rigid expectations of the child's behavior, and harsh punishment of a previous child.

After the children reached an age of one to two years, their medical charts were reviewed. A negative rating meant no signs of abuse. "Mild neglect" was signified by the mother's failure to provide sufficient medical care or her complaint that the baby was spoiled, difficult, or a poor feeder; "child neglect" was signified by the mother's failure to provide food, clothing, shelter, or supervision for the child or by the child's being "accident-prone" or failing to thrive; and "child abuse" was signified by the child's having broken bones, bruises, burns, or welts either verified or strongly suspected to have been inflicted by the parent. The Family Stress Checklist was 80 percent effective at predicting neglect and abuse. There were fewer false positives than in the previous study; the checklist was correct 89.4 percent of the time in predicting which parents would not be likely to be abusive. Variables such as age, marital status, and parenting experience did not significantly differentiate the high-risk mothers from those with low risk.

<u>Early</u> <u>Detection</u> <u>of</u> <u>Child</u> <u>Abuse:</u> <u>Injuries</u>

Johnson and Showers (1985) analyzed 616 child abuse reportings. Boys were reported abused more often than girls (56 percent to 44 percent), and black children were reported abused at a rate disproportionate to their population distribution and general hospitalization rate (p < .001). Also, although more men than women were reported for abuse (51 percent), mothers abuse their children more often. The type, cause, and location of the injuries varied with the child's age and race, but not sex. Johnson and Showers present a table with data on how injuries vary with age and race; this table is reproduced below.

How Injuries Vary with Age and Race

Child's Age	Highest Risk Type	Highest Risk Cause	Highest Risk Location
0-4 years	Broken Bones Hemorrhage Burns	Hot Liquid Grid/Heater Iron	Skull Brain Feet Genitalia Buttocks Hips
4-8	Erythema and marks	Cord Belt/Strap	Not significant
8-12	---	Foot Fist	---
12-17	Lacerations Pain-Tenderness Swelling	Foot Fist	Scalp Nose Neck
Blacks	Lacerations Erythema	Cord Belt/Strap Switch/Stick Knife Iron	Arms Thighs
Whites	Bruises	Board/Paddle Open Hand	Buttocks Face

TEACHING PRACTICE

Ask students to identify the tone of Laura's conclusion and discuss its appropriateness. What difference could another tone—for example, angry—make in this essay?

Conclusions

Overall, the findings of these studies seem to indicate that tests can be devised to predict potential child abusers. The study by Murphy, Orkow, and Nicola (1985), which relies less on subjective judgments, has a significantly lower false positive rate than the earlier study by Altemeier and associates (1984). Therefore, although such tests have not yet been perfected, they appear to be improving.

The two studies tried to integrate the complex relationships between child, parent, and environmental factors that are involved in child abuse. Ideally, if potential abusers could be identified early enough, they could undergo treatment even before the child is born. Of course, a parent could not be separated from a child on the basis of one test, and therefore, the results should remain confidential to avoid any potential for abuse of the test itself.

Whereas the tests look carefully at the parent's situation, the injury variables analyzed in the Johnson and Showers study (1985) focus attention on the child. If teachers or other people notice that children have frequent injuries (especially with the locations, types, and causes associated with different ages and races), abuse can be detected early and perhaps stopped.

References

Altemeier, W. A., O'Connor, S., Vietze, P., Sandler, H., & Sherrod, K. (1984). Prediction of child abuse: A prospective study of feasibiity. Child Abuse and Neglect: The International Journal, 8, 393–400.

Johnson, C. F., & Showers, J. (1985). Injury variables in child abuse. Child Abuse and Neglect: The International Journal, 9, 207–215.

USING CONVENTIONAL PATTERNS AND FORMATS

Murphy, S., Orkow, B., & Nicola, R. (1985). Prenatal
    prediction of child abuse and neglect: A prospective
    study. <u>Child Abuse and Neglect: The International
    Journal</u>, <u>9</u>, 225-235.

EXERCISE 42.6

On the basis of the essay about child abuse, make a list of the characteristics of a literature survey in psychology. Your list will constitute an initial set of criteria that you could use in writing a literature survey of your own.

▌ 2. Reporting research in the natural sciences

An introductory biology class was asked to write a report analyzing a genetic question about a particular species of crayfish: when a female heterozygous for red claws was mated with a male with black claws, the resulting offspring included 154 red claws, 235 black claws, and 43 blue claws. Students were asked to explain the results by constructing hypotheses and evaluating them through the use of the Chi-square test. They were to include in their explanation an elaboration on gene expression, and to refer to at least two scientific journals. In response to this assignment, a student writer produced the following report.

Determining the Genotype of One Parent--
When the Other Is Known--by Evaluation
of the Offspring Frequencies*

INTRODUCTION

The purpose of this experiment was to determine the genotype of a male crayfish with black claws that was mated with a red-clawed female known to be heterozygous for claw color. This determination was made by evaluating the frequencies of three different claw colors observed in the offspring. Hypotheses involving Mendelian principles of genetics and various possible hybrid crosses were proposed and either proven false or recognized as probable

---

* by Julie Slater

ANSWERS TO EXERCISE 42.6 (WILL VARY)

Characteristics include: identification of articles, titles, authors, publication information, and sources; a brief introduction to the subject or topics; a brief summary of the articles reviewed and a description of the general schools of thought on the subject; an evaluative comment on usefulness, weakness, and/or relevance of the sources; special vocabulary; development of the field and future possibilities; list of references.

TEACHING PRACTICE

This assignment and essay may well contain unfamiliar terms. Ask students to identify them and to then consult with a science major in the class. Are the unfamiliar terms used appropriately, or are they used to excess?

TEACHING PRACTICE

Note that this essay follows a prescribed structure common to many lab reports. Students can benefit by trying to organize it in some other way and seeing why this format is particularly effective.

by meeting the given stipulations of a black mated to a heterozygous red and the offspring frequencies.

METHODS AND MATERIALS

Two crayfish of a particular species complex were mated. The female, known to be heterozygous for the phenotype of red claws, was mated with a male that expressed black claws. The offspring were grouped according to claw color and counted. The data were analyzed statistically using a Chi-square test.

RESULTS

In the 432 offspring produced, three phenotypes were noted: 235 crayfish with black claws, 154 with red, and 43 with blue. The observed ratio was 5.4 : 3.6 : 1.

DISCUSSION

The ratio results, which were derived directly from the counting of color patterns, can be accounted for by only one type of mating. Other possibilities were evaluated, but only one passes the specificities of known female genotype along with the ratio results.

A monohybrid cross with one parent heterozygous for red claws and one homozygous for black produces a ratio of 1:1, which is not in accordance with the three different phenotypes expressed in the offspring. (See Figure 1.) Crossing two heterozygous parents would produce a phenotypic ratio of 3:1. (See Figure 2.) This again does not fit the observed ratio of the crayfish offspring, and it also contradicts the condition that one parent is heterozygous for red claws while the other shows black.

Because neither of the monohybrid crosses accounts for the observed ratio of the offspring, the next probable way to account for the male's genotype was dihybrid cross. A dihybrid cross involving two parents heterozygous for both gene pairs would produce a phenotypic ratio of 9:3:3:1. (See Figure 3.) However, such parents would themselves express the same claw color; in addition, only three different phenotypes were observed in the resulting offspring.

If the parent with red claws is heterozygous on both gene pairs and the one with black claws is homozygous recessive on the first gene pair and heterozygous on the second pair, the expected phenotypic ratio of the offspring would be 1:3:3:1 (See Figure 4.) This cross again produces too many phenotypes for the observed ratio. If, however, epistasis were involved in this cross, the expected ratio would be 4:3:1 (See Figure 5.) Epistasis occurs when a phenotype does not appear because one gene pair hides the effect of the other. In this cross, epistasis was hypothesized to function as follows. If one gene pair includes a dominant gene and the other is homozygous recessive, a black phenotype will be produced. To produce a red-clawed offspring, it is necessary to have a dominant gene on each gene pair. And for the blue phenotype to occur, both gene pairs must be homozygous recessive. The observed ratio approaches the ratio expected under these conditions. To further support this hypothesis, a Chi-square test was performed. The Chi-square value was 4.31 with two degrees of freedom. This value had a significance level between .2 and .1. For all these reasons, the hypothesis was accepted.

Even though a Mendelian dihybrid cross was found to be an acceptable hypothesis for the ratio observed in the offspring, the pigmentations on body surfaces cannot be explained solely by such a cross. There is substantial evidence that the genetic characteristic of coloring in other animals is governed by at least three to five loci (2). (As defined by Gardner (3), a locus is "a fixed position on a chromosome occupied by a given gene or one of its alleles.")

TEACHING PRACTICE

Call students' attention to the documentation style of this essay (number style) and to the fact that this system is widely used (with some variations) in the sciences.

According to Crow (4), it is also possible during meiosis for genes to subvert the process of equal selection by "cheating" so that their own survival is more likely. This cheating, which was shown in experiments with Drosophilia eye pigmentations, throws off the frequencies of the offspring phenotypes and thereby produces more difficult stipulations that have to be met and explained using Mendelian standards.

In addition to these possibilities, the frequencies of the offspring phenotypes can also be affected by the process assumed by the central dogma. (See Figure 6.) This dogma is the idea that information coded in the sequence of base pairs in DNA is passed on to new molecules of DNA, which transcribes codes for the production of mRNA, which then translates, by means of RNA, the information that will be coded into protein (5). At any stage of this process where information is passed on, there can be some form of interference that would prevent the achievement of the expected outcome. There could also be environmental factors that could possibly alter the phenotypes.

SUMMARY

The genotype of the male crayfish was determined as rrBb. This determination was made by using a dihybrid cross of RrBb x rrBb, where epistasis was taken into account, with an expected ratio of 4:3:1. It does not take into account the possibility that the offspring frequencies have been altered by interference during gene replication, transcription, or translation. Other knowledge that should be considered is the evidence that coloring of body surfaces is governed by at least three to five loci and that genes can actually "cheat" to ensure self-survival. Each of these possibilities could create a result that would require further extensive study into the chromosomal makeup of the species. Despite these

USING CONVENTIONAL PATTERNS AND FORMATS

possibilities, however, the genotype of the male was
proposed and accepted as rrBb.

MONOHYBRID CROSSES

Figure 1

```
Rr x rr →        1 Rr red
f,red m,black    1 rr black
f=female, m=male
```

Figure 2

```
Rr x Rr → 3 R_ ?
f,?  m,?  1rr ?
```

DIHYBRID CROSSES

Figure 3

```
RrBb x RrBb → 9/16 R_B_ ?
f,?     m,?    3/16 R_bb ?
               3/16 rrB_ ?
               1/16 rrbb ?
```

Figure 4

```
RrBb x rrBb →  3/8 R_B_ red
f,red  m,black 1/8 R_bb ?
               3/8 rrB_ black
               1/8 rrbb ?
```

Figure 5 (involving epistasis)

```
RrBb x rrBb →   3/8 R_B_ red
  f,red  m,black 1/8 R_bb black
                 3/8 rrB_ black
                 1/8 rrbb blue
```

CENTRAL DOGMA

Figure 6

```
replication
      DNA →           mRNA  → Protein
         transcription translation
                         involving
                            tRNA
```

TEACHING PRACTICE

These figures may be mysterious to some students.
Take the opportunity, then, to identify a science major in your class and ask that student to provide a
"reading" of these figures. Doing so will help the
student presenter to articulate prior knowledge and
will help the class enter the "conversation" of this
particular discipline.

LITERATURE CITED

1. Strickberger, Monroe W. 1968. Genetics. New York: Macmillan.

2. Branda, R. F., and J. W. Eaton. 1978. Skin color and nutrient photolysis: An evolutionary hypothesis. Sci. pp. 625–626.

3. Gardner, Eldon J. 1965. Principles of genetics. New York: Wiley.

4. Crow, James F. 1979. Genes that violate Mendel's rules. Sci. Amer.: pp. 134–146.

5. Purves, William K., and G. H. Orians. 1987. Life: The science of biology. Sunderland: Sinauer Associated Inc.

ANSWERS TO EXERCISE 42.7 (WILL VARY)

1. Characteristics include a prescribed format that accommodates all necessary information: Introduction (states purpose of the experiment or research); Methods and Materials (shows how the experiment or research was conducted); Results (lists data analysis); Summary (provides conclusions and explanations); Data (presents findings); Literature Cited.

2. The report should be factual, precise, and clearly stated. Vocabulary includes nominalizations and technical terminology. The report focuses on the empirical data and relies on evidence from outside sources. The style is formal; there is no authorial voice. The passive voice is used to give the impression of objective research, analysis, and presentation of the data and results. The focus on the data and procedures reinforces this impression. The format follows explicit guidelines; the writer knows exactly what information must be included and where it belongs. The sections are clearly labelled, for easy reference.

TEACHING PRACTICE

Using paragraph one as their text, ask students to identify the features of an introduction to a literary interpretation essay. Can they suggest ways to make the opening sentence more dramatic—perhaps by posing it as a question?

EXERCISE 42.7

1. On the basis of the paper about the crayfish genotype, make a list of the characteristics of a research report in biology. Your list will constitute an initial set of criteria that you could use in writing a report of your own.

2. Based on this paper, what can you surmise about the expectations, vocabulary, style, evidence, and conventional patterns or formats of this field?

3. Interpreting sources in the humanities

The following paper, written for a literature class, illustrates how a primary source can be analyzed and interpreted in one discipline. Notice that the writer assumes that a reader will need little plot review and will accept the interpretation of character and theme as appropriate concerns.

The Role of Men in The Third Life of Grange Copeland*

Many observers of American society charge that it has created a distorted definition of manhood and produced men who, in their need to assert control of their lives, release their frustration at the expense of women. In her novel The Third Life of Grange Copeland, Alice Walker addresses this theme from the point of view of black men

_____

* by Amy Dierst

USING CONVENTIONAL PATTERNS AND FORMATS   *dis*|42e

and women, for whom racism heightens the distortion and its consequences. She suggests that by stifling black men's sense of freedom and control, a racist society creates frustrations that are released in family violence and inherited by their children. Because his wife and children are the only aspect of the black man's life that he can control, they become the scapegoat upon which his frustrations are released. As Walker's title suggests, she sees redemption, or spiritual rebirth into a new life, as the best defense against society's injustice. Though Walker's male characters have been labeled as either heartlessly cruel or pathetically weak (Steinem 37), many of them, like Grange Copeland, do change during the course of a work. Individual transformation stimulates the potential for change in the social system as a whole.

In this novel, Walker shows how the social and economic system of the 1920s offered a futile existence to Southern black families. Grange Copeland, like most Southern black men of his era, lived and worked on a farm owned and operated by a white man. This system, called sharecropping, did not allow for future planning or savings, for everything earned was returned to the white man's pocket for rent. Thus sharecropping, like slavery before it, contributed to the black man's feelings of powerlessness. In his desperation and helplessness, Grange turns to exert power in the one place he is dominant, his home. He releases his frustration by abusing his family in a weekly cycle of cruelty:

> By Thursday, Grange's gloominess reached its
> peak and he grimaced respectfully, with veiled
> eyes, at the jokes told by the man who drove
> the truck [the white farm owner, Mr. Shipley].
> On Thursday night, he stalked the house from
> room to room pulled himself up and swung from

TEACHING PRACTICE
Call students' attention to the way the novel is used as *evidence* in this essay and ask them to compare this kind of evidence with the evidence presented in the two previous student essays.

663

TEACHING PRACTICE

One of the difficulties students often have in writing essays about literature is weaving quotations smoothly into the text of their own. Refer students back to the discussion of quotations in Chapter 39 and ask them to evaluate the use of quotations in this essay. Are they introduced clearly? Do they "fit in" to the preceding sentence? Does the student writer comment sufficiently on their significance?

the rafters. Late Saturday night Grange would come home lurching drunk, threatening to kill his wife and Brownfield [his son] stumbling and shooting his shotgun (Walker 12).

At other times, Grange displays his frustration through neglect, a more psychologically disturbing device that later affects Brownfield's emotional stability. Grange's inability to rise above his own discontent with his life and express feeling toward his son becomes his most abusive act. Eventually, he abandons his family completely for a new life in the North. Even when he says goodbye, "even in private and in the dark and with his son, presumably asleep, Grange could not bear to touch his son with his hand" (Walker 121).

Brownfield picks up where Grange left off, giving his father's violent threats physical form by beating his own wife and children regularly. Although he, too, blames the whites for driving him to brutality, Walker suggests that his actions are not excusable on these grounds. By the time he reaches adulthood, sharecropping is not a black man's only option in life and cannot be used as a scapegoat. Nevertheless, he chooses to relinquish his freedom and work for Mr. Shipley.

By becoming the overseer on Mr. Shipley's plantation, Brownfield positions himself for the same failure that ruined his father. Over time, his loss of control of his life turns his feelings of depression and lost pride into anger, and his own destructive nature turns him toward violence and evil (Harris, 240). Unable or unwilling to take responsibility for himself, Brownfield blames his own inadequacies on his wife, Mem, who bears the brunt of his anger:

> Brownfield beat his once lovely wife now, regu-
> larly, because it made him feel briefly good.

> Every Saturday night he beat her, trying to pin
> the blame for his failure on her by imprinting
> it on her face, and she . . . repaid him by
> becoming a haggard . . . witch. (Walker 55)

Brownfield demonstrates his power by stripping Mem, a former schoolteacher, of anything that would threaten his manhood. Reasoning that her knowledge is a power that he cannot have and therefore she does not deserve, he wants her to speak in her old dialect so that she will not appear to be more intelligent than he does. He also wants her to be ugly because her ugliness makes it easier for him to justify beating her. He wants her to reach a state of ultimate degradation where any strength of her character will be quickly extinguished by a blow to the face or a kick in the side. In fact, "he rather enjoyed her desolation because in it she had no hopes. She was totally weak, totally without view, without a sky" (Walker 59). In a final attempt to release his frustration, Brownfield kills Mem, literally and symbolically obliterating the remainder of her identity—her face (Theroux 2).

But in the face of this brutality and degradation, Walker raises the possibility of a different fate for black men and women. While in the North, Grange undergoes a spiritual rebirth and comes to understand that white injustice is not alone responsible for the cruelty of black men toward their families (Gasten 278). He also realizes that to weaken and destroy a wife and family is not a sign of manhood, saying:

> You gits just as weak as water, no feeling of
> doing nothing yourself, you begins to destroy
> everybody around you, and you blame it on crack-
> ers [whites]. Nobody's as powerful as we make
> out to be, we got our own souls, don't we?
> (Walker 207)

TEACHING PRACTICE

Ask students to identify the tone—or dominant impression—the writer of this essay creates and discuss how persuasive and effective they find the tone to be.

Grange redeems his spirit in his "third life" with his granddaughter, Ruth. His objective now is not to destroy what he loves but to cherish it. When a judge orders Ruth to go back to live with Brownfield after his release from prison, Grange kills him before this horror becomes a reality. Although he is shot to death as he tries to escape the police, he dies a redeemed man and passes his inner strength of hope on to his granddaughter.

The impact of the racist system of the South unquestionably pervades the lives of Walker's black characters. Nevertheless, she does not portray as justifiable the destructive need of black men to exert their strength at the expense of the weak. It is necessary to be aware of societal injustices and their effects but not to use them as excuses for individual cruelty. Through her characters, Walker gives us faith that cruelty turns back on itself. Some meet tragic endings, but the redemption of Grange shows Walker's faith in change. She envisions the children of tomorrow inheriting not hatred and selfishness but compassion and honesty. Her affirmative voice demonstrates the potential for social change through individual transformation.

Works Cited

Gaston, Karen C. "Women in the Lives of Grange Copeland." College Language Association Journal 24 (1981): 276–286.

Harris, Trudier. "Violence in The Third Life of Grange Copeland." College Language Association Journal 19 (1975): 238–247.

Steinem, Gloria. "Do You Know This Woman? She Knows You—A Profile on Alice Walker." Ms. June 1982: 89–94.

Theroux, Paul. Rev. of The Third Life of Grange Copeland, by Alice Walker. Bookworld 4 Sept. 1970: 2.

USING CONVENTIONAL PATTERN AND FORMATS

Walker, Alice. <u>The</u> <u>Third</u> <u>Life</u> <u>of</u> <u>Grange</u> <u>Copeland</u>. New
    York: Harcourt, 1970.

EXERCISE 42.8

1. On the basis of the paper about the Alice Walker novel, make a list of the characteristics of an interpretation of sources in literature. Your list will constitute an initial set of criteria that you could use in writing an interpretation in courses of your own.
2. On the basis of this paper, what can you surmise about the expectations, vocabulary, style, evidence, and conventional patterns or formats of this field?

FOR EXAMINING YOUR OWN WRITING IN A DISCIPLINE

Choose a piece of writing you have produced for a particular discipline—an essay on literature, a laboratory report, a review of the literature in the discipline, or any other assignment. Examine it closely for its use of that discipline's vocabulary, style, methods of proof, and conventional format. How comfortable are you in writing a piece of this kind? In what ways are you using the conventions of the discipline easily and well? What conventions of the discipline give you difficulty, and why? If you are keeping a writing log, make an entry in it on "What I would most like to know about how to write effectively in this discipline." Use this entry as the basis for interviewing an instructor in this field.

ANSWERS TO EXERCISE 42.8 (WILL VARY)

1. In literature studies, the work of literature is the primary focus of attention. Traditionally, writers focus on theme, character, plot, diction, and setting in order to explore values, ideas, and truths. Secondary critical sources serve to reinforce or guide analyses. Sources are listed in a Works Cited list.

2. Expectations of readers of this kind of paper include evidence of the writer's familiarity with the text and an ability to add something to the "conversation" of the discipline regarding the work discussed. Vocabulary includes language specific to discussions of literary texts. The style is fairly formal, but active voice is preferred. Evidence includes quotations from the text, and paraphrases, summaries, and quotations from outside sources. The paper is organized around a thesis, or a major point or idea. Format for the paper, particularly for parenthetical citations and the Works Cited list, follows guidelines set out by the Modern Language Association.

TEACHING PRACTICE

Ask students to bring the results of their examinations of their essays to class. Then group them according to discipline—all engineers together, sociology majors together and so forth. Ask them to compare notes and, as a group, to prepare a brief description of the conventions of writing in their particular discipline. Then ask each group to report back to the class as a whole.

43. Writing Essay Examinations

TEACHING PRACTICE

In their book, *Facts, Artifacts, and Counterfacts*, David Bartholomae and Anthony Petrosky suggest that asking students to write essay examinations is antithetical to the teaching of a drafting process of writing. Yet they hesitate to reject essay writing entirely. Exam writing "requires students to consolidate much of what they have learned in the course and to use their knowledge efficiently." But the emphasis can shift from ideas and organization to error control (101).

Given this hesitation, you may well wonder whether you should require essay exams. In many cases, however, exams are institutionally required and may even be institutionally composed, with the individual instructor having little choice in what goes into the test or how it is given—or sometimes how it is even graded. If the exams are institutionally imposed, you should find out as much as you can as early as you can in order to schedule preparation time, if needed.

If you are allowed the decision of whether or not to test a class, you need to clarify for yourself exactly what you expect your students to get out of it.

There are two reasons for giving such an exam. First, you may want to test your students' knowledge and abilities. In such a case, you will want to make sure that you either limit the topic or extend the time given so that students can complete the process—discover, narrow, and organize the topic; write, revise, and proofread the essay. Second, you may simply want to give your students experience writing under such conditions as practice for future exams in other college courses. In that case, you will want to actually spend class time on how to write under such conditions and then to simulate those conditions in an exam. In fact, essay writing is being used more frequently and in more and more disciplines. Instructors view essay examinations as better indicators of knowledge than multiple-choice tests and short-answer definitions.

"If you can't write it," says author and former college dean Arthur Adams, "you don't know it." While Adams's statement is debatable in some circumstances, it certainly applies to essay examinations, where writing is the way to demonstrate what you know.

Writing an effective essay examination requires two important abilities: recalling information and organizing the information in order to draw relevant conclusions from it. These conclusions form the thesis of the essay while the information serves as support. While this process sounds simple, writing an effective essay examination under pressure in limited time can be a daunting task. This chapter suggests ways to turn this sometimes daunting task into a perfectly manageable one.

43a. Preparing for essay examinations

In getting ready for an essay examination, nothing can take the place of knowing the subject well. You can, in other words, prepare for an essay examination throughout the term by taking careful notes of lectures, texts, and other assigned reading. You may want to outline a reading assignment, list its main points, list and define its key terms, or briefly summarize its argument or main points. A particularly effective method is to divide your notes into two categories. In a notebook, label the left-hand pages "Summaries and Quotations." Label the right-hand pages "Questions and Comments." Then as you read your text or other assigned material, use the left-hand page to record brief summaries of the major points made, the support offered for each point, and noteworthy quotations. On the right-hand page, record questions that your reading has not answered, ideas that are unclear or puzzling to you, and your own evaluative comments. This form of notetaking encourages active, hard-headed reading and, combined with careful

668

USEFUL READING

Bartholomae, David, and Anthony Petrosky. *Facts, Artifacts, and Counterfacts: Theory and Method for a Reading and Writing Course.* Upper Montclair, NJ: Boynton, 1986.

Greenberg, Karen, Harvey S. Weiner, and Richard A. Donovan. *Writing Assessment: Issues and Strategies.* New York: Longman, 1986. This collection includes twelve essays as well as an annotated bibliography of current research in assessment.

class notes, will do much to prepare you for the essay examination. Here is an entry from a student's notebook, written in response to Chapter 4 of this book.

Summaries and Quotations	Questions and Comments
-rhetoric—art of language (Aristotle) -all language is argumentative— purpose is to persuade	Maybe all language *is* persuasive, but if I greet people warmly, I don't *consciously* try to persuade them that I'm glad to see them. I just respond naturally (unless they're having an insecure day).
-to identify an *argument*, ask: 1. Does it try to persuade me? 2. Does it deal with a problem without a clear-cut answer? 3. Could I actually disagree with it?	Of all the statements that can be debated, I think the less absolute the possible answers, the more important the question (such as nuclear disarmament) and the harder to solve (otherwise the answer would be obvious—no problem).

In addition to taking careful, detailed notes, you can prepare for an essay examination by writing out essay answers to questions you think are likely to appear on the examination. Practicing ahead of time is usually more effective than last-minute cramming. Late-night cramming for a multiple-choice test may sometimes work, but it is almost sure to be unproductive for an essay examination. On the day of the exam, do ten to fifteen minutes of writing just before you go into the examination to get your thinking muscles "warmed up" and prepare you to do your best job of writing the examination.

▌ 43b. Analyzing essay examination questions

Before you begin writing, read the question over carefully several times, and *analyze* what it asks you to do. Most essay examination questions contain two kinds of terms, **strategy** terms that describe your task in writing the essay and **content** terms that define the scope and limits of the topic.

STRATEGY ┌──────── CONTENT ────────┐
Analyze Jesus' Sermon on the Mount.

669

─────────────────────────────

USEFUL READING

Berlin, James A. *Rhetoric and Reality: Writing Instruction in American Colleges, 1900–1985.* Carbondale and Edwardsville, IL: Southern Illinois UP, 1987.

————. *Writing Instruction in Nineteenth-Century American Colleges.* Carbondale and Edwardsville, IL: Southern Illinois UP, 1984.

(BACK)GROUNDING

Instructors have always wanted to assess the progress of their students, but writing tests are a rather new phenomenon in the history of education. Not until the mid-nineteenth century did writing tests become widespread. In 1874, Harvard led the way by introducing the first written entrance examination. Before that date, candidates were "promoted" on the basis of oral examinations. In the new test, students were required in an hour to produce a carefully thought out, carefully revised, unified, error-free essay on subjects such as a Shakespearean play, a novel like Scott's *Ivanhoe*, or dueling in the age of Queen Anne. Needless to say, many failed.

Ironically, before the institution of this exam, composition was not primarily considered a lower-level college or secondary school subject. Previously, it had been an upper-division course that the student took for three years. James Berlin suggests that the new entrance exam was one of several related events caused by the shift in educational priorities from rhetoric to poetics (*Rhetoric and Reality* 23). After 1874, essay exams proliferated in the schools and colleges.

TEACHING PRACTICE

How you give an essay exam depends upon how you view the function of exams. Before scheduling an exam, clarify in your own mind why you want to examine your students in this way. If you are interested in testing your students' writing abilities, consider these alternatives:

Schedule the exam over two class periods. Students come to class on the first exam day with nothing but a pen; you provide test booklets. The assignment includes several topic choices. The student spends the first day deciding upon a topic and a thesis, discovering support for that thesis, and writing a first draft. Take up all the exam booklets at the end of the period. On the second day, return the booklets to the students, and they rewrite and proofread and correct their essays. At the end of the second day, they turn in the exams.

Hand out topics several days ahead of time, assigning your students the task of deciding upon a topic, finding a thesis, and discovering support for that thesis before the time of the exam. On the day before the day of the exam, take up all of their preliminary work in order to insure that a student does not arrive with a fully written essay. On the day of the exam, they should arrive with nothing but a pen. You return their preliminary work to them with an exam booklet, and they write their essay during class.

TEACHING PRACTICE

If your intention in giving an essay exam is to give your students practice in taking such exams, you will want to simulate the conditions of such exams in as many ways as possible. Therefore, you will want to limit the exam to one class period.

No matter how you give an essay exam, you ought to prepare your class in two ways. First, you should make your expectations very clear to your students. A pre-exam class discussion of successful strategies, perhaps with reference to model exam essays, could help build confidence and calm fears. Second, you should allow your students practice runs. You might provide short in-class writings. You might even provide ungraded practice writings simulating exam conditions. If you give more than one exam, you might consider making the first one short and its grade less of the percentage of the overall grade.

WRITING TOGETHER

In the working world, groups of people often collaborate on a piece of writing and meet a certain deadline doing it. You might consider having groups of your students collaborate on an essay exam.

Or you might consider having groups of them prepare together for an essay exam on a common topic. They could then write separate essays on it.

STRATEGY ┌──────── CONTENT ────────┐
Describe the major effects of reconstruction.

STRATEGY ┌──────── CONTENT ────────┐
Discuss the function of the river in *Huckleberry Finn.*

STRATEGY ┌──────── CONTENT ────────┐
Explain the advantages of investing in government securities.

Words like *analyze, describe, discuss,* and *explain* tell what logical strategy to use and often help set the form of your essay answer. Since not all terms mean the same thing in every discipline, be sure you understand *exactly* what the term means in context of the material covered on the examination. In general, however, the most commonly used strategy terms have standard meanings.

ANALYZE   Divide an event, idea, or theory into its component elements, and examine each one in turn: *Analyze Milton Friedman's theory of permanent income.*

COMPARE AND/OR CONTRAST   Demonstrate similarities or dissimilarities between two or more events or topics: *Compare the portrayal of women in* The Great Gatsby *with that in* Pride and Prejudice.

DEFINE   Identify and state the essential traits or characteristics of something, differentiating it clearly from other things: *Define Hegelian dialectic.*

DESCRIBE   Tell about an event, person, or process in detail, creating a clear and vivid image of it: *Describe the dress of a medieval knight.*

EVALUATE   Assess the value or significance of the topic: *Evaluate the contribution of black musicians to the development of an American musical tradition.*

EXPLAIN   Make a topic as clear and understandable as possible by offering reasons, examples, and so on: *Explain the functioning of the circulatory system.*

SUMMARIZE   State the major points concisely and comprehensively: *Summarize the major arguments against using animals in laboratory research.*

Strategy terms give you important clues for the thesis of your essay answer. Sometimes, strategy terms are not explicitly stated in an essay

USEFUL READING

Guthrie, Warren. "The Development of Rhetorical Theory in America, 1636–1850," *Speech Monographs* 13 (1946): 14–22; 14 (1947): 38–54; 15 (1948): 61–71; 16 (1949): 98–113; 18 (1951): 17–30.

Kitzhaber, Albert R. *Rhetoric In American Colleges, 1850–1900.* Diss. U of Washington, 1953. Ann Arbor: UMI, 1978.

question. In these cases, you need to infer a strategy from the content terms. For example, a question that mentions two groups working toward the same goal may imply comparison and contrast, or a question referring to events in a given time period may imply summary. Once you understand which strategy to follow, make sure you understand the meanings of all content terms. Particularly in technical or advanced courses, specialized language may need to be clarified. *Romanticism*, for instance, means one thing in the context of an eighteenth-century literature course and something else in a class on modern art. Do not hesitate to ask for such clarification.

43c. Thinking through your answer and taking notes

During an essay examination, you may be tempted to begin writing at once. Time is precious—but so too are organizing and planning. You will profit, therefore, by spending some time—about 10 percent of the allotted time is a good rule of thumb—thinking through your answer.

Begin by deciding which major points you need to make and in what order to present them. Then jot down support or evidence for each point. Craft a clear, succinct *thesis* that satisfies the strategy term of the exam question. While in most writing situations you start from a working thesis in outlining your topic, when writing under pressure you will probably find it easier and more efficient to outline (or simply jot down) your ideas and craft your thesis from your outline. Suppose you were asked to define the three major components of personality, according to Freud. This is a clear question and, assuming that you have read the material and studied your notes, you should be able to make a brief outline as a framework for your answer.

> <u>Id</u>
> basic definition—what it *is* and *is* not
> major characteristics of
> functions of
>
> <u>Ego</u>
> basic definition—what it *is* and *is* not
> major characteristics of
> functions of

TEACHING PRACTICE

Choosing topics for an essay examination in a composition course can be tricky. Unless you specifically authorize your students to research the exam topic before the day of the writing, you must choose a topic with which they will be familiar. Also, you might consider looking for overlapping interests in your students' writings. Indeed, if you are ambitious, you could provide individualized exam questions for your students.

Responding to essay examinations is not the same as responding to a paper. Generally speaking, you cannot expect as much, both in quality and quantity, from in-class writings. After all, even an essay exam spread over two days is still limited to two class periods, which normally run less than an hour each.

Probably you will want to read generously in terms of mechanics and grammar unless the errors seriously affect the meaning of the writing. You can expect a clear thesis, clear support for that thesis, a fair amount of thoroughness in covering the topic, clear organization of the essay, and readable prose. The style may not be extraordinarily good; it may not even be up to the student's usual quality; but it still should be readable.

WRITING TOGETHER

After the examination but before you have returned these essays to your students, make sure that they have recorded the process by which they wrote their exam, perhaps in their writing logs. Consider having each of your students share his or her process with the rest of the class. Ask each student what he or she will do differently the next time. Are there invention strategies the student would use that he or she didn't use? After each student has shared his or her process, consider dividing the class into groups of three or four and having each group decide upon what they consider to be the best processes for each of the exam topics. Have each group share their ideal processes with the rest of the class. Finally, as a class, try to come to some sort of consensus on what the best processes would be.

TEACHING PRACTICE

Students react in a variety of ways to exams. Naturally, most become anxious at the thought of being tested, but in some, the pressure can cause such an emotional distress that a person may become physically ill and intellectually paralyzed. Such a condition is often referred to as "test anxiety," and it is much more common among students than instructors sometimes realize. Allen J. Ottens, a psychological counselor and author of numerous papers and a book on test anxiety, writes that such anxiety "is a significant problem affecting a substantial number of students" (1).

Of course, instructors cannot read their students' minds, and often those who suffer from such anxiety are not readily apparent. However, you should become aware of the following symptoms of test anxiety:

1. Frequent panicky talk by a student about the exam and its terrible consequences.
2. Frequent self-belittling by the student and comparisons of himself or herself with other students.
3. Reminiscences of previous tests in which the student performed badly.
4. Performing of irrelevant tasks that appear to be avoidance of performing tasks relevant to the test.
5. Attendance to what other students are doing during the test rather than attending to the student's own writing.
6. Too much clock-watching during an exam.
7. Physiological indicators, like trembling hands, unexplainable sweating, complaints of illness (which may be very real, by the way) on days when exams are scheduled.
8. Expressions or indications of embarrassment at asking questions.
9. A rushing through the exam so that the student misinterprets directions and/or does significantly worse than you expected.
10. Any other unusual behavior related to the exam.
11. And, of course, the student's explicit expression of fear of the exam.

Instructors themselves should not attempt to cure test anxiety in their students. It is a psychological problem, best dealt with by the student and a psychologist or psychoanalyst. However, instructors can help the student.

Your reassurance that the student can perform up to his or her abilities can go a long way in building self-confidence in the face of the exam. Of course, you must also be honest as well as supportive; you should not tell the student he or she can perform better than you really think he or she can.

Superego
basic definition—what it *is* and *is* not
major characteristics of
functions of

From this outline, you can develop a thesis:

> According to Freud, the human personality consists of three major and interlocking elements: the id, the ego, and the superego.

43d. Drafting your answer

Your goal in producing an essay examination answer is twofold: to demonstrate that you have mastered the course material and to communicate your ideas and information clearly, directly, and logically. During the drafting stage, follow your outline as closely as you can. Once you depart from it, you will lose time and perhaps have trouble returning to the main discussion. As a general rule, develop each major point into at least one paragraph. And make clear the connections among your main points by using transitions: "*The last element of the human personality, according to Freud, is the superego.*"

Besides referring to your outline for guidance, pause and read what you have written before going on to a new point. This kind of rereading may remind you of other ideas while you still have time to include them; it should also help you establish a clear connection with whatever follows. Write neatly, skip lines, and leave ample margins so you have space for changes or additions when you revise.

43e. Revising and editing your answer

Leave enough time (at least five to ten minutes) to read through your essay answer carefully. Consider the following questions.

- Is the thesis clearly stated? Does it answer the question?
- Are all the major points covered?
- Are the major points adequately developed and supported?
- Is each sentence complete?
- Are spelling, punctuation, and syntax correct?
- Is the handwriting legible?

The more familiar you become with the process of taking an essay exam, the better your answers will be.

USEFUL READING

Ottens, Allen J. *Coping with Academic Anxiety*. New York: Rosen Pub. Group, 1984. This book is one of several that describe what is usually referred to as "test anxiety," and offer suggestions for coping with it.

▌ 43f. Considering a sample essay answer

The following example illustrates how one student handled an essay and short-answer examination in a first-year American history course. She had fifty minutes to answer two of three essay questions and three of five short-answer questions. She chose to answer the following question first:

> Between 1870 and 1920, blacks and women were both struggling to establish certain rights in America. What did each group want? Briefly analyze their strategies for improvement, and indicate the degree of their success.

This student began her exam with this question because she knew the most about this topic. With another essay and three short answers to write, she decided to devote *no more than twenty minutes* to this essay.

First, she analyzed what the question asked her to do, especially noting the strategy terms. She decided that the first sentence of the question strongly *implied* comparison and contrast of the two struggles. The second sentence asked for an explanation of the goals of each group, and in the third sentence, she took *analyze* and *indicate* to mean "explain what each group did and how well it succeeded." As it turned out, this was a very shrewd reading of the question. In a post-exam discussion, the instructor remarked that those who had included a comparison and contrast produced better answers than those who did not. Note that, in this instance, the strategy the instructor expected is not stated explicitly in the question. Instead, class members were expected to read between the lines to infer the strategy.

After analyzing the strategy, the student then identified content terms around which to develop her answer: the groups—blacks and women—and their actions—goals, strategies, and degrees of success. Using these terms, she spent about three minutes producing the following outline.

<u>Introduction</u>
goals, strategies, degree of success

<u>Blacks</u>
want equality
two opposing strategies: Dubois and Washington
even with vote, great opposition

If you believe a student to have test anxiety, set up a private conference. You will want to talk to students about any problems they have without others around. In the conference, you can approach the subject directly, presenting the reasons you are concerned, and asking the student if he or she is aware of any cause for concern. A student might already be aware of and dealing with test anxiety. If not, you will want to suggest that the student see a school counselor. You should make it clear that while test anxiety is serious, it is also a common problem, and one that can be resolved. You might also suggest that the student check the library or local bookstores for books on test anxiety, such as Allen J. Ottens' *Coping with Academic Anxiety*. Finally, be reassuring, but honest. You cannot dismiss any student from work required of all other students in the class, but you might be able to compromise. Would the student cope with the exam better if he or she took it alone? In that case, you should be able to arrange a time and room in the same way you would a make-up exam. Perhaps, further conferences to discuss improvements in his or her writing generally and strategies for dealing with exams would help. Perhaps, the tests count little in the overall grade the student will receive; you could reassure the student of that. In addition, preparing for an exam in a peer group can help to reassure the student that he or she is able to contribute and do the work.

WRITERS ON WRITING

Although widely used, standardized tests measure only editorial skills—choosing the best sentence, recognizing correct usage, punctuation, and capitalization. At least for this reason, they are not valid measures of writing performance.

—CHARLES R. COOPER AND LEE ODELL

WRITERS ON WRITING

Since writing is an expressive human activity, we believe the best response to it is a receptive, sympathetic human response.

—CHARLES R. COOPER AND LEE ODELL

WRITERS ON WRITING

If a liberal education should teach students "how to think," not only in their own fields but in fields outside their own—that is, to understand "how the other fellow orders knowledge," then bulling, even in its purest form, expresses an important part of what a pluralist university holds dear, surely a more important part than the collecting of "facts that are facts" which schoolboys learn to do. Here, then, good bull appears not as ignorance at all but as an aspect of knowledge. It is both relevant and "true." In a university setting good bull is therefore of more value than "facts," which, without a frame of reference, are not even "true" at all.

—WILLIAM G. PERRY, JR.

<u>Women</u>
many ultimate goals (economic, political, educational equality), but focus on vote
use male rhetoric against them
use vote to achieve other goals

<u>Conclusion</u>
educational and economic differences between groups

From this outline, the student crafted the following thesis:

> In the years between 1870 and 1920, blacks and women were both fighting for equal rights, but in different ways.

Guided by these notes, she then wrote the following answer.

The years between 1870 and 1920 saw two major **THESIS** groups—blacks and women—demanding more rights, but the two groups approached the problem of inequality in different ways. Initially, women wanted the vote, equality **WOMEN** within the family, and equal job and education opportunities. Their attempts to achieve all these goals at once **GOALS** were unsuccessful, as men countered by accusing them of attacking the sanctity of the family institution. (Demanding equality in the family meant confronting traditional Christianity, which subordinated women to men.) With the lead of Carrie Chapman Catt, women narrowed their goal to a focus on the vote. They emphasized that **STRATEGY** they would vote to benefit middle-class Americans (like themselves), reduced the stridency of their rhetoric, and said that they would clean up an often corrupt goverment (they turned the men's strategy against them here by *emphasizing* their own purity and virtue). They also invited Wilson to talk at their conventions and won him to their side. Because of their specific focus and reorganization, **DEGREE OF** women did finally receive the vote which then gave them **SUCCESS** the power to work toward their other reform goals.

Less well organized and less formally educated than **BLACKS** middle-class women, American blacks often were unable to dedicate their full effort to the cause of equality because **GOAL** of severe economic problems. In addition, their leaders disagreed over strategy. Washington told the blacks to **STRATEGY** work hard and earn the vote and equality, while Dubois **(SPLIT)** maintained that blacks, like all other Americans, deserved it already. The blacks also had to overcome fierce racial

ANALYZING AND EVALUATING YOUR ANSWER

prejudice. Even after they finally won the vote, whites passed laws (literacy tests and grandfather clauses) and used force (particularly through the Ku Klux Klan) to keep blacks from voting. Therefore, even after the blacks got the vote in name, they had to fight to keep and use it.

DEGREE OF SUCCESS

Thus both blacks and women fought for (and are still fighting for) equal rights, but the women were more successful in late nineteenth-century America. Educated, organized, and financially secure, they concentrated their efforts on getting the vote as a means to higher political objectives, and they got it. Blacks, on the other hand, had to overcome great financial barriers that reduced access to education and worked against strong organization. Even after they received the vote, prejudicial laws and practices kept these Americans subjugated.

TWO GROUPS CONTRASTED

Although this essay answer is not perfect, as the student's commentary and analysis in 43g will make clear, it responded accurately and fully enough in its allotted fifteen to twenty minutes to receive a mark of A and only one criticism at the end: "No advances at all for blacks?— e.g. education."

43g. Analyzing and evaluating your answer

Although you will not have time to analyze your answers during an examination, you can improve your essay examination abilities by analyzing your own answers later. When the student who wrote the answer in 43f did so, she decided to go through her answer sentence by sentence to see how well she followed the guidelines in 43e and what additional points she might have covered. Lastly, she analyzed her answer with her instructor's comments in mind.

> *Thesis.* I think my thesis worked pretty well, but it probably would have been clearer if I had named specific kinds of rights rather than just saying "certain rights."
>
> *Major points.* I included all the points that I listed in my outline, but I should have developed more the term *equality* in my discussion of the blacks' struggle.
>
> *Spelling, punctuation, usage.* Would have been better to skim essay over for spelling and punctuation errors (as in the sixth sentence).
>
> *Additional points.* I could have talked much more about individual women's contributions—no time.

Response to instructor's comments. I should have listed the advances made for blacks, which I knew—my interpretation was too negative. I also know much more about Washington and Dubois than I showed on the exam.

Analyzing and evaluating her answer in this way allows her to see whether she tends to stray from the topic and whether she could improve certain elements—such as the thesis and strong topic sentences—in future examinations.

READING AN ESSAY ANSWER WITH A CRITICAL EYE

Here is question 3 on the examination described in this chapter, followed by the same student's answer. Using the checklist in 43e and the suggestions in 43g, analyze and evaluate her answer.

The United States, one might argue, entered the world arena in 1899 and moved to center stage in 1918. What were the landmarks of American entry into the world arena and what, according to George Kennan, were the major mistakes the United States made during those entry years?

The United States grew in power and land during the early twentieth century. We proved our strength in the War with Spain, and in the process, we acquired, at least temporarily, Cuba and the Philippines and tried to shape their governments. We also asserted ourselves in Hawaii, Guam, and Puerto Rico. Our entry into World War I showed our concern with, and entry into, World politics. The war probably would have been lost had we not entered when we did. We provided fresh soldiers who inspired the Europeans. We also provided financial assistance and military equipment to the allies throughout the war (although, initially we sold amunnitions to the Central Powers as well). According to Kennan, the Americans made many mistakes in their approach to the war. First, we did not recognize the importance of European affairs to our own safety. We said that WWI was none of our concern until the neutral rights issue came to a head. When we finally entered the war, we were unprepared. Kennan also states that Americans have a terrible approach to war. Democracies are slow to anger, but once they fight, they go for the kill, forgetting political objectives and focusing on hatred. Also, Kennan feels that we should not have gotten trapped into a war with Spain because of our involvement in Cuba. Finally, Kennan criticizes the Open Door Policy concerning China's regions of influence as being the work of a few elite men. By saying that all of the countries agreed, we took a big gamble. In conclusion, Kennan criticizes American politics because we fail to see the implications of world problems to ourselves; we are never prepared when we enter war; we focus on hatred rather than political objectives; and we take too many risks. Kennan wants us to learn from these mistakes and change our attitudes because, when you're dealing with nuclear war, you can't afford to make *any* mistakes.

FOR EXAMINING YOUR OWN ESSAY ANSWERS

Choose at least two of your recent answers to essay examination questions. Review each question, and then read your answer carefully. How could you improve the organization, content, and correctness of your answer? Make an entry in your writing log, if you are keeping one, noting any new strategies you can use for improving your essay exam answers.

PART TEN

Writing for Nonacademic Audiences

44. Writing for Business

Principles of effective business communication are rooted in ideas as old as civilization. In fact, anthropologists now suspect that the very earliest forms of writing record business transactions. Today, much of the world's commerce is conducted in writing—in proposals, reports, and correspondence, particularly memos and business letters. Such correspondence is at its best when it is succinct and clear. Cornelius Vanderbilt was legendary for his ability to write powerfully direct business letters. When the fifty-nine-year-old millionaire took his first vacation, he discovered that a pair of business associates had taken steps that challenged his interests. To them, he wrote this letter:

Gentlemen:

You have undertaken to cheat me. I won't sue you, for the law is too slow. I'll ruin you.

Yours truly,

Cornelius Vanderbilt

This chapter presents guidelines for effective business correspondence: letters, résumés, and memoranda.

44a. Following business style and format

Business communications are utilitarian documents, intended to produce results. An effective business letter is clear, concise, and polite; it also usually follows a conventional format and speaks in language its reader will readily understand.

(BACK)GROUNDING

In the twentieth century, English departments in universities still privilege belles lettres; composition courses, until recently, have also tended to focus on academic writing: "creative" writing (narratives, experience papers), the (academic) research paper, and the literary essay. Modern rhetoric, however, has expanded the realm of rhetoric to include all persuasion (Chaim Perelman focuses on legal discourse), all speech acts (J. L. Austin and John Searle), and all acts of identification (Kenneth Burke). Writing for nonacademic audiences, then, addresses a larger need of your students than writing for academic audiences. Much of the writing your students will do after they graduate will address nonacademic audiences (prospective employees and clients, customers, friends). Writing outside the academy may be less immediately important to either you or your students, but it will dominate your students' writing for most of their lives.

USEFUL READING

Lloyd-Jones, Richard. "Focus and Resolution." Rpt. in *The Writing Teacher's Sourcebook*. Eds. Gary Tate and Edward P. J. Corbett. New York: Oxford, 1981. Lloyd-Jones describes how English departments have eliminated much nonacademic reading and writing from their curriculums and offers five proposals for reform.

TEACHING PRACTICE

To help your students avoid jargon, consider providing them with the following rules, Richard Lanham's "Paramedic Method":

1. Circle the prepositions.
2. Circle the *is* forms.
3. Ask "Who is kicking Who?"
4. Put this "kicking" action in a simple (not compound) active verb.
5. Start fast—no mindless introductions.
6. Write out each sentence on a blank sheet of paper and mark off its basic rhythmic units with a slash (/).
7. Read the passage aloud with emphasis and feeling.
8. Mark off sentence lengths in the passage with a slash (/).

▌1. Writing clearly and concisely

It is best to use plain, straightforward language, avoiding long words unless they convey meaning precisely and are familiar to your reader.

Look at the following examples of inappropriate jargon—technical language used in unnecessarily complex, vague, or inflated ways. (See 26d5.) The revisions are not only more understandable, but more memorable.

JARGON	The biota marine exhibited a 100 percent mortality response.
REVISED	All the fish died.
JARGON	It is not inappropriate to know that all articles which coruscate do not necessarily possess a high intrinsic monetary value.
REVISED	All that glitters is not gold.

As you read this chapter, keep in mind these general principles of clear business writing.

- Keep sentences relatively short.
- Vary sentence length and structure.
- Prefer simple to complex words—for example *use* instead of *utilize*; *change* instead of *modification*; and *show* instead of *indicate*.
- Use concrete words—picture words and images—where possible, such as "the material springs back" instead of "the material possesses reversible extensibility."
- Use active verbs where possible, such as "waxing brightens the surface" instead of "when wax is applied to the surface, a brightness is achieved."
- Consider your readers at every point, avoiding unnecessary technical terms and relating your information to their experience.
- Write to *ex*press, not *im*press. If your writing is clearly expressive, it will make an impression.

▌2. Using a standard format

Business writers use several conventional letter formats which are easy to read and widely recognized. **Modified block** is the format most frequently used for business letters, probably because it is visually appealing on the page, with the whole letter centered vertically as well

---

USEFUL READING

Lanham, Richard. *Revising Prose.* 2d ed. New York: Macmillan, 1987. This is a concise, direct manual for shaping sentences and avoiding the bureaucratic style of writing.

————*Style: An Anti-Textbook.* New Haven: Yale UP, 1974. Clarity, according to Lanham, is a misleadingly simple and incomplete value in composition.

as horizontally. In this format, except for the return address, the date, and the signature block, all typed elements begin at the left-hand margin. The text of the letter is single-spaced but double-spaced between paragraphs and main sections so that they are clear and easy to read. (See 44b for a sample letter and envelope that illustrate this format.)

When you use the modified block format, first list your return address and the date, beginning each line at the center of the page. Should your stationery have a letterhead, type just the date, starting at the center several lines below the letterhead. Next, skip at least one line (or more to lengthen a short letter), and begin the inside address at the left-hand margin. List the recipient's name, title, and address just as on an envelope. Skip a line before the salutation, and follow the recipient's name with a colon. Skip another line, and begin the body of your letter. Separate paragraphs with double-spacing, but do not indent them.

At the end of the text of your letter, skip a line. Then, aligned with the return address and the date, begin the signature block with your complimentary close (followed by a comma). Four lines below, type your name, adding your title or phone number on the next line as needed. (The space above your typed name is for your handwritten signature.) Then, at the left-hand margin, note on separate lines the initials of the writer (in capitals) followed by those of the typist (in lower case), any enclosures (*Enclosure* or *Enc.*), and any copies (*cc*) forwarded to others. Mention enclosures, such as documents, photocopies, a check, or a résumé, in the text of your letter as well.

Traditional indented format resembles modified block format in every way except that the paragraphs, besides being double-spaced, are indented, generally five spaces. In **full block** format, all parts of the letter, including the heading and the signature block, are flush with the left-hand margin. **Simplified** format replaces the salutation with a subject line (typed in all capital letters) that announces the subject of the letter and omits the complimentary close. Although advocates of the simplified format argue that the salutation and the complimentary close add nothing to the content of the letter, most business people like the personal tone of these features.

▌ 44b. Writing letters of inquiry

Business letters often ask for information about job openings, products, services, fees, or prices. Like all business correspondence,

For John Kenneth Galbraith, writers should not wait for those "golden mornings [when] they are touched by the wand—are on intimate terms with poetry and cosmic truth." Writing demands a worklike attitude and dedication, a regular routine. Galbraith believes in revision, and claims (sardonically) that when he writes on a bad day, *without* being touched by the wand of poetry and cosmic truth, "no fewer than five revisions are required. However, when I'm greatly inspired, only four revisions are needed." According to Galbraith, first drafts focus either on ideas or on organization and style, and each succeeding draft allows the writer to combine these elements more successfully. The bottom line for Galbraith is: "Writing is difficult work."

USEFUL READING

Galbraith, John Kenneth. "Writing, Typing and Economics." Rpt. in *Writing in the Social Sciences*. Eds. Joyce S. Steward and Marjorie Smelstor. Glenview, IL: Scott, 1984. Galbraith's essay describes his writing process in a humorously ironic way.

(BACK)GROUNDING

Toward the end of "What Survey Research Tells Us about Writing at Work," Paul V. Anderson lists the implications for teaching that these surveys suggest. Career-related writing courses should do the following:

1. Explain to students that writing will probably play a large and important role in the students' careers, regardless of the students' majors.
2. Focus on general writing strategies that students can apply in a variety of work-related rhetorical situations.
3. Teach students to write communications that people in the workplace will perceive to be clear, concise, well-organized, and grammatically correct.
4. Provide students with instruction and practice in writing for a variety of kinds of readers.
5. Provide students with instruction and practice in writing a variety of kinds of communications.

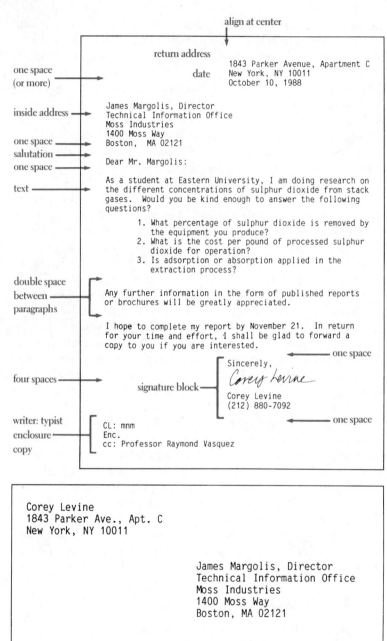

USEFUL READING

Anderson, Paul V. "What Survey Research Tells Us about Writing at Work." Rpt. in *Writing in Nonacademic Settings*. Eds. Lee Odell and Dixie Goswami. New York: Guilford, 1985. See pp. 75–77 where Anderson discusses the implications his research has for teaching career-related courses.

such letters of inquiry should be clear, concise, courteous, and correct. The most courteous way to begin a letter is to address the recipient by name (correctly spelled, of course). If you don't know the person's name, call the company, or check a business directory in your library. Unless you know that a woman prefers to be called *Miss* or *Mrs.*, address her either as *Ms.* or by her full name (*Dear Beverly Moss*).

Once you have identified the recipient, follow these principles for an effective letter of inquiry:

- Address the recipient politely.
- State your request clearly and specifically, including whatever details will help the reader to respond.
- Explain the reason for your request.
- Express your appreciation.
- Make a response as simple as possible by including your telephone number (with the best time to call if you are difficult to reach).
- If appropriate, include a self-addressed, stamped envelope.

Consider how the sample letter of inquiry on page 684 applies these principles. Note, too, that this letter illustrates standard modified block form.

44c. Writing letters of complaint

Complaint letters ask for satisfaction of some sort. The most effective complaint conveys the point, however, *without* sounding angry or whining. Such a letter treats the recipient with respect while firmly requesting satisfaction. It aims to evoke in the reader a willingness to please or help the writer without losing good will or violating self-respect. An effective complaint letter is courteous and businesslike, not antagonistic. It tells the recipient exactly what went wrong, what consequences resulted from the mistake, and what action the writer expects. Consider the following guidelines:

- Open cordially.
- Describe the problem clearly and concisely.
- Explain how the problem affected you.
- State what the recipient can do to make things right.
- Express confidence in the reader's ability to remedy the situation.
- Close with thanks.

685

(BACK)GROUNDING

In "Technical Communication in the Information Economy," Michael L. Keene helps put one part of nonacademic audiences, the field of "technical communication" (a generic term for technical writing/editing/speaking, science writing, medical writing, and other smaller areas), into perspective: the "academics," as measured by membership in the Association of Teachers of Technical Writing, number just over 1,000; the "practitioners," as measured by membership in the Society for Technical Communication, number 10,000. As instructors, we must note that most of the writing our students will do in their lifetimes will be for nonacademic audiences: resumes, job application letters, character references, personal letters, memos, reports, newsletters. To bridge the gap between our students' use of writing and writing in the academy, we must allow students to write in forms of discourse that they will use outside the academy.

WRITERS ON WRITING

What is our subject matter? In this broad context [an essay proposing to reform English department curriculums] the answer to the question should be equally broad: everything in writing is the product of the verbal imagination . . . the written word in all its forms.

—JOHN C. GERBER

We are not likely to rejoin journalism and speech, but we can work jointly with them and make sure that our own expository courses or our general courses include language which is informative about something other than literary topics and persuasive in a variety of ways.

—RICHARD LLOYD-JONES

USEFUL READING

Keene, Michael L. "Technical Information in the Information Economy." Rpt. in *Perspectives on Research and Scholarship in Composition*. Eds. Ben W. McClelland and Timothy R. Donovan. New York: Mod. Lang. Assoc., 1985. Keene reviews recent research in technical communication.

TEACHING PRACTICE

In "Making Information Accessible to Readers," Janice C. Redish, Robbin M. Battison, and Edward S. Gold argue that students need to develop overall organizational skills rather than sentence-level stylistic skills to improve nonacademic writing. As a result of their research, they argue that to help students produce documents in which information is easy to locate, instructors can

> have students write or revise a reference document. They can have students work on documents that are long enough to need informative headings, context-setting paragraphs, and other features that make information accessible. They can teach students general skills rather than ways to write within a prescribed format. They can provide more realistic assignments—ones that have consequences for readers other than themselves. They can send students out of the classroom to find documents that people need to have written or revised.

44d. Writing business memoranda

Business memos transmit information and record decisions made and actions taken. Like business letters, memos are typed, single-spaced, with double-spacing between paragraphs. They follow a conventional format using one-inch margins and full block form.

Follow these suggestions for any memos you need to write:

- Deal *only* with the subject specified.
- If the subject is complex, requiring a lengthy memo, add subheadings, subtopics, or numbers.
- Begin with the most important information, and move on from there.
- If you expect some action to be taken, end by stating exactly *what* that action should be and *when* it should occur.

The following example illustrates one standard form.

```
Memorandum

Date: May 7, 1988
To: Branch Managers
From: Melinda Russell, Director of Training
Subject: Customer Correspondence Seminars

Any of your personnel who participated in the Customer
Correspondence Seminar should schedule two follow-up
workshops. Please ask all participants to call my office
(ext. 280) during this next week to select dates and times
from the attached list of workshop sessions.

As requested at the last meeting of branch managers, the
workshops will last two hours, rather than three, and are
scheduled for alternating, rather than consecutive, days
to simplify arrangements for released time. Please contact
me personally should any scheduling problems arise.
```

44e. Writing job applications

Although a job application may contain a number of elements (writing samples, portfolios, autobiographical sketches, and so on), the résumé and the letter of application are part of nearly all applications.

1. Writing résumés

Résumé comes from the French word for "summary or epitome." A **résumé** summarizes your experience and qualifications and provides

---

USEFUL READING

Redish, Janice C., Robbin M. Battison, and Edward S. Gold. "Making Information Accessible to Readers." Rpt. in *Writing in Nonacademic Settings*. New York: Guilford, 1985. The authors argue that students need more experience revising organization rather than work on revising at the sentence level.

WRITING JOB APPLICATIONS

support for your letter. A **letter of application** or **cover letter,** on the other hand, emphasizes specific parts of the résumé, telling how your background is suited to a particular job.

An effective résumé is brief—a single, carefully planned page will usually suffice. Begin by brainstorming and taking notes, answering the following questions:

- What skills have you acquired in school, at work, and from your hobbies and interests? Try to find a common thread in all these experiences.
- What can you do well: draw, write, speak other languages, organize, lead, instruct, sell, solve problems, think creatively?
- Are you good at making decisions?
- Are you good at original thinking, at taking the initiative, or at following directions?
- Are you looking for security, excitement, money, travel, power, prestige, or something else?

Research reports that employers usually spend less than sixty seconds scanning a résumé. Remember that they are interested not in what they can do for you, but what you can do for them. They expect a résumé (1) to be typed or printed neatly on clean, high-quality paper; (2) to read easily, with clear headings, adequate spacing, and a conventional format; (3) to provide all the information necessary to make an interviewing decision.

Your résumé may be arranged chronologically or functionally—around your various skills or types of expertise, especially if you have considerable work experience in the field. Either way, you will probably include the following elements:

1. *Name and Address.* Begin with your name, which is usually centered. Supply your home, school, or work addresses, including dates or times you can be reached at each.
2. *Career Objective(s).* List long-range career goals, if appropriate, and specific jobs for which you realistically qualify.
3. *Educational Background.* Start with your most recent school, and list the others in reverse chronological order. Include degrees, diplomas, majors, and special programs or courses that pertain to your field of interest. Consider including your grade-point average if it is high. List notable honors, such as appearing on the Dean's List or receiving scholarships.
4. *Work Experience.* Place any relevant or extensive work experience *before* your education. List your jobs in reverse chronological order,

OPTIONAL EXERCISE

Consider asking students to prepare two résumés rather than one to emphasize how résumés can be changed to suit the position they are applying for. Allow students to select positions they want to apply for, or to choose want advertisements from a newspaper. Ask them to try to select advertisements that vary by duration of employment (full-time versus part-time) or by depth of experience needed (technical knowledge of a computer system versus keyboarding skills). Two contrasting advertisements are listed below:

OFFICE MANAGER
Immediate need—wants to hire this week. Meet and greet patients. Be the one who handles insurance and moderate secretarial duties. Small, stable office with very nice co-workers. Excellent benefits include free parking, health, pension, merit reviews.

CHILD CARE CENTER
Needs mature, energetic individual for part-time position from 2–6 P.M. with pre-school children. HS diploma required. Child care or early childhood development experience preferred.

```
                          Chris Saunders
                          247 Timber Trails
                       Corvallis, Oregon 97330
                          (503) 555-1365


OBJECTIVE:              Public relations position

EDUCATION:              Oregon State University
                        Bachelor of Arts in Journalism, December 1987
                        Major Sequence:  Public Relations
                        Major GPA: 3.0/4.0

COURSES RELATED
TO MAJOR:               Design Graphics
                        Reporter and editor for the campus newspaper


WORK EXPERIENCE:        Supervisor, The Sherwin-Williams Co.,
                        Portland, Oregon, June 1986 to June 1987.
                        Supervised the warehouse operations with
                        eight people working for me.  Ordered
                        supplies and stock with a computer.

                        Inside Sales, The Sherwin-Williams Co.,
                        Eugene, Oregon, summers 1981-1984.  Helped
                        walk-in customers, matched colors of paint,
                        and sometimes stocked shelves.


PROFESSIONAL CLUBS:     PRSS:  Public Relations Student Society
                        of America
                        SPJ/SDX:  Society of Professional Journalists/
                        Sigma Delta Chi


REFERENCES:             Available upon request
```

identifying each, noting dates and names of employers, and describing the nature of your duties. If a job is related to the one for which you are applying, give full details. Otherwise, be brief. Include any military experience in this category.

5. *Personal data.* It is illegal for an employer to discriminate on the basis of sex, religion, race, age, or natural origin. You don't need to provide this information or a photograph.

6. *Personal Interests, Activities, Awards, and Skills.* If space permits, list hobbies, offices held, dates and types of volunteer work, and any recognition for outstanding performance.

7. *References.* Choose references who know your work well and for whom you have worked successfully. Then ask these people if they are willing to serve as a reference. On your résumé, list the name, full title, and address of each reference, or note that your references are available on request.

Look at the résumé on page 688, noting in particular the use of space-saving phrases instead of full sentences.

2. Writing letters of application

A letter of application is the first "version" of you that a prospective employer will see. As your personal ambassador, it should be absolutely flawless—in format, spelling, grammar, punctuation, mechanics, and usage.

You may want to begin by reviewing your résumé, deciding which areas to emphasize and what information to add. Although each letter will take a somewhat different form, most letters of application consist of three main sections.

Introduction. State your reason for writing, and name the exact job for which you are applying. Tell the reader how you learned about the job.

Body. Describe, as specifically as possible, either your educational or work experience, whichever is more relevant.

Conclusion. Emphasize your interest in the position and your willingness to learn. Request an interview at the employer's convenience. Say when you will follow up with a telephone call if you plan to do so.

At this point you are ready for some constructive criticism. Ask friends, colleagues, or instructors to read your letter and suggest improvements. Read the letter aloud, or have someone else read it aloud to you so that you can listen to its rhythm and flow and catch needless repetitions. Then revise your letter carefully, and prepare the final copy, following these guidelines:

- Use high-quality bond paper and a good electric typewriter or word processor with a letter-quality printer.
- Follow a standard business letter format (see 44a).

TEACHING PRACTICE

Point out to your students that there are two kinds of letters of application: invited letters (either personally or through an advertisement), and the prospecting letter. In a prospecting letter the applicant does the following:

Demonstrates she or he is familiar with the company

Expresses a sincere desire to work for that company

Usually states that he or she is willing to travel and relocate

Distinguishes herself or himself from others, perhaps by linking experience to that employer's primary business

Requests an interview

An invited letter identifies where the advertisement and job description appeared, states the applicant's desire to be considered for the position, links the needs of the employer to the qualifications of the applicant (and usually refers to the résumé), and requests an interview.

USEFUL READING

Barnett, Marva T. *Writing for Technicians.* Albany: Delmar, 1982. Section six includes chapters on various kinds of letters, and also discusses résumés and application letters in detail.

WRITING FOR BUSINESS

247 Timber Trails
Corvallis, OR 97330
January 11, 1988

Suzanne Camdon
Director of Public Information
Northern California Bureau of Tourism
1421 Fairfax Street
San Francisco, CA 94120

Dear Ms. Camdon:

In response to the job description sent to the placement
office at Oregon State University, I am applying for the
position of public relations writer.

Having just completed my degree in journalism with a public
relations major, I am ready to begin a writing job. Besides
taking my courses, which included public relations writing
and case studies, I was a reporter for the campus newspaper
for two years and an editor in my senior year. During this
time, I learned to interview and collect information efficiently, to write and effective lead, to develop a story,
to engage a reader's interest, to meet deadlines, and to
accept an editor's revisions. Last year my feature on back-
packing grew into a series of columns, under my byline, on
student travel. These columns, and other writing samples,
are available should you wish to review them.

Given my background, I would very much enjoy a writing
position with the Northern California Bureau of Tourism.
I am available for an interview anytime, and I hope to hear
from you soon.

Sincerely,

Chris Saunders

Enc.   Chris Saunders

- Proofread at least twice—once to make sure no words are left out and to check syntax and once to check spelling and punctuation. Then ask at least one other qualified person to proofread your letter, too.
- Make a copy of the letter for your files.
- Prepare the envelope, and proofread it carefully.

Above is a sample letter of application.

WRITING JOB APPLICATIONS

▌ 3. Writing follow-up letters

Depending on the responses to your application letters, you may need to continue your correspondence with a potential employer. Should more information or materials be requested, send them along with a short letter explaining what you have enclosed. If you are interviewed, a brief thank-you letter, repeating your interest in the job, may work to your advantage. If you are offered a job, you will need to write a letter enthusiastically accepting or tactfully rejecting the offer. On the other hand, if you receive no response to an initial letter, especially to a large company, you may want to draft an inquiry, asking whether the opening remains or whether other jobs are available. You may want to use a similar letter to apply for a different job at a company that especially interests you but has not yet hired you.

Should you want other ideas about effective job-hunting correspondence as well as strategies for developing personal contacts within a business or industry, refer to the job-hunting books available at your college placement office, library, or bookstore. Whatever additional ideas you use, be sure to write clearly and concisely and to follow a standard format as the next letter does.

Dear Ms. Camdon:

Thank you once again for your helpful information about the many services provided by the Northern California Bureau of Tourism. After my interview with you yesterday, I am even more enthusiastic about the prospect of applying my training and experience as a writer on your staff. I hope to hear from you soon.

      Sincerely,

      Chris Saunders

      Chris Saunders

FOR EXAMINING YOUR OWN WRITING

Identify a job for which you think you are qualified and draft a job application letter. Review your letter using the guidelines presented in this chapter, and revise accordingly.

PART ELEVEN

Working with Your Text

45. Writing with a Computer

Imagine this scene: preparing to draft an essay, you begin gathering equipment. First, a quill pen or two. Then pen knives for trimming and sharpening the quill, ink, ink pots, blotting materials and containers, a stack of paper—which is *very* expensive—and perhaps a stationery stand. Finally, you begin. But the ink blots and runs, the quill splits and must be mended, you misspell a word. You will have to start all over again.

Until fairly recently, this scene described the plight of writers and explains why so many tended to concentrate on neatness, on getting things right the first time around. Producing drafts or recopying were very messy, very time-consuming tasks. Then came such advances as ball point pens, typewriters, copy machines, and—most recently and spectacularly—the computer. Today, writers can modify and revise drafts with the touch of a key, can turn out multiple neat, clean copies in a twinkling.

Regardless of its power and efficiency, however, a computer is only a tool. It cannot conduct research, limit a topic, establish a tone of voice, or devise a persuasive argument. Above all, it cannot think (yet). These tasks remain the writer's inescapable responsibility. As a labor saving device, however, the computer can free some of your time and effort—no more mopping up ink or mending pens—so that you can concentrate on the writing process rather than on the mechanics of producing a manuscript. This chapter suggests how to make the computer and three types of writing programs (invention, outlining, and word processing) work for you.

▌ 45a. Using a computer for planning

When it comes to writing, the **computer** is essentially a storage device. It takes the material you enter, manipulates it in certain

695

(BACK)GROUNDING

Computers evolved from the abacus, through mechanical calculators (designed to relieve astronomers from the boredom of extensive computations), analytical engines, and machines for automating the U.S. Census of 1890 into all-electronic machines—the machines that we call computers—designed to solve equations. In the 1960s the concept of *time sharing* (having several individuals use one computer simultaneously) allowed many more people to use these machines; time sharing encouraged people other than computer programmers to use these machines, and word processing became a leading "application" of computer technology. The exponential growth of personal computers owes much to our use of these machines to process texts.

In language classrooms, computers tend to be used in three ways: in tutorial programs that focus on practicing discrete skills, such as grammar drills; in interactive programs that guide students, such as programs that build outlines; and as word processors, with programs for processing, storing, and manipulating text. Most students, instructors, and writers regard the last use as the most important way that computers have changed writing habits. William Zinsser, for example, writes

> The word processor is God's gift, or at least science's gift, to the tinkerers and the refiners and the neatness freaks. For me it was obviously the perfect new toy. I began playing on page 1—editing, cutting and revising—and have been on a rewriting high ever since. The burden of the years has been lifted.

USEFUL READING

Schwartz, Helen J., and Lillian S. Bridwell-Bowles. "A Selected Bibliography on Computers in Composition: An Update." *CCC* 38 (1987): 453–57. This article is a useful, annotated bibliography of computer programs for writing classes that extends the earlier one—*CCC* 35 (1984): 71–77.

Selfe, Cynthia L. *Computer-Assisted Instruction in Composition: Create Your Own*. Urbana: NCTE, 1986. The "Introduction" discusses the history, possibilities, and limitations of computers in the classroom.

ways, and recalls it quickly. The computer cannot create your text, but it can, with appropriate software, help you plan material for an essay.

1. Using planning programs

Some specially designed **planning programs** can help you with preliminary writing tasks by asking a series of questions and recording your responses. After the questioning session, you can print your answers and use them to guide your composing. Some writers find planning programs helpful, but it is important to remember that the program can only *help* you think, not think for you.

2. Planning with a word processor

If you do not have access to a planning program, you can use your word processor (see 45c) to explore your topic as you would on paper, a technique that is especially helpful if you are accustomed to writing on a keyboard. You can key in notes, freewrite, make lists, write a series of loops, and answer questions (see 2e); you can then store all of these ideas in safe, yet easily accessible **files** on your data disk. By typing the name you have given that file, you return it to the screen and can consult, revise, and even print out **hard copy** if you want to work on it away from the computer, or if you are required to turn in all parts of your writing process.

45b. Using a computer for organizing and outlining

Outlining is an important step in organizing an essay, but it is sometimes difficult to do on paper. By its very nature, planning is a dynamic process, which changes as your ideas mature; often, however, as soon as you write an outline, it seems fixed and hard to change. For this reason, many writers find it convenient to outline with the help of a computer, since they can rearrange headings and subheadings freely.

1. Using outlining programs

Several commercial outlining or "idea-processing" programs can help you create a short, simple outline and gradually expand it into a full, multi-level sentence outline. You can experiment with your ideas,

---

OPTIONAL EXERCISE

If students have access to a planning program, have them try a session of at least twenty minutes on a topic they have been assigned. If no such program is available, have them try responding to a set of questions for exploring ideas on a word processor. Print the results and examine them for a potential topic or thesis.

OPTIONAL EXERCISE

If your students have access to an outlining program (or a word processing program that generates outlines), ask them to use the computer to develop an outline using the computer. Print the outline in two different forms, using two different organizational strategies.

USEFUL READING

Halpern, Jeanne, and Sarah Liggett. *Computers & Composing: How the New Technologies are Changing Writing.* Carbondale, IL: Southern Illinois UP, 1984. See Chapter Three, "Teachers Can Use Research about the New Systems in Freshman and Advanced Composition Courses."

Phillips, Martin. "CALL [computer assisted language learning] in its educational context." Rpt. in *Computers in English Language Teaching and Research.* London: Longman, 1986. Phillips discusses some ways computers challenge present theories of how we organize learning.

expanding a section of the outline by filling in more sub-levels; or you can condense a section by removing various levels from the screen until you wish to call them up again. Some word-processing programs also have this capability (see 45c).

2. Outlining with a word processor

If you do not have access to an outlining program, you can use word-processing software in much the same way, although it is less flexible. Start by making a list of the main topics you want to cover in your essay, and number them with roman numerals (I, II, III, and so on). Add subtopics as they occur to you, labeling subheadings with letters, the next level down with numbers, and so on (see 40b). Then use the **block insert** and **move** commands (see 45c2) to add, reorganize, or renumber subheadings. With these functions, you can easily move, add, or delete topics, and consider various arrangements of topics.

After completing an outline, you can print it out and examine it at leisure. You may find it helpful to work from hard copy, or printed version, of your outline when you begin to draft your essay. As new ideas come to mind, you can pencil them in. And, of course, you can always access your outline file, make your changes, and print out updated hard copy.

45c. Using the computer for drafting and revising

Word-processing programs, which allow you to enter and edit text in the computer, are most commonly used for drafting, revising, and editing. Ranging from simple data-entry programs to complex systems that can check spelling, display thesaurus entries, and search the text for specific words, word-processing software allows you to manipulate and edit text you might otherwise settle for in its first typed version.

Knowing basic word-processing functions

All good word-processing programs perform the same basic tasks. With them, you can write continuously without hitting a carriage return: the program automatically "wraps" from one line to another. With a single key (often called a **function key**), you can add, delete, or change letters, sentences, and entire paragraphs; move text from one page to another; and even define a block of text you've already typed

TEACHING PRACTICE
To help students adjust to using a computer, early in the term concentrate on making learning relaxed, not rushed; require that students write, but ask for informal rather than evaluated assignments. In your teaching, do not rely on a computer manual and program to present information—teach in person. To help students adjust to the machines, provide simple, straightforward handouts so that students can find technical answers easily. Keep working sessions on the computer brief and focused at the very start of the term so that students don't get frustrated. Finally, make sure that students know how to handle disks safely (don't remove them while the disk drive is operating) and that students save their files frequently.

USEFUL READING

Daiute, Colette. *Writing and Computers*. Reading: Addison-Wesley, 1985. See "Writers in College and Graduate School" for a discussion of how computers can be used in freshman composition.

Zinsser, William. *Writing with a Word Processor*. New York: Harper, 1973. See Chapters Sixteen and Seventeen for a description of how word processors affect the writing process.

WRITERS ON WRITING

In subtle, but important ways, computer conferences can make traditional composition classrooms more humane and egalitarian places than they have formerly been. Teachers can use these conferences to increase dialectic and dialogic exchanges in a forum under students' own control, increase students' egalitarian participation in such intellectual exchanges, accommodate a multiplicity of interpretive perspectives, and encourage both collaborative and divergent involvement in discourse production.

—CYNTHIA L. SELFE

and ask the computer to underline it or place it in bold letters. After completing a draft, you can store the text on a disk and work with it another time, or print a copy to see how the text looks on paper. Unlike typewriters, word processors allow you to rewrite, edit, and correct a draft without having to retype the entire document—whether you edit hard copy and then make your changes on screen or revise directly on the screen (see 45c3).

Learning the capabilities of your word processor

Many students learn to execute only the basic word-processing commands. Most systems, however, perform many other functions that further simplify your work as a writer. Some word-processing software, for example, can automatically format footnotes or endnotes. Some can generate tables of contents and indexes. Some have a built-in outlining feature similar to the programs described in 44b. While it may take a bit more of your time, investigating the capabilities of your program or those programs available to you on campus can make your writing process more efficient.

Using The St. Martin's Hotline

Accompanying this text is a software package that provides an on-line, abbreviated version of *The St. Martin's Handbook*, called *The St. Martin's Hotline*. Compatible with most word-processing systems, this program is loaded in conjunction with your writing program and "pops up" rules of grammar, punctuation, and style. Should you need to consult the handbook while you are writing, you need only press the "hot key" (**control-home**), and you are presented on the screen with lists (**menus**) of the handbook entries available to you. These lists are arranged hierarchically: each entry you select calls up a more specific list, until you have reached the particular entry, or rule, that you are looking for.

For instance, if you are puzzled about a particular use of the comma in your draft, you can immediately access the main menu, select *Punctuation*, then *Using commas*, and then *Following introductory elements*. Superimposed on your text will be the rule for using commas after introductory elements. After reading the rule, you can then return to your text, make any necessary changes, and proceed with your writing. You can also access the rule you need by typing in key words, in this case *comma* or *introductory element*. The *Hotline* should

USEFUL READING

Nancarrow, Paula, Donald Ross, and Lillian Bridwell. *Word Processors and the Writing Process.* Westport, CT: Greenwood, 1984. An excellent annotated bibliography of research on computers and composition.

Schwartz, Helen J. "Monsters and Mentors: Computer Applications for Humanistic Education." *College English* 44 (1982): 141–52. This article provides guidance on how to use computers to develop ideas and work collaboratively.

USING THE COMPUTER FOR DRAFTING AND REVISING   *com* 45c

be especially helpful as you revise (see 45c2); you may even want to wait until you have completed a draft before accessing your pop-up handbook so as not to lose momentum.

1. Drafting on a computer

Drafting on a computer is much like writing on paper, except that it is easier to make changes—so easy, in fact, that you may be tempted to spend too much time correcting errors during your early drafting. Because the text that appears on the screen and on the printout is neat and clean, mistakes are not hidden in the congenial messiness of a handwritten draft and tend to stand out more glaringly than they would in handwriting. Try not to interrupt your momentum and train of thought, however, by pausing frequently to correct mistakes. Concentrate first on setting down all your ideas, and second on revising and editing.

Once you become comfortable, drafting on a computer is so fast that you may find your eyes and mind getting tired. If so, stop for a moment, relax, and then return to the task. Many writers find that frequent short breaks help them work more efficiently at the computer.

Saving your text

Just as you can walk away from your handwritten or typewritten draft, you can let your word processed draft rest while you relax and revise a bit in your head. But before you step away from the computer or turn the machine off, you must save your text, using the **save** command. In fact, it is a good idea to save your text even after every few new paragraphs. The few seconds it takes you to save your text may save you hours of time and grief in the event of a power failure. Similarly, you should make a **back up copy** of the contents of your disk on another disk after each session at the computer. This way, should your working disk somehow get damaged, you will have another copy of your work.

It is also a good idea to print out your work at the end of each session. By looking over a printout of what you have written so far, you may discover the next point you should discuss or a different organization—ideas that didn't occur to you when you were looking at one page at a time on the screen. When you return to the computer you can incorporate these ideas and have all your changes in one place rather than on numerous handwritten inserts.

WRITING TOGETHER

Ask your students to draft a short essay on a computer, perhaps on the topic they outlined using the computer. As part of the assignment, have them keep notes, perhaps in their writing logs, describing how they spent their time writing. In class, have them compare experiences with each other. When they share experiences, encourage them to help solve technical difficulties (such as file saving) and direct discussion to how the computer directs or changes the way they write.

OPTIONAL EXERCISE

Ask students to revise the draft they created for the *Writing Together* exercise earlier in this chapter. Encourage them to use the insert, delete, and move commands. When they have finished, ask them to print the revised version and compare it with the original draft. In a class discussion, address the following questions: Have they changed their revision practices? Do they make more revisions? Do they feel their papers are better because they revised on a computer?

WRITERS ON WRITING

The computer is not, as some seem to think it is, an impartial 'delivery system,' that is, simply a medium which transmits a message without affecting it. On the contrary, the new technology has profound implications. . . . It brings into question quite fundamental notions such as the nature of the curriculum, the concept of the classroom itself, the locus of control over the learning process as well as the status of materials, the nature of language-training methodology, the role of the teacher and of teacher training.

—MARTIN PHILLIPS

TEACHING PRACTICE

Computers do not evaluate or respond to student writing well, but they can help students revise much more extensively, thoroughly, and quickly than traditional pen and paper technology. Before the papers pile up on your desk, consider structuring response to student writing in your class using these principles:

1. Establish peer-response groups to encourage students to evaluate each other, write together, and support each other.
2. Respond as a reader, rather than an evaluator or "instructor," to early drafts: don't worry about marking every error early in the drafting process.
3. Treat writing as a process, not a series of products (that is, do not treat each draft as a final product) that are to be evaluated—focus on discovery and change in the drafts, not correctness.

2. Revising on a computer

Some of the basic word-processing functions are especially helpful for revision: inserting, deleting, and moving. These functions allow you to reshape your text any number of times until you are completely satisfied with it.

Inserting text

The **insert** function found in most word-processing programs allows you to supply details, supporting evidence, transitional words and sentences, and other material without retyping the entire draft. With this function, added copy merely pushes apart the words and sentences around it, making a place for itself automatically.

Deleting text

When you **delete** text, the rest of the document closes around it so that only the desired copy remains. In some programs, the text is not truly erased, but rather relocated into a temporary memory, off the screen, from which it can be restored on command. If yours does not have this feature, be sure that you really do not want the text you are deleting. Should you want to replace the deleted copy, you must type it again. If you are at all unsure about whether you want to delete the text permanently, you may want to move the text temporarily.

Moving text

The **move** function permits you to move a block of text—a sentence, a paragraph, or an entire page—from one place in the essay to another. Because the original order is easily restored, this feature enables you to experiment with the organization of your draft without any retyping. You can even save the rearranged version under a new file name, print both the new file and the original one, and compare them to see which is more effective.

Revising from hard copy

Because you can print out a neat copy of your essay easily and often, you should use the opportunity to evaluate it often. After you have completed the first draft of your essay, print it out, double-spaced. Remember that the computer-printed draft needs just as much revision as a handwritten or typed draft. You need to scrutinize the printout carefully and reconsider all the decisions you made about content,

USING THE COMPUTER FOR DRAFTING AND REVISING 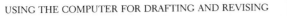 com 45c

organization, supporting evidence, transitions, sentence structure, and diction. Working from a clean, legible draft simplifies this task, for you can concentrate on what the paper says, not on how it looks. Revising from hard copy is particularly helpful, for it allows you to mark up the draft, insert notes, and see the entire essay spread out before you.

After marking up hard copy, you can then return to the screen and enter your revisions, taking advantage of the word processor's manipulation commands. You will probably want to save your printed drafts, in case your instructor asks you to turn in your preliminary work in addition to your final draft.

Getting responses to your draft

Another advantage to printing out your early drafts is that you can easily print out several copies, distribute them to some of your classmates, and receive a number of responses at the same time.

▌ 3. Editing and proofreading on a computer

Once you have revised your draft and are ready to edit and proofread, the speed and thoroughness with which computers operate can be a great advantage to you, especially through the tasks performed by the *search* and *search and replace* commands. In addition, a spell checker can ease your task of proofreading for misspelled words.

Searching text

The **search** command enables you to identify a character or string of characters, such as a mark of punctuation, a word, or several words. The program then scans the entire text, stopping every time it finds the designated characters, which you can then change or correct. For example, if you tend to place a comma before the word *and*, even when one is not called for, you can execute the search command and enter *and*. The screen will highlight each place *and* appears. You can then check to see if it follows a comma, and then decide whether the use is correct.

Replacing text

The **search and replace** command not only locates a character or string, but also replaces it automatically with another. If you find, for instance, that you have been writing *affect* for *effect*, you can use the search and replace command to find every occurrence of the word

WRITERS ON WRITING

The electronic word is going to revolutionize not only prose revision but prose itself, how we write it, read it, and theorize about it. Even in a short, practical, hands-on manual like this one [*Revising Prose*, 2nd ed.], we'll have to think for a moment about this revolution, simply because it has so transformed the subject that anyone who writes must know what has happened. And a lot more has happened than a mere change of means, from ink to electron.

—RICHARD LANHAM

OPTIONAL EXERCISE

Ask your students to print out a clean copy of the paper they revised for the last *Optional Exercise*. Then ask them to edit and proofread hard copy. Discuss any changes they may notice between revising on screen and on paper, and then have them compare their third draft with their first and second drafts by marking passages they changed on each draft. Discuss the sorts of changes they have made and ask each student to evaluate their own work—have the changes made their work better?

WRITERS ON WRITING

I wondered how this [impersonal, on-line editing] would affect the subtle relationship between writers and editors. I thought of all the times when a *Herald Tribune* editor brought over a piece of my copy to discuss changes he had made or wanted to make, and of all the times when I—as an editor or a teacher—had gone over my changes with a young writer or a student. To be apprenticed to a good editor is the best way to learn how to write. What would happen when all the editing was done on film by successive editors? Who would know who had done what? Who would remember what the original copy said? And who would be accountable for what had been changed?

—WILLIAM ZINSSER

USEFUL READING

Lanham, Richard. *Revising Prose*. New York: Macmillan, 1987. See Chapter Six, "Prose Composition and the Personal Computer," for some interesting experiments in typography.

affect and check to see whether it should really be *effect*. If you want to make the change, a keystroke will allow the computer to replace *affect* with *effect*. With search and replace you can also save time by abbreviating a long title or a phrase that occurs repeatedly in your paper: keyboard the abbreviation while drafting; after finishing the draft, use the search and replace command to find the abbreviation and replace it with the full word or phrase.

Using a spell checker

Spell checkers may be an integral part of your word-processing software; if not, they are available as separate add-on programs. Both work similarly: the program examines all the words in the text and tries to match each one against a word in its memory. If it cannot find a match, the program alerts you to the problem and you must examine the word yourself. Some spell checkers work as you type: the computer buzzes if you type a word it does not recognize. Others you must institute yourself after you have finished typing. A good spell checker not only has a large standard dictionary of words, which you can add to, but also helps you correct errors by displaying a choice of words similar to the one it cannot match. If the program does not have a correction feature, look up the word in a printed dictionary.

No matter how sophisticated the spell checker may be, the full responsibility of correction rests on you. If the program finds a word it cannot match in its memory, there may be several reasons. The word may in fact be misspelled, or it may not be in the program's dictionary. Many errors do not show up in a spell checker because the word, though incorrect in context, is nevertheless a recognizable English word: you may have used a permissible variant spelling, for example, *judgement* instead of *judgment*. The program also cannot tell that you meant to use *their* instead of *there*, *thorough* instead of *through*, or *either* instead of *ether*. Spell checkers can alert you to some misspellings and typographical mistakes, but only your own vigilance can produce an error-free paper.

Editing from hard copy

Even after using a spell checker and editing and proofreading on the screen, you should print out your essay and proofread hard copy meticulously. You may overlook errors on the screen (and so may your spell checker) that you may catch on hard copy. Furthermore, you can share your hard copy with classmates and have them check it over also.

USING THE COMPUTER FOR DRAFTING AND REVISING

Once you have found and marked all errors and changes on the printed copy, correct them on the screen; then you can print a final copy (see 45c4).

Using a text-analysis program

Text-analysis programs are designed to identify a variety of patterns in sentences. Some programs look for punctuation errors; others look at sentence length, and some even attempt to identify wordy or vague sentences. Some point out sentence fragments; still others search out passive constructions.

To use a text-analysis program, you must have a finished document to feed through the text analyzer. The program then creates a file of comments on your document. Depending upon the capabilities of your particular program, it will isolate long sentences; too frequent use of the verb *be* and other weak constructions; the passive voice; colloquialisms; and so on.

Text-analysis software is restricted, however, by the limited memory of personal computers. A computer is only a mechanism: its judgments are relatively simplistic and may even be wrong; it is not sophisticated enough to judge shades of meaning, tone, the effect of a passage on its intended audience, or other stylistic considerations that only you, the writer, can resolve. If you experiment with a text-analysis program, act on its comments only when your own judgment tells you that they are valid.

4. Formatting and printing on a computer

Formatting text

Before you print out your final draft, you will want to format it, or lay it out on the page. Your word-processing program enables you to specify the number of characters per inch, spaces per line, lines per page, justified (even) or ragged margins, and even fonts. Be conservative in the way you use different fonts, however; a mixture of underlining, boldface, and different size type can be dizzying if overdone. Be sure that whatever specifications you choose are in accordance with the style of your discipline and meet with your instructor's expectations.

Printing text

If your printer does not have **letter-quality** (fully formed letters) **capacity,** ask your instructor if he or she will accept **dot-matrix** (letters formed by lines of dots) **printing.** (You may even want to show your instructor a sample of the printing.) If you are printing on tractor-fed paper, always tear off the row of holes along the sides and separate the pages before turning in the paper.

FOR EXAMINING YOUR OWN USE OF COMPUTERS IN WRITING

Take the time to reflect on your use of technology in writing. If you do not yet use a computer/word processor, spend five minutes or so writing a list of those things a computer might help with in your writing. If you are using a computer, spend some time now analyzing how efficient that use is. What does the computer help most with in your writing? What is it the least help with? In what ways has the use of a computer changed or modified the way you go about writing an essay? What would you most like to improve about your ability to use the computer?

46. Preparing Your Manuscript

One of the most satisfying parts of the writing process is the preparation of your final manuscript. This step presents your work in a clean, neat, easy-to-read package, one you are happy to identify as your own.

46a. Following guidelines

Follow your instructor's guidelines carefully, and ask for more information if these are not clear to you. Most instructors expect type-written manuscripts, but some may accept neat, legible handwritten papers.

1. Typing your manuscript

A typewritten manuscript is far easier to read than a handwritten one. You should, therefore, type or print out a word-processed paper whenever possible, even if your instructor does not require doing so.

Selecting paper

Type or print your paper on medium-grade 8½″ × 11″ bond paper. Do not use legal-sized paper (8½″ × 14″), notebook paper, or mismatched, odd-sized sheets.

Onionskin or "erasable" paper is usually unacceptable because it is difficult for your instructor to write on. If you must use erasable paper, submit a photographic copy of your finished paper.

Select an appropriate quality of paper if you use a computer printer. Inexpensive grades are often too flimsy, and many leave stubs when the sheets are separated and the tractor holes are torn off. (Always

(BACK)GROUNDING

When addressing an audience, a speaker's presence is judged visually and aurally. The speaker's appearance, tone of voice, the degree to which he or she meets the audience's eyes, all create an impression. Our rhetorical sense tells us that we ought to dress appropriately when we go before a committee to be interviewed for a scholarship. Classical rhetoricians viewed this aspect of our behavior as one aspect of rhetoric's five arts or canons, *actio*, which we translate today as "delivery."

In classical rhetoric, *actio* referred exclusively to the delivery of a speech to an audience. In our literate culture today, however, rhetoric must also include written communications, where the audience is removed from the writer's immediate proximity. The writer has a different set of cues than the speaker on which to rely to get his or her image across to the reader. The primary cues, of course, must come from the writing itself: what it says, how it presents the writer's ideas and feelings, how it reflects him or her. But the physical appearance of the message also creates an impression. A manuscript that is carelessly typed on paper that is difficult to read gives the impression of someone who cares little if the reader really reads his or her work. Manuscript preparation, then, is another aspect of *ethos*, the persuasive appeal of the character of the writer. Seen in this light, its importance cannot be denied.

705

USEFUL READING

Connors, Robert J. "*Actio*: A Rhetoric of Manuscripts." *Rhetoric Review* 2 (September 1983): 64–73. Connors equates manuscript preparation with the last of the five lesser arts or canons of rhetoric. He discusses the rhetorical effects of typefaces, paper, and format.

TEACHING PRACTICE

It would be easy to neglect manuscript preparation. Yet, *actio* can be an important asset to your students' later writing. You should consider the importance of such preparation to your own writing and treat your students' manuscript preparation in the same way. Also, you need to make very clear your requirements concerning manuscript preparation—perhaps even spell them out in your syllabus.

WRITERS ON WRITING

I believe that composing on the typewriter has probably done more than anything else to deteriorate English prose.

—EDMUND WILSON

Some authors type their works, but I cannot do that. Writing is tied up with the hand, almost with a special nerve.

—GRAHAM GREENE

I write longhand and I type and I rewrite on typed pages.

—JOSEPH HELLER

I wrote in longhand at first, but I've lost it. I use two fingers on the typewriter.

—DOROTHY PARKER

tear computer-printed pages apart, and remove the tractor holes from the sides.)

Selecting typeface

Use a standard typeface, either **pica** (10-point) or **elite** (12-point). Because special typefaces, such as simulated script, are hard to read, avoid using them.

If you use a computer, a letter-quality printer is best. Check with your instructor before using a dot-matrix printer because some readers strongly object to reading low-quality dot-matrix print.

2. Handwriting your manuscript

If for some reason you cannot type your manuscript, write as clearly and legibly as you can, forming each word with care. Handwritten papers tend to contain more mechanical errors than do typed papers because they are more difficult to proofread. Thus you should devote extra care to the actual writing.

Selecting paper

Use white, ruled, 8½″ × 11″ loose-leaf notebook paper. Do not use spiral notebook paper, unlined paper, or paper with very narrow lines. Write on only one side of each piece of paper; ask your instructor whether you should write on every other line.

Selecting ink

Write neatly in dark blue or black ink, using a medium- or fine-point pen. Do not use pencil; it is hard to read and smears.

3. Positioning title and page numbers

The styles recommended for papers written in certain disciplines (MLA for many of the humanities; APA for many of the social sciences) specify the format for the title page. (See pp. 589 and 600 for examples of title pages for each style.) If your instructor does not specify a style, follow the standard format for the first page of a typed paper. One inch down from the top of the paper, type your name at the left margin, followed by the course number, your instructor's name, and the date. Double-space each line as well as your title, which is centered. Capitalize each major word in the title, but don't underline it or enclose it in quotation marks. If the title is very long, divide it into two double-

USING A READABLE PAGE FORMAT   *ms* 46b

spaced lines, and center each one. Put four spaces between the title and the first line of the essay.

If your essay is longer than two pages, number each page consecutively, beginning with the first page. Place page numbers in the upper right-hand corner, one-half inch from the top and flush with the right-hand margin. Use Arabic numerals, and do not use periods, slash marks, or parentheses with the page numbers. Type your name before each page number in case some of the pages are misplaced.

4. Including documentation and notes

Credit any sources you researched in writing your essay according to the style required by your instructor. (See Chapter 41 for examples of common documentation and note formats.)

46b. Using a readable page format

If your instructor asks you to follow a specific style manual in writing and preparing your paper, consult it for more specific details about format. Otherwise, use the following format.

Setting margins

White space helps readers understand how a page is set up. Standard guidelines call for one-inch margins top and bottom, left and right. (More generous margins, even one and one-half inches, make the page easier to read.) Begin each new page by measuring down one inch from the top of the paper.

Indenting paragraphs

Indent each new paragraph five spaces from the left margin. Do *not* leave an extra double-space between paragraphs. If you have only one line left at the bottom of a page, go to a new page to begin a new paragraph.

Double-spacing

Papers for college courses should be double-spaced unless you are specifically asked to do otherwise. Double-spaced type is much easier to read and proofread, and it leaves room for your instructor to make comments and suggestions. (See 31a1 for information about inserting long quotations.)

I publish a piece in order to kill it, so that I won't have to fool around with it any longer.

—WILLIAM GASS

Publication is a self-invasion of privacy.

—MARSHALL MCLUHAN

If you do not write for publication, there is little point in writing at all.

—GEORGE BERNARD SHAW

My schedule is flexible, but I am rather particular about my instruments: lined Bristol cards and well sharpened, not too hard, pencils capped with erasers.

—VLADIMIR NABOKOV

I revise the manuscript till I can't read it any longer, then I get somebody to type it. Then I revise the typing. Then it's retyped again. Then there's a third typing, which is the final one. Nothing should then remain that offends the eye.

—ROBERT GRAVES

(BACK)GROUNDING

Beyond the questions of unity, coherence, and paragraph development in general, paragraph breaks are also an element of *actio*. Fowler writes, "Paragraphing is also a matter of the eye. A reader will address himself more readily to his task if he sees from the start that he will have breathing-spaces from time to time than if what is before him looks like a marathon course" (434–35).

USEFUL READING

Fowler, H. W. A *Dictionary of Modern English Usage*. 2d ed. Rev. and ed. Sir Ernest Gowers. New York: Oxford UP, 1965. Fowler gives priority to the paragraph as "a unit of thought." But he does note the paragraph as an element of *actio*, as the quotation above indicates.

WRITING TOGETHER

Before allowing your students to hand in the final drafts of their papers, have them exchange these drafts for one final peer response, focusing purely on *actio*. In order to ensure that your students bring in a final typed draft, don't tell them ahead of time. Provide each student with a pencil and eraser. Proofreading marks should be made in pencil lightly so that the author of the paper can erase them, if he or she chooses. It is important that your students realize that making or not making the suggested corrections is their choice. If a student finds substantial changes need to be made, then he or she should be permitted to turn the paper in the next day.

TEACHING PRACTICE

Most style manuals agree that writers can make corrections by hand onto a manuscript—if they use discretion. Such corrections must go above the line. This "rule" comes from publishers who reserve margins for proofreaders' remarks and symbols. However, you might consider allowing your students to make such changes, as if they themselves were proofreaders, thus giving them experience with proofreaders' marks. *The MLA Style Manual* lists ways of correcting manuscripts that are *unacceptable* to publishers and typesetters, which you may wish to pass on to your students:

> Corrections made on the reverse of pages
> Corrections made in the margins
> Corrections on slips attached to pages
> Corrections pasted to the bottoms of pages
> Directions to insert a passage from another page
> Illegible corrections
> Drawing lines across the face of the text to indicate placement of a change.

Binding your manuscript

Unless your instructor asks you to use a binder, a folder, or staples, use only a paper clip to secure the pages of your paper.

▌46c. Putting your best product forward

Your final copy deserves care; proofread and correct it meticulously. A computer facilitates this job, allowing you to proofread from hard copy or on the screen, make changes, and then print out a clean draft. If you are typing your paper, however, try to make corrections as you go along, using white correction fluid or lift-off tape if your typewriter has a self-correcting mechanism. After you finish typing, go back and proofread each page. If possible, set the manuscript aside and look at it later with fresh eyes.

Correct minor typographical errors by applying correction fluid and retyping. If there is not enough room for the correction, delete the error with a single pen stroke. Then add the correction above the line, marking where it belongs with a caret (∧).

> What Meredith, or any author of a sonnet ∧ tries to do, *sequence*
> is to create a whole world of feelings.

If you must make more than two or three such corrections on a page, retype the page. Add any brackets, accent marks, or other symbols neatly in ink if they are not on your keyboard.

Finally, handle the finished product carefully, following those well-known directions: *do not fold, mutilate, or spindle.*

FOR EXAMINING YOUR OWN WRITING

Take a critical look at an essay you have just finished or have recently submitted. Using the guidelines presented in this chapter, assess your use of format and typing conventions. Note particularly those that you have not generally followed or those that are unfamiliar to you. Then annotate your essay, making corrections or noting the appropriate conventions in the margins or above the lines. Keep this annotated essay with your writing log, or make an entry, noting which conventions you need to check carefully when you next begin preparing a manuscript.

USEFUL READING

Achtert, Walter S., and Joseph Gibaldi. *The MLA Handbook for Writers of Research Papers.* 3rd. ed. New York: The Mod. Lang. Assoc., 1985.

The Chicago Manual of Style. 13th ed. Chicago: U of Chicago P, 1982. Two of the best and most commonly used style manuals.

Glossaries

Glossary of Grammatical Terms
Glossary of Usage

Glossary of Grammatical Terms

absolute phrase   See *phrase*.

abstract noun   See *noun*.

acronym   A word formed from the first letters of several words, such as *RADAR* for *radio detecting and ranging*.

active voice   See *voice*.

adjective   A word that modifies, quantifies, identifies, or describes a word or words acting as a noun. An **attributive** adjective precedes and a **predicative** adjective follows the noun or pronoun that it modifies (*a good book, the book is good*). Of the overlapping types of adjectives, **descriptive adjectives** identify a quality that is *common*, such as a type, color, or weight (*research paper, yellow paper, heavy paper*) or *proper*, derived from a proper noun (*English history, Jacobean drama, Homeric epic*). **Demonstrative adjectives** (*this, that, these,* and *those*) point out words acting as nouns (*this paper, those* papers). **Indefinite adjectives** define the specificity of the words they modify (*some research, any research, such research*). **Relative adjectives** qualify words bound directly to a modifying clause (*I know which research is yours*). **Interrogative adjectives** ask questions about the words they modify (*Whose research is finished? What research is she doing? Which research is in progress?*). **Limiting adjectives** are the articles *a, an,* and *the*. **Numerical adjectives** modify words with *cardinal* or *ordinal* numbers (*two girls in their tenth year*). **Participial adjectives** are verbals that act as adjectives (*a waiting car, a damaged package*). **Possessive adjectives** include *my, your, his, her, its, one's, our, your, their* (*her research, our research*) as well as proper possessives formed by adding an *-'s* to a proper noun (*Einstein's research, America's coastline*). See 6b4, 10a, 10b, and 10d.

adjective clause   See *clause*.

adjective forms   Changes in an adjective from the **positive** (simply *tall, good*) to **comparative** (comparing two—*taller, better*) or the **superlative** (comparing more than two—*tallest, best*). Short regular adjectives (*tall*) just add *-er* and

711

-est, but irregular adjectives (*good*) do not follow this pattern. Most longer adjectives form the comparative by adding *more* or *less* (*more beautiful, less beautiful*) and the superlative by adding *most* and *least* (*most beautiful, least beautiful*). Some adjectives (*only, forty*) do not change form.

adverb   A word that qualifies, modifies, limits, or defines a verb, an adjective, another adverb, or a clause, frequently answering the questions *where?, when?, how?, why?, to what extent?,* or *under what conditions?* Adverbs derived from adjectives and nouns commonly end in the suffix *-ly. She will <u>soon</u> travel <u>south</u> and <u>probably</u> visit her <u>very</u> favorite sister.* See also *conjunction.* See 6b5, 10c, and 10d.

adverb clause   See *clause.*

adverb forms   Changes in an adverb from the **positive** (simply *eagerly*) to the **comparative** (comparing two—*more eagerly*) or the **superlative** (comparing more than two—*most eagerly*). The forms of some adverbs and adjectives are identical (*fast, faster, fastest; little, less, least*). Most adverbs, however, add *more* or *less* in the comparative and *most* or *least* in the superlative (*quickly, more quickly, most quickly*).

agreement   The correspondence of a pronoun with its antecedent in person, number, and gender or of a verb with its subject in person and number. *Tina sings, and her fans go wild; the band members play, and the crowd goes wild.* See also *antecedent, gender, number, person.* See Chapter 9.

antecedent   A specific noun which a pronoun replaces and to which it refers. The two must agree in person, number, and gender. *<u>Fred Astaire</u> moved <u>his</u> feet as no else has.* The antecedent can sometimes follow the pronoun that refers to it. *Moving <u>his</u> feet as no one else has, <u>Fred Astaire</u> was a singular dancer.* See 6b3, 11a, and 11b.

appositive   One noun or noun phrase that parallels another, illuminating it with additional information. *Magic Johnson, <u>the best player in the NBA</u>, scored thirty-one points. The cruelest month, <u>April</u>, is my favorite.* See 6c3 and 27c3.

article   *A, an,* or *the,* the most common adjectives. *A* is used before consonants, *an* before vowels. Both are **indefinite** and do not specifically identify the nouns they modify. *<u>A</u> strange feeling came over me as <u>an</u> awful specter arose. The* is **definite** or specific. *<u>The</u> awful figure of my long-lost grandfather stood before me.*

auxiliary verb   A verb that combines with the base form or with the present or past participle of a main verb to form a verb phrase and to determine tense. The **primary** auxiliaries (*do, have, be*) have different forms and make verb phrases that are reasonably straightforward in terms of tense and mood (*I <u>did</u> think; I <u>had</u> thought; I <u>am</u> thinking*). **Modal** auxiliaries such as *can, may, shall, will, could, might, should, would,* and *ought* [*to*] have only one form and show

712

possibility, necessity, obligation, ability, capability, and so on. Some modals form uncomplicated verb phrases (*I shall (will) think*), but others achieve subtle variations in tense and mood (*I should have agreed with you had I not known better*). See 6b1 and 8a.

cardinal number A simple number that answers the question *how many?*—*seven, one hundred fifty*. Distinguished from *ordinal number*.

case The form of a noun or pronoun that reflects its grammatical role in a sentence. Nouns and indefinite pronouns can be **subjective, possessive,** or **objective**, but they change form only in the possessive case. *The dog* (subjective) *barked. The dog's* (possessive) *tail wagged. The mail carrier called the dog* (objective). The personal pronouns *I, he, she, we,* and *they,* as well as the relative or interrogative pronoun *who,* change form in all three cases. *We* (subjective) *will take the train to Chicago. Our* (possessive) *trip will last a week. Dr. Baker will meet us* (objective) *at the station.* See also *person; pronoun.* See Chapter 7.

clause A word cluster containing a subject and a predicate. An **independent** clause can stand alone as a sentence. *The car hit the tree.* A **dependent clause,** as the name suggests, is subordinate to an independent clause, linked to it by a subordinating conjunction or a relative pronoun. The dependent clause can function as an adjective, an adverb, or a noun. *The car hit the tree that stood at the edge of the edge of the road* (adjective clause). *The car, when it went out of control, hit the tree* (adverb clause). *The car hit what grew at the side of the road* (noun clause). See also *nonrestrictive element, restrictive element.* See 6c4.

collective noun See *noun.*

comma splice An error resulting from joining two independent clauses with only a comma. See Chapter 13 for ways of revising comma splices.

common noun See *noun.*

comparative See *adjective forms, adverb forms.*

complement A word or group of words completing the predicate in a sentence. A **subject complement** follows a linking verb and renames or describes the subject. It can be a **predicate noun** (*Anorexia is an illness.*) or a predicate adjective (*Karen Carpenter was anorexic.*). An object complement renames or describes a direct object (*We considered her a baby and her behavior infantile.*) See 6c2.

complete predicate See *predicate.*

complete subject See *subject.*

complex sentence See *sentence.*

compound adjective A combination of words (of whatever parts of speech)

713

that function as a single adjectival unit (*blue-green* sea, *ten-story* building, *get-tough* policy, *supply side* economics, *north by northwest* journey). Most, but not all, compound adjectives use hyphens to separate their individual elements.

compound-complex sentence   See *sentence*.

compound noun   A combination of words forming a unit that can function as a single noun (*go-getter, in-law, Johnny-on-the-spot, oil well, southeast*).

compound predicate   See *predicate*.

compound sentence   See *sentence*.

compound subject   See *subject*.

concrete noun   See *noun*.

conjunction   A word or words that join words, phrases, clauses, or sentences. A *coordinating conjunction* (such as *and, but, or,* or *yet*) joins elements that are grammatically comparable (*Marx and Engels wrote* [two nouns]; *Marx writing one essay, but Engels writing the other* [two phrases]; *Marx wrote one essay, yet Engels wrote the other* [two independent clauses]). **Correlative conjunctions** (such as *both, and; either, or;* or *not only, but* [*also*]) are used in pairs to connect elements that are grammatically equivalent (*neither Marx nor Engels, not only Marx, but also Engels*). A **subordinating conjunction** (such as *although, because, before, if, that, when, where,* or *why*) introduces a dependent clause, which it subordinates to an independent clause. *Marx wrote at the British Museum where he did most of his work. Before his association with Marx, Engels was already a social theorist.* A **conjunctive adverb** (such as *consequently, moreover,* or *then*) modifies one independent clause following another independent clause. A conjunctive adverb often generally follows a semicolon or colon and precedes a comma. *Thoreau lived simply at Walden; however, he regularly joined his aunt for tea in Concord.* See 6b7 and 13c.

coordination   The grammatical equality of two or more sentence elements. When elements are coordinate, they seem to express equally significant ideas. *She wanted both to stay and to go.* See also *subordination*. See 18a.

coordinating conjunction   See *conjunction*.

correlative conjunction   See *conjunction*.

count noun   See *noun*.

dangling modifier   A word, phrase, or clause that fails to modify the sentence element that it logically ought to. *Studying Freud, the subject of artistic creativity became complicated* (incorrect; the subject of artistic creativity was not studying Freud). *Studying Freud, the class appreciated the complicated nature of artistic creativity* (correct; the class was studying Freud). See 15c.

declension   See *case, inflection, number, person*.

degree   See *adjective forms, adverb forms*.

714

demonstrative adjective See *adjective*.

demonstrative pronoun See *pronoun*.

denotation The literal meaning of a term, as opposed to its **connotation** or associations. See 25b.

dependent clause See *clause*.

descriptive adjective See *adjective*.

determiner See *article*.

direct address A construction that uses a noun or pronoun naming whoever is spoken to. *Hey, Jack. You, get moving.*

direct discourse Quotation that reproduces a speaker's words exactly, using quotation marks. Jesse Jackson has often said, "I was born in the ghetto, but the ghetto wasn't born in me." See 31a and 31b.

direct object A noun or pronoun receiving the action of a **transitive verb** in an **active** construction. *McKellan recited Shakespearean soliloquies*. See also *indirect object*. See 6c2.

double comparative The incorrect use of a comparative to modify another comparative (*more better*; *less longer*). See also *adjective forms*, *adverb forms*.

double negative The incorrect use of more than one negative word to communicate a single negative idea. *I couldn't do nothing*; *I couldn't hardly do anything*.

double superlative The incorrect use of a superlative to modify another superlative (*most unkindest cut*; *least profoundest thought*). See also *adjective forms*, *adverb forms*.

expletive A construction that introduces a sentence with *there* or *it* and a form of *be*. Use *There are good reasons for having a physical exam* rather than *The reasons for having a physical exam are good* in formal writing.

finite verb A verb that can join a subject to form an independent clause without adding any auxiliary verb. *I breathe*. See 6c3, 8d, 8e, 8f, and 8g.

fused sentence An error in which two main clauses are run together without a coordinating conjunction or suitable punctuation. Also known as a *run-on* sentence. See Chapter 13.

future See *tense*.

gender The sexual classification of a noun or pronoun—*god, he* (masculine); *goddess, she* (feminine); *godliness, it* (neuter). To avoid sexist language, use words that can refer equally to members of either sex, as in *police officer* rather than *policeman* or *policewoman*.

gerund A verbal identical in form to the present participle but functioning as

715

a **noun.** *Studying is a bore* (gerund subject). *I enjoy studying* (gerund object). See 6c3.

gerund phrase See *phrase.*

helping verb An auxiliary verb. See *auxiliary verb.*

imperative mood The form of a verb expressing a command or urging an action. An imperative may or may not have a stated subject. *Leave. You be quiet. Do come in. Let's go.*

inconsistent structure The joining of two or more logically and grammatically incompatible elements in a single sentence.

indefinite adjective See *adjective.*

indefinite pronoun See *pronoun.*

independent clause See *clause.*

indicative mood The form of a verb expressing a fact, questioning a fact, or voicing an opinion or probability. *Washington crossed the Delaware on Christmas Eve. Did he defeat the Hessians?* See also *mood.*

indirect discourse A paraphrased quotation that does not repeat another's words verbatim and hence is not enclosed in quotation marks. *Coolidge said that, if elected, he would not run.*

indirect object A noun or pronoun identifying to or for whom or what a transitive verb's action is performed. The indirect object almost always precedes the direct object; it is usually the personal recipient of verbs of giving, showing, telling, and the like. *I handed the dean my application and told him that I needed financial aid.* See also *direct object.* See 6c2.

indirect question A sentence pattern in which a question is the basis of a subordinate clause. *Everyone wonders why young people continue to take up smoking.* (The question, phrased directly, is "Why do young people continue to take up smoking?")

infinitive The base form of a verb (*go, run, hit*), usually preceded by *to* (*to go, to run, to hit*). The *to* form is a verbal that can serve as a noun, adverb, or, occasionally, an adjective. *To go would be unthinkable* (noun, subject). *I do not wish to go* (noun, object). *I shall go to beg, to borrow, or to steal* (adverbs). *I'd like my sandwich to go* (adjective). An infinitive can be active (*to hit*) or passive (*to be hit*). Further, the infinitive has two tenses, present (*to [be] hit*) and perfect (*to have [been] hit*). Frequently an infinitive is preceded not by *to* but by a **modal auxiliary,** such as *can, may, must,* or *would,* or by the **primary auxiliary** *do* (*I can go, I did go*). An infinitive may be modified or take objects or complements as an **infinitive phrase.** See *phrase.* See 6b1, 6c3, and 8a.

inflection Changes in word forms to indicate person, number, gender, and case in pronouns; number, gender, and case in nouns; comparative and su-

716

perlative forms in adjectives and adverbs; and person, tense, voice, and mood in verbs.

intensifier A modifier that increases the emphasis of the word or words that it modifies. *I should very much like to go. I'm so happy.* Despite their name, intensifiers are stylistically weak; they are best avoided in formal writing.

intensive pronoun See *pronoun.*

interjection A grammatically independent word or group of words that is usually an exclamation of surprise, shock, dismay, or the like. *Help! We're losing control. My word, what do you think you're doing?*

interrogative adjective See *adjective.*

interrogative pronoun See *pronoun.*

intransitive verb A verb that does not need a direct object to complete its meaning. *The children raced up the path.* See also *verb.* See 6c2.

irregular verb A verb with a past tense and past participle that does not follow the usual *-ed* or *-d* pattern. Irregular verbs may be *strong,* with a vowel change in the past and a past participle ending in *-n* or *-en* (*see, saw, seen*), or *weak,* with other abnormalities (*go, went, gone; get, got, got/gotten*). See also *regular verb.* See 8b.

limiting adjective See *adjective.*

linking verb A linking verb joins a subject with a subject complement or complements. Common linking verbs are *appear, be, become, feel,* and *seem. The argument appeared sound. It was an exercise in logic.* See also *verb.* See 6c2.

main clause An independent clause. See *clause.*

mass noun See *noun.*

misplaced modifier A word, phrase, or clause confusingly positioned so that it fails to apply clearly to the expression intended. *With a credit card, the traveler paid for the motel room and opened the door. The traveler paid for the motel room and opened the door with a credit card.* Unless the writer intended to indicate that the traveler broke into a room already paid for, *with a credit card* should follow *paid* or *room.* See 15a.

modal auxiliaries See *auxiliary verb.*

modifier A word, phrase, or clause that acts as an adjective or an adverb and qualifies the meaning of another word, phrase, or clause. See also *adjective, adverb, clause, phrase.*

mood The form of a verb used to indicate whether an action or a state is a possible fact or to ask a question (*indicative*), to give a command (*imperative*), or to express a wish or condition contrary to fact (*subjunctive*). In other words, mood reflects the writer or speaker's attitude toward the idea expressed in the

717

verb. *The sea is turbulent* (indicative). *Be still, ye seas* (imperative). *Would that sea were calm* (subjunctive). See also *imperative mood, indicative mood, subjunctive mood.* See Chapter 8.

nominal   A word, phrase, or clause that acts as a noun.

nonfinite verb   See *verbal.*

nonrestrictive element   A word, phrase, or clause that modifies but does not limit or change the essential meaning of a sentence element. A nonrestrictive element is set off from the rest of the sentence with commas, dashes, or parentheses. *Quantum physics, a difficult subject, is fascinating. He addressed, acerbically, the failure of the system.* See also *restrictive element.* See 27c.

noun   A noun names a person, place, tangible object, concept, quality, action, or the like. Nouns serve as subjects, objects, complements, and appositives. Most nouns form the plural with the addition of *-s* or *-es* and the possessive with the addition of *'s* (see *number, case*). **Common nouns** name one (*rock, child, box*) or more (*rocks, children, boxes*) in a class or general group. **Proper nouns** begin with capital letters and name specifics such as a particular person, place, religion, time period, holiday, movement, or thing (*Angelou, Caesar, Florida, Jefferson Memorial, Elizabethan Age, July, Rosicrucianism, Ramadan*). Some proper nouns can form plurals (*Adamses, Caesars*). **Abstract nouns** name intangible qualities, concepts, actions, or states (*virtue, Virtue, peace, violence, evil, health, haste, time, inertia*). Some abstract nouns may be common or proper, depending on the sense that the writer wishes to communicate. Many abstract nouns have plural forms (*virtues, evils*), and as plurals they become increasingly *concrete*. **Concrete nouns** name people, places, or things and may be common or proper. In addition, **collective nouns** name coherent groups. In its singular form, a collective noun names a body or group of related elements; in its plural form, it names several such bodies or groups (*pride, prides* [of lions]; *family, families; Congress, Congresses*). **Count nouns** name people, places, and things that can be counted (*one woman, two women; one park, three parks; one tree, four trees; one Smith, five Smiths*). **Mass nouns** name concrete things that are not usually counted, although their plural forms are common (*sand, sands* [of Waikiki]; *rain,* [summer] *rains*). See 6b2.

noun clause   See *clause.*

noun phrase   See *phrase.*

number   The form of a noun, pronoun, demonstrative adjective, or verb that indicates whether it is singular or plural: *oak* is singular, *oaks* plural; *I* and *me* are singular, *we* and *us* plural; *he buys* is singular, *they buy* plural; *this book* is singular, *these books* plural. See 6b1, 6b2, Chapter 8 introduction, and 9a.

object   A word or words, acting as a noun or pronoun, influenced by a transitive verb, a verbal, or a preposition. See also *direct object, indirect object, object of a preposition.* See 6c2.

718

object complement See *complement*.

objective case See *case*.

object of a preposition A noun or pronoun connected to a sentence by a preposition, thus completing a **prepositional phrase**. *Johnson went to* <u>*Pembroke College*</u> *at* <u>*Oxford*</u>. *Thank you for* <u>*coming*</u>. See 6b6 and 6c3.

ordinal number The form of a number that expresses order or sequence (*first, seventeenth, twenty-third, two hundredth*). See also *cardinal number*.

participial adjective See *adjective*.

participial phrase See *phrase*.

participle A verbal with properties of both an adjective and a verb. Like an adjective, a participle can modify a noun or pronoun; like a verb, it has present and past tenses and can take an object. The **present** participle usually ends in *-ing*, the **past** participle in *-ed, d, -en*, or an irregular form. Without any auxiliary verbs, the present participle is active, the past participle passive. <u>*Reeling*</u>, *Spinks hit the canvas. The* <u>*torn*</u> *page was a clue.* See 6c3. With auxiliary verbs, present participles form the progressive tenses (I *am making*, I *was making*, I *will be making*, I *have been making*, I *had been making*, I *will have been making*). Similarly, past participles form the perfect tenses (I *have made*, I *had made*, I *will have made*). Further, past participles, with auxiliary verbs, are used to form the passive voice (I *am beaten*, I *was beaten*). These compound tenses are known as verb phrases. See also *adjective, phrase, tense, verbal, voice*.

parts of speech The eight grammatical categories into which words can be grouped depending on how they function in a sentence. Many words act as different parts of speech in different sentences. The parts of speech are *adjectives, adverbs, conjunctions, interjections, nouns, prepositions, pronouns*, and *verbs*. See 6b.

passive voice See *voice*.

past participle See *participle*.

past perfect tense See *tense*.

past tense See *tense*.

perfect tenses See *participle, tense, verb*.

person The relation between a subject and its corresponding verb, indicating whether the subject is speaking about itself (first person *I* or *we*), being spoken to (second person *you*), or being spoken about (third person *he, she, it*, or *they*). *Be* has several forms depending on the person (*am, is*, and *are* in the present tense plus *was* and *were* in the past). Other verbs change form in the present tense with a third-person singular subject (I *fall*, you *fall*, she <u>*falls*</u>, we *fall*, they *fall*). See 6b1, Chapter 8, and 9a. **Personal pronouns** also change form as subjects, objects, and possessives. See 6b3.

719

personal pronoun   See *pronoun*.

phrase   A group of words that functions as a single unit but lacks a subject, a finite verb in a predicate, or both. Phrases can be grouped not only by the parts of speech that govern or introduce them but also by their grammatical functions as adjectives, adverbs, nouns, or verbs. An **absolute phrase** modifies an entire sentence and thus is grammatically divorced from the sentence. It uses a noun or pronoun as its subject and a participle (possibly implied) or participial phrase as its predicate. *The party being over, everyone left. The party over, everyone left* (participle implied). A **gerund phrase** serves as a noun, acting as a subject, a complement, or an object. It is built around a gerund, the *-ing* form of a verb acting as a noun. *Exercising regularly and sensibly is a key to good health* (subject). *I dislike exercising regularly and sensibly* (direct object). *I am bored with exercising regularly and sensibly* (object of a preposition). An **infinitive phrase** may serve as an adjective, an adverb, or a noun and is governed by an infinitive. *The Pacific Coast is the place to be* (adjective). *She went to pay her taxes* (adverb). *To be young again is all I want* (noun). A **noun phrase**, including a noun and its modifiers, may serve as a subject, a complement, or an object. *A long, rough road* (subject) *crossed the barren desert* (object). *A raccoon is a resourceful animal* (complement). A **participial phrase** is governed by a present or past participle and functions as an adjective. *Breaking his leg, he stumbled. Having broken his leg, he stumbled.* A **prepositional phrase** is introduced by a preposition and may act as an adjective, an adverb, or a noun. *The gas in the laboratory is leaking* (adjective). *The firefighters went to the lab to check* (adverb). *Out of season is the least crowded time* (noun). A **verb phrase** is composed of a main verb and one or more auxiliaries, acting as a single verb in the sentence predicate. *I should have come to the review session.* See 6c3.

positive degree   See *adjective forms, adverb forms*.

possessive adjective   See *adjective, case*.

possessive case   See *case*.

predicate   The actual or implied finite verb and related words in a sentence. The predicate expresses what the subject does, experiences, or is. A **simple predicate** is a verb or a verb phrase that reflects on the subject. *For years the YMHA has been a cultural center in New York City.* A **compound predicate** has more than one simple predicate. *The athletes swam, cycled, and ran in the triathlon competition.* A **complete predicate** includes the simple predicate and any associated modifiers and objects. *I gave Sarah an engagement ring.* See 6c2.

predicate adjective   See *complement*.

predicate noun   See *complement*.

prefix   An addition (often derived from a Latin preposition or negative) to the beginning of a root word to alter its meaning (*preview, undress*). See 24d1.

720

preposition   A part of speech that indicates the position of a noun or pronoun in space or time and links it to other sentence elements. *He was at the top of the ladder before the other contestants had climbed to the fourth rung.* See *phrase.* See 6b6.

present participle   See *participle.*

present perfect   See *participle, tense, verb, verbal.*

present progressive   See *participle, tense, verb, verbal.*

present tense   See *tense, verb.*

progressive forms   See *participle, tense, verb.*

pronoun   A single-word noun substitute that refers to an actual or logical antecedent. **Demonstrative pronouns** (*this, that, these,* and *those*) point out particular nouns. *This is the article I read. Those are the books I bought.* **Indefinite pronouns** do not refer to specific nouns and include *any, each, everybody, everyone, some,* and similar words. *Never in the field of human conflict was so much owed by so many to so few.* Some indefinite pronouns have a possessive case. *Everyone's best interests will be served by a cure for AIDS.* **Intensive pronouns** (*myself, yourself, himself, herself, oneself, itself, ourselves, yourselves, themselves*) emphasize their antecedent nouns or personal pronouns, agreeing with them in person, number, and gender. *She herself knew that we ourselves were blameless. The fire did not damage the house itself.* **Interrogative pronouns** (*who, which,* and *what*) ask questions. *Which one would you like? What is going on?* **Personal pronouns** (*I, you, he, she, it, we, you,* and *they*) observe number, gender, and case as they refer to particular people or things. *He knew what was his and also what was best for him.* See also *case, gender, number.* **Reciprocal pronouns** (*each other, one another*) refer to the individuals included in a plural antecedent. *Holmes and Frazier fought each other. The candidates debated one another. Each other* is preferred in sentences involving two subjects, and *one another* in those involving more than two subjects. **Reflexive pronouns,** identical in form to intensive pronouns, refer back to the subject of the sentence or clause. *I washed myself* (direct object). *I gave myself a pat on the back* (indirect object). **Relative pronouns** (*who, whom, which, that, what, whoever, whomever, whichever,* and *whatever*) connect a dependent clause to a sentence. *I wonder who will win the prize.* See 6b3.

proper adjective   See *adjective.*

proper noun   See *noun.*

reciprocal pronoun   See *pronoun.*

reflexive pronoun   See *pronoun.*

regular verb   A verb with a past tense and past participle ending in *-d* or *-ed* (*care, cared, cared; look, looked, looked*). See also *irregular verb.* See 8b.

relative adjective   See *adjective.*

relative pronoun   See *pronoun*.

restrictive element   A word, phrase, or clause that limits the essential meaning of the sentence element it modifies. The restrictive element is not set off from the element that it modifies with commas, dashes, or parentheses. *The tree that I hit was an oak. The oak at the side of the road was a hazard.* See also *nonrestrictive element.* See 27c and 27i1.

run-on sentence   See *comma splice, fused sentence*.

sentence   The grammatically complete expression of an idea. In writing, a sentence begins with a capital letter and ends with a period, a question mark, or an exclamation point. A sentence may be **declarative** and make a statement (*The sun rose*), **interrogative** and ask a question (*Did the sun rise?*), **exclamatory** and indicate surprise or other strong emotion (*How beautiful the dawn is!*), or **imperative** and express a command (*Get up earlier tomorrow*). Besides having these functions, sentences are classified grammatically. A **simple** sentence is a single independent clause without dependent clauses. *I left the house.* Its subject, predicate, or both may be compound. *Sears and Roebuck founded a mail-order house and a chain of stores.* A **compound** sentence contains two or more independent clauses linked with a coordinating conjunction, a correlative conjunction, or a semicolon. *I did not wish to go, but she did. I did not wish to go; she did.* A **complex** sentence contains an independent clause and one or more dependent clauses. *After he had cleaned up the kitchen, Tom fell asleep in front of the television.* A **compound-complex** sentence contains at least two independent clauses and one or more dependent clauses. *We had hoped to go climbing, but the trip was postponed because she sprained her ankle.* See also *clause.* See 6a and 6d.

sentence fragment   An apparent sentence that fails to communicate a complete thought, usually because it lacks a subject or a finite verb. Often fragments are dependent clauses, introduced by a subordinating word but punctuated as sentences. Fragments should be revised to be complete sentences in formal writing. See Chapter 14 for ways of correcting sentence fragments.

simple predicate   See *predicate*.

simple sentence   See *sentence*.

simple subject   See *subject*.

simple tense   See *tense*.

split infinitive   The often awkward intrusion of an adverb between *to* and the base form of the verb in an infinitive construction (*to boldly go* rather than the preferable *to go boldly*). See 15b1.

squinting modifier   A misplaced word, phrase, or clause that could refer equally, but with different meanings, to words preceding or following it. *Playing poker often is dangerous.* The position of *often* fails to indicate whether

frequent poker playing is dangerous or whether poker playing is often dangerous. See 15a3.

subject The noun, pronoun, and related words that indicate who or what a
sentence is about. A **simple** subject is a single noun or pronoun. *Owls are
nocturnal birds.* A **complete** subject is the simple subject and its modifiers.
The timid gray mouse fled from the owl. (*Mouse* is the simple subject; *the timid
gray mouse* the complete subject.) Further, a subject may be **compound:** *The
mouse and the owl heard the fox.*

subject complement See *complement.*

subjective case See *case.*

subjunctive mood The form of a verb used to express a wish, a request, or a
condition that does not exist. The *contrary-to-fact subjunctive* using *were* is
the most common. *If I were president, I would change things.* The dependent
that clause expressing a command, demand, necessity, request, requirement
or suggestion is also common. *I asked that he come.* The subjunctive also
survives in many time-honored expressions. *Be that as it may. Suffice it to say
that I have had enough.* See 8h.

subordinate clause A dependent clause. See *clause.*

subordinating conjunction See *conjunction.*

subordination The grammatical dependence of one sentence element on another. *Because the corporal is subordinate to the sergeant, the sergeant is the
boss.* When one element is subordinate or dependent on another, instead of
being equal to it, the subordinate element seems less significant, and the independent element seems more significant. See also *clause, coordination.* See
18b.

substantive A word, phrase, or clause that serves a noun.

suffix An addition to the end of a word that alters the word's meaning or part
of speech—as in *migrate* (verb) and *migration* (noun) or *late* (adjective or
adverb) and *lateness* (noun). See 24d2.

superlative See *adjective forms, adverb forms.*

syntax The arrangement of words in a sentence in order to reveal the relation
of each to the whole and each to the other.

tense The verb forms that indicate the time at which an action takes place
or a condition exists. The times expressed by tense are basically present, past,
and future. Verbs have **simple** (I love), **perfect** (I have loved), **progressive** (I
am loving), and **perfect progressive** (I have been loving) forms that show tense
and, used in sequences, show the time relationships of actions and events. See
8d, 8e, 8f, and 8g.

transitive verb A verb that directs action toward a direct object and may
express action done to or for an indirect object. A transitive verb may be in

723

the active or passive voice. *The artist gave me the sketch.* See also *verb.* See 6c2.

verb   A word or group of words, essential to a sentence, that expresses what action the subject takes or receives, what the subject is, or what the subject's state of being is. Verbs change form to show tense, number, voice, and mood. A **transitive** verb takes an object or has passive forms. *Edison invented the incandescent bulb. The incandescent bulb was invented by Edison.* An **intransitive** verb does not take an object. *The bulb glowed.* **Linking** verbs join a subject and its complement. *Edison was pleased.* Depending upon its use in a sentence, a verb may sometimes belong to all three groups. *Evans grew oranges* (transitive). *The oranges grew well* (intransitive). *The oranges grew ripe* (linking). See also *auxiliary verb, irregular verb, mood, person, regular verb, tense, verbal, voice.* See 6b1 and Chapter 8.

verbal   A **gerund, participle,** or **infinitive** serving as a noun, an adjective, or an adverb. *Running is excellent exercise* (gerund/noun). *A running athlete is an exhilarating sight* (participle/adjective). *We went to the track to run* (infinitive/adverb). See also *gerund, infinitive, participle.* See 6c3.

verbal phrase   A phrase using a gerund, a participle, or an infinitive. See *phrase.*

verb phrase   A main verb and its auxiliary verbs. A verb phrase can act only as a predicate in a sentence. *She should have won the first race.* See *phrase.*

voice   The form of a transitive verb that indicates whether the subject is acting or being acted on. When a verb is **active,** the subject is the doer or agent. *Parker played the saxophone fantastically.* When a verb is **passive,** the subject and verb are transposed. Then the grammatical subject receives the action of the verb, action taken by the object of a preposition. *The saxophone was played fantastically by Parker.* The passive voice is formed with the appropriate tense of the verb *be* and the past participle of the transitive verb. See also *verb.* See Chapter 8.

724

Glossary of Usage

This glossary provides usage guidelines for some commonly confused words and phrases. Conventions of usage might be called the "good manners" of discourse. Just as our notions of good manners vary from culture to culture and time to time, so do conventions of usage. The word *ain't*, for instance, now considered bad manners in formal discourse, was once widely used by the most proper British speakers, and is still used normally in some spoken American dialects. So usage matters, like other choices you must make in writing, depend on what your purpose is and what is appropriate for a particular audience at a particular time. Matters of usage, especially those which are controversial or which seem to be changing, are treated in the body of this textbook. In addition, this glossary provides you, in brief form, with a guide to generally accepted usage in college writing and with a guide for distinguishing between words whose meanings are similar or which are easily confused. For fuller discussion of these matters, you may want to consult one of the usage guides listed in 23c.

a, an   Use *a* with a word that begins with a consonant, (*a forest*, *a book*), with a sounded *h* (*a hemisphere*), or with another consonant sound such as "you" or "wh" (*a euphoric moment*, *a one-sided match*). Use *an* with a word that begins with a vowel (*an umbrella*), with a silent *h* (*an honor*), or with a vowel sound (*an X-ray*).

accept, except   The verb *accept* means "receive" or "agree to." *Melanie will accept the job offer.* Used as a preposition, *except* means "aside from" or "excluding." *All the plaintiffs except Mr. Sneath decided to accept the settlement offered by the defendant.*

advice, advise   The noun *advice* means an "opinion" or "suggestion"; the verb *advise* means "offer or provide advice." *Charlotte's mother advised her to become a secretary, but Charlotte, who intended to become a dancer, ignored the advice.*

affect, effect   As a verb, *affect* means "influence" or "move the emotions of." *Effect* is a noun meaning "result" or, less commonly, a verb meaning "bring about." *A nuclear war would have far-reaching effects. Many people are deeply affected by this realization, and some join groups aimed at effecting arms reduction.*

aggravate Colloquially, *aggravate* means "irritate" or "annoy," but this usage should be avoided in formal writing. The formal meaning of *aggravate* is "make worse." *Having another mouth to feed aggravated their poverty.*

all ready, already *All ready* means "fully prepared." *Already* means "previously." *We were all ready for Lucy's party when we learned that she had already left.*

all right *All right* is always two words, not one.

all together, altogether *All together* means "all in a group" or "gathered in one place." *Altogether* means "completely," "in all," or "everything considered." *When the students were all together in the room, it was altogether filled.*

allude, elude *Allude* means "refer indirectly." *Elude* means "avoid" or "escape from." *The candidate frequently alluded to his immigrant grandparents who had come here to elude political oppression.*

allusion, illusion An *allusion* indirectly refers to something, as when a writer mentions or hints at a well-known event, person, story, quotation, or other information, assuming that the reader will recognize it (*a literary allusion*). An *illusion* is a false or misleading appearance (*an optical illusion*).

a lot *A lot* is not one word but two. Do not use it in formal writing to express "a large amount" or "a large number."

already See *all ready, already.*

alright See *all right.*

altogether See *all together, altogether.*

among, between In referring to two things or people, use *between*. In referring to three or more things or people, use *among*. *The relationship between the twins is different from that among the other three children.*

amount, number Use *amount* for quantities that you cannot count (singular nouns such as water, light, or power). Use *number* for quantities that you can count (usually plural nouns such as objects or people). *A small number of volunteers cleared a large amount of brush within a few hours.*

an See *a, an.*

and/or *And/or* should be avoided except in business or legal writing, where it is a short way of saying that one or both of two items apply. In other formal writing, take time and space to write out X, Y, *or both* rather than X *and/or* Y. If you mean *and* or *or*, use just that word.

any body, anybody, any one, anyone *Anybody* is an indefinite pronoun, as is *anyone*. *Although anyone could enjoy carving wood, not just anybody could make a sculpture like that. Any body* is two words, an adjective modifying a noun. *Any body of water has its own distinctive ecology. Any one* is two adjectives or a pronoun modified by an adjective. *Customers were allowed to buy only two sale items at any one time.*

726

anyplace, anywhere In formal writing, use *anywhere*, not *anyplace*. *She walked for an hour, not going <u>anywhere</u> in particular.*

anyway, anyways Use *anyway*, not *anyways*, in writing.

anywhere See *any place, any where.*

apt, liable, likely *Likely to* means "probably will," and *apt to* means "inclines or tends to," but either word will do in many instances. *During an argument, he is <u>apt</u> to yell while she is <u>likely</u> to slam doors. Liable to* is a more negative phrase that means "in danger of." *That dog is <u>liable</u> to dig up my garden. Liable* is also a legal term meaning "obligated" or "responsible for." *The dog's owners are <u>liable</u> for any damage that he causes.*

as Avoid using *as* for *because* or *when* in sentences where its meaning is not clear. For example, does *Carl left town <u>as</u> his father was arriving* mean *at the same time as his father was arriving* or *because his father was arriving?*

as, as if, like These expressions are used when making comparative statements. Use *as* when comparing two qualities that people or objects possess. *The box is <u>as</u> wide <u>as</u> it is long.* Also use *as* to identify equivalent terms in a description. *Gary served <u>as</u> moderator at the town meeting.* Use *like* to indicate similarity but not equivalency: *Hugo, <u>like</u> Jane, was a detailed observer.* In such instances, *like* acts as a preposition, followed by a noun or noun phrase, while *as* may act either as a preposition or as a conjunction introducing a clause. *The dog howled like a wolf, just <u>as if</u> she were a wild animal.*

assure, ensure, insure *Assure* means "convince" or "promise," and its direct object is usually a person or persons. *The candidate <u>assured</u> the voters he would not raise taxes. Ensure* and *insure* both mean "make certain," but *insure* is usually used in the specialized sense of protection against financial loss. *When the city began water rationing to <u>ensure</u> that the supply would last, the Browns found that they could no longer afford to <u>insure</u> their car wash business.*

as to *As to* should not be used as a substitute for *about. Phoebe was unsure <u>about</u>* (not *<u>as to</u>*) *Bruce's intentions.*

at, where See *where.*

awful, awfully The formal meanings of *awful* and *awfully* are "awe-inspiring" and "in an awe-inspiring way" respectively. Colloquial speech often dilutes *awful* to mean "bad" (*I had an <u>awful</u> day*) and *awfully* to mean "very" (*It was <u>awfully</u> cold*). In formal writing, avoid these casual usages.

awhile, a while The adverb *awhile* can be used to modify a verb. *A while*, however, is an article and a noun and can be the object of a preposition such as *for, in,* or *after. We drove <u>awhile</u> and then stopped for a <u>while</u>.*

bad, badly *Bad* is an adjective, used to modify a subject or an object or to follow a linking verb such as *be, feel,* or *seem. Badly* is an adverb, used to modify a verb. *The guests felt <u>bad</u> because the dinner was so <u>badly</u> prepared.*

727

because of, due to   Both phrases are used to describe the relationship between a cause and an effect. Use *due to* when the effect (a noun) is stated first and followed by the verb *be*. *His illness was due to malnutrition.* (*Illness*, a noun, is the effect.) Use *because of*, not *due to*, when the effect is a clause, not a noun. *He was sick because of malnutrition.* (*He was sick*, a clause, is the effect.)

being as, being that   These expressions are used colloquially as substitutes for *because*; avoid them in formal writing. *Because* (not *being as*) *Romeo killed Tybalt, he was banished to Padua.*

beside, besides   *Beside*, a preposition, means "next to." *Besides* is either a preposition meaning "other than" or "in addition to" or an adverb meaning "moreover." *No one besides Francesca knows whether the tree is still growing beside the house.*

between   See *among, between.*

breath, breathe   *Breath* is the noun, and *breathe* is the verb. *"Breathe," said the dentist, so June took a large breath of laughing gas.*

bring, take   *Bring* is comparable to *come*; *take* is comparable to *go*. Use *bring* when an object is moved from a farther place to a nearer one; use *take* when the opposite is true. *Please take my prescription to the pharmacist, and bring my medicine back to me.*

but, yet   Use these words separately, not together. *He is strong-minded but* (not *but yet*) *gentle.*

but that, but what   Avoid using these as substitutes for *that* in expressions of doubt. *Hercule Poirot never doubted that* (not *but that*) *he would solve the case.*

can, may   *Can* refers to ability and *may* to possibility or permission to do something. *Since I can ski the slalom well, I may win the race. May* (not *can*) *I leave early to practice?*

can't, couldn't   These are the contractions for *cannot* and *could not*. Avoid them, like other contractions, in formal writing. *If I couldn't complete it during the break, I certainly can't now.*

can't hardly, can't scarcely   Both *hardly* and *scarcely* are negatives; therefore, the expressions *can't hardly* and *can't scarcely* are redundant double negatives. *Tim is claustrophobic and can* (not *can't*) *hardly breathe in elevators.*

can't help but   This expression is wordy and redundant. Use the more formal *I cannot but go* or the less formal *I can't help going* instead of *I can't help but go.*

can't scarcely   See *can't hardly, can't scarcely.*

censor, censure   *Censor* means to remove material that is considered offensive for political, moral, personal, or other reasons. *Censure* means "formally reprimand." *The public censured the newspaper for censoring negative letters to the editor.*

728

center around   This idiom rarely if ever appears in formal writing. Use *center on* instead. *Their research centers on the disease-resistant hybrid varieties.*

compare to, compare with   *Compare to* means "describe one thing as similar to another." *Hillary compared the noise to the roar of a waterfall. Compare with* is the more general activity of noting similarities and differences between objects or people. *The detective compared the latest photograph with the old one, noting how the man's appearance had changed.*

complement, compliment   *Complement* means "go well with" or "enhance." *Compliment* means "praise." *Several guests complimented Julie on her marmalade which complemented the warm, buttered scones.*

comprise, compose   *Comprise* means "contain" (the whole *comprises* the parts). *Compose* means "make up" (the parts *compose* the whole). *The class comprises twenty students. Twenty students compose the class.*

conscience, conscious   *Conscience,* a noun, means "a sense of right and wrong." *Conscious,* an adjective, means "awake" or "aware." *After the angry argument, Lisa was conscious of her troubled conscience.*

consensus of opinion   Use *consensus* instead of this redundant phrase. *The family consensus was to sell the old house.*

consequently, subsequently   *Consequently* means "as a result" or "therefore." *Subsequently* just means "afterwards." *Roger lost his job, and subsequently I lost mine. Consequently, I was unable to pay my rent.*

continual, continuous   *Continual* describes an activity that is repeated at regular or frequent intervals. *Continuous* describes either an activity that is ongoing without interruption or an object that is connected without break. *The damage done by continuous erosion was increased by the continual storms.*

couple of   *Couple of* is used informally to mean either "two" or "a few." Avoid it in formal writing, and say specifically what you mean.

could of   See *have, of.*

criteria, criterion   *Criterion* means "a standard of judgment" or "a necessary qualification." *Criteria* is the plural form. *Many people believe that public image is the wrong criterion for choosing the next president of the United States.*

data   *Data* is the plural form of the Latin word *datum,* meaning "a fact" or "a result collected during research." Although colloquially *data* is used as either singular or plural, in formal writing it should be treated as plural. *These data indicate that fewer people smoke today than ten years ago.*

different from, different than   *Different from* is generally preferred in formal writing although both phrases are used widely. *Her lab results were no different from his.*

differ from, differ with   *Differ from* means "be unlike" in identity, appearance, or actions. *Differ with* means "disagree with" in opinion or belief. *Mr. Binns*

729

differs with Ms. White over the importance of class discussion. *Therefore, the way Mr. Binns conducts his class differs from the way she conducts hers.*

discreet, discrete *Discreet* means "tactful" or "prudent." *Discrete* means "distinct" or "separate." *The dean's discreet encouragement brought representatives of all the discrete factions to the meeting.*

disinterested, uninterested *Disinterested* means "unbiased" or "impartial." *It was difficult to find disinterested people for the jury.* *Uninterested* means "not interested" or "indifferent." *Cecile was uninterested in the outcome of the trial.*

distinct, distinctive *Distinct* means "separate" or "well defined." *The experiment involved separating the liquid into its five distinct elements.* *Distinctive* means "distinguishing from others" or "characteristic." *Even from a distance, everyone recognized Greg's distinctive way of walking.*

doesn't, don't *Doesn't* is the contraction for *does not* and should be used with *he, she, it,* and singular nouns. *Don't* is the contraction for *do not* and should be used with *I, you, we, they,* and plural nouns. In formal writing, however, avoid these and all other contractions.

due to See *because of, due to.*

effect See *affect, effect.*

elicit, illicit The verb *elicit* means "to draw out" or "evoke." The adjective *illicit* means "illegal." *The police tried to elicit from the criminal the names of others involved in his illicit activities.*

elude See *allude, elude.*

emigrate from, immigrate to, migrate *Emigrate from* means "move away from one's country." *Immigrate to* means "move to a foreign country and settle there." *My family emigrated from Norway in 1957. We immigrated to the United States.* *Emigration* and *immigration* are generally permanent actions; *migration* suggests movement that is temporary or seasonal and either *to* or *from* a place. *Every winter, whales off the Pacific coast migrate south from Alaska toward warmer water.*

ensure See *assure, ensure, insure.*

enthused, enthusiastic *Enthused* is used colloquially to mean "enthusiastic about." Avoid it in formal writing. *The students remained enthusiastic despite the rain and the mud that threatened to flood the excavation.*

equally as good Replace this redundant phrase with either *equally good* or *as good as. The two tennis players were equally good, each as good as the other.*

especially, specially *Especially* means "very" or "particularly." *Specially* means "for a special reason or purpose." *The audience especially enjoyed the new composition, specially written, for the holiday.*

every day, everyday *Everyday* is an adjective used to describe something as ordinary or common. *Every day* is an adjective modifying a noun, specifying

730

which particular day. *I ride the subway every day even though pushing and shoving are everyday occurrences.*

every one, everyone *Everyone* is an indefinite pronoun. *Every one* is a noun modified by an adjective, referring to each member of a group. *Because he began the assignment after everyone else, David knew that he could not finish every one of the selections.*

except See *accept, except.*

explicit, implicit *Explicit* means "directly or openly expressed." *Implicit* means "indirectly expressed or implied." *The explicit message of the ad urged consumers to buy the product while the implicit message promised popularity.*

farther, further *Farther* refers to physical distance. *How much farther is it to Munich? Further* refers to time or degree. *I want to avoid further delays and further misunderstandings.*

fewer, less Use *fewer* with objects or people that can be counted (plural nouns). Use *less* with amounts that cannot be counted (singular nouns). *The world would be safer with fewer bombs and less hostility.*

finalize *Finalize* is a pretentious way of saying "end" or "make final." *We closed* (not *finalized*) *the deal.*

firstly, secondly, thirdly These are old-fashioned and unwieldy words for introducing a series of points. Use *first, second,* and *third* instead.

flaunt, flout *Flaunt* means "show off." *Flout* means "mock" or "scorn." *The teens flouted convention by flaunting their multi-colored wigs.*

former, latter *Former* refers to the first and *latter* to the second of two things previously introduced. *Anna and Kim are both excellent athletes; the former plays tennis, and the latter has won several marathons.* See also *later, latter.*

further See *farther, further.*

good, well *Good* is an adjective and should not be used as a substitute for the adverb *well. Gabriel is a good host who cooks quite well.*

good and *Good and* is colloquial for "very"; avoid it in formal writing. *After Peter lost his sister's camera, he was very* (not *good and*) *sorry.*

half a, a half, a half a Both *half a* and *a half* are standard. *A half a* is wordy. *She ate half a* (or *a half* but not *a half a*) *sandwich.*

hanged, hung Of these two past forms of the verb *hang,* only *hanged* refers to executions while *hung* is used for all other meanings. *The old woman hung her head as she passed the tree where the murderer was hanged.*

hardly See *can't hardly, can't scarcely.*

has got to, has to These colloquial phrases for "must" should be avoided in formal writing. *She must* (not *has to*) *be intelligent.*

have, of *Have,* not *of,* should follow *could, would, should,* or *might. We should have* (not *of*) *invited them.*

731

herself, himself, myself, yourself   Do not use these reflexive pronouns as subjects or as objects in a prepositional phrase. *Tamara went with* <u>*me*</u> (not <u>*myself*</u>) *to see the pottery show.*

he/she, his/her   *He/she* and *his/her* are ungainly ways to avoid sexism in writing. Other solutions are to write out *he or she* or to alternate using *he* and *she*. Perhaps the best solutions are to eliminate the pronouns entirely or to make the subject plural (*they*), thereby avoiding all reference to gender. For instance, *Everyone should carry* <u>*his/her*</u> *driver's license with him or her* could be revised to <u>*Drivers*</u> *should carry driver's licenses at all times* or to <u>*People*</u> *should carry* <u>*their*</u> *driver's licenses with* <u>*them*</u>.

himself   See *herself, himself, myself, yourself.*

his/her   See *he/she, his/her.*

hisself   Replace *hisself* with *himself* in formal writing.

hopefully   *Hopefully* is widely misused to mean "it is hoped," but its correct meaning is "with hope." *Sam watched the roulette wheel* <u>*hopefully*</u>, not <u>*Hopefully*</u>, *Sam will win.*

hung   See *hanged, hung.*

if, whether   Use *whether* or *whether or not* to express an alternative. *She was considering* <u>*whether or not*</u> *to buy the new software.* Reserve *if* for the subjunctive case. <u>*If*</u> *it should rain tomorrow, our Tai Chi class will meet in the gym.*

illicit   See *elicit, illicit.*

illusion   See *allusion, illusion.*

immigrate to   See *emigrate from, immigrate to, migrate.*

impact   As a noun, *impact* means "a forceful collision." As a verb, it means "pack together." *Because they were* <u>*impacted*</u>, *Jason's wisdom teeth needed to be removed.* Avoid the colloquial use of *impact* as a weak and vague word meaning "to affect." *Population control may* <u>*reduce*</u> (not <u>*impact*</u>) *world hunger.*

implicit   See *explicit, implicit.*

imply, infer   To *imply* is to suggest. To *infer* is to make an educated guess. Speakers and writers *imply*; listeners and readers *infer*. *Beth and Peter's letter* <u>*implied*</u> *that they were planning a very small wedding; we* <u>*inferred*</u> *that we would not be invited.*

incident, instance   *Incident* refers to a specific occurrence. It should not be confused with *instance* which is an overused, though correct, word for "example" or "case." *The violent* <u>*incident*</u> *was just one* <u>*instance*</u> *of John's fiery temper.*

incredible, incredulous   *Incredible* means "unbelievable." *Incredulous* means "not believing." *When townspeople attributed the* <u>*incredible*</u> *events in their town to the presence of a UFO, Marina was* <u>*incredulous*</u>.

732

infer See *imply, infer.*

inside, inside of, outside, outside of Drop *of* after the prepositions *inside* and *outside. The class regularly met* outside (not *of*) *the building.*

instance See *incident, instance.*

insure See *assure, ensure, insure.*

interact with, interface with *Interface with* is computer jargon for "discuss" or "communicate." *Interact with* is a vague phrase meaning "doing something that somehow involves another person." Avoid these colloquial expressions.

irregardless, regardless *Regardless* is the correct word because *irregardless* is a double negative.

is when, is where These vague and faulty shortcuts should be avoided in definitions. *Schizophrenia is a psychotic condition* in which (not when or where) *a person withdraws from reality.*

its, it's *Its* is a possessive pronoun, even though it does not have an apostrophe. *It's* is a contraction for *it is*; avoid *it's* and other contractions in formal writing. It's (more formally, *it is*) *important to begin each observation just before the rat has* its *dinner.*

kind, sort, type As singular nouns, *kind, sort,* and *type* should be modified by *this* and followed by singular nouns. The plural forms, *kinds, sorts,* and *types* should be modified by *these* and followed by plural nouns. Write *this kind of dress* or *these kinds of dresses,* not *these kind of dress.* Use such phrases to classify or categorize, but leave them out otherwise.

kind of, sort of Avoid using these colloquial expressions as substitutes for "rather" or "somewhat." *Laura was somewhat* (not kind of) *tired after painting for several hours in the studio.*

later, latter *Later* means "more late" or "after some time." *Latter* refers to the last of two items mentioned and can be used to avoid repeating a subject twice. *Jackson and Chad won all their early matches, but the* latter *was injured* later *in the season.* See also *former, latter.*

latter See *former, latter* and *later, latter.*

lay, lie *Lay* means "place" or "put." Its forms are *lay, laid, laying, laid,* and *laid.* It generally has a direct object, specifying what has been placed. *She* laid *her books on the desk. Lie* means "recline" or "be positioned," and does not take a direct object. Its forms are *lie, lay, lain, lying. She* lay *awake until two, worrying about the exam.*

leave, let *Leave* means "go away" or "depart." *Let* means "allow." The expressions *leave alone* and *let alone,* however, are generally considered interchangeable. Let me leave *now, and* leave (or let) *me* alone *from now on!*

lend, loan In formal writing, use *loan* as a noun and *lend* as a verb. *Please* lend *me your pen so that I may fill out this application for a* loan.

733

less See *fewer, less.*

let See *leave, let.*

liable See *apt, liable, likely.*

lie See *lay, lie.*

like See *as, as if, like.*

like, such as Both *like* and *such as* may be used in a statement giving an example or a series of examples. *Like* means "similar to"; use *like* when comparing the subject mentioned to the examples. *A hurricane, like a flood or any other major disaster, may strain a region's emergency resources.* Use *such as* when the examples represent a general category of things or people. *Such as* is often a graceful alternative to *for example. A destructive hurricane, such as Gilbert in 1988, may drastically alter an area's economy.*

likely See *apt, liable, likely.*

literally *Literally* means "actually" or "exactly as it is written" and may be used to stress the truth of a statement that might otherwise be understood as figurative. *Literally* should not be used as an intensifier in a figurative statement. *Sarah was literally at the edge of her seat* may be accurate, but *Sarah was so hungry that she could literally eat a horse* is not.

loan See *lend, loan.*

loose, lose *Lose* is a verb meaning "misplace." *Loose*, as an adjective, means "not securely attached." *Sew on that loose button before you lose it.*

lots, lots of These informal expressions, meaning "much" or "many," should be avoided in formal writing.

man, mankind In the past, *man* and *mankind* were used to represent all human beings, but many people now consider these terms sexist because they do not mention women. Replace such words with *people, humans, humankind, men and women,* or similar all-encompassing phrases. Replace occupational terms ending with *-man* with gender-free phrasing such as *fire fighter* for *fireman, letter carrier* for *mailman,* and *minister* or *cleric* for *clergyman.*

may See *can, may.*

may be, maybe *May be* is a verb phrase. *Maybe*, the adverb, means "perhaps." *He may be the president today, but maybe he will lose the next election.*

media *Media*, the plural form of *medium*, takes a plural verb. *The media are* (not *is*) *going to cover the council meeting.*

might of See *have, of.*

migrate See *emigrate from, immigrate to, migrate.*

moral, morale A *moral* is a succinct lesson. *The unstated moral of the story is that generosity eventually is rewarded. Morale* is the spirit or mood of an individual or a group of people. *Office morale was low.*

734

Ms. A term invented in the 1960s to give women a title comparable to *Mr.* for men. Formerly, a woman was called either *Miss* or *Mrs.*, each term defining her in terms of her marital status, which is a private matter. Use *Ms.* unless the woman specifies another title. *Ms.* should appear before her first name, not before her husband's name: *Ms. Jane Tate*, not *Ms. John Tate*.

myself See *herself, himself, myself, yourself*.

nor, or Use *either* with *or* and *neither* with *nor*. *Cindy hopes to study abroad either next year or the year after. Neither her mother nor her father are very encouraging.*

number See *amount, number*.

of See *have*.

off of Use *off* rather than *off of*. *The spaghetti slipped off* (not *of*) *the plate*.

OK, O.K., okay All are acceptable spellings, but do not use the term in formal writing. Replace it with more exact language. *The performance was unpolished but enthusiastic* (not *OK*).

on, upon *Upon* is an old-fashioned and overly formal substitute for *on*. *My grade will depend on* (not *upon*) *how well I do on my final examination*.

on account of Use this substitute for *because of* sparingly or not at all. See also *because of, due to*.

or See *nor, or*.

outside, outside of See *inside, inside of, outside, outside of*.

owing to the fact that Avoid this and other unnecessarily wordy expressions for *because*.

per Use the Latin *per* only in standard technical phrases such as *miles per hour*. Otherwise, find English equivalents. *As mentioned in* (not *as per*) *the latest report, our town's average food expenses every week* (not *per week*) *are $40 per capita*.

percent, percentage These words identify a number as a fraction of one hundred. Because they show exact statistics, these terms should not be used casually to mean "portion," "amount," or "number." *Last year, 80 percent of the club's members were female*. Use *percent* after a figure. In formal writing, spell out *percent* rather than using its symbol (%). *Percentage* is not used with a specific number. *A large percentage of sales representatives are single*.

plenty *Plenty* means "enough" or "a great abundance." *Many immigrants consider America a land of plenty*. In formal writing, avoid its colloquial usage, meaning "very." *He was very* (not *plenty*) *tired*.

plus *Plus*, a preposition meaning "in addition to," often is used in the context of money. *My inheritance is enough to cover my debts plus yours*. Avoid using *plus* as a transitional adverb meaning "besides," "moreover," or "in addition." *That dress does not fit me. Besides* (not *plus*), *it is the wrong color*.

735

precede, proceed Both verbs, *precede* means "come before," and *proceed* means "continue" or "go forward," as in the related word *procession*. *Despite the storm that <u>preceded</u> the hallway flooding, we <u>proceeded</u> to class.*

pretty Avoid using *pretty* in formal writing as a substitute for *rather, somewhat,* or *quite*. *Bill was <u>quite</u>* (not *<u>pretty</u>*) *disagreeable.*

principal, principle These words are unrelated but are often confused because of their similar spellings. *Principal*, as a noun, refers to a head official or an amount of money loaned or invested. When used as an adjective, it means "most significant." The word meaning "a fundamental law, belief, or standard" is *principle*. *When Albert was sent to the <u>principal</u>, he defended himself with the <u>principle</u> of free speech.*

proceed See *precede, proceed.*

quotation, quote *Quote* is a verb, and *quotation* is a noun. In colloquial usage, *quote* is sometimes used as a short form of *quotation*. In formal writing, however, use *quotation* as the noun form. *He <u>quoted</u> the president, and the <u>quotation</u> was preserved in history books.*

raise, rise *Raise* means "lift" or "move upward." In the case of children, it means "bring up" or "rear." As a transitive verb, it takes a direct object— someone raises something. *The guests <u>raised</u> their glasses in good cheer. Rise* means "go upwards." It is not followed by a direct object; something rises by itself. *She saw the steam <u>rise</u> from the pan just as the soup bubbled into a boil.*

rarely ever In formal writing, use *rarely* by itself, or use *hardly ever*. *When we were poor, we <u>rarely</u> went to the movies.*

real, really The adjective *real* means "true" or "not artificial." The adverb *really*, in informal usage, means "very" or "extremely." Do not substitute *real* for *really*. *The old man walked <u>really</u>* (not *<u>real</u>*) *slowly.* In formal writing, avoid using *really* altogether. *The old man walked <u>very</u>* (not *<u>really</u>*) *slowly.*

reason is because This expression mixes *the reason is that* and *because*. Use one or the other but not both together. In general, use the less wordy *because* unless you want to give a statement the air of an explanation. *The reason the copier stopped <u>is that</u>* (not *<u>is because</u>*) *the paper jammed.*

regardless See *irregardless, regardless.*

relate to Avoid this vague colloquial expression in formal writing. *Relate to* loosely means "understand" or "appreciate." Write *I like the Rolling Stones* and explain why rather than writing *I can <u>relate to</u> the Rolling Stones*. Also see *regarding, in regard to, with regard to, relating to.*

respectfully, respectively *Respectfully* means "with respect." *Respectively* means "in the order given." *The brothers, <u>respectively</u> a juggler and an acrobat, <u>respectfully</u> greeted the audience.*

rise See *raise, rise.*

736

scarcely See *can't hardly, can't scarcely.*

secondly See *firstly, secondly, thirdly.*

set, sit *Set* means "put" or "place," and it is followed by a direct object—the thing that is placed. *Sit* does not take a direct object and refers to the action of taking a seat. *Amelia sat in the armchair and set her teacup on the table next to her.*

sexist language See *man/mankind; he/she, his/her.*

shall, will Today *shall* is used much more in British English than in American English. Use *shall* for polite questions in the first person ("*Shall we buy it?*" "*Shall I call a taxi?*"). Use *will* in all other cases involving the future tense.

should of See *have, of.*

since *Since* has two meanings. The first meaning shows the passage of time (*I have not eaten since Tuesday*); the second and more informal meaning is "because" (*Since you are in a bad mood, I will go away*). Be careful not to write sentences in which *since* is ambiguous in meaning. *Since I broke my leg, I have been doing nothing but sleeping.* (*Since* here could mean either "because" or "ever since." In order to avoid such problems some writers prefer not to use *since* to mean "because.")

sit See *set, sit.*

so, so that In formal writing, avoid using *so* by itself as an intensifier, meaning "very." Instead, follow *so* with *that* to show how the intensified condition leads to a result. *Aaron was so tired that he fell asleep at the wheel of his car.*

some body, somebody, some one, someone *Somebody* is an indefinite pronoun, as is *someone*. *When somebody comes walking down the hall, I always hope that it is someone I know.* *Some body* is two words, an adjective modifying a noun, while *some one* is two adjectives or a pronoun modified by an adjective. *In dealing with some body like the senate, arrange to meet consistently some one person who can represent the group.*

someplace, somewhere *Someplace* is informal for *somewhere*; use the latter in formal writing.

some time, sometime, sometimes *Some time* means "a length of time." *Please leave me some time to use the computer.* *Sometime* means "at some indefinite later time." *Sometime I will take you to the Orkney Islands.* *Sometimes* means "occasionally." *Sometimes I see him on my way to class.*

somewhere See *someplace, somewhere.*

sort See *kind, sort, type.*

sort of See *kind of, sort of.*

so that See *so, so that.*

specially See *especially, specially.*

737

stationary, stationery   *Stationary* is an adjective meaning "standing still." *Stationery* is a noun meaning "writing paper or materials." *When the bus was* <u>*stationary*</u> *at the light, Karen took out her* <u>*stationery*</u> *and wrote a quick note to a friend.*

subsequently   See *consequently, subsequently.*

such as   See *like, such as.*

supposed to, used to   Both of these expressions require the final *-d* indicating past tense. *He is* <u>*supposed*</u> *to bring his calculator to class.*

sure, surely   Avoid using *sure* as an intensifier in formal writing. Replace this colloquial expression with "certainly" or "without a doubt," or use the adverb *surely*, which means "it must be so." *Surely* is often used to express a hoped-for situation. <u>*Surely*</u> *John will go to a doctor.* It is also used persuasively. *We cannot go on a picnic.* <u>*Surely*</u> *it will rain.*

take   See *bring, take.*

than, then   Use the conjunction *than* in comparative statements. *The cat was bigger* <u>*than*</u> *the dog.* Use the adverb *then* when referring to a sequence of events or emotions. *Jim finished college, and* <u>*then*</u> *he joined the Peace Corps.*

that, which   *That*, always followed by a restrictive clause, singles out the object being described. *The trip* <u>*that*</u> *you took in Japan was expensive.* ("That you took to Japan" singles out the specific trip). *Which* may be followed by either a restrictive or a nonrestrictive clause but often is used only with the latter. The *which* clause may simply add more information about a noun or noun clause, and it is set off by commas. *The book,* <u>*which*</u> *is on the table, is a good one.* (This *which* clause simply adds extra, nonessential information about the book—its location. In contrast, *The book* <u>*that*</u> *is on the table is a good one* specifies or singles out the book on the table as opposed to the book on the chair or the book in some other particular place.)

their, there, they're   *Their* is a pronoun, the possessive form of *they*. *The gardeners held onto* <u>*their*</u> *hats as the helicopter flew over. There* refers to a place. <u>*There*</u>*, birds sing even at night. There* also is used with the verb *be* in expletive constructions (*there is, there are*). <u>*There is*</u> *only a short line at the cafeteria right now. They're* is a contraction of *they* and *are* and, like all contractions, it should be avoided in formal writing. <u>*They're*</u> *(more formally,* <u>*they are*</u>*) living in Japan.*

theirselves, themselves   Use *themselves* rather than *theirselves.*

then   See *than, then.*

thirdly   See *firstly, secondly, thirdly.*

'til, till, until   *Till* and *until* are both acceptable in formal writing, but some writers prefer the full word *until*. The older form *'til*, like all contractions, should be avoided in formal writing.

738

to, too, two *To* is a preposition, generally showing direction or nearness. *Stan flew to Cleveland.* Avoid using *to* after *where. Where are you flying* (not *flying to*)? *Too* means "also." *I am flying there too. Two* is the number. *We too are going to the meeting in two hours.*

to, where See *where.*

toward, towards *Toward* is generally preferred, but either word is acceptable.

try and, try to *Try and* is colloquial for *try to*; use *try to* in formal writing. *Try to have an expressive face.*

two See *to, too, two.*

type See *kind, sort, type.*

uninterested See *disinterested, uninterested.*

unique *Unique* means "the one and only." It describes an absolute state and therefore should not be used with adjectives that suggest degree, such as *very* or *most. Malcolm's hands are unique* (not *very unique*).

until See *'til, till, until.*

upon See *on, upon.*

used to See *supposed to, used to.*

very Avoid using *very* to intensify a weak adjective or adverb; instead, replace both words with one stronger, more precise, and more colorful word. Instead of *very nice*, for example, use *kind, warm, sensitive, endearing,* or *friendly,* depending on your precise meaning. Replace *very interesting* with a word such as *curious, fascinating, insightful, lively, provocative,* or *absorbing.*

way, ways When referring to distances, use *way*, not *ways. The Trivia Bowl championships were a long way* (not *ways*) *off.*

well See *good, well.*

when, where See *is when, is where.*

where Use *where* alone, not with prepositions such as *at* or *to. Where are you going?* (not *Where are you going to?*) *Where do you shop?* (not *Where do you shop at?*)

whether See *if, whether.*

which See *that, which.*

which, who When referring to ideas or things, use *which*. When referring to people, use *who*, not *which. My aunt, who was irritated, pushed on the door, which was still stuck.*

who, whom Use *who* if the following clause begins with a verb. *Monica, who smokes incessantly, is my godmother.* (*Who* is followed by the verb *smokes.*) *Monica, who is my godmother, smokes incessantly.* (*Who* is followed by the verb *is.*) Use *whom* if the following clause begins with a pronoun. *I have heard*

739

that Monica, whom I have not seen for ten years, wears only purple. (*Whom* is followed by the pronoun *I*). An exception occurs when a verbal phrase such as *I think* comes between *who* and the following clause. Ignore such a phrase as you decide which form to use. *Monica, who [I think] wears nothing but purple, is my godmother.* (Ignore *I think; who* is followed by the verb *wears.*)

who's, whose *Who's* is the contraction of *who* and *is.* Avoid *who's* and other contractions in formal writing. *Who's (more formally, Who is) in the garden? Whose* is a possessive form; it may be followed by the noun it modifies. *Whose sculpture is in the garden? Whose is on the patio?*

will See *shall, will.*

would of See *have, of.*

yet See *but, yet.*

your, you're *Your* shows possession. *Bring your sleeping bags along. You're* is the contraction of *you* and *are.* Avoid it and all other contractions in formal writing. *You're (more formally, You are) in the wrong room.*

yourself See *herself, himself, myself, yourself.*

740

Answers to Even-numbered Exercises

To help you check your progress as you work, here are answers to some exercises in Chapters 6–36. Specifically, you will find answers to even-numbered items of those exercises with predictable answers. Exercises with many possible answers—those asking you to imitate a sentence or to revise a paragraph, for example—are not answered here.

ANSWERS TO EXERCISE 6.1
The subject is set in italics, the predicate is in boldface.
2. *He* **was an army doctor, with . . . a rough voice.**
4. *The dog* **answered the sound with a whine.**

ANSWERS TO EXERCISE 6.2
2. ran, ran over (two-word verb)
4. can collect; might run; should finish
6. walked
8. will extend

ANSWERS TO EXERCISE 6.3
2. n-plagiarism
4. n-story; a-a; n-tale; n-theft; n-violation

ANSWERS TO EXERCISE 6.4
2. a-crowd; p-that; p-I
4. a-Celie; p-she; p-herself

ANSWERS TO EXERCISE 6.5
Adjectives are set in italics; adverbs are set in boldface.
2. **anxiously;** *my; long*
4. *Twenty; Italian; strong*
6. *Those;* **quite; happily;** *their; new*
8. **more; pessimistically;** *his*
10. *personal; political; relevant;* **not**

ANSWERS TO EXERCISE 6.6 (WILL VARY)
2. The beautiful, athletic heroine marries charming, bookish prince.
4. Only the best students are using the vast library holdings for scholarly research.

ANSWERS TO EXERCISE 6.7
2. through; across; into
4. from; beyond; toward

ANSWERS TO EXERCISE 6.8
2. conj-nevertheless
4. coor-but
6. corr-not only/but also
8. sub/until
10. corr-neither/nor; conj-therefore

ANSWERS TO EXERCISE 6.9
The complete subject is set in italics; the simple subject is set in boldface.
2. A *two-foot* **snowfall** *on April 13*
4. **Anyone** *who lives in a glass house*

ANSWERS TO EXERCISE 6.10
2. pred-made us a nation; trans-made; do-us; oc-nation
4. pred-shall rise again; inr-shall rise

ANSWERS TO EXERCISE 6.11
2. in his vocabulary
4. of the dugout

ANSWERS TO EXERCISE 6.12 (WILL VARY)
2. Without fear, Socrates faced death.
4. Except for a few of his followers, everyone thought Socrates was crazy.

ANSWERS TO EXERCISE 6.13
2. gerund-saving; n, object of prep
4. part-raised; adj, modifying "I"; part-exploring; adj, obj compl

ANSWERS TO EXERCISE 6.14
2. inf-To listen; prep-to Bruce Springsteen
4. part-Floating; prep-on my back
6. prep-of awe and excitement; app-a sensitive child
8. part-Basking; prep-in the sunlight; prep-in a reminiscence; prep-of golden birch trees
10. prep-of recreation; gerund-taking a nap

ANSWERS TO EXERCISE 6.15 (WILL VARY)
2. After soaking up the sun and eating good food, she looked healthy when he saw her the second time.
4. The Sunday afternoon dragged to an absolute halt.
6. In addition to kissing babies, posing for pictures, and eating boiled chicken, the candidates shook hands with the voters.
8. A late bloomer, Ben often thought regretfully about the past.
10. A young couple and their children, they lived in a trailer, crowded together like sardines.

ANSWERS TO EXERCISE 6.16 (WILL VARY)

2. Waiting to go through customs, we clutched our passports.
4. To annoy his parents, Michael had his ear pierced.

ANSWERS TO EXERCISE 6.17

2. dep-As a potential customer entered the store; sub conj-As; ind-Tony nervously attempted to retreat to the safety of the back room
4. dep-when she was deemed old enough to understand; sub conj-when; ind-she was told the truth; ind-she knew why; dep-her father had left home
6. ind-Mary and John decided to bake a chocolate cream pie; dep-which was Timothy's favorite; rel-which
8. ind-It was easier; dep-than she had expected
10. ind-I could see; dep-that he was very tired rel-that; dep-but I had to ask him a few questions

ANSWERS TO EXERCISE 6.18 (WILL VARY)

2. George was worried about his real estate investments ever since the representatives of the nuclear power plant had come to town for a site inspection.
4. Rob, who had an extensive collection of jazz records, always borrowed money from his friends.
6. We, who remembered the Grateful Dead and wanted tickets for their next performance, stood outside for an hour.
8. Because she was willing to stay home on weekends and study, Erin won the translation contest.
10. The man, whose memorial plaque hangs in the lobby, was killed in that mill in 1867.

ANSWERS TO EXERCISE 6.19

(The entire sentences are of course independent clauses.)

2. ind cl-Macmillan takes Strunk and me in our bare skins; ind cl-I want out; prep p-in our bare skins; n p-our bare skins
4. ind cl-Life in a zoo is just the ticket; prep p-in a zoo; n p-a zoo; n p-the ticket; prep p-for some animals and birds; n p-some animals and birds
6. ind cl-The way to read Thoreau is to enjoy him; inf p-to read Thoreau; inf p-to enjoy him; n p-his enthusiasms; n p-his acute perception
8. ind cl-No sensible writer sets out deliberately to develop a style; n p-no sensible writer; inf p-to develop; n p-a style; ind cl-all writers do have distinguishing qualities; v p-do have; n p-distinguishing qualities; ind cl-they become very evident; n p-very evident; dep cl-when you read the words; n p-the words
10. ind cl-A good many of Charlotte's descendants still live in the barn; prep p-of Charlotte's descendants; v p-still live; prep p-in the barn; n p-Charlotte's descendants; n p-the barn; dep cl-when the warm days of spring arrive; n p-the warm days; prep p-of spring; ind cl-there will be lots of tiny spiders; n p-tiny spiders; part p-emerging into the world; n p-the world

ANSWERS TO EXERCISE 6.20

2. complex, declarative
4. simple, declarative

743

6. complex, declarative
8. compound-complex, declarative
10. complex, declarative

ANSWERS TO EXERCISE 7.2 (WILL VARY)
2. hers
4. his

ANSWERS TO EXERCISE 7.3
2. whoever: subject of *faces*
4. whom: object of preposition, *with . . . whom we wanted*

ANSWERS TO EXERCISE 7.4
2. whom
4. he
6. she
8. whoever
10. whom, who

ANSWERS TO EXERCISE 7.5
2. I——→me
4. correct
6. him——→he
8. me——→I
10. whomever——→whoever

ANSWERS TO EXERCISE 8.1
2. have——→has
4. correct
6. be——→is
8. don't——→doesn't
10. is running

ANSWERS TO EXERCISE 8.2
2. come, found
4. lost/had lost; took/had taken
6. grew/have grown/could have grown
8. met, taken
10. met, thought, known

ANSWERS TO EXERCISE 8.3
2. sang——→sung
4. went——→gone

ANSWERS TO EXERCISE 8.4
2. laid
4. lying
6. sat

744

8. raise
10. rose

ANSWERS TO EXERCISE 8.5

2. have predicted/have been predicting—action begun in past continues
4. arrived/has arrived—started in past, may continue today
6. rode/was riding—past action, completed
8. will have watched—future action, completed by a certain time
10. rises—general truth

ANSWERS TO EXERCISE 8.7 (WILL VARY)

2. Having left England in December, the settlers arrived in Virginia in May.
4. Having cut off all contact with her parents, she did not know whom to ask for help.

ANSWERS TO EXERCISE 8.8

2. The storm uprooted huge pine trees.
4. For months, the mother kangaroo protects, feeds, and teaches her baby to survive.

ANSWERS TO EXERCISE 8.10

2. was———→were
4. was———→were

ANSWERS TO EXERCISE 9.1

2. am
4. supplies
6. were
8. holds
10. leaves

ANSWERS TO EXERCISE 9.2

2. correct, "talking and getting up" go together
4. correct
6. display———→displays; "neither/nor"
8. correct, "most" refers to a quantity
10. seem———→seems; "either/or" calls for a singular verb
12. correct, "only one" is singular
14. were———→was; *Our Tapes* is singular, a title
16. have———→has; "politics" is a collective noun
18. cause———→causes; "mumps" is singular
20. happen———→happens; "everything" is singular

ANSWERS TO EXERCISE 9.3 (WILL VARY)

2. Although roommates do not always get along, they can usually manage to tolerate each other temporarily.
4. Both Tom and Teresa are willing to lend us a car.
6. Every house and apartment has its advantages and its drawbacks.
8. Our team no longer wear their red and white uniforms.
10. Sometimes she turns on the bathroom fan and the infrared light and neglects to turn them off.

745

ANSWERS TO EXERCISE 10.2

2. negatively———→reacts
4. really———→cold
6. fully———→grown; well———→eating
8. surely———→have made
10. strictly———→brought

ANSWERS TO EXERCISE 10.4 (WILL VARY)

2. According to the article, walking is more healthful [not healthy] than jogging.
4. Women tend to live longer than men; hence, more of the elderly are women.
6. A research scientist from the Lunar and Planetary Laboratory, University of Arizona, argues that mining asteroids may well prove economically important.
8. The student cafeteria is operated by a college food service, part of a chain.
10. *Oedipus Rex* is a more successful play than *The Sandbox*.

ANSWERS TO EXERCISE 11.1 (WILL VARY)

2. Lear divides his kingdom between the two older daughters, Goneril and Regan, whose extravagant professions of love are more flattering than the simple affection of the youngest daughter, Cordelia. The consequences of this error in judgment soon become apparent, as the older daughters prove neither grateful nor kind to him.
4. New England helped to shape many aspects of American culture, including education, religion, and government. As New Englanders moved west, they carried their institutions with them.
6. Jimmy told Allen that his own mother was ill. Jimmy told Allen that Allen's mother was ill.
8. When drug therapy is combined with psychotherapy, the patients relate better and are more responsive to their therapists, and they are less vulnerable to what disturbs them.
10. If guns cause crimes, outlaw guns.

ANSWERS TO EXERCISE 11.2 (WILL VARY)

2. Texans often hear about the influence of big oil corporations on their political candidates.
4. After having a conversation with a Vietnam veteran, my friend saw the war differently.
6. The chair was delivered three weeks late, which, according to the store management, is a normal practice.
8. Many employees resented the company's no-smoking policy. (the no-smoking policy of the company)
10. Doctors can count on making their fortune within ten years of graduation.

ANSWERS TO EXERCISE 12.1 (WILL VARY)

2. Then, suddenly, the big day *arrived*. The children were still a bit sleepy, for their anticipation had kept them awake.
4. A cloud of snow powder rose as skis and poles *flew* in every direction.

746

ANSWERS TO EXERCISE 12.2 (WILL VARY)

2. I think it better that Grandfather die painlessly, bravely, and with dignity than that he *continue* to live in terrible pain.

4. The consultant recommended that the candidates tell more jokes and *smile* more during their speeches.

ANSWERS TO EXERCISE 12.3 (WILL VARY)

2. no change

4. The first thing *we see* as we start down the slope is a large green banner.

ANSWERS TO EXERCISE 12.4 (WILL VARY)

2. Workers with computer skills were in great demand, and a programmer could almost name *his or her* salary.

4. New parents often find it hard to adjust to having a baby around; *they* can't just get up and go someplace.

ANSWERS TO EXERCISE 12.5 (WILL VARY)

2. According to the article, the ozone layer is rapidly dwindling, *and the lives of future generations are endangered.*

4. Oscar Wilde wrote that books cannot be divided into moral and immoral categories, *and that books are either written well or badly.*

ANSWERS TO EXERCISE 13.1 (WILL VARY)

2. Film-makers today have no choice; therefore, they must use complicated electronic equipment.

4. My mother taught me to read, but my grandmother taught me to *love* to read.

ANSWERS TO EXERCISE 13.2 (WILL VARY)

2. The mother eagle called twice *before* the young eagle finally answered.

4. *After* the Soviet Union expelled Solzhenitsyn in 1974, he eventually settled in Vermont.

ANSWERS TO EXERCISE 14.1 (WILL VARY)

2. Americans yearn to live with gusto.

4. The climbers had two choices—to go over a four-hundred-foot cliff or to turn back—but they decided to make the attempt.

6. Westerners objected in particular to a law that limited traffic speed to fifty-five miles per hour.

8. Offering good pay, good working conditions, and the best equipment money can buy, organized crime has been able to attract graduates just as big business has.

10. Wollstonecraft believed in universal public education and in education that forms the heart and strengthens the body.

ANSWERS TO EXERCISE 14.2 (WILL VARY)

2. The researchers saw few, if any, teachers threaten students with bodily harm. Occasionally, though, they saw a teacher *resist* striking a student.

4. She scooped up the fur jacket which had been thrown into a heap on the dirt floor.

747

ANSWERS TO EXERCISE 14.3 (WILL VARY)

2. *verbal-phrase fragment:* The protagonist came to a decision to leave his family and go to London.
4. *subordinate-clause fragment:* Many senators from the West opposed the bill because of its restrictions on mining and oil drilling.
6. *appositive fragment:* Forster stopped writing novels after *A Passage to India*, one of the greatest novels of the twentieth century.
8. *compound-predicate fragment:* I loved Toni Morrison's *Beloved* and thought she deserved the Pulitzer prize.
10. *subordinate-clause fragment:* Because the younger generation often rejects the ways of its elders, one might say that rebellion is normal.

ANSWERS TO EXERCISE 15.1 (WILL VARY)

2. I heard my friends talk enthusiastically about their great weekends while I tried to finish my assignment.
4. On the day in question, the patient was not able to breathe normally.
6. He sat in his chair very quietly, rolling his eyes.
8. Vernon made an agreement with his father to pay the loan back.
10. The maintenance worker shut down the turbine that was revolving out of control.

ANSWERS TO EXERCISE 15.2 (WILL VARY)

2. I was glad to know that the money I had made for the night would stay in my pocket.
4. His doctor recommended a new, painless examination for heart disease.

ANSWERS TO EXERCISE 15.3 (WILL VARY)

2. The mayor promised that during her first term she would not raise taxes. During her first term, the mayor promised that she would not raise taxes.
4. Doctors can now restore limbs that have been partially severed to functioning condition. Doctors can now restore limbs that have been severed to partially functioning condition.

ANSWERS TO EXERCISE 15.4 (WILL VARY)

2. The exhibit attracted large audiences because it had been heavily publicized.
4. Bookstores sold fifty thousand copies in the first week after publication.

ANSWERS TO EXERCISE 15.5 (WILL VARY)

2. Given the sharp increase in the crime rate, many women feel that their safety is being threatened.
4. Women go to shooting ranges and gun clubs to train to use weapons.

ANSWERS TO EXERCISE 15.6 (WILL VARY)

2. While attending a performance at Ford's Theatre, Lincoln was shot by John Wilkes Booth.
4. Dreams are somewhat like a jigsaw puzzle: when put together in the correct order, both dreams and puzzles have organization and coherence.

ANSWERS TO EXERCISE 16.1 (WILL VARY)

2. Your dentist will usually tell you if you need braces. To find out if you need braces, ask your dentist.
4. By not prosecuting white-collar crime as vigorously as we prosecute violent crime, we encourage white-collar criminals to ignore the law. We must prosecute white-collar crime as vigorously as violent crime unless we want to encourage white-collar criminals to ignore the law.
6. People in love want to make each other happy. Love is often characterized by two people who want to make each other happy.
8. Oedipus has the "shock of recognition" when he suddenly realizes that he has killed his father and married his mother. The "shock of recognition" comes when Oedipus suddenly realizes that he has killed his father and married his mother.
10. Europeans discovered Australia, but the British made it into a penal colony. Although it was a European discovery, Australia became a British penal colony.

ANSWERS TO EXERCISE 16.2 (WILL VARY)

2. Argentina and Uruguay were originally colonized by Spain, and Brazil was colonized by Portugal.
4. During the football strike, fans were angrier at the players than they were at the management.
6. The picture made me think about whether Baby M's life would be more difficult than any other children's lives.
8. Nonsmokers and marijuana smokers have different personalities.
10. One way to develop a topic for an essay is to jot down whatever comes to mind on a sheet of paper.

ANSWERS TO EXERCISE 17.1 (WILL VARY)

2. Also notable throughout the story is the image of chrysanthemums.
4. Movie Indians always conjure up destructive stereotypes of drunkenness, horse thieves, and blood-thirsty war parties.

ANSWERS TO EXERCISE 17.2 (WILL VARY)

2. A prime example was the rescue attempt of the American hostages in Iran that resulted in the death of eight Marines.
4. I put on ten pounds immediately after I stopped exercising.
6. To check the engine, listen for rattling or pinging noises.
8. Randall exposes the injustices that confront American blacks.
10. Waitressing for six hours, followed by mopping and sweeping half a restaurant, can lead to exhaustion.

ANSWERS TO EXERCISE 18.3 (WILL VARY)

2. When Entwhistle and Townshend met singer and guitarist Roger Daltrey, they formed a group called the High Numbers.
4. *Working*, an important book by Studs Terkel, examines the situation of the American worker.

749

ANSWERS TO EXERCISE 19.2 (WILL VARY)

2. My favorite pastimes include reading, exercising, and talking with friends.
4. I want not only hot fudge but also whipped cream.

ANSWERS TO EXERCISE 19.3 (WILL VARY)

2. Most readers begin reading with an implicit faith that the text will be coherent and that the writer will convey meaning clearly.
4. Needing a new pair of shoes and not being able to afford them is enough to make anybody sensitive.
6. Too many students came to college to have fun, to find a husband or wife, or to put off having to go to work.
8. Her job was to show new products, to help Mr. Greer with sales, and to participate in advertising.
10. Stress can result in low self-esteem, total frustration, sleeplessness, nervousness, or eventually suicide.

ANSWERS TO EXERCISE 19.5 (WILL VARY)

2. There are three ways to apply Ninhydrin to the area to be examined: by brushing, spraying, or dipping.
4. There are two types of wallflowers: the male nerd and the female skeeve.

ANSWERS TO EXERCISE 20.3 (WILL VARY)

2. Once I mastered the problems which I had encountered at the beginning and once I had become thoroughly familiar with the stock, I became the best salesperson in our store.

ANSWERS TO EXERCISE 21.1 (WILL VARY)

2. I work for two brothers who own a hardware store.
4. The sweater feels soft and warm.

ANSWERS TO EXERCISE 21.4 (WILL VARY)

2. They started shooting pool, and before Marie knew it, ten dollars was owed to the kid. [Preference depends somewhat upon the context. The passive voice is unclear about who owes the kid ten dollars. Is Marie alone? Are she and the kid the "they" of the sentence, or is someone else involved? The active is clearer but might be incorrect, if others besides Marie owe the kid money.]
4. I adjusted more easily to living in a dorm than to living in an apartment. [Again, the active is preferred, since the passive adds nothing.]

ANSWERS TO EXERCISE 22.1

2. to; too
4. noticeable; until
6. believe; lose
8. affects; success; than; its
10. develop; truly; successful
12. where; and
14. businesses; dependent

750

16. experience; exercise
18. categories; final
20. occasion; whether; weather
22. woman's
24. It's; all right; sense

ANSWERS TO EXERCISE 22.3
2. conscience
4. leisure
6. caffeine
8. receive
10. heiress

ANSWERS TO EXERCISE 22.4
2. wholly
4. lonely
6. dyeing
8. continuous
10. outrageous

ANSWERS TO EXERCISE 22.5
2. fatally
4. finally

ANSWERS TO EXERCISE 22.6
2. carrying
4. studies
6. dutiful
8. obeyed
10. coyly

ANSWERS TO EXERCISE 22.7
2. fastest
4. reference
6. regrettable
8. drastically
10. weeping

ANSWERS TO EXERCISE 22.8
2. hooves
4. babies
6. stepchildren
8. miles per hour
10. phenomena
12. beaches
14. golf clubs

ANSWERS TO EXERCISE 23.2

2. student: from ME < L *studere*, to study
4. whine: from ME *whinen* < Indo-European *kwein*, to whiz, hiss, whistle
6. sex: from ME < L *sexus* < *secare*, to cut
8. tortilla: from Sp, diminutive of *torta*, cake
10. video: from L, I see < *videre*, to see

ANSWERS TO EXERCISE 23.5 (WILL VARY)

2. The *OED* lists to make strange or turn away from, to transfer ownership, and to change or alter something. *Webster's New World Dictionary* adds two slightly different meanings: to cause to be withdrawn from society, and to transfer affection.
4. The *OED* defines *hopefully* as an adverb: "In a hopeful manner; with a feeling of hope; with ground for hope, promisingly. *Webster's New World Dictionary* lists both adverb and adjective uses but notes that the adjectival use is "regarded by some as loose usage, but widely current."

ANSWERS TO EXERCISE 24.2 (WILL VARY)

2. subterranean: beneath earth; of or relating to under the surface of the earth.
4. monograph: to write one or a single writing; a learned treatise on a small area of learning.
6. superscript: to write over or above; a distinguishing symbol written immediately above or above and to the right of another character.
8. neologism: recent word or thought; a word, usage, or expression that is often disapproved because of its newness or barbarousness.
10. apathetic: without feeling or not suffering; having or showing little or no feeling or emotion, having or showing little or no interest or concern.

ANSWERS TO EXERCISE 25.1

2. rapturous
4. dramatically

ANSWERS TO EXERCISE 25.3 (WILL VARY)

2. *tragic*—distressing, alarming, disturbing; *consumes*—defeats, feeds on, erodes; *displays*—champions, thrives on, builds up, promotes; *drama*—excitement, tension, vitality; *expend*—commit; *greatest*—most challenging; *immediately*—instantly; *plunge*—dive; *incomprehensible*—unanticipated
4. *lightly*—carelessly; *held*—breathed; *keenness*—coolness, crispness; *twitch*—perk up; *surprise*—adventure, enterprise; *tremors*—chills; *run*—jet

ANSWERS TO EXERCISE 25.5 (WILL VARY)

2. Cooing, singing, twittering—the early morning beckoning of birds outside my window make it a treat to get up.
4. The valet stepped cautiously yet excitedly toward my Porsche.

ANSWERS TO EXERCISE 26.4 (WILL VARY)

2.   —destroys his victims with flashes of lightning (metaphor)
    —roasted her victims over a fire (metaphor): both of these metaphors suggest the

powerful effect that Pope's and Austen's words could have on the targets of their criticism or attacks; Pope's words were flashes of lightning, Austen's words made her victims feel as though they were being roasted over a fire

4.   —deep and soft like water moving in a cavern (simile): this simile compares the sound of her voice to water in a cavern

ANSWERS TO EXERCISE 26.6 (WILL VARY)

2. All candidates strive for the same results: they strive to discredit the opposition, and to persuade the majority of voters that they are qualified for the position.

4. The more angry she became over his actions, the more he rebelled and continued doing what he pleased.

ANSWERS TO EXERCISE 26.7 (WILL VARY)

2. total annihilation

4. to make peace

ANSWERS TO EXERCISE 27.1

  2. Unfortunately,

  4. If you follow instructions carefully,

  6. no comma needed

  8. no comma needed

10. Founded by Alexander the Great,

ANSWERS TO EXERCISE 27.2 (WILL VARY)

  2. Immigrants came to the United States with high hopes, *but* their illusions were often shattered.

  4. A basic quality of leather is stretchability, *so* it takes on the shape of a foot.

ANSWERS TO EXERCISE 27.3

2. *who laughs last* is a restrictive clause because only the *she* who has the last laugh can laugh best. The person who laughs first or second doesn't laugh best. Laughing best is restricted to the person who laughs last.

4. *smoked over an alder wood fire* is a restrictive appositive phrase because the meaning of the sentence is not complete without it. Only salmon that is smoked over an alder wood fire can have *a unique flavor*.

ANSWERS TO EXERCISE 27.4

  2. no comma needed.

  4. . . . power wire, which is usually red; . . . the ground wire, which is usually black.

  6. The Zunis, an ancient tribe dwelling in New Mexico,

  8. . . . was Karl Marx, who believed that his role as a social thinker . . .

10. aid, if one of them . . .

ANSWERS TO EXERCISE 27.5

  2. The social sciences include economics and psychology, political science, anthropology, and sociology.

  4. The daddy-long-legs's orange body resembled a colored dot amidst eight black legs.

6. Superficial observation does not provide accurate insight into people's lives—how they feel, what they believe in, how they respond to others.
8. I timidly offered to help a loud, overbearing, lavishly dressed customer.
10. These Cosell clones insist on calling every play, judging every move, and telling everyone within earshot exactly what is wrong with the team.

ANSWERS TO EXERCISE 27.6
2. The West, in fact, has become solidly Republican in presidential elections.
4. Fictions about race, not the facts, influence human relations.
6. no comma needed
8. And now, customers, follow along as I demonstrate the latest in video discs.
10. This is imported pâté, not chopped liver.

ANSWERS TO EXERCISE 27.7
2. Ithaca, New York, has a population of about 20,000.
4. The Modern Language Association headquarters recently moved to 10 Astor Place, New York, New York 10003.

ANSWERS TO EXERCISE 27.8
2. no change
4. "Neat people are lazier and meaner than sloppy people," according to Suzanne Britt.

ANSWERS TO EXERCISE 27.11
2. Observers watch and interpret facial expressions and gestures.
4. Our supper that evening consisted of stale bologna sandwiches, soggy cookies, and leftover trail mix.
6. As we sat around the campfire, we felt boredom and disappointment.
8. The photographer Edward Curtis is known for his depiction of the West.
10. Driving a car and talking on the car phone at the same time demand great care.

ANSWERS TO EXERCISE 28.1
2. City life offers many advantages; however, in many ways, life in a small town is much more pleasant.
4. Physical education forms an important part of many university programs; nevertheless, few students and professors clearly recognize its value.
6. Voltaire was concerned about the political implications of his skepticism; he warned his friends not to discuss atheism in front of the servants.
8. My high school was excessively competitive; virtually everyone went on to college, many to the top schools in the nation.
10. Propaganda is defined as the spread of ideas to further a cause; therefore, propaganda and advertisement are synonymous terms.

ANSWERS TO EXERCISE 28.4
2. If the North had followed up its victory at Gettysburg more vigorously, the Civil War might have ended sooner.
4. Our uniforms were unbelievably dingy, stained from being constantly splattered with food and often torn here and there.

ANSWERS TO EXERCISE 29.1
2. Cicero was murdered in 43 B.C.
4. In April 1981, NBC interviewed Dr. Spock.

ANSWERS TO EXERCISE 29.2
2. Are people with so many possessions really happy?
4. Correct, indirect question.

ANSWERS TO EXERCISE 29.3 (WILL VARY)
2. I screamed at Jamie, "You rat! You tricked me!"
4. Get away from that window right now!

ANSWERS TO EXERCISE 30.1
2. *CBS's* acquisition of the guitar company disappointed some musicians.
4. *Carol and Jim's* income dropped drastically after Jim quit his job.
6. Many smokers disregard the *surgeon general's* warnings.
8. The *governors'* attitude changed after the convention.
10. My *friend's* and my *brother's* cars have the same kind of stereo systems.

ANSWERS TO EXERCISE 30.3
2. That night I was escorted to the front row and placed on the *mourner's* bench with all the other young sinners. . . .
4. Then I was left all alone on the *mourner's* bench.

ANSWERS TO EXERCISE 31.2
2. In Flannery O'Connor's short story "Revelation," colors symbolize passion, violence, sadness, and even "God."
4. The "fun" of surgery begins before the operation ever takes place.
6. "Big Bill," the first section of Dos Passos's *U.S.A.*, opens with a birth.
8. Pink Floyd's song "Time" depicts the growth of technology and its impact on society.
10. This review will examine a TV episode entitled "48 Hours on Gang Street."

ANSWERS TO EXERCISE 31.4 (WILL VARY)
2. What is Hawthorne telling the readers in "Rappaccini's Daughter"?
4. This "typical American" is Ruby Turpin, who in the course of the story receives a message that brings about a change in her life.
6. One of Jackson's least-known stories is "Janice"; this story, like many of her others, leaves the reader shocked.
8. In his article, "How the Freeze Movement Was Born," Michael Kazin states that a freeze's "bilateral nature nullifies fears of a Soviet advantage."[1]
10. One thought flashed through my mind as I finished *In Search of Our Mothers' Garden:* "I want to read more of this writer's work."

ANSWERS TO EXERCISE 32.1
2. During my research, I found that a flat-rate income tax (a single-rate tax rate with no deductions) has its problems.
4. Many researchers used the Massachusetts Multiphasic Personal Inventory (MMPI) for hypnotizability studies.

ANSWERS TO EXERCISE 32.2

2. Even if smoking is harmful—and there is no real proof of this assertion—it is unjust to outlaw smoking while other harmful substances remain legal.
4. Many people would have ignored the children's taunts—but not Ace.

ANSWERS TO EXERCISE 32.3

2. Another example is taken from Psalm 139: 16.
4. Layton, Ed. *Martin Luther King: The Peaceful Warrior*, 3rd ed. Englewood Cliffs, NJ: Prentice, 1968.
6. Ghandi urged four things: tell the truth, even in business, adopt more sanitary habits, abolish caste and religious divisions, and learn English.
8. *Signs of Trouble and Erosion: A Report on Education in America* was submitted to Congress and the president in January 1984.
10. The article in *Time* reported that at 4:18 p.m. the surgeon, Dr. William DeVries, leaned over the heavily sedated man and said, "Everything went well—perfectly."

ANSWERS TO EXERCISE 33.1

2. Eating at a restaurant, whether it be a fast-food, Chinese, or Italian place, is always a treat.
4. The Council of Trent was convened to draw up the Catholic response to the Protestant Reformation.
6. I wondered if my new Lee jeans were faded enough and if I could possibly scuff up my new Nikes just a little more before I arrived for spring term.

ANSWERS TO EXERCISE 34.1

2. An MX missile is 71 feet long, 92 inches around, and weighs 190,000 pounds.
4. In 1955 the Reverend Martin Luther King, Jr., was elected president of the Montgomery Improvement Association.
6. Like black-and-white television, the five-cent candy bar is a relic of the past.
8. The Public Broadcasting System is promoting more and better programs in the arts throughout the country, not just in Los Angeles and New York City.
10. Dostoevsky was influenced by many European writers—for example, Dickens, Stendhal, and Balzac.

ANSWERS TO EXERCISE 34.2 (WILL VARY)

2. Some call it the handbook for the nineties.
4. I am writing in response to a letter submitted to the *Times-Picayune* on December 9, 1984, by George F. Lundy.
6. Educational broadcasting is at present available to 72 percent of the population.
8. In the thirty-five through forty-four age group, the risk is estimated to be about 1 in 2,500.
10. The ancient amulet measured 1⅛ by 2⅖ inches.

ANSWERS TO EXERCISE 35.1

2. When people think about the word *business*, they may associate it with people and companies that care about nothing but making money.
4. The word *veterinary* comes from the Latin *veterinarius*, meaning "of beasts of burden."

6. Flying the *Glamorous Glennis*, a plane named for his wife, Chuck Yeager was the first pilot to fly faster than the speed of sound.
8. *The Waste Land* is a long and difficult but ultimately rewarding poem.
10. My grandparents remember the sinking of the *Titanic*.

ANSWERS TO EXERCISE 36.1
2. re*tract; re-tract
4. mil*i*tar*y; mili-tary
6. oth*er*cen*tered; other-centered
8. dim*ming; dim-ming
10. at*ti*tude; atti-tude

ANSWERS TO EXERCISE 36.2
2. pre-World War II
4. correct
6. self-important
8. seven hundred thirty-three
10. correct

ANSWERS TO EXERCISE 36.3
2. McKuen began to write as an escape from his on-the-move life, which included various odd jobs ranging from ditch-digging to cookie-cutting.
4. Suicide among teenagers has tripled in the past thirty-five years, making it the third-leading cause of death among fifteen to twenty-four-year-olds.
6. Since the use of PCB's has been outlawed, environmentalists feel somewhat encouraged.
8. correct
10. The beautifully written essay earned high praise.

ACKNOWLEDGMENTS

Acknowledgments (continued from p. iv)

Emily Dickinson, "A Little Madness in the Spring" and "Much Madness Is Divinest Sense" reprinted by permission of the publishers and Trustees of Amherst College from *The Poems of Emily Dickinson*, edited by Thomas H. Johnson. Cambridge, Mass.: The Belknap Press of Harvard University Press. Copyright 1951, © 1955, 1979, 1983 by the Presidents and Fellows of Harvard College. Also from *The Complete Poems of Emily Dickinson*, edited by Thomas H. Johnson. Copyright 1914, 1942 by Martha Dickinson Bianchi. Reprinted by permission of Little, Brown and Company.

Dictionary of Modern English Usage, Second Edition, by H. W. Fowler and Sir Ernest Gowers, copyright © 1965, by permission of Oxford University Press.

Robert Francis, "The Pitcher." Copyright © 1953 by Robert Francis. Reprinted from *The Orb Weaver* by permission of Wesleyan University Press.

Robert Frost, "Fire and Ice." Copyright 1916, 1923 by Holt, Rinehart and Winston and renewed 1944, 1951 by Robert Frost. Reprinted from *The Poetry of Robert Frost*, edited by Edward Connery Latham, by permission of Henry Holt and Company, Inc.

Robert Frost, "The Road Not Taken." Copyright 1916, 1923 by Holt, Rinehart and Winston and renewed 1944, 1951 by Robert Frost. Reprinted from *The Poetry of Robert Frost*, edited by Edward Connery Latham, by permission of Henry Holt and Company, Inc.

Greenpeace advertisement. Produced by Greenpeace USA, 1436 U Street, NW, Washington, D.C., 20009.

Ellen Goodman, "Holiday Cheer Shouldn't End with the New Year." © 1988, the Boston Globe Newspaper Company/Washington Post Writers Group. Reprinted with permission.

A. E. Housman, "Loveliest of Trees." Copyright 1939, 1940, © 1965 by Holt, Rinehart and Winston. Copyright © 1967, 1968 by Robert E. Symons. Reprinted from *The Collected Poems of A. E. Housman* by permission of Henry Holt and Company, Inc.

Langston Hughes, "Harlem." Copyright © 1951 by Langston Hughes. Reprinted from *Selected Poems of Langston Hughes* by permission of Alfred A. Knopf, Inc.

Mathematics Dictionary, Fourth Edition, Glen James and Robert C. James, © 1976 by Van Nostrand Reinhold. All rights reserved. Reprinted by permission.

The Oxford English Dictionary, copyright © 1976, reprinted by permission of Oxford University Press.

Readers' Guide to Periodical Literature, August 1988, page 206, Copyright © 1988 by the H. W. Wilson Company. Material reproduced by permission of the publisher.

Karl Shapiro, "The Intellectual." Copyright © 1987 by Karl Shapiro. Reprinted from *New and Selected Poems 1940–1986* by permission of the University of Chicago Press and the author. All rights reserved.

John Updike, "Leaving Church Early." From *Tossing and Turning* by John Updike. Copyright © 1976 by John Updike. Reprinted by permission of Alfred A. Knopf, Inc.

758

ACKNOWLEDGMENTS

Webster's New Dictionary of Synonyms © 1984 by Merriam-Webster Inc., publisher of the Merriam-Webster dictionaries. Reprinted by permission.

Webster's New World Dictionary, Third College Edition, copyright © 1988 by Simon and Schuster, Inc. All rights reserved. Reprinted by permission.

Webster's Third New International Dictionary © 1986 by Merriam-Webster Inc., publisher of the Merriam-Webster ® dictionaries. Reprinted by permission.

The World Book Encyclopedia. Copyright © 1988 by World Book, Inc. "War of 1812" entry reprinted by permission.

World Wildlife Fund advertisement. Reprinted with permission of World Wildlife Fund.

Index of Authors and Titles

760

761

762

Subject Index

797

➤ THE TWENTY MOST COMMON ERRORS

The following list serves as a brief index of the error patterns most commonly found in college writing today. It can help you to recognize, understand, and overcome each one. Errors never exist in isolation, however; they are always part of some larger rhetorical context. This list can best serve you, then, as a means of identifying those patterns in your own writing that are problematic for you. Boldfaced pages feature guidelines to help you check your own writing for each of these common errors, including suggestions for ways to revise accordingly.